Student Loan Law

Collections, Intercepts, Deferments, Discharges, Repayment Plans, and Trade School Abuses

With CD-Rom

The Consumer Credit and Sales Legal Practice Series

Second Edition

Deanne Loonin

Contributing Author: John Rao

National Consumer Law Center

77 Summer Street, 10th Floor, Boston, MA 02110

www.consumerlaw.org

About NCLC

The National Consumer Law Center, a nonprofit corporation founded in 1969, assists consumers, advocates, and public policy makers nationwide who use the powerful and complex tools of consumer law to ensure justice and fair treatment for all, particularly those whose poverty renders them powerless to demand accountability from the economic marketplace. For more information, go to www.ConsumerLaw.org.

Ordering NCLC Publications

Publications Department, National Consumer Law Center, 77 Summer Street, Boston, MA 02110, www.consumerlaw.org, (617) 542-9595, FAX: (617) 542-8028, e-mail: publications@nclc.org.

Training and Conferences

NCLC participates in numerous national, regional, and local consumer law trainings. Its annual fall conference is a forum for consumer rights attorneys from legal services programs, private practice, government, and nonprofit organizations to share insights into common problems and explore novel and tested approaches that promote consumer justice in the marketplace. Contact NCLC for more information or see our web site.

Case Consulting

Case analysis, consulting and co-counseling for lawyers representing vulnerable consumers are among NCLC's important activities. Administration on Aging funds allow us to provide free consulting to legal services advocates representing elderly consumers on many types of cases. The Massachusetts Legal Assistance Corporation and other funds permit case assistance to advocates representing low-income Massachusetts and California consumers. Other funding may allow NCLC to provide very brief consultations to other advocates without charge. More comprehensive case analysis and research is available for a reasonable fee. See our web site for more information at www.ConsumerLaw.org.

Charitable Donations and Cy Pres *Awards*

NCLC's work depends in part on the support of private donors. Tax deductible donations should be made payable to National Consumer Law Center, Inc. For more information, contact NCLC's Development Office at (617) 542-8010 or scutler@nclc.org. NCLC has also received generous court-approved *cy pres* awards arising from consumer class actions to advance the interests of class members. For more information, contact Robert Hobbs (rhobbs@nclc.org) or Rich Dubois (rdubois@nclc.org) at (617) 542-8010.

Comments and Corrections

Write to the above address to the attention of the Editorial Department or e-mail consumerlaw@nclc.org.

About This Volume

This is the Second Edition of *Student Loan Law* with a 2002 companion CD-Rom, superseding the First Edition and its CD-Rom. Discard the 2001 First Edition and the 2001 CD-Rom. Continuing developments can be found in periodic supplements to this volume and in NCLC REPORTS.

Cite This Volume As

National Consumer Law Center, Student Loan Law (2d ed. 2002).

Attention

> *This publication is designed to provide authoritative information concerning the subject matter covered. Always use the most current edition and supplement, and use other sources for more recent developments or for special rules for individual jurisdictions. This publication cannot substitute for the independent judgment and skills of an attorney or other professional. Non-attorneys are cautioned against using these materials to conduct a lawsuit without advice from an attorney and are cautioned against engaging in the unauthorized practice of law.*

Copyright

About the Authors

Deanne Loonin is an NCLC staff attorney with a specialization in student loan law. She also specializes more generally in credit discrimination and consumer credit law, with an emphasis on issues affecting the elderly and new immigrants. She was formerly director a legal services attorney in Los Angeles specializing in consumer fraud cases. She is the author of the First Edition of this volume, co-author of *Credit Discrimination* (3rd ed. 2002) and *Surviving Debt* (2002).

John Rao is an NCLC attorney specializing in consumer bankruptcy and credit law. He is an editor of *Consumer Bankruptcy Law and Practice* (6th ed. 2000) co-author of *Repossessions and Foreclosures* (5th ed. 2002), and head of NCLC's Advice and Assistance Project. For 18 years, he had a bankruptcy and consumer law specialty at Rhode Island Legal Services, and was a managing attorney there. He is on the board of directors of the National Association of Consumer Bankruptcy Attorneys.

Acknowledgments: We are particularly grateful to Denise Lisio for editorial supervision; Shirlron Williams for assistance with cite checking; Shannon Halbrook for production assistance; Xylutions for typesetting services; and to Neil Fogarty of Law Disks for developing the CD-Rom.

We would also like to thank Elena Ackel, Irv Ackelsberg, Robert Bush, Elizabeth Costello, Kathryn Harlow, Jennifer Hartke, Steve Olden, Jane Stevens, Michael Tankersley, and Allen Agnitti for their substantive contributions to this edition. We also continue to thank all those who contributed to the First Edition, particularly Alan White for co-authoring Chapter 6, Carolyn Carter for her contributions to Chapter 4, and Jon Sheldon for authoring the student loans chapter in *Unfair and Deceptive Acts and Practices* which provided the springboard for this volume.

In memory of
Laurel Silverman

Her committment to excellence and her dedication to detail
have been reflected in our manuals for the past ten years
and serve as an inspiration for our future.

What Your Library Should Contain

The Consumer Credit and Sales Legal Practice Series contains 16 titles, updated annually, arranged into four libraries, and designed to be an attorney's primary practice guide and legal resource in all 50 states. Each manual includes a CD-Rom allowing information to be copied into a word processor.

Debtor Rights Library

2000 Sixth Edition, 2002 Cumulative Supplement, and 2002 Cumulative CD-Rom, Including Law Disk's Bankruptcy Forms

Consumer Bankruptcy Law and Practice: the definitive personal bankruptcy manual, with step-by-step instructions from initial interview to final discharge, and including consumers' rights as creditors when a merchant or landlord files for bankruptcy. Appendices and CD-Rom contain over 130 annotated pleadings, bankruptcy statutes, rules and fee schedules, an interview questionnaire, a client handout, and software to complete the latest versions of petitions and schedules.

2000 Fourth Edition, 2002 Cumulative Supplement, and 2002 Cumulative CD-Rom

Fair Debt Collection: the basic reference in the field, covering the Fair Debt Collection Practices Act and common law, state statutory and other federal debt collection protections. Appendices and companion CD-Rom contain sample pleadings and discovery, the FTC's Official Staff Commentary, *all* FTC staff opinion letters, and summaries of reported and unreported cases.

2002 Fifth Edition with CD-Rom

Repossessions and Foreclosures: unique guide to VA, FHA and other types of home foreclosures, servicer obligations, car and mobile home repossessions, threatened seizures of household goods, tax and other statutory liens, and automobile lease and rent-to-own default remedies. The CD-Rom reprints relevant UCC provisions and numerous key federal statutes, regulations, and agency letters, summarizes hundreds of state laws, and includes over 150 pleadings covering a wide variety of cases.

2002 Second Edition with CD-Rom

Student Loan Law: student loan debt collection and collection fees; discharges based on closed school, false certification, failure to refund, disability, and bankruptcy; tax intercepts, wage garnishment, and offset of social security benefits; repayment plans, consolidation loans, deferments, and non-payment of loan based on school fraud. CD-Rom and appendices contain numerous forms, pleadings, interpretation letters and regulations.

2001 Second Edition, 2002 Supplement, and 2002 Cumulative CD-Rom

Access to Utility Service: the only examination of consumer rights when dealing with regulated, de-regulated, and unregulated utilities, including telecommunications, terminations, billing errors, low-income payment plans, fuel allowances in subsidized housing, LIHEAP, and weatherization. Includes summaries of state utility regulations.

Credit and Banking Library

1999 Fourth Edition, 2002 Cumulative Supplement, and 2002 Cumulative CD-Rom

Truth in Lending: detailed analysis of *all* aspects of TILA, the Consumer Leasing Act, and the Home Ownership and Equity Protection Act (HOEPA). Appendices and the CD-Rom contain the Acts, Reg. Z, Reg. M, and their Official Staff Commentaries, numerous sample pleadings, rescission notices, and two programs to compute APRs.

National Consumer Law Center ■ 77 Summer Street ■ 10ᵗʰ Floor ■ Boston MA ■ 02110
(617) 542-9595 ■ FAX (617) 542-8028 ■ E-mail: publications@nclc.org ■ www.consumerlaw.org

2002 Fifth Edition with CD-Rom	**Fair Credit Reporting:** the key resource for handling any type of credit reporting issue, from cleaning up blemished credit records to suing reporting agencies and creditors for inaccurate reports. Covers credit scoring, privacy issues, identity theft, the FCRA, the Credit Repair Organizations Act, state credit reporting and repair statutes, and common law claims.
2002 Second Edition with CD-Rom	**Consumer Banking and Payments Law**: unique analysis of consumer law as to checks, money orders, credit, debit, and stored value cards, and banker's right of setoff. Also extensive treatment of electronic records and signatures, electronic transfer of food stamps, and direct deposits of federal payments. The CD-Rom and appendices reprint relevant agency interpretations and pleadings.
2000 Second Edition, 2002 Cumulative Supplement, and 2002 Cumulative CD-Rom	**The Cost of Credit: Regulation and Legal Challenges:** a one-of-a-kind resource detailing state and federal regulation of consumer credit in all fifty states, federal usury preemption, explaining credit math, and how to challenge excessive credit charges and credit insurance. The CD-Rom includes a credit math program and hard-to-find agency interpretations.
2002 Third Edition with CD-Rom	**Credit Discrimination**: analysis of the Equal Credit Opportunity Act, Fair Housing Act, Civil Rights Acts, and state credit discrimination statutes, including reprints of all relevant federal interpretations, government enforcement actions, and numerous sample pleadings.

Consumer Litigation Library

2002 Second Edition with CD-Rom	**Consumer Arbitration Agreements**: numerous successful approaches to challenge the enforceability of a binding arbitration agreement, the interrelation of the Federal Arbitration Act and state law, class actions in arbitration, the right to discovery, and other topics. Appendices and CD-Rom include sample discovery, numerous briefs, arbitration service provider rules and affidavits as to arbitrator costs.
2002 Fifth Edition with CD-Rom	**Consumer Class Actions: A Practical Litigation Guide**: makes class action litigation manageable even for small offices, including numerous sample pleadings, class certification memoranda, discovery, class notices, settlement materials, and much more. Includes contributions from seven of the most experienced consumer class action litigators around the country.
2002 Cumulative CD-Rom with Index Guide: ALL pleadings from ALL NCLC Manuals, including Consumer Law Pleadings Numbers One through Eight	**Consumer Law Pleadings on CD-Rom**: Over 650 notable recent pleadings from all types of consumer cases, including predatory lending, foreclosures, automobile fraud, lemon laws, debt collection, fair credit reporting, home improvement fraud, rent to own, student loans, and lender liability. Finding aids pinpoint the desired pleading in seconds, ready to paste into a word processing program.

Deception and Warranties Library

2001 Fifth Edition, 2002 Supplement, and 2002 Cumulative CD-Rom	**Unfair and Deceptive Acts and Practices**: the only practice manual covering all aspects of a deceptive practices case in every state. Special sections on automobile sales, the federal racketeering (RICO) statute, unfair insurance practices, and the FTC Holder Rule.
1998 First Edition, 2002 Cumulative Supplement, and 2002 Cumulative CD-Rom	**Automobile Fraud:** examination of odometer tampering, lemon laundering, sale of salvage and wrecked cars, undisclosed prior use, prior damage to new cars, numerous sample pleadings, and title search techniques.
2001 Second Edition, 2002 Supplement, and 2002 Cumulative CD-Rom	**Consumer Warranty Law:** comprehensive treatment of new and used car lemon laws, the Magnuson-Moss Warranty Act, UCC Articles 2 and 2A, mobile home and new home warranty laws, FTC Used Car Rule, tort theories, car repair and home improvement statutes, service contract and lease laws, with numerous sample pleadings.

NCLC's CD-Roms

Every NCLC manual comes with a companion CD-Rom featuring pop-up menus, PDF format, Internet-style navigation of appendices, indices, and bonus pleadings, hard-to-find agency interpretations and other practice aids. Documents can be copied into a word processing program. Of special note is *Consumer Law in a Box*:

December 2002 CD-Rom

Consumer Law in a Box: a CD-Rom combining *all* documents and software from 16 other NCLC CD-Roms. Quickly pinpoint the document from thousands found on the CD through key word searches and Internet-style navigation, links, bookmarks, and other finding aids.

Other NCLC Publications for Lawyers

issued 24 times a year

NCLC REPORTS covers the latest developments and ideas in the practice of consumer law.

2002 First Edition with CD-Rom

STOP Predatory Lending: A Guide for Legal Advocates: provides a roadmap and practical legal strategy for litigating predatory lending abuses, from small loans to mortgage loans. The CD-Rom contains a credit math program, pleadings, legislative and administrative materials, and underwriting guidelines.

National Consumer Law Center Guide Series are books designed for consumers, counselors, and attorneys new to consumer law:

2002 Edition

NCLC Guide to Surviving Debt: A great overview of consumer law. Everything a paralegal, new attorney, or client needs to know about debt collectors, managing credit card debt, whether to refinance, credit card problems, home foreclosures, evictions, repossessions, credit reporting, utility terminations, student loans, budgeting, and bankruptcy.

2002 Edition

NCLC Guide to Mobile Homes: what consumers and their advocates need to know about mobile home dealer sales practices and an in-depth look at mobile home quality and defects, with 35 photographs and construction details.

2002 Edition

NCLC Guide to Consumer Rights for Immigrants: an introduction to many of the most critical consumer issues faced by immigrants, including international wires, check cashing and banking, *notario* and immigration consultant fraud, affidavits of support, telephones, utilities, credit history discrimination, high-cost credit, used car fraud, student loans and more.

2000 Edition

Return to Sender: Getting a Refund or Replacement for Your Lemon Car: Find how lemon laws work, what consumers and their lawyers should know to evaluate each other, investigative techniques and discovery tips, how to handle both informal dispute resolution and trials, and more.

> Visit www.consumerlaw.org to find the full tables of contents and indices for all NCLC manuals.

Summary Contents

Contents

Chapter 3 The Consequences of Default

Chapter 4 Student Loan Collection

Chapter 5   Property and Asset Seizures

Chapter 6   Discharging Student Loan Obligations

Chapter 7   Discharging Student Loans in Bankruptcy

Chapter 8   Repayment Strategies for Getting Out of Default

Chapter 9

Challenging Trade School Abuses

Appendix A

Federal Student Loan Statutes

Appendix B

Federal Regulations

Appendix C

Department of Education Policy Guidance Letters

Appendix D

Student Assistance Forms

Chapter 1   Getting Started

1.1 Introduction

There is almost always something that borrowers can do to challenge student loan collection actions and either cancel a loan or set up an affordable monthly payment plan. Understanding borrower cancellation and repayment rights is the key to assisting clients with student loan problems. Resolving these problems is often a critical step in helping clients get back on their feet financially.

When threatened with tax refund intercepts, litigation, wage garnishment, and federal benefits offsets, many borrowers simply feel that they have no choice but to pay back the loans. To make matters worse, many of these borrowers received no value from their schooling, having attended for-profit scam vocational schools that were particularly prevalent in the late 1980s and early 1990s.

For these borrowers, education, initially seen as a way out of poverty, has led them into a cycle of endless debt. They find themselves in a trap. Student loan debt from the past keeps them from going back to school and moving into higher paying jobs. On the other hand, they cannot afford to go back to school and get additional training without some type of financial assistance.

Education is particularly critical for people entering the job force for the first time. This group includes many welfare-to-work clients, domestic violence survivors, and new immigrants. In addition, those re-entering the job force after lay-offs or hoping to transition into other types of work because of unemployment or disability also often look to education to move ahead. Although student loan debt is a problem that crosses class lines, low-income students tend to graduate with the highest levels of debt.[1]

An additional factor fueling the problem is the growth of private student loan products. Companies such as Sallie Mae offer an increasing number of private loans to supplement or even replace federal education assistance. Recent reports indicate that many schools steer low-income borrowers into these products. Because the government penalizes schools with high default rates, schools are particularly worried about less creditworthy borrowers taking out federal loans. On the other hand, schools do not have to worry about private loan defaults because the government does not count them when calculating school default rates.

It is critical for advocates to understand how best to counsel and represent student loan borrowers. An important first step is to learn about local educational options, particularly low-cost community colleges and other affordable programs. Advocates should also familiarize themselves with the range of government and private financing available.

Unfortunately, most clients do not seek legal help until long after they attended schools, took out loans, and defaulted on those loans. This manual focuses on assisting these clients, reviewing in detail the primary cancellation, repayment, bankruptcy, and other options available to challenge government collection efforts and help borrowers get out of default.

1.2 Using This Manual

1.2.1 Road Map

This manual is designed to help low-income advocates negotiate the world of federal student financial assistance, specifically federal student loan programs. Although geared toward low-income advocates, many of the same programs and remedies will apply to middle- and upper-income borrowers as well.

This manual deals almost exclusively with federal student loans. It does not cover private loans or private or public grants in any detail.[2]

Chapter 1 of this manual reviews the primary types of federal student assistance and how to help clients find out

---

1 *See* Tracey King and Ivan Frishberg, *Big Loans, Bigger Problems: A Report on the Sticker Shock of Student Loans* (The State PIRGs Mar. 2001); Tracey King and Ellynne Bannon, *The Burden of Borrowing: A Report on The Rising Rates of Student Loan Debt* (The State PIRG's Higher Education Project Mar. 2002). Both reports are available on-line at www.uspirg.org. *See also* Patricia M. Scherschel, *Student Debt Levels Continue to Rise* (Lumina Foundation June 2000), available on-line at www.luminafoundation.org.

2 Banks and other financial institutions make private loans without any direct financial backing from the federal government. They are not subsidized, meaning that interest starts to accrue at the time the loans are obtained. There are many different types of private loans, each program with specific rules and requirements. As noted earlier, the private student loan industry has been growing rapidly in the past few years. *See* § 1.1, *supra*.

1

what types of loans they have. Repayment plans for borrowers who have not yet fallen into default are also discussed in this chapter.

Chapter 2 covers deferment and forbearance options. Deferments are available only for borrowers who have not yet defaulted on their loans.

Chapters 3 through 5 focus on student loan collection issues. Chapter 3 covers the consequences of student loan default, including the elimination of the statute of limitations for student loan collections and credit reporting issues related to defaulted student loans. Chapter 4 focuses on the collection process, including collection fees and penalties. Chapter 4 also covers possible legal challenges to abusive student loan collection activity. Chapter 5 discusses property and asset seizures, including tax refund intercepts, administrative wage garnishments, and federal benefits offsets.

Chapter 6 presents the primary cancellation options available for borrowers, including closed school, false certification, unpaid refund, disability, and death cancellations. Cancellation of student loans may also be pursued in bankruptcy. The ways in which student loans can be discharged in bankruptcy are discussed in Chapter 7.

Chapter 8 includes information on repayment options, focusing on repayment strategies for low-income clients including loan consolidation and reasonable and affordable payment plans. This chapter also discusses the government's compromise and write-off authority. Finally, Chapter 9 presents information about suing schools and/or loan holders either affirmatively or defensively in response to collection actions.

The appendices to this manual reprint key student loan statutes and regulations and contain various practice aids. Appendix A includes critical federal student loan statutes. Key regulations can be found in Appendix B. Selected Department of Education policy guidance letters are included in Appendix C.

Appendices D, E and F contain a number of useful forms and pleadings for practitioners. Finally, Appendix G includes a current list of state guaranty agencies along with addresses and telephone numbers.

This volume also includes a CD-Rom containing the statutes, regulations, forms, and pleadings from the appendices, the index to this volume, and the quick reference to the entire National Consumer Law Center, Consumer Credit and Sales Legal Practices Series. The CD-Rom has numerous student loan-related pleadings as well as the latest regulations, and proposed regulations, issued by the Department of Education. See "About the CD-Rom" at the back of this volume for more information.

This volume will be supplemented, usually on an annual basis. Between supplements, new developments are reported in NCLC REPORTS, *Deceptive Practices and Warranties Edition*, published bimonthly. For subscription information, contact Publications Department, National Consumer Law Center, 77 Summer Street, 10th Floor, Boston, MA 02110, (617) 542-9595.

1.2.2 Clearinghouse Documents

Certain documents included in this manual are cited by a "Clearinghouse" number. The National Center on Poverty Law (formerly known as the National Clearinghouse for Legal Services) retains copies of these documents. Cases of special interest to low-income advocates, including unpublished cases, are frequently cited by a "Clearinghouse" number. Current case pleadings are available on the organization's website, www.povertylaw.org. Summaries are available to the general public. Subscribers can download the full text. Subscription fees are $25 per month or $200 per year. For older pleadings, call the National Center on Poverty Law at (312) 263-3830. A minimal copying and delivery fee will be charged.

1.3 Vocational School Issues

Unfair and deceptive vocational and correspondence school practices are a tremendous source of frustration, financial loss and loss of opportunity for consumers, particularly low-income consumers hoping to break out of poverty. Attracted by the financing provided by government student loan and grant programs, many vocational school scams and ill-conceived schools have exploited federally-funded student assistance programs.

This problem, for the most part, grew out of good intentions. In 1979, Congress amended the Higher Education Act (HEA) to encourage lenders to market loans to for-profit vocational school students.[3] Congress hoped to open up the student financial assistance market, particularly to non-high school graduates and others wishing to pursue vocational training.

Unfortunately, these changes not only opened the door to eager students, but also to unscrupulous for-profit schools and lenders. The federal student loan system became a victim of its own good intentions. Schools began to pressure vulnerable and low-income consumers into signing documents obligating them to thousands of dollars. Many schools promised that students would not have to repay

---

3 Higher Education Technical Amendments of 1979, Pub. L. No. 96-49, 93 Stat. 351 (1979). The 1979 amendments removed a ceiling on the federal interest subsidy paid to participating guaranteed student loan program lenders. Later amendments removed other limitations on student borrowers attending for-profit schools. *See* Education Amendments of 1980, Pub. L. No. 96-374, 94 Stat. 1367 (1980); Higher Education Amendments of 1986, Pub. L. No. 99-498, §§ 425, 1075(a), 100 Stat. 1268, 1359 (1986). *See also* discussion in Armstrong v. Accrediting Council for Continuing Education and Training, 168 F.3d 1362 (D.D.C. 1999).

loans until they got high paying jobs. The schools then literally took the money and ran, leaving loan collection to a third party.[4]

Throughout the late 1980s and early 1990s, vocational school abuses led to tremendous increases in student loan default rates. In 1968, the government paid $2 million to cover loan defaults; in 1987, default payments exceeded $1 billion; and by 1991, default claim payments reached $3.2 billion.[5] The overall default rate peaked at 22.4% in fiscal year 1990.[6] This rate decreased all the way to 5.6% in 1999.

The default rates for less than two-year proprietary schools have historically been much higher than the rates for other types of schools. The rate for these schools peaked in FY 1990 at 41.2%. By FY 1999, this rate had declined to 10.9%.

The government worked to lower the default rates by cracking down on some of the worst trade school offenders *and* by substantially expanding government collection powers. In addition, the government moved to suspend schools with excessive default rates from participating in federal student assistance programs.[7]

Although the situation has improved significantly, the abuses of the past are still relevant. Many clients still need help dealing with older student loan debt that may be preventing them from going back to school, from getting good credit, or even from buying a house. Unless addressed through loan cancellation, repayment, or other remedies, these problems can literally last forever due to the elimination of a statute of limitations for most student loan collection.[8] There are also new concerns for low-income students hoping to borrow money to attend trade schools.[9]

1.4 Introduction to Federal Student Assistance

1.4.1 General

This manual focuses on federally guaranteed student loans. Lenders have incentives to participate in these programs because the government lender reimburses them when borrowers default. Before getting reimbursed, lenders are required to make certain efforts to collect the loans.[10]

Often the original lender will sell the loan to another lender specializing in student loans, such as the Student Loan Marketing Association ("Sallie Mae"). Either the original or the subsequent lender can also contract with a servicing company to service the loan for the lender. In many cases, a loan servicing company such as Sallie Mae will also sell its own private loan products.

Although the student loan program is federal, it is mostly administered through state or private nonprofit agencies called guaranty agencies. Guaranty agencies pay off the lenders when borrowers default, and in turn, are reinsured by the Department of Education. In addition, when a loan held by a lender or other servicer goes into default, it is typically turned over to a guaranty agency for collection. At a later date, the United States, as an insurer on the loan, can take over the collection effort.[11]

There are general eligibility criteria that apply to most loan programs. In most cases, students must show financial need. Potential borrowers must also have a high school diploma or General Education certificate (GED), complete an approved home school education, or pass a test approved by the Department of Education. These tests are known as "ability to benefit" tests.[12]

Students must be enrolled in a degree, certificate or other approved program at an eligible school.[13] In addition, prospective borrowers must be United States citizens or eligible noncitizens. Eligible noncitizens primarily include permanent residents, refugees and asylees.[14] All borrowers must have valid Social Security numbers and must register with the Selective Service if required. Students convicted under federal or state law of sale or possession of illegal drugs are suspended from federal financial assistance programs.[15]

---

4 For more information on vocational school abuses, see Ch. 9, *infra.*

5 General Accounting Office, *Higher Education: Ensuring Quality Education From Proprietary Institutions*, GAO/T-HEHS-96-158 (June 1996).

6 Information on default rates is available on the Department of Education's website at www.ed.gov/offices/OSFAP/default-management/defaultrates.html. Default rates are defined as the percentage of borrowers who entered repayment in a certain year and defaulted before the end of the next year.

7 Since the inception of the program in 1991, according to the Department of Education, more than 1100 schools have lost student loan program eligibility. U.S. Department of Education, *Accountability for Results Works: College Loan Default Rates Continue to Decline*, Press Release (Sept. 19, 2001).

8 See § 3.2, *infra* (statute of limitations).

9 See § 9.1.3, *infra.*

---

10 34 C.F.R. §§ 682.411 (lender due diligence in collecting guaranty agency loans), 682.507.

11 A list of state guaranty agencies can be found at Appx. G, *infra.*

12 20 U.S.C. § 1091(d). For more on ability to benefit tests and false certification discharges, see § 6.3.2, *infra.*

13 20 U.S.C. § 1091(a)(1), (2).

14 20 U.S.C. § 1091(a)(5). Other eligible immigration categories include those on indefinite parole and/or humanitarian parole, Cuban-Haitian entrants with status pending, and conditional entrants (only if authorization issued before Apr. 1, 1980). Students in the United States with student visas only are not eligible for federal aid.

15 20 U.S.C. § 1091(r).

1.4.2 Federal Family Education Loans vs. Federal Direct Loans

The Higher Education Act Amendments of 1992 created a new generic name for the major forms of federal student loans.[16] Federal Family Education Loans (FFELs) include subsidized and unsubsidized Stafford Loans (formerly known as Guaranteed Student Loans or GSLs), Supplemental Loans for Students (SLSs), and parental (PLUS) loans.

It is usually important to keep track of whether a FFEL was disbursed before or after July 1, 1993. Many of the changes to the student loan programs instituted by the Higher Education Act Amendments of 1992 concerning deferments, repayment plans, and other topics apply only to FFELs disbursed after July 1, 1993.

Students can receive FFELs to attend most post-secondary schools, including private vocational schools. The Department of Education (DOE) does not review the educational quality of private vocational schools before certifying their eligibility to participate in the FFEL program. Instead, the DOE requires the schools to be licensed by a state agency and the Department recognizes various private accrediting agencies and associations whose job it is to review the educational standards of the school.[17]

The Student Loan Reform Act of 1993 significantly changed the student loan landscape by creating a new Federal Direct Loan program.[18] Federal Direct Loans (referred to throughout this manual as Direct Loans) are loans directly from the federal government to the student, with the assistance of the school or other entity that originates the loan. Lenders and guaranty agencies are cut out of the process.

The schools or other originators receive fees for originating the loans, but the Department selects which schools participate in the Direct Loan program. Other schools continue to participate in the FFEL program. Direct Loans have similar terms as FFELs, but the loans, when they become due, are immediately owed to the United States. As of 2000, over 1200 schools have joined Direct Lending, comprising about one third of new federal student loans.

There are four types of Direct Loans:

• Federal Direct Stafford/Ford Loans (Subsidized Loans);
• Federal Direct Unsubsidized Stafford/Ford Loans (Direct Unsubsidized Loans);
• Federal Direct PLUS Loans;
• Federal Direct Consolidation Loans.[19]

The relationship between the government and private lenders participating in the FFEL program is often strained. Throughout 2001 and 2002, Congress and the Bush Administration have expressed concern about the Direct Lending program, threatening to limit certain provisions. The Direct Loan program's Income Contingent Repayment Plan (ICRP) and the Direct Loan Consolidation program have been the target of much of this criticism.[20]

1.4.3 Types of Federal Student Assistance

1.4.3.1 Stafford Loans

Federal Stafford Loans are made to students through the Direct Loan program and the FFEL program (private lenders provide the funds). Direct Stafford and FFEL Stafford Loans have identical loan limits, and identical deferment and cancellation provisions. The major difference is that Direct Loans are originated by the government and FFEL loans by private lenders. There are also some differences in repayment options.

Stafford Loans are either subsidized or unsubsidized. Students can receive a subsidized and an unsubsidized loan for the same enrollment period.

A subsidized loan is awarded on the basis of financial need. The key difference between the two types of Stafford Loans is that for subsidized loans, borrowers are not charged any interest before the repayment period begins or during authorized periods of deferment. In essence, the government "subsidizes" the interest during these periods.

Unsubsidized loans are not awarded on the basis of financial need. Interest is charged from the time the loan is

---

16 Pub. L. No. 102-325, 106 Stat. 448 (1992).

17 For more information on accreditors, see § 9.4.1.2, *infra*.

18 Student Loan Reform Act of 1993, 107 Stat. 340, *enacted as* § 4021 of the Omnibus Budget Reconciliation Act of 1993, Pub. L. No. 103-66, 107 Stat. 312 (Aug. 10 1993).

19 Information about Direct Loans is available on the Department of Education website at www.ed.gov/DirectLoan. The phone number for information about direct loans is (800) 848-0979,

---

TDD: (800) 848-0983. The numbers for Direct Consolidation Loans are (800) 557-7392 and TDD: (800) 557-7395.

20 Much of the controversy, particularly in the Direct Loan consolidation program began after Congress amended the law in 1998 to allow borrowers with loans from different lenders to consolidate their loans with any eligible consolidation lender. 34 C.F.R. § 682.201(c)(iv)(B). This change stimulated competition and led to the growth of many new companies seeking to lure borrowers away from Sallie Mae (the largest FFEL consolidator) and the Direct Loan program. The large consolidation lenders such as Sallie Mae have begun to protest loudly against the "looser" consolidation rules. They argue that the third-party marketers and other consolidation lenders luring student loan borrowers into consolidating their loans will undermine the student loan originating industry. *See* Student Loan Fin. Corp. v. Paige, Case No: 1:00-CV-02660 (RWR) (D.D.C. 2000). *See also* General Accounting Office, *Student Loans: Direct Loan Default Rates*, GAO-01-68 (Oct. 2000) (focusing on higher default rates among Direct Loan consolidation borrowers with Income Contingent Repayment Plans. Private lenders have even filed a lawsuit against the Department of Education accusing the Department of illegally providing lower interest rates and other benefits to borrowers in the Direct Loan program).

disbursed until it is paid in full. Annual and aggregate loan limits are set out in the Department of Education regulations.[21]

Repayment for Stafford Loans begins after graduation, or after a student leaves school or drops below half-time enrollment. After one of these events, a borrower has six months to begin repayment.

1.4.3.2 Perkins Loans

Perkins Loans (formerly called National Direct Student Loans, and before that National Defense Student Loans) are not FFELs.[22] These are low-interest loans for both undergraduate and graduate students with exceptional financial need.

Perkins Loans are originated and serviced by participating schools and repaid to the school. The government does not insure the loans, but instead provides initial contributions to eligible institutions to partially capitalize a loan fund. Perkins Loans are administered by the school itself, at interest rates below Staffords. Repayment is postponed nine (or sometimes six) months after the student graduates or stops attending school.

If the student defaults, the school can seek collection through a lawsuit or otherwise. Perkins schools may assign loans to the United States when they cannot collect.[23] The United States will then seek collection from the defaulted borrower, using the full range of collection tools available.[24] However, the schools can no longer receive any of the funds collected after assignment.[25] In a few cases, such as review of disability discharges, schools are required to assign loans to the Department.[26]

Since Perkins Loans have different regulations than FFELs and Direct Loans, student rights and obligations are often different. However, the 1998 Higher Education Act contained a number of provisions that made the Perkins regulations much more like the FFEL and Direct Loan regulations. In particular, the closed school discharge for loans made on or after January 1, 1986 now applies to Perkins Loans as well.[27] Perkins Loan borrowers who make twelve consecutive monthly payments are also now allowed to rehabilitate defaulted loans.[28]

1.4.3.3 PLUS Loans

PLUS Loans allow parents to borrow to pay for the education of dependent undergraduate children enrolled in school at least half time. PLUS loans are available through both the Direct and FFEL programs. To be eligible for PLUS, parents are generally required to pass a credit check.[29] Repayment on PLUS Loans generally must begin within sixty days after the final loan disbursement for the period of enrollment for which the loan was borrowed.[30]

1.4.3.4 Older Loans

Prior to 1994, borrowers could also receive Supplemental Loans for Students (SLS). Effective July 1, 1994, SLS loans were no longer issued. The SLS program was merged into the unsubsidized component of the Stafford Loan program. However, many students obtained SLS loans before that date, and the conditions and benefits of those earlier loans remain unchanged.[31]

Many older loans are insured directly by the federal government, with no guaranty agency acting as intermediary. These loans are called Federally Insured Student Loans (FISLs). FISLs were made from 1966 to 1984. Unless specified otherwise, the term FFEL in this section includes FISLs.

1.4.3.5 Federal Grant Programs

A Basic Educational Opportunity Grant (BEOG), also called a Pell Grant,[32] and a Supplemental Educational Opportunity Grant (SEOG)[33] are not loans, and require no repayment (unless there is an overpayment).[34] The College Work Study program (CWS) provides salaries for students in exchange for work.[35] All of these assistance programs are

---

21 34 C.F.R. §§ 682.204(a) (FFEL), 685.203 (Direct Loan).

22 They are referred to in this chapter only as Perkins Loans. When this chapter refers to Direct Loans, the reference is to the Federal Direct Loan program. Statutory authority can be found at 20 U.S.C. §§ 1087aa–1087ii.

23 34 C.F.R. § 674.50.

24 The Department claims to have collection tools, such as administrative wage garnishment, federal offset, and Department of Justice litigation, that are not available to schools. It is unclear whether this statement accurately reflects current practice. Perkins schools can presumably refer accounts to the government for tax refund intercepts. They would seem to have authority to also refer accounts for federal benefits offset. However, the Department claims this is not current practice. *See* Department of Education, Dear Colleague Letter CB-02-05 (Apr. 2002). *See also* 34 C.F.R. § 674.41 (Perkins lender due diligence requirements). The situation is clearer for FFEL loans where guaranty agencies, in most cases, have specific authority to collect on behalf of the Department prior to assignment. *See generally* Ch. 5, *infra*.

25 *See* Department of Education, Dear Colleague Letter CB-02-05 (Apr. 2002).

26 *See* § 6.6 (disability discharges), *infra*.

27 34 C.F.R. § 674.33(g). *See* § 6.2, *infra*.

28 34 C.F.R. § 674.39.

29 34 C.F.R. §§ 682.201(b) (applies to FFEL PLUS loans made on or after July 1, 1993), 685.200 (Direct Loans).

30 34 C.F.R. §§ 682.209(a)(2)(i)(FFEL), 685.207(d) (Direct Loan).

31 SLSs were considered a part of the FFEL category of loans. Therefore FFEL regulations should apply to these loans as well.

32 20 U.S.C. § 1070a; 34 C.F.R. § 690.

33 20 U.S.C. § 1070b; 34 C.F.R. § 676.

34 *Id.*

35 42 U.S.C. §§ 2751–2756b; 34 C.F.R. § 675.

administered by the school. Students can have more than one form of student assistance, so that, for example, a student may participate in work-study, have a Pell Grant, a Stafford, and a PLUS Loan signed by his or her parents.

1.5 Repayment Options Prior to Default

1.5.1 FFEL Repayment

Standard repayment plans are the "typical" repayment plans that borrowers will get if they fail to choose another option.[36] Standard plans carry the highest monthly payments and borrowers generally pay the same amount for each installment period. The monthly amount may vary if there is a variable loan rate. Borrowers have at least five years, but not more than ten years to repay a FFEL loan with a standard plan.[37]

Graduated repayment plans are also available. Under these plans, payments start out low and increase every two years. As in the extended plan, discussed below, the repayment period will vary from twelve to thirty years, depending on the total amount borrowed.[38]

Graduated plans tend to work best for borrowers who are just starting out and are likely to see relatively quick increases in earnings over time. As with the standard plan, borrowers have at least five years, but not more than ten years to repay a FFEL loan with a graduated plan.[39]

Extended repayment plans are another option. These plans allow loan repayment to be extended over a period from generally twelve to thirty years, depending on the total amount borrowed. Borrowers still pay a fixed amount each month of at least $50, but monthly payments usually will be less than under the standard repayment plan. Borrowers will also usually pay more interest because the repayment period is longer.[40]

Most relevant to low-income client are the Income Sensitive Repayment Plans (ISRP).[41] With these plans, the amount of the borrower's installment payment is adjusted annually based on the borrower's expected total monthly gross income.

Borrowers are required to submit income information to the lender in order to establish an Income Sensitive Repayment Plan. If the documentation shows that the borrower will be unable to repay the loan within the maximum ten

year repayment period, the lender is required to grant forbearance to the borrower for up to five years.[42]

The ISRP plans with FFELs are generally much less affordable than the Income Contingent Repayment Plan (ICRP) available for Direct Loans and discussed below. This is because monthly payments under an ISRP, unlike an ICRP, must cover at least accruing interest.[43]

FFEL borrowers can switch plans, but in general, the maximum repayment period for the new plan must be longer than the amount of time the loans have already been in repayment.[44] Lenders must permit borrowers to change plans at least once a year, although they may do so more frequently at their discretion.[45]

1.5.2 Federal Direct Loan Repayment

The Direct Loan provisions for standard plans are similar to those for FFEL loans.[46] Borrowers are required to pay loans back on these plans within ten years. As with FFELS, the ten-year period is tolled during the time of any deferments or forbearances. The Direct Loan regulations require that a borrower pay a minimum of $50 per month under the standard repayment plan.[47]

For Direct Loan graduated and extended plans, the regulations set out specific repayment periods based on the amount of the loans. For example, borrowers with loan amounts less than $10,000 must complete repayment under a graduated or extended plan within twelve years.[48] The Direct Loan program also allows for alternative payment plans to accommodate a borrower's "exceptional circumstances."[49]

The more generous provisions of the Direct Loan Income Contingent Repayment Plan (ICRP) are particularly useful for low-income borrowers.[50] As with a FFEL Income Sensitive Plan, the ICRP allows borrowers to submit income documentation that is used to derive an affordable monthly payment. Unlike an ISRP, monthly payments under an ICRP do not need to cover monthly accruing interest. Monthly payments can be very low, even zero for borrowers with households incomes below the poverty level.[51]

Direct Loan borrowers may change repayment plans at any time after the loan has entered repayment.[52] However, borrowers with ICRPs cannot change plans unless they were

---

36 34 C.F.R. § 682.209(a)(7)(vi).

37 34 C.F.R. § 682.209(a)(8)(i).

38 *Id.*

39 34 C.F.R. § 682.209(a)(8)(i).

40 34 C.F.R. § 682.209(a)(7)(ix), (a)(8)(i).

41 34 C.F.R. § 682.209(a)(7)(viii).

42 34 C.F.R. § 682.209(a)(7)(viii)(D).

43 34 C.F.R. § 682.209(a)(7)(iv). ISRP and ICRP payments plans are discussed in detail at § 8.2.3.1, *infra*.

44 34 C.F.R. § 682.209(a)(7)(x).

45 34 C.F.R. § 682.209(a)(7)(x).

46 34 C.F.R. § 685.208.

47 34 C.F.R. § 685.208(b)(3).

48 34 C.F.R. § 685.208(e).

49 34 C.F.R. § 685.208(g).

50 34 C.F.R. §§ 685.208(f), 685.209.

51 *See* § 8.2.2.5, *infra*.

52 34 C.F.R. § 685.210(b).

required to and made payments under the plan in each of the prior three months or were not required to make payments but made three reasonable and affordable payments in the prior three months.[53]

1.5.3 Perkins Loan Repayment

Perkins repayment plans vary from FFELs and Direct Loans in several significant ways. The regulations set out minimum monthly repayment rates. For example, the rate is $30 for an NDSL loan or a Perkins Loan made before October 1, 1992 and $40 after that date.[54] Schools are allowed to extend the repayment period due to a borrower's prolonged illness or unemployment.[55] This extension can be up to an additional ten years if the borrower qualifies as a low-income individual.[56] Interest continues to accrue during any extension of a repayment period.

1.5.4 Interest Rates

The interest rates for FFELs, Direct Loans, and Perkins Loans are limited by federal regulations.[57] There are separate regulations for consolidation loan interest rates.[58] Each program has various repayment incentives that allow lenders to reduce interest rates for borrowers who make payments electronically and in other circumstances.[59]

1.6 Determining What Type of Loan a Client Has

1.6.1 National Student Loan Data System

The National Student Loan Data System (NSLDS), is the DOE's central database for student aid. It receives data from schools, agencies that guaranty loans, the Direct Loan program, the Pell Grant program, and other United States Department of Education programs. This information is available on the Internet at www.nslds.ed.gov.

Borrowers can use NSLDS to make inquiries about loans and grants using a personal identification number (PIN).[60]

---

53 34 C.F.R. § 685.210(b).
54 34 C.F.R. § 674.33(b)(6)(ii), (iii).
55 34 C.F.R. § 674.33(c).
56 34 C.F.R. § 674.33(c)(2).
57 34 C.F.R. §§ 682.202(a) (FFEL), 685.202(a) (Direct Loans), 674.31 (Perkins). Interest rates dropped to the lowest in decades in 2002. The rate was 4.06% effective July 1, 2002.
58 *See* Ch. 5, *infra*; 34 C.F.R. §§ 682.202(a)(4) (FFEL), 685.202(a)(3) (Direct Loans).
59 *See, e.g.*, 34 C.F.R. §§ 685.211(b), 674.33(f) (Perkins program allows reduction of interest rates for borrowers who make 48 consecutive monthly repayments and reductions on balances for loans paid before end of repayment period).
60 PINs can be ordered on-line but will be delivered by mail.

The site displays information on loan and/or grant amounts, outstanding balances, loan statuses, and disbursements.

Borrowers can also call the Federal Student Aid Information Center, 1-800-4-FED-AID, TDD 1-800-730-8913. The Center's counselors can help borrowers figure out what types of loans they have over the phone. There is a Direct Loan service center specifically for Direct Loan borrowers. Borrowers should call 1-800-848-0979 (1-800-557-7392 for Direct Consolidation Loans). The collection process, including the major collection players, is discussed in more detail in Chapter 4, *infra*.

1.7 Checklist for Handling Student Loan Issues

1.7.1 Loan Cancellation

Regardless of whether the client is in default, loan cancellation is the first option to consider. Cancellation provides the most complete remedy for student loan borrowers. Advocates should always review all of the various cancellation remedies for all clients. Clients may be eligible for more than one type of cancellation, but they can recover only once.

If eligible, the client's loan will not only be canceled, but also all payments made to date including monies seized will be returned and the client's credit report should be cleared. Cancellation options are discussed in detail in Chapter 6, *infra*.

Before reviewing cancellation options, it is important to know what type of loan the client has. Cancellation and other rights vary depending on the type of loan.[61] Some clients will have more than one type of loan. The next step is to determine when the loan was originated. Again, borrower rights differ depending on the date of origination.

In summary, before reviewing the cancellation and repayment options below, advocates should first determine:

- The type of loan;
- Loan origination date;
- Whether the client is already in default (if not in default, deferment should also be considered, particularly while the cancellation application is pending);
- Whether collection has begun (if so, what are the time deadlines for responding to the collection action? See Chapters 5 (defenses to tax refund intercepts, wage garnishments, and federal benefits offsets), 9 (defenses to collection lawsuits), 4 (possible fair debt violations), *infra*.); and
- The client's goals and financial situation.

---

61 *See* § 1.6, *supra*.

After considering these issues, advocates should determine whether the client is eligible for loan cancellation. The main cancellation programs are:

(1) Closed school. The closed school cancellation applies to FFELs, federal Direct Loans, and Perkins Loans (including NDSLs) received at least in part on or after January 1, 1986.[62] *See* § 6.2, *infra*.

(2) False Certification. Borrowers are entitled to a loan cancellation if they received at least part of a FFEL or Direct Loan after January 1, 1986 and if their eligibility to borrow was falsely certified by the school.[63] The cancellation does not apply to Perkins Loans, but students should be able to raise the school's misconduct as a defense to loan repayment because the school is the original lender.[64]

The Department recognizes only three bases for a false certification discharge:

- The school falsifies a non-high school graduate's ability to benefit from the program; or
- The school enrolls a student unable to meet minimum state employment requirements for the job for which the student is being trained; or
- The school forges or alters the student loan note or check endorsements. *See* § 6.3, *infra*.

(3) Disability cancellation. The borrower's permanent and total disability is grounds for a student loan discharge.[65] *See* § 6.6, *infra*.

(4) Death. The borrower's death is a defense to collection actions on Stafford, SLS, Perkins, and Federal Direct Loans.[66] The death of both parents (assuming both parents are obligated) or the death of the student discharges PLUS loans.[67] *See* § 6.7, *infra*.

(5) Bankruptcy. Some student loans may be discharged in bankruptcy. *See* Chapter 7, *infra*.

(6) Unpaid Refund. In November 1999, the Department of Education finalized regulations that provide an important new basis to discharge a student loan: that the school failed to make an owed refund to the student.[68] *See* § 6.4, *infra*. State tuition recovery funds should also be considered.[69]

Obtaining a loan cancellation can take a long time. In the meantime, advocates should request administrative forbearances to stop the collection efforts pending a decision.[70] If the client wants to go back to school before a decision on the cancellation is made, advocates should consider reviewing the repayment, loan rehabilitation, and consolidation options discussed in Chapter 8, *infra* and summarized below. It may best serve the client's goals to move forward with repayment, at least temporarily, while the cancellation application is pending.

1.7.2 Steps to Take If Cancellation Is Not Available

The next step depends on whether the client is already in default. Borrowers who are not yet in default are eligible for deferments. The various deferment programs detailed in Chapter 2, *infra* should be reviewed at this point. Forbearance, available both before and after default, should also be considered. Both deferment and forbearance options are discussed in Chapter 2.

If the client is not eligible for a deferment or is already in default, the next step depends on whether collection has begun, and if so, what type of collection. This is important because many defenses can be raised specifically in response to certain types of collection such as tax refund intercepts or administrative wage garnishments. Timing for these challenges is critical. At this point, advocates should be sure to check all notices and determine whether it is still possible to file a response to a collection action.

For tax refund intercepts, borrowers must make a written request to inspect a loan file within twenty days of the notice of offset.[71] To obtain a review, the borrower must file a request for review at the address specified in the notice by the *later* of sixty-five days after the date of the notice or fifteen days after the borrower's loan file is provided, if requested.[72] A borrower can request a later hearing, but only a timely hearing request will stop the intercept pending the hearing. These issues are discussed in § 5.2, *infra*.

Administrative wage garnishments cannot go forward if the borrower requests a hearing within fifteen days of the borrower's receipt of the garnishment notice (receipt is presumed within five days of mailing of the notice).[73] Administrative wage garnishment is discussed in detail at § 5.3, *infra*.

Clients may also have notices of federal benefits offsets. A key issue in these cases is whether the client's loan is at least ten years old. Borrower rights to challenge offsets, including a possible ten year limit on collection, are discussed at § 5.4, *infra*.

---

62 34 C.F.R. §§ 682.402(d) (FFEL), 685.214 (Direct Loans), 674.33(g) (Perkins).

63 34 C.F.R. §§ 682.402(e) (FFEL), 685.215 (Direct Loans).

64 *See* § 9.5.2.1, *infra*.

65 34 C.F.R. §§ 682.402(c) (FFEL), 685.213 (Direct Loans), 674.61 (Perkins). For a PLUS loan where both parents are obligated on the loan, the disability of only one parent does not discharge the loan. 34 C.F.R. § 682.402(a)(2). *See* § 6.6.1, *infra*.

66 34 C.F.R. §§ 674.61 (Perkins), 682.402 (FFEL), 685.212(a) (Direct Loans).

67 34 C.F.R. § 682.402(b)(1). Assuming the parents are co-borrowers, the death of only one of the two obligated parents does not discharge a PLUS loan. 34 C.F.R. § 682.402(a)(2). *See* § 6.7, *infra*.

68 34 C.F.R. §§ 682.402(l) (FFEL), 685.216 (Direct Loans).

69 *See* § 9.6.1, *infra*.

---

70 Forbearances are discussed at Ch. 2, *infra*.

71 34 C.F.R. § 30.33(c)(1).

72 34 C.F.R. § 30.33(d).

73 34 C.F.R. § 682.410(b)(9)(10)(i)(K).

The response date for lawsuits can be found on the summons. Possible defenses to student loan collection lawsuits are discussed in Chapter 9, *infra*.

Throughout this analysis, it is important to speak with clients about their goals. Do they want to go back to school? In that case, getting out of default as soon as possible is critical. If instead, they are primarily interested in stopping the collection efforts, it is then important to focus on challenging collection efforts as discussed in Chapters 5 and 9, *infra*. In addition possible fair debt collection violations, discussed in Chapter 4, *infra* should also be considered.

It is important to get a sense of the client's overall budget and in particular to determine whether the client is judgment proof. A client is judgment proof if she does not have any money or property that can legally be taken to pay the debt.

It is difficult, although not impossible, for a client to be completely protected from government student loan collection. Clients without significant federal benefits, without wages, without tax refunds, and with no other significant assets will most likely be safe from student loan collection, at least temporarily. However, as discussed in Chapter 3, *infra*, the elimination of a statute of limitations for student loan collections means that the debt may come back to haunt the client in the future.

1.7.3 Repayment Options

If a client is not eligible for a cancellation or cannot wait for a decision to get out of default, the next step is to consider the various repayment options. The primary strategies are:

- Loan Consolidation. Particularly for low-income clients, a Direct Loan consolidation with an Income Contingent Repayment Plan is an excellent strategy to get out of default and pay only minimal payments (or even 0) each month. *See* § 8.2, *infra*.
- Reasonable and Affordable Payment Plans. Borrowers can renew eligibility by setting up reasonable and affordable payment plans. Six consecutive, on-time monthly payments will renew eligibility. However, this option is a one-time deal. If a client sets up a reasonable and affordable plan and stops making payments, she will not be eligible again for a reasonable and affordable plan. *See* § 8.3, *infra*.
- Loan Rehabilitation. After making twelve reasonable and affordable monthly payments, a borrower can get out of default by rehabilitating a loan. *See* § 8.4, *infra*.

Once out of default, clients are not only eligible to return to school, but also for the deferment programs discussed in Chapter 2, *infra*.

1.8 Assistance Within the Department of Education

1.8.1 Student Loan Ombudsman

An ombudsman office has been established in the Department of Education specifically to help borrowers with difficult problems. The student loan ombudsman has a website and borrowers can submit problems on-line at www.sfahelp.ed.gov. The toll-free phone number is 877-557-2575.

The ombudsman's stated goal is to facilitate and provide creative options for borrowers needing assistance with federal loans, Direct, FFEL, SLS and Perkins Loans. The ombudsman will research problems and determine if borrowers have been treated fairly. They will also contact other offices within DOE, private lenders, and guaranty agencies to assist borrowers. However, the Ombudsman office strongly admonishes that they serve as a last resource, to be consulted only after a borrower has tried to resolve a problem on her own.

1.8.2 Additional Resources

The Department of Education's website is extensive and contains a great deal of useful information. In particular, the Direct Loan page allows borrowers to calculate monthly payments under the various repayment plans, including Income Contingent Repayment Plans. The site also contains useful addresses and phone numbers within the Department as well as collection agency and guaranty agency information.

The Department of Education also publishes a very useful "Student Guide" with information on all of the various student financial aid programs available through DOE. The Guide is updated each year and is available on-line or by calling the Federal Student Aid Information Center at 1-800-4-FED-AID.[74]

---

74 Also available at www.ed.gov/prog_info/SFA/StudentGuide and on the companion CD-Rom.

Chapter 2

Deferments and Forbearances

2.1 Introduction

This chapter covers the primary deferment and forbearance programs for federally guaranteed student loans. Deferments allow eligible borrowers to postpone paying back their loans in certain circumstances. This is an extremely useful option particularly since, in most cases, interest does not accrue on the loan during the deferment period. However, only borrowers who have not yet defaulted on their loans are eligible for deferments.

Also discussed in this chapter are forbearances. Like deferments, forbearances allow borrowers to temporarily postpone repayment. They are less optimal than deferments because interest continues to accrue during the forbearance period. Unlike deferments, forbearances may be granted to borrowers already in default.

Forbearances can be used to help borrowers avoid default in the first place. Borrowers may be able to get forbearances to postpone payments during periods of financial difficulty. Administrative forbearances are also available for borrowers who are waiting for decisions on cancellations, consolidation loan applications, or other matters pending with the Department or guaranty agencies.

2.2 Deferments

2.2.1 Benefits of Deferment

Student loan borrowers are legally entitled to defer payments in certain situations. Deferment rights vary depending on the type of loan and when the loan obligation was incurred. For example, deferment rights are different for Federal Family Education Loans (FFELs) issued before July 1, 1993 than FFELs issued after that date. Perkins Loans also have different rights than FFELs.[1]

For all of these types of loans, the right to a deferment is an important one. For "subsidized" student loans (where the United States pays the interest while the student is enrolled in school), a deferment not only postpones when a student must make payments, but interest obligations do not accrue during the deferment period. Instead, the federal government pays the interest portion of the loan and the student's payments on the principal are postponed until after the deferment expires.

For unsubsidized loans, where borrowers are responsible for interest accrued while they are in school, borrowers remain obligated for accrued interest during the deferment period. In this situation, lenders are encouraged to forbear and capitalize interest payments until after the deferment period.[2]

Deferments are designed to help borrowers who are financially unable to make loan payments, and thus are useful for borrowers who are unemployed or back in school. If a loan is being deferred, the loan is not in default, and the borrower will not be subject to debt collection attempts, lawsuits, tax intercepts, and will be eligible for additional educational assistance.

2.2.2 Borrower's Default Limits Eligibility for Deferment

An important limitation to the usefulness of the borrower's deferment right is that it exists only when borrowers are "delinquent" on the loan obligation, not when they are in "default."[3] If a borrower cannot qualify for a deferment because the loan is in default, the borrower can re-establish eligibility for a deferment by consolidating the loan into a new loan, or by rehabilitating the defaulted loan after twelve monthly payments.[4] The borrower can then apply for a deferment under the new loan.[5]

As a result, the borrower should first argue that a loan is only delinquent, and not technically in default. Default occurs where the Secretary or guarantee agency finds it reasonable to conclude that the borrower no longer intends to honor the obligation to repay *and* when the failure to pay persists for 270 days.[6]

---

1 For more information on how to figure out what kind of a loan a borrower has, see § 1.6, *supra*.

2 34 C.F.R. § 682.211(a)(4).

3 34 C.F.R. § 682.210(a)(7).

4 Consolidation and rehabilitation are discussed in §§ 8.2 (consolidation), 8.4 (rehabilitation), *infra*.

5 The borrower may also be eligible if she makes acceptable payments to the lender before the guaranty agency pays off a default claim. 34 C.F.R. § 682.210(a)(8).

6 34 C.F.R. § 682.200(b). Effective October 7, 1998, the definition of default was changed from the previous 180 days to 270 days

The 270-day period is based on the number of days the borrower has been delinquent until the onset of the *condition* justifying the deferment.[7] For example, if the borrower had been delinquent since January 1, and applied for a deferment on December 1, the 270 days would *not* have run if the condition justifying the deferment (e.g., economic hardship) occurred in June. It is the onset date of the condition and not the application date that is critical.

Previously, there was an important limitation to this rule for FFEL loans. Prior to 2000 amendments, a deferment period could begin no earlier than six months before the date the lender received the deferment application and relevant paperwork. The amendments eliminated this requirement, with a few exceptions.[8] First, the limit continues to apply to deferments for periods prior to July 1, 2001.[9] Second, the six-month limit continues to apply to unemployment deferments.[10] Thus, an initial unemployment deferment cannot begin more than six months before the date the holder receives a request for deferment and required documentation.[11]

2.2.3 Grounds for Seeking a Deferment

2.2.3.1 General

The various student loan programs have different rules about when the borrower qualifies for a deferment. Rules differ not only by the type of loan (e.g., Perkins or FFEL), but also by when the loan was extended. In particular, "economic hardship," an important deferment ground for low-income borrowers, is only available for Direct Loans or FFELs disbursed after July 1, 1993, and then only if the borrower had no outstanding FFEL balance on the date the borrower obtained the new loan.[12] Borrowers with earlier FFELs can usually qualify for this economic hardship deferment by consolidating the earlier FFEL into a new consolidation loan and then applying for a deferment based on the post-July 1, 1993 deferment rules.[13] Consolidation loans are discussed in detail in Chapter 8, *infra*.

Most deferments carry maximum time limits and each deferment has recertification requirements, generally every six months, for the borrower to remain eligible.[14]

The Department takes the position that the maximum length for deferments applies to the borrower, and not just to the specific loan. Consequently, borrowers may not receive more than the maximum deferment time under any given deferment category regardless of how many different types of loans they have or how much time has elapsed since they last sought a deferment.[15] For example, if a borrower is entitled to a two-year unemployment deferment, and uses that time up, the borrower may not later take out new loans and seek an additional unemployment deferment on those new loans.

2.2.3.2 Grounds for Direct Loans, FFELs and Consolidation Loans Extended After July 1, 1999

2.2.3.2.1 *Available deferments*

One set of criteria for deferment applies to Direct Loans, FFELs and most consolidation loans first disbursed on or after July 1, 1993. The available deferments for these loans are:[16]

- Student deferments for at least half-time study;[17]
- Graduate fellowship deferments;[18]
- Rehabilitation training program deferment;[19]
- Unemployment deferment not to exceed three years;[20]
- Economic hardship deferment, granted one year at a

---

past due for loans repayable in monthly installments. The period is now 330 days (previously 240) for loans repayable less frequently than in monthly installments. 34 C.F.R. § 682.200(b) (FFEL) and 34 C.F.R. § 685.102(b) (Direct loans).

7 34 C.F.R. §§ 682.210(a)(5), 682.210(a)(7).

8 65 Fed. Reg. 65, 616 (Nov. 1, 2000), *amending* 34 C.F.R. § 682.210(a)(5) (FFEL), 34 C.F.R. § 685.204 (Direct Loans).

9 *Id.*

10 34 C.F.R. § 682.210(a)(5).

11 34 C.F.R. § 682.210(a)(5). *See* § 2.2.3.2.3, *infra*.

12 34 C.F.R. § 682.210(s)(1) (FFEL); 34 C.F.R. § 685.204 (Direct Loans).

13 The "new" deferment rules apply to consolidation loans taken out after July 1, 1993 if the borrower has no other outstanding FFEL loans when the consolidation was made. 34 C.F.R. § 682.210(s)(1).

14 Effective July 1, 2001, the Department approved new deferment application forms for most deferment programs. For copies of the new forms, see Dear Colleague Letter G-01-331 (May 2001). The forms are also available on the Department of Education's web site, www.ed.gov and on this volume's companion CD-Rom. The FFEL economic hardship deferment form is also reprinted at Appx. D, *infra*.

15 34 C.F.R. § 682.210(a)(1)(ii).

16 In addition to the deferments listed here, the 1998 Higher Education Act amendments require the Secretary of Education to consult with the Secretary of Veterans Affairs to establish a deferment for disabled veterans. Pub. L. No. 105-244, § 490F (Oct. 7, 1998).

17 34 C.F.R. §§ 682.210(s)(2) (FFELs), 685.204(b)(1)(i)(A) (Direct Loans). The rules for this deferment are set out at 34 C.F.R. § 682.210(c).

18 34 C.F.R. §§ 682.210(s)(3) (FFELs), 685.204(b)(1)(i)(B) (Direct Loans). The rules for this deferment are set out at 34 C.F.R. § 682.210(d).

19 34 C.F.R. §§ 682.210(s)(4) (FFELs), 685.204(b)(1)(i)(C) (Direct Loans). The rules for this deferment are set out at 34 C.F.R. § 682.210(e).

20 34 C.F.R. §§ 682.210(s)(5) (FFELs), 685.204(b)(2)(i) (Direct Loans). The rules for this deferment are set out at 34 C.F.R. § 682.210(h). *See* § 2.2.3.2.3, *infra*.

time for a maximum of three years.[21]

In addition, in fall 2001, the Department issued guidance regarding deferments for borrowers called to active duty as a result of the September 11 terrorist attacks. These new requirements include:

- If a borrower's loans are in an in-school status, in-school deferment status, or in a grace period when the borrower is ordered to active duty or reassigned, the lender is required to maintain the loans in that status during the period of the borrower's active duty service or reassignment.[22] The status must also be maintained during the time necessary for the borrower to resume enrollment in the next available regular enrollment period if the borrower wishes to return to school.[23] This maintenance of loan status may not exceed a total of three years.[24]

2.2.3.2.2 Economic hardship deferment

The economic hardship deferment is the most complicated and usually the most important for low-income borrowers. The first three qualification categories are "automatic" as long as the borrower can provide supporting documentation. These three categories are:

1. Previous qualification for economic hardship deferment under another federal loan program.[25]
2. Receipt of federal or state public assistance benefits.[26] This includes anyone receiving payments under a federal or state public assistance program, such as TANF, SSI, Food Stamps, or state general public assistance.[27]

3. Peace Corps. The borrower qualifies if she is serving as a Peace Corps volunteer.[28]

The other categories to qualify for an economic hardship deferment require additional calculations. Individuals qualify for this deferment if they can pass any one of three tests relating to income:

1. *Full-time workers making less than a stated income level.* An individual qualifies for an economic hardship deferment if she is working full-time and her earnings from her full-time job (not including other sources of income) do not exceed the greater of the minimum wage or the federal poverty level for a family of two.[29]
2. *Full-time workers with high student loan debt burdens.* A borrower working full-time also qualifies for a deferment if: (1) the "federal education debt burden" is at least 20% of the borrower's total monthly gross income *and* (2) the borrower's income subtracted from the "federal education debt burden" is less than 220% of either the minimum wage or federal poverty level for a family of two, whichever is greater.[30] The term "federal education debt burden" is a defined term that calculates the debt assuming that the loan will be paid out over ten years, regardless of the actual length of the borrower's repayment schedule or the actual monthly payment (if any) that would be owed during the requested economic hardship deferment period.[31]

For example, an individual qualifies for a deferment with an income of $25,000 if the "federal education debt burden" on an annual basis is $5000. The difference between the two ($20,000) is less than 220% of the poverty level for a family of two ($11,940).[32]

3. *Those not working full-time with high student loan debt burdens.* This test applies only to a borrower whose *total* monthly gross income from all sources does not exceed twice the minimum wage or twice the poverty level for a family of two (whichever is

---

21 34 C.F.R. §§ 682.210(s)(6) (FFELs), 685.204(b)(3)(i) (Direct Loans). The economic hardship category includes deferments for Peace Corps volunteers. 34 C.F.R. § 682.210(s)(vi). *See* § 2.2.3.2.2, *infra.*

22 Dear Colleague Letter GEN-01-13, "Recent Terrorist Attacks: Persons Affected by Military Mobilization" (Sept. 2001).

23 *Id.*

24 This same September 2001 guidance also required lenders to grant forbearances to loans that are in repayment (other than those in an in-school deferment status) for the expected period of the borrower's active duty service. The borrower is required to request this forbearance, but it must be granted upon request. See Department of Education, Dear Colleague Letter GEN-01-13 (Sept. 2001). Lenders are also required to cease collection activities against borrowers in default for the expected period of the borrower's military service through September 14, 2002. The Department may extend this period. It is best to consult the Department web site, www.ed.gov, for updated information.

25 34 C.F.R. §§ 682.210(s)(6)(i) (FFEL), 685.204(b)(3)(i) (Direct Loan). The Direct Loan economic hardship deferment regulations specifically refer to the requirements in the FFEL regulations. The standards are the same for both loan programs.

26 34 C.F.R. § 682.210(s)(6)(ii).

27 34 C.F.R. §§ 682.210(s)(6)(ii) (FFELs), 685.204(b)(3)(ii) (Direct Loans).

28 34 C.F.R. § 682.210(s)(6)(vi).

29 34 C.F.R. §§ 682.210(s)(6)(iii) (FFELs), 685.204(b)(3)(ii) (Direct Loans).

30 34 C.F.R. §§ 682.210(s)(6)(iv) (FFELs), 685.204(b)(3)(ii) (Direct Loans).

31 34 C.F.R. § 682.210(s)(6)(vii). During spring 2002 negotiated rulemaking sessions, the negotiators and the Department of Education agreed to amend the regulations so that borrowers will be required to provide evidence that would allow the lender to determine the actual monthly payment that would have been owed by the borrower during the deferment period. The new rules will add 34 C.F.R. § 682.210(s)(vii)(A), (B), (C). Similar changes are proposed for the Perkins program. If the loan had been scheduled to be repaid in ten years or less, lenders may use the actual payment amount. *See* 67 Fed. Reg. 51036 (Aug. 6, 2002).

32 $11,940 is the 2002 poverty guideline for a family living in the contiguous states and D.C. The latest HHS Poverty Guidelines are found at 67 Fed. Reg. 6931–6933 (Feb. 14, 2002). These guidelines are adjusted annually.

higher).[33] Eligibility is determined by deducting the "federal education debt burden"[34] from income. The individual qualifies for a deferment if that difference does not exceed the greater of the minimum wage or the poverty level for a family of two.

An individual who is unemployed or only occasionally employed part-time will qualify for this deferment as long as that individual does not have significant sources of other income. An economic hardship deferment is thus a viable option for those who are unemployed, but not eligible for the unemployment deferment because they are unable or not ready to seek employment.[35]

For example:

Borrower A is not working but is not eligible for unemployment benefits and is not seeking new employment. The first test to determine eligibility for an economic hardship deferment is whether her monthly income is less than two times the minimum wage or two times the poverty level for a family of two (whichever is higher). Borrower A receives a monthly SSDI payment of $800. Her annual income of $9600 is less than the 2002 annual poverty level of $11,940.

The next step is to subtract her debt burden (her monthly loan payment amount (assuming that she is on a ten year repayment plan)[36] from her monthly income. Borrower A has a ten year repayment plan requiring payments of $150/month. This leaves her with $650/month. This is less than the monthly minimum wage and less than the poverty level for a family of two. Therefore, Borrower A is eligible for an economic hardship deferment.

2.2.3.2.3 *Unemployment deferment*

There are two ways to qualify for an unemployment deferment: the simpler route is for a borrower to provide proof that she is eligible to receive unemployment benefits;[37] alternatively, the borrower must show that she is conscientiously searching for full-time employment (defined as at least thirty hours per week and expected to last at least three months). Borrowers may qualify for this deferment whether or not they have been previously employed.[38]

To get a deferment based on the conscientious search requirement, borrowers must provide a written certificate

describing their search for full-time employment during the preceding six months.[39] A borrower requesting an initial period of unemployment deferment is not required to describe this search. The initial period of deferment can be granted for a period of unemployment that begins up to six months before the lender receives the borrower's request, and can be granted for up to six months after that date.[40]

To continue an unemployment deferment beyond the initial period, the borrower must provide written certification describing the borrower's diligent search for full-time employment during the preceding six months.[41] The borrower must also affirm that she has registered with a public or private employment agency if one is located within a fifty mile radius of the borrower's permanent or temporary address.[42] The deferment form requires the borrower to provide the name, address, and telephone number of the employment agency.[43]

2.2.3.3 Grounds for FFEL Deferments Extended Before July 1, 1993

A different set of rules applies to those with FFELs extended before July 1, 1993. The grounds for deferment under these loans include: unemployment for up to two years; full-time student at a participating school;[44] active-duty status in the United States Armed Forces;[45] the receipt

---

33 34 C.F.R. §§ 682.210(s)(6)(v) (FFELs), 685.204(b)(3)(ii) (Direct Loans).

34 *See Full-time workers with high student loan debt burdens*, test number 2, *above*.

35 There are also special rules to simplify the economic hardship deferment process for Peace Corps volunteers. 34 C.F.R. §§ 682.210(s)(vi) (FFEL), 674.34(6) (Perkins Loans).

36 For a discussion of the proposed change to the 10-year repayment period reporting rules, see note 31, *supra*.

37 34 C.F.R. §§ 682.210(h)(1) (FFEL), 685.204(b)(2)(i),(ii) (Direct Loans). The Direct Loan regulations specifically refer to the standards in the FFEL deferment regulations.

38 34 C.F.R. § 682.210(h)(3)(i).

39 34 C.F.R. § 682.210(h)(2).

40 34 C.F.R. § 682.210(h)(2)(i).

41 34 C.F.R. § 682.210(h)(2)(i). During spring 2002 negotiated rulemaking sessions, negotiators and the Department agreed to change this provision to require for all requests beyond the initial request that borrowers certify that they have made at least six diligent attempts during the preceding six-month period to secure full-time employment. *See* 67 Fed. Reg. 51036 (Aug. 6, 2002).

42 34 C.F.R. § 682.210(h)(2)(iii). Under proposed rules agreed to at spring 2002 negotiated rulemaking sessions, borrowers will be allowed to provide an "equivalent" to written certification that they have registered with a public or private employment agency. The Secretary must approve this "equivalent" proof. The Department is leaving open the possibility that borrowers will have registered, for example, by phone or on-line and will have proof other than written proof of these registrations. *See* 67 Fed. Reg. 51036 (Aug. 6, 2002).

43 The most recent forms, attached to Department of Education Dear Colleague Letter G-01-331, are available on the Department of Education web site and on the companion CD-Rom to this manual.

44 A borrower whose loan was obtained on or after July 1, 1987 and who has no outstanding FFEL balance on that date may obtain an in-school deferment for half-time study if the borrower also received or will receive a Stafford or SLS loan for the period during which deferment is sought. 34 C.F.R. § 682.210(c)(iii).

45 34 C.F.R. § 682.210(i). Borrowers on active duty in the United States Armed Forces are eligible for this deferment. "Armed Forces" is defined as the Army, Navy, Air Force, Marine Corps, and the Coast Guard. 34 C.F.R. § 682.210(i)(2). Borrowers enlisted in the reserves may qualify for the military deferment

of or the scheduled receipt of service under a program designed to rehabilitate disabled individuals; temporary total disability for up to three years; the provision of nursing or similar services to a spouse who is temporarily totally disabled; parental leave; and mothers of pre-school children starting work at no more than one dollar above the minimum wage.[46] The regulations set out detailed standards as to when a student is eligible for a deferment based on these grounds, particularly for unemployment, rehabilitation, temporary total disability, and spouse's temporary total disability.[47] Maximum deferment periods vary for each type of deferment.[48] Some can last indefinitely so long as the qualifying conditions or circumstances still apply.

The temporary total disability deferment can be especially critical for borrowers with disabilities that are not sufficiently permanent or severe to meet the requirements for a disability discharge.[49] In fact, advocates have proposed that the Department reinstate this deferment now that it is taking such a restrictive stance toward disability discharge applicants. The Department to date has refused to consider this possibility. The temporary disability deferment is still available only for pre-1993 loans. Although this is an advantage for some borrowers with older loans, these borrowers are not entitled to economic hardship deferments.

2.2.3.4 Grounds for Perkins Loans Deferments

Borrowers are entitled to defer Perkins Loan principal payments with interest not accruing in certain situations. As with FFELs, the specific qualifying circumstances depend on when the loan was made. For Perkins Loans made after July 1, 1993, deferments are available based on a number of grounds, including:

- Qualifying in-school status;[50]
- Full-time teaching in certain schools and in Head Start;[51]
- Full-time service in law enforcement or as correction officers in certain circumstances;[52]

- Certain military service;[53]
- Certain volunteer service such as the Peace Corps;[54]
- Seeking but unable to find full-time employment for a period not to exceed three years;[55] and
- Qualifying economic hardship conditions for a period not to exceed three years.[56] The Perkins economic hardship requirements are similar to those for FFEL and Direct loans.[57]

The government is also making the same provisions for Perkins borrowers affected by the September 11 terrorist attacks as for FFEL and Direct Loan borrowers.[58]

There are different criteria for Perkins Loans made before July 1, 1993.[59] Borrowers with these older loans are not eligible for economic hardship or unemployment deferments, but are eligible for temporary disability deferments, among others.

2.3 Forbearances

2.3.1 General

The Department of Education encourages the granting of forbearances to prevent borrowers from defaulting on their loans or to permit borrowers in default to resume "honoring" their loan obligations. Forbearance involves a loan holder agreeing to a temporary stoppage of payments, an extension of time for making payments, or acceptance of smaller payments.[60]

Forbearance is not as helpful for a borrower as a deferment because interest will continue to accrue while the loan payments are reduced or postponed. Consequently, the size of the outstanding obligation may actually increase during a forbearance period. A borrower not yet in default can use a forbearance agreement to delay going into default. The 270-day period before a delinquency is transformed to a default does not include periods of time when payments are subject to forbearance.

Forbearance is available even if the borrower is in default.[61] Forbearances will not remove students from default status. They will, however, obtain a temporary halt to

---

only for service on a full-time basis that is expected to last for a period of at least one year in length. Borrowers enlisted in the National Guard qualify for this deferment only while they are on active-duty status as a member of the U.S. Army or Air Force Reserves and meet the other requirements of § 682.210(i). There are new guidelines for military personnel activated in response to the September 11 terrorist attacks (and beyond). *See* § 2.2.3.2.1, *supra.*

46 20 U.S.C. § 1077(a)(2)(c); 34 C.F.R. § 682.210(b), (c), (e), (f), (g), (h), (i), (o), (r).

47 *See* 34 C.F.R. § 682.210(e), (f), (g), (h).

48 34 C.F.R. § 682.210(b).

49 *See* § 6.6 (disability discharges), *infra.*

50 34 C.F.R. § 674.34(b)(1).

51 34 C.F.R. § 674.34(c).

52 *Id.*

---

53 *Id.*

54 *Id.*

55 34 C.F.R. § 674.34(d). The Perkins unemployment deferment does not have the same documentation requirements as FFEL and Direct Loans. However, Perkins holders will require borrowers to provide certification supporting their applications.

56 34 C.F.R. § 674.34(e).

57 *See* § 2.2.3.2.2, *supra.*

58 *See* § 2.2.3.2.1, *supra.*

59 34 C.F.R. § 674.35.

60 34 C.F.R. § 682.211(a)(1) (FFELs); 34 C.F.R. § 685.205(a) (Direct Loans); 34 C.F.R. § 674.33(d) (Perkins).

61 34 C.F.R. § 682.211(a)(1). For a description of Perkins forbearance provisions, see § 2.3.4, *infra.*

collection actions such as tax refund intercepts, collection contacts and garnishments during the forbearance period.

2.3.2 Discretionary Forbearances

The FFEL regulations make a distinction between discretionary and mandatory forbearances. The Direct Loan program does not make this distinction. If a Direct Loan borrower qualifies for forbearance, the regulations provide that the Secretary will grant forbearance, with no reference to discretion on the Secretary's part.[62] The grounds for forbearance vary between the two programs in some respects.

Both the FFEL and Direct Loan regulations provide for forbearances if borrowers are in poor health or have other personal problems that affect the ability of the borrower to make the scheduled payments.[63] Forbearance for these reasons is discretionary under FFEL regulations.[64] The forbearance is granted up to a year at a time, but there are no limits to the number of years this type of forbearance may be granted.[65]

Both FFEL and Direct Loan regulations provide for administrative forbearances for various reasons such as while the lender is resolving a change in the loan's status or pending the resolution of a closed school or false certification discharge application.[66] With a few limited exceptions such as local or national emergencies, the FFEL administrative forbearances are discretionary.[67]

Both programs provide for forbearances in a number of similar circumstances, including:

- A properly granted period of deferment for which the lender learns the borrower did not qualify;[68]
- The period for which payments are overdue at the beginning of an authorized deferment period;[69]
- The period beginning when the borrower entered re-

payment until the first payment due date was established;[70]
- The period prior to the borrower's filing of a bankruptcy petition;[71]
- A period (not to exceed sixty days if a FFEL loan) after the lender receives information indicating that the borrower has died or has become disabled and until the lender receives documentation of death or disability;[72]
- Periods necessary to determine eligibility for discharge due to closed school or false certification;[73]
- Periods not to exceed sixty days while the lender collects and processes documentation supporting the borrower's request for a deferment, forbearance, change in repayment plan, or consolidation loan.[74]

If two individuals are jointly liable for repayment of a PLUS loan or a consolidation loan, the lender may grant forbearance on repayment only if both individuals cannot make the scheduled payments based on the same or different conditions.[75]

2.3.3 Mandatory Forbearances

The FFEL program provides for mandatory forbearances, based on a statutory right.[76] This right to forbearance is available even if a student is in default.[77] To obtain mandatory forbearance, the borrower must request a forbearance from the holder of the loan and provide sufficient supporting documentation.[78] Under current regulations, requests for forbearance do not need to be in writing, but the forbearance terms themselves need to be agreed to in writing.[79] Proposed rules agreed to in 2002 Department of Education negotiated rulemaking sessions will eliminate the requirement that the borrower and lender must agree to the terms of the forbear-

---

62   34 C.F.R. § 685.205(a).

63   34 C.F.R. §§ 682.211(a)(2)(i) (FFEL), 685.205(a)(1) (Direct Loans).

64   34 C.F.R. § 682.211(a)(2)(i).

65   34 C.F.R. §§ 682.211(c) (FFEL), 685.205(c) (Direct Loans).

66   34 C.F.R. §§ 682.211(f) (FFEL), 685.205(b) (Direct Loans).

67   During spring 2002 negotiated rulemaking sessions, negotiators and the Department agreed to expand a lender's authority to grant administrative forbearances beyond natural disaster circumstances. The new rules would allow forbearances for a period not to exceed three months not only for borrowers affected by natural disasters, but also for borrowers affected by local or national emergencies or military mobilization. *See* 67 Fed. Reg. 51036 (Aug. 6, 2002), *adding* 34 C.F.R. § 682.211(f)(11).

68   34 C.F.R. §§ 682.211(f)(1), 685.205(b)(1).

69   34 C.F.R. §§ 682.211(f)(2) (FFELs), 685.205(b)(2) (Direct Loans).

70   34 C.F.R. §§ 682.211(f)(3) (FFELs), 685.205(b)(3) (Direct Loans).

71   34 C.F.R. §§ 682.211(f)(4) (FFELs), 685.202(b)(4) (Direct Loans).

72   34 C.F.R. §§ 682.211(f)(5) (FFELs), 685.202(b)(5) (Direct Loans). Once the lender or holder has received the borrower's completed application for a disability discharge, she is required to cease collection. 34 C.F.R. § 682.402(c)(2). *See* § 6.6 (disability discharges), *infra*.

73   34 C.F.R. §§ 682.211(f)(6) (FFELs), 685.202(b)(6) (Direct Loans). Only closed school and false certification discharges are mentioned as grounds for administrative forbearances under these sections. Although the granting of administrative forbearances while unpaid refund applications are pending is not specifically mentioned, advocates should still argue that they should be available. *See* Ch. 6 (cancellation rights), *infra*.

74   34 C.F.R. §§ 682.211(f)(9) (FFEL), 685.202(b)(9) (Direct Loans).

75   34 C.F.R. § 682.211(a)(3).

76   20 U.S.C. § 1078(b)(1)(V).

77   20 U.S.C. § 1078(c)(3).

78   34 C.F.R. § 682.211(i)(3).

79   34 C.F.R. § 682.211(b).

ance in writing. Where the agreement is oral, the proposed rules will require lenders to notify the borrower (or endorser) of the terms within thirty days of the agreement.[80]

Most relevant for low-income borrowers are mandatory administrative forbearances for up to five years in cases where the borrower will not be able to repay the loan within the maximum repayment term.[81] For example, FFEL Standard, Graduated, and Income Sensitive Plans all generally require that the loan be repaid in not more than ten years.[82] If the documentation shows that the borrower will be unable to repay the loan within the maximum ten-year repayment period, the lender is required to grant forbearance to the borrower for up to five years.[83]

In addition, FFEL and Direct Loan forbearances are mandatory in increments up to one year for periods that collectively do not exceed three years if the amount of the borrower's monthly student loan payments collectively are equal to or greater than twenty percent of the borrower's total monthly income.[84] Borrowers are required to submit documentation of income and other relevant information. Forbearances are also mandatory for teachers who are performing teaching service that would qualify them for teacher loan forgiveness.[85]

The Department also issued special forbearance guidance to assist borrowers called to active duty in response to the September 11 terrorist attacks (and aftermath) or those who lived in or worked in the New York City declared disaster area. This guidance required lenders to grant forbearances to borrowers whose loans are in repayment (other than those with in-school deferments) for the expected period of the borrower's active duty service, beginning on the first day of active duty, not to exceed one year. Borrowers must request

these forbearances, but lenders must grant them if requested. Forbearances beyond the initial period require supporting documentation and a written agreement with the borrower.[86] These same rules apply to Perkins borrowers.

The Department also required mandatory forbearances for borrowers who lived or worked in the New York City designated disaster area. This period of mandatory forbearance was effective from September 11, 2001 through January 31, 2002. To get relief beyond that period, borrowers are required to submit supporting documentation for forbearance, deferment, or other relief.[87]

2.3.4 Perkins Provisions

Forbearances must be granted for Perkins borrowers under the following circumstances:

1. If the amount of the borrower's loan payments (for all Title IV loans) are equal to or greater than 20% of the borrower's total monthly income;[88] or
2. The borrower qualifies for a forbearance due to poor health or other "acceptable reasons;"[89] or
3. The Secretary authorizes forbearances due to a national military mobilization or other national emergency.[90]

To qualify for the first category, a borrower is required to submit documentation of her most recent total monthly gross income and evidence of the amount of her monthly loan payments.[91]

---

80 *See* 67 Fed. Reg. 51036 (Aug. 6, 2002), *amending* 34 C.F.R. § 685.211(b), (c).

81 34 C.F.R. § 682.211(i)(5)(ii).

82 *See* § 1.5 (pre-default repayment plans), *supra.*

83 34 C.F.R. § 682.209(a)(7)(viii)(D).

84 34 C.F.R. §§ 682.211(h)(2)(i) (FFEL), 685.205(a)(5) (Direct Loans).

85 34 C.F.R. § 682.211(h)(2)(ii)(C). Partial teacher loan forgiveness is available for FFEL and Direct Loan borrowers. Full and partial forgiveness is available for Perkins borrowers. *See* § 6.8 (teacher loan forgiveness), *infra.* The teacher loan forgiveness forbearance form and forgiveness application was released as an attachment to Dear Colleague Letter G-01-333 (Nov. 2001).

86 Department of Education, Dear Colleague Letter GEN-01-13, "Recent Terrorist Attacks-Persons Affected by Military Mobilization" (Sept. 2001). Note that the Department may issue additional guidance to extend these periods or otherwise supplement this guidance. Additional guidance will be available on the Department's web site, www.ed.gov.

87 *Id.* In 2002, Congress has also considered allowing loan forgiveness for certain surviving family members of September 11 victims. At the time this manual was printed, Congress had not yet passed this legislation.

88 34 C.F.R. § 674.33(d)(5)(i).

89 34 C.F.R. § 674.33(d)(5)(ii).

90 34 C.F.R. § 674.33(d)(5)(iii).

91 34 C.F.R. § 674.33(d)(6).

Chapter 3   The Consequences of Default

3.1 Student Loan Collections

3.1.1 General

In recent years, the Department of Education has significantly increased both its efforts to lower student loan default rates and its efforts to collect defaulted student loans. In FY 2000, the government collected over $4 billion on defaulted loans though a variety of collection methods, including:

- $920 million by offsetting federal income tax refunds and other federal offsets;
- Nearly $107 million through wage garnishment of defaulters;
- Nearly $2 billion by consolidating defaulted loans; and
- Almost $1.5 billion through other collection tools, including third-party private collection agencies.[1]

In FY 2001, through tax intercepts, wage garnishment, litigation, and other collection tools, the government collected over $2.5 billion.[2]

The growth in student loan recoveries can be attributed in large part to legislative changes giving student loan collectors enhanced collection powers. These powerful student loan collection tools, combined with aggressive government enforcement, make it increasingly difficult for even the lowest-income borrowers to ignore student loan debt.

The increased collection power also came about because of tremendous increases in student loan default rates throughout the 1980s and early 1990s.[3] In addition to increased collection powers, Congress also set up a program to sanction schools with very high default rates. Under this program, the Department has the authority to terminate high default schools from the federal student aid programs.[4] A brief description of this default management program is also included in this chapter, at § 3.1.3, *infra*.

---

1   U.S. Department of Education, *National Student Loan Default Rate Lowest Ever*, Press Release (Oct. 2, 2000).
2   U.S. Department of Education, *Accountability for Results Works: College Loan Default Rates Continue to Decline*, Press Release (Sept. 19, 2001).
3   *See* § 3.1.3, *infra*.
4   20 U.S.C. § 1085.

3.1.2 Road Map to Collection Issues Covered in This Manual

The 1993 elimination of the statute of limitations for student loan collection was one of the first in a series of Congressional actions to crack down on student loan defaulters. The implications of this change are discussed in this chapter. Also covered are possible challenges in cases where the government is suing to collect very old loans.

Section 3.3 of this chapter addresses credit reporting issues. For many clients, negative credit reports are some of the most long-lasting and severe consequences of student loan defaults. Limitations for reporting this information as well as strategies for cleaning up credit reports are discussed in § 3.3, *infra* of this chapter. The chapter also covers the ways student loans are reported to the major credit bureaus.

Chapters 4 and 5 also deal specifically with student loan collection matters. The major players in student loan collection are discussed in Chapter 4. In addition, Chapter 4 covers collection fee issues and the applicability of federal and state debt collection laws to student loan collectors.

Chapter 5 focuses on student loan collection tactics that lead to seizures of money or assets. Specific topics include tax intercepts, wage garnishments, and Social Security and federal benefit offsets. These non-litigation collection tactics often present severe consequences for low-income borrowers.

Chapter 9 focuses on substantive defenses to government collection actions. Chapter 9 is most relevant when assisting clients who have already been sued in student loan collection actions. In particular, Chapter 9 discusses when lenders are subject to defenses the borrower might have against the school.

The severity of these collection tactics and the government's increased willingness to go after even the lowest-income clients makes it more important than ever for advocates and borrowers to understand the range of available options. Chapter 6 covers student loan discharges, the most complete remedies for borrowers. Chapter 7 discusses bankruptcy options and Chapter 8 addresses renewal of eligibility and repayment plans.

3.1.3 *Penalties Against Schools With High Default Rates*

3.1.3.1 General

Throughout the late 1980s and early 1990s, vocational school abuses led to tremendous increases in student loan default rates. The overall default rate peaked at 22.4% in fiscal year 1990.[5] This rate fell all the way to 5.6% in FY 1999.

The default rates for less than two year proprietary schools have historically been much higher than the rates for other types of schools. The rate for these schools peaked in FY 1990 at 41.2%. By FY 1999, this rate had declined to 10.9%.[6]

The government worked to curb growing default rates by expanding collection powers, as discussed throughout this manual, and by initiating a program to punish schools with high default rates. Under this sanctions program, the Department has the authority to terminate high default schools from the federal student aid programs.[7] Since the inception of the program in 1991, according to the Department, more than 1100 schools have lost student loan program eligibility.[8]

The Department calculates default rates for institutions and may initiate proceedings against any institution with a FFEL, Direct Loan, or weighted average rate that is more than 40% for any fiscal year.[9] The rates are gathered for specific groups of borrowers during specific time periods. Each group is called a "cohort." Schools with cohort default rates of 25% or more for three consecutive years face loss of eligibility in the loan and Federal Pell Grant programs.[10]

The sanctions program and appeals process is described briefly below.[11]

3.1.3.2 How School Default Rates Are Calculated

For schools with thirty borrowers or more, the cohort default rate is the percentage of a school's borrowers who enter repayment on most FFEL and/or Direct Loans during a fiscal year and default before the end of the following fiscal year.[12] FFEL and Direct PLUS Loans, FISLs, and Perkins Loans are not included in the calculation. Perkins Loans have separate cohort default rate calculations.[13]

Consolidation loans are not directly included in the cohort rate calculation, but a defaulted consolidation loan may cause a borrower to be included in the calculation if the default occurs within the cohort default period applicable to the underlying loan. If the borrower rehabilitates the loan during the relevant period, it will not count toward the school default rate.[14] For schools with twenty-nine or fewer borrowers entering repayment during a fiscal year, the cohort rate data includes borrowers entering repayment over a three-year period.[15]

3.1.3.3 School Appeals Process

Schools have the right to appeal disciplinary action. Over the years, Congress has steadily expanded the grounds for appeal. In particular, provisions in the 1998 HEA allowed schools to appeal based on mitigating circumstances.[16] The "mitigating circumstance" most relevant for low-income clients is the exemption from sanctions for schools serving primarily low-income students. This is known as the "economically disadvantaged appeal."[17]

There are two types of economically disadvantaged appeals. The first applies to non-degree granting schools and is based on the percentage of low-income students at the school ("low income rate") and employment placement rate.[18] These schools must show that the low-income rate and the school's placement rate (generally, the percentage of students who became employed in the occupation for which the school trained them) is 44% or more.[19]

The second, applying to degree granting schools, is based on low-income rate and program completion rate.[20] Degree

---

5 Information on default rates is available on the Department of Education's web site at www.ed.gov/offices/OSFAP/defaultmanagement/defaultrates.html.

6 *Id.*

7 20 U.S.C. § 1085.

8 U.S. Department of Education, *Accountability for Results Works: College Loan Default Rates Continue to Decline*, Press Release (Sept. 19, 2001).

9 34 C.F.R. § 668.187(a)(1).

10 34 C.F.R. § 668.187(a)(2). Historically black colleges or universities, tribally controlled community colleges or Navajo community colleges are not subject to loss of eligibly as long as they meet certain requirements such as submission of a default management plan. 20 U.S.C. § 1085(a)(5); 34 C.F.R. § 668.198.

11 For more information, see U.S. Department of Education, *Cohort Default Rate Guide* (2001), available on the Department's web site, www.ed.gov.

12 34 C.F.R. § 668.183(d). Currently, the default rate also includes borrowers who received a Direct Loan to attend a non-degree granting proprietary school who, during the default period in question, were in repayment for 360 days under the ICRP plan with payments that were less than $15/month and less than the interest accruing on the loan. 34 C.F.R. § 668.183(c)(1)(iii). This provision was eliminated in the 2002 negotiated rulemaking session. 67 Fed. Reg. 51036, 51045, 51046 (Aug. 6, 2002) (proposed rules).

13 34 C.F.R. § 674.5.

14 34 C.F.R. § 668.183(c)(2)(i). There are a number of other special circumstances related to these calculations. For more information, see U.S. Department of Education, *Cohort Default Rate Guide* (2001), available on the Department's web site, www.ed.gov.

15 34 C.F.R. § 668.183(a)(1).

16 20 U.S.C. § 1085(a)(4)–(6).

17 34 C.F.R. § 668.194.

18 34 C.F.R. § 668.194(b), (d).

19 *Id.*

20 34 C.F.R. § 668.194(b), (c).

granting schools must show that the school's low-income rate is two-thirds or more and the school's completion rate (generally, the percentage of students who completed their program) is 70% or more.[21]

The low-income rate is defined as the percentage of students who are eligible to receive a federal Pell grant of at least one-half the maximum award, or have an adjusted gross income that, if added to the student's parents income (unless the student is an independent student), or added to the spouse's income if the student is a married independent student, is less than the poverty level for the student's family size.[22]

In determining the placement rate, students are considered "placed" if they were employed in a job for which the school provided training on the date following one year after their last date of attendance, or employed for at least thirteen weeks between the date they first enrolled and the date that is more than one year after the last date of attendance in a job for which the school provided training, or entered active military duty.[23] A student is not considered successfully placed if the school is the employer. Schools can also appeal based on errors or inaccuracies in the calculation of the default rate.[24]

It is important for advocates representing low-income clients to understand the cohort default appeals process. Vocational schools, particularly those in low-income communities, rely almost exclusively on federal assistance to stay in business.[25] They are very aware of the need to stay below the cohort default triggers. As a result, they may push borrowers into certain repayment options (such as consolidation) that may not make sense for a particular borrower. They also may try to mischaracterize certain types of employment as related to the student's program of study at the school. At a minimum, understanding these incentives is likely to give advocates additional leverage when negotiating with schools on behalf of low-income clients. It is also a good idea to check on a current school's default rate for a client who is complaining of problems with a particular school. A high default rate is usually a tip-off that there are serious problems with the school.

3.2 Statute of Limitations as Defense to Collection Action

3.2.1 Statute of Limitations Generally Eliminated

The Higher Education Technical Amendments of 1991 (HEA) eliminated all statutes of limitations for any collection action by a school, guaranty agency, or the United States under a federal loan program.[26] These amendments also eliminated all limitation periods for tax intercepts, wage garnishments, and other collection efforts.[27]

The elimination of the statute of limitations is probably the single most important obstacle student loan borrowers face. Without a statute of limitations, there seems to be no end to what the government can and will do to collect student loans. This is particularly true as the government has become more aggressive in collecting student loans, often suing for loans fifteen or twenty years after the borrower left school.[28]

The provision eliminating the statute of limitations applies retroactively, so that loans whose limitations period had expired even before 1991 are revived.[29] Courts have repeatedly rejected borrowers' due process and equal protection challenges to this retroactive change, finding that statutes of limitations are legislatively created defenses and not constitutionally protected property rights.[30]

Although nearly all borrower challenges to date have been unsuccessful, there may still be some hope for borrowers. The possibility of applying the laches doctrine to student loan collection is discussed in § 3.2.2, *supra*.

---

21 *Id.*

22 34 C.F.R. § 668.194(b).

23 34 C.F.R. § 668.194(d).

24 34 C.F.R. § 668.192 (erroneous data appeals).

25 The main barrier keeping schools from relying exclusively on student assistance revenue is the 90/10 (previously 85/15) rule. 34 C.F.R. § 600.5. This rule mandates that proprietary schools may not have more than 90% of their revenue derived from Title IV Higher Education Act program funds. The calculations under this rule are complex, 34 C.F.R. § 600.5(d). Changes were proposed during the spring 2002 negotiated rulemaking sessions but no action was taken. *See* 67 Fed. Reg. 51718 (Aug. 8, 2002); § 9.1.3.2, *infra*.

---

26 Pub. Law No. 102-26 eliminated the statute of limitations set out in 20 U.S.C. § 1091a(a). While the elimination of the limitations period was to have sunset on November 15, 1992, the Higher Education Amendments of 1992 § 1551, codified at 20 U.S.C. § 1091a, extended indefinitely the abolition of the statute of limitations for student loan collections.

27 *Id.*

28 There is some question whether the elimination of the statute of limitations applies to Social Security offsets. *See* § 5.4.3.3, *infra*.

29 *See, e.g,* United States v. Phillips, 20 F.3d 1005 (9th Cir. 1994); United States v. Hodges, 999 F.2d 341 (8th Cir. 1993); United States v. McLaughlin, 7 F. Supp. 2d 90 (D. Mass. 1998).

30 *See, e.g.,* United States v. Phillips, 20 F.3d 1005 (9th Cir. 1994); United States v. Hodges, 999 F.2d 341 (8th Cir. 1993); United States v. Glockson, 998 F.2d 896 (11th Cir. 1993); United States v. Dwelley, 59 F. Supp. 2d 115 (D. Me. 1999); United States v. McLaughlin, 7 F. Supp. 2d 90 (D. Mass. 1998); Sibley v. U.S. Dep't of Education, 913 F. Supp. 1181 (N.D. Ill. 1995), *aff'd without opinion*, 111 F.3d 133 (7th Cir. 1997) (rep. in full at 1997 U.S. App. LEXIS 6395 (7th Cir. 1997)); United States v. Davis, 817 F. Supp. 926 (M.D. Ala. 1993).

3.2.2 Laches

3.2.2.1 Barriers to Applying the Laches Doctrine in Student Loan Cases

One possible defense to a collection action instituted many years after a default is that the equitable doctrine of laches applies. There are a number of barriers to applying this doctrine in the student loan context.

First, it is possible that Congress eliminated equitable defenses when it eliminated the statute of limitations in student loan collections.[31] This is unclear. The Congressional amendments eliminating the statue of limitations state that Congress' purpose was to ensure that obligations to repay loans would be enforced without regard to any "statutory, regulatory, or administrative limitations."[32] Equitable defenses are not specifically mentioned. However, a number of courts have found that Congress did in fact intend to eliminate equitable defenses as well.[33]

Even if a court were to decide that Congress did not eliminate equitable defenses when it eliminated the statute of limitations, a second barrier is that the laches doctrine is generally inapplicable against the United States on the grounds of sovereign immunity.[34] Many courts hold to this rule absent a clear manifestation of congressional intent to the contrary. In student loan cases, these courts have found not only that there was no congressional intent to the contrary, but rather that Congress' retroactive elimination of all statutes of limitations appears to indicate the opposite intent.[35]

3.2.2.2 Exceptions to the Rule Barring Laches

A few courts have been willing to look beyond the traditional rule that the doctrine of laches is inapplicable against the United States. In a 1985 non-student loan case, *S.E.R. Jobs for Progress, Inc.*, the court noted that some relaxation of the principle that laches is not a defense against the government may be developing and that exceptions to the rule might be approved in certain cases.[36]

To invoke the doctrine of laches, a borrower must show: (1) a delay in asserting a right or claim; (2) that the delay was not excusable; and (3) that there was undue prejudice to the party against whom the claim is asserted.[37] Most courts that have considered this issue in the student loan context have found that the facts did not justify invoking an exception to the rule.[38]

Courts have rejected borrowers' claims for a variety of reasons. At least one court relied on the fact that prior to 1991, the government was bound by a six-year statute of limitations for student loan collections.[39] This court speculated that prior to the complete elimination of the statute, it was possible that the government was not actively collecting certain loans because they were barred by the existing statute of limitations. This argument should be considerably weaker now that more time has passed since the elimination of the student loan statute of limitations.

Even if borrowers can successfully persuade a court that the government was neglectful, they must also show that they were materially prejudiced by the delay. Borrowers have argued that they were prejudiced by years of inactivity on their student loan accounts, which allowed interest, penalties, and collection fees to pile up. Unfortunately for borrowers, most courts that have examined these arguments have found a lack of prejudice to borrowers.[40]

In a bright note for borrowers, at least one court, in *United States v. Rhodes*, found the doctrine of laches applicable in a student loan case.[41] The loan in this case was due in 1974.

---

31 *See* § 3.2, *infra*.
32 20 U.S.C. § 1091a(a)(1).
33 *See, e.g.*, United States v. Lawrence, 276 F.3d 193 (5th Cir. 2001), *citing* Millard v. U.S. Funds, 66 F.3d 252 (9th Cir. 195); U.S. v. Phillips, 20 F.3d 1005, 1007 (9th Cir. 1994); U.S. v. Glockson, 998 F.2d 896, 897 (11th Cir. 1993); United States v. Hodges, 999 F.2d 341 (8th Cir. 1993). *See also* United States v. Robbins, 819 F. Supp. 672 (E.D. Mich. 1993). The *Robbins* court also speculated that in eliminating equitable defenses, Congress might been swayed by the fact that student loans are not collectable after a borrower's disability or death. The court noted that this may have been sufficient to assuage any Congressional fears of a completely open-ended student loan collection process. *Id.* at 676. This is ironic given the restrictive stance taken by the Department toward disability, and even death, cancellations in recent years. *See* §§ 6.6 (disability), 6.7 (death), *infra*.
34 United States v. Summerlin, 310 U.S. 414, 60 S. Ct. 1019, 84 L. Ed. 2d 1283 (1940).
35 *See, e.g.*, United States v. McLaughlin, 7 F. Supp. 2d 90 (D. Mass. 1998); United States v. Davis, 817 F. Supp. 926 (M.D. Ala. 1993); United States v. Robbins, 819 F. Supp. 672 (E.D. Mich. 1993).

36 S.E.R. Jobs for Progress, Inc., 759 F.2d 1, 7 (Fed. Cir. 1985).
37 U.S. v. Davis, 817 F. Supp. 926, 929 (M.D. Ala. 1993), *citing* Envtl. Defense Fund. v. Alexander, 614 F.2d 474, 477–78 (5th Cir.), *cert. denied*, 449 U.S. 919 (1980).
38 *See, e.g.*, United States v. Durbin, 64 F. Supp. 2d 635 (S.D. Tex. 1999); United States v. Smith, 862 F. Supp. 257 (D. Haw. 1994); United States v. Davis, 817 F. Supp. 926 (M.D. Ala. 1993); United States v. Robbins, 819 F. Supp. 672 (E.D. Mich. 1993).
39 United States v. Davis, 817 F. Supp. 926 (M.D. Ala. 1993).
40 United States v. Durbin, 64 F. Supp. 2d 635 (S.D. Tex. 1999) (laches requires the person to have relied on the failure to enforce the right. In student loan cases, borrowers do all of their relying shortly after signing the note. In the years the government has not collected the debt, the borrower has done nothing with the money or about the debt); United States v. Dwelley, 59 F. Supp. 2d 115 (D. Me. 1999); United States v. McLaughlin, 7 F. Supp. 2d 90 (D. Mass. 1998) (no special hardship demonstrated sufficient to relax the laches rule); United States v. Robbins, 819 F. Supp. 672 (E.D. Mich. 1993).
41 United States v. Rhodes, 788 F. Supp. 339 (E.D. Mich. 1992).

The government began collection seventeen years later. The court found this to be a "blatant and unreasonable delay on the part of the lender and its assignees."[42] The court found further prejudice to the borrower as the school had closed during the seventeen year period of inactivity and the borrower no longer had access to any school records. The borrower had long since destroyed his own records.

Other courts have tended to distinguish the facts in *Rhodes*. A key distinction noted by other courts is that the borrower in *Rhodes* was defending the collection action on the grounds that he had already paid back the loan in full. Courts have tended to find this more sympathetic than "shakier" defenses such as lack of consideration or breach of contract.[43] Courts have also found it notable that because of the government's delay in collecting the loan in *Rhodes*, records were no longer available from the school or from the borrower, making it impossible for either side to show whether the debt was still owed.[44]

3.2.2.3 FISL Collection

Another possible use of the doctrine of laches involves Department of Education attempts to collect Federally Insured Student Loans (FISLs). Congress' elimination of the statute of limitations for student loan collections has resulted in collection attempts for some very old FISL loans, going back to the early 1970s. Many students subjected to such loans will have a solid defense—that federal law at the time allowed students to raise school-related claims.[45]

3.3 Reporting of Student Defaults to Credit Bureaus

3.3.1 Notice Required Prior to Reporting of Defaults to Credit Bureaus

The HEA requires that guaranty agencies, lenders, and the Secretary of Education regularly exchange information with credit reporting agencies about outstanding student loans.[46] No later than sixty days after defaulting, the guaranty agency is required to report default claims to all national credit bureaus.[47] Before a default may be reported, the borrower must be given notice that, unless the borrower enters into a repayment agreement, the information will be disclosed to a reporting agency. The repayment agreement must be on terms satisfactory to the guaranty agency (or Department if the Department holds the loan).[48] On the other hand, if the borrower simultaneously requests a reasonable and affordable repayment agreement to renew eligibility, the repayment agreement should in fact be reasonable and affordable based on the borrower's total financial circumstances.[49]

The notice must also inform the borrower of other rights, including the right to inspect and copy agency records concerning the loan obligation, and the opportunity for an administrative review of the legal enforceability or past-due status of the loan obligation.[50] The notice in addition provides certain basic information about the loan, such as the guarantor has taken assignment of the loan, the name of the lender and school, the loan's outstanding principal and interest, the rate of interest, the authority for and manner of calculating costs on the loan, the default will be reported to credit bureaus, the grounds on which the borrower may object that the loan obligation is not a legally enforceable debt, and any appeal rights and right to judicial review.[51] Although agencies have sixty days to report the default claim, they have only forty-five days after paying the claim to send this notice.[52]

The guaranty agency must give the borrower at least sixty days after the required notice is sent to request the hearing.[53] The guaranty agency official conducting the hearing cannot be an individual charged with the collection of loan obligations or compensated on the basis of collections on loan obligations.[54] Guaranty agencies may use the same procedures for this notice and hearing that they do for tax refund interceptions.[55] Guaranty agencies apparently can report default information to the credit bureaus even while a request for a hearing is pending.[56]

3.3.2 What Is Reported to the Credit Bureaus

The regulations specify the information to be supplied. The guaranty agency supplies—for that borrower—the total amount of loans extended, the remaining balance, the date of default, information concerning collection of the loan, in-

---

42 *Id.* at 343.
43 *See, e.g.,* United States v. Davis, 817 F. Supp. 926, 930 (M.D. Ala. 1993) (distinguishing the borrower's defense of lack of consideration to the borrower in *Rhodes* who alleged he had already repaid the loan).
44 *Id.*
45 *See* § 9.5.2.3, *infra.* It may also be possible to argue that the statute of limitations should not be eliminated for FFELs that have lost their guaranteed status, since neither a school, guaranty agency or the United States will be collecting on such a loan. *See also* § 9.5.3.2, *infra.*
46 20 U.S.C. § 1080a.

47 34 C.F.R. § 410(b)(5).
48 34 C.F.R. § 682.410(b)(5)(ii)(D).
49 *See* § 8.3, *infra.*
50 34 C.F.R. § 682.410(b)(5)(ii)(B), (C).
51 34 C.F.R. § 682.410(b)(5)(vi).
52 34 C.F.R. § 682.410(b)(6)(v). *See also* § 4.1.2, *infra.*
53 34 C.F.R. § 682.410(b)(5)(iv)(B).
54 34 C.F.R. § 682.410(b)(5)(v).
55 34 C.F.R. § 682.410(b)(5)(iii).
56 34 C.F.R. § 682.410(b)(5)(iv)(A).

cluding the repayment status of the loan, changes and corrections based on information after the initial report, and the date the loan is fully repaid or discharged by reason of death, bankruptcy, or disability.[57]

Schools that are holding loans (particularly true in Perkins Loans cases) are required to report any updated information to the original credit bureau to which it reported the account.[58] A March 1999 Federal Trade Commission staff letter clarified that pursuant to the Fair Credit Reporting Act, schools must report information to the original credit bureau even if the school no longer has a contractual relationship with that bureau.[59]

A defaulted student loan will be listed as a current debt that is in default. The default will also be listed in the historical section of the report, specifying the length of the default. If the borrower repays the debt in full, the debt will no longer be listed as a current debt in default, but the debt will still be listed on the report (for up to seven years) as a debt that was at one time in default. Perkins Loan defaults, however, can now be reported indefinitely.[60]

Because of the unique treatment often required for student loans, some standardized ways of furnishing information to consumer reporting agencies have been established. Below is a brief description of how student loan information is reported to the credit bureaus using the Metro 2 reporting format. Metro 2 is a software program used by student loan creditors (and other creditors) to provide information about consumer accounts to consumer reporting agencies.[61]

No distinction is made in Metro 2 between different types of student loans; they are all reported as education loans. A student loan may be reported in good status when payments are being made and also when payments are deferred with a future payment obligation. Deferred payment loans are further distinguished between those where repayment has never (yet) been made and those where the account was previously being repaid. When payments are deferred, the start date for making payments should be included in a specific segment of the program (called the K-4 segment) for specialized payments.

Student loans which are disbursed over a period of time are treated as a single account. The date opened is the date of the first disbursement, but the original loan amount, balance, and scheduled payment amounts increase appropriately as disbursements are made. If the loans are truly multiple loans, then each one is treated as a separate account. If multiple loans are consolidated, it is considered a new loan initially in good standing. The consolidated loans

should be recorded as paid or closed with zero balances, although a payment rating will reveal accounts which were not in good standing.

Status code 88 cases are those which have been referred to the Department of Education for payment of the insured balance on the loan. If the claim is denied, the lender or servicer must delete the account and furnish new information about the debt, using the original date opened, status, and other attributes. As is often the case, potential errors may result in the same student loan debt being reported twice.

Student loans can be cancelled for a variety of reasons, as discussed throughout this manual.[62] If the loan is cancelled due to a school closing, it should be deleted.[63] Similarly, in a false certification case, the loan report should also be deleted.[64] Cancellation for student disability may be reported one of two ways. If the loan never reached the repayment period, it too should be deleted.[65] However, if repayments had begun, the loan should be designated as paid or closed, and the balance or amount due recorded as zero. Teacher forgiveness is treated in the same manner.[66]

Student loans, like other debts, may be sold or transferred to others for collection. In general, the Metro 2 system relies upon the transferring creditor to delete the accounts from agency files and the new creditor or servicing agent to begin furnishing information about the account. The new furnisher does not start with a new open date, payment history, or status or date of first delinquency, but should retain prior information as furnished earlier on the account. A servicer, one who does not itself hold the note, must also continue to use the identification number of the holder. Mistakes when accounts are transferred can result in false or misleading information in consumer reports.[67]

If a student loan is transferred to a student loan guaranty agency, the agency is supposed to record the loan as seriously past due. If the consumer is nonetheless making payments, the debt is still coded as seriously past due but the balance due should decline. A code also exists for accounts paid off by the government or insurer, or forgiven because the student has become totally and permanently disabled. If the guaranty agency itself transfers the account to a debt collection agency or the United States government, it should use a code (DA) to delete the account from the records reported to the consumer reporting agencies. The collection agency or the government will then include the debt in its own Metro 2 submissions to the reporting agencies.

---

57 34 C.F.R. § 682.410(b)(5)(i).

58 34 C.F.R. § 674.45(b)(1).

59 Staff Letter from David Medine to Lee S. Harris, U.S. Department of Education, Clearinghouse No. 52,490 (Mar. 22, 1999).

60 *See* § 3.3.3, *infra.*

61 *See generally* National Consumer Law Center, Fair Credit Reporting (5th ed. 2002).

62 *See* Ch. 6 (loan cancellations), *infra.*

63 *See* § 6.2 (closed school discharges), *infra.*

64 *See* § 6.3 (false certification discharges), *infra.*

65 *See* § 6.6 (disability discharges), *infra.*

66 *See* § 6.8 (teacher loan forgiveness), *infra.*

67 In general, student loan holders are furnishers of information to credit bureaus and in some circumstances can be separately liable for submitting erroneous information. *See* National Consumer Law Center, Fair Credit Reporting (5th ed. 2002).

3.3.3 How Long Does Information Remain in the Consumer's File?

The HEA sets out special rules as to when reports on student loans become obsolete. With the notable exception of Perkins Loans, reports for most student loan defaults may be included in consumer reports for seven years from the later of three dates:

(1) When the Secretary or the guaranty agency pays a claim to the loan holder on the guaranty;

(2) When the Secretary, guaranty agency, lender, or any other loan holder first reported the account to the consumer reporting agency; or

(3) If a borrower re-enters repayment after defaulting on a loan, from the date the student subsequently goes into default again on the loan.[68]

Due to a change in the 1998 HEA, Perkins Loans, in contrast, may be reported indefinitely.[69] A small consolation for borrowers, passed at the same time, requires Perkins institutions to report to credit bureaus when a borrower has made six consecutive monthly payments on a defaulted loan, and to disclose promptly any changes to information previously disclosed.[70]

3.3.4 Cleaning Up the Consumer's Credit Record

Consumers can use various tactics to clean up credit files containing reports of defaulted student loans. As discussed above, a defaulted student loan will be listed as a current debt that is in default. The default will also be listed in the historical section of the report, specifying the length of the default. If the borrower repays the debt in full, the debt will no longer be listed as a current debt in default, but the debt will still be listed on the report (for up to seven years) as a debt that was at one time in default. Perkins Loan defaults, however, can now be reported indefinitely.[71]

Most creditors (such as mortgage companies or banks) will look more carefully at the current status of debts than the historical information in a file. For example, some mortgage lenders will not make loans to applicants that have any current loan defaults. Nevertheless, the historical information is reported to creditors and others authorized to see the consumer's file, and derogatory information there can

prove harmful to the consumer.[72]

If the borrower is eligible, the clearest way to remove the student loan default from *both* the current account information and the historical portion of the report is to obtain a closed school, false certification, or unpaid refund discharge.[73] The regulations state that the discharge should be reported to all credit reporting agencies to which the holder previously reported the status of the loan "so as to delete all adverse credit history assigned to the loan."[74] Consequently, the guarantor or Department should tell the reporting agency not only that the loan is no longer in default, but that the reporting of the loan as ever being in default was in error.

Borrowers can follow up a discharge by obtaining a copy of their credit report and determining if the current and historical information on the loan has been corrected.[75] If it has not been corrected, the borrower should first request the guarantor or the Department to report the debt's correct status to the reporting agency. They should also dispute the accuracy of the default with the reporting agency. The reporting agency will be required to verify the default with the loan holder.[76] The loan holder, in turn, should refuse to verify to the reporting agency that a default ever existed.

An alternative method of removing both the current and historical information on a student loan default is to dispute whether the debt is owed, based on forgery, fraud, school-related claims, or other defenses that go to the loan's enforceability.[77] As part of a settlement of such a claim, the loan holder may be willing to request that the reporting agency correct both the current and historical status of the debt.[78]

---

68 20 U.S.C. § 1080a.

69 Pub. L. No. 105-244 § 463(b) (Oct. 7, 1998), *amending* 20 U.S.C. § 1087cc(c)(3). The Secretary was given specific statutory authority to promulgate regulations establishing criteria under which a school can cease reporting the information before the loan is paid in full. 20 U.S.C. § 1087cc(c)(4)(B).

70 Pub. L. No. 105-244 § 463(b) (Oct. 7, 1998), *adding* 20 U.S.C. § 1087cc(c)(5), 34 C.F.R. § 674.45(b)(1).

71 *See* § 3.3.3, *infra*.

72 For more on clearing up credit, see generally National Consumer Law Center, Guide to Surviving Debt Ch. 7 (2002); National Consumer Law Center, Fair Credit Reporting (5th ed. 2002).

73 For unpaid refund discharges, it is possible that only a portion of the loan may be paid off. The credit report therefore may still show that the borrower is delinquent on a portion of the loan. *See* § 6.4, *infra*.

74 34 C.F.R. §§ 682.402(d)(2)(iv), 682.402(e)(2)(iv). A March 1999 Federal Trade Commission staff letter clarified that pursuant to the Fair Credit Reporting Act, schools must report information to the original credit bureau even if the school no longer has a contractual relationship with that bureau. *See* FTC Staff Letter from David Medine to Lee S. Harris, U.S. Department of Education, Clearinghouse No. 52,490 (Mar. 22, 1999).

75 For detailed information on how to obtain a copy of a credit report, see National Consumer Law Center, Fair Credit Reporting (5th ed. 2002).

76 For detailed information on how to dispute the accuracy of a credit report, and the reporting agency's responsibilities, see National Consumer Law Center, Fair Credit Reporting (5th ed. 2002).

77 *See* § 9.3, *infra*.

78 For detailed information on how to handle credit reporting issues as part of a settlement, including sample creditor letters to a reporting agency, see National Consumer Law Center, Fair Credit Reporting (5th ed. 2002).

It is easier to improve only the current status section of a credit report. A borrower can have the loan's current status changed so that it no longer indicates a default by taking any of the following steps:

- Repay the debt;
- Obtain a Consolidation Loan;[79]
- Rehabilitate the loan with twelve reasonable and affordable payments accompanied by the re-sale of the loan;[80] or
- Obtain a discharge based on total and permanent disability.[81]

The current status of the debt on a credit report will *not* be changed if the borrower merely enters into a reasonable and affordable payment plan, even after making six pay-

ments to renew eligibility for new loans. A payment agreement with a note holder will *not* remove a default from a student's credit record unless the loan holder explicitly agrees that it will take the loan out of default.

If a student loan is discharged in bankruptcy, the debt will no longer be treated as currently in default in the consumer's credit file. On the other hand, the fact that the consumer filed bankruptcy will be on the consumer's credit record for ten years.[82] Nevertheless, many experts believe that filing for bankruptcy will generally help a consumer's credit record in the long run. Certainly, the possibility of bankruptcy should not be rejected solely because of potential damage to the debtor's credit record.[83]

---

79 *See* § 8.2, *infra.*

80 *See* § 8.4, *infra.* There is some confusion whether rehabilitating a loan will also clean up the historical section of the student's credit rating.

81 *See* § 6.6, *infra.*

---

82 *See* National Consumer Law Center, Fair Credit Reporting (5th ed. 2002).

83 For a discussion of bankruptcy's positive and negative impacts on a consumer's credit rating, see National Consumer Law Center, Fair Credit Reporting (5th ed. 2002). For a discussion of the dischargeability of student loans in bankruptcy, see generally Ch. 7, *infra.*

Chapter 4   Student Loan Collection

4.1 The Collection Process

4.1.1 Pre-Default Collection

Borrowers are in default on Federal Family Education Loans (FFEL) or Direct Loans if they fail to make required payments for 270 days for loans repayable in monthly installments or 330 days for loans repayable less frequently than monthly.[1] This nine-month period is a relatively long time for borrowers to seek alternatives to default such as more affordable repayment plans, cancellation, deferment, and/or forbearance.[2]

During this period, the borrower is merely delinquent and not in default. This is an important distinction because as long as the borrower is not in default, she is still eligible for deferments and for flexible pre-default repayment options.

FFEL lenders are required to follow certain "due diligence" procedures in attempting to collect loans during the delinquency period. Delinquency begins on the first day after the due date of the first missed payment.[3] Once a loan becomes delinquent, lenders are required to provide the borrower with information about the availability of the Student Loan Ombudsman's office.[4]

Lenders are also required to engage in at least the following collection activities, depending on how long the borrower has been delinquent:

- 1–15 days delinquent: The lender must send at least one written notice or collection letter during this period informing the borrower of the delinquency and urging the borrower to make payments.[5] The notice or collection letter must at a minimum include a lender or servicer contact, a telephone number, and a prominent statement informing borrowers that assistance may be available if they are experiencing difficulty in making scheduled payments.[6]

- 16–180 days delinquent: During this period, the lender must make at least four diligent efforts to contact the borrower by telephone and send at least four collection letters.[7] At least one attempt to contact the borrower by phone must occur on or before, and another attempt must occur after, the 90th day of delinquency. Collection letters sent during this period must include, at a minimum, information regarding deferment, forbearance, income-sensitive repayment, loan consolidation, and other available options to avoid default.[8]

  At least two of the collection letters during this period must warn the borrower that if the loan is not paid, the lender will assign the loan to the guaranty agency. These letters must also inform the borrower that if assigned to a guaranty agency, a defaulted loan will be reported to all national credit bureaus and that the agency may institute tax refund offsets, offsets of other federal payments, wage garnishment, or assignment of the loan to the federal government for litigation.[9] Receipt of any payments from the borrower during this period allows the lender to hold off on some of the required collection activity.[10]

- 181–270 days delinquent: At a minimum, the lender during this period must provide information to the borrower regarding options to avoid default and the consequences of default.[11] On or after the 241st day of delinquency, the lender must send a final demand letter

---

1   34 C.F.R. §§ 682.200 (FFEL definition of default), 685.102(b) (Direct Loans). The rules are different for Perkins Loans where default is defined as the failure of a borrower to make an installment payment when due or to comply with other terms of the promissory note or written repayment agreement. 34 C.F.R. § 674.2. The collection process and due diligence requirements for Perkins Loans are set out at 34 C.F.R. §§ 674.41–.50. The collection procedures described in this section, unless otherwise noted, refer to FFEL and Direct Loans.

2   See § 1.5, *supra* (pre-default repayment plans); Ch. 2, *supra* (deferments and forbearances); Ch. 6, *infra* (loan cancellations).

3   34 C.F.R. § 682.411(b). For general Perkins due diligence requirements, see 34 C.F.R. § 674.41.

4   34 C.F.R. § 682.411(b)(3).

5   34 C.F.R. § 682.411(c).

6   *Id.*

7   34 C.F.R. § 682.411(d). Lenders are excused from further telephone efforts if after making diligent efforts, they are unable to obtain the correct telephone number of a borrower. 34 C.F.R. § 682.411(g).

8   *Id.*

9   34 C.F.R. § 682.411(d)(2). These collection methods are discussed in detail in Ch. 5, *infra*.

10   34 C.F.R. § 682.411(d)(3). The obligations differ if the lender receives a payment on the loan. 34 C.F.R. § 682.411(d)(3), (4).

11   34 C.F.R. § 682.411(e).

to the borrower.[12] The lender must give the borrower at least thirty days after the date the letter is mailed to respond and to bring the loan out of default.[13]

The lender is required to ensure that there is no gap in collection activity of more than forty-five days at any point during this delinquency period.[14]

4.1.2 Post-Default Collections

4.1.2.1 General

Lenders assign FFEL defaulted loans to the Department or to state guaranty agencies.[15] The Department and state guaranty agencies also contract with private collection agencies to administer many of their collection responsibilities.[16]

The regulations specify the efforts guaranty agencies must make to collect defaulted FFEL loans. These options include tax refund offsets, federal benefit offsets, wage garnishment, and litigation.[17]

Until 2001, the regulations prescribed specific behavior that guaranty agencies were required to follow. The rules were very detailed, listing specific collection activities for the first forty-five days through 181 days after default. The rules also restricted a guaranty agency's use of litigation in collecting defaulted loans.

Effective in 2001, the Department made a number of significant changes to these rules. In particular, guaranty agencies are no longer required to perform routine collection activities such as collection letters and phone calls.[18] Instead, the agencies are given discretion to design their own collection strategies as long as they perform at least one activity every 180 days to collect the debt, locate the borrower (if necessary) or determine if the borrower has the means to repay the debt.[19] The 2001 regulatory changes also eliminated the general prohibition against guaranty agencies suing borrowers.[20]

The changes followed previous amendments to the HEA placing greater financial responsibility for collection on guaranty agencies. As a result, guaranty agencies are now required to pay for collection activities using money in their own operating funds. Previously, agencies funded their col-

lection efforts with federal reserves. Congress hoped to decrease costs, assuming that agencies using their own funds would develop more cost efficient collection methods.[21] The Department argued that these financial incentives eliminated the need for prescriptive regulations.[22]

Although guaranty agencies have more freedom to develop collection strategies, certain requirements are still in place. These are summarized in the following subsections.

4.1.2.2 Credit Bureau Reporting and Collection Notices

No later than sixty days after default, the agency is required to report default claims to all national credit bureaus.[23] Prior to reporting the default and prior to assessing any collection costs, the agency must provide written notice containing the information described below. Although agencies have sixty days to report the default claim to the credit bureaus, they only have forty-five days after paying a lender's default claim to send this notice.[24]

The notice must:

Advise the borrower that the agency has paid a default claim filed by the lender and has taken assignment of the loan;

Identify the lender that made the loan and the school at which the loan was made;

List the outstanding principal, accrued interest, and any other charges owing on the loan;

Demand that the borrower immediately repay the loan;

Explain the rate of interest that will accrue on the loan, that all costs incurred to collect the loan will be charged to the borrower, the authority for assessing these costs, and the manner in which the agency will calculate the amount of these costs;

Notify the borrower that the agency will report the default to all national credit bureaus;

Explain the opportunities available to the borrower to request access to the agency's records on the loan, to request an administrative review of the legal enforceability or past-due status of the loan, and to reach a satisfactory repayment agreement, and methods for requesting this relief.[25]

Unless the agency uses a separate notice to advise the borrower of proposed enforcement actions, the notice with the information discussed above must also describe any other enforcement action, such as tax offsets or wage garnishment, that the agency intends to use to collect the debt, and explain the procedures available to the borrower prior to

---

12 34 C.F.R. § 682.411(f).

13 *Id.*

14 34 C.F.R. § 682.411(b)(2).

15 The Department is authorized to engage in the same types of collection activities as FFEL lenders to collect defaulted Direct Loans. 34 C.F.R. § 685.211(d)(3).

16 *See* § 4.2.1, *infra.*

17 All discussed in detail in Chapter 5, infra and §§ 4.1.2.3, 4.2.2.1, *infra.*

18 *See* 65 Fed. Reg. 46316, 46318 (July 27, 2000).

19 34 C.F.R. § 682.410(b)(6)(i).

20 *See generally* 65 Fed. Reg. 65621, 65650 (Nov. 1, 2000) (final rules).

21 65 Fed. Reg. 46316, 46318 (July 27, 2000) (proposed rules).

22 *Id.*

23 34 C.F.R. § 682.410(b)(5). *See* § 3.3, *supra.*

24 34 C.F.R. § 682.410(b)(6)(v).

25 34 C.F.R. § 682.410(b)(5)(vi).

these actions to access records, request administrative review, or to set up a payment plan.[26]

The initial notice must also describe the grounds on which the borrower may object that the loan obligation is not a legally enforceable debt and describe any appeal and judicial rights available to the borrower from an adverse decision regarding the legal enforceability or past-due status of the loan.[27] In addition, the notice must describe collection actions the agency may take in the future, including the filing of a lawsuit by the agency or by the Department of Education.[28]

During the first forty-five days after filing a default claim, agencies have the option of including even more information in the notice described above, or sending a separate notice explaining that if the borrower does not make acceptable repayment arrangements, the agency will promptly initiate collection procedures.[29] The various scenarios such as wage garnishment or civil suits must be listed.[30]

Given the volume of information in these collection notices, it is not surprising that borrowers are often confused about their rights. Recognizing this problem (although not necessarily solving it), the Department requires that the agency notify the borrower within forty-five days of paying a default claim that " . . . borrowers may have certain rights in the collection of debts, and that borrowers may wish to contact counselors or lawyers regarding those rights."[31] Within a reasonable time after all of this information is sent, the agency is also required to send borrowers at least one additional notice informing the borrower that the default has been reported to all national credit bureaus (if that is the case) and that the borrower's credit rating may thereby have been damaged.[32]

During the initial sixty-day period before the agency reports the claim to credit bureaus, borrowers must also be given an opportunity to inspect and copy agency records pertaining to the loan obligation and an opportunity for an administrative review of the legal enforceability of the debt and an opportunity to enter into a repayment agreement on terms "satisfactory to the agency."[33]

A collection agency's failure to follow these collection rules may violate the FDCPA.[34] Violations by guaranty agencies may also be actionable under the FDCPA.[35]

4.1.2.3 Allowable Post-Default Debt Collection Activities

Agencies are required to attempt an annual federal offset, including tax refund offsets as well as offsets of other federal payments.[36] However, before attempting offset, agencies must wait at least sixty days after sending the required collection notices described in the previous subsection.[37]

The agencies are also required to initiate administrative wage garnishment against all eligible borrowers.[38] The only exception to this requirement arises if the agency determines that litigation would be more effective in collecting the debt. In these circumstances, the agency may instead file a lawsuit against a borrower.[39] The regulations clarify that agencies have the discretion to file lawsuits instead of wage garnishment only if the borrower has no wages that can be garnished or the agency determines that the borrower has sufficient attachable assets or income that is not subject to administrative wage garnishment.[40] The regulations therefore reflect the Department's growing preference for extrajudicial collection methods.

Garnishment procedures are set out separately.[41] These procedures, including administrative review and hearing rights, are discussed in detail in Chapter 5, *infra*. For purposes of possible fair debt collection violations, it is important to note that the garnishment regulations require that guaranty agencies send notice of proposed garnishment to the borrower at least thirty days before initiating proceedings.[42]

---

26 34 C.F.R. § 682.410(b)(5)(vi)(H).

27 34 C.F.R. § 682.410(b)(5)(vi)(I), (J), (K).

28 34 C.F.R. § 682.410(b)(5)(vi)(L).

29 34 C.F.R. § 682.410(b)(6)(v).

30 *Id.*

31 34 C.F.R. § 682.410(b)(v).

32 34 C.F.R. § 682.410(b)(vi).

33 34 C.F.R. § 682.410(b)(5)(ii).

34 *See* §§ 4.3.2, 4.3.3, *infra*.

35 *See* § 4.3.3.6, *infra*.

36 34 C.F.R. § 682.410(b)(6)(ii). *See* §§ 5.2, 5.4, *infra*.

37 *Id.*

38 34 C.F.R. § 682.410(b)(6)(iii). *See* § 5.3, *infra*.

39 34 C.F.R. § 682.410(b)(6)(iv).

40 *Id.*

41 34 C.F.R. § 682.410(b)(9). For a detailed discussion on proposed changes to garnishment procedures, see § 5.3.3, *infra*.

42 34 C.F.R. § 682.410(b)(9)(i)(B). Class certification was granted in a 2001 case alleging that borrowers were not given the full thirty days to respond to the "Notice of Prior Wage Withholding." *See* Sanders v. OSI Educational Services, Inc., 2001 WL 883608 (N.D. Ill. Aug. 3, 2001) (granting class certification based on borrowers' allegations that student loan debt collector violated the Fair Debt Collection Practices Act). *See also* Kort v. Diversified Collection Services, 2001 WL 88149 (N.D. Ill. Aug. 2, 2001), *class cert. granted in part* 2001 WL 1617213 (N.D. Ill. Dec. 17, 2001) (denying class certification on plaintiffs' FDCPA claim regarding alleged insufficient time to respond to garnishment notice, but granting class certification on claim that defendants violated the FDCPA by falsely representing that borrowers have an affirmative duty to supply "written proof" of employment history to take advantage of garnishment exception). Both cases raised FDCPA violations related to defendants' requiring borrowers to affirmatively prove the exception to garnishment for borrowers who have been involuntarily separated from employment. *See* §§ 5.3.2.1, 5.3.3.1, *infra*.

4.2 Student Loan Collectors

4.2.1 Finding Out Who is Collecting the Loan

The first problem many borrowers face is figuring out which agency is collecting their loans. This information is critical to resolving student loan problems efficiently.

Defaulted loans may be held by the Department of Education, by a state guaranty agency, or by the school. The Department and state guaranty agencies also contract with private collection agencies to administer many of their collection responsibilities.[43]

A good place for borrowers to start is the federal student aid information center, 1-800-4-FED-AID (800-433-3243). The information center staff should be able to give borrowers the address and telephone number of the agency holding a defaulted loan. Borrowers with Direct Loans should contact the Direct Loan Servicing Center at (800) 848-0979. The number for information about Department-held loans is (800) 621-3115. More information is also available on the Department's website at *www.ed.gov*.[44]

It is best to contact the student loan ombudsman for help only after these other avenues have been exhausted. The toll-free phone number for the ombudsman is (877) 557-2575.[45]

4.2.2 The Department of Education As a Collector

4.2.2.1 Department-Held Loans

The Department of Education has two major roles concerning collection of student loans. The Department sets standards and supervises the collection of student loans held by other entities, such as guarantors, schools, lenders, and secondary market lenders. The Department also directly collects on loans that it holds.

The Department directly holds and thus directly collects on Direct Loans, Perkins Loans after the school assigns the note to the Department, and certain Stafford (GSL) Loans after the guaranty agency has assigned those loans to the Department.

Guaranty agencies or schools hold other defaulted student loans.[46] The Department generally does not collect on these loans, and it is important to distinguish whether the Department is collecting on a loan or supervising a guarantor or school's collection on the loan.

The types of activities third parties can use to collect student loans are different for different types of loans. The rules also vary depending on which collection tool they are using. For example, third parties acting as agents for the federal government are explicitly covered by the tax intercept statute.[47] The HEA wage garnishment statute also specifically applies to guaranty agencies.[48] However, in 2002, the Department published proposed rules that would allow them to begin garnishing under the Debt Collection Improvement Act (DCIA) authority rather than the HEA.[49] The DCIA, unlike the HEA, applies only to garnishment by the "heads" of executive, judicial, or legislative agencies.[50] This may mean that guaranty agencies will continue to garnish under HEA authority while the Department garnishes under the DCIA.[51]

Similar to the DCIA wage garnishment provisions, the federal benefits offset statute grants offset authority only to heads of agencies.[52] Despite this language, the Department's current policy is to allow guaranty agencies to refer debts to the Department of Treasury for offset after paying the lender, but before assigning loans.

The picture is less clear for Perkins Loans. Perkins schools are encouraged to assign defaulted loans to the Department.[53] The United States will then seek collection

---

43 The Department of Education website (*www.ed.gov*) lists the collection agencies with Department contracts. As of 2002, the Department contracted with the following agencies: Account Control Technology, Allied Interstate, Inc., Aman Collection Service, Credit Bureau Accounts, Diversified Collection Services, Education Credit Services, Education Debt Services, Equifax Risk Management, Financial Asset Management Systems, GC Services Limited Partnership, General Revenue Corp., Maximus, National Asset Management Enterprises, Nationwide Credit, NCO Group, OSI, Pioneer Credit Recovery, Progressive Financial Services, Recovery Bureau of America, St. Hill & Associates, Van Ru Credit Corp.

44 For information about using the national student loan data base to find out how many loans and what types of loans a borrower has, see § 1.6, *supra*. Borrowers may also use a LoanLocator service managed by the non-profit National Student Clearinghouse. Only loans from participating schools are listed. *See* www.studentclearinghouse.org.

45 For more information about the ombudsman program, see § 1.8, *supra*.

46 For a list of guaranty agencies and addresses, see Appx. G, *infra*.

47 31 U.S.C. § 3720A. This is significant because prior to the legislative change allowing interception of debts owed to agents of the federal government, authorization to intercept loans held by guaranty agencies was accomplished by the guarantors assigning the loans to the U.S. prior to interception. This posed practical problems for obligations that guarantors had already reduced to judgments, particularly since the interception program was not used to collect loans post-judgment. The interception program is now utilized to recover on debts pre- and post-judgment. *See* § 5.2, *infra*.

48 20 U.S.C. § 1095a(a).

49 *See* § 5.3.3, *infra*. Proposed rules are reprinted on the companion CD-Rom.

50 31 U.S.C. § 3720D(a).

51 *See generally* § 5.3.3, *infra*.

52 31 U.S.C. § 3716. *See* § 5.4, *infra*.

53 34 C.F.R. § 674.50 (assignment regulations). *See also* Department of Education, Dear Colleague Letter CB-02-05 (Apr. 2002).

from the defaulted borrower, using the full range of collection tools available. The Department claims to have collection tools, such as wage garnishment, federal offset, and Department of Justice litigation, which are not available to schools.[54] It is unclear to what extent this statement reflects actual practice.[55]

When the Department holds a defaulted loan, collection is by the Department's Debt Collection Service. That service has a small Washington office that establishes policy and three large regional offices that handle actual consumer files. However, most responsibilities for debt collection on Department-held loans are delegated to private debt collection agencies hired by the Department on a commission basis.[56]

The three regional offices—in Chicago, Atlanta, and San Francisco—handle closed-school and false-certification applications, rule on hearings concerning tax refund intercepts, garnishments and other matters, deal with loan consolidations and reinstatements, and supervise the collection agencies. Because assignment is not based on the student's residence, it is difficult to predict which of the three regional offices will be in charge of a loan. Loans are distributed based on which guaranty agency had guaranteed the loan.

4.2.2.2 Department's Responsibility for Loans Held by Others

If the Department is not holding a loan, it is generally *not* appropriate to initiate inquiries or make applications to the Department. Instead, borrowers should contact the party holding the loan—usually a guaranty agency on a FFEL and the school itself on a Perkins Loan. The guaranty agency or school may have hired a collector or servicer to deal with the loan.

Even though it is best to contact the holder directly, if problems arise, borrowers should also consider contacting the Department. The Department has responsibility for supervising the actions of guaranty agencies and setting standards for their conduct. Much of what guarantors do has first been approved by the Department.

The Department's division in charge of guarantor supervision is the Policy Development Division, Loans Branch. The Department also has offices in charge of policy concerning closed school discharges, false certification discharges, consolidation loans, and other issues of special importance to student loan advocates. Problems with guaranty agency handling of these issues could be forwarded to

those offices, but the right person to call for each of these offices changes too rapidly to specify in this volume.[57]

After all these avenues have been tried, borrowers should also consider contacting the student loan ombudsman by phone or through the Internet. The toll-free number for the Department of Education student loan ombudsman is (877) 557-2575. Assistance is available in both English and Spanish.[58]

4.3 Deceptive and Abusive Debt Collection Tactics

4.3.1 Factors That Foster Deception and Abuse in Student Loan Collections

The Department has turned over almost all student loans it holds to private collection agencies. Almost all guaranty agencies are doing the same. Consequently, one significant form of student loan collection is dunning letters and other contacts from private collection agencies.[59]

Student loan debt collection contacts, both by private collectors and guarantors, involve a remarkable amount of deceptive, unfair, and illegal conduct. There are several reasons for the extent of these abusive collection actions:

- Millions of student loan obligations are being handled on a "wholesale" basis, with little or no attention being paid to the facts of the individual borrower being dunned.
- Remedies available to collect on student loans are often both unique and misunderstood (e.g., federal tax refund intercepts, federal benefits offsets and non-judicial garnishments), and collectors often misrepresent the exact nature of these remedies when they send collection letters. By all reports, much false information is provided.
- The complexity of the student loan programs leads to much confusion about who is collecting on a debt, and makes it easy for an independent collector to misrepresent itself as the government.[60]

---

54 *See* Department of Education, Dear Colleague Letter CB-02-05 (Apr. 2002).

55 By many accounts, Perkins schools do in fact refer debts to the Department of Treasury for tax intercept. Presumably they could do the same for federal benefits offsets. However, the Department claims, at least with respect to benefits offsets, that this is not current practice.

56 See § 4.2.1, *supra* for a list of collection agencies contracted by the Department.

57 Contacts for some of these departments are available on the Department of Education website, www.ed.gov.

58 *See* § 1.8, *supra*.

59 The Department was particularly aggressive during the 1990s in referring cases out for collection. During FY 1999, there was a fifty-five percent increase in student loan default case filings in federal courts over 1997. *See* Edward Walsh, *Lawsuits Over Student Loans Rise: U.S. Hires More Collection Lawyers to Pursue Defaulters*, Washington Post, April 19, 1999 at A4. However, the growth of extra-judicial collection tools, such as administrative wage garnishment, tax offsets, and federal benefits offsets seems to have slowed this litigation trend.

60 *See* Brider v. Nationwide Credit, 1998 WL 729747 (N.D. Ill. June 24, 1998) (denying motion to dismiss of collector whose collection letter had large bold heading "U.S. Department of Education").

- Private collection agencies are delegated the responsibility for determining the size of a reasonable and affordable payment plan. In addition, these collection agencies help determine if students have defenses to wage garnishments and tax refund intercepts, even though the collection agencies' financial incentive is not to offer reasonable and affordable plans or to acknowledge defenses.[61]

4.3.2 Common Student Loan Debt Collection Abuses

4.3.2.1 Violations Unique to Student Loans

The special rules governing student loan collections lead to a number of collection abuses. This section discusses common fair debt collection violations, followed by a discussion in § 4.3.3 of whether the FDCPA and state debt collection laws apply in the student loan context.

Student loan borrowers routinely receive dunning letters threatening that the Department will garnish their wages without "legal action." These letters imply that the former student will receive no notice before the wage garnishment and that there will be no opportunity either to contest the validity of the student loan or to present defenses. In truth, the statute and regulations require both notice and an opportunity for an administrative hearing before an employer may be ordered to withhold any wages.[62]

Collectors may misrepresent a student's ability to obtain a closed school, unpaid refund, or false certification discharge. Collection agencies make no commissions from those obtaining the discharge, while they recover a set percentage on any payments made. These collectors thus have an incentive to discourage discharge applications. For this reason, the Department instructs them not to make any kind of determination concerning a student's eligibility, but instead to refer queries related to closed school, false certification, or unpaid refund discharges.[63]

Consequently, students may not even have to prove that a collector falsified a student's rights to a discharge. All the student need prove is that the student raised questions about any of the above-listed topics and the collector did not pass the file on to the Loan Discharge Unit.

There is likely to be even more confusion and misinformation as the Department gears up to implement federal benefits offsets to collect student loans.[64] For example, borrowers have reported numerous instances of collectors threatening to offset benefits even if the borrower receives SSI payments only. In fact, SSI benefits are completely exempt from offset.[65]

Borrowers have also reported that the Department routinely continues collection even after borrowers have submitted disability discharge applications. This practice also clearly violates Department regulations.[66]

In addition, collection agencies frequently mislead borrowers with respect to repayment options. In particular, agencies are often very aggressive in steering borrowers into loan consolidation or loan rehabilitation programs. These repayment strategies, as described in detail in Chapter 8, *infra*, benefit many, but not all, borrowers. Consolidation is equivalent to full payment of the existing obligation and collectors are compensated accordingly.

Typical private collection agency and Department collection letters make statements like the following to push these programs:

> We would like you to know that compliance with a mutually agreeable repayment arrangement will make your loan(s) eligible for loan "rehabilitation" or loan "consolidation," thus removing your loan(s) from default status, improving your credit rating and making you eligible for additional student financial assistance.
>
> Recent revisions in the loan consolidation and rehabilitation programs can give credit control back to you, the consumer. You can finally solve the credit problems crated by having defaulted student loans and bring them to a "current status." Participating in a refinance program can update, if necessary, your student loans negatives and could possibly allow you to make payment arrangements based on your current financial situation.[67]

---

61 *See, e.g.,* Arroyo v. Solomon & Solomon, 2001 U.S. Dist. LEXIS 21908 (E.D.N.Y. Nov. 16, 2001) (defendant's summary judgment motion denied in case alleging, among other FDCPA violations, that defendants demanded payments in amount more than borrower could reasonably afford).

62 *See* Sanders v. OSI Educational Services, Inc., 2001 WL 883608 (N.D. Ill. Aug. 3, 2001) (granting class certification based on borrowers' allegations that student loan debt collector violated the Fair Debt Collection Practices Act). *See also* Kort v. Diversified Collection Services, 2001 WL 88149 (N.D. Ill. Aug. 2, 2001), *class cert. granted in part* 2001 WL 1617213 (N.D. Ill. Dec. 17, 2001) (denying class certification on plaintiffs' FDCPA claim regarding alleged insufficient time to respond to garnishment notice, but granting class certification on claim that defendants violated the FDCPA by falsely representing that borrowers have an affirmative duty to supply "written proof" of employment history to take advantage of garnishment exception). Both cases raised FDCPA violations related to defendants' requiring borrowers to affirmatively prove the exception to garnishment for borrowers who have been involuntarily separated from employment. *See* §§ 5.3.2.1, 5.3.3.1, *infra*.

63 *Guidelines for Contract Collection Agencies Regarding Treatment of Borrowers Who Claim Relief Against Repayment Due to Closed School or False Certification*, Clearinghouse No. 51,942. *See generally* Ch. 6 (student loan discharges), *infra*.

64 *See* § 5.4, *infra*.

65 *See* § 5.4.1, *infra*.

66 34 C.F.R. § 682.402(c)(1)(iii)(C)(2). *See* § 6.6.2, *infra*.

67 This last sentence, taken directly from actual collection letters, is particularly confusing. It appears to be referring to the income sensitive and income contingent repayment plans available

As discussed in Chapter 8, *infra*, borrowers are also entitled to renew eligibility for financial assistance by making six consecutive reasonable and affordable payments. Here too, borrowers report frequent misrepresentations. Most commonly, collection agencies will insist, in violation of the federal statute and regulations, that borrowers are required to make minimum monthly payments.[68]

Collectors that charge excessive collection fees may also violate the FDCPA.[69] Widespread complaints about student loan collection activity are leading to more litigation. For example, one debt collector was required to pay the maximum $1000 Fair Debt Collection Practices Act (FDCPA) statutory damages and, under state law claims, another $1153 in actual damages, and $60,000 in punitive damages for contacting the borrower even after the borrower and the borrower's attorney had advised the collector that the debt had been discharged in bankruptcy.[70] In addition, a number of class actions have been brought in this area.[71]

Private FDCPA actions are in many cases the only way borrowers can get relief when collectors violate Department of Education collection regulations. Borrowers generally do not have a private right of action under the HEA.[72] However,

a collector's failure to follow the law or a collector's misrepresentation of applicable law may violate the FDCPA.

4.3.2.2 Illegal Debt Collection Activity Not Unique to Student Loans

The previous subsection outlined some special forms of illegal debt collection conduct relating solely to student loans. In addition, collectors may engage in a number of other basic forms of illegal debt collection practices that apply to collection of any type of consumer debt.

This subsection briefly lists a number of practices that are prohibited under the federal Fair Debt Collection Practices Act, and that can lead to actions for actual damages, up to $1000 in statutory damages, plus attorney fees.[73]

Examples of fair debt collection standards include:

- The collection agency must stop contacting the student if the student so requests in writing.[74]
- The collection agency, in its initial communication or within five days of that communication, must send the student a written notice identifying the debt and the creditor and giving the student the right to dispute the debt or to request the name and address of the original creditor, if different from the current one. If the student raises a dispute, the collector must suspend collection efforts on the disputed portion of the debt until the collector responds to the request.[75]

The following collection agency conduct also violates the FDCPA:

- Communicating with third parties, such as relatives, employers, friends, or neighbors, about a debt unless the student or a court has given the collector permission to do so. Several narrow exceptions to this prohibition apply. Collectors may contact creditors, attorneys, credit reporting agencies, cosigners, spouses, and parents if the student is a minor. Third-party contacts are also permit-

---

through loan consolidation. *See* §§ 8.2.2 (Direct consolidation loans), 8.2.3 (FFEL consolidation loans).

68 Misrepresentations about reasonable and affordable payment plans may violate the FDCPA. *See* Arroyo v. Solomon and Solomon, 2001 U.S. Dist. LEXIS 21908 (E.D.N.Y. Nov. 16, 2001) (defendant's summary judgment motion denied in case alleging, among other FDCPA violations, that defendants demanded payments in amounts more than borrower could reasonably afford). *See* § 8.3, *infra*.

69 *See, e.g.*, Padilla v. Payco General Am. Credits, Inc., 161 F. Supp. 2d 264 (S.D.N.Y. 2001) (plaintiff's summary judgment motion granted on claim that collection agency charged fees above the 18.5% allowable limit).

70 Miele v. Sid Bailey, Inc., 192 B.R. 611 (S.D.N.Y. 1996). *See also* Padilla v. Payco General Am. Credits, Inc., 161 F. Supp. 2d 264 (S.D.N.Y. 2001) (numerous FDCPA violations raised including charging of excessive collection fees and illegal contacts with the borrower).

71 *See e.g.*, Kort v. Diversified Collection Services, Inc., 2001 WL 88149 (N.D. Ill. Aug. 2, 2001), *class cert. granted in part* 2001 WL 1617213 (N.D. Ill. Dec. 17, 2001) (collector allegedly violated FDCPA by giving borrowers insufficient time to respond to wage garnishment notices and by requiring affirmative proof of unemployment exception to garnishment); Sanders v. OSI, 2001 WL 883608 (N.D. Ill. Aug. 3, 2001) (similar FDCPA violations alleged as those in Kort); Cliff v. Payco General Am. Credits, Inc., Clearinghouse No. 52,132 (M.D. Fla. 1998) (class action complaint) (suit alleges violation of due process rights in collection agencies' administration of wage garnishment procedures); Mitchell v. Educational Credit Management Corp., Clearinghouse No. 52,038 (N.D. Ill. Oct. 14, 1997) (complaint—class action); Sibley v. Diversified Collection Services, Clearinghouse No. 51,930 (N.D. Tex. Apr. 26, 1996) (first amended complaint—class action). Sample pleadings in cases challenging private collection agency conduct can be found at Appx. E, *infra*.

72 *See* § 9.3.5, *infra*.

73 For more detail, the best resource is National Consumer Law Center, Fair Debt Collection (4th ed. 2000 and Supp.), detailing what general collection practices are prohibited and available consumer remedies for such violations.

74 15 U.S.C. § 1692c(c). This provision, in particular, has been cited by collection agencies lobbying Congress to exempt student loan collectors from FDCPA coverage. They point out the conflict between federal student assistance due diligence provisions that require minimum contacts and the FDCPA prohibition against contacting borrowers in certain circumstances. Consumer advocates have responded with alternatives, including exempting collectors from the due diligence contact requirements in these cases, in lieu of wholesale exemption from the FDCPA. This issue is likely to arise again in future legislative sessions.

75 15 U.S.C. § 1692g. *See* Avila v. Rubin, 84 F.3d 222 (2d Cir. 1996) (student loan collector liable where other language overshadowed validation notice).

ted if the contacts are solely for the purpose of locating the student and do not reveal in any way the contact's underlying purpose.[76]

- Communicating with the student at unusual or inconvenient times or places. The times 8:00 a.m. to 9:00 p.m. are generally considered convenient, but daytime contacts with a consumer known to work a night shift may be inconvenient.[77]
- Contacting a student at work if the collector should know that the employer prohibits personal calls, or contacting the student at other inconvenient places, such as a friend's house or the hospital.[78]
- Contacting a student represented by a lawyer, unless the lawyer gives permission for the communication or fails to respond to the collector's communications.[79]
- Using obscene, profane, or abusive language.[80]
- Telephoning repeatedly and frequently with intent to annoy, abuse, or harass the student or other persons at the called number.[81]
- Telephoning without disclosing the collector's identity.[82]
- Making false, misleading or deceptive representations in collecting debts, such as pretending that letters carry legal authority or are from the government.[83]
- Falsely representing the character, amount or legal status of a debt, or of services rendered or compensation owed.[84]
- Falsely stating or implying a lawyer's involvement, such as form letters written on an attorney's letterhead and bearing an attorney's signature that in fact came from a collection agency and were not reviewed by a lawyer.[85]
- Stating that nonpayment will result in arrest, garnishment or seizure of property or wages, unless such actions are lawful, and unless the loan holder fully intends to take such action.[86]
- Using any false representation or other deception to collect or to attempt to collect any debt or to obtain

information about the student.[87]

- Failing to disclose in communications that the collector is attempting to collect a debt.[88]
- Using unfair or unconscionable means to collect debts.[89]
- Collecting fees or charges unless expressly authorized by the agreement creating the debt or permitted by law.[90]

4.3.3 Applicability of the FDCPA to Student Loan Collection Activity

4.3.3.1 General

The federal Fair Debt Collection Practices Act (FDCPA) is the key statute offering students protection from debt collection harassment.[91] The statute specifies numerous prohibited collection techniques, provides debtors with certain rights, and provides students with statutory and actual damages and attorney fees for violations.[92]

The key FDCPA issue for students is whether the Act applies to student loan collection activities. If it does, a student's attorney will often be able to pinpoint FDCPA violations leading to significant recoveries.

The FDCPA applies to collection of "debts" by "debt collectors." "Debt" is defined as "any obligation or alleged obligation of a consumer to pay money arising out of a transaction in which the money, property, insurance, or services which are the subject of the transaction are primarily for personal, family, or household purposes, whether or not such obligation has been reduced to judgment."[93] There is no question that student loan debts fall within this definition.[94]

---

76 15 U.S.C. §§ 1692b, 1692c(b).
77 15 U.S.C. § 1692c(a)(1).
78 15 U.S.C. § 1692c(a)(3).
79 15 U.S.C. § 1692c(a)(2); *see* Alger v. Ganick, O'Brien & Sarin, 35 F. Supp. 2d 148 (D. Mass. 1999) (contact with represented student loan debtor would be FDCPA violation).
80 15 U.S.C. § 1692d(2).
81 15 U.S.C. § 1692d(5).
82 15 U.S.C. § 1692d(6).
83 15 U.S.C. § 1692e(1), (4), (9), (10), (13); *see* Brider v. Nationwide Credit, 1998 U.S. Dist. LEXIS 22535 (N.D. Ill. June 24, 1998) (denying motion to dismiss of collector whose collection letter had large bold heading "U.S. Department of Education").
84 15 U.S.C. § 1692e(2)(A), (10).
85 15 U.S.C. § 1692e(3), (10); *see* Avila v. Rubin, 84 F.3d 222 (2d Cir. 1996) (collection letters on attorney's letterhead to student loan debtor misrepresented attorney's involvement).
86 *Id.*

87 15 U.S.C. § 1692e(10); *see* Alger v. Ganick, O'Brien & Sarin, 35 F. Supp. 2d 148 (D. Mass. 1999) (false statements to court that student loan debtor had not been making payments).
88 15 U.S.C. § 1692e(11).
89 15 U.S.C. § 1692f; *see* Alger v. Ganick, O'Brien & Sarin, 35 F. Supp. 2d 148 (D. Mass. 1999) (falsely telling process server that student loan debt was unpaid, and instructing him to notify debtor to appear in court would be violation).
90 15 U.S.C. § 1692f(1); *see* Alger v. Ganick, O'Brien & Sarin, 35 F. Supp. 2d 148 (D. Mass. 1999) (instructing process server to demand inflated amount on student loan debt would be violation); Padilla v. Payco General Am. Credits, Inc., 161 F. Supp. 2d 264 (S.D.N.Y. 2001) (plaintiff's summary judgment motion granted on claim that collection agency charged fees above the 18.5% allowable limit).
91 15 U.S.C. § 1692–1692o.
92 The Act is examined in great detail in another NCLC manual, Fair Debt Collection (4th ed. 2000 and Supp.).
93 15 U.S.C. § 1692a(5).
94 Brannan v. United Student Aid Funds, Inc., 94 F.3d 1260 (9th Cir. 1996), *cert. denied*, 521 U.S. 1111 (1997); Juras v. Aman Collection Service, Inc., 829 F.2d 739 (9th Cir. 1987), *cert. denied*, 488 U.S. 875 (1988); McComas v. Financial Collection Agencies, 1997 U.S. Dist. LEXIS 2725 (S.D. W. Va. Mar. 7,

More controversial, however, is the question whether an entity seeking to collect a student loan debt meets the FDCPA definition of "debt collector." The basic definition of "debt collector" is "any person who uses any instrumentality of interstate commerce or the mails in any business the principal purpose of which is the collection of any debts, or who regularly collects or attempts to collect, directly or indirectly, debts owed or due or asserted to be owed or due another."[95] There are many qualifications and exceptions to this definition. The analysis varies significantly depending on whether the entity is a private collector or attorney, a nonprofit guarantor, a state agency, or the Department.

4.3.3.2 Independent Collection Agencies and Attorneys

Independent collection agencies present the clearest example of coverage. There should be little question that an independent collection agency is covered by the FDCPA.[96] The FDCPA also applies to attorneys hired to sue or collect on student loans.[97] The FDCPA exception for "any officer or employee of the United States or any State"[98] does not apply to these collectors, since they are not governmental employees but private parties who have governmental contracts.[99]

4.3.3.3 Department of Education Employees

The FDCPA specifically excludes any officer or employee of the United States or any state to the extent that their activities are in the performance of their official duties.[100] The Department of Education is thus excluded if it collects its own debts.

4.3.3.4 Determining Who Sent the Collection Letter

For Department-held loans, the law is very clear. The Department's own actions are not covered, while actions by private collectors are. The problem in many cases though is determining who in fact engaged in the deceptive conduct—the private collector or the Department. While the Department has turned over almost all its defaulted loans to private collectors, the Department continues to assist those collectors. For example, many form letters appear to be joint efforts by the two. Determining the party responsible for illegal collection activity will often require careful discovery.

Even if the Department is partially responsible for deceptive collection practices, the debt collection agency doing the actual collection may still be liable under the FDCPA. For example, even if the Department actually sent deceptive dunning notices that instruct borrowers to make payments to a private debt collector, the letter may be viewed as an "indirect" attempt by the collection agency to collect a debt, which is within the scope of the FDCPA.[101]

4.3.3.5 Secondary Market Lenders and Servicing Agencies

The FDCPA does not apply to creditors collecting their own debts, but only to collection agencies and collection attorneys.[102] If a lender has not yet turned a FFEL over to the guarantor or a school is collecting on a Perkins Loan, and the lender or school is doing the collection activity through its own in-house staff, the FDCPA does not apply. Further, the FDCPA only applies if the third party collector obtained the debt after it had gone into default.[103] On the other hand, if the lender or school turns a defaulted loan over to a third party for collection, that third party is liable under the FDCPA.

Often a FFEL originating lender will sell the loan *before* default to Sallie Mae or some other secondary market lender. In other situations, a FFEL lender will hire a servicing company *before* default to service the loan payments for the

---

1997); Beaulieu v. American Nat'l Educ. Corp., CV 79-L-271, Clearinghouse No. 30,892 (D. Neb. 1981); Carrigan v. Central Adjustment Bur., Inc., 494 F. Supp. 824 (N.D. Ga. 1980); FTC Official Staff Commentary on the FDCPA, § 803(5), 53 Fed. Reg. 50097, 50102 (Dec. 13, 1988) [reprinted in National Consumer Law Center, Fair Debt Collection Appx. J (4th ed. 2000 and Supp.)].

95 15 U.S.C. § 1692a(6).

96 31 U.S.C. § 3718(a)(2); Richardson v. Baker, 663 F. Supp. 651 (S.D.N.Y. 1987) (FDCPA applies to collector servicing a tax intercept for the Department of Education); Marritz, FTC Informal Staff Letter (Nov. 6, 1978), included on companion CD-Rom to National Consumer Law Center, Fair Debt Collection Appx. I (4th ed. 2000 and Supp.). For a good discussion on using the FDCPA in student loan cases, see Arroyo v. Solomon & Solomon, 2001 U.S. Dist. LEXIS 21908 (E.D.N.Y. Nov. 16, 2001).

97 Alger v. Ganick, O'Brien & Sarin, 35 F. Supp. 2d 148 (D. Mass. 1999); Knight v. Schulman, 102 F. Supp. 2d 867 (S.D. Ohio 1999). *See also* 31 U.S.C. § 3718. *See generally* Heintz v. Jenkins, 514 U.S. 291, 115 S. Ct. 1489, 131 L. Ed. 2d 395 (1995).

98 15 U.S.C. § 1692a(6)(C).

99 Knight v. Schulman, 102 F. Supp. 2d 867 (S.D. Ohio 1999). *See also* Richardson v. Baker, 663 F. Supp. 651 (S.D.N.Y. 1987) (fact that collector sent letters at behest of Dept. of Education does not exempt it from FDCPA).

100 15 U.S.C. § 1692a(6)(C).

101 *See* 15 U.S.C. § 1692a(6) (" 'debt collector' means any person who . . . attempts to collect . . . *indirectly*, debts owed . . . another.") (emphasis added).

102 15 U.S.C. § 1692a(6)(A). *Cf.* Fischer v. Unipac Service Corp., 519 N.W.2d 793 (Iowa 1994) (FDCPA does not apply to loan servicer hired before default). *See generally* Pelfrey v. Educational Credit Management Corp., 71 F. Supp. 2d 1161 (N.D. Ala. 1999).

103 15 U.S.C. § 1692a(6)(F)(iii).

lender. In these situations the secondary market lender and servicer are not covered by the FDCPA, because they are not assigned the loan post-default, and are not taking the loan to collect on a default.[104]

Some advocates have argued that collection agencies should be covered by the FDCPA if they acquired the debt after it became "delinquent" as defined by the student loan regulations, even if it was not yet in "default" as defined by those regulations.[105] The ambiguity arises because the FDCPA does not provide a definition of "default."

The default period in the student loan regulations (previously 180 days, now 270)[106] is unusually long. Borrower advocates argue that allowing such a long period without FDCPA coverage is inconsistent with the purposes of the FDCPA. According to this argument, the definition of "default" in the FDCPA should be the same as "delinquent" in the student loan regulations. The FTC's Official Staff Commentary on the FDCPA lends support to this argument, as it states that the exemption "applies to parties such as mortgage service companies whose business is servicing *current* accounts."[107] Courts have, however, rejected these arguments and interpreted the definition of "default" for FDCPA coverage to be the same as the definition of "default" in the student loan regulations.[108]

4.3.3.6 FDCPA Applicability to Guaranty Agencies

Most collection on FFELs is conducted by guaranty agencies or collection agencies hired by the guarantor. If a guaranty agency hires a private collector, that collector is covered by the FDCPA just as a collector hired by the Department is covered.

Nevertheless, a significant amount of collection activity is still engaged in by the guarantor itself. State-created guaranty agencies may be exempt under the FDCPA's exclusion of state employees, depending upon the structure and authority given the agency by the state legislature.[109]

Private guaranty agencies should clearly fall into the general definition of "collector" under the FDCPA.[110] The governmental exemption does not apply to them, and the guaranty agency meets the other criteria for a debt collector under the FDCPA.[111] To be a debt collector, the guaranty agency's principal purpose must be the collection of debts or it must regularly collect debts owed another,[112] interpreted to mean *originally* owed another.[113]

Guaranty agencies devote most of their resources to collecting on defaulted loans, and their other functions are relatively minor, so there is a strong argument that collection of debts is their principal purpose.[114] Even if this argument

---

104 15 U.S.C. § 1692a(6)(F)(iii). *See* National Consumer Law Center, Fair Debt Collection § 4.3.9 (4th ed. 2000 and Supp.). *See also* Coppola v. Connecticut Student Loan Foundation, 1989 U.S. Dist. LEXIS 3415 (D. Conn. Mar. 21, 1989).

105 15 U.S.C. § 1692a(6)(F)(iii).

106 34 C.F.R. §§ 682.200(b) (FFEL) and 685.102(b) (Direct Loans). *See generally* § 4.1, *supra*.

107 FTC Official Staff Commentary on the FDCPA § 803-4(f), 53 Fed. Reg. 50097, 50103 (Dec. 13, 1988) (emphasis added).

108 *See* Brannan v. United Student Aid Funds, 94 F.3d 1260, 1262 n.3 (9th Cir. 1996), *cert. denied*, 521 U.S. 1106, 1111 (1997) (holding limited to guaranty agency not fitting within government actor exception and debt in this case obtained after default); Skerry v. Massachusetts Higher Education Assistance Corp., 73 F. Supp. 2d 47 (D. Mass. 1999); Jones v. Intuition, Inc., 12 F. Supp. 2d 775 (W.D. Tenn. 1998); *see also* Pelfrey v. Educational Credit Management Corp., 1999 U.S. Dist. LEXIS 16788 (N.D. Ala. 1999) (discussing issue, but finding collector exempt for other reasons), *aff'd*, 208 F.3d 945 (11th Cir. 2000); Games v. Cavazos, 737 F. Supp. 1368 (D. Del. 1990) (decision based on government actor exception); Coppola v. Connecticut Student Loan Foundation, 1989 U.S. Dist. LEXIS 3415 (D. Conn. Mar. 21, 1989) (servicing agency not covered because note not in default when transferred to secondary lender for whom agency serviced loan; facts suggest that plaintiff was current on payments at the time so loan was neither "delinquent" nor in "default.").

109 15 U.S.C. § 1692a(6)(C).

110 Brannan v. United Student Aid Funds, Inc., 94 F.3d 1260 (9th Cir. 1996), *cert. denied*, 521 U.S. 1106, 1111 (1997); Sibley v. Diversified Collection Services, Inc., 1997 U.S. Dist. LEXIS 23583 (N.D. Tex. June 10, 1997) (ruling on defendants' motion to dismiss). See Appx. F, *infra* for a complete list of state guaranty agencies and contact information.

111 Brannan v. United Student Aid Funds, Inc., 94 F.3d 1260 (9th Cir. 1996), *cert. denied*, 521 U.S. 1106, 1111 (1997); Student Loan Fund, Inc. v. Duerner, 951 P.2d 1272 (Idaho 1997), *cert. denied*, 525 U.S. 816 (1998) (court held that guaranty agency was a collector within meaning of FDCPA; guaranty agency "did not become a governmental employee by virtue of its contract with a government agency"); *see also* Spears v. Bowman, 875 F.2d 867 (6th Cir. 1989) (unpublished, full text available at 1989 U.S. App. LEXIS 6208) (reversing ruling that collection agency was exempt as de facto state employee; remanding for factual determination of legal relationship between it and state). *But see* Games v. Cavazos, 737 F. Supp. 1368 (D. Del. 1990) (USA Funds was performing essentially a governmental function in assisting the U.S. in the *tax intercept process* and, because other state guaranty agencies were in fact state entities, it made no sense to the court to distinguish between guaranty agencies that were private entities and those that were state agencies).

112 15 U.S.C. § 1692a(6). The guaranty agency is not a creditor because it is assigned the debt for the purposes of collecting the debt. *Id.* § 1692a(4).

113 *See* Games v. Cavazos, 737 F. Supp. 1368 (D. Del. 1990); Student Loan Fund, Inc. v. Duerner, 951 P.2d 1272 (Idaho 1997), *cert. denied*, 525 U.S. 816 (1998); *see generally* Kimber v. Federal Financial Corp., 668 F. Supp. 1480 (M.D. Ala. 1987). *But see* Trubek, FTC Informal Staff Letter (Sept. 12, 1988) (Great Lakes Higher Education Corp. not covered because it is a servicing company and is also a creditor because it owns the loans it guarantees).

114 *See* Games v. Cavazos, 737 F. Supp. 1368 (D. Del. 1990); Student Loan Fund, Inc. v. Duerner, 951 P.2d 1272 (Idaho 1997), *cert. denied*, 525 U.S. 816 (1998) (guaranty agency argued unsuccessfully that it should be excluded from FDCPA coverage because it was collecting a debt that it originated; court

is unsuccessful, it is clear that guaranty agencies regularly collect debts owed another and are therefore covered by the FDCPA.[115]

Consequently, the key initial issue in bringing an FDCPA action against a guarantor is determining whether the guarantor is a state or a private entity. Private agencies should clearly fall within the FDCPA's definition of "collector." State agencies, on the other hand, will likely be exempted under the FDCPA's exclusion of state employees.[116]

Advocates should not rely on the name or an agency's prior status as an indication that it is a state agency, but verify this independently. A number of guarantors recently have switched from state to private entities, or formed separate subsidiaries.[117] Agencies that appear to be public at first glance may in fact be private and therefore covered by the FDCPA.

A private guaranty agency may try to avoid coverage by arguing that it obtained the debt at the time the agency became the guarantor of the debt (at the initiation of the loan, when the loan was not in default) and that it is therefore exempt.[118] Courts have rejected this specious argument, holding that merely acting as guarantor does not amount to "obtaining" a debt.[119]

To avoid FDCPA coverage, state and private guaranty agencies may also argue that the numerous relationships and connections between the United States government and guaranty agencies place agencies in the position of fiduciaries for the government and thus the agencies fall within the exemption for bona fide fiduciaries. This provision of the FDCPA excludes from the definition of "debt collector" any person or agency attempting to collect a debt to the extent such activity is incidental to a bona fide fiduciary obligation

or a bona fide escrow arrangement.[120] At least a few courts have exempted nonprofit and private guaranty agencies on this basis.[121]

4.3.4 Applicability of State Debt Collection Law to Student Loans

While the FDCPA exempts creditors and government agencies from its scope, state law often does not. Thus, it is important to explore whether state debt collection laws apply to student loan collection.[122] In addition, state law may specifically prohibit certain collection activity not explicitly restricted by the FDCPA.

State laws that may apply include state debt collection statutes, state UDAP statutes, and common law tort theories. These legal challenges are described in detail in other NCLC manuals.[123]

In any state law challenge to student loan collection practices, advocates should expect a defense that the Higher Education Act's scheme of student loan collection preempts the state debt collection law. There can be no question that state law that directly conflicts with federal law is preempted. However, collectors even argue further that the federal scheme preempts *any* state regulation of student loan collectors.

Brannan v. United Student Aid Funds[124] supports the argument that the federal scheme "totally occupies the field" and thus all state regulation is preempted. In *Brannan*, the Oregon debt collection statute was found to be preempted by the federal scheme. The dissent, however, puts forth the better argument that the whole Oregon statute

---

held that the bank, not the agency, was the originator of the loans). *But see* Trubek, FTC Informal Staff Letter (Sept. 12, 1988) (Great Lakes Higher Education Corp. not covered because it is a servicing company and is also a creditor because it owns the loans it guarantees).

115 Games v. Cavazos, 737 F. Supp. 1368 (D. Del. 1990); Student Loan Fund, Inc. v. Duerner, 951 P.2d 1272 (Idaho 1997), *cert. denied*, 525 U.S. 816 (1998).

116 15 U.S.C. § 1692a(6)(C).

117 For example, in 1997 the California Student Aid Commission (CSAC) set up EDFUND as a separate nonprofit corporation. For a complete list of state guaranty agencies, see Appx. G, *infra*. This information is also available on the Department of Education's website at www.ed.gov.

118 *See* the exemption at 15 U.S.C. § 1692a(6)(F)(iii). *See generally* § 4.3.3.4, *infra*.

119 Sibley v. Diversified Collection Servs., Inc., 1997 U.S. Dist. LEXIS 23583 (N.D. Tex. June 10, 1997); *see also* Games v. Cavazos, 737 F. Supp. 1368 (D. Del. 1990) (fact that guaranty agency once held the debt does not exempt it, where it had transferred debt to Dept. of Education at time of collection activities).

120 15 U.S.C. § 1692a(6)(F)(i).

121 *See* Pelfrey v. Educational Credit Management Corp., 1999 U.S. Dist. LEXIS 16788 (N.D. Ala. 1999); Davis v. United Student Aid Funds, Inc., 45 F. Supp. 2d 1104 (D. Kan. 1998) (in granting motion to dismiss, court found that a nonprofit student loan guaranty agency was a fiduciary and therefore not a debt collector). The *Pelfrey* court repeatedly cited a declaration filed with the court by Larry Oxendine, Director of Guarantor and Lender Oversight Service with the Department of Education. This declaration is a useful summary of the various arguments guaranty agencies will use to support their position that they are exempt from the FDCPA. For a copy of the Oxendine declaration from another case, see Declaration of Larry Oxendine, Mitchell v. Educational Credit Management Corp., Clearinghouse No. 52492 (N.D. Ill. 1997).

122 Patzka v. Viterbo College, 917 F. Supp. 654 (W.D. Wis. 1996) (school barred from collecting interest where student not informed of interest rate; FDCPA and Wisconsin UDAP violations claimed); Sibley v. Firstcollect, Inc., 913 F. Supp. 469 (M.D. La. 1995).

123 National Consumer Law Center, Fair Debt Collection Chs. 8, 10, 11 (4th ed. 2000 and Supp.); National Consumer Law Center, Unfair and Deceptive Acts and Practices §§ 2.2.2, 5.1.1 (5th ed. 2001 and Supp.).

124 94 F.3d 1260 (9th Cir. 1996), *cert. denied*, 521 U.S. 1106, 1111 (1997).

should not be preempted, but only those prohibitions that specifically preempt a federal requirement.[125]

In a well-reasoned opinion, *McComas v. Financial Collection Agencies*,[126] a federal court in West Virginia has refused to follow the majority opinion in *Brannan*, and has held that the HEA preempts only those state debt collection provisions that specifically conflict with the federal scheme. The *McComas* court found that:

- The federal requirement that student loan collectors telephone debtors does not preempt state law prohibitions on abusive and deceptive telephone collection techniques;
- The federal requirement that guarantors sue debtors under certain conditions does not preempt a state law prohibition of a collector deceptively threatening legal action it does not intend to take;
- The federal requirement that a guarantor garnish wages in certain circumstances does not preempt a state law prohibition against threatening 33% wage garnishments without first informing the debtor that a court order must first be obtained; and
- The federal scheme does not preempt state laws prohibiting false statements that a collector is affiliated with the government.[127]

A second district court opinion agrees with *McComas* and rejects the notion that the HEA categorically preempts state debt collection laws.[128]

There are a number of reasons why *McComas* and the dissent in *Brannan* are correct. Federal law specifically requires that, when the Department contracts with debt collectors to recover indebtedness, the contract shall provide that the collector is subject to "the laws and regulations of the United States Government and State governments related to debt collection practices."[129] That is, private debt collectors agree in their own contracts to be subject to state debt collection laws.

In addition, the Department's own regulation preempts only state laws "that would conflict with or hinder satisfaction of the requirements of or frustrate the purposes of this section."[130] A subsequent Notice of Interpretation states that the Secretary "intended these provisions . . . to preempt contrary or inconsistent State law to the extent necessary to permit compliance with the Federal regulations."[131] *Bran-*

nan found other portions of this Notice of Interpretation to support its conclusion that the federal scheme occupies the field.[132] But *McComas* explains how *Brannan* took a particular passage out of context, and that the Notice of Interpretation relied on by *Brannan* actually says the exact opposite—that state law is preempted only to the extent it conflicts with the federal scheme.[133] The Notice of Interpretation suggests that state collection laws would be preempted to the extent that they conflict with:

- The Department's requirement that collectors complete a sequence of contacts with the borrower at specified intervals, using particular warnings about the consequences of default;
- The Department's requirement that guaranty agencies initiate suit and attempt to enforce a judgment (but all state law requirements about the manner of doing this are unaffected);
- The HEA requirement that holders report the status of loans to credit reporting agencies; and
- The HEA's imposition of liability upon borrowers for reasonable collection costs and its abrogation of the defense of infancy.

All other requirements of state law should be considered to continue in full force and effect.

4.3.5 Other Remedies for Government Agency Debt Collection Abuse

4.3.5.1 Other Federal Claims

In addition to the FDCPA and state debt collection law, borrowers may have other remedies for debt collection abuse. When the United States is the collector, potential claims include the Federal Tort Claims Act, the Privacy Act, the Administrative Procedure Act, and the Civil Rights Act.[134] A good example of a constitutional challenge to government student loan collection practices is *Williams v. Illinois State Scholarship Commission*,[135] in which the Illinois Supreme Court ruled that an Illinois statute[136] requiring guaranty agencies to sue only in Cook County violated the Due Process Clause. *Williams* also found violative of due process the guaranty agency's practice, even prior to the passage of the *special* Illinois venue statute, of bringing all its collection actions in Cook County.[137] However, in these

---

125 *Id.* at 1266 (opinion of J. Fletcher, concurring and dissenting).
126 1997 U.S. Dist. LEXIS 2725 (S.D. W. Va. Mar. 7, 1997).
127 *Id.*
128 Sibley v. Diversified Collection Services, Inc., 1997 U.S. Dist. LEXIS 23583 (N.D. Tex. June 10, 1997) (ruling on defendants' motion to dismiss) (court declined to follow majority in *Brannan* to the extent it holds that any state statute regulating debt collection practices is per se inconsistent with the collection requirements placed on guarantors by federal regulations).
129 31 U.S.C. § 3718(a)(2)(B).
130 34 C.F.R. § 682.411(n).
131 55 Fed. Reg. 40120, 40121 (1990).

132 Brannan v. United Student Aid Funds, Inc., 94 F.3d 1260 (9th Cir. 1996), *cert. denied*, 521 U.S. 1106, 1111 (1997).
133 McComas v. Financial Collection Agencies, 1997 U.S. Dist. LEXIS 2725 (S.D. W. Va. Mar. 7, 1997).
134 National Consumer Law Center, Fair Debt Collection § 13.4 (4th ed. 2000 and Supp.).
135 139 Ill. 2d 24, 563 N.E.2d 465 (1990).
136 Ill. Rev. Stat. 1988 Supp. 1, Par. 12.
137 Williams v. Illinois State Scholarship Comm'n, 139 Ill. 2d 24,

cases, plaintiffs will have to prove that the guaranty agency is a state actor in order to invoke constitutional due process protections.[138]

The guaranty agency in the Illinois case argued that it could bring its collection actions in Cook County because the state's *general* venue statute allows suit in any county with sufficient contacts with the transaction. The guaranty agency claimed it approved student loans from its Cook County offices. The court analyzed the loan process and found there to be insufficient contacts with Cook County.[139] Finally, the Illinois Supreme Court in *Williams* ruled that a venue waiver or forum selection clause found in the actual student loan agreement was against public policy and void.[140]

Similarly, if the Department is responsible for sending dunning letters that mislead students concerning the legal garnishment process (failing to disclose the right to a hearing and failing to disclose various limits to that garnishment right), an argument could be made that those who are misled into making a payment to avoid the garnishment are deprived of that property without notice of their right to a hearing, as required by the HEA and by the Due Process Clause of the Fifth Amendment. Such an argument could form the basis of a civil rights claim against the Department.

If a private collector is involved, advocates should also consider raising claims other than federal and state debt collection laws to challenge abusive collection behavior. There are numerous federal, state, and tort remedies that may apply.[141]

4.3.5.2 Complaining to the Department

Another response to debt collection abuse is to complain to the entity that hired the collection agency. This may not provide any relief to the borrower, but it may help others. If a collector is employed by the Department, borrowers should contact the Department Collection Services divisions or the student loan ombudsman to register complaints.[142]

If a guaranty agency holds a loan, the first place to complain about collection agency misconduct is the state guaranty agency. If the collection misconduct is by an employee of the guaranty agency, it is best to contact an official at a higher level of the agency. If a guaranty agency appears to be systematically failing to follow federal policy, advocates should send the Department or ombudsman the particulars of the complaint.

4.4 Collection Fees and Penalties

4.4.1 Department-Held Loans

4.4.1.1 How Collection Fees Work on Department-Held Loans

When the Department holds a loan and the loan has been in default for a period of time, the Department routinely turns the loan over to one of several major collection agencies with whom it has contracted.[143] The collection agency, in effect, is in charge of that loan throughout the remainder of the collection process. Whether the borrower believes payment is being sent to the Department or the collector, all payments on student loans go to the Department's National Payment Center. The Department then computes the commission owed to its collectors based on which collectors were collecting on which accounts that have paid.

The collector receives a commission on a payment as long as the collector has been assigned the file, whether or not the student's payment was instigated by that collector's actions. The Department then deducts an amount roughly equal to the commission it has paid its collector from the consumer's payment. Only the amount left over after the commission is paid is applied to interest and then principal, in that order.[144]

Consider the following example. Assume a borrower's current obligation, including principal and interest, on a loan is $10,000 and that the commission paid to collectors is 30% of the amount collected. Even if the borrower immediately pays the full $10,000, the Department will first apply the funds to pay the collection commission, leaving only $7,000 to apply to the outstanding balance. The borrower's obligation is thus lowered only to $3000. To pay off the $10,000 balance, the borrower must immediately pay $14,285.71. The Department will apply 30% of that amount (30% of $14,285.71 is $4285.71) to collection costs. The remainder ($10,000) pays off the loan.

---

563 N.E.2d 465 (1990). *But see* United States v. Frisk, 675 F.2d 1079 (9th Cir. 1982).

138 *See, e.g.*, George W. v. U.S. Dep't of Ed., 149 F. Supp. 2d 1195 (E.D. Cal. 2000) (in case raising constitutional violations for alleged unreasonable charging of collection fees, court found guaranty agency was not a state actor required to afford borrower due process).

139 Williams v. Illinois State Scholarship Comm'n, 139 Ill. 2d 24, 563 N.E.2d 465 (1990).

140 *Id.*

141 *See generally* National Consumer Law Center, Fair Debt Collection (4th ed. 2000 and Supp.).

142 *See* § 4.2.1, *supra.*

---

143 See § 4.2.1, *supra* for a list of private collection agencies that have contracts with the Department.

144 34 C.F.R. § 682.404(f) (payments are applied first to collection costs and then to other incidental charges such as late charges, then to interest and principal). *See* Padilla v. Payco General Am. Credits, Inc., 161 F. Supp. 2d 264 (S.D.N.Y. 2001) (defendant's summary judgment motion denied on plaintiff's claim that debt collector induced borrower to make a down payment by agreeing to apply, in violation of federal law, the payment toward principal only).

4.4.1.2 Avoiding Collection Agency Fees

There is no easy way to take an account away from a collection agency and avoid the collection fees. The fees will be assessed even if a borrower attempts to pay the Department directly. One exception is that no collection fees are assessed on amounts seized from tax refunds. Consequently, a borrower may be better off arranging to have a large tax refund due, and having that amount intercepted, rather than paying off the loan directly to a collection agency.

In general, funds from tax intercepts should be applied to principal and interest, not to collection fees.[145] Thus, the balance will decrease more rapidly through tax intercepts than through low monthly payment plans. Borrowers choosing this strategy should wait until the funds taken from the tax intercepts leave them with a small balance left on their loans. Once the borrower has paid down to a small balance, exclusive of collection fees, the Department will frequently agree at this point to compromise the remaining balance and accept a lump sum payment.[146] The Department will usually waive the collection fees when the principal and interest is paid in full. This strategy saves borrowers from paying the huge collection fees that accrue once an account is turned over to a collection agency.[147]

There are at least three other strategies a borrower can use to avoid paying collection costs once a loan has been turned over to a collection agency. The most complete remedy is to try to cancel the borrower's obligation on the loan. This can be done through a false certification, unpaid refund or closed school discharge, a bankruptcy discharge, through raising school-related defenses on the loan or if the student is totally and permanently disabled.[148] Making payments through a chapter 13 bankruptcy plan may also avoid collection fees.[149]

If the borrower is not eligible for cancellation, another possible solution is to consolidate the defaulted loan into a new Direct or FFEL loan. The consolidation loan will include an 18.5% collection fee from the old loan, but no further amounts will go to collection fees unless the consolidated loan goes into default.[150]

Third, the borrower can complain about the collection agency's illegal or improper conduct to the Department. The Department will sometimes take the loan away from the collector.[151]

4.4.1.3 Department Has Agreed to Limit Fees (Temporarily) to 25%

In 1995, borrowers sued the Department for assessing up to 43% collection fees on certain student loan borrowers whose loan notes specified 25% collection fees.[152] The Department admitted that it was in error to systematically charge the higher collection costs to those with the 25% provision in their notes.[153] It also admitted that it had no method for easily distinguishing those with the 25% collection provision from other borrowers.

Under the terms of the settlement agreement, the Department agreed to temporarily assess no more than 25% collection fees on all student loan payments. The agreement specified that this system would stay in place until the Department developed a way of distinguishing between collection fee limits in different loans.

The settlement agreement does not directly bind state guaranty agencies in their assessment of collection fees. However, federal regulations provide that guaranty agencies cannot charge more in collection fees than the Department can charge.[154] Therefore the guarantors should also not be charging more than 25% during the interim period. While the Department comes up with an alternative system, the guarantors will not in any case be able to charge more than that which is provided for in borrowers' promissory notes.

Through early 2001, the Department abided by the *Gibbons* settlement and did not publicly announce or implement an alternative system. For most of this time, the Department stated on its website that collection costs would be no more than 25%.[155]

---

145 The Department of Treasury regulations on tax intercepts specify only that offsets can be allocated for past due debts, less fees charged under 31 C.F.R. § 285.2(i). This section allows fees charged by the Financial Management Service (FMS) of the Department of Treasury and the IRS to be deducted from the amount collected. To the extent allowed by law, federal agencies may add these fees to the debt. Still, the fees deducted, if any, should be less than those charged by collection agencies. *See generally* § 5.2, *infra*.

146 *See* §§ 4.4.1.1, 4.4.1.5, *supra*. *See also Department of Education, Amendment to Agreement Pursuant to Section 428(b) of the Higher Education Act of 1965, as amended, with a State or Private Non-profit Institution or Organization for Coverage of its Student Loan Insurance Program under the Interest Benefits Provision of Section 428(a) of the Act*, Appendix I § 5.1, Clearinghouse No. 51,926 (July 11, 1994) (if borrower agrees to pay principal within 30 days, agency may enter into a repayment agreement that includes the compromise of interest owed).

147 *See* §§ 4.4.1.1, 4.4.1.5, *supra*.

148 *See generally* Chs. 6 (loan cancellations), 7 (bankruptcy), *infra*.

149 *See* 7.4, *infra*.

150 34 C.F.R. § 685.220(f)(iii), using amount in 34 C.F.R. § 682.401(b)(27) (FFEL). *See* § 8.2.4.4, *infra*.

151 *See* § 4.2.5.2, *supra*.

152 Clearinghouse No. 50,432C (E.D.N.Y. Nov. 9, 1994) (complaint filed).

153 Gibbons v. Riley, Clearinghouse No. 50,432 (E.D.N.Y. 1995) (stipulated extension of time for defendants to respond to complaint); *see also Letter of Fred J. Marinucci, Deputy Assistant General Counsel, to Andrew J. Cohen, Legal Assistance Foundation of Chicago*, Clearinghouse No. 50,423 (Oct. 18, 1994) (Department does not intend to collect any amount in excess of what is allowed by the loan agreement).

154 34 C.F.R. § 682.410(b)(2).

155 As of summer 2002, the website is not as clear, stating that the

In spring 2001, however, the Department began sending out notices to borrowers with loans that the Department had reviewed and determined that the collection fees charged the borrower did not exceed the promissory note. The notices state:

> The Department has discovered that some student loan debtors were charged an amount for collection costs that was higher than the limits on those costs set in their loan agreements (promissory notes). The Department has therefore just done a survey of collection costs it charged on student loans. Based on that survey, the Department believes that you were not charged more for collection costs than your note allowed.
>
> However, if you believe that you may have been charged more for collection costs than your loan agreement permits, on request, you may obtain a copy of your loan agreement and repayment history to review.
>
> If these records show that you were charged more than the loan agreement allowed, the department will adjust your account to give you credit for the overcharge, or, if your accounts are now closed, the Department will send you the amount of the overcharge by U.S. treasury check (unless the overcharge was less than $5,00). We will send the documents you request in any case.
>
> Please direct any requests for records to:
>
> U.S. Department of Education
> P.O. Box 4222
> Iowa City, IA 52244-4222.
>
> You may also obtain these documents and review by calling 1-800-621-3115. Please refer to code CCL to speed up your request.

As of 2002, the Department was still sending out these notices with plans to complete the process by the end of the year.[156]

4.4.1.4 United States Collection of Other Fees and Penalties

In some cases, the United States or private attorneys hired by the United States to collect on student loans attempt to collect court filing fees and penalties in addition to attorney fees and collection costs.[157] Because such collection actions

are usually uncontested, those fees are rarely questioned. The reality is that the United States may lack statutory authority to collect these amounts. For example, the United States need not pay filing fees, so any attempt to collect this amount, even by a private attorney collecting on behalf of the government, should be improper.[158]

Another dubious fee is a 6% per year penalty. Authority for this fee is explicitly found in federal regulations that allow the Secretary to impose a 6% per year penalty on the amount delinquent if the debtor does not make at least a partial payment on a debt within ninety days of the Secretary's demand for payment.[159]

However, the 6% penalty should not be a factor in the student loan context because it does not apply to obligations where either federal regulations or the loan agreement explicitly fixes the interest.[160] Since student loans charge interest while they are in default, the 6% penalty does not apply.[161] In addition, the penalty does not apply to loans executed before October 25, 1982.[162]

The Department appears to agree that it does not have authority to seek this fee because the promissory note limits the fees that may be charged the student. Nevertheless, certain pre-1986 NDSLs (now termed Perkins Loans) did specify a certain penalty or late charge in the promissory note.

Another federal statute, the Federal Debt Collection Procedures Act authorizes the United States to recover a surcharge of ten percent of the amount of the debt when collecting on the debt using pre-judgment remedies (such as attachment) or post-judgment remedies (such as writs of execution).[163] However, the statute does not apply to litigation to obtain a judgment on the debt, and the United States cannot assess the surcharge based on such litigation.[164]

4.4.1.5 Does the Department Have Legal Authority to Assess Collection Fees?

The Department has enacted regulations setting out when it will seek fees and the size of the collection fees it will seek

---

amount needed to satisfy a student loan debt collected by the Department's contractors will be up to 25 percent more than the principal and interest repaid by the borrower.

156 This is an area where there will likely be significant developments after the printing of this manual. Advocates should follow developments in NCLC's newsletter, NCLC REPORTS and possibly on the DOE website or through other DOE publications.

157 *See* United States v. Singer, 943 F. Supp. 9 (D.D.C. 1996), *aff'd in part, rev'd in part*, 132 F.3d 1482 (D.C. Cir. 1997) (Depart-

ment confessed error and the district court's ordering of 10% surcharge to Department as fees was reversed on appeal); United States v. Smith, 862 F. Supp. 257 (D. Haw. 1994); United States v. Spann, 797 F. Supp. 980 (S.D. Fla. 1992).

158 United States v. Spann, 797 F. Supp. 980 (S.D. Fla. 1992).

159 34 C.F.R. § 30.61(a). The authority for this regulation is 31 U.S.C. § 3717(e)(2).

160 31 U.S.C. § 3717(g)(1).

161 *See* United States v. Spann, 797 F. Supp. 980 (S.D. Fla. 1992).

162 31 U.S.C. § 3717(g)(2).

163 28 U.S.C. § 3011.

164 United States v. Singer, 943 F. Supp. 9 (D.D.C. 1996), *aff'd in part, rev'd in part*, 132 F.3d 1482 (D.C. Cir. 1997) (Department confessed error and the district court's ordering of 10% surcharge to Department as fees was reversed on appeal); United States v. Smith, 862 F. Supp. 257 (D. Haw. 1994) (proceeding did not involve pre- or post-judgment remedies and therefore government not entitled to 10% surcharge); U.S. v. Mauldin, 805 F. Supp. 35 (N.D. Ala. 1992).

Student Loan Law

from student loan defaulters.[165] Under these regulations, the Department may charge a debtor for costs associated with the collection of a particular debt, including but not limited to employee salaries, telephone and mailing costs, costs for reporting debts to credit bureaus or purchasing credit bureau reports, computer and record maintenance costs, bank charges, court costs, attorney fees, and collection agency costs.[166]

By far the most important of these costs are collection agency costs. This is computed as the commission rate the Department pays the collection agency or the average rate the Department pays all its collection agencies.[167]

This is an intuitively suspect method of calculating collection costs. It does not cost the collection agency $3000 to send out letters to collect on a $7000 loan where the collection agency does not institute any litigation. Students' attorneys should thus be able to challenge such unreasonable collection fees.[168]

This method of calculating collection costs is brought further into question by the regulation itself. The regulation specifies that the collection agency charge is not the actual cost associated with collection of a student's debt. As discussed below, advocates should argue that the collection agency charge is an arbitrary and excessive percentage of the student's outstanding debt, whereby students making payments to collection agencies are charged for costs associated with other students who do not make payments to collection agencies.

The first place to start in challenging the imposition of fees is the statutory authority for the Department's regulation. The regulation itself sets out as its statutory authority 20 U.S.C. §§ 1221e-3(a)(1), 1226a-1 and 31 U.S.C. §§ 3711(e), 3717(e)(1), 3718.[169] While none of the stated statutory provisions provide authority for the regulation, 20 U.S.C. § 1091a(b)(1) does authorize "reasonable collection costs." "Collection costs" traditionally refers to costs asso-

ciated with a lawsuit, such as attorney fees, and not costs just associated with a collection agency contacting debtors.[170] In any event, such costs can only be "reasonable," a standard the Department's regulation does not appear to meet.[171]

4.4.2 Guaranty Agency Collection Fees

4.4.2.1 Calculation of Fees

The Department's regulations require guaranty agencies to charge collection fees, whether or not provided for in the borrower's promissory note. The method of allocating students' payments to the fees must be the same as for Department-held loans.[172] Agencies must only charge amounts equal to reasonable costs incurred in collecting.[173]

The guaranty agency cannot assess an amount in advance for collection fees, but must instead apportion a percentage of each payment toward collection fees. The amount charged is the lesser of the amount that would be charged under the formula set out at 34 C.F.R. § 30.60 or the amount the borrower would be charged if the Department held the loan.[174]

34 C.F.R. § 30.60 allows collection charges equaling the costs associated with the collection of a *particular* debt. These costs may include salaries for employees, costs for computer operations and records maintenance, court costs, and attorney costs. Section 30.60 also sets out a formula for computing collection fees as a percentage of the debt *if* a collection agency is hired, based on the contingency fee arrangement contracted with that collection agency. The

---

165 34 C.F.R. §§ 30.60 –.62.

166 34 C.F.R. § 30.60(a).

167 34 C.F.R. § 30.60(c), (d).

168 *See, e.g.,* George W. v. U.S. Dep't of Ed., 149 F. Supp. 2d 1195 (E.D. Cal. 2000) (plaintiff's claim that even the 18.5% limit may be unreasonable was dismissed on procedural grounds).

169 None of these statutes provides such authority. 20 U.S.C. §§ 1221e-3(a)(1) and 1226a-1 and 31 U.S.C. § 3711(e) have nothing to do with collection fees. Moreover, § 3717(e)(1) of the Federal Claims Collection Act (FCCA) authorizes the Secretary to assess a "processing and handling" charge, hardly authority to charge 40% collection fees. Similarly, FCCA § 3718 does not authorize the Secretary to assess any charges. FCCA § 3718 specifies that collection agencies are subject to the FDCPA, 15 U.S.C. § 1692f(1), and other state law that *limits* collection charges. FCCA § 3718 also specifies that collection agencies can be paid out of the amounts they collect, but this clearly does not authorize an increase in the amounts they collect to offset the fees the collection agencies charge the United States. *See* Miller, FTC Informal Staff Letter (Dec. 30, 1988), Clearinghouse No. 44,337 and reprinted at National Consumer Law Center, Fair Debt Collection Appx. I (4th ed. 2000 and Supp.).

170 *See* National Consumer Law Center, Fair Debt Collection § 15.2 (4th ed. 2000 and Supp.).

171 *See* Trustees of Tufts College v. Ramsdell, 554 N.E.2d 34, 28 Mass. App. Ct. 584, *review denied*, 407 Mass. 1104 (1990) (college's request for $1400.00 (1/3) collection attorney fee denied as unreasonable on a $4198.27 Perkins student loan; $630 (15%) awarded where judgment obtained by default in municipal court. Federal student loan law did not preempt state trial court's authority to determine what amount is a reasonable attorney fee for enforcing a note. Regulation authorizing guarantee agency's recovery of contingent fees of collection agencies does not authorize the recovery of collection attorneys contingent fees for litigation if the contingent fee exceeds a reasonable amount).

172 34 C.F.R. § 682.410(b)(2).

173 *Id.*

174 *Id.* The only exception to these formulas are for defaulted FFEL loans being consolidated pursuant to 34 C.F.R. § 682.401(b)(27) or for loans being rehabilitated pursuant to 34 C.F.R. § 682.405(b)(i)(iv). In these cases, collection costs are limited to 18.5%. 34 C.F.R. § 685.220(f)(iii), using amount in 34 C.F.R. § 682.401(b)(27) (FFEL). *See* Padilla v. Payco General Am. Credits, Inc., 161 F. Supp. 2d 264 (S.D.N.Y. 2001) (plaintiff's summary judgment motion granted on claim that collection agency charged more than the 18.5% limit); George W. v. U.S. Dep't of Ed., 149 F. Supp. 2d 1195 (E.D. Cal. 2000) (plaintiff's claim that even the 18.5% limit may be unreasonable was dismissed on procedural grounds). *See* § 8.2.4.4, *infra*.

regulation does *not* authorize a percentage formula if a guaranty agency does not hire an independent collection agency.

Advocates should carefully scrutinize guaranty agency calculation of collection fees. Many guaranty agencies do not properly calculate collection costs, failing to assess fees as required by Department regulations. These guarantors often use a percentage average of total past costs divided by total past debts, which is most clearly not costs associated with a *particular* debt as specified in section 30.60. The regulation only allows use of a percentage formula when the holder uses "a collection agency to collect a debt on a contingent fee basis."[175]

In addition, many guaranty agencies force students to pay a collection fee even on amounts repaid by tax intercepts. This provides an extra windfall to guarantors that the Department does not charge students on Department-held loans.[176]

Under current methodology used by at least some guarantors, it is also critical to determine how the guarantor applies the student's payment between collection fees, interest and principal. If more than the pro-rata share goes to collection fees, then the amount the student must pay in interest for the exact same loan will be greater than if the Department holds the loan.[177]

As discussed throughout this section, guaranty agencies cannot charge more than what the Department would charge for collection fees.[178] The Department currently does not charge more than 25% in collection fees.[179] The same limit should therefore apply to guaranty agencies. In addition, a guaranty agency has authority to compromise the amount of collection fees charged if it receives all principal and interest in full.[180]

4.4.2.2 Do Guaranty Agencies Have Legal Authority to Assess Collection Fees?

Since guaranty agencies cannot charge more than the Department in assessing collection fees, all the criticisms

against the Department's collection of fees should apply equally to guarantors. Several other aspects of the guarantor assessment of fees are also particularly suspect.

First, there is the question of whether the contingent fee percentage set out by the guaranty agency is reasonable, as required by the regulations.[181] What constitutes "reasonable" is unclear, but the regulations do limit charges to those reasonably incurred.[182] Under the existing regulation, the fees charged must be the *lesser* of the amount the borrower should be charged under 34 C.F.R. § 30.60 or the amount the borrower would be charged if the Department held the loan.[183]

Advocates should make sure that the percentage assessed is not just what the Department uses or an arbitrary number, but a percentage that is no more than what the guarantor pays its collector.

The percentage contracted by the guarantors with its collectors should be significantly lower than the percentage contracted for by the Department, because the Department has older, more difficult loans to collect. Many guarantor-held loans have just recently gone into default, and should be much easier to collect than loans going back more than ten years. Thus the percentage the guarantor actually sets with a collector may also be challenged as excessive.

4.4.3 Collection Fees Sought by Lenders

The FFEL regulations set out what collection costs the lender can seek (that is, before the loan is turned over to the guarantor).[184] The lender can seek no collection costs unless such charges are authorized in the promissory note and such costs are actually incurred by the lender or its agent.[185] Even if incurred and authorized by contract, the regulation prohibits assessment of charges for "normal collection costs associated with preparing letters or notices or with making personal contacts with the borrower."[186]

---

175 34 C.F.R. § 30.60(b), (c).

176 *See generally* § 5.2, *infra.*

177 Greater amounts violate 34 C.F.R. § 682.410(b)(2).

178 34 C.F.R. § 682.410(b)(2).

179 *See* § 4.3.1.3, *infra.*

180 *See* § 8.5, *infra.*

181 34 C.F.R. § 682.410(b)(2).

182 34 C.F.R. § 682.410(b)(2). *See, e.g.,* George W. v. U.S. Dep't of Ed., 149 F. Supp. 2d 1195 (E.D. Cal. 2000) (plaintiffs claim that even the allowable 18.5% limit may be unreasonable was dismissed on procedural grounds).

183 34 C.F.R. § 682.410(b)(2).

184 34 C.F.R. § 682.202(g).

185 34 C.F.R. § 682.202(g)(1).

186 34 C.F.R. § 682.202(g)(2).

Chapter 5

Property and Asset Seizures

5.1 Introduction

The government collected over $4 billion on defaulted student loans in FY 2000 though a variety of methods, including:

- $920 million by offsetting federal income tax refunds and other federal offsets;
- Nearly $107 million through wage garnishment of defaulters;
- Nearly $2 billion by consolidating defaulted loans; and
- Almost $1.5 billion through other collection tools.[1] The government also began seizing certain federal benefits in 2001.[2]

These collection methods often break the budgets of low-income households. Those living on or near the poverty line simply cannot afford to lose a tax refund or hard-earned wages. It is therefore critical for advocates to explore possible ways to cancel, defer, or forebear clients' loans.[3] There may also be affordable repayment options available.[4]

It is also important for advocates to understand the strategies available to challenge property seizures themselves. This chapter focuses on these strategies, highlighting tax refund intercepts, administrative wage garnishments, and federal benefits offsets.

5.2 Tax Refund Interceptions

5.2.1 How Tax Refund Interceptions Work

The tax refund intercept program involves a blanket seizure of almost all tax refunds due to debtors who are in default on their student loans. There is no statute of limitations for such an offset.[5] In addition, a number of states have state laws that authorize state guaranty agencies to intercept state income tax refunds. This subsection, however, focuses exclusively on the federal tax refund interception program.

The federal statute requires an intercept when a debt is owed to a federal agency, including a debt administered by a third party acting as an agent for the federal government.[6] The Department uses this authority to delegate to guaranty agencies the authority to initiate intercepts for loans still held by the guaranty agency.[7] This is significant because prior to the legislative change allowing interception of debts owed to agents of the federal government, authorization to intercept loans held by guaranty agencies was accomplished by the guarantors assigning the loans to the United States prior to interception. This posed practical problems for obligations that guarantors had already reduced to judgments, particularly since the interception program was not used to collect loans post-judgment. The interception program is now utilized to recover on debts pre- and post-judgment.[8]

Whether the debt is owed to the Department or to the guarantor, the decision of which refunds to intercept is not done on an individual basis. Computer tapes of *all* students in default meeting certain general criteria are sent to the IRS and anyone on that list owed a refund will have that refund intercepted.

How to count the delinquency was once an issue of some concern (compare Grider v. Cavazos, 911 F.2d 1158 (5th Cir. 1990); Thomas v. Bennett, 856 F.2d 1165, 1169, n.4 (8th Cir. 1988) *with* Jones v. Cavazos, 889 F.2d 1043 (11th Cir. 1989); Roberts v. Bennett, 709 F. Supp. 222 (N.D. Ga. 1989)), but is now irrelevant. *See generally* § 3.2, *supra*. These cases, however, may still be relevant in determining whether the government is bound by a statute of limitations in federal benefits offsets. *See* § 5.4.3.3, *infra*.

6   31 U.S.C. § 3720A(a).

7   *But see* McAfee v. Unger & Associates Inc., 730 So. 2d 623 (Ala. Civ. App. 1998), *cert. denied*, 730 So. 2d 626 (Ala. 1999) (federal regulations provide that attachment of an income tax refund can be carried out only by federal government agencies. Borrower's attempt to sue a collection agency employed by the Department of Education failed because agency could not have been involved in the tax intercept process).

8   This is a key issue in litigation challenging the government's position that there is no statute of limitations for federal benefits offsets. *See* § 5.4.3.3, *infra*.

---

1   U.S. Department of Education, National Student Loan Default Rate Lowest Ever, Press Release, October 2, 2000.

2   *See* § 5.4, *infra*.

3   *See* Ch. 2 (deferments and forbearances), *supra*; Ch. 6 (cancellations), *infra*.

4   *See* Ch. 8, *infra*.

5   20 U.S.C. § 1091a(a). Prior to the elimination of the statute of limitations for student loan collections, debts that had been delinquent for more than 10 years were not subject to offset.

5.2.2 How to Challenge Tax Refund Intercepts

5.2.2.1 The Pre-Intercept Notice

The Secretary can refer a debt for offset only after complying with certain procedures.[9] The guarantor (or a computer services contractor for Department-held loans) mails to the borrower a written notice of the Secretary's intent to seek the tax intercept, using the borrower's current address, as determined from the guarantor's Department's records.[10] The notice informs the borrower of the intent to refer a past-due debt to the Secretary of the Treasury for offset, and provides the borrower with the opportunity to inspect and copy the records on the borrower's debt, obtain a review of the existence, amount, enforceability, or past-due status of the debt, or enter into a written repayment agreement.[11]

5.2.2.2 Inspection of the File and Requesting a Hearing

The borrower must make a written request to inspect a loan file within twenty days of the notice of offset.[12] To obtain a review, the borrower must file a request for review at the address specified in the notice by the *later* of sixty-five days after the date of the notice or fifteen days after the borrower's loan file is provided, if requested.[13] A borrower can request a later hearing, but only a timely hearing request will stop the intercept pending the hearing.

Most loans are held by guarantors, and for these loans the hearing is initially with the guarantor. Only Department-held loans are initially heard by a Department official. If the review is not by the Department, the borrower can request a subsequent review by the Department after receiving the guaranty agency decision. This request for further review must be made within seven days after the agency's initial determination.[14]

The timely request for a hearing stops the intercept until the hearing and any further requests for review have been exhausted. The statute specifies that no intercept can occur until there is a determination that a debt is owed.[15]

When requesting review, the borrower must file identifying information about herself and information about the particular debt, including the borrower's social security number and the name of the loan program. Borrowers must also explain their reasons for contesting debts and file any documents they wish to submit.[16] If the borrower wants an oral hearing, she must also submit the reasons why the review cannot be limited to a review of the documentary evidence and also submit a list of the witnesses the borrower wishes to call, the issues they will testify about, and the reasons why the testimony is necessary.[17] The Secretary has established detailed standards in the regulation about when an oral hearing will be granted and the rules to follow in that hearing.[18]

It is important for borrowers to send the guarantor or the Department of Education all relevant documentation. Even though the Department's file may not contain much useful information, it is still a good practice for borrowers to also request the Department or guaranty agency file.

5.2.2.3 Grounds to Contest a Tax Intercept

While many borrowers report frustration in raising even the most meritorious defenses to a tax intercept, the Department's stated policy is to consider the following types of defenses:[19]

- The borrower has repaid the loan or the Social Security Number is incorrect and the borrower does not owe the loan;
- The borrower has entered into a repayment agreement with the guaranty agency or the Department and the borrower is making payments as required;
- The borrower has filed for bankruptcy and the case is still open or the loan was discharged in bankruptcy;[20]
- The school failed to pay the borrower an owed refund;
- The borrower is dead or totally and permanently disabled;[21]
- The loan is not enforceable. The Department will apparently recognize forgery or alteration of the loan documents as a defense. It should also recognize school-related defenses on Perkins, Direct, and many

---

9 34 C.F.R. § 30.33(a).

10 34 C.F.R. § 30.22(a). *See also* Glover v. Brady, 1994 U.S. Dist. LEXIS 13211 (S.D.N.Y. 1994) (no due process violation found where letter was mailed twice to last known address); Setlech v. United States, 816 F. Supp. 161 (E.D.N.Y. 1993), *aff'd*, 17 F.3d 390, *cert. denied*, 511 U.S. 1085 (1994) (notice need not be received; reasonable efforts must be made in sending the notice; if reasonable efforts are not made, the court would require Department to provide the borrower with a hearing as to whether the debt was due).

11 34 C.F.R. § 30.33(b).

12 34 C.F.R. § 30.33(c)(1).

13 34 C.F.R. § 30.33(d).

14 34 C.F.R. § 30.33(d)(3).

15 31 U.S.C. § 3720A(b)(3).

16 34 C.F.R. § 30.24(b)(1), (2).

17 34 C.F.R. § 30.25.

18 34 C.F.R. § 30.26.

19 Department of Education, *Amendment to Agreement Pursuant to Section 428(b) of the Higher Education Act of 1965, as Amended, with a State or Private Non-profit Institution or Organization for Coverage of Its Student Loan Insurance Program under the Interest Benefits Provision of Section 428(a) of the Act*, Clearinghouse No. 51, 926 (July 11, 1994).

20 *See* Ch. 7, *infra*.

21 *See* § 6.6, *infra*.

FFEL Loans issued after January 1, 1994.[22] It is less clear whether the Department will consider school-related defenses (other than the failure to pay an owed refund) for FFELs issued before that date;[23]

- The borrower is eligible for a closed-school discharge;[24]
- The borrower is eligible for a false certification discharge.[25]

If the borrower checks the closed school or false certification box, the servicer should mail the borrower the applicable discharge form. The borrower must return the form within sixty days. The tax intercept servicer should not certify the loan for offset until and unless it determines that the borrower fails to qualify for the discharge.[26]

In addition, although not explicitly recognized by the Department as a defense, the enabling statute for tax intercepts explicitly states that an intercept cannot take place unless the Department has certified that reasonable efforts have been made by the agency to obtain payment of the debt.[27]

The failure to consider evidence should also be grounds to undo a tax intercept. The enabling statute for tax intercepts explicitly states that no intercept can take place until the Department "considers any evidence presented by such person and determines that an amount of such debt is past due and legally enforceable."[28]

5.2.2.4 Due Process Challenges

Unfortunately, there are widespread allegations that guarantors, or contractors hired by the Department ignore borrower requests for hearings, deny requests on inadequate grounds, ignore valid defenses, or simply fail to respond in any way to student requests concerning pending intercepts. At a minimum, borrowers should be prepared for delays and should be sure to send all correspondence return receipt requested. A file should be created with copies of all correspondence.

When hearings are offered, they often fail to meet even minimum due process standards. In-person hearings are arranged for the convenience of the guarantor or Department, and consequently can be thousands of miles from the borrower's residence. The Department has responded to this problem by offering telephone hearings in lieu of in-person.[29] The due process implications of preventing borrowers from presenting their cases in person has not been challenged to date.

There have, however, been challenges to some of the other features of the tax refund intercept program (TRIP). In *Jones v. Cavazos*,[30] the Eleventh Circuit threw out a due process challenge to the intercept procedure because the plaintiff lacked standing, concluding that the plaintiff had no meritorious defense to the tax refund intercept. The clear lesson is not to raise a constitutional challenge to a hearing procedure on behalf of an individual who has no claims to raise in the hearing.

Richardson v. Baker[31] was a more successful due process challenge to the notice and hearing procedures afforded debtors prior to the tax refund interception. The parties reached a settlement whereby the government modified TRIP procedures for student loan defaulters. The settlement only applies to New York students, but the case is instructive concerning the type of settlement attorneys are likely to reach in other states.

The settlement contains model documents which must be sent in advance of any potential offset of tax refunds, informing recipients in detail about their rights and possible defenses and the nature of their loan obligation. The Department of Education must also send out a form which simplifies and expedites students' requests for a pre-offset hearing. The hearings will be by telephone or in person in New York City. With certain exceptions, the same procedures will be followed for loans held by state guaranty agencies, although hearings will be by telephone or in the office of the guaranty agency. The settlement provides no protections for the residents of the other forty-nine states.

---

22 *See* § 9.5.2, *infra.*

23 The directions the Department provides guarantors concerning tax intercepts provides that school-related defenses will not be accepted except for: (1) the failure to make a refund discussed above; (2) where a state statute specifically provides such lender liability for a seller's conduct; (3) the school made the loan (e.g., a Perkins Loan); or (4) the lender and school are so closely related that under applicable law the lender is liable for the school's misconduct. *Department of Education, Amendment to Agreement Pursuant to Section 428(b) of the Higher Education Act of 1965, as Amended, with a State or Private Non-profit Institution or Organization for Coverage of Its Student Loan Insurance Program under the Interest Benefits Provision of Section 428(a) of the Act*, Appendix I § 2.4.10, Clearinghouse No. 51,926 (July 11, 1994).

24 *See* § 6.2, *infra.*

25 *See* § 6.3, *infra.*

26 *Department of Education, Amendment to Agreement Pursuant to Section 428(b) of the Higher Education Act of 1965, as Amended, with a State or Private Non-profit Institution or Organization for Coverage of Its Student Loan Insurance Program under the Interest Benefits Provision of Section 428(a) of the Act*, Appendix I §§ 2.4.6, 2.4.11, Clearinghouse No. 51,926 (July 11, 1994).

27 31 U.S.C. § 3720A(b)(5).

28 *Id.*

29 *Department of Education, Amendment to Agreement Pursuant to Section 428(b) of the Higher Education Act of 1965, as Amended, with a State or Private Non-profit Institution or Organization for Coverage of Its Student Loan Insurance Program under the Interest Benefits Provision of Section 428(a) of the Act*, Appendix I § 2.3.1, Clearinghouse No. 51,926 (July 11, 1994).

30 889 F.2d 1043 (11th Cir. 1989).

31 Clearinghouse No. 40,719 (S.D.N.Y. Feb. 9, 1990) (order of settlement).

A third case upheld the notice even though it did not list potential defenses, did not disclose the right to an attorney, and was arguably confusing.[32] The same court also found no due process violation where a pre-intercept hearing was offered, but never afforded because of a private contractor's negligence, not because of government policy.[33] An unreported district court case also upheld the pre-intercept procedures.[34]

5.2.2.5 Post-Intercept Challenges

The IRS takes the position that there is no right to an administrative review of the intercept within the IRS and courts do not have jurisdiction to hear challenges against the IRS based on the intercept.[35] As a consequence, any post-intercept challenge should be directed to the Department of Education, not the IRS.

The Department has not set out a formal administrative procedure to review intercepts after they have occurred, but has indicated that it will follow the pre-intercept hearing procedure even for hearings requested post-intercept. The only difference is that the intercept is not stayed pending the review.

Whether in fact guarantors or the Department will actually review such post-intercept requests is an open question. Such an administrative appeal may be prudent before filing suit to forestall the Department's argument that the student must first exhaust administrative remedies.[36]

If this request is ignored, the remaining approach, where the student loan is not owed, is to sue the Department of Education for return of the intercepted refund.[37] Such a challenge is generally advisable only if the borrower has a complete defense, because the Department can counterclaim on the student loan note.

5.2.2.6 Repayment Plan in Lieu of Intercept

Borrowers can request written agreements to repay debts if they do so within twenty days of receiving the notice of intent to offset.[38] The Secretary or guarantor provides a repayment schedule, and, to avoid the intercept, the borrower must make the first payment within the later of sixty-five days of receipt of the original notice or seven days after the Secretary's decision if a review of a guaranty agency's decision is requested.[39]

The regulations provide that the repayment agreement must be on terms acceptable to the Secretary.[40] It does not specifically require that the Secretary offer a reasonable and affordable payment plan.[41] However, borrowers may be able to argue that a reasonable and affordable plan should be available in these circumstances. At a minimum, borrowers should be able to make payments under plans agreed to by the Secretary and then later request reasonable and affordable plans.[42]

5.2.2.7 Can a State Law Exemption Prevent a Tax Refund Intercept?

The Eleventh Circuit overturned a federal district court determination that Alabama's $3000 personal exemption applies to tax refund intercepts.[43] The borrower had argued that the Federal Debt Collection Procedures Act allows debtors to raise state exemptions to federal collection actions.[44] The Eleventh Circuit assumed without any discussion that no exemptions applied under the federal tax intercept statutes,[45] and then determined that the tax intercept statutes, and not the Federal Debt Collection Procedures Act, applied.[46]

The court pointed out that the Federal Debt Collection Procedures Act indicates it does not "supersede or modify the operation of . . . statutory rights to set-off. . . ."[47] The court ruled that the intercept was such a set-off. In addition, state law cannot shape the federal tax intercept program. The court held that, where federal law conflicts with state exemption laws, the federal law prevails.[48]

The borrower in this case also argued that he was entitled to a "fairness" exception to the federal income tax offset

---

32 Games v. Cavazos, 737 F. Supp. 1368 (D. Del. 1990).

33 *Id.*

34 Downs v. McPherson, Clearinghouse No. 51,940 (D. Md. July 17, 1989).

35 26 C.F.R. § 301.6402-6(l); *see* Setlech v. United States, 816 F. Supp. 161 (E.D.N.Y. 1993), *aff'd*, 17 F.3d 390 (2d Cir.), *cert. denied*, 511 U.S. 1085 (1994); Richardson v. Baker, 663 F. Supp. 651 (S.D.N.Y. 1987); Sartorious v. United States Dep't of Treasury, 671 F. Supp. 592 (E.D. Wis. 1987); *In re* Blake, 235 B.R. 568 (Bankr. Md. 1998) (although action against Department of Treasury prohibited, borrower could bring suit against the Department of Education. Department ordered to return refund).

36 *Cf.* Bolden v. Equifax Accounts Receivable Services, 838 F. Supp. 507 (D. Kan. 1993) (suggesting, over the Department's objection, that administrative remedies need not first be exhausted).

37 *See, e.g., In re* Blake, 235 B.R. 568 (Bankr. Md. 1998).

38 34 C.F.R. § 30.27(a)(1).

39 34 C.F.R. § 30.33(f).

40 34 C.F.R. § 30.27(a).

41 *See* § 8.3 (reasonable and affordable payment plans), *infra.*

42 *Id.*

43 Bosarge v. U.S. Dept. of Education, 5 F.3d 1414 (11th Cir. 1993), *cert. denied*, 512 U.S. 1226 (1994).

44 28 U.S.C. §§ 3001–3308 (Debt Collection Procedures Act).

45 26 U.S.C. § 6402(d)(1); 31 U.S.C. § 3720A.

46 Bosarge v. U.S. Dept. of Education, 5 F.3d 1414 (11th Cir. 1993), *cert. denied*, 512 U.S. 1226 (1994).

47 28 U.S.C. § 3003(c)(6).

48 Bosarge v. U.S. Dept. of Education, 5 F.3d 1414 (11th Cir. 1993), *cert. denied*, 512 U.S. 1226 (1994).

statutes. The fairness argument was based on the fact that his refund consisted primarily of an earned income tax credit, a benefit available only to low-income families with dependent children.[49] The court rejected this argument as well.[50]

5.2.3 Preventing Intercepts

The only sure-fire method of avoiding a tax refund intercept for a borrower currently in default is to lower federal income tax withholding from earnings and any estimated tax payments. Then, at the end of the year, the taxpayer is not owed a refund, and there can be no interception.

This approach is partially available even for those receiving Earned Income Tax Credits (EITC).[51] Employees who are eligible for the EITC *and* who have a qualifying child are entitled to receive EITC payments in their pay during the year if they provide their employer with a completed IRS Form W-5, Earned Income Credit Advance Payment Certificate. The employee, though can only have a portion of the EITC paid during the year.[52]

A riskier strategy is to delay filing a refund. However, clients should be counseled on possible penalties associated with this option.

While most borrowers want to avoid interception of their tax refunds, borrowers who want to immediately pay off their loans may actually be better off having their tax refunds intercepted. Funds from tax intercepts should be applied to principal and interest, not to collection fees.[53] Thus, the balance will decrease more rapidly through tax intercepts than through low monthly payment plans. Borrowers choosing this strategy should wait until the funds taken from the tax intercepts leave them with a small balance left on their loans. Once the borrower has paid down to a small balance,

exclusive of collection fees, the Department will frequently agree at this point to compromise the remaining balance and accept a lump sum payment.[54] The Department will usually waive the collection fees when the principal and interest is paid in full. This strategy saves borrowers from paying the huge collection fees that accrue once an account is turned over to a collection agency.[55]

5.2.4 Using Bankruptcy Filing to Stave Off Intercept

Filing a personal bankruptcy petition *before* the intercept activates the United States Bankruptcy Code automatic stay provision.[56] The stay prohibits virtually all actions against the debtor's property, including intercepts of owed tax refunds. The Department claims it will always readily and promptly return any amount taken by an offset during a pending bankruptcy.

It may also be possible to file bankruptcy to protect an impending return and claim any Earned Income Tax Credit (EITC) due as exempt. The majority of courts have found the EITC to be part of the bankruptcy estate under federal law, available for distribution to creditors.[57] Even so, the EITC might be exempt under various state exemption schemes, particularly if a state exemption for "public benefits" is interpreted to include Earned Income Tax Credits.[58]

---

49 *Id.* at 1420.

50 *Id.* (court cannot hold that the earned income tax credit embodies a more valuable social policy than recovery of defaulted student loans). However, some bankruptcy courts have found the earned income tax credit to be a "public benefit" under state statutes and therefore exempt from the bankruptcy estate. *See* § 5.2.4, *infra.*

51 Courts have found that offsets may include the amount of an EITC owed. *See Sorenson v. Sec. of Treasury*, 475 U.S. 851 (1986) (U.S. has authority to seize earned income tax refund); *Bosarge v. U.S. Dep't of Education*, 5 F.3d 1414 (11th Cir. 1993), *cert. denied*, 512 U.S. 1226 (1994).

52 More information about the EITC is available on the IRS web site, www.irs.treas.gov and from the Center on Budget and Policy Priorities, www.cbpp.org, (202) 408-1080.

53 The Department of Treasury regulations on tax intercepts specify only that offsets can be allocated for past-due debts, less fees charged under 31 C.F.R. § 285.2(i). This section allows fees charged by the Financial Management Service (FMS) of the Department of Treasury and the IRS to be deducted from the amount collected. To the extent allowed by law, federal agencies may add these fees to the debt. Still, the fees deducted, if any, should be less than those charged by collection agencies. *See* § 4.4, *supra.*

54 *See* §§ 4.4.1.1, 4.4.1.5, *supra. See also Department of Education, Amendment to Agreement Pursuant to Section 428(b) of the Higher Education Act of 1965, as Amended, with a State or Private Non-profit Institution or Organization for Coverage of Its Student Loan Insurance Program under the Interest Benefits Provision of Section 428(a) of the Act*, Appendix I § 5.1, Clearinghouse No. 51,926 (July 11, 1994) (if borrower agrees to pay principal within 30 days, agency may enter into a repayment agreement that includes the compromise of interest owed).

55 *See* §§ 4.4.1.1, 4.4.1.5, *supra.*

56 11 U.S.C. § 362. *See generally* National Consumer Law Center, *Consumer Bankruptcy Law and Practice* § 2.5.2, Ch. 9, §§ 10.4.2.6.3 (bankruptcy preferences), 10.4.2.6.5 (post-petition transfers), 10.4.2.6.6 (set-off provisions) (6th ed. 2000 and Supp.).

57 *See, e.g., In re Johnston*, 222 B.R. 552 (6th Cir. B.A.P. 1998), *aff'd*, 209 F.3d 611 (6th Cir. 2000); *In re Ferns*, 232 B.R. 453 (Bankr. D. Ariz. 1999); *In re Meza*, 243 B.R. 538 (Bankr. M.D. Fla. 1999) (court agreed that an earned "earned income credit" is part of the debtor's bankruptcy estate, but credit was not part of the estate in this case because debtors had no cognizable interest in it at the commencement of the bankruptcy case).

58 *See, e.g., In re Jackson,* 2001 Bankr. LEXIS 1125 (Bankr. M.D. Ga. 2001); *In re Brasher*, 253 B.R. 484 (Bankr. M.D. Ala. 2000) (earned-income credit exempt under state "public assistance benefit" exemption); *In re* Longstreet, 246 B.R. 611 (Bankr. S.D. Iowa 2000) (Iowa exemption for any "public assistance benefit" is broad enough to include the federal earned-income credit); *In re Brockhouse*, 220 B.R. 623 (Bankr. C.D. Ill. 1998); *In re* Brown, 186 B.R. 224 (Bankr. W.D. Ky. 1995). *But see In re Collins*, 170 F.3d 512, 513 (5th Cir. 1999) (rejecting earned-income-credit exemption because the Louisiana statute specifically defined exempted assistance to mean "money payments

If the intercept has already occurred, borrowers can still recover that amount if they act quickly. If the borrower files a chapter 7 or 13 bankruptcy within ninety days of the intercept, she can recover the refund as a setoff under 11 U.S.C. § 553.[59]

5.2.5 Rights of Non-Obligated Spouses

When the United States intercepts a tax refund due on a joint return, the non-obligated spouse can recover *part* of the seized refund by filing an "injured spouse" claim with the Internal Revenue Service (IRS).[60] IRS regulations require that the United States notify any person who has filed a joint return with the obligated borrower concerning the steps that a non-obligated person can take to secure a proper partial refund.[61] If the non-obligated spouse files a separate return, the United States will seize no portion of a refund due on that return.

5.3 Wage Garnishment

5.3.1 Federal Statutes Authorize Limited, Non-Judicial Wage Garnishment

The Higher Education Act authorizes the Secretary and guaranty agencies to garnish borrowers' wages without first obtaining a court order.[62] Previously, the Department of Education was the only federal agency with this authority. However, the Debt Collection Improvement Act of 1996 (DCIA) extended the "privilege" to other federal agencies collecting debts owed to those agencies.[63]

The administrative wage garnishment provisions in the DCIA have muddied the waters considerably with respect to the existing Department of Education program. For a time, there was some question whether the Department would continue to operate under the authority of the HEA only, or whether it would try to conform to other agencies and operate under the authority of the DCIA. This is no longer a mystery. The Department in 2002 proposed rules to oper-

ate wage garnishment procedures under the authority of the DCIA.[64] Until these proposed rules become final, the Department should continue to operate under the HEA authority. It is also arguable that the DCIA will apply only when the Department is the garnishor and that guaranty agencies should continue to operate under the HEA.[65] Finally, it is possible that the Department's attempts to operate under the DCIA will be challenged, as discussed in § 5.3.3.3.

The significance of the switch from the HEA-authorized garnishment program to a DCIA-authorized program is discussed throughout this section. Although much of the Department's garnishment program should remain the same, there are a few critical changes that will occur if the Department begins to operate under the DCIA. In particular, the DCIA allows federal agencies to garnish up to 15% of a borrower's disposable income compared to the 10% limit in the HEA.

5.3.2 Current Wage Garnishment Program

5.3.2.1 General

The authority for the current program is derived from the HEA, 20 U.S.C. § 1095a. In its 2002 notice of proposed rulemaking, the Department claims that it has operated since 1993 under this statutory directive and that it never adopted implementing regulations.[66] This is misleading since the Department did in fact adopt regulations to govern guaranty agency garnishments.[67] The Department has at least paid lip service to following the guaranty agency garnishment regulations as well.

The Department encourages guaranty agencies to garnish debtor's wages. However, the Department no longer requires that agencies initiate proceedings by a certain date in the post-default process. Instead, agencies are under a general mandate to garnish wages of all eligible borrowers.[68] The only exception to this requirement arises if the agency determines that litigation would be more effective in col-

---

under this title"); *In re* Trudeau, 237 B.R. 803, 807 (B.A.P. 10th Cir. 1999) (Wyoming statute expressly exempts only public assistance and social services provided by the article); *In re* Rutter, 204 B.R. 57 (Bankr. D. Or. 1997). *See generally* National Consumer Law Center, Consumer Bankruptcy Law and Practice § 2.5.2 (6th ed. 2000 and Supp.).

59   *See, e.g., In re* Blake, 235 B.R. 568 (Bankr. Md. 1998) (Department of Education violated the automatic stay by causing improper IRS tax refund intercept. Court ordered the Department to refund set-off amount).

60   IRS forms are available on-line at www.irs.treas.gov. The injured spouse form is Form 8379.

61   26 C.F.R. § 301.6402-6(i).

62   20 U.S.C. § 1095a.

63   Pub. L. No. 104-134, § 31001(o)(1) (Apr. 26, 1996), *codified at* 31 U.S.C. § 3720D.

64   67 Fed. Reg. 18072 (Apr. 12, 2002). The switch to the DCIA occurred among other reasons because of criticism of the Department in a 2002 General Accounting Office (GAO) report. The GAO criticized the Department of Education and other federal agencies for failing to implement a wage garnishment program under the DCIA. In a letter to the GAO, the Department of Education complained that the report was misleading as it left the impression that no agency was conducting administrative wage garnishment. In fact, the Department of Education, as noted in this section, has used wage garnishment under the authority of the HEA since 1993. See United States General Accounting Office, Debt Collection Improvement Act of 1996: Status of Selected Agencies' Implementation of Administrative wage Garnishment, Report #GAO-02-313 (Feb. 2002).

65   *See* § 5.3.3.3, *infra.*

66   67 Fed. Reg. 18072 (Apr. 12, 2002).

67   34 C.F.R. § 482.410(b)(9).

68   34 C.F.R. § 682.410(b)(6)(iii).

lecting the debt.[69] The regulations clarify that agencies have the discretion to file lawsuits instead of wage garnishment only if the borrower has no wages that can be garnished or the agency determines that the borrower has sufficient attachable assets or income that is not subject to administrative wage garnishment.[70] The regulations therefore reflect the Department's growing preference toward using extrajudicial collection methods rather than filing suit.

There are a few substantive and procedural limits to this broad garnishment power in both the statute and the regulations. At least thirty days before beginning garnishment proceedings, agencies must mail borrowers a notice listing the nature and amount of the debt, the intention of the agency to collect the debt through deductions from pay, and an explanation of the borrower's rights.[71] Failure to follow these notice requirements as well as misrepresentations about the process may violate the FDCPA.[72]

In addition, the guarantor is required to offer the borrower an opportunity to enter into a repayment agreement, in lieu of the garnishment, on terms agreeable to the guarantor.[73] As with tax intercepts, there is no requirement that the payment plan be "reasonable and affordable." However, at a minimum, a borrower should be able to request a reasonable and affordable plan after making a few payments under the plan agreed to by the Secretary.

Garnishment is also prohibited if the borrower has been involuntarily separated from employment until the borrower has been re-employed continuously for twelve months. The regulations depart from the statute in authorizing garnishment unless the guarantor has *knowledge* that this exception applies to a particular borrower.[74] This places the burden on the borrower to notify the guarantor of the lack of continuous employment. The regulations also do not provide notice to the employer in the withholding order of the twelve months continuous employment requirement.[75]

Borrowers must inform loan holders that they qualify for the unemployment exception either by checking the appropriate box on the hearing form or by providing other written notice. However, borrowers should not also have to provide documentation or other proof that they qualify for the exception. Thus, collection letters requiring borrowers to submit affirmative proof of eligibility may violate the FDCPA.[76]

Many states place even greater restrictions on wage garnishment or prohibit the practice outright. These state law limitations on garnishment do not apply to garnishments to satisfy student loan obligations.[77] State procedural requirements prior to garnishment are not likely to apply either.[78] On the other hand, certain tribal law restrictions on garnishment should apply.[79]

5.3.2.2 The Maximum Amount That May Be Garnished

The Higher Education Act administrative wage garnishment statute and regulations allow garnishment of up to ten percent of "disposable pay."[80] Disposable pay is defined as pay remaining after deduction of any amounts required by law to be withheld.[81] The statute provides only that the amount deducted may not exceed 10%.[82] The Department's current regulations specify that the amount that can be garnished is the *lesser* of 10% of disposable income and 30 times the prevailing minimum wage (the amount permitted by 15 U.S.C. § 1673).[83] 15 U.S.C. § 1673 also limits total garnishments to 25% of disposable income, so that a student loan garnishment and other garnishments should not exceed 25% of income. Both the statute and regulations allow higher garnishments if the borrower gives written consent.[84]

At least one court has concluded that the maximum 10% deduction applies to holders of student loan notes individually rather than collectively.[85] The court allowed each holder of a defaulted loan to garnish up to 10% of the borrower's

---

69 34 C.F.R. § 682.410(b)(6)(iv).

70 *Id.*

71 34 C.F.R. § 682.410(b)(9)(i)(B).

72 *See, e.g.*, Kort v. Diversified Collection Services, Inc., 2001 WL 88149 (N.D. Ill. Aug. 2, 2001), *class cert. granted in part* 2001 WL 1617213 (N.D. Ill. Dec. 17, 2001) (alleging that collector violated FDCPA by giving borrowers insufficient time to respond to garnishment notices and by requiring affirmative proof of unemployment exception); Sanders v. OSI Educational Services, Inc., 2001 WL 883608 (N.D. Ill. Aug. 3, 2001). *See also* § 4.3, *supra.*

73 20 U.S.C. § 1095a(a)(4); 34 C.F.R. § 682.410(b)(9)(i)(D).

74 20 U.S.C. § 1095a(a)(d)(7); 34 C.F.R. § 682.410(b)(9)(i)(G).

75 *See* 59 Fed. Reg. 22,474, Comments 72, 73 (Apr. 29, 1994); 34 C.F.R. § 682.410(b)(10)(i)(I) (notice to employer must contain only the information necessary for the employer to comply with the withholding order).

76 *See, e.g.*, Kort v. Diversified Collection Services, Inc., 2001 WL 88149 (N.D. Ill. Aug. 2, 2001), *class cert. granted in part* 2001 WL 1617213 (N.D. Ill. Dec. 17, 2001) (alleging that collector violated FDCPA by giving borrowers insufficient time to respond to garnishment notices and by requiring affirmative proof of unemployment exception); Sanders v. OSI Educational Services, Inc., 2001 WL 883608 (N.D. Ill. Aug. 3, 2001).

77 20 U.S.C. § 1095a(a) (garnishment requirements are allowed notwithstanding any provisions of state law). *See, e.g.*, Clear v. Missouri Coordinating Board for Higher Education, 23 S.W.3d 896 (E.D. Mo. 2000); Nelson v. Diversified Collection Services Inc., 961 F. Supp. 863 (D. Md. 1997).

78 *See* Nelson v. Diversified Collection Services, Inc., 961 F. Supp. 863 (D. Md. 1997).

79 *See* 59 Fed. Reg. 22,473, Comment 63 (Apr. 29, 1994).

80 20 U.S.C. § 1095a; 34 C.F.R. § 682.410(b)(9)(i)(A).

81 20 U.S.C. § 1095a(e); 34 C.F.R. § 682.410(b)(9)(i)(A).

82 20 U.S.C. § 1095a(a)(1).

83 34 C.F.R. § 682.410(b)(9)(i)(A). The minimum wage can be found at 29 U.S.C. § 206(a)(1). The current minimum wage, as of October 1, 1997, is $5.15/hour. Therefore, 30 x $5.15 = $154.50 is protected per week.

84 20 U.S.C. § 1095a(a)(1); 34 C.F.R. § 682.410(b)(9)(i)(A).

85 Halperin v. Regional Adjustment Bureau, Inc., 206 F.3d 1063 (11th Cir. 2000).

wages as long as the total garnishments by all note holders did not exceed 25%.[86] Other courts have disagreed with this interpretation.[87]

5.3.2.3 The Right to a Hearing

Currently, the Secretary or guaranty agency must notify the borrower before the garnishment.[88] The borrower is entitled to a hearing with an independent official within the agency. "Independent official" is defined as someone not under the supervision or control of the head of the agency.[89]

The regulations allow the agency to establish the time and location of the hearing or to hold the hearing by telephone conference.[90] A location agreeable to the agency may be very inconvenient for the borrower, possibly thousands of miles away in another state. There is no requirement that the guarantor tape the hearing, although the agency may do so if it wishes.[91]

Instead of a hearing, the borrower can request that the holder review the borrower's written statement why the garnishment should not go forward. The borrower may (and is even encouraged by the Department's form letter) request copies of all documentation held by the loan holder on the

student loan before requesting the hearing or presenting a statement of the basis to the student's objection to the garnishment.

The Department suggests (for Department-held loans) that the borrower call the relevant collection agency to obtain copies of the file, and also contact the collection agency if the student wants to work out a repayment agreement in lieu of the garnishment. Hearings are reserved for claims that the borrower does not owe the debt in part or in whole.

Possible grounds for contesting the loan obligation include that the loan has already been repaid, that the social security numbers are wrong and the individual does not owe the loan, that the borrower is making repayments pursuant to a repayment agreement, that a bankruptcy proceeding is still pending or the loan was discharged in bankruptcy, that the borrower is totally and permanently disabled, that the school closed while the student was still enrolled, that the school falsely certified the student as eligible, that the school failed to refund money owed the student, that the loan is not enforceable, or that garnishment would result in extreme financial hardship.[92]

The extreme financial hardship defense was added in 1998.[93] Guaranty agencies have the option of sending the financial disclosure forms needed to prove hardship with all notices or only to those students who raise hardship as a defense.

If the borrower's written request for a hearing is received within fifteen days of the borrower's receipt of the garnishment notice (receipt is presumed within five days of mailing of the notice), no garnishment can issue until the hearing is provided.[94] The Department regulations require guaranty agencies to issue the hearing decision within sixty days.[95]

In some cases, agencies will be unprepared to offer borrowers proper hearings. As a result, in some cases, when borrowers have pushed for hearings, agencies have simply agreed to withdraw the garnishment order. Advocates should not rely on this possibility. However, borrowers are entitled to at least the procedural rights required in the regulations and should be prepared to aggressively advocate for these rights.[96]

If the borrower does not request a hearing, or if the borrower's objection is denied, the employer is notified to deduct the garnishment amount from the borrower's paycheck. If the borrower is late in requesting a hearing on the garnishment, the garnishment order will proceed, but the

---

86 *Id.*

87 *See* United States v. George, 144 F. Supp. 2d 161 (E.D.N.Y. 2001) (because the plaintiff had only one loan, the case was distinguishable from *Halperin*. However, court criticized the reasoning in *Halperin* as " . . . somewhat forced." Court stated in a footnote that a fair reading of the legislative history " . . . even as recounted in *Halperin*, supports an inference that any limitations on garnishment in the HEA . . . were intended to protect potential garnishees, who were often likely to be poor, from 'severe hardships.'"); Green v. Kentucky Higher Education Ass'n, 78 F. Supp. 2d 1259 (S.D. Ala. 1999) (interpreting 20 U.S.C. § 1095a to prevent multiple note holders from collectively garnishing more than 10%).

88 In 1998, the Department issued new "Notice Prior to Wage Withholding" and "Request for Hearing or Exemption" notices. These notices are attached to the Department's March 17, 1998 Dear Guaranty Agency Director letter, Clearinghouse No. 52,042.

89 34 C.F.R. § 682.410(b)(9)(i)(M).

90 34 C.F.R. § 682.410(b)(9)(i)(J). The telephone charges are the responsibility of the guaranty agency. In at least one case, a borrower challenged a collection agency's scheduling of a garnishment hearing in another state as a violation of the Fair Debt Collection Practices Act (FDCPA). *See* Lawson v. Management Adjustment Bureau, 1997 U.S. Dist. LEXIS 7275 (N.D. Ill. 1997) (plaintiff claimed that the scheduling of the hearing in another state violated 15 U.S.C. § 1692i(a)(2), the provision of the FDCPA that requires a collector to bring legal actions on a debt only in the judicial district in which the consumer signed the contract or where the consumer resides. The court granted defendant's motion to dismiss this claim, finding that an administrative wage garnishment hearing is not a "legal action" for purposes of the FDCPA venue requirement.).

91 *See* 59 Fed. Reg. 22,474, 22,475, Comment 75 (Apr. 29, 1994).

92 In 1998, the Department issued new "Notice Prior to Wage Withholding" and "Request for Hearing or Exemption" notices listing these defenses. These notices are attached to the Department's March 17, 1998 Dear Guaranty Agency Director letter, Clearinghouse No. 52,042.

93 *Id.*

94 34 C.F.R. § 682.410(b)(9)(i)(K).

95 34 C.F.R. § 682.410(b)(9)(i)(N).

96 Whether these procedures comport with due process is discussed in § 5.3.4, *infra.*

borrower should still receive a hearing and a decision within sixty days.[97] If the borrower prevails, the garnishment should be ordered to cease, and, if appropriate, amounts garnished should be returned. In addition, the guaranty agency has discretion to postpone a garnishment pending a hearing, even if the borrower's request for a hearing is late, if the borrower's delay was caused by factors over which she had no control or if the agency receives information that the agency believes justifies a delay.[98]

5.3.3 Proposed DCIA Wage Garnishment Program

5.3.3.1 Differences Between Garnishment Under the Debt Collection Improvement Act (DCIA) and the Higher Education Act (HEA)

The most significant difference between the two statutes is that the DCIA authorizes garnishment up to 15% and the HEA only up to 10%.[99] There are other, less significant, differences as well. These are summarized below.

The DCIA, like the HEA, prohibits garnishment if the borrower has been involuntarily separated from employment until the borrower has been re-employed continuously for twelve months.[100] As discussed in § 5.3.2.2, *supra*, the Department's garnishment regulations governing guaranty agencies departed from the statute in authorizing garnishment unless the guarantor has *knowledge* that this exception applies.[101] The Department's proposed garnishment regulations implementing the DCIA garnishment authority, in contrast, require that the borrower present credible evidence of involuntary separation from employment.[102] There is not much practical difference between these provisions. Under either garnishment scheme, borrowers have some burden to notify the loan holder of their unemployment status and to prove that they qualify for the unemployment exception.

There is a difference in the definition of "disposable pay." The HEA defines disposable pay as excluding only those amounts required by law to be withheld.[103] The DCIA has a similar definition.[104] However, the Department's proposed regulations follow the Department of Treasury's implementing regulations in defining "disposable pay" as amounts deducted from gross pay for health insurance premiums as well as amounts required by law to be withheld.[105]

In addition, the DCIA proposed regulations explicitly grant the Department authority to issue multiple garnishment orders even though there is no provision in the DCIA allowing this practice.[106] Hearing procedures under the DCIA are discussed in the next subsection.

5.3.3.2 The Right to a Hearing Under the DCIA

Like the HEA, the DCIA requires notice to the borrower before garnishment.[107] The notice provisions are similar.[108] Notice must be sent by mail to the last known address a minimum of thirty days before the initiation of garnishment procedures.[109] The notice must inform the borrower of the nature and amount of the debt, the agency's intention to initiate garnishment, and an explanation of the borrower's rights.[110]

The proposed regulations specify the borrower rights that must be revealed in the notice. These are: (1) right to inspect and copy records; (2) right to enter into a repayment agreement; and (3) right to request a hearing about the existence, amount, or current enforceability of the debt and the rate of withholding.[111]

The proposed regulations addressing the format of the hearings are similar to the HEA, with a few notable exceptions. As with the HEA, if the borrower requests a hearing on or before the fifteenth day following notice of garnishment, the garnishment should not proceed until after the hearing.[112] Borrowers can still request hearings after that date, but garnishment may proceed pending a hearing decision.[113]

The proposed regulations provide detail on the hearing process. First, borrowers who want an oral hearing must

---

97 34 C.F.R. § 684.410(b)(9)(i)(L).

98 *Id.*

99 31 U.S.C. § 3720D(b)(1)(DCIA); 20 U.S.C. § 1095a(1) (HEA).

100 31 U.S.C. § 3720D(b)(6).

101 34 C.F.R. § 682.410(b)(9)(i)(G). *See* § 5.3.2.1, *supra*.

102 67 Fed. Reg. 18072, 18079 (Apr. 12, 2002), *proposing to add* 34 C.F.R. § 34.23. Proposed regulations are available on the companion CD-Rom.

103 20 U.S.C. § 1095a(e).

104 31 U.S.C. § 3720D(g).

105 67 Fed. Reg. 18072 (Apr. 12, 2002), *proposing to add* 34 C.F.R § 34.3(a).

106 67 Fed. Reg. 18072 (Apr. 12, 2002), *proposing to add* 34 C.F.R. §§ 34.19, 34.20. For more on case decisions regarding multiple garnishments, see § 5.3.2.2, *supra*.

107 31 U.S.C. § 3720D(b)(2).

108 *See* § 5.3.2.3, *supra*.

109 31 U.S.C. § 3720D(b)(2).

110 *Id.*

111 67 Fed. Reg. 18072 (Apr. 12, 2002), *proposing to add* 34 C.F.R. §§ 34.5, 34.6.

112 31 U.S.C. § 3720D(c)(1).

113 31 U.S.C. § 3720D(c)(2). It is unclear whether borrowers requesting hearings after the fifteen days may also request in-person hearings. This issue was raised in comments submitted by the National Consumer Law Center, Community Legal Services, and Legal Aid Foundation of Los Angeles. See *Comments to the Department of Education* on proposed Administrative Wage Garnishment Regulations, submitted June 11, 2002 and available on the accompanying CD-Rom. (Hereafter "NCLC Wage Garnishment Comments").

request one and also must show good reason why the issues cannot be resolved on paper.[114] The oral hearing may be in-person or by telephone.[115]

The HEA regulations entitle borrowers to a hearing with an independent official from within the Department.[116] In contrast, the DCIA proposed regulations allow the hearing officer to be any "qualified employee" of the Department.[117] Unfortunately for borrowers, the Department does not provide any definition of "qualified employee" and does not explicitly state that the hearing officer must be independent or neutral. The National Consumer Law Center and other advocacy groups have argued that, at a minimum, employees of the collections division should not serve as hearing officers.[118]

The hearing officer is required to maintain a summary record and issue a written opinion.[119] Borrowers who object to the decision have the right to request a reconsideration.[120] Garnishment will continue pending a decision on reconsideration.[121] The regulations state that the Department will consider a request for reconsideration only if they determine that:

- The borrower's financial circumstances, as shown by evidence submitted with the request, have materially changed since issuance of the decision so that the amount to be garnished should be reduced; or
- The borrower submitted evidence that was not previously submitted and the evidence demonstrates that the Department should reconsider an objection to the existence, amount, or enforceability of the debt.[122] The Department may offer a hearing for reconsideration.[123]

There may be significant differences in the defenses available under the DCIA. The HEA defenses are spelled out in a Dear Guaranty Agency Director Letter from March 1998.[124] The DCIA proposed regulations are more limited. Only defenses related to the existence, amount, or enforceability or rate of withholding are allowed.[125] The latter category is similar to the current hardship waiver.[126] The National Consumer Law Center and others are advocating for more explicit defenses similar to those currently listed in the March 1998 letter. There are also some concerns about the Departments' proposed hardship defense.[127]

5.3.3.3 Challenges to the Department's Authority to Garnish under the DCIA

As discussed in the previous subsections, there are a number of conflicting provisions in the HEA and DCIA garnishment statutes. Most notably, the DCIA allows for garnishment of up to 15% of disposable pay whereas the HEA prescribes a maximum of 10% of disposable pay.[128] This subsection analyzes whether the Department is allowed to adopt the higher limits and other provisions of the DCIA without explicitly repealing the HEA garnishment statute.

The first question is whether the Department is intending to use the DCIA authority only for garnishments by the Department itself. It is arguable that the DCIA authority should, in fact, apply only in these circumstances. This is because the DCIA, unlike the HEA, applies only to garnishment by the "heads" of executive, judicial, or legislative agencies.[129] It does not specifically apply to agents of the federal departments. At a minimum, therefore, under this analysis, guaranty agencies engaging in administrative wage garnishment should continue to abide by the HEA statute and regulations even if the Department is allowed to garnish under the DCIA.[130]

The analysis is less clear when the Department is ordering garnishment. A search of the legislative history and statutory authority for the DCIA does not lead to any easy answers to

---

114   67 Fed. Reg. 18072 (Apr. 12, 2002), *proposing to add* 34 C.F.R. § 34.9. For a response to this proposal, See NCLC Wage Garnishment Comments, arguing that this requirement places an unfair burden on borrowers, many of whom are low-income and/or unsophisticated.

115   67 Fed. Reg. 18072 (Apr. 12, 2002), *proposing to add* 34 C.F.R. § 34.9.

116   34 C.F.R. § 682.410(b)(9)(i)(M). *See* § 5.3.2.3, *supra.*

117   67 Fed. Reg. 18072 (Apr. 12, 2002), *proposing to add* 34 C.F.R. § 34.13.

118   *See* NCLC Administrative Wage Garnishment Comments, objecting to the lack of any clear standards for hearing officers.

119   67 Fed. Reg. 18072 (Apr. 12, 2002), *proposing to add* 34 C.F.R. §§ 34.13, 34.16. *See also* NCLC Wage Garnishment Comments, noting that the regulations should require hearing officers to provide specific reasons for their decisions.

120   67 Fed. Reg. 18072 (Apr. 12, 2002), *proposing to add* 34 C.F.R. § 34.12.

121   67 Fed. Reg. 18072 (Apr. 12, 2002), *proposing to add* 34 C.F.R. § 34.12(b).

122   67 Fed. Reg. 18072 (Apr. 12, 2002), *proposing to add* 34 C.F.R. § 34.12(c).

123   67 Fed. Reg. 18072 (Apr. 12, 2002), *proposing to add* 34 C.F.R. § 34.12(d)(2)(ii).

124   Department of Education, Dear Guaranty Partner Letter, March 17, 1998, Clearinghouse No. 52,042. *See* § 5.3.2.3, *supra.*

125   67 Fed. Reg. 18072 (Apr. 12, 2002), *proposing to add* 34 C.F.R. § 34.6. *See* NCLC Wage Garnishment Comments, advocating that the Department amend the regulations to add explicit defenses similar to those listed in the March 1998 letter. The comments also express concern about the Department's proposed hardship defense.

126   *See* § 5.3.2.3, *supra.*

127   *Id.*

128   31 U.S.C. § 3720D(b)(1) (DCIA); 20 U.S.C. § 1095a(1) (HEA).

129   31 U.S.C. § 3720D(a). The HEA, in contrast, specifically applies to guaranty agencies as well as the Secretary of Education. 20 U.S.C. § 1095a(a).

130   *See* NCLC Wage Garnishment Comments, raising the question whether guaranty agencies will also be bound by the proposed regulations.

this conflict. There does not appear to be any explicit reference to the HEA garnishment procedures in either the legislation or statute.[131]

In a discussion of the Department of Education's wage garnishment procedures, the Department of Treasury specifically referred to the Department of Education's program as a similar program, but did not take the opportunity to clarify that the Treasury program was meant to repeal the Department program.[132] In fact, Treasury stated an important difference between the two programs, noting that the Department's wage garnishment program is applicable to the collection of one type of debt and is subject to a single statutory scheme.[133] The DCIA wage garnishment provision, in contrast, applies to all federal agencies collecting all types of debts and subject to a variety of statutory provisions.[134]

In addition, courts that have considered administrative wage garnishment in the student loan context since the passage of the DCIA have continued to refer only to the HEA statute and regulations, including the provision that only up to 10% of disposable pay may be garnished.[135] However, the Department of Education's proposal to implement the DCIA authority changes the picture considerably.[136] The decisions noted above were issued during the limbo period when the Department of Education was discussing garnishing the higher amount on its web site, for example, but had not yet taken any formal action.

The critical analysis therefore is whether the Department of Education can adopt the more recent DCIA authority without expressly repealing the HEA authority. This analysis requires an examination of principles of statutory construction.

As summarized below, there is no clear answer from this analysis either. There is strong support, however, for the argument that the HEA program should be governed by the HEA statute and regulations and that other federal agency garnishments should be governed by the DCIA statute and regulations.[137]

The starting point for statutory construction is the language of the statute itself.[138] The plain language doctrine, however, is not helpful since the DCIA does not explicitly refer to the HEA. In general, courts are reluctant to take the next step and find that the later statute implicitly repeals the earlier. The general principle is that federal courts do not assume that Congress used one statute to implicitly repeal an earlier one.[139]

When statutes conflict, the courts make an effort to protect both legislative objectives if possible.[140] When two statutes are capable of co-existence, it is the duty of the courts, absent a clearly expressed congressional intent to the contrary, to regard each as effective.[141]

In this case, it seems clear that the Department can continue to operate its garnishment program using the HEA statute and regulations without conflicting with other federal agencies implementing wage garnishments using the DCIA statute and regulations. Each federal agency is responsible only for debts owed to that agency. There should be no overlap between the garnishment programs administered by the various agencies. Since the two schemes can co-exist without conflict, there should be no need for judicial interference.

Because some courts might disagree with this conclusion, it is necessary to analyze the circumstances under which courts will implicitly repeal earlier statutes. Courts have recognized only two well-settled categories of implied repeals:

(1) where provisions in the two acts are in irreconcilable conflict, the later act, to the extent of the conflict, constitutes an implied repeal of the earlier one; and

(2) if the later act covers the whole subject of the earlier one and is clearly intended as a substitute, it will operate similarly as a repeal of the earlier act.[142]

The key question is whether the administrative wage provisions in the DCIA are irreconcilably in conflict with the HEA or whether the two can co-exist either wholly or partially. Again, there is no clear answer to this question.

As discussed above, there are a number of conflicts between the two statutes, most notably the difference in maximum allowable garnishment. There is an argument therefore that the later provisions repeal the earlier provisions at least with respect to this conflict, and perhaps others. On the other hand, there is also a strong argument that the

---

131 Pub. L. No. 104-134, 110 Stat. 1321–369 (Apr. 26, 1996).

132 63 Fed. Reg. 25, 136 (May 6, 1998) (final rules for DCIA administrative wage garnishment). The notice of proposed rulemaking was published at 62 Fed. Reg. 62,458 (Nov, 21, 1997).

133 *Id.*

134 *Id.*

135 *See, e.g.,* Halperin v. Regional Adjustment Bureau, Inc., 206 F.3d 1063 (11th Cir. 2000) (Department initiated garnishment); Clear v. Missouri Coordinating Board for Higher Education, 23 S.W.3d 896 (Mo. App. 2000) (guarantor initiated garnishment).

136 67 Fed. Reg. 18072 (Apr. 12, 2002).

137 The implementing regulations for DCIA garnishments can be found at 31 C.F.R. § 285.11.

138 United States v. DBB, Inc., 180 F.3d 1277, 1281 (11th Cir. 1999).

139 *See generally* Louis Fisher, *Symposium on Statutory Interpretation: Statutory Construction: Keeping a Respectful Eye on Congress,* 53 S.M.U. L. Rev. 49 (Winter 2000). *See, e.g.,* United States v. Langston, 118 U.S. 389, 393 (1886); Committee for Nuclear Responsibility, Inc. v. Seaborg, 463 F.2d 783, 785 (D.C. Cir. 1971).

140 Posadas v. National City Bank, 296 U.S. 497, 503 (1936).

141 Morton v. Mancari, 417 U.S. 535, 551 (1974).

142 Posadas v. National City Bank, 296 U.S. 497, 503 (1936); Radzanower v. Touche Ross & Co., 426 U.S. 148, 154 (1976) (rejecting argument that the Securities Exchange Act partially repealed the National Bank Act by implication because the two acts did not fall into either of the categories stated in *Posadas*).

two schemes can co-exist without conflict and that the more specific HEA provisions that apply only to student loan garnishment should remain. The answer is not clear.

5.3.4 Due Process Challenges to Garnishment

Serious due process questions are raised regardless of whether garnishment is authorized by the DCIA or HEA. This is particularly true when one considers these procedures in conjunction with the extraordinary statutory authorization for a state or even a private guaranty agency to conduct its own hearing and seize wages without judicial review.

One set of due process issues relates to the notices of hearing. Prior to the Department's issuance of standard notices for garnishment, borrowers challenged a number of misleading and confusing aspects of the withholding and request for hearing notices.[143] These challenges have been unsuccessful to date. For example, one court found that the failure to notify plaintiffs of several possible defenses to garnishment in the pre-hearing notice was not a violation of constitutional due process.[144] Even so, the Department later issued new notices that define more clearly the defenses available to borrowers.[145]

There are also many possible challenges to other aspects of the process including the failure to provide in-person hearings, questions about whether an official provided by the agency is truly an independent arbiter, among other possible violations. It is also very troubling that the Department does

not regulate the quality of hearing officers, by, for example, publishing minimum qualifications.[146]

In one case, the plaintiffs' due process challenges to the administrative hearing process based on absence of judicial review, inadequacy of hearing procedures and failure to ensure impartiality of hearing officers were ruled not ripe and dismissed.[147] The court found the claims not ripe because hearings were not actually held for either plaintiff. The court did consider plaintiffs' other due process claims, finding that the failure to offer borrowers the opportunity to appear in-person at the hearing did not violate constitutional due process standards.[148]

5.3.5 Participation of Private Collection Agencies in Garnishment

Under the current HEA program, the Department has issued guidance to guaranty agencies on the extent to which collection agencies can participate in the garnishment process.[149] The Department prohibits collection personnel from conducting hearings and requires that hearing officers must be independent not only of the guarantor, but also of the collector. The collector cannot issue withholding orders to employers and the order cannot appear to come from the collector.

Perhaps even more instructive is the type of collector conduct that the Department allows. This is a good indicator of what types of functions guarantors will turn over to collectors on a systematic basis. Just because the Department allows such involvement by collectors does not mean that the involvement complies with due process requirements.[150]

The Department authorizes collectors to send out the notice of garnishment, respond to debtor inquiries, negotiate

---

143 *See, e.g.,* Nelson v. Diversified Collection Services, Inc., 961 F. Supp. 863 (D. Md. 1997) (USA funds was the guarantor. The court found the notice adequate and the existence of pre- and post-intercept hearings before a "neutral" officer sufficient to meet procedural due process concerns. Court upheld the notice and hearing procedures, without addressing the issue that the administrative hearing procedure was entrusted to a non-governmental guaranty agency with a direct financial interest in the hearing's outcome); Lawson v. Management Adjustment Bureau, 1997 U.S. Dist. LEXIS 7275 (N.D. Ill. 1997) (collection agency notice not only stated valid defenses to garnishment, but also invalid defenses. Court found that borrower stated a claim for relief under the Fair Debt Collection Practices Act (FDCPA) and denied defendant's motion for summary judgment); Sibley v. Diversified Collection Services, Inc., 1997 U.S. Dist. LEXIS 23583 (N.D. Tex. June 10, 1997) (ruling on defendants' motion to dismiss). Class certification was denied on the remaining claims in the *Sibley* case. *See* Sibley v. Diversified Collection Services, 1998 U.S. Dist. LEXIS 9969 (N.D. Tex. June 30, 1998).

144 Sibley v. Diversified Collection Services, Inc., 1997 U.S. Dist. LEXIS 23583 (N.D. Tex. June 10, 1997) (ruling on defendant's motion to dismiss). Class certification was denied on the remaining claims. *See* Sibley v. Diversified Collection Services, 1998 U.S. Dist. LEXIS 9969 (N.D. Tex. June 20, 1998).

145 These notices are attached to the Department's March 17, 1998 Dear Guaranty Agency Director Letter, Clearinghouse No. 52,042.

146 This issue was raised in comments to the Department's notice or proposed rulemaking for administrative wage garnishment. *See* NCLC Wage Garnishment Comments.

147 Sibley v. Diversified Collection Services, Inc., 1997 U.S. Dist. LEXIS 23583 (N.D. Tex. June 10, 1997) (ruling on defendants' motion to dismiss). Class certification was denied on the remaining claims in the *Sibley* case. *See* Sibley v. Diversified Collection Services, 1998 U.S. Dist. LEXIS 9969 (N.D. Tex. June 30, 1998).

148 *Id.* For a more recent complaint challenging a collection agency's administration of the wage garnishment process, see Cliff v. Payco General Am. Credits, Inc., Clearinghouse No. 52,132 (M.D. Fla. 1998) (class action complaint).

149 Letter from Pamela Moran, Chief of the Loans Branch to Guaranty Agency Directors, Clearinghouse No. 50,424 (Nov. 1, 1994).

150 See Sibley v. Diversified Collection Services, Clearinghouse No. 51,930 (N.D. Tex. Apr. 26, 1996) (first amended complaint—class action) for an example of a challenge to collection agency participation in the garnishment process. Some aspects of the participation appear to exceed Department guidelines and some aspects appear to be consistent with Department guidelines.

repayment arrangements (consumers have a statutory right to avoid garnishment by entering into a repayment arrangement), and receive payments from employers. The contractor may assist in finding independent hearing officers, recommend that garnishment orders be issued, prepare the orders for review, and mail out the orders executed by the guarantor.[151]

In the proposed regulations to implement DCIA garnishment, the Department acknowledges that it cannot contract out "inherently government functions" related to wage garnishment.[152] These non-delegable functions include ruling on debtor's objections to garnishment, deciding to issue a garnishment letter order regarding an individual debtor, or causing a garnishment order to be issued.[153] However, the Department also states that they do (and will) make extensive use of collection contractors to collect by garnishment. The functions they explicitly envision include recommending garnishment action with respect to particular debtors, receiving and reviewing objections to garnishment and requests for hearing, attempting to secure missing information, analyzing financial statements under Department guidelines to determine affordable repayment amounts, and negotiating repayment agreements with debtors.[154] Finally, the Department states that they may use contracted services not only to analyze debtor objections to garnishment but also to propose appropriate findings for particular objections.[155]

5.3.6 Garnishment of Student Loan Funds

Student assistance funds, including loans, grants and work assistance may be garnished to collect debts owed to the Department of Education.[156] However, these funds (or property traceable to them) cannot be garnished by other collectors.[157] For example, a private collection agency pursuing a student for credit card debt cannot garnish or attach that student's federal student loan funds to collect the debt.

5.4 Seizure of Federal Benefits

5.4.1 General

In 1996, Congress further strengthened the debt collection powers of federal agencies.[158] Federal government agencies were given the authority to offset formerly exempt federal benefits to collect debts owed to the government, such as student loans.[159] The statute authorizes offset of the following federal benefits only:

- Social Security Act payments;
- Part B of the Black Lung Benefit Act;
- Railroad Retirement Benefits determined not to be Tier 2 benefits.[160]

Subsequent regulations specifically exempted SSI payments.[161] The legislation also exempted an annual amount of $9000.[162] In addition, the heads of the various benefit-granting programs were given authority to object to the offset program if it would "substantially interfere with or defeat" the purposes of the programs they administer.[163]

The Department of Treasury and Social Security Administration began implementing the offset process for Social Security payments in 2001.[164] As noted above, those affected include all recipients of Social Security payments, with the exception of Supplemental Security Income (SSI) recipients. Seniors receiving Social Security retirement benefits will be among the most affected by this change. These

---

151 Letter from Pamela Moran, Chief of the Loans Branch to Guaranty Agency Directors, Clearinghouse No. 50,424 (Nov. 1, 1994).

152 67 Fed. Reg. 18072, 18074 (Apr. 12, 2002).

153 *Id.*

154 *Id.*

155 *Id.*

156 20 U.S.C. § 1095a(d).

157 *Id.*

158 Debt Collection Improvement Act of 1996, Pub. L. No. 104-134 (1996) (Ch. 10).

159 31 U.S.C. § 3716.

160 31 U.S.C. § 3716(c)(3)(A)(ii).

161 31 C.F.R. § 285.4(b).

162 31 U.S.C. § 3716(c)(3)(A)(ii).

163 31 U.S.C. § 3716(c)(3)(B).

164 Information about the benefit payment offset program is available on the Department of Treasury web site at www.fms.treas.gov/news/factsheets/benefitoffset.html. The Department's Financial Management Service published a notice of proposed rulemaking and an interim rule concerning offsets on Aug. 21, 1998, 63 Fed. Reg. 44991, 44986, amending 31 C.F.R. Part 285 by adding § 285.4. The interim rule was adopted as final on December 16, 1998, becoming effective on January 22, 1999, 63 Fed. Reg. 71203 (Dec. 23, 1998). Federal agencies must either adopt regulations issued by the Departments of Treasury or Justice or adopt their own regulations consistent with those issued by Treasury or Justice. 31 U.S.C. § 3716(b). The Department of Education adopted regulations for administrative offset prior to the 1996 DCIA amendments. *See* 34 C.F.R. § 30.20 *et seq.* To date, the Department has not issued separate regulations addressing the new powers, including Social Security offsets, authorized by the 1996 amendments. The DOE appears to be following the Treasury regulations at least with respect to general issues regarding offset such as whether a ten year limit applies. The Treasury regulations can be found at 31 C.F.R. § 285.4 and 31 C.F.R. § 901.3, *reprinted at* Appx. B, *infra*.

seniors may have student loan debt, often from many years ago.[165]

Although this manual focuses on Department of Education's use of this authority to collect student loan debt, federal benefits recipients may also face offsets for collection of debts owed to other federal agencies. For example, the Department of Housing and Urban Development (HUD) has begun using the program to collect debts.[166] In addition, the Social Security Administration is using this power to collect Social Security overpayments. Other agencies have already begun, or are planning to develop, similar programs to collect debts owed to them.

5.4.2 Amount of Offset

The amount of the offset will be the lesser of:

- The amount of the debt;
- An amount equal to 15% of the monthly benefit payment; or
- The amount if any, by which the monthly benefit exceeds $750.[167]

The maximum amount that will be offset under any circumstances is 15% of the recipient's income. The Financial Management Service (FMS) of the Department of the Treasury provided the following examples:

Example 1: A debtor receives a monthly benefit payment of $850. The amount that is offset is the lesser of $127.50 (15% of 850) or $100 (the amount by which $850 exceeds $750). In this example, $100 would be offset.[168]

Example 2: A debtor receives a monthly benefit of $1250. The amount that is offset is the lesser of $187.50 (15% of 1250) or $500 (the amount by which 1,250 exceeds 750). In this example, the offset amount is $187.50 (assuming the debt is $187.50 or more).[169]

If the recipient receives $750 or less, nothing will be offset.[170]

5.4.3 Challenges to Offset

5.4.3.1 Notice and Hearing Rights

The offset process is managed by the Financial Management Service (FMS) of the Department of Treasury. Before referring a debt to FMS for collection, the federal agency is required to provide the debtor with a notice of intent to offset and an opportunity to review the basis for the debt.[171]

Since the 1996 amendments to the DCIA, the Department of Education has not issued new regulations addressing the additional powers authorized in the amendments. It is therefore unclear which regulations to follow to determine specific borrower rights. At present, the Department of Education appears to be following its existing administrative offset regulations, at least with respect to notice and hearing rights.[172]

The Department of Education regulations require borrowers to request a review within twenty days of receiving a notice of offset.[173] The borrower has the opportunity to first request the opportunity to review and copy relevant documents.[174] Borrowers have the right to request an oral hearing in lieu of a written review, but must submit an explanation of why a written review is insufficient.[175] As with other offsets, borrowers should have the right to set up a repayment plan acceptable to the Secretary prior to offset.[176] Borrowers also have a right to request a temporary hardship waiver, as discussed in the next subsection.

FMS has stated that once DOE (and other federal agencies) refer debts to them, they will subsequently notify the debtor twice, at sixty-day and thirty-day intervals, in writing of the anticipated offset.[177] However, according to the Treasury regulations, the offset remains legal even if the debtor does not receive the notices.[178]

Borrowers are likely to be confused regarding which agency to contact if they wish to challenge offsets or just have questions about them. The Department of Treasury explicitly requires borrowers to contact the "originating" agency (the Department of Education in student loan cases). The FMS notices for student loan administrative offsets list a number at the Department of Education for borrowers to

---

165 For a discussion of a possible ten year statute of limitations, see § 5.4.3.3, *infra*.

166 Note, however, that these agencies should clearly be bound by the ten year statute of limitations for federal benefits offsets. 31 U.S.C. § 3716(e)(1). This issue is less clear, at least in the government's view, for student loan collection. This issue is currently being litigated. *See* § 5.4.3.3, *infra*.

167 31 C.F.R. § 285.4(e).

168 31 C.F.R. § 285.4(e)(3)(i).

169 31 C.F.R. § 285.4(e)(3)(ii).

170 31 C.F.R. § 285.4(e)(3)(iii).

171 31 U.S.C. § 3716(a).

172 34 C.F.R. § 30.20 *et seq.* However, DOE is also referring to the more recent Treasury administrative offset regulations for guidance on issues such as whether a ten-year limit applies in the student loan context. *See* § 5.4.3.3, *infra*.

173 34 C.F.R. § 30.24(a)(1).

174 34 C.F.R. § 30.22(a)(3).

175 34 C.F.R. § 30.25(b)(1). The rules for oral hearings are set out at 34 C.F.R. § 30.26.

176 34 C.F.R. § 30.22(b)(3)(iii). Due process challenges to these review procedures are discussed at §§ 5.2.2.4 (tax refund intercepts), 5.3.4 (garnishment), *supra*.

177 *See* Department of Treasury web site at www.fms.treas.gov/news/factsheets/benefitoffset.html.

178 31 C.F.R. § 285.4(f)(3).

call. Borrowers can contact the FMS at 1-800-304-3107, but only to find out which agency to contact, particularly if they find that their benefits are being offset but they never received notice.

5.4.3.2 Hardship Waiver

Borrowers have the right to request a wavier of offset based on financial hardship. The Department of Education makes the determinations regarding financial hardship for student loan administrative offsets.

The Department requires borrowers to submit the following documents before they will review a claim of hardship:

- The notification of offset;
- The notification letter showing the amount of benefit;
- Proof of yearly income;
- A completed financial statement returned to DOE within ten days.[179] If the situation is an emergency, a borrower may submit equivalent information such as an eviction notice or a court order of foreclosure in writing with the completed financial statement;
- A letter explaining the exceptional circumstances that caused the financial hardship along with any other supporting documents.

The Department is currently setting up a review unit in the Chicago Service Center. This unit will examine the documents to determine whether the offset should be reduced partially or fully. Refunds may be granted as well. Documents should be sent to:

U.S. Department of Education
FMS OFFSET REVIEW UNIT
P.O. Box 617635
Chicago, IL 60661-8064[180]

The Unit will determine whether the borrower is entitled to a waiver and if so, whether the offset amount should be partially or fully reduced. If the Department denies the waiver, they will notify the borrower of the denial and continue offsetting. If the waiver is granted, the borrower may be entitled to a limited refund. The refund will only be for amounts offset above the newly determined offset amount and only for periods during which financial hardship can be shown.

Unfortunately for borrowers, the right to a hardship waiver is not listed in the notices sent by either DOE or FMS. Instead, borrowers will find out about the availability of the hardship wavier when they call the Department of Education number indicated on the notice of federal offset. If borrowers call that number, they will enter into a telephone menu requesting first that they provide identifying information such as name and social security number. After entering this information, borrowers are asked to press a number if they are disputing an offset or administrative wage garnishment. Once a borrower presses this option, they will at some point be asked if the offset is causing severe financial hardship. If the borrower is able to get this far in the process, she will receive information about how to submit an appeal of the offset in writing.

It is unclear how flexible the Department will be in granting these waivers, particularly with respect to the fifth "exceptional circumstances" category. Exceptional circumstances should clearly include pending evictions or foreclosures but might also include disability status or other "non-temporary" exceptional circumstances. The precise standards to prove financial hardship are also unclear at this point.

5.4.3.3 Statute of Limitations

5.4.3.3.1 Is there a 10-year limit on offsets?

The Debt Collection Improvement Act prohibits offset for claims that have been "outstanding" for more than ten years.[181] The issue of whether the ten-year statute of limitations in the DCIA applies to offsets for collection to student loan is currently being litigated.[182]

The government argues that the ten-year limit does not apply to student loans because of the separate Higher Education Act authority that eliminated the statute of limitations for student loan collections.[183] The plaintiffs agree that the HEA provision generally allows student loan collectors to pursue collection indefinitely. However, they claim that this unbridled authority does not apply in the Social Security context because of the explicit protections of the Social Security anti-assignment statute, 42 U.S.C. § 407. This statute can be abrogated only by statutes that expressly refer

---

179 A copy of this form is included at Appx. D, *infra* and on the companion CD-Rom.

180 The procedures are still in flux. In other documents, the DOE has stated that borrowers should send information to the TOP Hardship Review Unit at P.O. Box 4220, Iowa City, Iowa 52244-4220. It is probably best at this point to submit applications to both addresses and, as always, to keep copies. Requests should be sent return receipt requested.

181 31 U.S.C. § 3716(e)(1).

182 In December 2001, NCLC, along with Public Citizen Litigation Group and Oakland Livingston Legal Aid filed a lawsuit challenging the government's right to offset Social Security payments to collect old student loan debt. The lawsuit, filed in the Eastern District of Michigan, is an individual action, brought on behalf of three senior citizen plaintiffs. All three rely on Social Security retirement income as their main source of income. Each Plaintiff's benefits were being offset to collect old student loan. Both the Departments of Education and Treasury are named as defendants. *See* Guillermety v. U.S. Secretary of Education and U.S. Secretary of Treasury, Case #01-74904 (Complaint filed E.D. Mich. Dec. 20, 2001), available at Appx. E, *infra* and on the companion CD-Rom.

183 20 U.S.C. § 1091a(a)(1).

to it. The DCIA has an explicit reference to 42 U.S.C. § 407 and therefore meets this test. The HEA does not.

In a March 28, 2002 decision, the court agreed that plaintiffs had a substantial likelihood of prevailing on this statutory argument.[184] The court reasoned that the elimination of the statute of limitations in the HEA, although broad and general, was narrowly focused on a particular problem—the ability of the government to collect delinquent student loans through the offset of federal tax refunds. The judge found further that Congress did not and could not have anticipated that this would have any effect on the statute of limitations with respect to the offset of Social Security benefits since these offsets were strictly prohibited at the time the HEA provision was passed. When Congress did focus squarely on the Social Security offset issue, they explicitly kept the 10-year limit.

5.4.3.3.2 *Defining the 10-year period*

The court's agreement that the plaintiffs are likely to prevail on the statutory argument is only half the battle. The next key question is when the ten-year period begins to run. The statute merely refers to "outstanding" claims without defining what this means. The key question is whether the clock starts from the time the debt is incurred (as plaintiffs argued), or from the time the reinsurance claim is made or the loan is assigned to the Department of Education (as the government claims).

In a preliminary injunction decision, the judge concluded that the time period should run from either the date of assignment of the loan to the United States or the date on which the government paid the reinsurance claim. The court granted the injunction only for the one plaintiff whose loan was clearly older than ten years under this criterion.[185]

The ten-year issue is particularly critical because many holders of federal student loans, including schools in the case of Perkins Loans and guaranty agencies for FFEL loans, wait many years before assigning defaulted loans to the United States. In some cases, the loans are never assigned. For example, the sole plaintiff who was granted injunctive relief had one Perkins Loan from the 1970s.[186]

This loan was not assigned to the United States until 1990. The plaintiff never made any payments during this period. The other plaintiffs incurred loans during the mid-1980s and early 1990s. Because these loans were not assigned or reinsured ten years prior to the filing of the lawsuit, the court found that these loans were not yet "ten years old."

5.4.3.3.3 *Advice for clients with old loans*

Hopefully the litigation discussed in the previous subsection (and any similar cases) will ultimately be successful and all clients with old loans will be exempt from federal benefits offsets. In the interim, advocates should consider a number of options for clients facing Social Security offsets. One strategy is to file separate individual lawsuits for these clients.[187] It is necessary to first gather information on the type of loan the client has. If the loan is a Perkins Loan, advocates should find out the date the loan obligation was incurred, date of default, and date of assignment if any. For guaranteed loans, it is essential to determine the date of signing and default as well as reinsurance date and assignment date if any. If there is more than one loan, advocates will need to gather this information for each loan.

If the client is disabled, advocates should consider filing a disability discharge on the client's behalf. Although these are difficult to obtain, borrowers are entitled to this discharge if they are permanently and totally disabled.[188] It is not sufficient to show that a borrower has met the Social Security definition of disability. The Department of Education usually requires more (disability plus). However, many clients, particularly with the assistance of an aggressive advocate, will be able to get this discharge. This discharge is discussed in detail in Chapter 6, *infra*.

Once a disability discharge is granted, the loan is completely cancelled. While the application is pending, collection must cease.[189] Advocates should also consider other ways to cancel a client's loan.[190] Bankruptcy may also be an option for some clients.[191] In addition, some states have programs to assist certain student loan borrowers.[192]

If a client is not eligible for a cancellation, an affordable repayment plan or consolidation should be considered.

184　Guillermety v. U.S. Secretary of Education and U.S. Secretary of Treasury, Case #01-74904, Order Granting in Part and Denying in Part Plaintiffs' Motion for Preliminary Injunction, Clearinghouse No. 54561 (E.D. Mich. Mar. 28, 2002). An oral hearing on Plaintiffs' summary judgment motion occurred on July 30, 2002. The ruling was not yet available at the time this manual was printed.

185　Pleadings and discovery requests from this case are available at Appxs. E, F, *infra* and on the companion CD-Rom.

186　As discussed in Chapter 1, *supra*, unlike Federal FFEL loans, the government does not insure Perkins Loans. Instead, the government provides initial contributions to eligible institutions to partially capitalize a loan fund. It is in the school's discretion whether to assign defaulted loans to the U.S. Anecdotally, many Perkins lenders claim that they keep these loans in their port-

folios for as long as possible. Once they assign the loans, they do not receive any monies later recovered by the government. *See* 34 C.F.R. § 674.50. *See also* Department of Education, Dear Colleague Letter CB-02-05, Revised Policies and Procedures for Assigning Perkins Loans (Apr. 2002).

187　The counsel in the current case request that advocates considering filing litigation first consult with them so as to ensure coordination and communication. Pleadings and discovery requests from the *Guillermety* case are available at Appxs. E, F, *infra*.

188　34 C.F.R. § 682.402(c). *See* § 6.6, *infra*.

189　34 C.F.R. § 682.402(c)(2); *see* § 6.6, *infra*.

190　*See generally* Ch. 6, *infra*.

191　*See generally* Ch. 7, *infra*.

192　*See* § 9.6, *infra*.

These are discussed in Chapter 8, *infra*. Advocates should be aware of a few potential problems. First, consolidating the loan creates a new loan with a new promissory note. This means that if the litigation does succeed at some point and has national application, the client's loan will no longer be older than ten years and she will not be part of the group that gets relief from offset (at least not until another ten years goes by). Consolidation is not a good option in any case if the payments would be higher than the offset amount. Finally, even if there is no way to stop the offset, at a minimum, advocates should make sure that the government is only offsetting what they are entitled to offset.[193]

---

193 *See* § 5.4.2, *supra*.

Chapter 6   Discharging Student Loan Obligations

6.1 Introduction

Discharges provide the most powerful remedies for student loan borrowers. They offer complete relief as opposed to simply delaying the repayment obligation. After a cancellation, the borrower no longer owes anything on the loan and becomes eligible for new student loans and grants. In some cases, borrowers are also entitled to refunds of past loan payments, deletion of all negative references on their credit records, and renewed eligibility for federal financial aid.

Because these are such powerful remedies, advocates should always consider the various discharges first when evaluating a student loan case, regardless of whether a client is in default. Victims of trade school fraud, in particular, are likely to be eligible for at least one of these discharges.

The Higher Education Act (HEA) offers a six main ways to discharge or cancel a student loan obligation:

- The school's closure while the student was still enrolled;
- The school's false certification of the student's eligibility;
- The school's failure to pay a refund owed to a student;
- The borrower's permanent and total disability;
- The borrower's death; and
- The borrower's bankruptcy.

In addition, there are a number of cancellation and forgiveness programs, primarily for Perkins Loan borrowers as well as teacher forgiveness programs for certain Perkins, FFEL, and Direct Loan borrowers.[1]

This chapter considers all of these statutory bases for discharges with the exception of bankruptcy, which is discussed in Chapter 7, *infra*. This chapter also covers common law grounds for canceling student loan obligations.

---

[1] *See* § 6.8, *infra*.

6.2 The Closed School Discharge

6.2.1 The Closed School Discharge Applies to Specified Types of Loans

The closed school discharge applies to FFELs, federal Direct Loans, and Perkins Loans (including NDSLs) received at least in part on or after January 1, 1986.[2] The 1986 cut-off means that at least part of the loan must have been disbursed in 1986.[3] Even loans that have lost their guaranteed status because of a lender's failure to display due diligence or to comply with other program requirements are eligible.[4]

If a borrower consolidates multiple loans, only the portion of the consolidation attributable to the discharge-eligible loan(s) will be discharged. If a borrower consolidates a loan eligible for discharge, the borrower will receive a credit in the amount of the loan(s) relating to the closed school.[5]

---

[2] 34 C.F.R. §§ 682.402(d)(1)(i)) (FFEL), 685.214 (Direct Loans), 674.33(g). As the rules on the six main discharges are substantially the same for the different programs, citations hereafter refer mainly to FFEL rules. In particular, unless otherwise specified, Direct Loans have the same terms and conditions as FFELs. 20 U.S.C. § 1087e(a)(10). For a general description of the different loan programs, see § 1.4, *supra*.

[3] 34 C.F.R. § 682.402(d)(3)(A) (FFEL).

[4] *Id.* Borrowers with loans reduced to judgment should also qualify for the closed school and other federal discharges. The Department of Education grants discharges in these circumstances and has stated that they will continue to do so. This issue came up during spring 2002 negotiated rulemaking sessions with the Department of Education. Among other changes coming out of these sessions, the negotiators agreed to eliminate the rehabilitation right for borrowers with loans reduced to judgment. The Department stated in its explanation in the Federal Register that this change would not affect other rights for borrowers with judgments, including discharge rights. 67 Fed. Reg. 51036, 51038 (Aug. 6, 2002). *See also* § 8.4 (rehabilitation), *infra*.

[5] Dear Colleague Letter 94-G-256, Clearinghouse No. 50,422 (Sept. 1994), included at Appx. C, *infra*. *See* 34 C.F.R. § 685.220(k)(3) (Direct Consolidation Loans).

6.2.2 Determining if a Student Qualifies for a Closed School Discharge

6.2.2.1 Timing of School Closure

The HEA requires the Secretary to discharge a specified loan if the borrower was unable to complete the program due to the school's closure.[6] The regulations provide this discharge if the branch of the school at which the student attended closed.[7] For example, if the student goes to branch "A," there is no right to a discharge if only the main campus or branch "B" closed. On the other hand, if branch "A" closes, the student has a right to a discharge even if all other branches stay open. The closed school discharge applies to any school at which the student obtained a qualified loan, whether or not the school or branch was in fact an eligible institution under the program.[8]

The regulations provide a discharge if the student was still enrolled at the time of the school's closure or if the student withdrew from the school within ninety days before the school's closure.[9] A student on an approved leave of absence is treated as still enrolled.[10] The ninety-day period may be extended if the Secretary determines that exceptional circumstances related to the school's closing would justify an extension.[11] It also may be extended in some circumstances for students who attended correspondence schools.[12]

A school's closure date is the date at which it ceases offering *all* programs at a particular branch, not when it stops offering the particular program in which the student is enrolled.[13] Nevertheless, where a particular program at a location ceases four or five months before the branch closes, this would seem to be an appropriate situation for the Secretary to extend the ninety-day period because of the exceptional circumstances related to the school's closing.

Borrowers can obtain closed school discharges if the school closed before they completed a program, even if the school issued the borrower a diploma or other certificate.[14] On the other hand, if a student completes a program, there is no discharge even if the borrower never received a diploma or certificate.[15]

6.2.2.2 The Official School Closure Date

The Secretary determines the closure date, and for most situations, the borrower should rely on the Secretary's Cumulative List of Closed Schools to find out the official closure date. The Department continually updates this list. The easiest way to access the list is through the Department of Education's website. The site allows advocates to search for a specific school's closure date. The general Department website is www.ed.gov. The specific site for the list is www.ed.gov/offices/OSFAP/Students/closedschool/search.html.

Initially, numerous errors were reported concerning this list. This is less common now, but errors still appear. For this reason, advocates should not necessarily give up if their client has evidence of a different closing date that would affect eligibility.

Possible sources of evidence of a school's earlier closing date include dated newspaper articles or other media reports about the school's closure and declarations from other students, state regulators, or former school employees regarding the closure date. Advocates may submit a request to change a school closing date to the Department of Education's Closed School Section.[16] A change in a school closing date must be determined by the Department regardless of who holds the loan.

Official closure dates have been challenged both informally and in court.[17] In at least one case, the Department entered into a settlement agreeing to change the closure date,

---

6 20 U.S.C. § 1087(c)(1).

7 *See* 34 C.F.R. §§ 682.402(d)(1)(ii)(C) (FFEL), 685.214(a)(2)(ii) (Direct Loans).

8 *See* 34 C.F.R. § 682.402(d)(1)(ii)(C) (FFEL).

9 34 C.F.R. §§ 682.402(d)(1)(i) (FFEL), 685.214(c)(1)(ii) (Direct Loans), 674.33(g)(4)(i)(B) (Perkins). The "90 day rule" is not in the statute, only the regulations. The statute provides for discharges in certain circumstances if the borrower is unable to complete the program due to the closure of the institution. 20 U.S.C. § 1087(c). At least one court found that the plain language of the statute allowed for a closed school discharge even if the borrower was not enrolled at the time of closure or had not withdrawn within ninety days. *See* Sandler v. U.S. Dep't of Education, 2001 U.S. Dist. LEXIS 11179 (E.D. Pa. 2001) (school announced impending closure about a year ahead of time. Plaintiff still had over two years of coursework left to complete her program and could not transfer credits to a new location. Court found Plaintiff's situation fit squarely within the plain language of the statute and therefore court did not consider whether the regulations setting the limit at 90 days were arbitrary and capricious). Advocates should consider continuing to challenge this regulation in court.

10 The definition of an approved leave of absence is found at 34 C.F.R. § 668.22(d). The leave must usually be requested in writing, and is granted only once per year, and usually does not exceed 60 days, although it can last as long as six months in certain situations.

11 34 C.F.R. §§ 682.402(d)(1)(i) (FFEL), 685.214(c)(1)(ii) (Direct Loans).

12 *See* § 6.2.2.3, *infra*.

13 *See* 34 C.F.R. §§ 682.402(d)(1)(ii)(A) (FFEL), 685.214(a)(2)(i) (Direct Loans).

14 *See* United States Department of Education, Dear Colleague Letter GEN-94-256, Clearinghouse No. 50,422 (Sept. 1994), *reprinted at* Appx. C, *infra*.

15 *Id.*

16 United States Department of Education, SFAP/Closed School Unit, P.O. Box 23800, L'Enfant Plaza Station, Washington, D.C. 20026; (800) 4FED-AID. A list of regional closed school unit contacts is available at www.ed.gov/offices/OSFAP/Students/closedschool/assignmentlist.html (July 2002).

17 *See* Moorer v. Secretary of Education, Clearinghouse No. 51,931 (D.D.C. June 7, 1996) (complaint for declaratory and injunctive relief).

discharge the named plaintiff's loans, and provide notice of the new date to borrowers enrolled within 150 days of the new closure date.[18]

6.2.2.3 Correspondence Schools

There are often special problems when a student attended a correspondence school or a correspondence school with a final residential portion to the program. Such schools often stop corresponding with their students well before the school's official closure date. Even though the student's failure to submit lessons was caused by the school, the school's records may indicate, or the Department or guaranty agency might determine that the student had withdrawn from the school. Similarly, the school's failure to offer the student the residential portion of the program may be misinterpreted as the student dropping out.

In an attempt to address some of the problems associated with correspondence schools, the Department in July 1997 released a Dear Colleague letter extending the ninety-day period for students who attended and withdrew from specified correspondence schools.[19] These extended periods apply only to the ten closed correspondence schools listed below:

1. American Career Training Travel/Hart Secretarial School (ACT), Pompano Beach, FL, main location. Borrowers who enrolled in ACT and took out a loan with a loan period which began on or after March 1, 1988 may be eligible for the closed school discharge if they meet all other requirements.

For the other nine schools listed below, borrowers who took out loans with loan periods which began within twelve months of the closure date may be eligible for the closed school discharge:

2. AMS College, Home Study Division, Alpine, CA.
3. Columbia School of Broadcasting, Las Vegas, NV.
4. County Schools, Bridgeport, CT.
5. Global Academy, Atlanta, GA.
6. National Training Systems, Laurel, MD.
7. Northwest Schools, Portland, OR.
8. Superior Training Services, Phoenix, AZ.
9. United Schools, Clearwater, FL.
10. USA Training Academy Home Study, Newark, DE.[20]

The Dear Colleague Letter provides that guaranty agencies and lenders must review records to identify borrowers with loan periods that would qualify them for discharges under these extended periods. Agencies must reevaluate previously denied applications for borrowers identified in this process and mail out applications to all others. Previously denied applicants who meet all the other closed school discharge requirements should be granted discharges without the submission of new applications.

6.2.2.4 Teach-Outs

Students are barred from receiving a discharge if they completed the program through a "teach-out" at another school, or through transfer of credits or hours earned at the closed school to another school.[21] In a February 1998 decision in the *McComas* case, the United States District Court for the Southern District of West Virginia rejected the argument that the "teach out" bar to discharge contravened the meaning and purpose of the governing statute, 20 U.S.C. § 1087(c)(1). The court granted the Department's summary judgment motion.[22]

The statute states that in order to qualify for a closed school discharge, borrowers must be unable to complete the program in which they enrolled. The inability to complete the program must be due to school closure. The ambiguity, challenged in *McComas*, is whether "program" means only the program at the closed school or a general course of study that may be pursued at another school. In *McComas*, the plaintiff was able to transfer credits earned at the closed school to another school. The court agreed that the governing statute was susceptible to two different meanings, but did not find clear congressional intent to prohibit the Department's use of the "teach-out/transfer of credits" limitation.

6.2.3 Relief Available for Those Obtaining a Closed School Discharge

When a borrower receives a closed school discharge, the borrower (and any other obligor on the note) is no longer obligated to repay the loan or any charges or costs associated with the loan.[23] That is, the loan principal, interest charges, collection costs, and all other charges are forgiven.

In addition, the borrower is reimbursed all amounts paid to date on the loan, whether those payments were voluntary or involuntary, such as through tax intercepts or garnish-

---

18 Tello v. Secretary of Education, Clearinghouse No. 52,120B, Settlement Agreement and Stipulation of Dismissal (D. Md. Aug. 1998); Tello v. Secretary of Education, Clearinghouse No. 52,120A, Class Action Complaint (D. Md. 1997).

19 Dear Colleague Letter 97-G-300, Clearinghouse No. 52,043 (July 1997).

20 All locations listed here are the main locations. Closure dates are not listed because many of these schools had numerous locations, and closure dates vary by location. Closure dates are listed in the Dear Colleague Letter, 97-G-300, Clearinghouse No. 52,043 (July 1997) and The Secretary's Cumulative List of Closed Schools. *See* § 6.2.2.2, *infra*.

21 34 C.F.R. § 682.402(d)(3)(ii)(c).

22 McComas v. Riley, Clearinghouse No. 52,039 (S.D. W. Va. Feb. 27, 1998) (opinion and order granting defendants' renewed motion for summary judgment).

23 *See* 34 C.F.R. §§ 682.402(d)(2)(i) (FFEL), 685.214(b)(1) (Direct Loans), 674.33(g)(2)(i) (Perkins).

ments.[24] The borrower is no longer regarded in default, and is immediately eligible for new loans and grants.[25] The discharge of a FFEL must also be reported to all credit reporting agencies to which the holder previously reported the loan's status "so as to delete all adverse credit history assigned to the loan."[26]

6.2.4 How to Obtain a Closed School Discharge

6.2.4.1 General

It is rare for the Department and guaranty agencies to provide automatic discharges to those who appear eligible. Borrowers must apply for the discharge. Guarantors are required to inform those appearing eligible of their right to apply, with an application form, and the guarantors must forbear collecting from these individuals.[27] Presumably, the Department does the same on the loans it is collecting.

If a guaranty agency is holding a loan, borrowers should deal with the guaranty agency in obtaining a discharge. Only if the Department is holding the loan should the student apply directly to the Department. Department-held loans will almost invariably be handled by a private collection agency.

In cases where the borrower is initially dealing with a collection agency, the Department's policy is that once the borrower requests a closed school discharge, the file must be turned over immediately to Department staff. Thus it will be the Department staff, and not the collection agency, that processes the closed school discharge.

Nevertheless, advocates and borrowers must be prepared for collection agencies (working on a commission basis) to fail to turn accounts over to the Department and to discourage borrowers from seeking the discharge. There have been incidents of collection agencies advising consumers that they are obligated to repay a loan even if the school closed when they were enrolled. When a collection agency misrepresents a borrower's discharge rights, it violates the federal Fair Debt Collection Practices Act (FDCPA).[28]

6.2.4.2 Written Application for Discharge

With a few exceptions discussed below, a written application is required. To apply for a discharge, borrowers will typically fill out forms created by the loan holder, and submit the application to the loan holder. For example, if the Department holds the loan, the borrower should use the Department's closed school discharge application form and submit the form to the Department.[29] If a guaranty agency holds the loan, that guaranty agency's form should be used.

The borrower only needs to provide the minimum information required by the regulations, including:

- Whether the borrower has made a claim relating to the loan with a third party such as a state tuition recovery program or surety for the school, and if so the amount of any recovery;
- That the borrower received the loan proceeds after January 1, 1986;
- That the borrower did not complete the program because of the school's closing while the borrower was enrolled, or the borrower was on an approved leave of absence, or withdrew within ninety days of the school's closure;
- That the borrower did not complete the program through a teach out at another school or by transferring credits to another school (presumably this would only apply if the borrower received a credit toward tuition at the new school because of attendance at the closed school);
- That the borrower agrees to provide, if requested, other related documentation reasonably available to the borrower;
- That the borrower agrees to cooperate with the Secretary in any action to recover money relating to the loan from third parties, such as the school owners and the school's affiliates.[30]

The regulations contain no requirement that borrowers, in applying for a discharge, reaffirm their debt or waive other rights. If guaranty agencies provide discharge application forms with these extraneous provisions, borrowers should cross these provisions out, with their initials evidencing their intent to delete these items. The Department has also instructed guaranty agencies to process all requests for a

---

24　*See* 34 C.F.R. §§ 682.402(d)(2)(ii) (FFEL), 685.214(b)(2) (Direct Loans), 674.33(g)(2)(ii) (Perkins).

25　*See* 34 C.F.R. §§ 682.402(d)(2)(iii) (FFEL), 685.214(b)(3) (Direct Loans), 674.33(g)(2)(iii) (Perkins).

26　*See* 34 C.F.R. § 682.402(d)(2)(iv) (FFEL). The language in 34 C.F.R. § 685.214(b)(4) (Direct Loans) is not so extensive, solely requiring the Secretary to report the loan discharge to all credit bureaus to which the Secretary previously reported the status of the loan. *See generally* § 3.3, *supra*.

27　34 C.F.R. § 682.402(d)(6).

28　*See generally* Ch. 4, *supra*.

29　*See* Appx. D, *infra*. The form is also available on the Department of Education website: www.ed.gov. The Department issued new forms in June 2002. *See* Department of Education, Dear Partner Letter GEN-02-05, Approval of Loan Discharge Application Forms, (June 2002) (school closure discharge forms, false certification discharge forms). If the address to which the borrower is requested to send payments is the National Payment Center in Greenville, TX, borrowers should submit completed forms to U.S. Dept. of Ed., P.O. Box 4222, Iowa City, IA 52244-4222.

30　34 C.F.R. § 682.402(d)(3).

closed school discharge, even if the request is not on the agency's standard form.[31] In practice, however, it is generally most efficient to use the official agency form whenever possible.

6.2.4.3 Oral Applications

The 1998 HEA authorized the Department and guaranty agencies to grant closed school discharges without a written application in limited circumstances.[32] Specifically, a discharge may be granted without an application if (1) the borrower received a discharge of a different type of loan for the same program of study or (2) the Department or guaranty agency determines that the borrower qualifies for a discharge based on information in the Secretary or guaranty agency's possession. This may facilitate advocacy that a group of students be given a closed school discharge in settlement of an action, instead of requiring each student to submit an application.

6.2.4.4 Time Limits and Appeal Rights

There is no time limit on a borrower's eligibility for a discharge.[33] The Department expects guaranty agencies to respond to discharge requests within ninety days, although the Department has not set any time limits for its own response to discharge requests.

Decisions may take years to process. For this reason, advocates should be prepared to request administrative forbearances for borrowers so that collection activities will cease until the discharge has been granted or denied.[34] Guaranty agencies collecting FFEL loans should affirmatively suspend collection if the agency has information about a school not previously known to the Secretary.[35]

The regulations do not set out a review right for denial of a closed school discharge application. For a discussion on how to appeal an adverse decision, see § 6.9, *infra*.

6.2.5 *Effect of School Closure on FISLs and Older FFELs*

The closed school discharge applies only to loans disbursed after January 1, 1986. As a consequence, students whose loans were disbursed *in full* before that date will have to pursue other approaches.

Many loans from the 1970s and early 1980s were Federally Insured Student Loans (FISLs). There was no guaranty agency involvement with these loans. Instead, the lender or

even a school acting as lender made the loan, and the loan was directly insured by the United States. Department FISL regulations through 1986 stated that the school's closure while the student was enrolled provided a defense to repayment on the loan.[36]

The Stafford regulations never had such an explicit provision. Nevertheless, the Department had stated a policy, before the closed school discharge provision was enacted by Congress, encouraging guaranty agencies to excuse a portion or all of a student's Stafford Loan where the school closed while the student was still enrolled.[37]

Borrowers are excused from paying the percentage of the debt that equals the percentage of the loan period that the borrower was prevented from attending school because of the school closing. However, the borrower must agree to pay the remainder of the loan and assign to the guaranty agency any right to receive a refund from the school. In addition, the policy does not apply where a borrower has a "teach-out" available from another school.

Apparently, the Department agrees that this policy still applies to pre-1986 loans, although it is unlikely that collection agencies or most personnel hired by the Department or guarantors will be aware of it. Advocates may have to educate these personnel or find a knowledgeable person in the General Counsel's office or elsewhere in the Department such as the Ombudsman office.

Another avenue for pre-1986 Staffords is to raise the school's closure as a school-related claim that the student asserts as a defense to the loan.[38] A loan made directly by the school, such as a Perkins Loan, is subject to a straightforward breach of contract defense if the school closed before the educational services were provided.[39]

6.3 False Certification Discharge

6.3.1 *General*

Students are entitled to a loan discharge if they received at least part of a FFEL or Direct Loan after January 1, 1986[40] and if their eligibility to borrow was falsely certified by the school.[41] The discharge does not apply to Perkins Loans, but

---

31 Dear Colleague Letter 94-G-256, Clearinghouse No. 50,422 (Sept. 1994), *reprinted at* Appx. C, *infra*.

32 34 C.F.R. §§ 682.402(d)(8) (FFEL), 674.33(g)(3) (Perkins).

33 34 C.F.R. § 682.402(d)(6)(J).

34 34 C.F.R. § 682.211(f)(7). *See also* § 2.3.2, *supra*.

35 34 C.F.R. § 682.402(d)(6)(D).

36 34 C.F.R. § 518 (since rescinded). *See also* United States v. Griffin, 707 F.2d 1477 (D.C. Cir. 1983).

37 Department of Education letter titled, Compromise and Write-off Procedures 89-G-159, Clearinghouse No. 44,338 (May 1989).

38 *See* § 9.5.3.1, *infra*.

39 *See* § 9.5.2.1, *infra*.

40 A loan is dischargeable even if part of it was disbursed in 1985, as long as part was disbursed in 1986. 34 C.F.R. § 682.402(e)(3)(ii)(A).

41 20 U.S.C. § 1087(c)(1).

students should be able to raise the school's misconduct as a defense to loan repayment because the school is the original lender.[42]

The Department recognizes only three bases for a false certification discharge:

- The school falsifies a non-high school graduate's ability to benefit from the program;[43] or
- The school enrolls a student unable to meet minimum state employment requirements for the job for which the student is being trained;[44] or
- The school forges or alters the student loan note or check endorsements.[45]

6.3.2 Discharge Based on Ability-to-Benefit (ATB) Falsification

6.3.2.1 ATB Falsification Defined

Department regulations authorize a false certification discharge if the student was admitted to a school and the school falsified the student's ability to benefit from the program.[46] The school is required to test a student's ability to benefit only if the student did not have a high school diploma or its recognized equivalent prior to enrollment.[47] Therefore, borrowers who had high school diplomas or equivalencies at the time they enrolled will not be eligible for this type of false certification discharge. For enrollments between July 1, 1987 and June 30, 1991 only, both borrowers who had general education diplomas (GEDs) at the time of enrolling *and* those who received the diplomas before completing the program are deemed to have the ability to benefit from the program.[48]

The rules for schools to admit "Ability to Benefit" students changed in 1987, 1991, and 1996. For a school *not* to have falsified the ability of a student enrolled between July 1, 1987 and June 30, 1996[49] to benefit from the school, the student must have done at least one of the following:

- Passed an ability-to-benefit test, the test being approved by the accrediting agency[50] (or for enrollments after July 1, 1991, by the Secretary) and administered substantially in accordance with the test publisher's or accreditor's requirements for use of the test;[51] or
- Successfully completed a program of developmental or remedial education provided by the school.[52]

For periods of enrollment after July 1, 1996 and before June 30, 2000, the student must have done at least one of the following:

- Obtained within twelve months after the date the student initially received financial assistance, a passing score on an independently administered test;[53] or
- Enrolled in an eligible institution that participates in an alternative admissions process.[54] Alternative processes can be implemented by the states for some or all schools in that state. These processes must be approved by the Secretary of Education. In order to gain approval, the state must present certain information including proof of a minimum success rate.[55]

For periods of enrollment beginning on or after July 1, 2000, the student must meet one of the two conditions discussed above for July 1, 1996 through June 30, 2000, or meet the requirements for valid home schooling.[56]

A school not administering a valid test where one is required is a clear example of ATB fraud. The Department also considers the following testing errors, even if unintentional, proof of ATB falsification:[57]

---

42 *See* § 9.5.2.1, *infra.*

43 *See* § 6.3.2, *infra.*

44 *See* § 6.3.3, *infra.*

45 *See* § 6.3.4, *infra.*

46 34 C.F.R. §§ 682.402(e)(1)(i)(A), 685.215 (Direct Loans). For a thorough discussion of the false certification of ability to benefit discharge, see Alan White, *New Relief for Trade School Victims: Discharging Student Loans Based on False Certification of Ability to Benefit*, 29 Clearinghouse Rev. 1128 (Apr. 1996).

47 34 C.F.R. § 682.402(e)(1), (e)(13)(iv), citing student eligibility regulations in 34 C.F.R. § 668.32(e)(1) and ATB test requirements at 34 C.F.R. § 668.141(a).

48 34 C.F.R. § 682.402(e)(13)(i).

49 For students enrolled before that date, the school had to have developed and consistently applied criteria for determining whether students had the ability to benefit, and the school had to have been able to demonstrate that to the Secretary. *See* 34 C.F.R. § 682.402(e)(13)(ii)(A).

50 For an example of accrediting agency testing standards, see letter from President, ACCET to ACCET accredited schools re clarification of ATB requirements for all institutions utilizing a test to admit ability-to-benefit students, Clearinghouse No. 51,927 (Feb. 12, 1990). It should be noted that accreditors did not generally grant schools an explicit approval of their ATB tests. Instead, accreditors have guidelines that ATB tests must meet. While some schools were reviewed by accreditors and found to have violated accrediting agency ATB testing rules, the absence of an adverse finding by an accreditor is not tantamount to approval of a school's ATB test or test process.

51 34 C.F.R. § 682.402(e)(13)(ii)(B)(1), (2).

52 34 C.F.R. § 682.402(e)(13)(ii)(C).

53 34 C.F.R. § 682.402(e)(13)(ii)(D)(1). There are a number of requirements for independently administered tests including that the test be given at an assessment center by a test administrator who has no financial or ownership interest in the school. The regulations for independently administered tests are set out in 34 C.F.R. § 668, subpart J. 34 C.F.R. § 668.151 relates to the administration of tests. In addition, the test is not independently administered if the school pays a test administrator a bonus or other incentive. 34 C.F.R. § 668.151(c).

54 34 C.F.R. § 682.402(e)(13)(D)(2), citing regulations for approved state processes at 34 C.F.R. § 668.156.

55 34 C.F.R. § 668.156(b).

56 34 C.F.R. § 682.402(e)(13)(ii)(E)(1), (2). The home schooling regulations can be found at 34 C.F.R. § 668.32(e)(4).

57 Dear Colleague Letter Gen-95-42 from Elizabeth M. Hicks,

- A test requiring an independent test administrator was not so administered;
- The school allowed a student to retake the test earlier than the minimum prescribed waiting period or more frequently than allowed;
- The school allowed more time than permitted to take the test, did not use all required portions of the test, supplied answers to students, allowed students to discuss the answers among themselves, or passed a student whose score did not meet minimum standards;
- Starting after July 1, 1991, the test was not approved by the Department of Education.

Even if an approved ATB test is used, a false certification discharge may still be granted if the student was not given the appropriate portion of the approved test.[58] In *Pellot v. Riley*, a nursing assistant student who was given only the clerical portion of an approved test was found eligible on appeal for a false certification discharge. The accreditor guidelines and test publisher instructions made clear that a school should test aptitudes related to the course. In the case of a nursing assistant, this would include verbal and math ability, not just clerical matching skills.

6.3.2.2 Student No Longer Has to Prove Failure to Find Employment

In a significant victory for victims of school abuses and fraud, the Court of Appeals for the D.C. Circuit in November 1999 struck down the portion of the false certification discharge regulation that requires applicants to certify that they did not find employment after attending school.[59]

After this decision, the Department of Education agreed to extend the benefits of the ruling to borrowers nationwide. The Department's action was initially confirmed in a July 2000 Dear Colleague Letter and later formalized in new regulations effective July 1, 2001.[60]

In addition to streamlining the process for individual discharges, this change should make it easier to pursue group discharges. If it can be shown, for example, that a school used an improper test during a certain time period, all

non-high school graduates enrolled during that period should be eligible for false certification discharges. Advocates will no longer be forced to go through the tedious case-by-case process of proving that individual students did not find employment.

There are other new avenues for aggressive advocacy as well. For example, advocates should consider going through old files to look for previous false certification denials. If the basis of the denial was a failure to find or seek employment, the case should be resubmitted for consideration to the Department. The Department has not applied the change retroactively, but it should reopen files where a denial was based on a failure to find or seek employment.[61]

6.3.2.3 Using Independent Evidence to Prove ATB Falsification

6.3.2.3.1 Challenging Department denials based on lack of corroborating evidence

Often, the borrower's own statement on the discharge application form is the only available evidence of ATB falsification (e.g., the student certifying that no test was given or that the school helped the student pass the test). The Department is skeptical of such applications, and requires the presentation of additional, independent evidence of ATB falsification, such as a finding by an entity that had oversight responsibility, statements by school officials, or statements by other students, including statements made in other claims for discharge relief.[62] This is a huge obstacle for borrowers seeking false certification discharges.

The Department's practices in this area are ripe for legal challenge. One key issue is the level of review required once the Department receives a borrower's discharge application. The regulations provide that when a borrower applies for a false certification discharge, the guaranty agency shall " . . . review the borrower's request and supporting sworn statement in light of information available from the records of the agency and from other sources, including other guaranty agencies, state authorities, and cognizant accrediting associations."[63] However, in a 1995 Dear Colleague Letter, the Department directed guaranty agencies that an absence of

---

Deputy Assistant Secretary for Student Financial Assistance, Clearinghouse No. 51,675, pp.5, 6 (Sept. 1995), *reprinted at* Appx. C, *infra*.

58 Pellot v. Riley, Order, Clearinghouse No. 52,116A (E.D. Pa. 1998); Pellot v. Riley, Memorandum of Law in Support of Plaintiff's Motion for Summary Judgment, Clearinghouse No. 52,116B (E.D. Pa. 1998).

59 Jordan v. Secretary of Education, 194 F.3d 169 (D.C. Cir. 1999), *rev'g* 26 F. Supp. 173 (D.D.C. 1998). The relevant regulation is 34 C.F.R. § 682.402(e)(3)(ii)(C), *as amended* 65 Fed. Reg. 65,616, 65,620 (Nov. 1, 2000).

60 Department of Education, Dear Colleague Letter #G-00-01 (July 2000), *reprinted at* Appx. C, *infra*. The relevant regulation is 34 C.F.R. § 682.402(e)(3)(ii)(C), *as amended*, 65 Fed. Reg. 65,616, 65,620 (Nov. 1, 2000).

61 *See* 65 Fed. Reg. 65,617 (Nov. 1, 2000) (Department specifically rejected a regulatory change that would require guaranty agencies or the Department to review all applications for false certification discharge that had been denied based on the borrower's employment history. The Department decided that this issue was more appropriately addressed in ways other than regulation, claiming that it will work with the federal student loan community to determine how to make information about the change generally available to the public).

62 Dear Colleague Letter Gen-95-42 from Elizabeth M. Hicks, Deputy Assistant Secretary for Student Financial Assistance, Clearinghouse No. 51,675 (Sept. 1995), *reprinted at* Appx. C, *infra*.

63 34 C.F.R. § 682.402(e)(6)(iv).

findings of improper ATB practices by authorities with oversight powers " . . . raises an inference that no improper practices were reported because none were taking place."[64] The Department's reasoning in the Dear Colleague letter is that responsible authorities should have discovered ATB fraud, and the fact that these agencies did not issue such a report implies that no ATB fraud occurred. This is truly incredible. In fact, Congress in 1992 provided for the false certification discharge and overhauled the student loan system because such supervising authorities (including the Department) had failed to do their job.[65]

The Department's practices have been challenged in court in at least two separate cases.[66] There were two main issues raised in these cases. First, plaintiffs challenged the Department's assertion that the regulations require them only to look for *findings* from oversight agencies. The Department, at least in some cases, has stated that this means they do not need to examine other materials, such as student complaints.[67]

A second issue relates to Department practices after investigating a complaint. Even if the Department looks beyond investigative "findings, they will often not find evidence to support the borrower's statements. In these cases, the Department will deny the discharge and generally allow the borrower to respond by submitting any corroborating evidence. A typical Department denial under these circumstances states:

> This office has reviewed information from entities responsible for overseeing the school's compliance with ability-to-benefit regulations, and has concluded that either no evidence of ability-benefit-violations exist or the evidence does not support the issues raised in your discharge request. If you wish to contest this decision, it is your responsibility to present corroborating evidence that the school improperly determined your ability-to-benefit.[68]

In at least one case, plaintiffs argued that if the Department does not find evidence to contradict the borrower's state-

ment, the Department must grant the discharge.[69] These issues are critical areas for aggressive administrative, legislative and judicial advocacy.

6.3.2.3.2 Obtaining investigatory files through Freedom of Information Act requests

Lack of documentation has been the primary obstacle to the granting of false certification discharges. There is no magic solution to gathering evidence, but there are a number of sources to try.

One good source of information is state or federal regulators' investigatory files. The Department of Education's files on a school may be obtained through a Freedom of Information Act request. Important documents include the school's application for eligibility with accompanying documents, any program reviews, or reviews shared with the Department by guaranty agencies, state agencies, or accreditors.[70] It is also important to request any "Emergency Action" memos issued by the Department in relation to the school.

A separate request should be made to the Department's Inspector General, for audit and investigations concerning the school. State licensing agencies may also have files on schools, including investigation reports, which may be available under state sunshine laws.[71] Private accrediting agencies will not usually share files on schools without a subpoena.

The Freedom of Information Act contains standards for waiver of fees for search and duplication under the statute.[72] There is also a provision that the agency should not charge for the first 100 pages of copying.[73] The following language should be included in requests to obtain a wavier of fees:

> These records are not requested for any commercial purpose but to gather information on [how the agency has carried out its obligations in the area covered by the records]. Accordingly, I request that any fees be waived as disclosure of this information is in the public interest because it is likely to contribute significantly to public understanding of the operations or activities of the government. 5 U.S.C. § 552(a)(4)(A)(iii). If there are any proposed charges which are not waived and they exceed [Fill in amount], please notify me before they are incurred.

---

64 Department of Education, Dear Colleague Letter GEN-95-42 (Sept. 1995), reprinted at Appx. C, *infra*.

65 *See, e.g.*, United States Senate, *Abuses in Federal Student Grant Programs*, Hearings before the Permanent Subcommittee on Investigations of the Committee on Governmental Affairs (S. Hrg. 103-491, Oct. 1993). *See generally* Ch. 9 (challenging vocational school fraud), *infra*.

66 Two of these complaints, Cofan v. Paige, Civil Action No. 01-4239 (E.D. Pa. 2001) and Gill v. Riley, CV-00-5453 (E.D.N.Y. 2000) are reprinted at Appx. E, *infra*. The complaints and other documents from these cases are also available on the companion CD-Rom. The *Cofan* case settled and the *Gill* case was still pending at the time this manual was printed.

67 Gill v. Riley, CV-00-5453 (E.D.N.Y. 2000), available at Appx. E, *infra*.

68 This was the notice received by the plaintiff in the *Cofan* case, Cofan v. Paige, Civil Action No. 01-4239 (complaint filed E.D. Pa. 2001), available on the companion CD-Rom.

69 Gill v. Riley, CV-00-5453 (E.D.N.Y. 2000), available at Appx. E, *infra*.

70 Sample FOIA requests can be found at Appx. F, *infra*.

71 State licensing agency contact information can be found on the Department's website: www.ed.gov/offices/OSFAP/Students/closedschool/stateagency.html.

72 5 U.S.C. § 552(a)(4)(A)(iii).

73 *Id.*

For advocates seeking records to expose misconduct of a school operating under the loan program, it is important to emphasize the public benefit of disclosure concerning what the Department knew abut the school's operations and whether it acted effectively in enforcing HEA standards.

6.3.2.3.3 School files

Advocates should try to obtain copies of all the school's files on the student. This information is generally difficult to obtain directly from the school if it has already closed. In that case, students can often obtain the schools' student records from the state agency responsible for regulating the schools. Typically, a student has an academic file and a financial aid file. The academic file will be the more important. Information about state licensing agencies is available on the Department of Education website.[74]

Advocates should look for a copy of an admission test in the file or a description of the type of test used. The absence of a test or any reference to a test is evidence that the test was never given. In fact, for independent testing done after 1991, the Department regulations state that the school is liable to the Department for all funds disbursed if the school is unable to *document* that the student received a passing score on an approved test.[75]

6.3.2.3.4 Testing company information

If the file (or the school or state licensing agency) can identify the company giving the test, consider contacting the testing agency. The Wonderlic Company tests were widely used by trade schools for ATB testing. Wonderlic can provide appropriate information on whether a particular social security number matches one of its registered test results.[76] If the student was to have received the Wonderlic test, but if the test score is not registered, this may provide evidence that a proper test was not given. Wonderlic may also provide additional information about the validity of test scores at a particular school that administered the Wonderlic test for ATB purposes.

6.3.2.3.5 Information on specific schools

The National Consumer Law Center has compiled information on a few schools (unfortunately just a small fraction

of those involved in ATB falsification). Advocates should contact the Center if they need more information on any of the following schools:[77]

- National Business Academy, California, accredited by ACCET. State attorney general office submitted compilation of materials to California guaranty agency showing ATB fraud.
- National Technical College, accredited by ABHES and ACCT. Evidence shows, among other violations, that NTC routinely falsely certified students as having the ability to benefit from the training.
- PTC Career Institute, Philadelphia, Atlanta, Chicago, Baltimore, Newark, Cleveland, District of Columbia, accredited by ACCSCT/CCATTS (NATTS). Department's Office of Inspector General audit report finds ATB problems, as does an affidavit from Wonderlic Personnel Test, Inc. and an affidavit used to support application by Community Legal Services in Philadelphia for false certification discharges. The Department has authorized false certification discharges to PTC Philadelphia students during the audit period.
- United Business Institute, New York, Florida, Georgia, and New Jersey, accredited by SACCOE. New York State Education Department found ATB fraud.
- United Education and Software (UES) Schools in California includes National Technical Schools—Home Study, Pacific Coast Technical Institutes, and Pacific Coast Colleges, all accredited by CCATTS (NATTS). Court found systematic ATB fraud, as did two Department Office of Inspector General audits.

6.3.2.3.6 Other evidence of ATB fraud

Additional information can be provided by obtaining affidavits of other students who attended the same school as the client and who can testify that they were not tested or improperly tested. In cases where the client did not speak English at the time of enrollment or had a low reading aptitude, advocates should consider getting an official evaluation of the client's reading level.

For example, a monolingual Spanish-speaking client who dropped out of school in the fifth or sixth grade in her home country should submit an affidavit regarding her inability to speak English at the time of enrollment, that she dropped out of school, and that she was never tested or was improperly tested. This testimony, along with an official assessment of her reading level, should be strong evidence for an ATB discharge, even in the absence of official investigatory records.

---

74 See www.ed.gov/offices/OSFAP/Students/closedschool/stateagency.html.

75 34 C.F.R. § 668.154(c).

76 Call Wonderlic at 1-800-323-3742 and ask to talk to the ATB Department. Or mail a request to Wonderlic Personnel Test, Inc., 1795 N. Butterfield Rd., Libertyville, IL 60048; www.wonderlic.com. *See also* Tests in Print 6: An Index to Tests, Test Reviews, and the Literature on Specific Tests (Barbara Plake ed., July 2002) (providing a description of most tests and their appropriate uses, along with the addresses of the publishers).

77 Advocates should note that this list is much shorter than in the past. This is because a number of files were lost during NCLC's move to a new office. We hope to begin collecting the lost information (and more) in the next year or so. Please contact Deanne Loonin at NCLC for updates.

6.3.2.4 Group Discharges

The Department will provide false certification discharges upon proper application *without* independent evidence for a particular cohort of students (such as non-high school graduates who were admitted at a particular branch of a school during a certain time period) if *the Department* determines that a school committed pervasive and serious violations of ATB regulations.[78]

A partial list of group discharges provided by the Department in 1998 included the following schools:

1. 10/31/96, Draughon College, Oklahoma City. Approval of ATB borrowers enrolled from 7/1/87–6/30/91.

2. 12/20/96, National Technical Schools Home Study Division. Approval of ATB borrowers enrolled from 8/18/87–11/15/88.

3. 12/20/96, six branches of UES/Pacific Coast College. Approval of ATB borrowers enrolled from 2/1/87–5/31/89.

4. 5/20/97, Andover Tractor Trailer School. Approval of ATB borrowers enrolled from 6/1/86–4/30/89. This limited time period was successfully challenged in subsequent litigation. The group discharge should apply to any Andover borrower during any time period who did not have a high school diploma or GED at the time of enrollment and who otherwise meets the criteria for a false certification discharge.[79]

Another cohort of students is all loans currently or subsequently held by the Department related to enrollments at any PTC Career Institute[80] or USA Training Academy. The Department has also granted a group discharge for Cambridge Technical School students.[81]

This list is not exhaustive because to date the Department has not made a list of approved false certification group discharges widely available. There may be other schools where group discharges have been granted by the Department.

Another way to prove ATB falsification without evidence from an independent entity is to aggregate a number of students with ATB claims against the same school, and then send those applications in as a group with a cover letter. An alternative approach is to send in only one application, but refer to other previously filed applications in a cover letter. Each application should then serve as independent evidence for each of the other applications.

6.3.3 Discharge Based on Student's Inability to Meet Minimum State Job Requirements

Even students with a high school diploma can receive a false certification discharge if, *at the time of the student's enrollment*, "the student would not meet the requirements for employment (in the student's state of residence) in the occupation for which the training program supported by the loan was intended because of physical or mental condition, or age, or criminal record or other reason accepted by the Secretary."[82] According to the Department, "[t]hose provisions apply to all categories of students at all schools, including students for whom the school was not required to make ability-to-benefit determinations or for whom the school made such determinations properly."[83]

For example, students with less than a tenth-grade education should receive a false certification discharge if they attended a cosmetology school in one of a number of states (such as Pennsylvania and California) that requires licensed cosmetologists to have at least a tenth-grade education.[84] Other examples include those with felony records being trained as security guards or one-armed students being trained as truck-drivers where state law disqualifies those individuals from those occupations.

Monolingual Spanish students taught exclusively in Spanish are another example if the state licensing test is given only in English. Even absent a licensing exam requirement, it may be that a Spanish-speaking student would not "meet the requirements for employment" if the employment required the employee to be English speaking. The fact that the course was allegedly in English would not affect the fact that the student could only speak Spanish "at the time of the student's enrollment." The equities of this argument are even stronger where the school failed to provide promised English-as-a-second-language training. However, ac-

78 Requests to have schools treated in this way should be sent, with accompanying evidence, to Chief, General Provisions Branch, Policy, Training, and Analysis Service, Policy Development Division, U.S. Department of Education, 600 Independence Ave. SW, Washington D.C. 20202-5346; (202) 708-7888. *See* United States Department of Education, Dear Colleague Letter GEN-95-42, Clearinghouse No. 51,675 (Sept. 1995), *reprinted at* Appx. C, *infra*.

79 United States Department of Education, Letter from Carney M. McCollough to Irv Ackelsberg, Community Legal Services, Clearinghouse No. 52,135 (May 20, 1998). The deadline and other issues were challenged in White v. Riley, Clearinghouse No. 52,121 (E.D. Pa. 1998) (class action complaint).

80 PTC had schools in Philadelphia, Atlanta, Chicago, Baltimore, Newark, Cleveland, and the District of Columbia.

81 U.S. Department of Education, Letter from Carney M. McCollough to Stephen Olden, Legal Aid Society of Cincinnati, Clearinghouse No. 52,491 (Apr. 30, 1999).

82 34 C.F.R. § 682.402(e)(13)(iii)(B).

83 Dear Colleague Letter Gen-95-42 from Elizabeth M. Hicks, Deputy Assistant Secretary for Student Financial Assistance, Clearinghouse No. 51,675, p. 9 (Sept. 1995), *reprinted at* Appx. C, *infra*. That letter does state that a defense to the discharge would be evidence that the school asked the student about such a disqualifying condition and the student did not divulge it.

84 Apparently guaranty agencies are quite erratic in whether they require more than just the student's statement that the student did not complete the tenth grade. Guaranty agencies that require additional proof pose an interesting proof problem for the student to show the negative, that the student never completed the tenth grade at any school.

cording to anecdotal reports from advocates, the Department has generally, but not always, rejected this argument. To date, these denials have not been appealed.

The discharge should also apply where the school's program, instead of the student, does not meet minimum state requirements. For example, a discharge should be available where a program was not certified by the state, and graduation from a certified program is a precondition under state law for employment.

6.3.4 *Forgery*

A third important basis for a false certification discharge is if the student's signature was forged on the loan application, promissory note, loan check endorsement, or authorization for an electronic funds transfer.[85] Advocates may find more forged checks than loan applications, because students may have changed their enrollment decision after they signed the application, but before a first or subsequent check was cut, and thus not have been available or willing to endorse the check to the school.

It is essential to obtain copies not only of the loan application and promissory note, but of all canceled checks evidencing the indebtedness. If the borrower's signature appears forged, the student must submit five specimens of the student's own signature, two of which had to have been within one year of the forgery.[86]

A false certification discharge for a forged check is only available if the proceeds of the forged check went toward tuition payments which the student was not obligated to pay, such as that portion of tuition not owed under the applicable refund formula after the student had dropped out.[87] The regulations and a Dear Colleague letter appear to place the burden not on the student, but on the guaranty agency to determine whether the forged check proceeds went toward a legitimate student obligation or not.[88]

6.3.5 *Relief Available for Those Obtaining a False Certification Discharge*

The relief available is identical to that for a closed school discharge, as detailed in § 6.2.3, *supra*.

6.3.6 *How to Apply for a False Certification Discharge*

There is no time limit on a student's eligibility for a false certification discharge.[89] Whether a student seeks a discharge based on a disqualifying condition, ATB falsification, or a forged check, the application should be directed to the entity holding the loan. For a defaulted loan, the holder is almost always either a guaranty agency or the Department of Education. Guaranty agencies have their own forms and the Department has three different false certification discharge forms for loans it is holding, one relating to claims of a disqualifying condition, one for ATB fraud, and one for forgery claims.[90]

While it is important to fill out the forms in their entirety, it is useful to know what the regulations say is required of an application. According to the regulations, the student must submit a written request for a discharge and a sworn statement (not notarized, but sworn under the penalty of perjury) attesting:

(1) Whether the student has made a claim against another party on the loan (such as from a state tuition recovery fund);

(2) That at least part of the loan was disbursed after January 1, 1986;

(3) That the student agrees to provide, at the Secretary's request, additional information concerning the student's eligibility for a discharge; and

(4) That the student will cooperate with the Secretary in enumerated enforcement actions and to assign to the Secretary certain rights the student has to recover from third parties.[91]

For ATB falsification applications, students must also state that they had not graduated from high school before being admitted, and that they did not have the ability to benefit from the course.

For false certification discharges based on the school's forging of the student's signature on the loan application, the promissory note, a check endorsement, or electronic funds transfer authorization, the student must also state that a signature on one of these documents is not the student's and provides five signature specimens (two of which are within one year of the disputed signature).[92] Where the forgery is

---

85 34 C.F.R. § 682.402(e)(1)(i)(B), (e)(1)(ii).

86 34 C.F.R. § 682.402(e)(3)(iii), (iv).

87 34 C.F.R. § 682.402(e)(1)(ii).

88 Dear Colleague Letter 94-G-256 item 11, from Leo Kornfeld, Deputy Assistant Secretary for Student Financial Assistance Programs, Clearinghouse No. 51,670 (Sept. 1994).

89 34 C.F.R. § 682.402(e)(6)(v).

90 The Department of Education forms are *reprinted at* Appx. D, *infra*. They are also available on the Department's website: www.ed.gov. The Department released new forms in June 2002. See Department of Education, Dear Partner Letter Gen-02-05, Approval of Loan Discharge Application Forms, (June 2002).

91 34 C.F.R. § 682.402 (e)(3), (e)(4). There is questionable statutory authority for this requirement since the statute provides for assignment of rights only against the school and its affiliates and principals.

92 34 C.F.R. § 682.402(e)(3)(iii), (iv).

on a check endorsement or transfer authorization, the student must state that the student never received the loan proceeds and those proceeds were never credited to amounts owed to the school for that portion of the program that the student completed.[93]

The regulations contain no requirement that students, in applying for a discharge, reaffirm their debt or waive other rights. If guaranty agencies provide discharge application forms with these extraneous provisions, students should cross these provisions out, with their initials evidencing their intent to delete these items. The Department has also instructed guaranty agencies to process all requests for a discharge, even if the request is not on the agency's standard form.[94] In practice, however, it is generally expeditious to use the official agency form whenever possible. In addition, the loan may be discharged without a written application if the guaranty agency, with the Secretary's permission, determines that the borrower qualifies for a discharge based on information in its possession.[95]

In general, borrowers will find it difficult to obtain a false certification discharge. It will often be necessary to continue following up on applications and to dispute denials. Since discharge applications often take many years to process, advocates should be prepared to request administrative forbearances for students so that collection activities will cease until the discharge has been granted or denied.[96] The regulations do not specifically grant borrowers an automatic collection stay after applying for a discharge. Stays are granted only if the holder of the loan receives information it believes to be reliable indicating that a borrower is eligible or a discharge.[97] The borrower must respond within sixty days of receiving this notice in order to suspend collection.[98]

The Department expects guaranty agencies to respond to discharge requests within ninety days, although the Department has not set any time limits for its own response to discharge requests. The Department's delays in making decisions on false certification discharges were among the issues raised in a 1998 class action complaint. The complaint alleged that the Secretary had not assigned adequate staff to administer the program, resulting in a backlog of over 10,000 undecided applications, some of which had been pending for years.[99]

The student has a right to seek review by the Secretary of a guaranty agency denial of a false certification discharge application.[100]

---

93 34 C.F.R. § 682.402(e)(3)(iv).
94 Dear Colleague Letter 94-G-256, Clearinghouse No. 50,422 (Sept. 1994), *reprinted at* Appx. C, *infra*.
95 34 C.F.R. § 682.402(e)(14).
96 34 C.F.R. § 682.211(f)(7). *See also* § 2.3.2, *supra*.
97 34 C.F.R. § 682.402(e)(6)(ii).
98 34 C.F.R. § 682.402(e)(6)(iv).
99 White v. Riley, Clearinghouse No. 52,121 (E.D. Pa. 1998) (class action complaint).
100 *See* 34 C.F.R. § 682.402(e)(11). *See* § 6.9 (appeals), *infra*.

6.4 Discharge for Unpaid Refunds

6.4.1 General

In November 1999, the Department of Education finalized regulations that provide an important new basis to discharge a student loan: that the school failed to make an owed refund to the student.[101]

Failure to provide refunds was one of the most common complaints during the heyday of trade school fraud in the 1980s and early 1990s. Many borrowers signed up for schools, never attended classes, but were still charged the full amount of the loan. This new discharge should fill in some of the gaps left by the closed school and false certification discharges, which provide relief for many, but not all victims of trade school abuses.

6.4.2 Criteria for Unpaid Refund Discharge

The discharge applies to the following types of loans entered into after January 1, 1986: Guaranteed Student (Stafford) Loans, Unsubsidized Stafford Loans, Supplemental Loans for Students (SLSs), PLUS (parent borrower) loans, and Federal Direct Loans. Students already can raise an unpaid refund as a defense to the Perkins Loan collection action.[102] The unpaid refund discharge became effective as of July 1, 2000.[103]

The unpaid refund discharge applies to students who signed up for a school but never attended, or withdrew, or terminated within a time frame that entitled them to a refund, but who never received the refund from the school. Students who completed sixty percent or more of the loan period are not entitled to refunds and therefore not entitled to the discharge.[104] A student should not have to show written proof or other formal proof of withdrawal or termination in order to qualify.

Students who never received the owed refund are eligible to reduce their current obligations by the amount that should have been refunded plus interest and related charges. Based on previous experience with the closed school and false certification discharges, thousands of students who attended scam vocational schools will likely be eligible for this discharge. Implementation problems will arise in figuring out the amount of discharges due, pressuring the Department to grant the discharges in a timely manner, tracking down eligible borrowers, and educating them on this new right.

---

101 34 C.F.R. §§ 682.402(l) (FFEL), 685.216 (Direct Loans).
102 *See* § 9.5.2.1, *infra*.
103 64 Fed. Reg. 58,937–58,970 (Nov. 1, 1999).
104 34 C.F.R. § 682.402(o)(2)(iii).

6.4.3 Determining Amount of Discharge

The amount of the unpaid refund will be determined based on information the holder of the loan has or that the borrower can provide, or by applying the appropriate refund formula to information that the borrower provides or that is otherwise available to the agency. If the actual school refund formula is not available, the regulations set out a substitute formula to determine the amount eligible for discharge.[105]

In these circumstances, the guaranty agency is required to use the following formula to determine the amount eligible for discharge:

- In the case of a student who fails to attend or whose withdrawal of termination date is before October 7, 2000, and who completes less than 60 percent of the loan period, the guaranty agency discharges the lesser of the institutional charges unearned or the loan amount.[106] The guaranty agency determines the amount of the institutional charges unearned by (A) calculating the ratio of the amount of time in the loan period after the student's last day of attendance to the actual length of the loan period and (B) Multiplying the resulting factor by the institutional charges assessed the student for the loan period.[107]
- In the case of a student who fails to attend or whose withdrawal or termination date is on or after October 7, 2000 and who completes less than 60 percent of the loan period, the guaranty agency discharges the loan amount unearned. This is determined by (A) calculating the ratio of the amount of time remaining in the loan period after the student's last day of attendance to the actual length of the loan period and (B) multiplying the resulting factor by the total amount of title IV grants and loans received by the student, or if unknown, the loan amount.[108]

The borrower needs three pieces of information to calculate a refund: the tuition, the school's refund formula, and the percentage of the course or term the borrower completed. The school catalog or the written enrollment agreement will have the tuition, refund policy, and number of weeks per term. State licensing agencies sometimes have school catalogs and/or enrollment contract forms in their files for closed schools. The student must supply the enrollment date and last date of attendance to figure the percentage of the course completed. A refund is calculated based on the student's last date of attendance (LDA), regardless of whether the student notified the school of her withdrawal.

Federal rules have generally required that schools apply refunds of unearned tuition to loans first, and then to grants. This rule benefits the borrower, because even a partial tuition refund may eliminate the loan balance in full. For example, if the student was entitled to a 50% refund of a $5000 tuition, and had a $2500 loan and $2500 in grants, the entire loan should have been refunded by the school. The unpaid refund should be for 100% of the loan amount.

Students who completed sixty percent or more of the loan period are not entitled to refunds and therefore not entitled to the discharge.[109] On the other hand, most students who never attended classes at all were entitled to a full refund of their loan amount and therefore should get a full discharge of their loans.

6.4.4 Applying for the Discharge

The procedures and timing for a loan discharge are slightly different depending on whether the school is currently open or closed. If the school is still open, to qualify for the discharge, the borrower and guarantor must document that they attempted to resolve the problem within 120 days from the date that the borrower submitted a completed application for discharge.[110] This requirement does not apply if the school is closed.

Except where the guaranty agency (with the Department's approval) determines, based on information in its possession, that the borrower qualifies for a discharge, borrowers must submit written discharge applications.[111] Applications should be sent to the holder or guaranty agency. In most cases the holder will be the guaranty agency.[112]

The Department has developed a uniform application form.[113] In addition, the regulations require agencies to send discharge applications to potentially eligible borrowers.[114] Once they do so, they must cease collection until the application is resolved.[115] If the borrower does not return the application within sixty days, collection actions can resume.[116]

There is no time limit for the agency to make a decision. However, once an application is granted, the holder must

---

105 34 C.F.R. § 682.402(o)(2).
106 34 C.F.R. § 682.402(o)(2)(i).
107 *Id.*
108 34 C.F.R. § 682.402(o)(2)(ii).

109 34 C.F.R. § 682.402(o)(2)(iii).
110 34 C.F.R. § 682.402(l)(2)(ii).
111 34 C.F.R. § 682.402(l)(5)(iv).
112 The regulations are slightly different if the lender holds the loan. In these circumstances, lenders are required to provide the guaranty agency with documentation related to the borrower's qualification for discharge. 34 C.F.R. § 682.402(m).
113 *See* Department of Education, Dear Guaranty Agency Director Letter Gen-01-15 (Nov. 2001). The form is included at Appx. C, *infra* and available on the Department's website.
114 34 C.F.R. § 682.402(l)(5).
115 34 C.F.R. § 682.402(l)(5)(ii).
116 34 C.F.R. § 682.402(l)(5)(iii).

suspend collection within thirty days, discharge the appropriate amount, and inform the borrower of the determination.[117]

If the application is denied, the holder must notify the borrower in writing of the reason for the determination and of the borrower's right to request review within thirty days of the borrower's submission of additional documentation. Collection must be suspended during the review period.[118]

6.4.5 Relief Available for Those Obtaining a Discharge

Eligible borrowers will be granted a discharge in the amount of the unpaid refund including any accrued interest and any collection of other charges relating to the amount of the unpaid refund.[119] If the borrower has already paid off part of the loan, and the amount still owing on the loan is less than the unpaid refund, part of the unpaid refund will be used to fully discharge the loan. The rest of the unpaid refund will be paid the borrower in cash to the extent the borrower has made payments of that amount on the loan. The holder of the loan is also required to report the discharge to all credit reporting agencies to which the holder previously reported the status of the loan.[120]

6.5 Relationship Between Closed School, False Certification, and Unpaid Refund Discharges

Many victims of trade school fraud will be eligible for multiple discharges. The same borrower can apply for more than one discharge, but cannot obtain duplicate relief.

In practice, the closed school discharge has generally been easier to obtain than a false certification discharge. This is largely because the requirements for the closed school discharge are more straightforward. This may change to some extent now that false certification applicants no longer need to show proof of an employment search. Overall, however, the Department has granted greater numbers of closed school than false certification discharges.

Many clients who were truly victims of trade school fraud will not meet the criteria for one or more of the discharges. For this reason, it is always critical to consider all three. For example, many borrowers attended schools that closed, but the borrowers may not have been in attendance (or they cannot show they were in attendance) at the time the school closed or within ninety days of the closure. If a particular borrower is also a high school graduate, she may not be

eligible for either a closed school or false certification ability to benefit discharge even if the schooling was worthless. She may, however, be eligible to get at least partial relief from an unpaid refund discharge. Similarly, a borrower who withdrew from a school within a short period of enrolling, or who never attended classes, may have both a false certification by forgery and an unpaid refund claim.

Another avenue to consider, discussed in § 6.6, *infra* is a disability discharge. In addition, some states have tuition recovery funds that may reimburse all or part of a student's obligation.[121] Bankruptcy, discussed in detail in Chapter 7, *infra*, may also be a viable option, particularly for borrowers with bleak long-term financial prospects.

6.6 Disability Discharge

6.6.1 General

The borrower's permanent and total disability is grounds for a student loan discharge.[122] Prior to 1999, a disabled borrower simply had a licensed physician certify that the borrower was permanently disabled with an onset date after the date of the loan. This had to be done on the proper form and the discharge was almost always granted.

In 1999, the Department's Inspector General (IG) conducted a study that led to a Department crackdown on alleged fraud. The IG found that twenty-three percent of borrowers who received disability discharges in a specified time period worked and earned money after the disability determination was made or the loan was discharged.[123]

In response to these findings, the Department in November 1999 sent out a Dear Colleague letter detailing a more aggressive approach to the existing regulation.[124] It then made the disability discharge a focus of the 2000 round of negotiated rulemaking. Some of the new regulations that resulted from rulemaking went into effect July 1, 2001, although the most significant changes became effective July 1, 2002. The sections below describe the disability discharge program as effective July 1, 2002 and afterwards.

6.6.2 Determination of Disability

A borrower's FFEL, Direct Loan, and Perkins Loan may be discharged if she is found to be totally and permanently

---

117 34 C.F.R. § 682.402(l)(5)(vi).

118 34 C.F.R. § 682.402(l)(5)(vii). *See* § 6.9 (administrative appeals), *infra*.

119 34 C.F.R. § 682.402(l)(3)(i).

120 34 C.F.R. § 682.402(l)(3)(ii).

121 *See* § 9.6, *infra*.

122 34 C.F.R. §§ 682.402(c) (FFEL), 685.213 (Direct Loan), 674.61 (Perkins).

123 The report is cited in Dear Colleague Letter No. GEN- 99-36, Clearinghouse No. 52, 492 (Nov. 1999), *reprinted at* Appx. C, *infra*.

124 *Id.*

disabled.[125] For a PLUS loan, the disability of only one of two obligated parents does not discharge the debt.[126]

The new discharge is significantly different from the prior system in a number of ways. Most important, the new regulations set up a conditional discharge system. Under this system, even the most disabled borrowers will generally not be eligible for a final discharge until the end of a three-year waiting period.[127] This process is discussed in detail in the next subsection.

Similar to the system in place prior to July 2002, to qualify for a discharge, borrowers must provide certification from a physician that they are unable to work and earn money because of an illness or injury that is expected to continue indefinitely or result in death. The requirement that borrowers also not be able to attend school was removed, effective July 1, 2001.[128] A borrower is not considered disabled based on a condition that existed at the time she applied for the loan unless the condition substantially deteriorated after the loan was made.[129]

For consolidated loans, borrowers are considered disabled if they would meet the definition for all of the loans included in the consolidation loan.[130] The right to obtain a partial discharge of a consolidation loan applies only to borrowers who qualify for false certification, closed school, or unpaid refund discharges, not for disability. Expanding the partial discharge for disability was considered and rejected, during spring 2002 negotiated rulemaking sessions.[131] According to the Department, the only way that some, but not all, of a borrower's consolidated loans could be eligible for a disability discharge would be if the ineligible loans were made after the date the borrower became totally and permanently disabled. This would mean that the borrower was no longer totally and permanently disabled and therefore not eligible for a discharge on any of the loans.[132] However, the Department and negotiators agreed to allow partial discharges of joint consolidation loans in the case where one borrower becomes disabled, but the other borrower does not qualify for a discharge.[133]

The borrower is required to get a certification of disability from a physician of medicine or osteopathy. The Secretary may continue collection until receipt of the certification.[134] After that point, the loan holder should cease collection. This is a common problem as loan holders, including the Department, frequently continue collection efforts even after receiving a completed discharge application. The lender is also required to send back any payments received after the date that the borrower was certified as disabled.[135]

6.6.3 Post-July 2002 Evaluation Process

The Department initially set out a more restrictive approach to evaluating disability discharges in a November 1999 Dear Colleague letter.[136] A subsequent May 2002 Dear Colleague letter reiterated these standards and clarified the disability process under the new disability discharge regulations.[137]

The disability procedures under the new program are as follows:

The borrower applies to the loan holder for a discharge. The loan holder makes a preliminary determination as to whether the borrower meets the criteria for a disability discharge. For Perkins Loans, the school makes this determination. In the FFEL program, the current holder makes the determination. For Direct Loans, the Department's direct loan staff makes the decision.[138]

The Department intends for this preliminary determination to be a rigorous process. The Department's expectations were initially set out in the November 1999 Dear Colleague letter and affirmed in the May 2002 letter.

The Department requires guaranty agencies and others making preliminary disability determinations at a minimum to:

- Require additional information to support the borrower's application where the information provided is not definitive, is illegible, or incomplete.
- Reaffirm the physician's certification if the diagnosis and prognosis do not appear to reach the standard of total and permanent disability. (The Department emphasized that guaranty agencies should ensure that physicians understand that the FFEL definition of total and permanent disability is generally a higher standard than that used by other federal or state agencies for disability.)

---

125 34 C.F.R. §§ 682.402(c) (FFEL), 674.61 (Perkins), 685.213 (Direct Loans).

126 34 C.F.R. § 682.402(a)(2).

127 34 C.F.R. §§ 682.402(c)(1) (FFEL), 674.61(b) (Perkins), 685.213 (Direct Loans).

128 65 Fed. Reg. 65,680–65,695 (Nov. 1, 2000), *amending* 34 C.F.R. §§ 674.51(s) (Perkins), 682.200 (FFEL), 685.102 (Direct Loans). There is some indication that the Department is still using the old definition and requiring that borrowers also show they cannot attend school. *See, e.g.*, U.S. v. Norton, 2002 U.S. Dist. LEXIS 2691 (N.D. Iowa).

129 34 C.F.R. § 682.402(c)(1)(iii).

130 34 C.F.R. § 682.402(c)(iii)(A).

131 *See* 67 Fed. Reg. 51036, 51041 (Aug. 6, 2002).

132 *Id. See generally* § 6.6 (disability discharges), *supra*.

133 67 Fed. Reg. 51,036, 51,041 (Aug. 6, 2002), *proposing to amend* 34 C.F.R. §§ 682.402(a)(2), 685.220(l)(3)(ii).

134 34 C.F.R. § 682.402(c)(1)(iii)(3).

135 34 C.F.R. §§ 682.402(c)(1)(i), 682.402(r)(2), (3) (FFEL), 685.213(a)(2)(ii).

136 Dear Colleague Letter No. GEN-99-36, Clearinghouse No. 52, 492 (Nov. 1999), reprinted at Appx. C, *infra*.

137 Department of Education, Dear Colleague Letter No. GEN-02-03 (May 2002), reprinted at Appx. C, *infra*.

138 *Id.*

- Assist borrowers to obtain deferments or forbearances in cases when it does not appear that the borrower is totally and permanently disabled.[139]

The Department also suggests that agencies may want to seek the assistance of a qualified physician to evaluate discharge requests.[140] In addition, due to the increased responsibilities particularly for guaranty agencies, the Department is proposing to increase the time allowed for agencies to make preliminary decisions and to decide whether to pay a claim to the lender from forty-five to ninety days.[141]

For FFEL loans, the loan is assigned to the Disability Discharge Unit if both the loan holder and the guaranty agency, if different, decide that the borrower is eligible for discharge.[142] The loan holder is required to notify the borrower that the loan will be sent to the Department for further review. The Department suggests that the notice also explain the Department's procedures for reviewing discharges when preliminary approval has been granted and explain that the Department will be requesting information on the borrower's income from earnings during the conditional period.[143] If the application is denied, the loan holder is required to notify the borrower of the denial, including reasons for the decision.[144] In cases where preliminary approval is granted, Perkins Loans holders (schools) are required to assign the loans to the Department's Disability Discharge Unit and notify borrowers of the assignment.[145]

The Department will then review all preliminarily approved loans to affirm that the borrower meets the disability discharge criteria. If the Department agrees with the preliminary determination, the borrower is placed in a conditional discharge status for three years *beginning on the date the borrower became totally and permanently disabled.*[146]

It is important to note that the conditional period begins on the date the borrower is certified as disabled. This means that for many borrowers, the conditional period will have expired by the time they apply for a discharge. In these cases, an initial determination of eligibility will also be the final determination of eligibility. The borrower will not have to wait another three years to get a discharge.[147]

For example, Borrower A applies for a disability discharge in 2002. Her doctor certifies that the onset date of her disability was 1997. Since this is more than three years before the application date, if the Department agrees with the doctor's evaluation, Borrower A can immediately get a loan discharge. If the onset date was 2001 and she applied in 2002, she would have to wait two additional years (the conditional period) for a final discharge.

During this conditional time period, the Department will review the borrower's earnings records. It appears that the Department will primarily look at earnings records obtained from Social Security to determine whether borrowers lost their disability status during the three-year period. Borrowers will satisfy the criteria for a discharge after the three years if their annual earnings from employment during that time do not exceed 100 percent of the poverty line for a family of two and they did not receive a student loan during that time, except for a FFEL or Direct Consolidation Loan that does not include any loans that are in a conditional discharge status.[148] There is no requirement that the borrower obtain a medical review of her condition.

During the conditional period, borrowers are not required to make any payments on the loan. The loan is not considered past due or in default. Borrowers are required to notify the Department if their annual earnings exceed the poverty line limit.[149] If at any time during the three-year period, the Department finds that the borrower does not meet the eligibility requirements, the Department will resume collection. The borrower is not required to pay any interest that accrued on the loan from the date of the initial determination through the end of the conditional discharge.[150] Presumably if the Department finds evidence that the borrower is no longer disabled midway through the conditional period, interest will begin to accrue at the point that the conditional discharge is officially terminated.

If the borrower satisfies the criteria for a disability discharge during and at the end of the conditional discharge period, the balance of the loan will be discharged.[151] Any payments received after the date the borrower became disabled are to be returned.[152]

The Department has developed a new disability request form incorporating these changes.[153] Unfortunately, borrowers will often find that a discharge is denied even after they have submitted a properly completed physician's certifica-

---

139 Dear Colleague Letter No. GEN-99-36, Clearinghouse No. 52,492 (Nov. 1999); Dear Colleague Letter No. GEN-02-03 (May 2002), both *reprinted at* Appx. C, *infra.*

140 Dear Colleague Letter GEN-02-03 (May 2002), reprinted at Appx. C, *infra.*

141 67 Fed. Reg. 51036 (Aug. 6, 2002).

142 Dear Colleague Letter No. GEN-02-03 (May 2002). *See also* 34 C.F.R. § 682.402(c)(11).

143 Dear Colleague Letter No. GEN-02-03 (May 2002).

144 Dear Colleague Letter No. GEN-02-03 (May 2002). *See also* 34 C.F.R. § 682.402(c)(7).

145 34 C.F.R. § 674.61(b)(3).

146 34 C.F.R. §§ 682.402(c)(1) (FFEL), 674.61(b) (Perkins), 685.213(a) (Direct Loans).

147 Dear Colleague Letter No. GEN-02-03 (May 2002).

148 34 C.F.R. § 682.402(c)(1)(ii)(A), (B).

149 34 C.F.R. § 682.402(c)(14).

150 34 C.F.R. § 682.402(c)(16).

151 34 C.F.R. § 682.402(c)(15).

152 34 C.F.R. § 682.402(c)(1)(i), (r)(2), (3).

153 The form is available on the Department's website at http://ifap.ed.gov and reprinted at Appx. D, *infra.* The new form is attached to the Department's Dear Partner Letter Gen-02-04 (June 2002).

tion of total and permanent disability. Such denials may be appealed under the judicial review provision of the Administrative Procedures Act.[154]

6.6.4 Potential Problems

Legal services and other advocates argued that the conditional discharge was an exaggerated response to the IG report. An alternative revocation system was proposed. This would have allowed the Department to revoke discharges during a specified period of time. The Department would be able to revoke discharges if they found particular borrowers were no longer disabled. The Department disagreed with this proposal, claiming that final agency decisions cannot be changed based on events occurring after the decision.[155]

A second issue relates to the Department's assumption that minimal earnings are synonymous with a loss of disability status. In fact, it is possible that someone may be severely disabled, yet still find a way to earn minimal amounts of money. Many people in this situation will later have to stop working again due to their disability. Yet sufficient earnings even during one year of the three-year period can keep a disabled borrower from moving from conditional to final discharge status. That borrower will once again be fully responsible for paying back her loan.

This aspect of the conditional discharge appears to discourage rehabilitation efforts. Borrowers may be reluctant to try work for fear of losing their disabled status during the conditional period. Department regulations related to borrower eligibility, in contrast, recognize that a borrower who received a discharge at some point may be able at a later date to go back to school, either to pursue job training which medical or technological changes have now made feasible or to obtain a more general education.[156] Under these regulations, to regain eligibility, the borrower has to obtain a doctor's certificate that the student can engage in substantial gainful activity, and must sign a statement acknowledging that the new loan cannot be canceled in the future on the basis of any impairment present when the new loan is made, unless that impairment substantially deteriorates.[157]

Another issue of particular concern to many low-income borrowers is the Department's refusal to consider a Social Security disability determination as proof of disability. The Department considered in proposed rules whether to tie the determination to Social Security standards. The Department ultimately dropped this key proposal in the final rules,

finding that there is no documentation currently issued by SSA that would effectively establish disability under the Department's standards.[158]

Another concern is that the new system will add an expensive bureaucracy at the Department. As discussed above, initial determinations of disability are required to be forwarded to the Department from guaranty agencies. The Department is to monitor the loans during the three-year conditional period. In response to this concern, the Department has agreed that there are many operational details to work out but does not believe that the regulations will create undue administrative burden.[159]

One additional area that is ripe for legal challenge is the way in which the Department has developed the new disability discharge program. Although the switch to a conditional process came out of negotiated rulemaking sessions, there has been no corresponding revision in the HEA statute. In addition, the Department has issued much of its guidance on this issue through informal Dear Colleague letters instead of regulatory or statutory amendments.[160]

6.7 Discharge Based on Death

The borrower's death is a defense to collection actions on Stafford, SLS, Perkins, and Federal Direct Loans.[161] The death of both parents (assuming both parents are obligated) or the death of the student discharges PLUS loans.[162] The death of only one of the two obligated parents does not discharge a PLUS loan.[163] This is only the case if the parents were co-borrowers.

Currently, the regulations are slightly different for consolidation loans. Under current regulations, parent borrowers are not eligible for discharges if they consolidate their PLUS loans and the student for whom that loan was obtained dies. Proposed rules issued in August 2002 would close that loophole, allowing the portion of the consolidation loan attributable to that PLUS loan to be discharged.[164] In addition, the proposed rules will allow for the discharge of the applicable portion of a joint consolidation loan if one of the borrowers dies.[165]

Even the death discharge has become controversial in recent years. In the same IG report that found alleged disability discharge abuse, the Department of Education

---

154 *See* § 6.9, *infra*. For an example of a successful appeal, see U.S. v. Norton, 2002 U.S. Dist. LEXIS 2691 (N.D. Iowa) (denial of government's motion for summary judgment on disability discharge).

155 65 Fed. Reg. 65,678, 65,682 (Nov. 1, 2000).

156 34 C.F.R. §§ 682.201(a)(6) (FFEL), 685.200(a)(iv) (Direct Loans).

157 *Id.*

158 65 Fed. Reg. 65,678, 65,684 (Nov. 1, 2000).

159 65 Fed. Reg. 65,678, 65,682 (Nov. 1, 2000).

160 Sample complaints challenging the Department's process of adopting the new disability discharge program are included at Appx. E, *infra* and on the companion CD-Rom.

161 20 U.S.C. § 1087; 34 C.F.R. §§ 674.61(a), 682.402(b), 685.212(a).

162 34 C.F.R. § 682.402(b)(1).

163 34 C.F.R. § 682.402(a)(2).

164 67 Fed. Reg. 51036 (Aug. 6, 2002), *amending* 34 C.F.R. §§ 682.402(b)(6) (FFEL), 685.212(a)(3) (Direct Loans).

165 67 Fed. Reg. 51036 (Aug. 6, 2002), *amending* 34 C.F.R. §§ 682.402(a)(2) (FFEL), 685.220(l)(3) (Direct Loans).

concluded that some borrowers were continuing to live and work after receiving death discharges.[166] The Department has expressed concern that documentation used to support death discharges may be easily forged or may not provide definitive proof of death.

Under the new regulations, an original or certified copy of a death certificate will be required in most circumstances.[167] This new provision became effective for Perkins Loans by July 1, 2001 and for other loans on July 1, 2002.[168]

6.8 Other Loan Cancellations

Perkins Loans may be completely canceled in certain circumstances, including the debtor's service in Head Start or in the military service in an area "of hostilities."[169]

The Perkins program was also the first to provide for cancellations of loans for teachers in low-income school districts and for other service, including military and volunteer service.[170] Perkins cancellations are available even for borrowers in default in certain circumstances.[171]

The FFEL and Direct Loan programs recently added similar loan forgiveness regulations for teachers, effective July 1, 2001.[172] The teacher forgiveness or cancellation under FFEL and Direct Loans will repay up to a maximum of $5000 for individuals who are full-time teachers over five consecutive years in certain schools that serve low-income families.[173]

The FFEL and Direct Loan programs apply only to borrowers with no outstanding loan balances as of October 1, 1998 or later. Unlike the Perkins programs, FFEL and Direct Loan borrowers are not eligible for teacher loan forgiveness for defaulted loans unless they first make satisfactory repayment arrangements and reestablish loan eligibility.[174] Proposed rules issued in August 2002 for the Direct Loan program include new language stating that a joint

Direct Consolidation loan may be partially discharged if one of the borrowers qualifies for teacher loan forgiveness.[175]

6.9 Appealing Adverse Discharge Decisions

Before seeking judicial review of a discharge denial, student loan borrowers should be certain that they have presented a complete, fully documented application. If a discharge was denied for want of evidence that is now available, or on the basis of erroneous facts, the borrower should resubmit an accurate and complete application, rather than seeking judicial review. The Department will generally reconsider a prior discharge denial, particularly if circumstances have changed.

In addition, for false certification and unpaid refund discharges only, FFEL borrowers should first seek administrative review from the Department.[176] The closed school and disability discharge regulations do not provide for this type of "internal" review.

The Administrative Procedure Act governs judicial review of any informal agency adjudication, including denial of a student loan discharge by the Department of Education. The pertinent section provides that the court shall hold unlawful and set aside agency action, findings, and conclusions found to be

> (A) arbitrary, capricious, an abuse of discretion, or otherwise not in accordance with law. . . .[177]

Section 706 "require[s] the reviewing court to engage in a substantial inquiry."[178] In determining whether an agency's action was unlawful under section 706(2)(A), the court must "consider whether the decision was based on a consideration of the relevant factors and whether there has been a clear error in judgment."[179] If the court determines that the agency relied on factors Congress did not intend for it to consider, or has failed to consider an important aspect of the problem, the action should be set aside as arbitrary and capricious.[180]

---

166 *See* Dear Colleague Letter GEN-99-36 (Nov. 1999), *reprinted at* Appx. C, *infra*, citing an Office of Inspector General study that found that 2% of borrowers who received death discharges were working and earning money after the loan was discharged.

167 34 C.F.R. §§ 682.402(b)(2) (FFEL), 685.212(a)(3) (Direct Loans).

168 34 C.F.R. §§ 682.402(b)(2) (FFEL), 685.212(a) (Direct Loans), 674.61(a) (Perkins).

169 34 C.F.R. §§ 674.58 (Head Start cancellation), 674.59 (military cancellations).

170 34 C.F.R. §§ 674.55 (teacher cancellations), 674.56 (employment in certain professions such as nursing or medical technicians), 674.57 (law enforcement); 674.59 (military service), 674.60 (volunteer service including Peace Corps).

171 34 C.F.R. § 674.52(c).

172 34 C.F.R. §§ 682.215 (FFEL), 685.217 (Direct Loans).

173 65 Fed. Reg. 65,624 (Nov. 1, 2000), *adding* 34 C.F.R. §§ 682.215 (FFEL), 685.217 (Direct Loans). The Department has released teacher loan forgiveness and teacher forbearance forms, available on-line.

174 34 C.F.R. §§ 682.215(8), 685.217(8).

175 67 Fed. Reg. 51036 (Aug. 6, 2002), *amending* 34 C.F.R. § 685.220(l). According to the Department, similar changes were not made to FFEL consolidation regulations because the construction of those regulations already provides for a partial discharge under these circumstances.

176 34 C.F.R. §§ 682.402(e)(11)(ii) (false certification administrative appeals), 682.402(l)(5)(vii) (unpaid refund administrative appeals).

177 5 U.S.C. § 706(2)(A); *see also* Jordan v. Sec'y of Education of the U.S., 194 F.3d 169 (D.C. Cir. 1999).

178 Citizens to Preserve Overton Park, Inc. v. Volpe, 401 U.S. 402, 415 (1971); C.K. v. New Jersey Dep't of Health & Human Services, 92 F.3d 171, 182 (3d Cir. 1996).

179 *Overton Park*, 401 U.S. at 416 (citations omitted); *C.K.*, 92 F.3d at 182.

180 Frisby v. U.S. Dep't of Housing and Urban Development, 755

Discharging Student Loan Obligations

An agency is bound by its own regulations.[181] If an agency's action does not comport with its regulations, the action is contrary to law and should be reversed by a reviewing court.[182]

Because the Department of Education's decision to deny a student loan discharge is an informal adjudication, there is no formal record. The district court will consider all material that was presented to the Department by the borrower, and should also consider any other information or documents the Department relied on. The government will typically prepare and submit what it considers to be the administrative record. The borrower, however, is free to present to the court any additional evidence that had a bearing on the agency's decision. The guaranty agencies act as agents for the Department in reviewing discharge requests. Material submitted to the guaranty agencies should also be submitted as part of the agency record.[183]

An action for APA review is filed in federal district court. There is no time limit in the APA for seeking judicial review. Most courts have looked to 28 U.S.C. § 2401(a) as the relevant statute of limitations for appeals of agency decisions.[184] This section requires that civil actions against the United States be filed within six years after the right of action first accrued.

6.10 Forgery, Mistake, Infancy, and Other Defenses to Loan Enforceability

A student's obligation to pay a student loan is conditioned upon the loan agreement being enforceable under basic contract principles that affect a borrower's obligation on any note, such as forgery, mistake, and fraud. The only common law contract defense not available to student loan borrowers is infancy, that is, that the student was under age when signing the loan document. The HEA specifies that the United States and guaranty agencies, irrespective of state law on the issue, shall *not* be subject to a claim of infancy.[185]

The HEA does not limit other contract defenses. These defenses should therefore apply to student loans just as they do to any other type of loan. The Department on numerous occasions has stated that the student does not owe on a loan, and guaranty agencies should not seek payment, to the extent to which the loan obligation is not enforceable under state law.[186]

If a student did not sign a student loan note, and the student's signature was forged or altered, the student should have no liability under that note. It should make no difference whether the forger is the school or lender.

Similarly, when checks are presented to pay school tuition, the federal statute requires that the student's endorsement be included before the check is cashed.[187] Forgery of that endorsement or failure to obtain that endorsement should also void the student's liability for that check.

A 1993 letter from the Department of Education spells out student rights where a check lacks the student's endorsement or the endorsement is forged.[188] A student is not liable for the amount of a check where the student did not endorse the check, unless under state law the holder can show that the borrower is legally obligated for the amount disbursed. Holders cannot presume that a borrower who remained enrolled at a school after a check was cashed thereby received its proceeds or condoned the school's action in cashing the check.

According to the Department letter, if a student is not obligated on the amount involving the check without proper endorsement, the guarantor should correct the student's credit record to reflect that fact, must make sure that the failure to pay that amount is not causing the student to be ineligible for future loans and grants, and must return any amount collected concerning that check, including any tax intercept.

Where a promissory note or check endorsement is forged, the student may have two different approaches to discharging the loan. One is to apply for a false certification discharge based on the forgery, as described in § 6.3.4, *supra*. The other is to claim that the obligation is unenforceable under common law principles. In the appropriate case, both of these strategies should work, and the student can choose which way to proceed first.

Nevertheless, one can predict that the Department (as opposed to a court) in evaluating a claim based on the common law enforceability of the note, will adopt the same

---

F.2d 1052, 1055 (3d Cir. 1985), *citing* Motor Vehicle Mfrs. Ass'n v. State Farm Mut. Auto. Ins. Co., 463 U.S. 29, 43 (1983).

181 *See* United States v. Nixon, 418 U.S. 683, 696 (1974).

182 *See Frisby*, 755 F.2d at 1055–56; Kelly v. Railroad Retirement Board, 625 F.2d 486, 491–92 (3d Cir. 1980).

183 A sample APA appeal can be found at Appx. E, *infra*.

184 *See, e.g.*, Southwest Williamson County Community Ass'n, Inc. v. Slater, 173 F.3d 1033, 1036 (6th Cir. 1999); Chemical Weapons Work Group v. Department of Army, 111 F.3d 1485 (10th Cir. 1997); Village of Elk Grove Village v. Evans, 997 F.2d 328, 331 (7th Cir. 1993); Impro Products, Inc. v. Block, 722 F.2d 845 (D.C. Cir. 1983); Lewis v. Glickman, 104 F. Supp. 2d 1311 (Kan. 2000), *aff'd sub nom.* Jones v. Glickman, 2002 U.S. App. LEXIS 13269 (10th Cir. 2002) (rejecting government's claim that the statute of limitations should be 60 days pursuant to Fed. R. App. 4(a)).

185 20 U.S.C. § 1091a(b)(2). This provision only applies explicitly to FFELs, and not Perkins Loans. While the provision does not

mention Direct Loans, it will apply to Direct Loans because, unless otherwise specified, Direct Loans "shall have the same terms, conditions, and benefits" as FFELs. 20 U.S.C. § 1087e(a)(1).

186 A good enunciation of this policy is found in a letter from Acting Assistant Secretary Whitehead to Congressman Stephen Solarz, Clearinghouse No. 44,343 (May 19, 1988).

187 20 U.S.C. § 1078(b)(1)(O).

188 Letter of William Morant, Acting Deputy Assistant Secretary for Student Financial Assistance, Nos. 93-L-156, 93-G-236, Clearinghouse No. 49,163 (July 1993).

standards it uses for determining a false certification discharge based on forgery. That is, the Department may quickly settle a case if it would also grant a false certification discharge, while the student may have to litigate a forgery claim that would not be covered by the false certification regulations.

Fraud in obtaining the consumer's signature should also be a defense. For example, there are many reported cases of consumers signing promissory notes unaware that they were obligating themselves on a loan. The consumers typically thought they were just applying to a school or applying for a grant. The student never went to the school or realized the existence of the debt until much later when a lender tried to collect on the loan. While such facts should provide a valid defense on the note, advocates should be prepared for the Department and guaranty agencies to give little credibility to such claims.

Another type of loan defense relates to the consumer's claims and defenses against the school. The extent to which the consumer can raise these as grounds not to repay a student loan is discussed in Chapter 9, *infra*.

6.11 Connection Between Contract Defenses and Statutory Discharges

Any student entitled to a closed school (or false certification) discharge might also consider raising school-related claims as a defense on a loan, since, by definition, the student has serious claims against the school. In part because of Department regulations, students should demonstrate some care concerning the interrelationship of closed school (or false certification) discharges and raising school-related defenses.

The safest course is always to raise the discharge claim first, and then raise school-related defenses later. If borrowers are sued for collection, they should file an answer to the collection suit asserting the right to a discharge as a defense. The court should be asked not to enter judgment until the discharge application has been ruled on. If the Department of Education is suing, the United States Attorney will usually agree to stay the litigation until the Department rules on the discharge request.

It is also usually preferable, in response to a tax intercept or garnishment action, to raise the right to a discharge as a defense rather than raising school-related claims. The problem with raising school-related claims is that, if a guaranty agency, in the context of a tax intercept, garnishment, or

other administrative proceeding, determines a loan is unenforceable, the Department will not repay the guaranty agency on the discharge claim.[189] The regulations specify that for FFELs a loan "qualifies for payment" only if it is legally enforceable.[190] Presumably, the failure to receive reimbursement will mean the guaranty agency will refuse to process the discharge.

A student is not fully protected by the guaranty agency determination that a loan cannot be enforced. This may only temporarily stop a particular intercept or garnishment, providing no permanent loan cancellation. Obtaining a court ruling on a loan's enforceability may take years and extensive legal resources, during which time the very pendency of the lawsuit may prevent the student from obtaining a discharge.

Nevertheless, sometimes it is unavoidable that the student wants to raise a closed school or false certification discharge claim after the enforceability of the note has already been challenged, such as when the student is a member of a class action. The Secretary does have discretion to discharge loans even when a student is raising school-related defenses[191] or when a student who is potentially eligible for a discharge is sued for collection before the student has applied for a discharge. The best interpretation of the Department regulations is that the student should be fully protected, but that the guaranty agency will not be reimbursed for a closed school or false certification discharge if the loan is found to be unenforceable.

If a student has put the legal enforceability of a loan into question, but it has not yet been determined whether the loan is enforceable, the Secretary may authorize the payment of the claim to the guaranty agency. The guaranty agency will then have to refund the amount if the loan is later found to be unenforceable.[192] In most cases, the Secretary will authorize payment to the guarantor, and the student will receive the discharge.[193]

---

189 34 C.F.R. § 682.402(a)(4)(ii). The same is true if a court determines the loan to be unenforceable. *Id.* at 682.402(a)(4)(i).
190 34 C.F.R. § 682.402(a)(3). The Direct Loan regulations do not contain this requirement.
191 34 C.F.R. § 682.402(a)(4)(iii).
192 34 C.F.R. § 682.402(a)(4)(iii).
193 Even where the Secretary will not authorize payment, a literal reading of the regulation makes the issue irrelevant to students because it only deals with the Secretary paying guarantors if the student's loan is discharged. It does not limit the student's right to a discharge. This makes sense because even if a loan is later found to be unenforceable, the student assigns to the Secretary all rights to recover on the loan from third parties and the Secretary will charge back the guarantor in any event. 34 C.F.R. §§ 682.402(d)(5), 682.402(a)(4)(iii).

Chapter 7   Discharging Student Loans in Bankruptcy

7.1 About the Bankruptcy Option

Discharging student loans in bankruptcy is an important strategy for low-income consumers, either through a chapter 7 ("straight") or a chapter 13 ("wage earner plan") bankruptcy filing.[1] Though recent amendments to the Bankruptcy Code have made it more difficult to discharge student loans, it is still an option consumers struggling with debt may consider.[2] In addition, even when a student loan cannot be discharged in bankruptcy, a chapter 13 bankruptcy filing offers other important options for the student loan borrower.

Deciding whether to file for bankruptcy to deal with a student loan requires at least two decisions. The first decision—whether bankruptcy can effectively deal with a student loan—is described later in this chapter. The other issue is whether bankruptcy makes sense for a consumer in light of the consumer's total debt picture. This question is detailed in another NCLC manual,[3] and will only be briefly summarized here.[4]

In a chapter 7 bankruptcy, virtually all of a consumer's debts are eliminated (discharged) with no obligation to make payments, and the consumer will be able to keep exempt property. Non-exempt property, however, may be liquidated. It is therefore critical for a consumer's attorney to carefully study the consumer's exemption, redemption, and other rights if the consumer wishes to retain a home, car, or other significant asset. Nevertheless, exemption statutes will permit many low-income persons to retain all their assets in a chapter 7 proceeding.

If a consumer is concerned about his or her ability to retain a home, car, or other asset, a chapter 13 filing will often be a successful approach. In a chapter 13 bankruptcy, a debtor pays some portion (even if only 5 or 10%) of his or her unsecured debts in accordance with a court approved ("confirmed") plan, usually over a three-to-five year period.[5] At the conclusion of the plan, the remaining obligations on any unsecured debts are discharged.[6] The opportunity to cure defaults on or to restructure secured debt is also available.[7]

Another consideration is that filing a chapter 7 or chapter 13 bankruptcy instantly protects the student from most collection actions on claims arising before the bankruptcy. For example, the "automatic stay" would prevent a student loan creditor from continuing with an administrative wage garnishment.[8]

Currently, the fee for filing a chapter 7 is $200 and $185 for filing a chapter 13 bankruptcy. These fees generally cannot be waived, but the fee may be paid in installments.[9]

7.2 When Can a Student Loan Be Discharged in Bankruptcy?

7.2.1 Special Restriction on Dischargeability Applies to Most Student Loans

A chapter 7 or 13 discharge eliminates all of a debtor's unsecured debts, with certain statutory exceptions. While stu-

---

1 For a general introduction to bankruptcy law, see National Consumer Law Center, Consumer Bankruptcy Law and Practice Chs. 1–6 (6th ed. 2000 and Supp.).

2 Student loan debtors suffered a major setback in 1998 to their ability to discharge student loans. For all bankruptcy cases filed on or after October 7, 1998, the discharge of student loans which first became due more than seven years prior to the bankruptcy filing is no longer allowed. Pub. L. No. 105-244 § 971 (Oct. 7, 1998) (Higher Education Programs Authorization Extension Act).

3 National Consumer Law Center, Consumer Bankruptcy Law and Practice (6th ed. 2000 and Supp.).

4 As this manual goes to print, Congress is poised to enact sweeping revisions to the Bankruptcy Code that would make it harder for consumers to file bankruptcy and would undermine the relief currently available in the bankruptcy system. Though these amendments will affect a consumer's decision whether to file bankruptcy, they most likely will not have a significant impact on the issue of dischargeability of student loans discussed later in this chapter.

5 National consumer Law Center, Consumer Bankruptcy Law and Practice Ch. 4 (6th ed. 2000 and Supp.).

6 11 U.S.C. § 1328(c).

7 See National Consumer Law Center, Consumer Bankruptcy Law and Practice Ch. 11 (6th ed. 2000 and Supp.).

8 See 11 U.S.C. § 362. The automatic stay remains in effect while the bankruptcy case is pending or until such time as it is lifted by the court upon request by a creditor based on grounds specified in § 362 of the Bankruptcy Code. See § 5.2.4, *supra* for a discussion of the automatic stay in relation to tax intercepts.

9 Part of each fee is a mandatory noticing fee rather than a filing fee. That part of the fee is waivable in most jurisdictions. For more information about bankruptcy court fee waivers, see National Consumer Law Center, Consumer Bankruptcy Law and Practice §§ 7.2, 13.6 (6th ed. 2000 and Supp.).

dent loans are unsecured debts subject to discharge, the Bankruptcy Code restricts whether most types of student loans can be discharged in either a chapter 7 or chapter 13 bankruptcy. These educational loans can only be discharged if the consumer can show that payment of the debt "will impose an undue hardship on the debtor and the debtor's dependents."[10]

This special restriction on dischargeability applies to educational loans "made, insured or guaranteed by any governmental unit, or made under any program funded in whole or in part by a government unit or a nonprofit institution."[11] Consequently, the dischargeability of Stafford, SLS, Federal Direct, and Perkins loans are all restricted. Most courts find these limitations apply not only to student borrowers, but also to parents who cosign a student loan or take out a PLUS or other loan for their child's education.[12]

In addition, while the exception to discharge applies to loans by state agencies and nonprofit organizations,[13] loans made by for-profit institutions may be discharged.[14] The

restriction on dischargeability also applies to educational benefit overpayments (such as Pell grant overpayments) and obligations to repay funds received as educational benefits, scholarships or stipends.[15] The restriction on dischargeability should also apply in the same way to consolidation loans.[16] However, it does not apply to a student's nonpayment of tuition or room and board, where the charges are not incurred as an extension of credit or under an appropriate program.[17] In addition, the restriction may not apply to non-students who sign as co-obligors to finance a third party's education.[18]

10　11 U.S.C. § 523(a)(8).

11　11 U.S.C. §§ 523(a)(8), 1328(a)(2). In general, it is the purpose for which the loan was made that controls rather than the use of the loan proceeds. *In re* Murphy, 282 F.3d 868 (5th Cir. 2002) (student loans non-dischargeable even if portion used by debtor to purchase car, housing, food and other living expenses). *See also* National Consumer Law Center, Consumer Bankruptcy Law and Practice § 14.4.2 (6th ed. 2000 and Supp.) for a discussion on the dischargeability of student loans.

12　*See In re* Pelkowski, 990 F.2d 737 (3d Cir. 1993); *In re* Varma, 149 B.R. 817 (N.D. Tex. 1992); *In re* Wilcon, 143 B.R. 4 (D. Mass. 1992); Uterhark v. Great Lakes Higher Education Corp. (*In re* Uterhark), 185 B.R. 39 (Bankr. N.D. Ohio 1995); Owens v. Nebraska Higher Education Loan Program, Inc. (Matter of Owens), 161 B.R. 829 (Bankr. D. Neb. 1993). *But see In re* Kirkish, 144 B.R. 367 (Bankr. W.D. Mich. 1992); *In re* Behr, 80 B.R. 124 (Bankr. N.D. Iowa 1987). Courts have been less willing to find that the exception to discharge applies to co-signers who are not the student's parents. *See, e.g., In re* Pryor, 234 B.R. 716 (Bankr. W.D. Tenn. 1999) (exception not applicable to non-student co-signer); *In re* Meier, 85 B.R. 805 (Bankr. W.D. Wis. 1986) (exception not applicable to accommodation party).

13　*See* TI Federal Credit Union v. DelBonis, 72 F.3d 921 (1st Cir. 1995) (federally chartered credit union is a governmental unit for purposes of exception to discharge); *In re* Merchant, 958 F.2d 738 (6th Cir. 1992) (loan guaranteed by nonprofit institution was nondischargeable); *In re* Roberts, 149 B.R. 547 (C.D. Ill. 1993) (loan from nonprofit credit union nondischargeable). *Cf. In re* Reis, 274 B.R.46 (Bankr. D. Mass. 2002) (private student loan made by grandparents not excepted from discharge because not made pursuant to student loan program of governmental unit or by non-profit entity).

14　*In re* Jones, 242 B.R. 441 (Bankr. W.D. Tenn. 1999) (debt to for-profit trade school was not within scope of § 523(a)(8)); *In re* Shorts, 209 B.R. 818 (Bankr. D.R.I. 1997) (same); *In re* Simmons, 175 B.R. 624 (Bankr. E.D. Va. 1994) (credit union was not a nonprofit institution and loan was not made pursuant to a program within meaning of § 523(a)(8)); *In re* Pilcher, 139 B.R. 948 (Bankr. D. Ariz. 1992) (law school loans originated and funded by for-profit entities held dischargeable); *In re* Sinclair-Ganos, 133 B.R. 382 (Bankr. W.D. Mich. 1991) (credit union not a nonprofit institution within meaning of § 523(a)(8)). Readers should note that proposed legislation currently pending

in Congress would expand the nondischargeability provision to include some loans made by for-profit institutions.

15　11 U.S.C. § 523(a)(8). *In re* Burks, 244 F.3d 1245 (11th Cir. 2001) (obligation to repay stipend due to failure to fulfill stipend agreement to teach in "other race" institution after receiving degree was non-dischargeable); U.S. Dept. of Health and Human Servs. v. Smith, 807 F.2d 122 (8th Cir. 1986) (scholarship grants received to finance medical training in exchange for agreement to practice in designated physician shortage area non-dischargeable). *See also In re* Coole, 202 B.R. 518 (Bankr. D.N.M. 1996) (an "educational benefit overpayment" involves a program like the "GI Bill" where students receive payments based on their attendance at school and overpayment occurs when student continues to receive payments after leaving school).

16　*See In re* Flint, 238 B.R. 676 (E.D. Mich. 1999), *rev'g* 231 B.R. 611 (Bankr. E.D. Mich. 1999); *In re* Shaffer, 237 B.R. 617 (Bankr. N.D. Tex. 1999); *In re* Cobb, 196 B.R. 34 (Bankr. E.D. Va. 1996). *Cf. In re* Segal, 57 F.3d 342 (3d Cir. 1995) (when nonprofit hospital paid off debtor's student loans, replacing it with new loans, those new loans were dischargeable because they were not made under a "program" of giving educational loans).

17　Cazenovia College v. Renshaw, 222 F.3d 82 (2d Cir. 2000) (tuition debt not a loan); *In re* Nelson, 188 B.R. 32 (D.S.D. 1995) (debt for tuition, room and board to university was not a loan); *In re* Ray, 262 B.R. 544 (Bankr.D. Okla. 2001) (tuition debt was neither "loan" nor "obligation to repay funds received as an educational benefit"); *In re* Mehta, 262 B.R. 35 (D.N.J. 2001) (same); *In re* Pelzman, 233 B.R. 575 (Bankr. D.D.C. 1999) (room and board for first semester non-dischargeable because pursuant to program but not for remaining semesters where extension of credit violated school policy); *In re* Gordon, 231 B.R. 459 (Bankr. D. Conn. 1999) (residency program assistance not student loan); *In re* Feyes, 228 B.R. 998 (Bankr. N.D. Ohio 1998) (credit extension was dischargeable where school allowed student to attend classes on a credit basis and pay for them when he could and no promissory note was signed); *In re* Johnson, 222 B.R. 783 (Bankr. E.D. Va. 1998) (debt for tuition was not obligation for funds received on a loan and there was no "program"); *In re* Meinhart, 211 B.R. 750 (Bankr. D. Colo. 1997) (debt to school was not an obligation to repay "funds received" as required by statute); *In re* Coole, 202 B.R. 518 (Bankr. D.N.M. 1996) (debt to school for services rendered was not a loan); *In re* Alibatya, 178 B.R. 339 (Bankr. E.D.N.Y. 1995) (no loan where debtor failed to pay student housing rent under lease with university). *Cf. In re* DePasquale, 225 B.R. 830 (B.A.P. 1st Cir. 1998) (payment agreement for overdue tuition constituted "loan"); *In re* Johnson, 218 B.R. 449 (B.A.P. 8th Cir. 1998) (debtor who signed promissory note to college for unpaid tuition had student loan).

18　*See In re* Pryor, 234 B.R. 716 (W.D. Tenn. 1999) (exception not applicable to non-student codebtor); Kirkish v. Meritor Sav.

7.2.2 Discharging Student Loans Over Seven Years Old No Longer Allowed for Cases Filed After October 7, 1998

In 1998, student loan debtors suffered a major setback to their ability to discharge student loans. For all bankruptcy cases filed after October 7, 1998, the discharge of student loans that first became due more than seven years prior to the bankruptcy filing will no longer be allowed.[19] Cases filed before October 7, 1998 are not affected by the change in the law. The following discussion of discharges under the seven-year rule is still relevant for consumers who filed before the change in law and there remains a question as to whether a student loan was discharged.

For cases filed before October 7, 1998, if the first student loan installment became due more than seven years prior to the bankruptcy filing, then the entire loan and not just the first installment is discharged.[20] The most important issue in counting the seven-year period is that the seven years are "exclusive of any applicable suspension of the repayment period."[21] This means that a deferment or forbearance may lengthen the seven-year period if repayments were suspended during that period.[22] On the other hand, the seven-year period should not be lengthened just because the consumer was allowed to make reduced payments or entered into a reasonable and affordable repayment agreement, because payments were not suspended.[23] Consolidating one or more student loans, though, will likely start the seven-year period running all over again as of the date of the consolidated loan.[24]

7.2.3 Undue Hardship as Basis for Discharging Student Loan

7.2.3.1 General

A student loan may be discharged if payment of the debt "will impose an undue hardship on the debtor and the debtor's dependents."[25] There is no statutory definition of "undue hardship." Generally it means the consumer's present income is inadequate to pay the loan and this situation is not likely to change even after considering the consumer's future earning potential.

Many bankruptcy courts have adopted the three-prong test for determining undue hardship set forth in the Second Circuit decision in *Brunner v. New York State Higher Educ. Servs. Corp.*[26] The *Brunner* test requires a showing that: (1) the debtor cannot maintain, based on current income and expenses, a "minimal" standard of living for the debtor and the debtor's dependents if forced to repay the student loans; (2) additional circumstances exist indicating that this state of affairs is likely to persist for a significant portion of the repayment period of the student loans; and (3) the debtor has made good faith efforts to repay the loans.

While the *Brunner* test is widely followed, some courts have chosen to apply other tests or to consider other criteria.[27] Another commonly used test that preceded *Brunner*

Bank, 144 B.R. 367 (Bankr. W.D. Mich. 1992). *But see In re* Pelkowski, 990 F.2d 737 (3d Cir. 1993) (language of statute does not limit exception to discharge to exclude parent cosigners); *In re* Salter, 207 B.R. 272 (Bankr. M.D. Fla. 1997) (exception applies to co-maker as focus should be kind of debt involved rather than who signed); *In re* Varma, 149 B.R. 817 (N.D. Tex. 1992); *In re* Wilcon, 143 B.R. 5 (D. Mass. 1992).

19 Pub. L. No. 105-244 § 971 (Oct. 7, 1998) (Higher Education Programs Authorization Extension Act).

20 *See, e.g., In re* Nunn, 788 F.2d 617 (9th Cir. 1986).

21 11 U.S.C. § 523(a)(8)(A). U.S. Dep't of Ed. v. Scott (*In re* Scott), 147 F.3d 788 (8th Cir. 1998) (loan first became due after six-month grace period expired, not when student left school). *See also* National Consumer Law Center, Consumer Bankruptcy Law and Practice § 14.4.3.8 (6th ed. 2000 and Supp.).

22 *In re* Huber, 169 B.R. 82 (Bankr. W.D.N.Y. 1994) (deferment period counts even where debtor eventually found not eligible for deferment where repayment requirement was suspended); *In re* Barciz, 123 B.R. 771 (Bankr. N.D. Ohio 1990) (forbearance tolls running of period). *But see In re* Flynn, 190 B.R. 139 (Bankr. D.N.H. 1995) (a reference to a period of forbearance did not refer to a suspension of payment).

23 *In re* Salter, 207 B.R. 272 (Bankr. M.D. Fla. 1997) (stipulation changing amount of payments did not constitute a new obligation that would restart the seven-year time period); *In re* Marlewski, 168 B.R. 378 (Bankr. E.D. Wis. 1994) (repayment agreement does not toll period where agreement did not call for suspension of payments or lengthening of repayment period). *See also In re* Manriquez, 207 B.R. 890 (B.A.P. 9th Cir. 1996) (retroactive forbearance agreement signed after seven years had already run did not render loan nondischargeable).

24 *See, e.g.,* Hiatt v. Indiana State Student Assistance Comm'n, 36 F.3d 21 (7th Cir. 1994); United States v. McGrath, 143 B.R. 820 (D. Md. 1992); *In re* Cobb, 196 B.R. 34 (Bankr. E.D. Va. 1996); *In re* Hasselgrave, 177 B.R. 681 (Bankr. D. Or. 1995); *In re* Menendez, 151 B.R. 972 (Bankr. M.D. Fla. 1993); *In re* Martin, 137 B.R. 770 (Bankr. W.D. Mo. 1992). *But see In re* McKinney, 120 B.R. 416 (Bankr. N.D. Ohio 1990).

25 11 U.S.C. § 523(a)(8)(B).

26 *See* Brunner v. New York State Higher Education Services, 831 F.2d 395 (2d Cir. 1987).

27 Since the *Brunner* decision, courts have tended to "mix and match" both restrictive and less restrictive elements from various cases. *See* United Student Aid Funds v. Pena (*In re* Pena), 155 F.3d 1108 (9th Cir. 1998) (adopting *Brunner* test); *In re* Cheesman, 25 F.3d 356 (6th Cir. 1994) (no specific test adopted but *Brunner* analysis followed); *In re* Roberson, 999 F.2d 1132 (7th Cir. 1993) ("dischargeability of student loan should be based on certainty of hopelessness, not simply a present inability to fulfill financial commitment"); *In re* Faish, 72 F.3d 298 (3d Cir. 1995), *cert. denied,* 116 S. Ct. 2532 (1996); *In re* Mayer, 210 B.R. 677 (E.D. Pa. 1997), *aff'g* 198 B.R. 116 (Bankr. E.D. Pa. 1996). Still other courts have cited the more restrictive language in *Roberson* to deny discharges. *See, e.g., In re* Coveney, 192 B.R. 140 (Bankr. W.D. Tex. 1996); *In re* Walcott, 185 B.R. 721 (Bankr. E.D.N.C. 1995); *In re* Hawkins, 187 B.R. 294 (Bankr. N.D. Iowa 1995). *See generally* Andrew M. Campbell, *Bankruptcy Discharge of Student Loan on Ground of*

and is similar in some ways is the *Johnson* test.[28] Like *Brunner*, the *Johnson* test has three parts:

(1) The Mechanical Test: Courts will ask whether the debtor's future financial resources will be sufficient to support the debtor and dependents (similar to steps one and two of *Brunner*);

(2) The Good Faith Test: Here the courts ask whether the debtor was negligent or irresponsible in her efforts to maximize income and minimize expenses and if so, whether the absence of such negligence would have altered the answer to the mechanical test (similar to step three in *Brunner*);

(3) The Policy Test: The courts ask whether the circumstances, particularly the amount and percentage of total indebtedness of the student loan, indicate that the dominant purpose of the bankruptcy petition was to discharge the student debt. Courts will favor debtors who have truly fallen on hard times after incurring student loan debt and are unlikely to derive future benefits from the education financed with the loan.[29]

This third step, unlike the *Brunner* test, takes into account whether the debtor benefited or is likely to benefit financially from the education. Though this prong of the *Johnson* test can be restrictive, it should be more favorably applied to low-income students who have attended scam vocational schools and never benefited from the education.

Other courts have rejected the rigid tests set out in both *Brunner* and *Johnson*, choosing instead to use a more flexible test and consider the "totality of the debtor's circumstances."[30] This test does not necessarily conflict with *Brunner* and *Johnson* but expands the scope of factors a court may consider, taking into consideration more fully the student's personal circumstances.

In still other cases, courts have not necessarily rejected the *Brunner* or *Johnson* tests, but rather refined or expanded some of the prongs in making their decisions.[31] And at least one court has introduced a "poverty test" where a debtor's loans were presumptively considered nondischargeable if the debtor's income exceeded the federal poverty guidelines, unless the debtor could show extreme circumstances.[32]

Regardless of the test used, courts must ultimately engage in the discretionary determination of when "hardship" becomes "undue." Courts are generally in agreement that "ordinary" or "garden variety" hardship, however defined, is simply not sufficient. On the other extreme are courts that require extraordinary circumstances such as the total physical incapacity of the debtor. One court recently criticized these latter decisions, finding the requisite hardship to be more "mundane":

> To conclude that the debtor must demonstrate something approaching a "certainty of hopelessness" or "total incapacity" would be to sacrifice the notion of "fresh start" at the altar of "undue hardship."[33]

7.2.3.2 Applying the Hardship Tests

The Sixth Circuit decision in *In re Cheesman* provides an example of the application of the undue hardship standard. Though the Sixth Circuit did not adopt any specific test in *Cheesman*, it examined the three factors found in the *Brunner* test.

The court concluded first that the debtors could not maintain a minimal standard of living if they were required to repay their loans. The debtors, though college educated, were barely above poverty level; even a frugal budget would require $400 a month more in expenses than their anticipated income.[34]

Undue Hardship Under § 523(a)(8)(B) of Bankruptcy Code of 1978 (11 U.S.C.S. § 523(a)(8)(B) Discharge of Student Loans, 144 A.L.R. Fed. 1 (1998).

28 *In re* Johnson, 1979 U.S. Dist. LEXIS 11428, 5 B.C.D. 532 (Bankr. E.D. Pa. 1979). *See also In re* Roe, 226 B.R. 258 (Bankr. N.D. Ala. 1998); *In re* Taylor, 198 B.R. 700 (Bankr. N.D. Ohio 1996). For decisions comparing the *Brunner* and *Johnson* tests, see *In re* Kopf, 245 B.R. 731 (Bankr. D. Me. 2000); *In re* Lehman, 226 B.R. 805 (Bankr. D. Vt. 1998) (court chooses *Brunner* test and denies discharge); *In re* Holtorf, 204 B.R. 567 (Bankr. S.D. Cal. 1997); *In re* Hawkins, 187 B.R. 294 (Bankr. N.D. Iowa 1995) (*Brunner* test applied after discussing both *Brunner* and *Johnson* tests).

29 *In re* Johnson, 1979 U.S. Dist. LEXIS 11428, 5 B.C.D. 532 (Bankr. E.D. Pa. 1979).

30 *See, e.g.*, Tennessee Student Assistance Corp. v. Hornsby (*In re* Hornsby), 144 F.2d 433 (6th Cir. 1998) (declining to "adopt any one test"); *In re* Andresen, 232 B.R. 127 (B.A.P. 8th Cir. 1999) (rejection of *Brunner* test in favor of "totality of circumstances test"), *citing In re* Andrews, 661 F.2d 702 (8th Cir. 1981); *In re* Kopf, 245 B.R. 731 (Bankr. D. Me. 2000); *In re* Phelps, 237 B.R. 527 (Bankr. D.R.I. 1999); *In re* Clark, 240 B.R. 758 (Bankr. W.D. Mo. 1999) (applying the *Andrews* test); *In re* Law, 159 B.R. 287 (Bankr. D.S.D. 1993) (described as a "case-by-case approach that is fact sensitive").

31 *See, e.g., In re* Roberson, 999 F.2d 1132 (7th Cir. 1993); *In re* Faish, 72 F.3d 298 (3d Cir. 1995), *cert. denied*, 116 S. Ct. 2532 (1996).

32 *In re* Bryant, 72 B.R. 913, 916–17 (Bankr. E.D. Pa. 1987). *See also In re* Ekenasi, 271 B.R. 256 (S.D. W. Va. 2002) (adopting *Bryant* poverty guideline presumption).

33 *In re* Kopf, 245 B.R. 731, 744 (Bankr. D. Me. 2000).

34 *See also In re* Pena, 155 F.3d 1108 (9th Cir. 1998) (debtors' monthly deficit of $41 after deducting average expenses from net income cannot support minimal standard of living); *In re* Hornsby, 144 F.3d 433 (6th Cir. 1998) (debtors did not need to be at poverty level to show undue hardship); *In re* Ivory, 269 B.R. 890 (Bankr. N.D. Ala. 2001) (applying both a subjective and objective evaluation of debtor's income and expenses and citing studies showing that income far higher than poverty level needed for minimal standard of living). In considering a student's ability to repay a student loan in cases where the student does not file bankruptcy with his or her spouse, courts fre-

Second, the court concluded that it was not likely there would be significant improvement in their financial circumstances in the near future.[35] The court evaluated only realistic expectations rather than speculation concerning future prospects.[36] And finally, the court concluded that the consumers had acted in good faith, after limiting that inquiry to a finding that they had attempted to make minimal payments on the loan over a period of several years and that they had no prospect of embarking on lucrative careers in the private sector.[37]

However, in a more troubling aspect of the decision, the court concluded that a bankruptcy court has the discretion to defer making a final determination about the dischargeability of a student loan for as long as eighteen months after the case is heard in order to determine if the debtor's situation has improved. This conclusion is hard to accept as proper. A finding of undue hardship always calls for a prediction by a court. A deferral process shirks the courts' responsibility to make the necessary forecast and delays the debtors' ability to obtain a fresh start. Although, as the dissent points out, in some circumstances a delay may result in an improved opportunity to establish undue hardship, more often the delay will create an unnecessary uncertainty about the debtor's ongoing responsibilities.[38]

7.2.3.3 Other Hardship Factors

The student's undue hardship argument may be stronger where the student loan arose from a private vocational school that closed down or defrauded the student. Absent a meaningful educational experience, the student has no job skills and, because of the default, is ineligible for future government educational loans. If a discharge is not granted, the student will not be able to go back to school, and will not be able to obtain a decent paying job, making repayment now or in the future an undue hardship.

In addition, the nature of the schooling will be relevant to whether the education enabled or would enable the debtor to obtain substantially higher income.[39] Another bankruptcy

---

quently consider the non-filing spouse's income and contributions to household expenses. *See, e.g., In re* Dolan, 256 B.R. 230 (Bankr. D. Mass. 2000); *In re* Greco, 251 B.R. 670 (Bankr. E.D. Pa. 2000); *In re* Koch, 144 B.R. 959 (Bankr. W.D. Pa. 1992); *In re* Albert, 25 B.R. 98 (Bankr. N.D. Ohio 1982).

35 *See also* Queen v. Pennsylvania H.E.A.A., 210 B.R. 677 (E.D. Pa. 1997), *aff'd without op. sub nom In re* Mayer, 156 F.3d 1225 (3d Cir. 1998) (discharge granted to single parent manual laborer with uncompleted masters degree; any salary increase from full-time work would be offset by day care costs); *In re* Cline, 248 B.R. 347 (B.A.P. 8th Cir. 2000) (single woman unable to increase income would need decades to repay $53,000 in loans); *In re* Thomson, 234 B.R. 506 (Bankr. D. Mont. 1999) (discharge granted to veteran with permanent and total disability); *In re* Kasey, 227 B.R. 473 (Bankr. W.D. Va. 1998) (discharge granted for single mother suffering from depression with three young children, unlikely to finish education, had attempted payments); *In re* Bessette, 226 B.R. 103 (Bankr. D. Idaho 1998) (chapter 7 debtor had two minor dependents, limited job skills and limited potential for increasing income); *In re* Young, 225 B.R. 312 (Bankr. E.D. Pa. 1998) (discharge granted where court also considered race and age as factors in determining whether hardship conditions were likely to persist); *In re* Lebovits, 223 B.R. 265 (Bankr. E.D.N.Y. 1998) (discharge granted to parent with M.S.W. with seven children where religious convictions required parochial schooling); *In re* Doherty, 219 B.R. 665 (Bankr. W.D.N.Y. 1998) (chapter 7 debtor satisfied her burden of proving that her present inability to repay the debt was likely to continue, presenting undisputed evidence of an incurable mental illness which was the cause of present inability to earn a sufficient wage); *In re* Shankwiler, 208 B.R. 701 (Bankr. C.D. Cal. 1997); *In re* Dotson-Cannon, 206 B.R. 530 (Bankr. W.D. Mo. 1997) (student loans discharged where single 51 year old woman with B.S. in public administration was only able to obtain $7/hour clerical work); *In re* Coats, 214 B.R. 397 (Bankr. N.D. Okla. 1997); *In re* Windland, 201 B.R. 178 (Bankr. N.D. Ohio 1996); *In re* Derby, 199 B.R. 328 (Bankr. W.D. Pa. 1996); Hoyle v. Pennsylvania Higher Education Assistance Agency, 199 B.R. 518 (Bankr. E.D. Pa. 1996); *In re* Fuertes, 198 B.R. 379 (Bankr. S.D. Fla. 1996). *But see In re* Garybush, 265 B.R. 587 (Bankr. S.D. Ohio 2001) (no discharge where family income should improve because debtor can resume part-time employment when youngest child enters school); *In re* Vinci, 232 B.R. 644 (Bankr. E.D. Pa. 1999); *In re* Pantelis, 229 B.R. 716 (Bankr. N.D. Ohio 1999) (no discharge where no documentation of physical disability and no showing of effective job search); *In re* Elmore, 230 B.R. 22 (Bankr. D. Conn. 1999); *In re* Mitchell, 210 B.R. 139 (Bankr. W.D. Mo. 1997); *In re* McLeod, 197 B.R. 624 (Bankr. N.D. Ohio 1996).

36 *See also In re* Doherty, 219 B.R. 665 (Bankr. W.D.N.Y. 1998) (court took judicial notice of prognosis for debtor suffering from bipolar disorder).

37 The test requiring a good faith effort to pay the loan does not require that repayment actually occurred, although it may require some effort to deal with the loan prior to bankruptcy. *In re*

Ivory, 269 B.R. 890 (Bankr. N.D. Ala. 2001) (no bad faith where debtor never had ability to repay loan); *In re* Coats, 214 B.R. 397 (Bankr. N.D. Okla. 1997); *In re* Maulin, 190 B.R. 153 (Bankr. W.D.N.Y. 1995). *Cf.* Tennessee Student Assistance Corp. v. Hornsby (*In re* Hornsby), 144 F.3d 433 (6th Cir. 1998) (debtors had not made any payments; court holds that loan is non-dischargeable because they had not done everything possible to minimize expenses and maximize income).

38 *See In re* Shirzadi, 269 B.R. 664 (Bankr. S.D. Ind. 2001) (since hardship discharge denied under *Brunner* test because debtor failed to maximize income by pursuing child support, determination of whether debtor should be granted partial discharge deferred for 9 months to get update on her efforts to collect support); *In re* Jones v. Catholic University of America, 1997 Bankr. LEXIS 92, 1997 WL 52188 (Bankr. D.D.C. 1997) (debts discharged for 18 months, after which the debtor would become re-obligated; debtor could amend the judgment as the 18 months approached with proof that present financial situation would persist). *See also* § 7.2.3.5, *infra*.

39 United Student Aid Funds v. Pena (*In re* Pena), 155 F.3d 1108 (9th Cir. 1998) (value of education relevant to future ability to pay student loans); *In re* Evans, 131 B.R. 372 (Bankr. S.D. Ohio 1991) (trade school education in word-processing did not improve debtor's ability to repay her student loans); Price v. Bureau of Student Financial Assistance (*In re* Price), 25 B.R. 256, 258 (Bankr. W.D. Mo. 1982); *see also* Correll v. Union Nat'l Bank of Pittsburgh, 105 B.R. 302 (Bankr. W.D. Pa. 1989); Carter v. Kent State University (*In re* Carter), 29 B.R. 228 (Bankr. N.D. Ohio 1983); Love v. Department of Health, Edu-

court has put it this way:

> There is thus great pressure and temptation on the part of college authorities to encourage students to apply for loans and grant them when in effect it is not a sound economic thing to do. This should be a substantial factor in determining whether a student loan should be dischargeable. Was the student in-veigled into obtaining the loan and taking particular courses in college when the college authorities should have known that upon graduation from college the student had little chance of obtaining employment in that field?[40]

Yet another bankruptcy court has used an investment analysis. Education is an investment with the hope that the student will obtain a higher paying job in the future. For example, it would be inequitable for a doctor to discharge his medical school debts just before embarking on a well-paid career made possible because of his educational loans. But this exception should not apply where a student attends a cosmetology school and the schooling did not increase the student's job skills in any significant amount.[41]

The fact that the student was swindled by the school may also be relevant to the consumer's good faith in seeking to discharge the loan. The student may not have felt that the obligation was owed in circumstances where the school referred the consumer to the lender and the school had defrauded the student.

Courts have also considered whether there should be a different hardship test applied in chapter 13 cases. Sometimes creditors argue against a chapter 13 undue hardship discharge for a student loan on the basis that a debtor can only propose a chapter 13 plan if the debtor has disposable income. If the debtor has disposable income, can it be an undue hardship to repay the student loan? Courts generally

reject this argument and apply the same undue hardship standards for chapter 13 and 7 bankruptcies.[42]

Finally, debtors seeking a hardship discharge before a sympathetic bankruptcy court that is inclined to grant a discharge must still be vigilant in proving all the elements of the appropriate hardship test.[43] Appellate courts in several recent cases have reversed judgments in favor of the debtors on the basis that the record evidence failed to support findings that the debtors' financial circumstances were likely to persist.[44]

Evidence of the debtor's future financial prospects can be based on the debtor's own testimony. For example, courts have not required the introduction of expert testimony to prove that a debtor's financial outlook and earning capacity have been impaired by the debtor's psychological or emotional problems, or substance dependency problems.[45] But where the debtor can present corroborating testimony that his or her condition is not likely to improve, either from friends, family members or treating professionals, this certainly will improve the likelihood of obtaining a hardship discharge and having it survive on appeal.

7.2.3.4 Relevance of Older Loans (Seven Years or More) in Making Undue Hardship Claims

The elimination of the seven-year discharge rule means that more debtors will seek discharge based on undue hardship. There have been few hardship cases involving loans more than seven years old since previously these debtors were able to get discharges without a showing of

---

cation & Welfare (*In re* Love), 28 B.R. 475 (Bankr. S.D. Ind. 1983); Ford v. New York State Higher Education Services Corp. (*In re* Ford), 22 B.R. 442 (Bankr. W.D.N.Y. 1982); Littell v. State of Oregon (*In re* Littell), 6 B.R. 85 (Bankr. D. Or. 1980); *In re* Johnson, 5 B.C.D. 532 (Bankr. E.D. Pa. 1979). *But see In re* Chapman, 238 B.R. 450 (Bankr. W.D. Mo. 1999) (court rejected debtor's argument that his loans were not really student loans because he did not receive any educational benefit; in applying *Brunner* and totality of circumstances tests, court failed to find undue hardship.); *In re* O'Flaherty, 204 B.R. 793 (Bankr. N.D. Ala. 1997) (in applying *Brunner* test, court considered debtor's current income and expenses rather than his ability to utilize education he acquired through loan; debtor was unable to fulfill goal of ordination as Catholic priest).

40 Littell v. State of Oregon (*In re* Littell), 6 B.R. 85 (Bankr. D. Or. 1980); *see also* Correll v. Union Nat'l Bank of Pittsburgh, 105 B.R. 302 (Bankr. W.D. Pa. 1989).

41 Powelson v. Stewart School of Hairstyling, Inc., 25 B.R. 274 (Bankr. D. Neb. 1982). *See also In re* Law, 159 B.R. 287 (Bankr. D.S.D. 1993) (debtor obtained no benefit from $20,000 student loan for two and a half weeks of flight training).

42 *In re* Strauss, 216 B.R. 638 (Bankr. N.D. Cal. 1998); *In re* Oswalt, 215 B.R. 337 (Bankr. W.D.N.Y. 1997) (chapter 13 debtor entitled to undue hardship discharge); *In re* Goranson, 183 B.R. 52 (Bankr. W.D.N.Y. 1995); *In re* Evans, 131 B.R. 372 (Bankr. S.D. Ohio 1991); *see also In re* Elebrashy, 189 B.R. 922 (Bankr. N.D. Ohio 1995).

43 The debtor has the burden of proof on all elements of the hardship test. Goulet v. Educational Credit Management Corp., 284 F.3d 773 (7th Cir. 2002); *In re* Rifino, 245 F.3d 1083 (9th Cir. 2001); *In re* Faish, 72 F.3d 298 (3d Cir. 1995).

44 Goulet v. Educational Credit Management Corp., 284 F.3d 773 (7th Cir. 2002) (record devoid of evidence that debtor's problems with alcoholism and a felony conviction, which predated several of his student loan obligations, were "insurmountable," or that they prevented debtor from being gainfully employed); *In re* Rifino, 245 F.3d 1083 (9th Cir. 2001) (debtor failed to prove that her financial circumstances were likely to persist by rebutting creditor's testimony concerning the debtors' earning potential as a social worker); *In re* Brightful, 267 F.3d 324 (3d Cir. 2001) (debtor failed to introduce evidence that her mental and emotional condition prevented her from using her skills as a legal secretary to secure full-time employment).

45 *In re* Brightful, 267 F.3d 324 (3d Cir. 2001) (bankruptcy judge may make reasonable conclusions concerning debtor's emotional state without expert testimony); *In re* Cline, 248 B.R. 347 (B.A.P. 8th Cir. 2000) (court's findings were not unreliable simply because no expert testimony was presented that debtor was clinically disabled).

hardship. However, the fact that a loan remains unpaid after seven years should influence evaluation of the standards in several ways.

Previous inability to pay over seven years is solid evidence of the second factor discussed in *Brunner*, that financial problems are likely to persist into the future.[46] To the extent the court is being asked to make a prediction, there could be little evidence that is more relevant than past experience.

A debtor's history over seven years would also be important to the analysis of good faith (the *Brunner* third factor).[47] Presumably most debtors with older student loans will have made payment during some part of the seven-year period. Every effort should be made to explain why the debtor was able to make payments at one time, but is no longer able to do so now. The goal should be to establish that the debtor "tried but failed" to make payments for a valid reason.

Finally, judges may be more willing to discharge older student loans. Judges should be reminded that since there is no statute of limitations for collection of most student loans, failure to make an undue hardship discharge may mean that debtors take their student loans to their graves.

7.2.3.5 Partial Discharge or Modification of Student Loan

In cases involving large student loan debts owed by middle class debtors, courts have been exploring the possibility of offering a partial hardship discharge. The court may find that the student has future earnings potential, but that the amount of debt is still excessive. In this situation, several courts have discharged only part of the debt, and require the balance to be paid out over time.[48] Another approach is for the court to discharge some, but not all, of a debtor's individual student loans. This approach rejects a pro rata reduction, but still offers the debtor some relief by applying the hardship test on a loan-by-loan basis.[49]

Other courts have used the dischargeability proceeding to restructure the loan, reducing the amount owed and establishing a modified repayment schedule. For example, courts have discharged collection fees and accrued interest, and delayed for several years the obligation to make payments, during which time no further interest would accrue.[50]

Despite recent interest in partial discharges, the view most consistent with the statutory language is that courts should determine simply whether the debt is or is not dischargeable.[51] Courts that have created the middle ground approach of a partial discharge should not apply it to low-income

---

46 *See* note 35, *supra*.

47 At least one court has commented that the "good faith" and "policy" factors are less relevant following the elimination of the seven-year discharge rule, as courts previously were concerned that debtors who sought a discharge before the seven-year period had passed "might not yet have given repayment efforts a chance." *In re* Kopf, 245 B.R. 731, 741 (Bankr. D. Me. 2000).

48 *See In re* Hornsby, 144 F.3d 433 (6th Cir. 1998) (partial discharge is permitted under court's equitable powers); *In re* Saxman, 263 B.R. 342 (W.D. Wash. 2001); *In re* Nary, 253 B.R. 752 (N.D. Tex. 2000); *In re* Kapinos, 243 B.R. 271 (W.D. Va. 2000); *In re* Brown, 239 B.R. 204 (S.D. Cal. 1999); *In re* Muto, 216 B.R. 325 (N.D.N.Y. 1996); *In re* Ammirati, 187 B.R. 902 (D.S.C. 1995); *In re* Barron, 264 B.R. 833 (Bankr. E.D. Tex. 2001) (bankruptcy court may use equitable power under section 105(a) of Bankruptcy Code to grant partial discharge and restructure student loan debt); *In re* Lohr, 252 B.R. 84 (Bankr. E.D. Va. 2000) (discharge allowed for $30,500 out of $35,000 in student loans; recommendation that $4,500 balance be paid at 7% interest amortized over 10 years); *In re* Rivers, 213 B.R. 616 (Bankr. S.D. Ga. 1997) ($40,000 out of $55,000 consolidated student loans held nondischargeable); *In re* Wetzel, 213 B.R. 220 (Bankr. N.D.N.Y. 1996); *In re* Raimondo, 183 B.R. 677 (Bankr. W.D.N.Y. 1995); *In re* Fox, 189 B.R. 115 (Bankr. N.D.

Ohio 1995); *In re* Gammoh 174 B.R. 707 (Bankr. N.D. Ohio 1994). *See also* Graves v. Myrvang, 232 F.3d 1116 (9th Cir. 2000) (Ninth Circuit applies *Hornsby* analysis to dischargeability provision relating to child support).

49 *In re* Andresen, 232 B.R. 127 (B.A.P. 8th Cir. 1999) (affirms bankruptcy court's discharge of two of three loans); *In re* Morris, 277 B.R. 910 (Bankr.W.D. Ark. 2002) (largest student loan in amount of $65,912 discharged but not smaller loans totaling $41,741); *In re* Grigas, 252 B.R. 866 (Bankr. D.N.H. 2000) (based on court's finding that debtor could pay $224 per month for 15 years, debtor's 15 student loans should be analyzed in chronological order so that only those that can first be fully repaid within 15 years will be excepted from discharge); *In re* Shankwiler, 208 B.R. 701 (Bankr. C.D. Cal. 1997) (holding that each loan should be treated separately); *In re* Hinkle, 200 B.R. 690 (Bankr. W.D. Wash. 1996) (discharging three out of six student loans).

50 *See In re* Shirzadi, 269 B.R. 664 (Bankr. S.D. Ind. 2001) (court reduced monthly payment amount and suspended accrual of interest and late fees for 9 months pending rehearing on whether debtor entitled to partial discharge); *In re* Garybush, 265 B.R. 587 (Bankr. S.D. Ohio 2001) (court discharged all interest, costs and fees, granted 4-year deferment on payments, and set monthly amount to be paid on principal after deferment); *In re* Kapinos, 253 B.R. 709 (Bankr. W.D. Va. 2000) (discharging accrued interest and future interest for period of five years, at which time debtor may reopen case to seek further discharge relief); *In re* Griffin, 197 B.R. 144 (Bankr. E.D. Okla. 1996) (discharging accrued interest and attorney fees on loans, but not principal); *In re* Heckathorn, 199 B.R. 188 (Bankr. N.D. Okla. 1996) (court found debt nondischargeable but deferred repayment for five years and suspended accrual of interest for three years); *In re* O'Donnell, 189 B.R. 1 (Bankr. D.N.H. 1996); *In re* Mayes, 183 B.R. 261 (Bankr. E.D. Okla. 1995).

51 Courts rejecting partial discharges have done so largely based on a strict construction of section 523(a)(8), that the statutory language does not use the phrase "to the extent" as found in other sections providing for partial discharge. *In re* Taylor, 223 B.R. 747 (B.A.P. 9th Cir. 1998) (no partial discharge allowed). *See also In re* Pincus, 280 B.R. 303 (Bankr. S.D.N.Y. 2001) (no language in § 523(a)(8) permits granting of partial discharge); *In re* Brown, 249 B.R. 525 (Bankr. W.D. Mo. 2000) (court grants full discharge after determining that Bankruptcy Code precludes partial discharge); *In re* Young, 225 B.R. 312 (Bankr. E.D. Pa. 1998); *In re* Skaggs, 196 B.R. 865 (Bankr. W.D. Okla. 1996); *In re* Barrows, 182 B.R. 640 (Bankr. D.N.H. 1994); *In re* Hawkins, 187 B.R. 294 (Bankr. N.D. Iowa 1995).

debtors with limited future earnings potential. The partial discharge should be relevant only to debtors with significant future earnings potential, but with extremely large student loan debt loads, such as $50,000 to $100,000.[52] If repayment of a relatively small student loan will likely be a hardship for the foreseeable future, the debt should be completely discharged to allow the debtor a fresh start.

7.2.3.6 Effect of Income Contingent Repayment Plans

In recent cases, student loan authorities and the Department of Education have argued that courts need not find that repayment will impose an undue hardship on students because the Department's regulations provide for payment relief in the form of Income Contingent Repayment Plans (ICRP).[53] In granting only a partial discharge, one court found that the debtor had an ability to repay some of her student loans because she could enter into an ICRP providing for $56 per month payments for twenty-five years.[54] Other courts have found the availability of ICRPs relevant under the "good faith effort to repay" prong of the *Brunner* test[55] and as a factor under the "totality of the circumstances" test.[56]

While some courts may embrace arguments relating to the availability of these payment plans, the Bankruptcy Code undeniably provides an opportunity for a debtor to obtain an absolute and immediate discharge of student loans if the statutory conditions are met, and no comparable discharge is available under the Department's regulations and administrative collection programs.[57] At least one court has concluded that such payment plans should not present an opportunity for courts to abdicate their obligation to apply the bankruptcy law as written.[58]

In addition, students should present evidence of any obstacles they have faced in attempting to negotiate an affordable plan. An agency's claim of flexible payment arrangements will be undercut by testimony that the agency failed to cooperate with the student and ultimately demanded payments in excess of the student's ability to pay, or where the student was told that affordable payment plans simply do not exist.[59] Even where the debtor intends to argue that an ICRP should not be a substitute for a bankruptcy discharge, the debtor should review available payment options before the discharge hearing[60] and be prepared to present evidence where an ICRP is not feasible, particularly where the accrual of interest will effectively prevent any meaningful repayment of the loan. Since payments must be made under an ICRP if the debtor's income is even slightly above poverty level, the debtor should present evidence that making these payments will prevent the debtor from maintaining a minimal standard of living.

7.2.3.7 Special Rule for HEAL Loans

The limits on dischargeability of Health Education Assistance Loans (HEALs) are more severe than for other student loans. They can be discharged only if the court finds denial of discharge would be "unconscionable," and the student cannot seek a discharge during the first seven years

---

The *Taylor* decision has been effectively overruled by *dicta* in Graves v. Myrvang, 232 F.3d 1116 (9th Cir. 2000), which questioned the *Taylor* holding and applied the *Hornsby* analysis to another dischargeability provision in section 523 relating to child support. *See In re* Saxman (W.D. Wash. 2001) (case remanded for consideration of partial discharge based on *Myrvang's* disapproval of *Taylor* holding).

52 *Cf. In re* Heckathorn, 199 B.R. 188 (Bankr. N.D. Okla. 1996).
53 *See* 20 U.S.C. §§ 1078(m), 1087a; 34 C.F.R. § 685.209(a)(2)(i); and Ch. 8, *infra*.
54 *In re* Chambers, 239 B.R. 767 (Bankr. N.D. Ohio 1999).
55 *See, e.g., In re* Douglass, 237 B.R. 652 (Bankr. N.D. Ohio 1999) (debtor who failed to make any payments on student loans or negotiate an ICRP denied discharge based on lack of good faith effort to repay under *Brunner* test).
56 *In re* Standfuss, 245 B.R. 356 (Bankr. E.D. Mo. 2000) ("flexibility" of ICRP plan considered in determining debtors' ability to repay student loan). *See also In re* Ford, 269 B.R. 673 (B.A.P. 8th Cir. 2001) (availability of ICRP is merely one factor considered in totality of circumstances test and not determinative in case where ICRP would result in 62-year-old woman with arthritic condition carrying large and increasing debt that would not be forgiven until she is 87-years old).
57 If Congress had intended for the ICRP and other payment programs to meet all hardship situations, it would have repealed the hardship provisions in the Bankruptcy Code. In fact, Congress has not eliminated the bankruptcy hardship discharge

despite having made amendments to section 523(a)(8) since the student loan payment programs were enacted.
58 *In re* Kopf, 245 B.R. 731 (Bankr. D. Me. 2000) (no matter how flexible or "humanely executed" such programs may be, they simply are not the equivalent of a discharge). The *Kopf* court noted that even where a debtor's monthly payment obligation is reduced to zero under an ICRP, this will only "postpone repayment indefinitely and, unless interest is abated, permit additional interest accruals." *Id.* at 735. *See also In re* Long, 271 B.R. 322 (B.A.P. 8th Cir.) (bankruptcy court's finding that debtor would not be able to "retire or even reduce" student loan balance under ICRP was not erroneous even if obligation can be discharged after 25 years under ICRP program). An ICRP actually allows the loan balance to increase, with capitalization of some interest, and does not prevent the discharge of a remaining balance after 25 years from being deemed taxable income to the debtor. See generally § 8.2.2.6, *infra* for a discussion of the long-term consequences for borrowers making small payments under an ICRP.
59 *In re* Thomsen, 234 B.R. 506, 514 (Bankr. D. Mont. 1999) (debtor made three separate requests for affordable payment plans but DOE never sent application and instead demanded excessive payments contrary to rule for "satisfactory payment arrangements").
60 *See In re* Chambers, 239 B.R. 767 (Bankr. N.D. Ohio 1999) (debtor admitted on cross-examination that she was unaware of availability of ICRP before filing bankruptcy and that she would have participated in the payment program had she known).

of the loan repayment period.[61] The Sixth Circuit has concluded that the unconscionability standard for HEAL loans is "significantly more stringent" than the undue hardship standard.[62] This standard can be particularly harsh on students who never benefited from the HEAL loans.[63] However, under a plain language reading of 11 U.S.C. § 523(b), HEALs may be more easily dischargeable if the debtor receives a second bankruptcy discharge.[64]

7.3 The Dischargeability Determination

7.3.1 Procedure for Determining Dischargeability of Student Loan

Whether a student loan is discharged based on hardship is not automatically determined in the bankruptcy proceeding. The debtor must affirmatively seek such a determination. If the debtor fails to do so, and a loan holder subsequently attempts to collect on the loan, the loan's dischargeability can be resolved at that later date either by the bankruptcy court or by a state court in a proceeding relating to the note's collection. In general, it is best to resolve the loan's dischargeability in the bankruptcy court while the case is pending.

If there is no dispute about a student loan being dischargeable, it should be relatively easy to resolve this at the time of the bankruptcy. For example, if the loan was clearly over seven years old for cases filed before October 7, 1998, even accounting for all deferments, forbearances, consolidations, and the like, the guaranty agency or the Department will usually admit the loan's dischargeability.[65] A written stipulation of this sort may even make it unnecessary for the bankruptcy court to rule on the issue.

Requests for stipulations are usually fruitless when the student seeks a hardship discharge or where the seven-year period is in doubt. Guaranty agencies are strongly urged by the Department of Education to contest dischargeability.[66]

Schools making Perkins Loans are instructed to oppose dischargeability if they determine that legal costs are not expected to exceed one-third of the amount owed.[67]

Even when the student loan creditor intends to contest the loan's dischargeability, it is usually the best approach to resolve the loan's dischargeability at the time of the bankruptcy filing. The student may do this by bringing an adversary proceeding in the bankruptcy court seeking a declaratory judgment that a particular debt is dischargeable.[68] An "adversary proceeding" is a lawsuit within the bankruptcy case initiated by the filing of an adversary complaint. It is subject to rules almost identical to the Federal Rules of Civil Procedure, including those relating to discovery procedure.[69] For a more detailed discussion of adversary proceedings, see National Consumer Law Center, Consumer Bankruptcy Law and Practice (6th ed. 2000 and Supp.). In addition, sample adversary complaints and related pleadings in student loan cases are provided at Appendix E, *infra* and on the companion CD-Rom.[70]

An adversary proceeding to determine dischargeability of a student loan may be brought at any time and a bankruptcy case that has been closed may be reopened without payment of an additional filing fee in order to obtain a dischargeability determination.[71] Likewise, courts have held that since the denial of a hardship discharge is generally made without prejudice, a student may renew a request for discharge relief where there has been a change in circumstances.[72]

Since there are no time limitations on when the action can be filed, a student may consider reopening a bankruptcy case to seek a hardship discharge where the student's situation

---

61 42 U.S.C. § 294f(g).

62 *In re* Malloy, 155 B.R. 940 (E.D. Va. 1993), *aff'd* 23 F.3d 402 (4th Cir. 1994); *In re* Rice, 78 F.3d 1144, 1149 (6th Cir. 1996) (denial not unconscionable; nondischarge of the loan must be "shockingly unfair, harsh, or unjust"). *See also In re* Ascue, 268 B.R. 739 (Bankr. W.D. Va. 2001) (partial discharge, eliminating $300,000 in interest on National Health Service Corps loan for debtor whose earnings were limited).

63 *In re* Rogers, 250 B.R. 883 (Bankr. S.D. Ohio 2000) (debtor never received health education degree and employed as shipping clerk).

64 *In re* Tanski, 195 B.R. 408 (Bankr. E.D. Wis. 1996).

65 However, some prodding may be required. One or more letters requesting a stipulation that the loan is dischargeable can be followed up with a request for the court to determine the issue if no agreement is forthcoming. In any event, it is important to create a paper trail establishing the dischargeability in order to prevent later disputes.

66 34 C.F.R. § 682.402(f), (g), (h), (i). *See* note 97, *infra*.

67 34 C.F.R. § 674.49(c)(4).

68 *See* Fed. R. Bankr. P. 7001. The student has the burden to prove entitlement to a hardship discharge, though the student loan creditor generally has the initial burden to establish the existence of the debt. *In re* Kopf, 245 B.R. 731 (Bankr. D. Me. 2000); *In re* Green, 238 B.R. 727 (Bankr. N.D. Ohio 1999).

69 *See* Fed. R. Bankr. P. 7001–7087. Under the present fee schedule adopted by the Administrative Office of the federal courts, there is no filing fee for an adversary complaint brought by a debtor in a bankruptcy case.

70 For reasons discussed in § 7.3.3, *infra*, concerning sovereign immunity, in preparing the adversary complaint it is generally advisable to name the director of the student loan agency as a defendant in order to invoke the *Ex parte* Young doctrine.

71 *See* Fed. R. Bankr. P. 4007(b) and 11 U.S.C. § 350(b).

72 *In re* Andrews, 661 F.2d 702 (8th Cir. 1981) (recommending that the denial of a hardship discharge by bankruptcy courts should be made without prejudice to permit the debtor to seek relief under Rule 4007 where there has been a change in circumstances); *In re* Sobh, 61 B.R. 576 (E.D. Mich. 1986) (res judicata does not bar a debtor from filing a new complaint seeking a hardship discharge based on new facts). *But see In re* Kapsin, 265 B.R. 778 (Bankr. N.D. Ohio 2001) (change in circumstances one-and-one-half years later did not constitute "cause" for reopening bankruptcy). The Bankruptcy Code also provides that a student loan that was excepted from discharge in a prior bankruptcy may be discharged in a subsequent bankruptcy case if the debtor can satisfy the undue hardship test. *See* 11 U.S.C. § 523(b).

has taken a turn for the worse after the bankruptcy case is closed.[73] In some situations, a student may also defer filing the adversary proceeding until sometime after the bankruptcy is closed where the student's ability to prove the elements of the hardship test may improve with time.[74] Particularly where the student needs to file bankruptcy for other reasons, but may not be in a position to prove all of the elements of the applicable hardship test, the student should attempt to avoid a premature filing of the hardship adversary proceeding.[75] However, a consolidation loan entered into after the bankruptcy case has been closed may cut off the student's right to seek a hardship discharge of the original loans.[76]

If the student does not obtain a stipulation or court determination of a student loan's dischargeability at the time of the bankruptcy, then the loan's dischargeability is left in limbo—the lack of prosecution of the issue prejudices neither the debtor nor creditor's position. If the loan's dischargeability is not determined, the guaranty agency or Department can be expected to try to collect on the loan through tax intercepts, garnishments, and collection contacts. The student would then have to argue before a collection agency or in an administrative hearing that the debt is not owed because the loan was discharged by the bankruptcy. Such arguments may not go far in such proceedings even where the student can prove the application of the seven-year rule, but certainly will be of no avail where hardship is the basis for discharge.

The better approach is to apply to the bankruptcy court (even after the bankruptcy case has been closed) for a determination that the loan is discharged by the bankruptcy. Then the court determination can be presented to the collector or guarantor.

If the Department or other party is pressing a collection action on the note in state court, the student has two choices. The student can ask the state court judge to rule on the dischargeability of the debt. Alternatively, the student can seek to remove the action to the bankruptcy court for such a determination[77] (or request that the state action be stayed pending the reopening of the bankruptcy case).

7.3.2 Undue Hardship Determination in Chapter 13

Another way to obtain a student loan hardship determination is through the chapter 13 plan confirmation process. Courts are split on whether a provision in a confirmed chapter 13 plan allowing discharge based on undue hardship is enforceable against a student loan creditor based on the *res judicata* effect of a confirmed plan.[78] The key factor is whether an objection to the provision is made prior to or after plan confirmation. If an objection is made before confirmation, courts will generally deny the plan provision on the ground that dischargeability determinations should be made in an adversary proceeding.[79]

In general, there is probably no harm in including a plan provision concerning undue hardship if such a provision can be offered in good faith.[80] If no objection is raised and the plan is confirmed, the existence of the plan provision will constitute an additional ground to establish that the debt is dischargeable. If the court rules otherwise, an adversary proceeding can be filed at that time. In addition, a plan provision seeking to discharge post-petition interest, if it is not objected to and is given preclusive effect,[81] can be an effective way to ensure that a student who has paid a student loan claim in a chapter 13 plan does not emerge from the bankruptcy owing post-petition interest.[82]

Plan provisions should be drafted with care in order to preclude an argument that the plan did not give the creditor

---

73　*In re* Fisher, 223 B.R. 377 (Bankr. M.D. Fla. 1998) (debtor may reopen bankruptcy two years later where debtor's medical condition did not manifest until after case closed).

74　*See In re* Doherty, 219 B.R. 665 (Bankr. W.D.N.Y. 1998) (good faith shown where debtor tried to make payments for year and a half before reopening her case to bring discharge proceeding).

75　*In re* Kraft, 161 B.R. 82 (Bankr. W.D.N.Y. 1993) (hardship complaint filed too early as debtor could not prove good faith under *Brunner* test).

76　*In re* Clarke, 266 B.R. 301 (Bankr. E.D. Pa. 2001) (consolidation loan extinguishes original student loans).

77　28 U.S.C. § 1452; Fed. R. Bankr. P. 9027.

78　Great Lakes Higher Education Corp. v. Pardee (*In re* Pardee), 193 F.3d 1083 (9th Cir. 1999) (confirmation of chapter 13 plan providing that post-petition interest on student loan would be discharged bound the creditor); *In re* Andresen, 179 F.3d 1253 (10th Cir. 1998) (court found that confirmation of chapter 13 plan including a provision of undue hardship bound the creditor). *But see* Banks v. Sallie Mae Servicing Corp. (*In re* Banks), 2002 WL 1790145 (4th Cir. Aug. 5, 2002) (confirmed plan providing for discharge of post-petition interest violated student loan creditor's due process rights where creditor not served with adversary complaint and summons and therefore plan not given preclusive effect); *In re* Key, 128 B.R. 742 (Bankr. S.D. Ohio 1991) (plan provision cannot render claim dischargeable).

79　Kielisch v. Educational Credit Management Corp. (*In re* Kielisch), 258 F.3d 315 (4th Cir. 2001) (plan provision providing for non-accrual of post-petition interest not effective where debtor has not brought adversary proceeding to obtain hardship discharge); *In re* Webber, 251 B.R. 554 (Bankr. D. Ariz. 2000); *In re* Mammell, 221 B.R. 238 (Bankr. N.D. Iowa 1998).

80　Bad faith provisions may run afoul of 11 U.S.C. § 1325(c). Some courts have even sanctioned counsel for including such provisions. *See, e.g., In re* Evans, 242 B.R. 407 (Bankr. S.D. Ohio 1999).

81　*In re* Pardee, 193 F.3d 1083 (9th Cir. 1999); *In re* York, 250 B.R. 842 (Bankr. D. Del. 2000) (res judicata prevents student loan creditor from objecting to plan provision providing for discharge of post-petition interest).

82　*See* note 115, *infra*.

adequate notice of dischargeability.[83] Once the plan is filed, it should be served on the affected creditor to avoid the lack of notice argument.[84]

If the student does not seek a hardship determination as part of the initial chapter 13 confirmation process, the nondischargeability issue may be raised at any time during the three- to five-year period of the plan,[85] and similar timing considerations apply as discussed previously.[86] However, some courts have required that the student wait until the end of the chapter 13 plan before seeking a hardship discharge.[87]

7.3.3 Discharge of Student Loans Owed to State Agencies

Since the Supreme Court decision in *Seminole Tribe v. Florida*, state agencies collecting student loan debts have been aggressively asserting Eleventh Amendment immunity (sovereign immunity) as a way of barring debtors from discharging student loans in bankruptcy.[88]

The issue of sovereign immunity arises because debtors must affirmatively seek student loan discharges through an adversary proceeding. This proceeding, if characterized as a private suit in federal court against the state, may be barred by the Eleventh Amendment. The doctrine of sovereign immunity acts as a jurisdictional bar to suits filed by private individuals against unconsenting states.[89]

There are three exceptions to sovereign immunity that the courts rely on:

(1) Pursuant to the *Ex Parte Young* doctrine, suits against state officials in their individual capacities seeking prospective declaratory or injunctive relief for ongoing violations of federal law are not barred.[90] A number of bankruptcy courts have dismissed discharge actions against state agencies on sovereign immunity grounds subject to the debtor's possible use of the *Young* doctrine in bringing an action against a state official.[91]

However, some courts have begun to crack down on a perceived overuse of the *Young* doctrine.[92] These courts have found the doctrine inapplicable based on the premise that no ongoing violation of federal law can be asserted until the debtor has first prevailed in an affirmative action establishing dischargeability.[93] At least one court has recognized this Catch-22 trap that debtors first need a ruling on a discharge in order to assert improper collection, but that they cannot get this ruling if they are not allowed to sue the state.[94]

(2) The second exception to sovereign immunity is that Congress may abrogate it by unequivocally expressing an intent to do so and acting pursuant to a valid exercise of power.[95] While courts are in general agreement that Congress clearly intended to abrogate immunity through section 106(a) of the Bankruptcy Code, they are divided on whether this provision is valid.[96]

---

83 *See In re* Andresen, 215 B.R. 792 (B.A.P. 10th Cir. 1998), *aff'd*, 179 F.3d 1253 (10th Cir. 1999) for a good model plan provision. *Cf. In re* Loving, 269 B.R. 655 (Bankr. S.D. Ind. 2001) (no preclusive effect given where debtor's plan did not explicitly provide for discharge of student loans upon completion of plan payments).

84 Advocates may take note that the Fourth Circuit has held that although the mailing of a proposed plan, confirmation order and hearing notice satisfies the notice requirements of Bankruptcy Rule 2002, it is not sufficient to protect a student loan creditor's due process rights; a plan seeking discharge of interest requires the filing of an adversary complaint and service of process under Bankruptcy Rule 7004. Banks v. Sallie Mae Servicing Corp. (*In re* Banks), 2002 WL 1790145 (4th Cir. Aug. 5, 2002).

85 *In re* Ekenasi, 271 B.R. 256 (S.D. W. Va. 2002) (debtor need not wait until end of chapter 13 plan to bring dischargeability proceeding).

86 *See* § 7.3.1, *supra*.

87 *See, e.g., In re* Raisor, 180 B.R. 163 (Bankr. E.D. Tex. 1995).

88 Seminole Tribe v. Florida, 517 U.S. 44 (1996). *See generally* Patricia L. Barsalou & Scott A. Stengel, *Ex Parte Young: Relativity in Practice*, 72 Am. Bankr. L.J. 455 (1998); National Consumer Law Center, Consumer Bankruptcy Law and Practice § 13.3.2.2 (6th ed. 2000 and Supp.).

89 For a good summary of the doctrine in student loan case, see *In re* Greenwood, 237 B.R. 128 (N.D. Tex. 1999) (upholding state agency's sovereign immunity claim). For other cases where sovereign immunity was affirmed, *see, e.g.*, Murphy v. Michigan Guaranty Agency (*In re* Murphy), 271 F.3d 629 (5th Cir. 2001) (adversary proceeding seeking student loan discharge was "suit" against the state barred by Eleventh Amendment); *In re*

Kahl, 240 B.R. 524 (Bankr. E.D. Pa. 1999); *In re* Stout, 231 B.R. 313 (Bankr. W.D. Mo. 1999); *In re* Schmitt, 220 B.R. 68 (Bankr. W.D. Mo. 1998).

90 *Ex Parte* Young, 209 U.S. 123 (1908) (allowing federal court suit against state official acting *ultra vires* to proceed). *See also* Coeur d'Alene Tribe of Idaho, 521 U.S. 261 (1997).

91 *In re* Kahl, 240 B.R. 524 (Bankr. E.D. Pa. 1999) (case dismissed without prejudice to afford debtor opportunity to invoke the *Young* doctrine if relevant); *In re* Schmitt, 220 B.R. 68 (Bankr. W.D. Mo. 1998); *In re* Morrell, 218 B.R. 87 (Bankr. C.D. Cal. 1998) (granting debtors leave to amend in state franchise tax case to invoke *Young*).

92 *See, e.g., In re* Stout, 231 B.R. 313 (Bankr. W.D. Mo. 1999) (*Young* doctrine does not give blanket authorization for suits against state officials to obtain injunctive relief).

93 *In re* Holland, 230 B.R. 387 (Bankr. W.D. Mo. 1999); *In re* Perkins, 228 B.R. 431 (Bankr. E.D. Mo. 1998).

94 *In re* Stout, 231 B.R. 313, 317 (Bankr. W.D. Mo. 1999) ("Unfortunately, perhaps all the debtors can do is wait until the state seeks to collect the student loan balances and then seek relief in the state courts, thereby prolonging for months and perhaps years the uncertainty of whether they will have to pay the debts owed. Or, alternatively, the debtor may initiate a discharge action in the state courts, which have concurrent jurisdiction to determine such issues, though at some substantial additional expense and delay. Neither alternative is appealing.").

95 For a good discussion of this exception, see *In re* Innes, 184 F.2d 1275 (10th Cir. 1999) (case decided on waiver grounds).

96 *See In re* Sacred Heart Hospital of Norristown, 133 F.3d 237 (3d Cir. 1997) (section 106 not valid abrogation); *In re* Estate of Fernandez, 123 F.3d 241 (5th Cir. 1997) (section 106(a) violates the 11th Amendment and therefore unconstitutional); *In re*

(3) The third exception is that states may waive Eleventh Amendment immunity and therefore consent to suit in federal courts. For example, participation in the federal loan program may act as a waiver of the state's Eleventh Amendment immunity in bankruptcy or other federal proceedings.[97] Mere participation, however, is generally insufficient to waive sovereign immunity without some indication of affirmative assent to suit such as the state's filing of a proof of claim in bankruptcy.[98]

In an apparent response to court decisions where waiver has been found, the Department of Education amended the applicable regulations to make it less likely there will be a waiver by agreement.[99] Though not explicitly referencing sovereign immunity, these changes permit institutions or guaranty agencies to assert an Eleventh Amendment defense where appropriate.

Nevertheless, these amendments are confined to the specific regulations dealing with dischargeability determinations. The regulations governing Perkins Loans continue to require that participating colleges file a proof of claim upon notice that a borrower has filed bankruptcy (unless it is a no asset chapter 7).[100] The filing of a proof of claim by a college or guaranty agency can itself be a waiver of sovereign immunity.[101]

In addition, the amended regulations may still be used to support a waiver argument based on the conduct of the college or guaranty agency during the dischargeability litigation. Where the college or guaranty agency initially participates in the adversary proceeding without asserting the immunity defense, the student may argue that the college or guaranty agency must have determined that the discharge would be "more effectively opposed" by addressing the merits of the action.[102] This should bolster the debtor's argument that any subsequent assertion of the immunity defense, particularly when raised for the first time on the eve of trial or on appeal,[103] has been waived.[104]

Another issue that may arise in these cases is the threshold question of whether the state actor collecting the loan is truly an "arm of the state."[105] If not, the state actor should not be entitled to assert sovereign immunity.

Most circuit courts have established a multi-prong test to determine whether an agency is an "arm of the state."[106]

Creative Goldsmiths, 119 F.3d 1140 (4th Cir. 1997) *cert. denied*, 523 U.S. 1075 (1998); *Cf.* Wilson v. South Carolina State Educ. Assist. Auth., 2001 Bankr. LEXIS 57 (Bankr. S.D. Ga. 2001) (section 108 valid abrogation as enacted pursuant to privileges and immunities clause of the Fourteenth Amendment); *In re* Nelson, 254 B.R. 436 (Bankr. W.D. Wis. 2000); Lees v. Tennessee Student Assist. Corp., 252 B.R. 441 (W.D. Tenn. 2000), *aff'd on other grounds*, 264 B.R. 884 (W.D. Tenn. 2001). A few courts have held that the issue of whether immunity had been waived or abrogated need not be considered in regard to dischargeability proceedings because the states, in ratifying the Constitution, ceded their sovereignty over discharge matters to Congress. *In re* Hood, 262 B.R. 412 (B.A.P. 6th Cir. 2001) (student loan authority not immune from dischargeability proceeding); *In re* Bleimeister, 251 B.R. 383 (Bankr. D. Ariz. 2000), *aff'd on other grounds*, 2002 WL 1586907 (9th Cir. June 12, 2002).

97 *See In re* Innes, 184 F.2d 1275 (10th Cir. 1999) *cert. denied*, 120 S. Ct. 1530 (2000); *In re* Rose, 187 F.3d 926 (8th Cir. 1999); *In re* Huffine, 246 B.R. 405 (Bankr. E.D. Wash. 2000) (waiver found based on a review of Perkins loan program as a whole, including the statute, the participation contract and the governing regulations). *But see In re* Janc, 251 B.R. 525 (Bankr. W.D. Mo. 2000) (state guaranty agency did not waive sovereign immunity by participating in student loan program).

98 *See generally* College Sav. Bank v. Florida Prepaid Postsecondary Educ. Expense Bd., 527 U.S. 666 (1999) (rejecting doctrine of "constructive waiver"); Atascadero v. Scanlon, 473 U.S. 234 (1985). *See also In re* Innes, 184 F.2d 1275 (10th Cir. 1999); *In re* Rose, 187 F.3d 926 (8th Cir. 1999); *In re* Phelps, 237 B.R. 527 (Bankr. D.R.I. 1999) (waiver found where among other actions, creditor acknowledged it was a party to discharge proceeding and only raised immunity issue after unfavorable decision on hardship).

99 In both the Perkins and FFEL regulations, DOE added the following language, effective July 1, 2000, to the sections requiring a response to a borrower's request for a hardship discharge: "The [institution or guaranty agency] must use due diligence and may assert any defense consistent with its status under applicable law to avoid discharge of the loan." *See* 34 C.F.R. § 682.402(i)(1)(iv) and § 674.49(c)(1). In addition, a general qualification was added providing that an institution or guaranty agency must follow the specific procedures in the regulation "unless discharge would be more effectively opposed by avoiding that action."

100 34 C.F.R. § 674.49(b). The Department of Education has issued a proposed rule under the FFEL program, amending 34 C.F.R. § 682.402, that would provide that a guaranty agency that is a state agency and does not assign to other guaranty agencies loans affected by bankruptcy filings is not required to file a proof of claim, and may instruct lenders not to file proof of claims on loans it has guaranteed. *See* 67 Fed. Reg. 151 (Aug. 6, 2002).

101 *See* Gardner v. New Jersey, 329 U.S. 565 (1947); Rose v. Dep't of Educ., 187 F.3d 926 (8th Cir. 1999); *In re* Straight, 143 F.3d 1387 (10th Cir. 1998); Georgia Dept. of Revenue v. Burke, 146 F.3d 1313 (11th Cir. 1998), *cert. denied*, 119 S. Ct. 2410 (1999); *In re* Stanley, 273 B.R. 907 (Bankr. N.D. Fla. 2002) (state guaranty agency that waived sovereign immunity by filing proof of claim could not reinstate immunity defense by later withdrawing claim).

102 *See*, note 99, *supra.*

103 While sovereign immunity may be raised for the first time on appeal, it is not an ordinary limitation on subject matter jurisdiction, federal courts are not required to *sua sponte* consider a possible immunity defense. Wisconsin Dep't of Corrections v. Schacht, 118 S. Ct. 2047, 2053 (1998); Toll v. Moreno, 458 U.S. 1, 17–19 (1982), *see also* Parella v. R.I. Employee's Retirement Board, 173 F.3d 47, 55 (1st Cir. 1999).

104 Phelps v. Sallie Mae, 237 B.R. 527 (Bankr. D. R.I. 1999) (guaranty agency waived immunity defense through its actions during the adversary proceeding); *see also* Commonwealth of Virginia v. Collins (*In re* Collins), 173 F.3d 924 (4th Cir. 1999).

105 *See* Lake County Estates, Inc. v. Tahoe Regional Planning Agency, 440 U.S. 391 (1979).

106 *See, e.g.,* Duke v. Grady Municipal Schools, 127 F.3d 972 (10th Cir. 1997); Mancuso v. New York State Thruway Authority, 86 F.3d 289 (2d Cir. 1996); Hadley v. North Ark. Community Technical College, 76 F.3d 1437 (8th Cir. 1996); Christy v.

The foremost factor under these tests is whether the state will be financially burdened by the action in question.[107] This should be a strong argument in the student loan context where states are usually not responsible for guaranty agencies' financial obligations[108] because such entities typically have a legal existence distinct from the state.[109] Moreover, based on their contractual arrangement with the Department of Education, guaranty agencies are reimbursed by the federal government for most of the indebtedness on discharged loans.[110] One court has applied the various factors of the "arm of the state" test to a student loan authority and found that it was not entitled to claim sovereign immunity.[111]

7.3.4 Use of Older Dischargeability Standards Today Where Student's Pre-1998 Bankruptcy Did Not Determine Student Loan's Dischargeability

Unless the student or another party seeks a determination in the bankruptcy proceeding concerning a student loan's dischargeability, the loan's dischargeability will *not* be determined in a bankruptcy proceeding—the loan is neither ruled discharged nor enforceable. Instead, whether the loan has been discharged by the bankruptcy will not be determined until a later date, perhaps many years later, when a guarantor or the Department seeks to collect on that debt in court or when the student seeks a judicial determination of the loan's enforceability.

When a student loan's dischargeability is determined after the bankruptcy proceeding, the test will be whether the loan was dischargeable based on the Bankruptcy Code in effect at the time of the bankruptcy case, not at the time the loan's dischargeability is determined. This distinction may have a significant impact on whether the debt is dischargeable.

For example, the dischargeability exception for bankruptcies filed before November 1990, was that student loans more than *five* years old were dischargeable in chapter 7 bankruptcies (compared to the subsequent seven-year standard). Also, a chapter 13 discharge operated to discharge a student loan obligation, even one less than five years old (compared to the present where dischargeability is treated the same for chapter 13 and 7 cases).[112]

Thus, where a loan was first due in 1983, and the loan's dischargeability was not determined in a chapter 7 bankruptcy filed in 1989, a court today should determine that the loan was discharged by that bankruptcy.[113] While the loan is not dischargeable under the present seven-year test, it is dischargeable under the five-year test in place at that time. Likewise, a loan that first became due in 1990 was discharged in a bankruptcy filed in 1998 (before October 7, 1998) under the seven-year rule.

7.4 Advantages of a Chapter 13 Bankruptcy Where Student Loan Cannot Be Discharged

7.4.1 Separate Classification

If a student loan cannot be discharged based on undue hardship in a chapter 7 or 13 bankruptcy filing, there are still

---

Pennsylvania Turnpike Comm'n, 54 F.3d 1140 (3d Cir. 1995); Harter v. C.D. Vernon, 101 F.3d 334 (4th Cir. 1996); Metcalf & Eddy v. P.R. Aqueduct & Sewer Auth., 991 F.2d 935 (1st. Cir. 1993). For a more detailed discussion of this topic, see NCLC REPORTS, 19 Bankruptcy and Foreclosures Ed. (Nov/Dec. 2000).

107 *See* Metcalf & Eddy v. P.R. Aqueduct & Sewer Auth., 991 F.2d 935 (1st Cir. 1993).

108 The enabling statutes of guaranty agencies often provide that their bonds and loan guaranties are not an obligation of the state. *See, e.g.,* Iowa Code § 261.38; Mich. Comp. Laws § 390.1154; N.J. Stat. § 18A:71A-18 (same for New Jersey Higher Education Student Assistance Authority); N.C. Gen. Stat. § 116-202; 24 Pa. Cons. Stat. § 5105.1(b) (bonds and notes of Pennsylvania Higher Education Assistance Authority not debt of Pennsylvania); R.I. Gen. Laws § 16-57-12.

109 *See In re* Muir, 239 B.R. 213 (Bankr. D. Mont. 1999) (student loan guaranty agency failed to satisfy burden of demonstrating that it was an arm of the state and entitled to 11th Amendment immunity). *But see In re* Kahl, 240 B.R. 524 (Bankr. E.D. Pa. 1999) (finding Texas agency to be an arm of the state, but no waiver of sovereign immunity). *See generally* Duke v. Grady Municipal Schools, 127 F.3d 972 (10th Cir. 1997) (court must focus on legal liability for a judgment rather than practical or indirect impact a judgment would have on a state's treasury); Metcalf & Eddy v. P.R. Aqueduct & Sewer Auth., 991 F.2d 935 (1st Cir. 1993) (rejecting among other arguments the state agency's claim that it could claim immunity solely on the basis that judgments against it might absorb unrestricted funds donated by the state and in that way lead indirectly to the depletion of the state's treasury).

110 *See* 10 U.S.C. § 1087(b).

111 Lees v. Tennessee Student Assist. Corp., 264 B.R. 884 (W.D. Tenn. 2001).

112 Section 1328(a)(2) of the Bankruptcy Code was amended by Pub. L. No. 101-508, § 3007 (Nov. 5, 1990).

113 Similarly, between November 6, 1978 and August 14, 1979, there was no statutory restriction in place on the dischargeability of student loans. Thus students can argue today that any student loan listed as a debt in a bankruptcy during that period is discharged, no matter how recently the debt was first due before the bankruptcy proceeding. 20 U.S.C. § 1087-3, dealing with the discharge of student loans in bankruptcy, was repealed by the Bankruptcy Reform Act, Pub. L. No. 95-598 § 317 (1978). It was replaced as to cases filed on and after August 14, 1979 by the United States Bankruptcy Code. *See* S. Rep. No. 230, 96th Cong., 1st Sess. (1979) *reprinted in* 1979 U.S.C.C.A.N. 936, 938. *But see* Adamo v. New York State Higher Education Services Corp. (*In re Adamo*), 619 F.2d 216 (2d Cir. 1980), *cert. denied*, 449 U.S. 843 (1980).

strategic advantages to filing a chapter 13 bankruptcy.[114] One advantage is that the student's chapter 13 plan, not the loan holder, determines the size of a student's loan payments. For the three- to five-year life of the chapter 13 plan, the plan will determine how much the student pays each unsecured creditor, including student loan creditors.

For many plans, this would mean that only five or ten percent of the outstanding loan would be paid off over those three to five years. At the end of the plan, the student could seek a determination that repayment of the balance would cause an undue hardship. During the three- to five-year pendency of the plan, no collection action, garnishment, or tax intercepts can be taken against the student, though interest on the debt will continue to accrue.[115]

Nevertheless, if the remainder of the debt is not dischargeable after the plan has terminated, the student is then obligated to pay the remainder. When that is the case, it is in the student's interest to pay off as much of the student loan in the chapter 13 plan as possible, at the expense of other unsecured creditors—creditors whose remaining balance *will* be dischargeable after the plan is completed.

One way to pay more on the student loan than on other unsecured debts is to classify separately the student loan for payments at a higher percentage than other unsecured debts pursuant to 11 U.S.C. § 1322(b)(1). Recent cases have been divided, both in the means of analysis and the result, as to whether students can separately classify student loans; some allowing separate classification,[116] and some

not.[117] Some courts have even issued opinions providing guidance as to the amount of discrimination that will be allowed.[118]

A useful alternative to separate classification, in those jurisdictions where separate classification has not been approved, is to cure a default on the student loan pursuant to 11 U.S.C. § 1322(b)(5).[119] This allows the debtor to cure an arrearage on the student loan over time while maintaining the postpetition payments during the life of the plan. A number of courts have already permitted debtors to make ongoing student loan payments from income on this basis outside the plan.[120] An added benefit of this approach is that the ongoing payments will include postpetition interest that would not otherwise be paid as part of a claim under the plan.[121] By failing to give effect to section 1322(b)(5) as a

---

114 For more details, see National Consumer Law Center, Consumer Bankruptcy Law and Practice § 14.4.3.8.4 (6th ed. 2000 and Supp.).

115 If the student loan debt is nondischargeable, postpetition interest will not be discharged. *See* Kielisch v. Educational Credit Management Corp. (*In re* Kielisch), 258 F.3d 315 (4th Cir. 2001); *In re* Pardee, 218 B.R. 916 (B.A.P. 9th Cir. 1998), *aff'd*, 187 F.3d 548 (9th Cir. 1999); *In re* Jordan, 146 B.R. 31 (D. Colo. 1992). In addition, section 502(b)(2) of the Code provides that general unsecured creditors such as student loan creditors may not include unmatured, post-petition interest in their bankruptcy claims. Leeper v. Pennsylvania Higher Education Assistance Agency, 49 F.3d 98 (3d Cir. 1995) (interest accruing during pendency of plan not discharged, even though debtor paid prepetition debt in full through chapter 13 plan). One court has held that while unmatured, post-petition interest may not be included in the student loan creditor's claim, section 502(b) does not prevent the creditor from applying chapter 13 plan payments to accrued interest, including post-petition interest, on the nondischargeable debt. Kielisch v. Educational Management Corp. (*In re* Kielisch), 258 F.3d 315 (4th Cir. 2001).

116 *In re* Cox, 186 B.R. 744 (Bankr. N.D. Fla. 1995); *In re* Brown, 152 B.R. 232 (Bankr. N.D. Ill. 1993); *In re* Tucker, 159 B.R. 325 (Bankr. D. Mont. 1993); Matter of Foreman, 136 B.R. 532 (Bankr. S.D. Iowa 1992); *In re* Boggan, 125 B.R. 533 (Bankr. N.D. Ill. 1991); *In re* Freshley, 69 B.R. 96 (Bankr. N.D. Ga. 1987); *see also In re* Dodds, 140 B.R. 542 (Bankr. D. Mont. 1992); *In re* Sullivan, 195 B.R. 649 (Bankr. W.D. Tex. 1996).
     On the analogous question of whether nondischargeable child support debts may be separately classified, many courts have concluded in the affirmative. *E.g., In re* Leser, 939 F.2d 669 (8th

Cir. 1991); *In re* Whittaker, 113 B.R. 531 (D. Minn. 1990) (allowing a fresh start is sufficient to justify discriminatory classification in favor of nondischargeable support debt); *In re* Husted, 142 B.R. 72 (Bankr. W.D.N.Y. 1992).

117 *In re* Groves, 39 F.3d 212 (8th Cir. 1994) (plan could not discriminate in favor of student loans solely due to their nondischargeability); *In re* Bentley, 266 B.R. 229 (B.A.P. 1st Cir. 2001) (chapter 13 plan that favored student loan creditor failed unfair discrimination test by altering the "allocation of benefits and burdens" to detriment of other unsecured creditors); *In re* Sperna, 173 B.R. 654 (B.A.P. 9th Cir. 1994) (plan could not discriminate in favor of student loans solely due to their nondischargeability); *In re* Thibodeau, 248 B.R. 699 (Bankr. D. Mass. 2000) (plan was not proposed in non-discriminatory manner based on debtor's sizeable income and lack of good faith); *In re* Burns, 216 B.R. 945 (Bankr. S.D. Cal. 1998); *In re* Gonzalez, 206 B.R. 239 (Bankr. S.D. Fla. 1997); *In re* Coonce, 213 B.R. 344 (Bankr. S.D. Ill. 1997); *In re* Willis, 189 B.R. 203 (N.D. Okla. 1995), *rev'd and remanded*, 197 B.R. 912 (N.D. Okla. 1996); McCullough v. Brown, 162 B.R. 506 (N.D. Ill. 1994); *In re* Colfer, 159 B.R. 602 (Bankr. D. Me. 1993) (refusing to allow separate classification); *In re* Smalberger, 157 B.R. 472 (Bankr. D. Or. 1993); *In re* Chapman, 146 B.R. 411 (Bankr. N.D. Ill. 1992); *In re* Scheiber, 129 B.R. 604 (Bankr. D. Minn. 1991); *In re* Furlow, 70 B.R. 973 (Bankr. E.D. Pa. 1987) (separate classification of student loan debt not allowed without further explanation of reasons).

118 *In re* Williams, 253 B.R. 220 (Bankr. W.D. Tenn. 2000) (plan that provides for 100% repayment of student loan will be confirmed only if other unsecured creditors are paid at least 70%; debtors may show "unique circumstances" to justify confirmation of plans with more than 30% difference in repayment percentage).

119 Section 1322(b)(5) permits the curing of defaults under the plan and maintenance of ongoing payments, typically made outside the plan, on any secured or unsecured claims where the last payment on the debt is due after the final payment under the plan.

120 *See In re* Williams, 253 B.R. 220 (Bankr. W.D. Tenn. 2000); *In re* Chandler, 210 B.R. 898 (Bankr. D.N.H. 1997); *In re* Sullivan, 195 B.R. 649 (Bankr. W.D. Tex. 1996); *In re* Cox, 186 B.R. 744 (Bankr. N.D. Fla. 1995); *In re* Christophe, 151 B.R. 475 (Bankr. N.D. Ill. 1993) (plan can propose cure of student loan default pursuant to § 1322(b)(5)); *In re* Benner, 156 B.R. 631 (Bankr. D. Minn. 1993); *In re* Saulter, 133 B.R. 148 (Bankr. W.D. Mo. 1991).

121 *See*, note 115, *supra. In re* Williams, 253 B.R. 220 (Bankr. W.D. Tenn. 2000) (maintenance of ongoing payments on student

distinct plan provision, some courts have required debtors proposing to pay student loans outside the plan to satisfy the unfair discrimination test under section 1322(b)(1).[122]

A final approach might be to establish a five-year plan, not separately classify the student loan for the first three years of the plan, but then to classify it for greater payment during the plan's final two years.[123] The basis for this approach is the Bankruptcy Code provision that requires disposable income only to be paid out over three years.[124] Any amount that creditors receive in the final two years would be a bonus in any event. Courts have split on whether they will allow this separate classification of student loans in years four and five of a chapter 13 plan.[125]

7.4.2 Codebtor Stay

Another advantage of chapter 13 is that there is an additional type of "automatic stay" that goes into effect when the case is filed. This stay prohibits any act or legal action to collect a consumer debt of the debtor from a codebtor or coobligor.[126] Students who file under chapter 13 can thus protect from collection parents or other family members who may have cosigned a student loan as long as the student's plan provides for payment of the student loan.[127] In addition, the need to retain the codebtor stay may provide an additional justification for the separate classification of a student loan in a chapter 13 plan.[128]

7.4.3 Raising Defenses in Response to Creditor Claims

The chapter 13 claim allowance process may also present an opportunity for consumers to raise defenses to a student loan obligation. In addition to the various grounds for objections to creditors' claims that may be raised under the Bankruptcy Code,[129] no claim may be allowed to the extent that it is unenforceable against the debtor.[130] This means that the student may assert as objections any defenses, counter-claims or setoffs the debtor may have, including for instance defenses relating to the school's misconduct.[131] The objection will generally be treated by the bankruptcy court as a "contested matter."[132]

For students who are confronted with unlawful or excessive interest and collection fees, or the miscrediting of payments by loan servicers, this process also provides an opportunity for the student to challenge the amount owed on the student loan. A student loan creditor is bound by a determination disallowing collection costs as part of its claim in bankruptcy regardless of whether the student loan debt is nondischargeable. Student loan creditors may be denied collection costs and fees as part of their claims where no entitlement exists under the relevant regulations or contract provisions.[133]

7.5 Student's Rights After Bankruptcy Discharge

If there has been a judicial determination that a student loan is discharged in bankruptcy, the consumer is no longer liable for the obligation, and is protected from any attempt to collect the debt.[134] The lender should not accept any further payments on the loan, such as payments the lender may receive through a tax intercept program, or even those voluntarily made by the debtor. Department of Education regulations provide that if a guaranty agency receives payments on a discharged loan on which the Department previously paid a claim to the agency, the agency must return

---

loans under section 1322(b)(5) includes the payment of post-petition interest).

122 *In re* Labib-Kiyarash, 271 B.R. 189 (B.A.P. 9th Cir. 2001) (use of § 1322(b)(5) subject to debtor showing that classification if fair under § 1322(b)(1)); *In re* Edwards, 263 B.R. 690 (Bankr. R.I. 2001); *In re* Thibodeau, 248 B.R. 699 (Bankr. D. Mass. 2000).

123 *In re* Strickland, 181 B.R. 598 (Bankr. N.D. Ala. 1995) (court held nondischargeable student loan debt could not be treated more favorably than other unsecured claims for first 36 months of chapter 13 plan, but remaining 24 months could be devoted solely to payment of student loan).

124 11 U.S.C. § 1325(b)(1)(B).

125 *Compare In re* Stickland, 181 B.R. 598 (Bankr. N.D. Ala. 1995) (allowing separate treatment in years four and five); *In re* Rudy, 1993 WL 365370 (Bankr. S.D. Ohio 1993) (same) *with In re* Sullivan, 195 B.R. 649 (Bankr. W.D. Tex. 1996) (not allowing separate classification).

126 *See* 11 U.S.C. § 1301. For a more detailed discussion of the codebtor stay in chapter 13, *see* National Consumer Law Center, Consumer Bankruptcy Law and Practice § 9.4.4 (6th ed. 2000 and Supp.).

127 The Department of Education regulations acknowledge the chapter 13 codebtor stay by noting that guaranty agencies must suspend all collection efforts against a "co-maker or endorser" if the student borrower has filed under chapter 13. *See* 34 C.F.R. § 682.402(f)(2).

128 11 U.S.C. 1322(b)(1). *See* § 7.4.1, *supra*.

129 For a detailed discussion of objections to claims, *see* National Consumer Law Center, Consumer Bankruptcy Law and Practice § 13.4.3 (6th ed. 2000 and Supp.).

130 11 U.S.C. § 502(b)(1).

131 *See generally* Ch. 9, *infra*.

132 Such proceedings are governed by Fed. R. Bankr. P. 9014.

133 *In re* McAlpin, 254 B.R. 449 (Bankr. D. Minn. 2000), *rev'd on other grounds*, 263 B.R. 881 (B.A.P. 8th Cir. 2001), *aff'd* 278 F.3d 866 (8th Cir. 2002) (collection costs and fees disallowed, based on 34 C.F.R. § 674.45(e) *et seq.*, where creditor failed to prove they were reasonable and limited to actual or average cost incurred).

134 11 U.S.C. § 524(a)(2). Damages and attorney fees are available if improper collection activities occur. *See* National Consumer Law Center, Consumer Bankruptcy Law and Practice § 14.5.5.6 (6th ed. 2000 and Supp.).

the payments to the sender and notify the borrower that there is no obligation to pay the loan.[135]

Similarly, a school cannot withhold a former student's transcripts just because the debt has been discharged in bankruptcy.[136] The 1994 amendments to the Bankruptcy Code clarified this principle, prohibiting discrimination with respect to student loans or grants based upon discharge of a prior debt. Prior to this time, courts had split on whether schools could deny transcripts after discharge and also on whether schools could deny transcripts to students who filed for bankruptcy but had not yet received a discharge.[137] Some courts have continued to allow denial of transcripts in the latter situation where a debtor filed bankruptcy but has not yet been granted a discharge. The debtor's response in this situation should be that as soon as a bankruptcy is filed, acts such as withholding of transcripts are prohibited by the automatic stay.[138]

While the Department of Education in the early 1990s stated that students who discharged student loans in bankruptcy would not be eligible for new student loans,[139] the question of a student's eligibility for new loans and grants after discharging a student loan in bankruptcy has now been resolved by Congressional action. The Bankruptcy Reform Act of 1994 specifies that those discharging student loans in bankruptcy remain eligible for new loans and grants. The United States, guarantors, and lenders cannot discriminate against those who have not paid their student loans where those loans were discharged in bankruptcy.[140]

The Act's legislative history states that the "section clarifies the anti-discrimination provisions of the Bankruptcy Code to ensure that applicants for student loans or grants are not denied those benefits due to a prior bankruptcy. The section overrules *In re Goldrich*. . . ."[141]

The Department responded by changing its regulations so that students no longer have to reaffirm student loans discharged in bankruptcy to be eligible for new loans or grants. The Department states that such a reaffirmation requirement is no longer permissible because the Bankruptcy Reform Act prohibits denial of a loan or loan guarantee based on a bankruptcy discharge.[142] Consequently, the offending language has been deleted from the regulations.[143]

Nevertheless, the Department will look to a prior bankruptcy in considering an applicant's future creditworthiness in applying for PLUS Loans. A PLUS Loan is a specialized type of loan taken out by parents of the student, where, by statute, the Department is required to consider the parent(s)' creditworthiness. Thus applicants for PLUS Loans will be required to explain the bankruptcy or secure a credit-worthy endorser.

---

135 34 C.F.R. § 682.402(r)(1).

136 *Id. See also* National Consumer Law Center, Consumer Bankruptcy Law and Practice § 14.5.5.2 (6th ed. 2000 and Supp.).

137 *In re* Merchant, 958 F.2d 738 (6th Cir. 1992); Juras v. Aman Collection, 829 F.2d 739 (9th Cir. 1987), *cert. denied*, 488 U.S. 875, 977 (1988) (institutions cannot withhold transcripts from students who have had their loans discharged, who are making payments under chapter 13 plan, or who have filed for bankruptcy but not yet received a discharge); *In re* Gustafson, 111 B.R. 282 (B.A.P. 9th Cir. 1990); *In re* Carson, 150 B.R. 228 (Bankr. E.D. Mo. 1993) (protections of the automatic stay override creditor's ability to collect student loan debt until such time as debt is determined to be nondischargeable. Therefore, no withholding of transcripts until debt is found to be nondischargeable). *But see In re* Joyner, 171 B.R. 759 (Bankr. E.D. Pa. 1994); *In re* Najafi, 154 B.R. 185 (Bankr. E.D. Pa. 1993) (rejecting *Gustafson*, reasoning that it is unfair to the creditor if students can get transcripts up until the moment the debt is found to be nondischargeable. Court found that the college had a right comparable to a "security interest" in the transcript). Both the *Najafi* and *Joyner* courts ordered the colleges to release transcripts upon payment of $300 in each case by the students to the colleges. Both cases involved private colleges and in both cases, the student debts were found nondischargeable. *See generally* Ramares, *Annotation: Validity, Constructions, and Application of Statutes, Regulations, or Policies Allowing Denial of Student Loans, Student Loan Guarantees, or Educational Services to Debtors Who Have Had Student Loans Scheduled in Bankruptcy*, 107 A.L.R. Fed. 192 (1998).

138 Loyola v. McClarty, 234 B.R. 386 (E.D. La. 1999).

139 Its position was that the Bankruptcy Code's prohibition of governmental discrimination at 11 U.S.C. § 525(a) did not apply to the granting of credit, such as a student loan. *See, e.g., In re* Goldrich, 771 F.2d 28 (2d Cir. 1985) (student loan not within scope of § 525(a)). *But see, e.g., In re* Watts, 93 B.R. 350 (E.D. Pa. 1988). Of course, the Code discrimination prohibition will clearly apply to Pell and other student *grants*.

140 Pub. L. No. 103-394 § 313, amending 11 U.S.C. § 525 (Oct. 22, 1994). *See also* Cong. Rec. H 107771 (Oct. 4, 1994). While the Act applies to bankruptcies filed after October 22, 1994, unless otherwise noted, the language of § 313 makes clear a Congressional intent to apply that section to any student loan discharged in bankruptcy, even to student loans discharged under the Bankruptcy Act, i.e. discharged before 1979.

141 H.R. Rep. No. 103-835 (Judiciary Comm.) at 103d Cong. 2d Sess. 58 (1994), *reprinted in* 1994 U.S.C.C.A.N. 3340, 3367.

142 59 Fed. Reg. 61212 (Nov. 29, 1994) (FFEL loans); *see also* 59 Fed. Reg. 61667 (Dec. 1, 1994) (FDSL loans).

143 59 Fed. Reg. 61215 (Nov. 29, 1994), amending 34 C.F.R. § 682.201(4)(i).

Chapter 8

Repayment Strategies for Getting Out of Default

8.1 Introduction

Many low-income student loan defaulters have been placed in an impossible situation. Their inability to repay their student loans makes them ineligible for new student loans and grants which might help them pull themselves out of poverty. It also damages their credit ratings, leads to interception of Earned Income Tax Credits, wage garnishment, aggressive collection efforts, and assessment of high collection fees.

The primary goal for most of these borrowers is to get out of default. Some hope to go back to school. Others simply want to stop the government collection onslaught. Whatever their reasons, there are numerous possibilities for low-income borrowers to get out of default by making payments on their loans. In many cases, the payments will be very low and affordable.

This chapter reviews the primary repayment options for clients in default. These include loan consolidation, renewal of eligibility through reasonable and affordable payment plans, and loan rehabilitation. Some clients may have the ability to pay a lump sum to settle the loan. The Department's discretionary authority to compromise or even write off all or part of the loan is also discussed in this chapter. Pre-default repayment options are covered in Chapter 1, *supra*.

Discharges and bankruptcy will also renew eligibility. These options should be considered before attempting to set up payment plans. Discharge rights are discussed in Chapter 6, *supra*. Low-income victims of vocational school fraud will often qualify for discharges. Bankruptcy, as discussed in Chapter 7, *supra*, is a more remote possibility due to restrictions on when student loans can be discharged in bankruptcy. State tuition recovery funds, discussed in Chapter 9, *infra*, should also be considered where available.

Many borrowers, however, will not qualify for any of the federal or state discharges discussed in Chapters 6, *supra* and 9, *infra* and/or will be unable to discharge their loans in bankruptcy as discussed in Chapter 7, *supra*. Even if they do qualify for discharges, borrowers may still want to set up repayment plans pending resolution of their discharge applications. This may be preferable in some cases to the administrative forbearance options discussed in Chapter 2, *supra*.

8.2 Consolidation Loans

8.2.1 General

Consolidation can be a relatively quick, easy, and effective solution to get out of default.[1] Low-income borrowers can consolidate their defaulted student loans into a new Direct Consolidation Loan with an Income Contingent Repayment Plan (ICRP). An alternative is to obtain a Federal Family Education Consolidation Loan (FFEL) with an Income Sensitive Repayment Plan (ISRP).[2]

Consolidation loans with ICRPs or ISRPs are designed for those who cannot afford to repay their existing student loans. Borrowers with family incomes not exceeding the poverty line for their family size do not need to make any payments on Direct Consolidation Loans with ICRPs. Payments for borrowers with incomes above the poverty line are contingent on family income level and the size of the student loan.[3]

After obtaining a consolidation loan, the borrower obtains a fresh start, becoming eligible for new loans, grants, and even deferments. Borrowers will no longer be listed as currently in default on their credit records, and no longer subject to tax intercepts, garnishments, or other collection efforts.

8.2.2 Direct Consolidation Loans

8.2.2.1 How to Obtain a Direct Consolidation Loan Application

There are three categories of Direct Consolidation Loans:

---

1 Consolidation loans are also available prior to default for borrowers seeking to get better loan terms. Direct Consolidation Loans are even available while the borrower is still in school. 34 C.F.R. § 685.220(d)(ii)(A), (B).

2 Direct Consolidation Loans are discussed beginning at § 8.2.2, *infra*; FFEL Consolidation loans at § 8.2.3, *infra*. For a comparison of the two programs, see § 8.2.4, *infra*.

3 *See* § 8.2.2.5, *infra*.

(1) Direct Subsidized Consolidation Loans,[4] (2) Direct Unsubsidized Consolidation Loans,[5] and (3) Direct PLUS Consolidation Loans.[6] Even if a borrower has more than one type of consolidation loan, she can generally still make only one payment.

There is no charge to obtain a Direct Consolidation loan. The first step is to request an application by calling the current toll-free number, (800) 557-7392 or for TDD: (800) 557-7395. Borrowers can also apply for Direct Consolidation loans using the Internet. The website is www.ed.gov/DirectLoan.[7] The Direct Loan website has information about interest rates and payment plans for consolidation loans. It also provides a number of calculators to help borrowers estimate their monthly repayments under the various plans.

8.2.2.2 Which Loans Can Be Consolidated Under the Direct Loan Program?

Under the Direct Loan Consolidation Program, borrowers can consolidate Subsidized and Unsubsidized Stafford Loans, Supplemental Loans for Students (SLSs), Federally Insured Student Loans (FISLs), PLUS Loans, Direct Loans, Perkins Loans, Health Education Assistance Loans (HEALs), and just about any other type of federal student loan.[8]

Although all of these different loans may be consolidated, the borrower must have at least one outstanding FFEL or Direct Loan to obtain a Direct Consolidation Loan.[9] This means, for example, that a Perkins Loan on its own cannot be consolidated into a Direct Loan. If the "qualifying" loan is a FFEL loan, the borrower must also certify that she was

unable to obtain FFEL Consolidation or is unable to obtain a FFEL Consolidation Loan with acceptable income sensitive repayment terms and is eligible for the Income Contingent Repayment Plan.[10] Loans that are not eligible for consolidation include state or private loans that are not federally guaranteed, law, medical and graduate access loans, and graduate extension loans.

Borrowers can even obtain a Direct Consolidation Loan when they are still in school. In these circumstances, the borrower must be consolidating both FFEL and Direct Loans or if the borrower is consolidating FFEL loans only, she must be enrolled at a school participating in the Direct Loan program.[11] Borrowers can also consolidate if they are out of school but in repayment, or most important for many low-income borrowers, if they are already in default. Loans that have been reduced to judgment may be consolidated with the approval of the Department.[12] Department approval is also required to consolidate a defaulted Direct Consolidation Loan.[13]

Borrowers have the option to consolidate all, just some, or even just one of their existing student loans. There is no minimum or maximum size for a Direct Consolidation Loan. Married borrowers can choose to consolidate loans from both spouses or jointly consolidate the loans of either spouse. However, both borrowers must agree to be jointly and severally liable for repayment.[14] Thus, in order to defer, forebear or discharge a joint loan, each borrower must meet the applicable requirements.[15] For example, if one spouse becomes disabled and is eligible for a disability discharge, the other is still responsible for repayment as long as she is not also disabled.[16] In addition, the borrowers must agree to repay the joint loan regardless of any change in marital status.[17] As a result, consolidated loans cannot be "unconsolidated" after divorce. To avoid these risks, spouses may want to consolidate separately.

8.2.2.3 Borrower Certification That FFEL Consolidation Loan Is Not Satisfactory

Borrowers with outstanding balances on Direct Loans are eligible for Direct Loan Consolidation.[18] However, many borrowers, particularly low-income trade school students will not meet this requirement. This is primarily because the

---

4   Only subsidized loans may be consolidated into Direct Subsidized Consolidation Loans. Interest is not charged to the borrower during in-school grace and deferment periods. 34 C.F.R. § 685.102(b). *See generally* § 1.4.3, *supra.*

5   Borrowers are responsible for the interest that accrues during any period on these loans.

6   Parent Loans for Undergraduate Students, FFEL PLUS, Direct PLUS, and Direct PLUS Consolidation Loans may be consolidated into a Direct PLUS Consolidation Loan. Parent borrowers must pass a credit check for any PLUS portion of the consolidation request. 34 C.F.R. § 685.220(d)(v)(A). Credit requirements can be found at 34 C.F.R. § 685.200(b)(7)(ii). Borrowers with adverse credit histories must find a creditworthy endorser or produce documentation showing extenuating circumstances related to their credit problems. 34 C.F.R. § 685.220(d)(v)(B).

7   A copy of the most recent Direct Consolidation application form is reprinted at Appx. D, *infra.*

8   34 C.F.R. § 685.220(b). In addition, advocates should note that the Health Education Assistance Loan (HEAL) program has been phased out. *See* United States Department of Education, Dear Colleague Letter GEN-98-18, Clearinghouse No. 52,137 (Aug. 1998); United States Department of Education, Dear Colleague Letter GEN-96-14, Clearinghouse No. 52,133 (Aug. 1996). Recent Dear Colleague letters are available on the Department of Education web site: www.ed.gov.

9   34 C.F.R. § 685.220(d).

10   34 C.F.R. § 685.220(d)(1)(i). *See* § 8.2.2.3, *infra.*

11   34 C.F.R. § 685.220(d)(ii)(A), (B).

12   34 C.F.R. § 685.220(d)(vii). *See* § 8.2.2.7, *infra.*

13   34 C.F.R. § 685.220(d)(vi).

14   34 C.F.R. § 685.220(d)(2)(iii).

15   34 C.F.R. § 685.220(l)(1), (2), (3).

16   34 C.F.R. § 682.402(a)(2). *See* § 6.6 (disability discharges), *supra.*

17   34 C.F.R. § 685.220(d)(2)(iii).

18   34 C.F.R. § 685.220(d)(1)(i)(A).

Direct Loan program is relatively new and the number of schools participating in the program is limited.[19]

Fortunately, borrowers with FFEL loans are also eligible for Direct Consolidation Loans. However, these borrowers must meet one of the following two conditions: (1) The borrower must be unable to obtain a FFEL Consolidation Loan *or* (2) The borrower must be unable to obtain a FFEL Consolidation Loan with income-sensitive repayment terms acceptable to the borrower. To meet this second condition, the borrower must also be eligible for the Income Contingent Repayment Plan (ICRP) under the Direct Loan program.[20] Low-income borrowers generally will have no difficulty meeting the second alternative category. They do not also have to certify that they have first been turned down or even applied for a FFEL Consolidation (the first category).[21]

To meet the second category, the borrower must certify that he is unable to obtain a FFEL Consolidation Loan with acceptable income-sensitive repayment terms. This is a subjective assessment based on information about available FFEL Income Sensitive Repayment Plans compared to available Direct Loan Income Contingent Repayment Plans. The borrower determines what is acceptable, and for nearly all low-income borrowers, FFEL ISRP terms will not be as good as Direct Loan ICRP terms. FFELs at a minimum require payments that equal *all* interest as it accrues while Direct Loans can have even zero payment amounts.[22] The borrower is not required to present any special evidence or justification why the Direct Loan is more acceptable. To meet the second condition, the borrower must also certify that he is eligible for a Direct Loan ICRP. Again, most low-income borrowers will have no problem meeting this standard.[23]

Even though borrowers who can meet the second category are not required to show that they attempted to obtain a FFEL Consolidation Loan, many FFEL lenders will nevertheless claim that borrowers will be perjuring themselves if they do not apply for a FFEL loan prior to applying for a Direct Consolidation Loan. This is clearly not the case. Not only is actually applying for a FFEL Consolidation *not* a precondition for applying for a Direct Consolidation Loan, but the application may delay or even prevent the borrower from obtaining a Direct Consolidation Loan. Direct Consolidation applicants must certify that no other application to consolidate their loans is pending with any other lender.[24]

8.2.2.4 Filling Out the Direct Loan Consolidation Application

Within a week or two after the borrower calls the current toll-free number, (800) 557-7392, the Department will send an informational package with a projected payment schedule, application and various other forms to be completed. The borrower must return the filled-out application to the Department. It is important for Direct Loan Consolidation applicants to include accurate information about all loans to be consolidated. Borrowers may also apply on-line.[25]

For Department-held loans other than Direct Loans, one way for borrowers to obtain information about their loans is to call the Federal Student Aid Center, (800) 4-FED-AID. For guaranty agency-held loans, the borrower will generally have to obtain the loan information from the guaranty agency.

Another excellent resource is the Department's National Student Loan Data System (NSLDS). The system can be accessed on-line at www.nslds.ed.gov or by calling the federal student aid information center at (800) 4-FED-AID or TDD (800) 730-8913. The database includes information about all federal loans, regardless of who holds the loans, and Pell grants. Borrowers can find out about loan and/or grant amounts, outstanding balances, loan statuses, and disbursements. In order to use the data base, borrowers need to provide their social security numbers, first two digits of last name, date of birth, and a personal identification number (PIN).[26]

If the loan balances on the borrower's application are incorrect, the Department notifies the borrower of the correct amount. The Department sends out a promissory note with the correct loan amount only after the consolidation has been approved. The borrower is then required to sign and return this promissory note to the Department.

Once the information about the borrower's loans is compiled, the next step is to complete the application. Among other information, the application calls for two references. These individuals will not be financially obligated on the loan and do not have to possess good credit records. The references are used only if the Department cannot locate the borrower.

Virtually all low-income student loan defaulters will want an Income Contingent Repayment Plan. In fact, they must make this selection if they have not, prior to consolidation, made at least three consecutive reasonable and affordable payments.[27] Borrowers requesting ICRPs must complete the "Repayment Plan Selection" and "Income Contingent Re-

---

19 *See* § 1.4.2, *supra*.

20 34 C.F.R. § 685.220(d)(1)(i), (B).

21 *Id.*

22 34 C.F.R. § 682.209(a)(7)(iv) (FFEL). Those borrowers under an ISRP that cannot afford to pay all accrued interest can apply each year for forbearance or a deferment, but this is not an automatic part of the ISRP and the deferments or forbearance are usually limited to three years. *See generally* Ch. 2 (forbearances and deferments), *supra*.

23 *See* § 8.2.2.5 (Income Contingent Repayment Plans), *infra*.

24 34 C.F.R. § 685.220(d)(1)(iii).

25 The current web site to apply is www.ed.gov/DirectLoan/consolid2.html.

26 Borrowers can obtain their own PINs on-line through the National Student Loan Data System web site: www.nslds.ed.gov. PINs will be sent by mail. *See generally* § 1.6.1 (National Student Loan Data System), *supra*.

27 34 C.F.R. § 685.220(h)(2). *See* § 8.2.2.7, *infra*.

payment Plan Consent to Disclosure of Tax Information" forms that accompany the application and promissory note.[28] However, borrowers may not use the ICRP to repay Direct PLUS Consolidation loans.[29]

Within about two months (sometimes less) of the borrower sending in all the application papers, the Direct Consolidation Loan should be in effect. The holders of the prior loans also notify the borrower that the loans have been paid in full.

8.2.2.5 Calculating the Monthly Payment Under ICRP

The ICRP payment for a Direct Loan Consolidation can go up or down over time as the borrower's income changes. The monthly payment is based on annual income and the loan amount. The payments should be zero for families living at the poverty line or below.[30] The payments are minimal for those earning several thousand dollars more than that amount. The exact formulas for determining the ICRP are set out in Department regulations.[31]

In general, the annual amount payable under an ICRP is the lesser of:

(1) the amount the borrower would repay annually over 12 years using standard amortization multiplied by an income percentage factor that corresponds to the borrower's adjusted gross income (AGI) as shown in the income percentage factor table in a notice published annually by the Secretary in the *Federal Register*;[32] or

(2) 20% of discretionary income.

The Department provides information to help borrowers calculate the monthly payments. The following example was published in the 2002 *Federal Register*:[33]

> Example: This example assumes you are a single borrower with $15,000 in Direct Loans, the interest rate being charged is 8.25 percent, and you have an adjusted gross income (AGI) of $32,345.

Step 1: Determine your annual payments based on what you would pay over 12 years using standard amortization. To do this, multiply your loan balance by the constant multiplier for 8.25 percent interest (0.1315449).[34]

$0.1315449 \times \$15,000 = \$1,973.17$.

Step 2: Multiply the result of Step 1 by the income percentage factor shown in the income percentage factor table that corresponds to your income and divide that result by 100.[35]

88.77 (the income percentage factor) × $1,973.17/ 100 = $1,751.58.

Step 3: Determine 20 percent of your discretionary income. Because you are a single borrower, subtract the poverty level for a family of one, as published in the *Federal Register*[36] from your income and multiply the result by 20%.

$\$32,345 - \$8860 = \$23,485$.

$\$23,485 \times 0.20 = \$4,697.00$.

Step 4: Compare the amount from Step 2 with the amount from Step 3. The lower of the two will be your annual payment amount. In this example, you will be paying the amount calculated under Step 2. To determine your monthly payment amount, divide the annual amount by 12.

$\$1,751.58/12 = \$145.97$.

A married borrower who wants to make payments under the ICRP and who has filed a separate income tax return must provide her spouse's written consent to disclosure of tax information.[37] This requirement does not apply if the borrower and her spouse are separated. The adjustable gross income (AGI) for both spouses is used to calculate the monthly payment.[38] If both have loans, married borrowers may also choose to repay jointly.[39]

The following example for married borrowers is from the 2002 *Federal Register*[40]:

---

28 These forms are included on the CD-Rom accompanying this volume.

29 34 C.F.R. § 685.220(h)(1).

30 The HHS Poverty Guidelines are published every year, currently found at 67 Fed. Reg. 6931–6933 (Feb. 14, 2002). For example, the 2002 poverty income threshold for a family of two living in the contiguous 48 states is $11,940 and $18,100 for a family of four. The payment amounts are determined using a formula found at 34 C.F.R. § 685.209(a)(2).

31 Each year the Department publishes the income percentage factors, case examples of calculations, a constant multiplier chart, and sample first year monthly repayment tables for various income and debt levels in an annual notice to the Federal Register. *See* 67 Fed. Reg. 44817–44822 (July 5, 2002).

32 34 C.F.R. § 685.209(a)(2). For 2002 figures, see 67 Fed. Reg. 44817–44822 (July 5, 2002).

33 67 Fed. Reg. 44817–44822 (July 5, 2002).

---

34 The multipliers for various interest rates are included in a table in the annual Federal Register notice updating the ICRP formula. For 2002 figures, see 67 Fed. Reg. 44817–44822 (July 5, 2002). 8.25% is the maximum interest rate for all Direct Loans, except Direct Plus Loans. 34 C.F.R. § 685.202(a). *See* § 1.5.4, *supra*.

35 The income percentage factors are also included in the annual Federal Register update. For 2002 figures, see 67 Fed. Reg. 44817–44822 (July 5, 2002).

36 67 Fed. Reg. 44817–44822 (July 5, 2002).

37 34 C.F.R. § 685.209(b)(1).

38 *Id.*

39 34 C.F.R. § 685.209(b)(2).

40 67 Fed. Reg. 44817–44822 (July 5, 2002).

Example: This example assumes you are married. You and your spouse have a combined adjusted gross income (AGI) of $61,121 and are repaying your loans jointly under the Income Contingent Repayment Plan. You have no children. You have a Direct Loan balance of $10,000, and your spouse has a Direct Loan balance of $15,000. Your interest rate is 8.25%.

Step 1: Add your loan balances and your spouse's Direct Loan balances together to determine your aggregate loan balance:

$10,000 + $15,000 = $25,000

Step 2: Determine the annual payment based on what you would pay over 12 years using standard amortization. To do this, multiply your aggregate loan balance by the constant multiplier for 8.25% interest (0.1315449).

0.1315449 × $25,000 = $3,288.62

Step 3: Multiply the result of Step 2 by the income percentage factor shown in the income percentage factors table that corresponds to your and your spouse's income and then divide the result by 100.

109.40 × $3,288.62/100 – $3,597.75

Step 4: Determine 20 percent of your discretionary income. To do this, subtract the poverty level for a family of two from your aggregate income and multiply the result by 20 percent:

$61,121 – $11,940 = $49.181.00

$49.181 × 0.20 = $9,836.20.

Step 5: Compare the amount from Step 3 with the amount from Step 4. The lower of the two will be your annual payment amount. You and your spouse will pay the amount calculated under Step 3. To determine your monthly repayment amount, divide the annual amount by 12.

$3,597.75/12 = $299.81.

The Department website offers an excellent resource to help borrowers figure out their monthly payment amounts under an ICRP. Budget, monthly repayment, and Direct Consolidation Loan calculators are available on-line at www.ed.gov/DirectLoan/calc.html.

8.2.2.6 What Happens to the Loan Obligation While Borrower Makes Only Minimal Payments

Unlike a FFEL ISRP, a Direct Loan ICRP can create negative amortization. Even though the borrower makes all required payments, the minimal amount of the payment does not cover accrued interest, and the amount owed is increased to include this unpaid interest. Interest is then charged on the accrued interest ("capitalization"), resulting in the loan balance increasing beyond the original amount due.

Three features of the Direct Consolidation Loan Program mitigate the consequences of negative amortization. First, borrowers can seek loan deferments, during which period the United States pays for accrued interest.[41] Borrowers in school can obtain deferments for as long as they are in school. Borrowers may also be eligible for unemployment, economic, and other deferments for periods as long as three years.[42] Many low-income borrowers, even those in default on older loans, will qualify for these deferments as soon as they obtain Direct Consolidation Loans.

A second feature limiting negative amortization is the ICRP's limitation of interest capitalization to 10% of the loan amount.[43] Unpaid interest is capitalized until the outstanding principal amount is 10% greater than the original principal amount. After that point, interest continues to accrue but is not capitalized.

The third limit on negative amortization is that after twenty-five years of ICRP payments (even if the payment amount was zero over the whole twenty-five-year period), the remainder of the loan is cancelled.[44] Deferment or forbearance periods are excluded from the twenty-five-year ICRP period.

There may be negative consequences for borrowers if the loan is written off after twenty-five years. Most importantly, when the balance of the loan is forgiven, under current tax law, the amount forgiven will be taxable income for the borrower. This may not be particularly worrisome for many borrowers since they will not have to worry about the tax liability for twenty-five years.

However, the "25 year issue" is a legitimate concern for many advocates and their clients. At a minimum, clients should be counseled about the potential problems that may arise in the future. In addition, borrowers should be counseled that they may be able to avoid future tax consequences. In particular, they will not have to report the cancelled debt as income to the extent they are insolvent at the time the debt is written off.[45] To establish insolvency, a borrower must send the IRS a statement concerning the

---

41 This is the case for that portion of the consolidation loan whose underlying loans were GSLs, Staffords, FISLs, Perkins, Direct Loans, or other subsidized loans. Interest continues to accrue during a deferment period for that portion of the consolidation loan that derives from an unsubsidized loan, such as an SLS or Unsubsidized Stafford. See Ch. 2, *supra* for more information on deferments.

42 34 C.F.R. § 682.210. *See generally* Ch. 2, *supra* (deferments).

43 34 C.F.R. § 685.209(c)(5). Advocates should keep in mind that the original consolidation balance will often be much greater than the original loan amount.

44 34 C.F.R. § 685.209(c)(4)(iv).

45 26 U.S.C. § 108.

discharged debt along with a list that shows that, at the time of forgiveness, the borrower had more debts (including the forgiven debt) than assets.[46]

Even borrowers who are not insolvent may be able to escape the post-twenty-five year negative tax consequences. In particular, some borrowers may have only temporary financial difficulties that require them to repay loans using an ICRP. As their financial circumstances improve, they will be able to move to a different repayment plan that allows them to pay off their loans more quickly. These borrowers will not qualify for the twenty-five year loan write-off because they will not meet the condition that borrowers must be in repayment under an ICRP for twenty-five consecutive years.[47] A strict reading of this regulation leads to the conclusion that a borrower could choose another repayment plan at any point along the way, even after twenty-four years, and avoid having the debt forgiven.

Although it is possible that the tax code will be amended before many clients reach the twenty-five-year mark, it is still important to counsel clients on the drawbacks of ICRPs. In general, negative amortization or other low payment plans should be viewed, if possible, as temporary solutions. In practice, some clients will never be able to break out of the cycle of low monthly payments. It is still critical to consider other options for these clients. For example, if their financial hardship seems likely to continue into the future, they may be able to discharge their loans in bankruptcy.[48] As always, the cancellation options discussed in Chapter 6, *supra* should also be considered.

Borrowers should also be counseled that the low monthly payments may not last forever. ICRP payment amounts are reviewed annually.[49] If a borrower's financial situation improves, she will be required to make higher payments.

8.2.2.7 Consolidating Defaulted Loans Under the Direct Loan Program

To obtain a Direct Consolidation Loan, borrowers in default *either* have to make three reasonable and affordable payments based on their total financial circumstances (sometimes set as low as $5 a month) *or* agree to accept an Income Contingent Repayment Plan (ICRP) and consent to the IRS disclosing to the Department certain tax return information for the purposes of calculating a monthly repayment amount.[50] Through the Direct Loan Consolidation Program, a borrower can even consolidate a defaulted loan that has been reduced to judgment. In this instance, though,

the borrower must obtain the approval of the Secretary.[51] Consolidating a defaulted Direct Consolidation Loan also requires the Secretary's approval.[52]

The Direct Loan regulations state that, in consolidating defaulted loans, the Department imposes reasonable limits on the size of collection costs that can be added to the amount owed on the old loans and then added into the consolidation loan. These collection costs are limited to the same rate as those authorized under the FFEL program.[53]

8.2.3 FFEL Consolidation Loans

8.2.3.1 General

The rules for FFEL Consolidation Loans differ from Direct Loan Consolidations in important ways. First, FFEL Consolidation lenders do not have to include non-FFEL loans in the new consolidation loan. They may do so at their discretion.[54]

Similar to Direct Consolidation Loans, a borrower in default applying for a FFEL Consolidation Loan must first make three consecutive reasonable and affordable monthly payments or arrange to pay under an ISRP.[55] The difference is that the FFEL program's ISRP will require low-income borrowers to make higher monthly payments than the Direct Loan program's ICRP.[56]

Another difference between the two programs is that borrowers in the FFEL Consolidation Loan Program are not eligible for consolidation loans if they are subject to a judgment secured through litigation related to a student loan unless the judgment has been vacated.[57] Direct Consolidation Loans may include loans reduced to judgments at the Secretary's discretion.[58] Loans subject to an order of garnishment are also not eligible unless the order has been lifted.[59]

To obtain a FFEL Consolidation Loan, the best approach is to contact the party holding the note. That party will generally be eager to process the FFEL Consolidation Loan. In fact, there are instances where debt collectors hired by the

---

46 More information about reporting cancelled debts is available on the IRS web site, www.irs.gov. In particular, see Publication 908: Bankruptcy Tax Guide.

47 34 C.F.R. § 685.209(c)(4)(iv).

48 *See* Ch. 7, *supra.*

49 34 C.F.R. § 685.209(a)(5).

50 34 C.F.R. § 685.220(d)(1)(ii)(E), (F).

51 34 C.F.R. § 685.220(d)(1)(vii).

52 34 C.F.R. § 685.220(d)(1)(vi).

53 34 C.F.R. § 685.220(f)(iii). The Department presently limits these costs to 18.5% of the loan. 34 C.F.R. § 682.401(b)(27)(i). When Perkins Loans are consolidated, the costs may be higher.

54 34 C.F.R. § 682.201(d). For FFEL consolidations, eligible loans received prior to the date a consolidation loan was made and loans received during the 180-day period following the date a consolidation loan was made may be added to the consolidation loan upon request. This request must be made during the 180-day period after the consolidation loan was made.

55 *See* 34 C.F.R. §§ 682.200 (satisfactory repayment arrangement), 682.201(c)(1)(i)(3).

56 *See* § 8.2.4, *infra.*

57 34 C.F.R. § 682.201(c)(1)(B).

58 34 C.F.R. § 685.220(d)(1)(vii).

59 34 C.F.R. § 682.201(c)(1)(C).

Department have steered consumers to FFEL Consolidations where they would have been better off with a Direct Loan Consolidation from the Department. The Department has approved common loan forms for FFEL Consolidation Loans.[60]

However, borrowers should not assume that they will get the best deal from their original lenders. In fact, in 1998, Congress specifically moved to foster competition among lenders and give borrowers more options. Before 1998, borrowers trying to get a FFEL Consolidation Loan had to use one of the lenders who held their loans. As part of the 1998 HEA reauthorization, Congress amended the law to allow borrowers with loans from different lenders to consolidate their loans with any eligible consolidation lender.[61] Borrowers may also apply to any eligible consolidation lender if they have been unable to receive a consolidation loan from the holder of their outstanding loans or unable to receive a consolidation loan with income sensitive repayment terms.[62] Borrowers with loans all from a single lender still must consolidate with that lender.

This change stimulated competition and led to the growth of many new companies seeking to lure borrowers away from Sallie Mae (the largest FFEL consolidator) and the Direct Loan program.[63] Many of these companies are "third party marketers" that work as contractors for banks hoping to attract student loan borrowers. These third party marketers often use aggressive marketing techniques.

Loan consolidation is an increasingly controversial issue. In particular, the large consolidation lenders such as Sallie Mae have begun to protest loudly against the "looser" consolidation rules. They argue that the third party marketers and other consolidation lenders luring student loan borrowers into consolidating their loans will undermine the student loan originating industry. In their view, student loan originators will simply leave the loan program if they believe that their loan portfolios will be later "stolen" by other companies offering to consolidate loans at favorable terms. Sallie Mae and other lenders also argue that mainly middle and higher income borrowers consolidate their loans and that the government should not be providing "subsidies" to these wealthier borrowers.[64] At present, borrowers benefit from lower interest rates and better consolidation deals. However, advocates should continue to follow this issue for possible Congressional action.

8.2.4 Direct and FFEL Consolidations Compared

8.2.4.1 Advantages of Direct Consolidation Loans

Both the FFEL and Direct Loan Consolidation Programs technically allow borrowers in default to obtain the consolidation immediately. The FFEL program allows borrowers in default to either make three consecutive reasonable and affordable monthly payments or agree to pay under an ISRP.[65] Similarly, the Direct Consolidation program allows defaulted borrowers to make three reasonable and affordable monthly payments or agree to pay under an ICRP.[66]

The advantage of the Direct Consolidation program, particularly for low-income borrowers, is that the ICRP will almost always be a better deal. ISRP payments must at least cover accruing interest.[67] Under the ICRP, the monthly payment amount is zero for borrowers with incomes less than or equal to the United States poverty level for their family size. Payment amounts for borrowers with incomes only slightly above the poverty line will also be very low.[68]

At the Secretary's discretion, defaulted loans reduced to judgment can be consolidated under the Direct Loan program.[69] FFEL lenders cannot consolidate loans subject to judgments unless the judgments have been vacated.[70]

The Department of Education summarizes the difference between Direct and FFEL Consolidation loans as follows:

Lender Options. All eligible loans that an eligible borrower requests to be consolidated must be accepted by the Direct Consolidation Loan Program. FFEL Consolidation lenders may accept all eligible loans for their Consolidation loans, but some lenders may not consolidate some non-FFEL loans. For example, some FFEL lenders may not include a HEAL loan in their FFEL Consolidation loans but instead may offer a separate HEAL consolidation loan with different terms.

Repayment Plans. FFEL Consolidation lenders are required to offer the borrower a Standard Repayment Plan, a Graduated Repayment Plan, an Extended Repayment Plan for new borrowers after 1998 owing $30,000 or more, and an Income Sensitive Repayment Plan. The monthly payment amount under the Income Sensitive Repayment Plan is determined by taking into account the borrower's income and loan debt. The details of the plans may differ by FFEL lender.

---

60 *See* Department of Education, Dear Guaranty Agency Director Letter GEN-00-16, Approved Federal Consolidation Loan application forms for use within the Federal Family Education Loan Program (FFELP) (Oct. 2000). The forms are included on the CD-Rom accompanying this volume.

61 34 C.F.R. § 682.201(c)(iv)(B).

62 34 C.F.R. § 682.201(c)(iv)(B)(2).

63 *See generally* Stephen Burd, Facing Competition, Lenders Attack Loan Consolidation Program, The Chronicle of Higher Education (July 19, 2002) at A19.

64 *Id.*

65 34 C.F.R. § 682.201(c)(1)(i)(3).

66 34 C.F.R. § 685.220(d)(1)(ii)(E), (F).

67 34 C.F.R. § 682.209(a)(7)(iv).

68 34 C.F.R. § 685.209(a)(2). *See* § 8.2.2.5, *supra*.

69 34 C.F.R. § 685.220(d)(1)(vii).

70 34 C.F.R. § 682.201(c)(1)(B). *See* § 8.2.3.1, *supra*.

The Direct Loan program offers the borrower a Standard Repayment Plan, a Graduated Repayment Plan, an Extended Repayment Plan, and an Income Contingent Repayment Plan (ICRP). The monthly payment amount for the ICRP is based upon a formula that takes into account the borrower's income, family size, and total amount of the borrower's Direct Loans.

Assistance for Defaulted Borrowers. FFEL lenders may choose to make FFEL Consolidation Loans to borrowers who have defaulted on prior loans and may allow them to include a defaulted loan in the FFEL Consolidation Loan, but not all lenders do that. The Direct Loan program also has options for a defaulted loan borrower to consolidate his or her defaulted loans. Under either Consolidation Loan program, if the borrower consolidates all of his or her defaulted loans, he or she regains eligibility for federal student aid.

In-School Consolidation. The Direct Consolidation program allows a student borrower to consolidate while in school. Borrowers who are eligible to obtain an in-school consolidation may receive a six-month grace period and a lower interest rate. In some cases, even borrowers with only FFEL loans can obtain an in-school consolidation through the Direct Consolidation Loan program.

In the FFEL Consolidation program student borrowers may consolidate after they have left school and all of their loans are in grace or repayment.[71]

8.2.4.2 Raising School-Related Defenses After Consolidation

By consolidating a loan through either the FFEL or Direct Loan programs, the borrower's ability to raise school-related defenses may be muddled. Borrowers can still obtain a closed-school discharge for that portion of the Consolidation Loan that relates to an original loan that would be eligible for the closed-school discharge, and the same guidelines apply for false certification and unpaid-refund discharges.[72]

Currently the right to obtain a partial discharge of a consolidation loan applies only to borrowers who qualify for false certification, closed school, or unpaid refund discharges. Borrowers cannot get a partial discharge of a consolidation loan based on disability. This issue was considered, and rejected, during spring 2002 negotiated rulemaking sessions.[73] According to the Department, the only way that some, but not all, of a borrower's consolidated loans could be eligible for a disability discharge would be if the ineligible loans were made after the date the borrower became totally and permanently disabled. This would mean that the borrower was no longer totally and permanently disabled and therefore not eligible for a discharge on any of the loans.[74]

In contrast, the 2002 negotiating rulemaking process did lead to more favorable changes for PLUS Consolidation borrowers. Current regulations allow for the discharge of a PLUS Loan if the student on whose behalf the loan was obtained dies.[75] However, this discharge is not currently available to parents who consolidate a PLUS Loan and the student for whom the loan was obtained dies. The proposed rules would allow partial discharges of the portion of the consolidation loan attributable to that PLUS Loan.[76] The proposed rules also clarify that borrowers may receive partial discharges of consolidation loans to the extent they qualify for teacher loan forgiveness under either the FFEL or Direct Loan teacher forgiveness programs.[77]

The situation for other school-related claims is less clear. It is possible that a court would find that borrowers consolidating their loans waive their right to bring claims and defenses concerning the original loan.[78] The difference between FFEL and Direct Loan Consolidations is that FFEL Loans after January 1, 1994 contain the FTC Holder Notice making the note holder liable for school-related defenses where the school is for-profit and related to the lender. The Direct Consolidation Loan note does not include this notice. The issue of raising school-related defenses is discussed at Chapter 9, *infra*.

8.2.4.3 Interest Rates

With respect to interest rates, there is currently no difference between Direct Consolidation Loans and FFEL Consolidation Loans. For applications received between February 1, 1999 and June 30, 2003, the interest for Direct Consolidation Loans is fixed for the life of the loan at the weighted average of the interest rates on the loans being consolidated, rounded to the nearest higher one-eighth of one percent, not to exceed 8.25%. The same formula applies to FFEL Consolidation Loan applications received on or after October 1, 1998.[79]

---

71 *See* Department of Education, Direct Consolidation Loans: Frequently Asked Questions, available on the Department's web site, www.loanconsolidation.ed.gov/hfaq.shtml (last checked July 2002).

72 Dear Colleague Letter 94-G-256, Clearinghouse No. 50,422 (Sept. 1994), *reprinted at* Appx. C, *infra*. 34 C.F.R. § 685.216(l)(3).

73 *See* 67 Fed. Reg. 51036, 51041 (Aug. 6, 2002).

74 *Id. See generally* § 6.6 (disability discharges).

75 *See* § 6.7, *supra*.

76 67 Fed. Reg. 51036, 51041 (Aug. 6, 2002).

77 67 Fed. Reg. 51036, 51041 (Aug. 6, 2002). *See generally* § 6.8, *supra*.

78 *But see* Crawford v. The Am. Institute of Professional Careers, Inc., Clearinghouse No. 51,258 (D. Ariz. Feb. 8, 1996).

79 34 C.F.R. § 685.220(g) (Direct Loans), citing the rate established in 34 C.F.R. § 685.202(a)(3)(i) and (ii). In 2002, the Bush Administration proposed to convert the fixed consolidation loan interest rate to a variable rate. Many congresspeople opposed the proposal and the Administration withdrew. *See* Karen L. Werner, *Hearing Halted After Education Official Says No Plans*

8.2.4.4 General Considerations

There are some disadvantages to consolidation regardless of which program the borrower chooses. When a borrower in default consolidates a loan through either program, presently 18.5% is added to the amount due for collection fees.[80] This may be preferable to existing collection fees that may be as high as 43%.[81] However, borrowers have at least some hope of seeking a waiver of the collection fees before a consolidation. After the consolidation, the fees become part of the amount due on the new loan. Consolidation also may not be a wise strategy for borrowers who owe a lot of interest on their loans. Consolidating will end up converting much of that interest into principal.

Generally, borrowers should always first consider loan cancellation options.[82] Low-income borrowers with bleak financial prospects should also seriously consider filing bankruptcy to discharge student loan debt. Many of these borrowers will be able to meet the undue hardship test required to discharge student loans in bankruptcy.[83]

Another disadvantage to consolidation relates to credit reporting. Consolidation results in a notation on a borrower's credit report that the defaulted loan was paid in full. In contrast, rehabilitation removes the default notation completely.[84] This may be of concern to some clients. However, rehabilitation is not always an attractive option for low-income borrowers due to potentially higher monthly payments as well as proposed changes in the law that would eliminate the rehabilitation option for loans reduced to judgment.[85]

In addition, borrowers may have more opportunity to compromise the amount owed on an old loan than on a consolidation loan. However, this will usually require a lump sum payment of a significant portion of the loan, something that is rarely possible for most low-income consumers.[86]

8.3 Renewing Eligibility Through Reasonable and Affordable Payment Plans

8.3.1 Basic Requirements

Another option for FFEL and Direct Loan borrowers in default is to reschedule their payments through reasonable and affordable payment plans based on their total financial circumstances. The defaulted borrower has a statutory right to such a plan, and payments can be as low as $5 a month or less.[87] Whether the Department or a guaranty agency holds the loan, the borrower, to renew eligibility, must enter a satisfactory repayment arrangement, defined as six consecutive on-time monthly payments.[88]

A reasonable and affordable payment plan to renew eligibility must be sharply distinguished from a normal repayment plan where the student may be asked to pay hundreds of dollars a month. Payments under reasonable and affordable plans can be much lower, often not even covering interest payments.

If a borrower wants eventually to pay off a loan, monthly payments that at least equal accrued monthly interest will avoid negative amortization. Borrowers who cannot afford payments that high may still want to set up reasonable and affordable payments plans. They may not be particularly concerned about the total amount of interest that will accrue on the loan over time. It is for these borrowers that payments as low as $5 a month or less may provide the needed avenue back to school.

While the borrower will still technically be in default while making reasonable and affordable payments, the borrower will not be subject to tax intercepts, wage garnishments, collection contacts, or collection lawsuits. The borrower's credit record will most likely still show a default unless she rehabilitates the loan. Rehabilitation is discussed in § 8.4, *infra*.

---

to Alter Student Loan Consolidation, 78 Banking Report. 19 (May 13, 2002).

80 34 C.F.R. § 685.220(f)(iii), using amount in 34 C.F.R. § 682.401(b)(27) (FFEL).

81 *See generally* § 4.4, *supra.*

82 *See* Ch. 6, *supra.*

83 *See* Ch. 7, *supra.*

84 *See generally* § 8.4 (rehabilitation), *infra.* There is some confusion whether rehabilitating a loan will also clean up the historical section of the student's credit rating. *See* § 3.3.4, *supra.*

85 *See* § 8.4 (rehabilitation), *infra.*

86 *See* § 8.5, *infra.*

---

87 20 U.S.C. § 1078-6(b). The Conference Report for this provision states that it is intended to provide a second chance at educational loans and grants for low-income students previously defrauded by trade schools. *See* H.R. Conf. Rep. No. 630, 102d Cong., 2d Sess. 467 (1992). Although the statute refers to guaranty agencies, the Conference Report makes clear that the Secretary must offer the same opportunity to renew eligibility where the Department of Education is holding the loan.

88 The regulation that provides for reinstatement of borrower eligibility, 34 C.F.R. § 682.401(a)(4) (FFEL) requires the borrower to make satisfactory repayment arrangements as defined in § 682.200. Section 682.200 provides that the borrower must make six timely payments and that the amount must be reasonable and affordable. *See also* 34 C.F.R. §§ 685.200(c), 685.102 (definition of satisfactory repayment arrangement for purposes of regaining eligibility).

8.3.2 Eligible Borrowers

Borrowers who previously set up reasonable and affordable payment plans and became delinquent on their payments cannot renew eligibility through a new reasonable and affordable plan. Therefore, a borrower has only one chance to renew eligibility with a reasonable and affordable repayment agreement.[89]

Borrowers who stay current on the reasonable and affordable plan can apparently keep on the plan indefinitely at that level of payment. The level will change if the borrower's financial circumstances change. Although the regulations do not speak to the issue, the Department has stated that a student is eligible to obtain a reasonable and affordable repayment schedule even if the defaulted loan has been reduced to a court judgment.[90]

The problem with staying on a reasonable and affordable payment plan indefinitely is that borrowers will not be able to get out of default. To get out of default, they must rehabilitate or consolidate their loans.[91] Rehabilitation requires twelve consecutive reasonable and affordable payments. For FFEL loans, rehabilitation also requires finding a lender to buy the loan.

The main disadvantage of rehabilitation is that the payments may be higher than under a reasonable and affordable payment plan.[92] Instead of staying on the reasonable and affordable plan, however, borrowers who can make minimal monthly payments are better off consolidating their loans through the Direct Loan program and getting an Income Contingent Repayment Plan (ICRP).[93]

8.3.3 Determining a Reasonable and Affordable Payment Amount

A satisfactory repayment arrangement involves an amount that is determined to be reasonable and affordable based on the borrower's total financial circumstances.[94] To come up with that amount, the guaranty agency (and the Department on loans which it holds) must consider the borrower's and spouse's disposable income. Disposable income is defined as income from any source that remains after the deduction of any amounts required by law to be withheld (e.g., taxes and wage garnishments) or any child support or alimony payments under court order or legally enforceable agreement.[95]

The note holder must also consider the borrower's and spouse's necessary expenses, including, but not limited to, housing, utilities, food, medical costs, dependent-care costs, work-related expenses, and other student loan repayments.[96]

No formula is specified, but the note holder *cannot* establish a minimum payment amount for all borrowers, such as $50. That is, the amount must be less than $50 if that is what is determined to be reasonable and affordable based on the borrower's total financial circumstances.[97] However the guarantor must maintain documentation in the student's file if the amount is less than $50.[98]

An important document relating to the minimum repayment amount is a February 1, 1993 letter to the Secretary of Education from United States Representative Bruce F. Vento, who had originally introduced the renewed eligibility provisions in Congress.[99] The Congressman objected to a $50 minimum standard being use by certain guarantors, and indicated that Congress' intent was to require only "nominal payments well below $50 per month for those with very low incomes."

The regulations do not provide a specific formula for determining how to compute a reasonable and affordable repayment amount. Where a borrower's necessary expenses exceed income, advocates should argue that the reasonable and affordable amount is either nothing or a nominal amount, since the regulations require consideration of these necessary expenses.

On the other hand, some collectors and guarantors have demanded payment plans based on the size of the outstanding loan. Department officials have made it clear that this is wrong. The payment amount must be based on the borrower's ability to pay, and not on the size of the outstanding loan. Confusion arises because guarantors or collectors are allowed to base "normal" payment plans on the amount outstanding. Borrowers should clearly state to the collector or guarantor that they are not seeking a normal repayment agreement, but a special agreement to renew eligibility that is reasonable and affordable based on their total financial circumstances.

The guarantor, for its part, must provide the borrower with a written statement of the monthly payment amount, and provide the borrower with an opportunity to object to its terms.[100]

---

89 34 C.F.R. §§ 682.200 (FFEL) (definition of "satisfactory repayment arrangement"), 685.102 (Direct Loans).

90 Letter from Robert W. Evans, Director, Division of Policy Development, Policy, Training, and Analysis Service, Department of Education to Cornelius Foley, President of the New York State Higher Education Services Corporation, Clearinghouse No. 47,963 (Mar. 3, 1993).

91 *See* §§ 8.2 (consolidation), *supra*, 8.4 (rehabilitation), *infra*.

92 *See* § 8.4, *infra*.

93 *See* § 8.2, *supra*.

94 34 C.F.R. § 682.200 (satisfactory repayment arrangement).

95 34 C.F.R. § 682.200 (disposable income).

96 34 C.F.R. § 682.401(b)(4)(i)(A).

97 34 C.F.R. § 682.401(b)(4)(i)(B).

98 *Id.*

99 Letter of Representative Bruce F. Vento to the Honorable Rich Riley, Secretary of Education, Clearinghouse No. 47,962 (Feb. 1, 1993).

100 34 C.F.R. § 682.401(b)(4)(iii).

8.3.4 *How to Obtain a Reasonable and Affordable Payment Plan*

As a practical matter, the first step in seeking a reasonable and affordable repayment agreement is to determine who is servicing the loan. Since this right only applies to loans already in default, the entity is almost always a state guaranty agency or a collection agency hired by the Department of Education for Department-held loans. Most trade school loans ten years old or older are held by the Department and serviced by a collection agency. On the other hand, most loans taken out within the last six years are still held by a state guaranty agency.[101]

The next step is to contact the party servicing the loan to request a reasonable and affordable payment plan. It is typical for the loan servicer to tell a student that a repayment plan is not available or that the plan will require a down payment and minimum monthly payments. This is because the borrower has not specifically requested "a reasonable and affordable payment plan to renew eligibility" or words to that effect. However, the borrower should not have to use any "magic words" in order to get a reasonable and affordable payment plan.[102]

There have been widespread reports of guarantors and collectors still refusing to acknowledge the existence of the option for reasonable and affordable plans even after the borrower specifically requests one. This is a very serious matter. Collectors hired by the Department have been given lengthy training about this option and all guarantors have established such an option.

The refusal of a staffer to acknowledge the existence of such a plan or to misrepresent the requirements implies either deliberate deception by that individual or grossly deficient supervision and training of that individual. This conduct should rise to the level of a federal Fair Debt Collection Practices Act violation for collectors and private guarantors, and perhaps a due process or other violation for state employees.[103] More on actions against this type of misconduct is detailed at Chapter 4, *supra*.

The Department's regulations specify the type of documentation the borrower should provide in seeking a reasonable and affordable repayment agreement. The borrower should provide to the guarantor or to the Department's collector handling the debt documentation of income, expenses and the amount owed on all student loans. Evidence of current income might include proof of receipt of public assistance or the borrower's two most recent pay stubs. Expenses might be proved by filling in a form provided by the guaranty agency showing the borrower's monthly household budget.[104]

In theory, there is no reason for a borrower in default to accept another type of payment plan. However, in practice, it is often difficult for advocates and borrowers to convince loan holders that they must offer these plans. In many situations, consolidation will be an easier option.[105] In either case, borrowers should be advised to think seriously about whether they can make even minimal payments. If not, repaying student loan debt may not be possible until the borrower's financial circumstances improve and it might not be worth jeopardizing the one-time only option of a reasonable and affordable payment plan.

8.4 Loan Rehabilitation

8.4.1 *General*

A student can renew eligibility for new loans and grants and cure the loan default by "rehabilitating" the defaulted loan. Loan rehabilitation for FFELs and Direct Loans may be requested after the borrower has made twelve reasonable and affordable payments.[106] The rules for Perkins rehabilitation are discussed at § 8.4.3, *infra*.

The payment amount is determined by the guaranty agency (or the United States if it is holding the loan) in the same way as a reasonable and affordable payment plan to renew eligibility, described in the prior subsection.[107]

For FFEL loans, after the borrower makes twelve timely monthly payments under the new plan, and the borrower requests rehabilitation, the guarantor or the United States must attempt to secure a lender to purchase the loan.[108] If the loan is sold (it may not be if no lender agrees to purchase the loan), the loan is removed from default status and the borrower is eligible for new loans and grants.[109] According to the Department, it is an industry practice not to repur-

---

101 For a list of state guaranty agencies, see Appx. F, *infra*. See also § 8.2.2.4, *supra* for information on finding loan holders.

102 *See, e.g.,* Arroyo v. Solomon and Solomon, P.C., 2001 U.S. Dist. LEXIS 21908 (E.D.N.Y. 2001) (borrower's claim that collection agency violated the Fair Debt Collection Practices Act by misrepresenting the requirements for a reasonable and affordable payment plan survived summary judgment). *See* §§ 4.3.2, 4.3.3, *supra*.

103 *See* Arroyo v. Solomon and Solomon, P.C., 2001 U.S. Dist. LEXIS 21908 (E.D.N.Y. 2001) (borrower's claim that collection agency violated the Fair Debt Collection Practices Act by misrepresenting the requirements for a reasonable and affordable payment plan survived summary judgment). *See* §§ 4.3.2, 4.3.3, *supra*.

104 34 C.F.R. § 682.401(b)(4)(i)(C).

105 *See* § 8.2, *supra*.

106 34 C.F.R. § 682.405(b)(1). For Direct Loans, the 12 payments must be made directly to the Department.

107 20 U.S.C. § 1078-6(a)(1); 34 C.F.R. § 682.405(b)(1))(i)(B) (no minimum requirement for reasonable and affordable payment plan).

108 34 C.F.R. § 682.405(b)(1).

109 20 U.S.C. § 1078-6(a)(3); 34 C.F.R. § 682.405(a)(3).

chase FFEL program loans with a balance of less than $1500. If a FFEL loan cannot be resold, it will not be rehabilitated.[110]

The current regulation explicitly provides for rehabilitation of defaulted loans reduced to judgment, although in that case the borrower must sign a new promissory note prior to sale of the loan.[111] However, during spring 2002 negotiated rulemaking sessions, negotiators and the Department agreed to eliminate this right.[112]

This issue was very controversial during spring 2002 negotiated rulemaking. Perkins lenders originally suggested the change.[113] They argued that their efforts to collect defaulted loans through litigation are often wasted if they are later required to vacate judgments as part of rehabilitation plans. However, the Perkins lenders did not originally request a complete elimination of the right to rehabilitate for borrowers with judgments. Instead, they argued that lenders should be given the option to rehabilitate these loans. The Department responded that there was no statutory basis for providing a loan holder this option. Rehabilitating loans with judgments must either be mandatory, according to the Department, or not allowed at all. The Department and negotiators ended up with the latter option.

The FFEL lenders at the negotiating table had not requested this change. However, the Department argued that if they made this change for Perkins lenders, they would have to do the same for other lenders. Therefore, the proposed amendments to rehabilitation rights for borrowers with judgments apply not only to Perkins borrowers, but also to FFEL and Direct Loan borrowers.[114]

The proposed rules take away the rehabilitation right for borrowers with judgments.[115] However, the proposed regulations provide that a loan holder may, at its option, enter into agreements with these borrowers. An example cited in the *Federal Register* is that the lender could set up an agreement with the borrower that the lender would vacate the judgment if the borrower made twelve consecutive monthly payments. In essence, the lender would agree to extend the privileges of rehabilitation, but the lender would no longer be required to provide this service and would have more flexibility to define the terms of the repayment agreement.[116]

In addition, the proposed rules clarify that borrowers with judgments may still regain eligibility for financial assistance, but lenders will have greater flexibility in this area.

Under the proposed rules, a borrower with a judgment may regain eligibility if she repays the debt in full or makes at least six consecutive satisfactory repayment arrangements. This is similar to the current regulations covering renewed eligibility for borrowers in default.[117] The most significant change is that borrowers either in default or with judgments will have only one chance to reestablish eligibility.[118] Although this "one-time limit" currently applies to guaranty agencies reinstating borrower eligibility through reasonable and affordable payment plans, it does not currently appear in other regulations.[119]

It is important to note that the rehabilitation rules remain the same for borrowers with defaulted loans not yet subject to judgment. Only Perkins regulations limit borrowers to one chance at rehabilitation.[120]

8.4.2 Advantages and Disadvantages of Loan Rehabilitation

Loan rehabilitation has certain benefits. The defaulted student loan is stricken from the consumer's credit rating. Collection fees are reduced to 18.5% of the unpaid principal and accrued interest at the time of the sale.[121] All ill effects of having a defaulted loan are removed, and the borrower becomes eligible for all benefits afforded other borrowers, such as deferrals and forbearance.[122] Rehabilitation removes the default notation from the borrower's credit report.[123]

However, not all borrowers will be well served by loan rehabilitation as opposed to simply establishing renewed eligibility with six payments or consolidating the loan. After sale, the loan will be subject to repayment under the same terms as other loans of the same type, usually requiring repayment within ten years.[124] This requirement often results in a monthly payment amount after rehabilitation, which exceeds what is affordable for low-income borrowers.

---

110 Department of Education, Direct Consolidation Loan Guide for Schools at 11 (2000).

111 34 C.F.R. §§ 682.405(a)(4) (FFEL), 674.39 (Perkins), 685.211(f).

112 67 Fed. Reg. 51036 (Aug. 6, 2002) (proposed rules).

113 67 Fed. Reg. 51036, 51037 (Aug. 6, 2002).

114 67 Fed. Reg. 51036 (Aug. 6, 2002), *amending* 34 C.F.R. §§ 674.39(a) (Perkins), 682.405 (FFEL), 685.211(f) (Direct Loans), and 668.35 (Student Assistance General Provisions).

115 67 Fed. Reg. 51036 (Aug. 6, 2002).

116 67 Fed. Reg. 51036, 51038 (Aug. 6, 2002).

117 34 C.F.R. § 668.35(a). Reinstatement of borrower eligibility under a "reasonable and affordable payment plan" is covered at 34 C.F.R. § 682.401(a)(4). *See* 8.3.2, *supra.*

118 *Id.*

119 It is unclear at this point how the Department will treat the one-time right to renew eligibility under a reasonable and affordable payment plan with the more general right to renew eligibility when a borrower is in default or with a judgment. These regulations require borrowers to make payments "satisfactory to the loan holder." It is safest to assume that borrowers only have one chance in total to renew eligibility. *See also* § 8.3 (reasonable and affordable payment plans), *supra.*

120 34 C.F.R. § 674.39(e) (Perkins). *See* § 8.4.3, *infra.*

121 34 C.F.R. § 682.405(b)(1)(iv).

122 20 U.S.C. § 1078-6(a)(4); 34 C.F.R. § 682.405(a)(3), (b)(2) (removal of default from credit report).

123 There is some confusion whether rehabilitating a loan will also clean up the historical section of the student's credit rating. *See* § 3.3.4, *supra.*

124 *See* § 1.5, *supra.*

8.4.3 Perkins Rehabilitation

Perkins Loan borrowers may also rehabilitate defaulted loans.[125] The requirements are similar to the FFEL requirements. Borrowers must make twelve consecutive on-time payments as determined by the institution.[126] Currently, Perkins borrowers are also allowed to rehabilitate a loan when judgment has been entered as long as they sign a new promissory note.[127] As with FFEL and Direct Loans, this provision was eliminated for Perkins Loans during the 2002 negotiated rulemaking sessions.[128] Another difference between Perkins and the other loan rehabilitation programs is that Perkins regulations specify that defaulted loans may be rehabilitated only once.[129] Collection costs related to Perkins Loan rehabilitations cannot exceed 24%.[130]

8.5 Compromise and Write-Off Authority

8.5.1 Compromise

The Department has authority to compromise FFEL or Perkins Loans of any amount or to suspend or terminate collection of these loans.[131] The regulations state that the Department will use the standard set out by the Department of Treasury for compromise of federal claims.[132]

The Treasury regulations give federal agencies discretion to compromise debts if they cannot collect the full amount because:

(1) The debtor is unable to pay the full amount in a reasonable time, as verified through credit reports or other financial information;[133]

(2) The government is unable to collect the debt in full within a reasonable time by enforced collection proceedings;

(3) The cost of collecting the debt does not justify the enforced collection of the full amount;[134] or

(4) There is significant doubt concerning the government's ability to prove its case in court.[135]

Agencies are discouraged from accepting compromises payable in installments.[136] However, this is allowed as long as the agency obtains a legally enforceable written agreement providing that, in the event of default, the full original principal balance of the debt prior to compromise, less sums paid, is reinstated.[137] Agencies are also encouraged to obtain security for repayment.

The Department has also approved Standardized Compromise and Write-Off Procedures for use by all guaranty agencies for FFELs.[138] The compromise standards relate to a negotiated agreement between the student loan borrower and the guaranty agency to accept less than full payment as full liquidation of the entire debt.

This compromise will often, but not always, be binding on the United States. It is important for borrowers to secure written verification of this point to assure that the United States will not demand the student's balance at a later date.

1. *Collection costs* can be waived to obtain payment of all principal and interest in full. Guaranty agencies can make this determination through the supervisor directly charged with collections. In practice, many guaranty agencies will quickly agree to waive collection fees.

2. *30% of principal and interest owing* also can be waived to recover the remaining 70%. If the amount waived only involves interest, the determination can be made by the supervisor directly charged with collections. If principal is to be waived, then the next level of management must make the determination. Guaranty agencies are less likely to agree to compromise interest and principal, because the amounts compromised apparently will be taken out of the 30% guaranty agencies make on a loan collection. On the other hand, guaranty agencies still have an incentive to compromise up to 30%. If the guaranty agencies do not collect anything, they will eventually turn the loan over to the United States and keep none of the 30%.

3. *Compromises involving more than 30%* of outstanding principal and interest will bind only the guaranty agency, *not* the United States. Such compromises cannot waive the Secretary's right to collect the remaining balance due. The guaranty agency can compromise this larger amount as long

125 34 C.F.R. § 674.39.

126 34 C.F.R. § 674.39(a)(2).

127 34 C.F.R. § 674.39(a)(3).

128 67 Fed. Reg. 51036 (Aug. 6, 2002) (proposed rules). *See* § 8.4.1, *supra.*

129 34 C.F.R. § 674.39(e).

130 34 C.F.R. § 674.39(c)(1).

131 34 C.F.R. § 30.70(h). Compromises for other types of debts are set out in 34 C.F.R. § 30.70(a)–(f).

132 34 C.F.R. § 30.70(a), referring to 4 C.F.R. § 103 (regulations now found at 31 C.F.R. § 902).

133 Debtors are required to submit a current financial statement executed under penalty of perjury showing assets, liabilities, income and expenses. 31 C.F.R. § 902.2(g).

134 In these circumstances, agencies may impose an appropriate discount on the amount accepted in compromise for the administrative and litigative costs of collection, with consideration

given to the time it will take to effect collection. The regulations state that collection costs may be a substantial factor in the settlement of small debts. 31 C.F.R. § 902.2(e).

135 31 C.F.R. § 902.2(a).

136 31 C.F.R. § 902.2(f).

137 *Id.*

138 *See* Letter from Jean Frohlicher, President of the National Council of Higher Education Loan Programs, Inc. re Compromise and Write-Off Procedures (Nov. 7, 1993), with attached approval by Robert W. Evans, Director, Division of Policy Development (Nov. 24, 1993), and attached Standardized Compromise and Write-Off Procedures, all found at Clearinghouse No. 49,168.

as it can document the reasons for the action, the guaranty agency director approves the compromise, and the compromise does not bind the United States.

Perkins lenders have discretion to write off loan balances less than $5.00.[139]

---

[139] 34 C.F.R. § 674.47(h). During the spring 2002 negotiated rulemaking sessions, negotiators and the Department agreed to increase this write-off amount to $25. The amount was increased to $50 if the borrower has been billed (and not paid) the balance for at least two years. 67 Fed. Reg. 51036 (Aug. 6, 2002).

Chapter 9 — Challenging Trade School Abuses

9.1 Trade School Abuses

9.1.1 Brief History of Trade School Abuses

Unfair and deceptive vocational and correspondence school practices are a tremendous source of frustration, financial loss and loss of opportunity for consumers, particularly low-income consumers hoping to break out of poverty. Attracted by the financing provided by government student loan and grant programs, many vocational school scams and ill-conceived schools have exploited federally funded student assistance programs.

Abuses were particularly widespread during the 1980s and early 1990s when student financial assistance became more widely available for non-high school graduates and for vocational training.[1] The abuses were fueled by a federal student loan system that created a con artist's perfect dream. Schools were able to pressure vulnerable and low-income consumers into signing documents obligating them to thousands of dollars. Many schools promised that students would not have to repay loans until they got high paying jobs. The schools then literally took the money and ran, leaving loan collection to a third parties and the government.

The tragedy of trade school fraud is that it robs vulnerable people of their dreams. According to testimony given by a former truck driver training school owner, "In the proprietary school business what you sell is dreams and so ninety-nine percent of the sales were made in poor, black areas [at] welfare offices and unemployment lines, and in housing projects. My approach was that if [a prospect] could breathe, scribble his name, had a driver's license, and was over 18 years of age, he was qualified for North American's program."[2]

Although the situation has improved significantly,[3] the abuses of the past are still relevant. Many clients need help dealing with older student loan debt that may be preventing them from going back to school, from getting good credit or even from buying a house. Unless addressed through loan cancellation, repayment, or other remedies, these problems can literally last forever due to the elimination of a statute of limitations for most student loan collection.[4] In addition, as discussed in § 9.1.3, *infra*, there are many new concerns, threatening to open the door to future abuses.

9.1.2 Regulation of Trade Schools

The current regulatory structure for schools participating in federal financial assistance programs is often referred to as the "triad." The three "arms" of the triad consist of the federal Department of Education, state agencies, and accrediting agencies. The Department of Education relies heavily on the other two arms to determine program standards.[5] The federal Department mainly plays a gate keeping role, verifying institutions' eligibility, certifying their financial and administrative capacities, and granting recognition to accrediting agencies.

The state-based regulatory approach varies widely. Some states have developed standards setting, for example, minimum qualifications for trade school teachers. Others have created state tuition recovery funds.[6] Overall, nearly every state agency is understaffed and underfunded.

The role of the accrediting agencies has been particularly controversial.[7] During Senate hearings in the early 1990s,

---

1 For a good history of student financial assistance for vocational schools, see C. Mansfield, *The Federal Trade Commission Holder Rules and its Applicability to Student Loans—Re-Allocating the Risk of Proprietary School Failure*, 26 Wake Forest L. Rev. 635 (1991). In addition, although the issue was not briefed by the parties in the litigation, the *Armstrong* court on its own initiative summarized some of the changes that made federal student aid more widely available over time. *See* Armstrong v. Accrediting Council for Continuing Education and Training, 168 F. Rep. 3d 1362, 1364 (D.C. Cir. 1999).

2 Testimony from S. Rep. No. 102-58 at 12-13 (1991), *quoted in* Patrick F. Linehan, *Dreams Protected: A New Approach to*

Policing Proprietary Schools' Misrepresentations, 89 Geo. L.J. 753 (Mar. 2001).

3 Since the inception of the program in 1991, according to the Department of Education, more than 1100 schools have lost student loan program eligibility. U.S. Department of Education, *Accountability for Results Works: College Loan Default Rates Continue to Decline*, Press Release (Sept. 19, 2001). Individual school default rates are posted on the Department of Education website at www.ed.gov/offices/OSFAP/defaultmanagement/cdr.html. *See* § 3.1.3, *supra*.

4 *See* § 3.2, *supra*.

5 *See generally* General Accounting Office, *Higher Education: Ensuring Quality Education From Proprietary Institutions*, GAO/T-HEHS-96-158 (June 1996).

6 *See* § 9.6, *infra*.

7 *See, e.g.*, S. Rep. No. 102-58 at 20 (1991). For a summary of

the Senate noted the inherent conflict of interest in accreditation: once an agency approves a school for accreditation, the agency thereafter assumes the role of the school's advocate.[8] Despite these conflicts, the basic model persists, allowing for a buffer between trade schools and direct federal oversight.

9.1.3 Current Concerns

9.1.3.1 General

Trade school fraud is by no means only a legacy of the past. There is concern that new trade school abuses will emerge, particularly as welfare reform programs with school-based educational components offer lucrative sources of government education money. Other abuses, unfortunately, often go hand in hand with the growth of for-profit schools. The booming for-profit educational market is increasingly dominated by regional and even national franchises, many with stock shares traded on Wall Street. There are already many complaints about some of these "mega-schools."[9]

In many cases, the types of abuses have changed from the "old days" of trade school fraud. Whereas most of the fraud in the past occurred in schools serving non-high school graduates, much of the fraud today affects a different demographic. Complaints against schools offering longer courses and serving high school graduates are growing.[10]

Another problem is that even legitimate trade schools tend to offer courses in areas with bleak job prospects. A 1997 General Accounting Office (GAO) study found that a large percentage of the federal assistance money that goes to trade school students is used to train students for these low-demand jobs.[11] In some cases, the data was dramatic,

with students being trained for occupations where local supply exceeded demand by ratios of 10 to 1 or more. Common trade school courses, such as barbering/cosmetology and appliance/equipment repair were oversupplied for all states in the study.[12]

Despite the real potential for abuse, the strong trade school lobby argues that the bad schools from the past are gone and that the industry now deserves relief from strict regulation. This argument is striking a chord among many in the Bush Administration and in Congress.

An example of the new political reality is the 2001–2002 debate over incentive compensation. Existing law, enacted in response to prior abuses, prohibits commissions, bonuses, and other incentive payments by school recruiters when those payments are tied directly or indirectly to success in securing enrollments or financial aid.[13] Legislation pending in Congress in 2002 would have taken much of the bite out of this law.[14] However, the Department of Education bypassed the legislative process by proposing to enact many of the provisions in the Congressional bill (and more) during spring 2002 negotiated rulemaking sessions.[15]

9.1.3.2 Reliance on Federal Financial Aid Funds

The continued reliance of many for-profit trade schools on federal student assistance funds has been an issue of concern throughout the history of trade school regulation and fraud. The availability of these funds can bring the possibility of education to previously underserved low-income consumers. This is beneficial if the schools provide a service, but extremely harmful when these students attend scam schools. The main problem, according to a GAO study, is that proprietary schools that rely more heavily on student assistance tend to have poorer student outcomes, including lower completion and placement rates and higher default rates.[16] These schools are also more likely to push students into taking out loans that they will not be able to repay.

Congress passed the 85/15 (now 90/10) rule to address this problem. Enacted as part of the 1992 Higher Education Act reauthorization, the rule requires each school to limit the

newspaper articles exposing these issues as well as government investigations, see Patrick F. Linehan, *Dreams Protected: A New Approach to Policing Proprietary Schools' Misrepresentations*, 89 Geo. L.J. 753 (Mar. 2001). *See also* 9.4.1.4, *supra*.

8   S. Rep. No. 102-58 (1991).

9   The Chronicle of Higher Education keeps an index of for-profit education, noting changes in stock prices, profits and acquisitions. The index was developed by the Center for Research in Security Prices at the University of Chicago's Graduate School of Business.

10   Masters Institute provides an example of this new era. Masters was a private school offering classroom and distance education. It was for a short time part of the Department of Education Distance Education Pilot Project. *See* § 9.1.3.3, *supra*. The school closed very suddenly in 2001, but problems with course quality and other issues had surfaced long before then. *See* California Department of Consumer Affairs, News Release, *State Offers Help For Students Locked Out of Masters Institute in the South Bay, Mar. 7, 2001*; Cecily Barnes, *Masters of Deceit*, Metro Newspaper, Oct. 16–22, 1997 ed. (available on-line at www.metroactive.com).

11   *See* General Accounting Office, *Proprietary Schools: Millions Spent to Train Students for Oversupplied Occupations*, GAO/

HEHS-97-104 (June 1997). In contrast, several major federal job training programs restrict training to fields with favorable job projections. Most welfare to work programs also require welfare agencies to work with private industry councils and ensure that programs provided training for jobs likely to become available in the area. *See Id.*

12   General Accounting Office, *Proprietary Schools: Millions Spent to Train Students for Oversupplied Occupations*, GAO/HEHS-97-104 (June 1997).

13   20 U.S.C. § 1094(a)(20); 34 C.F.R. § 668.24.

14   S. 1445, Internet Equity and Education Act of 2001, 107th Congress, 1st session.

15   67 Fed. Reg. 51718 (Aug. 8, 2002) (Proposed Rules).

16   General Accounting Office, *Proprietary Schools: Poorer Student Outcomes at Schools That Rely More on Federal Student Aid*, GAO/HEHS-97-103 (June 1997).

percentage of revenues it receives from federal financial assistance.[17] Schools are required to calculate the federal student assistance dollars its students receive as the numerator, and total revenues from educational programs as the denominator. The maximum result (equaling the school's federal student assistance dollars as a percentage of total revenues) was initially set at 85%, and then increased to 90%.[18]

A 1997 GAO report affirmed the importance of this rule. Interestingly, the GAO suggested that decreasing the percentage from 85% would be more likely to reduce defaults. However, the Agency noted that this might lead to fewer low-income students enrolling in trade schools.[19] Instead, Congress went the other way, increasing the percentage to 90% (now known as the 90/10 rule).[20] In the spring 2002 negotiated rulemaking sessions, trade school negotiators and others tried unsuccessfully to further amend the rule to allow more funds to be counted as non-federal revenues.[21] This issue is very likely to come up again in the future.

9.1.3.3 Distance Education

Another area of concern is the growing field of distance education. While technological innovation may in some cases provide benefits for low-income students, there are also dangers that diminished classroom (or seat time) will lead to abuses by unscrupulous school operators.

Existing regulations limit schools' ability to receive federal financial assistance for distance education courses in a number of ways. These limits are tied to restrictions on correspondence courses. Schools offering bogus correspondence courses were guilty of some of the most abusive practices during the 1980s and early 1990s. As a result, Congress barred federal funding for most correspondence courses that are not part of programs leading to bachelors, associates or graduate degrees.[22] In addition, degree-granting schools that offer more than 50% of their courses by correspondence are not eligible to participate in the federal financial assistance programs.[23] These schools, even if otherwise eligible, are also considered ineligible if the school enrolls 50% or more of its regular students in correspondence courses.[24]

The rules are different for schools that offer "telecommunications" courses. The main difference between correspondence and telecommunications courses is that correspondence courses involve instruction for students who do not physically attend classes. This may include courses offered by videocassette and discs if the school does not offer comparable instruction to students physically attending classes.[25] In contrast, telecommunications courses are defined as courses offered principally through the use of television, audio, or computer transmission.[26] Telecommunication instruction is not necessarily offered in-person.

Most important, degree-granting schools (schools where at least 50% of the courses lead to a recognized degree) that offer telecommunications courses may participate in federal assistance programs as long as the total of correspondence and telecommunications courses do not equal or exceed 50%.[27]

The limits on telecommunications courses had little effect until recently as more schools began to offer "distance education" courses. The percentage of higher education institutions offering courses through distance education grew by one-third from 1995 to 1997–98 and continues to grow.[28] The regulations cited above are increasingly seen as barriers to integrating distance education into trade school course offerings.

The industry and others have made it a priority to expand funding to more schools offering telecommunications courses, also known as distance education.[29] This was the impetus for the distance education pilot project passed as part of the 1998 Higher Education Act (HEA) Amendments.[30] This project allows schools to apply for relief from the regulations, discussed above, that were passed in 1992 to curb the abuses of correspondence schools. In particular, the program provides waivers from two legislative provisions:

1. The statutory rule that currently bars institutions that enroll 50 percent or more of their students in distance education programs or that offer 50 percent or more of

---

17 34 C.F.R. § 600.5(a)(8). *See* Department of Education, Dear Colleague Letter Gen-99-33 (Oct. 1999).

18 34 C.F.R. § 600.5(a)(8), 600.5(d).

19 General Accounting Office, *Proprietary Schools: Poorer Student Outcomes at Schools That Rely More on Federal Student Aid*, GAO/HEHS-97-103 (June 1997).

20 34 C.F.R. § 600.5(a)(8).

21 *See* 67 Fed. Reg. 51718 (Aug. 8, 2002) (Proposed Rules).

22 20 U.S.C. § 1091(k).

23 34 C.F.R. § 600.7(a)(1)(i).

24 34 C.F.R. § 600.7(a)(1)(ii).

25 34 C.F.R. § 600.2.

26 20 U.S.C. § 1091(l)(4); 34 C.F.R. § 600.2.

27 20 U.S.C. § 1091(l)l; 34 C.F.R. § 600.7(b)(1).

28 National Center for Educational Statistics, Distance Education at Postsecondary Education Institutions: 1997–1998, December 1999, p.5, cited in U.S. Department of Education, Office of Postsecondary Education, Policy, Planning and Innovation, *Report to Congress on the Distance Education Demonstration Programs*, Washington, D.C. Jan. 2001.

29 For example, legislation introduced in Congress in the 107th Congress, S. 1445, *Internet Equity and Education Act of 2001*, proposed to exempt all telecommunications courses from the definition of correspondence courses for any school that had a cohort default rate for each of the three most recent years that was less than 10 percent. Similarly, a student enrolled in a school meeting that criteria would not count as a "correspondence course" student. The legislation was still pending at the time this manual was printed.

30 20 U.S.C. § 1093.

their courses via distance education from participation in the federal student aid programs;[31] and

2. The statutory rule that requires that an academic year provide a minimum of 30 weeks of instruction.[32]

To date, only a few of the schools participating in the pilot project are for-profit trade schools.[33] However, the numbers are likely to grow in the coming years. The challenge for low-income advocates is to help foster the positive aspects of technological innovation while ensuring that borrowers are protected.

9.1.3.4 Scholarship Scams

Companies that take advance payment from consumers to find them scholarships and grants is another growing form of abuse. These companies may send high school and college students postcards advertising that for an advance fee the service can find "unclaimed" scholarship and grant funds from private companies. They promise to refund the fee if the student does not receive a minimum amount. Nevertheless, these companies all too often provide neither the promised financial aid nor the promised refunds.[34] Other times, they claim a refund is not owing because the small print places onerous conditions on receiving a refund.[35] When they cannot get the student to send money up front, the companies may discover the student's checking account number and take money out of the account with an unauthorized demand draft or telecheck.[36]

Sometimes, these companies merely provide consumers with lists of financial aid sources to whom the consumers must apply on their own.[37] One company agreed to stop its practice of selling employment and financial aid directories that they misrepresented as programs that guaranteed students jobs with free room, board and transportation, or free financial aid.[38]

In 2000, Congress passed legislation specifically addressing this issue. The College Scholarship Fraud Prevention Act of 2000 required the United States Sentencing Commission to provide enhanced penalties for financial aid fraud.[39] The Act also requires the Departments of Education, Justice and Federal Trade Commission to coordinate enforcement and outreach activities in this area.[40]

9.2 Litigating Trade School Cases

9.2.1 *Affirmative vs. Defensive Claims*

In most cases, clients will seek legal help for student loans long after they have left or graduated from school. As noted above, the complete elimination of a statute of limitations for most student loans means that collection efforts can go on indefinitely.[41] Some clients may seek legal assistance for loans from ten, twenty, or even thirty years ago.

Although the majority of student loan cases will be defensive, affirmative suits may still be viable in some cases. In general, suing the school affirmatively puts the student in a better stance before the court. In fact, particularly for older, pre-1994 FFELs, some courts refuse to allow borrowers to raise school-related claims defensively. Affirmative claims may be the only available relief in these circumstances.[42]

Moreover, lenders will not always sue, but instead may subject the borrower to tax refund intercepts, debt collection contacts, non-judicial wage garnishments, and other collection tactics. It is usually difficult, although not impossible, to raise school-related claims to these collection actions.[43] Even if the borrower prevails with such defenses, the result

---

31 20 U.S.C. § 1091(l). Waiver authority provided at 20 U.S.C. § 1093(b)(2).

32 20 U.S.C. § 1093(b)(2) (waiver authority).

33 One for-profit school, Masters Institute, as noted earlier, closed in 2001 amidst widespread allegations of fraud. *See* § 9.1.3.1, *supra*. For more information on the pilot project, see www.ed.gov/offices/OPE/PPI/DistEd/index.html.

34 FTC v. National Scholarship Foundation, Inc., 5 Trade Reg. Rep. (CCH) ¶ 24,512 (S.D. Fla. 1998) (order for permanent injunction); FTC v. Deco Consulting Services, Inc., 5 Trade Reg. Rep. (CCH) ¶ 24,363 (S.D. Fla. 1998) (consent decree); FTC v. National Grant Foundation, Inc., 5 Trade Reg. Rep. (CCH) ¶ 24,427 (S.D. Fla. 1998) (proposed consent decree); FTC v. College Assistance Services, Inc., 5 Trade Reg. Rep. (CCH) ¶ 24,357 (S.D. Fla. 1998) (proposed consent decree); FTC v. Career Assistance Planning, Inc., 5 Trade Reg. Rep. (CCH) ¶ 24,218 (N.D. Ga. 1997) (consent decree); FTC v. Nwaigwe, 5 Trade Reg. Rep. (CCH) ¶ 24,253 (D. Md. 1997) (proposed consent decree).

35 FTC v. Student Aid Inc., 5 Trade Reg. Rep. (CCH) ¶ 24,312 (S.D.N.Y. 1997) (proposed consent decree).

36 *Id. See* National Consumer Law Center, Unfair and Deceptive Acts and Practices §§ 5.1.15, 5.1.16 (5th ed. 2001 and Supp.) for a discussion of demand drafts or telechecks.

37 FTC v. National Grant Foundation, Inc., 5 Trade Reg. Rep. (CCH) ¶ 24,427 (S.D. Fla. 1998) (proposed consent decree).

38 FTC v. Progressive Media, Inc., 5 Trade Reg. Rep. (CCH) ¶ 24,304 (W.D. Wash. 1997) (proposed consent decree). More information on the Department of Education's website, www.ed.gov.

39 Scholarship Fraud Prevention Act, Pub. Law No. 106-420, 114 Stat. 1867 (Nov. 1, 2000).

40 Project Scholarscam is the FTC's ongoing project to prevent and prosecute scholarship fraud. For more information, see www.ftc.gov/bcp/conline/edcams/scholarship/index.html. The Department of Education also has consumer education information to help borrowers avoid scholarship scams, available at www.ed.gov/studentaid or by calling 1-800-4FED-AID (1-800-433-3243). *See also* Department of Justice, Department of Education, Federal Trade Commission, *Scholarship Fraud Prevention Act of 2000: First Annual Report to Congress* (May 2002).

41 *See* § 3.2, *supra*.

42 *See* § 9.5, *infra*.

43 *See* § 5.2.2, *supra*.

may be that the guarantor or Department simply abandons that particular collection effort, but later renews other collection activity.

A major obstacle to affirmative litigation is that in many cases, the school will already be closed by the time the client seeks assistance. It is also very common for schools to close during the course of litigation. As a result, relying on a recovery from the school can be a frustrating endeavor.

The reality is that in many cases, affirmative litigation will simply not be an option. The statute of limitations for the various affirmative claims discussed in § 9.3, *infra* may have expired. In addition, the client may already be facing a collection lawsuit for the loan. In these circumstances, the borrower will be forced to raise the school-related claim by way of recoupment to an action to collect on the debt, or as a declaratory action that the debt is not owed.[44]

9.2.2 When a Government Agency Is Suing for Collection

A consumer sued on a loan by a guaranty agency or the United States should consider not just raising school-related defenses to the collection action, but also impleading the school if it is still solvent. Joining the school will also aid discovery and paint a clearer picture for the judge.

When the United States (as opposed to a state guaranty agency) is bringing the lawsuit, there should be little question of the student's right to implead the school or other parties against whom the student has student-loan related claims. The Federal Debt Collection Procedures Act authorizes debtors sued by the United States to join, as a defendant in the same lawsuit, any party owing the debtor money related to the same transaction that form the basis of the government's suit against the debtor.[45]

The Act not only permits students to implead the school,[46] but also authorizes the United States to do so as well. Where the student has neither the legal resources to implead the school nor the financial resources to satisfy a judgment, the United States' best course would be to implead the school and seek payment from that party.

Where no collection action has been brought against the student, but where tax refund intercepts and other collection contacts are threatened, and the school is insolvent, another approach is to bring an affirmative action for declaratory relief that the loan amount is not owed to the guarantors or the Department because of school-related claims.[47]

9.3 Legal Challenges to Trade School Abuse

9.3.1 General

Whether the student is suing the school, raising school-related claims as a defense to repayment of the student loan, or seeking a declaration that the loan amount is not owed because of school misconduct, an essential step is establishing viable claims against the school. This section sets out legal theories and strategies for bringing claims against the school and related entities. The ability to raise these school-related claims as a defense to loan repayment is examined at § 9.4, *infra*.

9.3.2 UDAP Theories to Challenge School Misconduct

9.3.2.1 General

Unfair and Deceptive Acts and Practices (UDAP) claims are generally well-suited to challenge trade school abuses. Oral and print misrepresentations can be deceptive; the failure to disclose can be deceptive; and enrolling students unable to benefit from a program can be unfair or unconscionable.[48] The student's proof burden is simplified with a UDAP claim because the student normally need not prove intent, scienter, or other components of a common law fraud claim.[49] Some states do, however, require proof of reliance on the deceptive statement or conduct.[50] UDAP remedies often offer multiple or punitive damages and attorney fees.[51]

Despite the existence of federal regulation of the student loan program, the Higher Education Act should generally not preempt UDAP claims against a school. Specifically, only state claims that conflict with the purposes or provisions of the HEA should be preempted.[52]

---

44 Defensive claims are discussed in § 9.5, *infra*.

45 28 U.S.C. § 3012.

46 *See* H.R. Rep. No. 736, 101th Cong., 2d Sess. 30 (Sept. 21, 1990), *reprinted in* 1991 U.S.C.C.A.N. 6638.

47 *See* § 9.5.3.1.7, *infra*.

48 *See generally* National Consumer Law Center, Unfair and Deceptive Acts and Practices §§ 4.3, 4.4 (5th ed. 2001 and Supp.).

49 *See id.* § 4.2.

50 *See id.* §§ 7.5.2, 10.5.2. *See, e.g.,* Finstad v. Wasburn University of Topeka, 845 P.2d 685 (Kan. 1993) (in UDAP case, court found students failed to demonstrate causation between school's false statement regarding accreditation and students' injuries; students did not claim they were induced to enroll by the false statement).

51 *See* National Consumer Law Center, Unfair and Deceptive Acts and Practices Ch. 8 (5th ed. 2001 and Supp.).

52 *See* Morgan v. Markerdowne Corp., 976 F. Supp. 301 (D.N.J. 1997) (HEA preempts only those state laws which are in conflict with it), *class cert. denied*, 201 F.R.D. 341 (D.N.J. 2001) (court found no typical and predominant questions whether the plaintiffs relied on school's misrepresentations in deciding to enroll); Williams v. National School of Health Technology, Inc., 836 F. Supp. 273 (E.D. Pa. 1993). *But see* Wilson v. Chism, 279 Ill. App. 3d. 934, 665 N.E.2d 446 (1996), *appeal denied*, 671

This section will detail existing UDAP precedent concerning trade school abuses, but other unfair or deceptive practices are equally actionable under a UDAP statute. Trade school abuses should be challenged even if the exact practice is not listed below.

9.3.2.2 FTC Guides and Rule

The FTC has issued guides concerning unfair and deceptive private vocational school practices.[53] The guides specify that schools cannot misrepresent, through their name or otherwise, that they are connected with government agencies or civil service commissions or that they are an employment agency or employer.[54]

Among other provisions, the FTC Guides require that schools disclose if the course is offered through correspondence.[55] It is deceptive for a school to misrepresent the nature of its approval or accreditation or the extent to which former students, employers, or counselors recommend a course.[56]

The FTC updated its vocational school guides in 1998, renaming them the "Guides for Private Vocational and Distance Education Schools."[57] The most significant change was a new provision addressing misrepresentations about a school's placement success following training. The guides now specifically state that it is deceptive for a school, in promoting a course of training, to misrepresent the availability of employment after graduation from a course, the success that the member's graduates have realized in obtaining such employment, or the salary that the member's graduates will receive in such employment.[58] The new guides also state that it is deceptive for a school to misrepresent that the lack of a high school education or prior training is not an impediment to successful completion of a course or obtaining employment.[59]

9.3.2.3 Other Precedent

Courts have identified a number of other trade school practices not enumerated in the FTC Guides as unfair or deceptive. State UDAP precedent and FTC case law provide important additional principles concerning job and earnings claims, student loans, and refund policies.

Schools may not deceive students with respect to the nature, terms or conditions of contractual obligations, veterans' educational benefits, and federally insured student loans.[60] A school may not misrepresent its refund policy or deceive students into attending additional classes before dropping out with the result that their contractual obligation is significantly increased under the refund formula.[61] Schools must also pay all owed refunds.[62]

N.E.2d 745 (1996) (where consumer's claim was based on school's false certification pursuant to HEA standards, the consumer's remedy was to seek a false certification discharge). [*Editor's note*: this case is wrong if it implies that the HEA generally preempts UDAP challenges to a school's admission of unqualified applicants.]

53 Guides for Private Vocational and Distance Education Schools, 16 C.F.R. §§ 254.0–254.10. In 1978, the FTC also promulgated a rule related to private trade school activities. Trade Regulation Rule Concerning Proprietary Vocational and Home-Study Schools, 43 Fed. Reg. 60,795 (Dec. 18, 1978). The Commission withdrew the Vocational School Rule's effective date pending further Commission action, and in 1988 finally terminated the Rule. 53 Fed. Reg. 29,482 (Aug. 5, 1988). Nevertheless, the Rule's Statement of Basis and Purpose, 43 Fed. Reg. 60,791 (Dec. 18, 1978) and the FTC staff report recommending the rule still provide a useful factual and legal background to vocational school issues. Bureau of Consumer Protection, Proprietary Vocational and Home-Study Schools, Final Report and Proposed Trade Regulation Rule, Clearinghouse No. 31,041 (1976).

54 16 C.F.R. § 254.2. *See also* FTC v. Couture School of Modeling, 5 Trade Reg. Rep. (CCH) ¶ 22,815 (D. Md. 1990) (injunction); United States v. Eyler, 5 Trade Reg. Rep. (CCH) ¶ 22,891 (M.D. Fla. 1990) (consent decree); People v. Wilshire Computer College, Clearinghouse No. 46,309B (Cal. Super. Ct. 1991) (preliminary injunction pursuant to stipulation).

55 16 C.F.R. § 254.2(c).

56 16 C.F.R. § 254.3. *See also* Malone v. Academy of Court Reporting, 64 Ohio App. 3d 588, 582 N.E.2d 54 (1990) (concealment of fact that school was not certified or accredited to issue promised associate degree violates UDAP); Cavaliere v. Duff's Business Institute, 605 A.2d 397 (Pa. Super. Ct. 1992); Webster College v. Speier, 605 S.W.2d 712 (Tex. Civ. App. 1980). *But see* Lidecker v. Kendall College, 550 N.E.2d 1121 (Ill. App. Ct. 1990) (failure to inform prospective students of nursing school's lack of accreditation not a UDAP violation where school did not intend that students rely on the omission, and the lack of accreditation did not cause the student harm).

57 63 Fed. Reg. 42,570 (Aug. 10, 1998) (amending 16 C.F.R. part 254), *corrections*, 63 Fed. Reg. 72,350 (Dec. 31, 1998).

58 16 C.F.R. § 254.4(d).

59 16 C.F.R. § 254.5.

60 Bell & Howell Co., 95 FTC 761 (1980) (consent order); People v. Wilshire Computer College, Clearinghouse No. 46,309B (Cal. Super. Ct. 1991) (preliminary injunction pursuant to stipulation); Manley v. Wichita Business College, 237 Kan. 427, 701 P.2d 893 (1985). *But see* Finstad v. Wasburn University of Topeka, 845 P.2d 685 (Kan. 1993) (overruling the holding in *Manley* that actual damages are not required in Kansas UDAP cases); Gamble v. University System of New Hampshire, 610 A.2d 357 (N.H. 1992) (university's imposition of mid-semester tuition increase due to fiscal crisis not a UDAP violation where it notified almost all affected students of possible increase in letter accompanying initial billing for semester).

61 People v. Wilshire Computer College, Clearinghouse No. 46,309B (Cal. Super. Ct. 1991) (preliminary injunction pursuant to stipulation); Manley v. Wichita Business College, 237 Kan. 427, 701 P.2d 893 (1985); Reynolds v. Sterling College, Inc., 750 A.2d 1020 (Vt. 2000) (summary judgment awarded to student on contractual claim, consumer fraud claim remanded. Change in refund policy after substantial tuition payments had been made found to be a unilateral modification of specific contractual term for which no consideration had been received). *But see* Finstad v. Wasburn University of Topeka, 845 P.2d 685 (Kan. 1993) (overruling the holding in *Manley* that actual damages are not required in Kansas UDAP cases).

62 United States v. Eyler, 5 Trade Reg. Rep. (CCH) ¶ 22,891 (M.D.

It is deceptive to misrepresent the amount of personalized instruction available in a correspondence course, or the difficulty of the correspondence courses themselves.[63] Schools cannot misrepresent students' ability to benefit from a course. Schools cannot fail to meet state entrance standards.[64] Nor can schools encourage students to falsify their identity or immigration status.[65]

Also deceptive are misrepresentations concerning the nature of school placement services.[66] For example, in one UDAP case, consumer recovery was based on the school's "admissions officers" (who worked on commission and made as much as $56,000 a year) promising 90 to 95% job placement when in fact the school was reporting to its accrediting agency job placement rates averaging only 47%. The school's higher 90 to 95% figure was derived only from students who kept in touch with the school's placement office, not the total number of the school's graduates.[67]

Another source of precedent on unfair or deceptive trade school practices may be found in a state's education statutes, such as California's Maxine Waters Student Protection Act.[68] In some cases, these statutes will provide for a private right of action. If not, a violation of these standards may be actionable under a state UDAP statute.

9.3.3 Other State and Common Law Claims

In some states, a state RICO claim may provide superior remedies than a UDAP claim, or the two together may provide more relief than just a UDAP claim.[69] For example, in Oregon one UDAP and state RICO case against a school resulted in a jury verdict of $320,000 in multiple and punitive damages for nine former computer school students.[70] On appeal, the state RICO recovery was reversed on technical grounds, but all the UDAP actual and punitive damages were affirmed, as was the award of attorney fees to the consumers.[71]

State UDAP claims are key to school cases, but other theories should also be considered. Common law fraud, in particular, should not be overlooked because of the possibility of punitive damages.[72]

However, fraud and negligence claims may be difficult to bring in trade school cases. To prove fraudulent misrepresentation, for example, plaintiffs must show that: (1) the defendant made a false representation; (2) acted with an intent to deceive; (3) the defendant made a representation directed at a particular person; (4) the plaintiff relied on the representation; and (5) the plaintiff was damaged as a result.

The first element may be particularly difficult as many trade school employees make representations that are clearly misleading, but often difficult to prove as false. For example, representations about job placement made before a student enrolls may be different when the student graduates due to many factors including unexpected changes in the labor market and the student's academic performance.[73] Proving causation can also be a problem if the plaintiff is trying to prove that his failure to learn marketable skills is the schools' fault.[74]

Similarly, a common problem with negligence claims is showing that the school had a duty of care to the plaintiff

---

Fla. 1990) (consent decree); People v. Wilshire Computer College, Clearinghouse No. 46,309B (Cal. Super. Ct. 1991) (preliminary injunction pursuant to stipulation). In addition, there is now a federal discharge program to reimburse students for unpaid refunds. *See* § 6.4, *supra*.

63 Bell & Howell Co., 95 FTC 761 (1980) (consent order).

64 People v. Wilshire Computer College, Clearinghouse No. 46,309B (Cal. Super. Ct. 1991) (preliminary injunction pursuant to stipulation).

65 *Id.*

66 Control Data Corp., 97 FTC 84 (1981) (consent order); Bell & Howell Co., 95 FTC 761 (1980) (consent order); Universal Training Service Inc., 94 FTC 167 (1979) (consent order); Art Instruction Schools Inc., 93 FTC 32 (1979) (consent order); Driver Training Institute Inc., 92 FTC 235 (1978) (consent order); Commercial Programming Unlimited Inc., 88 FTC 913 (1976) (consent order); Lafayette United Corp., 88 FTC 683 (1976) (consent order); Lear Siegler Inc., 86 FTC 860 (1975) (consent order); Weaver Airline Personnel School, 85 FTC 237 (1975) (consent order); Eastern Detective Academy Inc., 78 FTC 1428 (1971); Missouri College of Automation, 67 FTC 258 (1965) (consent order); People *ex rel.* Abrams v. New York Vocational School, Inc., Clearinghouse No. 43,088 (N.Y. Sup. Ct. 1987); Florida Rules of the Dept. of Legal Affairs, ch. 2-18, Contracts for Future Consumer Services.

67 Beckett v. Computer Career Institute, Inc. (Or. Cir. Ct. July 2, 1990), *aff'd in part and rev'd in part*, 120 Or. App. 143, 852 P.2d 840 (1993).

68 Cal. Educ. Code § 94850 (formerly § 94316). Most of the provisions in the California Student Protection Act apply only to violations that occurred after January 1, 1990. For some provisions, the effective date is January 1, 1991. There are some, more limited protections in the California Code for pre-1990 violations.

69 *See* National Consumer Law Center, Unfair and Deceptive Acts and Practices § 9.3 (5th ed. 2001 and Supp.).

70 Beckett v. Computer Career Institute, Inc. (Or. Cir. Ct. July 2, 1990), *aff'd in part and rev'd in part*, 120 Or. App. 143, 852 P.2d 840 (1993).

71 Beckett v. Computer Career Institute, Inc., 120 Or. App. 143, 852 P.2d 840 (1993).

72 *See* Moy v. Adelphi Institute, Inc., 866 F. Supp. 696 (E.D.N.Y. 1994) (misrepresentation and fraud claims survived motion to dismiss, but not claim for negligent misrepresentation or breach of fiduciary duty), related case at Moy v. Terranova, 1999 WL 118773 (E.D.N.Y.); Phillips College of Alabama, Inc. v. Lester, 622 So. 2d 308 (Ala. 1993) (a valid fraud claim asserted against school that had promised in written materials but failed to provide a specific number of hours of practical training); Craig v. Forest Institute of Professional Psychology, 713 So. 2d 967 (Ala. Civ. App. 1997).

73 *See generally* Patrick F. Linehan, *Dreams Protected: A New Approach to Policing Proprietary Schools' Misrepresentations*, 89 Geo. L. J. 753 (Mar. 2001).

74 *See, e.g.*, Idrees v. American University of the Caribbean, 546 F. Supp. 1342 (S.D.N.Y. 1982).

student. The main barrier to these claims is judicial academic abstention doctrine.[75] This doctrine developed from judicial concern that decisions about educational quality are often subjective. In addition, courts are hesitant to appear to be creating educational policy, preferring to leave this to educational experts.[76]

9.3.4 Contract Claims

9.3.4.1 General

Courts have also, on a variety of legal theories, rescinded enrollment agreements and directed schools to reimburse students for their tuition payments or student loan debts.[77]

The threshold question in contract claims against schools is whether there is an enforceable contractual promise. Courts are reluctant to enforce a school's representations that it will provide a "quality education" or other assertions about the value of the school's diploma because of the subjective inquiry involved.

In general, courts are more likely to find a breach of a contractual obligation if the student's claim is based, at least in part, on objective promises or guarantees, particularly if they are set forth in written materials, such as catalogs or advertisements.[78] School catalogs, bulletins, and regulations should be considered part of the contract between the school and its students.[79]

9.3.4.2 No Claim for Educational Malpractice

The general rule is that courts will not allow a claim for educational malpractice, but may allow a contract claim based on failure to provide any instruction or failure to provide a specific service.[80] This view is based on the belief that there is no clear standard of care in education.

For example, in one case, the court in reviewing student claims of breach of contract based on alleged unsuitable computer courses, held that an inquiry into whether the courses were appropriate was "best left to the educational community. A different situation might be presented if defendants were to provide 'no educational services' or failed to meet its contractual obligation to provide certain specified services, such as a designated number of hours of instruction. . . ."[81]

The difference between educational malpractice and a contract claim is not always clear. In general, the more limited the claim (for example, a school's failure to offer a particular promised course) and the more the claim is tied to written promises, the stronger the case.[82]

---

75 *See, e.g.,* Alsides v. Brown Inst., Ltd, 592 N.W.2d 468 (Minn. App. 1999) (rejecting claims against educational institutions outside of a contractual relationship); *see generally* Patrick F. Linehan, *Dreams Protected: A New Approach to Policing Proprietary Schools' Misrepresentations*, 89 Geo. L. J. 753 (Mar. 2001). *See also* § 9.3.4.2 (educational malpractice claims), *supra.*

76 *Id.*

77 André v. Pace University, 170 Misc. 2d 893, 655 N.Y.S.2d 777 (1996), *rev'g* 161 Misc. 2d 613, 618 N.Y.S.2d 975 (1994) (school's complete failure to provide course at promised level allows damages and rescission); Brown v. Hambric, 638 N.Y.S.2d 873, 168 Misc. 2d 502 (1995) (travel agents school found to be a deceptive pyramid scheme; rescission of contract warranted and failure to deliver the promised support and training was unconscionable and deceptive business practice); James v. SCS Business & Technical Institute, 595 N.Y.S.2d 885 (Civ. Ct. Cty. of New York 1992) (unconscionability and lack of consideration); Cavaliere v. Duff's Business Institute, 605 A.2d 397 (Pa. Super. Ct. 1992) (general claim of lack of quality education not actionable, but misrepresentation or breach of contract would be).

78 Another good source to establish a contractual relationship is a student handbook. *See generally* Idrees v. American Univ. of the Caribbean, 546 F. Supp. 1342 (S.D.N.Y. 1982) (inaccurate and misleading statements in a university brochure about facilities, equipment and faculty constituted fraudulent misrepresentation); Ralph D. Mawdsley, *Litigation Involving Higher Education Employee and Student Handbooks*, 109 Ed. Law. Rep. 1031 (1996); Claudia G. Catalano, *Liability of Private School or Educational Institution for Breach of Contract Arising From Provision of Deficient Educational Instruction*, 46 A.L.R.5th 581 (1997).

79 Ross v. Creighton University, 957 F.2d 410 (7th Cir. 1992)

(basic legal relationship between student and school is contractual in nature). *See also* Gally v. Columbia University, 22 F. Supp. 2d 199 (S.D.N.Y. 1998) (implied contract between students and school required university to act in good faith and students to satisfy academic requirements and comply with school procedures); Zumbrun v. University of So. Calif., 25 Cal. App. 3d 1, 101 Cal. Rptr. 499 (1972); Wickstrom v. North Idaho College, 725 P.2d 155 (Idaho 1986).

80 Ambrose v. New England Ass'n of Schools and Colleges, Inc., 2000 WL 1195363 (D. Me.), *aff'd*, 252 F.3d 488 (1st Cir. 2001); Whayne v. United States Dept. of Education, 915 F. Supp. 1143 (D. Kan. 1996) (allegation that education simply was not good enough insufficient to state a claim for breach of contract; educational malpractice claim rejected as a matter of state law); Cencor Inc. v. Tolman, 868 P.2d 396 (Colo. 1994) (although no claim for educational malpractice, plaintiff may have a claim for failure to provide a specific service); Page v. Klein Tools, Inc., 610 N.W.2d 900 (Mich. 2000) (explains policy considerations underlying various courts' rejection of educational malpractice claims); Alsides v. Brown Institute, 592 N.W.2d 468 (Minn. App. 1999) (courts may consider contract, fraud, and misrepresentation claims only if they do not require inquiry into the nuances of educational processes and theories); Andre v. Pace University, 170 Misc. 2d 893, 655 N.Y.S.2d 777 (1996), *rev'g* 161 Misc. 2d 613, 618 N.Y.S. 2d 975 (1994); Cavaliere v. Duff's Business Institute, 413 Pa. Super. 357, 605 A.2d 397 (1992) (if the contract with the school were to provide for certain specified services such as, for example, a designated number of hours of instruction and the school failed to meet its obligation, then a contract action with appropriate consequential damages might be viable).

81 Andre v. Pace University, 170 Misc. 2d 893, 655 N.Y.S.2d 777 (1996), *rev'g* 161 Misc. 2d 613, 618 N.Y.S.2d 975 (1994).

82 Dillon v. Ultrasound Diagnostic Schools, 1997 U.S. Dist. LEXIS 20795 (E.D. Pa. 1997) (plaintiff's complaints identified specific alleged benefits and services which defendants promised and failed to provide so as to state a claim for breach of educational contract); Grundlach v. Reinstein, 924 F. Supp. 684 (E.D. Pa. 1996) (no written contact between law school and

9.3.4.3 Other Contract Claims

Courts have found a lack of consideration in some education cases. For example, failure of consideration was found where the school accepted the student's tuition and failed to provide the promised educational services.[83] In another case, the court awarded summary judgment to a student, agreeing that a change in the school's refund policy after substantial tuition payments had been made was a unilateral modification of a specific contractual term for which no consideration had been received.[84]

Some courts have also allowed an implied contract theory.[85] Even when a contract claim is not viable, UDAP and/or common law fraud and negligence claims are often possible.[86]

9.3.5 Federal Claims

There are two primary federal claims against schools, which provide federal court jurisdiction—the federal RICO statute[87] and the federal Higher Education Act (HEA).[88] In general, the consumer should have a good reason to seek federal instead of state court jurisdiction, because there are serious drawbacks with RICO and particularly with HEA claims.

A RICO claim requires consumers to prove various technical elements, which will significantly complicate a case.[89] Nevertheless, RICO claims have proved successful in a number of vocational school cases.[90]

The HEA claim may be dismissed outright, because most courts find there is no implied private right of action under the statute.[91] The HEA also explicitly states that failure to

---

student, student failed to identify specific manner in which school breached contract); Cencor Inc. v. Tolman, 868 P.2d 396 (Colo. 1994) (court agreed that enrollment agreement and school catalog constituted the express terms of the contract and that students showed specific services which had not been provided; also found failure to provide qualified teacher); Wickstrom v. North Idaho College, 725 P.2d 155 (Idaho 1986); Alsides v. Brown Institute, 592 N.W.2d 468 (Minn. App. Ct. 1999) (allowing students to proceed with claims involving a computer school's promises to provide instruction on a particular software program and particular types of computers; frequent absences or tardiness of instructors; insufficient operable computers; outdated hardware and software; and failure to deliver the number of hours of instruction promised); Squires v. Sierra Nevada Ed. Foundation, 823 P.2d 256 (Nev. 1991); Brown v. Hambric, 638 N.Y.S.2d 873, 168 Misc. 2d 502 (1995); Ryan v. University of N.C. Hosps., 494 S.E.2d 789 (N.C. App. 1998) (court upheld claim for breach of contract); Britt v. Chestnut Hill College, 429 Pa. Super. 263, 632 A.2d 557 (Pa. Super. 1993); Thomas v. French, 30 Wash. App. 811, 638 P.2d 613 (1981), *rev'd on other grounds*, 99 Wash. 2d 95, 659 P.2d 1097 (1983) (viable contract claim where private cosmetology school's contract expressly required the school to prepare the students to take a state cosmetology exam).

83 James v. SCS Business & Technical Institute, 59 N.Y.S.2d 885 (Civ. Ct. Cty. of New York 1992).

84 Reynolds v. Sterling College, Inc., 750 A.2d 1020 (Vt. 2000).

85 Gally v. Columbia University, 22 F. Supp. 2d 199 (S.D.N.Y. 1998); Gupta v. New Britain Gen. Hospital, 687 A.2d 111 (Conn. 1996) (residency contract is an educational contract carrying an implied covenant of good faith and fair dealing. Resident failed to produce any evidence showing hospital showed bad faith or arbitrary manner in its dismissal of resident); Wickstrom v. North Idaho College, 725 P.2d 155 (Idaho 1986) (valid cause of action based on breach of implied contract where school failed to satisfy "objective criteria" such as number of hours). *But see* Harris v. Adler School of Professional Psychology, 723 N.E.2d 717 (Ill. App. Ct. 1999) (no cause of action in Illinois for breach of implied provision of good faith. Students dismissed from doctoral program on basis of failed exam had alleged school breached implied term in failing to have objective and articulable criteria for grading exams).

86 *See* § 9.3.2, *supra. See generally* Moy v. Adelphi Institute, 866 F. Supp. 696 (E.D.N.Y. 1994) (student stated prima facie cause of action in fraud by alleging reliance on school's recruitment statements and catalog concerning federal funding, educational facilities and job placement, especially in light of fact that most

students were welfare and public assistance recipients desperately seeking to improve themselves), related case at Moy v. Terranova, 1999 WL 118773 (E.D.N.Y.); Craig v. Forest Institute of Professional Psychology, 713 So. 2d 967 (Ala. Civ. App. 1997) (breach of contract and fraud claim actionable where school failed completely in providing promised educational services); Hellvig v. City of New York, 662 N.Y.S.2d 316 (App. Div. 1995) (while educational malpractice is not actionable, causes of action are recognized for fraud and other intentional torts if properly pled); Carol Crocca, *Liability of Private Vocational or Trade School for Fraud or Misrepresentation Including Student to Enroll or Pay Fees*, 85 A.L.R.4th 1079 (1991 and Supp.).

87 18 U.S.C. §§ 1961–1968. See National Consumer Law Center, Unfair and Deceptive Acts and Practices §§ 9.2, 9.3 (5th ed. 2001 and Supp.) for an analysis of the federal and state RICO statutes.

88 20 U.S.C. §§ 1001–1010. Truth in Lending does not apply to FFEL, Perkins, or Federal Direct Loans. *See* National Consumer Law Center, Truth in Lending § 2.4.5 (4th ed. 1999 and Supp.).

89 *See* National Consumer Law Center, Unfair and Deceptive Acts and Practices § 9.2 (5th ed. 2001 and Supp.).

90 *See* Rosario v. Livaditis, 963 F.2d 1013 (7th Cir. 1992), *cert. denied*, 506 U.S. 1051 (1993) (Illinois law); Rodriguez v. McKinney, 878 F. Supp. 744 (E.D. Pa. 1995); Moy v. Adelphi Institute, Inc., 866 F. Supp. 696 (E.D.N.Y. 1994), related case at Moy v. Terranova, 1999 WL 118773 (E.D.N.Y.); Gonzalez v. North American College, 700 F. Supp. 362 (S.D. Tex. 1988) (students sufficiently alleged RICO claim). *But see* Johnson v. Midland Career Institute, 1996 U.S. Dist. LEXIS 1308 (N.D. Ill. 1996).

91 *See* Labickas v. Arkansas State University, 78 F.3d 333 (8th Cir. 1996), *cert. denied*, 117 S. Ct. 395 (1997); Morgan v. Markerdowne Corp., 976 F. Supp. 301 (D.N.J. 1997); Bartels v. Alabama Commercial College, 918 F. Supp. 1565 (S.D. Ga. 1995), *aff'd without published op.*, 189 F.3d 483 (11th Cir. 1999), *cert. denied*, 528 U.S. 1074 (2000); Moy v. Adelphi Institute, Inc., 866 F. Supp. 696 (E.D.N.Y. 1994); Spinner v. Chesapeake Business Institute of Virginia, Clearinghouse No. 49,131A (E.D. Va. Feb. 5, 1993); Keams v. Tempe Technical Institute, 807 F. Supp. 569 (D. Ariz. 1992); Jackson v. Culinary School of Washington, 811 F. Supp. 714 (D.D.C. 1993) (claim dismissed based on summary judgment motion that students had not presented evidence of origination relationship), *aff'd on other grounds*, 27 F.3d 573 (D.C. Cir. 1994) (origination theory not

comply with its loan disclosure requirements does *not* provide a basis for a claim for civil damages.[92] Similarly, the school's failure to adhere to federal procedures and requirements, including collection provisions, is not a basis for affirmative damages or a defense to collection efforts.[93]

Federal court jurisdiction is the only benefit of an HEA claim. No multiple or statutory damages or attorney fees will be available. In addition, anything that violates the HEA should also be a UDAP, contract or tort violation. The RICO claim, at least, has the benefit of treble damages and attorney fees, and its structure is well-suited to bringing in as defendants the school, school personnel, lenders, accrediting associations, and other parties.

9.4 Affirmative Litigation Against Vocational Schools

9.4.1 Potential Defendants

9.4.1.1 When the School Is Bankrupt or Insolvent

If the school is already in bankruptcy, advocates should consider recovering a judgment in bankruptcy. Students may have a consumer priority, giving them first crack at any school assets ahead of unsecured creditors.[94] Another benefit arises if the student's attorney serves on a creditor's committee. In these cases, the attorney fees for that service will be paid out of the school's assets.[95]

Another possible approach to recover from a bankrupt school is to jump ahead of other creditors by means of a criminal restitution order. *United States v. Grundhoefer*[96] affirms an order of almost $1 million in criminal restitution to students victimized by a private vocational school. Brooklyn and Bronx Legal Services suggested to two different federal judges sentencing several principals of the school that all the criminal restitution go to defrauded students and not to the school's other creditors. The judges agreed, instructing the government and the legal services attorneys to work out a restitution plan. The school's bankruptcy trustee, representing the school's other creditors, appealed. The Second Circuit found no abuse of discretion in the restitution plan, and no standing by the other creditors to object to the courts' orders.[97]

When dealing with an insolvent school, advocates should also explore the following potential alternative defendants:

- *A bonding company or state tuition recovery fund*, since schools are licensed by many states, and a bond or contribution to a state tuition recovery fund is usually a pre-condition to licensure.[98]
- *The parent company or franchisor* is often a deep pocket and may aid or abet the school's misrepresentations.
- *Owners, officers,*[99]*and employees are responsible* for their own actions, even if they are acting as a corporate agent. Individuals dealing directly with a student, and those supervising those individuals are potential defendants, as is a school's owner to the extent the owner supervises the school or to the extent the corporate veil can be pierced.
- *Advertising agencies, accountants, lawyers, or others aiding and abetting a fraudulent scheme* are individually liable for their own misconduct.[100]

9.4.1.2 Claims Against Private Accrediting Agencies

9.4.1.2.1 General

A private accrediting association is responsible for monitoring the school's educational program, admissions procedures, advertising, and sales techniques. The school's ac-

---

enforceable against the Secretary), *vacated on other grounds*, 115 S. Ct. 2573 (1995) (appellate court used de novo instead of abuse of discretion standard to review district court's decision to decide state law issues in declaratory judgment action), *remanded to district court on state law claims, but affirming own ruling on origination*, 59 F.3d 254 (D.C. Cir. 1995) (to determine on what basis federal court decided to rule on state law issues), *motion dismissed*, 1995 U.S. App. LEXIS 22304 (D.C. Cir. 1995); Shorter v. Alexander, Clearinghouse No. 47,950 (N.D. Ga. Dec. 8, 1992); Graham v. Security Sav. & Loan, 125 F.R.D. 687 (N.D. Ind. 1989); *But see* Tipton v. Northeastern Business College, Clearinghouse No. 44,339 (S.D. W. Va. Jan. 8, 1988) (private right of action); Chavez v. LTV Aerospace Corp., 412 F. Supp. 4 (N.D. Tex. 1976) (private cause of action where school allegedly imposed illegal charges on students).

92 Student loan lenders are also not subject to Truth in Lending requirements. 20 U.S.C. § 1083(c).

93 *See, e.g.*, U.S. v. Lewis, 2001 U.S. Dist. LEXIS 9909 (D. Kan. 2001); Vanderbilt University v. Henderson, 2001 Tenn. App. LEXIS 762 (Ct. App. Tenn. 2001).

94 *See, e.g., In re* Longo, 144 B.R. 305 (Bankr. Md. 1992) (Maryland Higher Education Commission brought tuition recovery claims on behalf of student borrowers. Court granted consumer deposit priority pursuant to 11 U.S.C. § 507(a)(6). School president argued unsuccessfully that the school's services were business and not consumer in nature).

95 A more detailed analysis of a consumer creditor's rights where a company has filed for bankruptcy can be found in National Consumer Law Center, Unfair and Deceptive Acts and Practices

§ 6.8 (5th ed. 2001 and Supp.) and National Consumer Law Center, Consumer Bankruptcy Law and Practice Ch. 17 (6th ed. 2000 and Supp.).

96 916 F.2d 788 (2d Cir. 1990).

97 *Id.*

98 *See* § 9.6, *infra* (student tuition recovery funds).

99 *See* Goldsmith v. Rodano, Clearinghouse No. 50,943C (Cal. Super. Ct. Aug. 21, 1995) (former president agrees to pay $100,000 to 75 students and $30,000 to student's attorney).

100 *See* National Consumer Law Center, Unfair and Deceptive Acts and Practices § 6.5 (5th ed. 2001 and Supp.).

creditation makes a school eligible for government assistance programs, and the failure to adequately examine a school may be directly connected to the student's injury.

As outlined by the Department of the Education, the functions of accreditation include:

> Certifying that an institution or program has met established standards;
>
> Assisting students in identifying acceptable institutions;
>
> Assisting institutions in determining the acceptability of transfer credits;
>
> Creating goals for self-improvement of weaker programs and stimulating a general raising of standards among educational institutions;
>
> Establishing criteria for professional certification and licensure; and
>
> Identifying institutions and programs for the investment of public and private funds.[101]

The United States Department of Education does not review the educational quality of private vocational schools before certifying their eligibility to participate in the GSL program. Instead the Department of Education recognizes various private accrediting agencies and associations whose job it is to review the educational standards of the schools.

In general, the agency must have the administrative and fiscal capacity to carry out accrediting activities.[102] The agency is required to demonstrate that it has standards for accreditation that are sufficiently rigorous to ensure that the agency is a reliable authority on the quality of education or training in institutions it accredits.[103]

The Secretary of Education recognizes approximately 100 major national accrediting agencies, but only a few have accredited the majority of proprietary vocational schools over the last decade, including:

- The Accrediting Bureau for Health Education Schools (ABHES);
- The Accrediting Council for Continuing Education and Training (ACCET);
- The Association of Independent Colleges and Schools (AICS) (now joined with NATTS into the Accrediting Council for Independent Colleges and Schools);
- The National Association of Trade and Technical Schools (NATTS) (later joined with AICS into the Accrediting Council for Independent Colleges and Schools);
- The National Accrediting Commission of Cosmetology Arts and Sciences (NACCAS);

- The National Home Study Council (NHSC); and
- The Southern Association of Colleges and Schools, the Commission on Colleges.[104]

The process by which the Department of Education recognizes accrediting agencies has been severely criticized. The staff of the United States Senate Permanent Subcommittee on Investigations issued a report finding that owners "can get an unaccredited school accredited simply by buying an already accredited school and developing some connection, however tenuous, between the two."[105] Similarly, a small, accredited school can suddenly sprout dozens of branch schools all over the country, and the accrediting association will grant the branches automatic accreditation. Similar conclusions were reached by the Department of Education's own Inspector General.[106] Unfortunately, the Department rarely invokes its power to suspend or terminate an agency's recognition.[107]

9.4.1.2.2 Obstacles to suing accrediting agencies

Attorneys representing defrauded students may want to consider adding as a party to the lawsuit the private accrediting agency that accredited the defendant school. Although usually non-profit organizations, these agencies may be an important alternative source of assets particularly when schools are bankrupt or insolvent.

Advocates have met with mixed success in their attempts to hold agencies liable for the bad acts of schools they accredit. Most courts have found that accrediting agencies are not responsible for students damaged by inferior schools accredited by these agencies. For example, the Ninth Circuit found that accrediting agencies owed no tort law duty under state law to students who attended the schools accredited by those agencies.[108]

Students in another federal court action in the District of Columbia presented UDAP and common law claims against an accrediting agency. The court found that the District of Columbia UDAP statute did not apply to accrediting agen-

---

101 General Accounting Office, *Higher Education: Ensuring Quality Education From Proprietary Institutions*, GAO/T-HEHS-96-158 (June 1996).

102 34 C.F.R. § 602.15.

103 34 C.F.R. § 602.16.

104 The Department of Education publishes the lists of agencies applying for initial or renewed recognition as accreditors. *See, e.g.*, 67 Fed. Reg. 48450 (July 24, 2002).

105 *Abuses in Federal Student Aid Programs, Part 2: Licensing, Accreditation, Certification and Eligibility*, Clearinghouse No. 45,922 (Sept. 12, 1990).

106 *See* Statement of James Thomas, Jr., Department of Education Inspector General, before the Senate Permanent Subcommittee on Investigation, Clearinghouse No. 45,923 (Sept. 12, 1990).

107 The regulatory authority for revocation can be found at 34 C.F.R. §§ 602.40–.43.

108 Keams v. Tempe Technical Institute, 39 F.3d 222 (9th Cir. 1994), *appeal after remand*, 103 F.3d 138 (9th Cir. 1996), *redesignated as opinion*, 110 F.3d 44 (9th Cir. 1997) (students failed to identify a single decision where any court has held that accrediting agencies owe a tort law duty to students), *claims against all defendants dismissed*, 16 F. Supp. 2d 1119 (D. Ariz. 1998).

cies, but did allow the students to pursue common law claims for misrepresentation and fraud against the accrediting agency.[109]

Both sides sought summary judgment in the case. The students claimed that the accreditor fraudulently provided accreditation even though the accreditor had no knowledge of whether the school met the accreditor's standards. The court found that the students could go forward with their case to trial, having met all the prima facie elements of fraud.[110]

A settlement was reached with the accreditor in this case.[111] Without admitting any liability or fault, the accreditor agreed to make payments to members of the class. The amount paid to each class member varies depending on the total number of claims received.

A claim of negligence against an accrediting agency is even more difficult. The borrower has to show a duty of the accreditor to the student, reliance on the accreditor's certification, negligence in the accreditation process, causing proximate injury to the consumer. The little case law in this area generally relates to personal injury relating to products that received independent certification.[112] At least at few courts have considered the issue in the student loan context, and found that an accrediting agency did not owe a duty to the students upon which a negligence action could be brought.[113]

9.4.1.3 Claims Against the Department of Education

Another potential claim in the typical vocational school/student loan case is that the Department of Education failed to adequately supervise the school and improperly recognized the accrediting agency. The Federal Tort Claims Act[114] sharply limits a party's ability to recover *damages* from a federal agency, but the Act does not prevent the student from receiving reimbursement of amounts improperly paid or otherwise receiving money to be made whole.[115]

The Secretary is likely to argue that the Department has no responsibility to review the educational quality of the school. The counter-argument is that the Secretary has an obligation under the Higher Education Act to evaluate the financial responsibility of the school.[116]

An audit report of the Inspector General of the Department of Education faulted the Department for not requiring financially shaky vocational schools to provide adequate surety bonds before the Department certified them for participation in the guaranteed student loan program.[117] The report is a stinging indictment of the performance of the Department in monitoring schools' financial health, a key safeguard in avoiding students signing up for loans to attend schools likely to close.

At least one federal court decision found that students could proceed with claims directly against the Department of Education.[118] The court allowed the students to proceed to trial to try to prove any of the following: (1) that the Secretary acted arbitrarily and capriciously in certifying branch campuses to participate in the loan program; (2) that certain campuses were not affiliated with any other eligible school and thus never approved for participation in the program; or (3) that the courses did not provide education for a recognized occupation or "useful employment." The court also allowed the students to proceed in their mandamus action against the Secretary to force the school to repay program funds where the program failed to satisfy federal standards.

9.4.1.4 Claims Against State Licensing Agencies

Claims may be available against state licensing agencies that have even greater responsibility than the Department of Education to review a school's operation. For example, a New York appellate court allowed a claim to proceed where the students sought declaratory and injunctive relief that the

---

109 Armstrong v. Accrediting Council for Continuing Education & Training, Inc., 832 F. Supp. 419 (D.D.C. 1993).

110 Armstrong v. Accrediting Council for Continuing Education & Training, Inc., 961 F. Supp. 305 (D.D.C. 1997).

111 Armstrong v. Accrediting Council for Continuing Education & Training, Inc., Clearinghouse No. 52,040 (D.D.C. Mar. 30, 1998) (settlement agreement and order approving settlement).

112 *See* Jacobs, Certification and Accreditation Law Handbook Ch. 3 (1992 American Society of Association Executives).

113 Keams v. Tempe Technical Institute, 39 F.3d 222 (9th Cir. 1994), *appeal after remand*, 103 F.3d 138 (9th Cir. 1996), *redesignated as opinion*, 110 F.3d 44 (9th Cir. 1997), *claims against all defendants dismissed*, 16 F. Supp. 2d 1119 (D. Ariz. 1998); Ambrose v. New England Association of Schools and Colleges, 2000 WL 1195363 (D. Me. Aug. 7, 2000) (analogizing negligent accreditation claims to educational malpractice. Court found it improper for courts to make these subjective determinations. Summary judgment granted to defendant accrediting organization).

114 28 U.S.C. § 1346(b).

115 Florence County School District Four v. Carter, 510 U.S. 7 (1993); Burlington School Committee v. Massachusetts Dep't of Education, 471 U.S. 359 (1985); Army & Air Force Exchange Service v. Sheehan, 456 U.S. 728, 739 n.11 (1982); United States v. Testan, 424 U.S. 392, 401–02 (1976); Porter v. Warner Holding Co., 328 U.S. 395 (1946); Muller v. Commission on Sp. Educ. of E. Islip Sch. Dist., 145 F.3d 95 (2d Cir. 1998); Gadsby by Gadsby v. Grasmick, 109 F.3d 940 (4th Cir. 1997); Whayne v. United States Dep't of Education, 915 F. Supp. 1143 (D. Kan. 1996) (Federal Tort Claims cause of action dismissed due to plaintiff's failure to exhaust administrative remedies).

116 *See* 34 C.F.R. §§ 668.14, 668.15.

117 *See Financial Analysis Certification Process Not Adequate to Protect Students and Government*, Clearinghouse No. 44,845, Audit Control No. 11-80160 (Sept. 1989).

118 Hernandez v. Alexander, Clearinghouse No. 46,792 (D. Nev. May 18, 1992). *But see* Armand v. Secretary of Education, Clearinghouse No. 51,298 (S.D. Fla. July 19, 1995).

state education department fulfill its statutory obligation in supervising private vocational schools.[119]

9.4.2 Practical Considerations

9.4.2.1 Deciding Between Class and Individual Actions

9.4.2.1.1 General

An individual action is one way to pursue a trade school case. A second, and often more efficient, approach is to join a number of individual students as plaintiffs.[120] Sometimes it is easier to obtain punitive damages on behalf of a limited number of students than on behalf of a class. The case can easily be brought before a jury, where sympathetic facts on each individual plaintiff can be presented directly to the jury.[121] A class action, in contrast, might not allow as effective a presentation of each student's case, and might not result in a punitive damages award.

A class action against a trade school may also lead to successful results. For example, in one case a class action against a cosmetology school recovered $640,000 UDAP actual damages and $271,000 in UDAP attorney fees.[122]

Because each student may be subjected to a different oral sales presentation, the Rule 23(b)(2) commonality requirement may be a problem in vocational school class action litigation. However, courts may find that each of these individual presentations is sufficiently close to the school's standard sales script to present common issues of fact, and

the core issue in question may be whether the school operated pursuant to an ongoing scheme to defraud and deceive students.[123]

For example, one federal court certified a class of about 400 Native Americans recruited to attend the TTI trade school by one particular salesperson over a fifteen-month period.[124] Although the bulk of the evidence related to oral sales presentations, the court found enough commonality in the salesman's presentations to justify the class action.

At least in California, there is one additional alternative. Anyone can bring an action under California Business & Professional Code § 17200, seeking an injunctive action against any unfair, deceptive, or illegal business practice. Restitution can be sought as ancillary to the injunctive action.[125]

9.4.2.1.2 Class certification

When seeking a declaration that the student does not owe on a Federal Family Education Loan (FFEL) because of school-related defenses, it usually makes sense to do so on behalf of a class of students who were victimized by the same program and who took out FFELs to attend. To proceed as a class, it will be necessary to convince the court that the class action requirements have been met.

In theory, if an action meets that test, then issues of lender liability should be sufficiently common to the class that the class should be certified. In fact, the standards may even be easier for a declaratory judgment action than in a damage action against a school. At least one court has ruled that an action seeking to declare loans unenforceable is not a damage action, and that only the requirements of Rule 23(b)(2), not (b)(3), need be met.[126] Class actions seeking damages or restitution actions are often problematic in the trade school context.[127]

---

119 Figueroa v. Market Training Institute, Inc., 167 A.D.2d 503, 562 N.Y.S.2d 175 (App. Div. 1990).

120 *See, e.g.*, Cross v. Academy of Court Reporting, Inc., Clearinghouse No. 46,794 (Ohio Summit Cty. 1991) (thirty-four individual students brought an action against a trade school; all the students recovered actual damages, ranging from $2600 to $12,200, and punitive damages of either $2500 or $3000 each. Their total recovery exceeded $400,000), *aff'd in part and remanded in part sub nom.* Matulin v. Academy of Court Reporting, 1992 WL 74210 (Ohio Ct. App. Apr. 8, 1992) (upholding virtually all counts, but remanding the case for redetermination of the attorney fee award of $116,000, which it found to be inadequate); Beckett v. Computer Career Institute, Inc. (Or. Cir. Ct. July 2, 1990), *aff'd in part and rev'd in part*, 120 Or. App. 143, 852 P.2d 840 (1993) (significant recovery for nine students).

121 *See* Beckett v. Computer Career Institute, Inc. (Or. Cir. Ct. July 2, 1990), *aff'd in part and rev'd in part*, 120 Or. App. 143, 852 P.2d 840 (1993) (significant recovery for nine students).

122 Rosario v. Livaditis, Clearinghouse No. 47,927B (N.D. Ill. 1989), *aff'd*, 963 F.2d 1013 (7th Cir. 1992) (Illinois law). *See generally* National Consumer Law Center, Unfair and Deceptive Acts and Practices § 8.5 (5th ed. 2001 and Supp.).

123 *See* Shorter v. Riley, Clearinghouse No. 47,950B (N.D. Ga. Nov. 18, 1993).

124 Keams v. Tempe Technical Institute, 807 F. Supp. 569 (D. Ariz. 1992), *rev'd*, 39 F.3d 222 (9th Cir. 1994), *appeal after remand*, 103 F.3d 138 (9th Cir. 1996), *redesignated as opinion*, 110 F.3d 44 (9th Cir. 1997), *claims against all defendants dismissed*, 16 F. Supp. 2d 1119 (D. Ariz. 1998).

125 *See generally* National Consumer Law Center, Unfair and Deceptive Acts and Practices § 8.3.2.4.3 (5th ed. 2001 and Supp.). *See also* Payne v. National Collection Systems, Inc., 111 Cal. Rptr. 2d 260 (Ct. App. 2001) (case brought by plaintiffs who did not receive restitution under an action brought by the attorney general).

126 Shorter v. Riley, Clearinghouse No. 47,950B (N.D. Ga. Nov. 18, 1993). *See generally* National Consumer Law Center, Unfair and Deceptive Acts and Practices § 8.5 (5th ed. 2001 and Supp.); National Consumer Law Center, Consumer Class Actions: A Practical Litigation Guide (5th ed. 2002).

127 *See, e.g.*, Morgan v. Markerdowne Corp., 201 F.R.D. 341 (D.N.J. 2001).

9.4.2.2 Developing the Case

One of the best ways to develop evidence of school malfeasance is to find disgruntled former employees—both commissioned sales representatives and faculty. The names, addresses, and dates of employment of present and past school employees can be obtained through discovery. The names of disgruntled sales representatives may also be obtained from court records, since many of them must sue the school for their back commissions. Not only can these people provide crucial evidence, but the "educational" institution's use of commissioned enrollment officers probably will have an impact on the jury or judge. Clients may also remember instructors' names and/or be able to provide a school catalog with this information.

Advocates should also be sure to obtain the school's sales manuals, marketing memos, and sales training materials. It is critical to find out how the student was enrolled, e.g., outside a welfare office or in a high pressure door-to-door sale.

Other information can be found on file with private accrediting associations, state licensing agencies, and the Department of Education. Advocates should focus on drop-out and job placement rates.[128] A school's actual job placement statistics may be more readily available and can be crucial evidence in a case. For example, the National Association of Trade and Technical Schools, the largest accrediting association of trade and technical schools, requires that all schools it accredits submit annual reports of both job placement and school drop-outs. Other accrediting associations typically have the same requirements. While having these numbers can be invaluable, the numbers themselves often are wildly inflated. It is also important to compare admissions criteria with eligibility requirements for the jobs students are being trained for and to speak to potential employers about the school.

9.4.2.3 Proving Actual Damages

Student plaintiffs may have suffered a variety of actual damages as a result of vocational school fraud. In one case, the plaintiffs successfully argued that they would never have attended had they known of the school's actual placement rate, which was lower than represented. The students' actual damages were found to be their *total* tuition (even though most had graduated from the school) plus the students' lost wages incurred when they left their jobs to attend the school.[129]

Other damage claims to consider in these cases include child care and transportation expenses incurred while students attended school. In addition, many students were encouraged or required by schools to purchase equipment or materials. For example, many schools purporting to teach automobile mechanic skills required students to purchase their own tools. These costs can also be claimed as damages.

9.4.2.4 Settlements

Despite a reluctance by the Department and guaranty agencies to admit that students can raise school-related defenses, students who do so may be able to settle their claims. A settlement agreement in one case dismissed the loan obligations of six students, granted closed school discharges to three students, and provided for correction of all the students' credit records.[130] Pursuant to the settlement agreement, the lender is required to pay the United States $16,000, covering the costs of the government's insurance payments for these students.[131]

Another settlement agreement provided for discharge of the loan obligations of the six named plaintiffs.[132] The guaranty agencies, not the United States, absorbed the loss.[133]

Students have been less successful in obtaining class-wide relief. Generally, the only offer the United States makes class-wide (i.e., not just to named plaintiffs) is to process closed school and false certification discharges for individuals that meet the Department's standards concerning those discharges.

9.5 Raising School-Related Defenses Against Student Loan Collection Actions

9.5.1 Introduction

In many cases, defrauded students have no other practical recourse than to raise school-related defenses on their student loans. While it is almost always preferable to obtain a discharge than to raise school-related defenses, many defrauded students will not receive such discharges.[134] Simi-

---

128　For information on gathering evidence from state licensing agencies, including Freedom of Information Act requests, see § 6.3.2.3, *supra.*

129　Beckett v. Computer Career Institute, Inc. (Or. Cir. Ct. July 2, 1990), *aff'd in part and rev'd in part*, 120 Or. App. 143, 852 P.2d 840 (1993).

130　Spinner v. Chesapeake Business Institute of Virginia, Inc., Clearinghouse No. 49,131B (E.D. Va. May 6, 1993) (order of dismissal).

131　*Id.*

132　Hicks v. Riley, Clearinghouse No. 49,133 (N.D. Ga. May 27, 1993) (plaintiff's motion to approve settlement and brief in support thereof).

133　*Id. See also* Alberto v. School of Business Machines, Clearinghouse No. 46,755C (D.N.J. 1994) (consent order).

134　*See generally* Ch. 6, *supra* (discharges). At least one court found that borrowers seeking relief for false certification must use the federal discharge process rather than suing in state court. *See*

larly, most defrauded students will not want to file for bankruptcy or may not be able to obtain a bankruptcy discharge of their student loans.[135] Affirmative suits against the school raise many practical problems, not the least of which is that the school may now be insolvent, or insolvent by the time a judgment is entered against the school.[136]

Consequently, for millions of students defrauded by trade schools in the 1980s and 1990s, raising school-related defenses on their student loans is critical. This same right to raise seller-related claims on loans has proven essential for other defrauded consumers as well, such as those victimized by home improvement contractors or used car dealers. In most cases, where the seller refers the consumer to the lender or where the seller and lender have a business arrangement, these other consumers can successfully raise as a defense to their loans all claims and defenses they have against the seller.[137]

Unfortunately it is not as clear whether defrauded students can raise school-related defenses to their loans. The analysis depends at least initially on the type of student loan involved. Students can raise school-related defenses for Perkins Loans, Direct Loans, and usually on Federally Insured Student Loans (FISLs). They can also raise these defenses on FFELs extended on or after January 1, 1994 where a for-profit school has a referral or other business relationship with the lender.

The situation for earlier FFELs, on the other hand, is far from clear. In addition, special issues arise where an FFEL has lost its guaranteed status or where a student loan is consolidated into a new student loan.

This section sets out existing standards for raising school-related defenses for all of these types of loans. Advocates must properly match their client's type of loan with the appropriate discussion below.[138] The types of claims to raise defensively are similar to those that can be raised in affirmative cases. These issues are discussed in § 9.4, *supra*.

9.5.2 The Clearer Picture: Loans Where School-Related Defenses Should Be Available

9.5.2.1 Perkins Loans

Schools are the lender for Perkins Loans. In these cases, the lender (i.e. the school) should be subject to school-related defenses. In addition, the lender may *assign* the note to the United States for collection.[139] The United States, as assignee, should be subject to all defenses that could be raised against the assignor.[140] While this legal theory is straightforward and unassailable, few if any students have raised school-related defenses on Perkins Loans.

9.5.2.2 Direct Loans

The HEA specifies that, notwithstanding any other provision of state or federal law, the Secretary shall, for Direct Loans, specify in regulations when school misconduct may be asserted as a defense to loan repayment, but the student's recovery pursuant to such a defense cannot exceed the amount the borrower has repaid on the loan.[141]

The regulations state that in any proceeding to collect on a Direct Loan, the borrower may assert as a defense against repayment any act or omission of the school that would give rise to a cause of action against the school under applicable state law.[142] In addition, the Secretary may determine that all or part of amounts already paid on the loan should be refunded to the student and may also correct negative credit reports.[143] These defenses can be raised not only in litigation, but also in tax offset proceedings, wage garnishment proceedings, and other salary offset proceedings.[144]

9.5.2.3 FISLs

Federally Insured Student Loans (FISLs) usually date back to the 1970s or early 1980s. Loans from a bank or even from a school were insured directly by the United States. Students can raise many school-related defenses to FISLs because, until 1986 (when it was dropped without comment), an FISL regulation explicitly stated that the United States would not collect an FISL to the extent that a school had closed or students had certain school-related de-

---

Wilson v. Chism, 665 N.E.2d 446 (Ct. App. Ill. 1996). [*Editor's note*: this case is wrong if it implies that the HEA generally preempts UDAP challenges to a school's admission of unqualified applicants.] *See* § 9.3.2, *supra*.

135 *See* Ch. 7, *supra*.

136 *See* § 9.4, *supra*.

137 *See generally* National Consumer Law Center, Unfair and Deceptive Acts and Practices § 6.6 (5th ed. 2001 and Supp.).

138 For information on how to find out what type of loan a client has, see § 1.6, *supra*.

139 *See* 34 C.F.R. §§ 674.8(d), 674.50 (assignment of defaulted loans).

140 The note is not a negotiable instrument so that the United States cannot be a holder-in-due course. *See generally* National Consumer Law Center, Unfair and Deceptive Acts and Practices § 6.6 (5th ed. 2001 and Supp.).

141 20 U.S.C. § 1087e(h).

142 34 C.F.R. § 685.206(c)(1).

143 34 C.F.R. § 685.206(c)(2).

144 34 C.F.R. § 685.206(c)(1).

fenses.[145] This regulation should apply at least to FISLs entered into before 1986. Moreover, where the school was the originating lender, students should also be able to raise all defenses against the assignee (the United States) based on the same rationale as Perkins Loans.[146]

9.5.2.4 FFELs Extended After January 1, 1994

Starting on January 1, 1994, all FFELs use a common promissory note that is drafted by the United States Department of Education. The note includes an adaptation of the FTC Holder Notice:

> If this loan is made by the school, or if the proceeds of this loan are used to pay tuition and charges of a for-profit school that refers loan applicants to the lender, or that is affiliated with the lender by common control, contract or business arrangement, any holder of this Note is subject to all claims and defenses which I could assert against the school. My recovery under this provision shall not exceed the amount I paid on this loan.[147]

Students whose notes include this loan provision will be in a strong position to raise school-related claims. Nevertheless, this loan provision, by its very terms, only allows consumers to raise school-related defenses to a FFEL *if* the school is for-profit and *if* the school refers students to the lender or is affiliated with the lender by common control, contract or business arrangement. In raising school-related defenses, the student should thus allege that the school is for-profit and that it refers students or has a business arrangement with the lender.

The Department has issued a letter giving its interpretations when a referral relationship exists.[148] Such a relationship does not exist if the only relationship between school and lender is based on certain specific duties required of the school and lender by the Higher Education Act or regulations. Moreover, simply giving students a list of available lenders does not create a referral relationship.

On the other hand, if a school seeks out a lender to add to its list of lenders, such a relationship is more likely to exist. The relationship does not exist if the list of lenders is obtained from a third source, such as a guaranty agency or trade association.

There is a referral relationship where the school recommends a particular lender, but only where the lender knows about the recommendation. If a lender sends the school promotional material about its lending activity, the lender should expect that students seeking loans have been recommended by the school. On the other hand, credible assurances to a lender that the school will do no more than include its name on a list of willing lenders is not knowledge of the recommendation.

The Department statement concludes that FTC interpretations will ordinarily be dispositive as to whether a referral relationship exists. Interested parties should consider statements from the FTC staff on the Holder Rule's application.[149]

Advocates should also check to see if the lender waives origination fees the school must pay or otherwise provides special privileges to the school. This is excellent evidence of a business arrangement.

9.5.3 *The Murkier Picture: Where School-Related Defenses May Not Be Allowed*

9.5.3.1 FFELs Extended Before 1994

9.5.3.1.1 Introduction

It is quite frustrating to students that lenders, guaranty agencies, and the Department still, in large part, refuse to recognize legitimate school-related defenses for FFELs entered into before 1994. For these loans, the only undisputed right to relief is through a closed school, unpaid refund, or false certification discharge.[150]

The key question in determining whether students can raise school-related defenses to FFELs extended before 1994 is whether the originating lender (usually a bank) is subject to the student's claims against the school. If the bank is, then so are its assignees—a secondary market lender, a guaranty agency, and the United States.[151]

Unlike a Perkins Loan, the school is not the originating lender. While the school may assist the lender and refer the

---

145   34 C.F.R. § 518 (1985) (since rescinded). *See also* United States v. Griffin, 707 F.2d 1477 (D.C. Cir. 1983).

146   *See* § 9.5.2.1, *supra*. *Cf.* United States v. Griffin, 707 F.2d 1477 (D.C. Cir. 1983) (not ruling on whether the United States was an assignee or surety because Department regulations authorized students to raise defenses).

147   *See* Common Application Material and Promissory Note, Clearinghouse No. 47,974 (Apr. 16, 1993).

148   Division of Policy Development, Office of the Assistant Secretary for Postsecondary Education, Overview of the Federal Trade Commission Holder Rule, Clearinghouse No. 49,162 (July 2, 1993).

149   The Department statement particularly references 40 Fed. Reg. 53,506 (Nov. 18, 1975); 41 Fed. Reg. 43,594 (Aug. 16, 1976); 57 Fed. Reg. 28,814 (June 29, 1992).

150   *See* Ch. 6, *supra* (discharges).

151   There may be additional issues that arise in trying to hold secondary market purchasers liable for a school's fraud or negligence. *See* Crawford v. The American Institute of Professional Careers, Inc., 934 F. Supp. 335 (D. Ariz. 1996) (state law claims against secondary purchasers deemed preempted by the HEA. Court agreed that purchasers could not comply with state law and the anti-discrimination provisions of the HEA which require purchasers to purchase certain loans without any independent oversight or control over school programs. No separate fraud or wrongdoing alleged against purchaser in this case).

student to the lender, the loan goes directly from the bank or other lender to the student. Lenders argue that they have nothing to do with the school—they are not assignees of the school, do not guaranty school quality, and are not subject to any school-related defenses.

Nevertheless, in other analogous consumer transactions a direct lender is liable for the misconduct of a related seller, such as where a finance company arranges for a homeowner's payment to a home improvement contractor.[152] Well-established legal principles and statutes protect consumers in these situations. Where a seller refers the consumer to the lender or otherwise has an arrangement or course of dealing with that creditor, the creditor is generally subject to all the consumer's claims and defenses against the seller.[153]

An important avenue for relief for students would be if these general principles of lender liability for other con-

sumer transactions and for other student loans (including FFELs after January 1, 1994) also applied to FFELs prior to 1994. Since the lender would be liable for the school's misconduct, the same would be true for the guaranty agency and the Department, who are merely assignees of the lender.[154] Legal theories allowing the student to raise school-related claims and defenses against the lender, the guaranty agency, and the United States are set out below.

9.5.3.1.2 Agency and other common law theories

One ground for lender liability for school-related claims is that the lender has appointed the school its agent for certain functions, and that, under *respondeat superior*, the principal is liable for the acts of its agent within the actual or apparent scope of the agent's authority. Typically, in many vocational school enrollments, the school acts as the lender's agent in giving the loan papers to the student, filling out the lender's portion of the loan paperwork, helping the student fill out the student portion, and forwarding that paperwork to the lender.[155]

The key question is whether the federal regulatory scheme preempts application of the state or federal common law of *respondeat superior*. Unfortunately for borrowers, the current judicial trend favors federal preemption in these circumstances.[156]

---

152 Williams v. ITT Financial Services, 1997 Ohio App. LEXIS 2721 (Ohio App. June 25, 1997) (state appellate court upheld $1.5 million punitive damages award against finance company for failing to warn borrower that a home improvement contractor was fraudulent. Liability upheld even though home improvement contractor was not an agent of finance company and even though did not receive payment from company). The *Williams* court approach should apply in the student loan context both to argue for punitive damages against a lender in excess of the FTC Holder cap on liability and to create a claim against a direct lender where the FTC Holder notice is not contained in the loan documents.

153 *See* National Consumer Law Center, Unfair and Deceptive Acts and Practices § 6.6 (5th ed. 2001 and Supp.). There is a congressional intent that this general rule of lender liability apply to at least certain GSLs. The House version of the Higher Education Amendments of 1992 provided lenders with extensive immunity from students' school-related defenses, but the House acceded to the Senate version that provided no such immunity, indicating a Congressional intent that banks be liable in at least certain situations, as to be determined by the courts:

> The conferees are reluctant to legislate in this area while the issue is pending in the courts. The conferees have instead chosen to leave to the courts the complex determination as to when a student should and should not be able to raise the school's fraud or other misconduct as a defense to the student's loans. Courts will have to consider many factors, including the exact nature of the lender's relationship and dealings with the school. In deciding to leave this matter to the courts, the conferees weighed several important, but in some cases conflicting, considerations. Allowing victimized students to raise defenses on their loans may also have the salutary effect of causing increased scrutiny of schools, thereby effectively policing sham schools. At the same time, the ability of schools to refer students to lenders willing to make loans to them, the participation of national lenders and servicers, and cooperative efforts to improve service to students and reduce defaults are important to improve service to students and reduce defaults are important to achieving nationwide loan access. H.R. Conf. Rep No. 630, 102d Cong., 2d Sess. 508 (1992).

154 Guaranty agencies at one time argued, but appear to have given up arguing that, even if the lenders are liable for school-related claims, the guaranty agency enforcing that loan obligation is not. More common is for the guaranty agency to argue that it is not liable even if the lender is liable because the guaranty agency is not an assignee of the lender, but the students' "guarantor." At common law, a guarantor seeking reimbursement from the primary obligor is not subject to that primary obligor's defenses against the lender unless the guarantor had notice of those defenses before it paid off the lender.

There are three principal reasons why the common law rule protecting "guarantors" is not available in the student loan context: (1) At common law, the entities that are labeled "guarantors" would have been considered insurers under the HEA, not guarantors. Insurers were not covered by the rule that foreclosed borrower defenses if the loan was repaid without prior notice of the defense; (2) even under common law, the rule concerning prior notice was only available where the guarantor was acting to accommodate the borrower because of a relationship with the borrower. That relationship does not exist in the HEA where the guarantor becomes involved because of its contractual relationship with the lender; and (3) guarantors often have actual or constructive notice of the school-related claims before they pay off the insurance claims by the lenders.

155 *See* Shorter v. Riley, Clearinghouse No. 47,950B (N.D. Ga. Nov. 18, 1993); Hicks v. Riley, Clearinghouse No. 49,133 (N.D. Ga. May 27, 1993) (plaintiff's motion to approve settlement and brief in support thereof); Tillis v. Bank of America, Clearinghouse No. 49,932 (Cal. Super. Ct. Nov. 17, 1993).

156 *See, e.g.,* Keams v. Tempe Technical Institute, 39 F.3d 222 (9th Cir. 1994), *appeal after remand*, 103 F.3d 138 (9th Cir. 1996), *redesignated as opinion*, 110 F.3d 44 (9th Cir. 1997), *claims against all defendants dismissed*, 16 F. Supp. 2d 1119 (D. Ariz.

Even if the claim survives preemption, a weakness of the agency approach is that the principal will only be liable for acts within the actual or apparent authority of the agent. This will usually relate to the student's enrollment in the school, and not to the school's quality of teaching, equipment or placement services.

However, the principal should also be responsible for misrepresentations made by the agency. The strength of the agency approach therefore lies in misrepresentation, rather than contract, claims against the school. If the school makes misrepresentations to induce the student to enroll and sign the forms, those misrepresentations can be raised against the lender if the school had actual or apparent authority to make such representations.

Another agency argument is that the school was acting as the Department of Education's agent in administering the HEA, and that the Department should thus be estopped from collecting on a loan involving misconduct by its agent.[157] Other common law theories that may be applicable in some states include close connectedness and joint enterprise,[158] and that the enrollment contract and loan papers were integrated contracts, making the breach of the first a defense as to enforcement of the second.[159]

9.5.3.1.3 State lender liability statutes

A number of states have enacted statutes specifically requiring that lenders be liable for the acts of their related sellers, specifying in some detail the type of relationship between the seller and lender that is sufficient to allow the consumer to raise seller-related defenses on the loan.[160]

While these statutes in some states are vague,[161] they still may provide a basis for a student raising school-related defenses to a FFEL.[162]

The major obstacle yet again is federal preemption of the state statutes. In theory, the HEA should not preempt state laws because the Department of Education now requires that student loans provide for the same protection specified in these state laws.[163] Specifically, in post-1994 student loans containing the FTC Holder Notice, lenders should be liable for school-related claims.

Courts have generally agreed that the HEA does not expressly preempt state lender liability statutes, and that it does not implicitly preempt the field of lender liability.[164]

---

ceptive Acts and Practices § 6.6.4.9 (5th ed. 2001 and Supp).

161　Armstrong v. Accrediting Council for Continuing Education & Training, Inc., 84 F.3d 1452 (D.C. Cir. 1996), *on remand*, 950 F. Supp. 1 (D.D.C. 1996) (court maintained jurisdiction of pendent claims and found case to be appropriate for declaratory relief), *on further remand*, 980 F. Supp. 53 (D.D.C. 1997), *aff'd*, 168 F.3d 1362 (D.C. Cir. 1999) (state law claims preempted by pre-1992 federal policy to protect lenders; in essence, all state law claims prior to 1993 preempted unless there is an origination relationship), *cert. denied*, 528 U.S. 1073 (2000); Jackson v. Culinary School of Washington, 811 F. Supp. 714 (D.D.C. 1993) (summary judgment) (state statute required that lender act at express request of seller and seller receive compensation from lender; court found insufficient facts to establish such compensation), *aff'd on other grounds*, 27 F.3d 573 (D.C. Cir. 1994) (court declines to consider complex state law issues in declaratory judgment action), *affirmance vacated*, 115 S. Ct. 2573 (1995) (appellate court used de novo instead of abuse of discretion standard to review district court's decision to decide state law issues in declaratory judgment action), *remanded to district court on state law claims* 59 F.3d 254 (D.C. Cir. 1995) (to determine on what basis federal court decided to rule on state law issues), *motion dismissed by* 1995 U.S. App. LEXIS 22304 (D.C. Cir. 1995); Williams v. National School of Health Technology, Inc., 836 F. Supp. 273 (E.D. Pa. 1993) (state retail installment sales act applies to loans directly from a seller, not to loans directly from a lender. Student loan directly from lender was not structured to avoid this Pennsylvania law, but was structured pursuant to the federal scheme. Consequently, the installment sales act does not apply by its very terms and there is no reason to extend statute to third party student loans).

162　*See* Tipton v. Secretary of Education, 768 F. Supp. 540 (S.D. W. Va. 1991).

163　*See* § 9.5.2.5, *supra*.

164　Armstrong v. Accrediting Council for Continuing Education & Training, Inc., 84 F.3d 1452 (D.C. Cir. 1996), *on remand*, 950 F. Supp. 1 (D.D.C. 1996) (court maintained jurisdiction of pendent claims and found case to be appropriate for declaratory relief), *on further remand*, 980 F. Supp. 53 (D.D.C. 1997), *aff'd*, 168 F.3d 1362 (D.C. Cir. 1999) (state law claims preempted by pre-1992 federal policy to protect lenders; in essence, all state law claims prior to 1993 preempted unless there is an origination relationship), *cert. denied*, 528 U.S. 1073 (2000); Keams v. Tempe Technical Institute, 39 F.3d 222 (9th Cir. 1994), *appeal after remand*, 103 F.3d 138 (9th Cir. 1996), *redesignated as opinion*, 110 F.3d 44 (9th Cir. 1997), *claims against all defendants dismissed*, 16 F. Supp. 2d 1119 (D. Ariz. 1998); Jackson v. Culinary School of Washington, Ltd., 27 F.3d 573 (D.C. Cir. 1994), *vacated on other grounds*, 115 S. Ct. 2573 (1995)

1998); Morgan v. Markerdown Corp., 976 F. Supp. 301 (D.N.J. 1997) (New Jersey's law of agency and close connectedness preempted to the extent they would hold the lenders and guarantors liable for alleged misrepresentations by the school); Crawford v. American Institute of Professional Careers, 934 F. Supp. 335 (D. Ariz. 1996); Bartels v. Alabama Community College, 918 F. Supp. 1565 (N.D. Ga. 1995), *aff'd without published op.*, 189 F.3d 483 (11th Cir. Ga. 1999), *cert. denied*, 528 U.S. 1074 (2000) (only relationship between guarantors or secondary market holders and school were functions required by the HEA; liability based on such functions would conflict with the HEA; court never considered whether there were special functions delegated by the originating lender to the school); Bogart v. Nebraska Student Loan Program, 313 Ark. 656, 858 S.W.2d 78 (1993) (court finds that federal law preempts state law claim based on agency, the students apparently not bringing to court's attention various federal court rulings limiting preemption).

157　Spinner v. Chesapeake Business Institute of Virginia, Clearinghouse No. 49,131A (E.D. Va. Feb. 5, 1993).

158　Tillis v. Bank of America, Clearinghouse No. 49,932 (Cal. Super. Ct. Nov. 17, 1993).

159　*But see* Bartels v. Alabama Commercial College, 918 F. Supp. 1565 (S.D. Ga. 1995), *aff'd without published op.*, 189 F.3d 483 (11th Cir. 1999), *cert. denied*, 528 U.S. 1074 (2000); Shorter v. Alexander, Clearinghouse No. 47,950 (N.D. Ga. Dec. 8, 1992).

160　*See generally* National Consumer Law Center, Unfair and De-

Therefore, these state statutes should be preempted only if they are in actual conflict with federal requirements or objectives.[165]

The problem for students is that courts have generally found that some federal requirements or objectives conflict with the state statutory provisions. For example, state statutes finding lenders liable where the loan is conditioned on the proceeds going to a particular purpose or where the lender provides forms to the seller have been considered preempted.[166] These judicial interpretations have far-reach-

ing consequences since the HEA requires all lenders to condition the loan on the student using the money to go to school and all lenders must supply forms to schools.

Even more troubling for student litigants, though, is a judicial trend toward courts finding certain state statutory provisions to conflict with federal "objectives" that are not embodied in any statute or regulation. The 1999 *Armstrong* decision is illustrative of this trend. The loan at issue in that case was made in 1988. The *Armstrong* court refused to imply the FTC Holder Rule terms and concluded that state law claims were preempted.[167] The court found that state laws that would allow school-related defenses to be raised against lenders were preempted during the period that the FTC had decided not to enforce the Holder Rule with respect to student loans.[168]

In a blow to student advocates, the court stuck to this position even while acknowledging that the FTC and the Secretary of Education have since concluded that the Holder Rule does apply, and did apply during this period of non-enforcement.[169] The *Armstrong* court seemed uneasy about the result, acknowledging that students with these older loans are left "holding the bag," but claimed they had no authority to protect the students.[170]

9.5.3.1.4 Private remedy for failure to include FTC holder notice

As described above, all student loans extended on or after January 1, 1994 include a provision based on the FTC Holder Rule allowing students to raise school-related defenses where certain conditions are met.[171] Unfortunately for students, virtually no student loans before that date contained such a provision.

Federal law is clear that many of those pre-1994 FFELs should have included the FTC Holder Notice. The FTC

(appellate court used de novo instead of abuse of discretion standard to review district court's decision to decide state law issues in declaratory judgment action), *remanded to district court on state law claims* 59 F.3d 254 (D.C. Cir. 1995) (to determine on what basis federal court decided to rule on state law issues), *motion dismissed*, 1995 U.S. App. LEXIS 22304 (D.C. Cir. 1995); Spinner v. Chesapeake Business Institute of Virginia, Clearinghouse No. 49,131A (E.D. Va. Feb. 5, 1993); Jackson v. Culinary School of Washington, 811 F. Supp. 714 (D.D.C. 1993) (claim dismissed based on summary judgment motion that students had not presented evidence of origination relationship), *aff'd on other grounds*, 27 F.3d 573 (D.C. Cir. 1994) (origination theory not enforceable against the Secretary), *vacated on other grounds*, 115 S. Ct. 2573 (1995) (appellate court used de novo instead of abuse of discretion standard to review district court's decision to decide state law issues in declaratory judgment action), *remanded to district court on state law claims, but affirming own ruling on origination*, 59 F.3d 254 (D.C. Cir. 1995) (to determine on what basis federal court decided to rule on state law issues), *motion dismissed*, 1995 U.S. App. LEXIS 22304 (D.C. Cir. 1995); Hernandez v. Alexander, Clearinghouse No. 46,792 (D. Nev. May 18, 1992); Tipton v. Secretary of Education, Clearinghouse No. 45,765D (S.D. W. Va. Mar. 31, 1992) (denial of permission for an interlocutory appeal); Tipton v. Secretary of Education, 768 F. Supp. 540 (S.D. W. Va. 1991); Wilson v. Manufacturers Hanover Trust Co., Clearinghouse No. 45,921 (W. Va. Cir. Ct. Sept. 25, 1990).

165 *See* Armstrong v. Accrediting Council for Continuing Education & Training, Inc., 84 F.3d 1452 (D.C. Cir. 1996) (ruling on state law claims must first determine whether district court should exercise pendent jurisdiction and consider possibility of declaratory relief; if district court decides to proceed, it must revisit state law issues as to which state law applies, whether provision is preempted by federal law, and interpretation of state law), *on remand*, 950 F. Supp. 1 (D.D.C. 1996) (court maintained jurisdiction of pendent claims and found case to be appropriate for declaratory relief), *on further remand*, 980 F. Supp. 53 (D.D.C. 1997) (court determined that California law controls and invited plaintiff to amend complaint to assert claims and defenses under California consumer protection laws), *aff'd*, 168 F.3d 1362 (D.C. Cir. 1999) (state law claims preempted by pre-1992 federal policy to protect lenders; in essence, all state law claims prior to 1993 preempted unless there is an origination relationship), *cert. denied*, 528 U.S. 1073 (2000); Hernandez v. Alexander, Clearinghouse No. 46,792 (D. Nev. May 18, 1992); Jackson v. Culinary School of Washington, 788 F. Supp. 1233 (D.D.C. 1992), see note 58, *supra*, for subsequent history; Tipton v. Secretary of Education, 768 F. Supp. 540 (S.D. W. Va. 1991); Bogart v. Nebraska Student Loan Program, 1993 WL 284926 (Ark. 1993).

166 Tipton v. Secretary of Education, 768 F. Supp. 540 (S.D. W. Va. 1991).

167 Armstrong v. Accrediting Counsel for Continuing Education & Training, Inc., 168 F.3d 1362 (D.C. Cir. 1999), *cert. denied*, 528 U.S. 1073 (2000).

168 This period was from 1982–1993, or possibly from 1982–1991, depending on a court's historical interpretation. The court noted that a common promissory note with the FTC holder rule was instituted in 1993, although the FTC began enforcing the Rule again in 1991. Armstrong v. Accrediting Counsel for Continuing Education & Training, Inc., 168 F.3d 1362, 1365 (D.C. Cir. 1999), *cert. denied*, 528 U.S. 1073 (2000).

169 Armstrong v. Accrediting Council for Continuing Education & Training, Inc., 168 F.3d 1362, 1368 (D.C. Cir. 1999), *cert. denied*, 528 U.S. 1073 (2000).

170 *Id.* at 1370. As discussed below in § 9.5.3.1.5, the *Armstrong* court indicated that state law claims were not preempted, even during the period of FTC non-enforcement, where the school and lender had an "origination relationship" under federal law.

171 *See* § 9.5.2.4, *supra*. The Federal Trade Commission Trade Regulation Rule Concerning the Preservation of Consumers' Claims and Defenses, 16 C.F.R. § 433, discussed in detail at National Consumer Law Center, Unfair and Deceptive Acts and Practices § 6.6 (5th ed. 2001 and Supp.).

Student Loan Law

Holder Rule specifies that where a for-profit seller (such as a proprietary trade school) refers the consumer to a particular lender, then the FTC Holder Notice must be included in the promissory note.

The FTC staff in charge of enforcing the Holder Rule has unambiguously stated that the Holder Rule applies to FFELs.[172] The Secretary of Education[173] and a 1993 Congressional Conference Report[174] reach the same conclusion. These 1991, 1992, and 1993 interpretations supersede a few earlier courts that ruled otherwise.[175] Subsequent court rulings are in line with the FTC, Department, and Congressional interpretation that the Holder Rule does apply to FFELs.[176]

The problem for students is that, while courts may assume that the FTC Holder Notice should have been included in the GSL note, courts are leery of providing consumers with a *remedy* for the lenders' failure to include that notice. There is no direct private right of action for violation of an FTC Rule.[177] As a result, consumers must use state law theories to claim violations of the FTC Rule. To date, such state law claims have met with limited success.

In other contexts, courts have had little difficulty finding a violation of an FTC Rule to be a state UDAP violation.[178] Yet in the student loan context, courts have usually found ways to avoid UDAP liability for FFELs violating the FTC Holder Rule.[179]

---

172 *See* FTC Staff Letter from David Medine, Associate Director for Credit Practices, Clearinghouse No. 47,975 (Feb. 11, 1993); FTC Staff Opinion Letter to Jonathan Sheldon, National Consumer Law Center, Clearinghouse No. 46,752 (July 24, 1991). These letters reverse a prior letter on the subject, Esposito, FTC Informal Staff Letter, Clearinghouse No. 44,341 (Jan. 9, 1989). The full Federal Trade Commission, while not formally adopting the 1991 staff opinion, did refer to that opinion with apparent approval in 1992. In a Commission decision not to amend the Holder Rule, the Commission stated that "the Commission staff has provided NCLC with an opinion letter stating that such educational loans are not exempt from the Rule." 57 Fed. Reg. 28815, n.11 (June 29, 1992). *But see* Armstrong v. Accrediting Council for Continuing Education & Training, Inc., 168 F.3d 1362 (D.C. Cir. 1999), *cert. denied*, 528 U.S. 1073 (2000).

173 The introductory material to the Department's common promissory note, at page 7, states "The Secretary of Education has determined that the Governing Law and Notices section of the common promissory note must include the Federal Trade Commission (FTC) consumer defense clause as required by the FTC regulations, 16 CFR Section 433.2." *See* Common Application Material and Promissory Note, Clearinghouse No. 47,974 (Apr. 16, 1993).

174 "The Holder Rule applies to student loan borrowers attending for-profit institutions, and the new Federal Family Education Loan promissory note includes the required notice." Omnibus Budget Reconciliation Act of 1993, Conference Report to Accompany H.R. 2264, H.R. Rep. No. 213, 455, 103d Cong., 1st Sess. (Aug. 4, 1993). In addition, Congress, in the Higher Education Amendments of 1992, had an opportunity, by adopting the House version, to limit significantly the FTC Rule's applicability to GSLs. Instead, Congress decided to adopt the Senate version that would not limit the Holder Rule's applicability.

175 Veal v. First American Savings Bank, 914 F.2d 909 (7th Cir. 1990); *see also* McVey v. U.S. Training Academy, Clearinghouse No. 44,344 (Bankr. E.D. Ky. Aug. 25, 1988); Molina v. Crown Business Institute, Clearinghouse No. 45,920 (N.Y. Sup. Ct. 1990).

176 *See, e.g.*, Morgan v. Markerdowne Corp., 976 F. Supp. 301 (D.N.J. 1997); Jackson v. Culinary School of Washington, 788 F. Supp. 1233 (D.D.C. 1992) (see note 91, *supra*, for subsequent history); *see also* Spinner v. Chesapeake Business Institute of Virginia, Clearinghouse No. 49,131A (E.D. Va. Feb. 5, 1993); C. Mansfield, *The Federal Trade Commission Holder Rule and its Applicability to Student Loans—Re-allocating the Risk of Proprietary School Failure*, 26 Wake Forest L. Rev. 635 (1991).

But cf. Hernandez v. Alexander, Clearinghouse No. 46,792 (D. Nev. May 18, 1992).

177 *See* National Consumer Law Center, Unfair and Deceptive Acts and Practices § 6.6.2 (5th ed. 2001 and Supp.).

178 *See, e.g.*, Iron & Glass Bank v. Franz, 9 Pa. D. & C.3d 419, Clearinghouse No. 31,037 (C.P. Allegheny Cty. 1978). *See also* National Consumer Law Center, Unfair and Deceptive Acts and Practices § 6.6.4.7 (5th ed. 2001 and Supp.).

179 Armstrong v. Accrediting Council for Continuing Education & Training, Inc., 84 F.3d 1452 (D.C. Cir. 1996), *on remand*, 950 F. Supp. 1 (D.D.C. 1996) (court maintained jurisdiction of pendent claims and found case to be appropriate for declaratory relief), *on further remand*, 980 F. Supp. 53 (D.D.C. 1997) (court determined that California law controls and invited plaintiff to amend complaint to assert claims and defenses under California consumer protection laws), *aff'd*, 168 F.3d 1362 (D.C. Cir. 1999) (affirming district court's dismissal of claims), *cert. denied*, 528 U.S. 1073 (2000); Keams v. Tempe Technical Institute, Inc., 993 F. Supp. 714 (D. Ariz. 1997) (since student loan contracts did not include terms of Holder Rule, former vocational school students were not able to assert claims and defenses arising from school's behavior against assignee), *claims against all defendants dismissed*, 16 F. Supp. 2d 1119 (D. Ariz. 1998); Morgan v. Markerdowne Corp., 976 F. Supp. 301 (D.N.J. 1997); United States v. Ornecipe, Clearinghouse No. 51,941 (S.D. Fla. 1995) (Florida UDAP statute does not apply to banks); Jackson v. Culinary School of Washington, 811 F. Supp. 714 (D.D.C. 1993) (summary judgment) (court found insufficient facts to find UDAP liability), *aff'd on other grounds*, 27 F.3d 573 (D.C. Cir. 1994) (court declined to consider complex state law issue in declaratory judgment action), *vacated* 115 S. Ct. 2573 (1995) (appellate court used de novo instead of abuse of discretion standard to review district court's decision to decide state law issues in declaratory judgment action), *remanded to district court on state law claims* 59 F.3d 254 (D.C. Cir. 1995) (to determine on what basis federal court decided to rule on state law issues), *motion dismissed*, 1995 U.S. App. LEXIS 22304 (D.C. Cir. 1995); Williams v. National School of Health Technology, Inc., 836 F. Supp. 273 (E.D. Pa. 1993) (United States committed no wrongdoing, so no UDAP violation; court failed to consider that lender did engage in wrongdoing and that the United States is an assignee of the lender); Spinner v. Chesapeake Business Institute of Virginia, Clearinghouse No. 49,131A (E.D. Va. Feb. 5, 1993) (UDAP statute exempted practices authorized by federal laws or regulations and the court determined that the student loan contracts were authorized); Hernandez v. Alexander, Clearinghouse No. 46,792 (D. Nev. May 18, 1992). *But see* Keams v. Tempe Technical

Despite this judicial reluctance, in many states a consumer should be able to challenge a lender's systematic failure to comply with the FTC Holder Rule as a state UDAP violation.[180] This is particularly the case for loans entered into after April 16, 1993, when the Department of Education announced to lenders and guarantors that the FTC Holder Rule applies to student loans.[181] Lenders after that date had no excuse not to include the Holder Notice in their promissory notes, where applicable.

Another approach is to seek to enforce the Holder language as an implied term in the note even though the notice is not present.[182] This approach has not been successful in the student loan context.[183] Also not successful to date has been the argument that the lender should be estopped from taking advantage of the illegality in the note or that an illegal note cannot be enforced.[184]

It may also be possible to argue that the note without the FTC Notice is unconscionable and thus unenforceable, or that the Department, guaranty agency, or the lender had a fiduciary duty to the borrower or were engaged in constructive fraud. At least one federal court rejected the fiduciary duty argument but let go to trial both the arguments that the note involved constructive fraud and was unconscionable.[185] A RICO claim is another possibility.[186]

9.5.3.1.5 Origination theory

The Secretary of Education recognizes that students can raise school-related defenses to FFEL collection actions when the school is in an "origination relationship" with the lender.[187] Therefore, if an origination relationship can be proven, even loans from the period prior to the inclusion of the FTC Holder Notice should be subject to school-related defenses. The *Armstrong* court affirmed this concept, citing the origination relationship as a major exception to lenders' protection from student suits prior to re-enforcement of the FTC Holder Rule.[188]

Unfortunately for students, the District of Columbia Circuit has ruled that the Secretary has not sufficiently communicated an intention to be bound by the origination policy so as to create a legally enforceable right grounded in federal law.[189] The *Armstrong* decision, however, indicates that if

---

Institute, Inc., Clearinghouse No. 41,793J (D. Ariz. Oct. 19, 1995).

180 *See* Keams v. Tempe Technical Institute, 39 F.3d 222 (9th Cir. 1994), *appeal after remand*, 103 F.3d 138 (9th Cir. 1996), *redesignated as opinion*, 110 F.3d 44 (9th Cir. 1997), *claims against all defendants dismissed*, 16 F. Supp. 2d 1119 (D. Ariz. 1998); Jackson v. Culinary School of Washington, 788 F. Supp. 1233 (D.D.C. 1992) (see note 91, *supra* for the subsequent history in this case); Shorter v. Alexander, Clearinghouse No. 47,950 (N.D. Ga. Dec. 8, 1992). *But see* Armand v. Secretary of Education, Clearinghouse No. 51,298 (S.D. Fla. July 19, 1995) (Florida UDAP statute does not apply to banks).

181 Common Application Material and Promissory Note, Clearinghouse No. 47,974 (Apr. 16, 1993).

182 *See* Anderson v. Central States Waterproofing, Clearinghouse No. 40,627 (Minn. Dist. Ct. Hennepin Cty 1982). *See also* White, *Coping with Violations of the Federal Trade Commission's Holder In Due Course Rule*, 66 Temple L. Rev. 661 (1993).

183 Lee v. Riley, Clearinghouse No. 52,041 (W.D. Ky. Feb. 27, 1998) (memorandum opinion); Armstrong v. Accrediting Council for Continuing Education & Training, Inc., 84 F.3d 1452 (D.C. Cir. 1996), *on remand*, 950 F. Supp. 1 (D.D.C. 1996), *on further remand*, 980 F. Supp. 53 (D.D.C. 1997), *aff'd*, 168 F.3d 1362 (D.C. Cir. 1999), *cert. denied*, 528 U.S. 1073 (2000); Bartels v. Alabama Commercial College, 918 F. Supp. 1565 (S.D. Ga. 1995), *rev'd on other grounds*, 54 F.3d 702 (11th Cir. 1995); Spinner v. Chesapeake Business Institute of Virginia, Clearinghouse No. 49,131A (E.D. Va. Feb. 5, 1993); Jackson v. Culinary School of Washington, 788 F. Supp. 1233 (D.D.C. 1992) (see note 91, *supra*, for subsequent history in this case); Hernandez v. Alexander, Clearinghouse No. 46,792 (D. Nev. May 18, 1992); Shorter v. Alexander, Clearinghouse No. 47,950 (N.D. Ga. Dec. 8, 1992).

184 Armstrong v. Accrediting Council for Continuing Education & Training, Inc., 84 F.3d 1452 (D.C. Cir. 1996), *on remand*, 950 F. Supp. 1 (D.D.C. 1996), *on further remand*, 980 F. Supp. 53 (D.D.C. 1997), *aff'd*, 168 F.3d 1362 (D.C. Cir. 1999), *cert. denied*, 528 U.S. 1073 (2000); Spinner v. Chesapeake Business Institute of Virginia, Clearinghouse No. 49,131A (E.D. Va. Feb. 5, 1993).

185 Spinner v. Chesapeake Business Institute of Virginia, Clearinghouse No. 49,131A (E.D. Va. Feb. 5, 1993).

186 *See* §§ 9.3.3 (state RICO claims), 9.3.5 (federal RICO claims), *supra*.

187 A good enunciation of this policy is found in a letter from Acting Assistant Secretary Whitehead to Congressman Stephen Solarz, Clearinghouse No. 44,343 (May 19, 1988). In addition, a recent Department of Education regulation requires schools to warn students that students cannot raise school-related defenses against lenders "other than a loan made or originated by the school." 34 C.F.R. § 682.604(f)(2)(iii). See also 41 Fed. Reg. 4,496 (Jan. 29, 1976) for an explanation of the origins of this policy.

One early case dismissed the origination theory as applied to GSL because the plaintiffs had mistakenly relied on FISL regulations. *See* Veal v. First American Savings Bank, 914 F.2d 909 (7th Cir. 1990). The Department itself has stated that, while the FISL regulations do not regulate GSLs, the origination theory is independently applicable to GSLs. November 9, 1990 letter of Fred J. Marinucci, Department of Education Office of General Counsel to the Honorable John T. Copenhaver, Jr., federal district court judge, Clearinghouse No. 45,919.

188 Armstrong v. Accrediting Council for Continuing Education & Training, 168 F.3d 1362, 1365 (D.C. Cir. 1999) (as long as lenders avoided school origination relationships, they could make and sell loans without fear that students could assert school misconduct as a defense against repaying their loans), *cert. denied*, 528 U.S. 1073 (2000); Morgan v. Markerdown, 976 F. Supp. 301 (D.N.J. 1997) (origination relationship between lender and school subjects lenders and guarantors to school-related defenses).

189 Jackson v. Culinary School of Washington, Ltd., 27 F.3d 573 (D.C. Cir. 1994), *vacated on other grounds*, 115 S. Ct. 2573 (1995) (appellate court used de novo instead of abuse of discretion standard to review district court's decision to decide state law issues in declaratory judgment action), *remanded to district court on state law claims, but affirming ruling on origination*, 59 F.3d 254 (D.C. Cir. 1995) (to determine on what

there was an origination relationship, a state law theory of lender liability would not be preempted even during the period of FTC non-enforcement.[190]

Some courts have found the origination theory binding on the Department and guarantors,[191] based on the Department's statements that it expects guaranty agencies not to collect unenforceable loans where an origination relationship exists.[192] Other courts find that even if the Department's statements are binding on the Department, the statements have never been promulgated as a rule, and are not binding on guarantors.[193]

If a court allows a consumer to raise defenses where there is an origination relationship, the next step is to present sufficient proof of the relationship. Department regulations define origination as a special relationship where the lender delegates to the school substantial functions normally performed by lenders.[194] The regulations also, until 1994, gave three examples where the Secretary determined that an origination relationship exists:

- The school determines who receives a loan and the amount of the loan;
- The lender has the school verify the identity of the borrower; *or*
- The lender has the school complete forms normally completed by the lender.[195]

The burden of proving this relationship is on the student.[196]

9.5.3.1.6 Ineligible school

Where a guaranty agency or the Department is seeking collection on a guaranteed loan, a possible defense is that the loan never should have been guaranteed, and that the guarantor or the Department should not be collecting on the loan.[197]

In certain cases, the school was not an eligible institution when the loan was extended, so that, under federal law, the loan was not eligible for a federal guarantee. More common is the situation where the Department recognized a school as eligible where the school should not in fact have been found to be eligible. No court has yet found this as a basis to refuse to enforce an FFEL.[198]

---

basis federal court decided to rule on state law issues), *motion dismissed* 1995 U.S. App. LEXIS 22304 (D.C. Cir. 1995); Williams v. National School of Health Technology, Inc. 836 F. Supp. 273 (E.D. Pa. 1993), *aff'd without op.*, 37 F.3d 1491 (3d Cir. 1994); *see also* Bartels v. Alabama Commercial College, 918 F. Supp. 1565 (S.D. Ga. 1995), *aff'd without published op.*, 189 F.3d 483 (11th Cir. Ga. 1999), *cert. denied*, 528 U.S. 1074 (2000).

190 *See* § 9.5.3.1.3, *supra.* Armstrong v. Accrediting Council for Continuing Education & Training, Inc., 168 F.3d 1362 (D.C. Cir. 1999), *cert. denied*, 528 U.S. 1073 (2000).

191 Morgan v. Markerdowne Corp., 976 F. Supp. 301 (D.N.J. 1997); Tipton v. Secretary of Education, 768 F. Supp. 540 (S.D. W. Va. 1991). *See also* Hernandez v. Alexander, Clearinghouse No. 46,792 (D. Nev. May 18, 1992); Alberto v. School of Business Machines, Clearinghouse No. 46,755 (N.J. Super. Ct. July 26, 1991); *cf.* Armstrong v. Accrediting Council for Continuing Education & Training, Inc., Clearinghouse No. 46,789 (D.D.C. filed Apr. 1, 1992) (Plaintiff's Opposition to Motions to Dismiss of Defendants Bank of America, California Student Loan Finance Corp., the Higher Education Assistance Foundation, and the Secretary of Education).

192 *See, e.g.*, Letter from Acting Assistant Secretary Whitehead to Congressman Stephen Solarz, Clearinghouse No. 44,343 (May 19, 1988).

193 Armstrong v. Accrediting Council for Continuing Education & Training, Inc., 84 F.3d 1452 (D.C. Cir. 1996), *on remand*, 950 F. Supp. 1 (D.D.C. 1996), *on further remand*, 980 F. Supp. 53 (D.D.C. 1997), *aff'd*, 168 F.3d 1362 (D.C. Cir. 1999) (affirming district court's dismissal of claims), *cert. denied*, 528 U.S. 1073 (2000); Bartels v. Alabama Commercial College, 918 F. Supp. 1565 (S.D. Ga. 1995), *aff'd without published opinion*, 189 F.3d 483 (11th Cir. 1999), *cert. denied*, 528 U.S. 1074 (2000); Williams v. National School of Health Technology, Inc., 836 F. Supp. 273 (E.D. Pa. 1993); Spinner v. Chesapeake Business Institute of Virginia, Clearinghouse No. 49,131A (E.D. Va. Feb. 5, 1993); Shorter v. Alexander, Clearinghouse No. 47,950 (N.D. Ga. Dec. 8, 1992).

194 34 C.F.R. § 682.200(b) ("Origination").

195 *Id.* Morgan v. Markerdowne Corp., 976 F. Supp. 301 (D.N.J. 1997) (origination relationship existed where school chose the banks from which borrowers would obtain financing, obtained all of the necessary financial papers, either completed the papers or assisted borrowers in completing the papers, verified borrowers' information and had borrowers sign the documents).

196 Jackson v. Culinary School of Washington, 811 F. Supp. 714 (D.D.C. 1993) (claim dismissed based on summary judgment motion that students had not presented evidence of origination relationship), *aff'd on other grounds*, 27 F.3d 573 (D.C. Cir. 1994) (origination theory not enforceable against the Secretary), *vacated on other grounds*, 115 S. Ct. 2573 (1995) (appellate court used de novo instead of abuse of discretion standard to review district court's decision to decide state law issues in declaratory judgment action), *remanded to district court on state law claims, but affirming own ruling on origination*, 59 F.3d 254 (D.C. Cir. 1995) (to determine on what basis federal court decided to rule on state law issues), *motion dismissed*, 1995 U.S. App. LEXIS 22304 (D.C. Cir. 1995); Hernandez v. Alexander, 845 F. Supp. 1417 (D. Nev. 1993) (not sufficient to allege that the school determined the amount of the loan requested (but not the amount of the loan actually lent), verified the identity of the borrower (there being no requirement that the lender verify the borrower's identity, and filled in portions of the note normally filled in by the student and school (but not by the lender)); *see also* Armand v. Secretary of Education, Clearinghouse No. 51,298 (S.D. Fla. July 19, 1995). *But cf.* Shorter v. Riley, Clearinghouse No. 47,950B (N.D. Ga. Nov. 18, 1993) (question of whether there is an origination relationship must be decided at trial, and not based on either sides' summary judgment motions).

197 See § 9.5.3.2, *infra* for a discussion of loans that have lost their guaranteed status.

198 *But see* Hernandez v. Alexander, Clearinghouse No. 46,792 (D. Nev. May 18, 1992) (court appears to accept argument that loan could be unenforceable because school was improperly certified as eligible).

9.5.3.1.7 *How to raise school-related claims on older FFELs*

In some cases, the borrower may not be facing a collection lawsuit, but other collection methods such as tax intercepts and/or wage garnishments. It is difficult to raise school-related defenses in response to a threatened tax intercept, garnishment, or collection contact.[199]

One way to address this problem is for students to bring an affirmative action in state or federal court for declaratory relief that the student does not owe the loan. The student can then use the declaration as a defense in any tax intercept or other administrative collection action. An action for declaratory relief should not violate the HEA's anti-injunction provision.[200]

Care must be taken in selecting the defendants. For example, a New Jersey state court case demonstrates the dangers of bringing an action in state court without naming the Secretary of Education as a defendant.[201] After the judge ruled preliminarily in the students' favor, one of the defendants brought in the United States as a third party defendant, and the United States removed the case to federal court.

Naming the United States as a defendant initially will avoid this result. The United States will almost certainly remove the case immediately to federal court. Alternatively, the case can be brought in federal court, naming the United States as a defendant. The HEA contains an explicit grant of federal jurisdiction for suits against the Secretary of Education.[202] Yet another approach is to file bankruptcy and litigate the validity of the student loan within the bankruptcy court.

Since a class action seeking declaratory relief from student loans may drag on for years, it is tempting to seek preliminary injunctive relief to try to stop collection contacts, tax intercepts, and bad credit reports, and to allow students to qualify for additional student loans. Nevertheless, the HEA specifically states that no injunction shall be issued against the Secretary of Education.[203] This is not always fatal. In some cases, the guaranty agency will be the loan holder and an injunction can generally be crafted to

fully protect students without naming the Secretary. In other cases, additional agencies, such as the Department of Treasury, will be involved in collection efforts. These agencies should be named in cases seeking injunction relief.[204]

Nevertheless, courts are likely to be wary when treading on such complex issues as those involved in student loan cases, and may not grant preliminary relief until the legal principles are clarified. The best strategy may be to seek a voluntary agreement with the Secretary and the guaranty agency that they temporarily will cease certain actions.

A number of such class actions seeking declaratory relief have been certified.[205] Sometimes the court will create subclasses for each different guaranty agency involved.[206]

One special issue relating to cases seeking class actions to declare FFELs unenforceable is the interrelation of the class with the closed school and false certification discharge. The Department's regulations state that a student is eligible for a closed school and false certification discharge only where the loan is enforceable.[207] Class defendants can argue that there would be a conflict of interest between those class members entitled to a closed school or false certification discharge (who would not want to allege that the loans were unenforceable) and other class members who would want to prove that the loans were unenforceable.

At least one federal court was not persuaded by this argument, finding that those class members entitled to a discharge would not be prejudiced by pursuing the action. The court found that the Secretary was unlikely to punish students who are raising school-related defenses by excluding them from eligibility for closed school and false certification discharges.[208]

9.5.3.2 FFELs That Have Lost Their Guaranteed Status

A FFEL may lose its guaranteed status if a lender does not exercise due diligence, if the school was not an eligible institution, or for some other reason. While the promissory

---

199 *See* §§ 5.2.2.3 (tax offset), 5.3.3.2 (garnishment), *supra*.

200 Bank of America, NT & SA v. Riley, 940 F. Supp. 348 (D.D.C. 1996) (HEA's anti-injunctive provision does not apply to a declaratory judgment action against the Secretary). *See also* Thomas v. Bennett, 856 F.2d 1165 (8th Cir. 1988); Student Loan Marketing Ass'n v. Riley, 907 F. Supp. 464 (D.D.C. 1995); Pro Schools, Inc. v. Riley, 824 F. Supp. 1314 (E.D. Wis. 1993). A number of briefs filed on behalf of students have also persuasively countered the argument that the anti-injunctive provision applies to actions for declaratory relief.

201 Alberto v. School of Business Machines, Clearinghouse No. 46,755 (N.J. Super. Ct. July 26, 1991).

202 20 U.S.C. § 1082(a); *see also* Bartels v. Alabama Commercial College, Inc., 54 F.3d 702 (11th Cir. 1995), *aff'd without published opinion*, 189 F.3d 483 (11th Cir. 1999), *cert. denied*, 528 U.S. 1074 (2000).

203 *See* 20 U.S.C. § 1082(a)(2).

204 This issue was raised in litigation challenging the government's right to offset Social Security benefits for old student loans. *See* § 5.4.3.3, *supra*. Pleadings and discovery requests can be found at Appxs. E, F, *infra* and on the companion CD-Rom.

205 *See* Keams v. Tempe Technical Institute, 39 F.3d 222 (9th Cir. 1994), *appeal after remand*, 103 F.3d 138 (9th Cir. 1996), *redesignated as opinion*, 110 F.3d 44 (9th Cir. 1997), *claims against all defendants dismissed*, 16 F. Supp. 2d 1119 (D. Ariz. 1998); Shorter v. Riley, Clearinghouse No. 47,950B (N.D. Ga. Nov. 18, 1993); Genzale v. Zenzi's Beauty College, Clearinghouse No. 49,931 (Cal. Super. Ct. Apr. 19, 1993) (order certifying the class).

206 Shorter v. Riley, Clearinghouse No. 47,950B (N.D. Ga. Nov. 18, 1993).

207 *See* §§ 6.2, 6.3, *supra*.

208 Keams v. Tempe Technical Institute, 39 F.3d 222 (9th Cir. 1994), *appeal after remand*, 103 F.3d 138 (9th Cir. 1996), *redesignated as opinion*, 110 F.3d 44 (9th Cir. 1997), *claims against all defendants dismissed*, 16 F. Supp. 2d 1119 (D. Ariz. 1998).

note between the lender and student will not be automatically cancelled, the guaranty agency and the United States no longer back up the loan. Typically the lender will sell the loan to some private entity, and that entity (not a guaranty agency) will try to collect from the student on the loan.

When this private entity collects on what is now a private loan, state laws should apply as to the loan's enforceability. The state's applicable statute of limitations should apply. State common law and statutory theories of lender liability should also apply. There can no longer be any issue of preemption of state law because of a conflict with the HEA, since the loan is no longer part of the federal program.

The FTC Holder Rule should be inserted in the loan as well, and there is no excuse that the guaranty agency or the United States approved of a loan without such notice, since this is no longer a guaranteed loan. Thus state remedies for failure to comply with the Holder Notice should apply as well.

If the FFEL lost its guaranteed status because the school was never an eligible program, this should be raised as a defense on any collection of the now non-guaranteed loan. The school was almost certainly the original lender's agent in signing the student up for the school. The school's fraud in signing the student up for an ineligible loan should be imputed to its principal, and thus to all subsequent assignees of the loan.[209]

Moreover, if the loan lost its guaranteed status because of the lender's lack of due diligence, it may be possible to argue that this lack of due diligence also acts as a defense to the student's obligation to pay the loan.[210] Such loans may also be dischargeable in bankruptcy even though the loan does not meet the substantial hardship test because the loan is not insured by a government unit.[211] Even though a loan has lost its guaranteed status, the Department has stated the student is still eligible for a closed school or false certification discharge.[212]

9.5.3.3 Consolidation Loans

A loan consolidation has significant benefits for most student loan borrowers in default.[213] One problem is that consolidating a student loan may make it more difficult to raise school-related defenses on that loan. The lender may argue that the new consolidated loan is a novation, and that defenses to the old loan do not apply to the new loan. Even though the post-1994 FFEL loans contain the FTC Holder Notice, the Direct Consolidation Loan does not.

At least one federal court has rejected this argument, holding instead that a student does not waive her defenses to an original student loan by exchanging that loan for a federal consolidation loan.[214] The court found insufficient policy grounds to rule as a matter of law that the consolidation was a new loan extinguishing defenses to the old loan. The court also found unpersuasive the language in the loan consolidation that explicitly stated that the borrower was waiving all defenses on the original loan. The court found the waiver language not sufficiently conspicuous and not based on a knowing and voluntary agreement. The court found that there was no novation, because there was no mutual agreement that the student was waiving defenses.

Another argument why a consolidation loan does not waive student defenses is that the Department of Education has stated that the student can continue, despite the consolidation, to apply for a closed school, unpaid refund or false certification discharge.[215] The policy grounds for the ability to continue raising school-related defenses should apply with equal force.

9.6 Student Claims Against Tuition Recovery Funds

9.6.1 General

State tuition recovery funds (STRFs) can be a valuable source of relief for defrauded students where a school is insolvent and where the student cannot obtain a closed school or false certification discharge. STRFs contain deposits of money collected from schools approved to operate in the state. The funds are disbursed to victimized students under specified conditions.

Many states have either a STRF or a bond program to reimburse defrauded students. States with STRFs tend to have two different funds—one for degree-granting institutions, and one for schools that offer non-degree-granting vocational programs.[216]

---

209 *See* § 9.5.3.1.2, *supra.*

210 *See* United States v. Rhodes, 788 F. Supp. 339 (E.D. Mich. 1992).

211 *Id.*

212 Dear Colleague Letter 94-G-256, Clearinghouse No. 50,422 (Sept. 1994).

213 *See* § 8.2, *supra.*

214 Crawford v. The American Institute of Professional Careers, Inc., 934 F. Supp. 335 (D. Ariz. 1996).

215 *See* Dear Colleague Letter 94-G-256, Clearinghouse No. 50,422 (Sept. 1994). The right to obtain a partial discharge of a consolidation loan applies only to borrowers who qualify for false certification, closed school, or unpaid refund discharges, not for disability. This issue was considered, and expanding the partial discharge for disability was rejected, during spring 2002 negotiated rulemaking sessions. *See* 67 Fed. Reg. 51036, 51041 (Aug. 6, 2002); § 6.6, *supra.*

216 The following is a fairly current list of states which have STRFs, including contact information:
Arizona: Student Tuition Recovery Fund, 1400 W. Washington, Suite 260, Phoenix, AZ 85007. (602) 542-5709.
Arkansas: State Board of Higher Education, 114 E. Capital, Little Rock, Ark. 72201. (501) 371-2000.
California: Bureau for Private Postsecondary and Vocational

The STRF is an important student remedy because it will provide relief in situations where defrauded students cannot obtain a closed school, unpaid refund, or false certification discharge. The California STRF, for example, will pay claims where a student ceased attending a school because of a breach or anticipatory breach of the agreement for the course of instruction.[217] The California STRF also provides relief for students who have obtained judgments against schools for violations of the state student protection act provisions, but are unable to collect the judgment after diligent efforts.[218] The operation of STRFs varies significantly by state. Advocates will need to contact their own state regulatory agency concerning detailed information on their STRF.

9.6.2 Relationship of STRF to Closed School and False Certification Discharges

Quite often students entitled to relief under a STRF are also entitled under federal law to a closed school, unpaid refund, or false certification discharge.[219] For example, the California STRF pays claims to students who suffered losses as a result of the closure of an institution.[220]

Students entitled to recovery under the STRF and a federal discharge provision can expect to be placed in the middle of a tug-a-war between the state agency and the Department, as each agency tries to have the other pay for the student's loss. For example, the Department's closed school regulations require students to specify whether they have applied to a STRF and what payment they received from the STRF.[221] The applicant for a closed school discharge also assigns to the student all the student's rights to make a claim on STRF funds received from a private party.[222]

State agencies often respond by delaying processing on a STRF application until the closed school or false certification application is resolved. As a result, STRF applications are often held in limbo for long periods of time. Despite these delays, it is important for students to apply to the STRF in any case and keep records of application dates as the state STRF, unlike the federal discharge programs, may limit the time period for applications.[223] Students who do not apply to the STRF pending decisions on their federal discharge applications risk losing the tuition fund remedy. Students should also contact the STRF periodically to check on the status of their recovery fund applications.

Education, California Department of Consumer Affairs, Student Tuition Recovery Fund, 400 R Street, Suite 5000, Sacramento, CA 95814. (916) 445-3427.

Connecticut: Department of Higher Education, P.O. Box 2219, Hartford, CT 06145.

Delaware: Department of Education, 401 Federal St., P.O. Box 1402, Dover, DE 19903-1402. (302) 739-4601.

Georgia: Tuition Guaranteed Trust Fund, 2189 N. Lake Pkwy, Bldg. 10, Suite 100, Tucker, GA 30084. (770) 414-3300. Non-Public Post Secondary Commission, 2100 E. Exchange Pl. #203, Tucker, GA 30303. (770) 414-3302.

Louisiana: Student Protection Fund, P.O. Box 94064, Baton Rouge, LA 70804-4064.

Maryland: Guaranteed Student Tuition Fund, 16 Francis St., Annapolis, MD 21704.

Massachusetts: Board of Cosmetology, 239 Causeway Street, Boston, MA 02114. (617) 727-3067. Board of Higher Education, One Ashburton Pl, Suite 1401, Boston, MA 02108. (617) 727-7785. Private Postsecondary Schools, 350 Main St., Malden, MA 02148.

Nebraska: Department of Education, 310 Centennial Mall South, Lincoln, NE 68509. (402) 471-2295.

Nevada: State Board of Cosmetology, 1785 E. Sahara Ave., Suite 255, Las Vegas, NV 89104. (702) 486-6542. Student Tuition Indemnification Fund, 1820 E. Sahara, Suite 111, Las Vegas, NV 89104.

New Mexico: Commission on Higher Education, 5301 Central Northeast, Suite 1500, Albuquerque, NM 87108. (505) 841-6611. State Board of Barbers and Cosmetologists, 1599 St. Francis Dr., P.O. Box 251, Santa Fe, NM 87504. (505) 827-7550.

New York: Tuition Reimbursement Account, 116 W. 32d St., 14th Floor, New York, NY 10001. (212) 643-4760.

Ohio: Student Tuition Recovery Authority, 35 East Gay St., Suite 403, Columbus, OH 43215. (614) 446-2752.

Oklahoma: Board of Private Vocational Schools, 2200 North Classen Blvd, Oklahoma City, OK 73106. (405) 521-2225.

Oregon: Tuition Protection Fund, 255 Capital Street, NE, Salem, OR 97310-0203. (503) 378-3600. www.ode.state.or.us.

Tennessee: Tuition Guarantee Fund, 404 James Robertson Parkway, Suite 1900, Nashville, TN 37243. (615) 741-5293.

Texas: Tuition Protection Fund, 101 East 15th St., Austin, TX 78778. (512) 936-3253.

Vermont: Career and Lifelong Learning Department, 120 State St., Montpelier, VT 05620. (802) 828-5139. Vermont State Board of Cosmetology, 109 State St., Montpelier, VT 05609. (802) 828-2373.

Virginia: Student Tuition Recovery Fund, P.O. Box 2120, Richmond, VA 23218. (804) 225-2848.

Washington: Tuition Recovery Trust Fund, P.O. Box 43105, Olympia, WA 98504-3105. (360) 753-5673.

217 Cal. Educ. Code § 94944(a)(1)(A)(iv). The Act is scheduled to be repealed as of January 1, 2005. *See* Cal. Educ. Code § 94999.

218 Cal. Educ. Code § 94944(a)(2).

219 *See* Ch. 6 (loan cancellations), *supra*.

220 Cal. Educ. Code § 94944(a)(1)(i).

221 34 C.F.R. § 682.402(d)(3)(i).

222 34 C.F.R. § 682.402(d)(5)(i).

223 For example, *see* Cal. Educ. Code §§ 94944(d)(1)(F), 94944(d)(2).

Most of the statutory authority for federal student assistance can be found at 20 U.S.C. § 1070 *et seq.* Section 1070a (not reprinted here) relates to Pell grants. The Federal Family Education Loan Program (FFEL) statutory authority begins at § 1071. This appendix includes most of the relevant authority from these sections. It also includes selected authority for the Federal Direct Loan Program (§ 1087a *et seq.*). It also includes selected authority for the Federal Direct Loan Program (§ 1087a *et seq.*) and the Perkins Loan Program (§ 1087aa *et seq.*). Additional statutory sections for all of these programs can be found on the companion CD-Rom.

A.1 Federal Statutes

A.1.1 FFEL

20 U.S.C. sec.
1078-3. Federal consolidation loans.
1087.   Repayment by Secretary of loans of bankrupt, deceased, or disabled borrowers; treatment of borrowers attending closed schools or falsely certified as eligible to borrow

§ 1078-3. Federal consolidation loans

(a) Agreements with eligible lenders
(1) Agreement required for insurance coverage
For the purpose of providing loans to eligible borrowers for consolidation of their obligations with respect to eligible student loans, the Secretary or a guaranty agency shall enter into agreements in accordance with subsection (b) of this section with the following eligible lenders:

(A) the Student Loan Marketing Association or the Holding Company of the Student Loan Marketing Association, including any subsidiary of the Holding Company, created pursuant to section 1087-3 of this title;

(B) State agencies described in subparagraphs (D) and (F) of section 1085(d)(1) of this title; and

(C) other eligible lenders described in subparagraphs (A), (B), (C), (E), and (J) of such section.

(2) Insurance coverage of consolidation loans
Except as provided in section 1079(e) of this title, no contract of insurance under this part shall apply to a consolidation loan unless such loan is made under an agreement pursuant to this section and is covered by a certificate issued in accordance with subsection (b)(2) of this section. Loans covered by such a certificate that is issued by a guaranty agency shall be considered to be insured loans for the purposes of reimbursements under section 1078(c) of this title, but no payment shall be made with respect to such loans under section 1078(f) of this title to any such agency.

(3) Definition of eligible borrower
(A) For the purpose of this section, the term "eligible borrower" means a borrower who—

(i) is not subject to a judgment secured through litigation with respect to a loan under this subchapter and part C of subchapter I of chapter 34 of Title 42 or to an order for wage garnishment under section 1095a of this title; and

(ii) at the time of application for a consolidation loan—

(I) is in repayment status;

(II) is in a grace period preceding repayment; or

(III) is a defaulted borrower who has made arrangements to repay the obligation on the defaulted loans satisfactory to the holders of the defaulted loans.

(B)(i)[1] An individual's status as an eligible borrower under this section terminates upon receipt of a consolidation loan under this section, except that—

(I) an individual who receives eligible student loans after the date of receipt of the consolidation loan may receive a subsequent consolidation loan;

(II) loans received prior to the date of the consolidation loan may be added during the 180-day period following the making of the consolidation loan;

(III) loans received following the making of the consolidation loan may be added during the 180-day period following the making of the consolidation loan; and

(IV) loans received prior to the date of the first consolidation loan may be added to a subsequent consolidation loan.

(C)(i) A married couple, each of whom has eligible student loans, may be treated as if such couple were an individual borrowing under subparagraphs (A) and (B) if such couple agrees to be held jointly and severally liable for the repayment of a consolidation loan, without regard to the amounts of the respective loan obligations that are to be consolidated, and without regard to any subsequent change that may occur in such couple's marital status.

(ii) Only one spouse in a married couple applying for a consolidation loan under this subparagraph need meet any of the requirements of subsection (b) of this section, except that each spouse shall—

(I) individually make the initial certification that no other application is pending in accordance with subsection (b)(1)(A) of this section; and

(II) agree to notify the holder concerning any change of address in accordance with subsection (b)(4) of this section.

(4) "Eligible student loans" defined
For the purpose of paragraph (1), the term "eligible student loans" means loans—

(A) made, insured, or guaranteed under this part, including loans

---

1 So in original. No cl. (ii) has been enacted.

on which the borrower has defaulted (but has made arrangements to repay the obligation on the defaulted loans satisfactory to the Secretary or guaranty agency, whichever insured the loans);

(B) made under part D of this subchapter;

(C) made under part C of this subchapter;

(D) made under subpart II of part A of title VII of the Public Health Service Act (42 U.S.C. § 292 et seq.); or

(E) made under subpart II of part B of title VIII of the Public Health Service Act (42 U.S.C. § 297a et seq.).

(b) Contents of agreements, certificates of insurance, and loan notes

(1) Agreements with lenders

Any lender described in subparagraph (A), (B), or (C) of subsection (a)(1) of this section who wishes to make consolidation loans under this section shall enter into an agreement with the Secretary or a guaranty agency which provides—

(A) that, in the case of all lenders described in subsection (a)(1), the lender will make a consolidation loan to an eligible borrower (on request of that borrower) only if the borrower certifies that the borrower has no other application pending for a loan under this section and (i) the lender holds an outstanding loan of that borrower which is selected by the borrower for consolidation under this section, except that this clause shall not apply in the case of a borrower with multiple holders of loans under this part [20 U.S.C.A. § 1071 et seq.], or (ii) the borrower certifies that the borrower has sought and has been unable to obtain a consolidation loan with income-sensitive repayment terms from the holders of the outstanding loans of that borrower (which are so selected for consolidation);

(B) that each consolidation loan made by the lender will bear interest, and be subject to repayment, in accordance with subsection (c) of this section;

(C) that each consolidation loan will be made, notwithstanding any other provision of this part limiting the annual or aggregate principal amount for all insured loans made to a borrower, in an amount (i) which is not less than the minimum amount required for eligibility of the borrower under subsection (a)(3) of this section, and (ii) which is equal to the sum of the unpaid principal and accrued unpaid interest and late charges of all eligible student loans received by the eligible borrower which are selected by the borrower for consolidation;

(D) that the proceeds of each consolidation loan will be paid by the lender to the holder or holders of the loans so selected to discharge the liability on such loans;

(E) that the lender shall offer an income-sensitive repayment schedule, established by the lender in accordance with the regulations promulgated by the Secretary, to the borrower of any consolidation loan made by the lender on or after July 1, 1994; and

(F) such other terms and conditions as the Secretary or the guaranty agency may specifically require of the lender to carry out this section.

(2) Issuance of certificate of comprehensive insurance coverage

The Secretary shall issue a certificate of comprehensive insurance coverage under section 1079(b) of this title to a lender which has entered into an agreement with the Secretary under paragraph (1) of this subsection. The guaranty agency may issue a certificate of comprehensive insurance coverage to a lender with which it has an agreement under such paragraph. The Secretary shall not issue a certificate to a lender described in subparagraph (B) or (C) of subsection (a)(1) of this section unless the Secretary determines that such lender has first applied to, and has been denied a certificate of insurance by, the guaranty agency which insures the preponderance of its loans (by value).

(3) Contents of certificate

A certificate issued under paragraph (2) shall, at a minimum, provide—

(A) that all consolidation loans made by such lender in conformity with the requirements of this section will be insured by the Secretary or the guaranty agency (whichever is applicable) against loss of principal and interest;

(B) that a consolidation loan will not be insured unless the lender has determined to its satisfaction, in accordance with reasonable and prudent business practices, for each loan being consolidated—

(i) that the loan is a legal, valid, and binding obligation of the borrower;

(ii) that each such loan was made and serviced in compliance with applicable laws and regulations; and

(iii) in the case of loans under this part, that the insurance on such loan is in full force and effect;

(C) the effective date and expiration date of the certificate;

(D) the aggregate amount to which the certificate applies;

(E) the reporting requirements of the Secretary on the lender and an identification of the office of the Department of Education or of the guaranty agency which will process claims and perform other related administrative functions;

(F) the alternative repayment terms which will be offered to borrowers by the lender;

(G) that, if the lender prior to the expiration of the certificate no longer proposes to make consolidation loans, the lender will so notify the issuer of the certificate in order that the certificate may be terminated (without affecting the insurance on any consolidation loan made prior to such termination); and

(H) the terms upon which the issuer of the certificate may limit, suspend, or terminate the lender's authority to make consolidation loans under the certificate (without affecting the insurance on any consolidation loan made prior to such limitation, suspension, or termination).

(4) Terms and conditions of loans

A consolidation loan made pursuant to this section shall be insurable by the Secretary or a guaranty agency pursuant to paragraph (2) only if the loan is made to an eligible borrower who has agreed to notify the holder of the loan promptly concerning any change of address and the loan is evidenced by a note or other written agreement which—

(A) is made without security and without endorsement, except that if the borrower is a minor and such note or other written agreement executed by him or her would not, under applicable law, create a binding obligation, endorsement may be required;

(B) provides for the payment of interest and the repayment of principal in accordance with subsection (c) of this section;

(C)(i) provides that periodic installments of principal need not be paid, but interest shall accrue and be paid in accordance with clause (ii), during any period for which the borrower would be eligible for a deferral under section 1078(b)(1)(M) of this title, and that any such period shall not be included in determining the repayment schedule pursuant to subsection (c)(2) of this section; and

(ii) provides that interest shall accrue and be paid during any such period—

(I) by the Secretary, in the case of a consolidation loan for which the application is received by an eligible lender before November 13, 1997, that consolidated only Federal Stafford Loans for which the student borrower received an interest subsidy under section 1078 of this title;

(II) by the Secretary, in the case of a consolidation loan for which the application is received by an eligible lender on or after November 13, 1997 except that the Secretary shall pay such interest only on that portion of the loan that repays Federal Stafford Loans for which the student borrower received an interest subsidy under section 1078 of this title or Federal Direct Stafford Loans for which the borrower received an interest subsidy under section 1087e of this title; or

(III) by the borrower, or capitalized, in the case of a consolidation loan other than a loan described in subclause (I) or (II);

(D) entitles the borrower to accelerate without penalty repayment of the whole or any part of the loan; and

(E)(i) contains a notice of the system of disclosure concerning such loan to credit bureau organizations under section 1080a of this title, and (ii) provides that the lender on request of the borrower will provide information on the repayment status of the note to such organizations.

(5) Direct loans

In the event that a borrower is unable to obtain a consolidation loan from a lender with an agreement under subsection (a)(1) of this section, or is unable to obtain a consolidation loan with income-sensitive repayment terms acceptable to the borrower from such a lender, the Secretary shall offer any such borrower who applies for it, a direct consolidation loan. Such direct consolidation loan shall, as requested by the borrower, be repaid either pursuant to income contingent repayment under part C of this subchapter or pursuant to any other repayment provision under this section. The Secretary shall not offer such loans if, in the Secretary's judgment, the Department of Education does not have the necessary origination and servicing arrangements in place for such loans.

(6) Nondiscrimination in loan consolidation

An eligible lender that makes consolidation loans under this section shall not discriminate against any borrower seeking such a loan—

(A) based on the number or type of eligible student loans the borrower seeks to consolidate, except that a lender is not required to consolidate loans described in subparagraph (D) or (E) of subsection (a)(4) of this section or subsection (d)(1)(C)(ii) of this section;

(B) based on the type or category of institution of higher education that the borrower attended;

(C) based on the interest rate to be charged to the borrower with respect to the consolidation loan; or

(D) with respect to the types of repayment schedules offered to such borrower.

(c) Payment of principal and interest

(1) Interest rate

(A) Notwithstanding subparagraphs (B) and (C), with respect to any loan made under this section for which the application is received by an eligible lender on or after October 1, 1998, and before July 1, 2003, the applicable interest rate shall be determined under section 1077a(k)(4) of this title.

(B) A consolidation loan made before July 1, 1994, shall bear interest at an annual rate on the unpaid principal balance of the loan that is equal to the greater of—

(i) the weighted average of the interest rates on the loans consolidated, rounded to the nearest whole percent; or

(ii) 9 percent.

(C) A consolidation loan made on or after July 1, 1994, shall bear interest at an annual rate on the unpaid principal balance of the loan that is equal to the weighted average of the interest rates on the loans consolidated, rounded upward to the nearest whole percent.

(D) A consolidation loan for which the application is received by an eligible lender on or after November 13, 1997, and before October 1, 1998, shall bear interest at an annual rate on the unpaid principal balance of the loan that is equal to the rate specified in section 1077a(f) of this title, except that the eligible lender may continue to calculate interest on such a loan at the rate previously in effect and defer, until not later than April 1, 1998, the recalculation of the interest on such a loan at the rate required by this subparagraph if the recalculation is applied retroactively to the date on which the loan is made.

(2) Repayment schedules

(A) Notwithstanding any other provision of this part, to the extent authorized by its certificate of insurance under subsection (b)(2)(F) of this section and approved by the issuer of such certificate, the lender of a consolidation loan shall establish repayment terms as will promote the objectives of this section, which shall include the establishment of graduated or income-sensitive repayment schedules, established by the lender in accordance with the regulations of the Secretary. Except as required by such income-sensitive repayment schedules, or by the terms of repayment pursuant to income contingent repayment offered by the Secretary under subsection (b)(5) of this section, such repayment terms shall require that if the sum of the consolidation loan and the amount outstanding on other student loans to the individual—

(i) is less than $7,500, then such consolidation loan shall be repaid in not more than 10 years;

(ii) is equal to or greater than $7,500 but less than $10,000, then such consolidation loan shall be repaid in not more than 12 years;

(iii) is equal to or greater than $10,000 but less than $20,000, then such consolidation loan shall be repaid in not more than 15 years;

(iv) is equal to or greater than $20,000 but less than $40,000, then such consolidation loan shall be repaid in not more than 20 years;

(v) is equal to or greater than $40,000 but less than $60,000, then such consolidation loan shall be repaid in not more than 25 years; or

(vi) is equal to or greater than $60,000, then such consolidation loan shall be repaid in not more than 30 years.

(B) The amount outstanding on other student loans which may be counted for the purpose of subparagraph (A) may not exceed the amount of the consolidation loan.

(3) Additional repayment requirements

Notwithstanding paragraph (2)—

(A) a repayment schedule established with respect to a consolidation loan shall require that the minimum installment payment be an amount equal to not less than the accrued unpaid interest; and

(B) except as required by the terms of repayment pursuant to income contingent repayment offered by the Secretary under subsection (b)(5) of this section, the lender of a consolidation loan may, with respect to repayment on the loan, when the amount of a monthly or other similar payment on the loan is not a multiple of $5, round the payment to the next highest whole dollar amount that is a multiple of $5.

(4) Commencement of repayment

Repayment of a consolidation loan shall commence within 60 days after all holders have, pursuant to subsection (b)(1)(D) of this section, discharged the liability of the borrower on the loans selected for consolidation.

(5) Insurance premiums prohibited

No insurance premium shall be charged to the borrower on any consolidation loan, and no insurance premium shall be payable by the lender to the Secretary with respect to any such loan, but a fee may be payable by the lender to the guaranty agency to cover the costs of increased or extended liability with respect to such loan.

(d) Special program authorized

(1) General rule and definition of eligible student loan

(A) In general

Subject to the provisions of this subsection, the Secretary or a guaranty agency shall enter into agreements with eligible lenders described in subparagraphs (A), (B), and (C) of subsection (a)(1) of this section for the consolidation of eligible student loans.

(B) Applicability rule

Unless otherwise provided in this subsection, the agreements entered into under subparagraph (A) and the loans made under such agreements for the consolidation of eligible student loans under this subsection shall have the same terms, conditions, and benefits as all other agreements and loans made under this section.

(C) Definition

For the purpose of this subsection, the term "eligible student loans" means loans—

(i) of the type described in subparagraphs (A), (B), and (C) of subsection (a)(4) of this section; and

(ii) made under subpart I of part A of title VII of the Public Health Service Act (42 U.S.C. 292 et seq.).

(2) Interest rate rule

(A) In general

The portion of each consolidated loan that is attributable to an eligible student loan described in paragraph (1)(C)(ii) shall bear interest at a rate not to exceed the rate determined under subparagraph (B).

(B) Determination of the maximum interest rate

For the 12-month period beginning after July 1, 1992, and for each 12-month period thereafter, beginning on July 1 and ending on June 30, the interest rate applicable under subparagraph (A) shall be equal to the average of the bond equivalent rates of the 91-day Treasury bills auctioned for the quarter prior to July 1, for each 12-month period for which the determination is made, plus 3 percent.

(C) Publication of maximum interest rate

The Secretary shall determine the applicable rate of interest under subparagraph (B) after consultation with the Secretary of the Treasury and shall publish such rate in the Federal Register as soon as practicable after the date of such determination.

(3) Special rules

(A) No special allowance rule

No special allowance under section 1087-1 of this title shall be paid with respect to the portion of any consolidated loan under this subsection that is attributable to any loan described in paragraph (1)(C)(ii).

(B) No interest subsidy rule

No interest subsidy under section 1078(a) of this title shall be paid on behalf of any eligible borrower for any portion of a consolidated loan under this subsection that is attributable to any loan described in paragraph (1)(C)(ii).

(C) Additional reserve rule

Notwithstanding any other provision of this chapter, additional reserves shall not be required for any guaranty agency with respect to a loan made under this subsection.

(D) Insurance rule

Any insurance premium paid by the borrower under subpart I of part A of title VII of the Public Health Service Act (42 U.S.C. 292 et seq.) with respect to a loan made under that subpart and consolidated under this subsection shall be retained by the student loan insurance fund established under section 710 of the Public Health Service Act (42 U.S.C. 292i).

(4) Regulations

The Secretary is authorized to promulgate such regulations as may be necessary to facilitate carrying out the provisions of this subsection.

(e) Termination of authority

The authority to make loans under this section expires at the close of September 30, 2004. Nothing in this section shall be construed to authorize the Secretary to promulgate rules or regulations governing the terms or conditions of the agreements and certificates under subsection (b) of this section. Loans made under this section which are insured by the Secretary shall be considered to be new loans made to students for the purpose of section 1074(a) of this title.

(f) Interest payment rebate fee

(1) In general

For any month beginning on or after October 1, 1993, each holder of a consolidation loan under this section for which the first disbursement was made on or after October 1, 1993, shall pay to the Secretary, on a monthly basis and in such manner as the Secretary shall prescribe, a rebate fee calculated on an annual basis equal to 1.05 percent of the principal plus accrued unpaid interest on such loan.

(2) Special rule

For consolidation loans based on applications received during the period from October 1, 1998 through January 31, 1999, inclusive, the rebate described in paragraph (1) shall be equal to 0.62 percent of the principal plus accrued unpaid interest on such loan.

(3) Deposit

The Secretary shall deposit all fees collected pursuant to subsection (a) of this section into the insurance fund established in section 1081 of this title.

(Pub. L. 89-329, title IV, Sec. 428C, as added Pub. L. 99-498, title IV, Sec. 402(a), Oct. 17, 1986, 100 Stat. 1388; amended Pub. L. 100-50, Sec. 10(s), June 3, 1987, 101 Stat. 345; Pub. L. 102-325, title IV, Sec. 419, July 23, 1992, 106 Stat. 532; Pub. L. 102-408, title III, Sec. 306(a), (b), Oct. 13, 1992, 106 Stat. 2084, 2086; Pub. L. 103-66, title IV, Sec. 4046(a), (b)(2), 4106(a), Aug. 10, 1993, 107 Stat. 360, 363, 368; Pub. L. 103-208, Sec. 2(c)(33)-(37), Dec. 20, 1993, 107 Stat. 2466; Pub. L. 103-382, title III, Sec. 356, Oct. 20, 1994, 108 Stat. 3967; Pub. L. 104-208, div. A, title I, Sec.

101(e) (title VI, Sec. 602(b)(1)(A)(ii)), Sept. 30, 1996, 110 Stat. 3009-233, 3009-283; Pub. L. 105-33, title VI, Sec. 6104(3), Aug. 5, 1997, 111 Stat. 652; Pub. L. 105-78, title VI, Sec. 609(b)-(e), Nov. 13, 1997, 111 Stat. 1522, 1523; Pub. L. 105-244, title IV, Sec. 416(b)(2), 420, Oct. 7, 1998, 112 Stat. 1682, 1695.)

§ 1087. Repayment by Secretary of loans of bankrupt, deceased, or disabled borrowers; treatment of borrowers attending closed schools or falsely certified as eligible to borrow

(a) Repayment in full for death and disability

If a student borrower who has received a loan described in subparagraph (A) or (B) of section 1078(a)(1) of this title dies or becomes permanently and totally disabled (as determined in accordance with regulations of the Secretary), then the Secretary shall discharge the borrower's liability on the loan by repaying the amount owed on the loan.

(b) Payment of claims on loans in bankruptcy

The Secretary shall pay to the holder of a loan described in section 1078(a)(1)(A) or (B), 1078-1, 1078-2, 1078-3, or 1078-8 of this title, the amount of the unpaid balance of principal and interest owed on such loan—

(1) when the borrower files for relief under chapter 12 or 13 of title 11 [11 U.S.C.A. § 1201 et seq. or 1301 et seq.];

(2) when the borrower who has filed for relief under chapter 7 or 11 of such title [11 U.S.C.A. § 701 et seq. or 1101 et seq.] commences an action for a determination of dischargeability under section 523(a)(8)(B) of such title; or

(3) for loans described in section 523(a)(8)(A) of such title, when the borrower files for relief under chapter 7 or 11 of such title [11 U.S.C.A. § 701 et seq. or 1101 et seq.].

(c) Discharge
(1) In general

If a borrower who received, on or after January 1, 1986, a loan made, insured, or guaranteed under this part and the student borrower, or the student on whose behalf a parent borrowed, is unable to complete the program in which such student is enrolled due to the closure of the institution or if such student's eligibility to borrow under this part [20 U.S.C.A. § 1071 et seq.] was falsely certified by the eligible institution, or if the institution failed to make a refund of loan proceeds which the institution owed to such student's lender, then the Secretary shall discharge the borrower's liability on the loan (including interest and collection fees) by repaying the amount owed on the loan and shall subsequently pursue any claim available to such borrower against the institution and its affiliates and principals or settle the loan obligation pursuant to the financial responsibility authority under subpart 3 of part G [20 U.S.C.A. § 1099 et seq.]. In the case of a discharge based upon a failure to refund, the amount of the discharge shall not exceed that portion of the loan which should have been refunded. The Secretary shall report to the Committee on Education and the Workforce of the House of Representatives and the Committee on Labor and Human Resources of the Senate annually as to the dollar amount of loan discharges attributable to failures to make refunds.

(2) Assignment

A borrower whose loan has been discharged pursuant to this subsection shall be deemed to have assigned to the United States the right to a loan refund up to the amount discharged against the institution and its affiliates and principals.

(3) Eligibility for additional assistance

The period of a student's attendance at an institution at which the student was unable to complete a course of study due to the closing of the institution shall not be considered for purposes of calculating the student's period of eligibility for additional assistance under this subchapter and part C of subchapter I of chapter 34 of title 42.

(4) Special rule

A borrower whose loan has been discharged pursuant to this subsection shall not be precluded from receiving additional grants, loans, or work assistance under this subchapter and part C of subchapter I of chapter 34 of Title 42 for which the borrower would be otherwise eligible (but for the default on such discharged loan). The amount discharged under this subsection shall be treated the same as loans under section 1087ee(a)(5) of this title.

(5) Reporting

The Secretary shall report to credit bureaus with respect to loans which have been discharged pursuant to this subsection.

(d) Repayment of loans to parents

If a student on whose behalf a parent has received a loan described in section 1078-2 of this title dies, then the Secretary shall discharge the borrower's liability on the loan by repaying the amount owed on the loan.

(Pub. L. 89-329, title IV, Sec. 437, as added Pub. L. 99-498, title IV, Sec. 402(a), Oct. 17, 1986, 100 Stat. 1414; amended Pub. L. 102-325, title IV, Sec. 428, July 23, 1992, 106 Stat. 551; Pub. L. 103-208, Sec. 2(c)(63)-(65), Dec. 20, 1993, 107 Stat. 2469; Pub. L. 105-244, title IV, Sec. 431, Oct. 7, 1998, 112 Stat. 1709.)

A.1.2 *Direct Loans*

20 U.S.C. sec.
1087e. Terms and conditions of loans

§ 1087e. Terms and conditions of loans

(a) In general
(1) Parallel terms, conditions, benefits, and amounts

Unless otherwise specified in this part [20 U.S.C.A. § 1087a et. seq.], loans made to borrowers under this part shall have the same terms, conditions, and benefits, and be available in the same amounts, as loans made to borrowers under sections 1078, 1078-2, and 1078-8 of this title.

(2) Designation of loans

Loans made to borrowers under this part that, except as otherwise specified in this part, have the same terms, conditions, and benefits as loans made to borrowers under—

(A) section 1078 of this title shall be known as "Federal Direct Stafford Loans";

(B) section 1078-2 of this title shall be known as "Federal Direct PLUS Loans"; and

(C) section 1078-8 of this title shall be known as "Federal Direct Unsubsidized Stafford Loans".

(b) Interest rate
(1) Rates for FDSL and FDUSL

For Federal Direct Stafford Loans and Federal Direct Unsubsidized Stafford Loans for which the first disbursement is made on or after July 1, 1994, the applicable rate of interest shall, during any 12-month period beginning on July 1 and ending on June 30, be determined on the preceding June 1 and be equal to—

(A) the bond equivalent rate of 91-day Treasury bills auctioned at the final auction held prior to such June 1; plus

(B) 3.1 percent, except that such rate shall not exceed 8.25 percent.

(2) In school and grace period rules

(A) Notwithstanding the provisions of paragraph (1), but subject to paragraph (3), with respect to any Federal Direct Stafford Loan or Federal Direct Unsubsidized Stafford Loan for which the first disbursement is made on or after July 1, 1995, the applicable rate of interest for interest which accrues—

(i) prior to the beginning of the repayment period of the loan; or

(ii) during the period in which principal need not be paid (whether or not such principal is in fact paid) by reason of a provision described in section 1078(b)(1)(M) or 1077(a)(2)(C) of this title, shall not exceed the rate determined under subparagraph (B).

(B) For the purpose of subparagraph (A), the rate determined under this subparagraph shall, during any 12-month period beginning on July 1 and ending on June 30, be determined on the preceding June 1 and be equal to—

(i) the bond equivalent rate of 91-day Treasury bills auctioned at the final auction prior to such June 1; plus

(ii) 2.5 percent, except that such rate shall not exceed 8.25 percent.

(3) Out-year rule

Notwithstanding paragraphs (1) and (2), for Federal Direct Stafford Loans and Federal Direct Unsubsidized Stafford Loans made on or after July 1, 1998, the applicable rate of interest shall, during any 12-month period beginning on July 1 and ending on June 30, be determined on the preceding June 1 and be equal to—

(A) the bond equivalent rate of the security with a comparable maturity as established by the Secretary; plus

(B) 1.0 percent, except that such rate shall not exceed 8.25 percent.

(4) Rates for FDPLUS

(A) For Federal Direct PLUS Loans for which the first disbursement is made on or after July 1, 1994, the applicable rate of interest shall, during any 12-month period beginning on July 1 and ending on June 30, be determined on the preceding June 1 and be equal to—

(i) the bond equivalent rate of 52-week Treasury bills auctioned at final auction held prior to such June 1; plus

(ii) 3.1 percent, except that such rate shall not exceed 9 percent.

(B) For Federal Direct PLUS loans made on or after July 1, 1998, the applicable rate of interest shall, during any 12-month period beginning on July 1 and ending on June 30, be determined on the preceding June 1 and be equal to—

(i) the bond equivalent rate of the security with a comparable maturity as established by the Secretary; plus

(ii) 2.1 percent, except that such rate shall not exceed 9 percent.

(5) Temporary interest rate provision

(A) Rates for FDSL and FDUSL

Notwithstanding the preceding paragraphs of this subsection, for Federal Direct Stafford Loans and Federal Direct Unsubsidized Stafford Loans for which the first disbursement is made on or after July 1, 1998, and before October 1, 1998, the applicable rate of interest shall, during any 12-month period beginning on July 1 and ending on June 30, be determined on the preceding June 1 and be equal to—

(i) the bond equivalent rate of 91-day Treasury bills auctioned at the final auction held prior to such June 1; plus

(ii) 2.3 percent, except that such rate shall not exceed 8.25 percent.

(B) In school and grace period rules

Notwithstanding the preceding paragraphs of this subsection, with respect to any Federal Direct Stafford Loan or Federal Direct Unsubsidized Stafford Loan for which the first disbursement is made on or after July 1, 1998, and before October 1, 1998, the applicable rate of interest for interest which accrues -

(i) prior to the beginning of the repayment period of the loan; or

(ii) during the period in which principal need not be paid (whether or not such principal is in fact paid) by reason of a provision described in section 1078(b)(1)(M) or 1077(a)(2)(C) of this title, shall be determined under subparagraph (A) by substituting "1.7 percent" for "2.3 percent".

(C) PLUS loans

Notwithstanding the preceding paragraphs of this subsection, with respect to Federal Direct PLUS Loan for which the first disbursement is made on or after July 1, 1998, and before October 1, 1998, the applicable rate of interest shall be determined under subparagraph (A)—

(i) by substituting "3.1 percent" for "2.3 percent"; and

(ii) by substituting "9.0 percent" for "8.25 percent".

(6) Interest rate provision for new loans on or after October 1, 1998, and before July 1, 2006

(A) Rates for FDSL and FDUSL

Notwithstanding the preceding paragraphs of this subsection, for Federal Direct Stafford Loans and Federal Direct Unsubsidized Stafford Loans for which the first disbursement is made on or after October 1, 1998, and before July 1, 2006, the applicable rate of interest shall, during any 12-month period beginning on July 1 and ending on June 30, be determined on the preceding June 1 and be equal to—

(i) the bond equivalent rate of 91-day Treasury bills auctioned at the final auction held prior to such June 1; plus

(ii) 2.3 percent, except that such rate shall not exceed 8.25 percent.

(B) In school and grace period rules

Notwithstanding the preceding paragraphs of this subsection, with respect to any Federal Direct Stafford Loan or Federal Direct Unsubsidized Stafford Loan for which the first disbursement is made on or after October 1, 1998, and before July 1, 2006, the applicable rate of interest for interest which accrues—

(i) prior to the beginning of the repayment period of the loan; or

(ii) during the period in which principal need not be paid (whether or not such principal is in fact paid) by reason of a provision described in section 1078(b)(1)(M) or 1077(a)(2)(C) of this title, shall be determined under subparagraph (A) by substituting "1.7 percent" for "2.3 percent".

(C) PLUS loans

Notwithstanding the preceding paragraphs of this subsection, with respect to Federal Direct PLUS Loan for which the first disbursement is made on or after October 1, 1998, and before July 1, 2003, the applicable rate of interest shall be determined under subparagraph (A)—

(i) by substituting "3.1 percent" for "2.3 percent"; and

(ii) by substituting "9.0 percent" for "8.25 percent".

(D) Consolidation loans

Notwithstanding the preceding paragraphs of this subsection, any Federal Direct Consolidation loan for which the application is received on or after February 1, 1999, and before July 1, 2003, shall bear interest at an annual rate on the unpaid principal balance of the loan that is equal to the lesser of—

(i) the weighted average of the interest rates on the loans consolidated, rounded to the nearest higher one-eighth of one percent; or

(ii) 8.25 percent.

(E) Temporary rules for consolidation loans

Notwithstanding the preceding paragraphs of this subsection, any Federal Direct Consolidation loan for which the application is received on or after October 1, 1998, and before February 1, 1999, shall bear interest at an annual rate on the unpaid principal balance of the loan that is equal to—

(i) the bond equivalent rate of 91-day Treasury bills auctioned at the final auction held prior to such June 1; plus

(ii) 2.3 percent, except that such rate shall not exceed 8.25 percent.

(7) Interest rate provision for new loans on or after July 1, 2006

(A) Rates for FDSL and FDUSL

Notwithstanding the preceding paragraphs of this subsection, for Federal Direct Stafford Loans and Federal Direct Unsubsidized Stafford Loans for which the first disbursement is made on or after July 1, 2006, the applicable rate of interest shall be 6.8 percent on the unpaid principal balance of the loan.

(B) PLUS loans

Notwithstanding the preceding paragraphs of this subsection, with respect to any Federal Direct PLUS loan for which the first disbursement is made on or after July 1, 2006, the applicable rate of interest shall be 7.9 percent on the unpaid principal balance of the loan.

(C) Consolidation loans

Notwithstanding the preceding paragraphs of this subsection, any Federal Direct Consolidation loan for which the application is received on or after July 1, 2006, shall bear interest at an annual rate on the unpaid principal balance of the loan that is equal to the lesser of—

(i) the weighted average of the interest rates on the loans consolidated, rounded to the nearest higher one-eighth of one percent; or

(ii) 8.25 percent.

(8) Repayment incentives

(A) In general

Notwithstanding any other provision of this part [20 U.S.C.A. § 1087a et seq.], the Secretary is authorized to prescribe by regulation such reductions in the interest rate paid by a borrower of a loan made under this part as the Secretary determines appropriate to encourage on-time repayment of the loan. Such reductions may be offered only if the Secretary determines the reductions are cost neutral and in the best financial interest of the Federal Government. Any increase in subsidy costs resulting from such reductions shall be completely offset by corresponding savings in funds available for the William D. Ford Federal Direct Loan Program in that fiscal year from section 1087h of this title and other administrative accounts.

(B) Accountability

Prior to publishing regulations proposing repayment incentives, the Secretary shall ensure the cost neutrality of such reductions. The Secretary shall not prescribe such regulations in final form

unless an official report from the Director of the Office of Management and Budget to the Secretary and a comparable report from the Director of the Congressional Budget Office to the Congress each certify that any such reductions will be completely cost neutral. Such reports shall be transmitted to the Committee on Labor and Human Resources of the Senate and the Committee on Education and the Workforce of the House of Representatives not less than 60 days prior to the publication of regulations proposing such reductions.

(9) Publication

The Secretary shall determine the applicable rates of interest under this subsection after consultation with the Secretary of the Treasury and shall publish such rate in the Federal Register as soon as practicable after the date of determination.

(c) Loan fee

The Secretary shall charge the borrower of a loan made under this part [20 U.S.C.A. § 1087a et seq.] an origination fee of 4.0 percent of the principal amount of loan.

(d) Repayment plans

(1) Design and selection

Consistent with criteria established by the Secretary, the Secretary shall offer a borrower of a loan made under this part [20 U.S.C.A. § 1087a et seq.] a variety of plans for repayment of such loan, including principal and interest on the loan. The borrower shall be entitled to accelerate, without penalty, repayment on the borrower's loans under this part. The borrower may choose—

(A) a standard repayment plan, with a fixed annual repayment amount paid over a fixed period of time, consistent with subsection (a)(1) of this section;

(B) an extended repayment plan, with a fixed annual repayment amount paid over an extended period of time, except that the borrower shall annually repay a minimum amount determined by the Secretary in accordance with section 1078(b)(1)(L) of this title;

(C) a graduated repayment plan, with annual repayment amounts established at 2 or more graduated levels and paid over a fixed or extended period of time, except that the borrower's scheduled payments shall not be less than 50 percent, nor more than 150 percent, of what the amortized payment on the amount owed would be if the loan were repaid under the standard repayment plan; and

(D) an income contingent repayment plan, with varying annual repayment amounts based on the income of the borrower, paid over an extended period of time prescribed by the Secretary, not to exceed 25 years, except that the plan described in this subparagraph shall not be available to the borrower of a Federal Direct PLUS loan.

(2) Selection by Secretary

If a borrower of a loan made under this part [20 U.S.C.A. § 1087a et seq.] does not select a repayment plan described in paragraph (1), the Secretary may provide the borrower with a repayment plan described in subparagraph (A), (B), or (C) of paragraph (1).

(3) Changes in selections

The borrower of a loan made under this part may change the borrower's selection of a repayment plan under paragraph (1), or the Secretary's selection of a plan for the borrower under paragraph (2), as the case may be, under such terms and conditions as may be established by the Secretary.

(4) Alternative repayment plans

The Secretary may provide, on a case by case basis, an alternative repayment plan to a borrower of a loan made under this part [20 U.S.C.A. § 1087a et seq.] who demonstrates to the satisfaction of the Secretary that the terms and conditions of the repayment plans available under paragraph (1) are not adequate to accommodate the borrower's exceptional circumstances. In designing such alternative repayment plans, the Secretary shall ensure that such plans do not exceed the cost to the Federal Government, as determined on the basis of the present value of future payments by such borrowers, of loans made using the plans available under paragraph (1).

(5) Repayment after default

The Secretary may require any borrower who has defaulted on a loan made under this part [20 U.S.C.A. § 1087a et seq.] to—

(A) pay all reasonable collection costs associated with such loan; and

(B) repay the loan pursuant to an income contingent repayment plan.

(e) Income contingent repayment

(1) Information and procedures

The Secretary may obtain such information as is reasonably necessary regarding the income of a borrower (and the borrower's spouse, if applicable) of a loan made under this part that is, or may be, repaid pursuant to income contingent repayment, for the purpose of determining the annual repayment obligation of the borrower. Returns and return information (as defined in section 6103 of Title 26) may be obtained under the preceding sentence only to the extent authorized by section 6103(*l*)(13) of Title 26. The Secretary shall establish procedures for determining the borrower's repayment obligation on that loan for such year, and such other procedures as are necessary to implement effectively income contingent repayment.

(2) Repayment based on adjusted gross income

A repayment schedule for a loan made under this part [20 U.S.C.A. § 1087a et seq.] and repaid pursuant to income contingent repayment shall be based on the adjusted gross income (as defined in section 62 of Title 26 [26 U.S.C.A. § 62]) of the borrower or, if the borrower is married and files a Federal income tax return jointly with the borrower's spouse, on the adjusted gross income of the borrower and the borrower's spouse.

(3) Additional documents

A borrower who chooses, or is required, to repay a loan made under this part [20 U.S.C.A. § 1087a et seq.] pursuant to income contingent repayment, and for whom adjusted gross income is unavailable or does not reasonably reflect the borrower's current income, shall provide to the Secretary other documentation of income satisfactory to the Secretary, which documentation the Secretary may use to determine an appropriate repayment schedule.

(4) Repayment schedules

Income contingent repayment schedules shall be established by regulations promulgated by the Secretary and shall require payments that vary in relation to the appropriate portion of the annual income of the borrower (and the borrower's spouse, if applicable) as determined by the Secretary.

(5) Calculation of balance due

The balance due on a loan made under this part [20 U.S.C.A. § 1087a et seq.] that is repaid pursuant to income contingent repayment shall equal the unpaid principal amount of the loan, any

accrued interest, and any fees, such as late charges, assessed on such loan. The Secretary may promulgate regulations limiting the amount of interest that may be capitalized on such loan, and the timing of any such capitalization.

(6) Notification to borrowers

The Secretary shall establish procedures under which a borrower of a loan made under this part [20 U.S.C.A. 1087a et seq.] who chooses or is required to repay such loan pursuant to income contingent repayment is notified of the terms and conditions of such plan, including notification of such borrower—

(A) that the Internal Revenue Service will disclose to the Secretary tax return information as authorized under section 6103(*l*)(13) of Title 26 [20 U.S.C.A. § 6103(*l*)(13)]; and

(B) that if a borrower considers that special circumstances, such as a loss of employment by the borrower or the borrower's spouse, warrant an adjustment in the borrower's loan repayment as determined using the information described in subparagraph (A), or the alternative documentation described in paragraph (3), the borrower may contact the Secretary, who shall determine whether such adjustment is appropriate, in accordance with criteria established by the Secretary.

(f) Deferment

(1) Effect on principal and interest

A borrower of a loan made under this part [20 U.S.C.A. § 1087a et seq.] who meets the requirements described in paragraph (2) shall be eligible for a deferment, during which periodic installments of principal need not be paid, and interest—

(A) shall not accrue, in the case of a—

(i) Federal Direct Stafford Loan; or

(ii) a Federal Direct Consolidation Loan that consolidated only Federal Direct Stafford Loans, or a combination of such loans and Federal Stafford Loans for which the student borrower received an interest subsidy under section 1078 of this title; or

(B) shall accrue and be capitalized or paid by the borrower, in the case of a Federal Direct PLUS Loan, a Federal Direct Unsubsidized Stafford Loan, or a Federal Direct Consolidation Loan not described in subparagraph (A)(ii).

(2) Eligibility

A borrower of a loan made under this part shall be eligible for a deferment during any period—

(A) during which the borrower—

(i) is carrying at least one-half the normal full-time work load for the course of study that the borrower is pursuing, as determined by the eligible institution (as such term is defined in section 1085(a) of this title) the borrower is attending; or

(ii) is pursuing a course of study pursuant to a graduate fellowship program approved by the Secretary, or pursuant to a rehabilitation training program for individuals with disabilities approved by the Secretary, except that no borrower shall be eligible for a deferment under this subparagraph, or a loan made under this part [20 U.S.C.A. § 1087a et seq.] (other than a Federal Direct PLUS Loan or a Federal Direct Consolidation Loan), while serving in a medical internship or residency program;

(B) not in excess of 3 years during which the borrower is seeking and unable to find full-time employment;

(C) not in excess of 3 years during which the Secretary determines, in accordance with regulations prescribed under section 1085(*o*) of this title, that the borrower has experienced or will experience an economic hardship.

(3) Definition of borrower

For the purpose of this subsection, the term "borrower" means an individual who is a new borrower on the date such individual applies for a loan under this part for which the first disbursement is made on or after July 1, 1993.

(4) Deferments for previous part B loan borrowers

A borrower of a loan made under this part [20 U.S.C.A. § 1087a et seq.], who at the time such individual applies for such loan, has an outstanding balance of principal or interest owing on any loan made, insured, or guaranteed under part B of this subchapter [20 U.S.C.A. § 1071 et seq.] prior to July 1, 1993, shall be eligible for a deferment under section 1077(a)(2)(C) of this title or section 1078(b)(1)(M) of this title as such sections were in effect on July 22, 1992.

(g) Federal Direct Consolidation Loans

A borrower of a loan made under this part may consolidate such loan with the loans described in section 1078-3(a)(4) of this title. Loans made under this subsection shall be known as "Federal Direct Consolidation Loans".

(h) Borrower defenses

Notwithstanding any other provision of State or Federal law, the Secretary shall specify in regulations (except as authorized under section 1087g(a)(1) of this title) which acts or omissions of an institution of higher education a borrower may assert as a defense to repayment of a loan made under this part [20 U.S.C.A. § 1087a et seq.], except that in no event may a borrower recover from the Secretary, in any action arising from or relating to a loan made under this part, an amount in excess of the amount such borrower has repaid on such loan.

(i) Loan application and promissory note

The common financial reporting form required in section 1090(a)(1) of this title shall constitute the application for loans made under this part [20 U.S.C.A. § 1087a et seq.] (other than a Federal Direct PLUS loan). The Secretary shall develop, print, and distribute to participating institutions a standard promissory note and loan disclosure form.

(j) Loan disbursement

(1) In general

Proceeds of loans to students under this part [20 U.S.C.A. § 1087a et seq.] shall be applied to the student's account for tuition and fees, and, in the case of institutionally owned housing, to room and board. Loan proceeds that remain after the application of the previous sentence shall be delivered to the borrower by check or other means that is payable to and requires the endorsement or other certification by such borrower.

(2) Payment periods

The Secretary shall establish periods for the payments described in paragraph (1) in a manner consistent with payment of Federal Pell Grants under subpart 1 of part A of this subchapter [20 U.S.C.A. § 1070a et seq.].

(k) Fiscal control and fund accountability

(1) In general

(A) An institution shall maintain financial records in a manner consistent with records maintained for other programs under this subchapter [20 U.S.C.A. § 1070 et seq.].

(B) Except as otherwise required by regulations of the Secretary, or in a notice under section 1087g(a)(1) of this title, an institution

may maintain loan funds under this part in the same account as other Federal student financial assistance.

(2) Payments and refunds

Payments and refunds shall be reconciled in a manner consistent with the manner set forth for the submission of a payment summary report required of institutions participating in the program under subpart 1 of part A of this subchapter [20 U.S.C.A. § 1070a et seq.], except that nothing in this paragraph shall prevent such reconciliations on a monthly basis.

(3) Transaction histories

All transaction histories under this part shall be maintained using the same system designated by the Secretary for the provision of Federal Pell Grants under subpart 1 of part A of this subchapter [20 U.S.C.A. § 1070a et seq.].

(Pub. L. 89-329, title IV, Sec. 455, as added Pub. L. 99-498, title IV, Sec. 404, Oct. 17, 1986, 100 Stat. 1439; amended Pub. L. 102-325, title IV, Sec. 451, July 23, 1992, 106 Stat. 572; Pub. L. 103-66, title IV, Sec. 4021, Aug. 10, 1993, 107 Stat. 346; Pub. L. 103-382, title III, Sec. 359, Oct. 20, 1994, 108 Stat. 3968; Pub. L. 105-178, title VIII, Sec. 8301(c), June 9, 1998, 112 Stat. 498; Pub. L. 105-244, title IV, Sec. 401(g)(6), 452(a)(1), (b), (c), Oct. 7, 1998, 112 Stat. 1652, 1715-1717; Pub. L. 106-554, § 1(a)(1), Dec. 21, 2000, 114 Stat. 2763, 2763A-49; Pub. L. 107-139, § 1(b), (c), Feb. 8, 2002, 116 Stat. 9)

A.1.3 Perkins Loans

20 U.S.C. sec.
1087bb. Allocation of funds.
1087cc. Agreements with institutions of higher education.
1087dd. Terms of loans.

1087bb. Allocation of funds

(a) Allocation based on previous allocation

(1) From the amount appropriated pursuant to section 1087aa(b) of this title for each fiscal year, the Secretary shall first allocate to each eligible institution an amount equal to—

(A) 100 percent of the amount received under subsections (a) and (b) of this section for fiscal year 1999 (as such subsections were in effect with respect to allocations for such fiscal year), multiplied by

(B) the institution's default penalty, as determined under subsection (e) of this section, except that if the institution has a cohort default rate in excess of the applicable maximum cohort default rate under subsection (f) of this section, the institution may not receive an allocation under this paragraph.

(2)(A) From the amount so appropriated, the Secretary shall next allocate to each eligible institution that began participation in the program under this part after fiscal year 1999 but is not a first or second time participant, an amount equal to the greater of-

(i) $5,000; or

(ii) 100 percent of the amount received and expended under this part for the first year it participated in the program.

(B) From the amount so appropriated, the Secretary shall next allocate to each eligible institution that began participation in the program under this part after fiscal year 1999 and is a first or second time participant, an amount equal to the greatest of—

(i) $5,000;

(ii) an amount equal to (I) 90 percent of the amount received and used under this part in the second preceding fiscal year by eligible institutions offering comparable programs of instruction, divided by (II) the number of students enrolled at such comparable institutions in such fiscal year, multiplied by (III) the number of students enrolled at the applicant institution in such fiscal year; or

(iii) 90 percent of the institution's allocation under this part for the preceding fiscal year.

(C) Notwithstanding subparagraphs (A) and (B) of this paragraph, the Secretary shall allocate to each eligible institution which—

(i) was a first-time participant in the program in fiscal year 2000 or any subsequent fiscal year, and

(ii) received a larger amount under this subsection in the second year of participation,

an amount equal to 90 percent of the amount it received under this subsection in its second year of participation.

(D) For any fiscal year after a fiscal year in which an institution receives an allocation under subparagraph (A), (B), or (C), the Secretary shall allocate to such institution an amount equal to the product of—

(i) the amount determined under subparagraph (A), (B), or (C), multiplied by

(ii) the institution's default penalty, as determined under subsection (e) of this section, except that if the institution has a cohort default rate in excess of the applicable maximum cohort default rate under subsection (f) of this section, the institution may not receive an allocation under this paragraph.

(3)(A) If the amount appropriated for any fiscal year is less than the amount required to be allocated to all institutions under paragraph (1) of this subsection, then the amount of the allocation to each such institution shall be ratably reduced.

(B) If the amount appropriated for any fiscal year is more than the amount required to be allocated to all institutions under paragraph (1) but less than the amount required to be allocated to all institutions under paragraph (2), then—

(i) the Secretary shall allot the amount required to be allocated to all institutions under paragraph (1), and

(ii) the amount of the allocation to each institution under paragraph (2) shall be ratably reduced.

(C) If additional amounts are appropriated for any such fiscal year, such reduced amounts shall be increased on the same basis as they were reduced (until the amount allocated equals the amount required to be allocated under paragraphs (1) and (2) of this subsection).

(b) Allocation of excess based on share of excess eligible amounts

(1) From the remainder of the amount appropriated pursuant to section 1087aa(b) of this title after making the allocations required by subsection (a) of this section, the Secretary shall allocate to each eligible institution which has an excess eligible amount an amount which bears the same ratio to such remainder as such excess eligible amount bears to the sum of the excess eligible amounts of all such eligible institutions (having such excess eligible amounts).

(2) For any eligible institution, the excess eligible amount is the amount, if any, by which—

(A)(i) that institution's eligible amount (as determined under paragraph (3)), divided by (ii) the sum of the eligible amounts of all institutions (as so determined), multiplied by (iii) the amount appropriated pursuant to section 1087aa(b) of this title for the fiscal year; exceeds

(B) the amount required to be allocated to that institution under subsection (a) of this section, except that an eligible institution which has a cohort default rate in excess of the applicable maximum cohort default rate under subsection (f) of this section may not receive an allocation under this paragraph.

(3) For any eligible institution, the eligible amount of that institution is equal to—

(A) the amount of the institution's self-help need, as determined under subsection (c) of this section; minus

(B) the institution's anticipated collections; multiplied by

(C) the institution's default penalty, as determined under subsection (e) of this section;

except that, if the institution has a cohort default rate in excess of the applicable maximum cohort default rate under subsection (f) of this section, the eligible amount of that institution is zero.

(c) Determination of institution's self-help need

(1) The amount of an institution's self-help need is equal to the sum of the self-help need of the institution's eligible undergraduate students and the self-help need of the institution's eligible graduate and professional students.

(2) To determine the self-help need of an institution's eligible undergraduate students, the Secretary shall—

(A) establish various income categories for dependent and independent undergraduate students;

(B) establish an expected family contribution for each income category of dependent and independent undergraduate students, determined on the basis of the average expected family contribution (computed in accordance with part E of this subchapter) of a representative sample within each income category for the second preceding fiscal year;

(C) compute 25 percent of the average cost of attendance for all undergraduate students;

(D) multiply the number of eligible dependent students in each income category by the lesser of—

(i) 25 percent of the average cost of attendance for all undergraduate students determined under subparagraph (C); or

(ii) the average cost of attendance for all undergraduate students minus the expected family contribution determined under subparagraph (B) for that income category, except that the amount computed by such subtraction shall not be less than zero;

(E) add the amounts determined under subparagraph (D) for each income category of dependent students;

(F) multiply the number of eligible independent students in each income category by the lesser of—

(i) 25 percent of the average cost of attendance for all undergraduate students determined under subparagraph (C); or

(ii) the average cost of attendance for all undergraduate students minus the expected family contribution determined under subparagraph (B) for that income category, except that the amount computed by such subtraction for any income category shall not be less than zero;

(G) add the amounts determined under subparagraph (F) for each income category of independent students; and

(H) add the amounts determined under subparagraphs (E) and (G).

(3) To determine the self-help need of an institution's eligible graduate and professional students, the Secretary shall—

(A) establish various income categories for graduate and professional students;

(B) establish an expected family contribution for each income category of graduate and professional students, determined on the basis of the average expected family contribution (computed in accordance with part E of this subchapter) of a representative sample within each income category for the second preceding fiscal year;

(C) determine the average cost of attendance for all graduate and professional students;

(D) subtract from the average cost of attendance for all graduate and professional students (determined under subparagraph (C)), the expected family contribution (determined under subparagraph (B)) for each income category, except that the amount computed by such subtraction for any income category shall not be less than zero;

(E) multiply the amounts determined under subparagraph (D) by the number of eligible students in each category;

(F) add the amounts determined under subparagraph (E) for each income category.

(4)(A) For purposes of paragraphs (2) and (3), the term "average cost of attendance" means the average of the attendance costs for undergraduate students and for graduate and professional students, which shall include (i) tuition and fees determined in accordance with subparagraph (B), (ii) standard living expenses determined in accordance with subparagraph (C), and (iii) books and supplies determined in accordance with subparagraph (D).

(B) The average undergraduate and graduate and professional tuition and fees described in subparagraph (A)(i) shall be computed on the basis of information reported by the institution to the Secretary, which shall include (i) total revenue received by the institution from undergraduate and graduate tuition and fees for the second year preceding the year for which it is applying for an allocation, and (ii) the institution's enrollment for such second preceding year.

(C) The standard living expense described in subparagraph (A)(ii) is equal to 150 percent of the difference between the income protection allowance for a family of five with one in college and the income protection allowance for a family of six with one in college for a single independent student.

(D) The allowance for books and supplies described in subparagraph (A)(iii) is equal to $450.

(d) Anticipated collections

(1) An institution's anticipated collections are equal to the amount which was collected during the second year preceding the beginning of the award period, multiplied by 1.21.

(2) The Secretary shall establish an appeals process by which the anticipated collections required in paragraph (1) may be waived for institutions with low cohort default rates in the program assisted under this part.

(e) Default penalties

(1) Years preceding fiscal year 2000

For any fiscal year preceding fiscal year 2000, any institution with a cohort default rate that—

(A) equals or exceeds 15 percent, shall establish a default reduction plan pursuant to regulations prescribed by the Secretary, except that such plan shall not be required with respect to an institution that has a default rate of less than 20 percent and that has less than 100 students who have loans under this part in such academic year;

(B) equals or exceeds 20 percent, but is less than 25 percent, shall have a default penalty of 0.9;

(C) equals or exceeds 25 percent, but is less than 30 percent, shall have a default penalty of 0.7; and

(D) equals or exceeds 30 percent shall have a default penalty of zero.

(2) Years following fiscal year 2000

For fiscal year 2000 and any succeeding fiscal year, any institution with a cohort default rate (as defined under subsection (g) of this section) that equals or exceeds 25 percent shall have a default penalty of zero.

(3) Ineligibility

(A) In general

For fiscal year 2000 and any succeeding fiscal year, any institution with a cohort default rate (as defined in subsection (g) of this section) that equals or exceeds 50 percent for each of the 3 most recent years for which data are available shall not be eligible to participate in a program under this part for the fiscal year for which the determination is made and the 2 succeeding fiscal years, unless, within 30 days of receiving notification from the Secretary of the loss of eligibility under this paragraph, the institution appeals the loss of eligibility to the Secretary. The Secretary shall issue a decision on any such appeal within 45 days after the submission of the appeal. Such decision may permit the institution to continue to participate in a program under this part if—

(i) the institution demonstrates to the satisfaction of the Secretary that the calculation of the institution's cohort default rate is not accurate, and that recalculation would reduce the institution's cohort default rate for any of the 3 fiscal years below 50 percent; or

(ii) there are, in the judgment of the Secretary, such a small number of borrowers entering repayment that the application of this subparagraph would be inequitable.

(B) Continued participation

During an appeal under subparagraph (A), the Secretary may permit the institution to continue to participate in a program under this part.

(C) Return of funds

Within 90 days after the date of any termination pursuant to subparagraph (A), or the conclusion of any appeal pursuant to subparagraph (B), whichever is later, the balance of the student loan fund established under this part by the institution that is the subject of the termination shall be distributed as follows:

(i) The Secretary shall first be paid an amount which bears the same ratio to such balance (as of the date of such distribution) as the total amount of Federal capital contributions to such fund by the Secretary under this part bears to the sum of such Federal capital contributions and the capital contributions to such fund made by the institution.

(ii) The remainder of such student loan fund shall be paid to the institution.

(D) Use of returned funds

Any funds returned to the Secretary under this paragraph shall be reallocated to institutions of higher education pursuant to subsection (i) of this section.

(E) Definition

For the purposes of subparagraph (A), the term "loss of eligibility" shall be defined as the mandatory liquidation of an institution's student loan fund, and assignment of the institution's outstanding loan portfolio to the Secretary.

(f) Applicable maximum cohort default rate

(1) Award years prior to 2000

For award years prior to award year 2000, the applicable maximum cohort default rate is 30 percent.

(2) Award year 2000 and succeeding award years

For award year 2000 and subsequent years, the applicable maximum cohort default rate is 25 percent.

(g) "Cohort default rate" defined

(1)(A) The term "cohort default rate" means, for any award year in which 30 or more current and former students at the institution enter repayment on loans under this part (received for attendance at the institution), the percentage of those current and former students who enter repayment on such loans (received for attendance at that institution) in that award year who default before the end of the following award year.

(B) For any award year in which less than 30 of the institution's current and former students enter repayment, the term "cohort default rate" means the percentage of such current and former students who entered repayment on such loans in any of the three most recent award years and who default before the end of the award year immediately following the year in which they entered repayment.

(C) A loan on which a payment is made by the institution of higher education, its owner, agency, contractor, employee, or any other entity or individual affiliated with such institution, in order to avoid default by the borrower, is considered as in default for the purposes of this subsection.

(D) In the case of a student who has attended and borrowed at more than one school, the student (and his or her subsequent repayment or default) is attributed to the school for attendance at which the student received the loan that entered repayment in the award year.

(E) In determining the number of students who default before the end of such award year, the institution, in calculating the cohort default rate, shall exclude—

(i) any loan on which the borrower has, after the time periods specified in paragraph (2)—

(I) voluntarily made 6 consecutive payments;

(II) voluntarily made all payments currently due;

(III) repaid in full the amount due on the loan; or

(IV) received a deferment or forbearance, based on a condition that began prior to such time periods;

(ii) any loan which has, after the time periods specified in paragraph (2), been rehabilitated or canceled; and

(iii) any other loan that the Secretary determines should be excluded from such determination.

(F) The Secretary shall prescribe regulations designed to prevent an institution from evading the application to that institution of a cohort default rate determination under this subsection through the use of such measures as branching, consolidation, change of ownership or control or other means as determined by the Secretary.

(2) For purposes of calculating the cohort default rate under this subsection, a loan shall be considered to be in default—

(A) 240 days (in the case of a loan repayable monthly), or

(B) 270 days (in the case of a loan repayable quarterly), after the borrower fails to make an installment payment when due or to comply with other terms of the promissory note.

(h) Filing deadlines

The Secretary shall, from time to time, set dates before which institutions must file applications for allocations under this part.

(i) Reallocation of excess allocations

(1) In general

(A) If an institution of higher education returns to the Secretary any portion of the sums allocated to such institution under this section for any fiscal year, the Secretary shall reallocate 80 percent of such returned portions to participating institutions in an amount not to exceed such participating institution's excess eligible amounts as determined under paragraph (2).

(B) For the purpose of this subsection, the term "participating institution" means an institution of higher education that—

(i) was a participant in the program assisted under this part in fiscal year 1999; and

(ii) did not receive an allocation under subsection (a) of this section in the fiscal year for which the reallocation determination is made.

(2) Excess eligible amount

For any participating institution, the excess eligible amount is the amount, if any, by which—

(A)(i) that institution's eligible amount (as determined under subsection (b)(3) of this section), divided by (ii) the sum of the eligible amounts of all participating institutions (as determined under paragraph (3)), multiplied by (iii) the amount of funds available for reallocation under this subsection; exceeds

(B) the amount required to be allocated to that institution under subsection (b) of this section.

(3) Remainder

The Secretary shall reallocate the remainder of such returned portions in accordance with regulations of the Secretary.

(4) Allocation reductions

If under paragraph (1) of this subsection an institution returns more than 10 percent of its allocation, the institution's allocation for the next fiscal year shall be reduced by the amount returned. The Secretary may waive this paragraph for a specific institution if the Secretary finds that enforcing it is contrary to the interest of the program.

(Pub. L. 89-329, title IV, Sec. 462, as added Pub. L. 99-498, title IV, Sec. 405(a), Oct. 17, 1986, 100 Stat. 1440; amended Pub. L. 100-50, Sec. 13(a)-(d), June 3, 1987, 101 Stat. 348; Pub. L. 102-325, title IV, Sec. 462, July 23, 1992, 106 Stat. 576; Pub. L. 103-208, Sec. 2(f)(1)-(4), Dec. 20, 1993, 107 Stat. 2470, 2471; Pub. L. 105-244, title IV, Sec. 462(a)(1), (2), (b)-(e), Oct. 7, 1998, 112 Stat. 1720-1723.)

§ 1087cc. Agreements with institutions of higher education

(a) Contents of agreements

An agreement with any institution of higher education for the payment of Federal capital contributions under this part shall—

(1) provide for the establishment and maintenance of a student loan fund for the purpose of this part;

(2) provide for the deposit in such fund of—

(A) Federal capital contributions from funds appropriated under section 1087aa of this title;

(B) a capital contribution by an institution in an amount equal to one-third of the Federal capital contributions described in subparagraph (A);

(C) collections of principal and interest on student loans made from deposited funds;

(D) charges collected pursuant to regulations under section 1087dd(c)(1)(H) of this title; and

(E) any other earnings of the funds;

(3) provide that such student loan fund shall be used only for—

(A) loans to students, in accordance with the provisions of this part;

(B) administrative expenses, as provided in subsection (b) of this section;

(C) capital distributions, as provided in section 1087ff of this title; and

(D) costs of litigation, and other collection costs agreed to by the Secretary in connection with the collection of a loan from the fund (and interest thereon) or a charge assessed pursuant to regulations under section 1087dd(c)(1)(H) of this title;

(4) provide that where a note or written agreement evidencing a loan has been in default despite due diligence on the part of the institution in attempting collection thereon—

(A) if the institution has knowingly failed to maintain an acceptable collection record with respect to such loan, as determined by the Secretary in accordance with criteria established by regulation, the Secretary may—

(i) require the institution to assign such note or agreement to the Secretary, without recompense; and

(ii) apportion any sums collected on such a loan, less anamount not to exceed 30 percent of any sums collected to cover the Secretary's collection costs, among other institutions in accordance with section 1087bb of this title; or

(B) if the institution is not one described in subparagraph (A), the Secretary may—

(i) allow such institution to transfer its interest in such loan to the Secretary, for collection, and the Secretary may use any collections thereon (less an amount not to exceed 30 percent of any such sums collected to cover the Secretary's collection costs) to make allocations to institutions of additional capital contributions in accordance with section 1087bb of this title; or

(ii) allow such institution to refer such note or agreement to the Secretary, without recompense, except that any sums collected on such a loan (less an amount not to exceed 30 percent of any such sums collected to cover the Secretary's collection costs) shall be repaid to such institution no later than 180 days after collection by the Secretary and treated as an additional capital contribution;

(5) provide that, if an institution of higher education determines not to service and collect student loans made available from funds under this part, the institution will assign, at the beginning of the repayment period, notes or evidence of obligations of student loans made from such funds to the Secretary and the Secretary shall apportion any sums collected on such notes or obligations (less an amount not to exceed 30 percent of any such sums collected to cover that Secretary's collection costs) among other institutions in accordance with section 1087bb of this title;

(6) provide that, notwithstanding any other provision of law, the Secretary will provide to the institution any information with respect to the names and addresses of borrowers or other relevant information which is available to the Secretary, from whatever source such information may be derived;

(7) provide assurances that the institution will comply with the provisions of section 1087cc-1 of this title;

(8) provide that the institution of higher education will make loans first to students with exceptional need; and

(9) include such other reasonable provisions as may be necessary to protect the United States from unreasonable risk of loss and as are agreed to by the Secretary and the institution.

(b) Administrative expenses

An institution which has entered into an agreement under subsection (a) of this section shall be entitled, for each fiscal year during which it makes student loans from a student loan fund established under such agreement, to a payment in lieu of reimbursement for its expenses in administering its student loan program under this part during such year. Such payment shall be made in accordance with section 1096 of this title.

(c) Cooperative agreements with credit bureau organizations

(1) For the purpose of promoting responsible repayment of loans made pursuant to this part, the Secretary and each institution of higher education participating in the program under this part shall enter into cooperative agreements with credit bureau organizations to provide for the exchange of information concerning student borrowers concerning whom the Secretary has received a referral pursuant to section 1087gg of this title and regarding loans held by the Secretary or an institution.

(2) Each cooperative agreement made pursuant to paragraph (1) shall be made in accordance with the requirements of section 1080a of this title except that such agreement shall provide for the disclosure by the Secretary or an institution, as the case may be, to such organizations, with respect to any loan held by the Secretary or the institution, respectively, of—

(A) the date of disbursement and the amount of such loans made to any borrower under this part at the time of disbursement of the loan;

(B) information concerning the repayment and collection of any such loan, including information concerning the status of such loan; and

(C) the date of cancellation of the note upon completion of repayment by the borrower of any such loan, or upon cancellation or discharge of the borrower's obligation on the loan for any reason.

(3) Notwithstanding paragraphs (4) and (6)[2] of subsection (a) of section 1681c of title 15, a consumer reporting agency may make a report containing information received from the Secretary or an institution regarding the status of a borrower's account on a loan made under this part until the loan is paid in full.

(4)(A) Except as provided in subparagraph (B), an institution of higher education, after consultation with the Secretary and pursuant to the agreements entered into under paragraph (1), shall

---

2 Paragraph (6) of subsection (a) of section 1681c of title 15, referred to in subsec. (c)(3), was redesignated paragraph (5) of subsection (a) of section 1681c of title 15 by Pub. L. 105-347, Sec. 5(4), Nov. 2, 1998, 112 Stat. 3211.

Subsection (a)(5) of this section relating to due diligence, referred to in subsec. (e), was redesignated subsec. (a)(4), by Pub. L. 105-244, title IV, Sec. 463(a)(3), Oct. 7, 1998, 112 Stat. 1724.

disclose at least annually to any credit bureau organization with which the Secretary has such an agreement the information set forth in paragraph (2), and shall disclose promptly to such credit bureau organization any changes to the information previously disclosed.

(B) The Secretary may promulgate regulations establishing criteria under which an institution of higher education may cease reporting the information described in paragraph (2) before a loan is paid in full.

(5) Each institution of higher education shall notify the appropriate credit bureau organizations whenever a borrower of a loan that is made and held by the institution and that is in default makes 6 consecutive monthly payments on such loan, for the purpose of encouraging such organizations to update the status of information maintained with respect to that borrower.

(d) Limitation on use of interest bearing accounts

In carrying out the provisions of subsection (a)(9) of this section, the Secretary may not require that any collection agency, collection attorney, or loan servicer collecting loans made under this part deposit amounts collected on such loans in interest bearing accounts, unless such agency, attorney, or servicer holds such amounts for more than 45 days.

(e) Special due diligence rule

In carrying out the provisions of subsection (a)(5)[3] of this section relating to due diligence, the Secretary shall make every effort to ensure that institutions of higher education may use Internal Revenue Service skip-tracing collection procedures on loans made under this part.

(Pub. L. 89-329, title IV, Sec. 463, as added Pub. L. 99-498, title IV, Sec. 405(a), Oct. 17, 1986, 100 Stat. 1444; amended Pub. L. 100-50, Sec. 13(e), (f), June 3, 1987, 101 Stat. 349; Pub. L. 102-325, title IV, Sec. 463(a), (b), July 23, 1992, 106 Stat. 579; Pub. L. 103-208, Sec. 2(f)(5)-(7), Dec. 20, 1993, 107 Stat. 2471; Pub. L. 105-244, title IV, Sec. 463, Oct. 7, 1998, 112 Stat. 1724.)

§ 1087dd. Terms of loans

(a) Terms and conditions

(1) Loans from any student loan fund established pursuant to an agreement under section 1087cc of this title to any student by any institution shall, subject to such conditions, limitations, and requirements as the Secretary shall prescribe by regulation, be made on such terms and conditions as the institution may determine.

(2)(A) Except as provided in paragraph (4), the total of loans made to a student in any academic year or its equivalent by an institution of higher education from a loan fund established pursuant to an agreement under this part shall not exceed—

(i) $4,000, in the case of a student who has not successfully completed a program of undergraduate education; or

(ii) $6,000, in the case of a graduate or professional student (as defined in regulations issued by the Secretary).

(B) Except as provided in paragraph (4), the aggregate unpaid

principal amount for all loans made to a student by institutions of higher education from loan funds established pursuant to agreements under this part may not exceed—

(i) $40,000, in the case of any graduate or professional student (as defined by regulations issued by the Secretary, and including any loans from such funds made to such person before such person became a graduate or professional student);

(ii) $20,000, in the case of a student who has successfully completed 2 years of a program of education leading to a bachelor's degree but who has not completed the work necessary for such a degree (determined under regulations issued by the Secretary), and including any loans from such funds made to such person before such person became such a student; and

(iii) $8,000, in the case of any other student.

(3) Regulations of the Secretary under paragraph (1) shall be designed to prevent the impairment of the capital student loan funds to the maximum extent practicable and with a view toward the objective of enabling the student to complete his course of study.

(4) In the case of a program of study abroad that is approved for credit by the home institution at which a student is enrolled and that has reasonable costs in excess of the home institution's budget, the annual and aggregate loan limits for the student may exceed the amounts described in paragraphs (2)(A) and (2)(B) by 20 percent.

(b) Demonstration of need and eligibility required

(1) A loan from a student loan fund assisted under this part may be made only to a student who demonstrates financial need in accordance with part E of this subchapter, who meets the requirements of section 1091 of this title, and who provides the institution with the student's drivers license number, if any, at the time of application for the loan. A student who is in default on a loan under this part shall not be eligible for an additional loan under this part unless such loan meets one of the conditions for exclusion under section 1087bb(g)(1)(E) of this title.

(2) If the institution's capital contribution under section 1087bb of this title is directly or indirectly based in part on the financial need demonstrated by students who are (A) attending the institution less than full time, or (B) independent students, then a reasonable portion of the loans made from the institution's student loan fund containing the contribution shall be made available to such students.

(c) Contents of loan agreement

(1) Any agreement between an institution and a student for a loan from a student loan fund assisted under this part—

(A) shall be evidenced by note or other written instrument which, except as provided in paragraph (2), provides for repayment of the principal amount of the loan, together with interest thereon, in equal installments (or, if the borrower so requests, in graduated periodic installments determined in accordance with such schedules as may be approved by the Secretary) payable quarterly, bimonthly, or monthly, at the option of the institution, over a period beginning nine months after the date on which the student ceases to carry, at an institution of higher education or a comparable institution outside the United States approved for this purpose by the Secretary, at least one-half the normal full-time academic workload, and ending 10 years and 9 months after such date except that such period may begin earlier than 9 months after such date upon the request of the borrower;

---

3 Paragraph (6) of subsection (a) of section 1681c of title 15, referred to in subsec. (c)(3), was redesignated paragraph (5) of subsection (a) of section 1681c of title 15 by Pub. L. 105-347, Sec. 5(4), Nov. 2, 1998, 112 Stat. 3211.

Subsection (a)(5) of this section relating to due diligence, referred to in subsec. (e), was redesignated subsec. (a)(4), by Pub. L. 105-244, title IV, Sec. 463(a)(3), Oct. 7, 1998, 112 Stat. 1724.

(B) shall include provision for acceleration of repayment of the whole, or any part, of such loan, at the option of the borrower;

(C)(i) may provide, at the option of the institution, in accordance with regulations of the Secretary, that during the repayment period of the loan, payments of principal and interest by the borrower with respect to all outstanding loans made to the student from a student loan fund assisted under this part shall be at a rate equal to not less than $40 per month, except that the institution may, subject to such regulations, permit a borrower to pay less than $40 per month for a period of not more than one year where necessary to avoid hardship to the borrower, but without extending the 10-year maximum repayment period provided for in subparagraph (A) of this paragraph; and

(ii) may provide that the total payments by a borrower for a monthly or similar payment period with respect to the aggregate of all loans held by the institution may, when the amount of a monthly or other similar payment is not a multiple of $5, be rounded to the next highest whole dollar amount that is a multiple of $5;

(D) shall provide that the loan shall bear interest, on the unpaid balance of the loan, at the rate of 5 percent per year in the case of any loan made on or after October 1, 1981, except that no interest shall accrue (I) prior to the beginning date of repayment determined under paragraph (2)(A)(i), or (II) during any period in which repayment is suspended by reason of paragraph (2);

(E) shall provide that the loan shall be made without security and without endorsement;

(F) shall provide that the liability to repay the loan shall be canceled upon the death of the borrower, or if he becomes permanently and totally disabled as determined in accordance with regulations of the Secretary;

(G) shall provide that no note or evidence of obligation may be assigned by the lender, except upon the transfer of the borrower to another institution participating under this part (or, if not so participating, is eligible to do so and is approved by the Secretary for such purpose), to such institution, and except as necessary to carry out section 1087cc(a)(6)[4] of this title;

(H) pursuant to regulations of the Secretary, shall provide for an assessment of a charge with respect to the loan for failure of the borrower to pay all or part of an installment when due, which shall include the expenses reasonably incurred in attempting collection of the loan, to the extent permitted by the Secretary, except that no charge imposed under this subparagraph shall exceed 20 percent of the amount of the monthly payment of the borrower; and

(I) shall contain a notice of the system of disclosure of information concerning default on such loan to credit bureau organizations under section 1087cc(c) of this title.

(2)(A) No repayment of principal of, or interest on, any loan from a student loan fund assisted under this part shall be required during any period—

(i) during which the borrower—

(I) is pursuing at least a half-time course of study as determined by an eligible institution; or

(II) is pursuing a course of study pursuant to a graduate fellowship program approved by the Secretary, or pursuant to a rehabilitation training program for disabled individuals approved by the

Secretary, except that no borrower shall be eligible for a deferment under this clause, or loan made under this part while serving in a medical internship or residency program;

(ii) not in excess of 3 years during which the borrower is seeking and unable to find full-time employment;

(iii) not in excess of 3 years for any reason which the lender determines, in accordance with regulations prescribed by the Secretary under section 1085(o) of this title, has caused or will cause the borrower to have an economic hardship; or

(iv) during which the borrower is engaged in service described in section 1087ee(a)(2) of this title; and provides that any such period shall not be included in determining the 10-year period described in subparagraph (A) of paragraph (1).

(B) No repayment of principal of, or interest on, any loan for any period described in subparagraph (A) shall begin until 6 months after the completion of such period.

(C) An individual with an outstanding loan balance who meets the eligibility criteria for a deferment described in subparagraph (A) as in effect on October 7, 1998, shall be eligible for deferment under this paragraph notwithstanding any contrary provision of the promissory note under which the loan or loans were made, and notwithstanding any amendment (or effective date provision relating to any amendment) to this section made prior to the date of such deferment.

(3)(A) The Secretary is authorized, when good cause is shown, to extend, in accordance with regulations, the 10-year maximum repayment period provided for in subparagraph (A) of paragraph (1) with respect to individual loans.

(B) Pursuant to uniform criteria established by the Secretary, the repayment period for any student borrower who during the repayment period is a low-income individual may be extended for a period not to exceed 10 years and the repayment schedule may be adjusted to reflect the income of that individual.

(4) The repayment period for a loan made under this part shall begin on the day immediately following the expiration of the period, specified in paragraph (1)(A), after the student ceases to carry the required academic workload, unless the borrower requests and is granted a repayment schedule that provides for repayment to commence at an earlier point in time, and shall exclude any period of authorized deferment, forbearance, or cancellation.

(5) The institution may elect—

(A) to add the amount of any charge imposed under paragraph (1)(H) to the principal amount of the loan as of the first day after the day on which the installment was due and to notify the borrower of the assessment of the charge; or

(B) to make the amount of the charge payable to the institution not later than the due date of the next installment.

(6) Requests for deferment of repayment of loans under this part by students engaged in graduate or post-graduate fellowship-supported study (such as pursuant to a Fulbright grant) outside the United States shall be approved until completion of the period of the fellowship.

(7) There shall be excluded from the 9-month period that begins on the date on which a student ceases to carry at least one-half the normal full-time academic workload (as described in paragraph (1)(A)) any period not to exceed 3 years during which a borrower who is a member of a reserve component of the Armed Forces named in section 10101 of title 10 is called or ordered to active duty for a period of more than 30 days (as defined in section

---

4 Section 1087cc(a) of this title, referred to in subsec. (c)(1)(G), was amended by Pub. L. 105-244, title IV, Sec. 463(a)(3), Oct. 7, 1998, 112 Stat. 1724, which redesignated pars. (6) and (7) as (5) and (6), respectively.

101(d)(2) of such title). Such period of exclusion shall include the period necessary to resume enrollment at the borrower's next available regular enrollment period.

(d) Availability of loan fund to all eligible students

An agreement under this part for payment of Federal capital contributions shall include provisions designed to make loans from the student loan fund established pursuant to such agreement reasonably available (to the extent of the available funds in such fund) to all eligible students in such institutions in need thereof.

(e) Forbearance

The Secretary shall ensure that, upon written request, an institution of higher education shall grant a borrower forbearance of principal and interest or principal only, renewable at 12-month intervals for a period not to exceed 3 years, on such terms as are otherwise consistent with the regulations issued by the Secretary and agreed upon in writing by the parties to the loan, if—

(1) the borrower's debt burden equals or exceeds 20 percent of such borrower's gross income; or

(2) the institution determines that the borrower should qualify for forbearance for other reasons.

(f) Special repayment rule authority

(1) Subject to such restrictions as the Secretary may prescribe to protect the interest of the United States, in order to encourage repayment of loans made under this part which are in default, the Secretary may, in the agreement entered into under this part, authorize an institution of higher education to compromise on the repayment of such defaulted loans in accordance with paragraph (2). The Federal share of the compromise repayment shall bear the same relation to the institution's share of such compromise repayment as the Federal capital contribution to the institution's loan fund under this part bears to the institution's capital contribution to such fund.

(2) No compromise repayment of a defaulted loan as authorized by paragraph (1) may be made unless the student borrower pays—

(A) 90 percent of the loan under this part;

(B) the interest due on such loan; and

(C) any collection fees due on such loan;

in a lump sum payment.

(g) Discharge

(1) In general

If a student borrower who received a loan made under this part on or after January 1, 1986, is unable to complete the program in which such student is enrolled due to the closure of the institution, then the Secretary shall discharge the borrower's liability on the loan (including the interest and collection fees) and shall subsequently pursue any claim available to such borrower against the institution and the institution's affiliates and principals, or settle the loan obligation pursuant to the financial responsibility standards described in section 1099c(c) of this title.

(2) Assignment

A borrower whose loan has been discharged pursuant to this subsection shall be deemed to have assigned to the United States the right to a loan refund in an amount that does not exceed the amount discharged against the institution and the institution's affiliates and principals.

(3) Eligibility for additional assistance

The period during which a student was unable to complete a course of study due to the closing of the institution shall not be considered for purposes of calculating the student's period of eligibility for additional assistance under this subchapter and part C of subchapter I of chapter 34 of title 42.

(4) Special rule

A borrower whose loan has been discharged pursuant to this subsection shall not be precluded, because of that discharge, from receiving additional grant, loan, or work assistance under this subchapter and part C of subchapter I of chapter 34 of title 42 for which the borrower would be otherwise eligible (but for the default on the discharged loan). The amount discharged under this subsection shall be treated as an amount canceled under section 1087ee(a) of this title.

(5) Reporting

The Secretary or institution, as the case may be, shall report to credit bureaus with respect to loans that have been discharged pursuant to this subsection.

(h) Rehabilitation of loans

(1) Rehabilitation

(A) In general

If the borrower of a loan made under this part who has defaulted on the loan makes 12 ontime, consecutive, monthly payments of amounts owed on the loan, as determined by the institution, or by the Secretary in the case of a loan held by the Secretary, the loan shall be considered rehabilitated, and the institution that made that loan (or the Secretary, in the case of a loan held by the Secretary) shall request that any credit bureau organization or credit reporting agency to which the default was reported remove the default from the borrower's credit history.

(B) Comparable conditions

As long as the borrower continues to make scheduled repayments on a loan rehabilitated under this paragraph, the rehabilitated loan shall be subject to the same terms and conditions, and qualify for the same benefits and privileges, as other loans made under this part.

(C) Additional assistance

The borrower of a rehabilitated loan shall not be precluded by section 1091 of this title from receiving additional grant, loan, or work assistance under this subchapter and part C of subchapter I of chapter 34 of title 42 (for which the borrower is otherwise eligible) on the basis of defaulting on the loan prior to such rehabilitation.

(D) Limitations

A borrower only once may obtain the benefit of this paragraph with respect to rehabilitating a loan under this part.

(2) Restoration of eligibility

If the borrower of a loan made under this part who has defaulted on that loan makes 6 ontime, consecutive, monthly payments of amounts owed on such loan, the borrower's eligibility for grant, loan, or work assistance under this subchapter and part C of subchapter I of chapter 34 of title 42 shall be restored to the extent that the borrower is otherwise eligible. A borrower only once may obtain the benefit of this paragraph with respect to restored eligibility.

(i) Incentive repayment program

(1) In general

Each institution of higher education may establish, with the approval of the Secretary, an incentive repayment program designed to reduce default and to replenish student loan funds established under this part. Each such incentive repayment program may—

(A) offer a reduction of the interest rate on a loan on which the borrower has made 48 consecutive, monthly repayments, but in no event may the rate be reduced by more than 1 percent;

(B) provide for a discount on the balance owed on a loan on which the borrower pays the principal and interest in full prior to the end of the applicable repayment period, but in no event may the discount exceed 5 percent of the unpaid principal balance due on the loan at the time the early repayment is made; and

(C) include such other incentive repayment options as the institution determines will carry out the objectives of this subsection.

(2) Limitation

No incentive repayment option under an incentive repayment program authorized by this subsection may be paid for with Federal funds, including any Federal funds from the student loan fund, or with institutional funds from the student loan fund.

(Pub. L. 89-329, title IV, Sec. 464, as added Pub. L. 99-498, title IV, Sec. 405(a), Oct. 17, 1986, 100 Stat. 1448; amended Pub. L. 100-50, Sec. 13(i), June 3, 1987, 101 Stat. 349; Pub. L. 100-369, Sec. 7(c), July 18, 1988, 102 Stat. 837; Pub. L. 101-239, title II, Sec. 2002(a)(3), Dec. 19, 1989, 103 Stat. 2111; Pub. L. 102-325, title IV, Sec. 464, July 23, 1992, 106 Stat. 580; Pub. L. 103-208, Sec. 2(f)(9)-(11), Dec. 20, 1993, 107 Stat. 2471; Pub. L. 105-244, title IV, Sec. 464, Oct. 7, 1998, 112 Stat. 1725.)

A.1.4 General Provisions

20 U.S.C. sec.
1091.   Student eligibility.
1091a. Statute of limitations, and State court judgments.
1091b. Institutional refunds.
1095a. Wage garnishment requirements.

§ 1091. Student eligibility

(a) In general

In order to receive any grant, loan, or work assistance under this subchapter and part C of subchapter I of chapter 34 of Title 42, a student must—

(1) be enrolled or accepted for enrollment in a degree, certificate, or other program (including a program of study abroad approved for credit by the eligible institution at which such student is enrolled) leading to a recognized educational credential at an institution of higher education that is an eligible institution in accordance with the provisions of section 1094 of this title, except as provided in subsections (b)(3) and (b)(4) of this section, and not be enrolled in an elementary or secondary school;

(2) if the student is presently enrolled at an institution, be maintaining satisfactory progress in the course of study the student is pursuing in accordance with the provisions of subsection (c) of this section;

(3) not owe a refund on grants previously received at any institution under this subchapter and part C of subchapter I of chapter 34 of Title 42, or be in default on any loan from a student loan fund at any institution provided for in part D of this subchapter, or a loan made, insured, or guaranteed by the Secretary under

this subchapter and part C of subchapter I of chapter 34 of Title 42 for attendance at any institution;

(4) file with the Secretary, as part of the original financial aid application process, a certification,,[5] which need not be notarized, but which shall include—

(A) a statement of educational purpose stating that the money attributable to such grant, loan, or loan guarantee will be used solely for expenses related to attendance or continued attendance at such institution; and

(B) such student's social security number, except that the provisions of this subparagraph shall not apply to a student from the Republic of the Marshall Islands, the Federated States of Micronesia, or the Republic of Palau;[6]

(5) be a citizen or national of the United States, a permanent resident of the United States, able to provide evidence from the Immigration and Naturalization Service that he or she is in the United States for other than a temporary purpose with the intention of becoming a citizen or permanent resident,[7] a citizen of any one of the Freely Associated States.

(b) Eligibility for student loans

(1) In order to be eligible to receive any loan under this subchapter and part C of subchapter I of chapter 34 of Title 42 (other than a loan under section 1078-2 or 1078-3 of this title) for any period of enrollment, a student who is not a graduate or professional student (as defined in regulations of the Secretary), and who is enrolled in a program at an institution which has a participation agreement with the Secretary to make awards under subpart 1 of part A of this subchapter, shall—

(A) (i) have received a determination of eligibility or ineligibility for a Pell Grant under such subpart 1 for such period of enrollment; and (ii) if determined to be eligible, have filed an application for a Pell Grant for such enrollment period; or

(B) have (A) filed an application with the Pell Grant processor for such institution for such enrollment period, and (B) received from the financial aid administrator of the institution a preliminary determination of the student's eligibility or ineligibility for a grant under such subpart 1.

(2) In order to be eligible to receive any loan under section 1078-1[8] of this title for any period of enrollment, a student shall—

---

5 So in original.

6 So in original. Probably should be followed by "and".

7 So in original. Probably should be followed by "or".

8 Section 1078-1 of this title, referred to in subsec. (b)(2), was repealed by Pub. L. 103-66, title IV, Sec. 4047(b)-(d), Aug. 10, 1993, 107 Stat. 364, eff. July 1, 1994, except with respect to loans provided under that section as it existed prior to Aug. 10, 1993. Subsequently, a new section 1078-1, relating to voluntary flexible agreements with guaranty agencies, was enacted by Pub. L. 105-244, title IV, Sec. 418, Oct. 7, 1998, 112 Stat. 1691.

   Subsection (h) of this section, referred to in subsecs. (h)(2), (3) and (i), was redesignated subsec. (g) of this section by Pub. L. 103-208, Sec. 2(h)(25), Dec. 20, 1993, 107 Stat. 2477.

   Section 2471 of this title, referred to in subsec. (l)(1)(B)(i), was omitted in the general amendment of chapter 44 (Sec. 2301 et seq.) of this title by Pub. L. 105-332, Sec. 1(b), Oct. 31, 1998, 112 Stat. 3076.

   Section 1113 of Public Law 97-252, referred to in subsec. (n), amended section 462 of Title 50, Appendix, War and National Defense, and enacted provisions set out as a note under section 462 of Title 50, Appendix.

(A) have received a determination of need for a loan under section 1078(a)(2)(B) of this title;

(B) if determined to have need for a loan under section 1078 of this title, have applied for such a loan; and

(C) has applied for a loan under section 1078-8 of this title, if such student is eligible to apply for such a loan.

(3) A student who—

(A) is carrying at least one-half the normal full-time work load for the course of study that the student is pursuing, as determined by an eligible institution, and

(B) is enrolled in a course of study necessary for enrollment in a program leading to a degree or certificate,

shall be, notwithstanding paragraph (1) of subsection (a) of this section, eligible to apply for loans under part B or C of this subchapter. The eligibility described in this paragraph shall be restricted to one 12-month period.

(4) A student who—

(A) is carrying at least one-half the normal full-time work load for the course of study the student is pursuing, as determined by the institution, and

(B) is enrolled or accepted for enrollment in a program at an eligible institution necessary for a professional credential or certification from a State that is required for employment as a teacher in an elementary or secondary school in that State,

shall be, notwithstanding paragraph (1) of subsection (a) of this section, eligible to apply for loans under part B, C, or D of this subchapter or work- study assistance under part C of subchapter I of chapter 34 of Title 42.

(5) Notwithstanding any other provision of this subsection, no incarcerated student is eligible to receive a loan under this subchapter and part C of subchapter I of chapter 34 of Title 42.

(c) Satisfactory progress

(1) For the purpose of subsection (a)(2) of this section, a student is maintaining satisfactory progress if—

(A) the institution at which the student is in attendance, reviews the progress of the student at the end of each academic year, or its equivalent, as determined by the institution, and

(B) the student has a cumulative C average, or its equivalent or academic standing consistent with the requirements for graduation, as determined by the institution, at the end of the second such academic year.

(2) Whenever a student fails to meet the eligibility requirements of subsection (a)(2) of this section as a result of the application of this subsection and subsequent to that failure the student has academic standing consistent with the requirements for graduation, as determined by the institution, for any grading period, the student may, subject to this subsection, again be eligible under subsection (a)(2) of this section for a grant, loan, or work assistance under this subchapter and part C of subchapter I of chapter 34 of Title 42.

(3) Any institution of higher education at which the student is in attendance may waive the provisions of paragraph (1) or paragraph (2) of this subsection for undue hardship based on—

(A) the death of a relative of the student,

(B) the personal injury or illness of the student, or

(C) special circumstances as determined by the institution.

(d) Students who are not high school graduates

In order for a student who does not have a certificate of graduation from a school providing secondary education, or the recognized equivalent of such certificate, to be eligible for any assistance under subparts 1, 3, and 4 of part A and parts B, C, and D of this subchapter and part C of subchapter I of chapter 34 of Title 42, the student shall meet one of the following standards:

(1) The student shall take an independently administered examination and shall achieve a score, specified by the Secretary, demonstrating that such student can benefit from the education or training being offered. Such examination shall be approved by the Secretary on the basis of compliance with such standards for development, administration, and scoring as the Secretary may prescribe in regulations.

(2) The student shall be determined as having the ability to benefit from the education or training in accordance with such process as the State shall prescribe. Any such process described or approved by a State for the purposes of this section shall be effective 6 months after the date of submission to the Secretary unless the Secretary disapproves such process. In determining whether to approve or disapprove such process, the Secretary shall take into account the effectiveness of such process in enabling students without high school diplomas or the equivalent thereof to benefit from the instruction offered by institutions utilizing such process, and shall also take into account the cultural diversity, economic circumstances, and educational preparation of the populations served by the institutions.

(3) The student has completed a secondary school education in a home school setting that is treated as a home school or private school under State law.

(e) Certification for GSL eligibility

Each eligible institution may certify student eligibility for a loan by an eligible lender under part B of this subchapter prior to completing the review for accuracy of the information submitted by the applicant required by regulations issued under this subchapter and part C of subchapter I of chapter 34 of Title 42, if—

(1) checks for the loans are mailed to the eligible institution prior to disbursements;

(2) the disbursement is not made until the review is complete; and

(3) the eligible institution has no evidence or documentation on which the institution may base a determination that the information submitted by the applicant is incorrect.

(f) Loss of eligibility for violation of loan limits

(1) No student shall be eligible to receive any grant, loan, or work assistance under this subchapter and part C of subchapter I of chapter 34 of Title 42 if the eligible institution determines that the student fraudulently borrowed in violation of the annual loan limits under part B, part C, or part D of this subchapter in the same academic year, or if the student fraudulently borrowed in excess of the aggregate maximum loan limits under such part B, part C, or part D.

(2) If the institution determines that the student inadvertently borrowed amounts in excess of such annual or aggregate maximum loan limits, such institution shall allow the student to repay any amount borrowed in excess of such limits prior to certifying the

---

This chapter, referred to in subsec. (o), was in the original "this Act", meaning Pub. L. 89-329, as amended, known as the Higher Education Act of 1965. For complete classification of this Act to the Code, see Short Title note set out under section 1001 of this title and Tables.

student's eligibility for further assistance under this subchapter and part C of subchapter I of chapter 34 of Title 42.

(g) Verification of immigration status

(1) In general

The Secretary shall implement a system under which the statements and supporting documentation, if required, of an individual declaring that such individual is in compliance with the requirements of subsection (a)(5) of this section shall be verified prior to the individual's receipt of a grant, loan, or work assistance under this subchapter and part C of subchapter I of chapter 34 of Title 42.

(2) Special rule

The documents collected and maintained by an eligible institution in the admission of a student to the institution may be used by the student in lieu of the documents used to establish both employment authorization and identity under section 1324a(b)(1)(B) of Title 8 to verify eligibility to participate in work-study programs under part C of subchapter I of chapter 34 of Title 42.

(3) Verification mechanisms

The Secretary is authorized to verify such statements and supporting documentation through a data match, using an automated or other system, with other Federal agencies that may be in possession of information relevant to such statements and supporting documentation.

(4) Review

In the case of such an individual who is not a citizen or national of the United States, if the statement described in paragraph (1) is submitted but the documentation required under paragraph (2) is not presented or if the documentation required under paragraph (2)(A) is presented but such documentation is not verified under paragraph (3)—

(A) the institution—

(i) shall provide a reasonable opportunity to submit to the institution evidence indicating a satisfactory immigration status, and

(ii) may not delay, deny, reduce, or terminate the individual's eligibility for the grant, loan, or work assistance on the basis of the individual's immigration status until such a reasonable opportunity has been provided; and

(B) if there are submitted documents which the institution determines constitute reasonable evidence indicating such status—

(i) the State shall transmit to the Immigration and Naturalization Service either photostatic or other similar copies of such documents, or information from such documents, as specified by the Immigration and Naturalization Service, for official verification,

(ii) pending such verification, the institution may not delay, deny, reduce, or terminate the individual's eligibility for the grant, loan, or work assistance on the basis of the individual's immigration status, and

(iii) the institution shall not be liable for the consequences of any action, delay, or failure of the Service to conduct such verification.

(h) Limitations of enforcement actions against institutions

The Secretary shall not take any compliance, disallowance, penalty, or other regulatory action against an institution of higher education with respect to any error in the institution's determination to make a student eligible for a grant, loan, or work assistance based on citizenship or immigration status—

(1) if the institution has provided such eligibility based on a

verification of satisfactory immigration status by the Immigration and Naturalization Service,

(2) because the institution, under subsection (h)(4)(A)(i)[9] of this section, was required to provide a reasonable opportunity to submit documentation, or

(3) because the institution, under subsection (h)(4)(B)(i)[10] of this section, was required to wait for the response of the Immigration and Naturalization Service to the institution's request for official verification of the immigration status of the student.

(i) Validity of loan guarantees for loan payments made before immigration status verification completed

Notwithstanding subsection (h)[11] of this section, if—

---

9 Section 1078-1 of this title, referred to in subsec. (b)(2), was repealed by Pub. L. 103-66, title IV, Sec. 4047(b)-(d), Aug. 10, 1993, 107 Stat. 364, eff. July 1, 1994, except with respect to loans provided under that section as it existed prior to Aug. 10, 1993. Subsequently, a new section 1078-1, relating to voluntary flexible agreements with guaranty agencies, was enacted by Pub. L. 105-244, title IV, Sec. 418, Oct. 7, 1998, 112 Stat. 1691.

Subsection (h) of this section, referred to in subsecs. (h)(2), (3) and (i), was redesignated subsec. (g) of this section by Pub. L. 103-208, Sec. 2(h)(25), Dec. 20, 1993, 107 Stat. 2477.

Section 2471 of this title, referred to in subsec. (l)(1)(B)(i), was omitted in the general amendment of chapter 44 (Sec. 2301 et seq.) of this title by Pub. L. 105-332, Sec. 1(b), Oct. 31, 1998, 112 Stat. 3076.

Section 1113 of Public Law 97-252, referred to in subsec. (n), amended section 462 of Title 50, Appendix, War and National Defense, and enacted provisions set out as a note under section 462 of Title 50, Appendix.

This chapter, referred to in subsec. (o), was in the original "this Act", meaning Pub. L. 89-329, as amended, known as the Higher Education Act of 1965. For complete classification of this Act to the Code, see Short Title note set out under section 1001 of this title and Tables.

10 Section 1078-1 of this title, referred to in subsec. (b)(2), was repealed by Pub. L. 103-66, title IV, Sec. 4047(b)-(d), Aug. 10, 1993, 107 Stat. 364, eff. July 1, 1994, except with respect to loans provided under that section as it existed prior to Aug. 10, 1993. Subsequently, a new section 1078-1, relating to voluntary flexible agreements with guaranty agencies, was enacted by Pub. L. 105-244, title IV, Sec. 418, Oct. 7, 1998, 112 Stat. 1691.

Subsection (h) of this section, referred to in subsecs. (h)(2), (3) and (i), was redesignated subsec. (g) of this section by Pub. L. 103-208, Sec. 2(h)(25), Dec. 20, 1993, 107 Stat. 2477.

Section 2471 of this title, referred to in subsec. (l)(1)(B)(i), was omitted in the general amendment of chapter 44 (Sec. 2301 et seq.) of this title by Pub. L. 105-332, Sec. 1(b), Oct. 31, 1998, 112 Stat. 3076.

Section 1113 of Public Law 97-252, referred to in subsec. (n), amended section 462 of Title 50, Appendix, War and National Defense, and enacted provisions set out as a note under section 462 of Title 50, Appendix.

This chapter, referred to in subsec. (o), was in the original "this Act", meaning Pub. L. 89-329, as amended, known as the Higher Education Act of 1965. For complete classification of this Act to the Code, see Short Title note set out under section 1001 of this title and Tables.

11 Section 1078-1 of this title, referred to in subsec. (b)(2), was repealed by Pub. L. 103-66, title IV, Sec. 4047(b)-(d), Aug. 10, 1993, 107 Stat. 364, eff. July 1, 1994, except with respect to loans provided under that section as it existed prior to Aug. 10, 1993. Subsequently, a new section 1078-1, relating to voluntary

(1) a guaranty is made under this subchapter and part C of subchapter I of chapter 34 of Title 42 for a loan made with respect to an individual,

(2) at the time the guaranty is entered into, the provisions of subsection (h) of this section had been complied with,

(3) amounts are paid under the loan subject to such guaranty, and

(4) there is a subsequent determination that, because of an unsatisfactory immigration status, the individual is not eligible for the loan,

the official of the institution making the determination shall notify and instruct the entity making the loan to cease further payments under the loan, but such guaranty shall not be voided or otherwise nullified with respect to such payments made before the date the entity receives the notice.

(j) Assistance under subparts 1 and 3 of part A, and part C

Notwithstanding any other provision of law, a student shall be eligible until September 30, 2004, for assistance under subparts 1 and 3 of part A of this subchapter, and part C of subchapter 1 of chapter 34 of Title 42, if the student is otherwise qualified and—

(1) is a citizen of any one of the Freely Associated States and attends an institution of higher education in a State or a public or nonprofit private institution of higher education in the Freely Associated States; or

(2) meets the requirements of subsection (a)(5) of this section and attends a public or nonprofit private institution of higher education in any one of the Freely Associated States.

(k) Special rule for correspondence courses

A student shall not be eligible to receive grant, loan, or work assistance under this subchapter and part C of subchapter I of chapter 34 of Title 42 for a correspondence course unless such course is part of a program leading to an associate, bachelor or graduate degree.

(*l*) Courses offered through telecommunications

(1) Relation to correspondence courses

(A) In general of this title; and

A student enrolled in a course of instruction at an institution of higher education that is offered in whole or in part through telecommunications and leads to a recognized certificate for a program of study of 1 year or longer, or a recognized associate, baccalaureate, or graduate degree, conferred by such institution,

shall not be considered to be enrolled in correspondence courses unless the total amount of telecommunications and correspondence courses at such institution equals or exceeds 50 percent of the total amount of all courses at the institution.

(B) Requirement

An institution of higher education referred to in subparagraph (A) is an institution of higher education—

(i) that is not an institute or school described in section 2471(4)(C)[12]

(ii) for which at least 50 percent of the programs of study offered by the institution lead to the award of a recognized associate, baccalaureate, or graduate degree.

(2) Restriction or reductions of financial aid

A student's eligibility to receive grants, loans, or work assistance under this subchapter and part C of subchapter I of chapter 34 of Title 42 shall be reduced if a financial aid officer determines under the discretionary authority provided in section 1087tt of this title that telecommunications instruction results in a substantially reduced cost of attendance to such student.

(3) Special rule

For award years prior to July 23, 1992, the Secretary shall not take any compliance, disallowance, penalty, or other action against a student or an eligible institution when such action arises out of such institution's prior award of student assistance under this subchapter and part C of subchapter I of chapter 34 of Title 42 if the institution demonstrates to the satisfaction of the Secretary that its course of instruction would have been in conformance with the requirements of this subsection.

(4) "Telecommunications," defined

For the purposes of this subsection, the term "telecommunications" means the use of television, audio, or computer transmission, including open broadcast, closed circuit, cable, microwave, or satellite, audio conferencing, computer conferencing, or video cassettes or discs, except that such term does not include a course that is delivered using video cassette or disc recordings at such institution and that is not delivered in person to other students of that institution.

---

12 Section 1078-1 of this title, referred to in subsec. (b)(2), was repealed by Pub. L. 103-66, title IV, Sec. 4047(b)-(d), Aug. 10, 1993, 107 Stat. 364, eff. July 1, 1994, except with respect to loans provided under that section as it existed prior to Aug. 10, 1993. Subsequently, a new section 1078-1, relating to voluntary flexible agreements with guaranty agencies, was enacted by Pub. L. 105-244, title IV, Sec. 418, Oct. 7, 1998, 112 Stat. 1691.

Subsection (h) of this section, referred to in subsecs. (h)(2), (3) and (i), was redesignated subsec. (g) of this section by Pub. L. 103-208, Sec. 2(h)(25), Dec. 20, 1993, 107 Stat. 2477.

Section 2471 of this title, referred to in subsec. (l)(1)(B)(i), was omitted in the general amendment of chapter 44 (Sec. 2301 et seq.) of this title by Pub. L. 105-332, Sec. 1(b), Oct. 31, 1998, 112 Stat. 3076.

Section 1113 of Public Law 97-252, referred to in subsec. (n), amended section 462 of Title 50, Appendix, War and National Defense, and enacted provisions set out as a note under section 462 of Title 50, Appendix.

This chapter, referred to in subsec. (o), was in the original "this Act", meaning Pub. L. 89-329, as amended, known as the Higher Education Act of 1965. For complete classification of this Act to the Code, see Short Title note set out under section 1001 of this title and Tables.

---

flexible agreements with guaranty agencies, was enacted by Pub. L. 105-244, title IV, Sec. 418, Oct. 7, 1998, 112 Stat. 1691.

Subsection (h) of this section, referred to in subsecs. (h)(2), (3) and (i), was redesignated subsec. (g) of this section by Pub. L. 103-208, Sec. 2(h)(25), Dec. 20, 1993, 107 Stat. 2477.

Section 2471 of this title, referred to in subsec. (l)(1)(B)(i), was omitted in the general amendment of chapter 44 (Sec. 2301 et seq.) of this title by Pub. L. 105-332, Sec. 1(b), Oct. 31, 1998, 112 Stat. 3076.

Section 1113 of Public Law 97-252, referred to in subsec. (n), amended section 462 of Title 50, Appendix, War and National Defense, and enacted provisions set out as a note under section 462 of Title 50, Appendix.

This chapter, referred to in subsec. (o), was in the original "this Act", meaning Pub. L. 89-329, as amended, known as the Higher Education Act of 1965. For complete classification of this Act to the Code, see Short Title note set out under section 1001 of this title and Tables.

(m) Students with a first baccalaureate or professional degree

A student shall not be ineligible for assistance under parts B, C, and D of this subchapter and part C of subchapter I of chapter 34 of Title 42 because such student has previously received a baccalaureate or professional degree.

(n) Data base matching

To enforce the Selective Service registration provisions of section 1113 of Public Law 97-252, the Secretary shall conduct data base matches with the Selective Service, using common demographic data elements. Appropriate confirmation, through an application output document or through other means, of any person's registration shall fulfill the requirement to file a separate statement of compliance. In the absence of a confirmation from such data matches, an institution may also use data or documents that support either the student's registration, or the absence of a registration requirement for the student, to fulfill the requirement to file a separate statement of compliance. The mechanism for reporting the resolution of nonconfirmed matches shall be prescribed by the Secretary in regulations.

(o) Study abroad

Nothing in this chapter shall be construed to limit or otherwise prohibit access to study abroad programs approved by the home institution at which a student is enrolled. An otherwise eligible student who is engaged in a program of study abroad approved for academic credit by the home institution at which the student is enrolled shall be eligible to receive grant, loan, or work assistance under this subchapter and part C of subchapter I of chapter 34 of Title 42, without regard to whether such study abroad program is required as part of the student's degree program.

(p) Verification of social security number

The Secretary of Education, in cooperation with the Commissioner of the Social Security Administration, shall verify any social security number provided by a student to an eligible institution under subsection (a)(4) of this section and shall enforce the following conditions:

(1) Except as provided in paragraphs (2) and (3), an institution shall not deny, reduce, delay, or terminate a student's eligibility for assistance under this part because social security number verification is pending.

(2) If there is a determination by the Secretary that the social security number provided to an eligible institution by a student is incorrect, the institution shall deny or terminate the student's eligibility for any grant, loan, or work assistance under this subchapter and part C of subchapter I of chapter 34 of Title 42 until such time as the student provides documented evidence of a social security number that is determined by the institution to be correct.

(3) If there is a determination by the Secretary that the social security number provided to an eligible institution by a student is incorrect, and a correct social security number cannot be provided by such student, and a loan has been guaranteed for such student under part B of this subchapter, the institution shall notify and instruct the lender and guaranty agency making and guaranteeing the loan, respectively, to cease further disbursements of the loan, but such guaranty shall not be voided or otherwise nullified with respect to such disbursements made before the date that the lender and the guaranty agency receives such notice.

(4) Nothing in this subsection shall permit the Secretary to take any compliance, disallowance, penalty, or other regulatory action against—

(A) any institution of higher education with respect to any error in a social security number, unless such error was a result of fraud on the part of the institution; or

(B) any student with respect to any error in a social security number, unless such error was a result of fraud on the part of the student.

(q) Verification of income data

(1) Confirmation with IRS

The Secretary of Education, in cooperation with the Secretary of the Treasury, is authorized to confirm with the Internal Revenue Service the adjusted gross income, Federal income taxes paid, filing status, and exemptions reported by applicants (including parents) under this subchapter and part C of subchapter I of chapter 34 of Title 42 on their Federal income tax returns for the purpose of verifying the information reported by applicants on student financial aid applications.

(2) Notification

The Secretary shall establish procedures under which an applicant is notified that the Internal Revenue Service will disclose to the Secretary tax return information as authorized under section 6103(l)(13) of Title 26.

(r) Suspension of eligibility for drug-related offenses

(1) In general

A student who has been convicted of any offense under any Federal or State law involving the possession or sale of a controlled substance shall not be eligible to receive any grant, loan, or work assistance under this subchapter and part C of subchapter I of chapter 34 of Title 42 during the period beginning on the date of such conviction and ending after the interval specified in the following table:

If convicted of an offense involving:

The possession of a controlled substance:	Ineligibility period is:
First offense	1 year
Second offense	2 years
Third offense	Indefinite.
The sale of a controlled substance:	Ineligibility period is:
First offense	2 years
Second offense	Indefinite.

(2) Rehabilitation

A student whose eligibility has been suspended under paragraph (1) may resume eligibility before the end of the ineligibility period determined under such paragraph if—

(A) the student satisfactorily completes a drug rehabilitation program that—

(i) complies with such criteria as the Secretary shall prescribe in regulations for purposes of this paragraph; and

(ii) includes two unannounced drug tests; or

(B) the conviction is reversed, set aside, or otherwise rendered nugatory.

(3) Definitions

In this subsection, the term "controlled substance" has the meaning given the term in section 802(6) of Title 21.

(Pub.L. 89-329, Title IV, § 484, as added Pub.L. 99-498, Title IV, § 407(a), Oct. 17, 1986, 100 Stat. 1479, and amended Pub.L. 99-603, Title I, § 121(a)(3), Nov. 6, 1986, 100 Stat. 3388; Pub.L. 100-50, § 15(7) to (9), June 3, 1987, 101 Stat. 356, 357; Pub.L. 100-369, §§ 1, 2, 6, July 18, 1988, 102 Stat. 835, 836; Pub.L. 100-525, § 2(g), Oct. 24, 1988, 102 Stat. 2611; Pub.L. 101-508, Title III, § 3005(a), Nov. 5, 1990, 104 Stat. 1388- 27; Pub.L. 102-26, § 2(b), (c)(2), (d)(2)(A), Apr. 9, 1991, 105 Stat. 123, 124; Pub.L. 102-73, Title VIII, § 801(a), July 25, 1991, 105 Stat. 359; Pub.L. 102-325, Title IV, § 484(a), (b)(1), (c) to (h), July 23, 1992, 106 Stat. 615 to 619; Pub.L. 103-208, § 2(h)(13) to (25), Dec. 20, 1993, 107 Stat. 2476, 2477; Pub.L. 103-382, Title III, § 360A, Oct. 20, 1994, 108 Stat. 3969; Pub.L. 104-208, Div. C, Title V, § 507(b), Sept. 30, 1996, 110 Stat. 3009-673; Pub.L. 105-244, Title IV, § 483(a) to (f)(1), Oct. 7, 1998, 112 Stat. 1735, 1736.)

§ 1091a. Statute of limitations, and State court judgments

(a) In general

(1) It is the purpose of this subsection to ensure that obligations to repay loans and grant overpayments are enforced without regard to any Federal or State statutory, regulatory, or administrative limitation on the period within which debts may be enforced.

(2) Notwithstanding any other provision of statute, regulation, or administrative limitation, no limitation shall terminate the period within which suit may be filed, a judgment may be enforced, or an offset, garnishment, or other action initiated or taken by—

(A) an institution that receives funds under this subchapter and part C of subchapter I of chapter 34 of Title 42 that is seeking to collect a refund due from a student on a grant made, or work assistance awarded, under this subchapter and part C of subchapter I of chapter 34 of Title 42;

(B) a guaranty agency that has an agreement with the Secretary under section 1078(c) of this title that is seeking the repayment of the amount due from a borrower on a loan made under part B of this subchapter after such guaranty agency reimburses the previous holder of the loan for its loss on account of the default of the borrower;

(C) an institution that has an agreement with the Secretary pursuant to section 1087c or 1087cc(a) of this title that is seeking the repayment of the amount due from a borrower on a loan made under part C or D of this subchapter after the default of the borrower on such loan; or

(D) the Secretary, the Attorney General, or the administrative head of another Federal agency, as the case may be, for payment of a refund due from a student on a grant made under this subchapter and part C of subchapter I of chapter 34 of Title 42, or for the repayment of the amount due from a borrower on a loan made under this subchapter and part C of subchapter I of chapter 34 of Title 42 that has been assigned to the Secretary under this subchapter and part C of subchapter I of chapter 34 of Title 42.

(b) Assessment of costs and other charges

Notwithstanding any provision of State law to the contrary—

(1) a borrower who has defaulted on a loan made under this subchapter and part C of subchapter I of chapter 34 of title 42 shall be required to pay, in addition to other charges specified in this subchapter and part C of subchapter I of chapter 34 of title 42 reasonable collection costs; and

(2) in collecting any obligation arising from a loan made under part B of this subchapter, a guaranty agency or the Secretary shall

not be subject to a defense raised by any borrower based on a claim of infancy.

(c) State court judgments

A judgment of a State court for the recovery of money provided as grant, loan, or work assistance under this subchapter that has been assigned or transferred to the Secretary under this subchapter may be registered in any district court of the United States by filing a certified copy of the judgment and a copy of the assignment or transfer. A judgment so registered shall have the same force and effect, and may be enforced in the same manner, as a judgment of the district court of the district in which the judgment is registered.

(Pub. L. 89-329, title IV, Sec. 484A, as added Pub. L. 99-498, title IV, Sec. 407(a), Oct. 17, 1986, 100 Stat. 1482; amended Pub. L. 102-26, Sec. 3(a), Apr. 9, 1991, 105 Stat. 124; Pub. L. 105-244, title IV, Sec. 484, Oct. 7, 1998, 112 Stat. 1737.)

§ 1091b. Institutional refunds

(a) Return of title IV funds
(1) In general

If a recipient of assistance under this subchapter and part C of subchapter I of chapter 34 of Title 42 [42 U.S.C.A. § 2751 et seq.] withdraws from an institution during a payment period or period of enrollment in which the recipient began attendance, the amount of grant or loan assistance (other than assistance received under part C of subchapter I of chapter 34 of Title 42 [12 U.S.C.A. § 2751 et seq.]) to be returned to the title IV programs is calculated according to paragraph (3) and returned in accordance with subsection (b) of this section.

(2) Leave of absence
(A) Leave not treated as withdrawal

In the case of a student who takes a leave of absence from an institution for not more than a total of 180 days in any 12-month period, the institution may consider the student as not having withdrawn from the institution during the leave of absence, and not calculate the amount of grant and loan assistance provided under this subchapter [20 U.S.C.A. § 1070 et seq.] and part C of subchapter I of chapter 34 of Title 42 [42 U.S.C.A. § 2751 et seq.] that is to be returned in accordance with this section if—

(i) the institution has a formal policy regarding leaves of absence;

(ii) the student followed the institution's policy in requesting a leave of absence; and

(iii) the institution approved the student's request in accordance with the institution's policy.

(B) Consequences of failure to return

If a student does not return to the institution at the expiration of an approved leave of absence that meets the requirements of subparagraph (A), the institution shall calculate the amount of grant and loan assistance provided under this subchapter [20 U.S.C.A. § 1070 et seq.] and part C of subchapter I of chapter 34 of Title 42 [42 U.S.C.A. § 2751 et seq.] that is to be returned in accordance with this section based on the day the student withdrew (as determined under subsection (c).

(3) Calculation of amount of title IV assistance earned
(A) In general

The amount of grant or loan assistance under this subchapter [20 U.S.C.A. § 1070 et seq.] and part C of subchapter I of chapter 34 of Title 42 [42 U.S.C.A. § 2751 et seq.] that is earned by the recipient for purposes of this section is calculated by—

(i) determining the percentage of grant and loan assistance under this subchapter [20 U.S.C.A. § 1070 et seq.] and part C of subchapter I of chapter 34 of Title 42 [42 U.S.C.A. 2751 et seq.] that has been earned by the student, as described in subparagraph (B); and

(ii) applying such percentage to the total amount of such grant and loan assistance that was disbursed (and that could have been disbursed) to the student, or on the student's behalf, for the payment period or period of enrollment for which the assistance was awarded, as of the day the student withdrew.

(B) Percentage earned

For purposes of subparagraph (A)(i), the percentage of grant or loan assistance under this subchapter [20 U.S.C.A. § 1070 et seq.] and part C of subchapter I of chapter 34 of Title 42 [42 U.S.C.A. § 2751 et seq.] that has been earned by the student is—

(i) equal to the percentage of the payment period or period of enrollment for which assistance was awarded that was completed (as determined in accordance with subsection (d)) as of the day the student withdrew, provided that such date occurs on or before the completion of 60 percent of the payment period or period of enrollment; or

(ii) 100 percent, if the day the student withdrew occurs after the student has completed 60 percent of the payment period or period of enrollment.

(C) Percentage and amount not earned

For purposes of subsection (b), the amount of grant and loan assistance awarded under this subchapter [20 U.S.C.A. § 1070 et seq.] and part C of subchapter I of chapter 34 of Title 42 [42 U.S.C.A. § 2751 et seq.] that has not been earned by the student shall be calculated by—

(i) determining the complement of the percentage of grant or loan assistance under this subchapter and part C of subchapter I of chapter 34 of Title 42 that has been earned by the student described in subparagraph (B); and

(ii) applying the percentage determined under clause (i) to the total amount of such grant and loan assistance that was disbursed (and that could have been disbursed) to the student, or on the student's behalf, for the payment period or period of enrollment, as of the day the student withdrew.

(4) Differences between amounts earned and amounts received

(A) In general

If the student has received less grant or loan assistance than the amount earned as calculated under subparagraph (A) of paragraph (3), the institution of higher education shall comply with the procedures for late disbursement specified by the Secretary in regulations.

(B) Return

If the student has received more grant or loan assistance than the amount earned as calculated under paragraph (3)(A), the unearned funds shall be returned by the institution or the student, or both, as may be required under paragraphs (1) and (2) of subsection [20 U.S.C.A. § 1070 et seq.] (b), to the programs under this subchapter and part C of subchapter I of chapter 34 of title 42 [42 U.S.C.A. § 2751 et seq.] in the order specified in subsection (b)(3).

(b) Return of title IV program funds

(1) Responsibility of the institution

The institution shall return, in the order specified in paragraph (3), the lesser of—

(A) the amount of grant and loan assistance awarded under this subchapter [20 U.S.C.A. § 1070 et seq.] and part C of subchapter I of chapter 34 of Title 42 [42 U.S.C.A. § 2751] that has not been earned by the student, as calculated under subsection (a)(3)(C); or

(B) an amount equal to—

(i) the total institutional charges incurred by the student for the payment period or period of enrollment for which such assistance was awarded; multiplied by

(ii) the percentage of grant and loan assistance awarded under this subchapter and part C of subchapter I of chapter 34 of title 42 that has not been earned by the student, as described in subsection (a)(3)(C)(i)

(2) Responsibility of the student

(A) In general

The student shall return assistance that has not been earned by the student as described in subsection (a)(3)(C)(ii) in the order specified in paragraph (3) minus the amount the institution is required to return under paragraph (1).

(B) Special rule

The student (or parent in the case of funds due to a loan borrowed by a parent under part B or C of this subchapter [20 U.S.C.A. § 1071 et seq.]) shall return or repay, as appropriate, the amount determined under subparagraph (A) to—

(i) a loan program under this subchapter [20 U.S.C.A. § 1070] and part C of subchapter I of chapter 34 of Title 42 [42 U.S.C.A. § 2751 et seq.] in accordance with the terms of the loan; and

(ii) a grant program under this subchapter and part C of subchapter I of chapter 34 of title 42, as an overpayment of such grant and shall be subject to—

(I) repayment arrangements satisfactory to the institution; or

(II) overpayment collection procedures prescribed by the Secretary.

(C) Requirement

Notwithstanding subparagraphs (A) and (B), a student shall not be required to return 50 percent of the grant assistance received by the student under this subchapter [20 U.S.C.A. § 1070 et seq.] and part C of subchapter I of chapter 34 of Ttitle 42 [42 U.S.C.A. § 2751 et seq.], for a payment period or period of enrollment, that is the responsibility of the student to repay under this section.

(3) Order of return of title IV funds

(A) In general

Excess funds returned by the institution or the student, as appropriate, in accordance with paragraph (1) or (2), respectively, shall be credited to outstanding balances on loans made under this subchapter and part C of subchapter I of chapter 34 of title 42 to the student or on behalf of the student for the payment period or period of enrollment for which a return of funds is required. Such excess funds shall be credited in the following order:

(i) To outstanding balances on loans made under section 1078-8 of this title for the payment period or period of enrollment for which a return of funds is required.

(ii) To outstanding balances on loans made under section 1078 of this title for the payment period or period of enrollment for which a return of funds is required.

(iii) To outstanding balances on unsubsidized loans (other than parent loans) made under part C of this subchapter [20 U.S.C.A. 1087a et seq] for the payment period or period of enrollment for which a return of funds is required.

(iv) To outstanding balances on subsidized loans made under part C of this subchapter for the payment period or period of enrollment for which a return of funds is required.

(v) To outstanding balances on loans made under part D of this subchapter [20 U.S.C.A. § 1087a et seq.] for the payment period or period of enrollment for which a return of funds is required.

(vi) To outstanding balances on loans made under section 1078-2 of this title for the payment period or period of enrollment for which a return of funds is required.

(vii) To outstanding balances on parent loans made under part C of this subchapter for the payment period or period of enrollment for which a return of funds is required.

(B) Remaining excesses

If excess funds remain after repaying all outstanding loan amounts, the remaining excess shall be credited in the following order:

(i) To awards under subpart 1 of part A of this subchapter for the payment period or period of enrollment for which a return of funds is required.

(ii) To awards under subpart 3 of part A of this subchapter for the payment period or period of enrollment for which a return of funds is required.

(iii) To other assistance awarded under this subchapter and part C of subchapter I of chapter 34 of title 42 for which a return of funds is required.

(c) Withdrawal date

(1) In general

In this section, the term "day the student withdrew"—

(A) is the date that the institution determines—

(i) the student began the withdrawal process prescribed by the institution;

(ii) the student otherwise provided official notification to the institution of the intent to withdraw; or

(iii) in the case of a student who does not begin the withdrawal process or otherwise notify the institution of the intent to withdraw, the date that is the mid-point of the payment period for which assistance under this subchapter [20 U.S.C.A. § 1070 et seq.] and part C of subchapter I of chapter 34 of Title 42 [42 U.S.C.A. § 2751 et seq.] was disbursed or a later date documented by the institution; or

(B) for institutions required to take attendance, is determined by the institution from such attendance records.

(2) Special rule

Notwithstanding paragraph (1), if the institution determines that a student did not begin the withdrawal process, or otherwise notify the institution of the intent to withdraw, due to illness, accident, grievous personal loss, or other such circumstances beyond the student's control, the institution may determine the appropriate withdrawal date.

(d) Percentage of the payment period or period of enrollment completed

For purposes of subsection (a)(3)(B)(i), the percentage of the payment period or period of enrollment for which assistance was awarded that was completed, is determined—

(1) in the case of a program that is measured in credit hours, by dividing the total number of calendar days comprising the payment period or period of enrollment for which assistance is awarded into the number of calendar days completed in that period as of the day the student withdrew; and

(2) in the case of a program that is measured in clock hours, by dividing the total number of clock hours comprising the payment period or period of enrollment for which assistance is awarded into the number of clock hours—

(A) completed by the student in that period as of the day the student withdrew; or

(B) scheduled to be completed as of the day the student withdrew, if the clock hours completed in the period are not less than a percentage, to be determined by the Secretary in regulations, of the hours that were scheduled to be completed by the student in the period.

(e) Effective date

The provisions of this section shall take effect 2 years after October 7, 1998. An institution of higher education may choose to implement such provisions prior to that date.

(Pub. L. 89-329, title IV, Sec. 484B, as added Pub. L. 102-325, title IV, Sec. 485(a), July 23, 1992, 106 Stat. 619; amended Pub. L. 103-208, Sec. 2(h)(26), (27), Dec. 20, 1993, 107 Stat. 2477; Pub. L. 105-244, title IV, Sec. 485, Oct. 7, 1998, 112 Stat. 1737.)

§ 1095a. Wage garnishment requirement

(a) Garnishment requirements

Notwithstanding any provision of State law, a guaranty agency, or the Secretary in the case of loans made, insured or guaranteed under this subchapter [20 U.S.C.A. 1070 et seq.] and part C of subchapter I of chapter 34 of title 42 [42 U.S.C.A. § 2751 et seq.] that are held by the Secretary, may garnish the disposable pay of an individual to collect the amount owed by the individual, if he or she is not currently making required repayment under a repayment agreement with the Secretary, or, in the case of a loan guaranteed under part B of this subchapter on which the guaranty agency received reimbursement from the Secretary under section 1078(c) of this title, with the guaranty agency holding the loan, as appropriate, provided that—

(1) the amount deducted for any pay period may not exceed 10 percent of disposable pay, except that a greater percentage may be deducted with the written consent of the individual involved;

(2) the individual shall be provided written notice, sent by mail to the individual's last known address, a minimum of 30 days prior to the initiation of proceedings, from the guaranty agency or the Secretary, as appropriate, informing such individual of the nature and amount of the loan obligation to be collected, the intention of the guaranty agency or the Secretary, as appropriate, to initiate proceedings to collect the debt through deductions from pay, and an explanation of the rights of the individual under this section;

(3) the individual shall be provided an opportunity to inspect and copy records relating to the debt;

(4) the individual shall be provided an opportunity to enter into a written agreement with the guaranty agency or the Secretary, under terms agreeable to the Secretary, or the head of the guaranty agency or his designee, as appropriate, to establish a schedule for the repayment of the debt;

(5) the individual shall be provided an opportunity for a hearing in accordance with subsection (b) of this section on the determination of the Secretary or the guaranty agency, as appropriate, concerning the existence or the amount of the debt, and, in the case of an individual whose repayment schedule is established other than by a written agreement pursuant to paragraph (4), concerning the terms of the repayment schedule;

(6) the employer shall pay to the Secretary or the guaranty agency as directed in the withholding order issued in this action, and shall be liable for, and the Secretary or the guaranty agency, as appropriate, may sue the employer in a State or Federal court of

competent jurisdiction to recover, any amount that such employer fails to withhold from wages due an employee following receipt of such employer of notice of the withholding order, plus attorneys' fees, costs, and, in the court's discretion, punitive damages, but such employer shall not be required to vary the normal pay and disbursement cycles in order to comply with this paragraph;

(7) if an individual has been reemployed within 12 months after having been involuntarily separated from employment, no amount may be deducted from the disposable pay of such individual until such individual has been reemployed continuously for at least 12 months; and

(8) an employer may not discharge from employment, refuse to employ, or take disciplinary action against an individual subject to wage withholding in accordance with this section by reason of the fact that the individual's wages have been subject to garnishment under this section, and such individual may sue in a State or Federal court of competent jurisdiction any employer who takes such action. The court shall award attorneys' fees to a prevailing employee and, in its discretion, may order reinstatement of the individual, award punitive damages and back pay to the employee, or order such other remedy as may be reasonably necessary.

(b) Hearing requirements

A hearing described in subsection (a)(5) of this section shall be provided prior to issuance of a garnishment order if the individual, on or before the 15th day following the mailing of the notice described in subsection (a)(2) of this section, and in accordance with such procedures as the Secretary or the head of the guaranty agency, as appropriate, may prescribe, files a petition requesting such a hearing. If the individual does not file a petition requesting a hearing prior to such date, the Secretary or the guaranty agency, as appropriate, shall provide the individual a hearing under subsection (a)(5) of this section upon request, but such hearing need not be provided prior to issuance of a garnishment order. A hearing under subsection (a)(5) of this section may not be conducted by an individual under the supervision or control of the head of the guaranty agency, except that nothing in this sentence shall be construed to prohibit the appointment of an administrative law judge. The hearing official shall issue a final decision at the earliest practicable date, but not later than 60 days after the filing of the petition requesting the hearing.

(c) Notice requirements

The notice to the employer of the withholding order shall contain only such information as may be necessary for the employer to comply with the withholding order.

(d) No attachment of student assistance

Except as authorized in this section, notwithstanding any other provision of Federal or State law, no grant, loan, or work assistance awarded under this subchapter [20 U.S.C.A. 1070 et seq.] and part C of subchapter I of chapter 34 of Title 42 [42 U.S.C.A. § 2751 et seq.], or property traceable to such assistance, shall be subject to garnishment or attachment in order to satisfy any debt owed by the student awarded such assistance, other than a debt owed to the Secretary and arising under this subchapter and part C of subchapter I of chapter 34 of title 42.

(e) "Disposable pay" defined

For the purpose of this section, the term "disposable pay" means that part of the compensation of any individual from an employer remaining after the deduction of any amounts required by law to be withheld.

(Pub. L. 89-329, title IV, Sec. 488A, as added Pub. L. 102-164, title VI, Sec. 605(a), Nov. 15, 1991, 105 Stat. 1066; amended Pub. L. 105-244, title IV, Sec. 490A, Oct. 7, 1998, 112 Stat. 1753.)

A.1.5 Selected Debt Collection Statutes

The following is selected statutory authority from the federal Debt Collection Act. These provisions apply to all federal agencies including the Department of Education.

31 U.S.C. sec.
3716.   Administrative offset.
3720A. Reduction of tax refund by amount of debt.
3720D. Garnishment.

§ 3716. Administrative offset

(a) After trying to collect a claim from a person under section 3711(a) of this title, the head of an executive, judicial, or legislative agency may collect the claim by administrative offset. The head of the agency may collect by administrative offset only after giving the debtor—

(1) written notice of the type and amount of the claim, the intention of the head of the agency to collect the claim by administrative offset, and an explanation of the rights of the debtor under this section;

(2) an opportunity to inspect and copy the records of the agency related to the claim;

(3) an opportunity for a review within the agency of the decision of the agency related to the claim; and

(4) an opportunity to make a written agreement with the head of the agency to repay the amount of the claim.

(b) Before collecting a claim by administrative offset, the head of an executive, judicial, or legislative agency must either—

(1) adopt, without change, regulations on collecting by administrative offset promulgated by the Department of Justice, the General Accounting Office, or the Department of the Treasury; or

(2) prescribe regulations on collecting by administrative offset consistent with the regulations referred to in paragraph (1).

(c)(1)(A) Except as otherwise provided in this subsection, a disbursing official of the Department of the Treasury, the Department of Defense, the United States Postal Service, or any other government corporation, or any disbursing official of the United States designated by the Secretary of the Treasury, shall offset at least annually the amount of a payment which a payment certifying agency has certified to the disbursing official for disbursement, by an amount equal to the amount of a claim which a creditor agency has certified to the Secretary of the Treasury pursuant to this subsection.

(B) An agency that designates disbursing officials pursuant to section 3321(c) of this title is not required to certify claims arising out of its operations to the Secretary of the Treasury before such agency's disbursing officials offset such claims.

(C) Payments certified by the Department of Education under a program administered by the Secretary of Education under title IV of the Higher Education Act of 1965 shall not be subject to administrative offset under this subsection.

(2) Neither the disbursing official nor the payment certifying agency shall be liable—

(A) for the amount of the administrative offset on the basis that the underlying obligation, represented by the payment before the administrative offset was taken, was not satisfied; or

(B) for failure to provide timely notice under paragraph (8).

(3)(A)(i) Notwithstanding any other provision of law (including sections 207 and 1631(d)(1) of the Social Security Act (42 U.S.C. 407 and 1383(d)(1)), section 413(b) of Public Law 91-173 (30 U.S.C. 923(b)), and section 14 of the Act of August 29, 1935 (45 U.S.C. 231m)), except as provided in clause (ii), all payments due to an individual under—

(I) the Social Security Act,

(II) part B of the Black Lung Benefits Act, or

(III) any law administered by the Railroad Retirement Board (other than payments that such Board determines to be tier 2 benefits),

shall be subject to offset under this section.

(ii) An amount of $9,000 which a debtor may receive under Federal benefit programs cited under clause (i) within a 12-month period shall be exempt from offset under this subsection. In applying the $9,000 exemption, the disbursing official shall—

(I) reduce the $9,000 exemption amount for the 12-month period by the amount of all Federal benefit payments made during such 12-month period which are not subject to offset under this subsection; and

(II) apply a prorated amount of the exemption to each periodic benefit payment to be made to the debtor during the applicable 12-month period.

For purposes of the preceding sentence, the amount of a periodic benefit payment shall be the amount after any reduction or deduction required under the laws authorizing the program under which such payment is authorized to be made (including any reduction or deduction to recover any overpayment under such program).

(B) The Secretary of the Treasury shall exempt from administrative offset under this subsection payments under means-tested programs when requested by the head of the respective agency. The Secretary may exempt other payments from administrative offset under this subsection upon the written request of the head of a payment certifying agency. A written request for exemption of other payments must provide justification for the exemption under standards prescribed by the Secretary. Such standards shall give due consideration to whether administrative offset would tend to interfere substantially with or defeat the purposes of the payment certifying agency's program. The Secretary shall report to the Congress annually on exemptions granted under this section.

(C) The provisions of sections 205(b)(1), 809(a)(1), and 1631(c)(1) of the Social Security Act shall not apply to any administrative offset executed pursuant to this section against benefits authorized by title II, VIII, or title XVI of the Social Security Act, respectively.

(4) The Secretary of the Treasury may charge a fee sufficient to cover the full cost of implementing this subsection. The fee may be collected either by the retention of a portion of amounts collected pursuant to this subsection, or by billing the agency referring or transferring a claim for those amounts. Fees charged to the agencies shall be based on actual administrative offsets completed. Amounts received by the United States as fees under this subsection shall be deposited into the account of the Department of the Treasury under section 3711(g)(7) of this title, and shall be collected and accounted for in accordance with the provisions of that section.

(5) The Secretary of the Treasury in consultation with the Commissioner of Social Security and the Director of the Office of Management and Budget, may prescribe such rules, regulations, and procedures as the Secretary of the Treasury considers necessary to carry out this subsection. The Secretary shall consult with the heads of affected agencies in the development of such rules, regulations, and procedures.

(6) Any Federal agency that is owed by a person a past due, legally enforceable nontax debt that is over 180 days delinquent, including nontax debt administered by a third party acting as an agent for the Federal Government, shall notify the Secretary of the Treasury of all such nontax debts for purposes of administrative offset under this subsection.

(7)(A) The disbursing official conducting an administrative offset with respect to a payment to a payee shall notify the payee in writing of—

(i) the occurrence of the administrative offset to satisfy a past due legally enforceable debt, including a description of the type and amount of the payment otherwise payable to the payee against which the offset was executed;

(ii) the identity of the creditor agency requesting the offset; and

(iii) a contact point within the creditor agency that will handle concerns regarding the offset.

(B) If the payment to be offset is a periodic benefit payment, the disbursing official shall take reasonable steps, as determined by the Secretary of the Treasury, to provide the notice to the payee not later than the date on which the payee is otherwise scheduled to receive the payment, or as soon as practical thereafter, but no later than the date of the administrative offset. Notwithstanding the preceding sentence, the failure of the debtor to receive such notice shall not impair the legality of such administrative offset.

(8) A levy pursuant to the Internal Revenue Code of 1986 shall take precedence over requests for administrative offset pursuant to other laws.

(d) Nothing in this section is intended to prohibit the use of any other administrative offset authority existing under statute or common law.

(e) This section does not apply—

(1) to a claim under this subchapter that has been outstanding for more than 10 years; or

(2) when a statute explicitly prohibits using administrative offset or setoff to collect the claim or type of claim involved.

(f) The Secretary may waive the requirements of sections 552a(o) and (p) of title 5 for administrative offset or claims collection upon written certification by the head of a State or an executive, judicial, or legislative agency seeking to collect the claim that the requirements of subsection (a) of this section have been met.

(g) The Data Integrity Board of the Department of the Treasury established under 552a(u) of title 5 shall review and include in reports under paragraph (3)(D) of that section a description of any matching activities conducted under this section. If the Secretary has granted a waiver under subsection (f) of this section, no other Data Integrity Board is required to take any action under section 552a(u) of title 5.

(h)(1) The Secretary may, in the discretion of the Secretary, apply subsection (a) with respect to any past-due, legally-enforceable debt owed to a State if—

(A) the appropriate State disbursing official requests that an offset be performed; and

(B) a reciprocal agreement with the State is in effect which contains, at a minimum—

(i) requirements substantially equivalent to subsection (b) of this section; and

(ii) any other requirements which the Secretary considers appropriate to facilitate the offset and prevent duplicative efforts.

(2) This subsection does not apply to—

(A) the collection of a debt or claim on which the administrative costs associated with the collection of the debt or claim exceed the amount of the debt or claim;

(B) any collection of any other type, class, or amount of claim, as the Secretary considers necessary to protect the interest of the United States; or

(C) the disbursement of any class or type of payment exempted by the Secretary of the Treasury at the request of a Federal agency.

(3) In applying this section with respect to any debt owed to a State, subsection (c)(3)(A) shall not apply.

(Added Pub.L. 97-452, § 1(16)(A), Jan. 12, 1983, 96 Stat. 2471; amended Pub.L. 104-134, Title III, § 31001(c)(1), (d)(2), (e), (f), Apr. 26, 1996, 110 Stat. 1321-359, 1321-362; Pub.L. 106-169, Title II, § 251(b)(10), Dec. 14, 1999, 113 Stat. 1856.)

§ 3720A. Reduction of tax refund by amount of debt

(a) Any Federal agency that is owed by a person a past-due, legally enforceable debt (including debt administered by a third party acting as an agent for the Federal Government) shall, and any agency subject to section 9 of the Act of May 18, 1933 (16 U.S.C. 831h), owed such a debt may, in accordance with regulations issued pursuant to subsections (b) and (d), notify the Secretary of the Treasury at least once each year of the amount of such debt.

(b) No Federal agency may take action pursuant to subsection (a) with respect to any debt until such agency—

(1) notifies the person incurring such debt that such agency proposes to take action pursuant to such paragraph with respect to such debt;

(2) gives such person at least 60 days to present evidence that all or part of such debt is not past-due or not legally enforceable;

(3) considers any evidence presented by such person and determines that an amount of such debt is past due and legally enforceable;

(4) satisfies such other conditions as the Secretary may prescribe to ensure that the determination made under paragraph (3) with respect to such debt is valid and that the agency has made reasonable efforts (determined on a government-wide basis) to obtain payment of such debt; and

(5) certifies that reasonable efforts have been made by the agency (pursuant to regulations) to obtain payment of such debt.

(c) Upon receiving notice from any Federal agency that a named person owes to such agency a past-due legally enforceable debt, the Secretary of the Treasury shall determine whether any amounts, as refunds of Federal taxes paid, are payable to such person. If the Secretary of the Treasury finds that any such amount is payable, he shall reduce such refunds by an amount equal to the amount of such debt, pay the amount of such reduction to such agency, and notify such agency of the individual's home address.

(d) The Secretary of the Treasury shall issue regulations prescribing the time or times at which agencies must submit notices of past-due legally enforceable debts, the manner in which such notices must be submitted, and the necessary information that must be contained in or accompany the notices. The regulations shall specify the minimum amount of debt to which the reduction procedure established by subsection (c) may be applied and the fee that an agency must pay to reimburse the Secretary of the Treasury for the full cost of applying such procedure. Any fee paid to the Secretary pursuant to the preceding sentence may be used to reimburse appropriations which bore all or part of the cost of applying such procedure.

(e) Any Federal agency receiving notice from the Secretary of the Treasury that an erroneous payment has been made to such agency under subsection (c) shall pay promptly to the Secretary, in accordance with such regulations as the Secretary may prescribe, an amount equal to the amount of such erroneous payment (without regard to whether any other amounts payable to such agency under such subsection have been paid to such agency).

(f)(1) Subsection (a) shall apply with respect to an OASDI overpayment made to any individual only if such individual is not currently entitled to monthly insurance benefits under title II of the Social Security Act.

(2)(A) The requirements of subsection (b) shall not be treated as met in the case of the recovery of an OASDI overpayment from any individual under this section unless the notification under subsection (b)(1) describes the conditions under which the Commissioner of Social Security is required to waive recovery of an overpayment, as provided under section 204(b) of the Social Security Act.

(B) In any case in which an individual files for a waiver under section 204(b) of the Social Security Act within the 60-day period referred to in subsection (b)(2), the Commissioner of Social Security shall not certify to the Secretary of the Treasury that the debt is valid under subsection (b)(4) before rendering a decision on the waiver request under such section 204(b). In lieu of payment, pursuant to subsection (c), to the Commissioner of Social Security of the amount of any reduction under this subsection based on an OASDI overpayment, the Secretary of the Treasury shall deposit such amount in the Federal Old-Age and Survivors Insurance Trust Fund or the Federal Disability Insurance Trust Fund, whichever is certified to the Secretary of the Treasury as appropriate by the Commissioner of Social Security.

(g) In the case of refunds of business associations, this section shall apply only to refunds payable on or after January 1, 1995. In the case of refunds of individuals who owe debts to Federal agencies that have not participated in the Federal tax refund offset program prior to the date of enactment of this subsection, this section shall apply only to refunds payable on or after January 1, 1994.

(h)(1)[13] The disbursing official of the Department of the Treasury—

(1) shall notify a taxpayer in writing of—

(A) the occurrence of an offset to satisfy a past-due legally enforceable nontax debt;

(B) the identity of the creditor agency requesting the offset; and

(C) a contact point within the creditor agency that will handle concerns regarding the offset;

(2) shall notify the Internal Revenue Service on a weekly basis of—

(A) the occurrence of an offset to satisfy a past-due legally enforceable non-tax[14] debt;

---

13 So in original. Subsec. (h) contains two pars. designated (1) and (2).

14 So in original. Probably should not be hyphenated.

(B) the amount of such offset; and

(C) any other information required by regulations; and

(3) shall match payment records with requests for offset by using a name control, taxpayer identifying number (as that term is used in section 6109 of the Internal Revenue Code of 1986), and any other necessary identifiers.

(h)(2)[15] The term "disbursing official" of the Department of the Treasury means the Secretary or his designee.

(i) An agency subject to section 9 of the Act of May 18, 1933 (16 U.S.C. 831h), may implement this section at its discretion.

(Added Pub.L. 98-369, Title VI, § 2653(a)(1), July 18, 1984, 98 Stat. 1153, and amended Pub.L. 101-508, Title V, § 5129(b), Nov. 5, 1990, 104 Stat. 1388-287; Pub.L. 102-589, § 3, Nov. 10, 1992, 106 Stat. 5133; Pub.L. 103-296, Title I, § 108(j)(2), Aug. 15, 1994, 108 Stat. 1488; Pub.L. 104- 134, Title III, § 31001(u)(1), (v)(1), (w), Apr. 26, 1996, 110 Stat. 1321-375.)

§ 3720D. Garnishment

(a) Notwithstanding any provision of State law, the head of an executive, judicial, or legislative agency that administers a program that gives rise to a delinquent nontax debt owed to the United States by an individual may in accordance with this section garnish the disposable pay of the individual to collect the amount owed, if the individual is not currently making required repayment in accordance with any agreement between the agency head and the individual.

(b) In carrying out any garnishment of disposable pay of an individual under subsection (a), the head of an executive, judicial, or legislative agency shall comply with the following requirements:

(1) The amount deducted under this section for any pay period may not exceed 15 percent of disposable pay, except that a greater percentage may be deducted with the written consent of the individual.

(2) The individual shall be provided written notice, sent by mail to the individual's last known address, a minimum of 30 days prior to the initiation of proceedings, from the head of the executive, judicial, or legislative agency, informing the individual of—

(A) the nature and amount of the debt to be collected;

(B) the intention of the agency to initiate proceedings to collect the debt through deductions from pay; and

(C) an explanation of the rights of the individual under this section.

(3) The individual shall be provided an opportunity to inspect and copy records relating to the debt.

(4) The individual shall be provided an opportunity to enter into a written agreement with the executive, judicial, or legislative agency, under terms agreeable to the head of the agency, to establish a schedule for repayment of the debt.

(5) The individual shall be provided an opportunity for a hearing in accordance with subsection (c) on the determination of the head of the executive, judicial, or legislative agency concerning—

(A) the existence or the amount of the debt, and

(B) in the case of an individual whose repayment schedule is established other than by a written agreement pursuant to paragraph (4), the terms of the repayment schedule.

(6) If the individual has been reemployed within 12 months after

---

15 So in original. Subsec. (h) contains two pars. designated (1) and (2).

having been involuntarily separated from employment, no amount may be deducted from the disposable pay of the individual until the individual has been reemployed continuously for at least 12 months.

(c)(1) A hearing under subsection (b)(5) shall be provided prior to issuance of a garnishment order if the individual, on or before the 15th day following the mailing of the notice described in subsection (b)(2), and in accordance with such procedures as the head of the executive, judicial, or legislative agency may prescribe, files a petition requesting such a hearing.

(2) If the individual does not file a petition requesting a hearing prior to such date, the head of the agency shall provide the individual a hearing under subsection (a)(5) [FN1] upon request, but such hearing need not be provided prior to issuance of a garnishment order.

(3) The hearing official shall issue a final decision at the earliest practicable date, but not later than 60 days after the filing of the petition requesting the hearing.

(d) The notice to the employer of the withholding order shall contain only such information as may be necessary for the employer to comply with the withholding order.

(e)(1) An employer may not discharge from employment, refuse to employ, or take disciplinary action against an individual subject to wage withholding in accordance with this section by reason of the fact that the individual's wages have been subject to garnishment under this section, and such individual may sue in a State or Federal court of competent jurisdiction any employer who takes such action.

(2) The court shall award attorneys' fees to a prevailing employee and, in its discretion, may order reinstatement of the individual, award punitive damages and back pay to the employee, or order such other remedy as may be reasonably necessary.

(f)(1) The employer of an individual—

(A) shall pay to the head of an executive, judicial, or legislative agency as directed in a withholding order issued in an action under this section with respect to the individual, and

(B) shall be liable for any amount that the employer fails to withhold from wages due an employee following receipt by such employer of notice of the withholding order, plus attorneys' fees, costs, and, in the court's discretion, punitive damages.

(2)(A) The head of an executive, judicial, or legislative agency may sue an employer in a State or Federal court of competent jurisdiction to recover amounts for which the employer is liable under paragraph (1)(B).

(B) A suit under this paragraph may not be filed before the termination of the collection action, unless earlier filing is necessary to avoid expiration of any applicable statute of limitations period.

(3) Notwithstanding paragraphs (1) and (2), an employer shall not be required to vary its normal pay and disbursement cycles in order to comply with this subsection.

(g) For the purpose of this section, the term "disposable pay" means that part of the compensation of any individual from an employer remaining after the deduction of any amounts required by any other law to be withheld.

(h) The Secretary of the Treasury shall issue regulations to implement this section.

(Added Pub.L. 104-134, Title III, § 31001(o)(1), Apr. 26, 1996, 110 Stat. 1321-369.)

Appendix B   Federal Regulations

Reprinted below are selected regulations for the FFEL, Direct Loan and Perkins Loan programs, as well as general debt collection regulations. Additional regulations can be found on the companion CD-Rom. Key proposed regulations are also available on the companion CD-Rom.

B.1 Selected Debt Collection Procedures

B.1.1 Administrative Offset

34 C.F.R. sec.
30.20   To what do Secs. 30.20-30.31 apply?
30.21   When may the Secretary offset a debt?
30.22   What notice does the debtor receive before the commencement of offset?
30.23   How must a debtor request an opportunity to inspect and copy records relating to a debt?
30.24   What opportunity does the debtor receive to obtain a review of the existence or amount of a debt?
30.25   How may a debtor obtain an oral hearing?
30.26   What special rules apply to an oral hearing?
30.27   When does the Secretary enter into a repayment agreement rather than offset?
30.28   When may the Secretary offset before completing the procedures under §§ 30.22–30.27?
30.29   What procedures apply when the Secretary offsets to collect a debt owed another agency?
30.30   What procedures apply when the Secretary requests another agency to offset a debt owed under a program or activity of the Department?
30.31   How does the Secretary apply funds recovered by offset if multiple debts are involved?

§ 30.20 To what do §§ 30.20–30.31 apply?

(a)(1)(i) Sections 30.20–30.31 establish the general procedures used by the Secretary to collect debts by administrative offset.

(ii) The Secretary uses the procedures established under other regulations, including § 30.33, What procedures does the Secretary follow for IRS tax refund offsets?, 34 CFR part 31, Salary Offset for Federal Employees Who Are Indebted to the United States Under Programs Administered by the Secretary of Education, and 34 CFR part 32, Salary Offset to Recover Overpayments of Pay or Allowances from Department of Education Employees, if the conditions requiring application of those special procedures exists.

(2) The word "offset" is used in this subpart to refer to the collection of a debt by administrative offset.

(b) The Secretary does not rely on 31 U.S.C. 3716 as authority for offset if:

(1) The debt is owed by a State or local government;

(2) The debt, or the payment against which offset would be taken, arises under the Social Security Act;

(3) The debt is owed under:

(i) The Internal Revenue Code of 1954; or

(ii) The tariff laws of the United States; or

(4) The right to collect the debt first accrued more than ten years before initiation of the offset.

(c)(1) The Secretary may rely on 31 U.S.C. 3716 as authority for offset of a debt to which paragraph (b)(4) of this section would otherwise apply if facts material to the Government's right to collect the debt were not known and could not reasonably have been known by the official or officials of the Government who are charged with the responsibility to discover and collect the debt.

(2) If paragraph (c)(1) of this section applies, the Secretary may rely on 31 U.S.C. 3716 as authority for offset up to 10 years after the date that the official or officials described in that paragraph first knew or reasonably should have known of the right of the United States to collect the debt.

(d) The Secretary determines when the right to collect a debt first accrued under the existing law regarding accrual of debts such as 28 U.S.C. 2415.

(Authority: 20 U.S.C. 1221e-3(a)(1) and 1226a-1, 31 U.S.C. 3716(b))

[51 FR 24099, July 1, 1986, as amended at 51 FR 35646, Oct. 7, 1986; 53 FR 33425, Aug. 30, 1988; 54 FR 43583, Oct. 26, 1989]

§ 30.21 When may the Secretary offset a debt?

(a) The Secretary may offset a debt if:

(1) The debt is liquidated or certain in amount; and

(2) Offset is feasible and not otherwise prohibited.

(b)(1) Whether offset is feasible is determined by the Secretary in the exercise of sound discretion on a case-by-case basis, either:

(i) For each individual debt or offset; or

(ii) For each class of similar debts or offsets.

(2) The Secretary considers the following factors in making this determination:

(i) Whether offset can be practically and legally accomplished.

(ii) Whether offset will further and protect the interests of the United States.

(c) The Secretary may switch advance funded grantees to a reimbursement payment system before initiating an offset.

(Authority: 20 U.S.C. 1221e-3(a)(1) and 1226a-1, 31 U.S.C. 3716(b))

§ 30.22 What notice does the debtor receive before the commencement of offset?

(a)(1) Except as provided in §§ 30.28 and 30.29, the Secretary provides a debtor with written notice of the Secretary's intent to offset before initiating the offset.

(2) The Secretary mails the notice to the debtor at the current address of the debtor, as determined by the Secretary from information regarding the debt maintained by the Department.

(b) The written notice informs the debtor regarding:

(1) The nature and amount of the debt;

(2) The Secretary's intent to collect the debt by offset;

(3) The debtor's opportunity to:

(i) Inspect and copy Department records pertaining to the debt;

(ii) Obtain a review within the Department of the existence or amount of the debt; and

(iii) Enter into a written agreement with the Secretary to repay the debt;

(4) The date by which the debtor must request an opportunity set forth under paragraph (b)(3) of this section; and

(5) The Secretary's decision, in appropriate cases, to switch the debtor from advance funding to a reimbursement payment system.

(c)(1) In determining whether a debtor has requested an opportunity set forth under paragraph (b)(3) of this section in a timely manner, the Secretary relies on:

(i) A legibly dated U.S. Postal Service postmark for the debtor's request; or

(ii) A legibly stamped U.S. Postal service mail receipt for debtor's request.

(2) The Secretary does not rely on either of the following as proof of mailing;

(i) A private metered postmark.

(ii) A mail receipt that is not dated by the U.S. Postal Service.

NOTE: The U.S. Postal Service does not uniformly provide a dated postmark. Before relying on this method for proof of mailing, a debtor should check with its local post office.

(d) If a debtor previously has been notified of the Secretary's intent to offset or offered an opportunity to take any of the actions set forth in paragraph (b)(3) of this section in connection with the same debt, the Secretary may offset without providing the debtor with an additional notice of intent or opportunity to take any of those actions under these offset procedures.

(Authority: 20 U.S.C. 1221e-3(a)(1) and 1226a-1, 31 U.S.C. 3716(b))

§ 30.23 How must a debtor request an opportunity to inspect and copy records relating to a debt?

(a) If a debtor wants to inspect and copy Department documents relating to the debt, the debtor must:

(1) File a written request to inspect and copy the documents within 20 days after the date of the notice provided under § 30.22; and

(2) File the request at the address specified in that notice.

(b) A request filed under paragraph (a) of this section must contain:

(1) All information provided to the debtor in the notice under § 30.22 or § 30.33(b) that identifies the debtor and the debt, including the debtor's Social Security number and the program under which

the debt arose, together with any corrections of that identifying information; and

(2) A reasonably specific identification of the records the debtor wishes to have available for inspection and copying.

(c) The Secretary may decline to provide an opportunity to inspect and copy records if the debtor fails to request inspection and copying in accordance with this section.

(Approved by the Office of Management and Budget under control number 1880-0515)

(Authority: 20 U.S.C. 1221e-3(a)(1) and 1226a-1, 31 U.S.C. 3716(b))

[51 FR 24099, July 1, 1986, as amended at 51 FR 35646, Oct. 7, 1986]

§ 30.24 What opportunity does the debtor receive to obtain a review of the existence or amount of a debt?

(a) If a debtor wants a review within the Department of the issues identified in the notice under § 30.22(b)(3)(ii) or § 30.33(b)(3)(ii), the debtor must:

(1) File a request for review within 20 days after the date of the notice provided under § 30.22; and

(2) File a request at the address specified in that notice.

(b) A request filed under paragraph (a) of this section must contain:

(1) All information provided to the debtor in the notice under § 30.22 or § 30.33(b) that identifies the debtor and the particular debt, including the debtor's Social Security number and the program under which the debt arose, together with any corrections of that identifying information; and

(2) An explanation of the reasons the debtor believes that the notice the debtor received under § 30.22 or § 30.33(b) inaccurately states any facts or conclusions relating to the debt.

(c) The Secretary may decline to provide an opportunity for review of a debt if the debtor fails to request the review in accordance with this section.

(d)(1) The debtor shall:

(i) File copies of any documents relating to the issues identified in the notice under § 30.22(b)(3)(ii) or § 30.33(b)(3)(ii) that the debtor wishes the Secretary to consider in the review;

(ii) File the documents at the address specified in that notice, and

(iii) File the documents no later than:

(A) 20 days after the date of the notice provided under § 30.22; or

(B) If the debtor has requested an opportunity to inspect and copy records under § 30.23 within the time period specified in that section, 15 days after the date on which the Secretary makes available to the debtor the relevant, requested records.

(2) The Secretary may decline to consider any reasons or documents that the debtor fails to provide in accordance with paragraphs (b) and (d) of this section.

(e) If the Secretary bases the review on only the documentary evidence, the Secretary:

(1) Reviews the documents submitted by the debtor and other relevant evidence; and

(2) Notifies the debtor in writing of the Secretary's decision regarding the issues identified in the notice under § 30.22(b)(3)(ii) or § 30.33(b)(3)(ii) and, if appropriate, the question of waiver of the debt.

(Approved by the Office of Management and Budget under control number 1880-0515)

(Authority: 20 U.S.C. 1221e-3(a)(1) and 1226a-1, 31 U.S.C. 3716(b))

[51 FR 24099, July 1, 1986, as amended at 51 FR 35647, Oct. 7, 1986]

§ 30.25 How may a debtor obtain an oral hearing?

(a) If a debtor wants the Secretary to conduct the review requested under § 30.24 as an oral hearing, the debtor must file a written request for an oral hearing together with the request for review filed under § 30.24(a).

(b) A request filed under paragraph (a) of this section must contain the following in addition to the information filed under § 30.24(b):

(1) An explanation of reason(s) why the debtor believes the Secretary cannot resolve the issues identified in the notice under § 30.22(b)(3)(ii) or § 30.33(b)(3)(ii) through a review of the documentary evidence.

(2) An identification of:

(i) The individuals that the debtor wishes to have testify at the oral hearing;

(ii) The specific issues identified in the notice regarding which each individual is prepared to testify; and

(iii) The reasons why each individual's testimony is necessary to resolve the issue.

(c) The Secretary grants a debtor's request for an oral hearing regarding the issues identified in the notice under § 30.22(b)(3)(ii) or § 30.33(b)(3)(ii) only if:

(1)(i) A statute authorizes or requires the Secretary to consider waiver of the indebtedness involved;

(ii) The debtor files a request for waiver of the indebtedness with the request for review filed under paragraph (a)(1) of this section; and

(iii) The question of waiver of the indebtedness turns on an issue of credibility or veracity; or

(2) The Secretary determines that the issues identified in the notice under § 30.22(b)(3)(ii) or § 30.33(b)(3)(ii) cannot be resolved by review of only the documentary evidence.

(d) Notwithstanding paragraph (b) of this section, the Secretary may deny oral hearings for a class of similar debts if:

(1) The issues identified in the notice under § 30.22(b)(3)(ii) or 30.33(b)(3)(ii) for which an oral hearing was requested, or the issue of waiver, rarely involve issues of credibility or veracity; and

(2) The Secretary determines that review of the documentary evidence is ordinarily an adequate means to correct mistakes.

(e) The Secretary may decline to consider any reasons that the debtor fails to provide in accordance with paragraph (b)(1) of this section.

(Approved by the Office of Management and Budget under control number 1880-0515)

(Authority: 20 U.S.C. 1221e-3(a)(1) and 1226a-1, 31 U.S.C. 3716(b))

[51 FR 24099, July 1, 1986, as amended at 51 FR 35647, Oct. 7, 1986]

§ 30.26 What special rules apply to an oral hearing?

(a) The oral hearing under § 30.25 is not a formal evidentiary hearing subject to 5 U.S.C. 554, unless required by law.

(b) If the Secretary grants an oral hearing, the Secretary notifies the debtor in writing of:

(1) The time and place for the hearing;

(2) The debtor's right to representation; and

(3) The debtor's right to present and cross examine witnesses.

(c) If the Secretary grants an oral hearing, the Secretary designates an official to:

(1) Govern the conduct of the hearing;

(2) Take all necessary action to avoid unreasonable delay in the proceedings;

(3) Review the evidence presented at the hearing, the documents submitted by the debtor, and other relevant evidence; and

(4) After considering the evidence, notify the debtor in writing of the official's decision regarding the issues identified in the notice under § 30.22(b)(3)(ii) or § 30.33(b)(3)(ii) and, if appropriate, the question of waiver of the debt.

(d) The official designated under paragraph (c) of this section may decline to hear any witnesses or testimony not identified by the debtor in accordance with § 30.25(b)(2).

(e) The decision of the designated official under paragraph (c) of this section constitutes the final decision of the Secretary.

(Authority: 20 U.S.C. 1221-3(a)(1) and 1226a-1, 31 U.S.C. 3716(b))

§ 30.27 When does the Secretary enter into a repayment agreement rather than offset?

(a) If a debtor wants an opportunity to enter into a written agreement to repay a debt on terms acceptable to the Secretary, the debtor must:

(1) File a request to enter into such agreement within 20 days after the date of the notice provided under § 30.22; and

(2) File the request at the address specified in the notice.

(b) A request filed under paragraph (a) of this section must contain all information provided to the debtor in the notice under § 30.22 or § 30.33(b) that identifies the debtor and the debt, including the debtor's Social Security number and the program under which the debt arose, together with any corrections of that identifying information.

(c) If the Secretary receives a request filed in accordance with this section, the Secretary may enter into a written agreement requiring repayment in accordance with 4 CFR 102.11, instead of offsetting the debt.

(d) In deciding whether to enter into the agreement, the Secretary may consider:

(1) The Government's interest in collecting the debt; and

(2) Fairness to the debtor.

(e)(1) A debtor that enters into a repayment agreement with the Secretary under this section waives any right to further review by the Secretary of the issues relating to the original debt identified in the notice under § 30.22(b)(3)(ii) or § 30.33(b)(3)(ii).

(2) If a debtor breaches a repayment agreement, the Secretary may offset, or, under § 30.30, refer to another agency for offset:

(i) The amount owing under the agreement; or

(ii) The entire original debt, to the extent not repaid.

(Authority: 20 U.S.C. 1221-3(a)(1) and 1226a-1, 31 U.S.C. 3716(b))

[51 FR 24099, July 1, 1986, as amended at 51 FR 35647, Oct. 7, 1986]

§ 30.28 When may the Secretary offset before completing the procedures under §§ 30.22–30.27?

(a) The Secretary may offset before completing the procedures otherwise required by §§ 30.22–30.27 if:

(1) Failure to offset would substantially prejudice the Government's ability to collect the debt; and

(2) The amount of time remaining before the payment by the United States which is subject to offset does not reasonably permit completion of the procedures under §§ 30.22–30.27.

(b) If the Secretary offsets under paragraph (a) of this section, the Secretary:

(1) Promptly completes the procedures under §§ 30.22–30.27 after initiating the offset; and

(2) Refunds any amounts recovered under the offset that are later found not to be owed to the United States.

(Authority: 20 U.S.C. 1221e-3(a)(1) and 1226a-1, 31 U.S.C. 3716(b))

§ 30.29 What procedures apply when the Secretary offsets to collect a debt owed another agency?

The Secretary may initiate offset to collect a debt owed another Federal agency if:

(a) An official of that agency certifies in writing:

(1) That the debtor owes a debt to the United States;

(2) The amount of the debt; and

(3) That the agency has complied with 4 CFR 102.3; and

(b) For offsets under 31 U.S.C. 3716, the Secretary makes an independent determination that the offset meets the standards under § 30.21(a)(2).

(Authority: 20 U.S.C. 1221e-3(a)(1) and 1226a-1, 31 U.S.C. 3716(b))

§ 30.30 What procedures apply when the Secretary requests another agency to offset a debt owed under a program or activity of the Department?

(a) The Secretary may request another Federal agency to offset a debt owed under a program or activity of the Department if the Secretary certifies in writing to the other Federal agency:

(1) That the debtor owes a debt to the United States;

(2) The amount of the debt; and

(3) That the Secretary has complied with 4 CFR 102.3.

(b) Before providing the certification required under paragraph (a) of this section, the Secretary complies with the procedures in §§ 30.20–30.27.

(Authority: 20 U.S.C. 1221e-3(a)(1) and 1226a-1, 31 U.S.C. 3716(b))

§ 30.31 How does the Secretary apply funds recovered by offset if multiple debts are involved?

If the Secretary collects more than one debt of a debtor by administrative offset, the Secretary applies the recovered funds to satisfy those debts based on the Secretary's determination of the best interests of the United States, determined by the facts and circumstances of the particular case.

(Authority: 20 U.S.C. 1221e-3(a)(1) and 1226a-1, 31 U.S.C. 3716(b))

B.1.2 Tax Refund Offset

34 C.F.R. sec.

30.33 What procedures does the Secretary follow for IRS tax refund offsets?

§ 30.33 What procedures does the Secretary follow for IRS tax refund offsets?

(a) If a named person owes a debt under a program or activity of the Department, the Secretary may refer the debt for offset to the Secretary of the Treasury after complying with the procedures in §§ 30.20–30.28, as modified by this section.

(b) Notwithstanding § 30.22(b), the notice sent to a debtor under § 30.22 informs the debtor that:

(1) The debt is past due;

(2) The Secretary intends to refer the debt for offset to the Secretary of Treasury;

(3) The debtor has an opportunity to:

(i) Inspect and copy Department records regarding the existence, amount, enforceability, or past-due status of the debt;

(ii) Obtain a review within the Department of the existence, amount, enforceability, or past-due status of the debt;

(iii) Enter into a written agreement with the Secretary to repay the debt; and

(4) The debtor must take an action set forth under paragraph (b)(3) by a date specified in the notice.

(c) Notwithstanding § 30.23(a), if a debtor wants to inspect and copy Department records regarding the existence, amount, enforceability, or past-due status of the debt, the debtor must:

(1) File a written request to inspect and copy the records within 20 days after the date of the notice provided under § 30.22; and

(2) File the request at the address specified in that notice.

(d) Notwithstanding the time frame under § 30.24(a), if a debtor wants a review under that paragraph, the debtor must file a request for review at the address specified in the notice by the later of:

(1) Sixty-five days after the date of the notice provided under § 30.22;

(2) If the debtor has requested an opportunity to inspect and copy records within the time period specified in paragraph (c) of this section, 15 days after the date on which the Secretary makes available to the debtor the relevant, requested records; or

(3) If the debtor has requested a review within the appropriate time frame under paragraph (d) (1) or (2) of this section and the Secretary has provided an initial review by a guarantee agency, seven days after the date of the initial determination by the guarantee agency.

(e) Notwithstanding the time frames under § 30.24(d), a debtor shall file the documents specified under that paragraph with the request for review.

(f) Notwithstanding the time frame under § 30.27(a), a debtor must agree to repay the debt under terms acceptable to the Secretary and make the first payment due under the agreement by the latest of:

(1) The seventh day after the date of decision of the Secretary if the debtor requested a review under § 30.24;

(2) The sixty-fifth day after the date of the notice under § 30.22(b),

if the debtor did not request a review under § 30.24, or an opportunity to inspect and copy records of the Department under § 30.23; or

(3) The fifteenth day after the date on which the Secretary made available relevant records regarding the debt, if the debtor filed a timely request under § 30.23(a).

(Authority: 20 U.S.C. 1221e-3(a)(1) and 1226a-1, 31 U.S.C. 3720A)

* * *

B.1.3 Collection Costs and Penalties

34 C.F.R. sec.

30.60 What costs does the Secretary impose on delinquent debtors?

§ 30.60 What costs does the Secretary impose on delinquent debtors?

(a) The Secretary may charge a debtor for the costs associated with the collection of a particular debt. These costs include, but are not limited to—

(1) Salaries of employees performing Federal loan servicing and debt collection activities;

(2) Telephone and mailing costs;

(3) Costs for reporting debts to credit bureaus;

(4) Costs for purchase of credit bureau reports;

(5) Costs associated with computer operations and other costs associated with the maintenance of records;

(6) Bank charges;

(7) Collection agency costs;

(8) Court costs and attorney fees; and

(9) Costs charged by other Governmental agencies.

(b) Notwithstanding any provision of State law, if the Secretary uses a collection agency to collect a debt on a contingent fee basis, the Secretary charges the debtor, and collects through the agency, an amount sufficient to recover—

(1) The entire amount of the debt; and

(2) The amount that the Secretary is required to pay the agency for its collection services.

(c)(1) The amount recovered under paragraph (b) of this section is the entire amount of the debt, multiplied by the following fraction:

[Graphic Omitted]

(2) In paragraph (c)(1) of this section, cr equals the commission rate the Department pays to the collection agency.

(d) If the Secretary uses more than one collection agency to collect similar debts, the commission rate (cr) described in paragraph (c)(2) of this section is calculated as a weighted average of the commission rates charged by all collection agencies collecting similar debts, computed for each fiscal year based on the formula

[Graphic Omitted]

where—

(1) Xi equals the dollar amount of similar debts placed by the Department with an individual collection agency as of the end of the preceding fiscal year;

(2) Yi equals the commission rate the Department pays to that collection agency for the collection of the similar debts;

(3) Z equals the dollar amount of similar debts placed by the Department with all collection agencies as of the end of the preceding fiscal year; and

(4) N equals the number of collection agencies with which the Secretary has placed similar debts as of the end of the preceding fiscal year.

(e) If a debtor has agreed under a repayment or settlement agreement with the Secretary to pay costs associated with the collection of a debt at a specified amount or rate, the Secretary collects those costs in accordance with the agreement.

(f) The Secretary does not impose collection costs against State or local governments under paragraphs (a) through (d) of this section.

(Authority: 20 U.S.C. 1221e-3(a)(1) and 1226a-1, 31 U.S.C. 3711(e), 3717(e)(1), 3718)

§ 30.61 What penalties does the Secretary impose on delinquent debtors?

(a) If a debtor does not make a payment on a debt, or portion of a debt, within 90 days after the date specified in the first demand for payment sent to the debtor, the Secretary imposes a penalty on the debtor.

(b)(1) The amount of the penalty imposed under paragraph (a) of this section is 6 percent per year of the amount of the delinquent debt.

(2) The penalty imposed under this section runs from the date specified in the first demand for payment to the date the debt (including the penalty) is paid.

(c) If a debtor has agreed under a repayment or settlement agreement with the Secretary to pay a penalty for failure to pay a debt when due, or has such an agreement under a grant or contract under which the debt arose, the Secretary collects the penalty in accordance with the agreement, grant, or contract.

(d) The Secretary does not impose a penalty against State or local governments under paragraphs (a) and (b) of this section.

(Authority: 20 U.S.C. 1221e-3(a)(1) and 1226a-1, 31 U.S.C. 3711(e))

B.1.4 Compromise of Debts

34 C.F.R. sec.

30.70 How does the Secretary exercise discretion to compromise a debt or to suspend or terminate collection of a debt?

§ 30.70 How does the Secretary exercise discretion to compromise a debt or to suspend or terminate collection of a debt?

(a) The Secretary uses the standards in the FCCS, 4 CFR part 103, to determine whether compromise of a debt is appropriate if—

(1) The debt must be referred to the Department of Justice under this section; or

(2) The amount of the debt is less than or equal to $20,000 and the Secretary does not follow the procedures in paragraph (e) of this section.

(b) The Secretary refers a debt to the Department of Justice to decide whether to compromise a debt if—

(1) The debt was incurred under a program or activity subject to section 452(f) of the General Education Provisions Act and the initial determination of the debt was more than $50,000; or

(2) The debt was incurred under a program or activity not subject to section 452(f) of the General Education Provisions Act and the amount of the debt is more than $20,000.

(c) The Secretary may compromise the debt under the procedures in paragraph (e) of this section if—

(1) The debt was incurred under a program or activity subject to section 452(f) of the General Education Provisions Act; and

(2) The initial determination of the debt was less than or equal to $50,000.

(d) The Secretary may compromise a debt without following the procedure in paragraph (e) of this section if the amount of the debt is less than or equal to $20,000.

(e) The Secretary may compromise the debt pursuant to paragraph (c) of this section if—

(1) The Secretary determines that—

(i) Collection of any or all of the debt would not be practical or in the public interest; and

(ii) The practice that resulted in the debt has been corrected and will not recur;

(2) At least 45 days before compromising the debt, the Secretary publishes a notice in the Federal Register stating—

(i) The Secretary's intent to compromise the debt; and

(ii) That interested persons may comment on the proposed compromise; and

(3) The Secretary considers any comments received in response to the Federal Register notice before finally compromising the debt.

(f)(1) The Secretary uses the standards in the FCCS, 4 CFR part 104, to determine whether suspension or termination of collection action is appropriate.

(2) The Secretary—

(i) Refers the debt to the Department of Justice to decide whether to suspend or terminate collection action if the amount of the debt at the time of the referral is more than $20,000; or

(ii) May decide to suspend or terminate collection action if the amount of the debt at the time of the Secretary's decision is less than or equal to $20,000.

(g) In determining the amount of a debt under paragraphs (a) through (f) of this section, the Secretary excludes interest, penalties, and administrative costs.

(h) Notwithstanding paragraphs (b) through (f) of this section, the Secretary may compromise a debt, or suspend or terminate collection of a debt, in any amount if the debt arises under the Guaranteed Student Loan Program authorized under title IV, part B, of the Higher Education Act of 1965, as amended, or the Perkins Loan Program authorized under title IV, part E, of the Higher Education Act of 1965, as amended.

(i) The Secretary refers a debt to the General Accounting Office (GAO) for review and approval before referring the debt to the Department of Justice for litigation if—

(1) The debt arose from an audit exception taken by GAO to a payment made by the Department; and

(2) The GAO has not granted an exception from the GAO referral requirement.

(j) Nothing in this section precludes—

(1) A contracting officer from exercising his authority under applicable statutes, regulations, or common law to settle disputed claims relating to a contract; or

(2) The Secretary from redetermining a claim.

(Authority: 20 U.S.C. 1082(a) (5) and (6), 1087hh, 1221e-3(a)(1), 1226a-1, and 1234a(f), 31 U.S.C. 3711(e))

[53 FR 33425, Aug. 30, 1988]

B.1.5 Department of Treasury Debt Collection Regulations

34 C.F.R. sec.
285.4 Offset of Federal benefit payments to collect past-due, legally enforceable nontax debt.

§ 285.4 Offset of Federal benefit payments to collect past-due, legally enforceable nontax debt.

(a) *Scope.* (1) This section sets forth special rules applicable to the offset of Federal benefit payments payable to an individual under the Social Security Act (other than Supplemental Security Income (SSI) payments), part B of the Black Lung Benefits Act, or any law administered by the Railroad Retirement Board (other than payments that such Board determines to be tier 2 benefits) to collect delinquent nontax debt owed to the United States.

(2) As used in this section, benefit payments "due to" an individual, "payable to" an individual, and/or benefit payments "received by" an individual, refer to those benefit payments expected to be paid to an individual before any amounts are offset to satisfy the payee's delinquent debt owed to the United States. Nothing in these phrases, similar phrases, or this section is intended to imply or confer any new or additional rights or benefits on an individual with respect to his or her entitlement to benefit payments. The Financial Management Service (FMS), the Social Security Administration, the Railroad Retirement Board, and other payment agencies are not liable for the amount offset from an individual's benefit payment on the basis that the underlying obligation, represented by the payment before the offset was taken, was not satisfied. See 31 U.S.C. 3716(c)(2)(A).

(b) *Definitions.* As used in this section:

Administrative offset or *offset* means withholding funds payable by the United States (including funds payable by the United States on behalf of a State government) to, or held by the United States for, a person to satisfy a debt.

Agency or *Federal agency* means a department, agency, court, court administrative office, or instrumentality in the executive, judicial, or legislative branch of the Federal Government, including government corporations.

Covered benefit payment means a Federal benefit payment payable to an individual under the Social Security Act (other than SSI payments), part B of the Black Lung Benefits Act, or any law administered by the Railroad Retirement Board (other than payments that such Board determines to be tier 2 benefits). The amount of the covered benefit payment payable to a debtor for purposes of this section will be the amount after reduction or deduction required under the laws authorizing the program. Reductions to recover benefit overpayments are excluded from the covered benefit payment when calculating amounts available for offset.

Creditor agency means a Federal agency owed a debt that seeks to collect that debt through administrative offset.

Debt or *claim* means an amount of money, funds, or property which has been determined by an agency official to be due the United States from any person, organization, or entity except another Federal agency. Debt or claim does not include a debt or claim arising under the Internal Revenue Code of 1986 or the tariff laws of the United States.

Debtor means a person who owes a debt. The term "person" includes any individual, organization or entity, except another Federal agency.

Disbursing official means an official who has authority to disburse public money pursuant to 31 U.S.C. 3321 or another law, including an official of the Department of the Treasury, the Department of Defense, the United States Postal Service, or any other government corporation, or any official of the United States designated by the Secretary of the Treasury to disburse public money.

FMS means the Financial Management Service, a bureau of the Department of the Treasury.

Monthly covered benefit payment means a covered benefit payment payable to a payee on a recurring basis at monthly intervals that is not expressly limited in duration, at the time the first payment is made, to a period of less than 12 months.

Payee means a person who is due a payment from a disbursing official. For purposes of this section, a "payee" is a person who is entitled to the benefit of all or part of a payment from a disbursing official.

Taxpayer identifying number means the identifying number described under section 6109 of the Internal Revenue Code of 1986 (26 U.S.C. 6109). For an individual, the taxpayer identifying number generally is the individual's social security number.

(c) *Administrative offset, generally.* Disbursing officials shall offset payments to satisfy, in whole or in part, debts owed by the payee. Disbursing officials shall compare payment records with records of debts submitted to FMS for collection by administrative offset. A match will occur when the taxpayer identifying number and name of the payee (as defined in paragraph (b) of this section) on a payment record are the same as the taxpayer identifying number and name of the debtor on a debt record. When a match occurs and all other requirements for offset have been met, the disbursing official shall offset the payment to satisfy, in whole or in part, the debt. Any amounts not offset shall be paid to the payee. Covered benefit payments, i.e., payments made to individuals under the Social Security Act (other than Supplemental Security Income (SSI) payments), part B of the Black Lung Benefits Act, or any law administered by the Railroad Retirement Board (RRB) (other than tier 2 benefit payments) are among the types of payments which may be offset to collect debts owed to the United States. Offset of covered benefit payments are subject to the limitations contained in this section. Offsets of covered benefit payments will occur only if the name and taxpayer identifying number of the person who is entitled to the benefit of all or a part of the payment matches the name and taxpayer identifying number of the debtor.

(d) *Submission of debts to FMS for collection by administrative offset.* Creditor agencies must notify FMS of all past-due, legally enforceable debt delinquent for more than 180 days for purposes of collection by administrative offset. Creditor agencies may notify FMS of all debt delinquent for less than 180 days for purposes of collection by administrative offset. Prior to such notification, creditor agencies must certify to FMS that the debt is past-due, legally enforceable, and that the creditor agency has provided the debtor with notice and an opportunity for a review in accordance with the

provisions of 31 U.S.C. 3716(a) and other applicable law.

(e) *Offset amount.* (1) The amount offset from a monthly covered benefit payment shall be the lesser of:

(i) The amount of the debt, including any interest, penalties and administrative costs;

(ii) An amount equal to 15% of the monthly covered benefit payment; or

(iii) The amount, if any, by which the monthly covered benefit payment exceeds $750.

(2) A debtor shall not receive a refund of any amounts offset if the debtor's monthly covered benefit payments are reduced, suspended, terminated, or otherwise not received for a period of 12 months.

(3) *Examples.* (i) A debtor receives monthly Social Security benefits of $850. The amount offset is the lesser of $127.50 (15% of $850) or $100 (the amount by which $850 exceeds $750). In this example, the amount offset is $100 (assuming the debt is $100 or more).

(ii) A debtor receives monthly Social Security benefits of $1250. The amount offset is the lesser of $187.50 (15% of $1250) or $500 (the amount by which $1250 exceeds $750). In this example, the amount offset is $187.50 (assuming the debt is $187.50 or more).

(iii) A debtor receives monthly Social Security payments of $650. No amount will be offset because $650 is less than $750.

(f) *Notification of offset.* (1) Before offsetting a covered benefit payment, the disbursing official will notify the payee in writing of the date offset will commence. The notice shall inform the payee of the type of payment that will be offset; the identity of the creditor agency which requested the offset; and a contact point within the creditor agency that will handle concerns regarding the offset.

(2) The disbursing official conducting the offset will notify the payee in writing of the occurrence of the offset to satisfy, in whole or in part, a delinquent debt owed to the United States. The notice shall inform the payee of the type and amount of the payment that was offset; the identity of the creditor agency which requested the offset; and a contact point within the creditor agency that will handle concerns regarding the offset.

(3) Non-receipt by the debtor of the notices described in paragraphs (f)(1) and (f)(2) of this section shall not impair the legality of the administrative offset.

(g) *Fees.* A fee which FMS has determined to be sufficient to cover the full cost of the offset procedure, shall be deducted from each offset amount. Creditor agencies may add this fee to the debt if not otherwise prohibited by law.

(h) *Disposition of amounts collected.* The disbursing official conducting the offset will transmit amounts collected for debts, less fees charged under paragraph (g) of this section, to the appropriate creditor agency. If an erroneous offset payment is made to a creditor agency, the disbursing official will notify the creditor agency that an erroneous offset payment has been made. The disbursing official may deduct the amount of the erroneous offset payment from future amounts payable to the creditor agency. Alternatively, upon the disbursing official's request, the creditor agency shall return promptly to the disbursing official or the affected payee an amount equal to the amount of the erroneous payment. The disbursing official and the creditor agency shall adjust the debtor records appropriately.

[63 FR 44988, Aug. 21, 1998; 63 FR 71204, Dec. 23, 1998]

§ 901.3 Collection by administrative offset.

(a) *Scope.* (1) The term "administrative offset" has the meaning provided in 31 U.S.C. 3701(a)(1).

(2) This section does not apply to:

(i) Debts arising under the Social Security Act, except as provided in 42 U.S.C. 404;

(ii) Payments made under the Social Security Act, except as provided for in 31 U.S.C. 3716(c) (*see* 31 CFR 285.4, Federal Benefit Offset);

(iii) Debts arising under, or payments made under, the Internal Revenue Code (*see* 31 CFR 285.2, Tax Refund Offset) or the tariff laws of the United States;

(iv) Offsets against Federal salaries to the extent these standards are inconsistent with regulations published to implement such offsets under 5 U.S.C. 5514 and 31 U.S.C. 3716 (*see* 5 CFR part 550, subpart K, and 31 CFR 285.7, Federal Salary Offset);

(v) Offsets under 31 U.S.C. 3728 against a judgment obtained by a debtor against the United States;

(vi) Offsets or recoupments under common law, State law, or Federal statutes specifically prohibiting offsets or recoupments of particular types of debts; or

(vii) Offsets in the course of judicial proceedings, including bankruptcy.

(3) Unless otherwise provided for by contract or law, debts or payments that are not subject to administrative offset under 31 U.S.C. 3716 may be collected by administrative offset under the common law or other applicable statutory authority.

(4) Unless otherwise provided by law, administrative offset of payments under the authority of 31 U.S.C. 3716 to collect a debt may not be conducted more than 10 years after the Government's right to collect the debt first accrued, unless facts material to the Government's right to collect the debt were not known and could not reasonably have been known by the official or officials of the Government who were charged with the responsibility to discover and collect such debts. This limitation does not apply to debts reduced to a judgment.

(5) In bankruptcy cases, agencies should seek legal advice from their agency counsel concerning the impact of the Bankruptcy Code, particularly 11 U.S.C. 106, 362, and 553, on pending or contemplated collections by offset.

(b) *Mandatory centralized administrative offset.* (1) Creditor agencies are required to refer past due, legally enforceable nontax debts which are over 180 days delinquent to the Secretary for collection by centralized administrative offset. Debts which are less than 180 days delinquent also may be referred to the Secretary for this purpose. *See* § 901.3(b)(5) for debt certification requirements.

(2) The names and taxpayer identifying numbers (TINs) of debtors who owe debts referred to the Secretary as described in paragraph (b)(1) of this section shall be compared to the names and TINs on payments to be made by Federal disbursing officials. Federal disbursing officials include disbursing officials of Treasury, the Department of Defense, the United States Postal Service, other Government corporations, and disbursing officials of the United States designated by the Secretary. When the name and TIN of a debtor match the name and TIN of a payee and all other requirements for offset have been met, the payment will be offset to satisfy the debt.

(3) Federal disbursing officials will notify the debtor/payee in writing that an offset has occurred to satisfy, in part or in full, a past due, legally enforceable delinquent debt. The notice shall include a description of the type and amount of the payment from which the offset was taken, the amount of offset that was taken, the identity of the creditor agency requesting the offset, and a contact point within the creditor agency who will respond to questions regarding the offset.

(4)(i) Before referring a delinquent debt to the Secretary for administrative offset, agencies must have prescribed administrative offset regulations consistent with this section or have adopted this section without change by cross-reference.

(ii) Such regulations shall provide that offsets may be initiated only after the debtor:

(A) Has been sent written notice of the type and amount of the debt, the intention of the agency to use administrative offset to collect the debt, and an explanation of the debtor's rights under 31 U.S.C. 3716; and

(B) The debtor has been given:

(1) The opportunity to inspect and copy agency records related to the debt;

(2) The opportunity for a review within the agency of the determination of indebtedness; and

(3) The opportunity to make a written agreement to repay the debt.

(iii) Agency regulations may provide for the omission of the procedures set forth in paragraph (a)(4)(ii) of this section when:

(A) The offset is in the nature of a recoupment;

(B) The debt arises under a contract as set forth in *Cecile Industries, Inc. v. Cheney*, 995 F.2d 1052 (Fed. Cir. 1993) (notice and other procedural protections set forth in 31 U.S.C. 3716(a) do not supplant or restrict established procedures for contractual offsets accommodated by the Contracts Disputes Act); or

(C) In the case of non-centralized administrative offsets conducted under paragraph (c) of this section, the agency first learns of the existence of the amount owed by the debtor when there is insufficient time before payment would be made to the debtor/payee to allow for prior notice and an opportunity for review. When prior notice and an opportunity for review are omitted, the agency shall give the debtor such notice and an opportunity for review as soon as practicable and shall promptly refund any money ultimately found not to have been owed to the Government.

(iv) When an agency previously has given a debtor any of the required notice and review opportunities with respect to a particular debt (*see, e.g.,* § 901.2), the agency need not duplicate such notice and review opportunities before administrative offset may be initiated.

(5) Agencies referring delinquent debts to the Secretary must certify, in a form acceptable to the Secretary, that:

(i) The debt(s) is (are) past due and legally enforceable; and

(ii) The agency has complied with all due process requirements under 31 U.S.C. 3716(a) and the agency's regulations.

(6) Payments that are prohibited by law from being offset are exempt from centralized administrative offset. The Secretary shall exempt payments under means-tested programs from centralized administrative offset when requested in writing by the head of the payment certifying or authorizing agency. Also, the Secretary may exempt other classes of payments from centralized offset upon the written request of the head of the payment certifying or authorizing agency.

(7) Benefit payments made under the Social Security Act (42 U.S.C. 301 *et seq.*), part B of the Black Lung Benefits Act (30

U.S.C. 921 et seq.), and any law administered by the Railroad Retirement Board (other than tier 2 benefits), may be offset only in accordance with Treasury regulations, issued in consultation with the Social Security Administration, the Railroad Retirement Board, and the Office of Management and Budget. See 31 CFR 285.4.

(8) In accordance with 31 U.S.C. 3716(f), the Secretary may waive the provisions of the Computer Matching and Privacy Protection Act of 1988 concerning matching agreements and post-match notification and verification (5 U.S.C. 552a(o) and (p)) for centralized administrative offset upon receipt of a certification from a creditor agency that the due process requirements enumerated in 31 U.S.C. 3716(a) have been met. The certification of a debt in accordance with paragraph (b)(5) of this section will satisfy this requirement. If such a waiver is granted, only the Data Integrity Board of the Department of the Treasury is required to oversee any matching activities, in accordance with 31 U.S.C. 3716(g). This waiver authority does not apply to offsets conducted under paragraphs (c) and (d) of this section.

(c) *Non-centralized administrative offset.* (1) Generally, non-centralized administrative offsets are ad hoc case-by-case offsets that an agency conducts, at the agency's discretion, internally or in cooperation with the agency certifying or authorizing payments to the debtor. Unless otherwise prohibited by law, when centralized administrative offset is not available or appropriate, past due, legally enforceable nontax delinquent debts may be collected through non-centralized administrative offset. In these cases, a creditor agency may make a request directly to a payment authorizing agency to offset a payment due a debtor to collect a delinquent debt. For example, it may be appropriate for a creditor agency to request that the Office of Personnel Management (OPM) offset a Federal employee's lump sum payment upon leaving Government service to satisfy an unpaid advance.

(2) Before requesting a payment authorizing agency to conduct a non-centralized administrative offset, agencies must adopt regulations providing that such offsets may occur only after:

(i) The debtor has been provided due process as set forth in paragraph (b)(4) of this section; and

(ii) The payment authorizing agency has received written certification from the creditor agency that the debtor owes the past due, legally enforceable delinquent debt in the amount stated, and that the creditor agency has fully complied with its regulations concerning administrative offset.

(3) Payment authorizing agencies shall comply with offset requests by creditor agencies to collect debts owed to the United States, unless the offset would not be in the best interests of the United States with respect to the program of the payment authorizing agency, or would otherwise be contrary to law. Appropriate use should be made of the cooperative efforts of other agencies in effecting collection by administrative offset.

(4) When collecting multiple debts by non-centralized administrative offset, agencies should apply the recovered amounts to those debts in accordance with the best interests of the United States, as determined by the facts and circumstances of the particular case, particularly the applicable statute of limitations.

(d) *Requests to OPM to offset a debtor's anticipated or future benefit payments under the Civil Service Retirement and Disability Fund.* Upon providing OPM written certification that a debtor has been afforded the procedures provided in paragraph (b)(4) of this section, creditor agencies may request OPM to offset a debtor's anticipated or future benefit payments under the Civil Service

Retirement and Disability Fund (Fund) in accordance with regulations codified at 5 CFR 831.1801-831.1808. Upon receipt of such a request, OPM will identify and "flag" a debtor's account in anticipation of the time when the debtor requests, or becomes eligible to receive, payments from the Fund. This will satisfy any requirement that offset be initiated prior to the expiration of the time limitations referenced in paragraph (a)(4) of this section.

(e) *Review requirements.* (1) For purposes of this section, whenever an agency is required to afford a debtor a review within the agency, the agency shall provide the debtor with a reasonable opportunity for an oral hearing when the debtor requests reconsideration of the debt and the agency determines that the question of the indebtedness cannot be resolved by review of the documentary evidence, for example, when the validity of the debt turns on an issue of credibility or veracity.

(2) Unless otherwise required by law, an oral hearing under this section is not required to be a formal evidentiary hearing, although the agency should carefully document all significant matters discussed at the hearing.

(3) This section does not require an oral hearing with respect to debt collection systems in which a determination of indebtedness rarely involves issues of credibility or veracity and the agency has determined that review of the written record is ordinarily an adequate means to correct prior mistakes.

(4) In those cases when an oral hearing is not required by this section, an agency shall accord the debtor a "paper hearing," that is, a determination of the request for reconsideration based upon a review of the written record.

B.2 FFEL Regulations

§ 682.200 Definitions.

(a)(1) The definitions of the following terms used in this part are set forth in subpart A of the Student Assistance General Provisions, 34 CFR part 668:

Academic year
Campus-based programs
Dependent student
Eligible program
Eligible student

Enrolled
Federal Consolidation Loan Program
Federal Pell Grant Program
Federal Perkins Loan Program
Federal PLUS Program
Federal Work-Study (FWS) Program
Full-time student
Independent student
Leveraging Educational Assistance Partnership (LEAP) Program
National of the United States (Referred to as U.S. Citizen or National in 34 CFR 668.2)
Payment period
Supplemental Educational Opportunity Grant (SEOG) Program
Supplemental Loans for Students (SLS) Program

(2) The following definitions are set forth in the regulations for Institutional Eligibility under the Higher Education Act of 1965, as amended, 34 CFR part 600:

Accredited
Clock hour
Correspondence course
Educational program
Federal Family Education Loan Program (formerly known as the Guaranteed Student Loan (GSL) Program)
Institution of higher education (§ 600.4)
Nationally recognized accrediting agency
Postsecondary Vocational Institution
Preaccredited
Secretary
State

(3) The definition for cost of attendance is set forth in section 472 of the Act, as amended.

(b) The following definitions also apply to this part:

Act. The Higher Education Act of 1965, as amended, 20 U.S.C. 1071 et seq.

Actual interest rate. The annual interest rate a lender charges on a loan, which may be equal to or less than the applicable interest rate on that loan.

Applicable interest rate. The maximum annual interest rate that a lender may charge under the Act on a loan.

Authority. Any private non-profit or public entity that may issue tax-exempt obligations to obtain funds to be used for the making or purchasing of FFEL loans. The term "Authority" also includes any agency, including a State postsecondary institution or any other instrumentality of a State or local governmental unit, regardless of the designation or primary purpose of that agency, that may issue tax-exempt obligations, any party authorized to issue those obligations on behalf of a governmental agency, and any non-profit organization authorized by law to issue tax-exempt obligations.

Borrower. An individual to whom a FFEL Program loan is made.

Co-Maker: One of two married individuals who jointly borrow a Consolidation loan, each of whom are eligible and who are jointly and severally liable for repayment of the loan. The term co-maker also includes one of two parents who are joint borrowers as previously authorized in the PLUS Program.

Default. The failure of a borrower and endorser, if any, or joint borrowers on a PLUS or Consolidation loan, to make an installment payment when due, or to meet other terms of the promissory note, the Act, or regulations as applicable, if the Secretary or guaranty agency finds it reasonable to conclude that the borrower and endorser, if any, no longer intend to honor the obligation to repay, provided that this failure persists for—

(1) 270 days for a loan repayable in monthly installments; or

(2) 330 days for a loan repayable in less frequent installments.

Disbursement. The transfer of loan proceeds by a lender to a holder, in the case of a Consolidation loan, or to a borrower, a school, or an escrow agent by issuance of an individual check, a master check or by electronic funds transfer that may represent loan amounts for borrowers.

Disposable income. That part of an individual's compensation from an employer and other income from any source, including spousal income, that remains after the deduction of any amounts required by law to be withheld, or any child support or alimony payments that are made under a court order or legally enforceable written agreement. Amounts required by law to be withheld include, but are not limited, to Federal, State, and local taxes, Social Security contributions, and wage garnishment payments.

Endorser. An individual who signs a promissory note and agrees to repay the loan in the event that the borrower does not.

Escrow agent. Any guaranty agency or other eligible lender that receives the proceeds of a FFEL program loan as an agent of an eligible lender for the purpose of transmitting those proceeds to the borrower or the borrower's school.

Estimated financial assistance. (1) The estimated amount of assistance for a period of enrollment that a student (or a parent on behalf of a student) will receive from Federal, State, institutional, or other sources, such as, scholarships, grants, financial need-based employment, or loans, including but not limited to—

(i) Except as provided in paragraph (2)(iii) of this definition, national service education awards or post-service benefits under title I of the National and Community Service Act of 1990 and veterans' educational benefits paid under chapters 30, 31, 32, and 35 of title 38 of the United States Code;

(ii) Educational benefits paid under Chapters 106 and 107 of Title 10 of the United States Code (Selected Reserve Educational Assistance Program);

(iii) Reserve Officer Training Corps (ROTC) scholarships and subsistence allowances awarded under Chapter 2 of Title 10 and Chapter 2 of Title 37 of the United States Code;

(iv) Benefits paid under Pub.L. 97-376, section 156: Restored Entitlement Program for Survivors (or Quayle benefits);

(v) Benefits paid under Pub.L. 96-342, section 903: Educational Assistance Pilot Program;

(vi) Any educational benefits paid because of enrollment in a postsecondary education institution;

(vii) The estimated amount of other Federal student financial aid, including but not limited to a Federal Pell Grant, campus-based aid, and the gross amount (including fees) of a Federal Stafford, Unsubsidized Stafford and Federal PLUS loan.

(2) The estimated amount of assistance does not include—

(i) Those amounts used to replace the expected family contribution, including—

(A) Unsubsidized and nonsubsidized Stafford loan amounts for which interest benefits are not payable.

(B) PLUS loan amounts; and

(C) Private and state-sponsored loan programs;

(ii) Federal Perkins loan and Federal Work-Study funds that the school determines the student has declined; and

(iii) For the purpose of determining eligibility for a subsidized Stafford loan, veterans' educational benefits paid under chapter 30 of title 38 of the United States Code (Montgomery GI Bill—Active Duty) and national service education awards or post-service benefits under title I of the National and Community Service Act of 1990.

Expected family contribution. The amount a student and his or her spouse and family are expected to pay toward the student's cost of attendance.

Federal GSL programs. The Federal Insured Student Loan Program, the Federal Supplemental Loans for Students Program, the Federal PLUS Program, and the Federal Consolidation Loan Program. Federal Insured Student Loan Program. The loan program authorized by title IV-B of the Act under which the Secretary directly insures lenders against losses.

Foreign school. A school not located in a State.

Grace period. The period that begins on the day after a Stafford loan borrower ceases to be enrolled as at least a half-time student at an institution of higher education and ends on the day before the repayment period begins. See also "Post-deferment grace period." For an SLS borrower who also has a Federal Stafford loan on which the borrower has not yet entered repayment, the grace period is an equivalent period after the borrower ceases to be enrolled as at least a half-time student at an institution of higher education.

Graduate or professional student. A student who, for a period of enrollment—

(1) Is enrolled in a program above the baccalaureate level at an institution of higher education or is enrolled in a program leading to a first professional degree;

(2) Has completed the equivalent of at least three academic years of full-time study at an institution of higher education, either before entrance into the program or as part of the program itself; and

(3) Is not receiving aid under title IV of the Act ás an undergraduate student for the same period of enrollment. Guaranty agency. A State or private nonprofit organization that has an agreement with the Secretary under which it will administer a loan guarantee program under the Act.

Half-time student. A student who is enrolled in an institution of higher education, and is carrying an academic workload that amounts to at least one-half the workload of a full-time student, as determined by the school, and is not a full-time student as defined in 34 CFR 668.2. A student enrolled solely in an eligible correspondence course as defined in 34 CFR 668.8 is considered a half-time student.

Holder. An eligible lender owning an FFEL Program loan including a Federal or State agency or an organization or corporation acting on behalf of such an agency and acting as a conservator, liquidator, or receiver of an eligible lender.

Legal guardian. An individual appointed by a court to be a "guardian" of a person and specifically required by the court to use his or her financial resources for the support of that person.

Lender. (1) The term "eligible lender" is defined in section 435(d) of the Act, and in paragraphs (2)–(5) of this definition.

(2) With respect to a National or State chartered bank, a mutual savings bank, a savings and loan association, a stock savings bank, or a credit union—

(i) The phrase "subject to examination and supervision" in section 435(d) of the Act means "subject to examination and supervision in its capacity as a lender";

(ii) The phrase "does not have as its primary consumer credit function the making or holding of loans made to students under this part" in section 435(d) of the Act means that the lender does not, or in the case of a bank holding company, the company's wholly-owned subsidiaries as a group do not at any time, hold FFEL Program loans that total more than one-half of the lender's or subsidiaries' combined consumer credit loan portfolio, including home mortgages held by the lender or its subsidiaries.

(3) A bank that is subject to examination and supervision by an agency of the United States, making student loans as a trustee, may be an eligible lender if it makes loans under an express trust, operated as a lender in the FFEL programs prior to January 1, 1975, and met the requirements of this paragraph prior to July 23, 1992.

(4) The corporate parent or other owner of a school that qualifies as an eligible lender under section 435(d) of the Act is not an eligible lender unless the corporate parent or owner itself qualifies as an eligible lender under section 435(d) of the Act.

(5) The term "eligible lender" does not include any lender that the Secretary determines, after notice and opportunity for a hearing before a designated Department official, has—

(i) Offered, directly or indirectly, points, premiums, payments, or other inducements, to any school or other party to secure applicants for FFEL loans, except that a lender is not prohibited from providing assistance to schools comparable to the kinds of assistance provided by the Secretary to schools under, or in furtherance of, the Federal Direct Loan Program.

(ii) Conducted unsolicited mailings to a student or a student's parents of FFEL loan application forms, except to a student who previously has received a FFEL loan from the lender or to a student's parent who previously has received a FFEL loan from the lender;

(iii) Offered, directly or indirectly, a FFEL loan to a prospective borrower to induce the purchase of a policy of insurance or other product or service by the borrower or other person; or

(iv) Engaged in fraudulent or misleading advertising with respect to its FFEL program loan activities.

(6) The term eligible lender does not include any lender that—

(i) Is debarred or suspended, or any of whose principals or affiliates (as those terms are defined in 34 CFR part 85) is debarred or suspended under Executive Order (E.O.) 12549 (3 CFR, 1986 Comp., p. 189) or the Federal Acquisition Regulation (FAR), 48 CFR part 9, subpart 9.4;

(ii) Is an affiliate, as defined in 34 CFR part 85, of any person who is debarred or suspended under E.O. 12549 (3 CFR 1986 Comp., p. 189) or the FAR, 48 CFR part 9, subpart 9.4; or

(iii) Employs a person who is debarred or suspended under E.O. 12549 (3 CFR, 1986 Comp., p. 189) or the FAR, 48 CFR part 9, subpart 9.4, in a capacity that involves the administration or receipt of FFEL program funds.

Master promissory note (MPN). A promissory note under which the borrower may receive loans for a single period of enrollment or multiple periods of enrollment.

National credit bureau. A credit bureau with a service area that encompasses more than a single region of the country. Nonsubsidized Stafford loan. A Stafford loan made prior to October 1, 1992 that does not qualify for interest benefits under § 682.301(b) or special allowance payments under § 682.302.

Origination relationship. A special business relationship between a school and a lender in which the lender delegates to the school, or to an entity or individual affiliated with the school, substantial functions or responsibilities normally performed by lenders before making FFEL program loans. In this situation, the school is considered to have "originated" a loan made by the lender.

Origination fee. A fee that the lender is required to pay the Secretary to help defray the Secretary's costs of subsidizing the loan. The lender may pass this fee on to the Stafford loan borrower. The lender must pass this fee on to the SLS or PLUS borrower.

Participating school. A school that has in effect a current agreement with the Secretary under § 682.600. Period of enrollment. The period for which a Stafford, SLS, or PLUS loan is intended. The period of enrollment must coincide with a bona fide academic term established by the school for which institutional charges are generally assessed (e.g., semester, trimester, quarter, length of the student's program or academic year). The period of enrollment is also referred to as the loan period.

Post-deferment grace period. For a loan made prior to October 1, 1981, a single period of six consecutive months beginning on the day following the last day of an authorized deferment period. Repayment period. (1) For a Stafford loan, the period beginning on the date following the expiration of the grace period and ending no later than 10 years, or 25 years under an extended repayment schedule, from the date the first payment of principal is due from the borrower, exclusive of any period of deferment or forbearance.

(2) For unsubsidized Stafford loans, the period that begins on the day after the expiration of the applicable grace period that follows after the student ceases to be enrolled on at least a half-time basis and ending no later than 10 years or 25 years under an extended repayment schedule, from that date, exclusive of any period of deferment or forbearance. However, payments of interest are the responsibility of the borrower during the in-school and grace period, but may be capitalized by the lender.

(3) For SLS loans, the period that begins on the date the loan is disbursed, or if the loan is disbursed in more than one installment, on the date the last disbursement is made and ending no later than 10 years from that date, exclusive of any period of deferment or forbearance. The first payment of principal is due within 60 days after the loan is fully disbursed unless a borrower who is also a Stafford loan borrower but who, has not yet entered repayment on the Stafford loan requests that commencement of repayment on the SLS loan be delayed until the borrower's grace period on the Stafford loan expires. Interest on the loan accrues and is due and payable from the date of the first disbursement of the loan. The borrower is responsible for paying interest on the loan during the grace period and periods of deferment, but the interest may be capitalized by the lender.

(4) For Federal PLUS loans, the period that begins on the date the loan is disbursed, or if the loan is disbursed in more than one installment, on the date the last disbursement is made and ending no later than 10 years, or 25 years under an extended repayment schedule from that date, exclusive of any period of deferment or forbearance. Interest on the loan accrues and is due and payable from the date of the first disbursement of the loan.

(5) For Federal Consolidation loans, the period that begins on the date the loan is disbursed and ends no later than 10, 12, 15, 20, 25, or 30 years from that date depending upon the sum of the amount of the Consolidation loan, and the unpaid balance on other student loans, exclusive of any period of deferment or forbearance.

Satisfactory repayment arrangement. (1) For purposes of regaining eligibility under § 682.401(b)(4), the making of six (6) consecutive, on-time, voluntary full monthly payments on a defaulted loan. A borrower may only obtain the benefit of this paragraph with respect to renewed eligibility once.

(2) For purposes of consolidating a defaulted loan under 34 CFR 682.201(c)(1)(iii)(C), the making of three (3) consecutive, on-time, voluntary full monthly payments on a defaulted loan.

(3) The required full monthly payment amount may not be more than is reasonable and affordable based on the borrower's total financial circumstances. Voluntary payments are those payments made directly by the borrower, and do not include payments obtained by income tax off-set, garnishment, or income or asset execution. On-time means a payment received by the Secretary or a guaranty agency or its agent within 15 days of the scheduled due date.

School. (1) An "institution of higher education" as that term is defined in 34 CFR 600.4.

(2) For purposes of an in-school deferment, the term includes an institution of higher education, whether or not it participates in any Title IV program or has lost its eligibility to participate in the FFEL program because of a high default rate.

School lender. A school, other than a correspondence school, that has entered into a contract of guarantee under this part with the Secretary or, a similar agreement with a guaranty agency.

Stafford Loan Program. The loan program authorized by Title IV-B of the Act which encourages the making of subsidized and unsubsidized loans to undergraduate, graduate, and professional students and is one of the Federal Family Education Loan programs.

State lender. In any State, a single State agency or private nonprofit agency designated by the State that has entered into a contract of guarantee under this part with the Secretary, or a similar agreement with a guaranty agency.

Subsidized Stafford Loan: A Stafford loan that qualifies for interest benefits under § 682.301(b) and special allowance under § 682.302.

Temporarily totally disabled. The condition of an individual who, though not totally and permanently disabled, is unable to work and earn money or attend school, during a period of at least 60 days needed to recover from injury or illness. With regard to a disabled dependent of a borrower, this term means a spouse or other dependent who, during a period of injury or illness, requires continuous nursing or similar services for a period of at least 90 days.

Third-party servicer. Any State or private, profit or nonprofit organization or any individual that enters into a contract with a lender or guaranty agency to administer, through either manual or automated processing, any aspect of the lender's or guaranty agency's FFEL programs required by any statutory provision of or applicable to Title IV of the HEA, any regulatory provision prescribed under that statutory authority, or any applicable special arrangement, agreement, or limitation entered into under the authority of statutes applicable to Title IV of the HEA that governs the FFEL programs, including, any applicable function described in the definition of third-party servicer in 34 CFR part 668; originating, guaranteeing, monitoring, processing, servicing, or collecting loans; claims submission; or billing for interest benefits and special allowance.

Totally and permanently disabled. The condition of an individual who is unable to work and earn money because of an injury or illness that is expected to continue indefinitely or result in death.

Undergraduate student. A student who is enrolled at a school in a program of study, at or below the baccalaureate level, that usually does not exceed four academic years, or is up to five academic years in length, and is designed to lead to a degree or certificate at or below the baccalaureate level.

Unsubsidized Stafford loan. A loan made after October 1, 1992, authorized under section 428H of the Act for borrowers who do not qualify for interest benefits under § 682.301(b) but do qualify for special allowance under § 682.302.

Write-off. Cessation of collection activity on a defaulted FFEL loan due to a determination in accordance with applicable standards that no further collection activity is warranted.

(Approved by the Office of Management and Budget under control number 1845-0020)

(Authority: 8 U.S.C. 1101; 20 U.S.C. 1070 to 1087-2, 1088-1098, 1141; E.O. 12549 (3 CFR, 1986 Comp., p. 189), E.O. 12689 (3 CFR, 1989 Comp., p. 235))

[59 FR 22454, April 29, 1994; 59 FR 25744, May 17, 1994; 59 FR 32656, June 24, 1994; 59 FR 33348, June 28, 1994; 59 FR 61215, Nov. 29, 1994; 60 FR 32912, June 26, 1995; 60 FR 61756, Dec. 1, 1995; 61 FR 60608, Nov. 29, 1996; 64 FR 18975, April 16, 1999; 64 FR 58952, Nov. 1, 1999; 65 FR 38729, June 22, 2000; 65 FR 65691, Nov. 1, 2000]

§ 682.201 Eligible borrowers.

(a) **Student borrower**. Except for a refinanced SLS/PLUS loan made under § 682.209(e) or (f), a student is eligible to receive a Stafford loan, and an independent undergraduate student, a graduate or professional student, or, subject to paragraph (a)(3) of this section, a dependent undergraduate student, is eligible to receive an unsubsidized Stafford loan, if the student who is enrolled or accepted for enrollment on at least a half-time basis at a participating school meets the requirements for an eligible student under 34 CFR part 668, and—

(1) In the case of an undergraduate student who seeks a Stafford loan or unsubsidized Stafford loan for the cost of attendance at a school that participates in the Pell Grant Program, has received a final determination, or, in the case of a student who has filed an application with the school for a Pell Grant, a preliminary determination, from the school of the student's eligibility or ineligibility for a Pell Grant and, if eligible, has applied for the period of enrollment for which the loan is sought;

(2) In the case of any student who seeks an unsubsidized Stafford loan for the cost of attendance at a school that participates in the Stafford Loan Program, the student must—

(i) Receive a determination of need for a subsidized Stafford loan; and

(ii) If the determination of need is in excess of $200, have made a request to a lender for a subsidized Stafford loan;

(3) For purposes of a dependent undergraduate student's eligibility for an additional unsubsidized Stafford loan amount, as described at § 682.204(d), is a dependent undergraduate student for whom the financial aid administrator determines and documents in the school's file, after review of the family financial information provided by the student and consideration of the student's debt burden, that the student's parents likely will be precluded by exceptional circumstances (e.g., denial of a PLUS loan to a parent based on adverse credit, the student's parent receives only public

assistance or disability benefits, is incarcerated, or his or her whereabouts are unknown) from borrowing under the PLUS Program and the student's family is otherwise unable to provide the student's expected family contribution. A parent's refusal to borrow a PLUS loan does not constitute an exceptional circumstance;

(4)(i) Reaffirms any FFEL loan amount on which there has been a total cessation of collection activity, including all principal interest, collection costs, legal costs, and late charges that have accrued on that amount up to the date of reaffirmation.

(ii) For purposes of this section, reaffirmation means the acknowledgement of the loan by the borrower in a legally binding manner. The acknowledgement may include, but is not limited to, the borrower—

(A) Signing a new promissory note that includes the same terms and conditions as the original note signed by the borrower or repayment schedule; or

(B) Making a payment on the loan.

(5) The suspension of collection activity has been lifted from any loan on which collection activity had been suspended based on a conditional determination that the borrower was totally and permanently disabled under § 682.402(c).

(6) In the case of a borrower whose prior loan under title IV of the Act was discharged after a final determination of total and permanent disability, the student must—

(i) Obtain certification from a physician that the borrower is able to engage in substantial gainful activity;

(ii) Sign a statement acknowledging that the FFEL loan the borrower receives cannot be discharged in the future on the basis of any impairment present when the new loan is made, unless that impairment substantially deteriorates; and

(iii) In the case of a borrower whose previous loan under title IV of the Act was discharged due to a total and permanent disability on or after July 1, 2001 and before July 1, 2002, meets the requirements of paragraphs (a)(6)(i) and (a)(6)(ii) of this section. If the borrower applies for another loan within three years from the date that the borrower became totally and permanently disabled, as certified by the physician, the borrower must reaffirm the previously discharged loan before receiving the new loan.

(7) In the case of a borrower whose prior loan under title IV of the HEA was conditionally discharged based on an initial determination that the borrower was totally and permanently disabled, the borrower must—

(i) Comply with the requirements of paragraphs (a)(6)(i) and (a)(6)(ii) of this section; and

(ii) Sign a statement acknowledging that—

(A) The loan that has been conditionally discharged prior to a final determination of total and permanent disability cannot be discharged in the future on the basis of any impairment present when the borrower applied for a total and permanent disability discharge or when the new loan is made unless that impairment substantially deteriorates; and

(B) Collection activity will resume on any loans in a conditional discharge period, as described in paragraph 682.402(c)(16).

(8) In the case of any student who seeks a loan but does not have a certificate of graduation from a school providing secondary education or the recognized equivalent of such a certificate, the student meets the requirements under 34 CFR Part 668.32(e).

(9) Is not serving in a medical internship or residency program, except for an internship in dentistry.

(b)(1) *Parent borrower*. A parent borrower, is eligible to receive a PLUS Program loan, other than a loan made under § 682.209(e), if the parent—

(i) Is borrowing to pay for the educational costs of a dependent undergraduate student who meets the requirements for an eligible student set forth in 34 CFR Part 668;

(ii) Provides his or her and the student's social security number;

(iii) Meets the requirements pertaining to citizenship and residency that apply to the student in 34 CFR 668.33;

(iv) Meets the requirements concerning defaults and overpayments that apply to the student in 34 CFR 668.35 and meets the requirements of judgment liens that apply to the student under 34 CFR 668.32(g)(3);

(v) Except for the completion of a Statement of Selective Service Registration Status, complies with the requirements for submission of a Statement of Educational Purpose that apply to the student in 34 CFR part 668;

(vi) Meets the requirement of paragraphs (a)(4) and (a)(6), as applicable of this section;

(vii)(A) In the case of a Federal PLUS loan made on or after July 1, 1993, does not have an adverse credit history.

(B) For purposes of this section, the lender must obtain a credit report on each applicant from at least one national credit bureau. The credit report must be secured within a timeframe that would ensure the most accurate, current representation of the borrower's credit history before the first day of the period of enrollment for which the loan is intended.

(C) Unless the lender determines that extenuating circumstances existed, the lender must consider each applicant to have an adverse credit history based on the credit report if—

(1) The applicant is considered 90 or more days delinquent on the repayment of a debt;

(2) The applicant has been the subject of a default determination, bankruptcy discharge, foreclosure, repossession, tax lien, wage garnishment, or write-off of a Title IV debt, during the five years preceding the date of the credit report.

(D) Nothing in this paragraph precludes the lender from establishing more restrictive credit standards to determine whether the applicant has an adverse credit history.

(E) The absence of any credit history is not an indication that the applicant has an adverse credit history and is not to be used as a reason to deny a PLUS loan to that applicant.

(F) The lender must retain a record of its basis for determining that extenuating circumstances existed. This record may include, but is not limited to, an updated credit report, a statement from the creditor that the borrower has made satisfactory arrangements to repay the debt, or a satisfactory statement from the borrower explaining any delinquencies with outstanding balances of less than $500.

(viii) Obtains an endorser who has been determined not to have an adverse credit history as provided in paragraph (b)(1)(vii)(C) of this section.

(2) For purposes of paragraph (b)(1) of this section, a "parent" includes the individuals described in the definition of "parent" in 34 CFR 668.2 and the spouse of a parent who remarried, if that spouse's income and assets would have been taken into account when calculating a dependent student's expected family contribution.

(3) Meets the requirements pertaining to citizenship and residency that apply to the student in 34 CFR 668.7;

(c) *Consolidation program borrower.*

(1) An individual is eligible to receive a Consolidation loan if the individual—

(i) On the loans being consolidated—

(A) Is, at the time of application for a Consolidation loan—

(1) In a grace period preceding repayment;

(2) In repayment status;

(3) In a default status and has either made satisfactory repayment arrangements as defined in applicable program regulations or has agreed to repay the consolidation loan under the income-sensitive repayment plan described in § 682.209(a)(7)(viii);

(B) Not subject to a judgment secured through litigation, unless the judgment has been vacated; or

(C) Not subject to an order for wage garnishment under section 488A of the Act, unless the order has been lifted;

(ii) Certifies that no other application for a Consolidation loan is pending;

(iii) Agrees to notify the holder of any changes in address; and

(iv)(A) Certifies that the lender holds at least one outstanding loan that is being consolidated; or

(B) Applies to any eligible consolidation lender if the borrower—

(1) Has multiple holders of FFEL loans; or

(2) Has been unable to receive from the holder of the borrower's outstanding loans, a Consolidation loan or a Consolidation loan with income-sensitive repayment.

(2) A married couple is eligible to receive a Consolidation loan in accordance with this section if each—

(i) Agrees to be held jointly and severally liable for the repayment of the total amount of the Consolidation loan;

(ii) Agrees to repay the debt regardless of any change in marital status; and

(iii) Meets the requirements of paragraph (c)(1) of this section, and only one must have met the requirements of paragraph (c)(1)(iv) of this section.

(d) A borrower's eligibility to receive a Consolidation loan terminates upon receipt of a Consolidation loan except that—

(1) Eligible loans received prior to the date a Consolidation loan was made and loans received during the 180-day period following the date a Consolidation loan was made, may be added to the Consolidation loan based on the borrower's request received by the lender during the 180-day period after the date the Consolidation loan was made;

(2) A borrower who receives an eligible loan after the date a Consolidation loan is made may receive a subsequent Consolidation loan; and

(3) A Consolidation loan borrower may consolidate an existing Consolidation loan only if the borrower has at least one other eligible loan made before or after the existing Consolidation loan that will be consolidated.

(e) In the case of a married couple, the loans of a spouse that are to be included in a Consolidation loan are considered eligible loans for the other spouse.

(Authority: 20 U.S.C. 1077, 1078, 1078-1, 1078-2, 1078-3, 1082, and 1091)

[59 FR 25745, May 17, 1994; 59 FR 33349, June 28, 1994; 59 FR 61215, Nov. 29, 1994; 60 FR 32912, June 26, 1995; 60 FR 61756, 61815, Dec. 1, 1995; 62 FR 63433, Nov. 28, 1997; 64 FR 18975, 18976, April 16, 1999; 64 FR 58952, Nov. 1, 1999; 65 FR 65619, 65691, Nov. 1, 2000; 66 FR 44007, Aug. 21, 2001]

§ 682.202 Permissible charges by lenders to borrowers.

The charges that lenders may impose on borrowers, either directly or indirectly, are limited to the following:

(a) *Interest.* The applicable interest rates for FFEL Program loans are given in paragraphs (a)(1) through (a)(4) of this section.

(1) *Stafford Loan Program.*

(i) For loans made prior to July 1, 1994, if, the borrower, on the date the promissory note evidencing the loan is signed, has an outstanding balance of principal or interest on a previous Stafford loan, the interest rate is the applicable interest rate on that previous Stafford loan.

(ii) If the borrower, on the date the promissory note evidencing the loan is signed, has no outstanding balance on any FFEL Program loan, and the first disbursement is made—

(A) Prior to October 1, 1992, for a loan covering a period of instruction beginning on or after July 1, 1988, the interest rate is 8 percent until 48 months elapse after the repayment period begins, and 10 percent thereafter; or

(B) On or after October 1, 1992 and prior to July 1, 1994, the interest rate is a variable rate, applicable to each July 1-June 30 period, that equals the lesser of—

(1) The bond equivalent rate of the 91-day Treasury bills auctioned at the final auction prior to the June 1 immediately preceding the July 1-June 30 period, plus 3.10 percent; or

(2) 9 percent.

(iii) For a Stafford loan for which the first disbursement is made before October 1, 1992—

(A) If the borrower, on the date the promissory note is signed, has no outstanding balance on a Stafford loan but has an outstanding balance of principal or interest on a PLUS or SLS loan made for a period of enrollment beginning before July 1, 1988, or on a Consolidation loan that repaid a loan made for a period of enrollment beginning before July 1, 1988, the interest rate is 8 percent; or

(B) If the borrower, on the date the promissory note evidencing the loan is signed, has an outstanding balance of principal or interest on a PLUS or SLS loan made for a period of enrollment beginning on or after July 1, 1988, or on a Consolidation loan that repaid a loan made for a period of enrollment beginning on or after July 1, 1988, the interest rate is 8 percent until 48 months elapse after the repayment period begins, and 10 percent thereafter.

(iv) For a Stafford loan for which the first disbursement is made on or after October 1, 1992 but before December 20, 1993, if the borrower, on the date the promissory note evidencing the loan is signed, has no outstanding balance on a Stafford loan but has an outstanding balance of principal or interest on a PLUS, SLS, or Consolidation loan, the interest rate is 8 percent.

(v) For a Stafford loan for which the first disbursement is made on or after December 20, 1993 and prior to July 1, 1994, if the borrower, on the date the promissory note is signed, has no outstanding balance on a Stafford loan but has an outstanding balance of principal or interest on a PLUS, SLS, or Consolidation loan, the interest rate is the rate provided in paragraph (a)(1)(ii)(B) of this section.

(vi) For a Stafford loan for which the first disbursement is made on or after July 1, 1994 and prior to July 1, 1995, for a period of enrollment that includes or begins on or after July 1, 1994, the interest rate is a variable rate, applicable to each July 1-June 30 period, that equals the lesser of—

(A) The bond equivalent rate of the 91-day Treasury bills auctioned at the final auction prior to the June 1 immediately preceding the July 1-June 30 period, plus 3.10; or

(B) 8.25 percent.

(vii) For a Stafford loan for which the first disbursement is made on or after July 1, 1995 and prior to July 1, 1998 the interest rate is a variable rate applicable to each July 1-June 30 period, that equals the lesser of—

(A) The bond equivalent rate of the 91-day Treasury bills auctioned at the final auction prior to the June 1 immediately preceding the July 1-June 30 period, plus 2.5 percent during the in-school, grace and deferment period and 3.10 percent during repayment; or

(B) 8.25 percent.

(viii) For a Stafford loan for which the first disbursement is made on or after July 1, 1998, the interest rate is a variable rate, applicable to each July 1-June 30 period, that equals the lesser of—

(A) The bond equivalent rate of the 91-day Treasury bills auctioned at the final auction prior to the June 1 immediately preceding the July 1-June 30 period plus 1.7 percent during the in-school, grace and deferment periods and 2.3 percent during repayment; or

(B) 8.25 percent.

(2) *PLUS Program.*

(i) For a combined repayment schedule under § 682.209d), the interest rate i the weighted average of the rates of all loans included under that schedule.

(ii) For a loan disbursed on or after July 1, 1987 but prior to October 1, 1992, and for any loan made under § 682.209 (e) or (f), the interest rate is a variable rate, applicable to each July 1-June 30 period, that equals the lesser of—

(A) The bond equivalent rate of the 52-week Treasury bills auctioned at the final auction prior to the June 1 immediately preceding the July 1-June 30 period, plus 3.25 percent; or

(B) 12 percent.

(iii) For a loan disbursed on or after October 1, 1992 and prior to July 1, 1994, the interest rate is a variable rate, applicable to each July 1-June 30 period, that equals the lesser of—

(A) The bond equivalent rate of the 52-week Treasury bills auctioned at the final auction prior to the June 1 immediately preceding the July 1-June 30 period, plus 3.10 percent; or

(B) 10 percent.

(iv) For a loan for which the first disbursement is made on or after July 1, 1994 and prior to July 1, 1998, the interest rate is a variable rate applicable to each July 1-June 30 period, that equals the lesser of—

(A) The bond equivalent rate of the 52-week Treasury bills auctioned at the final auction prior to the June 1 immediately preceding the July 1-June 30 period, plus 3.10 percent; or

(B) 9 percent.

(v) For a loan for which the first disbursement is made on or after July 1, 1998, the interest rate is a variable rate, applicable to each July 1-June 30 period, that equals the lesser of—

(A) The bond equivalent rate of the 91-day Treasury bills auctioned at the final auction prior to the June 1 immediately preceding the July 1-June 30 period, plus 3.10 percent; or

(B) 9 percent.

(vi)(A) Beginning on July 1, 2001, the interest rate on the loans described in paragraphs (a)(2)(ii) through (iv) of this section is a variable rate applicable to each July 1-June 30, as determined on the preceding June 26, and is equal to the weekly average 1-year constant maturity Treasury yield, as published by the Board of Governors of the Federal Reserve System, for the last calendar week ending on or before such June 26; plus—

(1) 3.25 percent for loans described in paragraph (a)(2)(ii) of this section; or

(2) 3.1 percent for loans described in paragraphs (a)(2)(iii) and (iv) of this section.

(B) The interest rates calculated under paragraph (a)(2)(vi)(A) of this section shall not exceed the limits specified in paragraphs (a)(2)(ii)(B), (a)(2)(iii)(B), and (a)(2)(iv)(B) of this section, as applicable.

(3) *SLS Program.*

(i) For a combined repayment schedule under § 682.209(d), the interest rate is the weighted average of the rates of all loans included under that schedule.

(ii) For a loan disbursed on or after July 1, 1987 but prior to October 1, 1992, and for any loan made under § 682.209 (e) or (f), the interest rate is a variable rate, applicable to each July 1-June 30 period, that equals the lesser of—

(A) The bond equivalent rate of the 52-week Treasury bills auctioned at the final auction prior to the June 1 immediately preceding the July 1-June 30 period, plus 3.25 percent; or

(B) 12 percent.

(iii) For a loan disbursed on or after October 1, 1992, the interest rate is a variable rate, applicable to each July 1-June 30 period, that equals the lesser of—

(A) The bond equivalent rate of the 52-week Treasury bills auctioned at the final auction prior to the June 1 immediately preceding the July 1-June 30 period, plus 3.10 percent; or

(B) 11 percent.

(iv)(A) Beginning on July 1, 2001, the interest rate on the loans described in paragraphs (a)(3)(ii) and (iii) of this section is a variable rate applicable to each July 1-June 30, as determined on the preceding June 26, and is equal to the weekly average 1-year constant maturity Treasury yield, as published by the Board of Governors of the Federal Reserve System, for the last calendar week ending on or before such June 26; plus—

(1) 3.25 percent for loans described in paragraph (a)(3)(ii) of this section; or

(2) 3.1 percent for loans described in paragraph (a)(3)(iii) of this section.

(B) The interest rates calculated under paragraph (a)(3)(iv)(A) of this section shall not exceed the limits specified in paragraphs (a)(3)(ii)(B) and (a)(3)(iii)(B) of this section, as applicable.

(4) *Consolidation Program.*

(i) A Consolidation Program loan made before July 1, 1994 bears interest at the rate that is the greater of—

(A) The weighted average of interest rates on the loans consolidated, rounded to the nearest whole percent; or

(B) 9 percent.

(ii) A Consolidation loan made on or after July 1, 1994, for which the loan application was received by the lender before November 13, 1997, bears interest at the rate that is equal to the weighted average of interest rates on the loans consolidated, rounded upward to the nearest whole percent.

(iii) For a Consolidation loan for which the loan application was received by the lender on or after November 13, 1997 and before October 1, 1998, the interest rate for the portion of the loan that consolidated loans other than HEAL loans is a variable rate,

applicable to each July 1-June 30 period, that equals the lesser of—

(A) The bond equivalent rate of the 91-day Treasury bills auctioned at the final auction held prior to June 1 of each year plus 3.10 percent; or

(B) 8.25 percent.

(iv) For a Consolidation loan for which the application was received by the lender on or after October 1, 1998, the interest rate for the portion of the loan that consolidated loans other than HEAL loans is a fixed rate that is the lesser of—

(A) The weighted average of interest rates on the loans consolidated, rounded to the nearest higher one-eighth of one percent; or

(B) 8.25 percent.

(v) For a Consolidation loan for which the application was received by the lender on or after November 13, 1997, the annual interest rate applicable to the portion of each consolidation loan that repaid HEAL loans is a variable rate adjusted annually on July 1 and must be equal to the average of the bond equivalent rates of the 91-day Treasury bills auctioned for the quarter ending June 30, plus 3 percent. There is no maximum rate on this portion of the loan.

(5) *Actual interest rates under the Stafford loan, SLS, PLUS, and Consolidation Programs.* A lender may charge a borrower an actual rate of interest that is less than the applicable interest rate specified in paragraphs (a)(1)-(4) of this section.

(6) *Refund of excess interest paid on Stafford loans.*

(i) For a loan with an applicable interest rate of 10 percent made prior to July 23, 1992, and for a loan with an applicable interest rate of 10 percent made from July 23, 1992 through September 30, 1992, to a borrower with no outstanding FFEL Program loans—

(A) If during any calendar quarter, the sum of the average of the bond equivalent rates of the 91-day Treasury bills auctioned for that quarter, plus 3.25 percent, is less than 10 percent, the lender shall calculate an adjustment and credit the adjustment as specified under paragraph (a)(6)(i)(B) of this section if the borrower's account is not more than 30 days delinquent on December 31. The amount of the adjustment for a calendar quarter is equal to—

(1) 10 percent minus the sum of the average of the bond equivalent rates of the 91-day Treasury bills auctioned for the applicable quarter plus 3.25 percent;

(2) Multiplied by the average daily principal balance of the loan (not including unearned interest added to principal); and

(3) Divided by 4;

(B) No later than 30 calendar days after the end of the calendar year, the holder of the loan shall credit any amounts computed under paragraph (a)(6)(i)(A) of this section to—

(1) The Secretary, for amounts paid during any period in which the borrower is eligible for interest benefits;

(2) The borrower's account to reduce the outstanding principal balance as of the date the holder adjusts the borrower's account, provided that the borrower's account was not more than 30 days delinquent on that December 31; or

(3) The Secretary, for a borrower who on the last day of the calendar year is delinquent for more than 30 days.

(ii) For a fixed interest rate loan made on or after July 23, 1992 to a borrower with an outstanding FFEL Program loan—

(A) If during any calendar quarter, the sum of the average of the bond equivalent rates of the 91-day Treasury bills auctioned for that quarter, plus 3.10 percent, is less than the applicable interest rate, the lender shall calculate an adjustment and credit the adjustment to reduce the outstanding principal balance of the loan as specified under paragraph (a)(6)(ii)(C) of this section if the borrower's account is not more than 30 days delinquent on December 31. The amount of an adjustment for a calendar quarter is equal to—

(1) The applicable interest rate minus the sum of the average of the bond equivalent rates of the 91-day Treasury bills auctioned for the applicable quarter plus 3.10 percent;

(2) Multiplied by the average daily principal balance of the loan (not including unearned interest added to principal); and

(3) Divided by 4;

(B) For any quarter or portion thereof that the Secretary was obligated to pay interest subsidy on behalf of the borrower, the holder of the loan shall refund to the Secretary, no later than the end of the following quarter, any excess interest calculated in accordance with paragraph (a)(6)(ii)(A) of this section;

(C) For any other quarter, the holder of the loan shall, within 30 days of the end of the calendar year, reduce the borrower's outstanding principal by the amount of excess interest calculated under paragraph (a)(6)(ii)(A) of this section, provided that the borrower's account was not more than 30 days delinquent as of December 31;

(D) For a borrower who on the last day of the calendar year is delinquent for more than 30 days, any excess interest calculated shall be refunded to the Secretary; and

(E) Notwithstanding paragraphs (a)(6)(ii)(B), (C) and (D) of this section, if the loan was disbursed during a quarter, the amount of any adjustment refunded to the Secretary or credited to the borrower for that quarter shall be prorated accordingly.

(7) *Conversion to Variable Rate.*

(i) A lender or holder shall convert the interest rate on a loan under paragraphs (a)(6)(i) or (ii) of this section to a variable rate.

(ii) The applicable interest rate for each 12-month period beginning on July 1 and ending on June 30 preceding each 12-month period is equal to the sum of—

(A) The bond equivalent rate of the 91-day Treasury bills auctioned at the final auction prior to June 1; and

(B) 3.25 percent in the case of a loan described in paragraph (a)(6)(i) of this section or 3.10 percent in the case of a loan described in paragraph (a)(6)(ii) of this section.

(iii)(A) In connection with the conversion specified in paragraph (a)(6)(ii) of this section for any period prior to the conversion for which a rebate has not been provided under paragraph (a)(6) of this section, a lender or holder shall convert the interest rate to a variable rate.

(B) The interest rate for each period shall be reset quarterly and the applicable interest rate for the quarter or portion shall equal the sum of—

(1) The average of the bond equivalent rates of 91-day Treasury bills auctioned for the preceding 3-month period; and

(2) 3.25 percent in the case of loans as specified under paragraph (a)(6)(i) of this section or 3.10 percent in the case of loans as specified under paragraph (a)(6)(ii) of this section.

(iv)(A) The holder of a loan being converted under paragraph (a)(7)(iii)(A) of this section shall complete such conversion on or before January 1, 1995.

(B) The holder shall, not later than 30 days prior to the conversion, provide the borrower with—

(1) A notice informing the borrower that the loan is being converted to a variable interest rate;

(2) A description of the rate to the borrower;

(3) The current interest rate; and

(4) An explanation that the variable rate will provide a substantially equivalent benefit as the adjustment otherwise provided under paragraph (a)(6) of this section.

(v) The notice may be provided as part of the disclosure requirement as specified under § 682.205.

(vi) The interest rate as calculated under this paragraph may not exceed the maximum interest rate applicable to the loan prior to the conversion.

(b) *Capitalization.*

(1) A lender may add accrued interest and unpaid insurance premiums to the borrower's unpaid principal balance in accordance with this section. This increase in the principal balance of a loan is called "capitalization."

(2) Except as provided in paragraph (b)(4) of this section, a lender may capitalize interest payable by the borrower that has accrued—

(i) For the period from the date the first disbursement was made to the beginning date of the in-school period;

(ii) For the in-school or grace periods, or for a period needed to align repayment of an SLS with a Stafford loan, if capitalization is expressly authorized by the promissory note (or with the written consent of the borrower);

(iii) For a period of authorized deferment;

(iv) For a period of authorized forbearance; or

(v) For the period from the date the first installment payment was due until it was made.

(3) A lender may capitalize accrued interest under paragraphs (b)(2)(ii) through (iv) of this section no more frequently than quarterly. Capitalization is again permitted when repayment is required to begin or resume. A lender may capitalize accrued interest under paragraph (b)(2)(i) and (v) of this section only on the date repayment of principal is scheduled to begin.

(4)(i) For unsubsidized Stafford loans disbursed on or after October 7, 1998 and prior to July 1, 2000, the lender may capitalize the unpaid interest that accrues on the loan according to the requirements of section 428H(e)(2) of the Act.

(ii) For Stafford loans first disbursed on or after July 1, 2000, the lender may capitalize the unpaid interest—

(A) When the loan enters repayment;

(B) At the expiration of a period of authorized deferment;

(C) At the expiration of a period of authorized forbearance; and

(D) When the borrower defaults.

(5) For any borrower in an in-school or grace period or the period needed to align repayment, deferment, or forbearance status, during which the Secretary does not pay interest benefits and for which the borrower has agreed to make payments of interest, the lender may capitalize past due interest provided that the lender has notified the borrower that the borrower's failure to resolve any delinquency constitutes the borrower's consent to capitalization of delinquent interest and all interest that will accrue through the remainder of that period.

(c) **Fees for FFEL Program loans**.

(1) A lender may charge a borrower an origination fee on a Stafford loan not to exceed 3 percent of the principal amount of the loan. Except as provided in paragraph (c)(2) of this section, a lender must charge all borrowers the same origination fee.

(2)(i) A lender may charge a lower origination fee than the amount specified in paragraph (c)(1) of this section to a borrower whose expected family contribution (EFC), used to determine eligibility for the loan, is equal to or less than the maximum qualifying EFC for a Federal Pell Grant at the time the loan is certified or to a borrower who qualifies for a subsidized Stafford loan. A lender must charge all such borrowers the same origination fee.

(ii) With the approval of the Secretary, a lender may use a standard comparable to that defined in paragraph (c)(2)(i) of this section.

(3) If a lender charges a lower origination fee on unsubsidized loans under paragraph (c)(1) or (c)(2) of this section, the lender must charge the same fee on subsidized loans.

(4)(i) For purposes of this paragraph (c), a lender is defined as:

(A) All entities under common ownership, including ownership by a common holding company, that make loans to borrowers in a particular state; and

(B) Any beneficial owner of loans that provides funds to an eligible lender trustee to make loans on the beneficial owner's behalf in a particular state.

(ii) If a lender as defined in paragraph(c)(4)(i) charges a lower origination fee to any borrower in a particular state under paragraphs (c)(1) or (c)(2) of this section, the lender must charge all such borrowers who reside in that state or attend school in that state the same origination fee.

(5) Shall charge a borrower an origination fee on a PLUS loan of 3 percent of the principal amount of the loan;

(6) Shall deduct a pro rata portion of the fee (if charged) from each disbursement; and

(7) Shall refund by a credit against the borrower's loan balance the portion of the origination fee previously deducted from the loan that is attributable to any portion of the loan—

(i) That is returned by a school to a lender in order to comply with the Act or with applicable regulations;

(ii) That is repaid or returned within 120 days of disbursement, unless—

(A) The borrower has no FFEL Program loans in repayment status and has requested, in writing, that the repaid or returned funds be used for a different purpose; or

(B) The borrower has a FFEL Program loan in repayment status, in which case the payment is applied in accordance with § 682.209(b) unless the borrower has requested, in writing, that the repaid or returned funds be applied as a cancellation of all or part of the loan;

(iii) For which a loan check has not been negotiated within 120 days of disbursement; or

(iv) For which loan proceeds disbursed by electronic funds transfer or master check in accordance with § 682.207(b)(1)(ii)(B) and (C) have not been released from the restricted account maintained by the school within 120 days of disbursement.

(d) *Insurance Premium.* A lender may charge the borrower the amount of the insurance premium paid by the lender to the guarantor up to 1 percent of the principal amount of the loan, if that charge is provided for in the promissory note.

(e) *Administrative charge for a refinanced PLUS or SLS Loan.* A lender may charge a borrower up to $100 to cover the administrative costs of making a loan to a borrower under § 682.209(e) for the purpose of refinancing a PLUS or SLS loan to secure a variable interest rate.

(f) *Late charge.*

(1) If authorized by the borrower's promissory note, the lender may require the borrower to pay a late charge under the circum-stances described in paragraph (f)(2) of this section. This charge may not exceed six cents for each dollar of each late installment.

(2) The lender may require the borrower to pay a late charge if the borrower fails to pay all or a portion of a required installment payment within 15 days after it is due.

(g) *Collection charges.*

(1) If provided for in the borrower's promissory note, and notwithstanding any provisions of State law, the lender may require that the borrower or any endorser pay costs incurred by the lender or its agents in collecting installments not paid when due, including, but not limited to—

(i) Attorney's fees;

(ii) Court costs; and

(iii) Telegrams.

(2) The costs referred to in paragraph (g)(1) of this section may not include routine collection costs associated with preparing letters or notices or with making personal contacts with the borrower (e.g., local and long-distance telephone calls).

(h) *Special allowance.* Pursuant to § 682.412(c), a lender may charge a borrower the amount of special allowance paid by the Secretary on behalf of the borrower.

(Authority: 20 U.S.C. 1077, 1078, 1078-1, 1078-2, 1078-3, 1079, 1082, 1087-1, 1091a)

[59 FR 22475, April 29, 1994; 59 FR 25745, May 17, 1994; 59 FR 29543, June 8, 1994; 59 FR 35625, July 13, 1994; 59 FR 61427, Nov. 30, 1994; 60 FR 32912, June 26, 1995; 61 FR 60486, Nov. 27, 1996; 62 FR 63434, Nov. 28, 1997; 64 FR 18976, April 16, 1999; 64 FR 58953, Nov. 1, 1999; 66 FR 34762, June 29, 2001]

§ 682.209 Repayment of a loan.

(a) *Conversion of a loan to repayment status.*

(1) For a Consolidation loan, the repayment period begins on the date the loan is disbursed. The first payment is due within 60 days after the date the loan is disbursed.

(2)(i) For a PLUS loan, the repayment period begins on the date of the last disbursement made on the loan. Interest accrues and is due and payable from the date of the first disbursement of the loan. The first payment is due within 60 days after the date the loan is fully disbursed.

(ii) For an SLS loan, the repayment period begins on the date the loan is disbursed, or, if the loan is disbursed in multiple installments, on the date of the last disbursement of the loan. Interest accrues and is due and payable from the date of the first disbursement of the loan. Except as provided in paragraph (a)(2)(iii), (a)(2)(iv), and (a)(2)(v) of this section the first payment is due within 60 days after the date the loan is fully disbursed.

(iii) For an SLS borrower who has not yet entered repayment on a Stafford loan, the borrower who has not yet entered repayment on a Stafford loan, the borrower may postpone payment, consistent with the grace period on the borrower's Stafford loan.

(iv) If the lender first learns after the fact that an SLS borrower has entered the repayment period, the repayment begins no later than 75 days after the date the lender learns that the borrower has entered the repayment period.

(v) The lender may establish a first payment due date that is no more than an additional 30 days beyond the period specified in paragraphs (a)(2)(i)–(a)(2)(iv) of this section in order for the lender to comply with the required deadline contained in § 682.205(c)(1).

(3)(i) Except as provided in paragraphs (a)(4) and (5) of this section, for a Stafford loan the repayment period begins—

(A) For a borrower with a loan for which the applicable interest rate is 7 percent per year, not less than 9 nor more than 12 months following the date on which the borrower is no longer enrolled on at least a half-time basis at an eligible school. The length of this grace period is determined by the lender for loans made under the FISL Program, and by the guaranty agency for loans guaranteed by the agency;

(B) For a borrower with a loan for which the initial applicable interest rate is 8 or 9 percent per year, the day after 6 months following the date on which the borrower is no longer enrolled on at least a half-time basis at an institution of higher education and

(C) For a borrower with a loan with a variable interest rate, the day after 6 months following the date on which the borrower is no longer enrolled on at least a half-time basis at an institution of higher education.

(ii) The first payment on a Stafford loan is due on a date established by the lender that is no more than—

(A) 45 days following the first day that the repayment period begins;

(B) 45 days from the expiration of a deferment or forbearance period unless the borrower during this period has submitted payments with instructions that those payments are intended for future installment payments;

(C) 45 days following the end of the post deferment grace period;

(D) If the lender first learns after the fact that the borrower has entered the repayment period, no later than 75 days after the date the lender learns that the borrower has entered the repayment period; or

(E) An additional 30 days beyond the period specified in paragraphs (a)(3)(ii)(A)–(a)(3)(ii)(D) of this section in order for the lender to comply with the required deadlines contained in § 682.205(c)(1).

(4) For a borrower of a Stafford loan who is a correspondence student, the grace period specified in paragraph (a)(3)(i) of this section begins on the earliest of—

(i) The day after the borrower completes the program;

(ii) The day after withdrawal as determined pursuant to 34 CFR 668.22; or

(iii) 60 days following the last day for completing the program as established by the school.

(5) For a Stafford loan, the repayment period begins prior to the end of the grace period if the borrower requests in writing and is granted a repayment schedule that so provides. In this event, a borrower waives the remainder of the grace period.

(6) For purposes of establishing the beginning of the repayment period for Stafford and SLS loans, the grace periods referenced in paragraphs (a)(2)(iii) and (a)(3)(i) of this section exclude any period during which a borrower who is a member of a reserve component of the Armed Forces named in section 10101 of title 10, United States Code is called or ordered to active duty for a period of more than 30 days. Any single excluded period may not exceed three years and includes the time necessary for the borrower to resume enrollment at the next available regular enrollment period. Any Stafford or SLS borrower who is in a grace period when called or ordered to active duty as specified in this paragraph is entitled to a full grace period upon completion of the excluded period.

(7)(i) The repayment schedule may provide for substantially equal installment payments or for installment payments that increase or decrease in amount during the repayment period. If the loan has a variable interest rate that changes annually, the lender may establish a repayment schedule that—

(A) Provides for adjustments of the amount of the installment payment to reflect annual changes in the variable interest rate; or

(B) Contains no provision for an adjustment of the amount of the installment payment to reflect annual changes in the variable interest rate, but requires the lender to grant a forbearance to the borrower (or endorser, if applicable) for a period of up to 3 years of payments in accordance with § 682.211(i)(5) in cases where the effect of a variable interest rate on a standard or graduated repayment schedule would result in a loan not being repaid within the maximum repayment term.

(ii) If a graduated or income-sensitive repayment schedule is established, it may not provide for any single installment that is more than three times greater than any other installment. An agreement as specified in paragraph (c)(1)(ii) of this section is not required if the schedule provides for less than the minimum annual payment amount specified in paragraph (c)(1)(i) of this section.

(iii) Not more than six months prior to the date that the borrower's first payment is due, the lender must offer the borrower a choice of a standard, income-sensitive, graduated, or, if applicable, an extended repayment schedule.

(iv) The repayment schedule must require that each payment equal at least the interest that accrues during the interval between scheduled payments.

(v) The lender shall require the borrower to repay the loan under a standard repayment schedule described in paragraph (a)(7)(vi) of this section if the borrower—

(A) Does not select an income-sensitive, a graduated, or if applicable, an extended repayment schedule within 45 days after being notified by the lender to choose a repayment schedule; or

(B) Chooses an income-sensitive repayment schedule, but does not provide the documentation requested by the lender under paragraph (a)(7)(viii)(C) of this section within the time period specified by the lender.

(vi) Under a standard repayment schedule, the borrower is scheduled to pay either—

(A) The same amount for each installment payment made during the repayment period, except that the borrower's final payment may be slightly more or less than the other payments; or

(B) An installment amount that will be adjusted to reflect annual changes in the loan's variable interest rate.

(vii) Under a graduated repayment schedule—

(A)(1) The amount of the borrower's installment payment is scheduled to change (usually by increasing) during the course of the repayment period; or

(2) If the loan has a variable interest rate that changes annually, the lender may establish a repayment schedule that may have adjustments in the payment amount as provided under paragraph (a)(7)(i) of this section; and

(B) An agreement as specified in paragraph (c)(1)(ii) of this section is not required if the schedule provides for less than the minimum annual payment amount specified in paragraph (c)(1)(i) of this section.

(viii) Under an income-sensitive repayment schedule—

(A)(1) The amount of the borrower's installment payment is adjusted annually, based on the borrower's expected total monthly gross income received by the borrower from employment and from other sources during the course of the repayment period; or

(2) If the loan has a variable interest rate that changes annually, the lender may establish a repayment schedule that may have adjustments in the payment amount as provided under paragraph (a)(7)(i) of this section; and

(B) In general, the lender shall request the borrower to inform the lender of his or her income no earlier than 90 days prior to the due date of the borrower's initial installment payment and subsequent annual payment adjustment under an income-sensitive repayment schedule. The income information must be sufficient for the lender to make a reasonable determination of what the borrower's payment amount should be. If the lender receives late notification that the borrower has dropped below half-time enrollment status at a school, the lender may request that income information earlier than 90 days prior to the due date of the borrower's initial installment payment;

(C) If the borrower reports income to the lender that the lender considers to be insufficient for establishing monthly installment payments that would repay the loan within the applicable maximum repayment period, the lender shall require the borrower to submit evidence showing the amount of the most recent total monthly gross income received by the borrower from employment and from other sources including, if applicable, pay statements from employers and documentation of any income received by the borrower from other parties;

(D) The lender shall grant a forbearance to the borrower (or endorser, if applicable) for a period of up to 5 years of payments in accordance with § 682.211(i)(5) in cases where the effect of decreased installment amounts paid under an income-sensitive repayment schedule would result in a loan not being repaid within the maximum repayment term; and

(E) The lender shall inform the borrower that the loan must be repaid within the time limits specified under paragraph (a)(8) of this section.

(ix) Under an extended repayment schedule, a new borrower whose total outstanding principal and interest in FFEL loans exceed $30,000 may repay the loan on a fixed annual repayment amount or a graduated repayment amount for a period that may not exceed 25 years. For purposes of this section, a "new borrower" is an individual who has no outstanding principal or interest balance on an FFEL Program loan as of October 7, 1998, or on the date he or she obtains an FFEL Program loan after October 7, 1998.

(x) A borrower may request a change in the repayment schedule on a loan. The lender must permit the borrower to change the repayment schedule no less frequently than annually.

(xi) For purposes of this section, a lender shall, to the extent practicable require that all FFEL loans owed by a borrower to the lender be combined into one account and repaid under one repayment schedule. In that event, the word "loan" in this section shall mean all of the borrower's loans that were combined by the lender into that account.

(8)(i) Subject to paragraphs (a)(8)(ii) through (iv) of this section, and except as provided in paragraph (a)(7)(ix) a lender shall allow a borrower at least 5 years, but not more than 10 years, or 25 years under an extended repayment plan to repay a Stafford, SLS, or Plus loan, calculated from the beginning of the repayment period. Except in the case of a FISL loan for a period of enrollment beginning on or after July 1, 1986, the lender shall require a borrower to fully repay a FISL loan within 15 years after it is made.

(ii) If the borrower receives an authorized deferment or is granted forbearance, as described in § 682.210 or § 682.211 respectively, the periods of deferment or forbearance are excluded from determinations of the 5-, 10-, 15- and 25-year periods, and from the 10-, 12-, 15-, 20-, 25-, and 30-year periods for repayment of a Consolidation loan pursuant to § 682.209(h).

(iii) If the minimum annual repayment required in paragraph (c) of this section would result in complete repayment of the loan in less than 5 years, the borrower is not entitled to the full 5-year period.

(iv) The borrower may, prior to the beginning of the repayment period, request and be granted by the lender a repayment period of less than 5 years. Subject to paragraph (a)(8)(iii) of this section, a borrower who makes such a request may, by written notice to the lender at any time during the repayment period, extend the repayment period to a minimum of 5 years.

(9) If, with respect to the aggregate of all loans held by a lender, the total payment made by a borrower for a monthly or similar payment period would not otherwise be a multiple of five dollars, the lender may round that periodic payment to the next highest whole dollar amount that is a multiple of five dollars.

(b) *Payment application and prepayment.*

(1) The lender may credit the entire payment amount first to any late charges accrued or collection costs and then to any outstanding interest and then to outstanding principal.

(2)(i) The borrower may prepay the whole or any part of a loan at any time without penalty.

(ii) If the prepayment amount equals or exceeds the monthly payment amount under the repayment schedule established for the loan, the lender shall apply the prepayment to future installments by advancing the next payment due date, unless the borrower requests otherwise. The lender must either inform the borrower in advance using a prominent statement in the borrower coupon book or billing statement that any additional full payment amounts submitted without instructions to the lender as to their handling will be applied to future scheduled payments with the borrower's next scheduled payment due date advanced consistent with the number of additional payments received, or provide a notification to the borrower after the payments are received informing the borrower that the payments have been so applied and the date of the borrower's next scheduled payment due date. Information related to next scheduled payment due date need not be provided to borrower's making such prepayments while in an in-school, grace, deferment, or forbearance period when payments are not due.

(c) *Minimum annual payment.*

(1)(i) Subject to paragraph (c)(1)(ii) of this section and except as otherwise provided by a graduated, income-sensitive, or extended repayment plan selected by the borrower, during each year of the repayment period, a borrower's total payments to all holders of the borrower's FFEL Program loans must total at least $600 or the unpaid balance of all loans, including interest, whichever amount is less.

(ii) If the borrower and the lender agree, the amount paid may be less.

(2) The provisions of paragraphs (c)(1)(i) and (ii) of this section may not result in an extension of the maximum repayment period unless forbearance as described in § 682.211, or deferment described in § 682.210, has been approved.

(d) *Combined repayment of a borrower's student PLUS and SLS loans held by a lender.*

(1) A lender may, at the request of a student borrower, combine the borrower's student PLUS and SLS loans held by it into a single repayment schedule.

(2) The repayment period on the loans included in the combined repayment schedule must be calculated based on the beginning of repayment of the most recent included loan.

(3) The interest rate on the loans included in the new combined repayment schedule must be the weighted average of the rates of all included loans.

(e) *Refinancing a fixed-rate PLUS or SLS Program loan to secure a variable interest rate.*

(1) Subject to paragraph (g) of this section, a lender may, at the request of a borrower, refinance a PLUS or SLS loan with a fixed interest rate in order to permit the borrower to obtain a variable interest rate.

(2) A loan made under paragraph (e)(1) of this section—

(i) Must bear interest at the variable rate described in § 682.202(a)(2)(ii) and (3)(ii) as appropriate; and

(ii) May not extend the repayment period provided for in paragraph (a)(8)(i) of this section.

(3) The lender may not charge an additional insurance premium on the loan, but may charge the borrower an administrative fee pursuant to § 682.202(e).

(f) *Refinancing of a fixed-rate PLUS or SLS Program loan to secure a variable interest rate by a discharge of previous loan.*

(1) Subject to paragraph (g) of this section, a borrower who has applied for, but been denied, a refinanced loan authorized under paragraph (e) of this section by the holder of the borrower's fixed rate PLUS or SLS loan, may obtain a loan from another lender for the purpose of discharging the fixed-rate loan and obtaining a variable interest rate.

(2) A loan made under paragraph (f)(1) of this section—

(i) Must bear interest at the variable interest rate described in § 682.202(a)(2)(ii) and (3)(ii), as appropriate;

(ii) May not operate to extend the repayment period provided for in paragraph (a)(8)(i) of this section; and

(iii) Must be disbursed to the holder of the fixed-rate loan to discharge the borrower's obligation thereon.

(3) Upon receipt of the proceeds of a loan made under paragraph (f)(1) of this section, the holder of the fixed-rate loan shall, within five business days, apply the proceeds to discharge the borrower's obligation on the fixed-rate loan, and provide the refinancing lender with either a copy of the borrower's original promissory note evidencing the fixed-rate loan or the holder's written certification that the borrower's obligation on the fixed-rate loan has been fully discharged.

(4) The refinancing lender may charge the borrower an insurance premium on a loan made under paragraph (f)(1) of this section, but may not charge a fee to cover administrative costs.

(5) For purposes of deferments under § 682.210, the refinancing loan—

(i) Is considered a PLUS loan if any of the included loans is a PLUS loan made to a parent;

(ii) Is considered an SLS loan if the combined loan does not include a PLUS loan made to a parent; or

(iii) Is considered a loan to a "new borrower" as defined in § 682.210(b)(7), if all the loans that were refinanced were made on or after July 1, 1987, for a period of enrollment beginning on or after that date.

(g) *Conditions for refinancing certain loans.*

(1) A lender may not refinance a loan under paragraphs (e) or (f) of this section if that loan is in default, involves a violation of a condition of reinsurance described in § 682.406, or, in the case of a Federal SLS or Federal PLUS loan, is uninsured by the Secretary.

(2)(i) Prior to refinancing a fixed-rate under paragraph (f) of this section, the lender shall obtain a written statement from the holder of the loan certifying that—

(A) The holder has refused to refinance the fixed-rate loan under paragraph (e) of this section; and

(B) The fixed-rate loan is eligible for insurance or reinsurance under paragraph (g)(1) of this section.

(ii) The holder of a fixed-rate loan shall, within 10 business days of receiving a lender's written request to provide a certification under paragraph (g)(1)(i) of this section, provide the lender with that certification, or provide the lender and the guarantor on the loan with a written explanation of the reasons for its inability to provide the certification to the requesting lender.

(iii) The refinancing lender may rely in good faith on the certification provided by the holder of the fixed-rate loan under paragraph (g)(2)(ii) of this section.

(h) *Consolidation loans.*

(1) For a Consolidation loan, the repayment period begins on the day of disbursement, with the first payment due within 60 days after the date of disbursement.

(2) If the sum of the amount of the Consolidation loan and the unpaid balance on other student loans to the applicant—

(i) Is less than $7,500, the borrower shall repay the Consolidation loan in not more than 10 years;

(ii) Is equal to or greater than $7,500 but less than $10,000, the borrower shall repay the Consolidation loan in not more than 12 years;

(iii) Is equal to or greater than $10,000 but less than 20,000, the borrower shall repay the Consolidation loan in not more than 15 years;

(iv) Is equal to or greater than $20,000 but less than $40,000, the borrower shall repay the Consolidation loan in not more than 20 years;

(v) Is equal to or greater than $40,000 but less than $60,000, the borrower shall repay the Consolidation loan in not more than 25 years; or

(vi) Is equal to or greater than $60,000, the borrower shall repay the Consolidation loan in not more than 30 years.

(3) For the purpose of paragraph (h)(2) of this section, the unpaid balance on other student loans—

(i) May not exceed the amount of the Consolidation loan; and

(ii) With the exception of the defaulted title IV loans on which the borrower has made satisfactory repayment arrangements with the holder of the loan, does not include the unpaid balance on any defaulted loans.

(4) A repayment schedule for a Consolidation loan—

(i) Must be established by the lender;

(ii) Must require that each payment equal at least the interest that accrues during the interval between scheduled payments.

(5) Upon receipt of the proceeds of a loan made under paragraph (h)(2) of this section, the holder of the underlying loan shall promptly apply the proceeds to discharge fully the borrower's obligation on the underlying loan, and provide the consolidating lender with the holder's written certification that the borrower's obligation on the underlying loan has been fully discharged.

(i) *Treatment by a lender of borrowers' title IV, HEA program funds received from schools if the borrower withdraws.*

(1) A lender shall treat a refund or a return of title IV, HEA program funds under § 668.22 when a student withdraws received by the lender from a school as a credit against the principal amount owed by the borrower on the borrower's loan.

(2)(i) If a lender receives a refund or a return of title IV, HEA program funds under § 668.22 when a student withdraws from a school on a loan that is no longer held by that lender, or that has been discharged by another lender by refinancing under § 682.209(f) or by a Consolidation loan, the lender must transmit the amount of the payment, within 30 days of its receipt, to the lender to whom it assigned the loan, or to the lender that discharged the prior loan, with an explanation of the source of the payment.

(ii) Upon receipt of a refund or a return of title IV, HEA program funds transmitted under paragraph (i)(2)(i) of this section, the holder of the loan promptly must provide written notice to the borrower that the holder has received the return of title IV, HEA program funds.

(j) *Certification on loans to be repaid through consolidation.*

Within 10 business days after receiving a written request for a certification from a lender under § 682.206(f), a holder shall either provide the requesting lender the certification or, if it is unable to certify to the matters described in that paragraph, provide the requesting lender and the guarantor on the loan at issue with a written explanation of the reasons for its inability to provide the certification.

(Approved by the Office of Management and Budget under control number 1845-0020)

(Authority: 20 U.S.C. 1077, 1078, 1078-1, 1078-2, 1078-3, 1079, 1082, 1085)

[59 FR 33352, June 28, 1994; 59 FR 33593, June 29, 1994; 60 FR 30788, June 12, 1995; 60 FR 32912, June 26, 1995; 60 FR 61756, Dec. 1, 1995; 61 FR 16718, April 17, 1996; 62 FR 63434, Nov. 28, 1997; 64 FR 18977, April 16, 1999; 64 FR 58957, 59043, Nov. 1, 1999; 66 FR 34763, June 29, 2001]

§ 682.210 Deferment.

(a) *General.*

(1)(i) A borrower is entitled to have periodic installment payments of principal deferred during authorized periods after the beginning of the repayment period, pursuant to paragraph (b) of this section.

(ii) With the exception of a deferment authorized under paragraph (o) of this section, a borrower may continue to receive a specific type of deferment that is limited to a maximum period of time only if the total amount of time that the borrower has received the deferment does not exceed the maximum time period allowed for the deferment.

(2)(i) For a loan made before October 1, 1981, the borrower is also entitled to have periodic installments of principal deferred during the six-month period (post-deferment grace period) that begins after the completion of each deferment period or combination of those periods, except as provided in paragraph (a)(2)(ii) of this section.

(ii) Once a borrower receives a post-deferment grace period following an unemployment deferment, as described in paragraph (b)(1)(v) of this section, the borrower does not qualify for addi-

tional post-deferment grace periods following subsequent unemployment deferments.

(3) Interest accrues and is paid by the borrower during the deferment period and the post-deferment grace period, if applicable, unless interest accrues and is paid by the Secretary for a Stafford loan and for all or a portion of a qualifying Consolidation loan that meets the requirements under § 682.301.

(4) As a condition for receiving a deferment, except for purposes of paragraphs (c)(1)(ii) and (iii) of this section, the borrower must request the deferment, and provide the lender with all information and documents required to establish eligibility for a specific type of deferment.

(5) An authorized deferment period begins on the date that the holder determines is the date that the condition entitling the borrower to the deferment first existed, except that an initial unemployment deferment as described in paragraph (h)(2) of this section cannot begin more than 6 months before the date the holder receives a request and documentation required for the deferment.

(6) An authorized deferment period ends on the earlier of—

(i) The date when the condition establishing the borrower's eligibility for the deferment ends;

(ii) Except as provided in paragraph (a)(6)(iv) of this section, the date on which, as certified by an authorized official, the borrower's eligibility for the deferment is expected to end;

(iii) Except as provided in paragraph (a)(6)(iv) of this section, the expiration date of the period covered by any certification required by this section to be obtained for the deferment;

(iv) In the case of an in-school deferment, the student's anticipated graduation date as certified by an authorized official of the school; or

(v) The date when the condition providing the basis for the borrower's eligibility for the deferment has continued to exist for the maximum amount of time allowed for that type of deferment.

(7) A lender may not deny a borrower a deferment to which the borrower is entitled, even though the borrower may be delinquent, but not in default, in making required installment payments. The 270- or 330-day period required to establish default does not run during the deferment and post-deferment grace periods. Unless the lender has granted the borrower forbearance under § 682.211, when the deferment and, if applicable, the post-deferment grace period expire, a borrower resumes any delinquency status that existed when the deferment period began.

(8) A borrower whose loan is in default is not eligible for a deferment on that loan, unless the borrower has made payment arrangements acceptable to the lender prior to the payment of a default claim by a guaranty agency.

(9) The borrower promptly must inform the lender when the condition entitling the borrower to a deferment no longer exists.

(10) Authorized deferments are described in paragraph (b) of this section. Specific requirements for each deferment are set forth in paragraphs (c) through (s) of this section.

(11) If two individuals are jointly liable for repayment of a PLUS loan or a Consolidation loan, the lender shall grant a request for deferment if both individuals simultaneously meet the requirements of this section for receiving the same, or different deferments.

(b) *Authorized deferments.*

(1) Deferment is authorized for a FFEL borrower during any period when the borrower is—

(i) Except as provided in paragraph (c)(5) of this section,

engaged in full-time study at a school, or at a school that is operated by the Federal Government (e.g., the service academies), unless the borrower is not a national of the United States and is pursuing a course of study at a school not located in a State;

(ii) Engaged in a course of study under an eligible graduate fellowship program;

(iii) Engaged in a rehabilitation training program for disabled individuals;

(iv) Temporarily totally disabled, or unable to secure employment because the borrower is caring for a spouse or other dependent who is disabled and requires continuous nursing or similar services for up to three years; or

(v) Conscientiously seeking, but unable to find, full-time employment in the United States, for up to two years.

(2) For a borrower of a Stafford or SLS loan, and for a parent borrower of a PLUS loan made before August 15, 1983, deferment is authorized during any period when the borrower is—

(i) On active duty status in the United States Armed Forces, or an officer in the Commissioned Corps of the United States Public Health Service, for up to three years (including any period during which the borrower received a deferment authorized under paragraph (b)(5)(i) of this section);

(ii) A full-time volunteer under the Peace Corps Act, for up to three years;

(iii) A full-time volunteer under Title I of the Domestic Volunteer Service Act of 1973 (ACTION programs), for up to three years;

(iv) A full-time volunteer for a tax-exempt organization, for up to three years; or

(v) Engaged in an internship of residency program, for up to two years (including any period during which the borrower received a deferment authorized under paragraph (b)(5)(iii) of this section).

(3) For a borrower of a Stafford or SLS loan who has been enrolled on at least a half-time basis at an institution of higher education during the six months preceding the beginning of this deferment, deferment is authorized during a period of up to six months during which the borrower is—

(i)(A) Pregnant;

(B) Caring for his or her newborn child; or

(C) Caring for a child immediately following the placement of the child with the borrower before or immediately following adoption; and

(ii) Not attending a school or gainfully employed.

(4) For a "new borrower," as defined in paragraph (b)(7) of this section, deferment is authorized during periods when the borrower is engaged in at least half-time study at a school, unless the borrower is not a national of the United States and is pursuing a course of study at a school not located in a State.

(5) For a new borrower, as defined in paragraph (b)(7) of this section, of a Stafford or SLS loan, deferment is authorized during any period when the borrower is—

(i) On active duty status in the National Oceanic and Atmospheric Administration Corps, for up to three years (including any period during which the borrower received a deferment authorized under paragraph (b)(2)(i) of this section);

(ii) Up to three years of service as a full-time teacher in a public or non-profit private elementary or secondary school in a teacher shortage area designated by the Secretary under paragraph (q) of this section.

(iii) Engaged in an internship or residency program, for up to

two years (including any period during which the borrower received a deferment authorized under paragraph (c)(2)(v) of this section); or

(iv) A mother who has preschool-age children (i.e., children who have not enrolled in first grade) and who is earning not more than $1 per hour above the Federal minimum wage, for up to 12 months of employment, and who began that full-time employment within one year of entering or re-entering the work force. Full-time employment involves at least 30 hours of work a week and it expected to last at least 3 months.

(6) For a parent borrower of a PLUS loan, deferment is authorized during any period when a student on whose behalf the parent borrower received the loan—

(i) Is not independent as defined in section 480(d) of the Act; and

(ii) Meets the conditions and provides the required documentation, for any of the deferments described in paragraphs (b)(1)(i)–(iii) and (b)(4) of this section.

(7) For purposes of paragraph (b)(5) of this section, a "new borrower" with respect to a loan is a borrower who, on the date he or she signs and promissory note, has no outstanding balance on—

(i) A Stafford, SLS, or PLUS loan made prior to July 1, 1987 for a period of enrollment beginning prior to July 1, 1987; or

(ii) A Consolidation loan that repaid a loan made prior to July 1, 1987 and or a period of enrollment beginning prior to July 1, 1987.

(c) *In-school deferment.*

(1) Except as provided in paragraph (c)(5) of this section, the lender processes a deferment for full-time study or half-time study at a school, when—

(i) The borrower submits a request and supporting documentation for a deferment;

(ii) The lender receives information from the borrower's school about the borrower's eligibility in connection with a new loan; or

(iii) The lender receives student status information from the borrower's school, either directly or indirectly, indicating that the borrower's enrollment status supports eligibility for a deferment.

(2) The lender must notify the borrower that a deferment has been granted based on paragraph (c)(1)(ii) or (iii) of this section and that the borrower has the option to pay interest that accrues on an unsubsidized FFEL Program loan or to cancel the deferment and continue paying on the loan. The lender must include in the notice an explanation of the consequences of these options.

(3) The lender must consider a deferment granted on the basis of a certified loan application or other information certified by the school to cover the period lasting until the anticipated graduation date appearing on the application, and as updated by notice or SSCR update to the lender from the school or guaranty agency, unless and until it receives notice that the borrower has ceased the level of study (i.e., full-time or half-time) required for the deferment.

(4) In the case of a FFEL borrower, the lender shall treat a certified loan application or other form certified by the school or for multiple holders of a borrower's loans, shared data from the Student Status Confirmation Report, as sufficient documentation for an in-school deferment for any outstanding FFEL loan previously made to the borrower that is held by the lender.

(5) A borrower serving in a medical internship residency program, except for an internship in dentistry, is prohibited from receiving or continuing a deferment on a Stafford, or a PLUS (unless based on the dependent's status) SLS, or Consolidation loan under paragraph (c) of this section.

(d) *Graduate fellowship deferment.*

(1) To qualify for a deferment for study in a graduate fellowship program, a borrower shall provide the lender with a statement from an authorized official of the borrower's fellowship program certifying—

(i) That the borrower holds at least a baccalaureate degree conferred by an institution of higher education;

(ii) That the borrower has been accepted or recommended by an institution of higher education for acceptance on a full-time basis into an eligible graduate fellowship program; and

(iii) The borrower's anticipated completion date in the program.

(2) For purposes of paragraph (d)(1) of this section, an eligible graduate fellowship program is a fellowship program that—

(i) Provides sufficient financial support to graduate fellows to allow for full-time study for at least six months;

(ii) Requires a written statement from each applicant explaining the applicant's objectives before the award of that financial support;

(iii) Requires a graduate fellow to submit periodic reports, projects, or evidence of the fellow's progress; and

(iv) In the case of a course of study at a foreign university, accepts the course of study for completion of the fellowship program.

(e) *Rehabilitation training program deferment.*

(1) To qualify for a rehabilitation training program deferment, a borrower shall provide the lender with a statement from an authorized official of the borrower's rehabilitation training program certifying that the borrower is either receiving, or is scheduled to receive, services under an eligible rehabilitation training program for disabled individuals.

(2) For purposes of paragraph (e)(1) of this section, an eligible rehabilitation training program for disabled individuals is a program that—

(i) Is licensed, approved, certified, or otherwise recognized as providing rehabilitation training to disabled individuals by—

(A) A State agency with responsibility for vocational rehabilitation programs;

(B) A State agency with responsibility for drug abuse treatment programs;

(C) A State agency with responsibility for mental health services program;

(D) a State agency with responsibility for alcohol abuse treatment programs; or

(E) The Department of Veterans Affairs; and

(ii) Provides or will provide the borrower with rehabilitation services under a written plan that—

(A) Is individualized to meet the borrower's needs;

(B) Specifies the date on which the services to the borrower are expected to end; and

(C) Is structured in a way that requires a substantial commitment by the borrower to his or her rehabilitation. The Secretary considers a substantial commitment by the borrower to be a commitment of time and effort that normally would prevent an additional from engaging in full-time employment, either because of the number of hours that must be devoted to rehabilitation or because of the nature of the rehabilitation. For the purpose of this paragraph, full-time employment involves at least 30 hours of work per week and is expected to last at least three months.

(f) *Temporary total disability deferment.*

(1) To qualify for a temporary total disability deferment, a borrower shall provide the lender with a statement from a physician, who is a doctor of medicine or osteopathy and is legally authorized to practice, certifying that the borrower is temporarily totally disabled as defined in § 682.200(b).

(2) A borrower is not considered temporarily totally disabled on the basis of a condition that existed before he or she applied for the loan, unless the condition has substantially deteriorated so as to render the borrower temporarily totally disabled, as substantiated by the statement required under paragraph (f)(1) of this section, after the borrower submitted the loan application.

(3) A lender may not grant a deferment based on a single certification under paragraph (f)(1) of this section beyond the date that is six months after the date of certification.

(g) *Dependent's disability deferment.*

(1) To qualify for a deferment given to a borrower whose spouse or other dependent requires continuous nursing or similar services for a period of at least 90 days, the borrower shall provide the lender with a statement—

(i) From a physician, who is a doctor of medicine or osteopathy and is legally authorized to practice, certifying that the borrower's spouse or dependent requires continuous nursing or similar services for a period of at least 90 days; and

(ii) From the borrower, certifying that the borrower is unable to secure full-time employment because he or she is providing continuous nursing or similar services to the borrower's spouse or other dependent. For the purpose of this paragraph, full-time employment involves at least 30 hours of work per week and is expected to last at least three months.

(2) A lender may not grant a deferment based on a single certification under paragraph (g)(1) of this section beyond the date that is six months after the date of the certification.

(h) *Unemployment deferment.*

(1) A borrower qualifies for an unemployment deferment by providing evidence of eligibility for unemployment benefits to the lender.

(2) A borrower also qualifies for an unemployment deferment by providing to the lender a written certification—

(i) Describing the borrower's diligent search for full-time employment during the preceding 6 months, except that a borrower requesting an initial period of unemployment deferment is not required to describe his or her search for full-time employment at the time the deferment is granted. The initial period of unemployment deferment can be granted for a period of unemployment beginning up to 6 months before the date the holder receives the borrower's request and documentation for the deferment, and can be granted for up to 6 months after that date. For a continuation of an unemployment deferment following the initial period, the borrower's written certification must include information showing that the borrower made at least six diligent attempts to secure employment to support the prior 6-month period covered by the certification. This information could be the name of the employer contacted and the employer's address and telephone number, or other information acceptable to the holder showing that the borrower made six diligent attempts to obtain full-time employment;

(A) The name of the employer contacted;

(B) The employer's address and phone number; and

(C) The name or title of the person contacted;

(ii) Setting forth the borrower's latest permanent home address and, if applicable, the borrower's latest temporary address; and

(iii) Affirming that the borrower has registered with a public or private employment agency, if one is within a 50-mile radius of the borrower's permanent or temporary address, specifying the agency's name and address and date of registration.

(3) For purposes of obtaining an unemployment deferment under paragraph (h)(2) of this section, the following rules apply:

(i) A borrower may qualify for an unemployment deferment whether or not the borrower has been previously employed.

(ii) An unemployment deferment is not justified if the borrower refuses to seek or accept employment in kinds of positions or at salary and responsibility levels for which the borrower feels over qualified by virtue of education or previous experience.

(iii) Full-time employment involves at least 30 hours of work a week and is expected to last at least three months.

(iv) A lender may accept, as an alternative to the certification of employer contacts required under paragraph (h)(2)(i) of this section, comparable documentation the borrower has used to meet the requirements of the Unemployment Insurance Service, if it shows the same number of contacts and contains the same information the borrower would be required to provide under this section.

(4) A lender may not grant a deferment based on a single certification under paragraph (h)(1) or (h)(2) of this section beyond the date that is six months after the date the borrower provides evidence of the borrower's eligibility for unemployment insurance benefits under paragraph (h)(1) of this section or the date the borrower provides the written certification under paragraph (h)(2) of this section.

(i) *Military deferment.*

(1) To qualify for a military deferment, a borrower shall provide the lender with—

(i) A written statement from the borrower's commanding or personnel officer certifying—

(A) That the borrower is on active duty in the Armed Forces of the United States;

(B) The date on which the borrower's service began; and

(C) The date on which the borrower's service is expected to end; or

(ii)(A) A copy of the borrower's official military orders; and

(B) A copy of the borrower's military identification.

(2) For the purpose of this section, the Armed Forces means the Army, Navy, Air Force, Marine Corps, and the Coast Guard.

(3) A borrower enlisted in a reserve component of the Armed Forces may qualify for a military deferment only for service on a full-time basis that is expected to last for a period of at least one year in length, as evidenced by official military orders, unless an order for national mobilization of reservists is issued.

(4) A borrower enlisted in the National Guard qualifies for a military deferment only while the borrower is on active duty status as a member of the U.S. Army or Air Force Reserves, and meets the requirements of paragraph (i)(3) of this section.

(j) *Public Health Service deferment.* To qualify for a Public Health Service deferment, the borrower shall provide the lender with a statement from an authorized official of the United States Public Health Service (USPHS) certifying—

(1) That the borrower is engaged in full-time service as an officer in the Commissioned Corps of the USPHS;

(2) The date on which the borrower's service began; and

(3) The date on which the borrower's service is expected to end.

(k) *Peace Corps deferment.*

(1) To qualify for a deferment for service under the Peace Corps Act, the borrower shall provide the lender with a statement from an authorized official of the Peace Corps certifying—

(i) That the borrower has agreed to serve for a term of at least one year;

(ii) The date on which the borrower's service began; and

(iii) The date on which the borrower's service is expected to end.

(2) The lender must grant a deferment for the borrower's full term of service in the Peace Corps, not to exceed three years.

(*l*) *Full-time volunteer service in the ACTION programs.* To qualify for a deferment as a full-time paid volunteer in an ACTION program, the borrower shall provide the lender with a statement from an authorized official of the program certifying—

(1) That the borrower has agreed to serve for a term of at least one year;

(2) The date on which the borrower's service began; and

(3) The date on which the borrower's service is expected to end.

(m) *Deferment for full-time volunteer service for a tax-exempt organization.* To qualify for a deferment as a full-time paid volunteer for a tax-exempt organization, a borrower shall provide the lender with a statement from an authorized official of the volunteer program certifying—

(1) That the borrower—

(i) Serves in an organization that has obtained an exemption from taxation under section 501(c)(3) of the Internal Revenue Code of 1986;

(ii) Provides service to low-income persons and their communities to assist them in eliminating poverty and poverty-related human, social, and environmental conditions;

(iii) Does not receive compensation that exceeds the rate prescribed under section 6 of the Fair Labor Standards Act of 1938 (the Federal minimum wage), except that the tax-exempt organization may provide health, retirement, and other fringe benefits to the volunteer that are substantially equivalent to the benefits offered to other employees of the organization;

(iv) Does not, as part of his or her duties, give religious instruction, conduct worship services, engage in religious proselytizing, or engage in fund-raising to support religious activities; and

(v) Has agreed to serve on a full-time basis for a term of at least one year;

(2) The date on which the borrower's service began; and

(3) The date on which the borrower's service is expected to end.

(n) *Internship or residency deferment.*

(1) To qualify for an internship or residency deferment under paragraphs (b)(2)(v) or (b)(5)(iii) of this section, the borrower shall provide the lender with a statement from an authorized official of the organization with which the borrower is undertaking the internship or residency program certifying—

(i) That the internship or residency program is a supervised training program that requires the borrower to hold at least a baccalaureate degree prior to acceptance into the program;

(ii) That, except for a borrower that provides the statement from a State official described in paragraph (n)(2) of this section, the internship or residency program leads to a degree or certificate awarded by an institution of higher education, a hospital, or a health care facility that offers postgraduate training;

(iii) That the borrower has been accepted into the internship or residency program; and

(iv) The anticipated dates on which the borrower will begin and complete the internship or residency program, or, in the case of a borrower providing the statement described in paragraph (n)(2) of this section, the anticipated date on which the borrower will begin and complete the minimum period of participation in the internship program that the State requires be completed before an individual may be certified for professional practice or service.

(2) For a borrower who does not provide a statement certifying to the matters set forth in paragraph (n)(1)(ii) of this section to qualify for an internship deferment under paragraph (b)(2)(v) of this section, the borrower shall provide the lender with a statement from an official of the appropriate State licensing agency certifying that the internship or residency program, or a portion thereof, is required to be completed before the borrower may be certified for professional practice or service.

(o) *Parental-leave deferment.*

(1) To qualify for the parental-leave deferment described in paragraph (b)(3) of this section, the borrower shall provide the lender with—

(i) A statement from an authorized official of a participating school certifying that the borrower was enrolled on at least a half-time basis during the six months preceding the beginning of the deferment period;

(ii) A statement from the borrower certifying that the borrower—

(A) Is pregnant, caring for his or her newborn child, or caring for a child immediately following the placement of the child with the borrower in connection with an adoption;

(B) Is not, and will not be, attending school during the deferment period; and

(C) Is not, and will not be, engaged in full-time employment during the deferment period; and

(iii) A physician's statement demonstrating the existence of the pregnancy, a birth certificate, or a statement from the adoption agency official evidencing a pre-adoption placement.

(2) For purposes of paragraph (o)(1)(ii)(C) of this section, full-time employment involves at least 30 hours of work per week and is expected to last at least three months.

(p) *NOAA deferment.* To qualify for a National Oceanic and Atmospheric Administration (NOAA) deferment, the borrower shall provide the lender with a statement from an authorized official of the NOAA corps, certifying—

(1) That the borrower is on active duty service in the NOAA corps;

(2) The date on which the borrower's service began; and

(3) The date on which the borrower's service is expected to end.

(q) *Targeted teacher deferment.*

(1) To qualify for a targeted teacher deferment under paragraph (b)(5)(ii) of this section, the borrower, for each school year of service for which a deferment is requested, must provide to the lender—

(i) A statement by the chief administrative officer of the public or nonprofit private elementary or secondary school in which the borrower is teaching, certifying that the borrower is employed as a full-time teacher; and

(ii) A certification that he or she is teaching in a teacher shortage area designated by the Secretary as provided in paragraphs (q)(5) through (7) of this section, as described in paragraph (q)(2) of this section.

(2) In order to satisfy the requirement for certification that a borrower is teaching in a teacher shortage area designated by the Secretary, a borrower must do one of the following:

(i) If the borrower is teaching in a State in which the Chief State School Officer has complied with paragraph (q)(3) of this section

and provides an annual listing of designated teacher shortage areas to the State's chief administrative officers whose schools are affected by the Secretary's designations, the borrower may obtain a certification that he or she is teaching in a teacher shortage area from his or her school's chief administrative officer.

(ii) If a borrower is teaching in a State in which the Chief State School Officer has not complied with paragraph (q)(3) of this section or does not provide an annual listing of designated teacher shortage areas to the State's chief administrative officers whose schools are affected by the Secretary's designations, the borrower must obtain certification that he or she is teaching in a teacher shortage area from the Chief State School Officer for the State in which the borrower is teaching.

(3) In the case of a State in which borrowers wish to obtain certifications as provided for in paragraph (q)(2)(i) of this section, the State's Chief State School Officer must first have notified the Secretary, by means of a one-time written assurance, that he or she provides annually to the State's chief administrative officers whose schools are affected by the Secretary's designations and the guaranty agency for that State, a listing of the teacher shortage areas designated by the Secretary as provided for in paragraph (q)(5) through (7) of this section.

(4) If a borrower who receives a deferment continues to teach in the same teacher shortage areas as that in which he or she was teaching when the deferment was originally granted, the borrower shall, at the borrower's request, continue to receive the deferment for those subsequent years, up to the three-year maximum deferment period, even if his or her position does not continue to be within an area designated by the Secretary as a teacher shortage area in those subsequent years. To continue to receive the deferment in a subsequent year under this paragraph, the borrower shall provide the lender with a statement by the chief administrative officer of the public or nonprofit private elementary or secondary school that employs the borrower, certifying that the borrower continues to be employed as a full-time teacher in the same teacher shortage area for which the deferment was received for the previous year.

(5) For purposes on this section a teacher shortage area is—

(i)(A) A geographic region of the State in which there is a shortage of elementary or secondary school teachers; or

(B) A specific grade level or academic, instructional, subject-matter, or discipline classification in which there is a statewide shortage of elementary or secondary school teachers; and

(ii) Designated by the Secretary under paragraphs (q)(6) or (q)(7) of this section.

(6)(i) In order for the Secretary to designate on or more teacher shortage areas in a State for a school year, the Chief State School Officer shall by January 1 of the calendar year in which the school year begins, and in accordance with objective written standards, propose teacher shortage areas to the Secretary for designation. With respect to private nonprofit schools included in the recommendation, the Chief State School Officer shall consult with appropriate officials of the private nonprofit schools in the State prior to submitting the recommendation.

(ii) In identifying teacher shortage areas to propose for designation under paragraph (q)(6)(i) of this section, the Chief State School Officer shall consider data from the school year in which the recommendation is to be made, unless the data is not yet available, in which case he or she may use data from the immediately preceding school year, with respect to—

(A) Teaching positions that are unfilled;

(B) Teaching positions that are filled by teachers who are certified by irregular, provisional, temporary, or emergency certification; and

(C) Teaching positions that are filled by teachers who are certified, but who are teaching in academic subject areas other than their area of preparation.

(iii) If the total number of unduplicated full-time equivalent (FTE) elementary or secondary teaching positions identified under paragraph (q)(6)(ii) of this section in the shortage areas proposed by the State for designation does not exceed 5 percent of the total number of FTE elementary and secondary teaching positions in the State, the Secretary designates those areas as teacher shortage areas.

(iv) If the total number of unduplicated FTE elementary and secondary teaching positions identified under paragraph (q)(6)(ii) of this section in the shortage areas proposed by the State for designation exceeds 5 percent of the total number of elementary and secondary FTE teaching positions in the State, the Chief State School Officer shall submit, with the list of proposes areas, supporting documentation showing the methods used for identifying shortage areas, and an explanation of the reasons why the Secretary should nevertheless designate all of the proposed areas as teacher shortage areas. The explanation must include a ranking of the proposed shortage areas according to priority, to assist the Secretary in determining which areas should be designated. The Secretary, after considering the explanation, determines which shortage areas to designate as teacher shortage areas.

(7) A Chief State School Officer may submit to the Secretary for approval an alternative written procedure to the one described in paragraph (q)(6) of this section, for the Chief State School Officer to use to select the teacher shortage areas recommended to the Secretary for designation, and for the Secretary to use to choose the areas to be designated. If the Secretary approves the proposed alternative procedure, in writing, that procedure, once approved, may be used instead of the procedure described in paragraph (q)(6) of this section for designation of teacher shortage areas in that State.

(8) For purposes of paragraphs (q)(1) through (7) of this section—

(i) The definition of the term *school* in § 682.200(b) does not apply;

(ii) *Elementary school* means a day or residential school that provides elementary education, as determined under State law;

(iii) *Secondary school* means a day or residential school that provides secondary education, as determined under State law. In the absence of applicable State law, the Secretary may determine, with respect to that State, whether the term "secondary school" includes education beyond the twelfth grade;

(iv) *Teacher* means a professional who provides direct and personal services to students for their educational development through classroom teaching;

(v) *Chief State School Officer* means the highest ranking educational official for elementary and secondary education for the State;

(vi) *School year* means the period from July 1 of a calendar year through June 30 of the following calendar year;

(vii) *Teacher shortage area* means an area of specific grade, subject matter, or discipline classification, or a geographic area in which the Secretary determines that there is an inadequate supply of elementary or secondary school teachers; and

(viii) *Full-time equivalent* means the standard used by a State in defining full-time employment, but not less than 30 hours per week. For purposes of counting full-time equivalent teacher positions, a teacher working part of his or her total hours in a position that is designated as a teacher shortage area is counted on a pro rata basis corresponding to the percentage of his or her working hours spent in such a position.

(r) *Working-mother deferment.*

(1) To qualify for the working-mother deferment described in paragraph (b)(5)(iv) of this section, the borrower shall provide the lender with a statement certifying that she—

(i) Is the mother of a preschool-age child;

(ii) Entered or reentered the workforce not more than one year before the beginning date of the period for which the deferment is being sought;

(iii) Is currently engaged in full-time employment; and

(iv) Does not receive compensation that exceeds $1 per hour above the rate prescribed under section 6 of the Fair Labor Standards Act of 1938 (the Federal minimum wage).

(2) In addition to the certification required under paragraph (r)(1) of this section, the borrower shall provide to the lender documents demonstrating the age of her child (e.g., a birth certificate) and the rate of her compensation (e.g., a pay stub showing her hourly rate of pay).

(3) For purposes of this paragraph—

(i) A preschool-age child is one who has not yet enrolled in first grade or a higher grade in elementary school; and

(ii) Full-time employment involves at least 30 hours of work a week and is expected to last at least 3 months.

(s) *Deferments for new borrowers on or after July 1, 1993—*

(1) *General.* A new borrower who receives an FFEL Program loan first disbursed on or after July 1, 1993 is entitled to receive deferments under paragraphs (s)(2) through (s)(6) of this section. For purposes of paragraphs (s)(2) through (s)(6) of this section, a "new borrower" is an individual who has no outstanding principal or interest balance on an FFEL Program loan as of July 1, 1993 or on the date he or she obtains a loan on or after July 1, 1993. This term also includes a borrower who obtains a Federal Consolidation Loan on or after July 1, 1993 if the borrower has no other outstanding FFEL Program loan when the Consolidation Loan was made.

(2) *In-school deferment.* An eligible borrower is entitled to a deferment based on the borrower's at least half-time study in accordance with the rules prescribed in § 682.210(c), except that the borrower is not required to obtain a Stafford or SLS loan for the period of enrollment covered by the deferment.

(3) *Graduate fellowship deferment.* An eligible borrower is entitled to a graduate fellowship deferment in accordance with the rules prescribed in § 682.210(d).

(4) *Rehabilitation training program deferment.* An eligible borrower is entitled to a rehabilitation training program deferment in accordance with the rules prescribed in § 682.210(e).

(5) *Unemployment deferment.* An eligible borrower is entitled to an unemployment deferment in accordance with the rules prescribed in § 682.210(h) for periods that, collectively, do not exceed 3 years.

(6) *Economic hardship deferment.* An eligible borrower is entitled to an economic hardship deferment for periods of up to one year at a time that, collectively, do not exceed 3 years (except that

a borrower who receives a deferment under paragraph (s)(6)(vi) of this section is entitled to an economic hardship deferment for the lesser of the borrower's full term of service in the Peace Corps or the borrower's remaining period of economic hardship deferment eligibility under the 3-year maximum), if the borrower provides documentation satisfactory to the lender showing that the borrower is within any of the categories described in paragraphs (s)(6)(I) through (s)(6)(vi) of this section.

(i) Has been granted an economic hardship deferment under either the Direct Loan or Federal Perkins Loan Programs for the period of time for which the borrower has requested an economic hardship deferment for his or her FFEL loan.

(ii) Is receiving payment under a Federal or State public assistance program, such as Aid to Families with Dependent Children, Supplemental Security Income, Food Stamps, or State general public assistance.

(iii) Is working full-time and has a monthly income that does not exceed the greater of (as calculated on a monthly basis)—

(A) The minimum wage rate described in section 6 of the Fair Labor Standards Act of 1938; or

(B) An amount equal to 100 percent of the poverty line for a family of two, as determined in accordance with section 673(2) of the Community Services Block Grant Act.

(iv) Is working full-time and has a Federal education debt burden that equals or exceeds 20 percent of the borrower's monthly income, and that income, minus the borrower's Federal education debt burden, is less than 220 percent of the amount described in paragraph (s)(6)(iii) of this section.

(v) Is not working full-time and has a monthly income that—

(A) Does not exceed twice the amount described in paragraph (s)(6)(iii) of this section; and

(B) After deducting an amount equal to the borrower's Federal education debt burden, the remaining amount of the borrower's income does not exceed the amount described in paragraph (s)(6)(iii) of this section.

(vi) Is serving as a volunteer in the Peace Corps.

(vii) In determining a borrower's Federal education debt burden for purposes of an economic hardship deferment under paragraphs (s)(6)(iv) through (v) of this section, the lender shall count only the monthly payment amount (or a proportional share if the payments are due less frequently than monthly) that would have been owed on a Federal postsecondary education loan if the loan had been scheduled to be repaid in 10 years from the date the borrower entered repayment, regardless of the length of the borrower's actual repayment schedule or the actual monthly payment amount (if any) that would be owed during the period that the borrower requested an economic hardship deferment. The lender shall require the borrower to provide evidence that would enable the lender to determine the amount of the monthly payments that would have been owed by the borrower during the deferment period to other entities for Federal postsecondary education loans.

(viii) For an initial period of deferment granted under paragraphs (s)(6)(iii) through (v) of this section, the lender must require the borrower to submit evidence showing the amount of the borrower's monthly income.

(ix) To qualify for a subsequent period of deferment that begins less than one year after the end of a period of deferment under paragraphs (s)(6)(iii) through (v) of this section, the lender must require the borrower to submit—

(A) Evidence showing the amount of the borrower's monthly income or a copy of the borrower's most recently filed Federal income tax return; and

(B) For periods of deferment under paragraphs (s)(6)(iv) and (v) of this section, evidence that would enable the lender to determine the amount of the monthly payments to all other entities for Federal postsecondary education loans that would have been owed by the borrower during the deferment period.

(x) For purposes of paragraph (s)(6) of this section, a borrower's monthly income is the gross amount of income received by the borrower from employment and from other sources, or one-twelfth of the borrower's adjusted gross income, as recorded on the borrower's most recently filed Federal income tax return.

(xi) For purposes of paragraph (s)(6) of this section, a borrower is considered to be working full-time if the borrower is expected to be employed for at least three consecutive months at 30 hours per week.

(Approved by the Office of Management and Budget under control number 1845-0020)

(Authority: 20 U.S.C. 1077, 1078, 1078-1, 1078-2, 1078-3, 1082, 1085)

[58 FR 9120, Feb. 19, 1993; 59 FR 25746, May 17, 1994; 59 FR 33594, June 29, 1994; 59 FR 61215, Nov. 29, 1994; 60 FR 30788, June 12, 1995; 60 FR 32912, June 26, 1995; 60 FR 61756, Dec. 1, 1995; 61 FR 16718, April 17, 1996; 64 FR 18977, April 16, 1999; 64 FR 57531, Oct. 25, 1999; 64 FR 58626, Oct. 29, 1999; 64 FR 58958, Nov. 1, 1999; 65 FR 65619, Nov. 1, 2000; 66 FR 34763, June 29, 2001]

§ 682.211 Forbearance.

(a)(1) The Secretary encourages a lender to grant forbearance for the benefit of a borrower or endorser in order to prevent the borrower or endorser from defaulting on the borrower's or endorser's repayment obligation, or to permit the borrower or endorser to resume honoring that obligation after default. *Forbearance* means permitting the temporary cessation of payments, allowing an extension of time for making payments, or temporarily accepting smaller payments than previously were scheduled.

(2) Subject to paragraph (g) of this section, a lender may grant forbearance to payments of principal and interest under paragraphs (b), (c), and (d) of this section only if—

(i) The lender reasonably believes, and documents in the borrower's file, that the borrower or endorser intends to repay the loan but, due to poor health or other acceptable reasons, is currently unable to make scheduled payments; or

(ii) The borrower's payments of principal are deferred under § 682.210 and the Secretary does not pay interest benefits on behalf of the borrower under § 682.301.

(3) If two individuals are jointly liable for repayment of a PLUS loan or a Consolidation loan, the lender may grant forbearance on repayment of the loan only if the ability of both individuals to make scheduled payments has been impaired based on the same or differing conditions.

(4) Except as provided in paragraph (f)(9) of this section, if payments of interest are forborne, they may be capitalized as provided in § 682.202(b).

(b) A lender may grant forbearance if the lender and the borrower or endorser agree in writing to the terms of the forbearance, or, in the case of forbearance of interest during a period of deferment. If the lender informs the borrower at the time the deferment is granted that interest payments are to be forborne.

(c) A lender may grant forbearance for a period of up to one year at a time if both the borrower or endorser and an authorized official of the lender agree in writing to the terms of the forbearance.

(d) A guaranty agency may authorize a lender to grant forbearance to permit a borrower or endorser to resume honoring the agreement to repay the debt after default but prior to claim payment. The terms of the forbearance agreement in this situation must include a new signed agreement to repay the debt.

(e) Except in the case of forbearance of interest payments during a deferment period, if a forbearance involves the postponement of all payments, the lender must contact the borrower or endorser by telephone or send a written notice to the borrower or endorser at least once every three months during the period of forbearance to remind the borrower or endorser of the outstanding obligation to repay.

(f) A lender may grant forbearance, upon notice to the borrower or if applicable, the endorser, with respect to payments of interest and principal that are overdue—

(1) For a properly granted period of deferment for which the lender leans the borrower did not qualify;

(2) Upon the beginning of an authorized deferment period under § 682.210, or an administrative forbearance period as specified under paragraph (f)(10) or (i)(2) of this section;

(3) For the period beginning when the borrower entered repayment until the first payment due date was established;

(4) For the period prior to the borrower's filing of a bankruptcy petition as provided in § 682.402(f).

(5) For the periods described in § 682.402(c) in regard to the borrower's total and permanent disability;

(6) For a period not to exceed an additional 60 days after the lender has suspended collection activity for the initial 60-day period required pursuant to § 682.211(i)(6) and § 682.402(b)(3), when the lender receives reliable information that the borrower (or student in the case of a PLUS loan) has died;

(7) For periods necessary for the Secretary or guaranty agency to determine the borrower's eligibility for discharge of the loan because of an unpaid refund, attendance at a closed school or false certification of loan eligibility, pursuant to § 682.402(d) or (e), or the borrower's or, if applicable, endorser's bankruptcy, pursuant to § 682.402(f); or

(8) For a period of delinquency at the time a loan is sold or transferred, if the borrower or endorser is less than 60 days delinquent on the loan at the time of sale or transfer.

(9) For a period of delinquency that may remain after a borrower ends a period of deferment or mandatory forbearance until the next due date, which can be no later than 45 days after the period ends.

(10) For a period not to exceed 60 days necessary for the lender to collect and process documentation supporting the borrower's request for a deferment, forbearance, change in repayment plan, or consolidation loan. Interest that accrues during this period is not capitalized.

(11) For a period not to exceed 3 months for a borrower who is affected by a natural disaster.

(g) In granting a forbearance under this section, except for a forbearance under paragraph (i)(5) of this section, a lender shall grant a temporary cessation of payments, unless the borrower chooses another form of forbearance subject to paragraph (a)(1) of this section.

(h) *Mandatory forbearance.*

(1) *Medical or dental interns or residents.* Upon receipt of a request and sufficient supporting documentation, as described in § 682.210(n), from a borrower serving in a medical or dental internship or residency program, a lender shall grant increments (or a lesser period equal to the actual period during which the borrower is eligible) if the borrower has exhausted his or her eligibility for a deferment under § 682.210(n), or the borrower's promissory note does not provide for such a deferment—

(i) For the length of time remaining in the borrower's medical or dental internship or residency that must be successfully completed before the borrower may begin professional practice or service; or

(ii) For the length of time that the borrower is serving in a medical or dental internship or residency program leading to a degree or certificate awarded by an institution of higher education, a hospital, or a health care facility that offers postgraduate training.

(2) *Borrowers who are not medical or dental interns or residents, and endorsers.* Upon receipt of a request and sufficient supporting documentation from an endorser (if applicable), or from a borrower (other than a borrower who is serving in a medical or dental internship or residency described in paragraph (h)(1) of this section), a lender shall grant forbearance—

(i) In increments up to one year, for periods that collectively do not exceed three years, if—

(A) The borrower or endorser is currently obligated to make payments on Title IV loans; and

(B) The amount of those payments each month (or a proportional share if the payments are due less frequently than monthly) is collectively equal to or greater than 20 percent of the borrower's or endorser's total monthly income;

(ii) In yearly increments (or a lesser period equal to the actual period during which the borrower is eligible) for as long as a borrower—

(A) Is serving in a national service position for which the borrower receives a national service educational award under the National and Community Service Trust Act of 1993;

(B) Is performing the type of service that would qualify the borrower for a partial repayment of his or her loan under the Student Loan Repayment Programs administered by the Department of Defense under 10 U.S.C. 2171; or

(C) Is performing the type of service that would qualify the borrower for loan forgiveness and associated forbearance under the requirements of the teacher loan forgiveness program in § 682.215.

(3) *Documentation.*

(i) Before granting a forbearance to a borrower or endorser under paragraph (h)(2)(i) of this section, the lender shall require the borrower or endorser to submit at least the following documentation:

(A) Evidence showing the amount of the most recent total monthly gross income received by the borrower or endorser from employment and from other sources; and

(B) Evidence showing the amount of the monthly payments owed by the borrower or endorser to other entities for the most recent month for the borrower's or endorser's Title IV loans.

(ii) Before granting a forbearance to a borrower or endorser under paragraph (h)(2)(ii)(B) of this section, the lender shall require the borrower or endorser to submit documentation showing the beginning and ending dates that the Department of Defense considers the borrower to be eligible for a partial repayment of his or her loan under the Student Loan Repayment Programs.

(iii) Before granting a forbearance to a borrower under paragraph (h)(2)(ii)(C) of this section, the lender must require the borrower to—

(A) Submit documentation for the period of the annual forbearance request showing the beginning and anticipated ending dates that the borrower is expected to perform, for that year, the type of service described in § 682.215(c); and

(B) Certify the borrower's intent to satisfy the requirements of § 682.215(c).

(Approved by the Office of Management and Budget under control number 1845-0020)

(i) *Mandatory administrative forbearance.*

(1) The lender shall grant a mandatory administrative forbearance for the periods specified in paragraph (i)(2) of this section until the lender is notified by the Secretary or a guaranty agency that the forbearance period no longer applies. The lender may not require a borrower who is eligible for a forbearance under paragraph (i)(2)(ii) of this section to submit a request or supporting documentation, but shall require a borrower (or endorser, if applicable) who requests forbearance because of a military mobilization to provide documentation showing that he or she is subject to a military mobilization as described in paragraph (i)(4) of this section.

(2) The lender is not required to notify the borrower (or endorser, if applicable) at the time the forbearance is granted, but shall grant a forbearance to a borrower or endorser during a period, and the 30 days following the period, when the lender is notified by the Secretary that—

(i) Exceptional circumstances exist, such as a local or national emergency or military mobilization; or

(ii) The geographical area in which the borrower or endorser resides has been designated a disaster area by the president of the United States or Mexico, the prime minister of Canada, or by a governor of a state.

(3) As soon as feasible, or by the date specified by the Secretary, the lender shall notify the borrower (or endorser, if applicable) that the lender has granted a forbearance and the date that payments should resume. The lender's notification shall state that the borrower or endorser—

(i) May decline the forbearance and continue to be obligated to make scheduled payments; or

(ii) Consents to making payments in accordance with the lender's notification if the forbearance is not declined.

(4) For purposes of paragraph (i)(2)(i) of this section, the term "military mobilization" shall mean a situation in which the Department of Defense orders members of the National Guard or Reserves to active duty under sections 688, 12301(a), 12301(g), 12302, 12304, and 12306 of title 10, United States Code. This term also includes the assignment of other members of the Armed Forces to duty stations at locations other than the locations at which they were normally assigned, only if the military mobilization involved the activation of the National Guard or Reserves.

(5) The lender shall grant a mandatory administrative forbearance to a borrower (or endorser, if applicable) during a period when the borrower (or endorser, if applicable) is making payments for a period of—

(i) Up to 3 years of payments in cases where the effect of a variable interest rate on a standard or graduated repayment schedule would result in a loan not being repaid within the maximum repayment term; or

(ii) Up to 5 years of payments in cases where the effect of decreased installment amounts paid under an income-sensitive repayment schedule would result in the loan not being repaid within the maximum repayment term.

(6) The lender shall grant a mandatory administrative forbearance to a borrower for a period not to exceed 60 days after the lender receives reliable information indicating that the borrower (or student in the case of a PLUS loan) has died, until the lender receives documentation of death pursuant to § 682.402(b)(3).

(Approved by the Office of Management and Budget under control number 1845-0020)

(Authority: 20 U.S.C. 1077, 1078, 1078-1, 1078-2, 1078-3, 1080, 1082)

[58 FR 9120, Feb. 19, 1993; 59 FR 25746, May 17, 1994; 59 FR 33595, June 29, 1994; 60 FR 30788, June 12, 1995; 60 FR 32912, June 26, 1995; 60 FR 61756, Dec. 1, 1995; 61 FR 16718, April 17, 1996; 64 FR 18977, April 16, 1999; 64 FR 58626, Oct. 29, 1999; 64 FR 58959, Nov. 1, 1999; 65 FR 65627, Nov. 1, 2000; 66 FR 34763, June 29, 2001; 66 FR 44007, Aug. 21, 2001]

§ 682.402 Death, disability, closed school, false certification, unpaid refunds, and bankruptcy payments.

(a) *General.*

(1) Rules governing the payment of claims based on filing for relief in bankruptcy, and discharge of loans due to death, total and permanent disability, attendance at a school that closes, false certification by a school of a borrower's eligibility for a loan, and unpaid refunds by a school are set forth in this section.

(2) If a PLUS loan was obtained by two parents as co-makers, or a Consolidation loan was obtained by a married couple, and only one of the borrowers dies, becomes totally and permanently disabled, has collection of his or her loan obligation stayed by a bankruptcy filing, or has that obligation discharged in bankruptcy, the other borrower remains obligated to repay the loan unless that borrower would qualify for discharge of the loan under these regulations.

(3) Except for a borrower's loan obligation discharged by the Secretary under the false certification discharge provision of paragraphs (e)(1)(ii) of this section, a loan qualifies for payment under this section and as provided in paragraph (h)(1)(iv) of this section, only to the extent that the loan is legally enforceable under applicable law by the holder of the loan.

(4) For purposes of this section—

(i) The legal enforceability of a loan is conclusively determined on the basis of a ruling by a court or administrative tribunal of competent jurisdiction with respect to that loan, or a ruling with respect to another loan in a judgment that collaterally estops the holder from contesting the enforceability of the loan;

(ii) A loan is conclusively determined to be legally unenforceable to the extent that the guarantor determines, pursuant to an objection presented in a proceeding conducted in connection with credit bureau reporting, tax refund offset, wage garnishment, or in any other administrative proceeding, that the loan is not legally enforceable; and

(iii) If an objection has been raised by the borrower or another party about the legal enforceability of the loan and no determination has been made under paragraph (a)(4)(i) or (ii) of this section, the Secretary may authorize the payment of a claim under this section under conditions the Secretary considers appropriate. If the Secretary determines in that or any other case that a claim was paid under this section with respect to a loan that was not a legally enforceable obligation of the borrower, the recipient of that payment must refund that amount of the payment to the Secretary.

(b) *Death.*

(1) If an individual borrower dies, or the student for whom a parent received a PLUS loan dies, the obligation of the borrower and any endorser to make any further payments on the loan is discharged.

(2) A discharge of a loan based on the death of the borrower (or student in the case of a PLUS loan) must be based on an original or certified copy of the death certificate. Under exceptional circumstances and on a case-by-case basis, the chief executive officer of the guaranty agency may approve a discharge based upon other reliable documentation supporting the discharge request.

(3) After receiving reliable information indicating that the borrower (or student) has died, the lender must suspend any collection activity against the borrower and any endorser for up to 60 days and promptly request the documentation described in paragraph (b)(2) of this section. If additional time is required to obtain the documentation, the period of suspension of collection activity may be extended up to an additional 60 days. If the lender is not able to obtain an original or certified copy of the death certificate or other documentation acceptable to the guaranty agency, under the provisions of paragraph (b)(2) of this section, during the period of suspension, the lender must resume collection activity from the point that it had been discontinued. The lender is deemed to have exercised forbearance as to repayment of the loan during the period when collection activity was suspended.

(4) Once the lender has determined under paragraph (b)(2) of this section that the borrower (or student) has died, the lender may not attempt to collect on the loan from the borrower's estate or from any endorser.

(5) The lender shall return to the sender any payments received from the estate or paid on behalf of the borrower after the date of the borrower's (or student's) death.

(c) *Total and permanent disability.*

(1)(i) If the Secretary has made an initial determination that the borrower is totally and permanently disabled, as defined in § 682.200(b), the loan is conditionally discharged for up to three years from the date that the borrower became totally and permanently disabled, as certified by a physician. The Secretary suspends collection activity on the loan from the date of the initial determination of total and permanent disability until the end of the conditional period. If the borrower satisfies the criteria for a total and permanent disability discharge during and at the end of the conditional discharge period, the balance of the loan is discharged at the end of the conditional discharge period and any payments received after the date the borrower became totally and permanently disabled as certified under § 682.402(c)(2), are returned to the sender.

(ii) A borrower satisfies the criteria for a discharge of a loan based on a total and permanent disability if, during and at the end of the three-year period described in paragraph (c)(1)(i) of this section—

(A) The borrower's annual earnings from employment do not exceed 100 percent of the poverty line for a family of two, as determined in accordance with the Community Service Block Grant Act; and

(B) The borrower does not receive a new loan under the Perkins, FFEL, or Direct Loan programs, except for a FFEL or Direct Consolidation loan that does not include any loans that are in a conditional discharge status.

(iii) Except as provided in paragraph (c)(1)(iv)(A) of this section, a borrower is not considered totally and permanently disabled based on a condition that existed at the time the loan was made unless the borrower's condition substantially deteriorated.

(iv)(A) For a Consolidation Loan, a borrower is considered totally and permanently disabled if he or she would be considered totally and permanently disabled under paragraphs (c)(1)(i) through (iii) of this section for all of the loans that were included in the Consolidation Loan if those loans had not been consolidated.

(B) For the purposes of discharging a loan under paragraph (c)(1)(iv)(A) of this section, provisions in paragraphs (c)(1)(i) through (iii) of this section apply to each loan included in the Consolidation Loan, even if the loan is not a FFEL Program loan.

(C) If requested, a borrower seeking to discharge a loan obligation under paragraph (c)(1)(iv)(A) of this section must provide the lender with the disbursement dates of the underlying loans if the lender does not possess that information.

(2) After being notified by the borrower or the borrower's representative that the borrower claims to be totally and permanently disabled, the lender promptly requests that the borrower or the borrower's representative submit, on a form approved by the Secretary, a certification by a physician, who is a doctor of medicine or osteopathy and legally authorized to practice in a State, that the borrower is totally and permanently disabled as defined in § 682.200(b).

(3) The lender must continue collection activities until it receives either the certification of total and permanent disability from a physician or a letter from a physician stating that the certification has been requested and that additional time is needed to determine if the borrower is totally and permanently disabled. Except as provided in paragraph (c)(5) or (c)(7) of this section, after receiving the physician's certification or letter the lender may not attempt to collect from the borrower or any endorser.

(4) The lender must submit a disability claim to the guaranty agency if the borrower submits a certification by a physician and the lender makes a determination that the certification supports the conclusion that the borrower meets the criteria for a total and permanent disability discharge, as defined in § 682.200(b).

(5) If the lender determines that a borrower who claims to be totally and permanently disabled is not totally and permanently disabled, or if the lender does not receive the physician's certification of total and permanent disability within 60 days of the receipt of the physician's letter requesting additional time, as described in paragraph (c)(3) of this section, the lender must resume collection and is deemed to have exercised forbearance of payment of both principal and interest from the date collection activity was suspended. The lender may capitalize, in accordance with § 682.202(b), any interest accrued and not paid during that period.

(6) The guaranty agency must pay a claim submitted by the lender if the guaranty agency has reviewed the application and determined that it is complete and that it supports the conclusion that the borrower meets the criteria for a total and permanent

disability discharge, as defined in § 682.200(b).

(7) If the guaranty agency does not pay the disability claim, the guaranty agency must return the claim to the lender with an explanation of the basis for the agency's denial of the claim. Upon receipt of the returned claim, the lender must notify the borrower that the application for a disability discharge has been denied, provide the basis for the denial, and inform the borrower that the lender will resume collection on the loan. The lender is deemed to have exercised forbearance of both principal and interest from the date collection activity was suspended until the first payment due date. The lender may capitalize, in accordance with § 682.202(b), any interest accrued and not paid during that period.

(8) If the guaranty agency pays the disability claim, the lender must notify the borrower that the loan will be assigned to the Secretary for determination of eligibility for a total and permanent disability discharge.

(9) After receiving a claim payment from the guaranty agency, the lender must forward to the guaranty agency any payments subsequently received from or on behalf of the borrower.

(10) The Secretary reimburses the guaranty agency for a disability claim paid to the lender after the agency pays the claim to the lender.

(11) The guaranty agency must assign the loan to the Secretary after the guaranty agency pays the disability claim.

(12) If the Secretary determines that the certification and information provided by the borrower do not support the conclusion that the borrower meets the criteria for a total and permanent disability discharge, the Secretary notifies the borrower that the application for a disability discharge has been denied, and that the loan is due and payable under the terms of the promissory note.

(13) If the Secretary makes an initial determination that the borrower is totally and permanently disabled, the Secretary notifies the borrower that the loan is conditionally discharged and that the conditional discharge period will last for up to three years after the date the borrower became totally and permanently disabled as certified under § 682.402(c)(2). The notification identifies the conditions of the conditional discharge period specified in paragraphs (c)(13) through (c)(16) of this section and specifies that all or part of the three-year period may predate the Secretary's initial determination.

(14) During the conditional discharge period, the borrower—

(i) Is not required to make any payments on the loan;

(ii) Is not considered delinquent or in default on the loan, unless the borrower was delinquent or in default at the time the conditional discharge was granted;

(iii) Must promptly notify the Secretary of any changes in address or phone number;

(iv) Must promptly notify the Secretary if the borrower's annual earnings from employment exceed the amount specified in paragraph (c)(1)(ii)(A) of this section; and

(v) Must provide the Secretary, upon request, with additional documentation or information related to the borrower's eligibility for discharge under this section.

(15) If, during and at the end of the conditional discharge period, the borrower continues to satisfy the eligibility criteria for a total and permanent disability discharge, as described in § 682.402(c)(1)(ii), the balance of the loan is discharged.

(16) If, at any time during the three-year conditional discharge period, the borrower does not continue to meet the eligibility requirements for a total and permanent disability discharge, the

Secretary resumes collection activity on the loan. The Secretary does not require the borrower to pay any interest that accrued on the loan from the date of the initial determination described in paragraph (c)(13) of this section through the end of the conditional discharge period.

(d) *Closed school.*

(1) *General.*

(i) The Secretary reimburses the holder of a loan received by a borrower on or after January 1, 1986, and discharges the borrower's obligation with respect to the loan in accordance with the provisions of paragraph (d) of this section, if the borrower (or the student for whom a parent received a PLUS loan) could not complete the program of study for which the loan was intended because the school at which the borrower (or student) was enrolled, closed, or the borrower (or student) withdrew from the school not more than 90 days prior to the date the school closed. This 90-day period may be extended if the Secretary determines that exceptional circumstances related to a school's closing would justify an extension.

(ii) For purposes of the closed school discharge authorized by this section—

(A) A school's closure date is the date that the school ceases to provide educational instruction in all programs, as determined by the Secretary;

(B) The term "borrower" includes all endorsers on a loan; and

(C) A "school" means a school's main campus or any location or branch of the main campus, regardless of whether the school or its location or branch is considered eligible.

(2) *Relief available pursuant to discharge.*

(i) Discharge under paragraph (d) of this section relieves the borrower of an existing or past obligation to repay the loan and any charges imposed or costs incurred by the holder with respect to the loan that the borrower is, or was otherwise obligated to pay.

(ii) A discharge of a loan under paragraph (d) of this section qualifies the borrower for reimbursement of amounts paid voluntarily or through enforced collection on a loan obligation discharged under paragraph (d) of this section.

(iii) A borrower who has defaulted on a loan discharged under paragraph (d) of this section is not regarded as in default on the loan after discharge, and is eligible to receive assistance under the Title IV, HEA programs.

(iv) A discharge of a loan under paragraph (d) of this section must be reported by the loan holder to all credit reporting agencies to which the holder previously reported the status of the loan, so as to delete all adverse credit history assigned to the loan.

(3) *Borrower qualification for discharge.* Except as provided in paragraph (d)(8) of this section, in order to qualify for a discharge of a loan under paragraph (d) of this section, a borrower must submit a written request and sworn statement to the holder of the loan. The statement need not be notarized, but must be made by the borrower under the penalty of perjury, and, in the statement, the borrower must state—

(i) Whether the student has made a claim with respect to the school's closing with any third party, such as the holder of a performance bond or a tuition recovery program, and if so, the amount of any payment received by the borrower (or student) or credited to the borrower's loan obligation;

(ii) That the borrower (or the student for whom a parent received a PLUS loan)—

(A) Received, on or after January 1, 1986, the proceeds of any disbursement of a loan disbursed, in whole or in part, on or after January 1, 1986 to attend a school;

(B) Did not complete the educational program at that school because the school closed while the student was enrolled or on an approved leave of absence in accordance with § 682.605(c), or the student withdrew from the school not more than 90 days before the school closed; and

(C) Did not complete the program of study through a teach-out at another school or by transferring academic credits or hours earned at the closed school to another school;

(iii) That the borrower agrees to provide, upon request by the Secretary or the Secretary's designee, other documentation reasonably available to the borrower that demonstrates, to the satisfaction of the Secretary or the Secretary's designee, that the student meets the qualifications in paragraph (d) of this section; and

(iv) That the borrower agrees to cooperate with the Secretary or the Secretary's designee in enforcement actions in accordance with paragraph (d)(4) of this section, and to transfer any right to recovery against a third party in accordance with paragraph (d)(5) of this section.

(4) *Cooperation by borrower in enforcement actions.*

(i) In any judicial or administrative proceeding brought by the Secretary or the Secretary's designee to recover for amounts discharged under paragraph (d) of this section or to take other enforcement action with respect to the conduct on which those claims were based, a borrower who requests or receives a discharge under paragraph (d) of this section must cooperate with the Secretary of the Secretary's designee. At the request of the Secretary or the Secretary's designee, and upon the Secretary's or the Secretary's designee's tendering to the borrower the fees and costs as are customarily provided in litigation to reimburse witnesses, the borrower shall—

(A) Provide testimony regarding any representation made by the borrower to support a request for discharge; and

(B) Produce any documentation reasonably available to the borrower with respect to those representations and any sworn statement required by the Secretary with respect to those representations and documents.

(ii) The Secretary revokes the discharge, or denies the request for discharge, of a borrower who—

(A) Fails to provide testimony, sworn statements, or documentation to support material representations made by the borrower to obtain the discharge; or

(B) Provides testimony, a sworn statement, or documentation that does not support the material representations made by the borrower to obtain the discharge.

(5) *Transfer to the Secretary of borrower's right of recovery against third parties.*

(i) Upon discharge under paragraph (d) of this section, the borrower is deemed to have assigned to and relinquished in favor of the Secretary any right to a loan refund (up to the amount discharged) that the borrower (or student) may have by contract or applicable law with respect to the loan or the enrollment agreement for the program for which the loan was received, against the school, its principals, affiliates and their successors, its sureties, and any private fund, including the portion of a public fund that represents funds received from a private party.

(ii) The provisions of paragraph (d) of this section apply notwithstanding any provision of State law that would otherwise restrict transfer of such rights by the borrower (or student), limit or

prevent a transferee from exercising those rights, or establish procedures or a scheme of distribution that would prejudice the Secretary's ability to recover on those rights.

(iii) Nothing in this section shall be construed as limiting or foreclosing the borrower's (or student's) right to pursue legal and equitable relief regarding disputes arising from matters otherwise unrelated to the loan discharged.

(6) *Guaranty agency responsibilities—*

(i) *Procedures applicable if a school closed on or after January 1, 1986, but prior to June 13, 1994.*

(A) If a borrower received a loan for attendance at a school with a closure date on or after January 1, 1986, but prior to June 13, 1994, the loan may be discharged in accordance with the procedures specified in paragraph (d)(6)(i) of this section.

(B) If a loan subject to paragraph (d) of this section was discharged in part in accordance with the Secretary's "Closed School Policy" as authorized by section IV of Bulletin 89-G-159, the guaranty agency shall initiate the discharge of the remaining balance of the loan not later than August 13, 1994.

(C) A guaranty agency shall review its records and identify all schools that appear to have closed on or after January 1, 1986 and prior to June 13, 1994, and shall identify the loans made to any borrower (or student) who appears to have been enrolled at the school on the school closure date or who withdrew not more than 90 days prior to the closure date.

(D) A guaranty agency shall notify the Secretary immediately if it determines that a school not previously known to have closed appears to have closed, and, within 30 days of making that determination, notify all lenders participating in its program to suspend collection efforts against individuals with respect to loans made for attendance at the closed school, if the student to whom (or on whose behalf) a loan was made, appears to have been enrolled at the school on the closing date, or withdrew not more than 90 days prior to the date the school appears to have closed. Within 30 days after receiving confirmation of the date of a school's closure from the Secretary, the agency shall—

(1) Notify all lenders participating in its program to mail a discharge application explaining the procedures and eligibility criteria for obtaining a discharge and an explanation of the information that must be included in the sworn statement (which may be combined) to all borrowers who may be eligible for a closed school discharge; and

(2) Review the records of loans that it holds, identify the loans made to any borrower (or student) who appears to have been enrolled at the school on the school closure date or who withdrew not more than 90 days prior to the closure date, and mail a discharge application and an explanation of the information that must be included in the sworn statement (which may be combined) to the borrower. The application shall inform the borrower of the procedures and eligibility criteria for obtaining a discharge.

(E) If a loan identified under paragraph (d)(6)(i)(D)(2) of this section is held by the guaranty agency as a defaulted loan and the borrower's current address is known, the guaranty agency shall immediately suspend any efforts to collect from the borrower on any loan received for the program of study for which the loan was made (but may continue to receive borrower payments), and notify the borrower that the agency will provide additional information about the procedures for requesting a discharge after the agency has received confirmation from the Secretary that the school had closed.

(F) If a loan identified under paragraph (d)(6)(i)(D)(2) of this section is held by the guaranty agency as a defaulted loan and the borrower's current address is unknown, the agency shall, by June 13, 1995, further refine the list of borrowers whose loans are potentially subject to discharge under paragraph (d) of this section by consulting with representatives of the closed school, the school's licensing agency, accrediting agency, and other appropriate parties. Upon learning the new address of a borrower who would still be considered potentially eligible for a discharge, the guaranty agency shall, within 30 days after learning the borrower's new address, mail to the borrower a discharge application that meets the requirements of paragraph (d)(6)(i)(E) of this section.

(G) If the guaranty agency determines that a borrower identified in paragraph (d)(6)(i)(E) or (F) of this section has satisfied all of the conditions required for a discharge, the agency shall notify the borrower in writing of that determination within 30 days after making that determination.

(H) If the guaranty agency determines that a borrower identified in paragraph (d)(6)(i)(E) or (F) of this section does not qualify for a discharge, the agency shall notify the borrower in writing of that determination and the reasons for it within 30 days after the date the agency—

(1) Made that determination based on information available to the guaranty agency;

(2) Was notified by the Secretary that the school had not closed;

(3) Was notified by the Secretary that the school had closed on a date that was more than 90 days after the borrower (or student) withdrew from the school;

(4) Was notified by the Secretary that the borrower (or student) was ineligible for a closed school discharge for other reasons; or

(5) Received the borrower's completed application and sworn statement.

(I) If a borrower described in paragraph (d)(6)(i)(E) or (F) of this section fails to submit the written request and sworn statement described in paragraph (d)(3) of this section within 60 days of being notified of that option, the guaranty agency shall resume collection and shall be deemed to have exercised forbearance of payment of principal and interest from the date it suspended collection activity. The agency may capitalize, in accordance with § 682.202(b), any interest accrued and not paid during that period.

(J) A borrower's request for discharge may not be denied solely on the basis of failing to meet any time limits set by the lender, guaranty agency, or the Secretary.

(ii) *Procedures applicable if a school closed on or after June 13, 1994.*

(A) A guaranty agency shall notify the Secretary immediately whenever it becomes aware of reliable information indicating a school may have closed. The designated guaranty agency in the state in which the school is located shall promptly investigate whether the school has closed and, within 30 days after receiving information indicating that the school may have closed, report the results of its investigation to the Secretary concerning the date of the school's closure and whether a teach-out of the closed school's program was made available to students.

(B) If a guaranty agency determines that a school appears to have closed, it shall, within 30 days of making that determination, notify all lenders participating in its program to suspend collection efforts against individuals with respect to loans made for attendance at the closed school, if the student to whom (or on whose behalf) a loan was made, appears to have been enrolled at the school on the closing date, or withdrew not more than 90 days prior to the date the school appears to have closed. Within 30 days after receiving confirmation of the date of a school's closure from the Secretary, the agency shall—

(1) Notify all lenders participating in its program to mail a discharge application explaining the procedures and eligibility criteria for obtaining a discharge and an explanation of the information that must be included in the sworn statement (which may be combined) to all borrowers who may be eligible for a closed school discharge; and

(2) Review the records of loans that it holds, identify the loans made to any borrower (or student) who appears to have been enrolled at the school on the school closure date or who withdrew not more than 90 days prior to the closure date, and mail a discharge application and an explanation of the information that must be included in the sworn statement (which may be combined) to the borrower. The application shall inform the borrower of the procedures and eligibility criteria for obtaining a discharge.

(C) If a loan identified under paragraph (d)(6)(ii)(B)(2) of this section is held by the guaranty agency as a defaulted loan and the borrower's current address is known, the guaranty agency shall immediately suspend any efforts to collect from the borrower on any loan received for the program of study for which the loan was made (but may continue to receive borrower payments), and notify the borrower that the agency will provide additional information about the procedures for requesting a discharge after the agency has received confirmation from the Secretary that the school had closed.

(D) If a loan identified under paragraph (d)(6)(ii)(B)(2) of this section is held by the guaranty agency as a defaulted loan and the borrower's current address is unknown, the agency shall, within one year after identifying the borrower, attempt to locate the borrower and further determine the borrower's potential eligibility for a discharge under paragraph (d) of this section by consulting with representatives of the closed school, the school's licensing agency, accrediting agency, and other appropriate parties. Upon learning the new address of a borrower who would still be considered potentially eligible for a discharge, the guaranty agency shall, within 30 days after learning the borrower's new address, mail to the borrower a discharge application that meets the requirements of paragraph (d)(6)(ii)(B) of this section.

(E) If the guaranty agency determines that a borrower identified in paragraph (d)(6)(ii)(C) or (D) of this section has satisfied all of the conditions required for a discharge, the agency shall notify the borrower in writing of that determination within 30 days after making that determination.

(F) If the guaranty agency determines that a borrower identified in paragraph (d)(6)(ii)(C) or (D) of this section does not qualify for a discharge, the agency shall notify the borrower in writing of that determination and the reasons for it within 30 days after the date the agency—

(1) Made that determination based on information available to the guaranty agency;

(2) Was notified by the Secretary that the school had not closed;

(3) Was notified by the Secretary that the school had closed on a date that was more than 90 days after the borrower (or student) withdrew from the school;

(4) Was notified by the Secretary that the borrower (or student) was ineligible for a closed school discharge for other reasons; or

(5) Received the borrower's completed application and sworn statement.

(G) Upon receipt of a closed school discharge claim filed by a lender, the agency shall review the borrower's request and supporting sworn statement in light of information available from the records of the agency and from other sources, including other guaranty agencies, state authorities, and cognizant accrediting associations, and shall take the following actions—

(1) If the agency determines that the borrower satisfies the requirements for discharge under paragraph (d) of this section, it shall pay the claim in accordance with § 682.402(h) not later than 90 days after the agency received the claim; or

(2) If the agency determines that the borrower does not qualify for a discharge, the agency shall, not later than 90 days after the agency received the claim, return the claim to the lender with an explanation of the reasons for its determination.

(H) If a borrower fails to submit the written request and sworn statement described in paragraph (d)(3) of this section within 60 days of being notified of that option, the lender or guaranty agency shall resume collection and shall be deemed to have exercised forbearance of payment of principal and interest from the date it suspended collection activity. The lender or guaranty agency may capitalize, in accordance with § 682.202(b), any interest accrued and not paid during that period.

(I) A borrower's request for discharge may not be denied solely on the basis of failing to meet any time limits set by the lender, guaranty agency, or the Secretary.

(7) *Lender responsibilities.*

(i) A lender shall comply with the requirements prescribed in paragraph (d) of this section. In the absence of specific instructions from a guaranty agency or the Secretary, if a lender receives information from a source it believes to be reliable indicating that an existing or former borrower may be eligible for a loan discharge under paragraph (d) of this section, the lender shall immediately notify the guaranty agency, and suspend any efforts to collect from the borrower on any loan received for the program of study for which the loan was made (but may continue to receive borrower payments).

(ii) If the borrower fails to submit the written request and sworn statement described in paragraph (d)(3) of this section within 60 days after being notified of that option, the lender shall resume collection and shall be deemed to have exercised forbearance of payment of principal and interest from the date the lender suspended collection activity. The lender may capitalize, in accordance with § 682.202(b), any interest accrued and not paid during that period.

(iii) The lender shall file a closed school claim with the guaranty agency in accordance with § 682.402(g) no later than 60 days after the lender receives the borrower's written request and sworn statement described in paragraph (d)(3) of this section. If a lender receives a payment made by or on behalf of the borrower on the loan after the lender files a claim on the loan with the guaranty agency, the lender shall forward the payment to the guaranty agency within 30 days of its receipt. The lender shall assist the guaranty agency and the borrower in determining whether the borrower is eligible for discharge of the loan.

(iv) Within 30 days after receiving reimbursement from the guaranty agency for a closed school claim, the lender shall notify the borrower that the loan obligation has been discharged, and request that all credit bureaus to which it previously reported the status of the loan delete all adverse credit history assigned to the loan.

(v) Within 30 days after being notified by the guaranty agency that the borrower's request for a closed school discharge has been denied, the lender shall resume collection and notify the borrower of the reasons for the denial. The lender shall be deemed to have exercised forbearance of payment of principal and interest from the date the lender suspended collection activity, and may capitalize, in accordance with § 682.202(b), any interest accrued and not paid during that period.

(8) *Discharge without an application.* A borrower's obligation to repay an FFEL Program loan may be discharged without an application from the borrower if the—

(i) Borrower received a discharge on a loan pursuant to 34 CFR 674.33(g) under the Federal Perkins Loan Program, or 34 CFR 685.213 under the William D. Ford Federal Direct Loan Program; or

(ii) The Secretary or the guaranty agency, with the Secretary's permission, determines that the borrower qualifies for a discharge based on information in the Secretary or guaranty agency's possession.

(e) *False certification by a school of a student's eligibility to borrow and unauthorized disbursements—*

(1) *General.*

(i) The Secretary reimburses the holder of a loan received by a borrower on or after January 1, 1986, and discharges a current or former borrower's obligation with respect to the loan in accordance with the provisions of paragraph (e) of this section, if the borrower's (or the student for whom a parent received a PLUS loan) eligibility to receive the loan was falsely certified by an eligible school. For purposes of a false certification discharge, the term "borrower" includes all endorsers on a loan. A student's eligibility to borrow shall be considered to have been falsely certified by the school if the school—

(A) Certified the student's eligibility for a FFEL Program loan on the basis of ability to benefit from its training and the student did not meet the applicable requirements described in 34 CFR Part 668 and section 484(d) of the Act, as applicable and as described in paragraph (e)(13) of this section; or

(B) Signed the borrower's name without authorization by the borrower on the loan application or promissory note.

(ii) The Secretary discharges the obligation of a borrower with respect to a loan disbursement for which the school, without the borrower's authorization, endorsed the borrower's loan check or authorization for electronic funds transfer, unless the student for whom the loan was made received the proceeds of the loan either by actual delivery of the loan funds or by a credit in the amount of the contested disbursement applied to charges owed to the school for that portion of the educational program completed by the student. However, the Secretary does not reimburse the lender with respect to any amount disbursed by means of a check bearing an unauthorized endorsement unless the school also executed the application or promissory note for that loan for the named borrower without that individual's consent.

(2) *Relief available pursuant to discharge.*

(i) Discharge under paragraph (e)(1)(i) of this section relieves the borrower of an existing or past obligation to repay the loan certified by the school, and any charges imposed or costs incurred by the holder with respect to the loan that the borrower is, or was, otherwise obligated to pay.

(ii) A discharge of a loan under paragraph (e) of this section qualifies the borrower for reimbursement of amounts paid voluntarily or through enforced collection on a loan obligation discharged under paragraph (e) of this section.

(iii) A borrower who has defaulted on a loan discharged under paragraph (e) of this section is not regarded as in default on the loan after discharge, and is eligible to receive assistance under the Title IV, HEA programs.

(iv) A discharge of a loan under paragraph (e) of this section is reported by the loan holder to all credit reporting agencies to which the holder previously reported the status of the loan, so as to delete all adverse credit history assigned to the loan.

(v) Discharge under paragraph (e)(1)(ii) of this section qualifies the borrower for relief only with respect to the amount of the disbursement discharged.

(3) *Borrower qualification for discharge.* Except as provided in paragraph (e)(14) of this section, to qualify for a discharge of a loan under paragraph (e) of this section, the borrower must submit to the holder of the loan a written request and a sworn statement. The statement need not be notarized, but must be made by the borrower under penalty of perjury, and, in the statement, the borrower must—

(i) State whether the student has made a claim with respect to the school's false certification with any third party, such as the holder of a performance bond or a tuition recovery program, and if so, the amount of any payment received by the borrower (or student) or credited to the borrower's loan obligation;

(ii) In the case of a borrower requesting a discharge based on defective testing of the student's ability to benefit, state that the borrower (or the student for whom a parent received a PLUS loan)—

(A) Received, on or after January 1, 1986, the proceeds of any disbursement of a loan disbursed, in whole or in part, on or after January 1, 1986 to attend a school; and

(B) Was admitted to that school on the basis of ability to benefit from its training and did not meet the applicable requirements for admission on the basis of ability to benefit as described in paragraph (e)(13) of this section;

(iii) In the case of a borrower requesting a discharge because the school signed the borrower's name on the loan application or promissory note—

(A) State that the signature on either of those documents was not the signature of the borrower; and

(B) Provide five different specimens of his or her signature, two of which must be not earlier or later than one year before or after the date of the contested signature;

(iv) In the case of a borrower requesting a discharge because the school, without authorization of the borrower, endorsed the borrower's name on the loan check or signed the authorization for electronic funds transfer or master check, the borrower shall—

(A) Certify that he or she did not endorse the loan check or sign the authorization for electronic funds transfer or master check, or authorize the school to do so;

(B) Provide five different specimens of his or her signature, two of which must be not earlier or later than one year before or after the date of the contested signature; and

(C) State that the proceeds of the contested disbursement were not received either through actual delivery of the loan funds or by a credit in the amount of the contested disbursement applied to charges owed to the school for that portion of the educational

program completed by the student;

(v) That the borrower agrees to provide upon request by the Secretary or the Secretary's designee, other documentation reasonably available to the borrower, that demonstrates, to the satisfaction of the Secretary or the Secretary's designee, that the student meets the qualifications in paragraph (e) of this section; and

(vi) That the borrower agrees to cooperate with the Secretary or the Secretary's designee in enforcement actions in accordance with paragraph (e)(4) of this section, and to transfer any right to recovery against a third party in accordance with paragraph (e)(5) of this section.

(4) *Cooperation by borrower in enforcement actions.*

(i) In any judicial or administrative proceeding brought by the Secretary or the Secretary's designee to recover for amounts discharged under paragraph (e) of this section or to take other enforcement action with respect to the conduct on which those claims were based, a borrower who requests or receives a discharge under paragraph (e) of this section must cooperate with the Secretary or the Secretary's designee. At the request of the Secretary or the Secretary's designee, and upon the Secretary's or the Secretary's designee's tendering to the borrower the fees and costs as are customarily provided in litigation to reimburse witnesses, the borrower shall—

(A) Provide testimony regarding any representation made by the borrower to support a request for discharge; and

(B) Produce any documentation reasonably available to the borrower with respect to those representations and any sworn statement required by the Secretary with respect to those representations and documents.

(ii) The Secretary revokes the discharge, or denies the request for discharge, of a borrower who—

(A) Fails to provide testimony, sworn statements, or documentation to support material representations made by the borrower to obtain the discharge; or

(B) Provides testimony, a sworn statement, or documentation that does not support the material representations made by the borrower to obtain the discharge.

(5) *Transfer to the Secretary of borrower's right of recovery against third parties.*

(i) Upon discharge under paragraph (e) of this section, the borrower is deemed to have assigned to and relinquished in favor of the Secretary any right to a loan refund (up to the amount discharged) that the borrower (or student) may have by contract or applicable law with respect to the loan or the enrollment agreement for the program for which the loan was received, against the school, its principals, affiliates and their successors, its sureties, and any private fund, including the portion of a public fund that represents funds received from a private party.

(ii) The provisions of paragraph (e) of this section apply notwithstanding any provision of state law that would otherwise restrict transfer of such rights by the borrower (or student), limit or prevent a transferee from exercising those rights, or establish procedures or a scheme of distribution that would prejudice the Secretary's ability to recover on those rights.

(iii) Nothing in this section shall be construed as limiting or foreclosing the borrower's (or student's) right to pursue legal and equitable relief regarding disputes arising from matters otherwise unrelated to the loan discharged.

(6) *Guaranty agency responsibilities—general.*

(i) A guaranty agency shall notify the Secretary immediately whenever it becomes aware of reliable information indicating that a school may have falsely certified a student's eligibility or caused an unauthorized disbursement of loan proceeds, as described in paragraph (e)(3) of this section. The designated guaranty agency in the state in which the school is located shall promptly investigate whether the school has falsely certified a student's eligibility and, within 30 days after receiving information indicating that the school may have done so, report the results of its preliminary investigation to the Secretary.

(ii) If the guaranty agency receives information it believes to be reliable indicating that a borrower whose loan is held by the agency may be eligible for a discharge under paragraph (e) of this section, the agency shall immediately suspend any efforts to collect from the borrower on any loan received for the program of study for which the loan was made (but may continue to receive borrower payments), and inform the borrower of the procedures for requesting a discharge.

(iii) If the borrower fails to submit the written request and sworn statement described in paragraph (e)(3) of this section within 60 days of being notified of that option, the guaranty agency shall resume collection and shall be deemed to have exercised forbearance of payment of principal and interest from the date it suspended collection activity. The agency may capitalize, in accordance with § 682.202(b), any interest accrued and not paid during that period.

(iv) Upon receipt of a discharge claim filed by a lender or a request submitted by a borrower with respect to a loan held by the guaranty agency, the agency shall have up to 90 days to determine whether the discharge should be granted. The agency shall review the borrower's request and supporting sworn statement in light of information available from the records of the agency and from other sources, including other guaranty agencies, state authorities, and cognizant accrediting associations.

(v) A borrower's request for discharge and sworn statement may not be denied solely on the basis of failing to meet any time limits set by the lender, the Secretary or the guaranty agency.

(7) *Guaranty agency responsibilities with respect to a claim filed by a lender based on the borrower's assertion that he or she did not sign the loan application or the promissory note, or that the school failed to test, or improperly tested, the student's ability to benefit.*

(i) The agency shall evaluate the borrower's request and consider relevant information it possesses and information available from other sources, and follow the procedures described in paragraph (e)(7) of this section.

(ii) If the agency determines that the borrower satisfies the requirements for discharge under paragraph (e) of this section, it shall, not later than 30 days after the agency makes that determination, pay the claim in accordance with § 682.402(h) and—

(A) Notify the borrower that his or her liability with respect to the amount of the loan has been discharged, and that the lender has been informed of the actions required under paragraph (e)(7)(ii)(C) of this section;

(B) Refund to the borrower all amounts paid by the borrower to the lender or the agency with respect to the discharged loan amount, including any late fees or collection charges imposed by the lender or agency related to the discharged loan amount; and

(C) Notify the lender that the borrower's liability with respect to the amount of the loan has been discharged, and that the lender must—

(1) Immediately terminate any collection efforts against the borrower with respect to the discharged loan amount and any charges imposed or costs incurred by the lender related to the discharged loan amount that the borrower is, or was, otherwise obligated to pay; and

(2) Within 30 days, report to all credit reporting agencies to which the lender previously reported the status of the loan, so as to delete all adverse credit history assigned to the loan.

(iii) If the agency determines that the borrower does not qualify for a discharge, it shall, within 30 days after making that determination—

(A) Notify the lender that the borrower's liability on the loan is not discharged and that, depending on the borrower's decision under paragraph (e)(7)(iii)(B) of this section, the loan shall either be returned to the lender or paid as a default claim; and

(B) Notify the borrower that the borrower does not qualify for discharge, and state the reasons for that conclusion. The agency shall advise the borrower that he or she remains obligated to repay the loan and warn the borrower of the consequences of default, and explain that the borrower will be considered to be in default on the loan unless the borrower submits a written statement to the agency within 30 days stating that the borrower—

(1) Acknowledges the debt and, if payments are due, will begin or resume making those payments to the lender; or

(2) Requests the Secretary to review the agency's decision.

(iv) Within 30 days after receiving the borrower's written statement described in paragraph (e)(7)(iii)(B)(1) of this section, the agency shall return the claim file to the lender and notify the lender to resume collection efforts if payments are due.

(v) Within 30 days after receiving the borrower's request for review by the Secretary, the agency shall forward the claim file to the Secretary for his review and take the actions required under paragraph (e)(11) of this section.

(vi) The agency shall pay a default claim to the lender within 30 days after the borrower fails to return either of the written statements described in paragraph (e)(7)(iii)(B) of this section.

(8) *Guaranty agency responsibilities with respect to a claim filed by a lender based only on the borrower's assertion that he or she did not sign the loan check or the authorization for the release of loan funds via electronic funds transfer or master check.*

(i) The agency shall evaluate the borrower's request and consider relevant information it possesses and information available from other sources, and follow the procedures described in paragraph (e)(8) of this section.

(ii) If the agency determines that a borrower who asserts that he or she did not endorse the loan check satisfies the requirements for discharge under paragraph (e)(3)(iv) of this section, it shall, within 30 days after making that determination—

(A) Notify the borrower that his or her liability with respect to the amount of the contested disbursement of the loan has been discharged, and that the lender has been informed of the actions required under paragraph (e)(8)(ii)(B) of this section;

(B) Notify the lender that the borrower's liability with respect to the amount of the contested disbursement of the loan has been discharged, and that the lender must—

(1) Immediately terminate any collection efforts against the borrower with respect to the discharged loan amount and any charges imposed or costs incurred by the lender related to the discharged loan amount that the borrower is, or was, otherwise obligated to pay;

(2) Within 30 days, report to all credit reporting agencies to

which the lender previously reported the status of the loan, so as to delete all adverse credit history assigned to the loan;

(3) Refund to the borrower, within 30 days, all amounts paid by the borrower with respect to the loan disbursement that was discharged, including any charges imposed or costs incurred by the lender related to the discharged loan amount; and

(4) Refund to the Secretary, within 30 days, all interest benefits and special allowance payments received from the Secretary with respect to the loan disbursement that was discharged; and

(C) Transfer to the lender the borrower's written assignment of any rights the borrower may have against third parties with respect to a loan disbursement that was discharged because the borrower did not sign the loan check.

(iii) If the agency determines that a borrower who asserts that he or she did not sign the electronic funds transfer or master check authorization satisfies the requirements for discharge under paragraph (e)(3)(iv) of this section, it shall, within 30 days after making that determination, pay the claim in accordance with § 682.402(h) and—

(A) Notify the borrower that his or her liability with respect to the amount of the contested disbursement of the loan has been discharged, and that the lender has been informed of the actions required under paragraph (e)(8)(iii)(C) of this section;

(B) Refund to the borrower all amounts paid by the borrower to the lender or the agency with respect to the discharged loan amount, including any late fees or collection charges imposed by the lender or agency related to the discharged loan amount; and

(C) Notify the lender that the borrower's liability with respect to the contested disbursement of the loan has been discharged, and that the lender must—

(1) Immediately terminate any collection efforts against the borrower with respect to the discharged loan amount and any charges imposed or costs incurred by the lender related to the discharged loan amount that the borrower is, or was, otherwise obligated to pay; and

(2) Within 30 days, report to all credit reporting agencies to which the lender previously reported the status of the loan, so as to delete all adverse credit history assigned to the loan.

(iv) If the agency determines that the borrower does not qualify for a discharge, it shall, within 30 days after making that determination—

(A) Notify the lender that the borrower's liability on the loan is not discharged and that, depending on the borrower's decision under paragraph (e)(8)(iv)(B) of this section, the loan shall either be returned to the lender or paid as a default claim; and

(B) Notify the borrower that the borrower does not qualify for discharge, and state the reasons for that conclusion. The agency shall advise the borrower that he or she remains obligated to repay the loan and warn the borrower of the consequences of default, and explain that the borrower will be considered to be in default on the loan unless the borrower submits a written statement to the agency within 30 days stating that the borrower—

(1) Acknowledges the debt and, if payments are due, will begin or resume making those payments to the lender; or

(2) Requests the Secretary to review the agency's decision.

(v) Within 30 days after receiving the borrower's written statement described in paragraph (e)(8)(iv)(B)(1) of this section, the agency shall return the claim file to the lender and notify the lender to resume collection efforts if payments are due.

(vi) Within 30 days after receiving the borrower's request for review by the Secretary, the agency shall forward the claim file to the Secretary for his review and take the actions required under paragraph (e)(11) of this section.

(vii) The agency shall pay a default claim to the lender within 30 days after the borrower fails to return either of the written statements described in paragraph (e)(8)(iv)(B) of this section.

(9) *Guaranty agency responsibilities in the case of a loan held by the agency for which a discharge request is submitted by a borrower based on the borrower's assertion that he or she did not sign the loan application or the promissory note, or that the school failed to test, or improperly tested, the student's ability to benefit.*

(i) The agency shall evaluate the borrower's request and consider relevant information it possesses and information available from other sources, and follow the procedures described in paragraph (e)(9) of this section.

(ii) If the agency determines that the borrower satisfies the requirements for discharge under paragraph (e)(3) of this section, it shall immediately terminate any collection efforts against the borrower with respect to the discharged loan amount and any charges imposed or costs incurred by the agency related to the discharged loan amount that the borrower is, or was otherwise obligated to pay and, not later than 30 days after the agency makes the determination that the borrower satisfies the requirements for discharge—

(A) Notify the borrower that his or her liability with respect to the amount of the loan has been discharged;

(B) Report to all credit reporting agencies to which the agency previously reported the status of the loan, so as to delete all adverse credit history assigned to the loan; and

(C) Refund to the borrower all amounts paid by the borrower to the lender or the agency with respect to the discharged loan amount, including any late fees or collection charges imposed by the lender or agency related to the discharged loan amount.

(iii) If the agency determines that the borrower does not qualify for a discharge, it shall, within 30 days after making that determination, notify the borrower that the borrower's liability with respect to the amount of the loan is not discharged, state the reasons for that conclusion, and if the borrower is not then making payments in accordance with a repayment arrangement with the agency on the loan, advise the borrower of the consequences of continued failure to reach such an arrangement, and that collection action will resume on the loan unless within 30 days the borrower—

(A) Acknowledges the debt and, if payments are due, reaches a satisfactory arrangement to repay the loan or resumes making payments under such an arrangement to the agency; or

(B) Requests the Secretary to review the agency's decision.

(iv) Within 30 days after receiving the borrower's request for review by the Secretary, the agency shall forward the borrower's discharge request and all relevant documentation to the Secretary for his review and take the actions required under paragraph (e)(11) of this section.

(v) The agency shall resume collection action if within 30 days of giving notice of its determination the borrower fails to seek review by the Secretary or agree to repay the loan.

(10) *Guaranty agency responsibilities in the case of a loan held by the agency for which a discharge request is submitted by a borrower based only on the borrower's assertion that he or she did not sign the loan check or the authorization for the release of loan proceeds via electronic funds transfer or master check.*

(i) The agency shall evaluate the borrower's request and consider relevant information it possesses and information available from other sources, and follow the procedures described in paragraph (e)(10) of this section.

(ii) If the agency determines that a borrower who asserts that he or she did not endorse the loan check satisfies the requirements for discharge under paragraph (e)(3)(iv) of this section, it shall refund to the Secretary the amount of reinsurance payment received with respect to the amount discharged on that loan less any repayments made by the lender under paragraph (e)(10)(ii)(D)(2) of this section, and within 30 days after making that determination—

(A) Notify the borrower that his or her liability with respect to the amount of the contested disbursement of the loan has been discharged;

(B) Report to all credit reporting agencies to which the agency previously reported the status of the loan, so as to delete all adverse credit history assigned to the loan;

(C) Refund to the borrower all amounts paid by the borrower to the lender or the agency with respect to the discharged loan amount, including any late fees or collection charges imposed by the lender or agency related to the discharged loan amount;

(D) Notify the lender to whom a claim payment was made that the lender must refund to the Secretary, within 30 days—

(1) All interest benefits and special allowance payments received from the Secretary with respect to the loan disbursement that was discharged; and

(2) The amount of the borrower's payments that were refunded to the borrower by the guaranty agency under paragraph (e)(10)(ii)(C) of this section that represent borrower payments previously paid to the lender with respect to the loan disbursement that was discharged;

(E) Notify the lender to whom a claim payment was made that the lender must, within 30 days, reimburse the agency for the amount of the loan that was discharged, minus the amount of borrower payments made to the lender that were refunded to the borrower by the guaranty agency under paragraph (e)(10)(ii)(C) of this section; and

(F) Transfer to the lender the borrower's written assignment of any rights the borrower may have against third parties with respect to the loan disbursement that was discharged.

(iii) In the case of a borrower who requests a discharge because he or she did not sign the electronic funds transfer or master check authorization, if the agency determines that the borrower meets the conditions for discharge, it shall immediately terminate any collection efforts against the borrower with respect to the discharged loan amount and any charges imposed or costs incurred by the agency related to the discharged loan amount that the borrower is, or was, otherwise obligated to pay, and within 30 days after making that determination—

(iv) The agency shall take the actions required under paragraphs (e)(9)(iii) through (v) if the agency determines that the borrower does not qualify for a discharge.

(11) *Guaranty agency responsibilities if a borrower requests a review by the Secretary.*

(i) Within 30 days after receiving the borrower's request for review under paragraph (e)(7)(iii)(B)(2), (e)(8)(iv)(B)(2), (e)(9)(iii)(B), or (e)(10)(iv) of this section, the agency shall forward the borrower's discharge request and all relevant documentation to the Secretary for his review.

(ii) The Secretary notifies the agency and the borrower of a determination on review. If the Secretary determines that the borrower is not eligible for a discharge under paragraph (e) of this section, within 30 days after being so informed, the agency shall take the actions described in paragraphs (e)(8)(iv) through (vii) or (e)(9)(iii) through (v) of this section, as applicable.

(iii) If the Secretary determines that the borrower meets the requirements for a discharge under paragraph (e) of this section, the agency shall, within 30 days after being so informed, take the actions required under paragraph (e)(7)(ii), (e)(8)(ii), (e)(8)(iii), (e)(9)(ii), (e)(10)(ii), or (e)(10)(iii) of this section, as applicable.

(12) *Lender Responsibilities.*

(i) If the lender is notified by a guaranty agency or the Secretary, or receives information it believes to be reliable from another source indicating that a current or former borrower may be eligible for a discharge under paragraph (e) of this section, the lender shall immediately suspend any efforts to collect from the borrower on any loan received for the program of study for which the loan was made (but may continue to receive borrower payments) and, within 30 days of receiving the information or notification, inform the borrower of the procedures for requesting a discharge.

(ii) If the borrower fails to submit the written request and sworn statement described in paragraph (e)(3) of this section within 60 days of being notified of that option, the lender shall resume collection and shall be deemed to have exercised forbearance of payment of principal and interest from the date the lender suspended collection activity. The lender may capitalize, in accordance with § 682.202(b), any interest accrued and not paid during that period.

(iii) The lender shall file a claim with the guaranty agency in accordance with § 682.402(g) no later than 60 days after the lender receives the borrower's written request and sworn statement described in paragraph (e)(3) of this section. If a lender receives a payment made by or on behalf of the borrower on the loan after the lender files a claim on the loan with the guaranty agency, the lender shall forward the payment to the guaranty agency within 30 days of its receipt. The lender shall assist the guaranty agency and the borrower in determining whether the borrower is eligible for discharge of the loan.

(iv) The lender shall comply with all instructions received from the Secretary or a guaranty agency with respect to loan discharges under paragraph (e) of this section.

(v) The lender shall review a claim that the borrower did not endorse and did not receive the proceeds of a loan check. The lender shall take the actions required under paragraphs (e)(8)(ii)(A) and (B) of this section if it determines that the borrower did not endorse the loan check, unless the lender secures persuasive evidence that the proceeds of the loan were received by the borrower or the student for whom the loan was made, as provided in paragraph (e)(1)(ii). If the lender determines that the loan check was properly endorsed or the proceeds were received by the borrower or student, the lender may consider the borrower's objection to repayment as a statement of intention not to repay the loan, and may file a claim with the guaranty agency for reimbursement on that ground, but shall not report the loan to credit bureaus as in default until the guaranty agency, or, as applicable, the Secretary, reviews the claim for relief. By filing such a claim, the lender shall be deemed to have agreed to the following—

(A) If the guarantor or the Secretary determines that the borrower endorsed the loan check or the proceeds of the loan were received by the borrower or the student, any failure to satisfy due diligence requirements by the lender prior to the filing of the claim that would have resulted in the loss of reinsurance on the loan in the event of default will be waived by the Secretary; and

(B) If the guarantor or the Secretary determines that the borrower did not endorse the loan check and that the proceeds of the loan were not received by the borrower or the student, the lender will comply with the requirements specified in paragraph (e)(8)(ii)(B) of this section.

(vi) Within 30 days after being notified by the guaranty agency that the borrower's request for a discharge has been denied, the lender shall notify the borrower of the reasons for the denial and, if payments are due, resume collection against the borrower. The lender shall be deemed to have exercised forbearance of payment of principal and interest from the date the lender suspended collection activity, and may capitalize, in accordance with § 682.202(b), any interest accrued and not paid during that period.

(13) *Requirements for certifying a borrower's eligibility for a loan.*

(i) For periods of enrollment beginning between July 1, 1987 and June 30, 1991, a student who had a general education diploma or received one before the scheduled completion of the program of instruction is deemed to have the ability to benefit from the training offered by the school.

(ii) A student not described in paragraph (e)(13)(i) of this section is considered to have the ability to benefit from training offered by the school if the student—

(A) For periods of enrollment beginning prior to July 1, 1987, was determined to have the ability to benefit from the school's training in accordance with the requirements of 34 CFR 668.6, as in existence at the time the determination was made;

(B) For periods of enrollment beginning between July 1, 1987 and June 30, 1996, achieved a passing grade on a test—

(1) Approved by the Secretary, for periods of enrollment beginning on or after July 1, 1991, or by the accrediting agency, for other periods; and

(2) Administered substantially in accordance with the requirements for use of the test;

(C) Successfully completed a program of developmental or remedial education provided by the school; or

(D) For periods of enrollment beginning on or after July 1, 1996 through June 30, 2000—

(1) Obtained, within 12 months before the date the student initially receives title IV, HEA program assistance, a passing score specified by the Secretary on an independently administered test in accordance with subpart J of 34 CFR part 668; or

(2) Enrolled in an eligible institution that participates in a State process approved by the Secretary under subpart J of 34 CFR part 668.

(E) For periods of enrollment beginning on or after July 1, 2000—

(1) Met either of the conditions described in paragraph (e)(13)(ii)(D) of this section; or

(2) Was home schooled and met the requirements of 34 CFR 668.32(e)(4).

(iii) Notwithstanding paragraphs (e)(13)(i) and (ii) of this section, a student did not have the ability to benefit from training offered by the school if—

(A) The school certified the eligibility of the student for a FFEL Program loan; and

(B) At the time of certification, the student would not meet the requirements for employment (in the student's State of residence) in the occupation for which the training program supported by the loan was intended because of a physical or mental condition, age, or criminal record or other reason accepted by the Secretary.

(iv) Notwithstanding paragraphs (e)(13)(i) and (ii) of this section, a student has the ability to benefit from the training offered by the school if the student received a high school diploma or its recognized equivalent prior to enrollment at the school.

(14) Discharge without an application. A borrower's obligation to repay all or a portion of an FFEL Program loan may be discharged without an application from the borrower if the Secretary, or the guaranty agency with the Secretary's permission, determines that the borrower qualifies for a discharge based on information in the Secretary or guaranty agency's possession.

(f) *Bankruptcy*—

(1) *General.* If a borrower files a petition for relief under the Bankruptcy Code, the Secretary reimburses the holder of the loan for unpaid principal and interest on the loan in accordance with paragraphs (h) through (k) of this section.

(2) *Suspension of collection activity.*

(i) If the lender is notified that a borrower has filed a petition for relief in bankruptcy, the lender must immediately suspend any collection efforts outside the bankruptcy proceeding against the borrower and—

(A) Must suspend any collection efforts against any co-maker or endorser if the borrower has filed for relief under Chapters 12 or 13 of the Bankruptcy Code; or

(B) May suspend any collection efforts against any co-maker or endorser if the borrower has filed for relief under Chapters 7 or 11 of the Bankruptcy Code.

(ii) If the lender is notified that a co-maker or endorser has filed a petition for relief in bankruptcy, the lender must immediately suspend any collection efforts outside the bankruptcy proceeding against the co-maker or endorser and—

(A) Must suspend collection efforts against the borrower and any other parties to the note if the co-maker or endorser has filed for relief under Chapters 12 or 13 of the Bankruptcy Code; or

(B) May suspend any collection efforts against the borrower and any other parties to the note if the co-maker or endorser has filed for relief under Chapters 7 or 11 of the Bankruptcy Code.

(3) *Determination of filing.* The lender must determine that a borrower has filed a petition for relief in bankruptcy on the basis of receiving a notice of the first meeting of creditors or other proof of filing provided by the debtor's attorney or the bankruptcy court.

(4) *Proof of claim.* Unless instructed otherwise by the guaranty agency, the lender shall file a proof of claim with the bankruptcy court within—

(i) 30 days after the lender receives a notice of first meeting of creditors unless, in the case of a proceeding under Chapter 7, the notice states that the borrower has no assets; or

(ii) 30 days after the lender receives a notice from the court stating that a Chapter 7 no-asset case has been converted to an asset case.

(5) *Filing of bankruptcy claim with the guaranty agency.*

(i) The lender shall file a bankruptcy claim on the loan with the guaranty agency in accordance with paragraph (g) of this section, if—

(A) The borrower has filed a petition for relief under Chapters 12 or 13 of the Bankruptcy Code; or

(B) The borrower has filed a petition for relief under Chapters

7 or 11 of the Bankruptcy Code before October 8, 1998 and the loan has been in repayment for more than seven years (exclusive of any applicable suspension of the repayment period) from the due date of the first payment until the date of the filing of the petition for relief; or

(C) The borrower has begun an action to have the loan obligation determined to be dischargeable on grounds of undue hardship.

(ii) In cases not described in paragraph (f)(5)(i) of this section, the lender shall continue to hold the loan notwithstanding the bankruptcy proceeding. Once the bankruptcy proceeding is completed or dismissed, the lender shall treat the loan as if the lender had exercised forbearance as to repayment of principal and interest accrued from the date of the borrower's filing of the bankruptcy petition until the date the lender is notified that the bankruptcy proceeding is completed or dismissed.

(g) *Claim procedures for a loan held by a lender—*

(1) *Documentation.* A lender shall provide the guaranty agency with the following documentation when filing a death, disability, closed school, false certification, or bankruptcy claim:

(i) The original promissory note or a copy of the promissory note certified by the lender as true and exact.

(ii) The loan application, if a separate loan application was provided to the lender.

(iii) In the case of a death claim, an original or certified death certificate, or other documentation supporting the discharge request that formed the basis for the determination of death.

(iv) In the case of a disability claim, a copy of the certification of disability described in paragraph (c)(2) of this section.

(v) In the case of a bankruptcy claim—

(A) Evidence that a bankruptcy petition has been filed, all pertinent documents sent to or received from the bankruptcy court by the lender, and an assignment to the guaranty agency of any proof of claim filed by the lender regarding the loan; and

(B) A statement of any facts of which the lender is aware that may form the basis for an objection or exception to the discharge of the borrower's loan obligation in bankruptcy and all documents supporting those facts.

(vi) In the case of a closed school claim, the documentation described in paragraph (d)(3) of this section, or any other documentation as the Secretary may require;

(vii) In the case of a false certification claim, the documentation described in paragraph (e)(3) of this section.

(2) *Filing deadlines.* A lender shall file a death, disability, closed school, false certification, or bankruptcy claim within the following periods:

(i) Within 60 days of the date on which the lender determines that a borrower (or the student on whose behalf a parent obtained a PLUS loan) has died, or the lender determines that the borrower is totally and permanently disabled.

(ii) In the case of a closed school claim, the lender shall file a claim with the guaranty agency no later than 60 days after the borrower submits to the lender the written request and sworn statement described in paragraph (d)(3) of this section or after the lender is notified by the Secretary or the Secretary's designee or by the guaranty agency to do so.

(iii) In the case of a false certification claim, the lender shall file a claim with the guaranty agency no later than 60 days after the borrower submits to the lender the written request and sworn statement described in paragraph (e)(3) of this section or after the

lender is notified by the Secretary or the Secretary's designee or by the guaranty agency to do so.

(iv) A lender shall file a bankruptcy claim with the guaranty agency by the earlier of—

(A) 30 days after the date on which the lender receives notice of the first meeting of creditors or other information described in paragraph (f)(3) of this section; or

(B) 15 days after the lender is served with a complaint or motion to have the loan determined to be dischargeable on grounds of undue hardship, or, if the lender secures an extension of time within which an answer may be filed, 25 days before the expiration of that extended period, whichever is later.

(h) *Payment of death, disability, closed school, false certification, and bankruptcy claims by the guaranty agency.*

(1) *General.*

(i) The guaranty agency shall review a death, disability, or bankruptcy claim promptly and shall pay the lender on an approved claim the amount of loss in accordance with paragraph (h) of this section, not later than 45 days after the claim was filed by the lender.

(ii) In the case of a bankruptcy claim, the guaranty agency shall, upon receipt of the claim from the lender, immediately take those actions required under paragraph (i) of this section to oppose the discharge of the loan by the bankruptcy court.

(iii) In the case of a closed school claim or a false certification claim based on the determination that the borrower did not sign the loan application, the promissory note, or the authorization for the electronic transfer of loan funds, or that the school failed to test, or improperly tested, the student's ability to benefit, the guaranty agency shall document its determination that the borrower is eligible for discharge under paragraphs (d) or (e) of this section and pay the borrower or the holder the amount determined under paragraph (h)(2) of this section.

(iv) In reviewing a claim under this section, the issue of confirmation of subsequent loans under an MPN will not be reviewed and a claim will not be denied based on the absence of any evidence relating to confirmation in a particular loan file. However, if a court rules that a loan is unenforceable solely because of the lack of evidence of the confirmation process or processes, insurance benefits must be repaid.

(2)(i) The amount of loss payable—

(A) On a death or disability claim is equal to the sum of the remaining principal balance and interest accrued on the loan, collection costs incurred by the lender and applied to the borrower's account within 30 days of the date those costs were actually incurred, and unpaid interest up to the date the lender should have filed the claim.

(B) On a bankruptcy claim is equal to the unpaid balance of principal and interest determined in accordance with paragraph (h)(3) of this section.

(ii) The amount of loss payable to a lender on a closed school claim or on a false certification claim is equal to the sum of the remaining principal balance and interest accrued on the loan, collection costs incurred by the lender and applied to the borrower's account within 30 days of the date those costs were actually incurred, and unpaid interest determined in accordance with paragraph (h)(3) of this section.

(iii) In the case of a closed school or false certification claim filed by a lender on an outstanding loan owed by the borrower, on the same date that the agency pays a claim to the lender, the agency shall pay the borrower an amount equal to the amount paid on the loan by or on behalf of the borrower, less any school tuition refunds or payments received by the holder or the borrower from a tuition recovery fund, performance bond, or other third-party source.

(iv) In the case of a claim filed by a lender based on a request received from a borrower whose loan had been repaid in full by, or on behalf of the borrower to the lender, on the same date that the agency notifies the lender that the borrower is eligible for a closed school or false certification discharge, the agency shall pay the borrower an amount equal to the amount paid on the loan by or on behalf of the borrower, less any school tuition refunds or payments received by the holder or the borrower from a tuition recovery fund, performance bond, or other third-party source.

(v) In the case of a loan that has been included in a Consolidation Loan, the agency shall pay to the holder of the borrower's Consolidation Loan, an amount equal to—

(A) The amount paid on the loan by or on behalf of the borrower at the time the loan was paid through consolidation;

(B) The amount paid by the consolidating lender to the holder of the loan when it was repaid through consolidation; minus

(C) Any school tuition refunds or payments received by the holder or the borrower from a tuition recovery fund, performance bond, or other third-party source if those refunds or payments were—

(1) Received by the borrower or received by the holder and applied to the borrower's loan balance before the date the loan was repaid through consolidation; or

(2) Received by the borrower or received by the Consolidation Loan holder on or after the date the consolidating lender made a payment to the former holder to discharge the borrower's obligation to that former holder.

(3) *Payment of interest.* If the guarantee covers unpaid interest, the amount payable on an approved claim includes the unpaid interest that accrues during the following periods:

(i) During the period before the claim is filed, not to exceed the period provided for in paragraph (g)(2) of this section for filing the claim.

(ii) During a period not to exceed 30 days following the receipt date by the lender of a claim returned by the guaranty agency for additional documentation necessary for the claim to be approved by the guaranty agency.

(iii) During the period required by the guaranty agency to approve the claim and to authorize payment or to return the claim to the lender for additional documentation not to exceed—

(A) 45 days for death, disability or bankruptcy claims; or

(B) 90 days for closed school and false certifications.

(i) *Guaranty agency participation in bankruptcy proceedings—*

(1) *Undue hardship claims.*

(i) In response to a petition filed prior to October 8, 1998 with regard to any bankruptcy proceeding by the borrower for discharge under 11 U.S.C. 523(a)(8) on the grounds of undue hardship, the guaranty agency must, on the basis of reasonably available information, determine whether the first payment on the loan was due more than 7 years (exclusive of any applicable suspension of the repayment period) before the filing of that petition and, if so, process the claim.

(ii) In all other cases, the guaranty agency must determine whether repayment under either the current repayment schedule or any adjusted schedule authorized under this part would impose an undue hardship on the borrower and his or her dependents.

(iii) If the guaranty agency determines that repayment would not constitute an undue hardship, the guaranty agency must then determine whether the expected costs of opposing the discharge petition would exceed one-third of the total amount owed on the loan, including principal, interest, late charges, and collection costs. If the guaranty agency has determined that the expected costs of opposing the discharge petition will exceed one-third of the total amount of the loan, it may, but is not required to, engage in the activities described in paragraph (i)(1)(iv) of this section.

(iv) The guaranty agency must use diligence and may assert any defense consistent with its status under applicable law to avoid discharge of the loan. Unless discharge would be more effectively opposed by not taking the following actions, the agency must—

(A) Oppose the borrower's petition for a determination of dischargeability; and

(B) If the borrower is in default on the loan, seek a judgment for the amount owed on the loan.

(v) In opposing a petition for a determination of dischargeability on the grounds of undue hardship, a guaranty agency may agree to discharge of a portion of the amount owed on a loan if it reasonably determines that the agreement is necessary in order to obtain a judgment on the remainder of the loan.

(2) *Response by a guaranty agency to plans proposed under Chapters 11, 12, and 13.* The guaranty agency shall take the following actions when a petition for relief in bankruptcy under Chapters 11, 12, or 13 is filed:

(i) The agency is not required to respond to a proposed plan that—

(A) Provides for repayment of the full outstanding balance of the loan;

(B) Makes no provision with regard to the loan or to general unsecured claims.

(ii) In any other case, the agency shall determine, based on a review of its own records and documents filed by the debtor in the bankruptcy proceeding—

(A) What part of the loan obligation will be discharged under the plan as proposed;

(B) Whether the plan itself or the classification of the loan under the plan meets the requirements of 11 U.S.C. 1129, 1225, or 1325, as applicable; and

(C) Whether grounds exist under 11 U.S.C. 1112, 1208, or 1307, as applicable, to move for conversion or dismissal of the case.

(iii) If the agency determines that grounds exist to challenge the proposed plan, the agency shall, as appropriate, object to the plan or move to dismiss the case, if—

(A) The costs of litigation of these actions are not reasonably expected to exceed one-third of the amount of the loan to be discharged under the plan; and

(B) With respect to an objection under 11 U.S.C. 1325, the additional amount that may be recovered under the plan if an objection is successful can reasonably be expected to equal or exceed the cost of litigating the objection.

(iv) The agency shall monitor the debtor's performance under a confirmed plan. If the debtor fails to make payments required under the plan or seeks but does not demonstrate entitlement to discharge under 11 U.S.C. 1328(b), the agency shall oppose any requested discharge or move to dismiss the case if the costs of litigation together with the costs incurred for objections to the plan are not reasonably expected to exceed one-third of the amount of the loan to be discharged under the plan.

(j) *Mandatory purchase by a lender of a loan subject to a bankruptcy claim.*

(1) The lender shall repurchase from the guaranty agency a loan held by the agency pursuant to a bankruptcy claim paid to that lender, unless the guaranty agency sells the loan to another lender, promptly after the earliest of the following events:

(i) The entry of an order denying or revoking discharge or dismissing a proceeding under any chapter.

(ii) A ruling in a proceeding under chapter 7 or 11 that the loan is not dischargeable under 11 U.S.C. 523(a)(8) or other applicable law.

(iii) The entry of an order granting discharge under chapter 12 or 13, or confirming a plan of arrangement under chapter 11, unless the court determined that the loan is dischargeable under 11 U.S.C. 523(a)(8) on grounds of undue hardship.

(2) The lender may capitalize all outstanding interest accrued on a loan purchased under paragraph (j) of this section to cover any periods of delinquency prior to the bankruptcy action through the date the lender purchases the loan and receives the supporting loan documentation from the guaranty agency.

(k) *Claims for reimbursement from the Secretary on loans held by guarantee agencies.*

(1)(i) The Secretary reimburses the guaranty agency for its losses on bankruptcy claims paid to lenders after—

(A) A determination by the court that the loan is dischargeable under 11 U.S.C. 523(a)(8) with respect to a proceeding initiated under chapter 7 or chapter 11; or

(B) With respect to any other loan, after the agency pays the claim to the lender.

(ii) The guaranty agency shall refund to the Secretary the full amount of reimbursement received from the Secretary on a loan that a lender repurchases under this section.

(2) The Secretary pays a death, disability, bankruptcy, closed school, or false certification claim in an amount determined under § 682.402(k)(5) on a loan held by a guaranty agency after the agency has paid a default claim to the lender thereon and received payment under its reinsurance agreement. The Secretary reimburses the guaranty agency only if—

(i) The guaranty agency determines that the borrower (or the student for whom a parent obtained a PLUS loan or each of the co-makers of a PLUS loan) has died, or the borrower (or each of the co-makers of a PLUS loan) has become totally and permanently disabled since applying for the loan, or has filed for relief in bankruptcy, in accordance with the procedures in paragraphs (b), (c), or (f) of this section, or the student was unable to complete an educational program because the school closed, or the borrower's eligibility to borrow (or the student's eligibility in the case of a PLUS loan) was falsely certified by an eligible school. For purposes of this paragraph, references to the "lender" and "guaranty agency" in paragraphs (b) through (f) of this section mean the guaranty agency and the Secretary respectively;

(ii) In the case of a Stafford, SLS, or PLUS loan, the guaranty agency determines that the borrower (or the student for whom a parent obtained a PLUS loan, or each of the co-makers of a PLUS loan) has died, or the borrower (or each of the co-makers of a PLUS loan) has become totally and permanently disabled since applying for the loan, or has filed the petition for relief in bankruptcy within 10 years of the date the borrower entered repayment, exclusive of periods of deferment or periods of forbearance granted by the lender that extended the 10-year maximum repayment

period, or the borrower (or the student for whom a parent received a PLUS loan) was unable to complete an educational program because the school closed, or the borrower's eligibility to borrow (or the student's eligibility in the case of a PLUS loan) was falsely certified by an eligible school;

(iii) In the case of a Consolidation loan, the guaranty agency determines that the borrower (or each of the co-makers) has died, is determined to be totally and permanently disabled under Sec. 682.402(c), or has filed the petition for relief in bankruptcy within the maximum repayment period described in § 682.209(h)(2), exclusive of periods of deferment or periods of forbearance granted by the lender that extended the maximum repayment period;

(iv) The guaranty agency has not written off the loan in accordance with the procedures established by the agency under § 682.410(b)(6)(x), except for closed school and false certification discharges; and

(v) The guaranty agency has exercised due diligence in the collection of the loan in accordance with the procedures established by the agency under § 682.410(b)(6)(x), until the borrower (or the student for whom a parent obtained a PLUS loan, or each of the co-makers of a PLUS loan) has died, or the borrower (or each of the co-makers of a PLUS loan) has become totally and permanently disabled or filed a Chapter 12 or Chapter 13 petition, or had the loan discharged in bankruptcy, or for closed school and false certification claims, the guaranty agency receives a request for discharge from the borrower or another party.

(3) [Reserved]

(4) Within 30 days of receiving reimbursement for a closed school or false certification claim, the guaranty agency shall pay—

(i) The borrower an amount equal to the amount paid on the loan by or on behalf of the borrower, less any school tuition refunds or payments received by the holder, guaranty agency, or the borrower from a tuition recovery fund, performance bond, or other third-party source; or

(ii) The amount determined under paragraph (h)(2)(iv) of this section to the holder of the borrower's Consolidation Loan.

(5) The Secretary pays the guaranty agency a percentage of the outstanding principal and interest that is equal to the complement of the reinsurance percentage paid on the loan. This interest includes interest that accrues during—

(i) For death or bankruptcy claims, the shorter of 60 days or the period from the date the guaranty agency determines that the borrower (or the student for whom a parent obtained a PLUS loan, or each of the co-makers of a PLUS loan) dies, or filed a petition for relief in bankruptcy until the Secretary authorizes payment;

(ii) For disability claims, the shorter of 60 days or the period from the date the guaranty agency makes a preliminary determination that the borrower became totally and permanently disabled until the Secretary authorizes payment; or

(iii) For closed school or false certification claims, the period from the date on which the guaranty agency received payment from the Secretary on a default claim to the date on which the Secretary authorizes payment of the closed school or false certification claim.

(*l*) *Unpaid refund discharge.*

(1) *Unpaid refunds in closed school situations.* In the case of a school that has closed, the Secretary reimburses the guarantor of a loan and discharges a former or current borrower's (and any endorser's) obligation to repay that portion of an FFEL Program loan (disbursed, in whole or in part, on or after January 1, 1986) equal to the refund that should have been made by the school under

applicable Federal law and regulations, including this section. Any accrued interest and other charges (late charges, collection costs, origination fees, and insurance premiums) associated with the unpaid refund are also discharged.

(2) *Unpaid refunds in open school situations.* In the case of a school that is open, the guarantor discharges a former or current borrower's (and any endorser's) obligation to repay that portion of an FFEL loan (disbursed, in whole or in part, on or after January 1, 1986) equal to the amount of the refund that should have been made by the school under applicable Federal law and regulations, including this section, if—

(i) The borrower (or the student on whose behalf a parent borrowed) is not attending the school that owes the refund; and

(ii) The guarantor receives documentation regarding the refund and the borrower and guarantor have been unable to resolve the unpaid refund within 120 days from the date the guarantor receives a complete application in accordance with paragraph (l)(4) of this section. Any accrued interest and other charges (late charges, collection costs, origination fees, and insurance premiums) associated with the amount of the unpaid refund amount are also discharged.

(3) *Relief to borrower (and any endorser) following discharge.*

(i) If a borrower receives a discharge of a portion of a loan under this section, the borrower is reimbursed for any amounts paid in excess of the remaining balance of the loan (including accrued interest, late charges, collection costs, origination fees, and insurance premiums) owed by the borrower at the time of discharge.

(ii) The holder of the loan reports the discharge of a portion of a loan under this section to all credit reporting agencies to which the holder of the loan previously reported the status of the loan.

(4) *Borrower qualification for discharge.* To receive a discharge of a portion of a loan under this section, a borrower must submit a written application to the holder or guaranty agency except as provided in paragraph (l)(5)(iv) of this section. The application requests the information required to calculate the amount of the discharge and requires the borrower to sign a statement swearing to the accuracy of the information in the application. The statement need not be notarized but must be made by the borrower under penalty of perjury. In the statement, the borrower must—

(i) State that the borrower (or the student on whose behalf a parent borrowed)—

(A) Received the proceeds of a loan, in whole or in part, on or after January 1, 1986 to attend a school;

(B) Did not attend, withdrew, or was terminated from the school within a timeframe that entitled the borrower to a refund; and

(C) Did not receive the benefit of a refund to which the borrower was entitled either from the school or from a third party, such as a holder of a performance bond or a tuition recovery program.

(ii) State whether the borrower has any other application for discharge pending for this loan; and

(iii) State that the borrower—

(A) Agrees to provide upon request by the Secretary or the Secretary's designee other documentation reasonably available to the borrower that demonstrates that the borrower meets the qualifications for an unpaid refund discharge under this section; and

(B) Agrees to cooperate with the Secretary or the Secretary's designee in enforcement actions in accordance with paragraph (e) of this section and to transfer any right to recovery against a third party to the Secretary in accordance with paragraph (d) of this section.

(5) *Unpaid refund discharge procedures.*

(i) Except for the requirements of paragraph (l)(5)(iv) of this section related to an open school, if the holder or guaranty agency learns that a school did not pay a refund of loan proceeds owed under applicable law and regulations, the holder or the guaranty agency sends the borrower a discharge application and an explanation of the qualifications and procedures for obtaining a discharge. The holder of the loan also promptly suspends any efforts to collect from the borrower on any affected loan.

(ii) If the borrower returns the application, specified in paragraph (l)(4) of this section, the holder or the guaranty agency must review the application to determine whether the application appears to be complete. In the case of a loan held by a lender, once the lender determines that the application appears complete, it must provide the application and all pertinent information to the guaranty agency including, if available, the borrower's last date of attendance. If the borrower returns the application within 60 days, the lender must extend the period during which efforts to collect on the affected loan are suspended to the date the lender receives either a denial of the request or the unpaid refund amount from the guaranty agency. At the conclusion of the period during which the collection activity was suspended, the lender may capitalize any interest accrued and not paid during that period in accordance with § 682.202(b).

(iii) If the borrower fails to return the application within 60 days, the holder of the loan resumes collection efforts and grants forbearance of principal and interest for the period during which collection activity was suspended. The holder may capitalize any interest accrued and not paid during that period in accordance with § 682.202(b).

(iv) The guaranty agency may, with the approval of the Secretary, discharge a portion of a loan under this section without an application if the guaranty agency determines, based on information in the guaranty agency's possession, that the borrower qualifies for a discharge.

(v) If the holder of the loan or the guaranty agency determines that the information contained in its files conflicts with the information provided by the borrower, the guaranty agency must use the most reliable information available to it to determine eligibility for and the appropriate payment of the refund amount.

(vi) If the holder of the loan is the guaranty agency and the agency determines that the borrower qualifies for a discharge of an unpaid refund, the guaranty agency must suspend any efforts to collect on the affected loan and, within 30 days of its determination, discharge the appropriate amount and inform the borrower of its determination. Absent documentation of the exact amount of refund due the borrower, the guaranty agency must calculate the amount of the unpaid refund using the unpaid refund calculation defined in paragraph (o) of this section.

(vii) If the guaranty agency determines that a borrower does not qualify for an unpaid refund discharge, (or, if the holder is the lender and is informed by the guarantor that the borrower does not qualify for a discharge)—

(A) Within 30 days of the guarantor's determination, the agency must notify the borrower in writing of the reason for the determination and of the borrower's right to request a review of the agency's determination. The guaranty agency must make a determination within 30 days of the borrower's submission of additional documentation supporting the borrower's eligibility that was not considered in any prior determination. During the review period, collection activities must be suspended; and

(B) The holder must resume collection if the determination remains unchanged and grant forbearance of principal and interest for any period during which collection activity was suspended under this section. The holder may capitalize any interest accrued and not paid during these periods in accordance with § 682.202(b).

(viii) If the guaranty agency determines that a current or former borrower at an open school may be eligible for a discharge under this section, the guaranty agency must notify the lender and the school of the unpaid refund allegation. The notice to the school must include all pertinent facts available to the guaranty agency regarding the alleged unpaid refund. The school must, no later than 60 days after receiving the notice, provide the guaranty agency with documentation demonstrating, to the satisfaction of the guarantor, that the alleged unpaid refund was either paid or not required to be paid.

(ix) In the case of a school that does not make a refund or provide sufficient documentation demonstrating the refund was either paid or was not required, within 60 days of its receipt of the allegation notice from the guaranty agency, relief is provided to the borrower (and any endorser) if the guaranty agency determines the relief is appropriate. The agency must forward documentation of the school's failure to pay the unpaid refund to the Secretary.

(m) *Unpaid refund discharge procedures for a loan held by a lender.* In the case of an unpaid refund discharge request, the lender must provide the guaranty agency with documentation related to the borrower's qualification for discharge as specified in paragraph (l)(4) of this section.

(n) *Payment of an unpaid refund discharge request by a guaranty agency.*

(1) *General.* The guaranty agency must review an unpaid refund discharge request promptly and must pay the lender the amount of loss as defined in paragraphs (l)(1) and (l)(2) of this section, related to the unpaid refund not later than 45 days after a properly filed request is made.

(2) *Determination of the unpaid refund discharge amount to the lender.* The amount of loss payable to a lender on an unpaid refund includes that portion of an FFEL Program loan equal to the amount of the refund required under applicable Federal law and regulations, including this section, and including any accrued interest and other charges (late charges, collection costs, origination fees, and insurance premiums) associated with the unpaid refund.

(o)(1) *Determination of amount eligible for discharge.* The guaranty agency determines the amount eligible for discharge based on information showing the refund amount or by applying the appropriate refund formula to information that the borrower provides or that is otherwise available to the guaranty agency. For purposes of this section, all unpaid refunds are considered to be attributed to loan proceeds.

(2) If the information in paragraph (o)(1) of this section is not available, the guaranty agency uses the following formulas to determine the amount eligible for discharge:

(i) In the case of a student who fails to attend or whose withdrawal or termination date is before October 7, 2000 and who completes less than 60 percent of the loan period, the guaranty agency discharges the lesser of the institutional charges unearned or the loan amount. The guaranty agency determines the amount of the institutional charges unearned by—

(A) Calculating the ratio of the amount of time in the loan period

after the student's last day of attendance to the actual length of the loan period; and

(B) Multiplying the resulting factor by the institutional charges assessed the student for the loan period.

(ii) In the case of a student who fails to attend or whose withdrawal or termination date is on or after October 7, 2000 and who completes less than 60 percent of the loan period, the guaranty agency discharges the loan amount unearned. The guaranty agency determines the loan amount unearned by—

(A) Calculating the ratio of the amount of time remaining in the loan period after the student's last day of attendance to the actual length of the loan period; and

(B) Multiplying the resulting factor by the total amount of title IV grants and loans received by the student, or if unknown, the loan amount.

(iii) In the case of a student who completes 60 percent or more of the loan period, the guaranty agency does not discharge any amount because a student who completes 60 percent or more of the loan period is not entitled to a refund.

(p) *Requests for reimbursement from the Secretary on loans held by guaranty agencies.* The Secretary reimburses the guaranty agency for its losses on unpaid refund request payments to lenders or borrowers in an amount that is equal to the amount specified in paragraph (n)(2) of this section.

(q) *Payments received after the guaranty agency's payment of an unpaid refund request.*

(1) The holder must promptly return to the sender any payment on a fully discharged loan, received after the guaranty agency pays an unpaid refund request unless the sender is required to pay (as in the case of a tuition recovery fund) in which case, the payment amount must be forwarded to the Secretary. At the same time that the holder returns the payment, it must notify the borrower that there is no obligation to repay a loan fully discharged.

(2) If the holder has returned a payment to the borrower, or the borrower's representative, with the notice described in paragraph (q)(1) of this section, and the borrower (or representative) continues to send payments to the holder, the holder must remit all of those payments to the Secretary.

(3) If the loan has not been fully discharged, payments must be applied to the remaining debt.

(r)(1) *If the guaranty agency receives any payments from or on behalf of the borrower on or attributable to a loan that as been discharged in bankruptcy on which the Secretary previously paid a bankruptcy claim, the guaranty agency must return 100 percent of these payments to the sender.* The guaranty agency must promptly return, to the sender, any payment on a cancelled or discharged loan made by the sender and received after the Secretary pays a closed school or false certification claim. At the same time that the agency returns the payment, it must notify the borrower that there is no obligation to repay a loan discharged on the basis of death, bankruptcy, false certification, or closing of the school.

(2) If the guaranty agency receives any payments from or on behalf of the borrower on or attributable to a loan that has been assigned to the Secretary for determination of eligibility for a total and permanent disability discharge, the guaranty agency must forward those payments to the Secretary for crediting to the borrower's account. At the same time that the agency forwards the payments, it must notify the borrower that there is no obligation to make payments on the loan while it is conditionally discharged prior to a final determination of eligibility for a total and permanent

disability discharge, unless the Secretary directs the borrower otherwise.

(3) When the Secretary makes a final determination to discharge the loan, the Secretary returns to the sender any payments received on the loan after the date the borrower became totally and permanently disabled.

(4) The guaranty agency shall remit to the Secretary all payments received from a tuition recovery fund, performance bond, or other third party with respect to a loan on which the Secretary previously paid a closed school or false certification claim.

(5) If the guaranty agency has returned a payment to the borrower, or the borrower's representative, with the notice described in paragraphs (r)(1) or (r)(2) of this section, and the borrower (or representative) continues to send payments to the guaranty agency, the agency must remit all of those payments to the Secretary.

(s) *Applicable suspension of the repayment period.* For purposes of this section and 11 U.S.C. 523(a)(8)(A) with respect to loans guaranteed under the FFEL Program, an applicable suspension of the repayment period—

(1) Includes any period during which the lender does not require the borrower to make a payment on the loan.

(2) Begins on the date on which the borrower qualifies for the requested deferment as provided in § 682.210(a)(5) or the lender grants the requested forbearance;

(3) Closes on the later of the date on which—

(i) The condition for which the requested deferment or forbearance was received ends; or

(ii) The lender receives notice of the end of the condition for which the requested deferment or forbearance was received, if the condition ended earlier than represented by the borrower at the time of the request and the borrower did not notify timely the lender of the date on which the condition actually ended

(4) Includes the period between the end of the borrower's grace period and the first payment due date established by the lender in the case of a borrower who entered repayment without the knowledge of the lender;

(5) Includes the period between the filing of the petition for relief and the date on which the proceeding is completed or dismissed, unless payments have been made during that period in amounts sufficient to meet the amount owed under the repayment schedule in effect when the petition was filed.

(Approved by the Office of Management and Budget under control number 1845-0020)

(Authority: 20 U.S.C. 1078, 1078-1, 1078-2, 1078-3, 1082, 1087)

[58 FR 9120, Feb. 19, 1993; 59 FR 22476, April 29, 1994; 59 FR 25746, May 17, 1994; 59 FR 29543, June 8, 1994; 59 FR 35625, July 13, 1994; 59 FR 46175, Sept. 7, 1994; 59 FR 61216, Nov. 29, 1994; 59 FR 61428, Nov. 30, 1994; 60 FR 32912, June 26, 1995; 60 FR 61757, Dec. 1, 1995; 62 FR 63434, Nov. 28, 1997; 64 FR 18979, April 16, 1999; 64 FR 58628, Oct. 29, 1999; 64 FR 58960, Nov. 1, 1999; 65 FR 65620, 65691, Nov. 1, 2000; 66 FR 34763, June 29, 2001]

§ 682.405 Loan rehabilitation agreement.

(a) *General.*

(1) A guaranty agency that has a basic program agreement must enter into a loan rehabilitation agreement with the Secretary. The guaranty agency must establish a loan rehabilitation program for all borrowers with an enforceable promissory note for the purpose of rehabilitating defaulted loans so that the loan may be purchases, if practicable, by an eligible lender and removed from default status.

(2) A loan is considered to be rehabilitated only after the borrower has made one voluntary reasonable and affordable full payment each month and the payment is received by a guaranty agency or its agent within 15 days of the scheduled due date for 12 consecutive months in accordance with this section, and the loan has been sold to an eligible lender.

(3) After the loan has been rehabilitated, the borrower regains all benefits of the program, including any remaining deferment eligibility under section 428(b)(1)(M) of the Act, from the date of the rehabilitation.

(4) A borrower who wishes to rehabilitate a loan on which a judgment has been entered must sign a new promissory note prior to the sale of the loan to an eligible lender.

(b) *Terms of agreement.* In the loan rehabilitation agreement, the guaranty agency agrees to ensure that its loan rehabilitation program meets the following requirements at all times:

(1) A borrower may request the rehabilitation of the borrower's defaulted FFEL loan held by the guaranty agency. The borrower must make one on-time voluntary full payment each month for 12 consecutive months to be eligible to have the defaulted loans rehabilitated. For purposes of this section, "full payment" means a reasonable and affordable payment agreed to by the borrower and the agency. The required amount of such monthly payment may be no more than is reasonable and affordable based upon the borrower's total financial circumstances. Voluntary payments are those made directly by the borrower regardless of whether there is a judgment against the borrower, and do not include payments obtained by income tax off-set, garnishment, or income or asset execution. A guaranty agency must attempt to secure a lender to purchase the loan at the end of the twelve-(12-)month payment period.

(i) For purposes of this section, the determination of reasonable and affordable must—

(A) Include a consideration of the borrower's and spouse's disposable income and reasonable and necessary expenses including, but not limited to, housing, utilities, food, medical costs, work-related expenses, dependent care costs and other Title IV repayment;

(B) Not be a required minimum payment amount, e.g. $50, if the agency determines that a smaller amount is reasonable and affordable based on the borrower's total financial circumstances. The agency must include documentation in the borrower's file of the basis for the determination if the monthly reasonable and affordable payment established under this section is less than $50.00 or the monthly accrued interest on the loan, whichever is greater. However, $50.00 may not be the minimum payment for a borrower if the agency determines that a smaller amount is reasonable and affordable; and

(C) Be based on the documentation provided by the borrower or other sources including, but not be limited to—

(1) Evidence of current income (e.g., proof of welfare benefits, Social Security benefits, child support, veterans' benefits, Supplemental Security Income, Workmen's Compensation, two most recent pay stubs, most recent copy of U.S. income tax return, State Department of Labor reports);

(2) Evidence of current expenses (e.g., a copy of the borrower's monthly household budget, on a form provided by the guaranty agency); and

(3) A statement of the unpaid balance on all FFEL loans held by other holders.

(ii) The agency must include any payment made under § 682.401(b)(4) in determining whether the 12 consecutive payments required under paragraph (b)(1) of this section have been made.

(iii) A borrower may request that the monthly payment amount be adjusted due to a change in the borrower's total financial circumstances only upon providing the documentation specified in paragraph (b)(1)(i)(C) of this section.

(iv) A guaranty agency must provide the borrower with a written statement confirming the borrower's reasonable and affordable payment amount, as determined by the agency, and explaining any other terms and conditions applicable to the required series of payments that must be made before a borrower's account can be considered for repurchase by an eligible lender. The statement must inform borrowers of the effects of having their loans rehabilitated (e.g. credit clearing, possibility of increased monthly payments). The statement must inform the borrower of the amount of the collection costs to be added to the unpaid principal at the time of the sale. The collection costs may not exceed 18.5 percent of the unpaid principal and accrued interest at the time of the sale.

(v) A guaranty agency must provide the borrower with an opportunity to object to terms of the rehabilitation of the borrower's defaulted loan.

(2) The guaranty agency must report to all national credit bureaus within 90 days of the date the loan was rehabilitated that the loan is no longer in a default status and that the default is to be removed from the borrower's credit history.

(3) An eligible lender purchasing a rehabilitated loan must establish a repayment schedule that meets the same requirements that are applicable to other FFEL Program loans made under the same loan type and provides for the borrower to make monthly payments at least as great as the average of the 12 consecutive monthly payments received by the guaranty agency. For the purposes of the maximum loan repayment period, the lender must treat the first payment made under the 12 consecutive payments as the first payment under the applicable maximum repayment term, as defined under sections 682.209(a) or (h).

(Approved by the Office of Management and Budget under control number 1845-0020)

(Authority: 20 U.S.C. 1078-6)

[59 FR 33355, June 28, 1994; 60 FR 30788, June 12, 1995; 64 FR 18980, April 16, 1999; 64 FR 58965, Nov. 1, 1999; 66 FR 34764, June 29, 2001]

§ 682.410 Fiscal, administrative, and enforcement requirements.

(a) *Fiscal requirements—*

(1) *Reserve fund assets.* A guaranty agency shall establish and maintain a reserve fund to be used solely for its activities as a guaranty agency under the FFEL Program ("guaranty activities"). The guaranty agency shall credit to the reserve fund—

(i) The total amount of insurance premiums collected;

(ii) Funds received from a State for the agency's guaranty activities, including matching funds under section 422(a) of the Act;

(iii) Federal advances obtained under sections 422(a) and (c) of the Act;

(iv) Federal payments for default, bankruptcy, death, disability, closed schools, and false certification claims;

(v) Supplemental preclaims assistance payments;

(vi) Transitional support payments received under section 458(a) of the Act;

(vii) Funds collected by the guaranty agency on FFEL Program loans on which a claim has been paid;

(viii) Investment earnings on the reserve fund; and

(ix) Other funds received by the guaranty agency from any source for the agency's guaranty activities.

(2) *Uses of reserve fund assets.* A guaranty agency may not use the assets of the reserve fund established under paragraph (a)(1) of this section to pay costs prohibited under § 682.418, but shall use the assets of the reserve fund to pay only—

(i) Insurance claims;

(ii) Costs that are reasonable, as defined under § 682.410(a)(11)(iii), and that are ordinary and necessary for the agency to fulfill its responsibilities under the HEA, including costs of collecting loans, providing preclaims assistance, monitoring enrollment and repayment status, and carrying out any other guaranty activities. Those costs must be—

(A) Allocable to the FFEL Program;

(B) Not higher than the agency would incur under established policies, regulations, and procedures that apply to any comparable non-Federal activities of the guaranty agency;

(C) Not included as a cost or used to meet cost sharing or matching requirements of any other federally supported activity, except as specifically provided by Federal law;

(D) Net of all applicable credits; and

(E) Documented in accordance with applicable legal and accounting standards;

(iii) The Secretary's equitable share of collections;

(iv) Federal advances and other funds owed to the Secretary;

(v) Reinsurance fees;

(vi) Insurance premiums related to cancelled loans;

(vii) Borrower refunds, including those arising out of student or other borrower claims and defenses;

(vii)(A) The repayment, on or after December 29, 1993, of amounts credited under paragraphs (a)(1)(ii) or (a)(1)(ix) of this section, if the agency provides the Secretary 30 days prior notice of the repayment and demonstrates that—

(1) These amounts were originally received by the agency under appropriate contemporaneous documentation specifying that receipt was on a temporary basis only;

(2) The objective for which these amounts were originally received by the agency has been fully achieved; and

(3) Repayment of these amounts would not cause the agency to fail to comply with the minimum reserve levels provided by paragraph (a)(10) of this section, except that the Secretary may, for good cause, provide written permission for a payment that meets the other requirements of this paragraph (a)(2)(ix)(A).

(B) The repayment, prior to December 29, 1993, of amounts credited under paragraphs (a)(1)(ii) or (a)(1)(ix) of this section, if the agency demonstrates that—

(1) These amounts were originally received by the agency under appropriate contemporaneous documentation that receipt was on a temporary basis only; and

(2) The objective for which these amounts were originally

received by the agency has been fully achieved.

(ix) Any other costs or payments ordinary and necessary to perform functions directly related to the agency's responsibilities under the HEA and for their proper and efficient administration;

(x) Notwithstanding any other provision of this section, any other payment that was allowed by law or regulation at the time it was made, if the agency acted in good faith when it made the payment or the agency would otherwise be unfairly prejudiced by the nonallowability of the payment at a later time; and

(xi) Any other amounts authorized or directed by the Secretary.

(3) *Accounting basis.* Except as approved by the Secretary, a guaranty agency shall credit the items listed in paragraph (a)(1) of this section to its reserve fund upon their receipt, without any deferral for accounting purposes, and shall deduct the items listed in paragraph (a)(2) of this section from its reserve fund upon their payment, without any accrual for accounting purposes.

(4) *Accounting records.*

(i) The accounting records of a guaranty agency must reflect the correct amount of sources and uses of funds under paragraph (a) of this section.

(ii) A guaranty agency may reverse prior credits to its reserve fund if—

(A) The agency gives the Secretary prior notice setting forth a detailed justification for the action;

(B) The Secretary determines that such credits were made erroneously and in good faith; and

(C) The Secretary determines that the action would not unfairly prejudice other parties.

(iii) A guaranty agency shall correct any other errors in its accounting or reporting as soon as practicable after the errors become known to the agency.

(iv) If a general reconstruction of a guaranty agency's historical accounting records is necessary to make a change under paragraphs (a)(4)(ii) and (a)(4)(iii) of this section or any other retroactive change to its accounting records, the agency may make this reconstruction only upon prior approval by the Secretary and without any deduction from its reserve fund for the cost of the reconstruction.

(5) *Investments.* The guaranty agency shall exercise the level of care required of a fiduciary charged with the duty of investing the money of others when it invests the assets of the reserve fund described in paragraph (a)(1) of this section. It may invest these assets only in low-risk securities, such as obligations issued or guaranteed by the United States or a State.

(6) *Development of assets.*

(i) If the guaranty agency uses in a substantial way for purposes other than the agency's guaranty activities any funds required to be credited to the reserve fund under paragraph (a)(1) of this section or any assets derived from the reserve fund to develop an asset of any kind and does not in good faith allocate a portion of the cost of developing and maintaining the developed asset to funds other than the reserve fund, the Secretary may require the agency to—

(A) Correct this allocation under paragraph (a)(4)(iii) of this section; or

(B) Correct the recorded ownership of the asset under paragraph (a)(4)(iii) of this section so that—

(1) If, in a transaction with an unrelated third party, the agency sells or otherwise derives revenue from uses of the asset that are unrelated to the agency's guaranty activities, the agency promptly shall deposit into the reserve fund described in paragraph (a)(1) of

this section a percentage of the sale proceeds or revenue equal to the fair percentage of the total development cost of the asset paid with the reserve fund monies or provided by assets derived from the reserve fund; or

(2) If the agency otherwise converts the asset, in whole or in part, to a use unrelated to its guaranty activities, the agency promptly shall deposit into the reserve fund described in paragraph (a)(1) of this section a fair percentage of the fair market value or, in the case of a temporary conversion, the rental value of the portion of the asset employed for the unrelated use.

(ii) If the agency uses funds or assets described in paragraph (a)(6)(i) of this section in the manner described in that paragraph and makes a cost and maintenance allocation erroneously and in good faith, it shall correct the allocation under paragraph (a)(4)(iii) of this section.

(7) *Third-party claims.* If the guaranty agency has any claim against any other party to recover funds or other assets for the reserve fund, the claim is the property of the United States.

(8) *Related-party transactions.* All transactions between a guaranty agency and a related organization or other person that involve funds required to be credited to the agency's reserve fund under paragraph (a)(1) of this section or assets derived from the reserve fund must be on terms that are not less advantageous to the reserve fund than would have been negotiated on an arm's-length basis by unrelated parties.

(9) *Scope of definition.* The provisions of this § 682.410(a) define reserve funds and assets for purposes of sections 422 and 428 of the Act. These provisions do not, however, affect the Secretary's authority to use all funds and assets of the agency pursuant to section 428(c)(9)(F)(vi) of the Act.

(10) *Minimum reserve fund level.* The guaranty agency must maintain a current minimum reserve level of not less than—

(i) .5 percent of the amount of loans outstanding, for the fiscal year of the agency that begins in calendar year 1993;

(ii) .7 percent of the amount of loans outstanding, for the fiscal year of the agency that begins in calendar year 1994;

(iii) .9 percent of the amount of loans outstanding, for the fiscal year of the agency that begins in calendar year 1995; and

(iv) 1.1 percent of the amount of loans outstanding, for each fiscal year of the agency that begins on or after January 1, 1996.

(11) *Definitions.* For purposes of this section—

(i) *Reserve fund level* means—

(A) The total of reserve fund assets as defined in paragraph (a)(1) of this section;

(B) Minus the total amount of the reserve fund assets used in accordance with paragraphs (a)(2) and (a)(3) of this section; and

(ii) *Amount of loans outstanding* means—

(A) The sum of—

(1) The original principal amount of all loans guaranteed by the agency; and

(2) The original principal amount of any loans on which the guarantee was transferred to the agency from another guarantor, excluding loan guarantees transferred to another agency pursuant to a plan of the Secretary in response to the insolvency of the agency;

(B) Minus the original principal amount of all loans on which—

(1) The loan guarantee was cancelled;

(2) The loan guarantee was transferred to another agency;

(3) Payment in full has been made by the borrower;

(4) Reinsurance coverage has been lost and cannot be regained; and

(5) The agency paid claims.

(iii) *Reasonable cost* means a cost that, in its nature and amount, does not exceed that which would be incurred by a prudent person under the circumstances prevailing at the time the decision was made to incur the cost. The burden of proof is upon the guaranty agency, as a fiduciary under its agreements with the Secretary, to establish that costs are reasonable. In determining reasonableness of a given cost, consideration must be given to—

(A) Whether the cost is of a type generally recognized as ordinary and necessary for the proper and efficient performance and administration of the guaranty agency's responsibilities under the HEA;

(B) The restraints or requirements imposed by factors such as sound business practices, arms-length bargaining, Federal, State, and other laws and regulations, and the terms and conditions of the guaranty agency's agreements with the Secretary; and

(C) Market prices of comparable goods or services.

(b) *Administrative requirements—*

(1) *Independent audits.* The guaranty agency shall arrange for an independent financial and compliance audit of the agency's FFEL program as follows:

(i) With regard to a guaranty agency that is an agency of a State government, an audit must be conducted in accordance with 31 U.S.C. 7502 and 34 CFR part 80, appendix G.

(ii) With regard to a guaranty agency that is a nonprofit organization, an audit must be conducted in accordance with OMB Circular A-133, Audits of Institutions of Higher Education and Other Nonprofit Organizations and 34 CFR 74.61(h)(3). If a nonprofit guaranty agency meets the criteria in Circular A-133 to have a program specific audit, and chooses that option, the program specific audit must meet the following requirements:

(A) The audit must examine the agency's compliance with the Act, applicable regulations, and agreements entered into under this part.

(B) The audit must examine the agency's financial management of its FFEL program activities.

(C) The audit must be conducted in accordance with the standards for audits issued by the United States General Accounting Office's (GAO) Government Auditing Standards. Procedures for audits are contained in an audit guide developed by, and available from, the Office of the Inspector General of the Department.

(D) The audit must be conducted annually and must be submitted to the Secretary within six months of the end of the audit period. The first audit must cover the agency's activities for a period that includes July 23, 1992, unless the agency is currently submitting audits on a biennial basis, and the second year of its biennial cycle starts on or before July 23, 1992. Under these circumstances, the agency shall submit a biennial audit that includes July 23, 1992 and submit its next audit as an annual audit.

(2) *Collection charges.* Whether or not provided for in the borrower's promissory note and subject to any limitation on the amount of those costs in that note, the guaranty agency shall charge a borrower an amount equal to reasonable costs incurred by the agency in collecting a loan on which the agency has paid a default or bankruptcy claim. These costs may include, but are not limited to, all attorney's fees, collection agency charges, and court costs. Except as provided in §§ 682.401(b)(27) and 682.405(b)(1)(iv), the amount charged a borrower must equal the lesser of—

(i) The amount the same borrower would be charged for the cost of collection under the formula in 34 CFR 30.60; or

(ii) The amount the same borrower would be charged for the cost of collection if the loan was held by the U.S. Department of Education.

(3) *Interest charged by guaranty agencies.* The guaranty agency shall charge the borrower interest on the amount owed by the borrower after the capitalization required under paragraph (b)(4) of this section has occurred at a rate that is the greater of—

(i) The rate established by the terms of the borrower's original promissory note;

(ii) In the case of a loan for which a judgment has been obtained, the rate provided for by State law.

(4) *Capitalization of unpaid interest.* The guaranty agency shall capitalize any unpaid interest due the lender from the borrower at the time the agency pays a default claim to the lender.

(5) *Credit bureau reports.*

(i) After the completion of the procedures in paragraph (b)(5)(ii) of this section, the guaranty agency shall, after it has paid a default claim, report promptly, but not less than sixty days after completion of the procedures in paragraph (b)(6)(v) of this section, and on a regular basis, to all national credit bureaus—

(A) The total amount of loans made to the borrower and the remaining balance of those loans;

(B) The date of default;

(C) Information concerning collection of the loan, including the repayment status of the loan;

(D) Any changes or corrections in the information reported by the agency that result from information received after the initial report; and

(E) The date the loan is fully repaid by or on behalf of the borrower or discharged by reason of the borrower's death, bankruptcy, total and permanent disability, or closed school or false certification.

(ii) The guaranty agency, after it pays a default claim on a loan but before it reports the default to a credit bureau or assesses collection costs against a borrower, shall, within the timeframe specified in paragraph (b)(6)(v) of this section, provide the borrower with—

(A) Written notice that meets the requirements of paragraph (b)(5)(vi) of this section regarding the proposed actions;

(B) An opportunity to inspect and copy agency records pertaining to the loan obligation;

(C) An opportunity for an administrative review of the legal enforceability or past-due status of the loan obligation; and

(D) An opportunity to enter into a repayment agreement on terms satisfactory to the agency.

(iii) The procedures set forth in 34 CFR 30.20–30.33 (administrative offset) satisfy the requirements of paragraph (b)(5)(ii) of this section.

(iv)(A) In response to a request submitted by a borrower, after the deadlines established under agency rules, for access to records, an administrative review, or for an opportunity to enter into a repayment agreement, the agency shall provide the requested relief but may continue reporting the debt to credit bureaus until it determines that the borrower has demonstrated that the loan obligation is not legally enforceable or that alternative repayment arrangements satisfactory to the agency have been made with the borrower.

(B) The deadline established by the agency for requesting

administrative review under paragraph (b)(5)(ii)(C) of this section must allow the borrower at least 60 days from the date the notice described in paragraph (b)(5)(ii)(A) of this section is sent to request that review.

(v) An agency may not permit an employee, official, or agent to conduct the administrative review required under this paragraph if that individual is—

(A) Employed in an organizational component of the agency or its agent that is charged with collection of loan obligations; or

(B) Compensated on the basis of collections on loan obligations.

(vi) The notice sent by the agency under paragraph (b)(5)(ii)(A) of this section must—

(A) Advise the borrower that the agency has paid a default claim filed by the lender and has taken assignment of the loan;

(B) Identify the lender that made the loan and the school for attendance at which the loan was made;

(C) State the outstanding principal, accrued interest, and any other charges then owing on the loan;

(D) Demand that the borrower immediately begin repayment of the loan;

(E) Explain the rate of interest that will accrue on the loan, that all costs incurred to collect the loan will be charged to the borrower, the authority for assessing these costs, and the manner in which the agency will calculate the amount of these costs;

(F) Notify the borrower that the agency will report the default to all national credit bureaus to the detriment of the borrower's credit rating;

(G) Explain the opportunities available to the borrower under agency rules to request access to the agency's records on the loan, to request an administrative review of the legal enforceability or past-due status of the loan, and to reach an agreement on repayment terms satisfactory to the agency to prevent the agency from reporting the loan as defaulted to credit bureaus and provide deadlines and method for requesting this relief;

(H) Unless the agency uses a separate notice to advise the borrower regarding other proposed enforcement actions, describe specifically any other enforcement action, such as offset against federal or state income tax refunds or wage garnishment that the agency intends to use to collect the debt, and explain the procedures available to the borrower prior to those other enforcement actions for access to records, for an administrative review, or for agreement to alternative repayment terms;

(I) Describe the grounds on which the borrower may object that the loan obligation as stated in the notice is not a legally enforceable debt owed by the borrower;

(J) Describe any appeal rights available to the borrower from an adverse decision on administrative review of the loan obligation;

(K) Describe any right to judicial review of an adverse decision by the agency regarding the legal enforceability or past-due status of the loan obligation; and

(L) Describe the collection actions that the agency may take in the future if those presently proposed do not result in repayment of the loan obligation, including the filing of a lawsuit against the borrower by the agency and assignment of the loan to the Secretary for the filing of a lawsuit against the borrower by the Federal Government.

(vii) As part of the guaranty agency's response to a borrower who appeals an adverse decision resulting from the agency's administrative review of the loan obligation, the agency must provide the borrower with information on the availability of the Student Loan Ombudsman's office.

(6) *Collection efforts on defaulted loans.*

(i) A guaranty agency must engage in reasonable and documented collection activities on a loan on which it pays a default claim filed by a lender. For a non-paying borrower, the agency must perform at least one activity every 180 days to collect the debt, locate the borrower (if necessary), or determine if the borrower has the means to repay the debt.

(ii) A guaranty agency must attempt an annual Federal offset against all eligible borrowers. If an agency initiates proceedings to offset a borrower's State or Federal income tax refunds and other payments made by the Federal Government to the borrower, it may not initiate those proceedings sooner than 60 days after sending the notice described in paragraph (b)(5)(ii)(A) of this section.

(iii) A guaranty agency must initiate administrative wage garnishment proceedings against all eligible borrowers, except as provided in paragraph (b)(6)(iv) of this section, by following the procedures described in paragraph (b)(9) of this section.

(iv) A guaranty agency may file a civil suit against a borrower to compel repayment only if the borrower has no wages that can be garnished under paragraph (b)(9) of this section, or the agency determines that the borrower has sufficient attachable assets or income that is not subject to administrative wage garnishment that can be used to repay the debt, and the use of litigation would be more effective in collection of the debt.

(v) Within 45 days after paying a lender's default claim, the agency must send a notice to the borrower that contains the information described in paragraph (b)(5)(ii) of this section. During this time period, the agency also must notify the borrower, either in the notice containing the information described in paragraph (b)(5)(ii) of this section, or in a separate notice, that if he or she does not make repayment arrangements acceptable to the agency, the agency will promptly initiate procedures to collect the debt. The agency's notification to the borrower must state that the agency may administratively garnish the borrower's wages, file a civil suit to compel repayment, offset the borrower's State and Federal income tax refunds and other payments made by the Federal Government to the borrower, assign the loan to the Secretary in accordance with § 682.409, and take other lawful collection means to collect the debt, at the discretion of the agency. The agency's notification must include a statement that borrowers may have certain legal rights in the collection of debts, and that borrowers may wish to contact counselors or lawyers regarding those rights.

(vi) Within a reasonable time after all of the information described in paragraph (b)(6)(v) of this section has been sent, the agency must send at least one notice informing the borrower that the default has been reported to all national credit bureaus (if that is the case) and that the borrower's credit rating may thereby have been damaged.

(7) *Special conditions for agency payment of a claim.*

(i) A guaranty agency may adopt a policy under which it pays a claim to a lender on a loan under the conditions described in § 682.509(a)(1).

(ii) Upon the payment of a claim under a policy described in paragraph (b)(7)(i) of this section, the guaranty agency shall—

(A) Perform the loan servicing functions required of a lender under § 682.208, except that the agency is not required to follow the credit bureau reporting requirements of that section;

(B) Perform the functions of the lender during the repayment period of the loan, as required under § 682.209;

(C) If the borrower is delinquent in repaying the loan at the time the agency pays a claim thereon to the lender or becomes delinquent while the agency holds the loan, exercise due diligence in accordance with § 682.411 in attempting to collect the loan from the borrower and any endorser or co-maker; and

(D) After the date of default on the loan, if any, comply with paragraph (b)(6) of this section with respect to collection activities on the loan, with the date of default treated as the claim payment date for purposes of those paragraphs.

(8) *Preemption of State law.* The provisions of paragraphs (b)(2), (5), and (6) of this section preempt any State law, including State statutes, regulations, or rules, that would conflict with or hinder satisfaction of the requirements of these provisions.

(9) *Administrative Garnishment.*

(i) If a guaranty agency decides to garnish the disposable pay of a borrower who is not making payments on a loan held by the agency, on which the Secretary has paid a reinsurance claim, it shall do so in accordance with the following procedures:

(A) The employer shall deduct and pay to the agency from a borrower's wages an amount that does not exceed the lesser of 10 percent of the borrower's disposable pay for each pay period or the amount permitted by 15 U.S.C. 1673, unless the borrower provides the agency with written consent to deduct a greater amount. For this purpose, the term "disposable pay" means that part of the borrower's compensation from an employer remaining after the deduction of any amounts required by law to be withheld.

(B) At least 30 days before the initiation of garnishment proceedings, the guaranty agency shall mail to the borrower's last known address, a written notice of the nature and amount of the debt, the intention of the agency to initiate proceedings to collect the debt through deductions from pay, and an explanation of the borrower's rights.

(C) The guaranty agency shall offer the borrower an opportunity to inspect and copy agency records related to the debt.

(D) The guaranty agency shall offer the borrower an opportunity to enter into a written repayment agreement with the agency under terms agreeable to the agency.

(E) The guaranty agency shall offer the borrower an opportunity for a hearing in accordance with paragraph (b)(9)(i)(J) of this section concerning the existence or the amount of the debt and, in the case of a borrower whose proposed repayment schedule under the garnishment order is established other than by a written agreement under paragraph (b)(9)(i)(D) of this section, the terms of the repayment schedule.

(F) The guaranty agency shall sue any employer for any amount that the employer, after receipt of the garnishment notice provided by the agency under paragraph (b)(9)(i)(H) of this section, fails to withhold from wages owed and payable to an employee under the employer's normal pay and disbursement cycle.

(G) The guaranty agency may not garnish the wages of a borrower whom it knows has been involuntarily separated from employment until the borrower has been reemployed continuously for at least 12 months.

(H) Unless the guaranty agency receives information that the agency believes justifies a delay or cancellation of the withholding order, it shall send a withholding order to the employer within 20 days after the borrower fails to make a timely request for a hearing, or, if a timely request for a hearing is made by the borrower, within 20 days after a final decision is made by the agency to proceed with garnishment.

(I) The notice given to the employer under paragraph (b)(9)(i)(H) of this section must contain only the information as may be necessary for the employer to comply with the withholding order.

(J) The guaranty agency shall provide a hearing, which, at the borrower's option, may be oral or written, if the borrower submits a written request for a hearing on the existence or amount of the debt or the terms of the repayment schedule. The time and location of the hearing shall be established by the agency. An oral hearing may, at the borrower's option, be conducted either in-person or by telephone conference. All telephonic charges must be the responsibility of the guaranty agency.

(K) If the borrower's written request is received by the guaranty agency on or before the 15th day following the borrower's receipt of the notice described in paragraph (b)(9)(i)(B) of this section, the guaranty agency may not issue a withholding order until the borrower has been provided the requested hearing. For purposes of this paragraph, in the absence of evidence to the contrary, a borrower shall be considered to have received the notice described in paragraph (b)(9)(i)(B) of this section 5 days after it was mailed by the agency. The guaranty agency shall provide a hearing to the borrower in sufficient time to permit a decision, in accordance with the procedures that the agency may prescribe, to be rendered within 60 days.

(L) If the borrower's written request is received by the guaranty agency after the 15th day following the borrower's receipt of the notice described in paragraph (b)(9)(i)(B) of this section, the guaranty agency shall provide a hearing to the borrower in sufficient time that a decision, in accordance with the procedures that the agency may prescribe, may be rendered within 60 days, but may not delay issuance of a withholding order unless the agency determines that the delay in filing the request was caused by factors over which the borrower had no control, or the agency receives information that the agency believes justifies a delay or cancellation of the withholding order. For purposes of this paragraph, in the absence of evidence to the contrary, a borrower shall be considered to have received the notice described in paragraph (b)(9)(i)(B) of this section 5 days after it was mailed by the agency.

(M) The hearing official appointed by the agency to conduct the hearing may be any qualified individual, including an administrative law judge, not under the supervision or control of the head of the guaranty agency.

(N) The hearing official shall issue a final written decision at the earliest practicable date, but not later than 60 days after the guaranty agency's receipt of the borrower's hearing request.

(O) As specified in section 488A(a)(8) of the HEA, the borrower may seek judicial relief, including punitive damages, if the employer discharges, refuses to employ, or takes disciplinary action against the borrower due to the issuance of a withholding order.

(ii) References to "the borrower" in this paragraph include all endorsers on a loan.

(10) *Conflicts of interest.*

(i) A guaranty agency shall maintain and enforce written standards of conduct governing the performance of its employees, officers, directors, trustees, and agents engaged in the selection, award, and administration of contracts or agreements. The standards of conduct must, at a minimum, require disclosure of financial or other interests and must mandate disinterested decision-making. The standards must provide for appropriate disciplinary actions to be applied for violations of the standards by employees, officers, directors, trustees, or agents of the guaranty agency, and must include provisions to—

(A) Prohibit any employee, officer, director, trustee, or agent from participating in the selection, award, or decision-making related to the administration of a contract or agreement supported by the reserve fund described in paragraph (a) of this section, if that participation would create a conflict of interest. Such a conflict would arise if the employee, officer, director, trustee, or agent, or any member of his or her immediate family, his or her partner, or an organization that employs or is about to employ any of those parties has a financial or ownership interest in the organization selected for an award or would benefit from the decision made in the administration of the contract or agreement. The prohibitions described in this paragraph do not apply to employees of a State agency covered by codes of conduct established under State law;

(B) Ensure sufficient separation of responsibility and authority between its lender claims processing as a guaranty agency and its lending or loan servicing activities, or both, within the guaranty agency or between that agency and one or more affiliates, including independence in direct reporting requirements and such management and systems controls as may be necessary to demonstrate, in the independent audit required under § 682.410(b)(1), that claims filed by another arm of the guaranty agency or by an affiliate of that agency receive no more favorable treatment than that accorded the claims filed by a lender or servicer that is not an affiliate or part of the guaranty agency; and

(C) Prohibit the employees, officers, directors, trustees, and agents of the guaranty agency, his or her partner, or any member of his or her immediate family, from soliciting or accepting gratuities, favors, or anything of monetary value from contractors or parties to agreements, except that nominal and unsolicited gratuities, favors, or items may be accepted.

(ii) *Guaranty agency restructuring.* If the Secretary determines that action is necessary to protect the Federal fiscal interest because of an agency's failure to meet the requirements of § 682.410(b)(10)(i), the Secretary may require the agency to comply with any additional measures that the Secretary believes are appropriate, including the total divestiture of the agency's non-FFEL functions and the agency's interests in any affiliated organization.

(c) *Enforcement requirements.* A guaranty agency shall take such measures and establish such controls as are necessary to ensure its vigorous enforcement of all Federal, State, and guaranty agency requirements, including agreements, applicable to its loan guarantee program, including, at a minimum, the following:

(1) Conducting comprehensive biennial on-site program reviews, using statistically valid techniques to calculate liabilities to the Secretary that each review indicates may exist, of at least—

(i)(A) Each participating lender whose dollar volume of FFEL loans made or held by the lender and guaranteed by the agency in the preceding year—

(1) Equaled or exceeded two percent of the total of all loans guaranteed in that year by the agency;

(2) Was one of the ten largest lenders whose loans were guaranteed in that year by the agency; or

(3) Equaled or exceeded $10 million in the most recent fiscal year;

(B) Each lender described in section 435(d)(1)(D) or (J) of the Act that is located in any State in which the agency is the principal

guarantor as defined in § 682.800(d), and, at the option of each guaranty agency, the Student Loan Marketing Association; and

(C) Each participating school, located in a State for which the guaranty agency is the principal guaranty agency, that has a cohort default rate, as described in subpart M of 34 CFR part 668, for either of the 2 immediately preceding fiscal years, as defined in 34 CFR 668.182, that exceeds 20 percent, unless the school is under a mandate from the Secretary under subpart M of 34 CFR part 668 to take specific default reduction measures or if the total dollar amount of loans entering repayment in each fiscal year on which the cohort default rate over 20 percent is based does not exceed $100,000; or

(ii) The schools and lenders selected by the agency as an alternative to the reviews required by paragraphs (c)(1)(A)–(C) of this section if the Secretary approves the agency's proposed alternative selection methodology.

(2) Demanding prompt repayment by the responsible parties to lenders, borrowers, the agency, or the Secretary, as appropriate, of all funds found in those reviews to be owed by the participants with regard to loans guaranteed by the agency, whether or not the agency holds the loans, and monitoring the implementation by participants of corrective actions, including these repayments, required by the agency as a result of those reviews.

(3) Referring to the Secretary for further enforcement action any case in which repayment of funds to the Secretary is not made in full within 60 days of the date of the agency's written demand to the school, lender, or other party for payment, together with all supporting documentation, any correspondence, and any other documentation submitted by that party regarding the repayment.

(4) Adopting procedures for identifying fraudulent loan applications.

(5) Undertaking or arranging with State or local law enforcement agencies for the prompt and thorough investigation of all allegations and indications of criminal or other programmatic misconduct by its program participants, including violations of Federal law or regulations.

(6) Promptly referring to appropriate State and local regulatory agencies and to nationally recognized accrediting agencies and associations for investigation information received by the guaranty agency that may affect the retention or renewal of the license or accreditation of a program participant.

(7) Promptly reporting all of the allegations and indications of misconduct having a substantial basis in fact, and the scope, progress, and results of the agency's investigations thereof to the Secretary.

(8) Referring appropriate cases to State or local authorities for criminal prosecution or civil litigation.

(9) Promptly notifying the Secretary of—

(i) Any action it takes affecting the FFEL program eligibility of a participating lender or school;

(ii) Information it receives regarding an action affecting the FFEL program eligibility of a participating lender or school taken by a nationally recognized accrediting agency, association, or a State licensing agency;

(iii) Any judicial or administrative proceeding relating to the enforceability of FFEL loans guaranteed by the agency or in which tuition obligations of a school's students are directly at issue, other than a proceeding relating to a single borrower or student; and

(iv) Any petition for relief in bankruptcy, application for receivership, or corporate dissolution proceeding brought by or against a school or lender participating in its loan guarantee program.

(10) Cooperating with all program reviews, investigations, and audits conducted by the Secretary relating to the agency's loan guarantee program.

(11) Taking prompt action to protect the rights of borrowers and the Federal fiscal interest respecting loans that the agency has guaranteed when the agency learns that a participating school or holder of loans is experiencing problems that threaten the solvency of the school or holder, including—

(i) Conducting on-site program reviews;

(ii) Providing training and technical assistance, if appropriate;

(iii) Filing a proof of claim with a bankruptcy court for recovery of any funds due the agency and any refunds due to borrowers on FFEL loans that it has guaranteed when the agency learns that a school has filed a bankruptcy petition;

(iv) Promptly notifying the Secretary that the agency has determined that a school or holder of loans is experiencing potential solvency problems; and

(v) Promptly notifying the Secretary of the results of any actions taken by the agency to protect Federal funds involving such a school or holder.

(Approved by the Office of Management and Budget under control number 1845-0020)

(Authority: 20 U.S.C. 1078, 1078-1, 1078-2, 1078-3, 1080a, 1082, 1087, 1091a, and 1099)

[58 FR 9119, Feb. 19, 1993; 59 FR 22487, April 29, 1994; 59 FR 25747, May 17, 1994; 59 FR 33357, June 28, 1994; 59 FR 35625, July 13, 1994; 59 FR 46175, Sept. 7, 1994; 59 FR 60691, Nov. 25, 1994; 60 FR 32912, June 26, 1995; 61 FR 60436, 60486, Nov. 27, 1996; 64 FR 18980, April 16, 1999; 64 FR 58630, Oct. 29, 1999; 64 FR 58965, Nov. 1, 1999; 65 FR 65621, Nov. 1, 2000; 65 FR 65650, Nov. 1, 2000; 66 FR 34764, June 29, 2001]

§ 682.411 Lender due diligence in collecting guaranty agency loans.

(a) *General.* In the event of delinquency on an FFEL Program loan, the lender must engage in at least the collection efforts described in paragraphs (c) through (n) of this section, except that in the case of a loan made to a borrower who is incarcerated, residing outside a State, Mexico, or Canada, or whose telephone number is unknown, the lender may send a forceful collection letter instead of each telephone effort required by this section.

(b) *Delinquency.*

(1) For purposes of this section, delinquency on a loan begins on the first day after the due date of the first missed payment that is not later made. The due date of the first payment is established by the lender but must occur by the deadlines specified in § 682.209(a) or, if the lender first learns after the fact that the borrower has entered the repayment period, no later than 75 days after the day the lender so learns, except as provided in § 682.209(a)(2)(v) and (a)(3)(ii)(E). If a payment is made late, the first day of delinquency is the day after the due date of the next missed payment that is not later made. A payment that is within five dollars of the amount normally required to advance the due date may nevertheless advance the due date if the lender's procedures allow for that advancement.

(2) At no point during the periods specified in paragraphs (c), (d), and (e) of this section may the lender permit the occurrence of

a gap in collection activity, as defined in paragraph (j) of this section, of more than 45 days (60 days in the case of a transfer).

(3) As part of one of the collection activities provided for in this section, the lender must provide the borrower with information on the availability of the Student Loan Ombudsman's office.

(c) *1–15 days delinquent.* Except in the case in which a loan is brought into this period by a payment on the loan, expiration of an authorized deferment or forbearance period, or the lender's receipt from the drawee of a dishonored check submitted as a payment on the loan, the lender during this period must send at least one written notice or collection letter to the borrower informing the borrower of the delinquency and urging the borrower to make payments sufficient to eliminate the delinquency. The notice or collection letter sent during this period must include, at a minimum, a lender or servicer contact, a telephone number, and a prominent statement informing the borrower that assistance may be available if he or she is experiencing difficulty in making a scheduled repayment.

(d) *16–180 days delinquent (16-240 days delinquent for a loan repayable in installments less frequently than monthly).*

(1) Unless exempted under paragraph (d)(4) of this section, during this period the lender must engage in at least four diligent efforts to contact the borrower by telephone and send at least four collection letters urging the borrower to make the required payments on the loan. At least one of the diligent efforts to contact the borrower by telephone must occur on or before, and another one must occur after, the 90th day of delinquency. Collection letters sent during this period must include, at a minimum, information for the borrower regarding deferment, forbearance, income-sensitive repayment and loan consolidation, and other available options to avoid default.

(2) At least two of the collection letters required under paragraph (d)(1) of this section must warn the borrower that, if the loan is not paid, the lender will assign the loan to the guaranty agency that, in turn, will report the default to all national credit bureaus, and that the agency may institute proceedings to offset the borrower's State and Federal income tax refunds and other payments made by the Federal Government to the borrower or to garnish the borrower's wages, or to assign the loan to the Federal Government for litigation against the borrower.

(3) Following the lender's receipt of a payment on the loan or a correct address for the borrower, the lender's receipt from the drawee of a dishonored check received as a payment on the loan, the lender's receipt of a correct telephone number for the borrower, or the expiration of an authorized deferment or forbearance period, the lender is required to engage in only—

(i) Two diligent efforts to contact the borrower by telephone during this period, if the loan is less than 91 days delinquent (121 days delinquent for a loan repayable in installments less frequently than monthly) upon receipt of the payment, correct address, correct telephone number, or returned check, or expiration of the deferment or forbearance; or

(ii) One diligent effort to contact the borrower by telephone during this period if the loan is 91-120 days delinquent (121-180 days delinquent for a loan repayable in installments less frequently than monthly) upon receipt of the payment, correct address, correct telephone number, or returned check, or expiration of the deferment or forbearance.

(4) A lender need not attempt to contact by telephone any borrower who is more than 120 days delinquent (180 days delinquent for a loan repayable in installments less frequent than

monthly) following the lender's receipt of—

(i) A payment on the loan;

(ii) A correct address or correct telephone number for the borrower;

(iii) A dishonored check received from the drawee as a payment on the loan; or

(iv) The expiration of an authorized deferment or forbearance.

(e) *181–270 days delinquent (241-330 days delinquent for a loan repayable in installments less frequently than monthly).* During this period the lender must engage in efforts to urge the borrower to make the required payments on the loan. These efforts must, at a minimum, provide information to the borrower regarding options to avoid default and the consequences of defaulting on the loan.

(f) *Final demand.* On or after the 241st day of delinquency (the 301st day for loans payable in less frequent installments than monthly) the lender must send a final demand letter to the borrower requiring repayment of the loan in full and notifying the borrower that a default will be reported to a national credit bureau. The lender must allow the borrower at least 30 days after the date the letter is mailed to respond to the final demand letter and to bring the loan out of default before filing a default claim on the loan.

(g) *Collection procedures when borrower's telephone number is not available.* Upon completion of a diligent but unsuccessful effort to ascertain the correct telephone number of a borrower as required by paragraph (m) of this section, the lender is excused from any further efforts to contact the borrower by telephone, unless the borrower's number is obtained before the 211th day of delinquency (the 271st day for loans repayable in installments less frequently than monthly).

(h) *Skip-tracing.*

(1) Unless the letter specified under paragraph (f) of this section has already been sent, within 10 days of its receipt of information indicating that it does not know the borrower's current address, the lender must begin to diligently attempt to locate the borrower through the use of effective commercial skip-tracing techniques. These efforts must include, but are not limited to, sending a letter to or making a diligent effort to contact each endorser, relative, reference, individual, and entity, identified in the borrower's loan file, including the schools the student attended. For this purpose, a lender's contact with a school official who might reasonably be expected to know the borrower's address may be with someone other than the financial aid administrator, and may be in writing or by phone calls. These efforts must be completed by the date of default with no gap of more than 45 days between attempts to contact those individuals or entities.

(2) Upon receipt of information indicating that it does not know the borrower's current address, the lender must discontinue the collection efforts described in paragraphs (c) through (f) of this section.

(3) If the lender is unable to ascertain the borrower's current address despite its performance of the activities described in paragraph (h)(1) of this section, the lender is excused thereafter from performance of the collection activities described in paragraphs (c) through (f) and (l)(1) through (l)(3) and (l)(5) of this section unless it receives communication indicating the borrower's address before the 241st day of delinquency (the 301st day for loans payable in less frequent installments than monthly).

(4) The activities specified by paragraph (m)(1)(i) or (ii) of this section (with references to the "borrower" understood to mean

endorser, reference, relative, individual, or entity as appropriate) meet the requirement that the lender make a diligent effort to contact each individual identified in the borrower's loan file.

(i) *Default aversion assistance.* Not earlier than the 60th day and no later than the 120th day of delinquency, a lender must request default aversion assistance from the guaranty agency that guarantees the loan.

(j) *Gap in collection activity.* For purposes of this section, the term *gap in collection activity* means, with respect to a loan, any period—

(1) Beginning on the date that is the day after—

(i) The due date of a payment unless the lender does not know the borrower's address on that date;

(ii) The day on which the lender receives a payment on a loan that remains delinquent notwithstanding the payment;

(iii) The day on which the lender receives the correct address for a delinquent borrower;

(iv) The day on which the lender completes a collection activity;

(v) The day on which the lender receives a dishonored check submitted as a payment on the loan;

(vi) The expiration of an authorized deferment or forbearance period on a delinquent loan; or

(vii) The day the lender receives information indicating it does not know the borrower's current address; and

(2) Ending on the date of the earliest of—

(i) The day on which the lender receives the first subsequent payment or completed deferment request or forbearance agreement;

(ii) The day on which the lender begins the first subsequent collection activity;

(iii) The day on which the lender receives written communication from the borrower relating to his or her account; or

(iv) Default.

(k) *Transfer.* For purposes of this section, the term transfer with respect to a loan means any action, including, but not limited to, the sale of the loan, that results in a change in the system used to monitor or conduct collection activity on a loan from one system to another.

(l) *Collection activity.* For purposes of this section, the term collection activity with respect to a loan means—

(1) Mailing or otherwise transmitting to the borrower at an address that the lender reasonably believes to be the borrower's current address a collection letter or final demand letter that satisfies the timing and content requirements of paragraph (c), (d), (e), or (f) of this section;

(2) Making an attempt to contact the borrower by telephone to urge the borrower to begin or resume repayment;

(3) Conducting skip-tracing efforts, in accordance with paragraph (h)(1) or (m)(1)(iii) of this section, to locate a borrower whose correct address or telephone number is unknown to the lender;

(4) Mailing or otherwise transmitting to the guaranty agency a request for default aversion assistance available from the agency on the loan at the time the request is transmitted; or

(5) Any telephone discussion or personal contact with the borrower so long as the borrower is apprised of the account's past-due status.

(m) *Diligent effort for telephone contact.*

(1) For purposes of this section, the term *diligent effort with respect to telephone contact* means—

(i) A successful effort to contact the borrower by telephone;

(ii) At least two unsuccessful attempts to contact the borrower by telephone at a number that the lender reasonably believes to be the borrower's correct telephone number; or

(iii) An unsuccessful effort to ascertain the correct telephone number of a borrower, including, but not limited to, a directory assistance inquiry as to the borrower's telephone number, and sending a letter to or making a diligent effort to contact each reference, relative, and individual identified in the most recent loan application or most recent school certification for that borrower held by the lender. The lender may contact a school official other than the financial aid administrator who reasonably may be expected to know the borrower's address or telephone number.

(2) If the lender is unable to ascertain the borrower's correct telephone number despite its performance of the activities described in paragraph (m)(1)(iii) of this section, the lender is excused thereafter from attempting to contact the borrower by telephone unless it receives a communication indicating the borrower's current telephone number before the 211th day of delinquency (the 271st day for loans repayable in installments less frequently than monthly).

(3) The activities specified by paragraph (m)(1)(i) or (ii) of this section (with references to "the borrower" understood to mean endorser, reference, relative, or individual as appropriate), meet the requirement that the lender make a diligent effort to contact each endorser or each reference, relative, or individual identified on the borrower's most recent loan application or most recent school certification.

(n) *Due diligence for endorsers.*

(1) Before filing a default claim on a loan with an endorser, the lender must—

(i) Make a diligent effort to contact the endorser by telephone; and

(ii) Send the endorser on the loan two letters advising the endorser of the delinquent status of the loan and urging the endorser to make the required payments on the loan with at least one letter containing the information described in paragraph (d)(2) of this section (with references to "the borrower" understood to mean the endorser).

(2) On or after the 241st day of delinquency (the 301st day for loans payable in less frequent installments than monthly) the lender must send a final demand letter to the endorser requiring repayment of the loan in full and notifying the endorser that a default will be reported to a national credit bureau. The lender must allow the endorser at least 30 days after the date the letter is mailed to respond to the final demand letter and to bring the loan out of default before filing a default claim on the loan.

(3) Unless the letter specified under paragraph (n)(2) of this section has already been sent, upon receipt of information indicating that it does not know the endorser's current address or telephone number, the lender must diligently attempt to locate the endorser through the use of effective commercial skip-tracing techniques. This effort must include an inquiry to directory assistance.

(o) *Preemption of State law.* The provisions of this section preempt any State law, including State statutes, regulations, or rules, that would conflict with or hinder satisfaction of the requirements or frustrate the purposes of this section.

(Approved by the Office of Management and Budget under control number 1845-0020)

(Authority: 20 U.S.C. 1078, 1078-1, 1078-2, 1078-3, 1080a, 1082, 1087)

[58 FR 9119, Feb. 19, 1993; 59 FR 22489, April 29, 1994; 59 FR 25747, May 17, 1994; 59 FR 46175, Sept. 7, 1994; 60 FR 32912, June 26, 1995; 61 FR 60486, Nov. 27, 1996; 62 FR 13539, March 21, 1997; 64 FR 18981, April 16, 1999; 64 FR 58630, Oct. 29, 1999; 64 FR 58965, Nov. 1, 1999]

B.3 Direct Loan Regulations

34 C.F.R. sec.
685.102 Definitions.

* * *

685.200 Borrower eligibility.

* * *

685.204 Deferment.
685.205 Forbearance.
685.206 Borrower responsibilities and defenses.
685.207 Obligation to repay.
685.208 Repayment plans.
685.209 Income contingent repayment plan.
685.210 Choice of repayment plan.
685.211 Miscellaneous repayment provisions.
685.212 Discharge of a loan obligation.
685.213 Total and permanent disability discharge.
685.214 Closed school discharge.
685.215 Discharge for false certification of student eligibility or unauthorized payment.
685.216 Unpaid refund discharge.

§ 685.102 Definitions.

(a)(1) The definitions of the following terms used in this part are set forth in subpart A of the Student Assistance General Provisions, 34 CFR part 668:

Academic year
Campus-based programs
Dependent student
Disburse
Eligible program
Eligible student
Enrolled
Federal Consolidation Loan Program
Federal Direct Student Loan Program (Direct Loan Program)
Federal Pell Grant Program
Federal Perkins Loan Program
Federal PLUS Program
Federal Supplemental Educational Opportunity Grant Program
Federal Work-Study Program
Independent student
Leveraging Educational Assistance Partnership Program
One-third of an academic year
Parent
Payment period
State

Two-thirds of an academic year

U.S. citizen or national

(2) The following definitions are set forth in the regulations for Institutional Eligibility under the Higher Education Act of 1965, as amended, 34 CFR Part 600:

Accredited

Clock hour

Educational program

Eligible institution

Federal Family Education Loan (FFEL) Program

Institution of higher education

Nationally recognized accrediting agency or association

Preaccredited

Program of study by correspondence

Secretary

(3) The following definitions are set forth in the regulations for the Federal Family Education Loan (FFEL) Program, 34 CFR Part 682:

Act

Endorser

Expected family contribution

Federal Insured Student Loan (FISL) Program

Federal Stafford Loan Program

Foreign school

Full-time student

Graduate or professional student

Guaranty agency

Holder

Legal guardian

Lender

Totally and permanently disabled

Undergraduate student

(b) The following definitions also apply to this part:

Alternative originator: An entity under contract with the Secretary that originates Direct Loans to students and parents of students who attend a Direct Loan Program school that does not originate loans.

Consortium: For purposes of this part, a consortium is a group of two or more schools that interacts with the Secretary in the same manner as other schools, except that the electronic communication between the Secretary and the schools is channeled through a single point. Each school in a consortium shall sign a Direct Loan Program participation agreement with the Secretary and be responsible for the information it supplies through the consortium.

Default: The failure of a borrower and endorser, if any, to make an installment payment when due, or to meet other terms of the promissory note, if the Secretary finds it reasonable to conclude that the borrower and endorser, if any, no longer intend to honor the obligation to repay, provided that this failure persists for 270 days.

Estimated financial assistance: (1) The estimated amount of assistance for a period of enrollment that a student (or a parent on behalf of a student) will receive from Federal, State, institutional, or other sources, such as scholarships, grants, financial need-based employment, or loans, including but not limited to—

(i) Except as provided in paragraph (2)(iii) of this definition, veterans' educational benefits paid under chapters 30, 31, 32, and 35 of title 38 of the United States Code;

(ii) Educational benefits paid under chapters 106 and 107 of title 10 of the United States Code (Selected Reserve Educational Assistance Program);

(iii) Reserve Officer Training Corps (ROTC) scholarships and subsistence allowances awarded under chapter 2 of title 10 and chapter 2 of title 37 of the United States Code;

(iv) Benefits paid under Public Law 97-376, section 156: Restored Entitlement Program for Survivors (or Quayle benefits);

(v) Benefits paid under Public Law 96-342, section 903: Educational Assistance Pilot Program;

(vi) Any educational benefits paid because of enrollment in a postsecondary education institution;

(vii) The estimated amount of other Federal student financial aid, including but not limited to a Federal Pell Grant, campus-based aid, and the gross amount (including fees) of a Direct Subsidized, Direct Unsubsidized, and Direct PLUS Loan; and

(viii) Except as provided in paragraph (2)(iii) of this definition, national service education awards or post-service benefits under title I of the National and Community Service Act of 1990.

(2) Estimated financial assistance does not include—

(i) Those amounts used to replace the expected family contribution, including—

(A) Direct PLUS Loan amounts;

(B) Direct Unsubsidized Loan amounts; and

(C) Non-Federal loan amounts;

(ii) Federal Perkins loan and Federal Work-Study funds that the student has declined; and

(iii) For the purpose of determining eligibility for a Direct Subsidized Loan, veterans' educational benefits paid under chapter 30 of title 38 of the United States Code (Montgomery GI Bill—Active Duty) and national service education awards or post-service benefits under title I of the National and Community Service Act of 1990.

Federal Direct Consolidation Loan Program: A loan program authorized by title IV, part D of the Act that provides loans to borrowers who consolidate certain Federal educational loan(s), and one of the components of the Direct Loan Program. Loans made under this program are referred to as Direct Consolidation Loans. There are three types of Direct Consolidation Loans:

(1) *Direct Subsidized Consolidation Loans*. Subsidized title IV education loans may be consolidated into a Direct Subsidized Consolidation Loan. Interest is not charged to the borrower during in-school grace and deferment periods.

(2) *Direct Unsubsidized Consolidation Loans*. Certain Federal education loans may be consolidated into a Direct Unsubsidized Consolidation Loan. The borrower is responsible for the interest that accrues during any period.

(3) *Direct PLUS Consolidation Loans*. Parent Loans for Undergraduate Students, Federal PLUS, Direct PLUS, and Direct PLUS Consolidation Loans may be consolidated into a Direct PLUS Consolidation Loan. The borrower is responsible for the interest that accrues during any period.

Federal Direct PLUS Program: A loan program authorized by title IV, part D of the Act that provides loans to parents of dependent students attending schools that participate in the Direct Loan Program, and one of the components of the Direct Loan Program. The borrower is responsible for the interest that accrues during any period. Loans made under this program are referred to as Direct PLUS Loans.

Federal Direct Stafford/Ford Loan Program: A loan program authorized by title IV, part D of the Act that provides loans to undergraduate, graduate, and professional students attending Direct Loan Program schools, and one of the components of the Direct Loan Program. The Secretary subsidizes the interest while the borrower is in an in-school, grace, or deferment period. Loans made under this program are referred to as Direct Subsidized Loans.

Federal Direct Unsubsidized Stafford/Ford Loan Program: A loan program authorized by title IV, part D of the Act that provides loans to undergraduate, graduate, and professional students attending Direct Loan Program schools, and one of the components of the Direct Loan Program. The borrower is responsible for the interest that accrues during any period. Loans made under this program are referred to as Direct Unsubsidized Loans.

Grace period: A six-month period that begins on the day after a Direct Loan Program borrower ceases to be enrolled as at least a half-time student at an eligible institution and ends on the day before the repayment period begins.

Half-time student: A student who is not a full-time student and who is enrolled in an institution of higher education and is carrying an academic workload that is at least one-half the workload of a full-time student, as determined by the school. A student enrolled solely in an eligible program of study by correspondence is considered a half-time student.

Interest rate: The annual interest rate that is charged on a loan, under title IV, part D of the Act.

Loan fee: A fee, payable by the borrower, that is used to help defray the costs of the Direct Loan Program.

Master promissory note (MPN): A promissory note under which the borrower may receive loans for a single academic year or multiple academic years. Loans for multiple academic years may no longer be made under an MPN after the earliest of—

(i) The date the Secretary or the school receives the borrower's written notice that no further loans may be disbursed;

(ii) One year after the date of the borrower's first anticipated disbursement if no disbursement is made during that twelve-month period; or

(iii) Ten years after the date of the first anticipated disbursement except that a remaining portion of a loan may be disbursed after this date.

Period of enrollment: The period for which a Direct Subsidized, Direct Unsubsidized, or Direct PLUS Loan is intended. The period of enrollment must coincide with one or more academic terms established by the school (such as semester, trimester, quarter, academic year, and length of the program of study), for which institutional charges are generally assessed. The period of enrollment is also referred to in this part as the loan period.

Satisfactory repayment arrangement.

(1) For the purpose of regaining eligibility under section 428F(b) of the HEA, the making of six consecutive, voluntary, on-time, full monthly payments on a defaulted loan. A borrower may only obtain the benefit of this paragraph with respect to renewed eligibility once.

(2) For the purpose of consolidating a defaulted loan under 34 CFR 685.220(d)(1)(ii)(E), the making of three consecutive, voluntary, on-time, full monthly payments on a defaulted loan.

(3) The required monthly payment amount may not be more than is reasonable and affordable based on the borrower's total financial circumstances. "On-time" means a payment made within 15 days of the scheduled due date, and voluntary payments are those payments made directly by the borrower, regardless of

whether there is a judgment against the borrower, and do not include payments obtained by income tax offset, garnishment, or income or asset execution.

School origination option 1: In general, under this option the school performs the following functions: creates a loan origination record, transmits the record to the Servicer, prepares the promissory note, obtains a completed and signed promissory note from a borrower, transmits the promissory note to the Servicer, receives the funds electronically, disburses a loan to a borrower, creates a disbursement record, transmits the disbursement record to the Servicer, and reconciles on a monthly basis. The Servicer initiates the drawdown of funds for schools participating in school origination option 1. The Secretary may modify the functions performed by a particular school.

School origination option 2: In general, under this option the school performs the following functions: creates a loan origination record, transmits the record to the Servicer, prepares the promissory note, obtains a completed and signed promissory note from a borrower, transmits the promissory note to the Servicer, determines funding needs, initiates the drawdown of funds, receives the funds electronically, disburses a loan to a borrower, creates a disbursement record, transmits the disbursement record to the Servicer, and reconciles on a monthly basis. The Secretary may modify the functions performed by a particular school.

Servicer: An entity that has contracted with the Secretary to act as the Secretary's agent in providing services relating to the origination or servicing of Direct Loans.

Standard origination: In general, under this option the school performs the following functions: creates a loan origination record, transmits the record to the Servicer, receives funds electronically, disburses funds, creates a disbursement record, transmits the disbursement record to the Servicer, and reconciles on a monthly basis. The Servicer prepares the promissory note, obtains a completed and signed promissory note from a borrower, and initiates the drawdown of funds for schools participating in standard origination. The Secretary may modify the functions performed by a particular school.

(Authority: 20 U.S.C. 1087a et seq.)

[60 FR 61793, Dec. 1, 1995; 61 FR 29899, June 12, 1996; 61 FR 60610, Nov. 29, 1996; 64 FR 58965, Nov. 1, 1999; 65 FR 38729, June 22, 2000; 65 FR 65629, Nov. 1, 2000; 66 FR 34765, June 29, 2001]

* * *

§ 685.200 Borrower eligibility.

(a) *Student borrower.* (1) A student is eligible to receive a Direct Subsidized Loan, a Direct Unsubsidized Loan, or a combination of these loans, if the student meets the following requirements:

(i) The student is enrolled, or accepted for enrollment, on at least a half-time basis in a school that participates in the Direct Loan Program.

(ii) The student meets the requirements for an eligible student under 34 CFR Part 668.

(iii) In the case of an undergraduate student who seeks a Direct Subsidized Loan or a Direct Unsubsidized Loan at a school that participates in the Federal Pell Grant Program, the student has received a determination of Federal Pell Grant eligibility for the period of enrollment for which the loan is sought.

(iv)(A) In the case of a borrower whose prior loan under title IV of the Act was discharged after a final determination of total and permanent disability, the borrower—

(1) Obtains a certification from a physician that the borrower is able to engage in substantial gainful activity; and

(2) Signs a statement acknowledging that the Direct Loan the borrower receives cannot be discharged in the future on the basis of any impairment present when the new loan is made, unless that impairment substantially deteriorates.

(B) In the case of a borrower whose prior loan under title IV of the Act was discharged on or after July 1, 2001 and before July 1, 2002 after a final determination of total and permanent disability, the borrower—

(1) Complies with the requirements of paragraph (a)(1)(iv)(A) of this section; and

(2) If the borrower applies for another loan within three years from the date that the borrower became totally and permanently disabled, as certified by the physician, reaffirms the previously discharged loan before receiving the new loan. For the purposes of this paragraph, reaffirmation means the acknowledgement of the loan by the borrower in a legally binding manner. The acknowledgement may include, but is not limited to, the borrower signing a new promissory note that includes the same terms and conditions as the original note signed by the borrower, making a payment on the loan, or signing a repayment agreement.

(C) In the case of a borrower whose prior loan under title IV of the Act was conditionally discharged based on an initial determination that the borrower was totally and permanently disabled—

(1) The suspension of collection activity on the prior loan has been lifted;

(2) The borrower complies with the requirement in paragraph (a)(1)(iv)(A)(1) of this section;

(3) The borrower signs a statement acknowledging that neither the prior loan nor the Direct Loan that the borrower receives may be discharged in the future on the basis of any impairment present when the borrower applied for a total and permanent disability discharge or when the new loan is made, unless that impairment substantially deteriorates; and

(4) The borrower signs a statement acknowledging that the suspension of collection activity on the prior loan will be lifted.

(v) In the case of a student who seeks a loan but does not have a certificate of graduation from a school providing secondary education or the recognized equivalent of such a certificate, the student meets the requirements under 34 CFR 668.32(e)(2), (3), or (4).

(2)(i) A Direct Subsidized Loan borrower must demonstrate financial need in accordance with title IV, part F of the Act.

(ii) The Secretary considers a member of a religious order, group, community, society, agency, or other organization who is pursuing a course of study at an institution of higher education to have no financial need if that organization—

(A) Has as its primary objective the promotion of ideals and beliefs regarding a Supreme Being;

(B) Requires its members to forego monetary or other support substantially beyond the support it provides; and

(C)(1) Directs the member to pursue the course of study; or

(2) Provides subsistence support to its members.

(b)(1) *Parent borrower.* A parent is eligible to receive a Direct PLUS Loan if the parent meets the following requirements:

(i) The parent is borrowing to pay for the educational costs of a dependent undergraduate student who meets the requirements for an eligible student under 34 CFR Part 668.

(ii) The parent provides his or her and the student's social security number.

(iii) The parent meets the requirements pertaining to citizenship and residency that apply to the student under 34 CFR 668.33.

(iv) The parent meets the requirements concerning defaults and overpayments that apply to the student in 34 CFR 668.32(g).

(v) The parent complies with the requirements for submission of a Statement of Educational Purpose that apply to the student under 34 CFR Part 668, except for the completion of a Statement of Selective Service Registration Status.

(vi) The parent meets the requirements that apply to a student under paragraph (a)(1)(iv) of this section.

(vii)(A) The parent—

(1) Does not have an adverse credit history;

(2) Has an adverse credit history but has obtained an endorser who does not have an adverse credit history; or

(3) Has an adverse credit history but documents to the satisfaction of the Secretary that extenuating circumstances exist.

(B) For purposes of paragraph (b)(1)(vii)(A) of this section, an adverse credit history means that as of the date of the credit report, the applicant—

(1) Is 90 or more days delinquent on any debt; or

(2) Has been the subject of a default determination, bankruptcy discharge, foreclosure, repossession, tax lien, wage garnishment, or write-off of a debt under title IV of the Act during the five years preceding the date of the credit report.

(C) For the purposes of (b)(1)(vii)(A) of this section, the Secretary does not consider the absence of a credit history as an adverse credit history and does not deny a Direct PLUS loan on that basis.

(2) For purposes of paragraph (b)(1) of this section, a "parent" includes the individuals described in the definition of "parent" in 34 CFR 668.2 and the spouse of a parent who remarried, if that spouse's income and assets would have been taken into account when calculating a dependent student's expected family contribution.

(c) *Defaulted FFEL Program and Direct Loan borrowers.* Except as noted in § 685.220(d)(1)(ii)(F), in the case of a student or parent borrower who is currently in default on an FFEL Program or a Direct Loan Program Loan, the borrower shall make satisfactory repayment arrangements, as described in paragraph (2) of the definition of that term under § 685.102(b), on the defaulted loan.

(d) *Use of loan proceeds to replace expected family contribution.* The amount of a Direct Unsubsidized Loan, a Direct PLUS Loan, a State-sponsored loan, or another non-Federal loan obtained for a loan period may be used to replace the expected family contribution for that loan period.

(Authority: 20 U.S.C. 1087a *et seq.*)

[60 FR 61816, Dec. 1, 1995; 61 FR 29900, June 12, 1996; 65 FR 65629, 65693, Nov. 1, 2000; 66 FR 34765, June 29, 2001; 66 FR 44007, Aug. 21, 2001]

* * *

§ 685.204 Deferment.

(a)(1) A Direct Loan borrower whose loan is eligible for interest subsidies and who meets the requirements described in paragraph (b) of this section is eligible for a deferment during which periodic installments of principal and interest need not be paid.

(2) A Direct Loan borrower whose loan is not eligible for interest subsidies and who meets the requirements described in paragraph (b) of this section is eligible for a deferment during which periodic installments of principal need not be paid but interest does accrue and is capitalized or paid by the borrower.

(b) Except as provided in paragraph (d) and (e) of this section, a Direct Loan borrower is eligible for a deferment during any period during which the borrower meets any of the following requirements:

(1)(i) The borrower—

(A) Is carrying at least one-half the normal full-time work load for the course of study that the borrower is pursuing, as determined by the eligible school the borrower is attending;

(B) Is pursuing a course of study pursuant to a graduate fellowship program approved by the Secretary; or

(C) Is pursuing a rehabilitation training program, approved by the Secretary, for individuals with disabilities; and

(ii) The borrower is not serving in a medical internship or residency program, except for a residency program in dentistry.

(iii)(A) For the purpose of paragraph (b)(1)(i) of this section, the Secretary processes a deferment when—

(1) The borrower submits a request to the Secretary along with documentation verifying the borrower's eligibility;

(2) The Secretary receives information from the borrower's school indicating that the borrower is eligible to receive a new loan; or

(3) The Secretary receives student status information from the borrower's school, either directly or indirectly, indicating that the borrower is enrolled on at least a half-time basis.

(B)(1) Upon notification by the Secretary that a deferment has been granted based on paragraph (b)(1)(iii)(A)(2) or (3) of this section, the borrower has the option to continue paying on the loan.

(2) If the borrower elects to cancel the deferment and continue paying on the loan, the borrower has the option to make the principal and interest payments that were deferred. If the borrower does not make the payments, the Secretary applies a deferment for the period in which payments were not made and capitalizes the interest.

(2)(i) The borrower is seeking and unable to find full-time employment.

(ii) For purposes of paragraph (b)(2)(i) of this section, the Secretary determines whether a borrower is eligible for a deferment due to the inability to find full-time employment using the standards and procedures set forth in 34 CFR 682.210(h) with references to the lender understood to mean the Secretary.

(3)(i) The borrower has experienced or will experience an economic hardship.

(ii) For purposes of paragraph (b)(3)(i) of this section, the Secretary determines whether a borrower is eligible for a deferment due to an economic hardship using the standards and procedures set forth in 34 CFR 682.210(s)(6) with references to the lender understood to mean the Secretary.

(c) No deferment under paragraphs (b) (2) or (3) of this section may exceed three years.

(d) If, at the time of application for a borrower's first Direct Loan, a borrower has an outstanding balance of principal or interest owing on any FFEL Program loan that was made, insured, or guaranteed prior to July 1, 1993, the borrower is eligible for a deferment during—

(1) the periods described in paragraph (b) of this section; and

(2) the periods described in 34 CFR 682.210(b), including those periods that apply to a "new borrower" as that term is defined in 34 CFR 682.210(b)(7).

(e) A borrower whose loan is in default is not eligible for a deferment, unless the borrower has made payment arrangements satisfactory to the Secretary.

(Approved by the Office of Management and Budget under control number 1845-0021)

(Authority: 20 U.S.C. 1087a *et seq.*)

[60 FR 33345, June 28, 1995; 61 FR 29900, June 12, 1996; 64 FR 58968, Nov. 1, 1999]

§ 685.205 Forbearance.

(a) *General.* "Forbearance" means permitting the temporary cessation of payments, allowing an extension of time for making payments, or temporarily accepting smaller payments than previously scheduled. The borrower has the option to choose the form of forbearance. Except as provided in paragraph (b)(9) of this section, if payments of interest are forborne, they are capitalized. The Secretary grants forbearance if the borrower or endorser intends to repay the loan but requests forbearance and provides sufficient documentation to support this request, and—

(1) The Secretary determines that, due to poor health or other acceptable reasons, the borrower or endorser is currently unable to make scheduled payments;

(2) The borrower's payments of principal are deferred under § 685.204 and the Secretary does not subsidize the interest benefits on behalf of the borrower;

(3) The borrower is in a medical or dental internship or residency that must be successfully completed before the borrower may begin professional practice or service, or the borrower is serving in a medical or dental internship or residency program leading to a degree or certificate awarded by an institution of higher education, a hospital, or a health care facility that offers postgraduate training;

(4) The borrower is serving in a national service position for which the borrower is receiving a national service education award under title I of the National and Community Service Act of 1990; or

(5) The borrower—

(i) Is performing the type of service that would qualify the borrower for loan forgiveness under the requirements of the teacher loan forgiveness program in § 685.217; and

(ii) Is required, by the Secretary, before a forbearance is granted under § 685.205(a)(5)(i) to—

(A) Submit documentation for the period of the annual forbearance request showing the beginning and ending dates that the borrower is expected to perform, for that year, the type of service described in § 685.217(c); and

(B) Certify the borrower's intent to satisfy the requirements of § 685.217(c).

(6) For not more than three years during which the borrower or endorser—

(i) Is currently obligated to make payments on loans under title IV of the Act; and

(ii) The sum of these payments each month (or a proportional share if the payments are due less frequently than monthly) is equal to or greater than 20 percent of the borrower's or endorser's total monthly gross income.

(b) *Administrative forbearance*. In certain circumstances, the Secretary grants forbearance without requiring documentation from the borrower. These circumstances include but are not limited to—

(1) A properly granted period of deferment for which the Secretary learns the borrower did not qualify;

(2) The period for which payments are overdue at the beginning of an authorized deferment period;

(3) The period beginning when the borrower entered repayment until the first payment due date was established;

(4) The period prior to a borrower's filing of a bankruptcy petition;

(5) A period after the Secretary receives reliable information indicating that the borrower (or the student in the case of a Direct PLUS Loan) has died, or the borrower has become totally and permanently disabled, until the Secretary receives documentation of death or total and permanent disability;

(6) Periods necessary for the Secretary to determine the borrower's eligibility for discharge—

(i) Under § 685.214;

(ii) Under § 685.215;

(iii) Under § 685.216; or

(iv) Under § 685.217; or

(v) Due to the borrower's or endorser's (if applicable) bankruptcy;

(7) A period of up to three years in cases where the effect of a variable interest rate on a fixed-amount or graduated repayment schedule causes the extension of the maximum repayment term;

(8) A period during which the Secretary has authorized forbearance due to a national military mobilization or other local or national emergency; or

(9) A period of up to 60 days necessary for the Secretary to collect and process documentation supporting the borrower's request for a deferment, forbearance, change in repayment plan, or consolidation loan. Interest that accrues during this period is not capitalized.

(c) *Period of forbearance*. (1) The Secretary grants forbearance for a period of up to one year.

(2) The forbearance is renewable, upon request of the borrower, for the duration of the period in which the borrower meets the condition required for the forbearance.

(Authority: 20 U.S.C. 1087a *et seq.*)

[61 FR 29900, June 12, 1996; 64 FR 58968, Nov. 1, 1999; 65 FR 65629, Nov. 1, 2000; 66 FR 34765, June 29, 2001]

§ 685.206 Borrower responsibilities and defenses.

(a) The borrower shall give the school the following information as part of the origination process for a Direct Subsidized, Direct Unsubsidized, or Direct PLUS Loan:

(1) A statement, as described in 34 CFR Part 668, that the loan will be used for the cost of the student's attendance.

(2) Information demonstrating that the borrower is eligible for the loan.

(3) Information concerning the outstanding FFEL Program and Direct Loan Program loans of the borrower and, for a parent borrower, of the student, including any Federal Consolidation Loan or Direct Consolidation Loan.

(4) A statement authorizing the school to release to the Secretary information relevant to the student's eligibility to borrow or to have a parent borrow on the student's behalf (e.g., the student's enrollment status, financial assistance, and employment records).

(b)(1) The borrower shall promptly notify the Secretary of any change of name, address, student status to less than half-time, employer, or employer's address; and

(2) The borrower shall promptly notify the school of any change in address during enrollment.

(c) *Borrower defenses*. (1) In any proceeding to collect on a Direct Loan, the borrower may assert as a defense against repayment, any act or omission of the school attended by the student that would give rise to a cause of action against the school under applicable State law. These proceedings include, but are not limited to, the following:

(i) Tax refund offset proceedings under 34 CFR 30.33.

(ii) Wage garnishment proceedings under section 488A of the Act.

(iii) Salary offset proceedings for Federal employees under 34 CFR Part 31.

(iv) Credit bureau reporting proceedings under 31 U.S.C. 3711(f).

(2) If the borrower's defense against repayment is successful, the Secretary notifies the borrower that the borrower is relieved of the obligation to repay all or part of the loan and associated costs and fees that the borrower would otherwise be obligated to pay. The Secretary affords the borrower such further relief as the Secretary determines is appropriate under the circumstances. Further relief may include, but is not limited to, the following:

(i) Reimbursing the borrower for amounts paid toward the loan voluntarily or through enforced collection.

(ii) Determining that the borrower is not in default on the loan and is eligible to receive assistance under title IV of the Act.

(iii) Updating reports to credit bureaus to which the Secretary previously made adverse credit reports with regard to the borrower's Direct Loan.

(3) The Secretary may initiate an appropriate proceeding to require the school whose act or omission resulted in the borrower's successful defense against repayment of a Direct Loan to pay to the Secretary the amount of the loan to which the defense applies. However, the Secretary does not initiate such a proceeding after the period for the retention of records described in § 685.309(c) unless the school received actual notice of the claim during that period.

(Approved by the Office of Management and Budget under control number 1845-0021)

(Authority: 20 U.S.C. 1087a *et seq.*)

[60 FR 33345, June 28, 1995; 64 FR 58972, Nov. 1, 1999]

§ 685.207 Obligation to repay.

(a) *Obligation of repayment in general*. (1) A borrower is obligated to repay the full amount of a Direct Loan, including the principal balance, fees, any collection costs charged under § 685.202(e), and any interest not subsidized by the Secretary, unless the borrower is relieved of the obligation to repay as provided in this part.

(2) The borrower's repayment of a Direct Loan may also be

subject to the deferment provisions in § 685.204, the forbearance provisions in § 685.205, and the discharge provisions in § 685.212.

(b) *Direct Subsidized Loan repayment.* (1) During the period in which a borrower is enrolled at an eligible school on at least a half-time basis, the borrower is in an "in-school" period and is not required to make payments on a Direct Subsidized Loan unless—

(i) The loan entered repayment before the in-school period began; and

(ii) The borrower has not been granted a deferment under § 685.204.

(2)(i) When a borrower ceases to be enrolled at an eligible school on at least a half-time basis, a six-month grace period begins, unless the grace period has been previously exhausted.

(ii)(A) Any borrower who is a member of a reserve component of the Armed Forces named in section 10101 of title 10, United States Code and is called or ordered to active duty for a period of more than 30 days is entitled to have the active duty period excluded from the six-month grace period. The excluded period includes the time necessary for the borrower to resume enrollment at the next available regular enrollment period. Any single excluded period may not exceed 3 years.

(B) Any borrower who is in a grace period when called or ordered to active duty as specified in paragraph (b)(2)(ii)(A) of this section is entitled to a full six-month grace period upon completion of the excluded period.

(iii) During a grace period, the borrower is not required to make any principal payments on a Direct Subsidized Loan.

(3) A borrower is not obligated to pay interest on a Direct Subsidized Loan for in-school or grace periods unless the borrower is required to make payments on the loan during those periods under paragraph (b)(1) of this section.

(4) The repayment period for a Direct Subsidized Loan begins the day after the grace period ends. A borrower is obligated to repay the loan under paragraph (a) of this section during the repayment period.

(c) *Direct Unsubsidized Loan repayment.* (1) During the period in which a borrower is enrolled at an eligible school on at least a half-time basis, the borrower is in an "in-school" period and is not required to make payments of principal on a Direct Unsubsidized Loan unless—

(i) The loan entered repayment before the in-school period began; and

(ii) The borrower has not been granted a deferment under § 685.204.

(2)(i) When a borrower ceases to be enrolled at an eligible school on at least a half-time basis, a six-month grace period begins, unless the grace period has been previously exhausted.

(ii)(A) Any borrower who is a member of a reserve component of the Armed Forces named in section 10101 of title 10, United States Code and is called or ordered to active duty for a period of more than 30 days is entitled to have the active duty period excluded from the six-month grace period. The excluded period includes the time necessary for the borrower to resume enrollment at the next available regular enrollment period. Any single excluded period may not exceed 3 years.

(B) Any borrower who is in a grace period when called or ordered to active duty as specified in paragraph (c)(2)(ii)(A) of this section is entitled to a full six-month grace period upon completion of the excluded period.

(iii) During a grace period, the borrower is not required to make any principal payments on a Direct Unsubsidized Loan.

(3) A borrower is responsible for the interest that accrues on a Direct Unsubsidized Loan during in-school and grace periods. Interest begins to accrue on the day the first installment is disbursed. Interest that accrues may be capitalized or paid by the borrower.

(4) The repayment period for a Direct Unsubsidized Loan begins the day after the grace period ends. A borrower is obligated to repay the loan under paragraph (a) of this section during the repayment period.

(d) *Direct PLUS Loan repayment.* The repayment period for a Direct PLUS Loan begins on the day the loan is fully disbursed. Interest begins to accrue on the day the first installment is disbursed. A borrower is obligated to repay the loan under paragraph (a) of this section during the repayment period.

(e) *Direct Consolidation Loan repayment.* (1) Except as provided in paragraphs (e)(2) and (e)(3) of this section, the repayment period for a Direct Consolidation Loan begins and interest begins to accrue on the day the loan is made. The borrower is obligated to repay the loan under paragraph (a) of this section during the repayment period.

(2) A borrower who obtains a Direct Subsidized Consolidation Loan during an in-school period will be subject to the repayment provisions in paragraph (b) of this section.

(3) A borrower who obtains a Direct Unsubsidized Consolidation Loan during an in-school period will be subject to the repayment provisions in paragraph (c) of this section.

(f) *Determining the date on which the grace period begins for a borrower in a correspondence program.* For a borrower of a Direct Subsidized or Direct Unsubsidized Loan who is a correspondence student, the grace period begins on the earliest of the date—

(1) The borrower completes the program;

(2) The borrower falls 60 days behind the due date for submission of a scheduled assignment, according to the schedule required in § 685.302. However, a school may grant the borrower one restoration to in-school status if the borrower fails to submit a lesson within this 60-day period after the due date for submission of a particular assignment if, within the 60-day period, the borrower declares, in writing, an intention to continue in the program and an understanding that the required lessons must be submitted on time; or

(3) That is 60 days following the latest allowable date established by the school for completing the program under the schedule required under § 685.302.

(Authority: 20 U.S.C. 1087a *et seq.*)

[64 FR 58968, Nov. 1, 1999]

§ 685.208 Repayment plans.

(a) *General.* (1) A borrower may repay a Direct Subsidized Loan, a Direct Unsubsidized Loan, a Direct Subsidized Consolidation Loan, or a Direct Unsubsidized Consolidation Loan under the standard repayment plan, the extended repayment plan, the graduated repayment plan, or the income contingent repayment plan.

(2) A borrower may repay a Direct PLUS Loan or a Direct PLUS Consolidation Loan under the standard repayment plan, the extended repayment plan, or the graduated repayment plan.

(3) The Secretary may provide an alternative repayment plan in accordance with paragraph (g) of this section.

(4) All Direct Loans obtained by one borrower must be repaid together under the same repayment plan, except that a borrower of a Direct PLUS Loan or a Direct PLUS Consolidation Loan may repay the Direct PLUS Loan or the Direct PLUS Consolidation Loan separately from other Direct Loans obtained by that borrower.

(b) *Standard repayment plan.* (1) Under the standard repayment plan, a borrower shall repay a loan in full within ten years from the date the loan entered repayment by making fixed monthly payments.

(2) Periods of authorized deferment or forbearance are not included in the ten-year repayment period.

(3) A borrower's payments under the standard repayment plan are at least $50 per month, except that a borrower's final payment may be less than $50.

(4) The number of payments or the fixed monthly repayment amount may be adjusted to reflect changes in the variable interest rate identified in § 685.202(a).

(c) *Extended repayment plan.* (1) Under the extended repayment plan, a borrower shall repay a loan in full by making fixed monthly payments within an extended period of time that varies with the total amount of the borrower's loans, as described in paragraph (e) of this section.

(2) Periods of deferment and forbearance are not included in the number of years of repayment.

(3) A borrower makes fixed monthly payments of at least $50, except that a borrower's final payment may be less than $50.

(4) The number of payments or the fixed monthly repayment amount may be adjusted to reflect changes in the variable interest rate identified in § 685.202(a).

(d) *Graduated repayment plan.* (1) Under the graduated repayment plan, a borrower shall repay a loan in full by making payments at two or more levels within a period of time that varies with the total amount of the borrower's loans, as described in paragraph (e) of this section.

(2) Periods of deferment and forbearance are not included in the number of years of repayment.

(3) The number of payments or the monthly repayment amount may be adjusted to reflect changes in the variable interest rate identified in § 685.202(a).

(4) No scheduled payment under the graduated repayment plan may be less than the amount of interest accrued on the loan between monthly payments, less than 50 percent of the payment amount that would be required under the standard repayment plan, or more than 150 percent of the payment amount that would be required under the standard repayment plan.

(e) *Repayment period for the extended and graduated plans.* Under the extended and graduated repayment plans, if the total amount of the borrower's Direct Loans is—

(1) Less than $10,000, the borrower shall repay the loans within 12 years of entering repayment;

(2) Greater than or equal to $10,000 but less than $20,000, the borrower shall repay the loans within 15 years of entering repayment;

(3) Greater than or equal to $20,000 but less than $40,000, the borrower shall repay the loans within 20 years of entering repayment;

(4) Greater than or equal to $40,000 but less than $60,000, the borrower shall repay the loans within 25 years of entering repayment; and

(5) Greater than or equal to $60,000, the borrower shall repay the loans within 30 years of entering repayment.

(f) *Income contingent repayment plan.* (1) Under the income contingent repayment plan, a borrower's monthly repayment amount is generally based on the total amount of the borrower's Direct Loans, family size, and Adjusted Gross Income (AGI) reported by the borrower for the most recent year for which the Secretary has obtained income information. The borrower's AGI includes the income of the borrower's spouse. A borrower shall make payments on a loan until the loan is repaid in full or until the loan has been in repayment through the end of the income contingent repayment period.

(2) The regulations in effect at the time a borrower enters repayment and selects the income contingent repayment plan or changes into the income contingent repayment plan from another plan govern the method for determining the borrower's monthly repayment amount for all of the borrower's Direct Loans, unless—

(i) The Secretary amends the regulations relating to a borrower's monthly repayment amount under the income contingent repayment plan; and

(ii) The borrower submits a written request that the amended regulations apply to the repayment of the borrower's Direct Loans.

(3) Provisions governing the income contingent repayment plan are set out in § 685.209.

(g) *Alternative repayment.* (1) The Secretary may provide an alternative repayment plan for a borrower who demonstrates to the Secretary's satisfaction that the terms and conditions of the repayment plans specified in paragraphs (b) through (f) of this section are not adequate to accommodate the borrower's exceptional circumstances.

(2) The Secretary may require a borrower to provide evidence of the borrower's exceptional circumstances before permitting the borrower to repay a loan under an alternative repayment plan.

(3) If the Secretary agrees to permit a borrower to repay a loan under an alternative repayment plan, the Secretary notifies the borrower in writing of the terms of the plan. After the borrower receives notification of the terms of the plan, the borrower may accept the plan or choose another repayment plan.

(4) A borrower shall repay a loan under an alternative repayment plan within 30 years of the date the loan entered repayment, not including periods of deferment and forbearance.

(5) If the amount of a borrower's monthly payment under an alternative repayment plan is less than the accrued interest on the loan, the unpaid interest is capitalized until the outstanding principal amount is 10 percent greater than the original principal amount. After the outstanding principal amount is 10 percent greater than the original principal amount, interest continues to accrue but is not capitalized. For purposes of this paragraph, the original principal amount is the amount owed by the borrower when the borrower enters repayment.

(Authority: 20 U.S.C. 1087a *et seq.*)

[61 FR 31359, June 19, 1996; 62 FR 25515, May 9, 1997; 66 FR 34765, June 29, 2001]

§ 685.209 Income contingent repayment plan.

(a) *Repayment amount calculation.* (1) The amount the borrower would repay is based upon the borrower's Direct Loan debt when the borrower's first loan enters repayment, and this basis for calculation does not change unless the borrower obtains another Direct Loan or the borrower and the borrower's spouse obtain approval to repay their loans jointly under paragraph (b)(2) of this section. If the borrower obtains another Direct Loan, the amount the borrower would repay is based on the combined amounts of the loans when the last loan enters repayment. If the borrower and the borrower's spouse repay the loans jointly, the amount the borrowers would repay is based on both borrowers' Direct Loan debts at the time they enter joint repayment.

(2) The annual amount payable under the income contingent repayment plan by a borrower is the lesser of—

(i) The amount the borrower would repay annually over 12 years using standard amortization multiplied by an income percentage factor that corresponds to the borrower's adjusted gross income (AGI) as shown in the income percentage factor table in a notice published annually by the Secretary in the Federal Register; or

(ii) 20 percent of discretionary income.

(3) For purposes of this section, discretionary income is defined as a borrower's AGI minus the amount of the "HHS Poverty Guidelines for all States (except Alaska and Hawaii) and the District of Columbia" as published by the United States Department of Health and Human Services on an annual basis.[1] For residents of Alaska and Hawaii, discretionary income is defined as a borrower's AGI minus the amounts in the "HHS Poverty Guidelines for Alaska" and the "HHS Poverty Guidelines for Hawaii" respectively. If a borrower provides documentation acceptable to the Secretary that the borrower has more than one person in the borrower's family, the Secretary applies the HHS Poverty Guidelines for the borrower's family size.

(4) For exact incomes not shown in the income percentage factor table in the annual notice published by the Secretary, an income percentage factor is calculated, based upon the intervals between the incomes and income percentage factors shown on the table.

(5) Each year, the Secretary recalculates the borrower's annual payment amount based on changes in the borrower's AGI, the variable interest rate, the income percentage factors in the table in the annual notice published by the Secretary, and updated HHS Poverty Guidelines (if applicable).

(6) If a borrower's monthly payment is calculated to be greater than $0 but less than or equal to $5.00, the amount payable by the borrower shall be $5.00.

(7) For purposes of the annual recalculation described in paragraph (a)(5) of this section, after periods in which a borrower makes payments that are less than interest accrued on the loan, the payment amount is recalculated based upon unpaid accrued interest and the highest outstanding principal loan amount (including amount capitalized) calculated for that borrower while paying under the income contingent repayment plan.

(8) For each calendar year after calendar year 1996, the Secretary publishes in the Federal Register a revised income percentage factor table reflecting changes based on inflation. This revised table is developed by changing each of the dollar amounts contained in the table by a percentage equal to the estimated percentage changes in the Consumer Price Index (as determined by the Secretary)

_____

1 The HHS Poverty Guidelines are available from the Office of the Assistant Secretary for Planning and Evaluation, Department of Health and Human Services (HHS), Room 438F, Humphrey Building, 200 Independence Avenue, S.W., Washington, D.C. 20201

between December 1995 and the December next preceding the beginning of such calendar year.

(9) Examples of the calculation of monthly repayment amounts and tables that show monthly repayment amounts for borrowers at various income and debt levels are included in the annual notice published by the Secretary.

(b) *Treatment of married borrowers.* (1) A married borrower who wishes to repay under the income contingent repayment plan and who has filed an income tax return separately from his or her spouse must provide his or her spouse's written consent to the disclosure of certain tax return information under paragraph (c)(5) of this section (unless the borrower is separated from his or her spouse). The AGI for both spouses is used to calculate the monthly repayment amount.

(2) Married borrowers may repay their loans jointly. The outstanding balances on the loans of each borrower are added together to determine the borrowers' payback rate under (a)(1) of this section.

(3) The amount of the payment applied to each borrower's debt is the proportion of the payments that equals the same proportion as that borrower's debt to the total outstanding balance, except that the payment is credited toward outstanding interest on any loan before any payment is credited toward principal.

(c) *Other features of the income contingent repayment plan.* (1) *Alternative documentation of income.* If a borrower's AGI is not available or if, in the Secretary's opinion, the borrower's reported AGI does not reasonably reflect the borrower's current income, the Secretary may use other documentation of income provided by the borrower to calculate the borrower's monthly repayment amount.

(2) *First and second year borrowers.* The Secretary requires alternative documentation of income from borrowers in their first and second years of repayment, when in the Secretary's opinion, the borrower's reported AGI does not reasonably reflect the borrower's current income.

(3) *Adjustments to repayment obligations.* The Secretary may determine that special circumstances, such as a loss of employment by the borrower or the borrower's spouse, warrant an adjustment to the borrower's repayment obligations.

(4) *Repayment period.* (i) The maximum repayment period under the income contingent repayment plan is 25 years.

(ii) The repayment period includes periods in which the borrower makes payments under the standard repayment plan and under extended repayment plans in which payments are based on a repayment period that is up to 12 years. The repayment period does not include periods in which the borrower makes payments under the graduated and alternative repayment plans or periods of authorized deferment or forbearance. The repayment period also does not include periods in which the borrower makes payments under an extended repayment plan in which payments are based on a repayment period that is longer than 12 years.

(iii) If a borrower repays more than one loan under the income contingent repayment plan, a separate repayment period for each loan begins when that loan enters repayment.

(iv) If a borrower has not repaid a loan in full at the end of the 25-year repayment period under the income contingent repayment plan, the Secretary cancels the unpaid portion of the loan.

(v) At the beginning of the repayment period under the income contingent repayment plan, a borrower shall make monthly payments of the amount of interest that accrues on the borrower's Direct Loans until the Secretary calculates the borrower's monthly repayment amount on the basis of the borrower's income.

(5) *Limitation on capitalization of interest.* If the amount of a borrower's monthly payment is less than the accrued interest, the unpaid interest is capitalized until the outstanding principal amount is ten percent greater than the original principal amount. After the outstanding principal amount is ten percent greater than the original amount, interest continues to accrue but is not capitalized. For purposes of this paragraph, the original amount is the amount owed by the borrower when the borrower enters repayment.

(6) *Notification of terms and conditions.* When a borrower elects or is required by the Secretary to repay a loan under the income contingent repayment plan, the Secretary notifies the borrower of the terms and conditions of the plan, including—

(i) That the Internal Revenue Service will disclose certain tax return information to the Secretary or the Secretary's agents; and

(ii) That if the borrower believes that special circumstances warrant an adjustment to the borrower's repayment obligations, as described in § 685.209(c)(3), the borrower may contact the Secretary and obtain the Secretary's determination as to whether an adjustment is appropriate.

(7) *Consent to disclosure of tax return information.* (i) A borrower shall provide written consent to the disclosure of certain tax return information by the Internal Revenue Service (IRS) to agents of the Secretary for purposes of calculating a monthly repayment amount and servicing and collecting a loan under the income contingent repayment plan. The borrower shall provide consent by signing a consent form, developed consistent with 26 CFR 301.6103(c)-1 and provided to the borrower by the Secretary, and shall return the signed form to the Secretary.

(ii) The borrower shall consent to disclosure of the borrower's taxpayer identity information as defined in 26 U.S.C. 6103(b)(6), tax filing status, and AGI.

(iii) The borrower shall provide consent for a period of five years from the date the borrower signs the consent form. The Secretary provides the borrower a new consent form before that period expires. The IRS does not disclose tax return information after the IRS has processed a borrower's withdrawal of consent.

(iv) The Secretary designates the standard repayment plan for a borrower who selects the income contingent repayment plan but—

(A) Fails to provide the required written consent;

(B) Fails to renew written consent upon the expiration of the five-year period for consent; or

(C) Withdraws consent and does not select another repayment plan.

(v) If a borrower defaults and the Secretary designates the income contingent repayment plan for the borrower but the borrower fails to provide the required written consent, the Secretary mails a notice to the borrower establishing a repayment schedule for the borrower.

(Approved by the Office of Management and Budget under control number 1845-0021)

(Authority: 20 U.S.C. 1087a *et seq.*)

[60 FR 33345, June 28, 1995; 60 FR 61823, Dec. 1, 1995; 61 FR 24447, May 15, 1996; 61 FR 31359, June 19, 1996; 64 FR 29183, May 28, 1999; 64 FR 58972, Nov. 1, 1999]

§ 685.210 Choice of repayment plan.

(a) *Initial selection of a repayment plan.* (1) Before a Direct Loan enters into repayment, the Secretary provides the borrower a description of the available repayment plans and requests the borrower to select one. A borrower may select a repayment plan before the loan enters repayment by notifying the Secretary of the borrower's selection in writing.

(2) If a borrower does not select a repayment plan, the Secretary designates the standard repayment plan described in § 685.208(b) for the borrower.

(b) *Changing repayment plans.* (1) A borrower may change repayment plans at any time after the loan has entered repayment by notifying the Secretary. However, a borrower who is repaying a defaulted loan under the income contingent repayment plan under § 685.211(c)(3)(ii) may not change to another repayment plan unless—

(i) The borrower was required to and did make a payment under the income contingent repayment plan in each of the prior three (3) months; or

(ii) The borrower was not required to make payments but made three reasonable and affordable payments in each of the prior three months; and

(iii) The borrower makes and the Secretary approves a request to change plans.

(2)(i) A borrower may not change to a repayment plan that has a maximum repayment period of less than the number of years the loan has already been in repayment, except that a borrower may change to the income contingent repayment plan at any time.

(ii) If a borrower changes plans, the repayment period is the period provided under the borrower's new repayment plan, calculated from the date the loan initially entered repayment. However, if a borrower changes to the income contingent repayment plan, the repayment period is calculated as described in § 685.209(c)(4).

(Authority: 20 U.S.C. 1087a et seq.)

[65 FR 65629, Nov. 1, 2000]

§ 685.211 Miscellaneous repayment provisions.

(a) *Payment application and prepayment.* (1) The Secretary applies any payment first to any accrued charges and collection costs, then to any outstanding interest, and then to outstanding principal.

(2) A borrower may prepay all or part of a loan at any time without penalty. If a borrower pays any amount in excess of the amount due, the excess amount is a prepayment.

(3) If a prepayment equals or exceeds the monthly repayment amount under the borrower's repayment plan, the Secretary—

(i) Applies the prepaid amount according to paragraph (a)(1) of this section;

(ii) Advances the due date of the next payment unless the borrower requests otherwise; and

(iii) Notifies the borrower of any revised due date for the next payment.

(4) If a prepayment is less than the monthly repayment amount, the Secretary applies the prepayment according to paragraph (a)(1) of this section.

(b) *Repayment incentives.* To encourage on-time repayment, the Secretary may reduce the interest rate for a borrower who repays a loan under a system or on a schedule that meets requirements specified by the Secretary.

(c) *Refunds and returns of title IV, HEA program funds from schools.* The Secretary applies any refund or return of title IV, HEA program funds that the Secretary receives from a school under § 668.22 against the borrower's outstanding principal and notifies the borrower of the refund or return.

(d) *Default*. (1) *Acceleration*. If a borrower defaults on a Direct Loan, the entire unpaid balance and accrued interest are immediately due and payable.

(2) *Collection charges*. If a borrower defaults on a Direct Loan, the Secretary assesses collection charges in accordance with § 685.202(e).

(3) *Collection of a defaulted loan*. (i) The Secretary may take any action authorized by law to collect a defaulted Direct Loan including, but not limited to, filing a lawsuit against the borrower, reporting the default to national credit bureaus, requesting the Internal Revenue Service to offset the borrower's Federal income tax refund, and garnishing the borrower's wages.

(ii) If a borrower defaults on a Direct Subsidized Loan, a Direct Unsubsidized Loan, a Direct Unsubsidized Consolidation Loan or a Direct Subsidized Consolidation Loan, the Secretary may designate the income contingent repayment plan for the borrower.

(e) *Ineligible borrowers*. (1) The Secretary determines that a borrower is ineligible if, at the time the loan was made and without the school's or the Secretary's knowledge, the borrower (or the student on whose behalf a parent borrowed) provided false or erroneous information or took actions that caused the borrower or student—

(i) To receive a loan for which the borrower is wholly or partially ineligible;

(ii) To receive interest benefits for which the borrower was ineligible; or

(iii) To receive loan proceeds for a period of enrollment for which the borrower was not eligible.

(2) If the Secretary makes the determination described in paragraph (e)(1) of this section, the Secretary sends an ineligible borrower a demand letter that requires the borrower to repay some or all of a loan, as appropriate. The demand letter requires that within 30 days from the date the letter is mailed, the borrower repay any principal amount for which the borrower is ineligible and any accrued interest, including interest subsidized by the Secretary, through the previous quarter.

(3) If a borrower fails to comply with the demand letter described in paragraph (e)(2) of this section, the borrower is in default on the entire loan.

(4) A borrower may not consolidate a loan under § 685.220 for which the borrower is wholly or partially ineligible.

(f) *Rehabilitation of defaulted loans*. A defaulted Direct Loan is rehabilitated if the borrower makes 12 consecutive on-time, reasonable, and affordable monthly payments. The amount of such a payment is determined on the basis of the borrower's total financial circumstances. If a defaulted loan is rehabilitated, the Secretary instructs any credit bureau to which the default was reported to remove the default from the borrower's credit history.

(Authority: 20 U.S.C. 1087a *et seq*.)

[64 FR 57961, Oct. 27, 1999; 64 FR 59043, Nov. 1, 1999; 65 FR 65629, Nov. 1, 2000; 66 FR 34765, June 29, 2001]

§ 685.212 Discharge of a loan obligation.

(a) *Death*. (1) If a borrower (or the student on whose behalf a parent borrowed a Direct PLUS Loan) dies, the Secretary discharges the obligation of the borrower and any endorser to make any further payments on the loan based on an original or certified copy of the borrower's (or student's in the case of a Direct PLUS loan) death certificate.

(2) If an original or certified copy of the death certificate is not available, the Secretary discharges the loan only based on other reliable documentation that establishes, to the Secretary's satisfaction, that the borrower (or student) has died. The Secretary discharges a loan based on documentation other than an original or certified copy of the death certificate only under exceptional circumstances and on a case-by-case basis.

(b) *Total and permanent disability*. If a borrower meets the requirements in § 685.213(c), the Secretary discharges the obligation of the borrower and any endorser to make any further payments on the loan.

(c) *Bankruptcy*. If a borrower's obligation to repay a loan is discharged in bankruptcy, the Secretary does not require the borrower to make any further payments on the loan.

(d) *Closed schools*. If a borrower meets the requirements in § 685.214, the Secretary discharges the obligation of the borrower and any endorser to make any further payments on the loan. In the case of a Direct Consolidation Loan, the Secretary discharges the portion of the consolidation loan equal to the amount of the discharge applicable to any loan disbursed, in whole or in part, on or after January 1, 1986 that was included in the consolidation loan.

(e) *False certification and unauthorized disbursement*. If a borrower meets the requirements in § 685.215, the Secretary discharges the obligation of the borrower and any endorser to make any further payments on the loan. In the case of a Direct Consolidation Loan, the Secretary discharges the portion of the consolidation loan equal to the amount of the discharge applicable to any loan disbursed, in whole or in part, on or after January 1, 1986 that was included in the consolidation loan.

(f) *Unpaid refunds*. If a borrower meets the requirements in § 685.216, the Secretary discharges the obligation of the borrower and any endorser to make any further payments on the amount of the loan equal to the unpaid refund and any accrued interest and other charges associated with the unpaid refund. In the case of a Direct Consolidation Loan, the Secretary discharges the portion of the consolidation loan equal to the amount of the unpaid refund owed on any loan disbursed, in whole or in part, on or after January 1, 1986 that was included in the consolidation loan.

(g) *Payments received after eligibility for discharge*. (1) *For the discharge conditions in paragraphs (a), (c), (d), and (e) of this section*. Upon receipt of acceptable documentation and approval of the discharge request, the Secretary returns to the sender, or, for a discharge based on death, the borrower's estate, any payments received after the date that the eligibility requirements for discharge were met.

(2) *For the discharge condition in paragraph (b) of this section*. Upon making a final determination of eligibility for discharge based on total and permanent disability, the Secretary returns to the sender any payments received after the date the borrower became totally and permanently disabled, as certified under § 685.213(b).

(3) *For the discharge condition in paragraph (f) of this section*. Upon receipt of acceptable documentation and approval of the discharge request, the Secretary returns to the sender payments received in excess of the amount owed on the loan after applying the unpaid refund.

(h) *Teacher loan forgiveness program*. If a new borrower meets the requirements in § 685.217, the Secretary repays up to $5,000 of the borrower's Direct Subsidized Loans, Direct Unsubsidized Loans, and, in certain cases, Direct Consolidation Loans.

(Approved by the Office of Management and Budget under control number 1845-0021)

(Authority: 20 U.S.C. 1087a *et seq.*)

[61 FR 29900, June 12, 1996; 62 FR 30412, June 3, 1997; 62 FR 63435, Nov. 28, 1997; 63 FR 34816, June 26, 1998; 64 FR 58969, Nov. 1, 1999; 65 FR 65629, 65694, Nov. 1, 2000; 66 FR 34765, June 29, 2001]

§ 685.213 Total and permanent disability discharge.

(a) *General.* (1) If the Secretary makes an initial determination that a borrower is totally and permanently disabled, the Secretary—

(i) Notifies the borrower that the loan will be in a conditional discharge status for up to three years from the date that the borrower became totally and permanently disabled, as certified under 685.213(b). The Secretary also notifies the borrower of the conditions of the conditional discharge period, and that all or part of the three-year conditional discharge period may predate the Secretary's initial determination.

(ii) Suspends any efforts to collect on the loan from the date of the initial determination described in paragraph (a)(1) of this section until the end of the conditional discharge period.

(2) If the borrower continues to meet the eligibility requirements for total and permanent disability discharge during and at the end of the three-year conditional discharge period, the Secretary—

(i) Discharges the obligation of the borrower and any endorser to make any further payments on the loan at the end of that period; and

(ii) Returns to the borrower any payments received after the date the borrower became totally and permanently disabled, as certified under § 685.213(b).

(3) If the borrower does not continue to meet the eligibility requirements for a total and permanent disability discharge at any time during or at the end of the three-year conditional discharge period, the Secretary resumes collection activity on the loan. The Secretary does not require the borrower to pay any interest that accrued on the loan from the date of the initial determination described in paragraph (a)(1) of this section through the end of the conditional discharge period.

(4) Except as provided in paragraph (e)(1) of this section, a borrower is not considered totally and permanently disabled based on a condition that existed at the time the loan was made, unless the borrower's condition substantially deteriorated after the loan was made so as to render the borrower totally and permanently disabled.

(b) *Initial determination of total and permanent disability.* The Secretary makes an initial determination that a borrower is totally and permanently disabled if the borrower (or the borrower's representative) provides the Secretary with a certification (on a form approved by the Secretary) by a physician who is a doctor of medicine or osteopathy and legally authorized to practice in a State that the borrower is totally and permanently disabled as defined in 34 CFR 682.200(b).

(c) *Eligibility requirements for total and permanent disability discharge.* A borrower meets the eligibility requirements for total

and permanent disability discharge if, during and at the end of the three-year conditional discharge period described in paragraph (a)(1) of this section—

(1) The borrower's annual earnings from employment do not exceed 100 percent of the poverty line for a family of two, as determined in accordance with the Community Service Block Grant Act; and

(2) The borrower does not receive a new loan under the Perkins, FFEL, or Direct Loan programs, except for a FFEL or Direct consolidation loan that does not include any loans that are in a conditional discharge status.

(d) *Conditional discharge period.* During the conditional discharge period described in paragraph (a)(1) of this section, the borrower—

(1) Is not required to make any payments of principal or interest on the loan beginning on the date the Secretary makes an initial determination that the borrower is totally and permanently disabled;

(2) Is not considered to be delinquent or in default on the loan, unless the loan was delinquent or in default at the time the conditional discharge was granted;

(3) Must promptly notify the Secretary of any changes in the borrower's address or telephone number;

(4) Must promptly notify the Secretary if the borrower's annual earnings from employment exceed the amount specified in paragraph (c)(1) of this section; and

(5) Must provide the Secretary, upon request, with additional documentation or information related to the borrower's eligibility for discharge under this section.

(e) *Provisions for discharge of Direct Consolidation Loans.* (1) For a Direct Consolidation Loan, a borrower is considered totally and permanently disabled if he or she would be considered totally and permanently disabled under the provisions of this section for all of the loans that were included in the Direct Consolidation Loan if those loans had not been consolidated.

(2) For the purposes of discharging a loan under paragraph (e)(1) of this section, the provisions of this section apply to each loan included in the Direct Consolidation Loan, even if the loan is not a Direct Loan Program loan.

(3) If requested, a borrower seeking to discharge a loan obligation under paragraph (e)(1) of this section must provide the Secretary with the disbursement dates of the underlying loans.

(Authority: 20 U.S.C. 1087a *et seq.*)

[65 FR 65629, 65694, Nov. 1, 2000]

§ 685.214 Closed school discharge.

(a) *General.* (1) The Secretary discharges the borrower's (and any endorser's) obligation to repay a Direct Loan in accordance with the provisions of this section if the borrower (or the student on whose behalf a parent borrowed) did not complete the program of study for which the loan was made because the school at which the borrower (or student) was enrolled closed, as described in paragraph (c) of this section.

(2) For purposes of this section—

(i) A school's closure date is the date that the school ceases to provide educational instruction in all programs, as determined by the Secretary; and

(ii) "School" means a school's main campus or any location or branch of the main campus.

(b) *Relief pursuant to discharge.* (1) Discharge under this section relieves the borrower of any past or present obligation to repay the loan and any accrued charges or collection costs with respect to the loan.

(2) The discharge of a loan under this section qualifies the borrower for reimbursement of amounts paid voluntarily or through enforced collection on the loan.

(3) The Secretary does not regard a borrower who has defaulted on a loan discharged under this section as in default on the loan after discharge, and such a borrower is eligible to receive assistance under programs authorized by title IV of the Act.

(4) The Secretary reports the discharge of a loan under this section to all credit reporting agencies to which the Secretary previously reported the status of the loan.

(c) *Borrower qualification for discharge.* In order to qualify for discharge of a loan under this section, a borrower shall submit to the Secretary a written request and sworn statement, and the factual assertions in the statement must be true. The statement need not be notarized but must be made by the borrower under penalty of perjury. In the statement, the borrower shall—

(1) State that the borrower (or the student on whose behalf a parent borrowed)—

(i) Received the proceeds of a loan, in whole or in part, on or after January 1, 1986 to attend a school;

(ii) Did not complete the program of study at that school because the school closed while the student was enrolled, or the student withdrew from the school not more than 90 days before the school closed (or longer in exceptional circumstances); and

(iii) Did not complete the program of study through a teach-out at another school or by transferring academic credits or hours earned at the closed school to another school;

(2) State whether the borrower (or student) has made a claim with respect to the school's closing with any third party, such as the holder of a performance bond or a tuition recovery program, and, if so, the amount of any payment received by the borrower (or student) or credited to the borrower's loan obligation; and

(3) State that the borrower (or student)—

(i) Agrees to provide to the Secretary upon request other documentation reasonably available to the borrower that demonstrates that the borrower meets the qualifications for discharge under this section; and

(ii) Agrees to cooperate with the Secretary in enforcement actions in accordance with paragraph (d) of this section and to transfer any right to recovery against a third party to the Secretary in accordance with paragraph (e) of this section.

(d) *Cooperation by borrower in enforcement actions.* (1) In order to obtain a discharge under this section, a borrower shall cooperate with the Secretary in any judicial or administrative proceeding brought by the Secretary to recover amounts discharged or to take other enforcement action with respect to the conduct on which the discharge was based. At the request of the Secretary and upon the Secretary's tendering to the borrower the fees and costs that are customarily provided in litigation to reimburse witnesses, the borrower shall—

(i) Provide testimony regarding any representation made by the borrower to support a request for discharge;

(ii) Produce any documents reasonably available to the borrower with respect to those representations; and

(iii) If required by the Secretary, provide a sworn statement regarding those documents and representations.

(2) The Secretary denies the request for a discharge or revokes the discharge of a borrower who—

(i) Fails to provide the testimony, documents, or a sworn statement required under paragraph (d)(1) of this section; or

(ii) Provides testimony, documents, or a sworn statement that does not support the material representations made by the borrower to obtain the discharge.

(e) *Transfer to the Secretary of borrower's right of recovery against third parties.* (1) Upon discharge under this section, the borrower is deemed to have assigned to and relinquished in favor of the Secretary any right to a loan refund (up to the amount discharged) that the borrower (or student) may have by contract or applicable law with respect to the loan or the enrollment agreement for the program for which the loan was received, against the school, its principals, its affiliates and their successors, its sureties, and any private fund, including the portion of a public fund that represents funds received from a private party.

(2) The provisions of this section apply notwithstanding any provision of State law that would otherwise restrict transfer of those rights by the borrower (or student), limit or prevent a transferee from exercising those rights, or establish procedures or a scheme of distribution that would prejudice the Secretary's ability to recover on those rights.

(3) Nothing in this section limits or forecloses the borrower's (or student's) right to pursue legal and equitable relief regarding disputes arising from matters unrelated to the discharged Direct Loan.

(f) *Discharge procedures.* (1) After confirming the date of a school's closure, the Secretary identifies any Direct Loan borrower (or student on whose behalf a parent borrowed) who appears to have been enrolled at the school on the school closure date or to have withdrawn not more than 90 days prior to the closure date.

(2) If the borrower's current address is known, the Secretary mails the borrower a discharge application and an explanation of the qualifications and procedures for obtaining a discharge. The Secretary also promptly suspends any efforts to collect from the borrower on any affected loan. The Secretary may continue to receive borrower payments.

(3) If the borrower's current address is unknown, the Secretary attempts to locate the borrower and determines the borrower's potential eligibility for a discharge under this section by consulting with representatives of the closed school, the school's licensing agency, the school's accrediting agency, and other appropriate parties. If the Secretary learns the new address of a borrower, the Secretary mails to the borrower a discharge application and explanation and suspends collection, as described in paragraph (f)(2) of this section.

(4) If a borrower fails to submit the written request and sworn statement described in paragraph (c) of this section within 60 days of the Secretary's mailing the discharge application, the Secretary resumes collection and grants forbearance of principal and interest for the period in which collection activity was suspended. The Secretary may capitalize any interest accrued and not paid during that period.

(5) If the Secretary determines that a borrower who requests a discharge meets the qualifications for a discharge, the Secretary notifies the borrower in writing of that determination.

(6) If the Secretary determines that a borrower who requests a

discharge does not meet the qualifications for a discharge, the Secretary notifies that borrower in writing of that determination and the reasons for the determination.

(Approved by the Office of Management and Budget under control number 1845-0021)

(Authority: 20 U.S.C. 1087a *et seq.*)

[60 FR 33345, June 28, 1995; 64 FR 58972, Nov. 1, 1999; 65 FR 65629, Nov. 1, 2000; 66 FR 34765, June 29, 2001]

§ 685.215 Discharge for false certification of student eligibility or unauthorized payment.

(a) *Basis for discharge.* (1) *False certification.* The Secretary discharges a borrower's (and any endorser's) obligation to repay a Direct Loan in accordance with the provisions of this section if a school falsely certifies the eligibility of the borrower (or the student on whose behalf a parent borrowed) to receive the loan. The Secretary considers a student's eligibility to borrow to have been falsely certified by the school if the school—

(i) Certified the student's eligibility for a Direct Loan on the basis of ability to benefit from its training and the student did not meet the eligibility requirements described in 34 CFR part 668 and section 484(d) of the Act, as applicable;

(ii) Signed the borrower's name on the loan application or promissory note without the borrower's authorization; or

(iii) Certified the eligibility of a student who, because of a physical or mental condition, age, criminal record, or other reason accepted by the Secretary, would not meet the requirements for employment (in the student's State of residence when the loan was originated) in the occupation for which the training program supported by the loan was intended.

(2) *Unauthorized payment.* The Secretary discharges a borrower's (and any endorser's) obligation to repay a Direct Loan if the school, without the borrower's authorization, endorsed the borrower's loan check or signed the borrower's authorization for electronic funds transfer, unless the proceeds of the loan were delivered to the student or applied to charges owed by the student to the school.

(b) *Relief pursuant to discharge.* (1) Discharge for false certification under paragraph (a)(1) of this section relieves the borrower of any past or present obligation to repay the loan and any accrued charges and collection costs with respect to the loan.

(2) Discharge for unauthorized payment under paragraph (a)(2) of this section relieves the borrower of the obligation to repay the amount of the payment discharged.

(3) The discharge under this section qualifies the borrower for reimbursement of amounts paid voluntarily or through enforced collection on the discharged loan or payment.

(4) The Secretary does not regard a borrower who has defaulted on a loan discharged under this section as in default on the loan after discharge, and such a borrower is eligible to receive assistance under programs authorized by title IV of the Act.

(5) The Secretary reports the discharge under this section to all credit reporting agencies to which the Secretary previously reported the status of the loan.

(c) *Borrower qualification for discharge.* In order to qualify for discharge under this section, the borrower shall submit to the Secretary a written request and a sworn statement, and the factual assertions in the statement must be true. The statement need not be notarized but must be made by the borrower under penalty of perjury. In the statement, the borrower shall meet the requirements in paragraphs (c)(1) through (5) of this section.

(1) *Ability to benefit.* In the case of a borrower requesting a discharge based on defective testing of the student's ability to benefit, the borrower shall state that the borrower (or the student on whose behalf a parent borrowed)—

(i) Received a disbursement of a loan, in whole or in part, on or after January 1, 1986 to attend a school; and

(ii) Received a Direct Loan at that school on the basis of an ability to benefit from the school's training and did not meet the eligibility requirements described in 34 CFR Part 668 and section 484(d) of the Act, as applicable.

(2) *Unauthorized loan.* In the case of a borrower requesting a discharge because the school signed the borrower's name on the loan application or promissory note without the borrower's authorization, the borrower shall—

(i) State that he or she did not sign the document in question or authorize the school to do so; and

(ii) Provide five different specimens of his or her signature, two of which must be within one year before or after the date of the contested signature.

(3) *Unauthorized payment.* In the case of a borrower requesting a discharge because the school, without the borrower's authorization, endorsed the borrower's loan check or signed the borrower's authorization for electronic funds transfer, the borrower shall—

(i) State that he or she did not endorse the loan check or sign the authorization for electronic funds transfer or authorize the school to do so;

(ii) Provide five different specimens of his or her signature, two of which must be within one year before or after the date of the contested signature;

(iii) State that the proceeds of the contested disbursement were not delivered to the student or applied to charges owed by the student to the school.

(4) *Claim to third party.* The borrower shall state whether the borrower (or student) has made a claim with respect to the school's false certification or unauthorized payment with any third party, such as the holder of a performance bond or a tuition recovery program, and, if so, the amount of any payment received by the borrower (or student) or credited to the borrower's loan obligation.

(5) *Cooperation with Secretary.* The borrower shall state that the borrower (or student)—

(i) Agrees to provide to the Secretary upon request other documentation reasonably available to the borrower that demonstrates that the borrower meets the qualifications for discharge under this section; and

(ii) Agrees to cooperate with the Secretary in enforcement actions as described in § 685.214(d) and to transfer any right to recovery against a third party to the Secretary as described in § 685.214(e).

(6) *Discharge without an application.* The Secretary may discharge a loan under this section without an application from the borrower if the Secretary determines, based on information in the Secretary's possession, that the borrower qualifies for a discharge.

(d) *Discharge procedures.* (1) If the Secretary determines that a borrower's Direct Loan may be eligible for a discharge under this section, the Secretary mails the borrower a disclosure application and an explanation of the qualifications and procedures for obtaining a discharge. The Secretary also promptly suspends any efforts to collect from the borrower on any affected loan. The Secretary may continue to receive borrower payments.

(2) If the borrower fails to submit the written request and sworn statement described in paragraph (c) of this section within 60 days of the Secretary's mailing the disclosure application, the Secretary resumes collection and grants forbearance of principal and interest for the period in which collection activity was suspended. The Secretary may capitalize any interest accrued and not paid during that period.

(3) If the borrower submits the written request and sworn statement described in paragraph (c) of the section, the Secretary determines whether to grant a request for discharge under this section by reviewing the request and sworn statement in light of information available from the Secretary's records and from other sources, including guaranty agencies, State authorities, and cognizant accrediting associations.

(4) If the Secretary determines that the borrower meets the applicable requirements for a discharge under paragraph (c) of this section, the Secretary notifies the borrower in writing of that determination.

(5) If the Secretary determines that the borrower does not qualify for a discharge, the Secretary notifies the borrower in writing of that determination and the reasons for the determination.

(Approved by the Office of Management and Budget under control number 1845-0021)

(Authority: 20 U.S.C. 1087a *et seq.*)

[60 FR 33345, June 28, 1995; 61 FR 29900, June 12, 1996; 64 FR 58972, Nov. 1, 1999; 65 FR 65622, 65629, Nov. 1, 2000; 66 FR 34765, June 29, 2001]

§ 685.216 Unpaid refund discharge.

(a)(1) *Unpaid refunds in closed school situations.* In the case of a school that has closed, the Secretary discharges a former or current borrower's (and any endorser's) obligation to repay that portion of a Direct Loan equal to the refund that should have been made by the school under applicable law and regulations, including this section. Any accrued interest and other charges associated with the unpaid refund are also discharged.

(2) *Unpaid refunds in open school situations.* (i) In the case of a school that is open, the Secretary discharges a former or current borrower's (and any endorser's) obligation to repay that portion of a Direct Loan equal to the refund that should have been made by the school under applicable law and regulations, including this section, if—

(A) The borrower (or the student on whose behalf a parent borrowed) is not attending the school that owes the refund;

(B) The borrower has been unable to resolve the unpaid refund with the school; and

(C) The Secretary is unable to resolve the unpaid refund with the school within 120 days from the date the borrower submits a complete application in accordance with paragraph (c)(1) of this section regarding the unpaid refund. Any accrued interest and other charges associated with the unpaid refund are also discharged.

(ii) For the purpose of paragraph (a)(2)(i)(C) of this section, within 60 days of the date notified by the Secretary, the school must submit to the Secretary documentation demonstrating that the refund was made by the school or that the refund was not required to be made by the school.

(b) *Relief to borrower following discharge.* (1) If the borrower receives a discharge of a portion of a loan under this section, the borrower is reimbursed for any amounts paid in excess of the remaining balance of the loan (including accrued interest and other charges) owed by the borrower at the time of discharge.

(2) The Secretary reports the discharge of a portion of a loan under this section to all credit reporting agencies to which the Secretary previously reported the status of the loan.

(c) *Borrower qualification for discharge.* (1) Except as provided in paragraph (c)(2) of this section, to receive a discharge of a portion of a loan under this section, a borrower must submit a written application to the Secretary. The application requests the information required to calculate the amount of the discharge and requires the borrower to sign a statement swearing to the accuracy of the information in the application. The statement need not be notarized but must be made by the borrower under penalty of perjury. In the statement, the borrower must—

(i) State that the borrower (or the student on whose behalf a parent borrowed)—

(A) Received the proceeds of a loan, in whole or in part, on or after January 1, 1986 to attend a school;

(B) Did not attend, withdrew, or was terminated from the school within a timeframe that entitled the borrower to a refund; and

(C) Did not receive the benefit of a refund to which the borrower was entitled either from the school or from a third party, such as the holder of a performance bond or a tuition recovery program;

(ii) State whether the borrower (or student) has any other application for discharge pending for this loan; and

(iii) State that the borrower (or student)—

(A) Agrees to provide to the Secretary upon request other documentation reasonably available to the borrower that demonstrates that the borrower meets the qualifications for discharge under this section; and

(B) Agrees to cooperate with the Secretary in enforcement actions as described in § 685.214(d) and to transfer any right to recovery against a third party to the Secretary as described in § 685.214(e).

(2) The Secretary may discharge a portion of a loan under this section without an application if the Secretary determines, based on information in the Secretary's possession, that the borrower qualifies for a discharge.

(d) *Determination of amount eligible for discharge.* (1) The Secretary determines the amount eligible for discharge based on information showing the refund amount or by applying the appropriate refund formula to information that the borrower provides or that is otherwise available to the Secretary. For purposes of this section, all unpaid refunds are considered to be attributed to loan proceeds.

(2) If the information in paragraph (d)(1) of this section is not available, the Secretary uses the following formulas to determine the amount eligible for discharge:

(i) In the case of a student who fails to attend or whose withdrawal or termination date is before October 7, 2000 and who completes less than 60 percent of the loan period, the Secretary discharges the lesser of the institutional charges unearned or the loan amount. The Secretary determines the amount of the institutional charges unearned by—

(A) Calculating the ratio of the amount of time remaining in the loan period after the student's last day of attendance to the actual length of the loan period; and

(B) Multiplying the resulting factor by the institutional charges assessed the student for the loan period.

(ii) In the case of a student who fails to attend or whose withdrawal or termination date is on or after October 7, 2000 and who completes less than 60 percent of the loan period, the Secretary discharges the loan amount unearned. The Secretary determines the loan amount unearned by—

(A) Calculating the ratio of the amount of time remaining in the loan period after the student's last day of attendance to the actual length of the loan period; and

(B) Multiplying the resulting factor by the total amount of title IV grants and loans received by the student, or, if unknown, the loan amount.

(iii) In the case of a student who completes 60 percent or more of the loan period, the Secretary does not discharge any amount because a student who completes 60 percent or more of the loan period is not entitled to a refund.

(e) *Discharge procedures.* (1) Except as provided in paragraph (c)(2) of this section, if the Secretary learns that a school did not make a refund of loan proceeds owed under applicable law and regulations, the Secretary sends the borrower a discharge application and an explanation of the qualifications and procedures for obtaining a discharge. The Secretary also promptly suspends any efforts to collect from the borrower on any affected loan. The Secretary may continue to receive borrower payments.

(2) If a borrower who is sent a discharge application fails to submit the application within 60 days of the Secretary's sending the discharge application, the Secretary resumes collection and grants forbearance of principal and interest for the period in which collection activity was suspended. The Secretary may capitalize any interest accrued and not paid during that period.

(3) If a borrower qualifies for a discharge, the Secretary notifies the borrower in writing. The Secretary resumes collection and grants forbearance of principal and interest on the portion of the loan not discharged for the period in which collection activity was suspended. The Secretary may capitalize any interest accrued and not paid during that period.

(4) If a borrower does not qualify for a discharge, the Secretary notifies the borrower in writing of the reasons for the determination. The Secretary resumes collection and grants forbearance of principal and interest for the period in which collection activity was suspended. The Secretary may capitalize any interest accrued and not paid during that period.

(Approved by the Office of Management and Budget under control number 1845-0021)

(Authority: 20 U.S.C. 1087a *et seq.*)

[64 FR 58969, Nov. 1, 1999; 65 FR 65629, Nov. 1, 2000; 66 FR 34765, June 29, 2001]

B.4 Perkins Regulations

§ 674.33 Repayment.

(a) *Repayment Plan.* (1) The institution shall establish a repayment plan before the student ceases to be at least a half-time regular student.

(2) If the last scheduled payment would be $25 or less the institution may combine it with the next-to-last repayment.

(3) If the installment payment for all loans made to a borrower by an institution is not a multiple of $5, the institution may round that payment to the next highest dollar amount that is a multiple of $5.

(4) The institution shall apply any payment on a loan in the following order:

(i) Collection costs.

(ii) Late charges.

(iii) Accrued interest.

(iv) Principal.

(b) *Minimum monthly repayment—*(1) *Minimum monthly repayment option.* (i) An institution may require a borrower to pay a minimum monthly repayment if—

(A) The promissory note includes a minimum monthly repayment provision specifying the amount of the minimum monthly repayment; and

(B) The monthly repayment of principal and interest for a 10-year repayment period is less than the minimum monthly repayment; or

(ii) An institution may require a borrower to pay a minimum monthly repayment if the borrower has received loans with different interest rates at the same institution and the total monthly repayment would otherwise be less than the minimum monthly repayment.

(2) *Minimum monthly repayment of loans from more than one institution.* If a borrower has received loans from more than one institution, the following rules apply:

(i) If the total of the monthly repayments is equal to at least the minimum monthly repayment, no institution may exercise a minimum monthly repayment option.

(ii) If only one institution exercises the minimum monthly repayment option when the monthly repayment would otherwise be less than the minimum repayment option, that institution receives the difference between the minimum monthly repayment and the repayment owed to the other institution.

(iii) If each institution exercises the minimum repayment option, the minimum monthly repayment must be divided among the institutions in proportion to the amount of principal advanced by each institution.

(3) *Minimum monthly repayment of both Defense and NDSL or Federal Perkins loans from one or more institutions.* If the total monthly repayment is less than $30 and the monthly repayment on a Defense loan is less than $15 a month, the amount attributed to the Defense loan may not exceed $15 a month.

(4) *Minimum monthly repayment of loans with differing grace periods and deferments.* If the borrower has received loans with

different grace periods and deferments, the institution shall treat each note separately, and the borrower shall pay the applicable minimum monthly payment for a loan that is not in the grace or deferment period.

(5) *Hardship.* The institution may reduce the borrower's scheduled repayments for a period of not more than one year at a time if—

(i) It determines that the borrower is unable to make the scheduled repayments due to hardship (see § 674.33(c)); and

(ii) The borrower's scheduled repayment is the minimum monthly repayment described in paragraph (b) of this section.

(6) *Minimum monthly repayment rates.* For the purposes of this section, the minimum monthly repayment rate is—

(i) $15 for a Defense loan;

(ii) $30 for an NDSL or for a Federal Perkins loan made before October 1, 1992, or for a Federal Perkins loan made on or after October 1, 1992, to a borrower who, on the date the loan is made, has an outstanding balance of principal or interest owing on any loan made under this part; or

(iii) $40 for a Federal Perkins loan made on or after October 1, 1992, to a borrower who, on the date the loan is made, has no outstanding balance of principal or interest owing on any loan made under this part.

(7) The institution shall determine the minimum repayment amount under paragraph (b) of this section for loans with repayment installment intervals greater than one month by multiplying the amounts in paragraph (b) of this section by the number of months in the installment interval.

(c) *Extension of repayment period—*(1) *Hardship.* The institution may extend a borrower's repayment period due to prolonged illness or unemployment.

(2) *Low-income individual.* (i) For Federal Perkins loans and NDSLs made on or after October 1, 1980, the institution may extend the borrower's repayment period up to 10 additional years beyond the 10-year maximum repayment period if the institution determines during the course of the repayment period that the borrower is a "low-income individual." The borrower qualifies for an extension of the repayment period on the basis of low-income status only during the period in which the borrower meets the criteria described in paragraph (c)(2)(i)(A) or (B) of this section. The term *low-income individual* means the following:

(A) For an unmarried borrower without dependents, an individual whose total income for the preceding calendar year did not exceed 45 percent of the Income Protection Allowance for the current award year for a family of four with one in college.

(B) For a borrower with a family that includes the borrower and any spouse or legal dependents, an individual whose total family income for the preceding calendar year did not exceed 125 percent of the Income Protection Allowance for the current award year for a family with one in college and equal in size to that of the borrower's family.

(ii) The institution shall use the Income Protection Allowance published annually in accordance with section 478 of the HEA in making this determination.

(iii) The institution shall review the borrower's status annually to determine whether the borrower continues to qualify for an extended repayment period based on his or her status as a "low-income individual."

(iv) Upon determining that a borrower ceases to qualify for an extended repayment period under this section, the institution shall

amend the borrower's repayment schedule. The term of the amended repayment schedule may not exceed the number of months remaining on the original repayment schedule, provided that the institution may not include the time elapsed during any extension of the repayment period granted under this section in determining the number of months remaining on the original repayment schedule.

(3) Interest continues to accrue during any extension of a repayment period.

(d) *Forbearance.* (1) Forbearance means the temporary cessation of payments, allowing an extension of time for making payments, or temporarily accepting smaller payments than previously were scheduled.

(2) Upon receipt of a written request and supporting documentation, the institution shall grant the borrower forbearance of principal and, unless otherwise indicated by the borrower, interest renewable at intervals of up to 12 months for periods that collectively do not exceed three years.

(3) The terms of forbearance must be agreed upon, in writing, by the borrower and the institution.

(4) In granting a forbearance under this section, an institution shall grant a temporary cessation of payments, unless the borrower chooses another form of forbearance subject to paragraph (d)(1) of this section.

(5) An institution shall grant forbearance if—

(i) The amount of the payments the borrower is obligated to make on title IV loans each month (or a proportional share if the payments are due less frequently than monthly) is collectively equal to or greater than 20 percent of the borrower's total monthly gross income;

(ii) The institution determines that the borrower should qualify for the forbearance due to poor health or for other acceptable reasons; or

(iii) The Secretary authorizes a period of forbearance due to a national military mobilization or other national emergency.

(6) Before granting a forbearance to a borrower under paragraph (d)(5)(i) of this section, the institution shall require the borrower to submit at least the following documentation:

(i) Evidence showing the amount of the most recent total monthly gross income received by the borrower; and

(ii) Evidence showing the amount of the monthly payments owed by the borrower for the most recent month for the borrower's title IV loans.

(7) Interest accrues during any period of forbearance.

(8) The institution may not include the periods of forbearance described in this paragraph in determining the 10-year repayment period.

(e) *Compromise of repayment.* (1) An institution may compromise on the repayment of a defaulted loan if—

(i) The institution has fully complied with all due diligence requirements specified in subpart C of this part; and

(ii) The student borrower pays in a single lump-sum payment—

(A) 90 percent of the outstanding principal balance on the loan under this part;

(B) The interest due on the loan; and

(C) Any collection fees due on the loan.

(2) The Federal share of the compromise repayment must bear the same relation to the institution's share of the compromise repayment as the Federal capital contribution to the institution's

loan Fund under this part bears to the institution's capital contribution to the Fund.

(f)(1) *Incentive repayment program.* An institution may establish the following repayment incentives:

(i) A reduction of no more than one percent of the interest rate on a loan on which the borrower has made 48 consecutive, monthly repayments.

(ii) A discount of no more than five percent on the balance owed on a loan which the borrower pays in full prior to the end of the repayment period.

(iii) With the Secretary's approval, any other incentive the institution determines will reduce defaults and replenish its Fund.

(2) *Limitation on the use of funds.* (i) The institution must reimburse its Fund, on at least a quarterly basis, for money lost to its Fund that otherwise would have been paid by the borrower as a result of establishing a repayment incentive under paragraphs (f)(1)(i), (ii) and (iii) of this section.

(ii) An institution may not use Federal funds, including Federal funds from the student loan fund, or institutional funds from the student loan fund to pay for any repayment incentive authorized by this section.

(g) *Closed school discharge.* (1) *General.* (i) The holder of an NDSL or a Federal Perkins Loan discharges the borrower's (and any endorser's) obligation to repay the loan if the borrower did not complete the program of study for which the loan was made because the school at which the borrower was enrolled closed.

(ii) For the purposes of this section—

(A) A school's closure date is the date that the school ceases to provide educational instruction in all programs, as determined by the Secretary;

(B) "School" means a school's main campus or any location or branch of the main campus; and

(C) The "holder" means the Secretary or the school that holds the loan.

(2) *Relief pursuant to discharge.* (i) Discharge under this section relieves the borrower of any past or present obligation to repay the loan and any accrued interest or collection costs with respect to the loan.

(ii) The discharge of a loan under this section qualifies the borrower for reimbursement of amounts paid voluntarily or through enforced collection on the loan.

(iii) A borrower who has defaulted on a loan discharged under this section is not considered to have been in default on the loan after discharge, and such a borrower is eligible to receive assistance under programs authorized by title IV of the HEA.

(iv) The Secretary or the school, if the school holds the loan, reports the discharge of a loan under this section to all credit bureaus to which the status of the loan was previously reported.

(3) *Determination of borrower qualification for discharge by the Secretary.* The Secretary may discharge the borrower's obligation to repay an NDSL or Federal Perkins Loan without an application if the Secretary determines that—

(i) The borrower qualified for and received a discharge on a loan pursuant to 34 CFR 682.402(d) (Federal Family Education Loan Program) or 34 CFR 685.213 (Federal Direct Loan Program), and was unable to receive a discharge on an NDSL or Federal Perkins Loan because the Secretary lacked the statutory authority to discharge the loan; or

(ii) Based on information in the Secretary's possession, the borrower qualifies for a discharge.

(4) *Borrower qualification for discharge.* Except as provided in paragraph (g)(3) of this section, in order to qualify for discharge of an NDSL or Federal Perkins Loan, a borrower must submit to the holder of the loan a written request and sworn statement, and the factual assertions in the statement must be true. The statement need not be notarized but must be made by the borrower under penalty of perjury. In the statement the borrower must—

(i) State that the borrower—

(A) Received the proceeds of a loan to attend a school;

(B) Did not complete the program of study at that school because the school closed while the student was enrolled, or the student withdrew from the school not more than 90 days before the school closed (or longer in exceptional circumstances); and

(C) Did not complete and is not in the process of completing the program of study through a teachout at another school as defined in 34 CFR 602.2 and administered in accordance with 34 CFR 602.207(b)(6), by transferring academic credit earned at the closed school to another school, or by any other comparable means;

(ii) State whether the borrower has made a claim with respect to the school's closing with any third party, such as the holder of a performance bond or a tuition recovery program, and, if so, the amount of any payment received by the borrower or credited to the borrower's loan obligation; and

(iii) State that the borrower—

(A) Agrees to provide to the holder of the loan upon request other documentation reasonably available to the borrower that demonstrates that the borrower meets the qualifications for discharge under this section; and

(B) Agrees to cooperate with the Secretary in enforcement actions in accordance with paragraph (g)(6) of this section and to transfer any right to recovery against a third party to the Secretary in accordance with paragraph (g)(7) of this section.

(5) *Fraudulently obtained loans.* A borrower who secured a loan through fraudulent means, as determined by the ruling of a court or an administrative tribunal of competent jurisdiction, is ineligible for a discharge under this section.

(6) *Cooperation by borrower in enforcement actions.* (i) In order to obtain a discharge under this section, a borrower must cooperate with the Secretary in any judicial or administrative proceeding brought by the Secretary to recover amounts discharged or to take other enforcement action with respect to the conduct on which the discharge was based. At the request of the Secretary and upon the Secretary's tendering to the borrower the fees and costs that are customarily provided in litigation to reimburse witnesses, the borrower must—

(A) Provide testimony regarding any representation made by the borrower to support a request for discharge;

(B) Provide any documents reasonably available to the borrower with respect to those representations; and

(C) If required by the Secretary, provide a sworn statement regarding those documents and representations.

(ii) The holder denies the request for a discharge or revokes the discharge of a borrower who—

(A) Fails to provide the testimony, documents, or a sworn statement required under paragraph (g)(6)(i) of this section; or

(B) Provides testimony, documents, or a sworn statement that does not support the material representations made by the borrower to obtain the discharge.

(7) *Transfer to the Secretary of borrower's right of recovery against third parties.* (i) In the case of a loan held by the Secretary,

upon discharge under this section, the borrower is deemed to have assigned to and relinquished in favor of the Secretary any right to a loan refund (up to the amount discharged) that the borrower may have by contract or applicable law with respect to the loan or the enrollment agreement for the program for which the loan was received, against the school, its principals, its affiliates and their successors, its sureties, and any private fund, including the portion of a public fund that represents funds received from a private party.

(ii) The provisions of this section apply notwithstanding any provision of State law that would otherwise restrict transfer of those rights by the borrower, limit or prevent a transferee from exercising those rights, or establish procedures or a scheme of distribution that would prejudice the Secretary's ability to recover on those rights.

(iii) Nothing in this section limits or forecloses the borrower's right to pursue legal and equitable relief regarding disputes arising from matters unrelated to the discharged NDSL or Federal Perkins Loan.

(8) *Discharge procedures.* (i) After confirming the date of a school's closure, the holder of the loan identifies any NDSL or Federal Perkins Loan borrower who appears to have been enrolled at the school on the school closure date or to have withdrawn not more than 90 days prior to the closure date.

(ii) If the borrower's current address is known, the holder of the loan mails the borrower a discharge application and an explanation of the qualifications and procedures for obtaining a discharge. The holder of the loan also promptly suspends any efforts to collect from the borrower on any affected loan. The holder of the loan may continue to receive borrower payments.

(iii) In the case of a loan held by the Secretary, if the borrower's current address is unknown, the Secretary attempts to locate the borrower and determine the borrower's potential eligibility for a discharge under this section by consulting with representatives of the closed school or representatives of the closed school's third-party billing and collection servicers, the school's licensing agency, the school accrediting agency, and other appropriate parties. If the Secretary learns the new address of a borrower, the Secretary mails to the borrower a discharge application and explanation and suspends collection, as described in paragraph (g)(8)(ii) of this section.

(iv) In the case of a loan held by a school, if the borrower's current address is unknown, the school attempts to locate the borrower and determine the borrower's potential eligibility for a discharge under this section by taking steps required to locate the borrower under § 674.44.

(v) If the borrower fails to submit the written request and sworn statement described in paragraph (g)(4) of this section within 60 days of the holder of the loan's mailing the discharge application, the holder of the loan resumes collection and grants forbearance of principal and interest for the period during which collection activity was suspended.

(vi) If the holder of the loan determines that a borrower who requests a discharge meets the qualifications for a discharge, the holder of the loan notifies the borrower in writing of that determination.

(vii) In the case of a loan held by the Secretary, if the Secretary determines that a borrower who requests a discharge does not meet the qualifications for a discharge, the Secretary notifies that borrower, in writing, of that determination and the reasons for the determination.

(viii) In the case of a loan held by a school, if the school determines that a borrower who requests a discharge does not meet the qualifications for discharge, the school submits that determination and all supporting materials to the Secretary for approval. The Secretary reviews the materials, makes an independent determination, and notifies the borrower in writing of the determination and the reasons for the determination.

(ix) In the case of a loan held by a school and discharged by either the school or the Secretary, the school must reimburse its Fund for the entire amount of any outstanding principal and interest on the loan, and any collection costs charged to the Fund as a result of collection efforts on a discharged loan. The school must also reimburse the borrower for any amount of principal, interest, late charges or collection costs the borrower paid on a loan discharged under this section.

(Approved by the Office of Management and Budget under control number 1845-0019)

(Authority: 20 U.S.C. 425 and 1087dd, sec. 137(d) of Pub.L. 92-318)

[57 FR 32345, July 21, 1992; 57 FR 60706, Dec. 21, 1992; 58 FR 36870, 36871, July 9, 1993; 59 FR 61409, Nov. 30, 1994; 60 FR 61814, Dec. 1, 1995; 62 FR 50848, Sept. 26, 1997; 64 FR 58309, Oct. 28, 1999; 65 FR 18002, 18003, April 6, 2000; 65 FR 26136, May 5, 2000]

§ 674.34 Deferment of repayment—Federal Perkins loans, NDSLs and Defense loans.

(a) The borrower may defer making a scheduled installment repayment on a Federal Perkins loan, an NDSL, or a Defense loan, regardless of contrary provisions of the borrower's promissory note and regardless of the date the loan was made, during periods described in this section.

(b)(1) The borrower need not repay principal, and interest does not accrue, during a period after the commencement or resumption of the repayment period on a loan, when the borrower is—

(i) Enrolled and in attendance as a regular student in at least a half-time course of study at an eligible institution;

(ii) Enrolled and in attendance as a regular student in a course of study that is part of a graduate fellowship program approved by the Secretary;

(iii) Engaged in graduate or post-graduate fellowship-supported study (such as a Fulbright grant) outside the United States; or

(iv) Enrolled in a course of study that is part of a rehabilitation training program for disabled individuals approved by the Secretary as described in paragraph (g) of this section.

(2) No borrower is eligible for a deferment under paragraph (b)(1) of this section while serving in a medical internship or residency program, except for a residency program in dentistry.

(3) The institution of higher education at which the borrower is enrolled does not need to be participating in the Federal Perkins Loan program for the borrower to qualify for a deferment.

(4) If a borrower is attending an institution of higher education as at least a half-time regular student for a full academic year and intends to enroll as at least a half-time regular student in the next academic year, the borrower is entitled to a deferment for 12 months.

(5) If an institution no longer qualifies as an institution of higher

education, the borrower's deferment ends on the date the institution ceases to qualify.

(c)(1) The borrower of a Federal Perkins loan need not repay principal, and interest does not accrue, for any period during which the borrower is engaged in service described in §§ 674.53, 674.54, 674.56, 674.57, 674.58, 674.59, and 674.60.

(2) The borrower of an NDSL need not repay principal, and interest does not accrue, for any period during which the borrower is engaged in service described in §§ 674.53, 674.54, 674.56, 674.57, 674.58, and 674.59.

(d) The borrower need not repay principal, and interest does not accrue, for any period not to exceed 3 years during which the borrower is seeking and unable to find full-time employment.

(e) The borrower need not repay principal, and interest does not accrue, for periods of up to one year at a time (except that a deferment under paragraph (e)(6) of this section may be granted for the lesser of the borrower's full term of service in the Peace Corps or the borrower's remaining period of economic hardship deferment eligibility) that, collectively, do not exceed 3 years, during which the borrower is suffering an economic hardship, if the borrower provides documentation satisfactory to the institution showing that the borrower is within any of the categories described in paragraphs (e)(1) through (e)(6) of this section.

(1) Has been granted an economic hardship deferment under either the FDSL or FFEL programs for the period of time for which the borrower has requested an economic hardship deferment for his or her Federal Perkins loan.

(2) Is receiving payment under a federal or state public assistance program, such as Aid to Families with Dependent Children, Supplemental Security Income, Food Stamps, or state general public assistance.

(3) Is working full-time and earning a total monthly gross income that does not exceed the greater of—

(i) The monthly earnings of an individual earning the minimum wage described in section 6 of the Fair Labor Standards Act of 1938; or

(ii) An amount equal to 100 percent of the poverty line for a family of two, as determined in accordance with section 673(2) of the Community Service Block Grant Act.

(4) Is not receiving total monthly gross income that exceeds twice the amount specified in paragraph (e)(3) of this section and, after deducting an amount equal to the borrower's monthly payments on federal postsecondary education loans, as determined under paragraph (e)(9) of this section, the remaining amount of that income does not exceed the amount specified in paragraph (e)(3) of this section;

(5) Is working full-time and has a Federal education debt burden that equals or exceeds 20 percent of the borrower's total monthly gross income, and the borrower's income minus such burden is less than 220 percent of the amount calculated under paragraph (3) of this section.

(6) Is serving as a volunteer in the Peace Corps.

(7) For a deferment granted under paragraph (e)(4) or (e)(5) of this section, the institution shall require the borrower to submit at least the following documentation to qualify for an initial period of deferment—

(i) Evidence showing the amount of the borrower's most recent total monthly gross income, as defined in section 674.2; and

(ii) Evidence that would enable the institution to determine the amount of the monthly payments that would have been owed by the borrower during the deferment period to other entities for federal postsecondary education loans in accordance with paragraph (e)(9) of this section.

(8) To qualify for a subsequent period of deferment that begins less than one year after the end of a period of deferment under paragraphs (e)(3), (e)(4), or (e)(5) of this section, the institution shall require the borrower to submit a copy of the borrower's federal income tax return if the borrower filed a tax return within eight months prior to the date the deferment is requested.

(9) For purposes of paragraphs (e)(3) and (e)(5) of this section, a borrower is considered to be working full-time if the borrower is expected to be employed for at least three consecutive months at 30 hours per week.

(10) In determining a borrower's eligibility for an economic hardship deferment under paragraph (e) of this section, the institution shall count only the monthly payment amount (or a proportional share if the payments are due less frequently than monthly) that would have been owed on a federal postsecondary education loan if the loan had been scheduled to be repaid in 10 years from the date the borrower entered repayment, regardless of the length of the borrower's actual repayment schedule or the actual monthly payment amount (if any) that would be owed during the period that the borrower requested an economic hardship deferment.

(f) To qualify for a deferment for study as part of a graduate fellowship program pursuant to paragraph (b)(1)(ii) of this section, a borrower must provide the institution certification that the borrower has been accepted for or is engaged in full-time study in the institution's graduate fellowship program.

(g) To qualify for a deferment for study in a rehabilitation training program, pursuant to paragraph (b)(1)(iv) of this section, the borrower must be receiving, or be scheduled to receive, services under a program designed to rehabilitate disabled individuals and must provide the institution with the following documentation:

(1) A certification from the rehabilitation agency that the borrower is either receiving or scheduled to receive rehabilitation training services from the agency.

(2) A certification from the rehabilitation agency that the rehabilitation program—

(i) Is licensed, approved, certified, or otherwise recognized by one of the following entities as providing rehabilitation training to disabled individuals—

(A) A State agency with responsibility for vocational rehabilitation programs;

(B) A State agency with responsibility for drug abuse treatment programs;

(C) A State agency with responsibility for mental health services programs;

(D) A State agency with responsibility for alcohol abuse treatment programs; or

(E) The Department of Veterans Affairs; and

(ii) Provides or will provide the borrower with rehabilitation services under a written plan that—

(A) Is individualized to meet the borrower's needs;

(B) Specifies the date on which the services to the borrower are expected to end; and

(C) Is structured in a way that requires a substantial commitment by the borrower to his or her rehabilitation. The Secretary considers a substantial commitment by the borrower to be a commitment of time and effort that would normally prevent an individual from engaging in full-time employment either because of the number of hours that must be devoted to rehabilitation or because of the nature of the rehabilitation.

(h) The institution may not include the deferment periods described in paragraphs (b), (c), (d), (e), (f), and (g) of this section and the period described in paragraph (i) of this section in determining the 10-year repayment period.

(i) The borrower need not pay principal and interest does not accrue until six months after completion of any period during which the borrower is in deferment under paragraphs (b), (c), (d), (e), (f), and (g) of this section.

(Approved by the Office of Management and Budget under control number 1845-0019)

(Authority: 20 U.S.C. 1087dd)

[59 FR 61410, Nov. 30, 1994; 60 FR 31410, June 15, 1995; 60 FR 61815, Dec. 1, 1995; 62 FR 50848, Sept. 26, 1997; 64 FR 57531, Oct. 25, 1999; 64 FR 58311, Oct. 28, 1999; 65 FR 18003, April 6, 2000; 65 FR 26136, May 5, 2000]

* * *

§ 674.38 Deferment procedures.

(a)(1) Except as provided in paragraph (a)(2)of this section, a borrower must request the deferment and provide the institution with all information and documents required by the institution by the date that the institution establishes.

(2) In the case of an in school deferment, the institution may grant the deferment based on student enrollment information showing that a borrower is enrolled as a regular student on at least a half-time basis, if the institution notifies the borrower of the deferment and of the borrower's option to cancel the deferment and continue paying on the loan.

(3) If the borrower fails to meet the requirements of paragraph (a) (1) of this section, the institution may declare the loan to be in default, and may accelerate the loan.

(b)(1) The institution may grant a deferment to a borrower after it has declared a loan to be a default.

(2) As a condition for a deferment under this paragraph, the institution—

(i) Shall require the borrower to execute a written repayment agreement on the loan; and

(ii) May require the borrower to pay immediately some or all of the amounts previously scheduled to be repaid before the date on which the institution determined that the borrower had demonstrated that grounds for a deferment existed, plus late charges and collection costs.

(c) If the information supplied by the borrower demonstrates that for some or all of the period for which a deferment is requested, the borrower had retained in-school status or was within the initial grace period on the loan, the institution shall—

(1) Redetermine the date on which the borrower was required to commence repayment on the loan;

(2) Deduct from the loan balance any interest accrued and late charges added before the date on which the repayment period commenced, as determined in paragraph (c)(1) of this section; and

(3) Treat in accordance with paragraph (b) of this section, the request for deferment for any remaining portion of the period for which deferment was requested.

(d) The institution must determine the continued eligibility of a borrower for a deferment at least annually, except that a borrower engaged in service described in §§ 674.34(e)(6), 674.35(c)(3), 674.36(c)(2), 674.37(c)(2), and § 674.60(a)(1) must be granted a deferment for the lesser of the borrower's full term of service in the Peace Corps, or the borrower's remaining period of eligibility for a deferment under § 674.34(e), not to exceed 3 years.

(Approved by the Office of Management and Budget under control number 1845-0019)

(Authority: 20 U.S.C. 425, 1087dd)

[53 FR 49147, Dec. 6, 1988; 59 FR 61410, 61411, Nov. 30, 1994; 64 FR 57531, Oct. 25, 1999; 64 FR 58315, Oct. 28, 1999]

§ 674.39 Loan rehabilitation.

(a) Each institution must establish a loan rehabilitation program for all borrowers for the purpose of rehabilitating defaulted loans made under this part. The institution's loan rehabilitation program must provide that—

(1) A defaulted borrower is notified of the option and consequences of rehabilitating a loan; and

(2) A loan is rehabilitated if the borrower makes an on-time, monthly payment, as determined by the institution, each month for twelve consecutive months and the borrower requests rehabilitation; and

(3) A borrower who wishes to rehabilitate a loan on which a judgment has been entered must sign a new promissory note after rehabilitating the loan.

(b) Within 30 days of receiving the borrower's last on-time, consecutive, monthly payment, the institution must—

(1) Return the borrower to regular repayment status;

(2) Treat the first payment made under the 12 consecutive payments as the first payment under the 10-year repayment maximum; and

(3) Instruct any credit bureau to which the default was reported to remove the default from the borrower's credit history.

(c) Collection costs on a rehabilitated loan—

(1) If charged to the borrower, may not exceed 24 percent of the unpaid principal and accrued interest as of the date following application of the twelfth payment;

(2) That exceed the amounts specified in paragraph (c)(1) of this section, may be charged to an institution's Fund until July 1, 2002 in accordance with § 674.47(e)(5); and

(3) Are not restricted to 24 percent in the event the borrower defaults on the rehabilitated loan.

(d) After rehabilitating a defaulted loan and returning to regular repayment status, the borrower regains the balance of the benefits and privileges of the promissory note as applied prior to the borrower's default on the loan. Nothing in this paragraph prohibits an institution from offering the borrower flexible repayment options following the borrower's return to regular repayment status on a rehabilitated loan.

(e) The borrower may rehabilitate a defaulted loan only one time.

(Approved by the Office of Management and Budget under control number 1845-0023)

[53 FR 49147, Dec. 6, 1988; 57 FR 32346, July 21, 1992; 58 FR 36870, July 9, 1993; 59 FR 61410, 61411, Nov. 30, 1994; 64 FR 58311, Oct. 28, 1999; 65 FR 65614, Nov. 1, 2000]

§ 674.50 Assignment of defaulted loans to the United States.

(a) An institution may submit a defaulted loan note to the Secretary for assignment to the United States if—

(1) The institution has been unable to collect on the loan despite complying with the diligence procedures, including at least a first level collection effort as described in § 674.45(a) and litigation, if required under § 674.46(a), to the extent these actions were required by regulations in effect on the date the loan entered default;

(2) The amount of the borrower's account to be assigned, including outstanding principal, accrued interest, collection costs and late charges is $25.00 or greater; and

(3) The loan has been accelerated.

(b) An institution may submit a defaulted note for assignment only during the submission period established by the Secretary.

(c) The Secretary may require an institution to submit the following documents for any loan it proposes to assign—

(1) An assignment form provided by the Secretary and executed by the institution, which must include a certification by the institution that it has complied with the requirements of this subpart, including at least a first level collection effort as described in § 674.45(a) in attempting collection on the loan.

(2) The original promissory note or a certified copy of the original note.

(3) A copy of the repayment schedule.

(4) A certified copy of any judgment order entered on the loan.

(5) A complete statement of the payment history.

(6) Copies of all approved requests for deferment and cancellation.

(7) A copy of the notice to the borrower of the effective date of acceleration and the total amount due on the loan.

(8) Documentation that the institution has withdrawn the loan from any firm that it employed for address search, billing, collection or litigation services, and has notified that firm to cease collection activity on the loans.

(9) Copies of all pleadings filed or received by the institution on behalf of a borrower who has filed a petition in bankruptcy and whose loan obligation is determined to be nondischargeable.

(10) Documentation that the institution has complied with all of the due diligence requirements described in paragraph (a)(1) of this section if the institution has a cohort default rate that is equal to or greater than 20 percent as of June 30 of the second year preceding the submission period.

(d) Except as provided in paragraph (e) of this section, and subject to paragraph (g) of this section, the Secretary accepts an assignment of a note described in paragraph (a) of this section and submitted in accordance with paragraph (c) of this section.

(e) The Secretary does not accept assignment of a loan if—

(1) The institution has not provided the Social Security number of the borrower;

(2) The borrower has received a discharge in bankruptcy, unless—

(i) The bankruptcy court has determined that the loan obligation is nondischargeable and has entered judgment against the borrower; or

(ii) A court of competent jurisdiction has entered judgment against the borrower on the loan after the entry of the discharge order;

(3) The institution has initiated litigation against the borrower,

unless the judgment has been entered against the borrower and assigned to the United States; or

(4) The borrower has been granted cancellation due to death or has filed for or been granted cancellation due to permanent and total disability.

(f)(1) The Secretary provides an institution written notice of the acceptance of the assignment of the note. By accepting assignment, the Secretary acquires all rights, title, and interest of the institution in that loan.

(2) The institution shall endorse and forward to the Secretary any payment received from the borrower after the date on which the Secretary accepted the assignment, as noted in the written notice of acceptance.

(g)(1) The Secretary may determine that a loan assigned to the United States is unenforceable in whole or in part because of the acts or omissions of the institution or its agent. The Secretary may make this determination with or without a judicial determination regarding the enforceability of the loan.

(2) The institution shall reimburse the Fund for that portion of the outstanding balance on a loan assigned to the United States which the Secretary determines to be unenforceable because of an act or omission of that institution or its agent.

(3) Upon reimbursement to the Fund by the institution, the Secretary shall transfer all rights, title and interest of the United States in the loan to the institution for its own account.

(h) An institution shall consider a borrower whose loan has been assigned to the United States for collection to be in default on that loan for the purpose of eligibility for title IV financial assistance, until the borrower provides the institution confirmation from the Secretary that he or she has made satisfactory arrangements to repay the loan.

(Approved by the Office of Management and Budget under control number 1845-0019)

(Authority: 20 U.S.C. 424, 1087cc)

[53 FR 49147, Dec. 6, 1988; 57 FR 32347, July 21, 1992; 57 FR 60706, Dec. 21, 1992; 58 FR 36870, 36871, July 9, 1993; 59 FR 61412, Nov. 30, 1994; 64 FR 58315, Oct. 28, 1999; 65 FR 65614, Nov. 1, 2000]

§ 674.51 Special definitions.

The following definitions apply to this Subpart:

(a) *Academic year or its equivalent for elementary and secondary schools and special education*: (1) One complete school year, or two half years from different school years, excluding summer sessions, that are complete and consecutive and generally fall within a 12-month period.

(2) If such a school has a year-round program of instruction, the Secretary considers a minimum of nine consecutive months to be the equivalent of an academic year.

(b) *Academic year or its equivalent for institutions of higher education*: A period of time in which a full-time student is expected to complete—

(1) The equivalent of 2 semesters, 2 trimesters, or 3 quarters at an institution using credit hours; or

(2) At least 900 clock hours of training for each program at an institution using clock hours.

(c) Title I Children: Children of ages 5 through 17 who are counted under section 1124(c)(1) of the Elementary and Secondary

Education Act of 1965, as amended.

(d) *Children and youth with disabilities*: Children and youth from ages 3 through 21, inclusive, who require special education and related services because they have disabilities as defined in section 602(a)(1) of the Individuals with Disabilities Education Act.

(e) *Early intervention services*: Those services defined in section 672(2) of the Individuals with Disabilities Education Act that are provided to infants and toddlers with disabilities.

(f) *Elementary school*: A school that provides elementary education, including education below grade 1, as determined by—

(1) State law; or

(2) The Secretary, if the school is not in a State.

(g) *Handicapped children*: Children of ages 3 through 21 inclusive who require special education and related services because they are—

(1) Mentally retarded;

(2) Hard of hearing;

(3) Deaf;

(4) Speech and language impaired;

(5) Visually handicapped;

(6) Seriously emotionally disturbed;

(7) Orthopedically impaired;

(8) Specific learning disabled; or

(9) Otherwise health impaired.

(h) *High-risk children*: Individuals under the age of 21 who are low-income or at risk of abuse or neglect, have been abused or neglected, have serious emotional, mental, or behavioral disturbances, reside in placements outside their homes, or are involved in the juvenile justice system.

(i) *Infants and toddlers with disabilities*: Infants and toddlers from birth to age 2, inclusive, who need early intervention services for specified reasons, as defined in section 672(1) of the Individuals with Disabilities Education Act.

(j) *Local educational agency*: (1) A public board of education or other public authority legally constituted within a State to administer, direct, or perform a service function for public elementary or secondary schools in a city, county, township, school district, other political subdivision of a State; or such combination of school districts of counties as are recognized in a State as an administrative agency for its public elementary or secondary schools.

(2) Any other public institution or agency having administrative control and direction of a public elementary or secondary school.

(k) *Low-income communities*: Communities in which there is a high concentration of children eligible to be counted under title I of the Elementary and Secondary Education Act of 1965, as amended.

(l) *Medical technician*: An allied health professional (working in fields such as therapy, dental hygiene, medical technology, or nutrition) who is certified, registered, or licensed by the appropriate State agency in the State in which he or she provides health care services. An allied health professional is someone who assists, facilitates, or complements the work of physicians and other specialists in the health care system.

(m) *Nurse*: A licensed practical nurse, a registered nurse, or other individual who is licensed by the appropriate State agency to provide nursing services.

(n) *Qualified professional provider of early intervention services*: A provider of services as defined in section 672(2) of the Individuals with Disabilities Education Act.

(o) *Secondary school*: (1) A school that provides secondary education, as determined by—

(i) State law; or

(ii) The Secretary, if the school is not in a State.

(2) However, State laws notwithstanding, secondary education does not include any education beyond grade 12.

(p) *State education agency*: (1) The State board of education; or

(2) An agency or official designated by the Governor or by State law as being primarily responsible for the State supervision of public elementary and secondary schools.

(q) *Teacher*: (1) A teacher is a person who provides—

(i) Direct classroom teaching;

(ii) Classroom-type teaching in a non-classroom setting; or

(iii) Educational services to students directly related to classroom teaching such as school librarians or school guidance counselors.

(2) A supervisor, administrator, researcher, or curriculum specialist is not a teacher unless he or she primarily provides direct and personal educational services to students.

(3) An individual who provides one of the following services does not qualify as a teacher unless that individual is licensed, certified, or registered by the appropriate State education agency for that area in which he or she is providing related special educational services, and the services provided by the individual are part of the educational curriculum for handicapped children:

(i) Speech and language pathology and audiology;

(ii) Physical therapy;

(iii) Occupational therapy;

(iv) Psychological and counseling services; or

(v) Recreational therapy.

(r) *Teaching in a field of expertise*: The majority of classes taught are in the borrower's field of expertise.

(s) *Total and permanent disability*: The condition of an individual who is unable to work and earn money because of an injury or illness that is expected to continue indefinitely or result in death.

(Authority: 20 U.S.C. 425, 1087ee, 1141, and 1401(1))

[59 FR 61412, Nov. 30, 1994; 65 FR 65690, Nov. 1, 2000]

§ 674.52 Cancellation procedures.

(a) *Application for cancellation*. To qualify for cancellation of a loan, a borrower shall submit to the institution to which the loan is owed, by the date that the institution establishes, both a written request for cancellation and any documentation required by the institution to demonstrate that the borrower meets the conditions for the cancellation requested.

(b) *Part-time employment*. (1)(i) An institution may refuse a request for cancellation based on a claim of simultaneously teaching in two or more schools or institutions if it cannot determine easily from the documentation supplied by the borrower that the teaching is full-time. However, it shall grant the cancellation if one school official certifies that a teacher worked full-time for a full academic year.

(ii) An institution may refuse a request for cancellation based on a claim of simultaneous employment as a nurse or medical technician in two or more facilities if it cannot determine easily from the documentation supplied by the borrower that the combined employment is full-time. However, it shall grant the cancellation if one facility official certifies that a nurse or medical technician worked full-time for a full year.

(2) If the borrower is unable due to illness or pregnancy to complete the academic year, the borrower still qualifies for the cancellation if—

(i) The borrower completes the first half of the academic year, and has begun teaching the second half; and

(ii) The borrower's employer considers the borrower to have fulfilled his or her contract for the academic year for purposes of salary increment, tenure, and retirement.

(c) *Cancellation of a defaulted loan.* (1) Except with regard to cancellation on account of the death or disability of the borrower, a borrower whose defaulted loan has not been accelerated may qualify for a cancellation by complying with the requirements of paragraph (a) of this section.

(2) A borrower whose defaulted loan has been accelerated—

(i) May qualify for a loan cancellation for services performed before the date of acceleration; and

(ii) Cannot qualify for a cancellation for services performed on or after the date of acceleration.

(3) An institution shall grant a request for cancellation on account of the death or disability of the borrower without regard to the repayment status of the loan.

(d) *Concurrent deferment period.* The Secretary considers a Perkins Loan, NDSL or Defense Loan borrower's loan deferment under § 674.34(c) to run concurrently with any period for which cancellation under §§ 674.53, 674.54, 674.55, 674.56, 674.57, 674.58, 674.59, and 674.60 is granted.

(e) *National community service.* No borrower who has received a benefit under subtitle D of title I of the National and Community Service Act of 1990 may receive a cancellation under this subpart.

(Approved by the Office of Management and Budget under control number 1845-0019)

(Authority: 20 U.S.C. 425, 1087ee)

[53 FR 49147, Dec. 6, 1988; 57 FR 32347, July 21, 1992; 58 FR 36870, July 9, 1993; 59 FR 61413, Nov. 30, 1994; 62 FR 50848, Sept. 26, 1997; 64 FR 58313, Oct. 28, 1999; 65 FR 18003, April 6, 2000; 65 FR 26136, May 5, 2000]

* * *

§ 674.61 Discharge for death or disability.

(a) *Death.* An institution must discharge the unpaid balance of a borrower's Defense, NDSL, or Perkins loan, including interest, if the borrower dies. The institution must discharge the loan on the basis of an original or certified copy of the death certificate. Under exceptional circumstances and on a case- by-case basis, the chief financial officer of the institution may approve a discharge based upon other reliable documentation supporting the discharge request.

(b) *Total and permanent disability.* (1) If the Secretary has made an initial determination that the borrower is totally and permanently disabled, as defined in § 674.51(s), the loan is conditionally discharged for up to three years from the date that the borrower became totally and permanently disabled, as certified by a physician. The Secretary suspends collection activity on the loan from the date of the initial determination of total and permanent disability until the end of the three-year conditional period. If the

borrower satisfies the criteria for a total and permanent disability discharge during and at the end of the conditional discharge period, the balance of the loan is discharged at the end of the conditional discharge period and any payments received after the date the borrower became totally and permanently disabled as certified under § 674.61(b)(3) are returned to the sender.

(2) A borrower satisfies the criteria for a discharge of a loan based on a total and permanent disability if, during and at the end of the three-year conditional discharge period described in paragraph (b)(1) of this section—

(i) The borrower's annual earnings from employment do not exceed 100 percent of the poverty line for a family of two, as determined in accordance with the Community Service Block Grant Act; and

(ii) The borrower does not receive a new loan under the Perkins, FFEL or Direct Loan programs, except for a FFEL or Direct Consolidation Loan that does not include any loans that are in a conditional discharge status.

(3) If a borrower becomes totally and permanently disabled after receiving a Defense, NDSL, or Perkins loan, the institution must assign the loan to the Secretary if the borrower submits a certification by a physician and the institution reviewed the application and determined that it is complete and that it supports the conclusion that the borrower has a total and permanent disability as defined in § 674.51(s).

(4) At the time the loan is assigned to the Secretary the institution must notify the borrower that the loan has been assigned to the Secretary for determination of eligibility for a total and permanent disability discharge.

(5) If the Secretary determines that the certification provided by the borrower does not support the conclusion that the borrower meets the criteria for a total and permanent disability discharge, the Secretary notifies the borrower that the application for a disability discharge has been denied, and that the loan is due and payable under the terms of the promissory note.

(6) If the Secretary makes an initial determination that the borrower is totally and permanently disabled, the Secretary notifies the borrower that the loan will be in a conditional discharge status for a period of up to three years after the date the borrower became totally and permanently disabled as certified under § 674.61(b)(3). This notification identifies the conditions of the conditional discharge period specified in paragraphs (b)(6) through (b)(9) of this section and specifies that all or part of the three-year period may predate the Secretary's initial determination.

(7) During the conditional discharge period, the borrower—

(i) Is not required to make any payments on the loan;

(ii) Is not considered past due or in default on the loan, unless the loan was past due or in default at the time the conditional discharge was granted;

(iii) Must promptly notify the Secretary of any changes in address or phone number;

(iv) Must promptly notify the Secretary if the borrower's annual earnings from employment exceed the amount specified in paragraph (b)(2)(i) of this section; and

(v) Must provide the Secretary, upon request, with additional documentation or information related to the borrower's eligibility for discharge under this section.

(8) If, during and at the end of the conditional discharge period, the borrower continues to satisfy the eligibility criteria for a total and permanent disability discharge, as described in paragraph

(b)(2) of this section, the balance of the loan is discharged.

(9) If, at any time during or at the end of the three-year conditional discharge period, the borrower does not continue to meet the eligibility requirements for total and permanent disability discharge, the Secretary resumes collection activity on the loan. The Secretary does not require the borrower to pay any interest that accrued on the loan from the date of the initial determination described in paragraph (b)(6) of this section through the end of the conditional discharge period.

(10) If the institution receives any payments from or on behalf of the borrower on or attributable to a loan that has been assigned to the Secretary for determination of eligibility for a total and permanent disability discharge, the institution must forward those payments to the Secretary for crediting to the borrower's account. At the same time that the institution forwards the payment, it must notify the borrower that there is no obligation to make payments on the loan while it is conditionally discharged prior to a final determination of eligibility for a total and permanent disability discharge, unless the Secretary directs the borrower otherwise.

(11) When the Secretary makes a final determination to discharge the loan, the Secretary returns to the sender any payments received on the loan after the date the borrower became totally and permanently disabled.

(c) *No Federal reimbursement.* No Federal reimbursement is made to an institution for cancellation of loans due to death or disability.

(d) *Retroactive.* Cancellation for death or disability applies retroactively to all Defense, NDSL or Perkins loans.

(Approved by the Office of Management and Budget under control number 1845-0019)

(Authority: 20 U.S.C. 425 and 1087dd and sec. 130(g)(2) of the Education Amendments of 1976, Pub.L. 94-482)

[53 FR 49147, Dec. 6, 1988; 59 FR 61413, 61415, Nov. 30, 1994; 64 FR 58315, Oct. 28, 1999; 65 FR 18002, April 6, 2000; 65 FR 26136, May 5, 2000; 65 FR 65690, Nov. 1, 2000; 66 FR 44007, Aug. 21, 2001]

Department of Education Policy Guidance Letters

The Department of Education Office of Postsecondary Education periodically distributes "Dear Colleague" and "Dear Guaranty Agency" letters. These are used to communicate Department instructions and directives. This appendix contains a selection of Dear Colleague letters of particular significance for low-income borrowers. The most efficient way to obtain additional copies or to search for other Dear Colleague letters is through the Department of Education website at http://ifap.ed.gov/IFAPWebApp/currentDPCLettersPag.jsp. The general website is www.ed.gov. The letters are sorted on-line by publication year and by subject matter. Only letters from 1995 or later are available.

This letter explains the new procedures for disability discharges, effective July 1, 2002.

May 2002

GEN-02-03
CB-02-08
G-02-334
L-02-228

SUBJECT: New Total and Permanent Disability Discharge Procedures for Title IV Loans— Effective July 1, 2002

SUMMARY: This letter discusses implementation of the regulatory changes for total and permanent disability discharges in the Federal Perkins Loan, Federal Family Education Loan (FFEL), and the William D. Ford Federal Direct Loan programs. The final regulations were published on November 1, 2000. While some of the provisions went into effect on July 1, 2001, most of the regulatory changes become effective July 1, 2002. This letter provides guidance to Perkins school lenders, FFEL lenders, and guaranty agencies on the new procedures for processing total and permanent disability discharge requests.

Dear Colleague:

To address weaknesses in the procedures for granting total and permanent disability discharges on federal student loans identified in a June 1999 report issued by the Department's Inspector General, the Department conducted a negotiated rulemaking process with representatives from the higher education community from January to May 2000. All members of the negotiating committee could not reach agreement on the proposed regulatory changes, and the Department published proposed regulations for public comment on August 2, 2000.

After considering the public comments received on the proposed regulations and making changes where appropriate, the Department published final regulations on November 1, 2000, that significantly revise the process for granting disability discharges. In addition, as part of those regulations, the definition of total and permanent disability was changed, removing the requirement that a borrower be unable to attend school. This revised definition became effective July 1, 2001.

Under the changed definition, a borrower is totally and permanently disabled if the borrower: "is unable to work and earn money because of an injury or illness that is expected to continue indefinitely or result in death" [34 C.F.R. §§674.51(s), 682.200]. The final regulations also made significant changes to the process for evaluating disability discharge applications. Those changes will go into effect on July 1, 2002.

This Dear Colleague Letter provides a general overview of the disability discharge regulations and procedures that go into effect on July 1, 2002. In addition, Attachments 1 and 2 to this letter provide guidance specific to Perkins school lenders and FFEL lenders and guarantors. Attachment 3 outlines the role of the Department in the new process.

I. Overview of Regulatory Changes

The regulatory changes revising the process for granting total and permanent disability discharges are contained in 34 C.F.R. §674. 61(b) of the Perkins regulations, 34 C.F.R. §§682.402(c) and 682.402(r) of the FFEL regulations, and 34 C.F.R. §685.213 of the Direct Loan regulations. Under the new regulations, the disability discharge procedures are as follows:

1. The borrower applies to the loan holder (i.e., the current owner of the loan) for a disability discharge. For Perkins Loans, the loan holder is the Perkins school lender. For FFEL loans, the loan holder is a lender or, if the loan has gone into default, a guaranty agency. For Direct Loans and other Title IV loans assigned to the Department, the loan holder is the U.S. Department of Education.

The loan holder must make a preliminary determination as to whether the borrower meets the criteria for a total and permanent disability discharge. For Perkins loans, the preliminary determination is made by the school. In the FFEL Program, the current loan holder makes the determination. For Direct Loans, the preliminary determination is made by Direct Loan staff. For other loans held by the Department, the preliminary determination is made by the Department's Federal Student Aid (FSA) Collections. In addition, for FFEL loans, the guaranty agency conducts an independent evaluation of the discharge request after the FFEL lender makes a preliminary determination that the borrower qualifies for the discharge, except in the case where the guaranty agency is the current loan holder and the borrower submitted the discharge request directly to the guaranty agency.

2. If during the preliminary determination a loan holder, guaranty agency or the Department determines that the borrower does not meet the criteria for a disability discharge, the discharge request is denied, the loan is returned to its prior status and, as appropriate, collection activity or regular servicing resumes on the loan.

3. For Perkins Loans, if the school determines that a borrower meets the criteria for a disability discharge, it must assign the loan to the Department's Disability Discharge Unit. For FFEL loans, the loan is assigned to the Department's Disability Discharge Unit if both the loan holder and the guaranty agency determine that a borrower meets the criteria for a total and permanent disability discharge.

4. The Department reviews all assigned loans with discharge applications to affirm that the borrower meets the criteria for a discharge. If we affirm that the borrower meets the criteria for a total and permanent disability discharge, the loan is placed in a conditional discharge status for three years. During this conditional discharge period, the borrower is not required to make payments and interest does not accrue.

5. During this conditional discharge period, we will monitor whether the borrower has been able to work and earn money or has received a new Title IV loan in order to ensure that the borrower continues to qualify for the total and permanent disability discharge. At the end of the conditional discharge period, we will make a determination that the borrower has met the definition of total and permanent disability if he or she has not had annual earnings from work during the conditional discharge period in excess of the poverty level for a family of two, and has not received any new Title IV loans during the period. If these conditions are met throughout the conditional discharge period, we will grant a final discharge.

6. In some cases, a borrower may have become totally and permanently disabled, as determined by a physician, three or more years before the loan is assigned. In these cases, the initial determination of eligibility—based on the borrower's medical documentation—and the final determination of eligibility—based on the borrower's earnings and subsequent Title IV loan activity—will be conducted at the same time and we may immediately grant a final discharge.

During the discharge process, borrowers will be given a phone number to call and speak with a representative if they have any questions about their discharge requests. Borrowers will also be told that they may contact our Student Loan Ombudsman for assistance in resolving disputes. However, as with the current total and permanent disability discharge process, there is no formal appeals process for a borrower who is denied a discharge.

II. Application Availability and Effective Date For Use

Currently, disability discharge requests in the FFEL and Direct Loan Program are processed using the form titled "Loan Discharge Application: Total and Permanent Disability" [OMB Number 1845-0015]. Perkins school lenders do not currently use a Department of Education form for processing disability discharge requests, although they have a comparable application process. We have developed a new total and permanent disability discharge application for use in all three of the Title IV loan programs. This form is currently under review by the Office of Management and budget. After this new total and permanent disability discharge application form is approved by OMB in the next few weeks, we will make it immediately available to the financial aid community by posting it to the Information for Financial Aid Professionals (IFAP) web site as an attachment to a Dear Colleague Letter. The new disability discharge application must be provided to all borrowers who request total and permanent disability discharges on or after July 1, 2002. However, program participants may use the previous form for borrowers who were in the discharge process prior to July 1, 2002, but must follow the new standards and procedures for all disability discharge determinations made on or after July 1, 2002.

III. Triggering Date for Implementation of New Procedures

The new standards and procedures for granting total and permanent disability discharges resulting from the November 1, 2000 final regulations that are discussed in this letter go into effect on July 1, 2002.

For all disability discharge requests approved on or after July 1, 2002 based on the previously approved total and permanent disability discharge form (or a school form for Perkins borrowers), the loan holder must, in the preliminary determination letter, inform the borrower that the regulations governing disability discharges have changed and explain the new total and permanent disability eligibility criteria and discharge process.

IV. Department's Expectations for Holders' Preliminary Determinations

We expect loan holders and guaranty agencies to conduct rigorous evaluations of disability discharge requests. If the borrower's medical documentation does not support the conclusion that the borrower is unable to work and earn money because of an injury or illness that is expected to continue indefinitely or result in death, the discharge request should be denied. Loan holders and guarantors should follow the guidance for reviewing disability claims that was provided in Dear Guaranty Agency Director Letter 99-G-324, dated November 1999. This guidance states that loan holders are expected to:

1. Require additional documentation to support a borrower's application if the information provided by the borrower is not definitive, is illegible, or is incomplete.
2. Require the physician to affirm certification of disability if the diagnosis does not appear to satisfy the standard for discharge. If it appears that the physician has used a less rigorous standard in certifying the borrower's disability, loan holders should clarify the definition of "total and permanent disability" with the physician.

Loan holders may want to seek the assistance of a qualified physician to evaluate total and permanent disability discharge requests, as appropriate. Loan holders should also report to the Department's Office of Inspector General any questionable patterns related to physicians' certifying signatures or state licensing numbers regarding the legitimacy of the disability discharge request.

The Attachments to this letter provide more detailed information on the new eligibility criteria and procedures for granting total and permanent disability discharges.

We would like to thank the student financial aid community for its assistance in developing these new procedures and designing the new total and permanent disability discharge form. We look forward to continuing to work with you to ensure that only those borrowers who are eligible will continue to receive total and permanent disability discharges on their Title IV loans. Thank you for your cooperation in implementing these new safeguards and your continued support of the federal student financial assistance programs.

Sincerely,
Jeffrey R. Andrade
Deputy Assistant Secretary for
Policy, Planning, and Innovation
Office of Postsecondary Education
Greg Woods
Chief Operating Officer
Federal Student Aid

[*Editor's Note: Attachments not reprinted herein.*]
Attachment 1: Federal Perkins Loan Program
Attachment 2: FFEL Program
Attachment 3: Department of Education

This letter explains the Department's actions to eliminate the "employment attempt" provisions in the federal false certification ability-to-benefit discharge. 34 C.F.R. § 682.402(e)(3)(ii)(C).

July 2000

G-00-327

Dear Guaranty Agency Partner:

This letter is to inform you of a recent court decision and resulting Department policy change that affects the Department's implementation of the "employment attempt" provisions in the Federal Family Education Loan (FFEL) Program false certification—ability-to-benefit discharge (false certification discharge) regulations. 34 CFR 682.402(e)(3)(ii)(C).

On November 16, 1999, the U.S. Court of Appeals for the District of Columbia (Court of Appeals), in *Jordan v. Riley*, ruled invalid the employment attempt provisions in the false certification discharge regulations, finding that the relevant statute did not authorize such provisions. As explained more fully below, the Department has decided to extend the Court's ruling to all borrowers and no longer consider the borrower's employment attempts in resolving false certification discharge claims.

I. *Background*

Currently, the false certification discharge regulations requires a borrower first to demonstrate that the school for which the loan was intended certified his or her eligibility to borrow based on his or her ability-to-benefit from the program offered but did not comply with the Higher Education Act requirements in making that determination. If that requirement is met and the borrower did not complete the program, the borrower must show that he or she did not find employment in his or her field of study. A borrower who did complete the program must show that he or she made a reasonable attempt to obtain employment in his or her field of study but was unable to obtain such employment or obtained employment only after receiving additional training from another school. 34 CFR 682.402(e)(3)(ii)(B) & (C).

In *Jordan v. Riley*, a FFEL borrower who claimed that her ability-to-benefit was falsely certified by the school was denied a false certification discharge because she completed the school's program but failed to make a reasonable attempt to obtain employment. The borrower sued the Department, challenging the employment attempt requirements in the regulations that were the basis for her denial. The U.S. District Court for the District of Columbia upheld the Department's regulations; the borrower appealed to the Court of Appeals.

II. *Court of Appeals Decision*

The Court of Appeals found that section 437(c) of the Higher Education Act of 1965, as amended, 20 USC 1087(c), does not authorize the Secretary to include criteria in the regulations that attempt to measure whether, despite any deficient certification by the school, the student nevertheless had the ability-to-benefit from the program. The court believed that "a student's post-training employment experience is irrelevant to the truth or falsity of the certification." Rather, the court ruled that the statute only authorizes the Secretary to determine whether the student met "the objective criteria for certification before being admitted" (*e.g.*, the school properly tested the student and the student passed the test).

III. *Department's Policy Change*

As a legal matter, the Court of Appeals decision stands as a controlling interpretation of law only in the District of Columbia. The Department, however, has decided to extend the application of the decision and treat all borrowers who apply for a false certification discharge uniformly.

Therefore, in order to be eligible for a false certification discharge, a borrower will now *only* be required to demonstrate that the school admitted him or her and certified the borrower's eligibility to borrow based on his or her ability-to-benefit from the program offered at the school, but did so without complying with the statutory ability-to-benefit requirements in place at the time of the student's enrollment. 34 CFR 682.402(e)(3)(ii)(B). The borrower will no longer have to demonstrate that he or she meets the employment attempt requirements set forth in 34 CFR 682.402(e)(3)(ii)(C).

The Department is in the process of discussing necessary regulatory changes to reflect this change of policy. Effective as of the date of this letter, guaranty agencies should issue decisions on false certification applications consistent with the policy guidance set forth in this letter.

If you have any questions regarding this matter, feel free to contact Daniel Madzelan at 202-502-7816 or Pamela Moran or George Harris at 202-708-8242.

Sincerely,

A. Lee Fritschler

This letter details the Department's instructions to guaranty agencies to tighten up the disability and death discharge programs. The letter is in response to the Office of Inspector General study finding alleged abuse in these programs.

November 1999

GEN-99-36
99-G-324
00-L-217

Subject:　Revised Procedures Related to Death and Total and Permanent Disability Discharge Requests for the Federal Family Education Loan (FFEL) Program

Dear Guaranty Agency Director:

The Department of Education's Office of Inspector General (OIG) recently completed a study of the process for granting discharges of Federal Family Education Loan (FFEL) Program loans due to death or total and permanent disability. The OIG's audit report focused on FFEL loan discharges granted from July 1, 1994 through December 31, 1996. Through a match of all borrowers receiving these discharges during this period with the Social Security Administration's master earning records, the OIG found that 23 percent of borrowers who received disability discharges during this period worked and earned money after the disability determination was made or the loan was discharged. The OIG also found that 2 percent of borrowers who received a discharge of their loan based on death were working and earning money after the loan was discharged. The OIG concluded from its review that inappropriate discharges were being provided to borrowers because of weaknesses in the current system for determining eligibility for the discharges. After reviewing the OIG report we have decided to implement the following changes to strengthen control of the process for granting death and disability discharges.

Loan Discharges Due to Death

We are concerned that documentation used to support discharges based on death may be easily forged or may not provide definitive proof of death. Section 682.402(b)(2) of the FFEL program regulations provides that the lender (or guaranty agency) may rely on a death certificate or other proof of death that is acceptable under applicable state law. If such documentation is not available, the guaranty agency is authorized to discharge a loan only if it determines that other evidence establishes that the borrower (or dependent student on whose behalf a parent has borrowed a PLUS loan) has died.

In order to strengthen the process of evaluating applications for discharge of loans based on death, we have decided that it is appropriate to interpret the regulations to require, generally, that a death cancellation may only be granted based on an *original* or *certified* copy of the death certificate. We believe this interpretation is consistent with the language of the regulation since certified death certificates are generally the ultimate proof of death under state law. In situations where the guaranty agency is unable to obtain an original or certified copy of the death certificate, it should contact our Financial Partners Channel.

We understand that stricter documentation standards for discharges based on death may lengthen the period required for securing the death certificate. The regulations in Section 682.402(b)(3) require the loan holder to suspend collection activity on a loan for 60 days after receiving a request for a death discharge while attempting to obtain the documentation needed to grant the discharge. To be sensitive to the needs of the bereaved family, the Secretary will authorize guaranty agencies to extend the suspension of collection activities an additional 60 days if extra time is needed to obtain the necessary documentation.

Loan Discharges Due to Total and Permanent Disability

Under Section 682.200, an individual is considered totally and permanently disabled for loan discharge purposes only if the individual is "unable to work and earn money or attend school because of an injury or illness that is expected to continue indefinitely or result in death." To address the issue of individuals receiving total and permanent disability discharges for conditions that do not meet this regulatory definition, we are requesting guaranty agencies to implement a more rigorous evaluation process for determining if a borrower qualifies for a total and permanent disability discharge. This process should include at a minimum:

- Requiring additional documentation to support the borrower's application for loan discharge in cases where the information provided in the initial application is not definitive, is illegible or is incomplete. Loan holders may assist borrowers who are having difficulty paying their loans while their claims are being evaluated by granting forbearance or otherwise ceasing collection activities during the evaluation period.
- Reaffirming the physician's certification if the diagnosis and prognosis do not appear to reach the standard of total and permanent disability. A disability discharge should not be granted based solely on the physician's certification if there is a question of the borrower's eligibility for the discharge. In such cases, agencies should contact the physician and review with the physician the standard that must be met to certify that a borrower is totally and permanently disabled. The guaranty agency should ensure that physicians clearly understand that the FFEL definition of total and permanent disability ("unable to work and earn money or attend school because of an injury or illness that is expected to continue indefinitely or result in death") generally is a higher standard than that used by other federal or state agencies for disability related benefits or programs. Guaranty agencies are urged to consider retaining the services of a physician to assist them in evaluating claims for which there is a question related to the disabling medical condition and the prognosis for recovery. If a guaranty agency is still not satisfied that

a borrower qualifies for a total and permanent disability discharge, the guaranty agency may require the borrower to obtain a second opinion from another physician instead of simply denying the discharge claim.

- Assisting borrowers to obtain a deferment or forbearance in cases when it does not appear that the borrower is totally and permanently disabled, but there is evidence that the borrower's ability to repay has been impaired by a temporary disability. Although the temporary total disability deferment is not available to new borrowers after July 1, 1993, these borrowers may qualify for an economic hardship deferment as a result of economic difficulties stemming from the temporary disability.

We have revised the Total and Permanent Disability Cancellation Request form to ask the physician to identify whether he or she is a doctor of medicine or a doctor of osteopathy. The revised form also requires physicians to provide their state professional license number. The revised Total and Permanent Disability Cancellation Request form is currently available on our IFAP web site at http://ifap.ed.gov and on the NCHELP web site at www.nchelp.org.

Future Activities

In consultation with guaranty agencies, lenders, and other interested parties, we expect to propose further changes to the Total and Permanent Disability Cancellation Request form to collect additional information regarding the borrower's disabling condition and prognosis for recovery that will assist agency staff in their reviews. We will also begin discussions with program constituents on other possible options for overhauling the process of granting disability discharges.

We will continue to explore strategies for ensuring that ineligible claims for loan discharges due to death or total and permanent disability are not granted. We appreciate the suggestions you shared for implementing short-term solutions. We look forward to working with you to develop and implement a process that balances the need to ensure program integrity with the need for prompt decisions and sensitivity involving a minimum of burden for borrowers and their families.

Contact Person

Should you have questions or suggestions concerning the discharge process, please contact Cameron Ishaq. Mr. Ishaq will serve as the Department's contact person for guaranty agencies on issues related to death and total and permanent disability discharges. You can e-mail Mr. Ishaq at cameron_ishaq@ed.gov, telephone him at (202) 260-5076, or send him a FAX at (202) 708-8404.

Sincerely,

Jeff Baker, Director
Program Development Division
Enclosure A

September 1995
GEN-95-42

SUBJECT: Loan discharges based on improper determination that a student had the ability-to-benefit (ATB) from the school's training.

REFERENCE: 34 CFR 682.402(e) and §685.214(a)

Dear Colleague:

Section 437(c)(1) of the Higher Education Act of 1965, as amended (HEA) provides for the discharge of a borrower's loan obligation under the Federal Family Education Loan (FFEL) Program, and §455(a)(1) makes this relief available under the William D. Ford Federal Direct Loan Program, if the student's eligibility to borrow was falsely certified by the school. In September 1994, initial guidance concerning these loan discharges was provided in "Dear Colleague" Letter 94-L-166/G-256 issued to lenders and guaranty agencies in the

FFEL Program. However, in the area of discharges based on a school's defective determination of a student's ability-to-benefit (ATB), the "Dear Colleague" Letter promised more detailed guidance concerning those discharges.

This letter addresses some common questions about discharges based on improper ATB determinations that have been asked by borrowers, lenders, guaranty agencies, and other parties. The Department intends to apply the guidance in this letter to similar false certification discharges in the William D. Ford Federal Direct Loan Program.

Thank you for ensuring that the intent of the false certification discharge provision is achieved. For further information, you may contact the Department's Customer Support Inquiry Service between the hours of 9:00 AM and 5:00 PM Eastern Time, at 1-800-433-7327. After hours calls will be accepted by an automated voice response system. Callers leaving their name and phone number will receive a return call the next business day. You may FAX your inquiry to the Customer Support Inquiry Service at any time by calling (202) 260-4199.

Sincerely,

Elizabeth M. Hicks
Deputy Assistant Secretary for Student Financial Assistance

Enclosure
Enclosure A
SUMMARY OF ATB REQUIREMENTS[1]

For periods of enrollment beginning January 1, 1986[2] through June 30, 1987

The school could determine that the student had the ability to benefit from the school's training in accordance with the requirements of 34 CFR 668.6, as those regulations existed at that time. The school simply had to "develop and consistently apply criteria" to determine if regular students who did not have a high school diploma or GED, and who were beyond the age of compulsory attendance, had the ability to benefit from the school's training.

For periods of enrollment beginning July 1, 1987 through June 30, 1991

Schools were required to use one of the following standards for admission of students without a high school diploma or its equivalent on the basis of ATB in accordance with 34 CFR 668.7 as it was in effect at that time: (1) the student received a GED prior to the student's completion of the program or by the end of the first year of the program, whichever was earlier; (2) the student was counseled prior to admission and successfully completed the school's program of remedial or developmental education that did not exceed one academic year or its equivalent; (3) the student passed a nationally recognized, standardized, or industry-developed ATB test, subject to criteria developed by the school's accrediting association; or (4) if the student failed the ATB test, he or she successfully completed the school's program of remedial or developmental education that did not exceed one academic year or its equivalent.

For periods of enrollment beginning July 1, 1991 through July 22, 1992

A student who was not a high school graduate or did not have a GED at the time of enrollment must have passed an independently administered ATB test approved by the Department[3] before the student's receipt of Title IV aid.

---

1   This summary presents a brief overview of some of the major ATB requirements over time. The Department has issued several "Dear Colleague" Letters that explained ATB requirements in greater detail. The reader may find "Dear Colleague" Letters GEN-89-55 (December 1989), GEN-90-33 (September 1990), and GEN-91-20 (June 1991) to be particularly helpful.

2   Sections 437(c)(1) and 455(a)(1) of the HEA do not authorize loan discharges based on defective ATB determination for loans made before January 1, 1986.

3   Listings of approved tests were published in the Federal Register on December 19, 1990 and December 30, 1992, and in "Dear Colleague" Letter GEN-93-21 (August 1993). A comprehensive listing was published in Chapter 2 of the 1995-96 Federal Student Financial Aid Handbook.

For periods of enrollment beginning on or after July 23, 1992

A student who was not a high school graduate or did not have a GED at the time of enrollment must meet one of the following standards before receiving Title IV aid: (1) achieve a score specified by the Department on an independently administered ATB test approved by the Department; or (2) be considered to have the ability to benefit from the school's training in accordance with a process prescribed by the state in which the school is located.

GENERAL RULES FOR LOAN DISCHARGES BASED ON A SCHOOL'S DEFECTIVE DETERMINATION OF A STUDENT'S ATB

1. The regulations[4] require the borrower to certify, under penalty of perjury, that the school failed to determine (or improperly determined) the student's ability-to-benefit from the school's training.

2. A student may, nevertheless, be considered to have had the ability to benefit from the school's training even though the school failed to determine the student's ability or did so improperly. The regulations recognize that a student who obtains employment in the occupation for which the school's program was designed to prepare him or her has proved, on the basis of that employment, that he or she actually possessed the ability to benefit from that training, without regard to whether the school was negligent in its implementation of the Department's ATB regulations. Therefore, the borrower must further certify that the student did not secure employment in the occupation for which the school stated its program was designed to prepare the student, or if the student completed the training program, he or she either was not able to find employment in that occupation, despite a reasonable attempt, or was able to get a job in that occupation only after receiving training from another school.

3. The regulations also recognize that a student would not be regarded as having had the ability-to-benefit from the school's training, despite a school's conclusion that the student had such ability if, at the time the school certified the student's eligibility for a loan, the student would not meet the legal requirements for employment (in the student's state of residence) in the occupation for which the training program was intended because of a physical or mental condition, age, or criminal record or other reason accepted by the Secretary.[5]

QUESTIONS AND ANSWERS

No evidence

1. If a borrower asserts in a claim for discharge that the school improperly determined the student's ATB, and the borrower presents neither documentary evidence from an oversight authority nor any other information to support that claim, and the guaranty agency has no specific information about the ATB testing practices of the school the student attended, is the statement, by itself, sufficient to qualify the borrower for a false certification discharge?

In evaluating an application for discharge, a guaranty agency must consider the statements in the application together with other evidence about the testing and admission practices of the school, and inferences that can reasonably be drawn from that other evidence. Because several authorities with oversight responsibilities, including the Department, accrediting agencies, guarantors, state licensing bodies, and the school's own auditor, would typically have both the opportunity and responsibility to find and report improper ATB admission practices, the absence of any such finding in reports about a school raises an inference that no improper practices were reported because none were taking place.

A borrower's statement must be evaluated in light of such an inference and the possibility that the borrower's statement may be motivated or affected by the borrower's financial self-interest in obtaining relief from the debt. Thus, a borrower's statement that he or she (or the student, in the case of a PLUS Loan) was "falsely certified" or "improperly tested" would not ordinarily be persuasive, and would not therefore be sufficient to establish entitlement to

---

4   34 CFR 682.402(e) for the FFEL Program, and 34 CFR 685.214(c) for the William D. Ford Federal Direct Loan Program.

5   34 CFR 682.402(e)(13)(iii)(B), published November 29, 1994, and §685.214(a)(1)(iii), published December 1, 1994.

discharge, if it is not supported by some other evidence that as a result of improper ATB admissions practices, students were admitted on the basis of ATB who should not have been admitted. That supporting evidence can include a finding by an entity or organization that had oversight responsibility over the school's SFA administration or educational programs, statements or admissions by school officials with knowledge of the school's practices, or statements made by other students who attended the school that are both sufficiently detailed and consistent with each other to appear reliable. Those statements can include statements made in other claims for discharge relief.

The Department expects a guaranty agency to obtain existing documentation available from any public or private agency that reviewed or had oversight responsibility for the school. If the guaranty agency concludes that such documentation either does not exist or does not support the borrower's assertion, it becomes the responsibility of the borrower making the claim to produce persuasive evidence that would corroborate his or her allegation of improper ATB determination.

Testing violations

2. In those instances where a school used an ATB test to determine a student's eligibility, what violations of ATB testing procedures justify discharge of a borrower's loan obligation, assuming the borrower is otherwise eligible?[6]

Discharge is warranted only in those cases where the ATB test was not "administered substantially in accordance with the requirements for use of the test."[7] For periods of enrollment beginning prior to July 1, 1991, a violation of the requirements for the use of an ATB test will be considered to have occurred if the school: (1) failed to substantially comply with the school's accrediting agency standards for ATB testing; or (2) if no such accrediting agency standards existed, the school failed to substantially comply with the test publisher's requirements for the use of the test. For periods of enrollment beginning on or after July 1, 1991, compliance with the Department's ATB requirements could only be met if the ATB test was approved by the Department and was administered substantially in accordance with the test publisher's rules for the use of the test.

The following violations of the applicable testing procedures are substantial enough to invalidate the results of the test, even though the violation may not have been knowingly committed:

-A test that was required to have been administered by an independent test administrator was not administered by such an individual.

-A school permitted a student who failed an ATB test to retake the test earlier than the minimum waiting period prescribed.

-A school permitted a student who failed an ATB test to retake the test more frequently than allowed.

-A school allowed more time for students to complete their ATB tests than was permitted.

-A school considered a student to have passed an ATB test even though the student did not achieve a minimum passing score which was permissible under the statute, regulations, and Departmental guidance in effect at the time the test was given.

-The school administered only part of a multi-part test, unless giving less than the entire test was permissible under the school's accrediting agency standards.

-For ATB tests given for periods of enrollment beginning on or after July 1, 1991, the version of the test used by the school was a version not approved by the Department.

-A school supplied answers to the ATB test, or permitted students to discuss the questions among themselves, in violation of the testing rules.

3. Even though a guaranty agency determines that a school did not completely comply with

---

6   NOTE: A borrower who obtains employment in the occupation for which the school's training program was intended does not qualify for a loan discharge unless the borrower obtained employment only after receiving additional training at another school. See §682.402(e)(3)(ii)(C) and §685.214(c)(1)(iii).

7   34 CFR 682.402(e)(13)(ii)(B)(2).

the Department's ATB regulations with respect to the use of an ATB test during periods when a test was required, are there violations of those regulations that are not sufficient to justify discharge of a borrower's loan obligation because, despite those technical regulatory violations, the test was administered substantially in accordance with the requirements for use of the test? 682.402(e)(13)(ii)(B)(2).

The Department has identified three violations of an accrediting agency's or a test publisher's requirements that, in the Department's view, do not have the effect of helping the student pass the test. These violations are not substantial enough to justify loan discharge.

> -A school used photocopied versions of the ATB test.
> -A school used a version of an ATB test that was obsolete by less than one year.
> -A school used an ATB test that was approved by the U.S. Department of Education, but had not been approved by the school's accrediting agency.

Although some states have laws addressing the conditions under which postsecondary institutions may properly admit students who do not have a high school diploma or GED, violation of such state requirements does not make borrowers eligible for false certification loan discharge under §437(c) of the HEA. State ATB requirements address the institution's qualification for a state license, and not whether students attending such schools are eligible for federal aid.

Section 437(c) of the HEA provides for loan discharge where a student's eligibility to borrow was falsely certified by the school. Student eligibility to borrow under the FFEL and William D. Ford Federal Direct Loan Programs is defined by the HEA and implementing regulations, and not by state laws addressing ATB admission. The regulations implementing the false certification discharge provision provide, among other things, that a borrower is eligible for false certification discharge if he or she (or the student in the case of a PLUS Loan) did not meet the requirements for admission on the basis of ability to benefit under FEDERAL law. The regulations describe FEDERAL standards for ATB admission between 1986 and the present, and explicitly refer to the FEDERAL regulatory standards in place during those periods.

Foreign language ATB test

4. A school's program was taught entirely or substantially in English. The ATB test used by the school for periods of enrollment beginning July 1, 1991 or later was given in a language other than English. The school admitted such students who passed their non-English ATB tests. Would a non-English language ATB test given to these students be considered a valid determination of their ATB?

The answer depends on whether the student was enrolled in a program with an English as a Second Language ("ESL") component, and whether the test instrument selected by the school was appropriate. The Department has approved examinations for testing students enrolled in ESL programs, programs with an ESL component, or for testing non-native speakers of English enrolling in regular academic or vocational programs taught in English. The approved examinations expect some degree of functional literacy in English. Before selecting an appropriate test, schools are encouraged to consider whether the examinations can determine the degree of English language proficiency necessary to succeed in the student's particular program of study. Whether a particular test used by a school could appropriately be used for a non-native English speaking student depends on the scope of approval of the test. For example, some tests were approved for use if Spanish is both the student's native language and the language of instruction, while others were approved for use where the student's native language is Spanish and the language of instruction is English.

Remedial Program

5. If a school admitted students for periods of enrollment beginning during the period July 1, 1987—July 1, 1991, and the school chose the ATB option of enrolling students in a program of remedial or developmental education, what rules applied to those programs?

For a school to be considered as having complied with the ATB requirements if it chose this option,[8] the school had to ensure that the students enrolled in, and successfully completed, the institutionally prescribed program of remedial or developmental education. In addition, students had to be either: (1) counselled before admission; or (2) fail an ATB test administered by the school. Those programs may not exceed one academic year or its equivalent. [NOTE: Extensive discussions concerning remedial programs were contained in "Dear Colleague" Letters GEN-89-55, issued December 1989, and GEN-91-20, June 1991.]

Student unable to get a job

6. What documentation is required to show that a student whose ATB was improperly determined was unable to get a job in the occupation for which he or she was trained?[9]

The answer depends on whether the student completed the school's training program. If the student DID NOT COMPLETE the program, the student must simply certify that he or she did not find employment in that occupation. The student's sworn statement that he or she could not get a job in that occupation will be considered proof that the school's defective (or non-existent) determination of the student's ability-to-benefit harmed the student to the extent that a discharge is permissible.

If the student COMPLETED the school's training program, it appears that, notwithstanding the school's improper ATB determination, the student's ability to successfully comprehend the subject matter was equivalent to a student who had a high school diploma or GED. The student obtained the degree or certificate that he or she desired, and for which the loan was obtained. However, the Department's regulations recognize that it is also important to consider whether the student was able to obtain employment after completing the school's program. For this reason, the loan discharge regulations permit a discharge if the student is unable to obtain employment in the occupation for which he or she was trained by the school, despite making a "reasonable attempt" to obtain employment in that occupation.

To fairly balance the interests of the student and the federal taxpayer, the Department believes that a student who COMPLETED the school's training program and who claims that he or she was unable to obtain employment in that occupation because of the school's defective determination of his or her ATB, should be expected to provide evidence that he or she made a "reasonable attempt" to obtain employment in that occupation. Ordinarily, a person who makes a reasonable attempt to obtain employment does not limit his or her job search to only one such effort. More commonly, an individual will try several times to obtain employment in a specific occupation. Therefore, if there were no unusual circumstances faced by a specific individual, it would be reasonable for a guaranty agency to consider three separate attempts by the student to find a job as a persuasive indication of the student's good-faith effort.

The type of information about a job search that most people could readily recall would include the basic facts, such as the name and address of the employer contacted, the date the employer was contacted, the position applied for, and the reason (if any) given by the employer for not hiring the person. Other information (for example, the employer's phone number or the name or title of the person contacted) may be remembered by the student, and would support his or her claim. In situations where an employer contacted by a student routinely declined to hire individuals who were trained by the school attended by the student, a generic statement from the employer to that effect would serve as evidence of the student's reasonable attempt to obtain employment with that employer.

Student's age, mental or physical condition, or criminal record

7. Are the regulatory provisions with respect to factors such as the student's age, mental or physical condition, or criminal record applicable to all students at all schools?

Those provisions[10] apply to all categories of students at all schools, including students for

---

8   This option was not available to schools for periods of enrollment beginning on or after July 1, 1991.

9   34 CFR 682.402(e)(3)(ii)(C) and §685.214(c)(1)((iii).

10   34 CFR 682.402(e)(13)(iii)(B), published November 29, 1994, and §685.214(a)(1)(iii), published December 1, 1994.

whom the school was not required to make ability-to-benefit determinations or for whom the school made such determinations properly.

8. What documentation is required from a borrower who requests a discharge on the basis that the student's age, mental or physical condition, criminal record, or other reason accepted by the Secretary prohibited the student from meeting the requirements for employment in the student's state of residence in the occupation for which the student was trained?

The borrower must provide evidence that the student had that disqualifying status at the time of enrollment, and evidence that a STATE PROHIBITION (in the student's state of residence) against employment in that occupation based on that status also existed at the time of enrollment. However, a loan discharge is not authorized if it can be shown that the school asked the student if he or she had such a disqualifying status, but the student did not divulge that information.

9. To whom should information be sent if it is believed that a possible "other reason" (in addition to the student's age, mental or physical condition, or criminal record) should be accepted by the Secretary?

Those parties that wish to provide such information should submit it to:

Ms. Carney McCullough
Chief, General Provisions Branch
Policy, Training, and Analysis Service
Policy Development Division
U.S. Department of Education
600 Independence Avenue, S.W.
Washington, DC 20202-5345

The submitted information must include unambiguous evidence that a STATE PROHIBITION based on that "other reason" existed at the time of the student's enrollment that would prohibit employment (in the student's state of residence) in the occupation for which the student was trained.

Group discharges

10. Does the Department regard as reasonable the approval of discharges for all borrowers who fall within a specified group, for example, ATB students who enrolled in a school with serious and well-documented ATB violations that could be considered to have affected every student admitted to the school based on ATB? If so, would those borrowers still be required to complete discharge applications?

In some cases, discharge may be authorized by the Department for borrowers who demonstrate that they fall within a particular cohort of students and who are otherwise eligible for false certification discharge. Such borrowers may receive discharge without individually presenting proof of improper determination of ATB or admission. All borrowers will, however, still be required to request a discharge and sign the sworn statement prescribed by the regulations. The Department will inform guaranty agencies when it has made such a determination, and notify them of the requirements and procedures for handling such discharges as they occur.

The Department invites interested parties to notify it of such special circumstances that may justify this approach. The type of documentation described in response to question #1 will be considered if it shows that a school committed pervasive and serious violations of the Department's regulations during the time period covered by the documentation. Those parties who wish to provide such documentation should submit it to Ms. Carney McCullough, at the address given in question #9.

Suspected fraud

11. What steps should a guaranty agency take if it suspects that a borrower has made false statements on a discharge request, but the agency is unable to disprove those suspected false statements?

The agency should contact the Department's Inspector General for assistance (1-800-

MISUSED). Depending on the investigative strategy in a specific case, the agency will be advised whether it should grant the discharge.

Reporting school violations

12. The FFEL regulations [§682.402(e)(6)(i)] require a guaranty agency to notify the Department immediately whenever it becomes aware of reliable information indicating that a school may have falsely certified a student's eligibility. To what address should this notification be sent?

Guaranty agencies should notify the Guarantor and Lender Review Branch in the Department's regional office responsible for the state in which the school is located.

Former 34 CFR 668.6

13. The regulations state that for periods of enrollment beginning prior to July 1, 1987, a student's ATB was to be determined "in accordance with the requirements of 34 CFR 668.6." However, that section of the current regulations has nothing in it except the word "reserved." The text of §668.6 as it existed during the applicable time period follows:

§ 668.6. Ability to benefit.

(a) "Ability to benefit" means that a person admitted to an institution of higher education has the ability to benefit from the education or training he or she is to receive.

(b) (1) An institution that admits as regular students persons who do not have a high school diploma or the recognized equivalent of a high school diploma and who are beyond the age of compulsory school attendance in the State in which the institution is located, shall develop and consistently apply criteria for determining whether these students have the ability to benefit from the education or training offered.

(2) An institution must be able to demonstrate, upon request of the Secretary, that these students have the ability to benefit.

(Authority: 20 U.S.C. 1088, 1141)

September 1994

Summary: This letter provides guidance concerning closed school and false certification loan discharges and relief for unauthorized endorsements in the Federal Family Education Loan (FFEL) Program.

Dear Colleague:

On April 29, 1994, final regulations (effective July 1, 1994) affecting the FFEL program were published in the *Federal Register*. Sections 34 CFR 682.402(d) and (e) of those regulations prescribe the procedures for discharging the loan obligation of a borrower who received an FFEL loan on or after January 1, 1986. If the student was unable to complete his or her program of study because the school closed, or the borrower's (or the student's for whom a parent received a PLUS loan) eligibility to receive the loan was falsely certified by the school. The regulations also prescribe the procedures for providing relief for unauthorized endorsements. This letter provides guidance on implementing those regulations. Part I covers closed school loan discharges. Part II covers false certification discharges and relief for unauthorized endorsements. Part III provides guidance that applies to both types of discharges and unauthorized endorsements. Attachment A is the Department's "Cumulative List of Schools That Closed Since January 1, 1986."

The regulations give the guaranty agency initial decision-making authority on discharge claims. A formal appeal to the Department is provided under the rules only in false certification claims and unauthorized check endorsements. To review whether guarantor decisions to discharge loans comply with the regulations, the Department will use the review and audit procedures it currently uses to examine other guarantor decisions. The intent of this letter and future Department communications on this responsibility is to give guarantors an interpretation of the regulations or an explanation of the application of particular regulations to general fact patterns. In the future, more specific guidance may be given as the need arises with respect to particular schools or to specific fact patterns that come to light in litigation or otherwise.

We appreciate your assistance and cooperation as we work to implement these provisions.

Sincerely,

Leo Kornfeld
Deputy Assistant Secretary for
Student Financial Assistance Programs

Attachment
PART I *CLOSED SCHOOL DISCHARGES*

1. How is a school's closure date determined?

For purposes of the closed school discharge authorized under the regulations, a school's closure date is the date that the school ceases to provide educational instruction in all programs, as determined by the Secretary. *See* 34 CFR 682.402(d)(1)(ii)(A).

Attachment A to this letter is the "Cumulative List of Schools That Closed Since January 1, 1986." It lists the schools known by the Secretary to have closed on or after January 1, 1986. The Secretary intends to update the Cumulative List with monthly supplements as new information and corrections become available. Guaranty agencies will be responsible for using the most current information. For example, if a school's closure date is revised, guaranty agencies will be expected to use the new closure date after receiving the monthly supplement containing that correction.

For approximately two years, the Secretary has published a quarterly cumulative list of closed schools. The Secretary intends to discontinue publishing this quarterly list and give guaranty agencies and lenders access to an electronic computer database containing the information. Guaranty agencies and lenders will be able to access the computer database by modem using the telephone system, or update their records with the printed monthly supplements. Additional details will be provided at a later date.

2. What should guaranty agencies and lenders do with the listings of closed schools published by the Department?

Guaranty agencies and lenders should review Attachment A and the subsequent lists of closed schools and notify the Department's Closed School Section immediately at (202) 401-3462 if corrections are necessary or information is missing. If the guaranty agency receives documentation that it believes will affect the Secretary's determination of a school's closure date, it should notify the Closed School Section. Evidence indicating that a school's closure date may be incorrect may include a letter from the school or state licensing agency, or a newspaper article. The Secretary will determine whether the closure date needs to be revised. In the meantime, the guaranty agency should suspend collection activity on the loan until a determination is made by the Secretary.

It is important that the Department has the correct name, address, OPE-ID number, and closure date for each school, and that all schools are listed (including unauthorized branches and locations). Unless the Department has complete and accurate information, potentially qualifying borrowers may be prevented from receiving loan discharges, and ineligible borrowers may receive discharges to which they are not entitled. Any comments, corrections, or additions to the Cumulative List, or other information regarding closed schools, should be sent to: U.S. Department of Education, Closed School Section, P.O. Box 23800, L'Enfant Plaza Station, Washington, DC 20026, telephone number (202)708-6048.

Within 30 days of receiving confirmation of the date of a school's closure by means of Attachment A or a supplemental listing of closed schools from the Department, or confirmation of a school's closure date by any other means, a guaranty agency must review its records and identify borrowers who appear to be eligible for a closed school loan discharge. After the eligible borrowers have been identified, the guaranty agency must follow the notification procedures prescribed in § 682.402(d)(6).

3. What should a guaranty agency do when it is notified of a revised school closure date by the Department?

A guaranty agency must review its records to identify any borrower who received a loan discharge from that agency based on the former closure date. If the revised closure date is less than 90 days later than the closure date on which discharge decisions were made for individuals who claimed to have been in attendance on that earlier closure date, the guarantor can deem those students to have withdrawn within the qualifying 90-day pre-closure period and need not revise those decisions or demand additional information from the borrowers to confirm the discharge previously granted. For individuals who claim to have withdrawn within that 90-day period and received discharges on that basis, the agency must redetermine the borrowers' eligibility based on the new date. Within 30 days after making a determination that a previously discharged borrower does not qualify for a discharge based on the revised closure date, the agency should notify the borrower of the reasons for that determination. The agency must advise the borrower that he or she remains obligated to repay the loan, warn the borrower of the consequences of default, and explain that the borrower will be considered to be in default on the loan unless the borrower submits a written statement to the agency within 30 days stating that the borrower acknowledges the debt and, if payments are due, will begin or resume making those payments.

The Department derives the information on which it sets or revises the closure date from the most authoritative sources available, and it is unlikely that the borrower would have more reliable information about the date of the school's closure. However, because the guarantor must explain to the borrower the reasons for any reconsideration decision denying a discharge or revoking one previously given, the borrower will be able to contest that decision before being considered to be in default. If the borrower presents evidence that the guarantor considers sufficient to warrant changing the closure date, the guarantor can defer action on the loan with respect to that debtor, and should present that evidence, with its recommendation, to the Department.

Within 30 days after receiving the borrower's written statement, if the loan had been filed as a closed school claim by a lender, the agency shall treat the loan as a repurchase by the lender and return the claim file to the lender. The amount owed by the borrower will be the sum of the claim amount previously paid to the lender plus the amount of payments refunded to the borrower by the guaranty agency when it paid the claim. The lender should be instructed to resume collection efforts if payments are due. If the borrower fails to acknowledge the debt within 30 days, the agency shall consider the borrower to be in default. If the loan had been held by the agency as a defaulted loan when it was discharged, the agency should once again treat the loan as a defaulted loan owed by the borrower (including any refunded payments) to the agency. The lender or agency shall be deemed to have exercised forbearance of payment of principal and interest from the date collection activity had been suspended, and may capitalize, in accordance with § 682.202(b), any interest accrued and not paid during that period.

If an agency discovers that a borrower may have made a false certification on an application for a loan discharge, it should follow normal procedures for reporting cases of suspected fraud by contacting the Department's Office of Inspector General.

4. Does a borrower or student who attended a branch location ineligible under the Title IV programs potentially qualify for a closed school discharge?

For purposes of closed school loan discharges, a "school" means a school's main campus or any location or branch of the main campus, regardless of whether the school or its location or branch is considered eligible. *See* § 682.402(d)(1)(ii)(C). The Secretary will list closure dates for schools or locations that received funds under Title IV of the Higher Education Act, even though the school or location may have been ineligible for any of a variety of reasons, or because the location was never approved by the Secretary. In publicizing the closure date, the Secretary will use the OPE-ID number of the funding school as the OPE-ID number for ineligible locations.

5. Does a borrower or student who claims a last day of attendance that is more than 90 days prior to the school's closure date qualify for discharge?

Unless an exception has been made (see question 6), the guaranty agency should deny the claim and state the specific reasons for the denial.

6. How can a guaranty agency obtain an extension from the Department to the 90-day limit on the pre-closure withdrawal period?

The regulations provide that the Secretary may extend the 90-day period to allow a longer time period for discharge if the Secretary determines that exceptional circumstances related to a school's closing would justify an extension. Guaranty agencies that believe that exceptional circumstances justify an extension for a particular school should request an extension by contracting the Department's Closed School Section at the address previously provided. In its request, the guaranty agency should present facts it believes would justify an extension, and make whatever recommendation it deems appropriate. The Secretary will then decide whether to extend the 90-day timeframe, and notify all guaranty agencies if he determines that an extension is warranted.

7. Does a borrower or student who did not complete the program but received a diploma or a certificate qualify for discharge?

Before closing, some schools may have issued a diploma or certificate to students who did not complete the program of study. The issuance of a diploma to a student who did not complete the training program will not disqualify the borrower for discharge if the other requirements for discharge are satisfied.

8. What is a student completed the program but the school did not issue a diploma or certificate?

If a student completed the program, the issuance of a diploma or certificate is irrelevant. A borrower is eligible for a loan discharge only if the student was unable to complete a program of study.

9. How does a guaranty agency submit a request for reinsurance and report closed school activity to the Department?

The guaranty agency files a reinsurance request and reports closed school activity to the Department by using the revised Guaranty Agency Quarterly/Annual Report (ED Form 1130) and Guaranty Agency Monthly Claims and Collections Report (ED Form 1189). For guidance on completing these forms, please refer to "Dear Guaranty Agency Director" Letters 93-G-234 (June 1993), 94-G-250 (January 1994), and 94-G-253 (June 1994).

PART II *FALSE CERTIFICATION DISCHARGE AND RELIEF FOR UNAUTHORIZED ENDORSEMENTS*

10. If a borrower (or student) claims that he or she did not sign the application, promissory note, loan check, or electronic funds transfer authorization, how does a guaranty agency determine if the borrower's allegation is valid?

The agency should carefully compare the contested signature(s) with the examples of signatures submitted by the borrower in accordance with § 682.402(e)(3)(iii) or (lv), and to the best of the agency's ability decide if the preponderance of evidence supports the borrower's assertion.

11. What sources of information or evidence should a guaranty agency investigate, and what actions should it take in the case of a claim for relief based on the borrower's (or student's) assertion that he or she die not sign the loan check or electronic funds transfer authorization?

If the borrower presents evidence that the guarantor finds to be credible showing that the borrower did not endorse the loan check or authorize the EFT disbursements,the guarantor must determine whether the student or borrower nevertheless received the disbursement either directly or through a credit satisfying a school charge actually due an owed by the student [*i.e.*, the tuition and other charges net of any refund owed the student]. To make that judgment, the guarantor must consider relevant evidence in its possession and other information that may be available from other sources. These sources include, in the first instance, the school records pertaining to the student's account, which may be available from State agency record custodians if not from the school itself. Where the guarantor is presented with a claim by a lender, the lender should have presented with the claim evidence to support the contention that the student received the proceeds. A guaranty agency should contact the school, the Department's regional office, the school's state licensing agency, and any other party that the guaranty agency has reason to believe would have relevant evidence and attempt to obtain documentation to show whether the student or borrower received the proceeds of the loan.

Whether the guarantor's review of evidence presented by the lender or secured by its own efforts leads it to conclude that is more probable, based on that evidence or lack of evidence, that the borrower or student did not receive the proceeds of such a disbursement, the guarantor must conclude that the loan is not enforceable, and take the actions prescribed in the regulations to give relief to the borrower and to effect the return of funds paid by the Department with respect to that loan to the lender and to the guarantor.

12. If a borrower's application for a false certification loan discharge was denied by a guaranty agency, and the borrower appeals the agency's decision to the Secretary, to what address should the guaranty agency forward the borrower's request?

Appeals should be forwarded to: U.S. Department of Education, P.O. Box 422037, San Francisco, California 94142-2037. The appeal must be clearly identified as a "false certification appeal" and must contain all the information and documentation examined by the agency when making its determination. The Department representatives in San Francisco will acknowledge receipt of the appeal to the guaranty agency and respond to the appeal request promptly. Until the appeal request is acted upon and a final decision made by the Department, the guaranty agency should cease all collections activity on the account.

13. How should guaranty agencies evaluate a borrower's claim for loan discharge based upon an alleged failure of the school to properly apply ability-to-benefit (ATB) provisions at the time the student was admitted?

Because of the complexity created by the various statutory and regulatory changes to the ATB requirements over the period covered by the false certification provisions of the regulations, the Department is still developing specific guidance which can be used by guaranty agencies to determine the validity of ATB false certification claims by borrowers seeking discharge of their FFEL loans. We will provide more detailed guidance about these ATB requirements (including guidance about what constitutes improper ATB testing) within the next few weeks.

PART III *GENERAL*

14. Will the Department provide a standardized application form for borrowers to use to request a closed school (or false certification) discharge?

The Department is developing application forms for closed school and false certification student loan discharges for loans held by the Department. The Ad Hoc Standardization Committee, which is composed of members representing the Department and the student aid community, is developing standardized application forms for use by other entities holding FFEL Program loans eligible for discharge. The Department expects he forms to be available soon. Until forms are available, the Department encourages lenders and guaranty agencies either to develop and use their own forms, or to inform applicants of the regulatory requirements for discharge so that they can submit discharge requests without using application forms. A guaranty agency or lender may use one application for all discharges, or one application for closed school discharges and another for false certification discharges. Guaranty agencies must ensure that their discharge request/application forms require the borrower to provide the information and certifications specified in the regulations. Agencies using their own forms must submit them to the Department's FFEL Policy Section for review in accordance with 34 CFR 682.401(d).

The guaranty agency or lender must evaluate all discharge requests submitted by borrowers regardless of whether standardized forms are developed to determine if the applicants meet the regulatory requirements for discharge, and guarantors must ensure that sufficient information and supporting documents are secured to demonstrate whether the borrower qualifies for discharge.

15. What amount of a Federal Consolidation Loan is dischargeable?

The Federal Consolidation Loan is not itself dischargeable, but the Consolidation Loan proceeds used to pay off a loan that qualified for discharge are refunded to the borrower by means of a credit to the Consolidation Loan. The amount of the credit is the amount dischargeable on the FFEL Program loans paid off by the Consolidation Loan.

16. Is a payment history necessary to apply a discharge credit to a Federal Consolidation Loan?

Payment histories are necessary to determine that portion of the Consolidation Loan that was disbursed to pay off the discharged loan(s), and whether other payments were made reducing the discharged loan balance prior to the payoff from the Consolidation Loan. If the payment histories are not available from the prior lenders, the current lender must make reasonable attempts to obtain the information from other sources. If the lender is unable to obtain a payment history from other sources, the borrower will be required to submit evidence of payments made on the loan prior to the date of the Consolidation Loan. All payments made by the borrower on the old loan before that date are included in determining the discharge amount applied to the remaining balance of the Consolidation Loan. Post-consolidation interest should be calculated by the lender based on the balance of the closed school loan at the time the Consolidation Loan was made.

17. How should a discharge credit be applied to a Federal Consolidation Loan?

The total discharge credit amount shall fist be applied to reduce the outstanding balance of the Consolidation loan. If the entire outstanding Consolidation Loan balance is repaid by the discharge credit, any difference is returned to the borrower.

18. If the borrower fails to submit the written request and sworn statement within 60 days of being notified of this requirement, what action should the lender or guaranty agency take?

The lender or guaranty agency should resume collection activity on the loan. If the borrower submits the written request and sworn statement at a later date, the lender or guaranty agency must suspend collection activity and review the borrower's request. A borrowers' request for discharge may not be denied solely on the basis of failing to meet any time limits set by the lender, the guaranty agency, of the Department.

19. What should a lender do if a borrower's request for discharge is incomplete or contains information that would clearly make the borrower ineligible for the discharge?

The lender should not submit a claim to a guaranty agency, and must inform the borrower of the reasons why the borrower's request is inadequate within 30 days of the date the lender received the borrower's request. *See* § 682.208(c)(l). Some reasons will be more obvious than others, for example, the borrower's loan was disbursed before January 1, 1986. Because the eligibility requirements for a false certification discharge typically depend on information not generally known by the lender, it is likely that lenders will be unable to readily determine whether a borrower's request for a false certification discharge is insufficient unless the borrower's sworn statement is incomplete. In all cases where the borrower appears to meet the eligibility requirements described in the regulations, the lender must file a claim with the guaranty agency no later than 60 days after the lender received the borrower's written request and sworn statement or after the lender is notified by the Secretary or the Secretary's designee or by the guaranty agency to file a claim.

20. Can a loan that does not qualify for federal reinsurance be discharged?

Legally enforceable loans that have lost reinsurance, because of a violation of due diligence or other programmatic requirements by the lender or guaranty agency, are generally eligible for discharge if the borrower meets all of the requirements for a discharge. In such cases, the Secretary will use his authority pursuant to § 682.406(b) to waive his right to refuse to make a reinsurance payment on the loan.

Student Assistance Forms

The Department of Education prints forms for the various discharge programs as well as loan and deferment applications. Most of these forms are available on the Department's web site at http://www.ed.gov. Selected forms are reprinted below. Advocates should note that many state guaranty agencies prefer that borrowers use their discharge forms instead of the federal forms printed below. State guaranty agency forms are available from the individual agencies and are not reprinted here.

D.1 Discharge Forms

D.1.1 Closed School

LOAN DISCHARGE APPLICATION: SCHOOL CLOSURE

Federal Family Education Loan Program / William D. Ford Federal Direct Loan Program / Federal Perkins Loan Program

OMB No. 1845-0015
Form Approved
Exp. Date 06/30/2005

WARNING: Any person who knowingly makes a false statement or misrepresentation on this form or on any accompanying documents will be subject to penalties which may include fines, imprisonment or both, under the U.S. Criminal Code and 20 U.S.C. 1097.

SECTION 1: BORROWER IDENTIFICATION

Please enter or correct the following information. If a correction, check this box: ☐

SSN |___|___|___|–|___|___|–|___|___|___|___|

Name _____

Address _____

City, State, Zip _____

Telephone - Home (   ) _____

Telephone - Other (   ) _____

E-mail address (optional) _____

SECTION 2: STUDENT INFORMATION

Before responding, carefully read the entire form, including the instructions and other information on the following page. If you are a student borrower applying for loan discharge, begin with Item 3. If you are a parent borrower applying for a PLUS loan discharge, begin with Item 1.

1. Student's name (last, first, middle initial): _____

2. Student's SSN: |___|___|___|–|___|___|–|___|___|___|___|

3. Closed school's name: _____

4. Date school closed (if known): |___|___|–|___|___|–|___|___|___|___|

5. Closed school's address (street, city, state, zip): _____

6. Dates of attendance at the closed school: From |___|___|–|___|___|–|___|___|___|___| To |___|___|–|___|___|–|___|___|___|___|

7. Name of the program of study that you (or, for PLUS borrowers, the student) were enrolled in at the time the school closed: _____

8. Did you (or, for PLUS borrowers, the student) complete the program of study at the closed school? ☐ Yes   ☐ No
   If No, check all reasons that apply:
   ☐ The school closed while you (or, for PLUS borrowers, the student) were still enrolled.
   ☐ You (or, for PLUS borrowers, the student) withdrew from the school on: |___|___|–|___|___|–|___|___|___|___|
   ☐ You (or, for PLUS borrowers, the student) were on a approved leave of absence when the school closed:
   From |___|___|–|___|___|–|___|___|___|___| To |___|___|–|___|___|–|___|___|___|___|

   ☐ Other (please explain): _____

9. Did you (or, for PLUS borrowers, the student) complete the program of study or a comparable program of study at another school?
   ☐ Yes   ☐ No   If Yes, skip Item 10 and answer Items 11 and 12. If No, continue with Item 10.

10. Are you (or, for PLUS borrowers, the student) in the process of completing the program of study or a comparable program of study at another school?
    ☐ Yes   ☐ No   If Yes, answer Items 11 and 12. If No, skip to Item 13.

11. Did the other school give you (or, for PLUS borrowers, the student) credit for training received at the closed school by allowing transfer of credits or hours earned at the closed school, or by any other means? ☐ Yes   ☐ No

12. Were you (or, for PLUS borrowers, the student) required to start the program of study over from the beginning at the other school?
    ☐ Yes   ☐ No

13. Did the holder of your loan receive any money back (a refund) from the school on your behalf? ☐ Yes   ☐ No   ☐ Don't Know
    If yes, give the amount and explain why the money was refunded: _____

14. Did you (or, for PLUS borrowers, the student) make any monetary claim with, or receive any payment from, the school or any third party (see definition in Section 5) in connection with enrollment or attendance at the school: ☐ Yes   ☐ No   ☐ Don't Know   If yes, please provide the following information:
    (a) Name/address/telephone number of the party with whom the claim was made or from whom payment was received:

    _____

    (b) Amount/status of claim: _____   (c) Amount of payment received: $ _____
                                                              (Write "none" if no payment was received.)

SECTION 3: BORROWER CERTIFICATION

My signature below certifies that I have read and agree to the terms and conditions that apply to this loan discharge, as specified in Section 6 on the following page. Under penalty of perjury, I certify that all of the information I have provided on this form and in any accompanying documentation is true and accurate to the best of my knowledge and belief.

Borrower's Signature: _____   Date: _____

SECTION 4: INSTRUCTIONS FOR COMPLETING THE FORM

Type or print using dark ink. For all dates, give month, day (if known), and year. Show dates as MM-DD-YYYY (for example, "January 31, 2002" = "01-31-2002"). If you need more space to answer any of the items, continue on separate sheets of paper and attach them to this form. Indicate the number of the item(s) you are answering and include your name and social security number (SSN) on all attached pages.

Send the completed form and any attachments to the address in Section 8.

SECTION 5: DEFINITIONS

- The **Federal Family Education Loan (FFEL) Program** includes Federal Stafford Loans (both subsidized and unsubsidized), Federal Supplemental Loans for Students (SLS), Federal PLUS Loans, and Federal Consolidation Loans.
- The **William D. Ford Federal Direct Loan (Direct Loan) Program** includes Federal Direct Stafford/Ford Loans (Direct Subsidized Loans), Federal Direct Unsubsidized Stafford/Ford Loans (Direct Unsubsidized Loans), Federal Direct PLUS Loans (Direct PLUS Loans), and Federal Direct Consolidation Loans (Direct Consolidation Loans).
- The **Federal Perkins Loan (Perkins Loan) Program** includes Federal Perkins Loans and National Direct Student Loans (NDSL).
- The **date a school closed** is the date that the school stoped providing educational instruction in **all programs**, as determined by the U.S. Department of Education (the Department).
- The **holder** of a borrower's FFEL Program loan(s) may be a lender, a guaranty agency, or the Department. The holder of a borrower's Direct Loan Program loan(s) is the Department. The holder of a borrower's Perkins Loan Program loan(s) may be the Department or a school.
- **Loan discharge** due to school closure cancels the obligation of a borrower (and endorser, if applicable) to repay the remaining balance on a FFEL Program, Direct Loan Program, or Perkins Loan Program loan, and qualifies the borrower for reimbursement of any amounts paid voluntarily or through forced collection on the loan. For consolidation loans, only the amount of the underlying loans (the loans that were consolidated) that were used to pay for the program of study listed in Item 7 will be considered for discharge. The loan holder reports the discharge to all credit reporting agencies to which the holder previously reported the status of the loan.
- The **student** refers to the student for whom a parent borrower obtained a Federal PLUS Loan or Direct PLUS Loan.
- **Dates of attendance:** The "to" date means the last date that you (or, for PLUS borrowers, the student) actually attended the closed school.
- **Program of study** means the instructional program leading to a degree or certificate in which you (or, for PLUS borrowers, the student) were enrolled.
- **Third party** refers to any entity that may provide reimbursement for a refund owed by the school, such as a tuition recovery program or performance bond.

SECTION 6: TERMS AND CONDITIONS FOR LOAN DISCHARGE

- I received FFEL Program, Direct Loan Program, or Perkins Loan Program loan funds on or after January 1, 1986, to attend (or, if I am a PLUS borrower, for the student to attend) the school identified as "closed school" in Section 2 of this form. Those funds were either received by me directly, or applied as a credit to the amount owed to the school. I (or, if I am a PLUS borrower, the student) was enrolled at that school or on an approved leave of absence on the date that it closed, or withdrew from the school not more than 90 days before it closed (or longer if authorized by the Department). Due to the school's closure, I (or, if I am a PLUS borrower, the student) did not complete the program of study at that school. I (or, if I am a PLUS borrower, the student) did not complete and am not in the process of completing that program of study or a comparable program at another school by transferring credits or hours earned at the closed school to another school, or by any other means by which I (or, if I am a PLUS borrower, the student) benefited from the training provided by the closed school.
- I will provide, upon request, testimony, a sworn statement, or other documentation reasonably available to me that demonstrates to the satisfaction of the Department or its designee that I meet the qualifications for loan discharge based on school closure, or that supports any representation that I made on this form or on any accompanying documents.
- I agree to cooperate with the Department or its designee regarding any enforcement actions related to my request for loan discharge.
- I understand that my request for loan discharge may be denied, or my discharge may be revoked, if I fail to provide testimony, a sworn statement, or documentation upon request, or if I provide testimony, a sworn statement, or documentation that does not support the material representations I have made, or if I (or, if I am a PLUS borrower, the student) completed or am in the process of completing the program of study or a comparable program at another school through transfer of credits or hours from the closed school or by any other means by which I (or, if I am a PLUS borrower, the student) benefited from the training provided by the closed school.
- I further understand that if my loan(s) is discharged based on any false, fictitious, or fraudulent statements that I knowingly made on this form or on any accompanying documents, I may be subject to civil and criminal penalties under applicable federal law.
- I hereby assign and transfer to the Department any right to a refund on the discharged loan(s) that I may have from the school identified in Section 2 of this form and/or any owners, affiliates, or assigns of the school, and from any third party that may pay claims for a refund because of the actions of the school, up to the amounts discharged by the Department on my loan(s).

SECTION 7: IMPORTANT NOTICES

Privacy Act Notice: The Privacy Act of 1974 (5 U.S.C. 552a) requires that the following notice be provided to you:

The authorities for collecting the requested information from and about you are §428(b)(2)(A) *et seq.* §451 *et seq.* and §461 *et seq.* of the Higher Education Act of 1965, as amended (20 U.S.C. 1078(b)(2)(a) *et seq.* 20 U.S.C. 1087a *et seq.* and 20 U.S.C. 1087aa *et seq.*) and the authority for collecting and using your Social Security Number (SSN) is §484(a)(4) of the HEA (20 U.S.C. 1091(a)(4)). Participating in the Federal Family Education Loan (FFEL) Program, the William D. Ford Federal Direct Loan (Direct Loan) Program, or the Federal Perkins Loan (Perkins Loan) Program and giving us your SSN are voluntary, but you must provide the requested information, including your SSN, to participate.

The principal purposes for collecting the information on this form, including your SSN, are to verify your identity, to determine your eligibility to receive a loan or a benefit on a loan (such as a deferment, forbearance, discharge, or forgiveness) under the FFEL, Direct Loan and/or Perkins Loan Programs, to permit the servicing of your loan(s), and, if it becomes necessary, to locate you and to collect on your loan(s) if your loan(s) become delinquent or in default. We also use your SSN as an account identifier and to permit you to access your account information electronically.

The information in your file may be disclosed to third parties as authorized under routine uses in the appropriate systems of records. The routine uses of this information include its disclosure to federal, state, or local agencies, to other federal agencies under computer matching programs, to agencies that we authorize to assist us in administering our loan programs, to private parties such as relatives, present and former employers, business and personal associates, to credit bureau organizations, to educational institutions, and to contractors in order to verify your identity, to determine your eligibility to receive a loan or a benefit on a loan, to permit the servicing or collection of your loan(s), to counsel you in repayment efforts, to enforce the terms of the loan(s), to investigate possible fraud and to verify compliance with federal student financial aid program regulations, or to locate you if you become delinquent in your loan payments or if you default, to provide default rate calculations, to provide financial aid history information, to assist program administrators with tracking refunds and cancellations, or to provide a standardized method for educational institutions efficiently to submit student enrollment status.

In the event of litigation, we may send records to the Department of Justice, a court, adjudicative body, counsel, party, or witness if the disclosure is relevant and necessary to the litigation. If this information, either alone or with other information, indicates a potential violation of law, we may send it to the appropriate authority for action. We may send information to members of Congress if you ask them to help you with federal student aid questions. In circumstances involving employment complaints, grievances, or disciplinary actions, we may disclose relevant records to adjudicate or investigate the issues. If provided for by a collective bargaining agreement, we may disclose records to a labor organization recognized under 5 U.S.C. Chapter 71. Disclosures may also be made to qualified researchers under Privacy Act safeguards.

Paperwork Reduction Notice: According to the Paperwork Reduction Act of 1995, no persons are required to respond to a collection of information unless it displays a currently valid OMB control number. The valid OMB control number for this information collection is 1845-0015. The time required to complete this information collection is estimated to average 0.5 hours (30 minutes) per response, including the time to review instructions, search existing data resources, gather and maintain the data needed, and complete and review the information collection. *If you have any comments concerning the accuracy of the time estimate(s) or suggestions for improving this form, please write to:* U.S. Department of Education, Washington, DC 20202-4651

If you have any questions regarding the status of *your individual submission* of this form, contact your loan holder (see Section 8).

SECTION 8: WHERE TO SEND THE COMPLETED LOAN DISCHARGE APPLICATION

Send the completed loan discharge application and any attachments to:

(If no address is shown, return to your loan holder.)

If you need help completing this form, call:

D.1.2 False Certification: Ability to Benefit

LOAN DISCHARGE APPLICATION:
FALSE CERTIFICATION OF ABILITY TO BENEFIT

Federal Family Education Loan Program / William D. Ford Federal Direct Loan Program

OMB No. 1845-0015
Form Approved
Exp. Date 06/30/2005

WARNING: Any person who knowingly makes a false statement or misrepresentation on this form or on any accompanying documents will be subject to penalties which may include fines, imprisonment or both, under the U.S. Criminal Code and 20 U.S.C. 1097.

SECTION 1: BORROWER IDENTIFICATION

Please enter or correct the following information. If a correction, check this box: ☐

SSN |___|___|___|–|___|___|–|___|___|___|___|

Name _____

Address _____

City, State, Zip _____

Telephone - Home (   ) _____

Telephone - Other (   ) _____

E-mail address (optional) _____

SECTION 2: STUDENT INFORMATION

Before responding, carefully read the entire form, including the instructions and other information on the following page. If you are a student borrower applying for loan discharge, begin with Item 3. If you are a parent borrower applying for a PLUS loan discharge, begin with Item 1.

1. Student's name (last, first, middle initial): _____

2. Student's SSN: |___|___|___|–|___|___|–|___|___|___|___|

3. School's name: _____

4. School's address (street, city, state, zip): _____

5. Dates of attendance at school: From |___|___|–|___|___|–|___|___|___|___| To |___|___|–|___|___|–|___|___|___|___|

6. Name of program of study that you (or, for PLUS borrowers, the student) were enrolled in: _____

7. Did you (or, for PLUS borrowers, the student) have a high school diploma or GED at the time of enrollment at the school?
    ☐ Yes   ☐ No   *NOTE: If Yes, you are not eligible for a loan discharge based on false certification of ability to benefit.*

8. Did you (or, for PLUS borrowers, the student) receive a GED before completing the program of study at the school?
    ☐ Yes   ☐ No   If Yes date GED received: |___|___|–|___|___|–|___|___|___|___|

9. Before you (or, for PLUS borrowers, the student) were admitted to the school, did the school give any kind of entrance examination to test your (or, for PLUS borrowers, the student's) ability to benefit from the program of study listed in Item 6?
    ☐ Yes   ☐ No   ☐ Don't Know   If No or Don't Know, go to Item 10.
    (a) Give the date of the test if you know it: (b) Give the name of the test if you know it: (c) Give the score on the test if you know it:
    |___|___|–|___|___|–|___|___|___|___|

    (d) Did anything appear improper about the way the test was given or scored?   ☐ Yes   ☐ No
    If Yes, explain in detail what appeared improper, and provide the name, telephone number and address of anyone who can support your statement (if you need more space, see the instructions in Section 4): _____

10. Did you (or, for PLUS borrowers, the student) complete a developmental or remedial program at the school?
    ☐ Yes   ☐ No   ☐ Don't Know   If Yes, list the program name, dates, courses, and grades earned: _____

11. Did the holder of your loan receive any money back (a refund) from the school on your behalf?   ☐ Yes   ☐ No   ☐ Don't Know
    If Yes, give the amount and explain why the money was refunded: _____

12. Did you (or, for PLUS borrowers, the student) make any monetary claim with or receive any payment from the school or any third party (see definition in Section 5) in connection with enrollment or attendance at the school?   ☐ Yes   ☐ No   ☐ Don't Know   If Yes, please provide the following information:
    (a) Name/address/telephone number of the party with whom the claim was made or from whom payment was received:
    _____

    (b) Amount/status of claim: _____   (c) Amount of payment received: $ _____
                                                       (Write "none" if no payment was received.)

SECTION 3: BORROWER CERTIFICATION

My signature below certifies that I have read and agree to the terms and conditions that apply to this loan discharge, as specified in Section 6 on the following page. Under penalty of perjury, I certify that all of the information I have provided on this form and in any accompanying documentation is true and accurate to the best of my knowledge and belief.

Borrower's Signature: _____   Date: _____

SECTION 4: INSTRUCTIONS FOR COMPLETING THE FORM

Type or print using dark ink. For all dates, give month, day (if known), and year. Show dates as MM-DD-YYYY (for example, "January 31, 2002" = "01-31-2002"). If you need more space to answer any of the items, continue on separate sheets of paper and attach them to this form. Indicate the number of the item(s) you are answering and include your name and social security number (SSN) on all attached pages.

Send the completed form and any attachments to the address in Section 8.

SECTION 5: DEFINITIONS

- The **Federal Family Education Loan (FFEL) Program** includes Federal Stafford Loans (both subsidized and unsubsidized), Federal Supplemental Loans for Students (SLS), Federal PLUS Loans, and Federal Consolidation Loans.
- The **William D. Ford Federal Direct Loan (Direct Loan) Program** includes Federal Direct Stafford/Ford Loans (Direct Subsidized Loans), Federal Direct Unsubsidized Stafford/Ford Loans (Direct Unsubsidized Loans), Federal Direct PLUS Loans (Direct PLUS Loans), and Federal Direct Consolidation Loans (Direct Consolidation Loans).
- The **holder** of a borrower's FFEL Program loan(s) may be a lender, a guaranty agency, or the U.S. Department of Education (the Department). The holder of a borrower's Direct Loan Program loan(s) is the Department.
- **Loan discharge** due to false certification of ability to benefit cancels the obligation of a borrower (and endorser, if applicable) to repay the remaining balance on a FFEL Program or Direct Loan Program loan, and qualifies the borrower for reimbursement of any amounts paid voluntarily or through forced collection on the loan. For consolidation loans, only the amount of the underlying loans (the loans that were consolidated) that were used to pay for the program of study listed in Item 6 will be considered for discharge. The loan holder reports the discharge to all credit reporting agencies to which the holder previously reported the status of the loan.
- The **student** refers to the student for whom a parent borrower obtained a Federal PLUS Loan or Direct PLUS Loan.
- **Program of study** means the instructional program leading to a degree or certificate in which you (or, for PLUS borrowers, the student) were enrolled.
- **Third party** refers to any entity that may provide reimbursement for a refund owed by the school, such as a tuition recovery program or performance bond.

SECTION 6: TERMS AND CONDITIONS FOR LOAN DISCHARGE

- I received FFEL Program or Direct Loan Program loan funds on or after January 1, 1986, to attend (or, if I am a PLUS borrower, for the student to attend) the school identified in Section 2 of this form. Those funds were either received by me directly, or applied as a credit to the amount owed to the school.
- I will provide, upon request, testimony, a sworn statement, or other documentation reasonably available to me that demonstrates to the satisfaction of the Department or its designee that I meet the qualifications for loan discharge based on false certification of ability to benefit, or that supports any representation that I made on this form or on any accompanying documents.
- I agree to cooperate with the Department or its designee regarding any enforcement actions related to my request for loan discharge.
- I understand that my request for loan discharge may be denied, or my discharge may be revoked, if I fail to provide testimony, a sworn statement, or documentation upon request, or if I provide testimony, a sworn statement, or documentation that does not support the material representations I have made on this form or on any accompanying documents.
- I further understand that if my loan(s) is discharged based on any false, fictitious, or fraudulent statements that I knowingly made on this form or on any accompanying documents, I may be subject to civil and criminal penalties under applicable federal law.
- I hereby assign and transfer to the Department any right to a refund on the discharged loan(s) that I may have from the school identified in Section 2 of this form and/or any owners, affiliates, or assigns of the school, and from any third party that may pay claims for a refund because of the actions of the school, up to the amounts discharged by the Department on my loan(s).

SECTION 7: IMPORTANT NOTICES

Privacy Act Notice: The Privacy Act of 1974 (5 U.S.C. 552a) requires that the following notice be provided to you:

The authorities for collecting the requested information from and about you are §428(b)(2)(A) *et seq.* and §451 *et seq.* of the Higher Education Act of 1965, as amended (20 U.S.C. 1078(b)(2)(a) *et seq.* and 20 U.S.C. 1087a *et seq.*) and the authority for collecting and using your Social Security Number (SSN) is §484(a)(4) of the HEA (20 U.S.C. 1091(a)(4). Participating in the Federal Family Education Loan (FFEL) Program or the William D. Ford Federal Direct Loan (Direct Loan) Program and giving us your SSN are voluntary, but you must provide the requested information, including your SSN, to participate.

The principal purposes for collecting the information on this form, including your SSN, are to verify your identity, to determine your eligibility to receive a loan or a benefit on a loan (such as a deferment, forbearance, discharge, or forgiveness) under the FFEL and/or Direct Loan Programs, to permit the servicing of your loan(s), and, if it becomes necessary, to locate you and to collect on your loan(s) if your loan(s) become delinquent or in default. We also use your SSN as an account identifier and to permit you to access your account information electronically.

The information in your file may be disclosed to third parties as authorized under routine uses in the appropriate systems of records. The routine uses of this information include its disclosure to federal, state, or local agencies, to other federal agencies under computer matching programs, to agencies that we authorize to assist us in administering our loan programs, to private parties such as relatives, present and former employers, business and personal associates, to credit bureau organizations, to educational institutions, and to contractors in order to verify your identity, to determine your eligibility to receive a loan or a benefit on a loan, to permit the servicing or collection of your loan(s), to counsel you in repayment efforts, to enforce the terms of the loan(s), to investigate possible fraud and to verify compliance with federal student financial aid program regulations, or to locate you if you become delinquent in your loan payments or if you default, to provide default rate calculations, to provide financial aid history information, to assist program administrators with tracking refunds and cancellations, or to provide a standardized method for educational institutions efficiently to submit student enrollment status.

In the event of litigation, we may send records to the Department of Justice, a court, adjudicative body, counsel, party, or witness if the disclosure is relevant and necessary to the litigation. If this information, either alone or with other information, indicates a potential violation of law, we may send it to the appropriate authority for action. We may send information to members of Congress if you ask them to help you with federal student aid questions. In circumstances involving employment complaints, grievances, or disciplinary actions, we may disclose relevant records to adjudicate or investigate the issues. If provided for by a collective bargaining agreement, we may disclose records to a labor organization recognized under 5 U.S.C. Chapter 71. Disclosures may also be made to qualified researchers under Privacy Act safeguards.

Paperwork Reduction Notice: According to the Paperwork Reduction Act of 1995, no persons are required to respond to a collection of information unless it displays a currently valid OMB control number. The valid OMB control number for this information collection is 1845-0015. The time required to complete this information collection is estimated to average 0.5 hours (30 minutes) per response, including the time to review instructions, search existing data resources, gather and maintain the data needed, and complete and review the information collection. *If you have any comments concerning the accuracy of the time estimate(s) or suggestions for improving this form, please write to:* U.S. Department of Education, Washington, DC 20202-4651

If you have any questions regarding the status of *your individual submission* of this form, contact your loan holder (see Section 8).

SECTION 8: WHERE TO SEND THE COMPLETED LOAN DISCHARGE APPLICATION

Send the completed loan discharge application and any attachments to:

(If no address is shown, return to your loan holder.)

If you need help completing this form, call:

D.1.3 *False Certification: Disqualifying Status*

LOAN DISCHARGE APPLICATION:
FALSE CERTIFICATION (DISQUALIFYING STATUS)

OMB No. 1845-0015
Form Approved
Exp. Date 06/30/2005

Federal Family Education Loan Program / William D. Ford Federal Direct Loan Program

WARNING: Any person who knowingly makes a false statement or misrepresentation on this form or on any accompanying documents will be subject to penalties which may include fines, imprisonment or both, under the U.S. Criminal Code and 20 U.S.C. 1097.

SECTION 1: BORROWER IDENTIFICATION

Please enter or correct the following information. If a correction, check this box: ☐

SSN |___|___|___|–|___|___|–|___|___|___|___|

Name _____

Address _____

City, State, Zip _____

Telephone - Home (___) _____

Telephone - Other (___) _____

E-mail address (optional) _____

SECTION 2: STUDENT INFORMATION

Before responding, carefully read the entire form, including the instructions and other information on the following page. If you are a student borrower applying for loan discharge, begin with Item 3. If you are a parent borrower applying for a PLUS loan discharge, begin with Item 1.

1. Student's name (last, first, middle initial): _____

2. Student's SSN: |___|___|___|–|___|___|–|___|___|___|___|

3. School's name: _____

4. School's address (street, city, state, zip): _____

5. Dates of attendance at the school: From |___|___|–|___|___|–|___|___|___|___| To |___|___|–|___|___|–|___|___|___|___|

6. Name of the program of study that you (or, for PLUS borrowers, the student) were enrolled in when the school certified or originated the loan that you are requesting to have discharged: _____

7. To qualify for a loan discharge based on false certification due to a disqualifying status, you (or, for PLUS borrowers, the student) must have been unable – at the time the school certified or originated your loan – to meet the **legal requirements for employment** in your state of residence (or, for PLUS borrowers, in the student's state of residence) in the occupation for which the program of study was intended because of age, a physical or mental condition, criminal record, or other reason. Indicate your disqualifying status by checking the appropriate box(es) below:

☐ Age   ☐ Physical condition   ☐ Mental condition   ☐ Criminal record   ☐ Other (please specify):_____

You must provide documentation to prove that you (or for PLUS borrowers, the student) had the disqualifying status at the time the school certified or originated your loan. Also, provide as much information as possible about the state **legal requirements for employment** that you (or, for PLUS borrowers, the student) could not meet. Include the title and/or section number of the specific state law or regulation, or attach a copy of the law or regulation. You may obtain this information from the appropriate state agency, such as the consumer protection office or department of labor and employment, from a public library, or from an internet site that contains state laws and regulations. _____

8. (a) Before certifying or originating the loan, did the school ask you (or, for PLUS borrowers, the student) if the disqualifying status explained in Item 7 existed?
☐ Yes   ☐ No   ☐ Don't Know
(b) Did you (or, for PLUS borrowers, the student) inform the school of the disqualifying status before the loan was certified or originated?
☐ Yes   ☐ No

9. Did the holder of your loan receive any money back (a refund) from the school on your behalf? ☐ Yes   ☐ No   ☐ Don't Know
If Yes, give the amount and explain why the money was refunded: _____

10. Did you (or, for PLUS borrowers, the student) make any monetary claim with, or receive any payment from, the school or any third party (see definition in Section 5) in connection with enrollment or attendance at the school: ☐ Yes   ☐ No   ☐ Don't Know   If yes, please provide the following information:
(a) Name/address/telephone number of the party with whom the claim was made or from whom payment was received:

_____

(b) Amount/status of claim:_____   (c) Amount of payment received: $_____
(Write "none" if no payment was received.)

SECTION 3: BORROWER CERTIFICATION

My signature below certifies that I have read and agree to the terms and conditions that apply to this loan discharge, as specified in Section 6 on the following page. Under penalty of perjury, I certify that all of the information I have provided on this form and in any accompanying documentation is true and accurate to the best of my knowledge and belief.

Borrower's Signature: _____   Date: _____

Page 1 of 2

SECTION 4: INSTRUCTIONS FOR COMPLETING THE FORM

Type or print using dark ink. For all dates, give month, day (if known), and year. Show dates as MM-DD-YYYY (for example, "January 31, 2002" = "01-31-2002"). If you need more space to answer any of the items, continue on separate sheets of paper and attach them to this form. Indicate the number of the item(s) you are answering and include your name and social security number (SSN) on all attached pages.

Send the completed form and any attachments to the address in Section 8.

SECTION 5: DEFINITIONS

- The **Federal Family Education Loan (FFEL) Program** includes Federal Stafford Loans (both subsidized and unsubsidized), Federal Supplemental Loans for Students (SLS), Federal PLUS Loans, and Federal Consolidation Loans.
- The **William D. Ford Federal Direct Loan (Direct Loan) Program** includes Federal Direct Stafford/Ford Loans (Direct Subsidized Loans), Federal Direct Unsubsidized Stafford/Ford Loans (Direct Unsubsidized Loans), Federal Direct PLUS Loans (Direct PLUS Loans), and Federal Direct Consolidation Loans (Direct Consolidation Loans).
- The **holder** of a borrower's FFEL Program loan(s) may be a lender, a guaranty agency, or the U.S. Department of Education (the Department). The holder of a borrower's Direct Loan Program loan(s) is the Department.
- **Loan discharge** due to false certification (disqualifying status) cancels the obligation of a borrower (and endorser, if applicable) to repay the remaining balance on a FFEL Program or Direct Loan Program loan, and qualifies the borrower for reimbursement of any amounts paid voluntarily or through forced collection on the loan. For consolidation loans, only the amount of the underlying loans (the loans that were consolidated) that were used to pay for the program of study listed in Item 6 will be considered for discharge. The loan holder reports the discharge to all credit reporting agencies to which the holder previously reported the status of the loan.
- The **student** refers to the student for whom a parent borrower obtained a Federal PLUS Loan or Direct PLUS Loan.
- **Program of study** means the instructional program leading to a degree or certificate in which you (or, for PLUS borrowers, the student) were enrolled.
- **Certification** and **origination** are steps in a school's processing of a loan. In the FFEL Program, a loan is **certified** when the school signs a loan application or submits an electronic loan record to the lender or guaranty agency after determining that the borrower meets all loan eligibility requirements. In the Direct Loan Program, a loan is **originated** when the school creates an electronic loan origination record after determining that the borrower meets all loan eligibility requirements.
- **Third party** refers to any entity that may provide reimbursement for a refund owed by the school, such as a tuition recovery program or performance bond.

SECTION 6: TERMS AND CONDITIONS FOR LOAN DISCHARGE

- I received FFEL Program or Direct Loan Program loan funds on or after January 1, 1986, to attend (or, if I am a PLUS borrower, for the student to attend) the school identified in Section 2 of this form. Those funds were either received by me directly or applied as a credit to the amount owed to the school.
- I will provide, upon request, testimony, a sworn statement, or other documentation reasonably available to me that demonstrates to the satisfaction of the Department or its designee that I meet the qualifications for loan discharge based on false certification (disqualifying status), or that supports any representation that I made on this form or on any accompanying documents.
- I agree to cooperate with the Department or its designee regarding any enforcement actions related to my request for loan discharge.
- I understand that my request for loan discharge may be denied, or my discharge may be revoked, if I fail to provide testimony, a sworn statement, or documentation upon request, or if I provide testimony, a sworn statement, or documentation that does not support the material representations I have made on this form or on any accompanying documents.
- I further understand that if my loan(s) is discharged based on any false, fictitious, or fraudulent statements that I knowingly made on this form or on any accompanying documents, I may be subject to civil and criminal penalties under applicable federal law.
- I hereby assign and transfer to the Department any right to a refund on the discharged loan(s) that I may have from the school identified in Section 2 of this form and/or any owners, affiliates, or assigns of the school, and from any third party that may pay claims for a refund because of the actions of the school, up to the amounts discharged by the Department on my loan(s).

SECTION 7: IMPORTANT NOTICES

Privacy Act Notice: The Privacy Act of 1974 (5 U.S.C. 552a) requires that the following notice be provided to you:

The authorities for collecting the requested information from and about you are §428(b)(2)(A) *et seq.* and §451 *et seq.* of the Higher Education Act of 1965, as amended (20 U.S.C. 1078(b)(2)(a) *et seq.* and 20 U.S.C. 1087a *et seq.*) and the authority for collecting and using your Social Security Number (SSN) is §484(a)(4) of the HEA (20 U.S.C. 1091(a)(4). Participating in the Federal Family Education Loan (FFEL) Program or the William D. Ford Federal Direct Loan (Direct Loan) Program and giving us your SSN are voluntary, but you must provide the requested information, including your SSN, to participate.

The principal purposes for collecting the information on this form, including your SSN, are to verify your identity, to determine your eligibility to receive a loan or a benefit on a loan (such as a deferment, forbearance, discharge, or forgiveness) under the FFEL and/or Direct Loan Programs, to permit the servicing of your loan(s), and, if it becomes necessary, to locate you and to collect on your loan(s) if your loan(s) become delinquent or in default. We also use your SSN as an account identifier and to permit you to access your account information electronically.

The information in your file may be disclosed to third parties as authorized under routine uses in the appropriate systems of records. The routine uses of this information include its disclosure to federal, state, or local agencies, to other federal agencies under computer matching programs, to agencies that we authorize to assist us in administering our loan programs, to private parties such as relatives, present and former employers, business and personal associates, to credit bureau organizations, to educational institutions, and to contractors in order to verify your identity, to determine your eligibility to receive a loan or a benefit on a loan, to permit the servicing or collection of your loan(s), to counsel you in repayment efforts, to enforce the terms of the loan(s), to investigate possible fraud and to verify compliance with federal student financial aid program regulations, or to locate you if you become delinquent in your loan payments or if you default, to provide default rate calculations, to provide financial aid history information, to assist program administrators with tracking refunds and cancellations, or to provide a standardized method for educational institutions efficiently to submit student enrollment status.

In the event of litigation, we may send records to the Department of Justice, a court, adjudicative body, counsel, party, or witness if the disclosure is relevant and necessary to the litigation. If this information, either alone or with other information, indicates a potential violation of law, we may send it to the appropriate authority for action. We may send information to members of Congress if you ask them to help you with federal student aid questions. In circumstances involving employment complaints, grievances, or disciplinary actions, we may disclose relevant records to adjudicate or investigate the issues. If provided for by a collective bargaining agreement, we may disclose records to a labor organization recognized under 5 U.S.C. Chapter 71. Disclosures may also be made to qualified researchers under Privacy Act safeguards.

Paperwork Reduction Notice: According to the Paperwork Reduction Act of 1995, no persons are required to respond to a collection of information unless it displays a currently valid OMB control number. The valid OMB control number for this information collection is 1845-0015. The time required to complete this information collection is estimated to average 0.5 hours (30 minutes) per response, including the time to review instructions, search existing data resources, gather and maintain the data needed, and complete and review the information collection. *If you have any comments concerning the accuracy of the time estimate(s) or suggestions for improving this form, please write to:* U.S. Department of Education, Washington, DC 20202-4651

If you have any questions regarding the status of *your individual submission* of this form, contact your loan holder (see Section 8).

SECTION 8: WHERE TO SEND THE COMPLETED LOAN DISCHARGE APPLICATION

Send the completed loan discharge application and any attachments to:

(If no address is shown, return to your loan holder.)

If you need help completing this form, call:

D.1.4 False Certification: Unauthorized Signature/Unauthorized Payment

LOAN DISCHARGE APPLICATION:
UNAUTHORIZED SIGNATURE/UNAUTHORIZED PAYMENT

Federal Family Education Loan Program / William D. Ford Federal Direct Loan Program

OMB No. 1845-0015
Form Approved
Exp. Date 06/30/2005

WARNING: Any person who knowingly makes a false statement or misrepresentation on this form or on any accompanying documents will be subject to penalties which may include fines, imprisonment or both, under the U.S. Criminal Code and 20 U.S.C. 1097.

SECTION 1: BORROWER IDENTIFICATION

Please enter or correct the following information. If a correction, check this box: ☐

SSN |__|__|__|–|__|__|–|__|__|__|__|

Name _____

Address _____

City, State, Zip _____

Telephone - Home ( ) _____

Telephone - Other ( ) _____

E-mail address (optional) _____

SECTION 2: STUDENT INFORMATION

Before responding, carefully read the entire form, including the instructions and other information on the following page. If you are a student borrower applying for loan discharge, begin with Item 3. If you are a parent borrower applying for a PLUS loan discharge, begin with Item 1.

1. Student's name (last, first, middle initial): _____

2. Student's SSN: |__|__|__|–|__|__|–|__|__|__|__|

3. School's name: _____

4. School's address (street, city, state, zip): _____

5. Dates of attendance at the school: From |__|__|–|__|__|–|__|__|__|__| To |__|__|–|__|__|–|__|__|__|__| ☐ Did not attend

6. Did you sign the application, promissory note, master promissory note (MPN), or combined application/promissory note for your loan(s)? ☐ Yes ☐ No
   If No, on which document(s) did someone else sign your name? ☐ Application ☐ Promissory note ☐ MPN ☐ Combined application/promissory note

7. Did you endorse each loan check or sign your name on each electronic funds transfer authorization or master check authorization?
   ☐ Yes ☐ No ☐ Does Not Apply
   If No, on which document(s) did someone else sign your name? ☐ loan check ☐ electronic funds transfer authorization ☐ master check authorization
   If No, did you (or, for PLUS borrowers, the student) ever receive any money from the school, or did the school ever reduce the amount of money that you (or, for PLUS borrowers, the student) owed to the school? ☐ Yes ☐ No ☐ Don't Know If Yes, explain (give dates, amounts, and circumstances):
   _____

   If No or Don't Know, explain how you (or, for PLUS borrowers, the student) paid the tuition and fees owed to the school:
   _____

8. If you answered No to Iem 6 or Item 7, do you know who signed your name on the document(s) checked in Item 6 or 7?
   ☐ Yes ☐ No If Yes, identify the person who signed your name on the document(s).
   School employee or representative (name and position): _____
   Other person (name): _____
   Provide any other information about the circumstances under which another person signed your name:
   _____

> **IMPORTANT:** If you did not sign your name on one of the documents listed in Item 6 or Item 7, you must attach documents containing four other samples of your signature in addition to the signature on this application. At least two of these samples must clearly show that your signatures were written within one year before or after the date of the document on which someone else signed your name. Examples of documents that would include both a signature sample and the date that the signature was written include—but are not limited to—cancelled checks, tax returns, and driver's licenses. If you do not provide these signature samples, you cannot be considered for a loan discharge.

9. Did the holder of your loan receive any money back (a refund) from the school on your behalf? ☐ Yes ☐ No ☐ Don't Know
   If Yes, give the amount and explain why the money was refunded: _____

10. Did you (or, for PLUS borrowers, the student) make any monetary claim with, or receive any payment from, the school or any third party (see definition in Section 5) in connection with enrollment or attendance at the school: ☐ Yes ☐ No ☐ Don't Know If yes, please provide the following information:
    (a) Name/address/telephone number of the party with whom the claim was made or from whom payment was received:
    _____

    (b) Amount/status of claim: _____   (c) Amount of payment received: $ _____
    (Write "none" if no payment was received.)

SECTION 3: BORROWER CERTIFICATION

My signature below certifies that I have read and agree to the terms and conditions that apply to this loan discharge, as specified in Section 6 on the following page. Under penalty of perjury, I certify that all of the information I have provided on this form and in any accompanying documentation is true and accurate to the best of my knowledge and belief.

Borrower's Signature: _____   Date: _____

Page 1 of 2

SECTION 4: INSTRUCTIONS FOR COMPLETING THE FORM

Type or print using dark ink. For all dates, give month, day (if known), and year. Show dates as MM-DD-YYYY (for example, "January 31, 2002" = "01-31-2002"). If you need more space to answer any of the items, continue on separate sheets of paper and attach them to this form. Indicate the number of the item(s) you are answering and include your name and social security number (SSN) on all attached pages.

Send the completed form and any attachments to the address in Section 8.

SECTION 5: DEFINITIONS

- The **Federal Family Education Loan (FFEL) Program** includes Federal Stafford Loans (both subsidized and unsubsidized), Federal Supplemental Loans for Students (SLS), Federal PLUS Loans, and Federal Consolidation Loans.
- The **William D. Ford Federal Direct Loan (Direct Loan) Program** includes Federal Direct Stafford/Ford Loans (Direct Subsidized Loans), Federal Direct Unsubsidized Stafford/Ford Loans (Direct Unsubsidized Loans), Federal Direct PLUS Loans (Direct PLUS Loans), and Federal Direct Consolidation Loans (Direct Consolidation Loans).
- The **holder** of a borrower's FFEL Program loan(s) may be a lender, a guaranty agency, or the U.S. Department of Education (the Department). The holder of a borrower's Direct Loan Program loan(s) is the Department.
- **Unauthorized signature** means that the school, without the borrower's authorization, signed the borrower's name on a loan application or promissory note.
- **Unauthorized payment** means that the school, without the borrower's authorization, endorsed the borrower's loan check or signed the borrower's authorization for electronic funds transfer or master check, and did not give the loan proceeds to the borrower or apply the loan proceeds to charges owed by the student to the school.
- **Loan discharge** due to an unauthorized signature on a loan application or promissory note cancels the obligation of a borrower (and endorser, if applicable) to repay the remaining balance on a FFEL Program or Direct Loan Program loan, and qualifies the borrower for reimbursement of any amounts paid voluntarily or through forced collection on the loan. Discharge due to an unauthorized signature on a loan check, electronic funds transfer authorization, or master check authorization applies only to the amount of the unauthorized payment. For consolidation loans, only the loan amounts associated with the document listed in Section 2, Item 6 or Item 7, will be considered for discharge. The loan holder reports the discharge to all credit reporting agencies to which the holder previously reported the status of the loan.
- The **student** refers to the student for whom a parent borrower obtained a Federal PLUS Loan or Direct PLUS Loan.
- **Third party** refers to any entity that may provide reimbursement for a refund owed by the school, such as a tuition recovery program or performance bond.

SECTION 6: TERMS AND CONDITIONS FOR LOAN DISCHARGE

- The school identified in Section 2 of this form received FFEL Program or Direct Loan Program loan funds on or after January 1, 1986, for me to attend (or, if I am a PLUS borrower, for the student to attend) the school. I am applying for a discharge of my FFEL Program or Direct Loan Program loan(s) because the loan application, promissory note, master promissory note, combined application/promissory note, loan disbursement check, electronic funds transfer authorization, or master check authorization were not authorized for the reasons stated in this application.
- I will provide, upon request, testimony, a sworn statement, or other documentation reasonably available to me that demonstrates to the satisfaction of the Department or its designee that I meet the qualifications for loan discharge based on unauthorized signature/unauthorized payment, or that supports any representation that I made on this form or on any accompanying documents.
- I agree to cooperate with the Department or its designee regarding any enforcement actions related to my request for loan discharge.
- I understand that my request for loan discharge may be denied, or my discharge may be revoked, if I fail to provide testimony, a sworn statement, or documentation upon request, or if I provide testimony, a sworn statement, or documentation that does not support the material representations I have made on this form or on any accompanying documents.
- I further understand that if my loan(s) is discharged based on any false, fictitious, or fraudulent statements that I knowingly made on this form or on any accompanying documents, I may be subject to civil and criminal penalties under applicable federal law.
- I hereby assign and transfer to the Department any right to a refund on the discharged loan(s) that I may have from the school identified in Section 2 of this form and/or any owners, affiliates, or assigns of the school, and from any third party that may pay claims for a refund because of the actions of the school, up to the amounts discharged by the Department on my loan(s).

SECTION 7: IMPORTANT NOTICES

Privacy Act Notice: The Privacy Act of 1974 (5 U.S.C. 552a) requires that the following notice be provided to you:

The authorities for collecting the requested information from and about you are §428(b)(2)(A) *et seq.* and §451 *et seq.* of the Higher Education Act of 1965, as amended (20 U.S.C. 1078(b)(2)(a) *et seq.* and 20 U.S.C. 1087a *et seq.*) and the authority for collecting and using your Social Security Number (SSN) is §484(a)(4) of the HEA (20 U.S.C. 1091(a)(4). Participating in the Federal Family Education Loan (FFEL) Program or the William D. Ford Federal Direct Loan (Direct Loan) Program and giving us your SSN are voluntary, but you must provide the requested information, including your SSN, to participate.

The principal purposes for collecting the information on this form, including your SSN, are to verify your identity, to determine your eligibility to receive a loan or a benefit on a loan (such as a deferment, forbearance, discharge, or forgiveness) under the FFEL and/or Direct Loan Programs, to permit the servicing of your loan(s), and, if it becomes necessary, to locate you and to collect on your loan(s) if your loan(s) become delinquent or in default. We also use your SSN as an account identifier and to permit you to access your account information electronically.

The information in your file may be disclosed to third parties as authorized under routine uses in the appropriate systems of records. The routine uses of this information include its disclosure to federal, state, or local agencies, to other federal agencies under computer matching programs, to agencies that we authorize to assist us in administering our loan programs, to private parties such as relatives, present and former employers, business and personal associates, to credit bureau organizations, to educational institutions, and to contractors in order to verify your identity, to determine your eligibility to receive a loan or a benefit on a loan, to permit the servicing or collection of your loan(s), to counsel you in repayment efforts, to enforce the terms of the loan(s), to investigate possible fraud and to verify compliance with federal student financial aid program regulations, or to locate you if you become delinquent in your loan payments or if you default, to provide default rate calculations, to provide financial aid history information, to assist program administrators with tracking refunds and cancellations, or to provide a standardized method for educational institutions efficiently to submit student enrollment status.

In the event of litigation, we may send records to the Department of Justice, a court, adjudicative body, counsel, party, or witness if the disclosure is relevant and necessary to the litigation. If this information, either alone or with other information, indicates a potential violation of law, we may send it to the appropriate authority for action. We may send information to members of Congress if you ask them to help you with federal student aid questions. In circumstances involving employment complaints, grievances, or disciplinary actions, we may disclose relevant records to adjudicate or investigate the issues. If provided for by a collective bargaining agreement, we may disclose records to a labor organization recognized under 5 U.S.C. Chapter 71. Disclosures may also be made to qualified researchers under Privacy Act safeguards.

Paperwork Reduction Notice: According to the Paperwork Reduction Act of 1995, no persons are required to respond to a collection of information unless it displays a currently valid OMB control number. The valid OMB control number for this information collection is 1845-0015. The time required to complete this information collection is estimated to average 0.5 hours (30 minutes) per response, including the time to review instructions, search existing data resources, gather and maintain the data needed, and complete and review the information collection. *If you have any comments concerning the accuracy of the time estimate(s) or suggestions for improving this form, please write to:* U.S. Department of Education, Washington, DC 20202-4651

If you have questions regarding the status of *your individual submission* of this form, contact your loan holder (see Section 8).

SECTION 8: WHERE TO SEND THE COMPLETED LOAN DISCHARGE APPLICATION

Send the completed loan discharge application and any attachments to:

(If no address is shown, return to your loan holder.)

If you need help completing this form, call:

D.1.5 Disability

LOAN DISCHARGE APPLICATION:
TOTAL AND PERMANENT DISABILITY

OMB No. 1845-0065
Form Approved
Exp. Date 11/30/2002

Federal Family Education Loan Program / Federal Perkins Loan Program / William D. Ford Federal Direct Loan Program

WARNING: Any person who knowingly makes a false statement or misrepresentation on this form or on any accompanying documents will be subject to penalties which may include fines, imprisonment or both, under the U.S. Criminal Code and 20 U.S.C. 1097.

SECTION 1: BORROWER IDENTIFICATION

Please enter or correct the following information.

SSN | | | – | | | – | | | |

Name _____

Address _____

City, State, Zip _____

Telephone - Home ( ) _____

Telephone - Other ( ) _____

E-mail address (optional) _____

SECTION 2: BORROWER DISCHARGE REQUEST

Before signing, carefully read the entire form, including the instructions and other information on the following pages.

Borrower Request, Authorization, Understandings, and Certifications

I **request** that the U.S. Department of Education (ED) discharge my loan(s) made under the Federal Family Education Loan (FFEL) Program, the Federal Perkins Loan (Perkins Loan) Program, and/or the William D. Ford Federal Direct Loan (Direct Loan) Program.

I **authorize** any physician, hospital, or other institution having records about the disability that is the basis for my request for a loan discharge to make information from these records available to the holder(s) of my loan(s).

I **understand** that I must submit a separate discharge application to each holder of the loan(s) that I want to have discharged. I further understand that I am not eligible to receive a final discharge of my loan(s) unless I meet certain requirements during and at the end of a conditional discharge period, as explained in Sections 6 and 7. If I am a veteran, I understand that the certification by a physician on this form is only for the purposes of establishing my eligibility to receive a discharge of a FFEL Program, Perkins Loan Program, or Direct Loan Program loan and is not for purposes of determining my eligibility for or the extent of my eligibility for Department of Veterans Affairs benefits.

I **certify** that I have a total and permanent disability, as defined in Section 5. In addition, I certify that I have read and understand the information on the loan discharge process, the terms and conditions for discharge, the eligibility requirements for loan discharge, and the eligibility requirements to receive future loans as explained in Sections 6, 7 and 9.

_____
Signature of Borrower or Borrower's Representative   **Date**

Printed Name of Borrower's Representative (if applicable)

_____
Address of Borrower's Representative (if applicable)

Representative's Relationship to Borrower (if applicable)

SECTION 3: PHYSICIAN'S CERTIFICATION

Instructions for Physician: The borrower identified above is applying for discharge of his/her federal education loan(s) based on total and permanent disability. You should complete and sign the certification below only if you are a doctor of medicine or osteopathy legally authorized to practice in a State (see definition in Section 5) and **if the borrower's condition meets the definition of total and permanent disability in Section 5.** Provide all requested information and attach additional pages if necessary. **Type or print in dark ink. Please return the completed form to the borrower or the borrower's representative.** The holder(s) of the borrower's loan(s) (see definition in Section 5) may contact you for additional information or documentation.

> *Note: The standard for determining disability for discharge of the borrower's loan(s) may be different from standards used under other programs in connection with occupational disability or eligibility for social service benefits.*

1. Diagnosis/explanation of the borrower's present medical condition (identify the borrower's condition and explain how it prevents the borrower from working and earning money in any capacity). Do not use abbreviations or insurance codes.

_____

2. When did the borrower's medical condition begin? (MM-DD-YYYY) | | | – | | | – | | | |

3. a. Does this medical condition prevent the borrower from being able to work and earn money in any capacity? ❏ Yes ❏ No

 b. If Yes, when did the borrower become unable to work and earn money in any capacity? (MM-DD-YYYY) | | | – | | | – | | | |

I certify that, in my best professional judgment, the borrower identified above is unable to work and earn money because of an injury or illness that is expected to continue indefinitely or result in death. I understand that a borrower who is currently able or who is expected to be able to work and earn money, even on a limited basis, is not considered to have a total and permanent disability.

I am a doctor of (check one) ❏ medicine ❏ osteopathy legally authorized to practice in the state of _____ .

My professional license no. is _____ .
(Subject to verification through State records.)

_____
Physician's Signature (a signature stamp is not acceptable)   **Date**

Printed Name of Physician

_____
Address

City, State, Zip

( ) _____   ( ) _____
Telephone   Fax (optional)

E-mail address (optional)

SECTION 4: INSTRUCTIONS FOR COMPLETING THE FORM

Type or print in dark ink. A representative may sign on your behalf in Section 2 if you are unable to do so because of your disability. Have Section 3 completed and signed by a doctor of medicine or osteopathy. **If you are applying for discharge of more than one loan and your loans are held by more than one loan holder, you must submit a separate discharge application (original or copy) with any accompanying attachments to each holder. A "copy" means a photocopy of the original form completed by you (or your representative) and your physician. If you submit copies, each copy must include an original signature from you or your representative.**

SECTION 5: DEFINITIONS

■ The **Federal Family Education Loan (FFEL) Program** includes Federal Stafford Loans (both subsidized and unsubsidized), Federal Supplemental Loans for Students (SLS), Federal PLUS Loans, and Federal Consolidation Loans.

■ The **Federal Perkins Loan (Perkins Loan) Program** includes Federal Perkins Loans, National Direct Student Loans (NDSL), and National Defense Student Loans (NDSL).

■ The **William D. Ford Federal Direct Loan (Direct Loan) Program** includes Federal Direct Stafford/Ford Loans (Direct Subsidized Loans), Federal Direct Unsubsidized Stafford/Ford Loans (Direct Unsubsidized Loans), Federal Direct PLUS Loans (Direct PLUS Loans), and Federal Direct Consolidation Loans (Direct Consolidation Loans).

■ A **conditional discharge** due to a total and permanent disability allows you (and, if applicable, any endorser) to stop making payments on your loan(s) during the conditional discharge period (see definition) while ED evaluates your eligibility for a final discharge. A conditional discharge is granted when ED makes an initial determination that you have a total and permanent disability as defined in this section. See also Sections 6 and 7.

■ The **conditional discharge period** begins on the date that you became totally and permanently disabled, as certified by the physician who completes Section 3, and lasts for up to three years. The conditional discharge period ends when ED either grants a final discharge or determines that you do not qualify for a final discharge. During the conditional discharge period, ED will monitor your eligibility for a final discharge. See also Sections 6 and 7.

■ A **final discharge** due to a total and permanent disability condition cancels your obligation (and, if applicable, any endorser's obligation) to repay the remaining balance on your FFEL Program, Perkins Loan Program, and/or Direct Loan Program loan. ED grants a final discharge if you meet certain conditions during and at the end of the conditional discharge period. See Section 7.

■ The **holder** of your FFEL Program loan(s) may be a lender, a guaranty agency, or the U.S. Department of Education (ED). The holder of your Perkins Loan Program loan(s) may be a school you attended or ED. The holder of your Direct Loan Program loan(s) is ED.

■ **State** includes the 50 United States, the District of Columbia, American Samoa, the Commonwealth of Puerto Rico, Guam, the Virgin Islands, the Commonwealth of the Northern Mariana Islands, the Republic of the Marshall Islands, the Federated States of Micronesia, and the Republic of Palau.

■ If you have a **total and permanent disability**, this means that you are unable to work and earn money because of an injury or illness that is expected to continue indefinitely or result in death. **NOTE: (1)** This standard may be different from standards used under other programs in connection with occupational disability or eligibility for social service benefits. **(2)** You cannot be considered to have a total and permanent disability if your condition existed at the time your loan(s) was made, unless your condition has substantially deteriorated so that you are now totally and permanently disabled.

SECTION 6: LOAN DISCHARGE PROCESS / TERMS AND CONDITIONS FOR LOAN DISCHARGE

1. If your loan holder (other than ED) determines, based on a review of your loan discharge application, that you appear to meet the eligibility requirements for a loan discharge based on total and permanent disability, your loan(s) will be assigned to ED. For FFEL Program loans currently held by a lender, this determination will be made by both your lender and guaranty agency. ED will be your new loan holder.

2. After receiving your loan(s), ED will review the physician's certification in Section 3 and other information relating to your application for loan discharge. Based on the results of this review, ED will make an initial determination on your application. If ED determines that you have a total and permanent disability, you will be notified that a conditional discharge has been granted for a period of up to three years from the date that you became totally and permanently disabled. If ED determines that you do not have a total and permanent disability, you will be notified of that determination and you must resume repayment of your loan(s).

3. During the conditional discharge period: **(A)** you are not required to make any payments on your loan(s); **(B)** you are not considered to be delinquent or in default on your loan(s), unless you were delinquent or in default at the time the conditional discharge was granted; **(C)** you must promptly notify ED if your annual earnings from employment exceed the poverty line amount for a family of two; **(D)** you must promptly notify ED of any changes in your address or telephone number; and **(E)** if requested, you must provide ED with additional documentation or information related to your eligibility for loan discharge. This may include, but is not limited to, documentation of your annual earnings from employment.

4. If you meet the conditions described in Section 7, Item 4, during and at the end of the conditional discharge period, ED will grant a final discharge of your loan(s) at the end of the conditional discharge period. The discharge will be reported to credit bureaus, and any payments you made after the date you became totally and permanently disabled will be returned to you.

5. If you do not meet the conditions described in Section 7, Item 4, at any time during or at the end of the conditional discharge period, the conditional discharge period will end and you will not receive a final discharge. This means that you will be responsible for repaying your loan(s) in accordance with the terms of your promissory note(s). However, you will not be required to pay interest that accrued on your loan(s) from the date ED made an initial determination that you were totally and permanently disabled until the date the conditional discharge period ended. ED will continue to be your loan holder.

SECTION 7: ELIGIBILITY REQUIREMENTS FOR LOAN DISCHARGE

1. Your condition must not have existed at the time your loan(s) was made, unless your condition has substantially deteriorated so that you are now totally and permanently disabled.

2. If you are applying for discharge of a consolidation loan, your condition must not have existed at the time any of the loan(s) you consolidated were made, unless your condition has substantially deteriorated so that you are now totally and permanently disabled. If requested, you must provide the holder of your consolidation loan(s) or ED with the disbursement dates of the loan(s) you consolidated.

3. To qualify for a **conditional discharge**, you must have a total and permanent disability, as defined in Section 5. This must be certified by a physician in Section 3.

4. To qualify for a **final discharge**, you must meet the following conditions during and at the end of the conditional discharge period described in Section 6:
   (A) your annual earnings from employment must not exceed the poverty line amount for a family of two in your state (regardless of your actual family size), and **(B)** you must not receive a new loan under the FFEL Program, the Perkins Loan Program, or the Direct Loan Program.
   NOTE: A physician cannot certify that you have a total and permanent disability if, at the time of the physician's certification, you are able to work and earn money in any capacity. However, if you attempt to work during the conditional discharge period, you may earn up to the poverty line amount each year during that period. This standard allows you to try to work without being disqualified from receiving a final discharge. The poverty line amounts are updated annually. ED will notify you of the current poverty line amounts during each year of the conditional discharge period.

SECTION 8: WHERE TO SEND THE COMPLETED LOAN DISCHARGE APPLICATION

Send the completed loan discharge application and any attachments to:
(If no address is shown, return to your loan holder.)

If you need help completing this form, call:

1. If you are granted a final discharge due to total and permanent disability, you are not eligible to receive future loans under the FFEL, Perkins Loan, or Direct Loan programs unless: **(A)** you obtain a certification from a physician that you are able to engage in substantial gainful activity, and **(B)** you sign a statement acknowledging that the new loan you receive cannot be discharged in the future on the basis of any injury or illness present at the time the new loan is made, unless your condition substantially deteriorates so that you are again totally and permanently disabled.

2. If you are granted a conditional discharge of your loan(s), based on a total and permanent disability and you request a new FFEL, Perkins Loan, or Direct Loan program loan during the conditional discharge period, you are not eligible to receive the new loan unless: **(A)** you obtain a certification from a physician that you are able to engage in substantial gainful activity; **(B)** you sign a statement acknowledging that neither the previous conditionally discharged loan(s) nor the new loan you receive can be discharged in the future on the basis of any injury or illness present when you applied for a total and permanent disability discharge or at the time the new loan is made, unless your condition substantially deteriorates so that you are again totally and permanently disabled; **(C)** you sign a statement acknowledging that the conditionally discharged loan(s) will be removed from conditional discharge status; and **(D)** ED has removed the conditionally discharged loan(s) from conditional discharge status (see Section 6, Item 5).

SECTION 10: IMPORTANT NOTICES

Privacy Act Notice. The Privacy Act of 1974 (5 U.S.C. 552a) requires that the following notice be provided to you:

The authorities for collecting the requested information from and about you are §428(b)(2)(A) *et seq.*, §451 *et seq.* and §461 *et seq.* of the Higher Education Act of 1965, as amended (20 U.S.C. 1078(b)(2)(A) *et seq.* 20 U.S.C. 1087a *et seq.*, and 20 U.S.C. 1087aa *et seq.*) and the authority for collecting and using your Social Security Number (SSN) is §484(a)(4) of the HEA (20 U.S.C. 1091(a)(4)). Participating in the Federal Family Education Loan (FFEL) Program, the William D. Ford Federal Direct Loan (Direct Loan) Program, or the Federal Perkins Loan (Perkins Loan) Program and giving us your SSN are voluntary, but you must provide the requested information, including your SSN, to participate.

The principal purposes for collecting the information on this form, including your SSN, are to verify your identity, to determine your eligibility to receive a loan or a benefit on a loan (such as a deferment, forbearance, discharge, or forgiveness) under the FFEL, Direct Loan, and/or Perkins Loan Programs, to permit the servicing of your loan(s), and, if it becomes necessary, to locate you and to collect on your loan(s) if your loan(s) become delinquent or in default. We also use your SSN as an account identifier and to permit you to access your account information electronically.

The information in your file may be disclosed to third parties as authorized under routine uses in the appropriate systems of records. The routine uses of this information include its disclosure to federal, state, or local agencies, to other federal agencies under computer matching programs, to agencies that we authorize to assist us in administering our loan programs, to private parties such as relatives, present and former employers, business and personal associates, to credit bureau organizations, to educational institutions, and to contractors in order to verify your identity, to determine your eligibility to receive a loan or a benefit on a loan, to permit the servicing or collection of your loan(s), to counsel you in repayment efforts, to enforce the terms of the loan(s), to investigate possible fraud and to verify compliance with federal student financial aid program regulations, or to locate you if you become delinquent in your loan payments or if you default, to provide default rate calculations, to provide financial aid history information, to assist program administrators with tracking refunds and cancellations, or to provide a standardized method for educational institutions efficiently to submit student enrollment status.

In the event of litigation, we may send records to the Department of Justice, a court, adjudicative body, counsel, party, or witness if the disclosure is relevant and necessary to the litigation. If this information, either alone or with other information, indicates a potential violation of law, we may send it to the appropriate authority for action. We may send information to members of Congress if you ask them to help you with federal student aid questions. In circumstances involving employment complaints, grievances, or disciplinary actions, we may disclose relevant records to adjudicate or investigate the issues. If provided for by a collective bargaining agreement, we may disclose records to a labor organization recognized under 5 U.S.C. Chapter 71. Disclosures may also be made to qualified researchers under Privacy Act safeguards.

Paperwork Reduction Notice. According to the Paperwork Reduction Act of 1995, no persons are required to respond to a collection of information unless it displays a currently valid OMB control number. The valid OMB control number for this information collection is 1845-0065. The time required to complete this information collection is estimated to average 0.5 hours (30 minutes) per response, including the time to review instructions, search existing data resources, gather and maintain the data needed, and complete and review the information collection. **If you have comments concerning the accuracy of the time estimate(s) or suggestions for improving this form, please write to:** U.S. Department of Education, Washington, DC 20202-4651. *Do not send the completed loan discharge application to this address.*

If you have comments or concerns regarding the status of *your individual submission* **of this form, contact your loan holder (see Section 8).**

LOAN DISCHARGE APPLICATION: UNPAID REFUND

Federal Family Education Loan Program/William D. Ford Federal Direct Loan Program

OMB No. 1845-0058
Form Approved
Exp. Date 10/31/2004

WARNING: Any person who knowingly makes a false statement or misrepresentation on this form or on any accompanying documents shall be subject to penalties which may include fines, imprisonment or both, under the U.S. Criminal Code and 20 U.S.C. 1097.

SECTION 1: BORROWER IDENTIFICATION

Please enter or correct the following information. If you make a correction, check this box: ❑

SSN |___|___|___| – |___|___| – |___|___|___|___|

Name _____

Address _____

City, State, Zip _____

Telephone - Home (____) _____

Telephone - Other (____) _____

E-mail (optional) _____

SECTION 2: LOAN AND SCHOOL INFORMATION

Before responding, carefully read the entire form, including the instructions and other information on the following page. *If you are a student borrower applying for loan discharge, begin with Item 3. If you are a parent borrower applying for a PLUS loan discharge, begin with Item 1.*

1. Student's name (last, first, middle initial):	2. Student's SSN:
	|___|___|___| – |___|___| – |___|___|___|___|

3. Name and address (street, city, state, zip) of the school that you believe owes you a refund:	4. Is this school still open? ❑ Yes ❑ No ❑ Don't Know
	5. If this school closed, were you (or, for PLUS borrowers, was the student) attending when it closed? ❑ Yes ❑ No

6. a. Do you have any other application for discharge, pending or approved, for a loan you obtained to attend this school? ❑ Yes ❑ No

   b. Has your school or any third party (see definition of "third party" in Section 6, on the following page) made a payment for any loan for which you are requesting a discharge, or is any such payment being considered? ❑ Yes ❑ No

7. If your answers to Items 6a and 6b are "No," proceed to Section 3. If your answer to Item 6a or 6b is "Yes," provide the information requested in Items 7a, 7b, and 7c for each discharge or payment, if known (use a separate sheet of paper if you need to report more than one discharge or payment).

a. Reason for discharge or payment:	b. From whom (include telephone number) was the discharge or payment requested?	c. Amount received or anticipated: $_____

SECTION 3: REFUND INFORMATION

If you have documentation from the school showing the amount of the unpaid refund, attach a copy to this form. *If you agree with the amount, go on to Section 4. If you don't agree with the amount or you don't have this documentation, complete Items 8 through 13. If you don't know the response to an Item in this section, write "Don't Know."*

8. What amount do you believe the school owes you? $ _____	9. Why do you believe the school owes you this amount?

10. Your (or, for PLUS borrowers, the student's) first and last dates of attendance at the school: |___|___| – |___|___| – |___|___|___|___| to |___|___| – |___|___| – |___|___|___|___| *OR* ❑ Never Attended	11. Your (or, for PLUS borrowers, the student's) program of study at the school:

12. This Item requests the total amounts related to the period of enrollment for which the loan was intended. For example, if you received a loan for the spring quarter only and you left school during the spring quarter, provide an amount for that quarter only. However, if the loan was received for the winter and spring quarters, provide the total amount for both quarters.

   a. If your (or, for PLUS borrowers, the student's) last date of attendance was before October 7, 2000, enter the amount of the school's charges for the period of enrollment for which the loan was intended. Include tuition, fees, and other school charges in the amount.* $ _____

   b. If your (or, for PLUS borrowers, the student's) last date of attendance was on or after October 7, 2000, enter the total amount of federal grants and loans received for any part of the period of enrollment for which the loan was intended.* $ _____

   * If the unpaid refund is for more than one loan and the loans were intended for different periods of enrollment, provide the amounts requested in Item 12a or 12b for each period of enrollment separately, using a separate sheet of paper for your additional response(s).

13. Attach a copy of any documentation that supports your responses to Items 8 though 12. Examples of documentation may include, but are not limited to, the school's catalog, refund policy, tuition bill(s), enrollment contract, student account statement, registration forms, withdrawal form, attendance records, and any correspondence from the school that contains information about the refund you believe the school owes you.

SECTION 4: BORROWER CERTIFICATION

My signature below certifies that –

- Each loan for which I am requesting a discharge was received by me, in whole or in part, on or after January 1, 1986. Those funds were either received by me directly or applied as a credit to my (or, for PLUS borrowers, the student's) school account to pay the amount owed to the school.

- I (or, for PLUS borrowers, the student) did not attend the school or, within the timeframe that would entitle me to a refund, withdrew or was terminated from the school. Except as identified in Section 2, Items 6 and 7, I have not received this refund, or any benefit of a refund to which I am entitled, from the school or any third party.

- I have read and agree to the terms and conditions that apply to this unpaid refund discharge, as specified in Section 7 on the following page.

- Under penalty of perjury, all of the information I have provided on this application and in any accompanying documentation is true and accurate to the best of my knowledge and belief.

_____   **Date** _____

Borrower's Signature   *Page 1 of 2*

Before you complete this application, you need to know that –

■ If the school is currently open, you may not apply for this type of discharge unless you have first contacted the school and attempted to resolve the issue. If the issue is not resolved, you may then apply for this type of discharge.

■ You may not apply for this type of discharge if you are currently attending the school. If you (or, for PLUS borrowers, the student) are still attending the school, you should contact the school about the refund.

■ If your school closed while you were enrolled (or if you withdrew from the school within 90 days before the school closed) and you did not complete your program of study at another school, you may wish to apply for a loan discharge based on the school's closure rather than a discharge based on the unpaid refund. If you are unsure about which type of loan discharge is most appropriate for you, contact your loan holder at the address shown in Section 9.

When completing this form, type or print using dark ink. For all dates, give month, day (if known), and year. Show dates as MM-DD-YYYY (for example, "July 01, 2001" = "07-01-2001"). If you need more space to answer any of the Items, continue on separate sheets of paper and attach them to this form. Indicate the number of the Item(s) you are answering and include your name and social security number (SSN) on all attached pages. If a refund is owed for more than one student or from more than one school, use separate forms for each student or school.

Return the completed form and any attachments to the address shown in Section 9.

SECTION 6: DEFINITIONS

■ The **Federal Family Education Loan (FFEL) Program** includes Federal Stafford Loans (both subsidized and unsubsidized), Federal Supplemental Loans for Students (SLS), Federal PLUS Loans, and Federal Consolidation Loans.

■ The **William D. Ford Federal Direct Loan (Direct Loan) Program** includes Federal Direct Stafford/Ford Loans (Direct Subsidized Loans), Federal Direct Unsubsidized Stafford/Ford Loans (Direct Unsubsidized Loans), Federal Direct PLUS Loans (Direct PLUS Loans), and Federal Direct Consolidation Loans (Direct Consolidation Loans).

■ **Loan discharge** due to an unpaid refund cancels your obligation (and any endorser's obligation) to repay the portion of the loan that should have been refunded. Any accrued interest and other charges associated with the unpaid refund will also be discharged, and you will be reimbursed for any amount that you have repaid that exceeds the remaining balance of the loan after the discharge. The loan holder reports the discharge to all credit reporting agencies to which the loan holder previously reported the status of the loan.

■ The **student** refers to the student for whom a parent borrower obtained a Federal PLUS Loan or Direct PLUS Loan.

■ **Third party** refers to the holder of a performance bond, a State or other agency offering a tuition recovery program, or any other entity that may reimburse you for a refund that you are owed.

SECTION 7: TERMS AND CONDITIONS FOR LOAN DISCHARGE BASED ON UNPAID REFUND

■ I agree to cooperate with the U.S. Department of Education (the Department) or the Department's designee in any enforcement action related to this application and to provide to the Department or the Department's designee, upon request, other documentation reasonably available to me that demonstrates that I meet the qualifications for an unpaid refund discharge.

■ I assign and transfer to the Department any right to recovery on the amount discharged that I may have from the school identified in Section 2 of this form and/or any owners, affiliates or assigns of the school, and from any party that may pay claims for a refund because of the actions of the school, up to the amounts discharged by the Department on my loan(s).

■ I understand that this request may be denied, or my discharge may be revoked, if I fail to cooperate, provide documentation, or meet any of the other terms of my agreement on this form.

■ I understand that if my loan is discharged based on any false, fictitious, or fraudulent statements that I knowingly made on this form or on any accompanying documents, I may be subject to civil and criminal penalties under applicable federal law.

SECTION 8: IMPORTANT NOTICES

Privacy Act Notice: The Privacy Act of 1974 (5 U.S.C. 552a) requires that the following notice be provided to you:

The authorities for collecting the requested information from and about you are 428(b)(2)(A) *et seq.* and 451 *et seq.* of the Higher Education Act of 1965, as amended (20 U.S.C. 1078(b)(2)(A) *et seq.* and 20 U.S.C. 1087a *et seq.*) and the authority for collecting and using your Social Security Number (SSN) is 484(a)(4) of the HEA (20 U.S.C. 1091(a)(4)). Participating in the Federal Family Education Loan (FFEL) Program or the William D. Ford Federal Direct Loan (Direct Loan) Program and giving us your SSN are voluntary, but you must provide the requested information, including your SSN, to participate.

The principal purposes for collecting the information on this form, including your SSN, are to verify your identity, to determine your eligibility to receive a loan or a benefit on a loan (such as a deferment, forbearance, discharge, or forgiveness) under the FFEL Program and/or Direct Loan Program, to permit the servicing of your loan(s), and, if it becomes necessary, to locate you and to collect on your loan(s) if your loan(s) becomes delinquent or in default. We also use your SSN as an account identifier and to permit you to access your account information electronically.

The information in your file may be disclosed to third parties as authorized under routine uses in the appropriate systems of records. The routine uses of this information include its disclosure to federal, state, or local agencies, to other federal agencies under computer matching programs, to agencies that we authorize to assist us in administering our loan programs, to private parties such as relatives, present and former employers, business and personal associates, to credit bureau organizations, to educational institutions, and to contractors in order to verify your identity, to determine your eligibility to receive a loan or a benefit on a loan, to permit the servicing or collection of your loan(s), to counsel you in repayment efforts, to enforce the terms of the loan(s), to investigate possible fraud and to verify compliance with federal student financial aid program regulations, to locate you if you become delinquent in your loan payments or if you default, to provide default rate calculations, to provide financial aid history information, to assist program administrators with tracking refunds and cancellations, or to provide a standardized method for educational institutions efficiently to submit student enrollment status.

In the event of litigation, we may send records to the Department of Justice, a court, adjudicative body, counsel, party, or witness if the disclosure is relevant and necessary to the litigation. If this information, either alone or with other information, indicates a potential violation of law, we may send it to the appropriate authority for action. We may send information to members of Congress if you ask them to help you with federal student aid questions. In circumstances involving employment complaints, grievances, or disciplinary actions, we may disclose relevant records to adjudicate or investigate the issues. If provided for by a collective bargaining agreement, we may disclose records to a labor organization recognized under 5 U.S.C. Chapter 71. Disclosures may also be made to qualified researchers under Privacy Act safeguards.

Paperwork Reduction Notice: According to the Paperwork Reduction Act of 1995, no persons are required to respond to a collection of information unless it displays a currently valid OMB control number. The valid OMB control number for this information collection is 1845-0058. The time required to complete this information collection is estimated to average 0.5 hours (30 minutes) per response, including the time to review instructions, search existing data resources, gather and maintain the data needed, and complete and review the information collection. **If you have any comments concerning the accuracy of the time estimate(s) or suggestions for improving this form, please write to:** U.S. Department of Education, Washington, DC 20202-4651

If you have any comments or concerns regarding the status of your individual submission of this form, write directly to the address shown below.

SECTION 9: WHERE TO SEND THE COMPLETED LOAN DISCHARGE APPLICATION

Return the completed loan discharge application and any attachments to:
(If no address is shown, return to your loan holder.)

If you need help completing this form, call:
(If no phone number is shown, call your loan holder.)

D.2 Other Department of Education Forms

D.2.1 *Federal Direct Consolidation Loan Application and Instructions*

Federal Direct Consolidation Loan
Instructions for Application and Promissory Note

OMB No. 1845-0053
Form Approved
Exp. Date 1/31/2005

Before beginning, you will need to gather all of your loan records, account statements, and bills so that you will have on hand all the information you will need to complete the application and promissory note.

The form should be printed in blue or black ink or typewritten, and it must be signed and dated by the applicant(s). If you cross out anything and write in new information, put your initials beside the change.

Incorrect or incomplete information may delay processing.

Items 1 and 2: Enter the information requested.

Item 3: Enter your permanent home street address. If your mailing address is an RFD, post office box, or general delivery, you must list **both** the street address and mailing address.

Items 4 - 6: Enter the information requested. Note, Items 5 and 6 are optional.

Item 7: Enter any former names under which one or more or your loans may have been made. (If none, enter "none.")

Item 8: Enter the information requested.

Item 9: First, enter in the parentheses the two letter abbreviation for the state that issued your driver's license. Then, enter your driver's license number. (If none, enter "none.")

Items 10 - 12: Enter the information requested. If none, enter "none."

Item 13: If married, check "Yes" or "No" to indicate whether you want to consolidate your loan(s) with your spouse's loan(s).

Item 14: See instructions provided in the section.

Note: Complete this section only if you are married and wish to consolidate your loans with those of your spouse. Remember, if you do this, you are both responsible for repaying the total consolidation loan, even if you become separated or divorced or if one spouse dies.

Items 15 - 17: Enter the information requested.

Item 18: First, enter in the parentheses the two letter abbreviation for the state that issued your spouse's driver's license. Then, enter your spouse's driver's license number. (If none, enter "none.")

Item 19: Enter the information requested. Note, this item is optional.

Item 20: Enter any former names under which one or more of your spouse's loans may have been made. (If none, enter "none.")

Item 21: Enter the information requested. Note, this item is optional.

Items 22 - 24: Enter the information requested. (If none, enter "none.")

This section asks about your education loans. List **all** your education loans in Section D, including your Direct Loans and loans you are **not** consolidating. To find the information you will need to answer these items, there are several places you can look, such as:

- the last monthly billing statement you received,
- your quarterly interest statement or annual statement,
- your coupon book, or
- the Internet site of your loan holder or servicer.

If you are currently in school, you can contact the financial aid administrator at your school.

Item 25: Enter the information requested. You must give us at least the name, city, and state of your loan holder or servicer. Use the resources listed above to find this information. For example, on your statement, there might be two addresses: first, the address where you send your payment, and second, an address that is sometimes called the "correspondence address." For Item 25, we want you to give us the "correspondence address." If there is only one address on your documents, give us that address. If you cannot find this information on your documents, call the telephone number on the statement or use the other resources listed. For each loan, send a photocopy of the document where you found the information.

Item 26: Enter the letter that corresponds to the loan type from the chart provided. If you are not sure about the loan type, leave this item blank.

Item 27: Tell us whether the loan was made to you, to your spouse, or to both of you by entering:
B - for borrower   **S** - for spouse   **J** - for loans to both of you
You **must** complete this item, even if you are not married.

Item 28: Enter the account number for each loan (the number should be on your statement or in your payment book). If you cannot find the account number, leave this item blank.

Item 29: Enter the current balance for each loan as of your last payment. You **must** complete this item. Use the amount on your last statement or give us an approximate amount.

Item 30: Tell us whether you wish to consolidate this loan by entering "Y" in the "Yes" column or "N" in the "No" column. You **must** answer this item.

Note: If you need additional space to list all of your loans, complete the Federal Direct Consolidation Loan Additional Loan Listing Sheet and return it with your application and promissory note. Be sure to write your name and social security number in the spaces provided.

Item 31: See instructions provided in the section.

Note: Read the entire promissory note (pages 3 and 4) and the accompanying Borrower's Rights and Responsibilities before signing and dating the promissory note as indicated.

Do not make any changes to this section. Changes will void the terms and agreements of the promissory note. This is a legally binding contract.

Item 32: Sign and date the promissory note in blue or black ink. If you and your spouse are applying for a joint consolidation loan, you both must sign and date the promissory note. If you fail to do so, your application will not be processed.

Review all the information on your Direct Consolidation Loan Application and Promissory Note. When complete, make a copy for your records and mail the original to us in the envelope provided.

As soon as we receive your completed application and promissory note and supporting documents, we will begin processing. During this time, we might call you with questions. We will be sending you a notice before we pay off your loan(s).

In the meantime, if you currently are required to make payments on your loan(s), continue to do so. You will need to continue making payments until you receive written notification that your loan(s) has been successfully consolidated and it is time to start paying your Direct Consolidation Loan. If you are having difficulty making payments on your loan(s), contact the correspondence address or telephone number on your current loan statement(s) to find out ways you might be able to postpone loan payments; ask specifically about your "deferment" or "forbearance" options.

Types of Education Loans and Their Codes

Subsidized Loans	Unsubsidized Loans
A Subsidized Federal Stafford Loans	**G** Unsubsidized Federal Stafford Loans (including
B Guaranteed Student Loans (GSL)	Non-Subsidized Stafford Loans made prior to 10/1/92)
C Federal Insured Student Loans (FISL)	**H** Federal Supplemental Loans for Students (SLS)
D Federal Direct Stafford/Ford Loans	**J** Unsubsidized Federal Consolidation Loans
E Federal Direct Subsidized	**K** Federal Direct Unsubsidized Consolidation Loans
Consolidation Loans	**L** Federal Direct Unsubsidized Stafford/Ford Loans
F Federal Perkins Loans	**P** Auxiliary Loans to Assist Students (ALAS)
M National Direct Student Loans (NDSL)	**Q** Health Professions Student Loans (HPSL)
N National Defense Student Loans (NDSL)	**R** Health Education Assistance Loans (HEAL)
O Subsidized Federal Consolidation Loans	**S** Federal PLUS Loans
	T Parent Loans for Undergraduate Students (PLUS)
	U Federal Direct PLUS Loans
Note: You must consolidate at least one	**V** Federal Direct PLUS Consolidation Loans
Direct Loan or FFEL Program Loan.	**Y** Nursing Student Loans (NSL)
	Z Loans for Disadvantaged Students (LDS)
	W Other education loans ineligible for consolidation

For assistance when completing this form, call the Loan Origination Center's Consolidation Department at 1-800-557-7392.

For the hearing impaired, the TDD number is 1-800-557-7395.

Federal Direct Consolidation Loan
Important Notices

Privacy Act Disclosure Notice

The Privacy Act of 1974 (5 U.S.C. 552a) requires that we disclose to you the following information:

The authority for collecting this information is §451 et seq. of the Higher Education Act of 1965, as amended (the HEA) (20 U.S.C. §1087a et seq.). The principal purposes for collecting this information are to determine your eligibility for a Federal Direct Consolidation Loan that is made under the William D. Ford Federal Direct Loan (Direct Loan) Program, to document your agreement to repay this loan, and to identify and locate you if it is necessary to enforce the loan.

We ask that you provide the information requested on this Federal Direct Consolidation Loan Application and Promissory Note (application and promissory note) on a voluntary basis. However, you must provide all of the requested information that is available to you so the Department may process this application and promissory note because the Department needs the information to consolidate your loans into a Federal Direct Consolidation Loan.

The information in your file may be disclosed to third parties as authorized under routine uses in the Privacy Act notices called "Title IV Program Files" (originally published on April 12, 1994, Federal Register, Vol. 59, p. 17351) and "National Student Loan Data System" (originally published on December 20, 1994, Federal Register, Vol. 59, p. 65532). Thus, this information may be disclosed to parties that we authorize to assist us in administering the Federal student aid programs, including contractors that are required to maintain safeguards under the Privacy Act. Disclosures may also be made for verification of information, determination of eligibility, enforcement of conditions of the loan or grant, debt collection, and the prevention of fraud, waste, and abuse and these disclosures may be made through computer matching programs with other Federal agencies. Disclosures may be made to determine the feasibility of entering into computer matching agreements. We may send information to members of Congress if you ask them in writing to help you with Federal student aid questions. If we are involved in litigation, we may send information to the Department of Justice (DOJ), a court, adjudicative body, counsel, or witness if the disclosure is related to financial aid and certain other conditions are met. If this information, either alone or with other information, indicates a potential violation of law, we may send it to the appropriate authority for consideration of action and we may disclose to DOJ to get its advice related to the Title IV, HEA programs or questions under the Freedom of Information Act. Disclosures may be made to qualified researchers under Privacy Act safeguards. In some circumstances involving employment decisions, grievances, or complaints or involving decisions regarding the letting of a contract or making of a grant, license, or other benefit, we may send information to an appropriate authority. In limited circumstances, we may disclose to a Federal labor organization recognized under 5 U.S.C. Chapter 71.

Because we request your social security number (SSN), we must inform you that we collect your SSN on a voluntary basis, but section 484(a)(4) of the HEA (20 U.S.C. 1091(a)(4)) provides that, in order to receive any grant, loan, or work assistance under Title IV of the HEA, a student must provide his or her SSN. Your SSN is used to verify your identity, and as an account number (identifier) throughout the life of your loan(s) so that data may be recorded accurately.

Financial Privacy Act Notice

Under the Right to Financial Privacy Act of 1978 (12 U.S.C. 3401-3421), ED will have access to financial records in your student loan file maintained in compliance with the administration of the Direct Loan Program.

Paperwork Reduction Notice

According to the Paperwork Reduction Act of 1995, no persons are required to respond to a collection of information unless it displays a currently valid OMB control number. The valid OMB control number for this information collection is 1845-0053. The time required to complete this information collection is estimated to average 1.0 hour (60 minutes) per response, including the time to review instructions, search existing data resources, gather and maintain the data needed, and complete and review the information collection. **If you have any comments concerning the accuracy of the time estimate(s) or suggestions for improving this form, please write to:** U.S. Department of Education, Washington, DC 20202-4651. **If you have any comments or concerns regarding the status of** *your individual submission* **of this form, write directly to:**

U.S. Department of Education
Consolidation Department
Loan Origination Center
P.O. Box 242800
Louisville, KY 40224-2800

Direct Loans
William D. Ford Federal Direct Loan Program

Federal Direct Consolidation Loan
Application and Promissory Note

WARNING: Any person who knowingly makes a false statement or misrepresentation on this form shall be subject to penalties which may include fines, imprisonment, or both, under the U.S. Criminal Code and 20 U.S.C. 1097.

OMB No. 1845-0053
Form Approved
Exp. Date 1/31/2005

Before You Begin

This form should be printed in blue or black ink or typewritten and must be signed and dated by the applicant(s). If you cross out anything and write in new information, put your initials beside the change.

Section A: Borrower Information

1. Last Name First Name Middle Initial	2. Social Security Number
3. Permanent Street Address (if P.O. box, see instructions)	4. Home Area Code/Telephone Number ( )
City State Zip Code	5. Fax Number (Optional) ( )	6. E-Mail Address (Optional)
7. Former Name(s)	8. Date of Birth	9. Driver's License Number (put state abbreviation first) ( )
10. Employer's Name	11. Employer's Address	
12. Employer's Area Code/Telephone Number ( )	City State Zip Code	

13. If you are married, does your spouse have an eligible loan(s) (see instructions) that you want to consolidate with your loan(s)? Yes ☐   No ☐
    If yes, complete Section C, include your spouse's loan(s) in Section D, and have your spouse sign and date Item 32 in Section F.

Section B: Reference Information

14. References: Enter the requested information for two relatives or acquaintances who do not live with you and who have known you for at least three years. References may not live outside the United States.

Name   1._____   2._____

Permanent Address   _____   _____

City, State, Zip Code   _____   _____

Area Code/Telephone Number ( ) _____   ( ) _____

Section C: Spouse Information   To be completed only if you responded "Yes" to Item 13.

15. Last Name First Name Middle Initial	16. Social Security Number
17. Date of Birth	18. Driver's License Number (put state abbreviation first) ( )	19. Fax Number (Optional) ( )
20. Former Name(s)		21. E-Mail Address (Optional)
22. Employer's Name	23. Employer's Address	
24. Employer's Area Code and Telephone Number ( )	City State Zip Code	

Page 1

283

Borrower's Name _____

Borrower's Social Security Number _____

Section D: Education Loan Indebtedness		(See instructions before completing this section.)				
25. Loan Holder/Servicer's Name, Address, and Area Code/Telephone Number	26. Loan Type	27. B=Borrower S=Spouse J=Joint	28. Account Number	29. Current Balance	30. To Be Consolidated? Yes	No
( )						
( )						
( )						
( )						
( )						
( )						
( )						
( )						

Page 2

Borrower's Name_____

Borrower's Social Security Number_____

Section E: Repayment Plan Selection

Carefully read the repayment plan information in "Direct Consolidation Loans" that accompanies this application and promissory note to understand your repayment plan options. Then, complete this section to select your repayment plan. Remember--

- All student loans must be repaid under the same repayment plan. Parent PLUS loans may be repaid under a different repayment plan.
- If you select the Income Contingent Repayment Plan, you must complete the "Repayment Plan Selection" and "Income Contingent Repayment Plan Consent to Disclosure of Tax Information" forms that accompany this application and promissory note. Your selection cannot be processed without these forms.
- **If you want to consolidate a defaulted student loan(s) and you have not made a satisfactory repayment arrangement with your current holder(s), you must select the Income Contingent Repayment Plan.**

31. Place an "X" in the box that corresponds to your repayment plan selection for each loan type. Note that Direct PLUS Consolidation Loans cannot be repaid under the Income Contingent Repayment Plan.

	Income Contingent	Standard	Extended	Graduated
STUDENT LOANS *Direct Subsidized and Unsubsidized Consolidation Loans*	☐	☐	☐	☐
PARENT LOANS *Direct PLUS Consolidation Loans*	Not Available	☐	☐	☐

Section F: Promissory Note (Continued on reverse side)   To be completed and signed by borrower and spouse, if applicable.

Promise to Pay:

I promise to pay to the U.S. Department of Education (ED) all sums (hereafter "loan" or "loans") disbursed under the terms of this Promissory Note (note) to discharge my prior loan obligations, plus interest, and other fees that may become due as provided in this note. If I fail to make payments on this note when due, I will also pay collection costs including but not limited to attorney's fees and court costs. If ED accepts my application, I understand that ED will on my behalf send funds to the holder(s) of the loan(s) selected for consolidation in order to pay off this loan(s). I further understand that the amount of this loan will equal the sum of the amount(s) that the holder(s) of the loan(s) verified as the payoff balance(s) on that loan(s) selected for consolidation. My signature on this note will serve as my authorization to pay off the balance(s) of the loan(s) selected for consolidation as provided by the holder(s) of such loan(s).

This amount may be more or less than the estimated total balance I have indicated in Section D. Further, I understand that if any collection costs are owed on the loans selected for consolidation, these costs may be added to the principal balance of the consolidation loan.

I understand that this is a Promissory Note. I will not sign this note before reading it, including the text on the reverse side, even if I am advised not to read the note. I am entitled to an exact copy of this note and a statement of the Borrower's Rights and Responsibilities. My signature certifies that I have read, understand, and agree, to the terms and conditions of this note, including the Borrower Certification and Authorization printed on the reverse side and the accompanying Borrower's Rights and Responsibilities.

If consolidating jointly with my spouse, we agree to the same terms and conditions contained in the Borrower Certification and Authorization. In addition, we confirm that we are legally married to each other and understand and agree that we are and will continue to be held jointly and severally liable for the entire amount of the debt represented by the Federal Direct Consolidation Loan without regard to the amounts of our individual loan obligations that are consolidated and without regard to any change that may occur in our marital status. We understand that this means that one of us may be required to pay the entire amount due if the other is unable or refuses to pay. We understand that the Federal Direct Consolidation Loan we are applying for will be cancelled only if both of us qualify for cancellation. We further understand that we may postpone repayment of the loan only if we provide ED with written requests that confirm Federal Direct Consolidation Loan Program deferment or forbearance eligibility for both of us at the same time.

I UNDERSTAND THAT THIS IS A FEDERAL LOAN THAT I MUST REPAY.

Promissory Note (continued)

Governing Law and Notices

This Promissory Note (note) applies to Federal Direct Consolidation Loans (Direct Consolidation Loans). In this note, the Higher Education Act of 1965, as amended, 20 U.S.C. 1070 et seq., and applicable U.S. Department of Education (ED) regulations are referred to as "the Act." The terms of this note will be interpreted according to the Act and other applicable federal statutes and regulations. Applicable state law, except as preempted by federal law, may provide for certain borrower rights, remedies, and defenses in addition to those stated in this note.

Disclosure of Terms

When the loan(s) that I am consolidating is paid off, I will be sent a Disclosure Statement and Repayment Schedule (disclosure). The disclosure will identify my Direct Consolidation Loan amount and additional terms of my loan. If I have questions about the information disclosed, I will contact ED. If the information in this note conflicts with the information in the disclosure, the disclosure will be controlling.

Important additional terms of this loan are disclosed in the statement of Borrower's Rights and Responsibilities accompanying this note.

I understand that my Direct Consolidation Loan may consist of up to three separate loan identification numbers depending on the loan(s) I choose to consolidate. These loan identification numbers will represent prior subsidized loans, prior unsubsidized loans, and prior parent PLUS loans. The Borrower's Rights and Responsibilities identifies which eligible loans are included in each of these categories. Each applicable loan identification number is represented by this note.

Interest

Except for interest ED does not charge me during an in-school, grace, or deferment period, I agree to pay interest on the principal amount of my Direct Consolidation Loan from the date of disbursement until the loan is paid in full or discharged. ED may add interest that accrues but is not paid when due to the unpaid principal balance of this loan, as provided under the Act. This is called capitalization.

Interest will be calculated according to the applicable formulas provided for by the Act.

The interest rate on my Direct Consolidation Loan will be based on the weighted average of the interest rates on the loans being consolidated, rounded to the nearest higher one-eighth of one percent, but shall not exceed 8.25%. This is a fixed interest rate, which means that the rate will remain the same throughout the life of the loan.

Late Charges and Collection Costs

If I fail to make any part of an installment payment within 30 days after it becomes due, ED may collect from me a late charge that will not exceed six cents for each dollar of each late installment. If I default on the loan, I will pay reasonable collection fees and costs, plus court costs and attorney's fees associated with collection of the debt.

Grace Period

My Direct Consolidation Loan will receive a grace period if I meet all of the following conditions: (1) I have at least one William D. Ford Federal Direct Loan (Direct Loan) Program loan or attend a Direct Loan school, (2) at least one Direct Loan or Federal Family Education Loan (FFEL) Program loan that I am consolidating is in an in-school period, and (3) my application for a Direct Consolidation Loan is received by ED prior to the end of my in-school period. A six-month grace period begins the day after I cease to be enrolled at least half time at an eligible school. (If my enrollment status changes to less than half time after I apply but before the first disbursement of my Direct Consolidation Loan, I will not have to make payments on my Direct Consolidation Loan for the number of months remaining in my grace period at the time the first disbursement is made.)

Repayment

Unless my Direct Consolidation Loan is in an in-school or grace period when it is disbursed, I must select a repayment plan. If I do not select a repayment plan, ED will choose a plan for me in accordance with ED's regulations. My first payment will be due within 60 days of the first disbursement of my Direct Consolidation Loan unless it is in an in-school, grace, or deferment period. A repayment schedule will be furnished to me and will establish repayment terms, including my payment amount and the length of my repayment period. Payments will be scheduled in monthly installments. The amount of my monthly payment may be adjusted to reflect changes in the variable interest rate. ED may adjust my repayment schedule if ED learns that any of the loans listed herein is not eligible to be consolidated. My repayment period will be up to 30 years in length, depending on the amount of my student loan indebtedness and my repayment plan. Any period for which ED has granted a deferment or forbearance will not be included in determining my repayment period.

I may prepay all or any part of the unpaid balance on my loan at any time without penalty. I agree to accept written notification of such pay off in lieu of receiving the original note.

Acceleration and Default

At the option of ED, the entire unpaid balance shall become immediately due and payable when either of the following events occurs: (i) I make false representation that results in my receiving a loan for which I am not eligible, or (ii) I default on the loan.

The following events shall constitute a default on a loan: (i) I fail to pay the entire unpaid balance after ED has exercised its option under the preceding paragraph; or (ii) I fail to make installment payments when due, or fail to comply with other terms of the loan, and ED reasonably concludes I no longer intend to honor my repayment obligation. My failure must have persisted for at least 270 days. If I default, ED will capitalize all outstanding interest into a new principal balance.

If I default, this will be reported to national credit bureau organizations and will significantly and adversely affect my credit rating. I acknowledge that a default shall have additional adverse consequences to me as disclosed in the Borrower's Rights and Responsibilities.

Following default, the loan may at ED's option, be subject to income contingent repayment in accordance with the Act.

Any notice required to be given to me will be effective when mailed by first class mail to the latest address that ED has for me. I will immediately notify ED of any change of my address. Failure by ED to enforce or insist on compliance with any term on this note shall not waive any right of ED. No provision of this note may be changed or waived except in writing by ED. If any provision of this note is determined to be unenforceable, the remaining provisions shall remain in force.

Borrower Certification and Authorization

I declare under penalty of perjury that the following is true and correct:

(1) I certify that the information provided by me and my spouse, if applicable, in this note is true, complete, and correct to the best of my knowledge and belief and is made in good faith.

(2) I certify that I do not now owe a refund on a Federal Pell Grant, Basic Educational Opportunity Grant, Federal Supplemental Educational Opportunity Grant, or a State Student Incentive Grant, or if I owe a refund, I have made satisfactory arrangements with the holder to repay the amount owed. I further certify that I am not now in default on any loan I am consolidating or, if I am in default, I have either made a satisfactory repayment arrangement with the holder of that defaulted loan, or I will repay under the income contingent repayment plan. I understand that income contingent repayment is not available for the parent PLUS loan portion of my Direct Consolidation Loan.

(3) I certify that all of the loans selected have been used to finance my education, my spouse's education, or my child's education.

(4) I certify that I do not have any other application pending for a Federal Consolidation Loan with any other lender. If my student loans are in a grace or repayment period and if none of the loans I am consolidating is a Direct Loan Program loan, I further certify that I have sought and been unable to obtain a Federal Consolidation Loan from a FFEL Program lender, or a lender would not provide me with a Federal Consolidation Loan with income-sensitive repayment terms acceptable to me. If I have parent PLUS loans and none of the loans I am consolidating is a Direct Loan Program loan, I further certify that I have sought and been unable to obtain a Federal Consolidation Loan from a FFEL Program lender. If, however, I am consolidating jointly with my spouse, only one borrower, my spouse or I, must have sought a Federal Consolidation Loan from a FFEL Program lender.

(5) I understand that this loan shall, to the extent used to discharge loans that I have selected, count against the applicable aggregate loan limits under the Act.

(6) I understand that the amount of my Direct Consolidation Loan is the sum of the balance(s) of my outstanding eligible loan(s) that I have chosen to consolidate. My outstanding balance on each loan to be consolidated includes unpaid principal, unpaid accrued interest, and late charges as defined by federal regulations and as certified by each holder. Collection costs may also be included. For a Direct Loan or FFEL Program loan that is in default, ED limits collection costs that may be charged to the borrower to no more than those currently authorized under the FFEL Program and may impose reasonable limits on collection costs paid to the holder. If the amount ED advances to my holder(s) exceeds the amount needed to pay off the balance(s) of the selected loan(s), I understand that the holder will refund the excess to ED for application against the outstanding balance of this loan. If the amount that ED advances to my holder(s) is less than the amount needed to pay off the balance(s) of the loan(s) selected for consolidation, ED will include the remaining amount in this loan unless I pay the remaining balance myself.

(7) I authorize ED to contact the holder(s) identified on my application to determine the eligibility and/or payoff amount for the loan(s) I have identified. I further authorize release to ED or its agent any information required to consolidate my education loan(s) pursuant to the Act.

(8) I authorize ED to issue the proceeds of my Direct Consolidation Loan to the holder(s) of the loan(s) so selected to discharge the debt.

(9) I authorize ED to investigate my credit record and report information concerning my loan status to proper persons and organizations authorized to receive this information.

(10) I authorize the release of information pertinent to this loan: (i) by my school(s) and ED, to members of my immediate family unless I submit written direction otherwise; and (ii) by and amongst my school(s), ED, and their agents.

(11) I authorize my school(s), ED, and their agents, to verify my social security number with the Social Security Administration (SSA) and, if the number on my loan record is incorrect, then I authorize SSA to disclose my correct social security number to these parties.

Page 4

D.2.2 FFEL Economic Hardship Deferment Form

Other selected deferment forms can be found on the companion CD-Rom.

HRD

ECONOMIC HARDSHIP DEFERMENT REQUEST

Federal Family Education Loan Program

USE THIS FORM ONLY IF **ALL** OF YOUR OUTSTANDING FEDERAL FAMILY EDUCATION LOAN PROGRAM LOANS WERE MADE ON OR AFTER JULY 1, 1993.

WARNING: Any person who knowingly makes a false statement or misrepresentation on this form or on any accompanying documents shall be subject to penalties which may include fines, imprisonment or both, under the U.S. Criminal Code and 20 U.S.C. §1097.

OMB No. 1845-0005
Form Approved
Exp. Date 06/30/2002

SECTION 1: BORROWER IDENTIFICATION

Please correct or, if information is missing, enter below. If a correction, check this box: ☐

SSN ⎸__⎸__⎸__⎸ – ⎸__⎸__⎸ – ⎸__⎸__⎸__⎸__⎸

Name _____

Address _____

City, State, Zip _____

Telephone - Home ( ) _____

Telephone - Other ( ) _____

SECTION 2: DEFERMENT REQUEST

Before answering any questions, carefully read the entire form, including the instructions and other information in Sections 4, 5, and 6.

■ I meet the qualifications stated in Section 6 for the Economic Hardship Deferment checked below and request that my loan holder defer repayment of my loan(s) beginning ⎸__⎸__⎸ – ⎸__⎸__⎸ – ⎸__⎸__⎸__⎸__⎸. To qualify, I must meet **one** of the conditions listed below and must provide the required documentation, as described in Section 6, for only that condition. *Check one:*

(1) ☐ I have been granted an economic hardship deferment under the William D. Ford Federal Direct Loan (Direct Loan) Program or the Federal Perkins Loan Program for the same period of time for which I am requesting this deferment. **I have attached documentation of the deferment.**

(2) ☐ I am receiving or received payments under a federal or state public assistance program, such as Aid to Families with Dependent Children (AFDC), Supplemental Security Income (SSI), Food Stamps, or state general public assistance. **I have attached documentation of these payments.**

(3) ☐ I am serving as a Peace Corps volunteer. **I have attached documentation certifying my period of service in the Peace Corps.**

(4) ☐ I work full-time **and** my monthly income, as defined in Section 5, does not exceed the **larger of** (A) the Federal Minimum Wage Rate, or (B) the Poverty Line income for a family of two for my state (regardless of my actual family size), as listed below. **I have attached documentation of this income.**

My monthly income is $ _____ .

(A) Federal Minimum Wage Rate (monthly amount, based on $5.15 an hour) $ 892.66

(B) Poverty Lines for a Family of Two (monthly amounts)
- All states and the District of Columbia (except Alaska and Hawaii) $ 967.50
- Alaska $1,209.17
- Hawaii $1,113.33

(5) ☐ I do **not** work full-time **and** my monthly income, as defined in Section 5, does not exceed the **larger of** (A) **two times** the Federal Minimum Wage Rate, or (B) **two times** the Poverty Line income for a family of two for my state (regardless of my actual family size), as listed above under condition (4). In addition, after deducting the total monthly payments that I am making on all of my federal education debts from my monthly income, the amount remaining does not exceed the **larger of** (A) the Federal Minimum Wage Rate, or (B) the Poverty Line income for a family of two for my state, as listed above under condition (4). My total monthly federal education debt payments must be adjusted, if necessary, to reflect a minimum 10-year repayment period. **I have attached documentation of my monthly income and my federal education loan debt.**

NOTE: *A worksheet to help you determine whether you meet this condition is available from your loan holder. Completion of the worksheet is optional. Your loan holder will determine whether you qualify based on the income and education debt information that you provide below.*

My monthly income is $ _____ .

The total amount I borrowed for all of my federal education loans now in repayment (including loans for which I am requesting this deferment) is $ _____ .

(6) ☐ I work full-time **and** the total amount of my monthly payments on all of my federal education loans in repayment is equal to or larger than 20% of my monthly income, as defined in Section 5. In addition, after deducting the total amount of my monthly payments on my federal education loans in repayment from my monthly income, the amount remaining is less than 220% of the **larger of** (A) the Federal Minimum Wage rate, or (B) the Poverty Line income for a family of two for my state (regardless of my actual family size), as listed above under condition (4). My total monthly federal education loan payments must be adjusted, if necessary, to reflect a minimum 10-year repayment period. **I have attached documentation of my monthly income and my federal education loan debt.**

NOTE: *A worksheet to help you determine whether you meet this condition is available from your loan holder. Completion of the worksheet is optional. Your loan holder will determine whether you qualify based on the income and education debt information that you provide below.*

My monthly income is $ _____ .

The total amount I borrowed for all of my federal education loans now in repayment (including loans for which I am requesting this deferment) is $ _____ .

SECTION 3: BORROWER INTEREST SELECTION AND CERTIFICATION

■ Principal payments will be deferred, but if I have an unsubsidized loan, I am responsible for paying the interest that accrues. I have the option of making interest payments on my unsubsidized loan(s) during my deferment. I may choose to make interest payments by checking the box below; unpaid interest that accrues will be capitalized by my loan holder.

☐ I wish to make interest payments on my unsubsidized loan(s) during my deferment.

■ **I certify that** the information I provided in Sections 1 and 2 above is true and correct, and that I have read, understand, and meet the terms and conditions and eligibility criteria of the deferment for which I have applied, as explained in Section 6.

Borrower's Signature _____   **Date** _____

SECTION 4: INSTRUCTIONS FOR COMPLETING THE FORM

Type or print using dark ink. Report dates as month-day-year (MM-DD-YYYY). For example, 'January 1, 1999' = '01-01-1999'. Include your name and social security number (SSN) on any documentation that you are required to submit with this form. If you need help completing this form, contact your loan holder.

Return the completed form and any required documentation to the address shown in Section 7.

SECTION 5: DEFINITIONS

- The **Federal Family Education Loan (FFEL) Program** includes Federal Stafford Loans (both subsidized and unsubsidized), Federal Supplemental Loans for Students (SLS), Federal PLUS Loans, and Federal Consolidation Loans.

- The **William D. Ford Federal Direct Loan (Direct Loan) Program** includes Federal Direct Stafford/Ford (Direct Subsidized) Loans, Federal Direct Unsubsidized Stafford/Ford (Direct Unsubsidized) Loans, Federal Direct PLUS (Direct PLUS) Loans, and Federal Direct Consolidation (Direct Consolidation) Loans.

- The **holder** of my FFEL Program loan(s) may be a lender, guaranty agency, secondary market, or the U.S. Department of Education.

- A **deferment** is a period during which I am entitled to postpone repayment of the principal balance of my loan(s). The federal government pays the interest that accrues during an eligible deferment for all subsidized Federal Stafford Loans and for Federal Consolidation Loans for which the Consolidation loan application was received by my loan holder **(1)** on or after January 1, 1993 but before August 10, 1993, **(2)** on or after August 10, 1993, if it includes **only** Federal Stafford Loans that were eligible for federal interest subsidy, or **(3)** on or after November 13, 1997, for that portion of the Consolidation loan that paid a subsidized Federal Stafford Loan or a Federal Direct Stafford/Ford (Direct Subsidized) Loan. I am responsible for the interest that accrues during this period on all other FFEL Program loans.

- **Monthly income** is either:

  (1) the amount of my monthly income from employment and other sources before taxes and other deductions, **or** (2) one-twelfth of the amount of my income reported as "adjusted gross income" on my most recently filed Federal Income Tax Return.

  I may choose either of these income amounts for the purpose of reporting my monthly income on this deferment request.

- **Full-time** employment is defined as working at least 30 hours per week in a position expected to last at least three consecutive months.

- Eligible **federal education loans** that may be included in determining the total amount I borrowed for deferment conditions (5) and (6) in Section 2 are listed below. I may include defaulted loans only if I have made satisfactory repayment arrangements with the holder of those loans.

  - All **FFEL Program** loans listed above
  - All **Direct Loan Program** loans listed above
  - Guaranteed Student Loans (GSL)
  - Federal Insured Student Loans (FISL)
  - Federal Perkins Loans

  - National Direct Student Loans (NDSL)
  - National Defense Student Loans (NDSL)
  - Auxiliary Loans to Assist Students (ALAS)
  - Parent Loans for Undergraduate Students (PLUS)
  - Health Education Assistance Loans (HEAL)

  - Health Professions Student Loans (HPSL)
  - Loans for Disadvantaged Students (LDS)
  - Primary Care Loans (PCL)
  - Nursing Student Loans (NSL)

- **Minimum 10-year repayment period** (for deferment conditions (5) and (6) in Section 2) refers to the period that is 10 years from the date I entered repayment, regardless of the actual length of my repayment schedule. If the length of my repayment schedule is more than 10 years, my payment amounts must be adjusted to show the estimated monthly amount that I would owe if my loan were scheduled to be repaid in fixed installments within a 10-year period.

- **Forbearance** means permitting the temporary cessation of payments, allowing an extension of time for making payments, or temporarily accepting smaller payments than previously scheduled. I am responsible for paying the interest on my loan(s) during a forbearance.

- **Capitalization** is the addition of unpaid interest to the principal balance of my loan. This will increase the principal and the total cost of my loan.

SECTION 6: ELIGIBILITY CRITERIA / TERMS AND CONDITIONS FOR ECONOMIC HARDSHIP DEFERMENT

- If **ALL** of my outstanding FFEL Program loans were made **on or after July 1, 1993**, I may defer repayment of my loan(s) while I meet one of the economic hardship conditions listed in Section 2.

- If my economic hardship deferment eligibility is based on condition (1), as described in Section 2, I must provide my loan holder with documentation of the deferment that has been granted under the Direct Loan Program or the Federal Perkins Loan Program (for example, correspondence from my loan holder showing that I have been granted a deferment).

- If my economic hardship deferment eligibility is based on condition (2), as described in Section 2, I must provide my loan holder with documentation confirming that I am receiving or received payments under a federal or state public assistance program.

- If my economic hardship deferment eligibility is based on condition (3), as described in Section 2, I must provide my loan holder with documentation which certifies the beginning and anticipated ending dates of my service in the Peace Corps and which is signed and dated by an authorized Peace Corps official.

- If my economic hardship deferment eligibility is based on conditions (4), (5) or (6), as described in Section 2, I must provide my loan holder with documentation of my monthly income as defined in Section 5. If I am reporting monthly income from employment and other sources, I must provide documentation such as pay stubs. If I am reporting one-twelfth of my adjusted gross income. I must provide a copy of my most recently filed Federal Income Tax Return.

- If my economic hardship deferment eligibility is based on condition (5) or condition (6), as described in Section 2, I must provide my loan holder with documentation of the total amount I borrowed for all federal education loans that are now in repayment, such as disclosure statements or current repayment schedules. This must include the monthly payment amount, beginning loan balance, and repayment terms. If my total federal education loan debt includes defaulted loans, I must provide documentation that I have made repayment arrangements satisfactory to the holder(s) of the defaulted loans.

- If my economic hardship deferment eligibility is based on conditions (4), (5), or (6), as described in Section 2, and I am not currently residing in the United States, I will use the Poverty Line amounts for my last state of residence in the United States.

- I will provide additional documentation to my loan holder, as required, to support my deferment status.

- I will notify my loan holder immediately when the condition that qualified me for the deferment ends.

- My deferment will begin on the date the deferment condition began.

- My deferment will end on the earlier of the date that the condition that establishes my deferment eligibility ends or the certified deferment end date.

Section 6 continued on Page 3.

SECTION 6 (Continued)

■ My maximum cumulative eligibility for an economic hardship deferment is 36 months.

■ My loan holder will not grant this deferment request unless all applicable sections of this form are completed and any additional required documentation is provided.

■ If my deferment does not cover all my past due payments, my loan holder may grant me a forbearance for all payments due before the begin date of my deferment. If the period for which I am eligible for a deferment has ended, my loan holder may grant me a forbearance for all payments due at the time my deferment request is processed.

■ My loan holder may grant me a forbearance on my loans for up to 60 days, if necessary, for the collection and processing of documentation related to my deferment request. Interest that accrues during the forbearance will not be capitalized.

SECTION 7: WHERE TO SEND THE COMPLETED DEFERMENT REQUEST

RETURN THE COMPLETED DEFERMENT REQUEST AND ANY REQUIRED DOCUMENTATION TO:
(IF NO ADDRESS IS SHOWN, RETURN TO YOUR LOAN HOLDER)

SECTION 8: IMPORTANT NOTICES

Privacy Act Disclosure Notice

The Privacy Act of 1974 (5 U.S.C. §552a) requires that we disclose to you the following information:

The authority for collecting this information is §421 *et seq.* of the Higher Education Act of 1965, as amended (the HEA) (20 U.S.C. §1071 to 1087-2). The principal purpose for collecting this information is to determine whether you are eligible for a deferment on your loan(s) under the Federal Family Education Loan (FFEL) Program.

We ask that you provide the information requested on this deferment request on a voluntary basis. However, you must provide all of the requested information so that the holder(s) of your loan(s) can determine whether you qualify for a deferment.

The information in your file may be disclosed to third parties as authorized under routine uses in the Privacy Act notices called "Title IV Program Files" (originally published on April 12, 1994, *Federal Register*, Vol. 59, p. 17351) and "National Student Loan Data System" (originally published on December 20, 1994, *Federal Register*, Vol. 59, p. 65532). Thus, this information may be disclosed to parties that we authorize to assist us in administering the federal student aid programs, including contractors that are required to maintain safeguards under the Privacy Act. Disclosures may also be made for verification of information, determination of eligibility, enforcement of conditions of the loan or grant, debt collection, and the prevention of fraud, waste, and abuse and these disclosures may be made through computer matching programs with other federal agencies. Disclosures may be made to determine the feasibility of entering into computer matching agreements. We may send information to members of Congress if you ask them in writing to help you with federal student aid questions. If we are involved in litigation, we may send information to the Department of Justice (DOJ), a court, adjudicative body, counsel, or witness if the disclosure is related to financial aid and certain other conditions are met. If this information, either alone or with other information, indicates a potential violation of law, we may send it to the appropriate authority for consideration of action and we may disclose to DOJ to get its advice related to the Title IV, HEA programs or questions under the Freedom of Information Act. Disclosures may be made to qualified researchers under Privacy Act safeguards. In some circumstances involving employment decisions, grievances, or complaints or involving decisions regarding the letting of a contract or making of a grant, license, or other benefit, we may send information to an appropriate authority. In limited circumstances, we may disclose to a federal labor organization recognized under 5 U.S.C. Chapter 71.

Because we request your social security number (SSN), we must inform you that we collect your SSN on a voluntary basis, but section 484(a)(4) of the HEA (20 U.S.C. §1091(a)(4)) provides that, in order to receive any grant, loan, or work assistance under Title IV of the HEA, a student must provide his or her SSN. Your SSN is used to verify your identity, and as an account number (identifier) throughout the life of your loan(s) so that data may be recorded accurately.

Paperwork Reduction Notice

According to the Paperwork Reduction Act of 1995, no persons are required to respond to a collection of information unless it displays a currently valid OMB control number. The valid OMB control number for this information collection is 1845-0005. The time required to complete this information collection is estimated to average 0.16 hours (10 minutes) per response, including the time to review instructions, search existing data resources, gather and maintain the data needed, and complete and review the information collection. *If you have any comments concerning the accuracy of the time estimate(s) or suggestions for improving this form, please write to:*

U.S. Department of Education, Washington, DC 20202-4651.

If you have any comments or concerns regarding the status of your individual submission of this form, write directly to the address shown in Section 7.

ECONOMIC HARDSHIP DEFERMENT
WORKSHEET A

Use this worksheet to determine if you are eligible for an economic hardship deferment based on condition (5) in Section 2 of the Economic Hardship Deferment Request form. Completion of this worksheet is optional — if you check condition (5), your loan holder will determine your eligibility based on the income and federal education debt documentation that you provide.

DO NOT RETURN THIS WORKSHEET WITH THE DEFERMENT REQUEST — KEEP IT FOR YOUR RECORDS.

STEP 1

Are you working full-time?

☐ Yes   You do not qualify for an economic hardship deferment based on condition (5). Do not continue with this worksheet.

☐ No   Go to Step 2.

STEP 2

(1) Line 1. Enter the amount listed below for your state: $ _____

(2) Line 2. $ __1,785.32__

(3) Line 3. Enter the **larger** of Line 1 or Line 2: $ _____

(4) Line 4. Enter your **MONTHLY INCOME**: $ _____
(see the definition of "Monthly income" in Section 5 of
the Economic Hardship Deferment Request)

(5) Is the amount on Line 4 **larger** than the amount on Line 3?

☐ Yes   You do not qualify for an economic hardship deferment based on condition (5). Do not continue with this worksheet.

☐ No   Go to Step 3.

Amounts for Line 1, above:

$1,935.00   (if you live in any state or the District of Columbia, *except* Alaska or Hawaii).

$2,418.34   (if you live in Alaska).

$2,226.66   (if you live in Hawaii).

NOTE: *If you are not currently living in the United States, use the amount for your last state of residence in the United States.*

STEP 3

Determine the total amount you borrowed in federal education loans that are now in repayment by adding together the amounts owed for the federal education loans listed below. You may include defaulted loans only if you have made satisfactory repayment arrangements with the holder of the loans.

Loan Type	Total Amount You Owed When Your Loans Entered Repayment
Federal Stafford Loans (subsidized and unsubsidized)	$ _____
Direct Subsidized and Direct Unsubsidized Loans	+ $ _____
Federal PLUS Loans	+ $ _____
Direct PLUS Loans	+ $ _____
Federal SLS Loans	+ $ _____
Federal Consolidation Loans	+ $ _____
Direct Consolidation Loans	+ $ _____
Federal Perkins Loans and/or National Direct Student Loans	+ $ _____
Other eligible federal education loans listed in Section 5	+ $ _____
TOTAL AMOUNT BORROWED:	= $ _____

Worksheet A continued on Page 2.

Worksheet A
Page 1 of 2

ECONOMIC HARDSHIP DEFERMENT
WORKSHEET A (Continued)

STEP 4

(1) Circle the current interest rate for your FFEL Program loan(s) in the chart below. If your exact interest rate is not listed, choose the next highest interest rate. If you have loans with different interest rates, circle the rate for the loan with the highest interest rate.

Interest Rate	7.0%	7.25%	7.43%	7.5%	7.75%	8.0%	8.25%	8.38%	8.5%	8.75%	9.0%
Constant Multiplier	.0116108	.0117401	.0118337	.0118702	.0120011	.0121328	.0122653	.0123345	.0123986	.0125237	.0126676

(2) Multiply the **TOTAL AMOUNT BORROWED** from Step 3 by the constant multiplier listed directly below the interest rate that you circled in the chart above:

TOTAL AMOUNT BORROWED (from Step 3)   **Constant multiplier** (from the chart above)   **ESTIMATED MONTHLY PAYMENT***

$ _____   **X**   _____   **=** $ _____

* This is an estimate of the amount that you would pay each month on your federal education loans if all of your loans were scheduled to be repaid in fixed installments over a 10-year period, regardless of the actual repayment period for your loans.

STEP 5

(1) Line 1. Enter your **MONTHLY INCOME** (from Step 2): $ _____

(2) Line 2. Enter your **ESTIMATED MONTHLY PAYMENT** (from Step 4): $ _____

(3) Line 3. Subtract Line 2 from Line 1: $ _____

(4) Line 4. Enter the amount listed below for your state: $ _____

(5) Line 5. $ ___892.66___

(6) Line 6. Enter the **larger** of Line 4 or Line 5: $ _____

(7) Line 7. Enter the amount from Line 3: $ _____

(8) Is the amount on Line 7 larger than the amount on Line 6?

   ❐ Yes   You do not qualify for an economic hardship deferment based on condition (5).

   ❐ No   You meet the qualifications for an economic hardship deferment based on condition (5). Check the box for condition (5) in Section 2 of the deferment request.

Amounts for Line 4, above:

  $ 967.50 (if you live in any state or the District of Columbia, *except* Alaska or Hawaii).

  $1,209.17 (if you live in Alaska).

  $1,113.33 (if you live in Hawaii).

NOTE: *If you are not currently living in the United States, use the amount for your last state of residence in the United States.*

ECONOMIC HARDSHIP DEFERMENT
WORKSHEET B

Use this worksheet to determine if you are eligible for an economic hardship deferment based on condition (6) in Section 2 of the Economic Hardship Deferment Request form. Completion of this worksheet is optional — if you check condition (6), your loan holder will determine your eligibility based on the income and federal education debt documentation that you provide.

DO NOT RETURN THIS WORKSHEET WITH THE DEFERMENT REQUEST — KEEP IT FOR YOUR RECORDS.

STEP 1

Are you working full-time?

❒ Yes   Go to Step 2.

❒ No   You do not qualify for an economic hardship deferment based on condition (6). Do not continue with this worksheet.

STEP 2

Determine the total amount you borrowed in federal education loans that are now in repayment by adding together the amounts owed for the federal education loans listed below. You may include defaulted loans only if you have made satisfactory repayment arrangements with the holder of the loans.

Loan Type	Total Amount You Owed When Your Loans Entered Repayment
Federal Stafford Loans (subsidized and unsubsidized)	$ _____
Direct Subsidized and Direct Unsubsidized Loans	+ $ _____
Federal PLUS Loans	+ $ _____
Direct PLUS Loans	+ $ _____
Federal SLS Loans	+ $ _____
Federal Consolidation Loans	+ $ _____
Direct Consolidation Loans	+ $ _____
Federal Perkins Loans and/or National Direct Student Loans	+ $ _____
Other eligible federal education loans listed in Section 5	+ $ _____
TOTAL AMOUNT BORROWED:	= $ _____

STEP 3

(1) Circle the current interest rate for your FFEL Program loan(s) in the chart below. If your exact interest rate is not listed, choose the next highest interest rate. If you have loans with different interest rates, circle the rate for the loan with the highest interest rate.

Interest Rate	7.0%	7.25%	7.43%	7.5%	7.75%	8.0%	8.25%	8.38%	8.5%	8.75%	9.0%
Constant Multiplier	.0116108	.0117401	.0118337	.0118702	.0120011	.0121328	.0122653	.0123345	.0123986	.0125237	.0126676

(2) Multiply the **TOTAL AMOUNT BORROWED** from Step 2 by the constant multiplier listed directly below the interest rate that you circled in the chart above:

TOTAL AMOUNT BORROWED (from Step 2)	**Constant multiplier** (from the chart above)	**ESTIMATED MONTHLY PAYMENT***
$ _____ X	_____ =	$ _____

* This is an estimate of the amount that you would pay each month on your federal education loans if all of your loans were scheduled to be repaid in fixed installments over a 10-year period, regardless of the actual repayment period for your loans.

Worksheet B continued on Page 2.

ECONOMIC HARDSHIP DEFERMENT
WORKSHEET B (Continued)

STEP 4

(1) Line 1. Enter your monthly income: $ _____

(see the definition of "Monthly income" in Section 5 of
the Economic Hardship Deferment Request)

(2) Line 2. Multiply the amount on Line 1 by .20 (= 20%): $ _____

(3) Line 3. Enter your **ESTIMATED MONTHLY PAYMENT** (from Step 3): $ _____

(4) Is the amount on Line 3 **equal to or larger than** the amount on Line 2?

◻ Yes   Go to Step 5.

◻ No   You do not qualify for an economic hardship deferment based on condition (6). Do not continue with this worksheet.

STEP 5

(1) Line 1. Enter your monthly income: $ _____

(2) Line 2. Enter your **ESTIMATED MONTHLY PAYMENT** (from Step 3): $ _____

(3) Line 3. Subtract Line 2 from Line 1: $ _____

(4) Line 4. Enter the amount listed below for your state: $ _____

(5) Line 5. $ __1,964.00__

(6) Line 6. Enter the **larger** of Line 4 or Line 5: $ _____

(7) Line 7. Enter the amount from Line 3: $ _____

(8) Is the amount on Line 7 **less than** the amount on line 6?

◻ Yes   You meet the qualifications for an economic hardship deferment based on condition (6). Check the box for condition (6) in Section 2
of the deferment request.

◻ No   You do not qualify for an economic hardship deferment based on condition (6).

Amounts for Line 4, above:

$2,128.50 (if you live in any state or the District of Columbia, *except* Alaska or Hawaii).

$2,660.17 (if you live in Alaska).

$2,449.33 (if you live in Hawaii).

NOTE: *If you are not currently living in the United States, use the amount for your last state of residence in the United States.*

D.2.3 Statement of Financial Status Form

The Department of Education uses this form to assess a borrower's eligibility for affordable payment plans as well as hardship waivers for various collection programs.

STATEMENT OF FINANCIAL STATUS

YOUR NAME _____ YOUR SSN _____

1. AMOUNT YOU ARE PROPOSING TO PAY EACH MONTH: $_____

**************** HOUSEHOLD AND EMPLOYMENT INFORMATION ****************

2. YOUR ADDRESS   _____

     _____

     _____

3. COUNTY IN WHICH YOU LIVE:_____ HOME PHONE _____

4. EMPLOYER'S NAME   _____

5. EMPLOYER'S
   ADDRESS   _____

     _____

6. EMPLOYER'S PHONE _____ YOUR JOB TITLE _____

7. NUMBER OF DEPENDENTS (AS DEFINED BY IRS) INCLUDING SELF: _____

8. MARITAL STATUS (MARRIED, SINGLE, DIVORCED):   _____

9. SPOUSE'S NAME AND SSN: _____

*********************** MONTHLY INCOME ***********************

NOTE: GROSS INCOME IS INCOME BEFORE ANY DEDUCTIONS SUCH AS TAXES. NET INCOME IS YOUR TAKE-HOME PAY. INCLUDE RECENT PAY STUBS AND TAX RETURNS.

10. YOUR AVERAGE MONTHLY INCOME   GROSS $_____ NET $_____
11. YOUR SPOUSE'S AVG MONTHLY INCOME   GROSS $_____ NET $_____
12. OTHER CONTRIBUTING RESIDENT(S) AVG MONTHLY INCOME   NET $_____
13. OTHER(ALIMONY, ETC. DESCRIBE_____)NET $_____

********************* MONTHLY EXPENSES *********************

14. RENT/MORTGAGE   (TO WHOM:_____)$_____
15. PROPERTY TAX $_____
16. HOME/RENTER'S INSURANCE $_____
17. FOOD $_____
18. CLOTHING $_____
19. ELECTRICITY $_____
20. NATURAL GAS/HEATING OIL/PROPANE $_____
21. WATER/SEWER/TRASH DISPOSAL $_____

CONTINUED ON PAGE 2 –

- STATEMENT OF FINANCIAL STATUS PAGE 2 – MONTHLY EXPENSES CONTINUED

22. BASIC PHONE SERVICE $_____
23. CAR PAYMENT (FIRST CAR) $_____
24. CAR PAYMENT (SECOND CAR) $_____
25. AUTO FUEL AND MAINTENANCE $_____
26. PUBLIC TRANSPORTATION $_____
27. AUTO INSURANCE $_____
28. MEDICAL INSURANCE PAYMENTS NOT DEDUCTED FROM PAYCHECK $_____
29. MEDICAL CO-PAYMENTS AND EXPENSES NOT COVERED BY INSURANCE $_____
30. CHILD CARE EXPENSES (NUMBER OF CHILDREN:_____) $_____
31. CHILD SUPPORT (NUMBER OF CHILDREN:_____) $_____

LIST ANY OTHER MONTHLY EXPENSES BELOW:

32. _____ $_____
33. _____ $_____
34. _____ $_____

****************************** ASSETS ******************************

35. BANK ACCOUNT 1 (BANK NAME:_____) $_____
36. BANK ACCOUNT 2 (BANK NAME:_____) $_____
37. BANK ACCOUNT 3 (BANK NAME:_____) $_____
38. STOCKS/BONDS (BANK NAME:_____) $_____
39. HOME VALUE:$_____ OWED:$_____
40. OTHER REAL ESTATE VALUE:$_____ OWED:$_____
41. CAR 1 (YR,MAKE,MODEL:_____) VALUE:$_____ OWED:$_____
42. CAR 2 (YR,MAKE,MODEL:_____) VALUE:$_____ OWED:$_____

************************ SWORN STATEMENT ************************

I DECLARE UNDER PENALTIES PROVIDED BY 18 U.S.C. SECTION 1001, THAT THE
ANSWERS AND STATEMENTS CONTAINED HEREIN ARE TO THE BEST OF MY KNOWLEDGE
AND BELIEF TRUE, CORRECT AND COMPLETE.

43. SIGNATURE:_____ DATE:_____

SOCIAL SECURITY NUMBER: _____

WARNING: 18 U.S.C. 1001 PROVIDES THAT "WHOEVER...KNOWINGLY AND WILLFULLY
FALSIFIES, CONCEALS OR COVERS UP BY ANY TRICK, SCHEME, OR DEVICE A
MATERIAL FACT, OR MAKES ANY FALSE, FICTITIOUS OR FRAUDULENT STATEMENTS
OR REPRESENTATION.., SHALL BE FINED NOT MORE THAN $10,000.00, OR
IMPRISONED NOT MORE THAN FIVE YEARS, OR BOTH".

RETURN THIS FORM AND ALL REQUIRED DOCUMENTATION TO:

        U.S. DEPARTMENT OF EDUCATION
        PO BOX 4222
        IOWA CITY, IA 52244-4222

STATEMENT OF FINANCIAL STATUS
INSTRUCTIONS

THIS STATEMENT OF FINANCIAL STATUS FORM HAS BEEN SENT IN RESPONSE TO YOUR REQUEST TO ESTABLISH A MONTHLY PAYMENT PLAN. IN ORDER TO DETERMINE A PAYMENT AMOUNT THAT IS BOTH AFFORDABLE FOR YOU AND REASONABLE BASED ON THE AMOUNT YOU OWE, YOU MUST COMPLETE AND RETURN IT.

1. IMMEDIATELY BEGIN SENDING THE AMOUNT YOU PROPOSE TO PAY EACH MONTH TO:

    U.S. DEPARTMENT OF EDUCATION
    PO BOX 4169
    GREENVILLE, TX 75403-4169

INCLUDE YOUR NAME AND SOCIAL SECURITY NUMBER ON YOUR CHECK OR MONEY ORDER. DO NOT SEND CASH.

2. COMPLETE EVERY FIELD ON THIS FORM. IF AN ANSWER IS ZERO, WRITE ZERO.

3. INCLUDE PROOF OF YOUR HOUSEHOLD INCOME FOR BOTH YOU AND YOUR SPOUSE (TWO MOST RECENT PAY STUBS AND FEDERAL INCOME TAX RETURNS), AND PROOF OF YOUR EXPENSES (SUCH AS COPIES OF MONTHLY BILLS AND/OR CANCELLED CHECKS).

4. DO NOT INCLUDE MONTHLY PAYMENTS ON CREDIT CARDS IF THE ITEMS PURCHASED BY THAT CREDIT CARD FIT UNDER AN EXPENSE CATEGORY LISTED. INCLUDE THOSE COSTS UNDER THAT EXPENSE CATEGORY. FOR EXAMPLE, PAYMENTS ON CREDIT CARDS USED TO PURCHASE CLOTHING SHOULD BE LISTED UNDER CLOTHING EXPENSES.

5. IF YOU ARE PAYING SOME EXPENSES QUARTERLY OR ANNUALLY, SUCH AS AUTOMOBILE INSURANCE, CALCULATE THE AMOUNT THAT WOULD BE DUE IF THESE EXPENSES WERE PAID MONTHLY AND PUT THAT AMOUNT IN THE SPACE PROVIDED.

6. RETURN THE COMPLETED FORM TO: U.S. DEPARTMENT OF EDUCATION
                                     PO BOX 4222
                                     IOWA CITY, IA 52244-4222

7. WE WILL NOTIFY YOU IN WRITING ONCE WE DETERMINE AN ACCEPTABLE MONTHLY PAYMENT AMOUNT. YOU MAY CONTACT US AT 800-621-3115 FOR FURTHER ASSISTANCE.

PRIVACY ACT NOTICE

THIS REQUEST IS AUTHORIZED UNDER 31 U.S.C. 3711, 20 U.S.C. 1078-6, AND 20 U.S.C. 1095A. YOU ARE NOT REQUIRED TO PROVIDE THIS INFORMATION. IF YOU DO NOT, WE CANNOT DETERMINE YOUR FINANCIAL ABILITY TO REPAY YOUR STUDENT AID DEBT. THE INFORMATION YOU PROVIDE WILL BE USED TO EVALUATE YOUR ABILITY TO PAY. IT MAY BE DISCLOSED TO GOVERNMENT AGENCIES AND THEIR CONTRACTORS, TO EMPLOYERS, LENDERS, AND OTHERS TO ENFORCE THIS DEBT; TO THIRD PARTIES IN AUDIT, RESEARCH, OR DISPUTE ABOUT THE MANAGEMENT OF THIS DEBT; AND TO PARTIES WITH A RIGHT TO THIS INFORMATION UNDER THE FREEDOM OF INFORMATION ACT OR OTHER FEDERAL LAW OR WITH YOUR CONSENT. THESE USES ARE EXPLAINED IN NOTICE IN THE STUDENT FINANCIAL ASSISTANCE COLLECTION FILES, NO 18-11-07; WE WILL SEND A COPY AT YOUR REQUEST.

E.1 Request for Reasonable and Affordable Repayment Agreement

[Date]
[Name]
Administrative Assistant
Pennsylvania Higher Education Assistance Agency
1200 N. 7th St.
Harrisburg, PA 17102

Dear Ms. [Name]:

On behalf of my client Kristi Brown [Address], [Social Security Number], I hereby request that PHEAA establish a reasonable and affordable payment plan for her so that she can renew her eligibility for student loans and grants under Higher Education Act Section 428F(b). A statement of her income, which is entirely derived from Public Assistance and Food Stamps, is enclosed.

In light of Ms. Brown's poverty-level income, I request that her monthly payment be set at $5.00.

Ms. Brown's first payment of $5.00, for the month of November 1994, is enclosed.

Ms. Brown is a young woman with two children who is on public assistance but is working with the Single Point of Contact Program in Adams County to complete her education and develop job skills. Establishing a reasonable and affordable payment plan for her existing student loans will enable her to achieve these goals.

Thank you for your consideration of this request.

Sincerely,

[Attorney for Student]

STATEMENT OF INCOME AND EXPENSES

1. My name is Kristi Brown. My address is [Address]. My Social Security number is [Social Security Number].

2. My monthly income consists entirely of Public Assistance benefits: $401.50 in cash assistance under the AFDC program, and $223.00 in Food Stamps. In the past, $50 in child support paid by my husband, from whom I am separated, was passed through to me by the Department of Public Welfare, but he has not paid child support and I have not received a pass-through in a number of months.

3. I have to use all of my Food Stamps every month for food for myself and my children. My monthly expenses over and above the amount I receive in Food Stamps are as follows, totalling $402.20: $55.00, household items not covered by Food Stamps (e.g. soap, toothpaste, toilet paper); $25.00, telephone; $20.00, clothing;

$74.20, storage (my furniture is in storage because I am living in the basement of my father's residence because I cannot afford my own residence); $50.00, payments on debts (credit cards); $50.00, food over and above that covered by my food stamps; $60.00, gasoline and car repairs; $60.00, laundry; $10.00, school expenses; $5.00, medical and vision care expenses not covered by Medical Assistance.

4. My two children, ages 5 and 7, live with me and are dependent upon me for support.

5. Understanding that a false statement herein would subject me to the penalties of 18 Pa.C.S. Sec. 4904, relating to unsworn falsification to authorities, I verify that the facts set forth in the foregoing statement are true and correct, to the best of my knowledge, information, and belief.

[Student]

Dated:

E.2 Discharge-related Pleadings

E.2.1 Group False Certification Discharge Request

Note that proof of an employment search is no longer a requirement for a false certification ability to benefit discharge. *See* § 6.3.2.2, *supra*.

[Date]
John Smith
Coordinator, Policy and Reports
PHEAA
1200 North Seventh Street
Harrisburg, PA 17102-1444

Re: PTC Career Institute
    False Certification Discharges

Dear Mr. Smith:

I am enclosing with this letter 14 additional individual applications for false certification discharges. Attached is an alphabetical list of the sixteen individuals with social security numbers and date of their "ability to benefit" testing. These are the first applications I have submitted to you for borrowers who were administered ability to benefit (ATB) tests *after* the audit period covered by the Inspector General's report, i.e., after June 30, 1990. (By my count, this brings to 35 the total number of individual PTC false certification applications I have submitted to you.)

In contrast to the previously submitted applications—covering the period January 1, 1986 to June 30, 1990—student files are still in existence, in the custody of the Inspector General. As a result of the assistance provided by the Inspector General's office, I have been able to review these files and obtain copies of documents pertaining to the "ability to benefit" (ATB) determination made in each of these cases. Those documents are attached to the individual applications.

In addition to the individual documentation, I am enclosing copies of test instructions from the publisher of the Wonderlic test, which was utilized by PTC during 1991 and 1992; the accrediting criteria of the Accrediting Commission of Career Schools and Colleges of Technology (previously "NATTS"), the accreditor of PTC; and the following three sworn statements:

1. *Vincent Jones.* Mr. Jones was a commissioned recruiter for PTC during 1990. He describes how testing was done during that year, in particular, how admissions personnel routinely assisted students in taking the ATB tests. In his words, "[M]oney, not qualifications, was what we were about . . . [T]esting was just a formality we had to go through."

2. *Eliot Short.* Mr. Short is a vice president of Wonderlic Personnel Test, Inc., the publisher of the Wonderlic test. During the years 1991-92 PTC principally relied on the Wonderlic for its ATB determinations. Mr. Short explains in detail why the Wonderlics administered at PTC-Philadelphia are not valid tests and states that the whole PTC chain was terminated from the Wonderlic system due to "severe problems" in its testing practices.

3. *William Copley* .During the years 1991-92 Mr. Copley was employed by PTC as its "independent" ATB tester. He used a variety of ATB tests, mainly the Wonderlic, but also the PARS and CPAT. His statement makes clear that from January 1991 until it closed—i.e., during the period that PTC was required by the Education Department to use an independent tester for its ATB testing—PTC never had a truly independent tester. On the contrary, the testers were employees of the school, and, although functioning separate from the admissions department, were under constant pressure to produce passing scores, regardless of the real qualifications of student applicants. Hines was fired because his passing rate was not, in the view of his employer, high enough.

Your office has stated to me previously on several occasions that the Inspector General audit report was not sufficient evidence of ATB fraud warranting discharge of PTC loans. At least for loans disbursed during the audit period, I continue to believe that your decision is wrong and that the IG report is more than sufficient to support discharges under 20 U.S.C. § 1087(c) and the 1994 regulations. However, with these submissions, along with the various individual statements previously sent, you now have the additional evidence you asked for. This additional evidence clearly shows both that PTC continued to engage in systematic ATB fraud *after* the I.G. made his findings and that those findings concerning the earlier testing practices were indicative of an ongoing intent by PTC to defraud students and Title IV.

Moreover, in the event you investigate the PTC situation in PHEAA's own investigative files or with the Pennsylvania Board of Private Licensed Schools, I am sure that you will find ample confirmation that PTC was more in the nature of a racketeering operation than an academic institution.

I note in your letter to me dated December 19, 1994 that PHEAA believes that "criteria for evaluating improper testing has not been published." I believe you are mistaken. The Department of Edu-cation issued final regulations on April 29, 1994 which clearly set forth substantive standards for deciding false certification discharge applications and which give to guarantee agencies the responsibility of deciding these applications. In a letter to me dated February 22, 1995 your counsel, Peggy Shedden, acknowledges that the Department "does not have plans to issue any new information or instructions for guarantors regarding PTC borrowers." Since PHEAA has the obligation to decide these applications, and since no further guidance from Washington is forthcoming, it would be wrong for PHEAA to continue to deny these applications out of hand, especially in light of the additional evidence I have submitted over and above the Inspector General Report.

Applicable Standards for Measuring Whether Applicants Were Falsely Certified

The substantive standard you must apply is found at 34 C.F.R. § 682.402(e)(13). For enrollments up to July 1, 1987, you are to determine whether the school conducted ability-to-benefit determinations in accordance with 34 C.F.R. § 668.6. For those after July 1, 1987 you must determine a) whether the school was using an admissions test approved by the Department or by the school's accrediting commission; b) whether tests were administered substantially in accordance with the requirements for use of the test; and c) whether the borrower achieved a passing score.

For the period after July 1, 1987 you are to start with the school's accrediting criteria and then, after January 1, 1991, you are to look to the testing requirements imposed directly by the Secretary of Education. I have attached the accrediting criteria of NATTS, the accreditor of PTC. The pertinent criteria, at Section VIII (Admissions Policies and Practices), are as follows:

1. The school must document in writing the basis of its determination that the applicant is capable of benefitting from the training offered.
2. The school actually establishes admissions qualifications and "determines, with reasonable certainty, in advance of acceptance of the enrollment that the applicant has proper qualifications to complete the training."
3. In the case of an ATB admission, the school must maintain "documentation of the applicant's achievement of an approved score on a test or *tests that have been reviewed by a qualified independent third party for appropriateness of the instrument and specific score levels required for admission.* The acceptable score ensures that students will benefit from the training provided and a substantial number of students will complete the training and be employed in the field for which training was provided." (emphasis added)
4. Periodic studies are conducted to document the effectiveness of the admissions requirements.

For testing conducted after July 1, 1991, the specific tests and passing scores had to be taken from the approved list published by the Department, and, in addition, had to be administered by an independent test administrator, which *could not be* an employee of the school. 57 Fed. Reg. 62440 (Dec. 30, 1992). ATB test results are invalid if not independently administered, or not administered in accordance with test publisher requirements.

Established Facts

For period January 1986 to July 1, 1987 you need go no further than the Inspector General report in concluding that the PTC did not conduct ability-to-benefit determinations in accordance with 34 C.F.R. § 668.6. The rule in effect at that time required schools to "develop and consistently apply criteria for determining whether these students have the ability to benefit from the education or training offered" and required them to "be able to demonstrate, upon request of the Secretary, that these students have the ability to benefit." 1980 Final Rule, 45 Fed. Reg. 86854, 86857 (December 31, 1980). This was further refined in 1986 to require schools to maintain documentation supporting such ability-to-benefit determinations for five years. 1986 Final Rule preamble, 51 Fed. Reg. 41920 (Nov. 19, 1986). The Inspector General made a clear finding—unrebutted by any evidence you have pointed to—that such determinations were not being made at PTC and that the kind of documentation required by ATB rule did not exist. (As previously mentioned to you, a former PTC vice president, Ronald Beall, will confirm to you, if asked, that the testing practices of PTC—i.e., their reliance on the ABLE reading test analyzed by the I.G.—were in place as early as 1984. Mr. Beall can be reached at the ACT school in Upper Darby, where he is the director.)

For the period July 1, 1987 to June 30, 1990—during which, according to the false certification regulation, the relevant standard is the accrediting criteria under which PTC operated—the Inspector General report is more than adequate evidence that the NATTS accrediting criteria were not being followed at PTC. NATTS specifically required PTC to use tests and cutoff scores provided to it by an independent expert, to conduct periodic evaluations of the effectiveness of this testing, and to maintain documentation supporting its system. However, according to the I.G., none of this was occurring at PTC. PTC was using the reading test only of the ABLE test, which, according to the test publisher, was designed for adults who have not completed the eighth grade and was to be given as part of a battery of several tests. Under the NATTS criteria, it was up to PTC to establish and to maintain documentation supporting its conclusion that the ABLE reading test alone was sufficient to establish "ability to benefit" from its courses and documentation confirming the effectiveness of the results of such testing. According to the I.G., when asked how it concluded that a passing score of 48 on the ABLE reading test was an appropriate measure of "ability to benefit,"

> PTC officials indicated they talked with officials from other schools and consulted with educators. However, when asked, they were not able to present any record of their consultations. . . . It is clear from the information obtained during our audit, and from the arguments presented in its response, that PTC did not perform studies or research to establish the basis for [its use of testing procedures different from those recommended by the test publisher]. . . . PTC was unable to produce any documentation to support the development of the cut-off scores that were used to gauge applicant success. . . .
>
> PTC has also stated that "its ATB testing procedures] have proven to be valid predictors of ability to benefit based upon PTC's completion and placement rates during the period in which the ABLE test was in use." We strongly disagree with this statement. . . . During our audit period we

attempted to verify the accuracy of PTC's completion and placement rates, only to find that no audit trail was available. Audit Report at 9, 11, 12, 16.

In your letter to me of December 19, 1994 you characterize these findings as the "*opinions* of the Office of Inspector General" (your emphasis), as opposed to being a final determination by "appropriate Education Department officials." Unless you are challenging the credibility of the Inspector General, these findings are his reports of what PTC officials stated to him in response to his requests. While the "appropriate officials" in the Department apparently chose to do little, if anything, with this information, that does not turn facts into opinions. Even in a court of law, this report, *including the conclusions contained therein,* would be regarded under the Federal Rules of Evidence as *admissible evidence* of ATB fraud at PTC. *See* Rule 803(8) (exception to hearsay rule for reports setting forth findings resulting from an investigation made pursuant to authority granted by law). Since a federal court would consider this report to be evidence, I do not understand how PHEAA can regard it as something less than evidence.

For the period of time covering the end of the audit period (July 1, 1990) to the closing of the school in January 1994, the supplemental evidence provided to you certainly is supportive of our contention that ATB fraud continued at PTC. Moreover, this evidence is relevant to the audit period as well, in so far as it shows the existence of an ongoing intent to ignore ATB requirements. Summarizing some of the additional evidence you now have before you:

— *Coaching and test fabrication by testers.* The Vincent Johnson statement provides direct evidence of systematic coaching, which supplements the I.G.'s conclusion that the ABLE test form itself was an inappropriate testing instrument. This is further confirmed by a few of the individual applications, included here or previously submitted. Yvette Prophet (SSN [Social Security Number]), whose application was submitted last week, stated that the admissions representative gave her the test in August 1987, "hurrying me along, telling me not to worry about whatever I put down, and occasionally telling me which answer to fill in." Tracey Johnson (SSN [Social Security Number]), one of applications enclosed herein, remembers that when she was administered the CPAT test in 1993 "the tester sat beside me and helped me do it." Crystal Ball (SSN [Social Security Number]), whose application is enclosed herein, was tested in November 1990 by her admissions representative, who gave her only a "clerical test" (probably the Minnesota Clerical Test listed in her file); she was never even given the ABLE, also noted in her file, so the

PARS answer sheet which appears in her file was apparently fabricated.

— *Use of invalid ATB tests.* The Eliot Long statement reveals that during 1991 PTC utilized invalid versions of the Wonderlic tests, apparently created by PTC. Moreover, contrary to the publisher's mandatory security system, individual test sheets were never submitted to the company for analysis. One so-called "independent" tester, William Hines, registered with the testing company months after he began testing, but operated totally outside the test registration system. The other tester, Art Adams, was unknown to the company, which requires all its testers to be registered. The 12-minute time limit was routinely ignored, and Hines "do[es] not recall" deducting 6 points from untimed tests as the publisher's instructions require. Also contrary to the publisher's instructions, he routinely gave retests on the exact same test form.

— *Tests administered by nonindependent testers.* As of July 1, 1991 testing had to be administered by individuals who met the Department's criteria of "independence." As the William Hines statement reveals, the testers at PTC were effectively employees of the school who administered tests chosen by the school. They were in competition with each other to see who could produce the highest pass/fail ratio, and any failure had to be specially justified to the school director. The Long statement is clear evidence that the Wonderlic testing during 1991 and 1992 certainly did not comply with the publisher's criteria for independence either. The Hines statement also makes clear that the "independence" of the tester continued to be tainted after PTC decided to switch to the CPAT in 1992, and actually the integrity of the testing worsened as sales pressures intensified. The other tester took over for him by reason of his ability to produce a higher level of "passes," a level Hines believed could not be produced by legitimate testing, especially given the fact that the qualification level of recruits was actually deteriorating.

— *Use of "approved" passing scores to mask obvious lack of qualifications.* The Hines statement explains how the tester was expected to cast a blind eye to an applicant's apparent lack of academic skills. He actually was reprimanded by the school director for going beyond the ATB test score and probing the reading capacity of an applicant who appeared to lack basic reading skills. Among those he tested and were admitted after supposedly achieving an "approved" score were Charlene Curry (SSN [Social Security Number]), a 45 year old woman who receives SSI for mental illness and who never completed *elementary* school, and Alfred Stewart, a 68 year-old, retired and disabled man who never attended high school and who was admitted into a security guard

program despite putting on the application that he suffered from shortness of breath and a bad back.

— *Frequent use of retestings.* Hines also admits to routinely giving retests using the exact same test form, a practice encouraged by the school director and specifically disallowed in the Wonderlic manual. This, too, illustrates the school's intent to produce an "approved" score at all costs. The Hines reference to retesting is confirmation of the I.G. finding of a "high percentage" of retesting (40 percent tested at least twice and 24 percent tested twice during the same day). For examples of retestings, see Tracey Johnson (SSN [Social Security Number]) and Wanda Matos (SSN [Social Security Number]).

— *Unusual volume of ATB admissions.* The large volume of false certification applications from PTC is itself evidence of the fact that PTC was little more than an "ATB mill," where admissions requirements were virtually nonexistent and lack of high school credentials was more the rule than the exception. The low-skill nature of the PTC student population is confirmed by both the Hines ("the school was depending . . . on admissions of people at the bottom of the ladder, meaning those functioning at an elementary school level") and Johnson statements ("one student . . . could not read at all. There were homeless people recruited literally off the street or out of shelters.") The I.G. report itself quotes from a post-audit memorandum by PTC's Vice President of Operations which described PTC's enrollment policies as follows:

"We (PTC) have enrolled people from shelters, people who need to satisfy parole conditions, addicts, persons who cannot read, write or speak, etc. We have also enrolled people who do not qualify for Financial Aid and/or are unable to make payments. The bottom line people, is that we are enrolling just numbers—not students serious about getting job training. Why? More than likely you are doing it to keep (PTC President) and (PTC Vice President) from ripping your backsides for not making budgeted numbers. These are excuses that are unacceptable." I.G. Report at 20.

I believe that we have provided an extraordinary amount of evidence to support our request for discharges of all PTC ATB borrowers. At the very least, we have provided you with "reliable information" sufficient to warrant class-wide forbearance and notice to individual PTC borrowers of their right to apply for a discharge on account of what you know about ATB testing at PTC. I am hereby advising PHEAA that I intend to initiate federal court litigation, including a request for class-wide relief, if PHEAA continues to fail to honor this request.

I realize that the Department of Education shares considerable blame for the continued absence of action in this case. For that reason, I intend to sue the Department, as well, for its failure to discharge these loans and for the continual mixed signals it has provided to guarantee agencies in general regarding false certification and in particular regarding PTC. Accordingly, I am copying officials of the Department with this correspondence.

Sincerely,

[*Attorney for Plaintiff*]

E.2.2 *Request for Discharge of All Students*

REQUEST FOR DOE DETERMINATION OF ATB FRAUD
BY CAMBRIDGE TECHNICAL INSTITUTE, INC. FOR USE
IN STUDENT LOAN DISCHARGE APPLICATIONS

I. Introduction

This memorandum provides the basis for the U.S. Department of Education (DOE) to rule that Cambridge Technical Institute, Inc., a for-profit, proprietary vocational school formerly operating four campuses in Ohio, committed such pervasive fraud and unlawful actions in its determination of students' ability to benefit (ATB) from Cambridge's courses, that all applications for a loan discharge, based on improper ATB determination, will be granted to otherwise-eligible Cambridge students, without independent evidence of ATB fraud. This request for DOE's decision as to Cambridge's improper determination of ATB status for students is being submitted pursuant to DOE's "Dear Colleague" letter GEN-95-42, Section 10. Included herewith are: 1) previous decisions of DOE on former Cambridge students' ATB discharge applications, 2) deposition and affidavit testimony by former students and employees of Cambridge, 3) findings by the Ohio Attorney General's Office, 4) a sample of Cambridge's ATB admissions scores compared with the requirements established by DOE, the accreditation agency for Cambridge, and the ATB test publisher, 5) findings by the Ohio State Board of Proprietary School Registration, and 6) generalized evidence of the widespread fraudulent and unlawful business practices of Cambridge, as set forth in various newspaper articles over the years.

The Legal Aid Society of Cincinnati represented students in a class-action lawsuit against Cambridge in the late 1980's. That lawsuit resulted in a consent decree whereby Cambridge agreed to close its Cincinnati campus as of October, 1990. Following that, the murder of Cambridge's president, and the criminal indictment of one of Cambridge's other officers (who ultimately pleaded guilty), the other three campuses (in Middletown, Dayton, and Cleveland) were also closed or sold. As a result, Cambridge long ago closed its doors in Ohio. Nevertheless, hundreds of students who were lured into Cambridge's classrooms with a promise of a good education and a good job, are now in a worse position than they were when they first heard about Cambridge. Many of them have had their self-esteem harmed and their credit records ruined, and they continue to be dunned for thousands of dollars allegedly owed on their defaulted student loans. Many of those students never should have attended Cambridge to begin with, given their inability to benefit from what Cambridge offered them. DOE now should facilitate the loan discharge process for them by issuing an administrative decision whereby it declares Cambridge's ATB testing and admissions procedures so pervasively fraudulent as to provide across-the-board proof that any applicant for a student loan discharge, based on ATB fraud, will have his or her application granted, provided he or she is otherwise eligible.

II. Numerous Former Students Already Have Received a Discharge of Their Loans Based on Cambridge's False Certification of Their Ability to Benefit.

The U.S. Department of Education already has granted a discharge of student loans to numerous former Cambridge students, based on Cambridge's false certification of their ability to benefit. The following is a partial list of former Cambridge students who have had their loans discharged based on such false certification. See the series A exhibits, attached hereto [*not reprinted herein*].

1. Nelson Muntz: He did not possess a high school diploma or a GED. He was given a ten-question admissions test, which is not consistent with Wonderlic's (the test developer's) test manual procedures. (Wonderlic ATB tests contain 24 or 50 questions). According to Mr. Muntz, "everyone" he heard of passed the exam. After completing the Cambridge course, he could not get a job because of his extensive criminal record.

2. Selma Bouvier: She did not have a high school diploma or a GED. She took a test, but she did not answer many questions. At the time of enrollment, she was suffering from the side effects of brain surgery.

3. Martin Prince: He was not given any admissions test, even though he did not have a high school diploma or a GED.

4. Elizabeth Hoover: She was not given any admissions test, even though she had no high school diploma or GED.

5. Wendell Borton: He had three different Cambridge loans (all discharged). He did not have a high school diploma or a GED, yet was not given any admissions test. Mr. Borton was 67 years old, had a glass eye and back problems, and weighed about 100 pounds when he was enrolled for the private security course at Cambridge.

6. Maude Flanders: She stated that she took the test with a group and they all were told they had passed the test even before it was graded. She did not have a high school diploma or a GED.

7. Doris Lunchlady: She had no high school diploma or GED. She was given an admissions test in a room with several other students also taking the test. The person giving the test left the room once the test started, and there was no time limit imposed.

8. Otto Mans: He was not given an admissions test nor did he possess a high school diploma or a GED. He also had an extensive criminal record of theft and drug abuse.

9. Jessica Lovejoy: She did not have a high school diploma or a GED, and was not given an admissions test before enrolling.

10. Ned Flanders: He was not given an admissions test, nor did he have a high school diploma or a GED.

11. Lisa Simpson: She had neither a high school diploma nor a GED when she enrolled. She had only the equivalent of a fifth grade education and did not take an admissions test.

12. Jackie Bouvier: She was not given an admissions test, nor did she have a high school diploma or a GED.

See the enclosed Request for Discharge (False Certification of Ability to Benefit) applications and decisions, Exhibits A-1 through A-12 [*not reprinted herein*].

III. Sworn Testimony of Numerous Former Cambridge Students Shows a Pattern of Testing and Admissions Fraud.

In the course of litigating *Brown, et al. v. Cambridge Technical Institute, Inc., et al.*, substantial pre-trial discovery took place. Depositions were taken of former students, and affidavits were obtained from others. Although the lawsuit did not raise directly the ability-to-benefit issue, information given by former students to the attorneys shows that Cambridge's test procedures were very lax and, at times, unlawful or fraudulent. The following are summaries of the ATB problems revealed through depositions and/or affidavits given by the listed individuals. See the series B exhibits, attached hereto [*not reprinted herein*].

1. Patty Brown (a former student and named plaintiff in the lawsuit): She could not read. She could not spell much, including her address. When she took the admissions test, a lady from Cambridge had to read the questions to her. Ms. Brown was taking medication (Cogentin and Prolixin) for her nerves at that time and was being followed by a case manager at the Mental Health Services West office. Although the application form for Ms. Brown states that she went to Taft High School, she did not; she did go to West High. She did not graduate from West High School or any high school. Her last years in school were spent at Gilford School (a school for developmentally delayed students). Ms. Brown is not good at math and numbers. Ms. Brown has a guardian, but she could not remember her name. Ms. Brown does not know the difference between a positive experience and a negative experience. Of all the questions on the Wonderlic admissions test, Ms. Brown completed only six of them. She does not know who filled in the other blanks. When she handed in her test, there were only six answers given by her on her paper. She does not know what happened after that. Ms. Brown was admitted to Cambridge after the test, and enrolled for custodial maintenance, electronics, and computers. After she attended school for a few days, she stopped going.

2. Marvin Monroe (a former student and former employee of Cambridge): Mr. Monroe states: "At the Cambridge Admissions Office, I was told that I would have to take an admissions test. When I told [the Cambridge person] that I didn't have time to take the test, he said he would take it for me, and he proceeded to do that."

3. Marge Simpson (a former student): While attending Cambridge, she met another student filling out loan papers. This other student had been enrolled for private security, but had only one leg and had a deformed left hand with only two fingers on it. Ms. Simpson also heard another student boasting, in a serious way, that she had given birth last week to a baby which was going to be stuck "back up inside her like all her other babies." This person did not "seem to know where she was." Another student Ms. Simpson met seemed very slow or retarded. He would sit near the back window and stare into space. The instructors stated that he flunked every test.

4. Clancy Wiggum (a former student): Ms. Wiggum was given the admissions test. The woman at Cambridge giving the test gave Ms. Wiggum "the answers to the first five questions."

See the enclosed deposition excerpts and affidavits, Exhibits B-1 through B-4 [*not reprinted herein*].

IV. The Ohio Attorney General Found Evidence of Admissions Test Fraud by Cambridge.

The Ohio Attorney General also filed a separate lawsuit against Cambridge for its operations at the Cleveland "campus." In its investigation of Cambridge's practices at that campus, the Ohio Attorney General's office determined that serious admissions test fraud had occurred. See the series C exhibits, attached hereto [*not reprinted herein*].

In responding to civil discovery requests propounded by Cambridge's attorneys, the Ohio Attorney General stated the following in response to one of the interrogatories regarding admissions testing: "The defendants [Cambridge] administered the test without supervision to students en masse. The test was an altered and simplified version of a valid test. Students were allowed to discuss the test with each other. The test was written, but illiterate students passed the test. The test was administered without time constraint."

Additionally, in this same litigation, the Ohio Attorney General filed a memorandum with the court opposing Cambridge's motion to dismiss the lawsuit. Attached as exhibits to that memorandum were excerpts from depositions of Cambridge officials and affidavits from various other people. The depositions of the Cambridge officials discussed examples of Cambridge enrolling students who obviously could not benefit from instruction. One discussion involved the enrollment of a student when, by Cambridge's own admission, it was "obvious the student should not have been enrolled." The Cambridge official went on to testify that the student was "extremely childlike, he did not seem to be able to carry through in conversation, communication skills were very poor." The student's "mannerisms and inability to communicate and comprehend in general conversation" were acknowledged, as well as the fact that the student, when asked a question, would not respond or would talk about something that was totally different and unrelated to the conversation. Another example testified to in deposition involved a Cambridge instructor reporting a second-quarter student whom the instructor had by then determined "could not read his text books and could not read or comprehend the content of the mid-term examination."

The Attorney General also submitted affidavits executed by two former students of the Cleveland branch of Cambridge. Each details improper testing procedures, including administering the test in a crowded room of other students, giving no explanation of the exam or test procedures, and allowing students to receive assistance on the test.

See the enclosed excerpts from the Attorney General's Supplemental Answers to Defendant's Interrogatories and Appendix thereto, with attachments, and excerpts from the Attorney General's court memorandum, with attachments, and affidavits (note: the above information has been "highlighted" for easy reference), Exhibits C-1 through C-2 [*not reprinted herein*].[1]

---

1 In a separate forum, Cambridge officials of the Cleveland campus admitted that Ernest Hall, the first example of improperly admitted students cited in the deposition, took his admissions test simultaneously with several other individuals and that his sister not only attended the admissions test with him, but actually helped him with the answers. The deposed official also conceded that the testing employee of Cambridge did not notice any of this during the exam (or, apparently, chose not to do anything about it). This is documented in Cambridge's own letter to a media reporter. See the enclosed Cambridge letter of 3/15/88, Exhibit C-3 [*not reprinted herein*].

V. Cambridge's Own Testing Documents Show Ability-to-Benefit Fraud and Other Irregularities.

Even a cursory review of Cambridge's admissions testing, taken from individual Cambridge files of former students, shows significant violations of the proper test procedures, scoring requirements, and remedial instruction options permitted by DOE and Cambridge's accreditation agency. See the series D exhibits, attached hereto [*not reprinted herein*].

In the 1980's, DOE promulgated regulations regarding the ability-to-benefit standards and the testing to be used by schools to determine whether prospective students actually had the ability to benefit from the school's training. The DOE summarized the ATB requirements in its September, 1995 "Dear Colleague" letter, GEN-95-42. Briefly, for enrollment periods from January 1, 1986 through June 30, 1987, a school could determine that a student had an ability to benefit in accordance with DOE regulations by using a fairly simple procedure. The school only had to:

> *develop and consistently apply criteria* to determine if regular students who did not have a high school diploma or GED, and who were beyond the age of compulsory attendance, had the ability to benefit from the school's training. [Emphasis added].

For periods of enrollment from July 1, 1987 through June 30, 1991, the DOE required more stringent evaluation of students. During this time period, a school had to use standard admissions practices for any applicants without a high school diploma or a GED. These practices required the school to determine the following:

> (1) the student received a GED prior to the student's completion of the program or by the end of the first year of the program, whichever was earlier; (2) the student was counseled prior to admission *and successfully completed the school's program of remedial or developmental education* that did not exceed one academic year or its equivalent; (3) the student passed a nationally recognized, standardized, or industry-developed ATB test, *subject to criteria developed by the school's accrediting association*; or (4) if the student failed the ATB test, he or she *successfully completed the school's program of remedial or developmental education* that did not exceed one academic year or its equivalent. [Emphasis added].

See the enclosed "Dear Colleague" letter GEN-95-42, page 2, Exhibit D-1 [*not reprinted herein*]. See also 34 C.F.R. § 668.7.

After June 30, 1987, DOE required that all ATB tests be used "subject to criteria developed by the institution's nationally recognized accrediting agency or association." 34 C.F.R. § 668.7(b)(1)(i). Cambridge was accredited by the Accrediting Council for Continuing Education and Training (ACCET), in Richmond, Virginia. ACCET standards for its accredited schools required that the admissions policy for all students be "based on the institution's stated objectives; it must be administered for all applicants as written and published." ACCET also required each institution to document each student's ability to benefit from the training offered. Finally, the school "must determine a student's

aptitude to complete successfully the . . . education *by following the applicable standards, procedures, and scores established by the publisher. . . . No deviation in scoring or testing procedures are allowed without written approval* of the test publisher and written concurrence by the ACCET Accrediting Commission." [Emphasis added]. See the enclosed 2/12/90 ACCET memorandum, with attachments of "Document 32" (June, 1989), p. 1, and "Document 32A" (February, 1990), p. 2, Exhibit D-2 [*not reprinted herein*]. Note that both of these memos state that they provide "clarification" (and thus do not change any policy); their instructions therefore are applicable back to 1986. See Exhibit D-2.

Cambridge published its admissions policy in its Policy and Procedures Manual. It eventually published the policy on a separate document. See Learning to Learn document, Exhibit D-3. This document represented Cambridge's ATB policy, written to comply with DOE's and ACCET's standards. However, the policy failed to use the cut-off scores "established by the publisher." Further, its scores did not "correspond with an appropriate grade level of the materials utilized in the instructional program" because people admitted with scores as low as Cambridge permitted do not learn well from formalized training and often need to be "explicitly taught" through an apprenticeship program rather than from "booklearning." This is explained next.

In determining the threshold scores needed to show an ability to benefit, Cambridge set scores far below the minimum suggested by the test manufacturer, Wonderlic. The following chart shows five programs offered by Cambridge, Cambridge's "conditional" passing scores on the ATB test, Cambridge's "unconditional" passing scores on the ATB test, and the test publisher's (Wonderlic's) minimum passing scores. As explained in Cambridge's admissions policy, prospective students scoring in the "conditional" range would be required to take the Learn to Learn course to gain admission. Those scoring in the "unconditional" range or higher would be admitted without conditions. However, the conditional scores fall below the scores set by Wonderlic in its testing manual:

Program	Cambridge's Conditional *Qualifying Score*	Cambridge's Unconditional *Qualifying Score*	Wonderlic's *Passing Score*
Custodial Maintenance	8	14	12
Data Entry	9	15	12
Law Enforcement/ Security	9	15	10
Nursing Assistant	9	15	11
Word Processing	9	15	15

See Exhibit D-3 and the enclosed Wonderlic ATB Test Score Registration Manual, pp. 11, 12, and 17, Exhibit D-4 [*not reprinted herein*]. Further, the test publisher recommends that schools "recruit and select students that score well above the minimum." See the enclosed Wonderlic ATB Test Score Registration Manual, p. 5, Exhibit D-5 [*not reprinted herein*].

The reason for these suggested scores and recommendations are based on Wonderlic's extensive testing and research to demonstrate its tests' validity, correlation, and reliability. Based on this research, including reviews with employers hiring people for various positions, Wonderlic explains that people in the test score ranges being used by Cambridge would not benefit from a formal training setting and would likely not find employment. Students from these ranges of scores need to be "explicitly taught," as with an apprenticeship program rather than attempting to learn through books and classroom training. See the enclosed Wonderlic User's Manual, p. 26, Exhibit D-6 [*not reprinted herein*].

As a result of Cambridge's own cut-off scores for admission, many students admitted did not have the requisite ability to benefit from the programs offered. The following examples are taken from Cambridge's own files.

1. Apu Nahasapeemapetelon: Mr. Nahasapeemapetelon was admitted in December, 1986 without having taken any admissions test. His enrollment agreement and application papers show he attended a high school, but the "Highest Grade Completed" and "Grad Date" blanks have no answers. Similar blanks for this information appear on the student's untitled data sheet containing background data with the courses, credit hours, and grades given. No high school diploma or transcript appears in the file.

2. Jo Quimby. Ms. Quimby enrolled in Cambridge in October, 1987, and received a grade of 10 on the admissions test. Accordingly, she was required to take the Learn to Learn course, but she never did take that course. A review of the file shows no indication, on any document, of her enrolling, much less completing, the remedial learning program offered by Cambridge.[2]

3. Lionel Hutz: Mr. Hutz had to take the test twice in order to achieve what appears to be a passable score to gain admittance to Cambridge's custodial maintenance program. On his first try, Mr. Hutz scored a 7; on his second attempt he moved up to an 8. However, serious concerns exist as to whether Mr. Hutz, himself, actually filled in all of the answers which appear on the second test. Mr. Hutz' handwriting in forming

the numbers 1, 2, 3, and 4 can be gleaned from looking at the few answers he provided on the first test and most of the answers he provided on the second test. Comparing that to the two answers appearing in the second test for questions 21 and 22, it is seen that the handwriting is much lighter and the numbers are less "shaky"—those two answers appear to have been written by a person with more graceful writing. Significantly, both of those answers are correct and bring what otherwise would have been a score of 6 (failing) to an 8 (barely within the passing range). Also significant is that this appears on the second, and last, test which Mr. Hutz would be permitted to take.

Further, because the score of 8 was the absolute minimum score, and left Mr. Hutz in the "conditional" range of passing scores, he was required to take the remedial instruction program offered by Cambridge in order to qualify for admission and federal loan assistance. This remedial course, entitled "Learn to Learn," is nowhere noted in Mr. Hutz' file or on the enrollment agreement or test cover sheet. This is in contrast to the next example below, Mr. Duncan, and other student files discussed later in which the Learn to Learn program is clearly documented.

4. Julius Hubbert: Mr. Hubbert sought admittance into Cambridge's custodial maintenance program with a score of 8. This is the absolute minimum score for eligibility, and it requires that the student also take the Learn to Learn program. The Learn to Learn program is documented (as "LL"), but only for the second quarter. Inexplicably, Mr. Hubbert was not required to enroll in the Learn to Learn program for the first quarter. This violates Cambridge's own policy—promulgated to comply with DOE and ACCET mandates—which requires the student to take the instruction "in the first quarter of enrollment." The Learn to Learn program is also documented on the test cover sheet itself (as "L&L"), again, in contrast to Mr. Hutz' file.

5. Hans Moleman: Mr. Moleman was admitted in November, 1988, after scoring only a 7 on his admissions test. A score of 7 does not meet Cambridge's own admission requirements. Nevertheless, Mr. Moleman was admitted into the custodial maintenance program (and apparently required to take Learn to Learn, as documented on the Master Attendance Record appearing in his file).

6. Troy McClure: Mr. McClure scored an 11 on his admissions test, thus requiring that he take the Learn to Learn program in addition to the custodial maintenance courses he wished to attend. However, his Master Attendance Record, which notes the Learn to Learn program, indicates Mr. McClure would not have to take the remedial course until the following quarter. This violated Cambridge's own policy which requires the student to take the instruction "in the first quarter of enrollment."

7. Dewey Largo: Mr. Largo took his admissions exam in December, 1988, and scored only a 6. Nevertheless, he was admitted into the custodial maintenance program for three quarters, beginning January 2, 1989. A score of 6 does not even meet the "conditional" eligibility minimum score set by Cambridge.

See the enclosed student files, Exhibits D-9 through D-15 [*not reprinted herein*].

---

2 With regard to the students who were in the "conditional" range, and thus required to take the Learn to Learn course, it is evident that where a file does not note the Learn to Learn program, the student did not take that course. Included herewith are examples from other student files which do indicate that the student was enrolled in the Learn to Learn program. For example, see the enclosed Cambridge files of Patty Marie Smith and Anthony Adams, Exhibits D-7, D-8 [*not reprinted herein*]. For ease of reference, documents indicating the student was enrolled in Learn to Learn have been highlighted.

It is interesting to note, however, that even when students did take this course, many of them routinely withdrew with a failing grade. Thus, it is clear that Cambridge did not satisfy the requirement for the ability-to-benefit standard set forth in 34 C.F.R. § 668.7(b)(3): "successfully completes a remedial . . . program. . . ." Both Mr. Adams and Ms. Smith, though ostensibly receiving remedial instruction, withdrew from the Learn to Learn course. In fact, they each took the course twice, the second time after already withdrawing from it in an earlier quarter or semester. Neither, however, took a second admissions test, notwithstanding the fact that they were only conditionally eligible and had not satisfactorily completed the Learn to Learn program which they had been required to take in order to be admitted. Again, Cambridge's practices show an across-the-board disregard for DOE's ATB requirements. Even when given the chance to admit students who failed the ATB test, Cambridge played "fast and loose" with the rules.

VI. Cambridge Conducted its Overall Business Practices in an Unlawful and Fraudulent Manner, Resulting in Revocation of Its License by the State of Ohio.

In late 1990, the Ohio State Board of Proprietary School Registration (SBPSR), the licensing and oversight agency for proprietary, for-profit schools in Ohio, revoked the Certificate of Registration for Cambridge and imposed a civil penalty for Cambridge's violations of various sections of the Ohio Revised Code governing proprietary schools. By the time of the license revocation, Cambridge's default rate for mature student loans was an astounding 83.8%. See the enclosed SBPSR letter of 12/5/90, the SBPSR Final Resolution of 1/23/91, and the Higher Education Assistance Foundation letter of 5/12/89, Exhibits E-1 through E-3 [*not reprinted herein*].

VII. Cambridge, and Its Officers, Have Been Involved in Other Fraud and Criminal Activity.

Over the years, the Cincinnati newspapers and other media have documented numerous incidents of fraud and criminal activity by Cambridge and its employees or officers. See the series F exhibits, attached hereto [*not reprinted herein*]. Timothy Lovejoy, the former president of Cambridge, was reported by CNN as having defrauded the U.S. government out of $5 million. It was alleged that he submitted information to the DOE which falsely represented more students attending Cambridge than was true. It was further alleged that Mr. Lovejoy kept the loan monies of students who had dropped out of Cambridge instead of returning it to the banks and/or DOE. In late 1990, Mr. Lovejoy was murdered in a telephone booth at a local airport before these allegations could be brought to trial. That murder remains unsolved to this day. Pete McCallister, another officer of Cambridge, was indicted on numerous counts of bribery, conspiracy to defraud, and lying to a grand jury, to cover up student aid fraud. Mr. McCallister was tried in federal court and eventually pleaded guilty to one count of conspiracy; he was sentenced to two years in prison. Former Ohio Congressman Donald "Buz" Lukens also was indicted on various federal charges, some related to Cambridge, and was tried in federal court. He was convicted of accepting bribes from Cambridge.

The newspaper also reported that former Cambridge employees falsified student records before DOE investigators arrived at the school to check on various allegations of fraud. These employees also stated that many student records were destroyed. Additionally, numerous students complained over the years of sharp recruitment practices, unqualified teachers, problems with the school equipment, problems with attendance and books, as well as describing their experiences in job-hunting. Many, many students were told by prospective employers that their Cambridge certificates were worthless. Cambridge's high loan repayment default rate can be attributed to its poor educational quality as well as its poor administrative and business practices.

Further, physical violence was used against a former employee who went public with some of the fraudulent practices at Cambridge. Mr. Lovejoy was accused of hiring two people to physically assault Mark McClure in April, 1990 because Mr. McClure was talking to the media about Cambridge and was aiding the Legal Aid Society of Cincinnati in its litigation against the school. These two men were sentenced to jail for beating Mr. McClure. And, as was explained earlier, the lawsuit filed by the Legal Aid Society was only the first—the Attorney General's Office filed its own. Both lawsuits succeeded in having Cambridge close its doors.

See the enclosed copies of newspaper articles, Exhibits F-1 through F-8 [*not reprinted herein*].

CONCLUSION

As has been demonstrated, Cambridge's admissions practices were fraudulent across the board. The pervasive fraud and unlawful practices included all areas of the mandatory testing of students for their ability to benefit from Cambridge's purported educational programs. DOE already has seen numerous instances of Cambridge's ATB fraud from individual students and thus has granted those students a discharge of their loans. These individual cases are merely representative of Cambridge's broader approach to education, namely enrolling as many students as could be fit into classrooms, with no regard to the students' ability to learn from the programs. The Ohio State Board of Proprietary School Registration and the Ohio Attorney General found numerous instances of ATB fraud by Cambridge. Numerous former students and employees have testified to the same unlawful practices. It is time for DOE to declare Cambridge's admissions and testing practices so pervasively fraudulent and unlawful as to render their ATB certification meaningless for each and every one of its former students. DOE now should consider any application for a school loan discharge based on improper determination of the student's ability to benefit as proven, so long as that former student did not have a high school diploma or a GED at the time of attending Cambridge.

[Attorney for Plaintiff]

E.2.3 Class Action Complaint Challenging Department of Education's False Certification Discharge Procedures

UNITED STATES DISTRICT COURT
EASTERN DISTRICT OF NEW YORK

[Plaintiffs], individually and on behalf of all others similarly situated,	))))
Plaintiffs,	)
	)
v.	))
RICHARD W. RILEY, in his official capacity as Secretary of the United States Department of Education, and the UNITED STATES DEPARTMENT OF EDUCATION,	))))))
Defendant.	))

COMPLAINT

PRELIMINARY STATEMENT

1. This is a class action pursuant to the Administrative Procedure Act, 5 U.S.C. § 701 *et seq.*, for declaratory and injunctive relief on behalf of individuals who have been denied discharges of their federally guaranteed student loans arbitrarily, capriciously and in violation of 20 U.S.C. § 1087(c), the Higher Education Act Amendments ("HEAA"). The statute mandates that the defendant Secretary of Education grant discharges of student loans if the schools attended by the students falsely certified that the students had the ability to benefit from the programs for which their loans were taken (hereinafter "ability-to-benefit discharge"). Instead of carefully considering the evidence of false certification presented by the plaintiffs, the defendant Secretary denied their requests for discharges arbitrarily and capriciously, on the basis of unsupported assumptions and inferences.

JURISDICTION

2. This court has jurisdiction under the Administrative Procedure Act 5 U.S.C. § 701 *et seq.*, 28 U.S.C. § 1331, § 1361, and 20 U.S.C. § 1082(a)(2).

3. Venue is proper in this district pursuant to 28 U.S.C. § 1391(e) because the named plaintiffs reside in this district.

PARTIES

4. Plaintiff 1 resides, and at all relevant times has resided, in Brooklyn, New York.

5. Plaintiff 2 resides, and at all relevant times has resided, in Brooklyn, New York

6. Defendant RICHARD W. RILEY is the Secretary of the United States Department of Education (hereafter "the Secretary" when speaking of Defendant Riley; and "U.S. ED" when referring to the Department), and as such is responsible for administration of the Federal Family Educational Loan program (hereafter "FFEL"), known until 1992 as the Guaranteed Student Loan Program (hereafter "GSLP"). Defendant Riley is sued only in his official capacity.

CLASS ACTION ALLEGATIONS

7. The named plaintiffs 1 and 2, bring this action, pursuant to Rule 23 of the Federal Rules of Civil Procedure, on behalf of themselves and as representatives of all individuals with federally guaranteed student loans obtained to attend for-profit vocational schools licensed by the New York State Department of Education, who have been or will be denied an ability-to-benefit discharge by the Secretary, without consideration of the facts in their individual cases, but rather in reliance upon an absence of findings by oversight agencies about the certification practices of the schools they attended.

8. The class is so numerous that joinder of all members is impracticable.

9. There are questions of law or fact common to the class which predominate over any questions affecting only the individual plaintiffs, including, but not limited to whether the defendant arbitrarily and capriciously relies on information provided by other agencies or on the absence of such information instead of examining the actual facts of the plaintiffs' cases.

10. The claims of the individual named plaintiff as to the legality of the defendant's practices are typical of the claims of all class members, in that each has had her request for an ability-to-benefit discharge denied arbitrarily and capriciously, without examination by the defendant of the individual facts of her case.

11. The named plaintiffs will adequately and fairly protect the interests of all members of the class, because they have the requisite personal interest in the outcome of this action, have no interest antagonistic to others in the class, and they are represented by the Social Justice Project at BLS Legal Services Corp., counsel experienced in class action litigation generally, and specifically including the rights of people with guaranteed student loan debts.

12. The prosecution of separate actions by individual members of the class would create a risk of inconsistent or varying adjudications with respect to the practices at issue in this action. Separate actions would be, as a practical matter, dispositive of the interests of other individual members of the class and would substantially impair their abilities to protect their interests. Defendants have acted on grounds generally applicable to the class in failing to make individual determinations based on the facts in each case in determining plaintiffs' eligibility for loan discharges. A class action is superior to other available methods for the fair and efficient adjudication of this controversy.

STATUTORY SCHEME

13. The Higher Education Act, 20 U.S.C. § 1071, *et seq.*, authorizes the Secretary to administer a federal student financial aid program (formerly known as the Guaranteed Student Loan (GSL) Program, now known as the Federal Family Education Loan (FFEL) Program).

14. Under the FFEL program, lenders make loans for "eligible borrowers" to attend "eligible" post-secondary institutions; state and private guaranty agencies insure the loans; and the Secretary reinsures the agencies. 20 U.S.C. §1071 *et seq.*.

15. Through the program, a student may obtain guaranteed student loans to attend a proprietary vocational school if the school (1) admits eligible students, (2) is legally authorized to provide vocational training, (3) has been in existence for at least two years, (4) is accredited by an agency approved by the Secretary, and (5) has a cohort default rate less than the statutorily specified threshold. 20 U.S.C. §§ 1002 (b), 1085 (a).

16. To qualify for a guaranteed student loan, a student must meet various requirements, including the "ability-to-benefit" requirement. The specific requirements have changed slightly during the life of the program, but at all times relevant to this case, have required that to be considered to have the ability to benefit from the program of study, the student must have a high school diploma, or a recognized equivalent (GED), or pass a standardized test given by the school prior to admission of the student, or receive a GED prior to graduation from the course of study or before the end of the first year of study, or be enrolled in and successfully complete an institutionally prescribed program of remedial education not to exceed one year. 20 U.S.C. § 1091; 34 C.F.R. § 668.6; § 682.402(e)(13); §685.214(c).

17. The Higher Education Act Amendments and implementing regulations provide that the Secretary must discharge a student loan (including interest and collection fees) of a borrower who received a loan after January 1, 1986, if a school falsely certified the

borrower as having the ability to benefit from the program of study. 20 U.S.C. § 1087(c).

18. Regulations promulgated by the Secretary require guaranty agencies to send discharge applications to all borrowers who, based on information acquired by the Secretary, may be eligible for such discharge. 34 C.F.R. § 682.402 (e) (i).

19. In evaluating the borrower's request for an ability-to-benefit discharge, the agency holding the loan must consider the information and supporting sworn statement provided by the borrower, "in light of information available from the records of the agency and from other sources, including other guaranty agencies, state authorities, and cognizant accrediting associations." 34 C.F.R. § 682.402 (e) (6) (iv).

20. If the agency determines that the borrower satisfies the requirements for an ability-to-benefit discharge, the agency must (1) pay off the loan debt; (2) notify the borrower that her liability has been suspended; (3) refund to the borrower all amounts paid by the borrower to the lender or agency with respect to the discharged amount; and (4) notify the lender that the borrower's liability with respect to the amount of the loan has been discharged. 34 C.F.R. § 682.402(e)(7)(ii).

21. If the guaranty agency decides that the borrower is not entitled to a discharge, a borrower can request a review of that decision by the Secretary. If a borrower does request a review of the guaranty agency's decision, the agency shall forward the borrower's discharge request and all relevant documentation to the Secretary. 34 C.F.R. § 682.402(e)(11)(i).

22. Discharge of a student loan under 20 U.S.C. § 1087(c), entitles the borrower to:

(a) relief from any existing or past obligation to repay the loan and any charges imposed or cost incurred by the holder with respect to the loan that the borrower is or was otherwise obligated to pay. 20 U.S.C. § 1087(c)(1).

(b) restoration of the borrower's eligibility to receive federal assistance under Title IV of the Higher Education Act Amendments. 20 U.S.C. § 1087(c)(3)–(4).

(c) correction of all adverse credit reports by reporting to all credit bureaus to which the holder previously reported the delinquent status of the loan that all adverse credit history assigned to the loan should be deleted. 20 U.S.C. § 1087(c)(5).

23. The Administrative Procedure Act ("APA"), 5 U.S.C. § 706(2)(A), specifically creates a cause of action to "hold unlawful and set aside agency action, findings, and conclusions found to be arbitrary and capricious, an abuse of discretion, or otherwise not in accordance with the law."

24. The APA also creates a cause of action to "hold unlawful and set aside agency action, findings, and conclusions found to be–in excess of statutory jurisdiction, authority, or limitations, or short of statutory rights." 5 U.S.C. § 706(2)(C).

FACTS PERTAINING TO THE CLASS

25. The Secretary denies ability-to-benefit discharges, without adequate consideration of the facts of individual students, based upon the inference that the absence of recorded findings of improper ability-to-benefit admissions practices by particular schools means the school was not engaged in improper ability-to-benefit practices.

26. The Secretary administers the guaranteed student loan pro-

gram in part through giving directions to the guaranty agencies that are the first line of insurance of the federally guaranteed student loans. These directions are sent to the guarantee agencies in the form of memoranda referred to as "Dear Colleague" letters.

27. The Secretary has issued several Dear Colleague letters about ability-to-benefit discharges.

28. In September 1995, in Dear Colleague letter Gen-95-42 (attached hereto as Exhibit A), the Secretary advised guaranty agencies about how to evaluate requests for ability-to-benefit discharges, stating that the absence of findings of improper ATB practices by authorities with oversight responsibilities "raises an inference that no improper practices were reported because none were taking place." *Id.* at 4.

29. In his own actions in administering guaranteed student loans held by U.S. ED, the Secretary follows the practices outlined in the Dear Colleague letter.

30. The Secretary supports and relies on such an inference even though Congress created the ability-to-benefit discharge specifically because agencies with oversight responsibilities have failed "to detect and or take action" regarding abuses such as failure to honestly assess students' ability to benefit from vocational programs. *Senate Permanent Subcommittee on Investigations* (hereinafter the "Committee"), *Abuses in Federal Student Aid Programs*, S. Rep. No. 102-58, (1991) (hereinafter "the Nunn Report").

31. Between 1989 and 1991, the United States Senate Permanent Subcommittee on Investigations, chaired by Senator Sam Nunn, studied the rapid increase of defaulted guaranteed student loans obtained for study at vocational schools. S. Rep. No. 102-58, at 23 (1991).

32. The Nunn Report revealed a national epidemic of fraud by proprietary trade schools, including the practice of fraudulently certifying students' ability to benefit from the schools' programs. *See id* at 12.

33. The Nunn Report found that "one of the most widely abused areas of trade school practices was admissions and recruitment, in particular the admission of students who had not finished high school under the so-called "ability-to-benefit" or "ATB" rule. *Id.* at 12.

34. The Nunn Report also found evidence of a failure "by state and federal authorities to detect and or take action" regarding the abuse of GSLP rules and regulations. *Id.* at 23.

35. The Nunn Report stated U.S. ED "has effectively abdicated its GSLP oversight responsibilities to private accrediting bodies, State licensing authorities, and guaranty agencies. Experience has proven that those bodies have neither the motivation nor the capabilities to effectively police the program." *Id.* at 32.

36. The mandate, in the Higher Education Act Amendments, that the Secretary discharge the loans of students who had been admitted into proprietary schools despite their lack of an ability to benefit from the programs, was a response to Congressional findings that "institutions falsely certified the eligibility of students for Federal loans. . . . students were left without the skills needed to obtain employment and consequently did not have the means to repay the loans." *Report of the House Committee on Education and Labor*, H. Rep. No. 102-447, at 116 (1992).

FACTS REGARDING NAMED PLAINTIFFS

PLAINTIFF 1

37. Plaintiff 1 was enrolled in the Robert Fiance Hair Design Institute (hereafter "RFHD") branch at [Address] (hereafter "[Address 1]").

38. RFHD is a for-profit vocational school.

39. Plaintiff 1 was enrolled in a course that was scheduled to run from March 10, 1988 to December 8, 1988.

40. Plaintiff 1 financed her studies at RFHD by taking out guaranteed student loans under the Guaranteed Student Loan Program.

41. Plaintiff 1 received the proceeds of the disbursement of her loan on March 10, 1988.

42. At the time of her application to RFHD, Plaintiff 1 did not have, and reported to RFHD that she did not have a high school diploma or a GED.

43. RFHD did not require Plaintiff 1 to take an admission test, and did not enroll her in a GED course or other program of remedial education.

44. Plaintiff 1 attended classes at [Address 1] from March 1988 to early fall 1988.

45. Plaintiff 1 did not receive the training and education for which she was contracted due to her inability to benefit from the program.

46. The guaranteed student loans obtained by Plaintiff 1 for her studies at RFHD were placed in default status by U.S. ED.

47. On December 30, 1999, Plaintiff 1 applied to the Secretary for a discharge of her guaranteed student loans based on the school's false certification of her ability to benefit from the program.

48. On April 10, 2000, the Secretary acknowledged the receipt of Plaintiff 1's loan discharge application and stated that Plaintiff 1 was not entitled to an ability-to-benefit loan discharge because authorities with oversight responsibilities had made no findings or adverse reports relating to false certification of ability-to-benefit at RFHD (Letter attached as Exhibit B [*not reprinted herein*]).

PLAINTIFF 2

49. Plaintiff 2 was enrolled at Commercial Programming Unlimited (hereafter CPU), at [Address].

50. CPU is a for profit vocational school.

51. Plaintiff 2 financed her education at CPU by taking out guaranteed student loans under the Guaranteed Student Loan Program.

52. At the time of her application to CPU, Plaintiff 2 did not have, and informed CPU that she did not have a high school diploma or a GED.

53. CPU did not require Plaintiff 2 to take an admission test and did not enroll her in a GED course or any other course of remedial education.

54. Plaintiff 2 began taking classes at CPU in August of 1988. She was enrolled in courses for computer programming.

55. Plaintiff 2 attended classes at CPU for approximately two months.

56. Plaintiff 2 discontinued her studies at CPU because of the difficulty of the course material, inadequate teaching, and over-crowded classrooms, and but she did not formally withdraw from CPU.

57. The guaranteed student loans obtained by Plaintiff 2 for her studies at CPU were placed in default status by the Secretary.

58. Plaintiff 2 applied to the Secretary for a discharge of her guaranteed student loans based on the school's false certification of her ability-to-benefit from the program.

59. In a letter dated March 8, 2000, the Secretary acknowledged the receipt of Plaintiff 2 loan discharge application and stated that Plaintiff 2 was not entitled to an ability-to-benefit discharge because authorities with oversight responsibilities had made no findings or adverse reports relating to false certification of ability-to-benefit at CPU. (Letter attached as Exhibit C [*not reprinted herein*]).

FIRST CAUSE OF ACTION

60. Defendant Secretary's adoption of the policy, stated in the September 1995 Dear Colleague letter, that the absence of findings of improper ATB practices by authorities with oversight responsibilities "raises an inference that no improper practices were reported because none were taking place," and his own reliance on that inference in denying requests for ATB discharges, without adequate consideration of the facts presented by students seeking discharges, is arbitrary and capricious and in violation of 5 U.S.C. § 706(2)(A).

SECOND CAUSE OF ACTION

61. Defendant Secretary's adoption of the policy, stated in the September 1995 Dear Colleague letter, that the absence of findings of improper ATB practices by authorities with oversight responsibilities "raises an inference that no improper practices were reported because none were taking place," and his own reliance on that inference in denying requests for ATB discharges, without adequate consideration of the facts presented by students seeking discharges, is in excess of his statutory authority, in violation of 5 U.S.C. § 706(2)(C).

PRAYER FOR RELIEF

WHEREFORE, plaintiffs respectfully request the court to:

1. Enter an order certifying this action as a class action pursuant to Rule 23(b)(2) of the Federal Rules of Civil Procedure, with the class consisting of all individuals with federally guaranteed student loans obtained to attend for-profit vocational schools licensed by the New York State Department of Education, who have been or will be denied an ability-to-benefit discharge by the Secretary, without consideration of the facts in their individual cases, in reliance upon an absence of findings by oversight agencies about the certification practices of the schools they attended.

2. Enter a judgement against the defendant

   a. declaring that the Secretary's practice of denying requests for ability-to-benefit discharges based solely on the absence of findings by oversight agencies of prior wrongdoing by a school, without consideration of the facts of a debtor's individual circumstances, is arbitrary and capricious and not in accordance with the law.

b. directing the defendant to
   i. Review the facts of each debtor's request for an ability-to-benefit discharge;
   ii. Discontinue the practice of relying on the absence of reports by oversight agencies;
   iii. Provide debtors with the supporting evidence relied upon by the Secretary in determining that they are not entitled to a loan discharge, including but not limited to a copy of the properly administered and nationally recognized ATB exam or evidence of enrollment in a remedial program of education;
   iv. discharge the loans of Plaintiffs 1 and 2;
   v. cease collection efforts on the loans of Plaintiffs 1 and 2;
   vi. correct any reports to credit agencies or eligible institutions that the loans of Plaintiffs 1 or 2 are in default or delinquent;
   vii. return all money paid voluntarily or involuntarily by Plaintiffs 1 and 2;
   viii. provide notice, within a reasonable time not to exceed 90 days from the date of a resolution favorable to the plaintiff, in a form to be agreed upon by the parties, to all student borrowers denied an a false certification of an ability-to-benefit discharge that they may be eligible for a discharge of their student loans; and providing to them all information in the possession of the Secretary relating to their eligibility for discharge, the procedures for requesting a discharge, and a form on which to request such discharge;
   ix. make determinations, and issue written decisions, on all requests for ability-to-benefit discharges, within 60 days of receipt of the requests;
c. ordering defendant to pay the cost of this action, together with reasonable attorneys' fees pursuant to the Equal Access to Justice Act, 28 U.S.C. § 2412(d)(1)(A), as determined by the court; and
d. granting such other and further relief as the Court may deem just and proper.

Dated:

Respectfully submitted,
[Attorney for Plaintiffs]

E.2.4 Individual Complaint Challenging Disability Discharge Denial

A preliminary injunction motion for this case as well as a similar pleading in another case can be found on the companion CD-Rom.

IN THE UNITED STATES DISTRICT COURT
FOR THE SOUTHERN DISTRICT OF GEORGIA
WAYCROSS DIVISION

JANE SMITH,	)
Plaintiff,	)
	)
v.	)
	)
ROD PAIGE, SECRETARY,	)
UNITED STATES DEPART-	)
MENT OF EDUCATION,	)
Defendant.	)

COMPLAINT

INTRODUCTION

1. Plaintiff brings this action for judicial review of the United States Secretary of Education's decision denying her application for a discharge of her federally-guaranteed student loan. Plaintiff seeks declaratory and injunctive relief against the Department of Education's new ad hoc, unpublished, and unreasonable standards for evaluating requests to discharge student loans based on the borrower's permanent disability.

I. JURISDICTION

2. This court has jurisdiction under 28 U.S.C. §1331 (federal question), 20 U.S.C. §1082 (suits against Secretary of Education), and the federal Administrative Procedure Act, 5 U.S.C. §§ 701 *et seq.* With respect to Plaintiff's request for declaratory relief, this Court has jurisdiction under 28 U.S.C. §2201.

II. PARTIES

3. Plaintiff Jane Smith, an individual who resides at [Address] signed up for a federally-guaranteed student loan by the Riley Training Institute in Waycross in February 1981.

4. Defendant Rod Paige, Secretary of the United States Department of Education, is responsible for the administration of the federally-guaranteed student loan program.

5. The United States Department of Education(DOE) is an agency within the meaning of the federal Administrative Procedure Act, 5 U.S.C. §§ 701 *et seq.*

6. The Riley Training Institute in Waycross, Georgia was a proprietary trade school that was certified as an eligible institution to participate in federal financial aid programs under the Higher Education Act until it closed in May of 1991.

III. STATEMENT OF FACTS

7. Plaintiff Jane Smith is a 45-year-old single mother of one who resides in [Address], Georgia.

8. Plaintiff graduated from high school in 1975 and enrolled at Okefenokee Technical College for a six weeks nurse's aide course.

9. Plaintiff was successfully employed as a nurse's aide for a period of ten years, 1975 until 1985.

10. In 1989 Plaintiff enrolled in Riley Training Institute to study retail sales management.

11. Upon her acceptance at Riley Training Institute also located in Waycross, Georgia, Plaintiff applied for a federally guaranteed loan in February 1989.

12. Plaintiff Smith received a student loan from Florida Federal Savings in the amount of $2,625.00.

13. Plaintiff attended Riley Training Institute but did not complete her studies.

14. After being successfully gainfully employed for a period of ten years and attending school for a short while, Jane Smith suffered severe physical and mental impairments.

15. In 1995, Plaintiff applied for Social Security disability and/or Supplemental Security Income (SSI) and was determined to be permanently and totally disabled by the Social Security Administration (hereinafter "SSA").

16. Plaintiff began receiving SSI benefits in the amount of $458.00 in 1995.

17. In 1999, some four years after receipt of SSI benefits, Satilla Community Mental Health, where Ms. Smith sought assistance, recommended her for participation in the SSI work incentive subsidized/supportive employment program.

18. The subsidized work program pays benefits and wages above the amount that Ms. Smith actually earns. She is able to work because she has a job coach and accommodations are made on a daily basis in consideration of both her physical and mental disability.

19. The accommodations made on a daily basis are substantial and include the ability to leave work when necessary, to return home during the day, to work fewer hours than other employees due to fatigue and to have frequent rest periods during the day.

20. On or before December 1999, Plaintiff Smith began receiving collection notices from the Department of Education indicating that she was in arrears on her student loan payment and directing her to pay her arrearage in full to Defendant's intermediary, Pioneer Credit Recovery, Inc.

21. On or about June 29, 2000, Defendant received notice that Defendant intended to garnish her income if she did not contact Pioneer Credit Recovery, Inc. to make arrangements to pay her student loan arrearage.

22. The Department of Education has demanded from Plaintiff a loan payment in the amount of $6,004.98.

23. In response to said collection notices, Plaintiff Smith filed an application for student loan discharge due to her disability.

24. The Higher Education Act provides that an individual who is unable to work because of an injury or illness that is expected to continue indefinitely or result in death is entitled to have the federally guaranteed student loan discharged. 20 U.S.C.§ 1087(a).

25. In conjunction with her application for discharge due to a disability, Ms. Smith informed the Department of Education that she was totally and permanently disabled because she has full-blown AIDS and other complicating medical conditions.

26. Ms. Smith also informed the Agency that she received treatment for AIDS and other medical conditions from her primary care physician of many years.

27. Ms. Smith completed the Department of Education form to request a disability discharge, and, additionally, her physician completed the "Physician's Certification of Borrowers and Total Permanent Disability" listing AIDS, insulin-dependent diabetes mellitus, high blood pressure and the side-effects resulting from several AIDS medications as contributing to Plaintiff's inability to work in a genuine work place without accommodations. (*See* attached Exhibit "A" [*not reprinted herein.*])

28. In addition to notifying the Agency in July 2000 that she was disabled and making an application for a loan discharge due to disability, Plaintiff sent in a request for a hearing along with an administrative wage garnishment disclosure form.

29. Plaintiff's request for an application to cancel the school loan obligation was denied. However, a request for a hearing was granted and scheduled for February 13, 2001. The hearing was held by telephone.

30. At the outset of the hearing, Jacqueline Hughley-Leonard, a Department of Education hearing officer, stated that Plaintiff could present her argument but could not qualify for a disability discharge because she was working.

31. Ms. Hughley-Leonard refused to consider evidence of the completed application for discharge due to disability with the attached physician's certification of disability during the hearing.

32. Upon request from counsel for Plaintiff, Ms. Hughley-Leonard recused herself from the hearing because of her refusal as Hearing Officer to even consider Ms. Smith's evidence. Hearing Officer Irene Ford then joined Ms. Hughley-Leonard in the hearing and allowed Ms. Smith's counsel to present evidence of her disability.

33. On February 26, Defendant Department of Education denied Plaintiff's application for a disability discharge stating, "Receiving Social Security disability benefits does not automatically qualify a borrower for total and permanent disability cancellations." (*See* decision attached as Exhibit "B" p. 2 [*not reprinted herein.*])

34. Said February 26 opinion also stated, "A borrower is not considered totally and permanently disabled based on a condition that existed before he or she applied for the loan." (*See* Ex. "B" p.2)

35. Said recitation of fact was a factual error and despite Plaintiff's protestation to the Agency, said correction has not been made. (*See* Plaintiff's letter attached as Exhibit "C" [*not reprinted herein*]).

36. Defendant Agency also requested that Plaintiff Jane Smith provide financial evidence regarding whether or not she had sufficient funds for garnishment.

37. Said final decision (Ex. "B" p. 2) stated the intention of Defendant to garnish Ms. Smith's income. Defendant's decision stated, however, that it would stay the garnishment for six months because Ms. Smith did not have sufficient monthly income to pay the amount.

38. As a result of an additional collection activity related to this loan, Plaintiff Smith's 2000 tax return, of $262.00 and her August 2001 tax rebate in the amount of $300.00 were both intercepted.

39. Ms. Smith's income has not improved subsequent to the date of Defendant's decision, but has worsened because her tax refund and rebate were intercepted.

40. In addition to her own expenses, the Plaintiff is attempting

to provide a minimum amount of income on a monthly basis to her son who is in school.

41. Garnishment of Ms. Smith's income would render her unable to moderately function on a monthly basis, and would result in her being unable to participate in her subsidized work program.

42. On June 26, 2001, Plaintiff wrote to Defendant submitting her request for reconsideration of her claim asserting that the denial appeared to be based on the mistake of fact among other issues.

43. Defendant refused to clarify or explain his decision. Defendant's decision constituted Agency action that is reviewable under the Administrative Procedure Act.

44. Defendant's decision also stated, "Our findings are conclusive and represent the Department of Education's final decision on your objections. If you disagree with this decision, you may have this decision reviewed by bringing a lawsuit in federal district court." (*See* Ex. "B" p. 1)

45. Defendant's decision denying Plaintiff's application for discharge due to disability is based on no applicable or discernible law, statute or regulation.

46. Additionally, the ad hoc decision does not contain a statement of fact or an analysis of the facts to the regulation or to the applicable law governing and controlling how a disability discharge should be resolved.

47. Defendant's refusal to discharge Plaintiff Smith's student loan is arbitrary and capricious and not in accordance with the law. Plaintiff's application for disability discharge met all of the statutory and regulatory provisions found at 34 C.F.R. § 682.402.

48. Ms. Smith's loan balance approximates Five Thousand, Eight-Hundred Eighty dollars and 64/100 Dollars ($5,880.64).

49. Ms. Smith has no adequate remedy at law.

50. Ms. Smith, has already had her tax refund and rebate intercepted and has also been threatened with imminent garnishment against her earnings.

51. Defendant recently contacted counsel for Plaintiff requesting additional financial information so that it could move ahead to start garnishing her monthly benefit amount.

IV. DEFENDANT'S PRACTICES

52. Defendant has stated that its adverse decision dated February 26, 2001 in Plaintiff's case is "conclusive" and "final" (*See* Ex. "B" p. 1), and therefore constitutes final agency action as defined by 5 U.S.C. § 704.

53. Defendant has persisted in its attempts to collect on Ms. Smith's loan, most recently seizing her year 2000 tax refund and 2001 tax rebate.

54. Defendant's actions have resulted in its applying new, more restrictive standards to Ms. Smith's request for a disability discharge.

55. On or about June 7, 1999, the Inspector General of the U.S. Department of Education issued a report entitled "Improving the Process for Forgiving Student Loans" (Hereinafter "IG Report"), which included findings that certain individuals who were allegedly not disabled, had received student loan disability discharges. (*See* attached report as Exhibit "D")

56. In response to the IG report, the Defendant began applying stricter criteria to requests for disability discharges, including but not limited to the following changes:

A. Defendant ceased its prior practice of granting a disability discharge on the basis of a properly completed physician's certification of disability submitted on the Defendant's approved form;

B. Defendant notified its employees and agents that physicians should be informed that eligibility for disability benefits under the Social Security Act would not be sufficient basis to establish eligibility for a student loan disability discharge and that the student loan discharge standard for disability was a "higher standard" than the Social Security standard; and,

C. Defendant directed its employees and agents, who have no medical training, to make an independent determination of whether a physician's certification of disability is definitive, or if the diagnosis and prognosis do not appear to reach the standard of total and permanent disability.

57. Some, but not all, of the Defendant's new policies and rules regarding disability discharges were set forth in a "Dear Colleague letter," designated GEN-99-36 (hereinafter the "Dear Colleague letter"). (*See* attached letter as Exhibit "E")

58. The Dear Colleague letter was not published in the Federal Register for notice and comment.

59. The new rules are set forth in the Dear Colleague letter as absolute requirements for eligibility for disability discharges rather than as guidelines to decision-makers.

60. The substantive changes set forth in the Dear Colleague letter are arbitrary and capricious and not in accordance with the law.

61. The Defendant's adverse decision has caused and will continue to cause substantial and irreparable harm to Ms. Smith.

V. CLAIMS FOR RELIEF

COUNT I: DEFENDANT'S DECISION VIOLATES THE DISABILITY DISCHARGE PROVISIONS FOUND IN 20 U.S.C.S. § 1087(A)

62. Plaintiff incorporates paragraphs 1 through 61 of her Complaint as if set forth fully herein.

63. The determination that Ms. Smith is permanently and totally disabled was made and certified by a medical doctor, following a personal examination.

64. Defendant's determination that Ms. Smith is not permanently and totally disabled was based solely upon nonmedical considerations.

65. Defendant's determination that Ms. Smith is not permanently and totally disabled was made by nonmedical personnel.

66. Defendant's total failure to consider Ms. Smith's documented physical disability in determining whether to grant a discharge pursuant to 20 U.S.C.S. § 1087(a) violates the Congressional mandate to provide debt relief to persons who suffer from debilitating and terminal illnesses.

COUNT II: DEFENDANT'S RELIANCE ON A MISTAKE OF FACT RESULTED IN A FINAL DECISION THAT IS ARBITRARY AND CAPRICIOUS AND VIOLATES 5 U.S.C. §706(2)(A)

67. Plaintiff incorporates paragraphs 1 through 61 of her Complaint as if set forth fully herein.

68. Ms. Smith's application seeking discharge of her student loan liability was filed under 20 U.S.C.S. § 1087(a), alleging permanent and totally disability.

69. In determining that Ms. Smith was not entitled to a discharge of her student loan obligation, Defendant failed to address any substantive considerations related to Ms. Smith's disability status.

70. Defendant relied upon a mistake of fact regarding Ms. Smith's disability onset date when it ruled against Ms. Smith.

71. Defendant has been asked to either rectify its mistake or to clarify its holding and has refused to do so, stating that its decision is final.

72. Defendant's adverse decision on Ms. Smith's application is arbitrary, capricious and not in accordance with law, and, therefore, violates 5 U.S.C. § 706(2)(a).

COUNT III: DEFENDANT FAILED TO FOLLOW ITS OWN REGULATIONS IN MAKING ITS DECISION TO DENY PLAINTIFF'S DISCHARGE APPLICATION AND, THEREFORE, THE DECISION IS UNLAWFUL UNDER 5 U.S.C. § 706.

73. Plaintiff incorporates paragraphs 1 through 61 of her Complaint as if set forth fully herein.

74. Defendant sets forth the procedures that must be followed by which a borrower becomes entitled to a disability discharge in 34 C.F.R. § 682.402.

75. Defendant's above-cited regulations require that a discharge be granted upon written certification of permanent and total disability by a physician, submitted upon a form approved by Defendant.

76. Ms. Smith submitted the required medical certification of her permanent and total disability.

77. Defendant has refused to approve Ms. Smith's discharge application in contravention of its own regulations.

COUNT IV: BY APPLYING AN UNPUBLISHED STANDARD OF REVIEW ARTICULATED IN A "DEAR COLLEAGUE" LETTER, DEFENDANT VIOLATED THE NOTICE AND COMMENT REQUIREMENTS FOUND IN 5 U.S.C. § 552.

78. Plaintiff incorporates paragraphs 1 through 61 of her Complaint as if set forth fully herein.

79. Defendant sets forth the procedures that must be followed by which a borrower becomes entitled to a disability discharge in 34 C.F.R. § 682.402.

80. Ms. Smith complied with the above-referenced procedures, and should have been entitled to a discharge.

81. In making its adverse decision, Defendant applied a different standard to Ms. Smith's application than authorized by statute or regulation.

82. Defendant ignored its formal regulations to apply different eligibility rules set forth in a Dear Colleague letter.

83. The above-mentioned letter was not submitted to a negotiated rule-making process, nor was it widely published, which violates the Administrative Procedure Act requirement, 5 U.S.C. § 552 that regulations be published in the Federal Register for notice and comment prior to being applied by federal agencies.

WHEREFORE, Plaintiff respectfully requests that the Court grant the following relief:

1. Assume jurisdiction over this case;

2. Enter an order declaring that Defendant's new more restrictive standards violate 20 U.S.C.S. § 1087(A), 34 C.F.R. § 682.402 and the requirements of the Administrative Procedure Act;

3. Grant a preliminary and permanent injunction enjoining Defendant from implementing its more restrictive disability discharge standards as set forth in unpublished rules and ordering Defendant to reevaluate any discharge requests denied under the new restrictive standard;

4. Grant a preliminary and permanent injunction enjoining Defendant and its agents from intercepting federal income tax refunds and rebates, garnishing wages or bank accounts, or otherwise collecting the balance of the Plaintiff's student loan.

5. That the Court enter an order reversing the Department's action in denying Plaintiff's discharge request;

6. That the Court enter an order directing Defendant to refund with interest all monies withheld, garnished, or unlawfully collected from Plaintiff; 7. That the Court enter an order awarding Plaintiff costs; and 8. That the Court enter an order granting any other and further relief as is just and proper.

[Dated]

Respectfully submitted,
[Attorneys for the Plaintiff]

E.3 Challenge to Student Loan Collection Letters

E.3.1 Complaint

IN THE UNITED STATES DISTRICT COURT
FOR THE MIDDLE DISTRICT OF LOUISIANA

Mary Johnson, on behalf of herself and all others similarly situated,	))))
Plaintiff,	))
v.	))
The Premier Collectors, Inc.,	)
Defendant.	))

CLASS ACTION COMPLAINT

Plaintiff Mary Johnson, on her own behalf and on behalf of the class defined below, complains as follows against defendant The Premier Collectors, Inc.:

INTRODUCTION

1. This action is brought to remedy defendant's violations of the federal Fair Debt Collection Practices Act, 15 U.S.C. §1692 et seq. ("FDCPA").

JURISDICTION AND VENUE

2. This Court has jurisdiction under 15 U.S.C. §1692k(d) and 28 U.S.C. §1331.

PARTIES

3. Plaintiff Mary Johnson is an individual who resides in Baton Rouge, Louisiana. She is a "consumer" as defined by the FDCPA, 15 U.S.C. §1692a(3).

4. The Premier Collectors, Inc. ("Premier Collectors") is a Delaware corporation registered to do business in the state of Louisiana. Its registered agent and address are AB Corporation Systems, 1000 Main Street, Baton Rouge, Louisiana.

5. Premier Collectors is regularly engaged for profit in the collection of debts allegedly owed by consumers. It is a "debt collector" as defined in the FDCPA, 15 U.S.C. §1692a(6).

FACTUAL ALLEGATIONS OF MS. JOHNSON

6. On or about August 11, 1993, Ms. Johnson was mailed a collection letter from Defendant for $11,417.31 allegedly owing to the U.S. Department of Education. (Attached hereto as *Exhibit A*) [*not reprinted herein*].

7. On or about April 20, 1994, Ms. Johnson was mailed a collection letter from Defendant for $10,706.14 allegedly owing to the U.S. Department of Education. (Attached hereto as *Exhibit B*) [*not reprinted herein*].

8. On or about May 5, 1994, Ms. Johnson was mailed a collection letter from Defendant for $10,732.65 allegedly owing to creditor U. S. Department of Education. (Attached hereto as *Exhibit C*) [*not reprinted herein*].

9. These collection letters were mailed in an attempt to collect alleged debts arising from transactions primarily for personal, family, or household purposes.

10. Defendant is not affiliated with the U.S. Department of Education.

11. In *Exhibits A-C*, Defendant lists the principal balance as $5650.49, interest varying from $2,242.59 to $1,744.71, and fees and costs varying from $3,524.23 to $3,310.94.

12. Defendant did not and does not determine the course of legal action taken by the U.S. Department of Justice with regard to such debts.

13. Neither Defendant, the U.S. Department of Justice, nor anyone else, has filed suit against Ms. Johnson to collect this debt.

DEFENDANT'S PRACTICES

14. Defendant regularly mails, or causes to be mailed, collection letters bearing the name of the U.S. Department of Education to Louisiana residents in an effort to collect consumer debts.

15. Defendant seeks to recover a collection fee of "42.84%", which is neither "reasonable" nor "enforceable".

16. Defendant states in the collection letters "OUR STAFF AND CLIENT WILL DETERMINE THE APPROPRIATE COURSE OF LEGAL ACTION", suggesting that The Premier Collectors, Inc. will participate in directing the initiation of litigation by the U.S. Department of Justice against the consumer.

17. Defendant states in the collection letters that The Premier Collectors, Inc. will conduct an investigation of the of the plaintiff's income, savings, employment, real estate ownership and personal assets.

18. Defendant states in the collection letter that a suit by the U.S. Department of Justice may result in garnishment, attachment and/or judgment liens without notifying the consumer of the right to be heard and the necessity of entry of judgement prior to such action.

19. Defendant's collection letter implies that it is "vouched for, bonded by, or affiliated with the United States".

20. Defendant places the validation notice and debt collection warning on the back of the collection letters without reference thereto.

DAMAGES SUFFERED

21. As a result of Defendant's practices, Plaintiff and the class are entitled to statutory damages pursuant to the Fair Debt Collection Practices Act.

VIOLATIONS OF FDCPA

22. Defendant violated the FDCPA by mailing collection letter without proper validation notice or debt collection warning, in violation of 15 U.S.C. §1692g(a)and e(11).

23. Defendant violated the FDCPA by seeking to collect fees of "42.84%", which are neither "reasonable" nor "enforceable", in violation of 15 U.S.C. §1692e(2)(A) and f(1).

24. Defendant states in the collection letters "OUR STAFF AND CLIENT WILL DETERMINE THE APPROPRIATE COURSE OF LEGAL ACTION", suggesting that The Premier Collectors, Inc. direct the U.S. Department of Justice to file suit against the consumer in violation of 15 U.S.C. §1692e and f.

25. Defendant states in the collection letters that The Premier Collectors, Inc. will conduct an investigation of the of the consumer's income, savings, employment, real estate ownership and personal assets, in violation of 15 U.S.C. §1692e(4), (5) and (10).

26. Defendant states in the collection letter that a suit by the U.S. Department of Justice may result in garnishment, attachment and/or judgment liens without notifying the consumer of the right to be heard and the necessity of entry of judgement prior to such action in violation of 15 U.S.C. §1692e(4), (5) and (10).

27. Defendant's violated 15 U.S.C. §1692e(1) and (10) by implying that it is "vouched for, bonded by, or affiliated with the United States".

CLASS ALLEGATIONS

28. Ms. Johnson brings this action on behalf of a class of all other persons similarly situated. The class consists of all persons who satisfy the following criteria:

All Louisiana residents who received a notice from Defendant similar to *Exhibit A*, *Exhibit B*, or *Exhibit C*, regarding an alleged debt incurred for personal, family, or household purposes, subsequent to one year prior to the filing of the present litigation.

29. On information and belief, based on the fact that a large number of persons are so contacted by Defendant, the class is sufficiently numerous that joinder of all members is impractical.

30. There are questions of law and fact common to the class, which questions predominate over any questions peculiar to individual class members. The common questions include:

a. Whether Defendant is a "debt collector".

b. Whether Defendant's collection notice fails to provide a proper validation notice and debt collection warning.

c. Whether Defendant's collection notices seek to collect an amount which is not owed.

d. Whether Defendant's collection notices threaten action which is not intended to be taken or cannot legally be taken.

e. Whether Defendant's collection notices falsely represent or imply the seizure, garnishment, attachment or sale of the consumer's property which is not lawful or intended to be taken.

f. Whether Defendant's collection notices falsely represents or implies that it is vouched for, bonded by, or affiliated with the United states.

31. Ms. Johnson has the same claims as the members of the class. All of the claims are based on the same factual and legal theories.

32. Ms. Johnson will fairly and adequately represent the interest of the class members. Ms. Johnson has retained counsel experienced in prosecuting class actions and in consumer protection matters. There is no reason why Ms. Johnson and her counsel will not vigorously pursue this matter.

33. Certification of a class pursuant to Fed.R.Civ.P. 23(b)(3) is appropriate. A class action is the only appropriate means of resolving this controversy because the class members are not aware of their rights. In the absence of a class action, a failure of justice will result.

WHEREFORE, plaintiff Mary Johnson requests that the Court grant the following relief in her favor and on behalf of the class and against Defendant:

A. The maximum amount of statutory damages provided under 15 U.S.C. §1692k.

B. Attorney's fees, litigation expenses and costs.

C. Such other and further relief as is appropriate.

JURY DEMAND

Plaintiff Mary Johnson demands trial by jury.

[Attorney for Plaintiff]

E.3.2 Motion for Class Certification

IN THE UNITED STATES DISTRICT COURT
FOR THE MIDDLE DISTRICT OF LOUISIANA

```
                                    )
Mary Johnson, on behalf of          )
herself and all others similarly    )
situated,                           )
                       Plaintiff,   )
                                    )
v.                                  )
                                    )
The Premier Collectors, Inc.,       )
                       Defendant.   )
                                    )
```

PLAINTIFF'S MOTION FOR CLASS CERTIFICATION

Plaintiff, Mary Johnson ("Ms. Johnson"), respectfully requests

that the Court enter an order certifying that this action be allowed to proceed as a class action pursuant to Fed.R.Civ.P. 23. The class is defined as all Louisiana residents who received a notice from defendant, The Premier Collectors, Inc. ("PCI"), similar to *Exhibit A*, *Exhibit B*, or *Exhibit C* [*not reprinted herein*], regarding an alleged debt incurred for personal, family or household purposes, on or after August 2, 1993.

In support of this motion, Ms. Johnson states:

1. Plaintiff filed this class action under the Fair Debt Collection Practices Act, 15 U.S.C §1692 *et seq.* ("FDCPA"). The complaint alleges that defendant PCI engaged in the following violations of the FDCPA:

a. PCI sent printed form collection letters without the "validation notice" required by 15 U.S.C. §1692g(a) or the debt collection warning required by 15 U.S.C. §1692e(11).

b. PCI added to the principal amount of the alleged debt collection fees of "42.84%", which are neither "reasonable" nor "enforceable", in violation of 15 U.S.C. §§1692e(2)(A) and 1692f(1).

c. PCI states in its printed form collection letters "OUR STAFF AND CLIENT WILL DETERMINE THE APPROPRIATE COURSE OF LEGAL ACTION". This suggests to unsophisticated consumers that PCI would direct the Government to file suit against the consumer. The suggestion is unfounded, and therefore making it violates 15 U.S.C. §§1692e and 1692f.

d. PCI states in its form collection letters that PCI will conduct an investigation of the consumer's income, savings, employment, real estate ownership and personal assets. This statement is not true, and making it violates 15 U.S.C. §1692e(4), (5) and (10).

e. PCI states in its form collection letters that nonpayment may result in garnishment, attachment and/or judgment liens. The consumer is not told that such action must be preceded by the right to be heard and the entry of judgment. By misrepresenting the imminence of garnishment, attachment and liens, PCI violates 15 U.S.C. §1692e(4), (5) and (10).

f. PCI violated 15 U.S.C. §1692e(1) and (10) by implying that it is "vouched for, bonded by, or affiliated with the United States".

2. All requirements of Rule 23 of the Federal Rules of Civil Procedure have been met.

3. The class is so numerous that joinder of all members is impractical. PCI is one of the largest collection agencies in the United States, with $800 million in annual placements. *Collection Agency Directory* (First Detroit Corporation), 1994 ed., p. 15 (*Exhibit D*) [*not reprinted herein*]. Furthermore, student loans, which were the subject of the form letters at issue, are one of four collection specialties of PCI. *Id.* It is therefore reasonable to infer that the number of members of the proposed class exceeds the 20-40 required for certification.

4. There are questions of law and fact common to the class, which predominate over any questions affecting only individual class members. The principal questions presented by this action are:

a. Whether PCI is a "debt collector".

b. Whether PCI's form collection notices fail to provide a proper validation notice and debt collection warning.

c. Whether PCI's form collection notices seek to collect an amount which is not owed.

d. Whether PCI's form collection notices threaten action which is not intended to be taken or cannot legally be taken.

e. Whether PCI's form collection notices falsely represent or imply the seizure, garnishment, attachment or sale of the consumer's property, when such action is not lawful or intended to be taken.

f. Whether PCI's form collection notices falsely represent or imply that PCI is vouched for, bonded by, or affiliated with the United States.

5. There are no individual questions, other than whether a class member was subjected to one or more of the practices complained of, which can be determined by ministerial inspection of PCI's records.

6. Ms. Johnson will fairly and adequately protect the interests of the class. She is committed to vigorously litigating this matter.

7. Plaintiff's claim is typical of the claims of the class. All arise from the same operative facts and are based on the same legal theories.

8. A class action is a superior method for the fair and efficient adjudication of this controversy in that:

a. Congress specifically contemplated FDCPA class actions as a principal means of enforcing the statute. 15 U.S.C. §1692k.

b. Most of the consumers who receive the notices undoubtedly believe that they are receiving a letter from the U.S. Department of Justice, and have no knowledge that their rights are being violated by illegal collection practices.

c. The interest of class members in individually controlling the prosecution of separate claims against defendant is small because the maximum damages in an individual action are $1,000.

d. Management of this class action is likely to present significantly fewer difficulties than those presented in many class claims, *e.g.*, for securities fraud.

These grounds are further explained and supported by the accompanying memorandum of law.

WHEREFORE, plaintiff requests that this action be certified as a class action.

[Attorney for Plaintiff]

E.3.3 *Memorandum in Support of Class Certification*

IN THE UNITED STATES DISTRICT COURT
FOR THE MIDDLE DISTRICT OF LOUISIANA

```
——————————————————  )
                                  )
Mary Johnson, on behalf of        )
herself and all others similarly  )
situated,                         )
                 Plaintiff,  )
                                  )
v.                                )
                                  )
The Premier Collectors, Inc.,     )
                 Defendant.  )
——————————————————  )
```

MEMORANDUM IN SUPPORT OF PLAINTIFF'S
MOTION FOR CLASS CERTIFICATION

I. NATURE OF THE CASE

Plaintiff filed this class action under the Fair Debt Collection Practices Act, 15 U.S.C. §1692 *et seq.* ("the FDCPA"). The complaint seeks redress for a number of illegal practices of defendants in connection with the collection of debts.

Specifically, the complaint alleges that The Premier Collectors, Inc. ("PCI") engages in the following practices through the use of printed form letters:

a. PCI sent printed form collection letters without the "validation notice" required by 15 U.S.C. §1692g(a) or the debt collection warning required by 15 U.S.C. §1692e(11).

b. PCI added to the principal amount of the alleged debt collection fees of "42.84%", which are neither "reasonable" nor "enforceable", in violation of 15 U.S.C. §§1692e(2)(A) and 1692f(1).

c. PCI states in its printed form collection letters "OUR STAFF AND CLIENT WILL DETERMINE THE APPROPRIATE COURSE OF LEGAL ACTION". This suggests to unsophisticated consumers that PCI would direct the Government to file suit against the consumer. The suggestion is unfounded, and therefore making it violates 15 U.S.C. §§1692e and 1692f.

d. PCI states in its form collection letters that PCI will conduct an investigation of the consumer's income, savings, employment, real estate ownership and personal assets. This statement is not true, and making it violates 15 U.S.C. §1692e(4), (5) and (10).

e. PCI states in its form collection letters that nonpayment may result in garnishment, attachment and/or judgment liens. The consumer is not told that such action must be preceded by the right to be heard and the entry of judgment. By misrepresenting the imminence of garnishment, attachment and liens, PCI violates 15 U.S.C. §1692e(4), (5) and (10).

f. PCI violated 15 U.S.C. §1692e(1) and (10) by implying that it is "vouched for, bonded by, or affiliated with the United States".

II. THE FAIR DEBT COLLECTION PRACTICES ACT

The FDCPA states that its purpose, in part, is "to eliminate abusive debt collection practices by debt collectors", 15 U.S.C. §1692(e). It is designed to protect consumers from unscrupulous collectors, whether or not there is a valid debt. *Baker v. G.C. Services Corp.*, 677 F.2d 775, 777 (9th Cir. 1982). The FDCPA broadly prohibits unfair or unconscionable collection methods; conduct which harasses, oppresses or abuses any debtor; and any false, deceptive or misleading statements, in connection with the collection of a debt. 15 U.S.C. §§1692d, 1692e, and 1692f.

Courts have generally held that whether a communication or other conduct violates the FDCPA is to be determined by analyzing it from the perspective of the "least sophisticated consumer" or "least sophisticated debtor." *Clomon v. Jackson*, 988 F.2d 1314, 1318-20 (2d Cir. 1993); *Graziano v. Harrison*, 950 F.2d 107, 111 (3d Cir. 1991); *Swanson v. Southern Oregon Credit Service, Inc.*, 869 F.2d 1222, 1225-26 (9th Cir. 1988); *Jeter v. Credit Bureau, Inc.*, 760 F.2d 1168 (11th Cir. 1985). "The basic purpose of the least-sophisticated-consumer standard is to ensure that the FDCPA protects all consumers, the gullible as well as the shrewd." *Clomon v. Jackson, supra* at 1318.

The violations alleged in this case include the following:

A. IMPROPER VALIDATION NOTICE

PCI's placement of the §1692g validation notice and §1692e(11) debt collection warning on the back of the collection letters without proper reference thereto on the front is in violation of 15 U.S.C. §§1692g(a) and 1692e(11). Among the decisions holding that similar conduct violates the FDCPA are *Rabideau v. Management Adjustment Bureau*, 805 F.Supp. 1086 (W.D.N.Y. 1992); *Riveria v. MAB Collections, Inc.*, 682 F.Supp. 174 (W.D.N.Y.1988); and *Ost v. Collection Bureau, Inc.*, 493 F.Supp. 701 (D.N.D. 1980).

B. DIRECTING THE COURSE OF LEGAL ACTION

PCI states in the collection letters "OUR STAFF AND CLIENT WILL DETERMINE The APPROPRIATE COURSE OF LEGAL ACTION," suggesting that PCI directs the filing of lawsuits against the consumer. In fact, the U.S. Department of Justice must decide to file suit against the consumer. The false statement that PCI has that authority violates 15 U.S.C. §§1692e and 1692f.

Misrepresenting the imminence of and authority to institute legal action against the consumer is a violation of the FDCPA. *Pipiles v. Credit Bureau of Lockport, Inc.*, 886 F.2d 22 (2d Cir. 1989).

C. INVESTIGATION OF THE CONSUMER'S ASSETS

PCI states in the collection letters that it will conduct an investigation of the consumer's income, savings, employment, real estate ownership and personal assets. It doesn't. The false statement is a violation of 15 U.S.C. §1692e(4), (5) and (10). *Rosa v. Gaynor*, 784 F.Supp. 1, 5 (D.Conn. 1989); *Woolfolk v. Van Ru Credit Corp.*, 783 F.Supp. 724 (D.Conn. 1990); *Cacace v. Lucas*, 775 F.Supp. 502 (D.Conn. 1990).

D. PADDING DEBTS WITH "UNREASONABLE" CHARGES

PCI, in violation of 15 U.S.C. §1692e(2)(A) and f(1), adds collection fees of "42.84%" to the principal amount of the debt. Such fees are neither "reasonable" nor "enforceable". *Jenkins v. Heintz*, 25 F.3d 536 (7th Cir. 1994); *Strange v. Wexler*, 796 F.Supp. 1117 (N.D.Ill. 1992).

E. GARNISHMENT WITHOUT NOTIFICATION OF RIGHTS

PCI states in its collection letters that a suit by the U.S. Department of Justice may result in garnishment, attachment and/or judgment liens, without notifying the consumer of the right to be heard and the necessity of entry of judgment prior to such action. This is a misrepresentation of the consequences of nonpayment, and violates 15 U.S.C. §1692e(4), (5) and (10). *Woolfolk v. Van Ru Credit Corp., supra*; *Cacace v. Lucas, supra*; *Rosa v. Gaynor, supra*.

F. IMPLYING AFFILIATION WITH THE UNITED STATES

PCI also violated 15 U.S.C. §1692e(1) and (10) by implying that it is "vouched for, bonded by or affiliated with the United States".

Gammon v. GC Services, 27 F.3d 1254 (7th Cir. 1994).

III. STANDARD FOR CLASS CERTIFICATION

In determining whether a class will be certified, the merits of the case are not examined and the substantive allegations of the complaint should be taken as true, except to the extent that they are contradicted by evidence. *Blackie v. Barrack*, 524 F.2d 891, 901 n. 16 (9th Cir. 1975); *Heastie v. Community Bank of Greater Peoria*, 125 F.R.D. 669, 671 n. 2 (N.D.Ill. 1989); *Riordan v. Smith Barney*, 113 F.R.D. 60, 62 (N.D.Ill. 1986). The Seventh Circuit has said that "Rule 23 must be liberally interpreted" and read to "favor maintenance of class actions". *King v. Kansas City Southern Industries*, 519 F.2d 20, 25-26 (7th Cir. 1975).

Class actions are essential to enforce laws protecting consumers. As the Illinois Appellate Court stated in *Eshaghi v. Hanley Dawson Cadillac Co.*, 214 Ill.App.3d 995, 574 N.E.2d 760 (1st Dist. 1991):

> Even without resort to the relaxed standards of proof envisioned by the Consumer Fraud Act, Illinois has been hospitable to maintenance of class actions and has been willing to recognize that common questions of law and fact predominate in a great many situations. . . . In a large and impersonal society, class actions are often the last barricade of consumer protection. . . . To consumerists, the consumer class action is an inviting procedural device to cope with frauds causing small damages to large groups. The slight loss to the individual, when aggregated in the coffers of the wrongdoer, results in gains which are both handsome and tempting. The alternatives to the class action — private suits or governmental actions — have been so often found wanting in controlling consumer frauds that not even the ardent critics of class actions seriously contend that they are truly effective. The consumer class action, when brought by those who have no other avenue of legal redress, provides restitution to the injured, and deterrence of the wrongdoer. (574 N.E.2d at 764, 766)

Congress expressly recognized the propriety of a class action under the FDCPA by providing special damage provisions and criteria in 15 U.S.C. §§1692k(a) and (b) for FDCPA class action cases. *Brewer v. Friedman*, 152 F.R.D. 142 (N.D.Ill. 1993); *Zanni v. Lippold*, 119 F.R.D. 32, 35 (C.D.Ill. 1988); *Beasley v. Blatt* 1994 U.S.Dist. LEXIS 9383 (N.D.Ill., July 14, 1994); *West v. Costen*, 558 F.Supp. 564, 572-573 (W.D. Va. 1983) (FDCPA class certified re unauthorized charges). Plaintiff's counsel also were involved in two FDCPA class actions that were settled. *Cramer v. First of America Bank Corp.*, 93 C 3189 (N.D.Ill.) (*Exhibit E*); *Boddie v. Meyer*, 93 C 2975 (N.D.Ill.) (*Exhibit F*).

IV. THE PROPOSED CLASS MEETS THE REQUIREMENTS FOR CERTIFICATION
A. RULE 23(A)(1)— NUMEROSITY

Fed.R.Civ.P. 23(a)(1) requires that the class be "so numerous that joinder of all members is impracticable." "When the class is large, numbers alone are dispositive. . . ." *Riordan v. Smith Barney*,

113 F.R.D. 60, 62 (N.D.Ill. 1986). Where the class numbers at least 40, joinder is usually impracticable. *Cypress v. Newport News General & Nonsectarian Hosp. Ass'n*, 375 F.2d 648, 653 (4th Cir. 1967) (18 sufficient); *Swanson v. American Consumer Industries*, 415 F.2d 1326, 1333 (7th Cir. 1969) (40 sufficient); *Riordan v. Smith Barney, supra*, 113 F.R.D. 60, 62 (N.D.Ill. 1986) (10-29 sufficient); *Blatt v. Beasley, supra* (25 sufficient in FDCPA case); *Sala v. National Railroad Passenger Corp.*, 120 F.R.D. 494, 497 (E.D.Pa. 1988) (40-50 sufficient); *Scholes v. Stone, McGuire & Benjamin*, 143 F.R.D. 181, 184 (N.D.Ill. 1992) (about 70). It is not necessary that the precise number of class members be known. *McCleery Tire Service, Inc. v. Texaco, Inc.*, 1975-2 Trade Cas. (CCH) ¶60,581 (E.D.Pa. 1975). "A class action may proceed upon estimates as to the size of the proposed class." *In re Alcoholic Beverages Litigation*, 95 F.R.D. 321 (E.D.N.Y. 1982); *Lewis v. Gross*, 663 F.Supp. 1164, 1169 (E.D.N.Y. 1986).

Here, it is reasonable to infer that the numerosity requirement is satisfied because the actions complained of were carried out by one of the largest collection agencies in the United States through the use of standard, preprinted form documents. This fact alone indicates that the numerosity requirement is satisfied. *Swiggett v. Watson*, 441 F.Supp. 254, 256 (D.Del. 1977) (in action challenging transfers of title pursuant to Delaware motor vehicle repairer's lien, fact that Department of Motor Vehicles issued printed form for such transfer in and of itself sufficient to show that numerosity was satisfied). Plaintiff has propounded discovery to determine the exact number of class members (*Exhibit G*).

B. RULE 23(A)(2)—COMMONALITY

Fed.R.Civ.P. 23(a)(2) requires that there be a common question of law *or* fact. Not all factual or legal questions raised in the litigation need be common so long as at least one issue is common to all class members. *Spencer v. Central States Pension Fund*, 778 F.Supp. 985, 989 n.2 (N.D.Ill. 1991). Where a question of law involves "standardized conduct of the defendants toward members of the proposed class, a common nucleus of operative facts is typically presented, and the commonality requirement . . . is usually met." *Franklin v. City of Chicago*, 102 F.R.D. 944, 949 (N.D.Ill. 1984); *Patrykus v. Gomilla*, 121 F.R.D. 357, 361 (N.D.Ill. 1988).

There are common questions of law and fact common to the class, which questions predominate over any questions affecting only individual class members. These questions include:

a. Whether PCI is a "debt collector".

b. Whether PCI's collection notice fails to provide a proper validation notice and debt collection warning.

c. Whether PCI's collection notices seek to collect an amount which is not owed.

d. Whether PCI's collection notices threaten action which is not intended to be taken or cannot legally be taken.

e. Whether PCI's collection notices falsely represent or imply the seizure, garnishment, attachment or sale of the consumer's property which is not lawful or intended to be taken.

f. Whether PCI's collection notices falsely represents or implies that it is vouched for, bonded by, or affiliated with the United states.

Each of these questions is concerned solely with the conduct of PCI. The only individual issue is the identification of the class members affected by each practice.

C. RULE 23(A)(3)—TYPICALITY

The rule requires that the claims of the named plaintiff be typical of the claims of the class:

> A plaintiff's claim is typical if it arises from the same event or practice or course of conduct that gives rise to the claims of other class members and his or her claims are based on the same legal theory. The typicality requirement may be satisfied even if there are factual distinctions between the claims of the named plaintiffs and those of other class members. Thus, similarity of legal theory may control even in the face of differences of fact.

De La Fuente v. Stokely-Van Camp, Inc., 713 F.2d 225, 232 (7th Cir. 1983) (citation omitted); *see also, Rosario v. Livaditis*, 963 F.2d 1013, 1018 (7th Cir. 1992).

In the instant case, typicality is inherent in both of the class definitions. By definition, each of the class members was subjected to the same violations as the named plaintiff. All class members' claims arise from the same practices of PCI's which gave rise to the named plaintiff's claims.

D. RULE 23(A)(4)—ADEQUACY OF REPRESENTATION

The rule also requires that the named plaintiff provide fair and adequate protection for the interests of the class. That protection involves two factors: "(a) the plaintiff's attorney must be qualified, experienced, and generally able to conduct the proposed litigation; and (b) the plaintiff must not have interests antagonistic to those of the class." *Rosario v. Livaditis*, 963 F.2d 1013, 1018 (7th Cir. 1992).

The qualifications of plaintiff's counsel are set forth in *Exhibits H and I*. Mr. Bragg is widely experienced in FDCPA litigation and class actions. He is the co-author of National Consumer Law Center, *Fair Debt Collection* (2d ed. 1991 and Supp.). Mr. Ridge has litigated several FDCPA cases in Louisiana.

The second relevant consideration under Rule 23(a)(4) is whether the interests of the named plaintiff are coincident with the general interests of the class. Both Ms. Johnson and the class members seek money damages as the result of PCI's unlawful collection notice. Given the identity of claims between the plaintiff and the class members, there is no potential for conflicting interests in this action. There is no antagonism between the interests of the named plaintiff and those of the class.

E. RULE 23(B)(3)— COMMON QUESTIONS OF LAW OR FACT PREDOMINATE

Rule 23(b)(3) requires that the questions of law or fact common to all members of the class predominate over questions pertaining to individual members. This criterion is normally satisfied when there is an essential common factual link between all class members and the defendants for which the law provides a remedy. *Halverson v. Convenient Food Mart, Inc.*, 69 F.R.D. 331 (N.D.Ill. 1974).

In this case, the "common nucleus of operative fact," *Id.* at 335, is that all class members, by definition, were subjected to the same violations as plaintiff.

Cases dealing with the legality of standardized documents and practices, are generally appropriate for resolution by class action because the document is the focal point of the analysis. *Halverson v. Convenient Food Mart, Inc.*, *supra*; *Brooks v. Midas-International Corp.*, 47 Ill.App.3d 266, 361 N.E.2d 815 (1st Dist. 1977) (claim that advertising conveyed meaning that exhaust systems would be replaced free of charge); *Spirek v. State Farm Mut. Auto. Ins. Co.*, 65 Ill.App.3d 440, 382 N.E.2d 111 (1st Dist. 1978) (propriety of insurer's practice in requiring execution of subrogation agreements before paying medical benefits); *Haynes v. Logan Furniture Mart, Inc.*, 503 F.2d 1161 (7th Cir. 1974) (propriety of disclosure documents under Truth in Lending Act); *Haroco v. American Nat'l Bk. & Tr. Co.*, 121 F.R.D. 664, 669 (N.D.Ill. 1988) (improper computation of interest); *Kleiner v. First Nat'l Bank of Atlanta*, 97 F.R.D. 683 (N.D.Ga. 1983) (same); *Heastie v. Community Bank of Greater Peoria*, 125 F.R.D. 669 (N.D.Ill. 1989) (execution of home improvement financing documents in sequence that evaded consumers' rescission rights). This is true even though the nature and amount of damages may differ among the members of the class. *Heastie v. Community Bank of Greater Peoria*, *supra*.

An FDCPA claim challenging the propriety of a form letter is similar to a Truth in Lending disclosure claim, which has frequently been certified as a class actions. *Haynes v. Logan Furniture Mart, Inc.*, 503 F.2d 1161 (7th Cir. 1974); *Adiel v. Chase Fed. S. & L. Ass'n*, 810 F.2d 1051 (11th Cir. 1987); *Hughes v. Cardinal Fed. S. & L. Ass'n*, 566 F.Supp. 834 (S.D.Ohio 1983); *Fetta v. Sears, Roebuck & Co.*, 77 F.R.D. 411 (D.R.I. 1977); *Bantolina v. Aloha Motors, Inc.*, 419 F.Supp. 1116, 1122 (D.Haw. 1976); *Jones v. Goodyear Tire & Rubber Co.*, 442 F.Supp. 1157 (E.D.La. 1977); *Simon v. World Omni Leasing*, 146 F.R.D. 197 (S.D.Ala. 1992); *Johnson v. Steven Sims Suburu Leasing*, 1993 U.S.Dist. LEXIS 8078 (N.D.Ill., June 9, 1993) (Magistrate Judge's recommendation).

FDCPA actions have been certified as class actions on several occasions. *Zanni v. Lippold*, 119 F.R.D. 32, 35 (C.D.Ill.1988); *Brewer v. Friedman*, 152 F.R.D. 142 (N.D.Ill. 1993); *Beasley v. Blatt*, 1994 U.S.Dist. LEXIS 9383 (N.D.Ill., July 14, 1994); *West v. Costen*, 558 F.Supp. 564, 572-73 (W.D.Va.1983).

Because of the standardized nature of the defendant's conduct, common questions predominate. The only individual issue is the identification of the consumers who received the letters, a matter capable of ministerial determination from PCI's records. This is not the kind of problem that is a barrier to class certification. *Heastie v. Community Bank of Greater Peoria*, 125 F.R.D. 669, 678 (N.D.Ill. 1989). The commonality requirement is therefore met.

F. RULE 23(B)(3) — CLASS ACTION IS SUPERIOR TO OTHER AVAILABLE METHODS TO RESOLVE THIS CONTROVERSY.

Efficiency is the primary focus in determining whether the class action is the superior method for resolving the controversy presented. *Eovaldi v. First Nat'l Bank*, 57 F.R.D. 545 (N.D.Ill. 1972). The Court is required to determine the best available method for resolving the controversy in keeping with judicial integrity, convenience, and economy. *Scholes*, *supra*, 143 F.R.D. at 189; *Hurwitz v. R.B. Jones Corp.*, 76 F.R.D. 149 (W.D. Mo. 1977). It is proper for a court, in deciding the "best" available method, to consider the

" . . . inability of the poor or uninformed to enforce their rights, and the improbability that large numbers of class members would possess the initiative to litigate individually." *Haynes v. Logan Furniture Mart, Inc.*, *supra*, 503 F.2d 1161 (7th Cir. 1974).

In this case there is no better method available for the adjudication of the claims which might be brought by each individual debtor subjected to PCI's practice. The special efficacy of the consumer class action has been noted by the courts and is applicable to this case:

> A class action permits a large group of claimants to have their claims adjudicated in a single lawsuit. This is particularly important where, as here, a large number of small and medium sized claimants may be involved. In light of the awesome costs of discovery and trial, many of them would not be able to secure relief if class certification were denied. . . .

In re Folding Carton Antitrust Litigation, 75 F.R.D. 727, 732 (N.D.Ill. 1977) (citations omitted). Class certification of a FDCPA damage action will provide an efficient and appropriate resolution of the controversy. *Zanni v. Lippold*, *supra*, 119 F.R.D. 32, 35-36 (C.D.Ill. 1988); *West v. Costen*, *supra*, 558 F.Supp. 564, 572-73 (W.D.Va. 1983); *Beasley v. Blatt*, *supra*, 1994 U.S. Dist. LEXIS 9383 (N.D.Ill., July 14, 1994); *Brewer v. Friedman*, 152 F.R.D. 142 (N.D.Ill. 1993); *Vaughn v. CSC Credit Services, Inc.*, 1994 U.S.Dist. LEXIS 2172 (N.D.Ill., March 1, 1994); *Duran v. Credit Bureau of Yuma, Inc.*, 93 F.R.D. 607 (D. Ariz. 1982); *Boddie v. Meyer*, *supra*, 93 C 2975 (N.D.Ill.); and *Cramer v. First of America Bank Corporation*, *supra*, 93 C 3189 (N.D.Ill.).

CONCLUSION

The proposed class meets the requirements of Rules 23(a) and (b)(3). Plaintiff respectfully requests that the Court certify this action as a class action.

[Attorney for Plaintiff]

E.4 Challenges to Student Loan Debt Collection Procedures

E.4.1 Class Action Complaint Challenging Wage Garnishment Procedures

IN THE UNITED STATES DISTRICT COURT
FOR THE MIDDLE DISTRICT OF FLORIDA
FORT MYERS DIVISION

Pedro Martinez, Individually and on behalf of all others similarly situated,
 	
       Plaintiff,
 	
 v.
 	
 Payco General American Credits, Inc., Great Lakes Higher Education Guaranty Corporation, and Richard W. Riley, Secretary of the United States Department of Education
 	
       Defendants.
	))))))))))))))))

SECOND AMENDED COMPLAINT—CLASS ACTION

TO THE HONORABLE JUDGE OF THE COURT:

Plaintiff Pedro Martinez ("Plaintiff" or "Martinez") complains of Payco General American Credits, Inc. ("Payco"), Great Lakes Higher Education Guaranty Corporation ("Great Lakes") [jointly called "Private Defendants"], and Richard W. Riley, Secretary of the United States Department of Education ("Secretary"), by way of a class action, and shows the Court the following:

INTRODUCTION

This is a class action for damages and injunctive relief for the Private Defendants' violations of the federal Fair Debt Collection Practices Act, 15 U.S.C. § 1692 *et seq.* ("FDCPA") and the Florida Consumer Collection Practices Act, Florida Statutes § 559.55 *et seq.* ("Florida Act"). This action also seeks to enjoin violations of 20 U.S.C. § 1095a *et seq.* and to challenge the constitutionality of that statute, along with interpretive regulations issued by the Secretary.

Martinez brings this class action on behalf of himself and on behalf of all other consumers who have been subjected to similar practices, seeking declaratory relief, damages, restitution, and a permanent injunction forcing the Private Defendants to stop their illegal efforts to collect student loans. Martinez seeks limited declaratory and injunctive relief against the Secretary.

Payco is one of the largest collection agencies in the country. Its success is in large part founded on its willingness to violate both state and federal laws regulating the conduct of debt collectors, by engaging in a variety of abusive and deceptive practices. This case is an example of its wrongful practices. This suit seeks damages and injunctive relief against Payco.

Great Lakes serves the dual role of guaranteeing student loans and acting as a collection agency for some of those loans. Under 20 U.S.C. § 1095a *et seq.*, it is authorized to garnish wages under certain circumstances. In violation of the constitutional guarantees of due process of law, it has unlawfully delegated its authority to private collection agencies such as Payco. This suit seeks damages and injunctive relief against Great Lakes.

The Secretary has failed to insure that collections of student loan debts through garnishment meet minimal constitutional due process requirements. The Secretary is sued in his official capacity seeking declaratory and injunctive relief only.

JURISDICTION AND VENUE

Jurisdiction of this Court arises under 15 U.S.C. § 1692k(d) and 28 U.S.C. § 1331. Supplemental jurisdiction exists for the state law claims pursuant to 28 U.S.C. § 1367(a).

Venue is proper in the Middle District of Florida, under 28 U.S.C. § 1391(b), (c) & (e).

PARTIES

Plaintiff Pedro Martinez is a natural person who resides in Naples, Florida. Martinez and each of the other members of the classes are "consumers" as defined in FDCPA and the Florida Act.

Defendant Payco is a for-profit Delaware corporation that regularly does business in this judicial district and elsewhere in this state. Payco regularly collects or attempts to collect debts owed or due or asserted to be owed or due another. Payco is a "debt collector" as defined by FDCPA and the Florida Act. Payco has appeared in this action.

Defendant Great Lakes is a non-profit Wisconsin corporation. Great Lakes is engaged in the practice of guaranteeing and collecting student loans in this judicial district and elsewhere in this state. It regularly collects or attempts to collect debts owed or due or asserted to be owed or due another. Great Lakes is a "debt collector" as defined by FDCPA and the Florida Act. Great Lakes has appeared in this action.

Richard W. Riley, sued in his official capacity as Secretary of the United States Department of Education, has appeared in this action.

CLASS ACTION ALLEGATIONS

Martinez sues on his own behalf and, as class representative, sues on behalf of two classes of people, defined as follows:

Class I

Consumers residing in Florida who have been the victims of the illegal acts of Payco and/or Great Lakes in violation of the Florida Act, as detailed below, beginning four years prior to the date the original Complaint was filed.

Class II

Consumers residing in any of the United States, including Florida, who have been the victims of the illegal acts of the Secretary, Payco and/or Great Lakes in violation of the FDCPA and/or the United States Constitution, as detailed below, beginning one year prior to the date the original Complaint was filed.

Whenever this Complaint simply refers to the "class" or "classes" it includes both Class I and Class II.

Martinez brings this lawsuit as a class action because (1) the classes are so numerous that joinder of all members is impracticable, (2) there are questions of law and fact common to the classes, (3) Martinez's claims are typical of the claims of the classes, and (4) Martinez can and will fairly and adequately protect the interests of the classes. Questions of whether, and to what extent, the Private Defendants engaged in the practices described herein, whether they did so intentionally or knowingly, and whether they thereby violated the law will be common to all members of the classes.

It is appropriate to maintain this lawsuit as a class action for injunctive relief pursuant to Federal Rule of Civil Procedure 23(b)(2) because all defendants acted on grounds generally applicable to the classes, thereby making injunctive and declaratory relief appropriate with respect to each class as a whole.

It is also appropriate to maintain this lawsuit as a class action for damages pursuant to Federal Rule of Civil Procedure 23(b)(3) because questions of law and fact common to the members of the classes predominate over questions affecting only individual members and because a class action is superior to other available methods for the fair and efficient adjudication of the controversy.

Martinez's claims are typical of the claims of both classes as a whole. He can and will fairly and adequately protect the interests of the classes, because he has retained experienced counsel to represent the classes, he has no conflict of interest with the classes, and he brings this lawsuit specifically for the protection of consumers who have been and will be harmed by these practices, and not solely to recover his personal damages. Acts of Agents

Whenever in this Complaint it is alleged that a defendant did any act, it is meant that the defendant performed or participated in the act, or the officers, agents, or employees of the defendant performed or participated in the act on behalf of and under the actual, vicarious, or apparent authority of the defendant. Conditions Precedent

All conditions precedent to the filing of this case have been performed, have occurred, or have been satisfied.

FACTS

Pedro Martinez accumulated approximately $29,000.00 in several student loans during his seven years of college and law school. In 1988, he consolidated those loans through a federal consolidation program run by the Student Loan Marketing Association ("Sallie Mae") on which Great Lakes was a guarantor. Sallie Mae is a financial services corporation that specializes in funding education. It currently funds approximately 40% of all insured student loans, by purchasing loans from lenders to replenish their funds. Sallie Mae is headquartered in Reston, Virginia, and maintains education loan servicing centers around the country.

After consolidation, Martinez received periodic offers from Sallie Mae to defer his loan for up to six months. In the fall of 1995, Martinez accepted an offer of deferral in order to finance his upcoming wedding. Sallie Mae told him that no additional documentation was required for this deferment and that he would be notified by mail when to resume payments.

Instead of a notice to resume payments, the next notice Martinez received from anyone relating to his student loan was a notice of default from Great Lakes. When he contacted Great Lakes by telephone to attempt to clear up the misunderstanding, Great Lakes refused to discuss his loan and insisted that he contact Payco.

Martinez telephoned Payco, which advised him that his only option was to enter into a rehabilitation program. Since he was told that this was his only option, Martinez took it.

Payco included in the repayment amount, without Martinez's authorization, approximately $5,000.00 in collection fees. When Martinez tried to contest these fees, he was rebuffed.

In October, 1997, Martinez received a communication ostensibly from Great Lakes, but possibly generated by Payco, styled "NOTICE PRIOR TO WAGE WITHHOLDING," that was "issued" on October 22, 1997 ("Notice"). The Notice represented that Martinez currently owed $35,935.61 and told Martinez that unless he established a new written repayment agreement with Payco on or before November 21, 1997, Martinez's employer would be ordered to begin garnishment of Martinez's wages.

The Notice advised Martinez that he could request a hearing concerning *only* (1) the existence of the debt, (2) the amount of the debt, or (3) the terms of his repayment schedule. Although federal law provides for other bases for cancelling or deferring a debt, the Notice did not advise Martinez of those rights. By stating only these three limited grounds for requesting a hearing, the Notice misrepresented Martinez's rights under the law.

Martinez timely sought a telephone hearing before garnishment, by completing and returning to Payco a form provided with the Notice. In that form, he stated that he wished to be heard regarding the terms of his repayment schedule and that he contested the amount of the debt because of the inclusion of the collection fees.

Despite the fact that Martinez timely sought a pre-garnishment hearing, Payco sent Martinez a letter dated December 16, 1997, which "denied" Martinez's request for a hearing without explanation and further represented to Martinez that nonpayment of the alleged debt would result in an "Administrative Wage Garnishment" without further opportunity for a hearing unless he made other arrangements. This letter stated that the amount of the debt was now $36,326.48 and was going up daily. This amount included $4,981.24, which the letter represented was *required* by federal regulation. This representation is false.

This letter did not advise Martinez of his rights pursuant to FDCPA § 1692g to dispute the debt and receive verification of the debt. On information and belief, Martinez never received the notice advising him of those rights.

On or about January 20, 1998, Payco issued an "ORDER OF WITHHOLDING FROM EARNINGS" ("Order") and served it on Martinez's employer. The Order directed the employer to garnish Martinez's wages and to send the money direct to Payco.

Martinez's employer began withholding his wages in the amount of $110.00 per week in February 1998, pursuant to the garnishment Order. The weekly garnishment continues to this day.

The Order deceptively advises the employer to withhold "10% of debtor's disposable pay" or an amount permitted by 15 U.S.C. § 1673. This method of withholding conflicts with federal law, and will result in overwithholding in many instances. Congress enacted limitations on wage garnishment, providing that the maximum amount of disposable earnings "subjected to garnishment may not exceed . . . (2) the amount by which his disposable earnings for that week exceed thirty times the Federal minimum hourly wage prescribed by section 206(a)(1) of Title 29 in effect at the time the earnings are payable . . . ." 15 U.S.C. § 1673. The effect of this law is to reduce the permissible amount withheld below the 10%

required by Payco, for many debtors. For example, although 10% of Martinez's weekly disposable pay (and the amount currently being withheld weekly pursuant to the Garnishment Order) is $110.00, which is within the limits of 29 U.S.C. § 206, on information and belief many other members of the classes will have excessive amounts of their earnings subject to garnishment.

The practices of Payco and Great Lakes violated the the due process guarantees of the United States Constitution; the protections against wrongful garnishment provided by the Higher Education Act of 1965, 20 U.S.C. 1095a; various provisions of the Fair Debt Collection Practices Act, 15 USC 1692 *et seq.*; and various provisions of the Florida Consumer Collection Practices Act, Florida Statutes § 559.55 *et seq.* By enactment of policies that encourage and permit these practices, the Secretary has exceeded his lawful authority and has contributed to the denial of due process.

On information and belief, the practices of Payco and Great Lakes in collecting Martinez's debt are typical of their student loan garnishment practices in general.

FIRST CAUSE OF ACTION

Request For Relief Pursuant To Florida Consumer Collection Practices Act

By the actions set forth above, Payco and Great Lakes violated the Florida Act Section 559.72(9), which was the proximate or producing cause of damages to Martinez and the other members of Class I.

As a result of the above violations of the Florida Act, Payco and Great Lakes are liable to Martinez for his actual damages, statutory damages, and costs and reasonable attorneys' fees.

On behalf of himself and of each Class I member, Martinez seeks statutory damages of $500.00 for each violation of the Florida Act by Payco and Great Lakes.

On behalf of himself and of each Class I member, Martinez seeks orders, for which he hereby prays, enjoining future violations of the Florida Act by Payco and Great Lakes.

SECOND CAUSE OF ACTION

Request For Relief Pursuant To FDCPA

By the actions set forth above, Payco and Great Lakes violated the FDCPA, which was the proximate or producing cause of damages to Martinez and the other Class II members. These violations include, but are not limited to:

a. Violating FDCPA Section 1692(e)(2) by falsely representing the character, amount or legal status of a debt or the compensation which may be lawfully received by the debt collector.

b. Violating FDCPA Section 1692e(4) by the representation or implication that nonpayment of a debt will result in the garnishment of wages when such action is not lawful or the debt collector does not intend to take such action.

c. Violating FDCPA Section 1692e(5) by threatening to take action that cannot legally be taken or that is not intended to be taken.

d. Violating FDCPA Section 1692e(10) by using false representations and deceptive means to collect and to attempt to collect a debt or to obtain information concerning a consumer.

e. Violating FDCPA Section 1692e(11) by failing to disclose clearly in the initial communication made to collect a debt or to obtain information about a consumer that the debt collector is attempting to collect a debt and that any information will be used for that purpose.

f. Violating FDCPA Section 1692f(1) by collecting amounts that are not expressly authorized by the agreement creating the debt or permitted by law.

g. Violating FDCPA Section 1692g by failing to give the notices and to take the actions required by that Section.

h. Violating FDCPA Section 1692i by bringing legal action (including a garnishment) on a debt in a judicial district or similar legal entity that is neither the one in which the consumer signed the contract sued upon or in which the consumer resides at the time of commencement of the action.

As a result of the above violations of the FDCPA, Payco and Great Lakes are liable to Martinez for his actual damages, statutory damages, and costs and reasonable attorneys' fees.

On behalf of himself and of each Class II member, Martinez seeks an order of the Court directing Payco and Great Lakes to restore to him and all other Class II members all money obtained by Payco or Great Lakes through garnishment or the threat of garnishment.

In addition, Martinez seeks on behalf of all other Class II members, without regard to minimum individual recovery, an award in the amount of the lesser of $500,000.00 or 1% of the separate net worths of Payco and Great Lakes.

SUMMARY OF RELIEF SOUGHT

Martinez individually seeks to recover his actual damages sustained as the result of Private Defendants' illegal acts, as well as statutory civil penalties, for which he hereby prays. Martinez also seeks equitable relief.

On behalf of himself and the class members, Martinez seeks statutory damages, restitution, and equitable relief from the Private Defendants.

On behalf of himself and the class members, Martinez seeks a declaratory judgment from this Court pursuant to 28 U.S.C. §§ 2201 & 2202, declaring that, as to Payco: (1) Payco regularly engages in the practices described herein, and (2) Payco's practices violate the FDCPA and the Florida Act.

On behalf of himself and the class members, Martinez seeks a declaratory judgment from this Court pursuant to 28 U.S.C. §§ 2201 and 2202, declaring that, as to Great Lakes, (1) Great Lakes regularly engages in the practices described herein; (2) Great Lakes' practices violate the FDCPA and the Florida Act, and (3) Great Lakes unlawfully delegated its administrative wage garnishment authority and violated 20 U.S.C. § 1095a *et seq.*, thereby violating the Fifth Amendment's requirement of due process of law.

On behalf of himself and the class members, Martinez seeks a declaratory judgment from this Court pursuant to 28 U.S.C. §§ 2201 and 2202, declaring that the federal statute codified at 20 U.S.C. § 1095a *et seq.* is unconstitutional on its face and as applied under the circumstances of this case, because it violates procedural due process requirements of the Fifth Amendment.

On behalf of himself and the class members, Martinez seeks an

injunction directing the Secretary to retract all policies and procedures that fail to meet the procedural due process requirements of
the Fifth Amendment and to refrain in the future from conduct that
encourages or permits violations of the law by Payco, Great Lakes,
or any other debt collector or guaranty agency.

Martinez seeks attorneys' fees for himself and the classes that
are reasonable in relation to the amount of work expended, and his
costs.

PRAYER

THEREFORE, plaintiff respectfully prays that this Court:

a. Upon notice and hearing, but at the earliest possible date,
certify this action as a class action.
b. Upon final trial of this cause, enter a Declaratory Judgment
declaring that the practices complained of herein are illegal
and a Permanent Injunction as sought herein.
c. Upon final trial of this cause, award plaintiff and the members
of the classes judgment for their damages and statutory civil
penalties as set forth herein. Plaintiff further prays that these
damages be multiplied pursuant to the provisions of the law.
d. Award punitive damages in an amount necessary to punish
the Private Defendants for their conduct, in amount not less
than $1,000,000.00.
e. Award plaintiff and the class attorneys' fees and costs of
court.
f. Award pre-judgment and post-judgment interest at the maximum rate permitted at law or at equity.
g. Grant plaintiff and the classes all other relief to which they
may show themselves and the classes entitled.

DEMAND FOR JURY TRIAL

Please take notice that Plaintiff demands trial by jury in this
action for all claims against the Private Defendants, but not as to
the claims against the Secretary.

Respectfully submitted,

[Attorney for Plaintiff]

E.4.2 *Individual Action Challenging Federal Benefit Offsets to Collect Old Student Loans*

E.4.2.1 Complaint

Discovery requests for this case can be found at Appx. F.1.2, *infra.*
Additional pleadings for this case are included on the companion
CD-Rom.

UNITED STATES DISTRICT COURT
FOR THE EASTERN DISTRICT OF MICHIGAN

[Student One] [Address]	))))
[Student Two] [Address]	)))
[Student Three] [Address]	)))
Plaintiffs,	)))
v.	))
Secretary of Education of the United States 400 Maryland Ave., SW Washington, D.C. 20202	) Case No.) Honorable:)))
and	)))
Secretary of Treasury of the United States 1500 Pennsylvania Ave., NW Washington, D.C. 20220	))))
Defendants.	))

Complaint for Declaratory and Injunctive Relief

Introduction

1. In this action, plaintiffs challenge the government's unauthorized attachment of Social Security funds to collect student
loans that have been outstanding for more than ten years. The
1996 Debt Collection Improvement Act ("DCIA") (31
U.S.C. §3716, as amended by P.L. 104-134, Title III §31001,
April 26, 1996) grants the Secretary of Education the authority to refer certain debts to the Department of Treasury
for collection by offset of federal benefits, including Social
Security. However, the DCIA explicitly prohibits offsets for
debts that have been outstanding for more than ten years. (31
U.S.C. §3716(e)(1)). The Secretaries of Education and Treasury have gone beyond the power authorized in the DCIA by
offsetting Social Security benefits to collect student loans that
have been outstanding for more than ten years.

2. Plaintiffs seek a judgment i) declaring offsets of Social Security benefits for student loans that have been outstanding for more than ten years to be illegal, ii) prohibiting additional offsets, and iii) directing that all funds taken from plaintiffs by offset be returned.

Jurisdiction

3. This Court has jurisdiction under 28 U.S.C. §§1331, 1346, and 1361, 20 U.S.C. §1082(a)(2), and 28 U.S.C. §§2201 and 2202.

Parties

4. Plaintiff [Student One] is 65 years old and is living on a fixed income of approximately $1117 per month in Social Security retirement benefits. She resides in Birmingham, Michigan.

5. Plaintiff [Student Two] is 65 years old and is living on a fixed income of approximately $827.00 per month in Social Security retirement benefits. He resides in Westville, Oklahoma.

6. Plaintiff [Student Three] is 77 years old and is living on a fixed income of approximately $991 per month in Social Security retirement benefits. He resides in Hamden, Connecticut.

7. Defendant Secretary of Education is sued in his official capacity as head of the Department of Education. The Secretary of Education is responsible for collection of defaulted student loans under Title IV of the Higher Education Act and the Federal Claim Collections Act.

8. Defendant Secretary of Treasury is sued in his official capacity as head of the Department of Treasury. The Secretary of Treasury is responsible for collecting debts on behalf of Federal agencies, including the Secretary of Education, by administrative offset of Social Security funds under the DCIA.

Background

Collection of Student Loans Through Social Security Offsets

9. The Social Security "anti-attachment statute," 42 U.S.C. §407, provides that a person's right to payment of benefits under the Social Security Act is not subject to execution, levy, attachment, garnishment, or other legal process . . . Other laws may limit, supersede, or modify this protection of Social Security payments only if they do so by express reference to the anti-attachment statute. *Id.* § 407(b).

10. The DCIA, enacted in 1996, grants the Secretary of Education, authority to refer certain debts to Treasury for collection by offset of federal benefits, including Social Security benefits. 31 U.S.C. §3716. The DCIA authorizes offset of payments under the Social Security Act ("SSA") by expressly referring to the SSA anti-assignment statute. 31 U.S.C. §3716(c)(3)(A)(i).

11. The DCIA specifically does not apply to claims that have been outstanding for more than ten years. 31 U.S.C. §3716(e)(1).

Plaintiffs' Loans

12. The Secretary of Education has certified to the Secretary of the Treasury that plaintiffs [Student One], [Student Two] and [Student Three] have unpaid student loan debts that are subject to collection under the DCIA.

13. In September 2001, the Secretary of the Treasury withheld $167.55 of [Student One]'s Social Security benefits by imposing an administrative offset under the DCIA to pay the Secretary of Education. A second offset for the same amount occurred in November 2001.

14. The federally guaranteed student loans that were the basis for offsetting [Student One]'s Social Security benefits were taken out on or before January 1991 to finance her coursework at St. Mary's College and the University of Detroit. Plaintiff ceased her coursework after the spring semester in 1991 due to health problems. The student loan debt that is the basis for offsetting the Social Security benefits of [Student One] has been outstanding for more than ten years.

15. In September 2001, the Secretary of the Treasury began to withhold $77.00 of [Student Two]'s Social Security benefits by imposing an administrative offset under the DCIA to pay the Secretary of Education.

16. The federally guaranteed student loans that were the basis for offsetting [Student Two]'s Social Security benefits were taken out around 1977 to attend Northeastern State University in Tahlequah, Oklahoma. [Student Two] stopped his coursework around November 1977 due to personal matters and because he needed to get a job. The student loan debt that is the basis for offsetting the Social Security benefits of [Student Two] has been outstanding for more than ten years.

17. In October 2001, the Secretary of the Treasury began to withhold $147.80 of [Student Three]'s Social Security benefits each month by imposing an administrative offset under the DCIA to pay the Secretary of Education.

18. The federally guaranteed student loan that is the basis for offsetting [Student Three]'s Social Security benefits is a "PLUS" loan obtained in September 1991 to help finance the education of [Student Three]'s son. The student loan debt that is the basis for offsetting the Social Security benefits of [Student Three] has been outstanding for more than ten years.

19. The Secretary of Treasury intends to continue to impose offsets on each plaintiffs' Social Security payments until the debts certified by the Secretary of Education for each plaintiff are satisfied.

Department of Education's Failure To Cease Offsets

20. [Student One], through her counsel, wrote to the DOE on November 27, 2001 informing them that [Student One]'s loans have been outstanding for more than ten years and therefore should not be offset under the DCIA. A copy of this letter is attached hereto as Exhibit A. [*Not reprinted here in.*]

21. On December 14, 2001 Plaintiff's counsel received a response to the November 27 letter. This response dated December 11, 2001 and attached hereto was written by Diane Spadoni, Regional Director, Chicago Service Center

of DOE. A copy of this letter is attached hereto as Exhibit B. [*Not reprinted here in.*]

22. The Department of Education's December 11, 2001 letter contends that the 10 year limit for administrative offsets in the DCIA does not apply to educational loans because of Section 484A of the Higher Education Act and 20 U.S.C. §1091a(a)(2).

23. The Section 484A of the Higher Education Act provides that most student loans are not subject to a statute of limitations. However, Section 484A does not exempt student loans from the provision of the DCIA which states that 31 U.S.C. 3716 does not apply to claims that have been outstanding for more than ten years.

24. Section 484A of the Higher Education Act cannot modify the protections of the Social Security anti-assignment statute (42 U.S.C. §407) because it does not expressly refer to the anti-assignment statute.

25. [Student Two] wrote to the DOE (through Legal Services of Eastern Oklahoma) on December 13, 2001 informing them that [Student Two]'s loan has been outstanding for more than ten years and therefore should not be offset. A copy of this letter is attached hereto as Exhibit C. [*Not reprinted here in.*] Plaintiff has not yet received a response.

26. [Student Three] wrote to the DOE (through Greater Hartford Legal Assistance) on December 11, 2001 informing them that [Student Three]'s loan has been outstanding for more than ten years and therefore should not be offset. A copy of this letter is attached hereto as Exhibit D. [*Not reprinted here in.*] Plaintiff has not yet received a response.

Claim for Relief

27. Plaintiffs reallege each of paragraphs 3 through 26 above as if fully set forth herein.

28. Plaintiffs' rights to payment of benefits under the Social Security Act is specifically protected from execution, levy, attachment, garnishment, or other legal process, unless Congress expressly limits, supersedes, or otherwise modifies the provisions of 42 U.S.C. § 407 by express reference to that section.

29. The DCIA does not provide authority for the Secretary of the Treasury, at the request of the Secretary of Education, to limit plaintiffs' rights to payments under the Social Security Act because the claims upon which the Secretary of Education seeks to collect are more than 10 years old.

30. The offsets of plaintiffs' Social Security payments that have been taken to date, and all future offsets that the Secretary of Treasury may seek to impose, are contrary to law and unauthorized.

31. Plaintiffs depend on their monthly Social Security payments for basic necessities, including food, housing and transportation.

32. Defendants' actions have irreparably injured plaintiffs by withholding payments that plaintiffs depend upon to pay for food, housing, transportation and other necessities.

33. Plaintiffs are entitled to reimbursement of all funds that have been withheld from their Social Security payments in violation of 42 U.S.C. § 407.

WHEREFORE, Plaintiffs request that the Court:

1. Enter a declaratory judgment that:

(a) The offset of Social Security benefits for debts that have been outstanding for more than ten years is unlawful under 31 U.S.C. §3716(e)(1),

(b) That the Secretary of Education is obligated to cease referring student loan debts that have been outstanding for more than ten years to the Department of Treasury for offset and that the Secretary is obligated to cease offset on the loans of plaintiffs [Student One, Student Two and Student Three] and reimburse plaintiffs for amounts improperly offset, and

(c) that the Secretary of Treasury is obligated to cease offsetting Social Security benefits for debts that have been outstanding for more than ten years and that the Secretary is obligated to cease offset on the loans of plaintiffs [Student One, Student Two and Student Three] and reimburse plaintiffs for amounts improperly offset.

2. Direct the Secretaries of Education and Treasury to cease offset on the loans of plaintiffs [Student One, Student Two and Student Three].

3. Restore all Social Security payments taken by offset from Plaintiffs [Student One, Student Two and Student Three].

4. Award plaintiffs their costs and reasonable attorneys' fees in their action; and

5. Grant such other and further relief as the Court may deem just and proper.

[Attorneys for Plaintiffs]

E.4.2.2 Brief in Support of Plaintiff's Motion for Summary Judgment

UNITED STATES DISTRICT COURT
FOR THE EASTERN DISTRICT OF MICHIGAN

[STUDENT ONE],	)
[STUDENT TWO]	)
and	)
[STUDENT THREE]	)
Plaintiffs,	)
	)
v.	)
	)
SECRETARY OF EDUCATION	)
OF THE UNITED STATES, and	)
THE SECRETARY OF THE	)
TREASURY OF THE UNITED	)
STATES,	)
Defendants.	)

BRIEF IN SUPPORT OF PLAINTIFFS' MOTION FOR SUMMARY JUDGMENT

Issues Presented

This action challenges the government's seizure of Social Security funds to pay debts that are over ten years old, despite an express statutory limitation that prohibits the use of Social Security payments to offset such debts.

Plaintiffs are three senior citizens whose primary source of income is Social Security. These payments are immune from legal process unless a statute expressly supersedes the protections of 42 U.S.C. § 407, commonly referred to as the Social Security "anti-attachment" statute. In an unusual step, Congress has provided that other laws may not be construed to limit this immunity unless they expressly reference the anti-attachment statute. 42 U.S.C. § 407(b).

Nonetheless, in recent months, the Department of the Treasury, acting at the request of the Department of Education, has reduced Plaintiffs' main source income by seizing part of their Social Security payments based on the Department's claims for collection of student loans that are over ten years old. Defendants' only authority for seizing these Social Security funds is the 1996 Debt Collection Improvement Act, 31 U.S.C. § 3716 ("DCIA"), which permits the Secretary of the Treasury to offset Social Security payments for certain debts, but expressly prohibits offsets for the collection claims that have been outstanding for more than ten years. *See id.* § 3716(e)(1).

The government apparently maintains that a provision in the Higher Education Act, 20 U.S.C. § 1091a, overrides the ten year limit in the DCIA and authorizes offsets of Social Security payments to collect student loan debts *no matter how long the loans have been outstanding.* Plaintiffs urge this Court to reject this claim because, unlike the DCIA, 20 U.S.C. §1091a does not explicitly supersede the anti-attachment statute. Because this dispute presents a purely legal issue, Plaintiffs hereby move for summary judgment. In particular, Plaintiffs ask the Court to declare that Defendants may not rely on the DCIA to collect on student loans that have been outstanding for more than ten years, and to direct the Secretary of the Treasury to restore the funds that have already been improperly taken from Plaintiffs.

Authority for Relief Sought

42 U.S.C. § 407, 31 U.S.C. § 3716, FRCP Rule 56.

BACKGROUND

Federal statutes authorize federal agencies, and the Secretary of Education in particular, to employ a number of means to collect debts owed to the United States. In addition to filing suit to obtain or collect a judgment, the Secretary of Education may collect student loan debts through extra-judicial means. For example, even if the government has not obtained a judgment, federal law allows agencies to collect a debt owed by a federal employee by deducting part of the employee's salary. 5 U.S.C. § 5514. Federal agencies, including the Department of Education, may also collect debts for which there have been no judicial proceedings by directing the Department of the Treasury to intercept tax refunds. 31 U.S.C. § 3720A. The Department of Education has also been given special authority to garnish the wages of private employees by issuing administrative garnishment orders. 20 U.S.C. § 1095a.

Until 1996, the Secretary of Education had no authority to collect loan debts by seizing Social Security income payments. This is because, since 1935, the Social Security Act has provided that an individual's right to payments under the Act cannot be infringed by attachment, garnishment or other legal process. 42 U.S.C. § 407(a). In 1983, Congress strengthened the immunity provided by this anti-attachment statute by mandating that:

> No other provision of law, enacted before, on, or after April 20, 1983, may be construed to limit,

supersede, or otherwise modify the provisions of this section except to the extent that it does so by express reference to this section.

42 U.S.C. § 407(b).

In 1996, Congress limited the protection of Section 407 in provisions of the "Debt Collection Improvement Act." 31 U.S.C. § 3716, Pub.L. 104-134, Title III, §31001(a)(2), 110 Stat. 1321-358—1321-362 (1996). 31 U.S.C. § 3716 authorizes collecting certain debts by withholding funds that the United States would otherwise pay to the debtor, a process know as "administrative offset." 31 U.S.C. § 3701(a)(1); 31 C.F.R. § 285.4(c) (describing offset program); 63 Fed. Reg. 44986 (1998)(same). Federal agencies that have been unable to collect claims against a debtor certify nontax debts that are over 180 days delinquent to be collected by administrative offset, and the officials disbursing federal payments to the debtor withhold funds to pay the claim. *Id.* § 3716(a), (c)(1),(6). The 1996 amendments to this statute added provisions that expressly refer to the Social Security anti-attachment statute to authorize withholding Social Security payments through administrative offset. *Id.* § 3716(c)(3). However, Section 3716 also imposes a number of limitations on administrative offsets. For example, the first $9,000 of Social Security or other payments covered by 3716(c)(3)is exempt from offset. *Id.* § 3716(c)(A)(ii). Although the Secretary of the Treasury may use administrative offset to collect debts owed to states, the Secretary may not offset Social Security payments and payments under certain other federal benefit programs to collect state debts. *Id.* § 3716(h). Furthermore, administrative offsets may only be imposed after the debtor has been given notice of the agency's claim and the opportunity to contest the debt in administrative review, or an opportunity to negotiate an agreement for repayment. *Id.* § 3716(a). Most importantly for this suit, the statute authorizing administrative offset does not apply "to a claim under this subchapter that has been outstanding for more than 10 years." *Id.* § 3716(e)(1).

Despite this express limitation, the Departments of the Treasury and Education have begun using administrative offset to collect student loan debts that are over ten years old. As a result, each of the Plaintiffs in this action have had portions of the Social Security payments on which they depend withheld by the government, and face the prospect of further seizures if the Defendants' actions continue.

Specifically, plaintiff [Student One] is 65 years old and lives on an income of approximately $1,117 per month in Social Security retirement income. *See* Declaration of [Student One]. In September 2001, the Secretary of the Treasury withheld $167.55 of her monthly income by imposing an administrative offset requested by the Secretary of Education. An additional offset of the same amount was taken in November 2001. The only federally-insured student loans that could provide the basis for the Secretary of Education's claim have been outstanding since early 1991, over ten years prior to the first offset. At that time, [Student One] withdrew from the college that she was attending for health reasons.

Plaintiff [Student Two] lives on Social Security retirement benefits of $827.00 per month. *See* Declaration of [Student Two]. The only federally guaranteed student loans that plaintiff [Student Two] signed date back to approximately 1977, when plaintiff [Student Two] attended Northeastern State University in Tahlequah, Oklahoma. In September 2001, the Secretary of the Treasury began to withhold $77.00 of plaintiff [Student Two]'s Social Security benefits, and he has continued to withhold this amount in each month since September 2001.

Finally, plaintiff [Student Three] is 77 years old and lives on the approximately $991 of Social Security retirement benefits that he receives each month. *See* Declaration of [Student Three]. The federally guaranteed student loan that is the basis for offsetting his Social Security benefits was obtained in September 1991 to help finance the education of Plaintiff [Student Three]'s son. In October 2001, over ten years from the date plaintiff incurred the loan, the Secretary of the Treasury began to withhold $147.80 of plaintiff [Student Three]'s Social Security benefits each month by imposing an administrative offset to pay the Secretary of Education. The Treasury has taken the same offset from plaintiff [Student Three]'s monthly income in each succeeding month.

In correspondence concerning the offset of plaintiff [Student One]'s and plaintiff [Student Two]'s payments, the Department of Education contends that the Social Security anti-attachment Act does not apply to collection of student loans that are more than ten years old because 20 U.S.C. § 1091a eliminates the ten-year limitation. *See* Complaint ¶¶ 21, 22. That statute exempts student loan collection from statutes of limitation by providing that, "[n]otwithstanding any other provision of statute, regulation or administrative limitation, no limitation shall terminate the period within which suit may be filed, a judgment may be enforced, or an offset, garnishment or other action initiated or taken . . ." Section 1091a contains no reference to the Social Security anti-attachment provision.

ARGUMENT
DEFENDANTS' WITHHOLDING OF PLAINTIFFS' SOCIAL SECURITY PAYMENTS TO COLLECT DEBTS THAT ARE OVER TEN YEARS OLD IS BARRED BY THE SOCIAL SECURITY ANTI-ATTACHMENT STATUTE

Plaintiffs are entitled to summary judgment in their favor because 42 U.S.C. § 407 and 31 U.S.C. § 3716, preclude Defendants, as a matter of law, from offsetting Social Security payments to collect debts that have been outstanding for more than ten years. The legal analysis supporting Plaintiffs' challenge to the offsets is straightforward: 42 U.S.C. § 407 imposes a broad bar on interference with Social Security payments that may be abrogated *only* by laws that expressly refer to the anti-attachment provision. The 1996 amendments to 31 U.S.C. § 3716 contain such an express reference, but represent a limited exception to the anti-attachment provision which is explicitly confined to claims that have not been outstanding over ten years. The government's claim that Section 1091a allows the Department of Education to ignore this ten-year limitation on offsets is without merit because 20 U.S.C. § 1091a does not contain any reference to the anti-attachment statute. Only offsets that comply with 31 U.S.C. § 3716 are exempt from the anti-attachment statute.

The Supreme Court has observed that 42 U.S.C. § 407 "imposes a broad bar against the use of any legal process to reach all social security benefits." *Philpott v. Essex County Welfare Bd.*, 409 U.S. 413, 417(1973); *accord In re Buren*, 725 F.2d 1080, 1084 (6th Cir.), *cert. denied*, 469 U.S. 818 (1984). The anti-attachment provision recognizes that, because Social Security payments are intended to meet the beneficiaries' most basic needs, these funds must be immune from creditors—including government claims—unless Congress has expressly provided otherwise. *See In re Buren*, 725

F.2d at 1084 (citing legislative history); *Dionne v. Bouley*, 757 F.2d 1344, 1355 (1st Cir. 1985).

The protection afforded by 42 U.S.C. § 407 applies to offsets like those that the government has employed here. Indeed, it appears that Defendants to not dispute that, without the authority provided by the 1996 amendments to Section 3716, the anti-attachment statute's prohibition on "execution, levy, attachment, garnishment, or other legal process," 42 U.S.C. § 407, would bar *any* effort by the Secretary of Education to collect student loans by withholding plaintiffs' Social Security payments. Courts interpreting the anti-attachment provision have construed its broad prohibition on use of any "legal process" to apply to offsets and other mechanisms for collecting funds without judicial proceedings. *See, e.g., Tom v. First American Credit Union*, 151 F.3d 1289, 1291-93 (10th Cir. 1998); *Crawford v. Gould*, 56 F.3d 1162, 1166-67 (9th Cir. 1995). The precedents also make clear that efforts by federal and state agencies to circumvent the anti-attachment statute's protections are unlawful. *See, e.g., Brinkman v. Rahm*, 878 F.2d 263, 265 (9th Cir. 1989) (state policy of seizing funds to pay for care of institutionalized patients is unlawful); *Gorrie v. Heckler*, 624 F.Supp. 85, 90 (D.Minn.1985) (federal rule affecting availability of payments held unlawful).

Under the 1996 DCIA, Congress expressly authorized limited administrative offset of Social Security payments by referencing 42 U.S.C. § 407. 31 U.S.C. § 3716(c)(3)(A)(i). This authorization must be narrowly construed. By its own terms, this authorization does not apply to debts that have been outstanding for more than ten years. 31 U.S.C. § 3716(c), (e)(1). Thus, the DCIA does not provide authority for the government's decision to ignore the anti-attachment statute when collecting student loans that are more than ten years old.

The government's disregard for the anti-attachment statute could pass legal muster if, but only if, 20 U.S.C. § 1091a is construed to nullify *both* the ten year limitation in 31 U.S.C. § 3716(e)(1) *and* the protections of the anti-attachment statute. Three considerations show that, although Section 1091a may remove the ten year limitations on an offset of payments that are not subject to special protection like that in 42 U.S.C. § 407, Section 1091a cannot plausibly be construed to limit the protections of the Social Security anti-attachment statute.

First, Section 1091a(a)(2) does not expressly reference the anti-attachment statute. Subpart (b) of the anti-attachment statute sets forth an unusual and clear requirement that no provision of law may be construed to modify or supersede the immunity afforded to Social Security payments unless "it does so by express reference to this section." 42 U.S.C. § 407(b). In enacting this provision, Congress imposed an extraordinary requirement that the anti-attachment statute may only be limited by laws in which Congress has explicitly stated its intention to do so.

Section 1091a(a)(2) plainly does not meet this demanding standard. Instead, it generally provides that time limitations on collection actions do not apply to collection of debts arising from federal educational assistance. It contains no specific reference to 42 U.S.C. § 407, and it does not directly address the Social Security Act or payments under that Act. Thus, Section 1091a(a)(2) is precisely the type of general provision that Congress determined would *not* supersede the anti-attachment statute when it mandated that an "express reference to this section" is required to modify the anti-attachment provisions.

Second, principles of statutory construction dictate that statutory provisions that most specifically address a topic take precedence over more general provisions. *See Morales v. Trans World Airlines, Inc.*, 504 U.S. 374, 384 (1992) ("It is a commonplace of statutory construction that the specific governs the general."); *Busic v. U. S.*, 446 U.S. 398, 406 (1980) ("a more specific statute will be given precedence over a more general one, regardless of their temporal sequence.") In reconciling laws enacted over time, "a specific policy embodied in a later federal statute should control our construction of the [earlier] statute, even though it ha[s] not been expressly amended." *Food and Drug Admin. v. Brown & Williamson Tobacco Corp.*, 529 U.S. 120, 143 (2000) (*quoting United States v. Estate of Romanini*, 523 U.S. 517, 530-31 (1998)). The theory underlying this rule is that, when enacting the specific statute, "the mind of the legislator has been turned to the details of a subject," and, thus, the specific statute reflects Congress' conclusion concerning the detailed rules that should govern that subject. *Radzanower v. Touche Ross & Co.*, 426 U.S. 148, 153 (1976); [1A Sutherland, Statutes and Statutory Construction § 23.15].

Accordingly, the three statutes at issue here are properly reconciled by finding that the government's ability to withhold Social Security payments is governed by the specific provisions of the anti-attachment statute and 31 U.S.C. § 3716—not by the general provisions of Section 1091a(a)(2). In enacting the anti-attachment statute and the 1996 amendments to 31 U.S.C. § 3716, Congress specifically focused on the extent to which Social Security payments should be subject to legal process for collecting debts. Those amendments show that Congress contemplated that such payments should be subject to offset where the specific limitations of 31 U.S.C. § 3716 are satisfied, including the requirement that the government may only impose an offset if its claim has been outstanding for less than ten years. There is no indication that when Congress amended 31 U.S.C. § 3716 to permit offset of Social Security payments it contemplated that the ten year provision would be nullified by Section 1091a so that the Secretary of Education could offset Social Security payments regardless of how old or stale the claim had become. Where, as in this case, "there is no clear intention otherwise, a specific statute will not be controlled or nullified by a general one." *Morton v. Mancari*, 417 U.S. 535, 550-51 (1974).

Courts have resolved similar tensions in statutory provisions by concluding that specific statutes control over general. For example, in *United States v. Estate of Romanini*, the Supreme Court addressed a provision of the Debt Collection Act that requires that federal claims be paid first when a decedent's estate is insolvent. 31 U.S.C. § 3713(a). The federal government argued that this statute required that its tax claims be given priority over secured creditors, even though a separate statute provides that federal tax liens are *not* given priority over secured creditors unless the government has perfected its lien by filing notice. 523 U.S. at 521 n.3 (*quoting Federal Tax Lien Act of 1966*, 26 U.S.C. §§ 6321, 6323). The Supreme Court rejected the federal government's argument that the general debt collection statute controlled, and held that the tax lien statute governs the priority of federal tax claims because the tax lien statute was enacted later, was more specific, and "[i]t represented Congress' detailed judgment as to when the Government's claims for unpaid taxes should yield to many different sorts of interests." *Id.* at 1487. *See also Radzanower v. Touche Ross & Co.*, 426 U.S. at 153-55 (specific venue provisions of the National Bank Act, rather than the general venue provisions of the Securities Exchange Act, govern the venue for action alleging violation of security laws by a national bank)

The Sixth Circuit applied a similar analysis to reject the argument that provisions of the Bankruptcy Act implicitly repealed the protections of the Social Security anti-attachment provision. *In re Buren* addressed whether the bankruptcy law or the anti-attachment provision should govern in a case that arose before the anti-attachment provision was amended in 1983 to require an "express reference to this section" to limit the immunity of Social Security payments from legal process. 725 F.2d at 1087. Even though the relevant provisions of the bankruptcy law had been enacted after the Social Security anti-attachment provision, the Sixth Circuit concluded that the more targeted anti-attachment provision controlled. *Id.* at 1087. The Court recognized that "the 1935 [Social Security] Act is addressed wholly to the topic of social security benefits and through section 407 specifically prevents judicial intrusion into the benefit payment process." *Id.* at 1086. The relevant bankruptcy statute, "on the other hand, addresses the rights and duties of debtors" and addresses social security beneficiaries only incidentally. *Id.*

Similarly, the issue presented in this case, namely whether the Social Security payments may be offset to satisfy government claims, is specifically addressed by the anti-attachment statute and 31 U.S.C.§ 3716—not by Section 1091a(a)(2). Offset of Social Security payments should be permitted only where they comply with the specific conditions imposed by Congress when it expressly authorized offsets in the 1996 amendments to 31 U.S.C. § 3716.

Third, the government's claim that the administrative offset of Social Security payments is permitted for student loans over ten years old attributes to Congress a policy that is illogical. Under the government's construction of Section 1091a(a)(2), the Secretary would be allowed to collect loans extra-judicially that he could not collect judicially.

If the Secretary of Education were to go to court to collect loan debts over ten years old and obtained a judgment in his favor, he could not enforce the judgment against Social Security payments because anti-attachment bars such attaching or garnishing these funds. However, under the government's construction, the Secretary would be allowed to seize Social Security payments claims using administrative offset procedures, in which the risk of an erroneous collection is far greater than if the claims were subject to scrutiny in judicial review. This counter-intuitive result provides another reason for rejecting the government's effort to limit the protection of Social Security payments. As the Tenth Circuit observed in rejecting the argument in *Tom* that the anti-attachment statute should be construed to permit extra-judicial collection procedures:

> We can see no reason why Congress would, on the one hand, choose to protect Social Security beneficiaries from creditors who utilized the judicial system, a system that is built upon principles of fairness and protection of the rights of litigants, yet, on the other hand, leave such beneficiaries exposed to creditors who devised their own extra-judicial methods of collecting debts.... Such a construction of § 407 would run contrary to both logic and the spirit underlying the Social Security Act.

151 F.3d at 1292 (citation omitted).

In addition, because the offsets imposed by Defendants in recent months based on debts over ten years old were not authorized by statute, Plaintiffs are entitled to restoration of the Social Security payments that have been unlawfully withheld. Restitution of funds that the government is obligated to pay by statute is available as a remedy under the Administrative Procedure Act. *See Bowen v. Massachusetts*, 487 U.S. 879, 893-900 (1988); *Ohio Student Loan Com'n v. Cavazos*, 900 F.2d 894, 898 fn. 1 (6th Cir.1990). Moreover, the Department of Treasury's own regulations provide for prompt refund of funds that have been improperly taken by offset. 31 C.F.R. §§ 5.38, 285.4(h) (2001).

CONCLUSION

The Court should grant summary judgment for Plaintiffs and enter a judgment declaring that Defendants have acted unlawfully in withholding Plaintiffs' Social Security payments because it is unlawful for the Secretary of the Treasury to offset Social Security payments in order to collect for debts that have been outstanding for more than ten years.

Respectfully submitted,

[Attorneys for Plaintiffs]

E.5 Cases Challenging Trade School Abuses

E.5.1 Individual Student's State Court Complaint Against School

COURT OF COMMON PLEAS
PHILADELPHIA COUNTY

SARAH WILLIAMS	)
	)
v.	)
	)
NATIONAL SCHOOL OF	)
HEALTH TECHNOLOGY, INC.	)

COMPLAINT

1. This is a damage action against a for-profit trade school by a former student of the school for breach of contract, for misrepresentation, conversion and fraud, as well as for treble damages and other appropriate relief under the Pennsylvania Unfair Trade Practices and Consumer Protection Law, 73 P.S. § 201-9.2.

2. Plaintiff Sarah Williams is a 44-year old individual who resides at [*Address*] but who is preparing to move to [*Address*]. She has an 11th-grade education and for several days in 1989 was a student at National Health Technology, Inc.

3. Defendant National Health Technology, Inc. (hereinafter "NSHT") is a corporation doing business at 801 Arch Street, Philadelphia, PA as a trade school licensed by the Pennsylvania Board of Private Licensed Schools to conduct vocational training

courses in a variety of medical fields.

4. During the early part of 1989 defendant advertised its on television in the Philadelphia area, including in such advertising representations (a) linking completion of defendant's course with eventual employment in the medical industry and (b) the availability of government grants and loans to pay for the course.

5. Plaintiff, who had some prior work history as a nurse's aide and who was interested in obtaining a state certification to enable her to return to that line of work, saw the said commercial. Because her prior employment as a nurse's aide was at or near the minimum wage, she was particularly swayed by the impression communicated in the ad that those graduating from defendant's program were earning wages significantly greater than the minimum wage.

6. Plaintiff called the telephone number listed in the said television ad and, as a result of her call, was contacted by a representative of NSHT and was given an appointment to visit the school. At that initial meeting with defendant's sales representative, she informed him of her interest to return to work as a nurse's aide. He represented to her, among other things,

    a. that completion of the course would entitle her to jobs earning in excess of $9.00/hour;

    b. that she would gain such employment through the placement assistance offered to graduates as part of the service offered by NSHT and,

    c. that, due to the professional reputation of NSHT, a graduation certificate from NSHT would provide plaintiff with enhanced job opportunities.

7. The salesman gave her an admissions test, which she failed, and invited her to return in several days to retake the same test. Plaintiff could not complete a substantial portion of the test, especially the part that involved mathematics. Nonetheless, on her second attempt plaintiff was told that she had passed the test with a nearly a perfect score and could enroll in the school.

8. On or about February 4, 1989 plaintiff entered into an enrollment agreement with defendant for enrollment in a twenty-six (26) week program, divided into two thirteen (13) week terms. A copy of the enrollment agreement is attached hereto as Exhibit A.

9. The enrollment agreement provided for a total cost to plaintiff of $3,228.35, payable entirely from a federal grant and from a guaranteed student loan. Thus, the total cost for each of the two terms was approximately $1,614. Defendant arranged for the entire financial aid package.

10. During the orientation session plaintiff attended during the first week of classes, the employees conducting the session repeatedly represented to the students that a good performance in the course would enable a graduate to obtain employment far in excess of the minimum wage. There were, in addition, repeated references to the placement services provided to students upon graduation.

11. Plaintiff attended classes for only one full week. Having not attended academic classes for approximately 25 years, she had considerable difficulty with the material covered. Prior to beginning her classes at the beginning of the second week, she was summoned to meet with an executive committee of the school which informed her that, due to her unacceptable academic performance, she would have to withdraw from her class and would have to repeat the first week with the next group of students.

12. Plaintiff returned to defendant's school several weeks later and repeated the first two days of the course. During the second day she was called from the school to deal with an emergency in her

home and she did not resume attendance. On the third day of her absence she was told by defendant not to return.

13. Concerned about her loan and grants—checks from which defendant had already had her endorse—plaintiff contacted the school and was assured that she would incur no financial liability under the enrollment agreement. Several months later, after she began receiving a bank bill for a student loan obligation, she contacted the school again and this time was informed that she was responsible for the loan.

14. Plaintiff believes and therefore avers that defendant received grant and loan proceeds on plaintiff's behalf in an amount equal to or in excess of the $3,228 total cost referred to in paragraph 7, *supra*. She is currently being dunned for a student loan debt of $2,700 arising out of her brief enrollment in defendant's school. She does not know how much defendant retained in government grants received on her behalf.

15. Under the enrollment agreement and under state law, *see* 22 Pa. Code § 73.134, defendant was required to refund to plaintiff at least 75% of the first term's portion of the tuition and lab fees. Defendant was entitled to retain at most (a) the remaining 25%, or $375, plus (b) an enrollment fee of $150, for a total of $525. Moreover, as to this maximum allowable retention, the agreement provides that in the event a student is subject to "circumstances that make it impractical for the student to complete the program, the shall make a settlement that is reasonable and fair to the student."

16. Despite plaintiff's demand, defendant has refused to refund her anything and has, on the contrary, retained all monies received on her behalf.

17. Contrary to the representations made by defendant,
   a. most students enrolling in defendant's program do not obtain employment as nurse's aides nor in other related fields;
   b. those that do find employment as nurse's aides earn wages at or near the minimum wage;
   c. defendant offers little, if any, placement assistance and
   d. a graduation certificate issued by defendant provides job applicants with little, if any, enhancement in job opportunities.

18. Contrary to the representations made by defendant to plaintiff, defendant does not provide a legitimate and useful educational service to students who are unskilled and who lack a high school diploma or its equivalent. For such students, the "school" is little more than a business stratagem to obtain student grant and loan proceeds by inducing low-income, unemployed and unskilled individuals to sign enrollment agreements like the one signed by plaintiff.

19. Defendant lures prospective students with express and implied promises of future employment at levels significantly above those they are living at (a) with little or no concern for the academic skills of the prospective students and through the use of meaningless and deceptive admissions standards; (b) with minimal contacts and/or credibility among relevant employers and with insignificant success in placing graduates in relevant work and (c) with the knowledge that relevant wage levels for nurse's aides (or equivalent positions) are at or near the minimum wage and that those lucky enough to find work in this field will be unlikely to have the ability to afford the student loan debt they have incurred.

Count I
(Contract)

20. All previous allegations are realleged and are incorporated by this reference.

21. By retaining all funds received on plaintiff's behalf, defendant has breached the enrollment agreement including, but not limited to,
   a. the terms at page 2, paragraphs C(1) and (2), which required defendant to return all but 25% of one term's portion of tuition and lab fees;
   b. the terms at page 2, paragraph C(3), which required defendant to "make a settlement that is reasonable and fair to the student" and
   c. the terms at page 3 which required defendant to refund the money within thirty (30) days of plaintiff's separation from the school.

22. Plaintiff is entitled to recover an amount equal to all funds obtained by defendant on her behalf, less the $150 enrollment fee, plus interest.

Count II
(Unfair or Deceptive Acts or Practices)

23. All previous allegations are realleged and are incorporated by this reference.

24. Defendant's conduct constituted unfair or deceptive acts or practices within the meaning of the Pennsylvania Unfair and Deceptive Practices and Consumer Protection Law, 73 P.S. § 201-1 et seq. including, but not limited to, the following:
   a. Making misleading and deceptive representations as to the efficacy of its training course, as to the economic value of an NSHT certificate, as to the school's professional reputation in the community and as to endorsements from former students and from employers;
   b. Making misleading and deceptive representations concerning the nature and extent of employment placement assistance offered to graduates and of defendant's success rate in this regard;
   c. Making misleading and deceptive representations concerning the wage levels which course graduates are likely to earn;
   d. Failing to endeavor to establish the qualifications which a prospective student should have in order to assimilate successfully the subject matter of the course, failing to inform prospective students of such qualifications and enrolling prospective students whether or not they are so qualified;
   e. Employing unfair, misleading and deceptive admissions tests and procedures which are designed to encourage prospective students to sign enrollment agreements regardless of their academic abilities and regardless of other factors relevant to success in defendant's course;
   f. Employing unfair, misleading, deceptive and fraudulent representations and practices regarding the prices charged students for tuition, books, lab fees and other charges and regarding the total ultimate cost to the student;
   g. Failing to supply prospective students with written, detailed and accurate disclosures concerning
      1. defendant's policy and regulations relative to make-up work and to delinquency in meeting course requirements,

2. the standards required of the student for achieving satisfactory progress, including class attendance,

3. the extent, nature and success rate of defendant's placement service and

4. other materials facts concerning the school and the program of instruction which are reasonably likely to affect the decision of the student to enroll therein;

h. Utilizing stricter academic and other standards after NSHT has received the proceeds of a student's financial aid package than it does before receiving them;

i. Failing to provide academic remediation to those students who are admitted despite failing to meet industry-accepted admissions requirements and

j. Failing to make prompt and accurate refunds to students who withdraw or who are terminated in accordance with defendant's contractual and regulatory obligations.

25. Plaintiff is entitled to damages equalling three times her economic loss, plus "other appropriate relief," 73 P.S. § 201-9.2, including attorney's fees.

Count III
(Misrepresentation, Fraud and Conversion)

26. All previous allegations are realleged and are incorporated by this reference.

27. Defendant having obtained plaintiff's grants and loan proceeds through knowingly false pretenses and representations upon which plaintiff relied, and having retained said funds without legal right despite her demand, defendant has committed the intentional torts of misrepresentation and conversion.

28. In addition to the lost tuition and lab fees, plaintiff incurred additional economic loss as a result of defendant's conduct, including, but not limited to the following:

a. The enrollment fee;

b. Book costs and

c. Uniform costs.

29. In addition to said economic loss defendant caused plaintiff to suffer severe humiliation and emotional distress.

30. Plaintiff is entitled to compensatory and punitive damages. WHEREFORE, plaintiff seeks the following relief:

a. Compensatory, treble and punitive damages not in excess of $20,000 and

b. A reasonable attorney's fee to her attorney.

[Attorney for Plaintiff]

E.5.2 Class Actions

E.5.2.1 Class Action Complaint Against Department of Education

UNITED STATES DISTRICT COURT
EASTERN DISTRICT OF PENNSYLVANIA

HOMER SIMPSON,	)
MONTGOMERY BURNS,	)
PATTY BOUVIER and	)
WAYLON SMITHERS, on	)
behalf of themselves and all	)
others similarly situated,	)
Plaintiffs,	)
	)
v.	)
	)
MOE SZYSLAK, Secretary,	)
United States Department of	)
Education,	)
Defendant.	)

AMENDED COMPLAINT—CLASS ACTION

PRELIMINARY STATEMENT

1. Plaintiffs Homer Simpson, Montgomery Burns, Patty Bouvier and Waylon Smithers bring this class action on behalf of several classes of student loan borrowers who were victimized by a fraudulent truck-driving-by-correspondence school and who have been wrongfully denied relief mandated by federal law. Congress expressly mandated that the Secretary of Education "shall discharge" the loan obligations of all borrowers whose eligibility for financial aid was "falsely certified" by schools participating in the financial aid system. 20 U.S.C. § 1087(c). Plaintiffs are eligible for a false certification discharge because, among other things, Andover falsely certified their "ability to benefit" from the particular course of study. Plaintiffs seek declaratory and injunctive relief to enforce the said statutory mandate, including, a reversal of the Secretary's denial of their applications for loan discharges, notification to class members that may be entitled to discharges and an order remedying his inaction on applications already submitted but not acted upon.

JURISDICTION AND VENUE

2. This court has jurisdiction under 28 U.S.C. § 1331 (federal question) and 20 U.S.C. § 1082 (suits against Secretary of Education). Venue is proper because a) this is a civil action in which the defendant is an officer of the United States, b) a substantial part of the events or omissions giving rise to the claims occurred in this judicial district and c) the plaintiffs reside in this district. 28 U.S.C. § 1391(e).

PARTIES

3. Plaintiff Homer Simpson is an individual residing at [Address]. He currently owes a student loan obligation that purportedly was used to pay the costs for participating in a commercial truck driving program run by a now-defunct trade school known as Andover Tractor Trailer School (hereinafter "Andover"). He never attended the school or participated in any such studies.

4. Plaintiff Montgomery Burns is an individual residing at [Address]. He currently owes a student loan obligation that purportedly was used to pay the costs for participating in a commercial truck driving program run by Andover. He never attended the school or participated in any such studies.

5. Plaintiff Patty Bouvier is an individual residing at [Address]. She currently owes a student loan obligation that purportedly was used to pay the costs for participating in a commercial truck driving program run by Andover. She never attended the school or participated in any such studies.

6. Plaintiff Waylon Smithers is an individual residing at [Address]. He currently owes a student loan obligation that purportedly was used to pay the costs for participating in a commercial truck driving program run by Andover. He never attended the school or participated in any such studies.

7. Defendant Moe Szyslak, the Secretary of the United States Department of Education (hereinafter "the Secretary"), is responsible as the chief executive of the Department of Education (hereinafter "the Department") for the administration of the student financial aid programs established by Title IV of the Higher Education Act, 20 U.S.C. § 1070 *et seq.*, including the Federal Family Education Loan ("FFEL") program (formerly "Guaranteed Student Loan Program," or "GSL"). Among other things, he and his predecessors were responsible for, among other things, approving and monitoring the Title IV eligibility of the so-called "school" that perpetrated the underlying fraud, for enforcing the eligibility requirements for student borrowers, and for administering the loan discharge program enacted by Congress for the purpose of extending relief to FFEL borrowers victimized by fraudulent schools.

CLASS ACTION ALLEGATIONS

8. Plaintiffs bring this action on behalf of the following four classes of similarly situated individuals:

   a. *Class A*: All individuals who incurred FFEL obligations to attend Andover Tractor Trailer School and who did not, at the time of their enrollment, have a high school or high school equivalency diploma;

   b. *Class B*: All individuals who incurred FFEL obligations to attend Andover Tractor Trailer School and who did not, at the time of their enrollment, have a valid driver's license;

   c. *Class C*: All student loan borrowers who incurred FFEL obligations to attend correspondence courses accredited by the National Home Study Council (now known as the Distance Education and Training Council) and who did not, at the time of their enrollment, have a high school or high school equivalency diploma;

   d. *Class D*: All FFEL borrowers who have submitted applications for false certification loan discharges or requests for review of denials of such applications to the United States Department of Education and who have not obtained a

decision from the Department within ninety (90) days of such submission.

9. As to each of the above-specified classes, and for the reasons set forth below:

   a. The class is so numerous that joinder is impracticable. Plaintiffs believe there are thousands of individuals in Classes A and B and tens of thousands of individuals in Classes C and D.

   b. There are questions of law and fact common to the class, as more fully set forth below.

   c. The claims of the named plaintiffs are typical of the claims of the class in that they all carry student loan obligations purportedly the result of attending the bogus truck driving program at Andover. Two of them (Simpson and Smithers) did not have high school credentials at the time they were admitted; all four were not licensed drivers; three (Simpson, Bouvier and Burns) were denied false certification discharges by the U.S. Department of Education and one of them (Smithers) filed an application for such a discharge but never got a decision rendered on the application.

   d. Plaintiffs will fairly and adequately assert and protect the interests of the class, in that:

      i. The attorney for Plaintiffs is an experienced litigator, an expert in the federal student loan program and has successfully managed consumer class actions before;

      ii. Neither plaintiff nor counsel have any conflict of interest in the maintenance of the class action

      iii. Plaintiffs and their counsel have adequate financial resources available to ensure competent and aggressive representation of the class, namely the resources of Community Legal Services, Inc., a well-established, public-interest legal services organization with an annual operating budget of approximately $5.5 million.

FACTUAL ALLEGATIONS OF THE NAMED PLAINTIFFS

Homer Simpson

10. Sometime during the summer of 1989, Plaintiff Homer Simpson, who was at the time homeless and addicted to drugs, signed what he now believes were enrollment and financial aid documents and course test sheets for a combined correspondence and resident commercial truck driving program supposedly being offered by a Massachusetts trade school named Andover Tractor Trailer School ("Andover"). He received $35 from an Andover recruiter in return for his signatures.

11. Mr. Simpson did not have a high school or GED diploma at the time he signed the various papers at the Andover recruiting office. His formal schooling ended during the tenth grade. He also did not have a driver's license at the time so could not have legally participated in a truck driving course.

12. Plaintiff assumes and therefore avers that Andover received proceeds from a FFEL loan made on his behalf, despite the fact that he never attended Andover and never participated in any home study program.

13. Andover falsely certified Mr. Simpson's eligibility for the student loans based on his "ability to benefit" from a postsecondary course in commercial truck driving. Among the reasons this certification was false was that it implied his having passed a valid admission test or having completed a remedial course, federal

requirements for obtaining financial aid on behalf of a student who does not have a high school or equivalency diploma. He was not administered a test and did not complete any remedial course. In addition, the enrollment ignored the fact that he was not a licensed driver and, therefore, could not legally get behind the wheel of a truck.

14. Andover also falsely certified on the guaranteed student loan application that Mr. Simpson was in attendance at the school and was making satisfactory progress in his studies. This certification is a material part of the certification process since it is an eligibility requirement under Title IV that the student borrower be in attendance at a school and that he be making satisfactory progress. 20 U.S.C. § 1091(a)(2).

15. Years later, after he had recovered and was gainfully employed, Mr. Simpson began receiving student loan collection notices from a FFEL guaranty agency, American Student Assistance ("ASA") and, in 1995, $2,284 owed to him for a tax refund was taken and applied to the student loan obligation.

16. On March 3, 1995, Mr. Simpson submitted a sworn statement requesting a discharge of the student loan to ASA under 11 U.S.C. § 1087(c).

17. While his application was pending before ASA, Mr. Simpson also began a correspondence with the Department regarding his request for discharge. In particular, on November 6, 1995, he wrote to the official designated by the Secretary to accept requests for "group discharges" requesting that she consider granting a false certification discharge to all student loan borrowers whose loans originated from Andover's fraudulent Philadelphia recruiting office.

18. On March 11, 1996, after receiving no response from ASA and then, after learning that ASA could not locate his request for discharge, Mr. Simpson submitted the request again, this time on a form supplied by ASA. He asserted four separate grounds for discharge: 1) the absence of an ability-to-benefit admissions test; 2) his lack of a driver's license; 3) the school's false certification of his enrollment status; and 4) likely forgery of the loan proceeds check.

19. On March 21, 1996 ASA advised Mr. Simpson that his loan had been assigned to the Defendant Secretary and that the request for discharge had also been referred to the Secretary.

20. In the months that followed, Mr. Simpson contacted the Department various times in order to try to get some action on the pending discharge request. As part of one of these contacts, he submitted proof on August 1, 1996 that Andover's accrediting agency, the National Home Study Council ("NHSC"), required its accredited schools to obtain advance approval of admissions tests or remedial programs they intended to use to admit students without high school credentials, and that Andover had never obtained such approval. He also followed up on the earlier request for group discharge, submitting in October and November 1996 investigative material from the criminal investigation surrounding Andover, audits and reviews by ASA and additional declarations of other student loan borrowers who also had incurred their obligations under circumstances similar to those described by Mr. Simpson.

21. On or about May 20, 1997, in response to the materials submitted by Mr. Simpson, the Secretary notified him that he had indeed proved that Andover had engaged in "serious and well-documented violations" of the Department's "ability-to-benefit" regulations, but, for reasons not stated, the Secretary also concluded that these violations occurred only during the time period June 1, 1986 to April 30, 1989.

22. On or about October 22, 1997, the Secretary issued a decision that Mr. Simpson is not eligible for a false certification discharge and that he is responsible for paying any outstanding balance on the loan. The Secretary's stated reason for denying the discharge request was that the loan was issued in July 1989, i.e., after the April 30, 1989 cut-off referred to in the May 20, 1997 letter, and that, in the absence of any official reports or audits pertaining to activities after such date, "[i]t is reasonable to conclude that . . . the school met the ability to benefit requirements for the enrollment period in question." The decision made no mention of the evidence submitted showing that Andover's accrediting agency had failed to approve any ability-to-benefit admissions by Andover.

23. In addition, the Secretary stated that lack of a driver's license was not a relevant "ability to benefit" factor. He made no decision on the additional false certification claims based on the false certification of his enrollment status or on the likely forgery of the check. (A copy of the October 22, 1997 decision letter is attached hereto as Exhibit A. [*not reprinted herein*])

24. In the October 22, 1997 decision, the Secretary invited Mr. Simpson to contest the decision by submitting corroboration in the form of "statements made by other students who attended the school that are both sufficiently detailed and consistent with each other to appear reliable."

25. On August 18, 1998 Mr. Simpson submitted to the Secretary nine separate statements by individuals who were victimized during the summer of 1989 by the fraudulent recruiting office operated by Andover in North Philadelphia during that period.

26. The Secretary's adverse decision has caused and will continue to cause substantial harm to Mr. Simpson. He had his income tax refunds seized and is threatened by seizure of future refunds and earned income tax credits. In addition, because of his default he has adverse credit history barring him access to credit and is ineligible for further financial aid to pursue legitimate education or job training.

Montgomery Burns

27. Like Mr. Simpson, Plaintiff Burns was, during 1989, a homeless addict and he, too, was induced by the same fraudulent recruiting operation to sign papers pertaining to an enrollment into Andover's commercial truck driving program. He was paid $25 to sign the papers.

28. At the time, he did have a high school diploma. However, he did not have a driver's license.

29. Mr. Burns assumes and therefore avers that Andover received proceeds from a FFEL loan made on his behalf, despite the fact that he never attended Andover and never participated in any home study program.

30. Andover falsely certified Mr. Burns's eligibility for the student loans based on his "ability to benefit" from a postsecondary course in commercial truck driving in that it ignored the fact that he was not a licensed driver and therefore could not legally get behind the wheel of a truck.

31. Andover also falsely certified on the guaranteed student loan application that Mr. Burns was in attendance at the school and was making satisfactory progress in his studies. This certification is a material part of the certification process since it is an eligibility

requirement under Title IV that the student borrower be in attendance at a school and that he be making satisfactory progress. 20 U.S.C. § 1091(a)(2).

32. Mr. Burns is now recovered and is being dunned by ASA on a account of student loan obligation. He is also now gainfully employed and, therefore, faces the prospect of wage garnishments and tax refund intercepts to enforce that obligation.

33. On December 20, 1996, Mr. Burns submitted a sworn statement to ASA, requesting a discharge of the student loan under 11 U.S.C. § 1087(c).

34. On January 21, 1997 ASA denied the loan discharge request on the grounds that, according to the Secretary, a false certification discharge application could not be based solely on the absence of a driver's license. (A copy of that decision is attached hereto as Exhibit B [*not reprinted herein*].)

35. On January 27, 1997 Mr. Burns submitted a request for review of ASA's decision to the Secretary.

36. On May 23, 1997 the Secretary issued a written decision, denying Mr. Burns' request for a loan discharge, on the grounds that the lacking of a valid driver's license could not be the basis for a false certification discharge. While acknowledging that a borrower would be eligible for a false certification discharge if he "would not meet the requirements for employment . . . in the occupation for which the training program supported by the loan was intended because of a physical or mental condition, age, or criminal record *or other reason accepted by the Secretary*," 34 C.F.R. § 682.402(e)(13)(iii)(B) (emphasis added), the Secretary decided that not having a driver's license before enrolling in a commercial truck driving course was not an acceptable reason. (A copy of the May 23, 1997 decision is attached hereto [*not reprinted herein*].)

37. The Secretary's adverse decision has caused and will continue to cause substantial harm to Mr. Burns. He faces the threat of wage garnishments and tax refund intercepts and, because of his default, has an adverse credit history that bars him access to credit and renders him ineligible for further financial aid to pursue legitimate education or job training.

Patty Bouvier

38. Like Mr. Simpson, Plaintiff Bouvier was, during 1989, a homeless addict and she, too, was induced by the same fraudulent recruiting operation to sign papers pertaining to an enrollment into Andover's commercial truck driving program. She was paid $25 to sign the papers.

39. At the time, she did have a high school diploma. However, she did not have a driver's license.

40. Ms. Bouvier assumes and therefore avers that Andover received proceeds from a FFEL loan made on her behalf, despite the fact that she never attended Andover and never participated in any home study program.

41. Andover falsely certified Ms. Bouvier's eligibility for the student loans based on her "ability to benefit" from a postsecondary course in commercial truck driving in that it ignored the fact that she was not a licensed driver and therefore could not legally get behind the wheel of a truck.

42. Andover also falsely certified on the guaranteed student loan application that Ms. Bouvier was in attendance at the school and was making satisfactory progress in her studies. This certification is a material part of the certification process since it is an eligibility

requirement under Title IV that the student borrower be in attendance at a school and that she be making satisfactory progress. 20 U.S.C. § 1091(a)(2).

43. Years later, after she had recovered and was gainfully employed, Ms. Bouvier began receiving student loan collection notices from a student loan guaranty agency, American Student Assistance ("ASA") and, in 1996 her tax refunds began getting seized and being applied to the student loan obligation. Over the last three years, she estimates that at least $5,000 has been paid on account of this loan obligation from tax refunds owing to her. She believes that a balance still exists on the loan obligation and that, therefore, she continues to face seizure of future tax refunds.

44. On March 26, 1997, Ms. Bouvier submitted a sworn statement to ASA, requesting a discharge of the student loan under 11 U.S.C. § 1087(c).

45. On September 11, 1997 ASA denied the loan discharge request on the grounds that, according to the Secretary, a false certification discharge application could not be based solely on the absence of a driver's license. (A copy of that decision is attached hereto as Exhibit C [*not reprinted herein*].)

46. Ms. Bouvier did not request the Secretary to review her case, since such a request for review would have been fruitless, given that the Secretary had already decided that Andover borrowers who had high school diplomas could not obtain false certification discharges based on their lacking valid driver's licenses.

47. The Secretary's final decision regarding Andover borrowers has caused and will continue to cause substantial harm to Ms. Bouvier. She had her income tax refunds seized and is threatened by seizure of future refunds and earned income tax credits, as well as wage garnishments. In addition, because of her default, she has adverse credit history barring her access to credit and is ineligible for further financial aid to pursue legitimate education or job training.

Waylon Smithers

48. Like Mr. Simpson, Plaintiff Smithers was, during 1989, a homeless addict and he, too, was induced by the same fraudulent recruiting operation to sign papers pertaining to an enrollment into Andover's commercial truck driving program. He was paid about $20 to sign the papers.

49. At the time, he did not have a high school diploma or a G.E.D., nor did he have a driver's license.

50. Mr. Smithers assumes and therefore avers that Andover received proceeds from a FFEL loan made on his behalf, despite the fact that he never attended Andover and never participated in any home study program.

51. Andover falsely certified Mr. Field's eligibility for the student loan based on his "ability to benefit" from a postsecondary course in commercial truck driving. Among the reasons this certification was false was that it implied his having passed a valid admission test or having completed a remedial course, federal requirements for obtaining financial aid on behalf of a student who does not have a high school or equivalency diploma. He was not administered a test and did not complete any remedial course. In addition, the enrollment ignored the fact that he was not a licensed driver and, therefore, could not legally get behind the wheel of a truck.

52. Andover also falsely certified on the guaranteed student loan application that Mr. Smithers was in attendance at the school and

was making satisfactory progress in his studies. This certification is a material part of the certification process since it is an eligibility requirement under Title IV that the student borrower be in attendance at a school and that he be making satisfactory progress. 20 U.S.C. § 1091(a)(2).

53. Mr. Smithers is now recovering and is being billed by an agent of either the Secretary or ASA regarding a FFEL obligation. He has already lost the benefit of a substantial tax refund was seized several years ago on account of the student loan. He faces the prospect of wage garnishments and tax refund intercepts to enforce the balance of that obligation.

54. During 1998 he learned from Plaintiff Simpson about the false certification discharge program and about his efforts to get the Secretary to discharge the loans of Andover borrowers. Upon information and belief, Plaintiff avers that the Secretary did not attempt to notify him of the fact that his loan, because it was originated by Andover, was potentially dischargeable.

55. On August 17, 1998, Mr. Smithers submitted a sworn statement to the Secretary on his own behalf, requesting a discharge of the student loan under 11 U.S.C. § 1087(c). By this time the Secretary should have either acted on his request, or, if the loan is held by ASA rather than the Secretary, should have been forwarded to ASA for its action. Upon Plaintiff's information and belief, the Secretary has done neither.

FACTUAL ALLEGATIONS PERTAINING TO THE CLASS

A. The Title IV System

56. Title IV of the Higher Education Act, 20 U.S.C. § 1070 et. seq., created a comprehensive program of educational grants and loans in which the Secretary, who is empowered to prescribe such regulations as may be necessary to carry out the Congressional purpose, 20 U.S.C. § 1082, coordinates the extension of Title IV grants and loans to certain eligible students for education at certain eligible institutions, and also coordinates the collection of such loan obligations.

57. Under Title IV of the HEA, financial assistance in the form of loans and grants is made available to students who enroll in a recognized "institution of higher education," 20 U.S.C. § 1091(a). Originally designed to provide student aid to those attending the nation's colleges and universities, Title IV was amended several times during the 1970's and 1980's so as to include within the definition of eligible institutions proprietary vocational and trade schools (hereinafter "trade schools") offering training programs often less than a year in duration.

58. Title IV grants ("Pell" and "SEOG" grants) are generally issued directly from the federal treasury to the approved educational institution. FFEL program loans, on the other hand, are generally issued by eligible lenders, guaranteed by approved guaranty agencies such as ASA, and then reinsured by the Secretary. Lenders receive direct interest subsidies from the Secretary and, in the event of default, receive repayment of the loans from the guaranty agencies, who, in turn, can by repaid by the Secretary.

59. The Secretary has contracted with ASA and the other guaranty agencies to administer the FFEL program, including the collection of defaulted loans, the handling of inquiries from participants in the program and the conducting of program reviews of participating schools.

60. Under Title IV "eligible students" are students with high school diplomas or General Education Development certificates (GEDs). A student failing to meet this requirement may nonetheless qualify to receive a FFEL loan to attend an eligible vocational institution if that institution certifies that the student has the "ability to benefit" from the school's training. 20 U.S.C. §§ 1085(c) (1990) and 1091(d) (1997). In 1989, when Plaintiffs incurred their education loans, institutions determined "ability to benefit" based on the student's performance on a test, or based on the student's successful completion of a remedial education program provided by the institution. 34 C.F.R. §§ 668.7(b). ("Ability to benefit" will occasionally be referred to hereafter as "ATB.")

61. An additional student eligibility requirement is that the student actually be in attendance at an eligible school and that he be making satisfactory progress in a program of study. 20 U.S.C. § 1091(a)(2).

62. Around 1990, Congress began investigating widespread allegations of fraud and abuse by vocational institutions that wrongfully obtained Title IV funds by enrolling ineligible students who were not capable of benefitting from the training. *See* United States Senate, Permanent Subcommittee on Investigations of the Senate Committee on Governmental Affairs, "Abuses in Federal Student Aid Programs," Senate Rep. No. 58, 102d Congress, 1st Session (1991) ("Victimized by unscrupulous profiteers and their fraudulent schools, students have received neither the training nor the skills they hoped to acquire and, instead, have been left burdened with debts they cannot repay.").

63. Congress responded to this problem in the 1992 reauthorization of the Higher Education Act. The 1992 amendments mandated that the Secretary of Education discharge liability on a FFEL loan received on or after January 1, 1986 if the "student's eligibility to borrow . . . was falsely certified by the eligible institution." 20 U.S.C. § 1087(c)(1).

64. In April 1994, the Secretary published regulations implementing the new false certification loan discharge provision. 34 C.F.R § 682.402(e). Among those borrowers identified in the regulation as being eligible for the new discharge were those whose "ability to benefit" from the educational program was falsely certified by the school they attended.

65. The Secretary's "false certification" regulation provides that borrowers a) who were admitted without a high school diploma or G.E.D. and without a proper determination of ability to benefit, and b) those who would not meet the requirements for employment in the occupation for which the training program supported by the loan was intended because of a condition or legal status approved by the Secretary, are entitled to have their student loans discharged upon submission of a sworn statement establishing their eligibility. 34 C.F.R. § 682.402(e)(3), (13).

66. Under the regulation, a student borrower who was enrolled during the relevant time period in Title-IV-funded education based on his having the requisite "ability to benefit" would meet the definition of "false certification" if he was admitted without a) passing an admissions test approved by the school's accrediting agency, or b) successfully completing a program of developmental or remedial education provided by the school. 34 C.F.R. § 682.402(e)(13)(ii).

67. The regulation does not deal separately with a situation where a school enrolls individuals with the intent of not teaching them and signs FFEL certifications that the student is making satisfactory progress in an educational program. Accordingly, under the regulation, only such students who did not have high school

credentials could obtain a false certification discharge even where the school falsely certified the fact that a high school graduate was in attendance making satisfactory progress in his studies.

68. Under the Secretary's regulations, in order to qualify for discharge of a "falsely certified" student loan, a borrower is required to submit to the holder of the loan a written request that sets forth, under penalty of perjury, the factual basis for the request. 34 C.F.R. § 682.402(e)(3). Within 90 days, a decision must be rendered on the request for discharge, § 682.402(e)(6)(iv).

69. Where a loan is held by a guaranty agency, a discharge request is submitted to such agency which has the power to make the eligibility determination in the first instance. In the event the guaranty agency denies the request, the borrower can seek a *de novo* review by the Secretary. 34 C.F.R. § 682.402(e)(9), (11).

70. Under his regulation, the Secretary has an independent obligation to gather information about groups of borrowers who might be eligible for a loan discharge and to notify such borrowers where reliable information suggests a pattern of false certification. *See* 34 C.F.R. § 682.402(e)(6)(I)–(ii).

71. In September 1995, as part of a "Dear Colleague" letter to participants in the Title IV system, the Secretary announced the designation of a Department official who would accept and decide requests for group discharges for borrowers who are members of a cohort of students that were signed up by a school "with serious and well-documented ATB violations that could be considered to have affected every student admitted to the school based on ATB." Borrowers covered by such group discharges do not have to submit any additional evidence that the school was falsely certifying students and, assuming they provide a sworn statement that conforms to the other requirements of the regulation, are entitled to a discharge of their loan.

B. The Andover Correspondence Course in Commercial Truck Driving

72. Andover Tractor Trailer School, Inc. was one of the most blatant and extensive trade school frauds perpetrated on the Title IV system. When it closed in 1990, it was taking in over $3 million annually in Title IV grants and loans, for the most part, for "students" who were not participating in any educational program. Most, if not all of the FFEL loans arranged by Andover were guaranteed by the Massachusetts guaranty agency, ASA.

73. The essence of the Andover scheme was to recruit "students" by paying commissions to recruiters and to the "students" themselves, for a Commercial Tractor Trailer Driving course supposedly consisting of a correspondence segment and a residential on-the-road driving segment at the school's facility in Methuen, Massachusetts and supposedly designed to enable graduates to sit for the commercial truck driving exam. The owners did not intend for more than 10% of the "students" to show up in Massachusetts and purposely targeted their recruitment efforts to disadvantaged, vulnerable individuals who had no intention of enrolling in a course of study. Employees were trained, among other things, in falsifying driver's license information, forging financial aid documentation and completing correspondence lessons on behalf of the "students."

74. A 1990 audit by the Inspector General of the Department of Education determined that the academic content of the correspondence segment was bogus. While Title IV requires such courses to involve at least 440 clock hours of study, the IG determined that the

course material would take a student only 50 hours to complete. The audit also determined that 86% of sampled students withdrew before completing the course.

75. A 1990 program review by ASA noted that of an estimated 942 individuals scheduled to complete the Tractor Trailer Driving course, at most 87 graduated, and four allegedly found jobs, although the agency found no evidence that any of these four individuals were in fact employed as truck drivers. In this review the agency also found that Andover did not determine the ability-to-benefit of students enrolled without high school credentials.

76. In 1992 a federal grand jury in Boston indicted five former employees of Andover. *U.S. v. Cotter et al.*, Crim. Act. 92-10297K (D.Mass.). The grand jury included, as part of the indictment, the following charge:

> 39. It was further part of the conspiracy to ignore student eligibility requirements for federal financial aid, including, but not limited to, whether a student possessed a valid motor vehicle license; whether a student possessed a high school diploma or GED equivalent and whether a student could successfully complete an "ability to benefit" examination.

The indictment further charged the defendants with fabricating driver's license numbers as part of the enrollment process. The defendants ultimately plead guilty and were sentenced.

77. During 1990–91 Andover lost its eligibility to participate in Title IV, ceased operations and filed for bankruptcy.

78. Andover's Commercial Tractor Trailer Driving course was accredited by a national accrediting commission called the National Home Study Council ("NHSC") (now "Distance Education and Training Council"). During the relevant time period, the NHSC prohibited its accredited schools from admitting "ability-to-benefit" students, i.e., those lacking high school credentials, unless the school received prior approval for an admissions test or for a remedial course. No such approval was ever given to any school accredited by the NHSC.

C. The Department's Actions regarding Plaintiffs' Applications for Relief

79. On October 9, 1996 counsel for Plaintiffs submitted to the appropriate agent of the Secretary documentation supporting a request that Andover be designated as a "group discharge" school. This documentation consisted for the most part of documents already in the possession of the Secretary, including the Massachusetts indictment, investigative memos from the Inspector General, and excerpts from the IG audit and the ASA program reviews mentioned above.

80. Counsel also submitted individual false certification discharge requests to ASA or to the Secretary (depending on who was holding the particular loan) in addition to the above-mentioned applications submitted by the named Plaintiffs. Some were, like Plaintiffs, denied. One (Seymour Skinner) was approved in November 1996 and another (Milhouse Van Houten) has been awaiting a decision from the Secretary since October 1996. In total, the Secretary has at least nine sworn statements of Andover borrowers from Philadelphia who described circumstances surrounding their

incurring of a FFEL obligation similar to those described by the Plaintiffs.

81. In August 1996 counsel also advised the Secretary of the facts surrounding ability-to-benefit admissions by correspondence programs accredited by NHSC, namely, that, according to the NHSC, it had never provided the required advance approval for either a testing or remedial program for ATB admissions to any of its schools and, therefore, that any ATB admission in a NHSC-accredited program was by definition a "false certification" within the meaning of the Secretary's regulation.

82. On February 6, 1997 the Secretary's representative in charge of group discharges wrote to counsel for Plaintiffs, advising him that the Department was conducting a mass mailing directed to all FFEL borrowers "who received loans from Andover Tractor Trailer School between January 1986 and August 1990," to inform them about the existence of the false certification discharge program and to provide them with an application form. "In addition," she advised, "we are examining the information you provided" in support of a request for a group discharge. (A copy of this letter is attached as Exhibit D [*not reprinted herein*].)

83. Plaintiffs believe and therefore aver that this mass mailing was mailed to only a fraction of the borrowers who should have received it. More specifically, they believe that the Secretary did not notify any borrowers whose loans are held by guaranty agencies, such as ASA.

84. On May 20, 1997 the Secretary's representative issued a decision on the group discharge request. (A copy of this letter is also attached as Exhibit E [*not reprinted herein*].) First, she approved the group discharge of borrowers enrolled as ATB students, on the grounds that the submitted documentation did support a finding of widespread ATB fraud by Andover, but she limited the scope of the discharge to cover only borrowers enrolled by Andover between June 1, 1986 and April 30, 1989. Since Plaintiff Simpson and the other known victims of Andover's Philadelphia recruiting operation were enrolled after April 30, 1989, the decision effectively denied them the benefit of the Secretary's group discharge approval. The decision did not reveal the significance of the mentioned dates, nor did it refer to any evidence supporting an inference that Andover changed its practices after April 30, 1989.

85. The May 20, 1997 decision also rejected one of the additional claims asserted in support of the request for a group discharge, namely, the argument that it constituted a false certification of financial aid eligibility to fabricate driver's licenses for individuals lacking valid licenses and to enroll them into a commercial truck driving program that assumed students were already licensed drivers. The Secretary's representative determined that the lack of a driver's license of a student enrolling in a commercial truck driving course is not a "reason accepted by the Secretary" to discharge a loan under 34 C.F.R. § 682.402(e)(13)(iii)(B).

86. The Secretary has yet to render any decision regarding the additional claim that NHSC-accredited correspondence schools were not authorized to admit ATB students and that, therefore, ATB enrollments at such schools constitute false certifications within the meaning of the Department's regulation, nor did he consider the additional argument that Andover falsely certified that its students were in attendance making satisfactory progress.

87. Plaintiffs believe and therefore aver that even the inexplicably limited discharge approval, for enrollments between June 1, 1986 and April 30, 1989, has not been implemented in terms of actually notifying borrowers and discharging individual loans.

88. Thousands of FFEL borrowers, who, like the Plaintiffs, went to fraudulent trade schools have applied to the Secretary for a false certification discharge or have requested the Secretary review a discharge denial by a guaranty agency.

89. Despite the statutory mandate that falsely certified loans be discharged and despite the Department's own regulation that imposes a 90-day decision period, the Secretary has not assigned adequate staff to administer the program, resulting in a backlog of over 10,000 undecided applications that have been pending, in some cases, for years.

90. The discharge regulations provide that FFEL borrowers who are eligible for a loan discharge are entitled to a refund of any payments made on the loan, including those made by enforced collection action, and to rehabilitation of their credit record. 34 C.F.R. § 682.402(e)(2). The Secretary's adverse decision and/or his inaction has deprived Plaintiffs and class members of these important rights.

CLAIMS FOR RELIEF

COUNT I
(Failure to Grant Discharge to Andover ATB Students—Class A)

91. Plaintiffs reaver all previous allegations and incorporate them by this reference.

92. The Secretary's duty to discharge "falsely certified" loans is a mandatory and clear statutory duty.

93. Class members are suffering ongoing harm and the real threat of future harm by the Secretary's actions and inaction in complying with this duty. Since the targets of trade school fraud, in general, and in the Andover fraud, in particular, tend to be those living at the bottom of the economic scale, this harm is having substantial impact on the health and welfare of class members. Such harm includes having to pay student loan obligations they no longer owe out of their meager incomes; the continued threat of collection actions against them, including wage garnishments and the seizure of their tax refunds and earned income credits; bad credit reports; and an inability to obtain further Higher Education Act assistance, often critical to self-improvement efforts to move out of poverty.

94. The Secretary's failure to act for the benefit of plaintiff and the class constitutes reviewable, final agency action within the meaning of the Administrative Procedures Act ("APA"), 5 U.S.C. § 704. Plaintiff and class members can compel agency action wrongfully withheld via an action under the APA or, alternatively, under the Mandamus Act, 28 U.S.C. § 1361.

95. The Secretary's adverse decision on Plaintiff Simpson's application for a false certification discharge of his loan was arbitrary, capricious, and not in accordance with law, and/or unsupported by substantial evidence and should be reversed under the Administrative Procedure Act, 5 U.S.C. §§ 702 and 706.

96. The Secretary's adverse decision on Plaintiffs' request for a group discharge covering all of Andover's ATB enrollments, was arbitrary, capricious, and not in accordance with law, and/or unsupported by substantial evidence and should therefore be reversed under the Administrative Procedure Act, 5 U.S.C. § 706(2). Alternatively, the Secretary's failure to implement a group discharge for Andover borrowers should be compelled as being unlawfully withheld or unreasonably delayed, under § 706(1).

COUNT II
(Failure to Grant Discharge to Andover Students Who Lacked Driver's License—Class B)

97. Plaintiffs reaver all previous allegations and incorporate them by this reference.

98. The Secretary's adverse decision on Plaintiff's applications for a false certification discharge, based on their being enrolled into a truck driving course and the school fabricating a driver's license to justify the enrollment, was arbitrary, capricious, and not in accordance with law, and should be reversed under the Administrative Procedure Act, 5 U.S.C. §§ 702 and 706.

99. The Secretary's adverse decision on Plaintiffs' request for a group discharge covering all of Andover's students who lacked driver's licenses, was arbitrary, capricious, and not in accordance with law, and should be reversed under the Administrative Procedure Act, 5 U.S.C. §§ 702 and 706. Alternatively, the Secretary's failure to implement a group discharge for Andover borrowers should be compelled as being unlawfully withheld or unreasonably delayed, under § 706(1).

COUNT III
(Failure to Treat Andover's False Certification that Borrowers Were Actually in Attendance and Making Satisfactory Progress as Sufficient to Trigger a Right to Discharge—Classes A and B)

100. Plaintiffs reaver all previous allegations and incorporate them by this reference.

101. In pursuit of their criminal scheme, the employees of Andover repeatedly and systematically certified that FFEL applicants were participating in an educational program in which said applicants were making satisfactory progress. These certifications were false when made.

102. The Secretary's determination that such a false certification does not trigger his obligation to discharge falsely certified loans is arbitrary, capricious, and not in accordance with the law. Alternatively, his failure to consider such a claim is unlawful and unreasonable.

COUNT IV *(Failure to Grant Discharge to ATB Borrowers that Enrolled in Correspondence Programs—Class C)*

103. Plaintiffs reaver all previous allegations and incorporate them by this reference.

104. The Secretary's failure to take any action to extend the benefits of his obligation to discharge falsely certified loans to ATB borrowers whose loans are attributable to correspondence programs accredited by the National Home Study Council is unlawful and unreasonable.

COUNT V
(Failure to Act on Submitted Applications for Discharge—Class D)

105. Plaintiffs reaver all previous allegations and incorporate them by this reference.

106. The Secretary's failure to act on submitted applications for discharge is unlawful and unreasonable.

PRAYER FOR RELIEF

WHEREFORE, Plaintiffs request that this Honorable Court grant the following relief for themselves and for the class:

A. Take jurisdiction and certify the four classes;

B. Declaratory and injunctive relief, (i) requiring the Secretary to grant discharges and/or provide appropriate notices, (ii) imposing a deadline for the Secretary to act on pending discharge requests, and/or (iii) granting interim relief to class members so as to protect them from further harm pending the action by the Secretary on their request for discharges;

C. An award of attorney's fees and costs pursuant to the Equal Access for Justice Act; and

D. Such other appropriate relief the Court deems necessary and proper.

[Attorney for Plaintiff]

E.5.2.2 Memorandum of Law Supporting Summary Judgment

UNITED STATES DISTRICT COURT
EASTERN DISTRICT OF PENNSYLVANIA

EDNA KRABAPPLE,	)
Plaintiff	)
	)
v.	)
	)
MOE SZYSLAK, Secretary,	)
United States Department of	)
Education,	)
Defendant.	)

MEMORANDUM OF LAW IN SUPPORT OF PLAINTIFF'S MOTION FOR SUMMARY JUDGMENT

Plaintiff Edna Krabapple brought this action for a discharge of her federally-guaranteed student loans, pursuant to 20 U.S.C. § 1087(c), because the trade school she attended falsely certified her as eligible for the loans. Ms. Krabapple did not have a high school diploma or G.E.D. when she enrolled in a Nurse Assistant training program at the American Institute of Design ("AID"), a for-profit trade school that at the time did business in Philadelphia. She thus was ineligible under the Higher Education Act and regulations of the defendant Secretary of Education ("the Department") to participate in the financial aid program unless AID determined through proper testing that she had the "ability to benefit" from the training program. The test that AID administered to Ms. Krabapple to make this determination was a simple alphabetizing and number-comparison test that was completely unrelated to her Nurse Assistant training. This test was not administered in accordance with the test publisher's instructions, nor in accordance with the requirements of AID's accrediting agency. According to the Department's regulations, therefore, AID's falsely certified Ms. Krabapple's ability to benefit from its training. Hence, the Department's denial of Ms. Krabapple's request for a discharge of her student loans pursuant to the 1992 amendments to the Higher Education Act was arbitrary, capricious, and contrary to law. Ms. Krabapple seeks a judgment that she is entitled to a discharge of her student loans.

I. REGULATORY BACKGROUND AND FACTS OF THE CASE

A. HOW TRADE SCHOOLS PARTICIPATING IN THE FEDERAL FINANCIAL AID PROGRAM CAN ADMIT STUDENTS WHO LACK HIGH SCHOOL CREDENTIALS

Title IV of the Higher Education Act of 1965 ("HEA" or "Title IV"), as amended, 20 U.S.C. § 1070 *et seq.*, creates various educational grant and loan programs designed to assist students in paying the cost of postsecondary education. The guaranteed student loan ("GSL") program, now known as the Federal Family Education Loan Program ("FFEL"), is one of those Title IV programs, providing loans for students to attend postsecondary institutions, including colleges, universities, and vocational training schools. The loans are issued by banks and other lenders, guaranteed in most cases by a state or nonprofit guarantee agency such as the Pennsylvania Higher Education Assistance Agency ("PHEAA") or United Student Aid Funds ("USAF," now USA-Group Guarantee Services, Inc.) and ultimately reinsured by the federal government. If a student does not repay the loan, the United States eventually pays the holder of the loan, and then attempts to collect the unpaid amount from the student, often using the guarantee agencies as collection agents. 20 U.S.C.A. §§ 1078, 1080 (1998).

To qualify for a GSL, the student must be an eligible student, *id.* § 1091; 34 C.F.R. §§ 668.31–668.39 (1997) (formerly § 668.7), and the school must be an eligible institution, 34 C.F.R. §§ 600.1–600.11 (1997), under the Department's regulations. Ordinarily, one would expect students to obtain a high school diploma or its equivalent before enrolling in postsecondary education. However, many proprietary trade schools, and some community colleges, admit students without high school diplomas or the equivalent. In the late 1970s and early 1980s the Higher Education Act was amended to allow more students without a high school diploma or G.E.D., and the schools that admit them, to qualify for financial aid by showing that the students had the "ability to benefit" ("ATB") from postsecondary education or training. 20 U.S.C. § 1091(d). The "ability to benefit" rules for financial aid eligibility have gotten progressively more strict, but they have generally allowed schools to use standardized ATB tests to determine whether a prospective student without high school credentials had the requisite "ability to benefit." In July 1988, when plaintiff Edna Krabapple enrolled at AID, the statute required that the student first be

> administered a nationally recognized, standardized or industry developed test, subject to criteria developed by the appropriate accrediting association, measuring the applicant's aptitude to complete successfully the program to which the applicant has applied. . . .

20 U.S.C.A. § 1091(d)(3)(A) (1990).[3]

Thus, during the time period at issue in this case, a trade school seeking to obtain financial aid for students lacking high school credentials was required to use entrance testing procedures that complied with two general requirements. First, the school's choice of tests was limited to only "nationally recognized, standardized or industry-developed" ATB tests. And second, to the extent the school's accrediting criteria imposed additional requirements, those requirements, too, had to be followed.

AID, the school involved in this case, was accredited by the National Association of Trade and Technical Schools ("NATTS").[4] As of July 1988, the NATTS accrediting criteria pertaining to ATB testing provided as follows:

> If the school enrolls a person who does not have a high school diploma or a GED, but admits the individual based on "ability to benefit," the school must document the basis on which ability is determined. The documentation is left to the discretion of the institution and may use one or more of the following: standardized test, practicum examination, interview, prior work experience, or other measurement indicators. *Periodic studies are to be conducted to document the reliability of the entrance requirements for all students.*

Accrediting Commission, National Association of Trade and Technical Schools, Standards for Accreditation, Document C, Section VI (A)(7) (Jan. 28, 1997) (emphasis added). Administrative Record ("A.R.") 32 (as referenced at A.R. 7).[5] Adding these criteria to the federal financial aid requirement that mandated the use of an established ATB test, AID was operating within a relatively clear regime for its ATB determinations. First, it had to follow the instructions accompanying the "nationally recognized, standardized or industry developed" test itself. Second, it had to conduct "periodic studies . . . to document the reliability" of the test as an effective measure of students' ability to benefit from the school's training programs, i.e., it had to study the extent to which the individuals it admitted ultimately were able to complete the pro-

---

3 In 1988, ATB students could also pass the eligibility threshold under two alternative methods: a student was eligible if she completed a program of remedial education from her school or if she obtained a G.E.D. before completing the program. 20 U.S.C.A. § 1091(d)(1), (2) (1990). It is undisputed that AID used testing, rather than one of these alternative mechanisms, to determine "ability to benefit."

4 This organization is currently named the Accrediting Commission of Career Schools of Colleges of Technology ("ACCSCT"). A.R. 1. It is one of seven accrediting entities that accredit the vast majority of trade schools receiving federally-guaranteed loan funds. *See* United States Senate, Permanent Subcommittee on Investigations of the Committee on Governmental Affairs, *Abuses in Federal Student Aid Programs*, S. Rep. 102-58, at 4 (1991) ("Nunn Report") (attached hereto as Exhibit 1).

5 As can be seen by these criteria, NATTS did not itself require ATB testing, and instead listed testing as one of several allowable methods for making entrance decisions regarding ATB students, including, apparently, a bare interview. It did, however, require ongoing assessment by the school that measured whether the particular method used was effectively admitting only those individuals who had the "ability to benefit." Of course, if a NATTS school wanted to obtain federal financial aid on the student's behalf, its choice of methods was limited to those allowed by Title IV rules.

gram and obtain employment in their field of training. As will be demonstrated, AID failed to comply with each of these requirements.

B. CONGRESSIONAL ENACTMENT OF THE "FALSE CERTIFICATION" DISCHARGE PROGRAM AS A RESPONSE TO WIDESPREAD ADMISSIONS ABUSES BY TRADE SCHOOLS

From 1989 to 1991, the U.S. Senate Subcommittee on Investigations of the Committee on Governmental Affairs, chaired by Senator Sam Nunn, studied the rapid escalation of loan default costs in the GSL program in the 1980s. United States Senate, Permanent Subcommittee on Investigations of the Committee on Governmental Affairs, *Abuses in Federal Student Aid Programs*, S. Rep. 102-58 (1991) ("Nunn Report") (attached hereto as Exhibit 1).[6] The Subcommittee focused on fraud and abuse by the for-profit trade schools, which accounted for a disproportionate share of GSL default dollars. The Subcommittee's report identified several trade school practices that contributed to fraud, abuse, and waste of GSL funds, including fraudulent admission of "ability to benefit" students. Nunn Report at 13.

The Subcommittee concluded that "the mechanism on which [Guaranteed Student Loan Program] oversight of schools depends—the Triad of licensure, accreditation, and certification/eligibility—provides little or no assurance that schools are educating students efficiently and effectively." *Id.* at 33. Among the Subcommittee's recommendations were the following:

(2) Congress and the Administration must hold the U.S. Department of Education accountable for the regulation and oversight of the [Guaranteed Student Loan Program]. In the past, the Department has effectively abdicated its GSLP oversight responsibilities to private accrediting bodies, State licensing authorities, and guaranty agencies. Experience has proven that those bodies have neither the motivation nor the capabilities to effectively police the program.

. . . .

(15) The Department of Education must develop ways to assist those students who continue to be victimized by fraud and abuse within the GSLP. Because the Department's oversight systems have failed, students who have not received the education promised have been left responsible for loans that they cannot repay and, therefore, on which they all too often default. The Department must not only increase efforts to prevent this type of abuse in the future, but also work with students to ease financial burdens imposed as a result of past abuse.

Id. at 34, 37.

In response to the growing evidence of ATB fraud, as noted by the Nunn Committee and similar findings of the General Accounting Office and the Education Department's Inspector General,[7]

Congress began tightening the ATB eligibility rules in the early 1990s, mandating that admissions tests be administered by an independent tester. Congress also took review of ATB testing out of the hands of the accrediting agencies and mandated that the Department itself approve the tests and the cutoff scores to be used. 20 U.S.C.A. § 1091(d)(1) (1998). As required, the Department has since published lists of tests it has approved for determining a student's ability to benefit from training. 55 Fed. Reg. 52160 (Dec. 19, 1990); 57 Fed. Reg. 62440 (Dec. 30, 1992); 61 Fed. Reg. 55542 (Oct. 25, 1996).[8]

In 1992 Congress also acted on the Nunn Report's recommendation regarding help for victims of admissions fraud by enacting the false certification loan discharge provision. Higher Education Act Amendments of 1992, Pub. L. 102-325, § 428, 106 Stat. 551 (1992). The law as amended in 1993 provides that:

If a borrower who received, on or after January 1, 1986, a loan made, insured, or guaranteed under this part and the student borrower, or the student on whose behalf a parent borrowed, is unable to complete the program in which such student is enrolled due to the closure of the institution or *if such student's eligibility to borrow under this part was falsely certified by the eligible institution*, then the Secretary *shall discharge* the borrower's liability on the loan (including interest and collection fees) by repaying the amount owed on the loan and shall subsequently pursue any claim available to such borrower against the institution and its affiliates and principals or settle the loan obligation pursuant to the financial responsibility authority under subpart 3 of part G.

20 U.S.C.A. § 1087(c)(1) (1998) (emphasis added). The law also provides that students entitled to this discharge "shall not be precluded from receiving additional grants, loans, or work assistance . . . for which the borrower would be otherwise eligible (but for the default on such discharged loan)," and requires the Secretary to report the discharges to credit bureaus. *Id.* § 1087(c)(4), (5).

In 1994, the Department issued regulations implementing the "false certification" provision of section 1087(c). These regulations provide that

[t]he Secretary reimburses the holder of a loan received by a borrower on or after January 1, 1986, and discharges a current or former borrower's obligation with respect to the loan . . . if the borrower's . . . eligibility to receive the loan was falsely certified by an eligible school. . . . A student's eligibility to borrow shall be considered to have been falsely certified by the school if the school

(A) Certified the student's eligibility for a FFEL Program loan on the basis of ability to benefit from its training and the student did not meet the appli-

---

6 The court may take judicial notice of this report. Overfield v. Pennroad Corp., 146 F.2d 889, 898 (3d Cir. 1944); *see also, e.g.,* Carolene Products Co. v. United States, 323 U.S. 18, 21 (1944).

7 *See, e.g.,* United States General Accounting Office, GAO/HRD-

91-82BR, *Student Loans: Characteristics of Defaulted Borrowers in the Stafford Student Loan Program* (1991); Office of Inspector General (United States Education Department) Audit Report 03-00001 (1991) (audit of PTC Career Institute).

8 Not surprisingly, the "Roeder" test—the test involved in this case—was not among the tests approved by the Department.

cable requirements described in 34 CFR Part 668 and section 484(d) of the Act, as applicable and as described in paragraph (e)(13) of this section. . . .

34 C.F.R. § 682.402(e)(1)(i) (1997).

Paragraph (e)(13) of section 682.402 then sets forth the relevant requirements for eligibility for federally-guaranteed student loans based on "ability to benefit" from training. Students such as the plaintiff in this case, who enrolled in training after July 1, 1987, are considered to have had the ability to benefit from training if they

> achieved a passing grade on a test—
>
> > (1) Approved by the Secretary, for periods of enrollment beginning on or after July 1, 1991, or by the accrediting agency for other periods; and
> >
> > (2) Administered substantially in accordance with the requirements for use of the test. . . .

Id. § 682.402(e)(13)(ii)(B). Under the Department's regulation, requests for false certification discharges must be directed at the first step to the guarantee agency holding the applicant's loan. In the event the application is denied, the borrower can request a *de novo* review by the Department. *Id.* § 682.402(e)(9).

C. PLAINTIFF'S ADMISSION INTO A NURSE ASSISTANT PROGRAM BASED ON HER PERFORMANCE ON A CLERICAL APTITUDE TEST

Plaintiff Edna Krabapple enrolled in a 6-month Nurse Assistant program at AID on July 22, 1988. A.R. 137–38. According to the school catalogue, the purpose of the program was to prepare students to work as a nurse assistant or home health care aide for a hospital or other health care facility. A.R. 126. At the time she enrolled, she was 17 years old, had only an eighth grade education, and was dependent on public assistance for her income. A.R. 183, 440. She was attracted to the school by a flyer inviting people without high school degrees to apply. A.R. 183, 214. When she applied she was administered a brief test (described by AID as "an aptitude evaluation," A.R. 189), ostensibly for the purpose of determining her ability to benefit from the Nurse Assistant course. A.R. 183. She correctly answered 57 of 64 questions on this test. A.R. 190–93. Based on plaintiff's performance on this test, the school enrolled her, arranged a financial aid package, and, as a result, obtained approximately $5,000 in Title IV funds. A.R. 397, 449. The financial aid package included two GSLs, one guaranteed by PHEAA and one guaranteed by United Student Aid Funds (now USAGroup Guarantee Services, Inc.). (A.R. 231, 419, 421, 426).[9]

The "aptitude evaluation" used by AID was part of a commercially purchased series of tests called the Aptitude Tests for Occupations devised by Wesley S. Roeder (the "Roeder tests"). A.R. 190. These tests were not designed by their author as ATB tests; instead, they were "devised as aids in the vocational counseling of high school students, college students, and adults." A.R. 197. The overall test consisted of six parts, each part measuring a distinct area of aptitude: "personal-social," "mechanical," "general sales," "clerical routine," "computational," and "scientific" apti-

tude. A.R. 198. The manual for using the Roeder tests lists patterns of occupations related to each of the six areas of aptitude, and to combinations of aptitudes. A.R. 201–03. The manual instructs that the test user to consider the occupations listed under each area of aptitude, or the combination of aptitudes, on which examinee scores the highest. A.R. 204.

AID administered only the "clerical routine" portion of the Roeder tests to Ms. Krabapple. A.R. 37. This test measures four types of skills: name-checking, number-checking, alphabetizing, and spelling. A.R. 198. Not surprisingly, the occupations listed in the test manual as being related to this form of aptitude are entirely clerical; none is related in any way to nursing or to health care. A.R. 201–02. Although the occupational patterns list does not include Nurse Assistant, it does include the similar occupations of Dentist's Assistant, Doctor's Assistant, and Nurse; each of these occupations is listed as related to "personal-social" or "scientific" aptitudes, or to both. *Id.*

Ms. Krabapple completed her training, which involved the study of geriatrics, nursing procedures, anatomy, and physiology. A.R. 270, 126. However, she had difficulty in understanding and performing clinical tasks involving measuring because of her weakness in basic math skills. A.R. 183. In searching for a job after completing the AID program, she discovered that prospective employers were not interested in hiring a 17-year-old without a high school education. AID referred her to a nursing home for a try-out, but she was unable to remain at that position because the nursing home expected her to do things she did not know how to do, such as taking blood pressure. A.R. 183–84. Later testing revealed that Ms. Krabapple's grade equivalent in "number operations" was 7.9, meaning she had less than an eighth grade ability in this area. A.R. 184, 194.

D. THE DEPARTMENT'S DENIAL OF PLAINTIFF'S REQUEST FOR A FALSE CERTIFICATION DISCHARGE

On June 29, 1995, Ms. Krabapple applied for a false certification discharge to the two guarantee agencies holding her loans, USA-Group Guarantee Services, Inc. (formerly United Student Aid Funds) and the Pennsylvania Higher Education Assistance Authority. A.R. 176, 301. In support of her applications, she submitted, among other things, a declaration concerning her admission, a copy of the Roeder test that was administered to her and her answer sheet, correspondence with AID, a news articles concerning AID, copies of NATTS accrediting material, and an explanatory letter by her counsel. A.R. 176–220, 301–344. Both of these agencies denied her application, A.R. 70, 291. Ms. Krabapple appealed both denials to the Department. A.R. 1, 76. On January 17, 1997, the Department issued a final decision denying Ms. Krabapple's application for a false certification discharge. A.R. 1 (also attached as Exhibit A to the Complaint).

The Department gave several reasons for its denial. It concluded that NATTS did not impose any requirements on AID regarding its use of the Roeder tests, and that the Roeder manual itself allows one of the six test batteries to be used without using others. It also relied on the facts that Ms. Krabapple ultimately completed the program and, upon completion, seemed satisfied with her experience at AID. Finally, after obtaining copies of reviews of AID conducted by NATTS and by PHEAA, the Department stated that it "is aware of no reviews conducted in 1988 which made adverse findings about the ATB testing at AID," apparently relying on this

---

9 In 1992 alone, nearly $2.3 million in Title IV loans and grants were paid to AID. More than 47 percent of the school's students defaulted on their loans that year, giving the school the dubious distinction of having the 5th highest default rate among career

fact as evidence that AID was in fact complying with Title IV ATB requirements.[10] As a result of this decision, the Department advised Ms. Krabapple that she will continue to be responsible for repayment of her loans. This appeal followed.

II. ARGUMENT

THE DEPARTMENT'S ACTION, IN DENYING PLAINTIFF'S REQUEST FOR A FALSE CERTIFICATION DISCHARGE, WAS ARBITRARY AND CAPRICIOUS AND CONTRARY TO LAW BECAUSE THE DEPARTMENT DID NOT PROPERLY APPLY ITS OWN FALSE CERTIFICATION REGULATION AND BECAUSE THE DEPARTMENT RELIED ON IMPERMISSIBLE CONSIDERATIONS.

Judicial review of informal agency adjudication, such as the Department's decision to deny Ms. Krabapple's request for a false certification discharge, is governed by the Administrative Procedure Act. The pertinent section provides that the court shall

> hold unlawful and set aside agency action, findings, and conclusions found to be—
> (A) arbitrary, capricious, an abuse of discretion, or otherwise not in accordance with law. . . .

5 U.S.C.A. § 706(2)(A) (1998).

Section 706 "require[s] the reviewing court to engage in a substantial inquiry." *Citizens to Preserve Overton Park, Inc. v. Volpe,* 401 U.S. 402, 415 (1971); *C.K. v. New Jersey Dep't of Health & Human Services,* 92 F.3d 171, 182 (3d Cir. 1996). In determining whether an agency's action was unlawful under § 706(2)(A), the court must "consider whether the decision was based on a consideration of the relevant factors and whether there has been a clear error in judgment." *Overton Park,* 401 U.S. at 416 (citations omitted); *C.K.,* 92 F.3d at 182.

> If the court determines that the agency relied on factors Congress did not intend for it to consider, or has failed to consider an important aspect of the problem, then the action should be set aside as arbitrary and capricious.

Frisby v. U.S. Dep't of Housing and Urban Development, 755 F.2d 1052, 1055 (3d Cir. 1985) (citing *Motor Vehicle Mfrs. Ass'n v. State Farm Mut. Auto. Ins. Co.,* 463 U.S. 29, 43 (1983)).

An agency is bound by its own regulations. *See United States v. Nixon,* 418 U.S. 683, 696 (1974). If an agency's action does not comport with its regulations, the action is contrary to law and should be reversed by a reviewing court. *See Frisby,* 755 F.2d at 1055–56; *Kelly v. Railroad Retirement Board,* 625 F.2d 486, 491–92 (3d Cir. 1980).

The governing standard for evaluating plaintiff's request for a false certification discharge under 20 U.S.C. § 1087(c) is found at 34 C.F.R. § 682.402(e)(13)(ii)(B) (1997). For the time period corresponding to AID's enrollment of Plaintiff, the ATB test used to measure her "ability to benefit" must have been (1) "[a]pproved . . . by the accrediting agency," and it must have been (2)

"[a]dministered substantially in accordance with the requirements for use of the test." *Id.* If the ATB test administered to her failed to meet either of these criteria, then, under the Department's regulation, AID falsely certified her eligibility for Title IV funding, and she is entitled to a discharge.

In denying plaintiff's application for a false certification discharge, the Department acted arbitrarily and capriciously and contrary to law by failing to follow its own regulation. It ignored the regulation's plain language and, instead, used an analysis that rendered the regulation meaningless. The Department's analysis also departed from the statutory directions and intent concerning ATB admissions practices and concerning the consideration of false certification discharge applications. That this was an arbitrary and capricious departure from governing law is demonstrable in several ways. First, the Department collapsed the required inquiry into compliance with the standardized test publisher's instructions into the totally separate inquiry into accrediting agency approval, effectively rendering the former inquiry meaningless. Second, the Department failed to analyze the accrediting agency's ATB requirements and so ignored AID's failure to comply with the NATTS requirement that schools conduct periodic studies documenting the reliability of their entrance testing practices. Finally, the Department improperly considered factors that were irrelevant to the criteria set forth in the regulation entitling students to a discharge.

1. The Department Made a Clear Error in Judgment in Determining That the Roeder Test Was "Administered Substantially in Accordance with the Requirements for the Use of the Test."

Ms. Krabapple is entitled to a false certification discharge if AID did not administer the Roeder test to her "substantially in accordance with the requirements for the use of the test." 34 C.F.R. §§ 682.402(e)(1)(i)(A), (e)(13)(ii)(B)(2) (1997).[11] As she demonstrated in her application, AID used a commercial test that on its face was not designed as an ATB test, and then ignored the test publisher's explicit instructions regarding which parts of the test measure aptitude for which kinds of jobs. For a training program designed to prepare unskilled people for work as nurse assistants in nursing homes or hospitals, the school used only the "Clerical Routine" part of the Roeder test, testing such "aptitudes" as the ability to recognize which listed name or number matches a given name or number, A.R. 191, and the ability to alphabetize four listed names, A.R. 192. AID chose not to use the "Scientific" and "Personal-Social" parts of the Roeder test, despite these being the parts that the test publisher stated were appropriate for measuring aptitude for jobs in health care fields. AID was seemingly more interested in making sure ATB applicants were admitted into the school—and in collecting students' financial aid awards—than in conducting any sort of serious evaluation of their capabilities. As a result, Ms. Krabapple enrolled in the six month course, incurring $5,000 in student loan debt, only to learn upon graduating that health care facilities were not interested in hiring a teenage high school dropout who, among other things, could not take simple measurements on medical equipment.

---

10 The Department also rejected an additional argument made by plaintiff regarding AID's failure to follow the time requirements for administering the Roeder test. This aspect of the Department's decision is not being appealed.

11 Under the regulation, proper ATB testing in July 1988 was contingent on *both* the "approval" of the accrediting agency *and* on using the test in a manner "substantially in accordance" with the test requirements. Thus, if AID fell short regarding either of these factors, Ms. Krabapple is entitled to a discharge.

The Department's explanation for denying Ms. Krabapple's claim for a discharge on the basis that AID did not administer its ATB test "substantially in accordance with the requirements for use of the test" was as follows:

> You also argue that your loans should be discharged because AID did not comply with the test publisher's requirements for use of the test as the school used the Roeder Clerical test to test students for admission on the basis of ATB. You suggest the school should have used the Personal Social and Scientific tests rather than the clerical test. . . . NATTS did not mandate how a school used the test instruments it selected in July, 1988. The manual for the Aptitude Test for Occupations submitted with your discharge application provides that the tests, [*sic*] can be used as a basis for aiding the selection of subjects in high school and colleges. While the Aptitude Test for Occupations can be used as a battery of six tests, the manual states that "[a]ny one test or a combination of test [*sic*] may be administered." Test Manual at 3.
>
> . . . .
>
> Based on a review of the accrediting agency standards and the materials submitted with your application, the Department cannot conclude that you were not tested substantially in accordance with the requirements for use of the test.

A.R. 2.

Thus, the Department gave two reasons for concluding that AID had substantially complied with the requirements of the Roeder test. The first was that "NATTS did not mandate how a school used the test instruments it selected in July, 1988." The second was that the Roeder manual stated that it was possible to use one of the parts of the test or a combination of parts. Both of these reasons are patently capricious and contrary to law.

As to the first reason articulated, the Department's analysis collapses into the inquiry regarding compliance with the requirements for the use of the test a second inquiry of whether the accrediting agency disapproved the test. Having found no accrediting agency disapproval, the Department apparently concluded that AID was essentially free to do what whatever it wanted. Under the Department's interpretation, a school could administer an untimed typing test, despite requirements built into the test that it be timed, as long as the accrediting agency never explicitly told the school not to. However, the structure of the regulation itself makes the accrediting agency's approval or disapproval a separate question from whether the test requirements were followed.

The Department's own regulations make clear that a test is not properly administered if it is not administered in accordance with the test publisher's requirements. The current regulation governing ATB testing requires that tests be "properly administered," 34 C.F.R. § 668.151(a)(2) (1997), and define that term as follows:

> [t]he Secretary considers that a test is properly administered if the test administrator—
>
> . . .
>
> (2) Administers the test in accordance with instructions provided by the test publisher, and in a manner that ensures the integrity and security of the test. . . .

Id. § 668.151(d).

Thus, it is the Roeder manual itself, not the action or inaction of NATTS, that provides the source material for determining whether or not AID administered the Roeder test "substantially in accordance with the requirements of the test." Contrary to the Department's out-of-context quotation from the manual, the Roeder test instructions provide no basis for using the "clerical routine" test to assess a student's ability to benefit from training to be a Nurse Assistant. The design of the Roeder test is to test students for various aptitudes, so that students may consider occupations in the areas of their strengths. The publisher's manual instructs examiners to convert the student's raw scores into percentile ranks. A.R. 204. Then,

> [i]f an examinee has only one high percentile rank, the vocations in that particular field should be considered. If, for instance, he ranks high in Test 3, the occupational patterns listed under the number 3, on page 6 should be considered.
>
> If an examinee has two high percentile ranks, the numbers of the two fields in which he ranked highest should be combined, placing the smaller number first. For instance, if he is high in the Clerical Routine and Computational fields (numbers 4 and 5), the numbers of these two fields should be combined into the number 4–5. Therefore, the occupational patterns listed under 4, 5, and 4–5 should be used by the counselor.

Id. The instructions conclude that "Regardless of where an individual's profile falls, the jobs of the occupational pattern list in which he has the highest aptitude should be considered." *Id.*

The jobs in the occupational pattern listed as related to the clerical routine aptitude for which Ms. Krabapple was tested are, of course, clerical jobs with no relationship to the training in geriatrics, anatomy, physiology, and nursing procedures that AID provided. Although the occupation of Nurse Assistant does not appear on Roeder's list of occupational patterns, the closely-related occupations of Nurse, Dentist's Assistant, and Doctor's Assistant appear under "scientific" or "personal-social" aptitude, or a combination of these aptitudes. A.R. 201–02. If any of the Roeder tests—tests not designed to measure ability to benefit from training at all, but rather designed for vocational counseling—were to be used to measure ability to benefit from Nurse Assistant training, it should have been the tests measuring these wholly different aptitudes.

Although, as the Department notes, the manual does state that "[a]ny one test or any combination of tests may be administered," the manual gives no suggestion that examiners could use one test to measure aptitude for unrelated occupations. Certainly, if a student shows an interest in a particular occupation, an examiner might choose to administer only one test to determine whether the student shows aptitude in the area of her interest. However, that one test tells nothing about the student's aptitude for other occupations. The Department's logic would yield absurd results: if the score on one test used in isolation can demonstrate ability to benefit from training in an unrelated field, then a school could use the "general sales" portion of the Roeder test to measure ability to benefit from training as an "aeronautical engineer," or could use the "mechanical'' aptitude test for to show ability to benefit from training to be a "taxation accountant."

Because the "requirements for the use" of the Roeder test instruct that each test only be used to measure aptitude for the related list of occupations, and because the occupation of Nurse Assistant is unrelated to "clerical routine" aptitude, the test given Ms. Krabapple was not "administered substantially in accordance with the requirements for use of the test." The test therefore did not meet the requirements of 34 C.F.R. § 682.402(e)(13)(ii)(B)(2). By focusing only on the single statement in the manual that "any one test . . . may be administered," the Department essentially ignored the manual's clear directions regarding which single test parts or combination of parts were relevant to measuring aptitude for which jobs. The conclusion that the Roeder publisher endorsed the practice of giving a simple clerical test to applicants for a health care training program was without any reasonable basis whatsoever, and, as such, was "capricious" and contrary to law.

2. The Department Made a Clear Error in Judgment in Determining that the Clerical Routine Portion of the Roeder Tests Was Approved by AID's Accrediting Agency.

The false certification regulation provides that a student is not considered to have had the requisite ability to benefit unless she "achieved a passing grade on a test . . . [a]pproved . . . by the accrediting agency." 34 C.F.R. § 682.402(e)(13)(ii)(B)(1) (1997). In this case, as of July 1988, AID's accrediting agency had neither approved nor disapproved the school's use of the Roeder "clerical routine" as an appropriate instrument for measuring ability to benefit. The meaning of this accrediting "approval" consideration, however, comes from the ability-to-benefit rule that was in effect at the time of Plaintiff's admission to AID. The relevant statutory language limited ATB enrollments to those individuals passing "a nationally recognized, standardized or industry developed test, *subject to criteria developed by the appropriate accrediting association.*" 20 U.S.C.A. § 1091(d)(3)(A) (1988) (emphasis added). The false certification regulation, by requiring separate reviews of the test publisher's instructions and of the accrediting commission "approval," corresponds to the statute's two-part requirement for schools' use of testing to admit ATB students, that the test be an established test (and administered in accordance with the requirements that accompany the test) and that it be used in a way that conforms to applicable accrediting criteria.

In its denial of Ms. Krabapple's application, the Department implicitly agreed that the analysis of whether the accrediting agency "approved" the use of a particular ATB test involves a determination of whether the school complied with applicable accrediting criteria regarding ATB testing. However, rather than actually applying the appropriate criteria to this case, the Department did little more than refute what plaintiff believed, at the time of her application, to be the relevant accrediting criteria. A proper analysis of the actual NATTS standards shows that AID did not comply with even the lenient accrediting criteria in effect when it admitted Ms. Krabapple into the school.

The Department, AID, and plaintiff's counsel have had some difficulty identifying NATTS's ATB requirements at the time of Ms. Krabapple's application. After Ms. Krabapple applied for a false certification discharge, the Department obtained a chronology from NATTS of its ATB requirements. This chronology provides

the following "summary" of the ATB requirements at the relevant time:

> Document C, Section VI(A)(7) of the Accrediting Standards describes the criteria the Commission uses to determine a school's compliance with accrediting standards. The Commission does not wish to be prescriptive in either the method or materials that a school may use and encourages all accredited schools to carefully study and select the most appropriate process for its students.

A.R. 7. The referenced Section VI(A)(7)—not provided to the Department by NATTS but included in an AID submission to the Department—provides:

> If the school enrolls a person who does not have a high school diploma or a GED, but admits the individual based on "ability to benefit," the school must document the basis on which ability is determined. The documentation is left to the discretion of the institution and may use one or more of the following: standardized test, practicum examination, interview, prior work experience, or other measurement indicators. Periodic studies are to be conducted to document the reliability of the entrance requirements for all students.

A.R. 32. Thus, at the time of Ms. Krabapple's enrollment at AID, NATTS required schools seeking accreditation to conduct "periodic studies . . . to document the reliability of the entrance requirements for all students." *See also* A.R. 6–7 (another statement of NATTS's ATB criteria, including the requirement to conduct periodic studies).[12]

The Department's response to Ms. Krabapple's application for a discharge on the grounds that NATTS did not approve AID's use of the Roeder test was as follows:

> During July, 1988 NATTS did not require schools it accredited to have ATB tests or scores reviewed by an independent third party. NATTS standards in effect at the time did not mandate the use of a particular test, and did not mandate that standardized or industry developed tests be used in a particular way. NATTS stated that it "does not wish to be prescriptive in either the method or materials

---

12 In January 1989, NATTS amended its accreditation criteria to require that ATB tests be "reviewed by a qualified third-party, such as an expert in tests and measurements, for both the appropriateness of the test and the specific score levels required for admission into each program." A.R. 34. When in 1993 plaintiff's counsel requested documentation from AID that its testing of Ms. Krabapple had complied with accrediting agency requirements, A.R. 186, AID stated that "Ability to Benefit prior to the current regulations allowed schools to use a test which had been evaluated by an independent third party." A.R. 187. AID also provided what now appears to be the January 1989 NATTS revision to its accrediting criteria, along with two letters purporting to satisfy the third-party evaluation requirement. A.R. 212, 213. Plaintiff's application to the Department for a false certification discharge assumed that AID had accurately described the applicable accrediting criteria.

that a school may use and encourages all accredited schools to carefully study and select the most appropriate process for its students." The requirement cited in your discharge application that the school have its test reviewed by a third party was not adopted until after you enrolled. Therefore, the fact that the third party validations used by the school were dated after you enrolled is not a basis to determine that the school failed to comply with accrediting agency requirements.

A.R. 2. This analysis does not actually address the accrediting criteria that were in effect at the time Ms. Krabapple enrolled at AID. In particular, the Department does not address the requirement that schools conduct periodic studies to document the reliability of their entrance requirements. The Department's only reference to NATTS's ATB requirements is a reference to a statement in the "summary" that the Department quotes as supporting its position that AID complied with NATTS's accrediting criteria. However, even this quoted statement encourages schools to "carefully study and select the most appropriate process" for testing their students. The record contains no evidence that AID ever studied the reliability of the Roeder test to measure ability to benefit.

Although given a full opportunity to do so, AID did not produce any documentation demonstrating that it conducted any periodic studies regarding the reliability of its use of the Roeder "clerical routine" as its ATB test. Both the Department and plaintiff's counsel solicited documentation from AID that it had complied with the applicable accrediting criteria. A.R. 49, 186. The Department also solicited such information from NATTS. A.R. 48. The only reasonable inference from NATTS's and AID's failure to provide such documentation is that AID did not conduct the required studies. The absence of any documentation that AID complied with the requirement to conduct periodic studies of the reliability of its entrance requirements is compelling evidence that AID was not in compliance with NATTS's criteria for use of the ATB tests. Consequently, the test was not "approved" by the accrediting agency, and AID did not satisfy the requirements of 34 C.F.R. § 682.402(e)(13)(ii)(B)(1).

Rather than inferring from this absence of evidence of reliability studies that AID failed to comply with the NATTS criteria, the Department came to precisely the opposite conclusion: it essentially treated the absence of an explicit finding by NATTS that AID was in violation of its ATB requirements as NATTS "approval" of AID's ATB testing. In other words, the Department failed to conduct its own independent analysis of whether AID was complying with its accrediting criteria, and, instead looked to the absence of some affirmative disapproval by NATTS as the critical fact. This was a clear departure from the kind of inquiry that the false certification regulation contemplates and, therefore, constituted an error of law.

As will now be discussed, this complete reliance on the assumed integrity of oversight by the accrediting agencies is also unreasonable given the legislative context that gave rise to the false certification discharge in the first place. Specifically, Congress's adoption of the false certification discharge to provide relief to victimized students stemmed in part from the conclusion of the Nunn Report that accrediting commissions had turned blind eyes to ATB abuses by trade schools.

3. The Department Relied on Irrelevant Factors in Denying Plaintiff's Application for a False Certification Discharge.

In addition to its errors in judgment in considering the regulatory factors governing its decision whether to grant a false certification discharge, the Department also considered factors that are irrelevant to its decision. Its reliance on irrelevant factors constitutes separate grounds for setting aside its action as arbitrary and capricious. *Frisby v. U.S. Dep't of Housing and Urban Development*, 755 F.3d 1052, 1055 (3d Cir. 1985).

Section 1087(c)(1) entitles students whose eligibility for student loans was falsely certified by their schools to a discharge of their loans. 20 U.S.C.A. § 1087(c)(1) (1998). The Department's implementing regulations interpret this entitlement to apply to students whose eligibility for student loans was based on purported ability to benefit from training, and who were administered a test that either (1) was not approved by the school's accrediting agency or (2) was not administered substantially in accordance with the requirements for use of the test. 34 C.F.R. § 682.402(e)(1)(i)(A), (e)(13)(ii)(B) (1997). These criteria, addressing only whether the test given the student was appropriately selected and administered, are the only factors that the statutory and regulatory scheme makes relevant to a decision whether to discharge a student's loans.[13]

The Department's decision denying Ms. Krabapple's application for a false certification discharge states that

> I also note that you did well at the school and graduated. In an evaluation of the school in your academic file you answered "yes" to the questions "If you had it to do over again would you enroll in the same program?" and "Are the text books easy to understand?"

A.R. 2. Ms. Krabapple's completion of the nurse assistant program and her stated satisfaction—before she started her job search and discovered that her training was not sufficient to get work as a nurse assistant—have no bearing on whether the test administered to Ms. Krabapple was proper.[14] Indeed, the false certification regulation itself considers actual employment, not but graduation from the program, to undercut a claim of improper ATB admission. See 34 C.F.R. § 682.402(3)(3)(ii)(C) (borrower who completes program and makes a reasonable, but unsuccessful, attempt to obtain employment is still eligible for discharge if ATB testing was improper). The Department should not have relied on these irrelevant comments as a basis for denying Ms. Krabapple's application.

The Department's denial letter also states that

---

13 The Department's regulations also authorize discharges for other false certifications besides false certification of ability to benefit, but these other forms of false certification are not at issue in Ms. Krabapple's case. 34 C.F.R. § 682.402(e)(1)(i)(B), (ii) (1997).

14 The Department reliance on Ms. Krabapple's statements in her student evaluation was highly selective: in response to other questions, Ms. Krabapple stated that she found the school to be "sort of" as it was represented to her when she enrolled, and that "maybe" she would recommend the school to her friends. A.R. 147. The Department also neglected the context in which Ms. Krabapple's comments were given: Ms. Krabapple was jobless and was relying on AID to find her a job; she consequently would' have been reluctant to offend the school.

[b]ecause entities with oversight responsibility would typically have both the opportunity and responsibility to find and report improper ATB admission practices, the absence of such findings raises an inference that improper practices were not reported because none were taking place.

Id. In other words, the fact that the Department did not turn up any reference to improper ATB practices in the program reviews of AID that it obtained from NATTS, PHEAA, and its own files was determined to outweigh the actual evidence of improper practices contained in plaintiff's submissions.

This is a remarkable inference. The actual text of the Department's program reviews, which the Department cites as evidence of an absence of ATB fraud at AID, reject any inference that its failure to identify particular forms of abuse means that such abuses did not occur:

> Although the review was thorough, it cannot be assumed to be all-inclusive. The absence of statements in the report concerning the institution's specific practices and procedures must not be construed as acceptance, approval or endorsement of those specific practices and procedures. Furthermore, it does not relieve the institution of its obligation to comply with all of the statutory or regulatory provisions governing the Title IV programs.

A.R. 462, 493; *see also* A.R. 453, 475, 481 (similar disclaimers in PHEAA reviews). Moreover, the Department's assumption that program reviews were comprehensive and can be relied on to have uncovered any wrongdoing represents a complete inversion of the facts as Congress found them to be at the time the false certification discharge program was enacted. As stated in the Nunn Report,

> the mechanism on which [Guaranteed Student Loan Program] oversight of schools depends—the Triad of licensure, accreditation, and certification/eligibility—provides little or no assurance that schools are educating students efficiently and effectively. Similarly, the investigation disclosed that the lure of fast and easy program profits, coupled with no effective government oversight, had already had devastating effects on the program's financial intermediaries, with similar problems likely in the future. Lastly, the Subcommittee found that through gross mismanagement, ineptitude, and neglect in carrying out its regulatory and oversight functions, the Department of Education had all but abdicated its responsibility to the students it is supposed to service and the taxpayers whose interests it is charged with protecting.

Nunn Report at 33.[15] As a direct result of this collapse in regulatory oversight, Congress felt compelled to extend relief to some of the

---

15 The Nunn Report specifically questioned the validity of Departmental and accrediting agency program reviews, noting testimony that both agency and NATTS review staff allowed schools to provide them with student files. This practice permitted schools to alter the student records or to hide problem cases. Nunn Report at 19, 32.

student victims who were left with worthless educations and loans they could not afford to repay. It would be a miscarriage of legislative intent if the failure of oversight agencies to notice that AID was ignoring Title IV ATB rules was used to defeat plaintiff's convincing case for a false certification discharge. If the court does not order the Department to discharge Ms. Krabapple's student loans pursuant to 34 C.F.R. § 682.402(e)(1)(i)(A) and § 682.402(e)(13)(ii)(B), the court should nonetheless remand this matter to the Department for redetermination without considering these irrelevant factors.

III. CONCLUSION

For the foregoing reasons, Ms. Krabapple is entitled to a judgment that the Department's action was arbitrary and capricious and not in accordance with law. The court should therefore set the defendant's action aside as unlawful pursuant to 5 U.S.C. § 706(2)(A). This matter should be remanded to the Department for a discharge of her student loans and a refund of any payments made, with interest.

[Attorney for Plaintiff]

E.6 Raising School's Fraud in Bankruptcy Proceeding

E.6.1 *Complaint to Determine Dischargeability of Student Loan*

UNITED STATES BANKRUPTCY COURT
EASTERN DISTRICT OF PENNSYLVANIA

```
———————————————————  )
IN RE: [Debtor]                    )
                       Debtor  )
[Debtor],                          )
                      Plaintiff  )
                                   )
v.                                 )
                                   )
[Director, Higher Education        )
Assistance Agency]                 )
                    Defendant  )
———————————————————  )
```

**COMPLAINT TO DETERMINE DISCHARGEABILITY
OF STUDENT LOAN**

1. The Debtor filed this case under chapter 7 of the Bankruptcy Code on September 1, 2000. This Court thus has jurisdiction over this action under 28 U.S.C. § 1334. This proceeding is a core proceeding.

2. One of the unsecured debts owing by the Debtor and listed in Schedule F is a student loan owing to [*creditor*].

3. The Defendant [*director*] is the executive director of the [*creditor*] and is responsible for the overall operation of the guaranteed student loan program.

4. This loan was incurred to pay expenses at [*school*].

5. Subsequent to beginning coursework at that school, the

Debtor learned that the school had lost its accreditation and that none of its recent graduates had obtained the employment for which they were trained due to that loss.

6. The Debtor was unable to transfer to any other educational program, and was also refused any refund of the tuition paid by the student loan.

7. Since that time, the Debtor has been unemployed, and the sole source of income for herself and her two children has been public assistance in the amount of $[*amount*], which barely suffices for the necessities of life.

8. The Debtor has no current or anticipated available income or resources with which to pay the aforementioned loan and any payments on that loan could be made only at great hardship to the Debtor and her children.

WHEREFORE, the Debtor prays that this Court enter an Order declaring the student loan debt of the Debtor to be dischargeable in this bankruptcy case.

Date:

[Attorney for Debtor]

E.6.2 *Dischargeability Complaint Raising School's Fraud*

UNITED STATES BANKRUPTCY COURT
EASTERN DISTRICT OF PENNSYLVANIA

```
————————————————  )
In re: MAE N. WEST,          )
                   Debtor    )
MAE N. WEST,                 )
                   Plaintiff )
                             )
v.                           )
                             )
PENNSYLVANIA HIGHER          )
EDUCATION ASSISTANCE         )
AGENCY, PHILADELPHIA         )
SAVINGS FUND SOCIETY and     )
LAMAR ALEXANDER,             )
Secretary, United States     )
Department of Education,      )
                  Defendants  )
Stephen Raslavich,           )
              Interim Trustee )
————————————————  )
```

DEBTOR'S COMPLAINT TO DETERMINE DISCHARGEABILITY OF STUDENT LOAN

PRELIMINARY STATEMENT

1. This is an adversary proceeding brought under the Bankruptcy Code, 11 U.S.C. § 523(a)(8), to determine the dischargeability of an educational loan made, insured or guaranteed by a governmental unit. The debtor also raises various claims under applicable nonbankruptcy law against the defendants.

JURISDICTION

2. Jurisdiction of the bankruptcy court in this matter is provided by 28 U.S.C. §§ 1334 and 157 and the Order of the United States District Court for this district dated July 25, 1984.

3. This is a core proceeding.

PARTIES

4. Plaintiff is an adult individual who resides at [Address]. She is the debtor in above-captioned chapter 7 case.

5. Defendant Pennsylvania Higher Education Assistance Agency ("PHEAA") is an instrumentality of the Commonwealth of Pennsylvania, doing business at [Address].

6. Defendant Philadelphia Savings Fund Society ("PSFS") is a Pennsylvania corporate financial institution whose local student loan operations are located at [Address].

7. Defendant Lamar Alexander is the Secretary of the Department of Education ("ED") and as such is the chief executive official of an agency of the United States (hereinafter "the Secretary.")

8. Stephen Reynolds is the interim trustee in this bankruptcy case and is a nominal party to this action.

FACTUAL ALLEGATIONS

9. In November, 1988 plaintiff enrolled in a data entry course at a proprietary trade school in Philadelphia named Commercial Programming Unlimited. Plaintiff, who had never graduated high school, was at the time 55 years old. She was induced to enroll by sales representatives of the school who promised her a) that she would obtain job training and a GED diploma at the school, b) that upon graduation she would receive job placement assistance and c) that the entire cost of this service would be financed by federal financial aid programs.

10. The school arranged a financial aid package for plaintiff which totalled $6,225 for a nine-month course. Included in this package were approximately $5,500 in loans provided by PSFS, guaranteed by PHEAA and insured by ED under the Guaranteed Student Loan (GSL) and Supplemental Loan (SLS) programs established by Subchapter IV of the Higher Education Act, 20 U.S.C. § 1077 et seq.

11. Plaintiff attended classes at the school for approximately one month, at which time, due to dissatisfaction with the quality of the teaching, she transferred to another trade school in the next building, the Palmer Business School. As with the first school, Palmer representatives assured her of a GED, job training and placement and a financial aid package covering all costs. The second package, like the first, was arranged by the school through PSFS and was guaranteed and insured, respectively, by PHEAA and ED.

12. In the case of all the above-mentioned student loans, plaintiff did not obtain the loans by herself, nor did she have any direct dealings whatsoever with PSFS. On the contrary, PSFS had the schools, among other things, verify plaintiff's identity, complete all the forms ordinarily completed by the lender, explain the transaction to plaintiff, and obtain her signature on all documents relating to the loans.

13. Plaintiff graduated from Palmer in the summer of 1989. She did not receive a GED, and, on the contrary, learned that she had to contact the School District of Philadelphia in order to take the test and to receive whatever additional GED training she needed.

At the one job interview Palmer arranged for plaintiff, she discovered that a GED was a requirement for the job. Soon after this interview Palmer went out of business.

14. Plaintiff's present indebtedness on her student loans is approximately $5,524.

CAUSES OF ACTION

Count I—Undue Hardship

15. Plaintiff-debtor's present income consists of approximately $600/month earned from a small beauty shop she rents. This amount is not even adequate for her to afford the basic necessities of life.

16. She lacks the resources to repay the student loans and any payments she would make would be at a great hardship. Excepting the loans from discharge would impose an undue hardship on her.

17. The above-described student loan debts are dischargeable under 11 U.S.C. § 523(a)(8)(B).

Count II—Breach of Contract

18. The purpose of the above-described loans, which the two schools arranged, was to finance the costs of a GED course, job training and job placement services purportedly provided by the school. Thus, plaintiff agreed to repay her indebtedness in consideration for the schools' agreement to provide her with the said services.

19. The schools never provided her the said services and, as a result, failed to perform in accordance with the above-described contract and breached said contract.

20. Plaintiff has been injured by this breach by the indebtedness involved in this case.

21. PSFS had an "origination relationship," *see* 34 C.F.R. §682.200, with each of the two schools plaintiff attended. Therefore, PSFS, PHEAA and the Secretary are subject to plaintiff's claims and defenses.

Count III—Fraud, Misrepresentation and/or Unfair Trade Practices

22. Both of the trade schools induced plaintiff to enroll and to continue in these so-called academic programs through a number of misleading, deceptive or fraudulent representations, including but not limited to representations concerning the quality, value and usefulness of the offered training, concerning the qualifications needed to benefit from the training and to obtain employment, concerning the ability to earn a GED after successful completion of the course, concerning the nature and wage levels of possible employment, and concerning the success rate of students completing the training.

23. The debtor relied on these representations, enrolled in the schools and then maintained herself in good standing until graduation.

24. The defendants are subject to plaintiff's claims and defenses as a result of the "origination relationship" that existed between the schools and PSFS.

Count IV—Violation of Higher Education Act

25. The underlying student loans are void and unenforceable in

that, in addition to defrauding students as described above, the schools also violated numerous federal regulatory requirements, including but not limited to, enrolling plaintiff into the program when she did not have the "ability to benefit" from the training as defined by federal law and failing to maintain standards and procedures for determining whether any applicants for admission had such an "ability to benefit."

WHEREFORE, plaintiff-debtor requests the this Court:

1. Assume jurisdiction of this case;
2. Declare the subject student loans dischargeable under 11 U.S.C. § 523(a)(8);
3. Declare the loan void;
4. Award the debtor damages;
5. Award the debtor's counsel reasonable attorney's fees and
6. Grant the debtor any other appropriate relief.

[Attorney for Plaintiff]

E.6.3 Complaint to Enjoin Discriminatory Denial of Guaranteed Student Loan

UNITED STATES BANKRUPTCY COURT
EASTERN DISTRICT OF PENNSYLVANIA

IN RE: [Debtor]	)
Debtor	)
[Debtor],	)
Plaintiff	)
	)
v.	)
	)
[Director, Higher Education	)
Assistance Agency]	)
Defendant	)

COMPLAINT

I. PRELIMINARY STATEMENT

1. This is an action brought by Plaintiff [*debtor*], a bankruptcy debtor who has received his discharge, seeking declaratory and injunctive relief to invalidate certain policies of and regulations promulgated by the Higher Education Assistance Agency ("HEAA") as violative of federal bankruptcy law, 11 U.S.C. § 525(c), 42 U.S.C. § 1983 and the Supremacy Clause of the United States Constitution.

II. JURISDICTION

2. Jurisdiction for this action is conferred by 28 U.S.C. § 1334. This proceeding is a core proceeding.

III. PARTIES

3. [*Debtor*] is an individual residing at [*address*].

4. Defendant HEAA is a public corporation and government instrumentality of the Commonwealth of [*state*] whose corporate purpose is to improve the higher education opportunities of [*state*]

residents by granting scholarships and guaranteeing loans to such persons to assist them in meeting their expenses of higher education. [*cite provision(s) of state law*].

5. Defendant [*defendant—director*] is the Executive Director of HEAA and is responsible for the overall operations of HEAA, including the enforcement of HEAA regulations codified at [*cite provision(s) of state law*].

6. Defendant [*defendant—deputy director*] is the Deputy Director of HEAA and is responsible for the operation of HEAA's guaranteed student loan program, including the enforcement of HEAA regulations codified at [*cite provision(s) of state law*].

IV. FACTS

7. Plaintiff attended undergraduate school at the University of [*name*] from the fall term of 1988 to the spring term of 1990.

8. During this period, Plaintiff received student loans guaranteed by HEAA in the total amount of approximately $5,874.00.

9. After leaving school, Plaintiff was financially unable to repay his student loans.

10. On March 12, 1996, Plaintiff filed a voluntary petition in bankruptcy under chapter 13 of the Bankruptcy Code, Bkr. No. [*number*].

11. By Order dated June 29, 1999, the Bankruptcy Court ordered Plaintiff released from all his dischargeable debts, including his obligation to HEAA.

12. During the spring term of 1999 Plaintiff returned to the University of [*name*] to complete the twelve credits he needed for his undergraduate degree.

13. To finance his education, Plaintiff applied for an HEAA higher education grant.

14. HEAA denied Plaintiff's grant application based upon section [*number*] of its regulations, [*cite provision of state law*].

15. In 1999, Plaintiff also applied for an HEAA guaranteed student loan.

16. Plaintiff graduated from the University of [*name*] in May 2000, with a B.A. in political science and philosophy.

17. When this action was filed, Plaintiff had been accepted for admission into several law schools commencing the fall term of 2000.

18. On or about June 21, 2000, Plaintiff filed an application through [*name*] Bank, [*address*], for an HEAA guaranteed student loan to assist the financing of his law school education at University of [*name*] Law School. The application has been approved by [*name*] Bank and is pending before HEAA.

19. On August 11, 2000, Plaintiff was accepted for admission into the University of [*name*] Law School.

20. Plaintiff has applied for financial aid from the University of [*name*] Law School.

21. The University of [*name*] Law School will provide $4,000.00 assistance in loans and grants and requires that Plaintiff obtain a guaranteed student loan of at least $4,700.00.

22. Plaintiff is in the process of applying for an HEAA student loan for the University of [*name*] Law School and expects that the application will be received by HEAA by August 31, 2000.

23. Pursuant to [*cite provision(s) of state law*], Plaintiff is ineligible for an HEAA guaranteed student loan due to his debt on the prior loans, even though his obligation has been discharged in bankruptcy.

24. Unless Plaintiff obtains a guaranteed student loan he will be unable to attend law school and he will suffer irreparable harm.

V. STATEMENT OF CLAIMS

A. First Claim

25. Defendants' policy of denying guaranteed student loans to individuals who have discharged in bankruptcy prior student loans which were in default constitutes discrimination against Plaintiff because he was a debtor under the Bankruptcy Code or because Plaintiff has not paid a debt that was discharged under the Bankruptcy Code, in violation of 11 U.S.C. § 525(c).

B. Second Claim

26. Defendants' policy of denying guaranteed student loans to individuals who have discharged in bankruptcy prior student loans which were in default violates 11 U.S.C. § 524 in that it fails to give Plaintiff a "fresh start" and it fails to treat Plaintiff as if he had never had a liability arising from that debt. Therefore, the policy violates the Supremacy Clause of the United States Constitution, Article VI, Clause 2.

27. By denying Plaintiff his rights guaranteed by federal law, i.e., the Bankruptcy Code and the United States Constitution, Defendants acting under color of law, have violated 42 U.S.C. § 1983.

VI. PRAYER FOR RELIEF

WHEREFORE, Plaintiff requests that this Court:

a. Take jurisdiction of this case;

b. Enter judgment and grant relief declaring that [*cite provision(s) of state law*] and Defendants' practice of denying guaranteed student loans to individuals who have discharged prior student loans in bankruptcy violates:
   i. 11 U.S.C. § 525(c);
   ii. 42 U.S.C. § 1983;
   iii. 11 U.S.C. § 524; and
   iv. The Supremacy Clause of the United States Constitution.

c. Enjoin Defendants from continuing the practice of denying Plaintiff guaranteed student loans, pursuant to [*cite provision(s) of state laws*], due to his prior loans which have been discharged in bankruptcy;

d. Order Defendants to process Plaintiff's application for a guaranteed student loan without consideration of or discrimination based upon Plaintiff's prior loans which have been discharged in bankruptcy;

e. Award Plaintiff's counsel a reasonable attorney's fee; and

f. Grant Plaintiff all such other relief as shall be just and proper.

Date: [Attorney for Plaintiff]

DECLARATION

I, [*debtor*], the Plaintiff in the above-captioned action, certify under penalty of perjury that the foregoing is true and correct to the best of my knowledge, information and belief.

Date: [Debtor]

Sample Discovery and Freedom of Information Act Requests

F.1 Discovery in Student Loan Collection Cases

F.1.1 Interrogatories and Requests for Admissions and Production of Documents in Case Challenging Student Loan Collection Letters

IN THE UNITED STATES DISTRICT COURT
FOR THE MIDDLE DISTRICT OF LOUISIANA

	)
Mary Johnson, on behalf of	)
herself and all others similarly	)
situated,	)
Plaintiff,	)
	)
v.	)
	)
The Premier Collectors, Inc.,	)
Defendant.	)
	)

PLAINTIFF'S FIRST DISCOVERY REQUEST

Plaintiff hereby requests that defendant respond to the following requests for admission, interrogatories and document requests. Throughout this request:

A. If defendant's response to any of the requests for admissions submitted herewith is anything other than an unqualified admission, describe in detail the basis for the inability to make such admission.

B. If any document requested in the document requests submitted herewith was but no longer is in defendant's possession, custody or control, state: the date of its disposition; the manner of its disposition (e.g., lost, destroyed, transferred to a third party); and the circumstances surrounding the disposition of the document including the identity of the person who disposed of it, the reason for its disposal, the identity of anyone who may have copies of it, the identity of anyone ordering or requesting its disposal, and whether its disposal was in compliance with defendant's document destruction policies.

C. Unless otherwise specified in a particular paragraph, the "relevant time period" covered by this request is August 1, 1993 to the present.

D. PCI means The Premier Collectors, Inc.

E. These requests are subject to the instructions and definitions attached hereto as *Exhibit 1 [reprinted at the end this section]*.

REQUESTS FOR ADMISSION

PLEASE TAKE NOTICE THAT, pursuant to Federal Rules of Civil Procedure 26 and 36, plaintiff hereby requests that defendant admit or deny the truth of the following matters in writing within 30 days after service of this request.

1. The Premier Collectors, Inc. ("PCI") is regularly engaged for profit in the collection of debts allegedly owed by consumers.
RESPONSE:

2. PCI is a "debt collector" as defined in the Fair Debt Collection Practices Act, 15 U.S.C. §1692a(6).
RESPONSE:

3. On or about August 11, 1993, PCI mailed to plaintiff a collection letter demanding $11,417.31 allegedly owing to the U.S. Department of Education. *Exhibit A* is a copy of the letter [*not reprinted infra*].
RESPONSE:

4. On or about April 20, 1994, PCI mailed to plaintiff a collection letter demanding $10,706.14 allegedly owing to the U.S. Department of Education. *Exhibit B* is a copy of the letter [*not reprinted infra*].
RESPONSE:

5. On or about May 5, 1994, PCI mailed to plaintiff a collection letter demanding $10,732.65 allegedly owing to the U.S. Department of Education. *Exhibit C* is a copy of the letter [*not reprinted infra*].
RESPONSE:

6. *Exhibit A-C* were mailed in an attempt to collect alleged debts arising from transactions primarily for personal, family, or household purposes, namely, an alleged student loan.
RESPONSE:

7. Defendant is not affiliated with U.S. Department of Education.
RESPONSE:

8. Defendant did not and does not determine the course of legal action, if any, taken by the United States Government with respect to student loans.
RESPONSE:

9. Neither PCI, the U.S. Department of Justice, nor anyone else, has filed suit against plaintiff to collect the alleged debt referred to in *Exhibits A-C*.
RESPONSE:

10. PCI regularly mails, or causes to be mailed, collection letters

bearing the name of the U.S. Department of Education to Louisiana residents in an effort to collect consumer debts.

RESPONSE:

11. Between August 1, 1993 and the present, PCI mailed more than 20 letters prepared on the same form as *Exhibit A* to Louisiana residents in an effort to collect student loans.

RESPONSE:

12. Between August 1, 1993 and the present, PCI mailed more than 20 letters prepared on the same form as *Exhibit B* to Louisiana residents in an effort to collect student loans.

RESPONSE:

13. Between August 1, 1993 and the present, PCI mailed more than 20 letters prepared on the same form as *Exhibit C* to Louisiana residents in an effort to collect student loans.

RESPONSE:

14. Between August 1, 1993 and the present, PCI sought to recover collection fees exceeding 20% of the principal debt from more than 20 Louisiana residents who allegedly owed money on student loans.

RESPONSE:

15. PCI does not in fact conduct an investigation of the income, savings, employment, real estate ownership and personal assets of each person to whom *Exhibit B* is sent.

RESPONSE:

16. PCI has not in fact conducted an investigation of the income, savings, employment, real estate ownership and personal assets of any person to whom *Exhibit B* was sent. [not reprinted *infra*]

RESPONSE:

17. A suit by the U.S. Department of Justice on a student loan may not result in garnishment, attachment or judgment liens until the consumer is heard in court and a judgment entered against the consumer.

RESPONSE:

INTERROGATORIES

PLEASE TAKE NOTICE THAT, pursuant to Federal Rules of Civil Procedure 26 and 33, plaintiff propounds the following Interrogatories to be answered by defendant under oath, within 30 days of service hereof.

1a. Describe the method, procedure, or general approach which defendant presently uses in the preparation and mailing of collection notices which are eventually sent to persons who allegedly owe money on student loans. Include in your answer a description of all letters or any series of letters that PCI sends to such persons.

ANSWER:

b. State when the method, procedure or general approach described in response to (a) was adopted;

ANSWER:

c. Describe all other methods, procedures or general approaches defendant uses in the preparation of and mailing of collection letters eventually sent to such persons.

ANSWER:

2a. How many notices, using the same form as *Exhibit A*, were sent to Louisiana residents between August 1, 1993 and the present [*not reprinted infra*].

ANSWER:

b. State the names and addresses of each such person.

ANSWER:

3a. How many notices, using the same form as *Exhibit B*, were

sent to Louisiana residents between August 1, 1993 and the present [*not reprinted infra*].

ANSWER:

b. State the names and addresses of each such person.

ANSWER:

4a. How many notices, using the same form as *Exhibit C*, were sent to Louisiana residents between August 1, 1993 and the present [*not reprinted infra*].

ANSWER:

b. State the names and addresses of each such person.

ANSWER:

5. Describe all reports, recommendations for action, or other advice provided by PCI to the United States Government with respect to alleged student loan debts which PCI is unable to collect.

ANSWER:

6. Identify all instances in which PCI has filed suit or caused suit to be filed to collect an alleged student loan debt owed to the U. S. Department of Education.

ANSWER:

7. Describe any basis which PCI has in contract, regulation, or otherwise for demanding a 42.84% collection fee from plaintiff, and how the amount of such fee was determined.

ANSWER:

8. State whether any person to whom PCI has ever (before or during the class period) sent a letter using the same form as *Exhibit B* has had their salary garnished, equity or bank accounts attached, or liens placed against their real estate without a judgment being first entered against that person by a court.

ANSWER:

9. Describe all investigations of income, bank accounts, business and employment information, real estate ownership, automobile ownership and personal assets which PCI has conducted of persons who were sent letters using the same form as *Exhibit B*, identifying each person who was investigated:

ANSWER:

REQUESTS FOR PRODUCTION OF DOCUMENTS

PLEASE TAKE NOTICE THAT, pursuant to Federal Rules of Civil Procedure 26 and 34, plaintiff hereby requests that defendant produce to plaintiff's counsel for examination, inspection and copying all of the documents specified herein in its possession, custody or control, within 30 days of service of this request.

1. All documents showing the number of Louisiana residents to whom PCI sent collection letters using the same forms as *Exhibit A-C* during any portion of the period between August 1, 1993 and the present [*not reprinted infra*]. If no documents showing the number of Louisiana residents exists, produce all documents showing the number of persons to whom PCI sent such letters during such period, without regard to residence.

RESPONSE:

2. All documents showing the names and addresses of Louisiana residents who were sent a collection letter prepared using the same forms as *Exhibit A-C*, during any portion of the period between August 1, 1993 and the present.

RESPONSE:

3. A copy of each form collection letter sent to Louisiana residents by PCI on or after August 1, 1993.

RESPONSE:

4. All documents purporting to authorize or justify the 42.84%

collection fee referred to in *Exhibit C*.

RESPONSE:

5. All reports, recommendations for action, or other advice provided by PCI to the United States Government with respect to alleged student loan debts which PCI is unable to collect.

RESPONSE:

6. All documents relating to any instance in which PCI has filed suit or caused suit to be filed to collect an alleged student loan debt owed to the U. S. Department of Education.

RESPONSE:

7. All documents relating to any instance (before or during the class period) in which a person to whom PCI sent a letter using the same form as *Exhibit B* has had their salary garnished, equity or bank accounts attached, or liens placed against their real estate without a judgment being first entered against that person by a court.

RESPONSE:

8. All documents relating to investigations of income, bank accounts, business and employment information, real estate ownership, automobile ownership and personal assets which PCI has conducted of persons who were sent letters using the same form as *Exhibit B*.

RESPONSE:

9. All documents relied on by PCI in answering any of the accompanying interrogatories or in responding to any of the accompanying requests for admission.

RESPONSE:

[*Attorney for Plaintiff*]

EXHIBIT 1

INSTRUCTIONS AND DEFINITIONS

Instructions

1. All documents within your possession, custody, or control or that of your agents, employees, or attorneys shall be produced. Without limitation of the term "control" as used in the preceding sentence, a document is deemed to be in your control if you have the right to secure the document or a copy thereof from another person having actual possession thereof.

2. To the extent any paragraph is objected to, set forth all reasons for your objection.

3. If you prefer, you may provide legible copies of documents that reflect all markings, notations and highlighting on the originals.

4. Documents to be produced shall be either (1) organized as they are kept in the ordinary course of business or (2) organized and labelled to correspond with the paragraphs of the request for production or interrogatory to which they are responsive.

5. The singular includes the plural number and vice versa. The masculine includes the feminine and neuter genders. The past tense includes the present tense where the clear meaning is not distorted by change of tense.

6. To the extent that any document cannot be furnished, such documents as are available shall be supplied, together with a description of the documents not furnished and the reason for not furnishing them.

7. "And" as well as "or" are used either disjunctively or conjunctively as necessary to bring information within the scope of the request that might otherwise be outside the scope of the request.

8. Plaintiff requests that documents be produced as they become ready and that defendant does not wait until all documents are ready to start production.

Definitions

1. The term "document" is used in the broadest sense permitted and includes, by way of illustration only and not by way of limitation, the following, whether printed or reproduced by any process, or written or produced by hand: ledgers; notes; correspondence; communications of any nature; telegrams; memoranda; notebooks of any character; summaries or records of personal conversations; diaries; reports; publications; photographs; microfilm, microfiche and similar media; minutes and records of meetings; transcripts of oral testimony and statements; reports and summaries of interviews; reports and summaries of investigations; court papers; brochures; pamphlets; press releases; drafts of, revisions of drafts of and translations of any document; tape recordings; dictation belts; invoices; bills; accounting records; telephone toll records; and disks, tapes and other magnetic or electronic information storage media. Any document or reproduction of a document bearing on any sheet or side thereof any marks, including by way of illustration only and not by way of limitation initials, stamped indicia or any comment or any notation of any character and not a part of the original text, is to be considered a separate document. Where it is uncertain whether something is a document, this definition shall be construed to include it.

2. References to "you" or any named entity or individual include agents, employees and attorneys of that person, whether or not acting within the scope of their authority; all other persons acting on behalf of the person referred to; and in the case of an entity its merged or acquired predecessors.

3. "Person" includes any individual, corporation, partnership, joint venture, firm, association, proprietorship, governmental agency, board, authority, commission and other entity.

4. "Communication" includes every manner or means of disclosure, transfer or exchange of information, whether orally or by document or whether face-to-face, by telephone, mail, personal delivery or otherwise.

5. "Relates," "refers," and "reflects" include constitutes, describes, contains, discusses, reflects, refers to, and logically pertains to.

6. "Identify" or "identification," when used with respect to a document, means to state the general nature of the document (*i.e.,* letter, memorandum, etc.); the name of the author or originator; each addressee; all individuals designated on the document to receive a copy or otherwise known to have received a copy; the date, title and general subject matter of the document; the present custodian of each copy thereof and the last known address of each such custodian; and the date of the making of the document.

7. "Identify" or "identification," when used with respect to a communication, means to state the date of the communication; the type of communication (*i.e.,* telephone conversation, meeting, etc.); the place where the communication took place; the identification of the person who made the communication; the identification of each person who received the communication and of each person present when it was made; and the subject matter discussed.

8. "Identify" or "identification," when used with respect to a person, means state the name, last known business and home addresses and telephone numbers, occupation, job titles and Social Security Number of the person being identified.

F.1.2 Request for Production of Documents and Interrogatories in Case Challenging Administrative Offset to Collect Old Student Loans

UNITED STATES DISTRICT COURT
FOR THE EASTERN DISTRICT OF MICHIGAN

[STUDENT ONE],	)
[STUDENT TWO]	)
and	)
[STUDENT THREE],	)
Plaintiffs,	)
	)
v.	)
	)
SECRETARY OF EDUCATION	)
OF THE UNITED STATES, and	)
THE SECRETARY OF THE	)
TREASURY OF THE UNITED	)
STATES,	)
Defendants.	)

PLAINTIFFS' FIRST REQUEST FOR PRODUCTION OF DOCUMENTS

Pursuant to Rule 34 of the Federal Rules of Civil Procedure, Plaintiffs, by and through her undersigned attorneys, request that Defendant Secretary of Education (hereinafter "Department") produce the following documents at the law offices of [Attorneys for Plaintiffs], [Address], at 10:00 a.m. on July 1, 2002, or at a mutually agreeable alternative time and/or place.

I. DEFINITIONS

Unless otherwise stated, the following definitions apply to all of the requests herein:

A. "*Documents*" or "*Documentation*" shall mean any kind of written, recorded or graphic matters, however produced or reproduced, of any kind or description whether sent or received, including originals, non-identical copies and drafts of both sides thereof, and including, but not limited to, papers, books, letters, correspondence, telegrams, bulletins, notices, announcements, instructions, charts, manuals, brochures, schedules, internal memoranda, notes, notations, transcripts, minutes, agendas, reports and recordings of telephonic or other conversations, interviews, conferences or other meetings, affidavits, statements, summaries, opinions, reports, studies, analyses, computer printouts, data processing input/output, microfilms and all other records kept by electronic means, photographic or mechanical means, and other things similar to any of the foregoing.

B. "*Refer*" or "*Relate to*" shall mean to make a statement about, discuss, describe, reflect, constitute, identify, deal with, consist of, establish, comprise, list, evidence, substantiate or in any way pertain, in whole or in part, to the subject.

II. DOCUMENTS AND DOCUMENTATION REQUESTED

1. Any documents that were consulted or otherwise used to determine the answers set forth in response to Interrogatories Nos. 1, 2, 3, 4, 5 and 8.
2. For each student loan that the Department seeks to enforce in its counterclaim, all documents that relate to assignment of the loan and when such assignments were made.
3. For each student loan under the guaranty programs authorized under Title IV of the Higher Education Act of 1965 that the Department seeks to enforce in its counterclaims, all documents showing that reinsurance or insurance claims were paid with respect to the loans and when such claims were paid.
4. For each student loan that the Department seeks to enforce in its counterclaim, all documents that relate to demands for payment of the loans.
5. For each student loan that the Department seeks to enforce in its counterclaims, all documents that relate to voluntary and involuntary payments made on the loans.
6. All documents that relate to correspondence or communications between the Department and plaintiffs or plaintiffs' representatives. (Correspondence includes any notices of offset).
7. All documents that relate to correspondence or communications between the Department and the Department of Treasury that relate to student loans that the Department seeks to enforce in its counterclaims.
8. All documents that relate to communications with Plaintiff [Student One] concerning a hardship waiver and any documents that relate to consideration of such a waiver.
9. All documents setting out the procedures or policies used by the Department or any agent of the Department in deciding whether to grant hardship waivers.
10. All documents that relate to communications with Plaintiff [Student Two] or his representatives concerning a disability discharge and any documents concerning consideration of such a discharge.
11. All documents setting out the procedures or policies used by the Department or any agent of the Department in processing applications for disability discharge.
12. All reports discussing the reliability and validity of loan information entered into the Debt Management Collection System and the National Direct Student Loan Database System.
13. All documents setting forth the procedures for entering and verifying the accuracy of information on individual student loans in the Debt Management Collection System and the National Direct Student Loan Database System.

Respectfully submitted,

[Attorneys for Plaintiffs]

UNITED STATES DISTRICT COURT
FOR THE EASTERN DISTRICT OF MICHIGAN

```
——————————————————  )
                    )
[STUDENT ONE],      )
[STUDENT TWO]       )
   and              )
[STUDENT THREE],    )
        Plaintiffs, )
                    )
v.                  )
                    )
SECRETARY OF EDUCATION  )
OF THE UNITED STATES, and )
THE SECRETARY OF THE    )
TREASURY OF THE UNITED  )
STATES,                 )
        Defendants.     )
——————————————————  )
```

PLAINTIFFS' FIRST SET OF INTERROGATORIES TO DEFENDANT SECRETARY OF EDUCATION

Pursuant to Federal Rules of Civil Procedure, Rule 33, Plaintiffs request that Defendant Secretary of Education ("Department") answer, in writing and under oath, the following interrogatories within thirty (30) days.

1. For each student loan that the Department seeks to enforce in its counterclaim, state the date and amount of any disbursement of loan proceeds, the lender and guaranty agency, the period of attendance, the first payment due date, the date of default, the current holder and balance outstanding.

2. For each student loan that the Department seeks to enforce in its counterclaim, state the dates and amounts of all payments on the loan and the manner in which the payments were collected.

3. Describe the basis for the calculation of the amounts owed set forth in paragraphs 11, 15 and 19 of the Department's counterclaim.

4. For each student loan that the Department seeks to enforce in its counterclaim that have been assigned, state the date(s) that the loan was assigned and the identity of the assignee.

5. For each student loan that the Department seeks to enforce in its counterclaim that was reinsured by the Secretary of Education, state the date the Department paid a reinsurance claim and the amount of reinsurance paid.

6. Identify the government agency, subdivision, contractor or other entity that is responsible for making decisions on waivers of offset based on hardship.

7. Describe any criteria that are used in deciding whether to grant waivers of offset based on hardship.

8. State whether the Department or its agents notified Plaintiff [Student One] or her representatives that she could request a hardship waiver and, if so, state the dates and form of notification, and identify the person or persons who made these communications.

9. Identity all individuals from which Department intends to present testimony to establish the admissibility of documents supporting the Department's counterclaim.

10. Identify the individuals who were consulted in the prepa-

ration of the answers to these interrogatories (other than counsel who have entered an appearance for defendants in this case) and specify the particular areas of their knowledge.

Respectfully submitted,

[Attorneys for Plaintiffs]

F.2 Discovery Directed to Trade Schools

F.2.1 First Interrogatories and Requests for Production of Documents from a School

COURT OF COMMON PLEAS PHILADELPHIA COUNTY

```
——————————————————  )
                    )
PAULA WILLIAMS      )
                    )
v.                  )
                    )
NATIONAL SCHOOL OF  )
HEALTH TECHNOLOGY, INC.  )
——————————————————  )
```

PLAINTIFF'S FIRST SET OF INTERROGATORIES AND REQUESTS FOR PRODUCTION DIRECTED TO DEFENDANT

Pursuant to Rules 4005, 4006 and 4009, Pa. Rules of Civil Procedure, defendant demands response within thirty (30) days to the following interrogatories and requests for production of documents:

DEFINITIONS

a. "Defendant" or "the school" shall refer to National School of Health Technology, its agents, officers, or employees.

b. "Plaintiff" shall refer to Paula Williams.

c. "Document" is used in the broadest possible sense permissible under the rules of civil procedure. Such term shall refer to any mechanism of preserving or transmitting any information, whether it be written, printed, photographed, electronically recorded, or otherwise made and maintained. It shall include all tangible items of any nature, both originals and copies, and all attachments and appendices thereto, and all drafts thereof, including but not limited to, agreements, contracts, communications, correspondence, letters, telegrams, faxes, memoranda, records, reports, books, summaries or other records of meetings and conferences, summaries or other records of negotiations, diaries, calendars, statistical data or statements, work papers, charts, accounts, brochures, circulars, press releases, marginal notations, bills, invoices, journals, lists, files and file jackets, printouts, compilations, minutes, checks, envelopes or folders or similar containers, vouchers, transcripts, articles, tape or disc recordings, photographs and including any information contained in a computer, although not yet printed out, within the possession, custody or control of defendant.

d. "Trial" includes arbitration hearings.

e. "State board" means the Pennsylvania Board of Private Licensed Schools.

f. "And" as well as "or" shall be construed either disjunctively or conjunctively as necessary to bring within the scope of the following interrogatories and requests information and documents that might otherwise be construed to be outside their scope; and as used herein the singular shall include the plural and the plural shall include the singular except as the context may otherwise dictate.

INTERROGATORIES

1. State the date of defendant's incorporation, the state(s) in which it is incorporated and the name of the incorporators.

Answer:

2. State the number of outstanding shares of stock and identify the owners of said stock, including the numbers of shares owned by each person.

Answer:

3. Identify by name, home address and occupation all members of defendant's board of directors on a) January 1, 1985, b) January 1, 1987, c) January 1, 1989 and d) January 1, 1991.

Answer:

4. Identify by name, home address and occupation the officers of defendant corporation as of a) January 1, 1985, b) January 1, 1987, c) January 1, 1989 and d) January 1, 1991.

Answer:

5. Identify by name and home address all individuals who have served as the chief administrator of the school between January 1, 1985 and the present, stating for each the time period during which they served and their salaries during that period.

Answer:

6. a. Is defendant the subsidiary of any other corporation?

    b. Does defendant own any subsidiaries?

    c. If the answer to either a. or b. is affirmative, identify and explain.

Answer:

7. Has defendant undergone any ownership changes since 1980? If so, explain such changes and identify the dates and the parties involved.

Answer:

8a. When did the school at 801 Arch Street open its doors?

b. When did the (i) Nurse's Aide and (ii) Medical Assistant programs begin?

c. Is the school at 801 Arch Street a branch of some other school? If so, identify the branching institution.

d. Describe the relationship, if any, between the school at 801 Arch Street and school of the same name in Northeast Philadelphia.

Answer:

9. Identify all institutional accreditations and all program accreditations pertaining to the Nurse's Aide or Medical Assistant programs which defendant has received since 1980, including the commencement and expiration dates and the accrediting agency.

Answer:

10. Have any past or present employees, directors or officers of defendant served on or been associated with an accreditation commission or agency? If so, identify the person, his/her relationship to defendant, the accrediting institution, position held at the accrediting institution and relevant dates.

Answer:

11. List the fee schedules for a) the Nurse's Aide and b) the Medical Assistant programs for each year since 1985, including all components of that schedule, and for each component explain what it is and, where applicable, the reason for increases.

Answer:

12. List the names, home addresses and positions of all employees or representatives of defendant who, during the time period 1988 to the present worked in the marketing, admissions or financial aid component of defendant's organization, and for each specify the particular job responsibilities held and, as to each position held, the time period applicable and the name and position of the individual's immediate supervisor. In addition, identify which, if any, individuals are still associated with defendant.

Answer:

13. State the names, home addresses, and positions of all officials or employees of defendant which had any policy-making responsibility concerning the standards and procedures employed by admissions personnel at the school during the time period 1988 to the present, and as to each, state what, if any, other positions the individual has had in defendant's organization and the relevant dates of such positions.

Answer:

14. State the names and home addresses of all individuals who made decisions or who participated in making decisions during the time period 1988 to the present to admit prospective students under the school's "ability-to-benefit" standards.

Answer:

15. List all academic instructors who taught courses in either the Nurse's Aide or Medical Assistant program during the years 1988 to the present and for each specify:

    a. The courses taught and the applicable time period;

    b. The individual's degrees, certifications and prior teaching experience;

    c. His/her last known address and telephone number.

Answer:

16. State the names, and, if not previously listed, their last known addresses and phone numbers, of all individuals who participated in the development of the curriculum of either the Nurse's Aide or Medical Assistant program and, in addition, as to each of them:

    a. List their academic and professional credentials;

    b. Describe the nature of the participation; and

    c. Specify all positions, with applicable dates, that they have held in defendant's organization.

Answer:

17. Regarding defendant's pleading that "admissions representatives . . . disclose to applicants the range of hourly rates earned by past graduates based upon the school's placement data," *Answer* ¶ 6(a),

    a. Specify the range of rates which were disclosed to applicants in the Nurse's Aide and Medical Assistant programs during the period 1988 to the present and

    b. Identify the data and the source of such data upon which the said disclosures were based.

Answer:

18. Identify the name and position of all representatives of defendant who interviewed plaintiff prior to her first day of class and specify the dates and purposes of such interviews.

Answer:

19a. Describe defendant's policy(ies) in effect during the years 1987-89 regarding the payment of commissions to sales representatives, financial aid employees or students?

b. Was any individual paid a commission as a result of plaintiff's enrollment, financial aid award or attendance? If so, identify the person by name and relationship to defendant and explain the terms and amount of such commission.

c. What documents were examined for purpose of answering "b?".

Answer:

20a. State the dates in which plaintiff actually attended classes at the school.

b. State the date plaintiff was terminated from the school.

c. If the date of termination is different from the last date of attendance, explain how defendant determined the date of termination.

Answer:

21a. State the amount defendant refunded to plaintiff.

b. State the date paid and the method of payment.

c. Explain how the amount refunded was calculated.

Answer:

22a. Specify the amounts of all financial aid which defendant received on plaintiff's behalf, including the specific aid program under which funds were received, the payor of such funds and the date received.

b. Specify the amounts of all financial aid funds received on plaintiff's behalf which defendant refunded to a lender, guarantee agency, or the United States government and as to each refund specify the program, the payee and the date payment was sent.

Answer:

23. State the names, positions and, if not previously stated, the home addresses of all individuals who were responsible to assist prospective or enrolled students in obtaining information concerning the matters covered in document request # 17, *infra*, with the relevant dates.

Answer:

24. For years ending December 31, 1986, 1988 and 1990, identify by name and itemized dollar figures the four highest paid employees or officers of defendant, including salary, fees, commissions or any other form of direct compensation and also including any payments for expenses such as automobiles or travel.

Answer:

DOCUMENT REQUESTS

1. Organizational charts for defendant's organization which exhibit the chain of authority and responsibility.

2. Any and all advertisements, mailings and marketing literature employed by defendant during the period 1988 to the present which was targeted either to prospective students or to prospective employees, including the scripts of all television commercials broadcast during said period.

3. All internal memoranda, training manuals, scripts, documents or writings of any kind which pertain to the standards, procedures or marketing tips or strategies employed by the school's admissions personnel or which instruct, advise, set policy, train or otherwise advise, educate or set guidelines for agents, representatives, officers or employees of defendant, which were in use or which applied to the time period 1987 to the present.

4. All documents involved in, referring to or relating to studies or surveys pertaining to or used in connection with defendant's recruitment of new students.

5. Any and all admissions tests administered by defendant for admission into its Nurse's Aide and Medical Assistant programs during the time period 1988 to the present, and as to each:

a. Identify the source for the test and

b. Produce copies of all applicable written criteria or correspondence from the school's accrediting commission pertaining to the school's use of the particular test.

6. The entire contents of plaintiff's admission file, including file jacket and all documents, notes, and other writings contained therein, including, but not limited to, admissions tests, enrollment agreements, "How Our Students Are Doing" disclosures, interview notes, financial aid inquiries and internal memoranda concerning the plaintiff's application or admission and defendant's decision to admit her.

7. The entire contents of plaintiff's academic and disciplinary files including the file jacket and all documents, notes, and other writings contained therein, including, but not limited to, transcripts, evaluations, internal memoranda, letters and notes of conversations.

8. Any and all account cards, ledger sheets or other documents showing debits, credits, and/or a running balance, pertaining to charges, payments, refunds and other financial transactions involving plaintiff.

9. Any and all documents, not covered by another section of this request, that are signed by plaintiff or that relate to the transaction in question.

10a. Course outlines and reading lists for any remedial courses offered by defendant for "ability to benefit" students during the period 1988 to the present.

b. Names and addresses of all individuals who taught such courses and relevant time periods that they did so.

11. Any and all applications and supporting documents sent to a third-party accrediting agency or commission and all accrediting documents received regarding the defendant's school in general or regarding in particular the Nurse's Aide or Medical Assistant programs.

12. The raw data, regardless of the form in which it is kept, from which defendant reported to the state board its Nurse's Aide or Medical Assistant enrollments, completions, withdrawals and the employment of graduates for years ending June 30, 1987 to the present.

13. Any and all application forms and all supporting documents submitted by defendant to the United States Department of Education and all eligibility notifications received by defendant concerning a) the school's status as an "eligible institution" to participate in federal financial aid program, and b) the school's designation as a participant in individual programs administered by the Department of Education.

14. All applications and supporting documents submitted by defendant to the state board pertaining to the licensing of its Nurse's Aide and Medical Assistant programs and all documents received from the state board pertaining to same.

15. All site visit and monitoring reports concerning any aspect of defendant's operation which was performed by the state board,

by an accrediting institution or by the United States Department of Education since 1985.

16. All written policies and all documents pertaining to such policies in effect during the period 1988 to the present regarding the school's definition of satisfactory academic progress and regarding student appeal rights concerning determinations of unsatisfactory progress and for each identify a) all persons (and their positions) who were responsible for developing these policies and b) their effective dates.

17. All written policies and all documents pertaining to such policies in effect at the school during the time period 1988 to the present regarding student refunds and regarding the application of such refunds to appropriate financial aid accounts.

18. All written materials which defendant disseminated to prospective and enrolled students in the Nurse's Aide or Medical Assistant program during the period 1988 to the present regarding a) financial aid eligibility criteria and the criteria and methods employed for making award determinations, b) itemized course costs, c) the refund policy, d) standards for progress, attendance and other student regulations, e) the academic content of and faculty for each program, f) the extent, nature and success rate of the placement service, g) the pass rates of former students, h) the rate of employment by former students, i) completion rates by former students and j) information regarding starting salaries and job availability in relevant fields.

19. For each document produced in response to request #18, identify a) the source for the document, b) the source of all data which would be contained in a form designed to be filled out, d) all individuals who participated in preparing the document and their positions, e) the time period during which it was used and f) all individuals who would have provided any data contained in a completed form.

20. All documents from which the data referred to in interrogatory #17, *supra*, were obtained.

21. Defendant's annual, audited financial reports for years ending December 31, 1986-1990.

22. Any and all professional articles written by present or past employees or officers of defendant.

23. All documents referring or relating to defendant's document retention policy.

24. All court pleadings pertaining to litigation between defendant and a former student or former employee which were filed on behalf of the former student or employee.

25. Any and all documents defendant intends to introduce at trial.

[Attorney for Plaintiff]

F.2.2 Additional Interrogatories and Request for Production of Documents from a School

UNITED STATES DISTRICT COURT
EASTERN DISTRICT OF PENNSYLVANIA

PAULA WILLIAMS, on behalf of herself and of others similarly situated,	))))
Plaintiffs,	))
v.	)))
NATIONAL SCHOOL OF HEALTH TECHNOLOGY, INC., UNITED STUDENT AID FUNDS and MERITOR SAVINGS BANK/PSFS, on behalf of themselves and of others similarly situated, and LAMAR ALEXANDER, SECRETARY OF THE UNITED STATES DEPARTMENT OF EDUCATION,	)))))))))))))
Defendants	))

PLAINTIFF'S FIRST SET OF INTERROGATORIES AND REQUESTS FOR PRODUCTION TO DEFENDANTS FRANCE AND ROBERTS

Plaintiff Sarah Williams, by her undersigned counsel, propounds the following Interrogatories and Requests for Production of Documents to defendants Diane France and Elizabeth Roberts pursuant to Fed.R.Civ.P. 26, 33 and 34. Each Interrogatory must be answered separately and full in writing under oath, and the answers must be signed by the person making them. A copy of defendants' answers, together with any objections, must be served upon plaintiffs no later than thirty (30) days after the service of these Interrogatories and Document Requests. Defendants are requested to produce for inspection and copying, within thirty (30) days from the date of service hereof, at the offices of below-signed counsel, any and all documents described in the Document Requests below.

INSTRUCTIONS

1. In answering, defendants are requested to identify separately and in a manner suitable for use in a subpoena all sources of information (whether human, documentary or other) and all records maintained by them, by National School of Health Technology or any by any other person, entity or organization on which defendants rely in answering the Interrogatories or which pertain or relate to the information called for by the Interrogatories.

2. The Interrogatories and Document Requests are to be considered continuing, and supplemental answers and documents must be filed by defendants upon discovering or becoming aware of additional responsive documents or of information rendering prior answers or any part thereof inaccurate, incomplete or untrue.

3. If any information called for by any Interrogatory is not available in the full detail requested, such Interrogatory shall be deemed to require the setting forth of the information related to the subject matter of the request in such detailed manner as is available.

4. If defendants withhold any requested information or identification and production of any document on the basis of privilege, please so state, and for each such document provide:

(a) The nature of the privilege(s) claimed;

(b) The type of document;

(c) The general subject matter of the document;

(d) The date of the document; and

(e) Such other information as is sufficient to identify the document for a subpoena duces tecum including, where appropriate, the author of the document, the addressee of the document, any other recipients of the document and, where not apparent, the relationship of the author addressee and any recipients to one another.

5. If any requested document has been misplaced, destroyed or discarded, or otherwise disposed of, please so state, and for each such document provide:

(a) Its date;

(b) The identity of the person(s) who prepared the document;

(c) The identity of all persons who participated in preparing the document, to whom the document was sent or who have otherwise seen the document;

(d) The length of the document;

(e) The subject matter of the document;

(f) If misplaced, the last time and place it was seen and a description of efforts made to locate the document;

(g) If disposed of, the date of and reason for disposal, the identity of the person(s) who authorized disposal and the identity of the person who disposed of the document.

6. If defendants are currently without information necessary to respond to any Interrogatory or Document Request, such Interrogatory or Document Request shall be deemed to require a reasonable investigation and any response thereto shall set forth the facts surrounding such investigation, including the identity of other individuals with knowledge.

7. Unless otherwise noted, the time period for the Interrogatories is 1987 through the present.

DEFINITIONS

1. The terms "you" or "your" shall include Diane Holland, Ilse Lobel and all individuals who were employees, officers or agents of National School of Health and Technology. Reference to "the school" means National School of Health and Technology.

2. The term "document" is used in the broadest possible sense and means, without limitation, any written, printed, typed, photostated, photographic, computerized, recorded or otherwise reproduced communication or representation, whether comprised of letters, words, numbers, pictures, sounds or symbols, or any combination thereof. This definition includes copies or duplicates of documents contemporaneously or subsequently created that have any non-nonconforming notes or other markings. Without limiting the generality of the foregoing, the term "document" includes, but is not limited to, correspondence, memoranda, notes, records, letters, envelopes, file folders, telegrams, messages, studies, reports, analyses, contracts, agreements, forms, working papers, summaries, statistical statements, financial statements or work papers, accounts, analytical records, trade letters, press releases, comparisons, books, calendars, diaries, logs, articles, magazines, newspapers, booklets, brochures, pamphlets, circulars, bulletins, notices, drawing, diagrams, instructions, notes or minutes of meetings, reports and/or summaries of investigations, or other communications of any type, including inter and intra-office communications, questionnaires, surveys, charts, graphs, recordings, films, tapes, computer and word processor disks, data cells, drums, print-outs, all other data compilations from which information can be obtained (translated, if necessary, into usable forms), and any preliminary versions, drafts or revisions of any of the foregoing.

3. The term "identify" when used in connection with a natural person means to state his or her:

(a) Full name and any aliases;

(b) Last known address and phone number;

(c) Last known business address and phone number;

(d) Employment, title, and job description during the time of their employment at the school; and

(e) Present employment and job description.

4. The term "identify" or "identity" when used in connection with a "document" or "documents" means to state the following:

(a) Its date;

(b) The identity of its author;

(c) The identity of its sender;

(d) The identity of the person to whom it was addressed;

(e) The identity of the recipient;

(f) Its format;

(g) Its title;

(h) The number of pages or other measure of length or size; and

(i) The identity of each person known or believed to have possession, custody, control of or access to any copy of the document having writings, notations, corrections or markings unique to such copy.

5. The phrase "identify the factual basis" for a denial or an Interrogatory answer means to state:

(a) Each and every fact which you believe supports the denial or Interrogatory answer;

(b) The identity of each and every person having knowledge of facts which you believe supports the denial or Interrogatory answer, along with a summary of such facts which that person knows; and

(c) The identity of each and every document which you believe supports the denial or Interrogatory answer.

INTERROGATORIES

1. Do you contend that plaintiff Williams had the "ability to benefit" from the school's Medical Assistant course, within the meaning of federal financial aid regulations? If the answer is "yes," identify the factual basis for this contention.

2. Identify all former students of the school who were admitted without a high school or equivalency diploma and on whose behalf the school obtained any federal grants or loans and, for each, also provide the following information:

a. The date of the enrollment agreement;

b. The course of study;

c. Whether or not the student completed the course;

d. The relevant dates the student withdrew or graduated;

e. All grants obtained (not counting refunds);

f. All grant refunds made to the Government;

g. All loan proceeds obtained (not counting refunds);

h. All loan refunds made to a lender or guarantee agency; and

i. If the student was placed in a job related to the course of study, identify the employer and the starting salary paid.

3. As to the individuals identified in response to Interrogatory #1, do you contend that these individuals had "the ability to benefit" from the course you enrolled them in? If the answer is "yes," identify the factual basis for this contention.

4. Identify all "ability to benefit" tests which the school administered to admissions applicants who lacked a high school or GED diploma from 1986 until the closing. As to each test, also provide the following information, and, if different tests or scores were used for different courses of study, provide all relevant information for each:

a. The dates during which the test was used;

b. The author of the test (if purchased from a third party, the name of the entity that produced the test);

c. The cutoff scores used to determine whether an applicant was qualified for admission;

d. How such cutoff scores were established, including a description of the methodology and identification of those individuals or entities who participated in making the decision to set a particular cutoff;

e. The name, address and telephone number of every person who was authorized to administer the test, including the relevant time period for each.

5. Did the school ever study or analyze the relationship between performance on an admission test or "ability to benefit test," on the one hand, and academic success and job placement, on the other? If the answer is "yes," describe the method used to study or analyze the relationship, as well as the system employed for maintaining data on this relationship, and identify all documents which pertain to such studies, analyses and data.

6. Identify all individuals who administered "ability to benefit" tests and the relevant time periods for each.

7. For the years ending December 31, 1986, 1988 and 1990, identify the four highest paid employees or officers of the school, and for each itemize the relevant figures for salary, fees, commissions and other form of compensation, including payments for automobiles or other expenses.

8. For the years 1986-92 identify all payments made by the school to Ilse Lobel, including for each year a description of the factual basis for such payments.

9. For the years 1986-92 identify all automobiles owned or leased by the school including for each:

a. The year, make and model;

b. The date of acquisition;

c. The identity of the person who primarily used the vehicle;

d. The purchase price or monthly lease payment;

e. A description of any customization which was done and the cost of such customization; and

f. A description of the disposition of the vehicle including the date and the reason the school lost possession of the vehicle.

10. During the years 1987-91 did the School arrange loans through guarantee agencies and lenders other than United Student Aid Funds and Meritor Savings Bank? If so, identify the entities and the approximate volume of such dealings.

11. Regarding the averment in defendant Holland's answer to the original complaint (at ¶ 17) that "students were told about the school's placement rate and the range of salaries that recent graduates received,"

a. Describe in detail the system that existed at the school for ensuring that this information was communicated accurately, including, but not limited to, identification of the roles of the various individuals involved, the methods of communication used between school departments and between the school and students, and any procedures used to ensure and monitor the accuracy of the information.

b. Identify what, if any, statistics or other information the school maintained concerning placement and salary levels of graduates, including, but not limited to identification of the roles of the various individuals involved, the methods used to obtain and record this information and the manner of maintaining such records.

c. Identify what, if any statistics or other information the school provided to prospective students and which substantiated the accuracy and truthfulness of such claims, including, but not limited to identification of the roles of the various individuals involved and a description of the form, manner and timing of such disclosures.

REQUESTS FOR PRODUCTION OF DOCUMENTS

1. All documents pertaining to the transfer of ownership and control in the School in December, 1986 from Ilse Lobel to Diane Holland and James Lupfer.

2. The most current resumes or personnel data sheets in your possession for the following individuals:

a. Diane Holland;

b. Ilse Lobel;

c. James Lupfer;

d. William Lorman;

e. Theodore Kaczorowski;

f. Joseph Paprzycki;

f. Phil Sherr;

g. Marge Ross and

h. Kim Wilcox.

3. All "ability to benefit" tests which the school administered to admissions applicants who lacked a high school or GED diploma from 1986 until the closing and all instruction books for each test.

4. All documents pertaining to the selection of particular tests, the procedures used in administering the tests, and the selection by the school of particular cutoff scores used to determine success or failure on the test.

5. All invoices, purchase orders, cancelled checks or other documents pertaining to the purchase of "ability to benefit" tests from vendors or testing companies.

6. All data or records pertaining to the relationship between performance on admission tests and academic/employment success, including, if they exist, summary reports produced by the testing companies.

7. All annual reports to accrediting commissions, including both NATTS and ABHES, for the years 1985-91.

8. All correspondence between the school and its accrediting commissions during the years 1986-1992.

9. Copies of site visit reports, reviews, show-cause orders or audits pertaining to the school, covering the years 1987-91, which were prepared by either an accrediting commission, the State Board of Private Licensed Schools, or the United States Depart-

ment of Education, and copies of any responses thereto.

10. Copies of the accrediting criteria of NATTS and of ABHES, which were applicable to the accreditation of the school and/or to the school's Medical Assistant course.

11. The school's annual, audited financial reports for the years 1986-90.

[Attorney for Plaintiff]

F.3 Discovery in Bankruptcy Proceeding to Determine Dischargeability of Student Loan

UNITED STATES BANKRUPTCY COURT
DISTRICT OF NEW JERSEY, CAMDEN VICINAGE

```
———————————————————  )
                                     )
IN RE: [Debtor]                      )
                          Debtor  )
[Debtor],                            )
                        Plaintiff  )
                                     )
v.                                   )
                                     )
United States Department of          )
Education                            )
                       Defendant  )
———————————————————  )
```

PLAINTIFF'S INTERROGATORIES TO DEFENDANT U.S. DEPARTMENT OF EDUCATION

To: Defendant U.S. Department Of Education

By and through its attorney of record

A. Defendant is hereby required to answer in writing, under oath in accordance with Rule 7033 of the Rules of this court, the interrogatories attached hereto.

B. In answering these interrogatories, furnish all information in the possession of Defendant, its officers, agents and employees and its attorneys and investigators for its attorneys.

C. If Defendant cannot answer the following interrogatories in full after exercising due diligence to secure the information to do so, state the answer to the extent possible specifying your inability to answer the remainder, and state whatever information or knowledge Defendant has concerning the unanswered portion.

D. Each interrogatory is considered continuing, and if Defendant obtains information which renders its answers or one of them, incomplete or inaccurate, Defendant is obligated to serve amended answers on the undersigned.

E. Insofar as may be applicable, and except as otherwise indicated, the term "document" or "documents" shall refer to any and all writings and recorded materials, of any kind whatsoever, that is or has been in the possession, control or custody of Defendant or of which Defendant has knowledge, whether originals or copies, including but not limited to contracts, documents, notes, rough drafts, interoffice memoranda, memoranda for the files, letters, research materials, correspondence, logs, diaries, forms, bank statements, tax returns, card files, books of account, journals, ledgers, invoices, blueprints, diagrams, drawings, computer print-outs or tapes, reports, surveys, statistical computations, studies, pictures, maps, graphs, charts, minutes, manuals, pamphlets, or books of any nature or kind whatsoever; and all other materials handwritten, printed, typed, mimeographed, photocopied or otherwise reproduced; and slides or motion pictures, television tapes; all tape recordings (whether for computer, audio or visual replay) or other written, printed or recorded matter or tangible things on which words, phrases, symbols or information are affixed.

F. A request to "identify" a document is a request to state (insofar as may be applicable):

1. The date of such document.
2. The type of document or written communication it is.
3. The names and present addresses of the person or persons who prepared such document and of the signers, addressors and addressees of such document.
4. The name of any principal whom or which the signers, addressors and preparers of such document were thereby representing.
5. The present location of such document.
6. The name and present address of the person now having custody of the document.
7. Whether you possess or control the original or a copy thereof and if so, the location and name of the custodian of such original or copy.
8. A brief description of the contents of such document.

G. A request to "describe" any oral statement or communication is a request to state:

1. The name and present address of each individual making such statement or communication.
2. The name of any principal or employer whom or which such individual was thereby representing and the position in which such individual was then employed or engaged by such principal or employee.
3. The name and present address of the individual or individuals to whom the oral statement or communication was made, and the name of any principal or employer whom such person or persons were representing at the time of and in connection with such oral statement or communication, as well as the employment position in which they were then employed or engaged.
4. The names and present addresses of any other individuals present when such oral statement or communication was made or who heard or acknowledged hearing the same.
5. The place where such oral statement or communication was made.
6. A brief description of the contents of such oral statement or communication.

H. A request to "cite" portions or provisions of any document is a request to state, insofar as applicable with reference to such portion or provision, the title, date, division, page, sheet, charge order number, and such other information as may be necessary to accurately locate the portion or provision referenced.

I. The term "person" shall include a natural person, partnership, corporation, association, or other group however organized.

J. Whenever a request is made to "identify" a natural person, it shall mean to supply all of the following information:

1. His/her full name.
2. His/her employer and position at the time.

3. The name of any person or entity (natural or artificial) whom she/he is claimed to have represented in connection with the matter to which the interrogatory relates.

4. His/her last known address, telephone number, and employer.

5. His/her present employer.

K. A request to "explain fully" any answer, denial or claim is a request (insofar as may be applicable) to:

1. State fully and specifically each fact and/or contention in support of your answer, denial or claim; and

2. For each such fact or contention, to identify each person who has knowledge relative to that fact or contention, each document that tends to support that fact or contention; and each document that tends to dispute that fact or contention.

L. A request in any of the enclosed interrogatories to "identify" any document is a request to attach said document to answers to these interrogatories. If documents are attached to answers to these interrogatories, they must be marked to identify which interrogatory they refer to. In identifying documents you

(a) how many hours each loan agent spent under such instruction;

(b) whether such instruction was mandatory or voluntary;

(c) the subject matter of the instruction.

INTERROGATORIES

IMPORTANT: All questions containing the terms "document," "documents," "identify," "describe," "cite," "person" or "explain fully" must be answered in accordance with the definitions of those terms contained in the attached instructions.

1. Please identify the person answering each of these interrogatories.

2. Identify each person Defendant may call as a witness in this case.

3. Identify each document which Defendant may introduce into evidence in this case.

4. State the total amount Defendant alleges to be owing as of the date of the filing of this lawsuit.

5. Itemize the total amount Defendant alleges to be owing by unpaid amounts financed, accrued finance charge, and other charges, as applicable.

6. Please identify any and all persons known to Defendant who have personal knowledge concerning the instant loans. Please specify which of these people are agents of Defendant or were agents of Defendant at the time of the instant transaction.

7. State the total amount of dollars in cash that Plaintiff has paid to Defendant. Identify each payment individually and state the date of payment.

8. List separately all persons to whom and charges, fees, or any other amounts were paid in connection with these loans, including the name and address of the payee, the amount disbursed to each, the date of dispersal, and the check number for each dispersal.

9. State whether you received any requests for deferment of loans from Plaintiff. If so, please specify when each request was made.

10. If you identified any requests in interrogatory 9, please provide your response to Plaintiff's requests.

11. State whether you received any requests for forbearance of loans from Plaintiff. If so, please specify when each request was made.

12. If you identified any requests in interrogatory 11, please provide your response to Plaintiff's requests.

13. Identify your procedures for granting of deferment and forbearance of loans at all relevant times.

14. State any policies and/or programs, outside of traditional deferment and forbearance of loans policies, in which plaintiff may have been qualified to participate.

15. If you identified any such policies and/or programs in interrogatory 14, please provide any information relating to Plaintiff's participation.

16. Please state each and every fact which is the basis for your contention in the Second Affirmative Defense of your Answer and Affirmative Defenses that "Debtor has not made a good faith effort to repay the loan and would not qualify for a discharge on the basis of undue hardship," and for each and every fact, please list the name, address, and telephone number of all witnesses with the knowledge relevant to the fact and all documents, giving the document description, date, and custodian, which touches upon or relates to that fact.

17. Please specify all amounts received from Plaintiff, and when such amounts were received, from the total sum identified in your Ninth Affirmative Defense of your Answer and Affirmative Defenses.

18. Please identify all policies relating to deferment and forbearance of loans, utilized by loan guarantors, the [Guaranty Agency].

19. Identify all documents containing information about the instant loans. State which, if any, of the above documents were given to Plaintiff, including where and when each document was given to Plaintiff.

20. Identify each telephone contact made to Plaintiff by Defendant or Defendant's agent regarding the loans. Describe the substance of each such telephone conversation.

21. Identify each document, including each notice, that Defendant mailed or otherwise delivered to Plaintiff concerning the instant loans. For each document, state the address it was mailed to and whether it was received by Plaintiff.

PLEASE TAKE NOTICE that a copy of the answers to the attached interrogatories and the requested documents must be served upon the undersigned within the time allowed by Rule 7033 of the Rules of this Court.

[Attorney for Plaintiff]

F.4 Freedom of Information Act Sample Requests

[Date]

Office of the Inspector General
U. S. Department of Education
400 Maryland Avenue, S.W.
Washington, D.C. 20202-1510

Attn: FOIA Request Officer—Inspector General's Office

Dear Sir or Madam:

This is a request for copies of public records under the Freedom of Information Act, 5 U.S.C. § 552 *et seq.* As you know, this Act requires public bodies to make available for inspection and copying all public records, except certain exempt records, within ten working days of receipt of a written request.

Please provide copies of any and all records, reports, forms, writings, letters, memoranda, books, papers, maps, photographs, microfilms, cards, tapes, recordings, electronic data processing records, recorded information and all other documentary material, regardless of physical form or characteristics, having been prepared or having been or being used, received, possessed or under control of the U.S. Department of Education pertaining to **any and all investigations, inquiries, audits, inspections, findings, administrative actions, or other determinations from** *1985 to the present* **regarding violations of local, state, or federal law, regulations, or guidelines involving** *"ability to benefit" determinations, testing, admissions or the false certification of student eligibility* **for the following school:**

[School]
[Address]

If you determine that any of the information requested is exempt from release, please delete the material which you determine to be exempt and send me copies of the remaining nonexempt material within ten working days. If you do withhold any part of the requested material, please advise me as to which exemption(s) you believe to be applicable.

I am requesting a fee waiver regarding this material. In support of a waiver, I am advising you of the following:

1. The subject of this request concerns the operations or activities of the government, namely, the administration of Title IV by the Department, and in particular the determination of eligibility of institutions which received Title IV funds.

2. The disclosure is likely to contribute to an understanding of the above-mentioned governmental operations and activities both by us and by the indigent clients we represent.

3. The disclosure is likely to contribute to a public understanding of these matters through our work as public interest lawyers for the poor.

4. Neither I nor my office has any commercial interest which would be furthered by disclosure. On the contrary, we are salaried employees of a government-funded program which provides free legal assistance to the poor.

5. The information we obtain will be disseminated and shared with other members of the public. We continue to provide information to other legal aid and community service agencies, as well as to the general media, on problem schools participating in Title IV financial aid programs. We expect to make some of the materials obtained available through the National Center on Poverty Law, publishers of the Clearinghouse Review, which makes such documents available at no charge to subscribing legal services agencies around the country, as well as to other individuals and organizations, in both paper and computer-readable forms.

If you have any questions concerning this request, I may be reached at (312) 347-8307.

Sincerely,

[Attorney for Plaintiff]

[Date]

Freedom of Information Act Officer

U.S. Department of Education
Washington, D.C. 20002

Re: *Freedom of Information Act Request*
School Name: [School]
OPE-ID: [Number]

Dear Sir or Madam:

This is a request pursuant to the Freedom of Information Act, 5 U.S.C. §552 ("FOIA"). I would like to receive a copy of the following documents (including any original, reproduction or copy of any kind, whether recorded, drafted, printed, written or documentary matters, including without limitation, correspondence, memoranda, reports, records, studies, computer tapes or other computer storage mediums, compilations, and/or summaries of data and other information) and any other written or printed material evidencing, relating to, or commenting upon the following matters at Tri-State Beauty College, referred to hereinafter as the "College," from January 1, 1985 through the present:

1. Pre-admission testing of students who did not have a high school diploma or GED, including efforts to comply with ability-to-benefit requirements promulgated by DOE;

2. Assessments and decisions made regarding students' ability to benefit ("ATB") from the courses and programs offered by the College;

3. Complaints made by any person or organization to DOE, other organization, or the College itself regarding any aspect of the College's admission's process;

4. All inspections, audits, assessments, evaluations, and findings made by any person or organization as to any aspect of the College operations;

5. All litigation or administrative proceedings brought by or against the College;

6. All information regarding College closure dates established by DOE for each branch of the College, including all materials that relate to how each such date was determined;

7. As to student loan closed school discharge applications filed with DOE, the number:
   a) granted
   b) denied
   c) pending

8. As to student loan ability to benefit false certification discharge applications filed with DOE, the number:
   a) granted
   b) denied
   c) pending

9. Default rates of former students and any default reduction plans, programs, and agreements;

10. All applications and documentation submitted by any former student of the College receiving a discharge of a student loan based on false ATB certification by the College; and

11. Any and all "Emergency Action" memoranda relating to the College.

To the extent that you determine that the release of certain requested documents or records would constitute a clearly unwarranted invasion of the personal privacy of third parties, I ask that you proceed according to 5 U.S.C. §552(b). For each such document or record, please delete or redact the names, addresses, and SSNs of applicants, loan recipients, students and other persons before producing it so as to remove any risk of invading someone's privacy. *See, Norwood v. Federal Aviation Administration*, 993 F.2d 570, 574-576 (Sixth Cir. 1993) (requiring disclosure after names, SSNs, and other information which, by itself, would identify an individual, had been redacted.)

I request a waiver of fees in connection with this request. Disclosure of these records is in the public interest because it will contribute significantly to public understanding of the activities of this proprietary voc-ed College which received federal monies and federally guaranteed loan monies. I will receive no business, commercial, or financial benefit from this request. Release of this information will serve the public interest because it pertains to the operations of the College and the possible discharge of certain student loans. Disclosure of this information also will benefit a large segment of the population, namely those persons in Ohio who attended the College and who have applied or may apply in the future for discharge of their student loans.

The Legal Aid Society of Greater Cincinnati is a federally funded legal services office. As such, it is a non-profit organization that exists to represent low income people both locally and, when appropriate, state-wide in matters such as federally supported education programs. By law, this office represents only clients who cannot afford to pay for legal assistance; they also cannot afford the cost associated with this request. I intend to use the requested information to assist clients.

I look forward to your response within the time frame described in the FOIA. Please contact me at the above number if you have any questions. Thank you for your assistance.

Yours truly,

[Attorney for Plaintiff]

Appendix G   Directory of Guaranty Agencies

Alabama
Kentucky Higher Education Assistance
Authority 1050 U.S. 127 South
Frankfort, KY 40601-4323
(502) 696-7200
(800) 928-8926
FAX: (502) 696-7496
E-Mail: *webmaster@kheaa.com*
URL: *http://www.kheaa.com/*

Alaska
No Entry

Arizona
USA Funds
P.O. Box 6028
Indianapolis, IN 46206-6028
(317) 849-6510
(888) 272-5543
TTY: (800) 331-2357
FAX: (317) 806-1203
E-Mail: *contact@usafunds.org*
URL: *http://www.usafunds.org/*

Arkansas
Student Loan Guarantee Foundation of
Arkansas
219 South Victory
Little Rock, AR 72201-1884
(501) 372-1491
(800) 622-3446
FAX: (501) 688-7675
E-Mail: *glangford@slgfa.org*
URL: *http://www.slgfa.org/*

California
California Student Aid Commission
P. O. Box 419026
Rancho Cordova, CA 95741-9026
(916) 526-8999
(888) 224-7268
E-Mail: *custsvcs@csac.ca.gov*
URL: *http://www.csac.ca.gov/*

Colorado
Colorado Student Loan Program
Suite 425
999 18th Street
Denver, CO 80202-2471
(303) 305-3000
(800) 727-9834
TTY: (800) 727-5343
FAX: (303) 294-5076
E-Mail: *cbergquist@cslp.org*
URL: *http://www.cslp.org/*

Connecticut
Connecticut Student Loan Foundation
525 Brook Street
Rocky Hill, CT 06067
(860) 257-4001
(800) 237-9721
FAX: (860) 257-1743
E-Mail: *mvalent@mail.cslf.org*
URL: *http://www.cslf.com/*

Delaware
American Education Services/PHEAA
1200 North Seventh Street
Harrisburg, PA 17102-1444
(717) 720-2800
(877) 603-3010
TTY: (800) 654-5988
FAX: (717) 720-3903
E-Mail: *info@aessuccess.org* or
kwoollam@aessuccess.org
URL: *http://www.aessuccess.org/*

District of Columbia
American Student Assistance
330 Stuart Street
Boston, MA 02116-5292
(617) 426-9434
(800) 999-9080
TTY: (800) 999-0923
FAX: (617) 521-6249
E-Mail: *webmaster@amsa.com*
URL: *http://www.amsa.com/*

Florida
Bureau of Student Financial Assistance
(Florida)
Department of Education
Suite 70
1940 North Monroe Street
Tallahassee, FL 32303-4759
(850) 410-5200
(800) 366-3475
FAX: (850) 488-3612
URL: *http://www.firn.edu/*

Georgia
Georgia Higher Education Assistance
Corporation Suite 220
2082 East Exchange Place
Tucker, GA 30084
(770) 724-9130
(800) 776-6878
FAX: (770) 724-9131
E-Mail: *gheacweb@mail.gsfc.state.ga.us*
URL: *http://www.gsfc.org/main.cfm*

Hawaii
USA Funds
P.O. Box 6028
Indianapolis, IN 46206-6028
(317) 849-6510
(888) 272-5543
TTY: (800) 331-2357
FAX: (317) 806-1203
E-Mail: *contact@usafunds.org*
URL: *http://www.usafunds.org/*

Idaho
Northwest Education Loan Association
Suite 300
190 Queen Anne North
Seattle, WA 98109
(206) 461-5300
(800) 562-3001
FAX: (206) 461-5449
E-Mail: *cheryll@nela.net*
URL: *http://www.nela.net/*

Illinois
Illinois Student Assistance Commission
1755 Lake Cook Road
Deerfield, IL 60015-5209
(847) 948-8500
(800) 899-4722
FAX: (847) 831-8549
E-Mail: *cssupport@isac.org* or
hrtech@isac.org
URL: *http://www.isac-online.org/*

Indiana
USA Funds
P.O. Box 6028
Indianapolis, IN 46206-6028
(317) 849-6510
(888) 272-5543
TTY: (800) 331-2357
FAX: (317) 806-1203
E-Mail: *contact@usafunds.org*
URL: *http://www.usafunds.org/*

Iowa
Iowa College Student Aid Commission
Fourth Floor
200 10th Street
Des Moines, IA 50309-3609
(515) 281-3501
(800) 383-4222
FAX: (515) 242-3389
E-Mail: *icsac@max.state.ia.us*
URL: *http://www.state.ia.us/collegeaid/*

Kansas
USA Funds
P.O. Box 6028
Indianapolis, IN 46206-6028
(317) 849-6510
(888) 272-5543
TTY: (800) 331-2357
FAX: (317) 806-1203
E-Mail: *contact@usafunds.org*
URL: *http://www.usafunds.org/*

Kentucky
Kentucky Higher Education Assistance
Authority
1050 U.S. 127 South
Frankfort, KY 40601-4323
(502) 696-7200
(800) 928-8926
FAX: (502) 696-7496
E-Mail: *webmaster@kheaa.com*
URL: *http://www.kheaa.com/*

Louisiana
Louisiana Office of Student Financial
Assistance
P.O. Box 91202
Baton Rouge, LA 70821-9202
(225) 922-1012
(800) 259-5626

FAX: (225) 922-0790
E-Mail: *gwales@osfa.state.la.us*
URL: *http://www.osfa.state.la.us/*

Maine
Maine Education Assistance Division
Finance Authority of Maine
5 Community Drive
P.O. Box 949
Augusta, ME 04332-0949
(207) 623-3263
(800) 228-3734
TTY: (207) 626-2717
FAX: (207) 623-0095
E-Mail: *info@famemaine.com*
URL: *http://www.famemaine.com/*

Maryland
USA Funds
P.O. Box 6028
Indianapolis, IN 46206-6028
(317) 849-6510
(888) 272-5543
TTY: (800) 331-2357
FAX: (317) 806-1203
E-Mail: *contact@usafunds.org*
URL: *http://www.usafunds.org/*

Massachusetts
American Student Assistance
330 Stuart Street
Boston, MA 02116-5292
(617) 426-9434
(800) 999-9080
TTY: (800) 999-0923
FAX: (617) 521-6249
E-Mail: *webmaster@amsa.com*
URL: *http://www.amsa.com/*

Michigan
Michigan Higher Education Assistance
Authority
Office of Michigan Guaranty Agency
P. O. Box 30047
Lansing, MI 48909-7547
(517) 373-0760
(800) 642-5626
FAX: (517) 335-6703
E-Mail: *mga@state.mi.us*
URL: *http://www.michigan.gov/
mistudentaid/*

Minnesota
Great Lakes Higher Education
Corporation
P.O. Box 7658
2401 International Lane
Madison, WI 53704
(608) 246-1800
(800) 236-5900
E-Mail: *service@glhec.org*
URL: *http://www.glhec.org/*

Mississippi
USA Funds
P.O. Box 6028
Indianapolis, IN 46206-6028
(317) 849-6510
(888) 272-5543
TTY: (800) 331-2357
FAX: (317) 806-1203
E-Mail: *contact@usafunds.org*
URL: *http://www.usafunds.org/*

Missouri
Missouri Student Assistance Resource
Services
3515 Amazonas Drive
Jefferson City, MO 65109
(573) 751-3940
(800) 473-6757
TTY: (800) 735-2966
FAX: (573) 751-6635
E-Mail: *icweb@mocbhe.gov*
URL: *http://www.cbhe.state.mo.us/*

Montana
Montana Guaranteed Student Loan
Program
P.O. Box 203101
Helena, MT 59620-3101
(406) 444-0638
(800) 537-7508
FAX: (406) 444-1869
E-Mail: *custserv@mgslp.state.mt.us* or
scholars@mgslp.state.mt.us
URL: *http://www.mgslp.state.mt.us/*

Nebraska
National Student Loan Program
(Nebraska)
P.O. Box 82507
Lincoln, NE 68501-2507
(402) 475-8686
(800) 735-8778
TTY: (800) 735-8778
FAX: (402) 479-6658
E-Mail: *rodl@nslp.org* or
NancyW@nslp.org
URL: *http://www.nslp.org/*

Nevada
USA Funds
P.O. Box 6028
Indianapolis, IN 46206-6028
(317) 849-6510
(888) 272-5543
TTY: (800) 331-2357
FAX: (317) 806-1203
E-Mail: *contact@usafunds.org*
URL: *http://www.usafunds.org/*

New Hampshire
New Hampshire Higher Education
Assistance Foundation

P.O. Box 877
4 Barrell Court
Concord, NH 03302-0877
(603) 225-6612
(800) 525-2577
FAX: (603) 224-2581
E-Mail: *resourcectr@gsmr.org*
URL: *http://www.nhheaf.org/*

New Jersey
New Jersey Higher Education Student
Assistance Authority
P.O. Box 540
Trenton, NJ 08625-0540
(609) 588-3214
(800) 792-8670
TTY: (609) 588-2526
FAX: (609) 588-7389
E-Mail: *osacs@hesaa.org*
URL: *http://www.hesaa.org/intro.asp*

New Mexico
New Mexico Student Loan Guarantee
Corporation
3900 Osuna NE
Albuquerque, NM 87199-2230
(505) 345-8821
(800) 279-3070
FAX: (505) 344-3631
E-Mail: *guarantee@nmslgc.org*
URL: *http://www.nmslgc.org/*

New York
New York State Higher Education
Services Corporation
99 Washington Avenue
Albany, NY 12255
(518) 473-7087
(888) 697-4372
TTY: (800) 445-5234
FAX: (518) 474-2839
E-Mail: *webmail@hesc.com*
URL: *http://www.hesc.com/*

North Carolina
North Carolina State Education
Assistance Authority
P. O. Box 13663
Research Triangle Park, NC 27709
(919) 549-8614
(800) 700-1775
FAX: (919) 549-8481
E-Mail: *information@ncseaa.edu*
URL: *http://www.ncseaa.edu/*

North Dakota
Student Loans of North Dakota—
Guarantor Bank of North Dakota
P.O. Box 5524
Bismarck, ND 58506-5524
(701) 328-5754
(800) 472-2166

TTY: (800) 643-3916
FAX: (701) 328-5716
E-Mail: *bndsl@state.nd.us* or
bndga@state.nd.us
URL: *http://mystudentloanonline.com/index.jsp*

Ohio
Great Lakes Higher Education
Corporation
P.O. Box 7658
2401 International Lane
Madison, WI 53704
(608) 246-1800
(800) 236-5900
E-Mail: *service@glhec.org*
URL: *http://www.glhec.org/*

Oklahoma
Oklahoma Guaranteed Student Loan
Program
P.O. Box 3000
Oklahoma City, OK 73101-3000
(405) 234-4300
(800) 442-8642
TTY: (405) 234-4511
FAX: (405) 234-4390
E-Mail: *info@ogslp.org*
URL: *http://www.ogslp.org/*

Oregon
Oregon Student Assistance Commission
Suite 100
1500 Valley River Drive
Eugene, OR 97401
(541) 687-7375
(800) 452-8807
TTY: (541) 687-7357
FAX: (541) 687-7426
E-Mail: *public_information@mercury.osac.state.or.us*
URL: *http://www.osac.state.or.us/*

Pennsylvania American Education
Services/PHEAA
1200 North Seventh Street
Harrisburg, PA 17102-1444
(717) 720-2800
(877) 603-3010
TTY: (800) 654-5988
FAX: (717) 720-3903
E-Mail: *info@aessuccess.org* or
kwoollam@aessuccess.org
URL: *http://www.aessuccess.org/*

Rhode Island
Rhode Island Higher Education
Assistance Authority
560 Jefferson Boulevard
Warwick, RI 02886-1320
(401) 736-1100
(800) 922-9855

TTY: (401) 222-6195
FAX: (401) 732-3541
E-Mail: *gjsilva@riheaa.org*
URL: *http://www.riheaa.org/*

South Carolina
South Carolina Student Loan Corporation
P.O. Box 210219
Suite 200, Interstate Center
Columbia, SC 29221
(803) 798-0916
(800) 347-2752
FAX: (803) 772-9410
E-Mail: *mfox@slc.sc.edu*
URL: *http://www.slc.sc.edu/*

South Dakota
Education Assistance Corporation (South
Dakota)
115 First Avenue SW
Aberdeen, SD 57401
(605) 225-6423
(800) 592-1802
TTY: (800) 752-3949
FAX: (605) 225-5722
E-Mail: *eac@eac-easci.org*
URL: *http://www.eac-easci.org/*

Tennessee
Tennessee Student Assistance Corporation
Suite 1950, Parkway Towers
404 James Robertson Parkway
Nashville, TN 37243-0820
(615) 741-1346
(800) 342-1663
Toll Free Restrictions: TN residents only
FAX: (615) 741-6101
E-Mail: *stephanie.aylor@state.tn.us* or
TSAC@mail.state.tn.us
URL: *http://www.state.tn.us/tsac/*

Texas
Texas Guaranteed Student Loan
Corporation
P. O. Box 201725
Austin, TX 78720-1725
(512) 219-5700
(800) 845-6267
TTY: (512) 219-4560
FAX: (512) 219-4633
E-Mail: *cust.assist@tgslc.org*
URL: *http://www.tgslc.org/*

Utah
Utah Higher Education Assistance
Authority
60 South 400 West
Salt Lake City, UT 84101-1284
(801) 321-7200
(800) 418-8757
FAX: (801) 321-7299
E-Mail: *uheaa@utahsbr.edu*

URL: *http://www.uheaa.org/*

Vermont
Vermont Student Assistance Corporation
P.O. Box 2000
Champlain Mill
Winooski, VT 05404-2601
(802) 655-9602
(800) 642-3177
TTY: (802) 654-3766
FAX: (802) 654-3765
E-Mail: *info@vsac.org*
URL: *http://www.vsac.org/*

Virginia
Educational Credit Management
Corporation (Virginia)
Suite 200
7325 Beaufont Springs Drive
Richmond, VA 23225
(804) 267-7100
(888) 775-3262
TTY: (804) 267-7104
FAX: (804) 267-7159
URL: *http://www.ecmc.org/*

Washington
Northwest Education Loan Association
Suite 300
190 Queen Anne North
Seattle, WA 98109

(206) 461-5300
(800) 562-3001
FAX: (206) 461-5449
E-Mail: *cheryll@nela.net*
URL: *http://www.nela.net/*

West Virginia
American Education Services/PHEAA
1200 North Seventh Street
Harrisburg, PA 17102-1444
(717) 720-2800
(877) 603-3010
TTY: (800) 654-5988
FAX: (717) 720-3903
E-Mail: *info@aessuccess.org* or
kwoollam@aessuccess.org
URL: *http://www.aessuccess.org/*

Wisconsin
Great Lakes Higher Education
Corporation
P.O. Box 7658
2401 International Lane
Madison, WI 53704
(608) 246-1800
(800) 236-5900
E-Mail: *service@glhec.org*
URL: *http://www.glhec.org/*

Wyoming
USA Funds

P.O. Box 6028
Indianapolis, IN 46206-6028
(317) 849-6510
(888) 272-5543
TTY: (800) 331-2357
FAX: (317) 806-1203
E-Mail: *contact@usafunds.org*
URL: *http://www.usafunds.org/*

Territories

American Samoa
No Entry

**Commonwealth of the Northern
Mariana Islands**
No Entry

Federated States of Micronesia
No Entry

Guam
USA Funds
P.O. Box 6028
Indianapolis, IN 46206-6028
(317) 849-6510
(888) 272-5543
TTY: (800) 331-2357
FAX: (317) 806-1203
E-Mail: *contact@usafunds.org*
URL: *http://www.usafunds.org/*

Index

References are to sections

References are to sections

WAGE GARNISHMENTS (*cont.*)
procedures, 5.3.2 (*cont.*)
  hearings, 5.3.3.2
  maximum amount, 5.3.2.2
restrictions, 5.3.1
sample class action complaint, Appx. E.4
school-related claims, raising, 9.5.3.1.7
statute of limitations eliminated, 3.2.1

WAIVERS
defenses, consolidation loan as, 9.5.3.3
loan obligations, *see* COMPROMISES

WEB RESOURCES
closed school list, 6.2.2.2

Direct Loans, 1.4.2, 1.8.2
  consolidation loans, 8.2.2.1
  monthly payments, 8.2.2.5
DOE forms, Appx. D
DOE policy guidance letters, Appx. C
NSLDS, 1.6.1
Student Guide, 1.8.2
student loan default rates, 1.3
Student Loan Ombudsman, 1.8.1

WONDERLIC TESTS
ATB testing, 6.3.2.3.4

WRITE-OFFS
see COMPROMISES

Quick Reference to the Consumer Credit and Sales Legal Practice Series

References are to sections in *all* manuals in NCLC's Consumer Credit and Sales Legal Practice Series.

This Quick Reference pinpoints where to find specific consumer law topics analyzed in the NCLC manuals. References are to individual manual or supplement sections from the National Consumer Law Center's Consumer Credit and Sales Legal Practice Series. For more information on other volumes, see *What Your Library Should Contain* at the beginning of this volume.

This Quick Reference is a speedy means to locate key terms in the appropriate NCLC Manual. More detailed indices are found at the end of the individual NCLC volumes. The detailed contents pages at the beginning of each volume provide further elaboration once the appropriate manual is identified by use of this Quick Reference.

Pleadings, statutes, regulations, agency interpretations, legislative history, and other appendix material are also found on the CD-Roms that are included with the specified volume. In addition, everything found on the sixteen individual CD-Roms is also included on NCLC's *Consumer Law in a Box* CD-Rom. **NCLC strongly recommends that those searching for pleadings refer to the *Index Guide* that accompanies *Consumer Law Pleadings on CD-Rom* (2002), and not to this *Quick Reference*.**

Abbreviations

AUS	=	Access to Utility Service (2d ed. 2001 and 2002 Supp)
Auto	=	Automobile Fraud (1998 and 2002 Supp)
Arbit	=	Consumer Arbitration Agreements (2d ed. 2002)
CBPL	=	Consumer Banking and Payments Law (2d ed. 2002)
Bankr	=	Consumer Bankruptcy Law and Practice (6th ed. 2000 and 2002 Supp)
CCA	=	Consumer Class Actions: A Practical Litigation Guide (5th ed. 2002)
CLP8	=	Consumer Law Pleadings Number Eight (2002)
CLP7	=	Consumer Law Pleadings Number Seven (2001)
CLP6	=	Consumer Law Pleadings Number Six (2000)

CLP5	=	Consumer Law Pleadings Number Five (1999)
CLP4	=	Consumer Law Pleadings Number Four (1998)
CLP3	=	Consumer Law Pleadings Number Three (1997)
CLP2	=	Consumer Law Pleadings Number Two (1995)
CLP1	=	Consumer Law Pleadings Number One (1994)
COC	=	The Cost of Credit (2d ed. 2000 and 2002 Supp)
CD	=	Credit Discrimination (3d ed. 2002)
FCR	=	Fair Credit Reporting (5th ed. 2002)
FDC	=	Fair Debt Collection (4th ed. 2000 and 2002 Supp)
Repo	=	Repossessions and Foreclosures (5th ed. 2002)
Stud	=	Student Loan Law (2d ed. 2002)
TIL	=	Truth in Lending (4th ed. 1999 and 2002 Supp)
UDAP	=	Unfair and Deceptive Acts and Practices (5th ed. 2001 and 2002 Supp)
Warr	=	Consumer Warranty Law (2d ed. 2001 and 2002 Supp)

Abandonment of Apartment Building in Bankruptcy—Bankr § 17.8.2
Abbreviations Commonly Used by Debt Collectors—FDC App M
Abuse of Process—UDAP § 5.1.4; FDC § 10.6
Acceleration—COC §§ 5.6.2, 5.7.1; Repo § 4.1
Accessions—Repo § 3.5.3.2
Accord and Satisfaction—CBPL § 1.7.3
Account Aggregation—CBPL § 4.10
Accountants—UDAP § 5.12.8
Accrediting Agencies, Student Loans—Stud § 9.4.1.2
Accurate Information in Consumer Reports—FCR § 7.8
Actual Damages—*See* Damages
Actuarial Rebates—COC § 5.6.3.4
Adhesion Contracts—UDAP § 5.2.3
Adjustable Rate Mortgages—TIL § 4.6.4; COC § 4.3.6
Administration of Lawsuit, Class Action—CCA Ch 13; CLP1
Admissibility of Other Bad Acts—Auto § 9.7.1.1
Advertisements as Warranties—Warr § 3.2.2.5
Advertising by Attorneys on the Internet—CLP4 Ch 10
Advertising Credit Terms—TIL §§ 5.13, 9.4
Affordability Programs, Utilities—AUS Ch 9, App F
After-Acquired Property—Repo § 3.4.5.2

References are to sections in *all* manuals in NCLC's Consumer Credit and Sales Legal Practice Series

References are to sections in *all* manuals in NCLC's Consumer Credit and Sales Legal Practice Series

References are to sections in *all* manuals in NCLC's Consumer Credit and Sales Legal Practice Series

References are to sections in *all* manuals in NCLC's Consumer Credit and Sales Legal Practice Series

References are to sections in *all* manuals in NCLC's Consumer Credit and Sales Legal Practice Series

References are to sections in *all* manuals in NCLC's Consumer Credit and Sales Legal Practice Series

References are to sections in *all* manuals in NCLC's Consumer Credit and Sales Legal Practice Series

References are to sections in *all* manuals in NCLC's Consumer Credit and Sales Legal Practice Series

NOTES

NOTES

NOTES

NOTES

About the Companion CD-Rom

CD-Rom Supersedes All Prior CD-Roms

This CD-Rom supersedes the CD-Rom accompanying *Student Loan Law* (2001). Discard the 2001 CD. The 2002 CD contains everything found on the 2001 CD and contains much additional material.

What Is on the CD-Rom

This CD-Rom features:

- Key Federal Student Loan Statutes, Regulations, and Department of Education Policy Guidance Letters (Appendices A–C and additional materials *not* found in the book)
- Department of Education Forms to Apply for Loan Discharges and for Consolidation Loans (Appendix D)
- Department of Education Forms to Apply for Deferment or Forbearance (many *not* found in the book)
- Sample Letters Seeking Reasonable Repayment Plan, Group False Certification Discharge, and Legal Pleadings re Collection Abuse, Garnishment, and Trade School Fraud as a Defense (Appendix E and additional letters *not* found in the book)
- Complaints of Discovery in Student Loan Collection Abuse Cases (Appendix F and additional pleadings *not* found in the book)
- Directory of Guaranty Agencies (Appendix G)
- 2002-2003 Department of Education Student Financial Aid Guide, in English and in Spanish (*not* found in the book)
- The Table of Contents of this and all other NCLC manuals
- A Cumulative Index to the manual and the Quick Reference to the complete series
- Consumer Education Brochures, and
- Acrobat Reader 5.

How to Use the CD-Rom

The CD's pop-up menu quickly allows you to use the CD—just place the CD into its drive and click on the "Start NCLC CD" button that will pop up in the middle of the screen. You can also access the CD by clicking on a desktop icon that you can create using the pop-up menu.[1] For detailed installation instructions, see *One-Time Installation* below.

All the CD-Rom's information is available in PDF (Acrobat) format, making the information:

- Highly readable (identical to the printed pages in the book);
- Easily navigated (with bookmarks, "buttons," and Internet-style forward and backward searches);
- Easy to locate with keyword searches and other quick-search techniques across the whole CD-Rom; and
- Easy to paste into a wordprocessor.

While much of the material is also found on the CD-Rom in word processing format, we strongly recommend you use the material in PDF format—not only because it is easiest to use, contains the most features, and includes more material, but also because you can easily switch back to a word processing format when you prefer.

Acrobat Reader 5 comes free of charge with the CD-Rom. **We strongly recommend that new Acrobat users read the Acrobat tutorial on the Home Page. It takes two minutes and will really pay off.**

How to Find Documents in Word Processing Format

The CD-Rom presents several options to find documents in word processing format, if that is preferred to the PDF format for a certain task. One option is simply to open a document on the CD-Rom from your standard word processing program, such as WordPerfect or Word. All word processing documents are in the D:\WP_Files directory, if "D:" is the CD-Rom drive.[2] Each document in that directory corresponds to an appendix in the book, and is named in the directory accordingly.

Another option is to navigate the CD in PDF format, and, when a particular document is on the screen, click on the corresponding bookmark for the "WordPerfect version

---

1 Alternatively, click on the D:\Start.pdf file on "My Computer" or open that file in Acrobat—always assuming "D:" is the CD-Rom drive on your computer.

2 The CD-Rom drive could be any letter following "D:" depending on your computer's configuration.

of . . ." This will automatically run WordPerfect for Windows, MS Word, or *any other word processor* that is associated with the ".WPD" extension, and then open the word processing file that corresponds to the Acrobat document on the screen.[3]

Important Information Before Opening the CD-Rom Package

Before opening the CD-Rom package, please read this information. Opening the package constitutes acceptance of the following described terms. In addition, the *book* is not returnable once the seal to the *CD-Rom* has been broken.

The CD-Rom is copyrighted and all rights are reserved by the National Consumer Law Center, Inc. No copyright is claimed to the text of statutes, regulations, excerpts from court opinions, or any part of an original work prepared by a United States Government employee.

You may not commercially distribute the CD-Rom or otherwise reproduce, publish, distribute or use the disk in any manner that may infringe on any copyright or other proprietary right of the National Consumer Law Center. Nor may you otherwise transfer the CD-Rom or this agreement to any other party unless that party agrees to accept the terms and conditions of this agreement. You may use the CD-Rom on only one computer and by one user at a time.

The CD-Rom is warranted to be free of defects in materials and faulty workmanship under normal use for a period of ninety days after purchase. If a defect is discovered in the CD-Rom during this warranty period, a replacement disk can be obtained at no charge by sending the defective disk, postage prepaid, with information identifying the purchaser, to National Consumer Law Center, Publications Department, 77 Summer Street, 10th Floor, Boston, MA 02110. After the ninety-day period, a replacement will be available

on the same terms, but will also require a $15 prepayment.

The National Consumer Law Center makes no other warranty or representation, either express or implied, with respect to this disk, its quality, performance, merchantability, or fitness for a particular purpose. In no event will the National Consumer Law Center be liable for direct, indirect, special, incidental, or consequential damages arising out of the use or inability to use the disk. The exclusion of implied warranties is not effective in some states, and thus this exclusion may not apply to you.

System Requirements

Use of this CD-Rom requires a Windows-based PC with a CD-Rom drive. (Macintosh users report success using NCLC CDs, but the CD has been tested only on Windows-based PCs.) The CD-Rom's features are optimized with Acrobat Reader 5 (2002), which is included free on this CD-Rom—you should install Acrobat Reader 5 even if you already have an earlier version of Acrobat. Much of the material on the CD-Rom can also be used with any word processor released after 1989.

One-Time Installation

When the CD-Rom is inserted in its drive, a menu will pop up automatically. (Please be patient if you have a slow CD-Rom drive; this will only take a few moments.) If you do not already have Acrobat Reader 5, first click the "Install Acrobat Reader" button. Do not reboot, but then click on the "Make Shortcut Icon" button. (You need not make another shortcut icon if you already have done so for another NCLC CD.) Then reboot and follow the *How to Use the CD-Rom* instructions above.

[*Note*: If the pop-up menu fails to appear, go to "My Computer," right-click "D:" if that is the CD-Rom drive, and select "Open." Then double-click on "Read_Me.txt" for alternate installation and use instructions.]

---

3 For instructions on how to associate MS Word to the ".WPD" extension, go to the CD-Rom's home page and click on "Word-Perfect Files and MS Word."